THE CIVIL COURT PRACTICE
2013

Procedure and Guidance

FOR REFERENCE

ONLY

LexisNexis®

THE CIVIL COURT PRACTICE
2013

PROCEDURE AND GUIDANCE

Members of the LexisNexis Group worldwide

United Kingdom	LexisNexis Butterworths, a Division of Reed Elsevier (UK) Ltd, Halsbury House, 35 Chancery Lane, London, WC2A 1EL, and London House, 20–22 East London Street, Edinburgh EH7 4BQ
Australia	LexisNexis Butterworths, Chatswood, New South Wales
Austria	LexisNexis Verlag ARD Orac GmbH & Co KG, Vienna
Benelux	LexisNexis Benelux, Amsterdam
Canada	LexisNexis Canada, Markham, Ontario
China	LexisNexis China, Beijing and Shanghai
France	LexisNexis SA, Paris
Germany	LexisNexis GmbH, Dusseldorf
Hong Kong	LexisNexis Hong Kong, Hong Kong
India	LexisNexis India, New Delhi
Italy	Giuffrè Editore, Milan
Japan	LexisNexis Japan, Tokyo
Malaysia	Malayan Law Journal Sdn Bhd, Kuala Lumpur
New Zealand	LexisNexis NZ Ltd, Wellington
Poland	Wydawnictwo Prawnicze LexisNexis Sp, Warsaw
Singapore	LexisNexis Singapore, Singapore
South Africa	LexisNexis Butterworths, Durban
USA	LexisNexis, Dayton, Ohio

First published in 1899
© Reed Elsevier (UK) Ltd 2013

Published by LexisNexis
This is a Butterworths title

Printed in the UK by CPI William Clowes Beccles NR34 7TL

Visit LexisNexis Butterworths at www.lexisnexis.co.uk

PREFACE

The Procedural Tables have, for many years, been updated and revised by Alan Simons, a long-serving District Judge at Swindon. Under his watchful eye the Tables grew to include references not only to Rules, Forms and Directions, but also to case law and articles in the legal press. On his retirement from the Editorial Board earlier this year he left behind a treasury of legal wisdom and sound practical advice, for which we are extremely grateful.

We have taken this opportunity to combine the booklet of Procedural Tables with official guidance covering the same ground, that has been moved from Volume 1: Admiralty and Commercial Courts Guide, Chancery Guide, Mercantile Court Guide, Patents Court Guide, Patents County Court Guide, Queen's Bench Guide and Technology and Construction Court Guide. However, the Senior Courts Costs Office Guide, which was revised in October 2013, will remain in Volume 1, where it appears alongside the costs rules (CPR 44-CPR 48).

At the same time the Procedural Tables have been updated and trimmed by the excision of material that has less relevance today than when it was first included. The result, now styled the Procedure and Guidance Supplement, is a handbook of manageable size to which the litigating practitioner can turn for practical guidance on all the various claims, appeals and applications that are the daily fare of the civil courts.

TABLE OF CONTENTS

PROCEDURAL TABLES

Preface v

TAB 1   Start of Proceedings Under Part 7 1

TAB 2   Start of Proceedings for Part 8 Claims 17

TAB 3   Sanctions, Avoidance and Relief 21

TAB 4   Service of Claim Forms within the Jurisdiction or in specified circumstances within the EEA 25

TAB 5   Service of Claims Form outside the Jurisdiction 35

TAB 6   Acknowledgment of Service of Part 7 Claim 41

TAB 7   Acknowledgment of Service of Part 8 Claim 43

TAB 8   Admissions and Judgment upon Admissions 45

TAB 9   Judgments in Default and Applications to Set them Aside . . 53

TAB 10   Summary Judgment 59

TAB 10A   Low value personal injury claims in Road Traffic Accidents . 67

TAB 11   Defence and Reply 81

TAB 12   Counterclaims, claims for Contribution of Indemnity and other Additional claims 83

TAB 13   Allocation 89

TAB 14   Applications 91

TAB 15   Disclosure and Inspection 97

TAB 16   Expert Evidence 109

TAB 17   Small Claims 117

TAB 18   Fast Track 127

TAB 19   Multi-track 137

TAB 20   Offers to Settle 187

TAB 21   Recovery of Possession of Land – Claims by Landlord, Mortgagee, Licensor, Person Entitled to Possession against Trespassers 199

TAB 22   Accelerated Possession Procedure – Housing Act 1988 s 21 . 253

TAB 23   Interim Possession Orders – Recovery of Possession of Land from Trespassers 259

TAB 24   Anti-Social Behaviour Orders under the Crime and Disorder Act 1998 263

TAB 24A   Change of Solicitor 273

TAB 25   Appeals to a Circuit Judge from a District Judge in a county court or an appeal to a High Court Judge from the county court or from a Master/District Judge in the High Court 277

TAB 26   Court of Appeal.................................... 285

TAB 27   Appeal to the Supreme Court 295

TAB 28   Appeal to the Judicial Committee of the Privy Council...... 303

Admiralty and Commercial Court Guide 313

Chancery Guide........................ 419

Mercantile Court Guide................................... 591

Patents Court Guide 631

Patents County Court Guide..................... 645

Guide to the Patents County Court Small Claims Track........ 667

Queen's Bench Guide................................... 677

Technology and Construction Court Guide.............. 779

TABLE 1—START OF PROCEEDINGS UNDER PART 7

TAB 1

	Form No	CPR	PD
1. Preliminary			
1.1 Pre-action Conduct and pre-action protocol			
Before issue, the claimant should comply with the Practice Direction (Pre-Action Conduct) and any relevant **pre-action protocol** (of which there are presently ten) The court **will** take this into account when it gives directions.		3.1(4)	Practice Direction (Pre-Action Conduct), para 4 Protocol 1, para 4.1–4.10
1.2 Alternative Dispute Resolution			
Before issue, the claimant should consider **Alternative Dispute Resolution** (**'ADR'**) with particular reference to the Protocols Practice Direction at para 4.7 noting the statement that the court may 'require evidence that alternative means of resolving their dispute were considered' and that 'The Courts take the view that litigation should be a last resort'.			
1.3 Letter before action			
1.3.1 Before issue, the claimant should write a **letter before action**; in *Phoenix Finance Ltd v Federation International de l'Automobile* [2002] EWHC 1028 (Ch), (2002) Times, 27 June it was stressed that nothing in the CPR removed the necessity of doing so			
1.3.2 Failure to write a letter before action will not necessarily relieve an unsuccessful defendant of his liability for costs. If the court finds such a letter would have had no effect on the defendant's conduct it is not likely in the exercise of its discretion to refuse the claimant's application for costs; *Merial Ltd v Sankyo Co Ltd* [2004] EWHC 3077 (Pat), [2004] All ER (D) 272 (Dec)			
1.3.3 If such letters before action are 'oppressive and unacceptable' sending them is capable of amounting to harassment falling within the Protection from Harassment Act 1997: *Ferguson v British Gas Trading Ltd* [2009] EWCA Civ 46, [2009] All ER (D) 80 (Feb), (2009 NLJ, Civil Way, 27 February, page 304. Clearly, care should be taken as to the content of such letters. See further **TAB 24A**, para 8.10 below.			
1.3.4 Where individuals are represented by Citizens Advice the SRA has warned solicitors that they risk breaching the Code of Conduct by contacting them directly: see Gazette (2012), 2 February, page 4.			
1.4 Funding arrangement			

TAB 1 PROCEDURAL TABLES

	Form No	CPR	PD
Before issue, the claimant should inform other potential parties if he enters into a **funding arrangement**. This must be done as soon as possible and in any event within 7 days of entering into the funding arrangement. If the funding arrangement was entered into before sending a letter of claim, in the letter of claim.			
If the funding arrangement was entered into prior to the issue of proceedings, the information set out in form N251 must be provided to the court when filing the claim form and if the court is to serve the claim form sufficient extra copies must be filed for service on all other parties.			
2. The Appropriate Court			
2.1 High Court or county court			
Restrictions on where proceedings may be started are set out in the relevant practice directions supplementing Part 7		7.1	7A
Subject to the provisions of the Practice Direction to CPR Pt 7, where both High Court and the county court have jurisdiction, the proceedings may be started in the High Court or a county court			7A, para 1
Claims which **must** be issued in the High Court: business from which county courts are excluded, eg admiralty, libel, slander, judicial review, patent infringement, human rights declarations of incompatibility, equity cases where the worth of the trust or estate is more than £30,000 *But note:*		58 (Commercial Court) 59 (Mercantile Courts)	7A, para 2.9 49 (specialist proceedings)
(a) as to Mercantile Courts – the Central London County Court		60 (Technology and Construction Court claims)	
(b) as to Technology and Construction Court Claims – county courts specified in the Practice Direction		61 (Admiralty claims)	
(c) as to Patent Court business – see Patents County Court		62 (Arbitration claims)	
But note also: Probate claims in the county court must only be brought where there is also a Chancery district registry or in the Central London County Court. See County Courts Act 1984 s 32 as to probate claims which may be heard in the county courts.		57.2	72.2.2
But note also that there is no monetary limit to the jurisdiction of the county court under the Trusts of Land and Appointment of Trustees Act 1996: see art 2(1)(a) of the High Court and County Courts Jurisdiction Order 1991.			
Claims which **should** be issued in the High Court: where the claimant believes			

	Form No	CPR	PD
that the claim ought to be heard by a High Court judge by reason of:			
(a) financial value and the amount in dispute, and/or			
(b) complexity of facts, legal issues, remedies or procedures involved, and/or			
(c) the importance of the outcome to the public in general			7A, para 2.4
Claims which **must** be issued in the county court:			
(a) proceedings whether for damages or a specific sum where the value is not more than £25,000			7A, para 2.1
(b) proceedings which include a claim for damages for personal injuries unless the value of the claim is £50,000 or more. For the definition of "value" see art 9 of the High Court and County Court Jurisdiction Order 1991 (SI 1991/724) as amended and note in particular that contributory negligence is not taken into account unless it is admitted (art 9(4)(b)) nor is interest unless it is contractual (art 9(2)(b))			7A, para 2.2
(c) where an enactment so requires			7A, para 2.3
2.2 Jurisdiction by agreement			
(a) Actions other than those which if issued in the High Court would have been assigned to the Chancery Division or to the Family Division or involved the exercise of the High Court's Admiralty jurisdiction, see para II CCA [10]			
(b) As to those proceedings within the High Court's equity jurisdiction, see para II CCA [12]			
2.3 Human Rights			
A claim under s 7(1)(a) of the Human Rights Act 1998 in respect of a judicial act can only be brought in the High Court. Any other claim under s 7(1)(a) may be brought in any court		7.11	
2.4 Allocation to levels of Judiciary			
Judges, Masters and District Judges may exercise any function of the court except where an enactment rule or practice direction provides otherwise.		2.4	2B
3. Venue			
The general rule is to allow the issue of Part 7 proceedings in any county court, with the following exceptions:			
In all **designated money claims** (as defined in the Preface to these tables), that is Part 7 claims for money only other than a claim issued through the bulk centre or Money Claims Online, practice form N1 must be **sent to**: County Court Money Claims Centre, PO Box 527, M5 0BY (CCMCC). The claim will then be			

TAB 1 PROCEDURAL TABLES

	Form No	CPR	PD
issued in Northampton County Court. The claimant must specify the **preferred court** (defined in the Preface to these tables), that is the court specified by the claimant in form N1 as the court to which the proceedings should be transferred if necessary.			7.A1–2
For **bulk issue in a Production Centre** and generally see CPR PD 7C; there is a varying scale of discounts for claims issued through the Claims Production Centre. A claim form will only be issued if the claim is for a specified sum under £100,000 and where the defendant's address for service is in England and Wales (there are a number of other conditions).		7.10	7C
Money Claim Online enables certain types of claim forms to be issued and other specified documents to be filed electronically via the Court Service website. The claimant must give an address for service in the United Kingdom. The address for service for the defendant must be an address for service within England and Wales. Claims started using MCOL will be issued by Northampton County court (for address see CPR PD 7 MCOL, para 1.4 (at para **CPR PD 7E** above)) and will proceed in that court unless they are transferred to another court. Judgment in default of acknowledgement of claim or defence and judgment on admission of the whole claim can be entered and a warrant of execution can be issued electronically. Where particulars of claim are served separately from the claim form a certificate of service in form N215 must be filed within 14 days of the service of the particulars of claim on the defendant. The electronic record of the progress of the claim may be viewed.		7.12	7E MCOL, paras 1.4, 1.5, 1.6 and para 13
4. Completion of the claim form			
This applies whether the claim is started in the High Court or a county court. Similarly, it applies whether the claim is likely to be allocated to the multi-, fast or small claims track			7A
The **claim form** will be issued under CPR Pt 7 unless:		8.1(2)	
(a) it is unlikely there will be a substantial dispute of fact, or		8.1(2)(a)	
(b) a Rule or Practice Direction permits the use of the Part 8 procedure		8.1(2)(b)	
The claim form must normally be in the practice form N1 prescribed to start a Part 7 claim but exceptions include	N1		
(a) Admiralty	ADM1 and 1A		
(b) Arbitration	8		
(c) Probate	N2		
(d) Possession of land; Tab 22	N5 N5A		

	Form No	CPR	PD
	N5B		
	N119		
	N120		
	N121		
5. Contents of the claim form			
For requirements for contents of the claim form, see	N1	16.2–16.3	16, para 2
Note:			
• The claim from must include an address at which the claimant resides or carries on business. This is the case even if the claimant's address for service is the business address of his solicitor. As to inclusion of a postcode or its equivalent in any EEA state, see CPR PD 2.4.			16, paras 2.2 and 2.4
• A defendant may be identified by description rather than name: *Bloomsbury Publishing Group Ltd v News Group Ltd* [2003] EWHC 1205 (Ch), [2003] 3 All ER 736			
• The **name** of the court should be specified but the court office will insert the claim number			
• In all designated money claims the claimant must specify the preferred court on practice form N1			
• In civil proceedings against the Crown for contents of the claim form see		16.2(1A)	
• For guidance as to the name and title of the claimant and of the defendant see "Notes for claimant on completing a claim form"	N1A		
• Where a partnership has a name, unless it is inappropriate to do so, claims must be brought in or against the name under which that partnership carried on business at the time the cause of action accrued		7.2A	7A, para 5A.3
• Where a person carries on business in a name other than his own ('the business name') the claim may be brought against the business name as if it were the name of a partnership		7.2A	7A, paras 5.1 and 5.1
• A written statement of the names and last known places of residence of all partners who were partners at the time when the cause of action accrued can be required (a 'partnership membership statement')		7.2A	7A, para 5B
• The claim form requires **brief details of the claim** and there should be inserted a concise statement of the nature of the claim and a statement of the remedy sought. These should be sufficient to iden-			

TAB 1   PROCEDURAL TABLES

	Form No	CPR	PD
tify the claim and inform the defendant of its nature and the remedy sought			
For example:			
"The claim is for damages for personal injuries and loss and damage caused by the **negligence** of the defendant in the driving of motor car [registration number] at [location] on or about [date and time] and interest thereon pursuant to [section 35A of the Senior Courts Act 1981] [section 69 County Court Act 1984]"			
"The claim is for damages for **nuisance** by noise from the defendant's house [address] and interest thereon . . . (continue as above)"			
"The claim is for the price of **goods** [describe nature of goods] **sold** and delivered by the claimant to the defendant on [specify date] and interest thereon . . . continue as above)"		16.2(1)(a) and (b)	
Note: The court may grant any remedy to which the claimant is entitled, even if that remedy is not specified in the claim form		16.2(5)	
• The claim form or the particulars of claim must contain a statement whether Sections III and IV of the Practice Direction (Pre-action Conduct) and any relevant protocol have been complied with.			Practice Direction (Pre-action Conduct), para 9.7
• Where the claimant is making a claim for money, he must state:			
(i) the amount of money he is claiming			
(ii) that he expects to recover not more than £10,000, more than £10,000 but not more than £25,000 or more than £25,000, or			
(iii) that the claimant cannot say how much he expects to recover		16.3	
The space opposite "value" can conveniently be completed:			
"The claimant expects to recover more than £10,000 but not more than £25,000 (or as the case may be) and, claims £X inclusive of £Y interest to the date of issue (when the claim can be so quantified)"			
This formula fits in appropriately with the calculation required in the claim form, where the only claim is for a specified sum, and on the form Notice of Issue (specified amount) when requesting judgment	N205A		
The matters to be disregarded by the claimant in calculating the amount he expects to recover are set out		16.3(6)	

	Form No	CPR	PD
In a claim for **personal injuries**, the claimant must also state in the claim form whether the amount the claimant expects to recover as general damages for pain, suffering and loss of amenity is or is not more than £1,000		16.3(4)	
• If the particulars of claim are not contained in or served with the claim form, there must be a statement in the claim form that **particulars of claim will follow**		16.2(3)	
• The claim form must also contain such matters as may be set out in a **Practice Direction**		16.2(1)(a)	
• Chancery business in the High Court should be marked in the top right hand corner of the claim forms "Chancery Division" and if issued in a county court, it should be marked "Chancery Business". If a chancery-type case is brought in a county court which does not coincide with a Chancery District Registry (usually described as a Chancery county court) and it needs specialist experience consideration will be given to its transfer to a Chancery county court for case management or trial or both.			7A, para 2.5
• Where a claim is for compensation for **mesothelioma** the claim form must be headed 'Living Mesothelioma claim' or 'Fatal Mesothelioma Claim'		3.1	3D, Mesothelioma Claims, para 3.1
• For the marking where a mercantile claim is intended to be entered in the business list of an authorised county court, see			59, para 2.2
• For the marking of a claim form in specialist proceedings generally, see		49	
• If the claim is to be served in Scotland, Northern Ireland or out of the United Kingdom where the permission of the court is not required the claimant must:			
(a) File with the claim form a notice stating the grounds on which the claimant is entitled to serve the claim form out of the jurisdiction; and			
(b) Serve a copy of that notice with the claim form. See **TAB 5** below.	N510	6.32–6.34	6B, para 2.1
• The claim form must be verified by a **statement of truth** whether or not separate particulars of claim incorporating a statement of truth are served			

TAB 1 PROCEDURAL TABLES

	Form No	CPR	PD
The statement of truth can be signed by the claimant or his litigation friend or his solicitors, provided in each case they are duly authorised by the claimant to sign		2.3(1) 22	
Where a person is unable to read or sign a document to be verified by a statement of truth see			22, para 3A and Annex 1
Statements of truth are not simply formalities and witnesses must be made aware of the consequence that permission will be given for contempt proceedings to be brought against the maker of a false statement of truth: see *KJM Superbikes v Hinton* [2008] EWCA 1280, [2008] All ER (D) 200 (Nov) in particular per Moore-Bick LJ. The case is discussed in detail at (2008) NLJ 28 November at page 1679 in an article by Janna Purdie and reported in the same edition of the NLJ at page 1683			
As to the mechanical signature of a document, see		5.3	
As to **electronic communication and filing of documents** see PD 5B (Electronic Communications and Filing of Documents) which applies to claims in specified courts only. Section I of the Practice Direction provides for parties to communicate with the court and file specified documents by e-mail; Section II provides for parties to file specified documents electronically via an online forms service; and Section III contains general provisions that apply to sections I and II. For user guidance and protocols see PREMA (Preston E-mail Application Service), User Guide and Protocols. See also **TAB 1**, section 11, last para.		5.5	5B
As to the **electronic working scheme** (EWS) which came into operation on 1 April 2010 and will operate in the Admiralty, Commercial and London Mercantile Courts, the Chancery Division of the High Court at the Royal Courts of Justice (including the Patents and the Bankruptcy and Companies Court) see:		5.5, 7.12	5C
The EWS has an official website at http://www.electronic working.org.			
It is intended that the PD should continue to apply to these jurisdictions when they transfer to the Rolls Building and to the Bankruptcy jurisdiction of the Central London County Court.			
The scheme applies to all claims started on or after 1 April 2010 and to claims started or continued electronically under the pilot scheme which ran from 1 April 2009 to 31 March 2010.			
6. Other documents to be filed with the claim form			
(a) A party who seeks to recover an additional liability under a fund-			

	Form No	CPR	PD
ing arrangement must give other parties information about this claim	N251		44, section 19
(b) Where the claim is by a **child** (a person under 18 years old) or **protected party** (a party or intended party who lacks capacity to conduct the proceedings) a certificate of suitability and a certificate of its service must be filed if a person becomes a litigation friend without a court order.	N235		
If, however, a deputy has been appointed by the Court of Protection under the Mental Health Act 2005 with power to conduct proceedings only an official copy of the order need be filed.		21.1(2)(d), 21.5(3) and 21.5(4)(a) and (b)	21 paras 2.1–2.4
The certificate of service is as to service on a parent, guardian etc of the certificate of suitability.		21.5(4)(a) and (b)	
For the procedure where a person becomes a litigation friend by order of the court, see		21.8, 21.10	21 paras 3.1–3.4
For the ability for a litigation friend to recover expenses out of the child's or protected party's estate, see		21.12 and 46.4(2)	21 paras 11.1 and 11.2
Where damages do not exceed £5,000 the litigation friend's recovery is limited to 25%; the court may increase this but not beyond 50%		21.12(6)	
For the court to adopt the **'show cause'** procedure in mesothelioma cases at the first case management conference, the claimant must file and serve any witness statements about liability as are available either at the time of serving the claim form and particulars of claim or in any even not less than 7 days before the case management conference.			
The relevant mesothelioma PD paras are			
• as to the filing of witness statements and starting proceedings			3D, para 3.2
• claimants with severely limited life expectancy			3D, para 4
• fixing case management conferences for cases that do not fall within para 4			3D, para 5
• the 'show cause' procedure			3D, para 6
• setting trial date			3D, para 7
• evidence by deposition			3D, para 8
• pre-action protocols			3D, para 7
Note that the present amount of a 'standard interim payment' is £50,000			3D, para 2(b)
(d) A response pack comprising			
(i) form for defending the claim			
(ii) form for admitting the claim			

TAB 1 PROCEDURAL TABLES

	Form No	CPR	PD
(iii) form for acknowledging service			
should be provided for service with the particulars of claim	N9	7.8(1)	
7. Particulars of claim			
Particulars of claim must be served with the claim form or within 14 days thereafter, but in any event no later than the latest time for serving the claim form (generally 4 months, 6 months if served out of the jurisdiction)		7.4(1), 7.4(2), 7.5(2) and (3)	
If the particulars of claim are served separately from the claim form a copy must be filed within 7 days of service		7.4(3)	
The court does have a **discretion to extend time for service** of the particulars of claim where the claim form was served within the time prescribed: *Totty v Snowden* [2001] EWCA Civ 1415, [2001] 4 All ER 577. See also *Austin v Newcastle Chronicle and Journal Ltd* [2001] All ER (D) 243 (May)			
Where the application to extend time for service of the particulars of claim pursuant to CPR 3.1(2)(a) is made before the time for compliance has expired, the judge in deciding whether to exercise his discretion is not required to consider the checklist in CPR 3.9(1); *Robert v Momentum Services Ltd* (2003) Times, 13 February, CA. The prejudice to be considered is that arising from the failure to file the particulars not pre-existing prejudice. The rule 3.9(1) check list must be applied where the application to serve the particulars of claim out of time is made after the time for service has expired.		3.9(1)	
An extension of time may be granted subject to conditions; see *Price v Price* [2003] EWCA Civ 888, [2003] 3 All ER 911, where time was extended on conditions including a condition limiting the claim			
Powers in the CPR to extend time, remedy and error in procedure and dispense with service cannot be used to extend a statutory time limit or to avoid service required by statute unless the statute expressly provides: *Mucelli v Government of Albania* [2009] UKHL 2, [2009] All ER (D) 135 (Jan), (2009) Times, 27 January.			
The matters that must be included in the particulars of claim are set out in		16.4(1)	
There must be a **concise statement of the facts** on which the claimant relies. It must be constantly kept in mind that the circumstances in which an unpleaded issue would be considered by the court would be rare. See *Pantelli Associates Ltd v Corporate City Developments Number Two Ltd* [2010] EWHC 3189 (TCC) (a professional negligence case)			

	Form No	CPR	PD
where a counterclaim 'read as if the pleader had simply taken each relevant contract term and then added "failing to" or "failing adequately or at all" . . . '. Toulson LJ drew attention to CPR 16.4(1)(a) which required particulars of claim to include a concise statement of the facts on which the claimant relies; see case note in 'Update: construction' (2011) Sol Jo, 8 February, page 26.			
If interest is claimed that must be stated and it must be further stated if it is claimed pursuant to statute (and if so which), pursuant to the contract or some other basis (and if so which)		16.4(1)(b), 16.4(2)	
If the claim for interest is for a specified amount of money, (i) the percentage rate claimed; (ii) date from which it is claimed; (iii) the date to which it is calculated (not being later than the date of issue); (iv) the total amount of interest claimed to the date of calculation; and (v) the daily rate must be set out			
No interest can be awarded on debts before proceedings			
Unless there is entitlement to interest by statute eg Taxes Management Act 1970, the award of interest is discretionary as to award, rate and period. The court has statutory power to award interest on debt and damages			
For interest in personal injury claims and its calculation, see Rodney Nelson Jones update, which appears in the Gazette annually.			
If a claim is for interest under the Late Payment of Commercial Debts (Interest) Act 1998 as amended, if both contracting parties have been acting n the course of a business, see CPR 16.4 [5.16] and CPR 16.4 [5.17], and for a precedent see BCCP B[7]. Note the ability to obtain a penalty as well as interest (£40 on a debt up to £1,000; £70 on a debt up to £10,000; and £100 above that figure). The rate of interest is 8% above bank base rate, which is currently 0.5%.			
An error in an invoice does not prevent there being a liability for late interest: *Ruttle Plant Hire Ltd v Secretary of State for the Environment, Food and Rural Affairs (No 3)* [2009] EWCA Civ 97, (2009) Times, 4 March, (2009) Sol Jo, Lawbrief 10 March, page 27.			
For 'remittal' (reduction in whole or part) under s 5 of the 1998 Act see the judgment in *Ruttle* and Lawbrief, above.			
For a case where the contract rate of interest was allowed although it had been negotiated at a time (2001) when			

TAB 1   PROCEDURAL TABLES

	Form No	CPR	PD
interest rates were considerably higher than those payable in the current climate, see *Taiwan Scot Ltd v The Master Golf Co Ltd* [2009] EWCA Civ 685, [2009] All ER (D) 221 (Jul).			
For the circumstances in which compound interest may be claimed see *Sempra Metals Ltd v IRC* [2007] UKHL 34, (2007) Times, 25 July and *Constantgreen v Customs Comrs* [2007] UKVAT V20303 where the test was expressed to be whether the taxpayer had to borrow to replace that which had been withheld. The effect of these decisions is not restricted to tax cases; for detailed consideration see article 'Bad pennies' by Crossley and Walsh in New Law Journal 14 September 2007, page 1254			
See further as to interest see **CPR 16.4** [0] to **CPR 16.4** [17] and articles in Gazette (2007) 18 October, page 29 and 25 October, page 29			
For interest on judgment debts in the county court see the County Courts (Interest on Judgment Debts) Order 1991, SI 1991/1184.			
If **aggravated damages, exemplary damages** or **provisional damages** are claimed, that must be stated and the ground for claiming them set out		16.4(1)(c) and (d)	
As a matter of pleading practice a claim for **disadvantage on the labour market** should be included in the particulars of injury but if omitted it will not be fatal where it is otherwise apparent from the pleadings: *Thorn v Powergen plc* [1997] PIQR Q71, CA; see also '*Smith v Manchester* awards', Butterworths Personal Injury Newsletter, October 2009, Vol 1, issue 8			
Any matters required to be set out in a **Practice Direction** must be included		16.4(1)(e)	
If the particulars of claim are separate from the claim form they must be verified by a **statement of truth**		22.1	
Besides the mandatory contents there are **additional requirements in particular cases:**			
personal injury claims – note that a schedule of details of any past and future losses claimed must be attached and the schedule of loss must be verified by a statement of truth. Further if the claimant is relying on the evidence of a medical practitioner the claimant must attach to or serve with his particulars of claim a medical report			16, para 4 and 22 para 1.5
fatal accident claims			16, para 5
hire purchase claims			16, para 6
injunction or declaration in respect of land, its possession, etc			16, para 7.1
return of goods			16, para 7.2

	Form No	CPR	PD
claim based on written agreement (unless claim issued from the Production Centre)			16, para 7.3 and 7, para 1.4(4)
claim based on oral agreement			16, para 7.4
claim based on agreement by conduct			16, para 7.5
consumer credit claim			16, para 7.6 7B, paras 7.1–7.4
It should be noted that where the agreement is regulated it is not appropriate to make an allowance for accelerated payment in the claim form. Judgment should be sought for the full amount; any refund will be given on settlement or enforcement of the judgment: *Forward Trust Ltd v Whymark* [1990] 2 QB 670, [1989] 3 All ER 915. For precedents see **BCCP K[1486]** and **BCCP K[1487]**			
where s11 or s12 of Civil Evidence Act 1968 is relied upon			16, para 8.1
where certain specific allegations, eg fraud or illegality are made			16, para 8.2
Besides the mandatory requirements and the additional requirement, the **particulars of claim may include:**			
(a) any point of law on which the claim is based			
(b) names of any witnesses			
(c) supporting documents (including an expert's report) attached			16, para 14.3
This provision enables particulars of claim to be "shaped" for the particular track to which the case is likely to be allocated. A small claim is given very little judicial case management and the particulars of claim can be drafted to cover, as much as is sensible of the claimant's statement, the aspects of which are supported by other evidence and the essential documents. If a point of law is involved this can also be dealt with. This will not be necessary on the fast track and on the multi-track, where disclosure and requests for information will be part of the normal procedure. The optional additions to the particulars of claim should be used sparingly on these tracks *Note: Morris v Bank of America National Trust* [2000] 1 All ER 954			
Contradictory statements are not permitted: *Clarke (Executor of the Will of Francis Bacon) v Marlborough Fine Arts (London) Ltd* [2002] 1 WLR 1731			
If the claim is to be served in Scotland, Northern Ireland or out of the United Kingdom without permission under rule 6.32 or 6.33 the statement required giving the grounds on which permission is not required must be filed with copies for service.		6.34	6B, para 2.1
8. Issue of the claim			
The claim form duly completed with notes for the defendant must be lodged			

TAB 1 PROCEDURAL TABLES

	Form No	CPR	PD
at or sent to the court office with a copy for sealing and return and a copy for each defendant. If the particulars of claim are attached (as opposed to endorsed) a similar number of copies is required	N1		
Unless the claimant is entitled to full or part remission or applies successfully for remission of the fees by reason of undue hardship, the **court fee on issue** must be paid. For sanctions for non-payment of fees see			3B
For county court fees see the Civil Proceedings Fees Order 2008, SI 2008/1053, Schedule 1 at FEE 1.8 in Volume 1 (fees were increased to their present level from 4 April 2011 and vary from £35 where the claim does not exceed £300 to £1,670 where the claim exceeds £300,000 or is unlimited),	EX50		
For full or part remission of fees see the Civil Proceedings (Fees) Order 2008, Schedule 2 at FEE 1.9 in Volume 1.	EX160A		
The proceedings are issued on or started on the issue date entered by the court staff on the claim form, but where the claim form was received in the court office before the date it is issued by the court, the claim is brought for the purposes of the Limitation Act 1980 and any relevant statute on that earlier date		7.2	7A, para 5.1
See further *Barnes v St Helens Metropolitan Borough Council* [2006] EWCA Civ 1372, (2006) Times, 17 November, [2007] 3 All ER 525 and article by Andrew Williams in New Law Journal 1 December 2006 1826			
The court date stamps the claim form held on the court file or the letter that accompanied it with the date of receipt			7A, para 5.2
Where issue is shortly before the expiry of any relevant limitation period, the claimant is best advised to lodge the forms with the court for issue and make his own note of the time and date of lodgment and the name of the court clerk who received the documents			7A, para 5.4
8.1 Procedure on issue of a money claim online			
The procedure to be followed on issue of, and when responding to, a claim electronically are set out in the PD			
Since 6 April 2009 where MCOL is being used or issue is through a production centre if the particulars of claim are too long to fit into the space available electronically, ie they exceed 1,080 characters including spaces, it is possible to serve them separately but the claimant must state the detailed particulars of claim will follow and include a brief summary of the claim.			
8.2 Fees			

	Form No	CPR	PD
Cheques and postal orders are required for designated money claims and cheques should be made payable to HM-CTS. Exemption from paying the fees, or paying only part, is explained in Leaflet EX160A. It is necessary to complete and submit form EX160 as evidence of means. Where exemption is claimed on the ground of receiving certain benefits a letter from DWP proving the current entitlement to the benefit has to be submitted in support.	EX160		

TABLE 2—START OF PROCEEDINGS FOR PART 8 CLAIMS

TAB 2

	Form No	CPR Rule	PD
1. Preliminary			
1.1 CPR Pt 8 provides an alternative procedure for use where:			
(a) the claimant seeks the court's decision on a question which is unlikely to involve a substantial dispute of fact, or		8.1(2)	
(b) where a Practice Direction permits or requires its use for the type of proceedings in question (although that Practice Direction may modify or disapply the Part 8 procedure and if so that Practice Direction must be complied with)		8.1(2) and (6)	
1.2 'Schedule rules' means rules previously contained in RSC or CCR			8, para 1
1.3 CPR PD 8 para 3 is divided into sections A, B and C			8, para 2.1
(i) Section A contains general provisions about Part 8 claims and applications (paras 3.1-3.5)			
(ii) Section B comprises a table listing claims etc which **must** be made under Part 8			
(iii) Section C contains variations to the Part 8 procedure that apply to the claims and applications identified			
Note:			
• Practice Direction to CPR Pt 21, para 6.1 provides that a claim by or against a child or protected party or brought solely to obtain the approval of the court must be made using the Part 8 procedure			8, section A, para 3.1(1)
• CPR PD 8, Section A, para 3.1(2) provides that a claim for provisional damages which has been settled prior to proceedings but is to be the subject of a consent judgment, may be made under CPR Pt 8 (but see CPR PD 41 para 4.1)			8, section A, para 3.1(2)
• The court may at any stage order the claim to continue as if the claimant had not used the Part 8 procedure and give any directions it considers appropriate. The directions may include allocation to track. For the consequences of not so allocating see para **CPR 8 [8]**		8.1(3)	
• The defendant may object to the use of the Part 8 procedure and must state the reasons for his ob-			

TAB 2 PROCEDURAL TABLES

		Form No	CPR Rule	PD
	jection when he files his acknowledgment		8.8 and 8.8(1)	8, section A, para 5.3
2. The contents of the claim form				
A Part 8 claim form must be used and must state:				
(a)	that CPR Pt 8 applies		8.2(a)	
(b)	(i) the question which the claimants wants the court to decide or		8.2(b)	
	(ii) the remedy which the claimant is seeking and the legal basis for the claim to that remedy			
(c)	if the claim is being made under an enactment, what that enactment is		8.2(c)	
(d)	if the claimant is claiming in a representative capacity, what the capacity is		8.2(d)	
(e)	if the defendant is sued in a representative capacity, what that capacity is		8.2(e)	
(f)	if the claim is to be served in Scotland, Northern Ireland or out of the United Kingdom without permission under rule 6.32 or 6.33 the statement required giving the grounds on which permission is not required must be filed with the copies for service.		6.34	6B, para 2.1
(g)	the claim form or the particulars of claim must contain a statement whether Sections III and IV of the Practice Direction (Pre-action Conduct) and any relevant protocol have been complied with.			Practice Direction (Pre-action conduct), para 9.7
The claim form must be verified by a statement of truth			Part 22	
Where the claimant seeks to recover an additional liability, information about the funding arrangement must be provided with the claim form and a copy of any notice of funding should be filed with copies for service.			44.15	6A, para 8.2
3. Special provisions				
The claimant must use the Part 8 procedure if the claim, petition or application is listed in the table in Section B, para 9.3 but where the listed claim is identified as one to which particular provisions of Section C apply the Part 8 procedure shall apply subject to the additions and modifications set out in the relevant paragraph in Section C				
4. Issuing the claim				
The general provisions of CPR Pt 7 and the Practice Direction that accompanies it will apply to Part 8 claims where appropriate				8, para 4.1
The Part 8 claim form must be used		N208		
The claimant must file any written evidence on which he intends to rely when he files his claim form: this must be				

	Form No	CPR Rule	PD
served on the defendant with the claim form unless an extension of time is granted		8.5(1) and (2)	8, paras 7.4 and 7.5
Information about funding arrangements must be filed with the claim form			
See also		44.15	6A, para 8.2
5. Defendant			
For the procedure to be followed by the defendant, see **TAB 7**			

TABLE 3—SANCTIONS, AVOIDANCE AND RELIEF

TAB 3

	Form No	CPR Rule	PD
1. Imposition of sanctions and types of sanction			
1.1 The long-standing power of the court to include in an order a sanction on default is reflected and repeated by CPR 3.1(3)(b) which provides that there is power to specify the consequences of non-compliance		3.1(3)(b)	
1.2 An order containing such a provision is frequently called an 'unless order'			
1.3 The consequence of non-compliance is frequently that the case of the defaulting party be struck out or do stand struck out in whole or in part.			
2. Consequences of non-compliance			
2.1 In *Marcan Shipping* (see above) it was clearly stated a sanction should not be imposed unless the consequences can be justified			
2.2 Those consequences of default are that the sanctions will: • take effect if there is not complete compliance: *Jani-King (GB) Ltd v Prodger* [2007] EWHC 712 (QB), [2007] All ER (D) 505 (Mar) • take effect automatically without the necessity of a further order, see *E Group Ltd v Bay Baker* [2008] EWHC 2349 (TCC), (2008) 18 September, unreported (Coulson J) • prevent any argument that it is not an appropriate consequence of the non-compliance			3A, para 1.9
2.3 Where a claim has been struck out for the claimant's failure to comply with an 'unless' order the claimant can no longer accept a Part 36 offer to settle: *Joyce v West Bus Coach Services* (2012) Times, 21 May (QB), Kenneth Parker J.			
2.4 For a recent case in which the Court of Appeal upheld the striking out of a claim under CPR 3.4(2)(c) for failure to comply with an unless order for specific disclosure, exchange of statements and delivery of a trial bundle see *Maqsood v Mahmood* [2012] EWCA Civ 251.			
3. Avoidance of the sanction			
3.1 The sanction can only be prevented from taking effect by complete performance by the date specified. It is almost invariably the case that failure to comply with the date specified is the breach relied on			

TAB 3 PROCEDURAL TABLES

	Form No	CPR Rule	PD
3.2 Besides the necessity of making a diary note of the date for compliance it is also necessary to note an earlier date when an assessment must be made of whether the time limit can be met. That earlier date must be sufficiently before the compliance date to allow steps to be taken to avoid non-compliance			
3.3 The most obvious step is to seek to agree with the opposing party an extension of time for compliance; if agreement is forthcoming the court should be informed		2.11	
If the time limit is part of a management timetable and the extension will necessitate a change in the date for delivery of the pre-trial check list, the trial window or the trial, an application, albeit by consent, will be necessary	N244	28.4 and 29.5	
3.4 If the opposing party refuses to agree the extension an application on notice should be made to the court for an extension supported by evidence of why it is required, the extra time required and how this has been calculated and the disproportionate effect of refusal taking into account the overriding objective. It is vital to seek a realistic extension of time for an extension to a date that will be insufficient to achieve complete compliance will be of no value to the applicant; it will merely be putting off the evil day.			
For forms of judgment for failure to comply with an 'unless' order see	PF 85A and 85B		
The court has power to extend the time for compliance with a court order and grant relief from a sanction contained in it even when the order was made by consent: *Pannone v Aardvark Digital Ltd* [2011] EWCA Civ 803, (2011) Times, 30 August. In this case the sanction was expressed to apply on the failure of the claimant to file documents. It was a few minutes late when the documents were received by fax; the court granted relief and extended time.			
4. Review of the position where sanction is likely to take effect			
Where it is apparent that it is unlikely that it will be possible to comply with an unless order the party adversely affected should:			
(a) carefully consider whether the unless order was **defective** by reason of impossibility of performance when it was made, eg where the unless order is simply to comply with an earlier order within, say, 14 days of service. If the time specified for compliance had already passed when the unless order was made clearly the unless order would be defective and could be set aside.			

	Form No	CPR Rule	PD
(b) consider an appeal.			
5. Where an unless order has not been complied with – application for relief			
5.1 See *Sayers v Clarke Walker (a firm)* [2002] EWCA Civ 645, [2002] 3 All ER 490, [2002] 1 WLR 3095 where Brooke LJ stated that in the event of non-compliance a defaulting party has to seek relief from the sanction by an **application under CPR 3.8** and in that event the court will consider all the matters raised in CPR 3.9 as far as they are relevant.			
5.2 The court has power to dispense with the filing of an application notice and grant relief, see *Keen Philips (a firm) v Field* [2006] EWCA Civ 1524, [2007] 1 WLR 686 where the court did dispense with the application notice, granted relief against the sanction and extended the time for compliance.			
5.3 In the case of *Supperstone v Hurst* [2008] EWHC 735 (Ch) after stating:			
'If a party does not have a good explanation or the other side is prejudiced by the failure relief from sanctions will normally be refused. It is vitally important that rules of procedure are observed.'			
Mr Justice Floyd provided practical guidelines for those seeking or opposing an application for relief against sanctions imposed by the rules. Two points in particular are to be noted:			
(i) the exercise of the discretion in accordance with the rules to grant or refuse relief, which is not flawed, is not open to challenge by appeal;			
(ii) if the defendant maintains he has been prejudiced he must put in evidence to that effect. He cannot rely on the applicant's failure to prove there is no prejudice.			
5.4 Where the sanction imposed was a stay of proceedings the claimant cannot avoid the stay by bringing fresh proceedings on facts that are not new and were capable of being pursued in the original stayed action. The second action would be struck out as an abuse of process: *Watson v Irwin Mitchell* [2009] EWHC 441 (QB), [2009] All ER (D) 113 (Mar).			
5.5 In *Azeez v Momson* [2009] EWCA Civ 202, [2009] All ER (D) 193 (Mar) the application for relief again failed. One of the grounds was based on Article 6 of the European Convention on Human Rights but although the refusal of relief would deprive the Appellant of a trial the court held it served a 'legitimate claim' since the order was made to achieve a fair trial of the claim.			
6. Service of the application for relief and evidence in support			

TAB 3 PROCEDURAL TABLES

	Form No	CPR Rule	PD
6.1 The filing, notice and service of the application must be in accordance with CPR 23; see **TAB 14**, para 3 below			
6.2 The application must be supported by written evidence and it is not open to the applicant to argue against the propriety of the terms of the order or the sanction; see para 4.1(b) above. The evidence should be prepared keeping in mind that the court will take into account the circumstances listed in CPR 3.9 and it is sensible to shape the evidence to deal with those considerations in turn: see, for example, the judgment of Mackay J in *Jani-King (GB) Ltd v Prodger* [2007] EWHC 712 (QB) at para 22. This was a case where the unless order was made and where having described an unless order as giving a 'last chance' the judge granted relief on terms.			
6.3 The evidence should also make it clear what has been done in an attempt to comply with the order and what has so far been achieved. It should also set out any obstacles that have arisen since the making of the order which were not then envisaged.			
6.4 The evidence should set out what time will be required to comply if relief is granted and should show how that period of time has been calculated.			
6.5 The evidence should include an apology for the failure to comply but stress that the default was not contumelous. Costs should in almost all cases be conceded			
7. Costs			
It is almost inevitable that the party in default will be liable for the costs			

TABLE 4—SERVICE OF CLAIM FORMS WITHIN THE JURISDICTION AND EEA

TAB 4

	Form No	CPR Rule	PD
Preliminary			
It is important to remember that it is not necessary to serve particulars of claim, schedule of loss and medical report with the claim form. If the limitation period is about to expire and the documents to accompany the claim form are not available the claim form should be served and an application made pursuant to CPR 3.1(2)(a) for an extension of time for service of the particulars of claim. The court has greater flexibility on such an application than on an application to extend time for the service of the claim form under CPR 7.6		3.1(2)(a)	
1. Service by the court			
1.1 Subject to Part IV and the rules in this section relating to service out of the jurisdiction on solicitors, European lawyers and parties, if the claimant notifies the court that he wishes to serve, the court will serve the claim form unless the court otherwise orders or directs		6.4(1)	
Service must be within the jurisdiction unless it is being effected by service on a solicitor in Scotland or Northern Ireland or EEA state other than the United Kingdom (r 6.7(2)) or on a European lawyer or in any EEA state (r 6.7(3)) or by a contractually agreed method pursuant to r 6.11 or unless the provisions for service out of the jurisdiction (see **TAB 5** below) are complied with.		6.6(1)	
The claimant must include in the claim form an address for service including a full postcode or its EEA equivalent.		6.6(2)	
The court will decide upon the method of service which will normally be first class post.		6.4(2)	6A, para 8.1
Where the court is to serve the claimant must file a copy of the claim form for each defendant in addition to the copy for the court.		6.4(3)	
1.2 Where the court serves a claim for the court will send to the claimant a notice which will include the date of deemed service under rule 6.14; see para 4 of this **TAB** below.			
• Note where the claimant serves the claim form the claimant must file a certificate in accordance with rule 6.17(2) and (3), unless all defendants have filed acknowledgments within 21 days of service of the par-			

TAB 4 PROCEDURAL TABLES

	Form No	CPR Rule	PD
ticulars of claim. Judgment in default of acknowledgment cannot be obtained unless a certificate of service has been filed.		6.17(2)	6A, para 7
1.3 Where the court serves the claim form by post and it is returned to the court the court will notify the claimant of its return but the claim form will be deemed to have been served unless the address for the defendant on the claim form is not the relevant address for the purposes of rules 6.7 to 6.10.		6.18	
1.4 Where the bailiff is to serve a claim form and is unable to do so the court will so notify the claimant.		6.19	
1.5 The court will not make further efforts to serve after it has notified the claimant of the outcome of postal service or given notice of non-service by the bailiff.			
2. Methods of service			
2.1 Must be within the jurisdiction – save as set out in this TAB at 1.1 above		6.6(1)	
2.2 **Personal service** is mandatory where any other part, Practice direction or court order provides this method must be used.		6.3(a) 6.5(1)	
Personal service of a claim form may be effected (except where rule 6.7, service on a solicitor, or rule 6.10, service on the crown, apply)		6.5(2)	
(a) on an individual by leaving it with that individual		6.5(3)(a)	
(b) on a company or other corporation by leaving it with a person holding a senior position (defined in Practice Direction 6A)		6.5(3)(b)	6A, para 6.2
(c) on a partnership where partners are being sued in the firm name by leaving it with a partner or a person who, at the time of service has control or management of the partnership business at its principal place of business.		6.5(3)(c)	6A, para 4
2.3 **First class post, document exchange** or other service providing for delivery on the next business day in accordance with Practice Direction 6A		6.3(1)(b)	
for 'document exchange' see			6A, para 2.1
2.4 **Leaving it** at		6.3(1)(c)	
(a) **the business address of a solicitor or European lawyer** within the jurisdiction or in any other EEA state where the provisions of 6.7(1)(a) or (b) are satisfied. These are **Solicitor within the jurisdiction** — subject to r 6.5(1) where: (i) the defendant has given in writing the business address		6.7(1)	

		Form No	CPR Rule	PD
	within the jurisdiction of a solicitor as an address at which the defendant may be served with the claim form; or			
(ii)	a solicitor acting for the defendant has notified the claimant in writing that the solicitor is instructed by the defendant to accept service of the claim form on behalf of the defendant at a business address within the jurisdiction			
	the claim form must be served at the business address of that solicitor.		6.2(d)	
•	Note the extended definition of solicitor in the preliminary paragraphs of this TAB			
•	Note also that, subject to rule 6.5(1) above, where rule 6.7 applies service must be effected in accordance with its provisions and not in any other way.			
(aa)	**Solicitor in Scotland of Northern Ireland or EEA state other than the United Kingdom** — subject to r 6.5(1) where:		6.7(2)	
(i)	the defendant has given in writing the business address in Scotland or Northern Ireland of a solicitor as an address at which the defendant may be served with the claim form;			
(ii)	a solicitor acting for the defendant has notified the claimant in writing that the solicitor is instructed by the defendant to accept service of the claim form on behalf of the defendant at a business address within Scotland or Northern Ireland;			

TAB 4 PROCEDURAL TABLES

			Form No	CPR Rule	PD
	(iii)	the claimant has given in writing the business address within any other EEA state of a solicitor as an address at which the defendant may be served with the claim form;			
	(iv)	a solicitor acting for the defendant has notified the claimant in writing that the solicitor is instructed by the defendant to accept service of the claim form on behalf of the defendant at a business address within any other EEA state, the claim form must be served at the business address of that solicitor.			
(ab)	**European lawyer in any EEA state:** see 6.7(3) and its footnote as to Production Centre Claims, Money Claims Online and Possession Claims online			6.7(3)	
(b)	Where rules 6.5(1) and 6.7 above do not apply and subject to the provisions of Section IV, at an address at which the defendant resides or carries on business within the United Kingdom or any other EEA state that the defendant has given before service for the purpose of being served with the proceedings or (in a claim by a tenant) the address given by a landlord under s 48 of the Landlord and Tenant Act 1987. See the footnote to rule 6.8 as to the Production Centre, Money Claims Online and Possession Claims Online.			6.8	
(c)	where rules 6.5(1), 6.7 and 6.8 do not apply and the defendant does not give an address for service he must be served at the appropriate place for the defendant given by the table set out in rule 6.9(2); provided that if the claimant has reason to believe the defendant is an individual and no longer resides at the address shown in the table to the belief of the claimant, he must take reasonable steps to ascertain the defendant's current residence or place of business and serve there.			6.9, 6.9(3)	
2.5 By fax or other electronic means in accordance with				6.3(d)	

	Form No	CPR Rule	PD
2.6 On a **company** by any method under CPR Part 6 (see however *SSL International plc v TTK LIG Ltd* [2011] EWCA Civ 1170, in which it was held if a company does not carry on business and is not present within the jurisdiction personal service of a claim form may not be effected by leaving it with a person holding a 'senior position within the company') or in accordance with the methods of service permitted under **Companies Act 1985** or the **Companies Act 2006**		6.3(2)	6A, para 6
2.7 A **limited liability partnership** may be served by any of the methods of service permitted by CPR Part 6 or by any of the methods of service permitted under the Companies Act 2006 as applied with modifications by regulations made under the Limited Liability Partnership Act 2000.		6.3(3)	
2.8 For service on an **overseas company** under s 685 of the Companies Act 1985, s 685A of the Companies Act 1985 (inserted in 1992) or s 1139(2) of the Companies Act 2006, see **CPR 6.3 [2]**; to discover whether a person resident in the UK has been nominated to accept service on the company's behalf and if so the registered address of the person so nominated, communicate with Companies House which will supply the information on the telephone.			
2.9 **Special cases:**			
(a) in proceedings against the Crown see		6.10	
(b) by a contractually agreed method for the effect of a contractual term that service should be 'either delivered personally or . . . ' see *Primus Build Ltd v Pompey Centre* [2009] EWHC 1487 (TCC), [2009] All ER (D) 14 (Jul).		6.11	
(c) in relation to a contract no an agent of a principal who is out of the jurisdiction see		6.12	
(d) on children and protected persons see		6.13	
(e) on members of the regular forces see			6A, para 5 and Annex
3. Place of service			
3.1 The claim form must be served within the jurisdiction save as set out in this TAB at para 1.1 above.			
Unless the court under rule 6.15, see below at para 5 of this **TAB**, specified the place or method of service the claimant must include in the claim form an address, complete with postcode or its equivalent in any EEA state, if appropriate, at which the defendant may be served.		6.6(2)	
4. Deemed service			

TAB 4 PROCEDURAL TABLES

	Form No	CPR Rule	PD
A claim form served within the United Kingdom is deemed to be served on the **second business day** after completion of the relevant step contained in the table set out in rule 7.5(1):		6.14	

Method of service	Step required
First class post, document exchange or other service which provides for delivery on the next business day	Posting, leaving with, delivering to or collection by the relevant service provider
Delivery of the document to or leaving it at the relevant place	Delivering to or leaving the document at the relevant place
Personal service under rule 6.5	Completing the relevant step required by rule 6.5(3)
Fax	Completing the transmission of the fax
Other electronic method	Sending the e-mail or other electronic transmission

	Form No	CPR Rule	PD
For business day see the definition at rule 6.2(b)			
5. Service of the claim form by an alternative method or at an alternative place			
Where there appears to the court there is good reason to do so it may make an order for service of the claim form by an alternative method or at an alternative place.		6.15	
An order can be sought by application supported by evidence and may be made without notice.	N244	6.15(1)	
On an application under this rule the court may order that steps already taken to bring the claim form to the defendant's attention by an alternative method or alternative place is good service. It should be noted that this is a power to make a retrospective order.		6.15(2)	
An order under this rule must specify: (a) the method or place of service (b) the place of service (c) the period for filing, acknowledgment and admission or defence			6A, para 9
Where service by an alternative method or at an alternative place is permitted by an order under rule 6.15 the fixed cost allowed for each individual served is £52.25.		45.5, Table 4	
6. Dispensing with service			
6.1 The court may dispense with service of a claim form in exceptional circumstances.		6.9	
6.2 An application seeking such an order should be made in accordance with			

	Form No	CPR Rule	PD
CPR Part 23 and must be supported by evidence. See further paras 7.6 and 7.7 of this **TAB**	N244	6.16	
7. Time for service and extension of time for the service of claim form			
7.1 Service within the jurisdiction must be effected before 12.00 midnight on the calendar day 4 months after the date of issue (ie the time for service runs from the day after issue) but the period is extended where the claim is for service out of the jurisdiction to 'within 6 months of the date of issue'		7.5	
7.2 The claimant may apply for an order to extend the time for serving a claim form. The general rule is that an application to extend time for compliance **must** be made within the period for serving the claim form under CPR 7.5 or when an order extending time has already been made, within the extended time allowed.			
7.3 If the claimant applies to extend time **after the time for compliance under rule 7.5** or under an order under this rule, the court can **only** make an order under this rule if:			
(a) the court has failed to serve the claim form, or			
(b) the claimant has taken all reasonable steps to effect service in accordance with rule 7.5 but has been unable to do so, and			
(c) In either case the claimant has acted promptly in making the application.			
These are mandatory requirements and in their absence the court has no discretion to extend time.			
7.4 Any application to extend time must be supported by evidence and may be made without notice. Rule 23.8 also permits the courts to deal with an application without a hearing. For the position where the application is refused or not granted in full on paper see *Leeson v Marsden, Glass v Surrendram and conjoined appeals* (2006) Times, 3 February, CA. The court stressed the danger of important applications made without notice being dealt with without a hearing		7.6(4)	
7.5 The court in *Dickins v Solicitors Indemnity Fund* [2007] EWHC 2754 (Ch), [2007] All ER (D) 298 (Oct) at paragraph 26 stated that on a rehearing '. . . the proper question is whether the order under re-consideration should have been made at the time it was made'.			
7.6 It was held in *Godwin v Swindon Borough Council* [2001] EWCA Civ 1478, [2001] 4 All ER 641, [2001] 1 WLR 997, CA that **the power to dis-**			

TAB 4 PROCEDURAL TABLES

	Form No	CPR Rule	PD
pense with service pursuant to CPR 6.9 (from 1 October 2008 replaced by CPR 6.16) should not be used to circumvent the restrictions on the grant of extensions of time imposed by CPR 7.6(3). See also *Mutifa Kuenyebia v International Hospitals Group Ltd* [2006] EWCA Civ 21 (para 26), (2006) Times, 17 February where the court considered Godwin and the case of Wilkey, see para 7.8 of this TAB above, and gave the following guidance:			
(a) an exceptional case will be required for the court to dispense with service where the time for service has expired;			
(b) the power is unlikely to be exercised save where either the claimant has made an ineffective attempt to serve in time or has served in a manner which involved a minor departure from one of those permitted methods of service;			
(c) it would not be possible to give an exhaustive list of the circumstances where an order dispensing with service could be properly made.		6.16 (formerly 6.9)	
7.7 In *Anderton v Clwyd County Council* [2002] EWCA Civ 933, [2002] 3 All ER 813 it was stated that generally applications for retrospective orders to dispense with service would be dealt with in accordance with *Godwin* (see 7.6 above) but exceptionally it might be appropriate to dispense with service. There were different considerations where the claimant had made no effort to serve as opposed to cases where claimant had already made ineffective attempts to serve by one of the permitted methods.			
7.8 In *Wilkey v BBC* [2002] EWCA Civ 1561, [2002] 4 All ER 1177 it was held that in cases involving late deemed service after the decision in *Anderton* ie after 3 July 2002 (see paragraph 7.6 above) the dispensing power will not ordinarily be exercised in the claimant's favour. For the power to be exercised in the claimant's favour the circumstances must be truly exceptional as perhaps for some very minor departure from the permitted method of service. For a case where the circumstances were considered to be exceptional and the power to dispense under CPR r 6.9 was exercised in favour of the claimant see *Olafsson v Gissurarson (No 2)* [2006] EWHC 3214 (QB), (2006) Times, 22 December following *Phillips v Nussberger* [2006] EWCA Civ 654, [2006] 3 All ER 838.			
7.9 It may well be that as a result of the new CPR 7.6(3) which came into force			

	Form No	CPR Rule	PD
on 1 October 2008 that in cases involving late deemed service the dispensing power will not be exercised save where the court would be prepared to extend time under rule 7.6(1).			
7.10 The court's power to extend time, dispense with service and correct a procedural error cannot be used to extend a statutory time limit or requirement as to service: *Mucelli v Government of Albania* [2009] UKHL 2, [2009] 3 All ER 1035, [2009] 1 WLR 276			

TABLE 5—SERVICE OF CLAIM FORM OUTSIDE THE JURISDICTION

TAB 5

	Form No	CPR Rule	PD
1. Preliminary			
• as to service of a claim form on an agent of a principal who is overseas see:		6.12	
1.1 Information concerning service out of the jurisdiction can be obtained from the Foreign Process Section, Room E02, Royal Courts of Justice, Strand, London, WC2A 2LL (tel: 020 7947 6691)			
1.2 CPR Part 6 Section IV contains rules as to:		6.30	
(a) service out of the jurisdiction;			
(b) obtaining permission of the court to serve out of the jurisdiction when that is required; and			
(c) the procedure for serving out of the jurisdiction			
2. Definitions			
2.1 For definitions generally see		6.31	
2.2 In particular note that for the purposes of CPR (and of this table):			
• 'the 1982 Act' means the Civil Jurisdiction and Judgments Act 1982		6.31(b)	
• 'claim form' includes petition and any application notice made before action or to commence proceedings		6.2(c)	
• 'Civil Procedure Convention' means the Brussels and Lugano Conventions (as defined in s 1(1) of the 1982 Act) and any other Convention (including the Hague Convention) entered into by the UK regarding service out of the jurisdiction		6.31(c)	
• the 'Judgments Regulation' means Council Regulation (EC) No 44/2001 of 22 December 2000		6.31(d)	
• the 'Service Regulation' means Council Regulation (EC) No 1393/2007 on service in member states of judicial and extra judicial documents in civil or commercial matters		6.31(e)	
3. Service out of the jurisdiction where the permission of the court is not required – Scotland and Northern Ireland		6.32	
3.1 The claimant may serve the claim form on a defendant in Scotland or Northern Ireland where each claim is a claim which the court has the power to determine under the 1982 Act and:			

TAB 5 PROCEDURAL TABLES

	Form No	CPR Rule	PD
(a) no proceedings between the parties concerning the same are pending in the courts of any other part of the United Kingdom; and			
(b) (i) the defendant is domiciled in the United Kingdom;			
(ii) the proceedings are within para 11 of Sch 4 to the 1982 Act; or			
(iii) the defendant is a party to an agreement conferring the jurisdiction within para 12 of Sch 4 to the 1982 Act.		6.32(1)	
3.2 The claimant may serve the claim form on a defendant in Scotland or Northern Ireland where each claim is a claim which the court has the power to determine under **any enactment other than the 1982 Act** notwithstanding that:			
(a) the person against whom the claim is made is not within the jurisdiction; or			
(b) the facts giving rise to the claim did not occur within the jurisdiction.		6.32(2)	
4. Service of the claim form where permission is not required out of the United Kingdom			
4.1 For claims that the court has power to determine under the 1982 Act or the Lugano Convention see		6.33(1)	
4.2 For claims that the court has power to determine under the Judgments Regulation see		6.33(2)	
4.3 For claims that the court has power to determine other than under the 1982 Act or the Lugano Convention or the Judgments Regulation see		6.33(3)	
5. Notice of statement of grounds where permission is not required for service			
5.1 Where a claimant intends to serve a claim under rule 6.32 (Scotland or Northern Ireland) or 6.33 (outside the UK) the claimant must:			
(a) file with the claim form a notice containing a statement of the grounds on which the claimant is entitled to serve the claim form out of the United Kingdom;			
(b) serve a copy of that notice with the claim form	N510	6.34(1)	6B, para 2.1
Until the claimant files the notice the claim form can only be served with the court's permission		6.34(2)	
6. Period for responding to a claim form when permission is not required			
6.1 The periods for filing and acknowledgment of service, an admission or a defence to a claim form served out of the jurisdiction under rules 6.32 and 6.33 (above) are			

	Form No	CPR Rule	PD
(a) on a defendant in Scotland or Northern Ireland as set out in		6.35(2)	
(b) on a defendant in a Convention territory within Europe or a Member State under rule 6.33 as set out in		6.35(3)	
(c) on a defendant in a Convention territory outside Europe under rule 6.33 as set out in		6.35(4)	
(d) on a defendant elsewhere as set out in		6.35(5)	
7. Service out of the jurisdiction where the permission of the court is required			
7.1 In any proceedings to which 6.32 or 6.33 above (service of the claim form) do not apply the claimant may serve a claim form out of the jurisdiction with the permission of the court if any of the grounds set out in para 3.1 of Practice Direction 6B apply.		6.36	6B, para 3.1(1)–(20)
7.2 There are 20 grounds (often referred to as 'jurisdictional gateways') set out in PD 6B, para 3.1, divided into 11 groups			
8. Application for permission to serve the claim form out of the jurisdiction			
8.1 The application must set out:			
(a) which paragraph of PD 6B, para 3.1 is relied on;			
(b) that the claimant believes the claim has a reasonable prospect of success; and			
(c) the defendant's address or, if not known, in what place the defendant is, or is likely to be, found		6.37(1)	
8.2 Where the application is made in respect of a claim referred to in para 3.1(3) of PD 6B (service on another person who is a necessary or proper party) the application must also state the grounds on which the claimant believes that there is between the claimant and the defendant a real issue which is reasonable for the court to try.		6.37(2)	
8.3 The court will not give permission unless satisfied that England and Wales is the proper place to bring the claim			
8.4 Where permission is sought to serve a claim form in Scotland or Northern Ireland and it appears the claimant may also be entitled to as remedy there, in deciding whether to give permission the court will:			
(a) compare the relative costs and convenience; and			
(b) (where relevant) have regard to the relative powers and jurisdiction.		6.37(4)	
8.5 When the court gives permission to serve a claim form out of the jurisdiction it will specify the periods within which the defendant may:			
(a) file an acknowledgment of service;			

TAB 5 PROCEDURAL TABLES

	Form No	CPR Rule	PD
(b) file or serve an admission;			
(c) file a defence; or			
(d) file any other response or document required by a rule in another Part, any other enactment or a practice direction			
and the court may			
(a) give directions about the method of service; and			
(b) give permission for other documents in the proceedings to be served out of the jurisdiction			
9. Methods of service of a claim form on a party out of the jurisdiction			
9.1 Where a claim form is served on a party **in Scotland or Northern Ireland** he must be served by a method permitted in Section II of CPR 6 (serving a claim form within the jurisdiction)		6.40(2)	
9.2 Where a **party out of the United Kingdom** is to be served with a claim form it my be served:			
(a) (i) in accordance with the Service Regulations as provided by rule 6.41;			
(ii) through foreign government, judicial authorities and British Consular authorities as provided by rule 6.44			
(iii) CPR 6.27 (service on a State) or			
(b) by any method permitted by a Civil Procedure Convention; or Treaty; or			
(c) by any other method permitted by the law of the country in which it is to be served.		6.40(3)	
But it is specifically provided that nothing in rule 6.40(3) above or in any court order authorises or requires any person to do anything which is contrary to the law of the country where the claim form is to be served.		6.40(4)	
10. Service in accordance with the Service Regulation			
10.1 The Service Regulation is annexed to CPR PD 6B.			
10.2 Where a party wishes to serve the claim form under the Service Regulation the claimant must file:			
(a) the claim form;			
(b) any transaction; and			
(c) any other documents required by the Service Regulation.			
The court officer will forward the relevant document to the Senior Master			
Rule 6.47 (proof of service before obtaining judgment) does not apply to service in accordance with this Regulation.			

	Form No	CPR Rule	PD
The Regulation prevails over other provisions contained in any other agreement or arrangement concluded by Member States. The Regulation does nto apply to service in the EEA states that are not Member States fo the EU.		6.41 (parenthesis)	
11. Service through foreign governments, judicial authorities and British Consular authorities		6.42	
11.1 Where service of the claim form on a party is to be effected in any country which is a party to a Civil Procedure Convention or Treaty see		6.42(1)	
11.2 Where service of the claim form on a party is to be effected in any country with respect to which there is no Civil Procedure Convention or Treaty see		6.42(2)	
11.3 Where service of the claim form on a party is to be effected in: (a) any Commonwealth state which is not a party to the Hague Convention or is such a party but HM Government has not declared acceptance, (b) the Isle of Man or Channel Islands, or (c) any British overseas territory			
The methods of service under 11.1, ie 6.42(1), and 11.2, ie 6.42(2), are not available and the claimant or claimant's agent must effect service direct unless PD 6B provides otherwise.		6.42(3)	
12. The procedure where service is through foreign governments, judicial authorities and British Consular authorities		6.43	
12.1 Rule 6.43 applies where the party wishes to serve a claim form under rule 6.42(1) or 6.42(2) (see 11.1 and 11.2 above)		6.43(2)	
12.2 A party must provide the documents listed in PD 6B, para 4.1 for each party to be served out of the jurisdiction.			6B, para 4
12.3 The court on filing will seal the copy of the claim form and forward the documents to the Senior Master		6.43(3)	
12.4 When service has been effected an official certificate will be issued pursuant to rule 6.43(5) which is evidence of the facts stated in the certificate		6.43(5)	
13. Service of a claim form on a State see		6.44	
14. Translation of Claim Form see		6.45	
14.1 Every copy of a claim form filed under rule 6.43 (service through foreign governments, judicial authorities, etc) or 6.44 (service on a State) must be accompanied by a translation of the claim form; but the translation is not required where the claim form is to be served: (a) in a country of which English is an official language		6.45(2)	

TAB 5 PROCEDURAL TABLES

	Form No	CPR Rule	PD
(b) on a British citizen unless a Civil Procedure Convention or Treaty requires a translation		6.45(4)	
14.2 The party is not required to file a translation of a claim form under 6.44 (service of a claim form on a State) where English is an official language of the State in which the claim form is to be served.			
• The Service Regulation contains provision about the service of documents.		6.45(5)	
15. Undertaking to be responsible for expenses			
15.1 Every request for service under rule 6.43 (service through foreign governments, judicial authorities, etc) or 6.44 (service on a State) must contain an undertaking by the person making the request:			
(a) to be responsible for all expenses incurred by the Foreign and Commonwealth Officer or foreign judicial authority; and			
(b) to pay those expenses on being informed of their amount.		6.46	
16. Proof of service			
16.1 When:			
(a) a hearing is fixed when the claim is issued			
(b) a defendant is served with the claim form out of the jurisdiction and			
(c) that defendant does not appear at the hearing			
the claimant may take not obtain judgment until he files written evidence that the claim form has been duly served in accordance with Part IV of CPR 6.			
This rule does not apply where service is effected under the Service Regulation. The 'receiving agency' is required to effect service and to complete and file a certificate at the court.			
17. Extension of time for service out of jurisdiction			
For the principles to be applied when an application is made for an extension of time for service outside the jurisdiction, ie 6 months from issue, see *Sodastream Ltd (in liq) v Coates* [2009] EWHC 1936 (Ch), [2009] All ER (D) 22 (Aug), 13 July, unreported.		7.5(2)	

TABLE 6—ACKNOWLEDGMENT OF SERVICE OF PART 7 CLAIM

TAB 6

	Form No	CPR Rule	PD
1. Preliminary			
A defendant may file an acknowledgment of service		10.1(3)	
• if he is not able to file a defence within the time allowed		15.4	
• if he disputes the court's jurisdiction		Part 11	
2. Completion of the form			
The form of acknowledgment is included in the Response Pack served on the defendant	N9		
The defendant must set out his full name (if it is different to the name given on the claim form) and the address within the jurisdiction to which documents should be sent to him. Any reference and the telephone number are to be included and, if applicable, fax number, DX number and e-mail details			10, para 5.1
A party's address for service must be:		6.23	
(1) the business address within the United Kingdom or any other EEA state of the solicitor of the party to be served; and			
(2) where there is no solicitor acting an address within the United Kingdom where the party resides or carries on business.			
Where the defendant's name has been incorrectly stated in the claim, after stating his correct name the defendant should add "described as" and the incorrect name			
The defendant must "tick" the appropriate box from:			
"I intend to defend all of this claim"			
"I intend to defend part of this claim"			
"I intend to contest jurisdiction"			10, para 5.2
3. Signature of the forms			
The form must be signed by the defendant or the defendant's legal representative. Where the acknowledgment is signed by a legal representative, the address for service must be the legal representative's business address. Otherwise the address for service that is given should be as set out in r 6.5 and Practice Direction 6B (r 6.23).		2.3	
Where the defendant is a company or other corporation, a person holding a senior position in the company or corporation may sign the form on the defen-			

TAB 6   PROCEDURAL TABLES

	Form No	CPR Rule	PD
dant's behalf, but he must state the position he holds			10, para 4.2
For a "person holding a senior position", see			10, para 4.3
Where the defendant is a partnership:			
(a) service must be acknowledged in the name of the partnership on behalf of all persons who were partners at the time the cause of action arose and			
(b) the acknowledgment of service may be signed by any of those partners or by any person authorised by any of those partners to sign it			10, para 4.4
Children or protected parties can only acknowledge service by their litigation friend or legal representative, unless the court otherwise orders			10, para 4.5
4. Period for filing			
Where the particulars of claim are served with the claim form the period for filing the acknowledgment of service is 14 days from service of the claim. If the particulars of claim are served subsequently, the time for filing the acknowledgment will be 14 days from their service		10.3(1)	
Note, however:			
(a) where service is effected on the agent of an overseas principal, or		6.12(3)	
(b) where claim form is served out of the jurisdiction without the permission of the court under CPR 6.32 or 6.33		6.35	
(c) where the claim form is served out of the jurisdiction with permission of the court see		6.37(5) and 10.3(2)(c)	
The court will give notice to the claimant that the defendant has filed an acknowledgment		10.4	
The court will also serve or deliver a copy of any notice of finding that has been filed with the acknowledgement of service provided copies were filed for service.			6A, para 8.2
5. Effect of filing			
If an acknowledgment is filed in accordance with CPR Pt 10, the period for filing a defence is extended from 14 days after service of the particulars of claim to 28 days after service of the particulars of claim. Accordingly, the period before which the claimant can apply for judgement in default of defence (where CPR Pt 12 allows it) is extended		15.4	
Acknowledgment of Part 8 claim see **TAB 7**			

TABLE 7—ACKNOWLEDGMENT OF SERVICE OF PART 8 CLAIM

TAB 7

	Form No	CPR Rule	PD
Where Part 8 procedure applies			
(a) The provisions of CPR Pt 15 (defence and reply) do not apply when a Part 8 claim is served			8, section A, para 5.1
The defendant who wishes to respond to the claim must file an **acknowledgment of service** which should be in Form N210	N210 N210A (Part 8 costs-only claim)		8, section A, para 5.2
(b) The general rule is that the acknowledgment must be filed not later than **14 days** after service of the claim form and a copy must be served on the claimant and any other party		10.3(1)	
The general rule under r 10.3(1) is subject to the exceptions listed at		10.3(2)	
Where the particulars of claim are not served with the claim form, see		10.3(1)(a)	
If the claim form is served out of the jurisdiction, see		10.3(2)	
(c) The acknowledgment must state:			
(i) whether the defendant contests the claim, and			
(ii) if the defendant seeks a different remedy from that set out in the claim form, what that remedy is		8.3(2)	
It must be signed by the defendant or his legal representative and include the defendant's address for service		10.5	
If the defendant disputes the use of the Part 8 procedure he must state the reasons in writing when he files the acknowledgment of service. If the statement of reasons include matters of evidence, it should be verified by a statement of truth			8, section A, para 5.3
(d) An acknowledgment of a claim started by the Part 8 procedure must be verified by a statement of truth.		22.1	22 para 1.1
(e) A defendant who wishes to rely on **written evidence** must file it with the acknowledgment of service and at the same time serve a copy on the other party		8.5(3) and (4)	
If the defendant does not do so he can only rely on written evidence if the court gives permission		8.6(1)	

TABLE 8—ADMISSIONS AND JUDGMENT UPON ADMISSIONS

TAB 8

	Form No	CPR Rule	PD
1. Making an admission before commencement			
From 6 April 2007 pre-action admissions are governed by the CPR. A person may by giving notice in writing admit the truth of the whole or part of another party's case before the commencement of proceedings (a pre-action admission)		14.1A(1)	14, para 1.4
In proceedings to which any one of the protocols			
(a) for personal injury claims;			
(b) for clinical disputes;			
(c) for disease and illness claims,			
applies, if a pre-action admission is made			
(a) after the party making it has received a letter before claim in accordance with the Practice Direction (Pre-Action Conduct) or any relevant pre-action protocol; or			
(b) before such a letter before claim has been received but it is stated to be made under Part 14,		14.1A(2)	14, para 1.1(2)
it may be withdrawn by the party making it by notice in writing			
(i) before the commencement of proceedings with the agreement of the party to whom the admission was made		14.1A(3)(a)	
(ii) after the commencement of proceedings if all the parties to the proceedings consent or with the permission of the court		14.1A(3)(b)	
After the commencement of proceedings			
(i) any party may apply for judgment on the pre-action admission, and			
(ii) the party who made the admission may apply to withdraw it		14.1A(4)	
Either of the applications referred to in the last paragraph must be made by an application in accordance with Part 23 or may be by cross application		14.1A(5)	
When deciding whether to give permission for the withdrawal of an admission the court must have regard to all the circumstances including those set out in			14, para 7.2
2. Making an admission after the commencement of proceedings			
A party may admit the truth of the whole or part of the other party's case by giving notice in writing		14.1 (1) and (2)	

TAB 8 PROCEDURAL TABLES

	Form No	CPR Rule	PD
Where the **only remedy sought is the payment of money**, the defendant can		14.1(3)	
(a) admit the whole of a claim for a specified amount (by service direct to the claimant)	N9A	14.4	
(b) admit (by filing at the court) part of the claim for a specific amount	N9A	14.5	
(c) admit (by filing at the court) the whole of a claim for unspecified amount, or	N9C	14.6	
(d) admit (by filing at the court) liability to pay a claim for an unspecified amount and offer a sum in satisfaction of the claim	N9C	14.7	
If a claimant files a request for judgment for an amount of money to be decided by the court in accordance with rule 14.6 or 14.7 and the claim is a designated money claim (defined in the Preface to these tables), the court will transfer to the preferred court (also defined in the Preface to these tables)		14.7A	
Note: The defendant may also file a defence			14, para 3.3
3. Time for returning or filing an admission under rr 14.4 to 14.7 (only remedy sought being the payment of money)			
The period is 14 days after service of the claim if particulars of claim are served with it or if they are not 14 days after service of the particulars but if an admission is returned or filed late it will be effective if default judgment has not been entered. See as to 14 day period		14.2(3) and (4)	
(a) If the claim form is served out of jurisdiction under CPR 6.32 or 6.33		6.35	
(b) If the court has specified a period for responding		6.12(3)	
4. Effect of an admission – where the claim is not for money only			
Any other party may apply for judgment on an admission by notice under r 14.1(1) and (2). The application will fall to be made under Part 23.		14.1(1) and (2)	
Judgment shall be such judgment as it appears to the court that the applicant is entitled to on the admission		14.3(1)	
This provision will be relied on only when the claim is for some other remedy or includes a claim for some other remedy than money		14.3(2)	
"Any other party" includes a party under a Part 20 claim			
5. Effect of an admission – claim for unspecified sum of money only			
(a) The claimant may obtain judgment (subject to CPR 14.1(4)(a) and (b) where a party is a child or protected person) by filing a request if the defendant **does not**			

	Form No	CPR Rule	PD
offer a specified amount in satisfaction of the claim	N226	14.6	
The court will serve a copy of the admission on the claimant and if the claimant does not file a request for judgment within 14 days the claim will be stayed until he does file a request for judgment		14.6(3), 14.6(5)	
Judgment will be for an amount to be fixed by the court plus costs. The court will, on entering judgment, give directions leading to the disposal hearing to fix the amount of the damages		14.6(7) and (8)	26
The court will not normally consider it to be appropriate to allocate to track (other than the small claims track) unless the amount payable is disputed on grounds which appear to be substantial or the dispute is not suitable to be dealt with at a **disposal hearing.**			26 para 12.2 and 12.3
A disposal hearing is one			
(i) which will normally not last longer than 30 minutes, and			
(ii) at which the court will not normally hear oral evidence			26 para 4(1)
It will be only the most straightforward of disposals where the damages exceed the small claims limit that are not allocated to track			
(b) If the defendant not only admits the claim but offers a sum in satisfaction of the claim			
The court will serve a notice on the claimant requiring him to state whether or not he accepts the amount offered by the defendant in satisfaction of his claim. If the claimant does not file the notice in 14 days after its service on him the claim is stayed until he does so		14.7(3) and (4)	
If the claimant accepts the amount offered he can obtain judgment (subject to CPR 14.1(4)(a) and (b) where a party is a child or protected person) by filing the appropriate form payable by such date or instalments as he specifies. If no date or instalments are specified the judgment will be for payment immediately	N226	14.7(5) and (6)	
If the defendant makes an offer acceptable but makes a proposal for instalment payments which is not, judgment can be obtained for the amount offered and accepted and the rate of payment will be determined by the court as set out in para 8 of this Table	N226	14.9–14.12	
If the claimant does not accept the amount offered he can obtain judgment for an amount to be decided by the court and costs by lodging the appropriate form. Subsequent procedure will be as under 5(a) above.	N226	14.7(9) and (10)	
6. Effect of admission of claim for specified amount of money only			
Where the admission is of the whole amount claimed the claimant may obtain			

TAB 8 PROCEDURAL TABLES

	Form No	CPR Rule	PD
judgment (subject to CPR 14.1(4)(a) and (b) where a party is a child or protected person) by filing the relevant form and, if the defendant has **not requested time to pay**, specify the date for payment or the time and amount of instalments. The judgment will be for the amount of the claim (less payments made) and costs	N225 or N205A	14.4(3) and (6)	
Where the **admission is of the whole amount but the defendant's proposal for payment is not acceptable to the claimant**, the claimant may obtain judgment (subject to CPR 14.1(4)(a) and (b) where a party is a child or protected person) for the amount claimed plus costs, and cause the rate of payment to be determined by the court by giving notice that the defendant's proposal is not acceptable	N225 or N205A	14.10	
Where the admission is of **part of a claim for a specified sum of money** the court will serve a notice on the claimant requiring him to return it stating whether:		14.5(3)	
(a) he accepts the amount admitted in satisfaction of the claim			
(b) he does not accept the amount admitted and wishes the claim to continue, or			
(c) if the defendant requests time to pay, he accepts the amount admitted in satisfaction but not the payment proposals			
The claimant must return the notice and serve a copy on the defendant in 14 days and if he does not, the claim will be stayed until he complies		14.5(4)	
If the claimant accepts the amount admitted and there is **no proposal for instalment payments** he can obtain judgment for the amount admitted (less payments made) and costs by such date instalments as he shall specify or, if none is specified, immediately	N225A	14.5(6) and (7)	
If the claimant **accepts the amount admitted but not the instalments,** the claimant may obtain judgment for the amount admitted and costs and cause the rate of payment to be determined by so requesting in the notice returned	N225A		
If the claimant **does not accept the amount admitted** the proceedings continue and the procedure is that set out in CPR Pt 26			
7. Interest			
The judgment will include interest to the date of judgment if the particulars of claim include the details required by CPR 16.4 and the claimant's request for judgment includes a calculation of interest between the date of issue and that of the request for judgment. The rate of interest on judgment debts has been 8% since 1 April 1993.		14.14	

	Form No	CPR Rule	PD
8. Determination of rate of payment		14.10	
A court officer may determine the time and rate of payment where the amount outstanding (including costs) does not exceed £50,000. He must do so without a hearing			
Where a judge is to make the determination he may do so without a hearing. If he directs that there be a hearing, and the claim is for a specified sum of money, if the defendant is an individual the proceedings will be transferred automatically to the defendant's home court		14.12	
For cases where transfer is automatically made, see		14.12(2)	
Where the judge is to determine the time and rate of payment at a hearing, the proceedings will be transferred automatically to the preferred court (defined in the Preface to these tables) if: (a) the only claim is for a specified amount of money; (b) the claim is a designated money claim (again, defined in the Preface to these tables); (c) the defendant is not an individual; and (d) the claim has not been transferred to another court.		14.12(2A)	
If there is to be a hearing to determine the time and rate of payment the court will give each party at least 7 days notice of the hearing.		14.12(3)	
The general rule is that a party must comply with a money judgment or order within 14 days of that judgment or order (CPR 40.11) and when the court is exercising its discretion under CPR 14.10 to extend that period, particularly when the parties are business entities, it will only do so exceptionally and only where the judgment debtor is solvent and then only for a short period: *Gulf International Bank v Al Ittefaq Steel Products Co* [2010] EWHC 2601 (QB).			
9. Redetermination			
Either party may apply for redetermination by a judge within 14 days after the service of the determination on him		14.3(2)	
On an application for redetermination the proceedings will be automatically transferred if the defendant is an individual		14.13(3)	
Where an application for redetermination is made, the proceedings will be transferred to the preferred court (defined in the Preface to these tables) if: (a) the only claim (apart from a claim for interest or costs) is for a specified amount of money;		14.13(3A)	

TAB 8 PROCEDURAL TABLES

	Form No	CPR Rule	PD
(b) the claim is a designated money claim (again, defined in the Preface to these tables);			
(c) the defendant is not an individual; and			
(d) the claim has not been transferred to another court.			
If the decision was made by a court officer, the redetermination may take place without a hearing unless a hearing is requested in the application notice			14, para 5.3
If the decision was made by a judge, the redetermination must be at a hearing unless the parties agree otherwise			14, para 5.4
In deciding the rate and time of payment the court will take into account:			
(a) the defendant's statement of means			
(b) the claimant's objections			
(c) any other factor			14, para 5.1
10. Withdrawal or amendment of admission			
The permission of the court is required to amend or withdraw an admission. The court's power is discretionary and CPR PD 14, para 7 provides that the court will consider all the circumstances including those listed in para 14.7.2(a)-(g). CPR 3.1(3) permits the court to attach conditions to the order. See *Soffit v DJ Broady* [2000] CPLR 259, CA and *Hamilton v Hertfordshire County Council* [2003] EWHC 3018 (QB), [2003] All ER (D) 260 (Dec)			
11. Pre-action admissions made on or after 6 April 2007		14.1A	14, para 1.4
From 6 April 2007 pre-action admissions are governed by the CPR. A person may by giving notice in writing admit the truth of the whole or part of another party's case before the commencement of proceedings (a pre-action admission)			
In proceedings to which any one of the protocols			
(a) for personal injury claims			
(b) for clinical disputes			
(c) for disease and illness claims			
applies, if a pre-action admission is made			
(a) after the party making it has received a letter before claim in accordance with the Practice Direction (Pre-Action Conduct) or any relevant pre-action protocol; or			
(b) before such a letter before claim has been received but it is stated to be made under Part 14,		14.1A(2)	14, para 1.1(2)
it may be withdrawn by the party making it by notice in writing			

		Form No	CPR Rule	PD
(i)	before the commencement of proceedings with the agreement of the party to whom the admission was made		14.1A(3)(a)	
(ii)	after the commencement of proceedings if all the parties to the proceedings consent or with the permission of the court		14.1A(3)(b)	
After the commencement of proceedings				
(i)	any party may apply for judgment on the pre-action admission, and			
(ii)	the party who made the admission may apply to withdraw it		14.1A(4)	
Either of the applications referred to in the last paragraph must be made by an application in accordance with Part 23 or may be by cross application.			14.1A(5)	
When deciding whether to give permission for the withdrawal of an admission the court must have regard to all the circumstances.				14, para 7.2

TABLE 9—JUDGMENTS IN DEFAULT AND APPLICATIONS TO SET THEM ASIDE

TAB 9

	Form No	CPR Rule	PD
1. Preliminary			
See **CPR 12 [1]–CPR 12 [6]** and note in particular:			
(a) where judgment in default is wrongly obtained it must be set aside irrespective of merits		13.2	
(b) special provisions requiring an application for default judgment where claim is against a child or protected party, claim is by one spouse against the other or claim is against the Crown		12.11(3)	
(c) default judgment may be obtained in respect of **default of filing of defence to counterclaim** but not on claims between defendants for contribution or indemnity		12.3(2)	
2. Meaning and where it is not available			
"**Default Judgment**" means judgment without a trial where the defendant:			
(a) has failed to file an acknowledgment of service or			
(b) has failed to file a defence		12.1	
It may include **interest** to the date of judgment where the particulars of claim include the details required by CPR 16.4 and any interest from issue to the date of request for judgment is calculated in the form of request. Interest may be added at the judgment rate, presently 8%, but if interest is sought at any higher rate the default judgment will be for an amount of interest to be decided by the court.			
It may also include **fixed costs**; if any other type of costs are sought, an application under CPR Pt 23 should be made for judgment and for the type of costs sought		12.6 12.9(1)	
If the claim is for a **specified sum of money**, judgment may be for the sum claimed less any sums paid in reduction. It will be payable by the date or at the rate specified by the claimant and if neither is specified it will be payable immediately		12.5(2)	
3. Conditions to be satisfied			
Claimant may only obtain **judgment in default of an acknowledgment of service** if the defendant has not filed an acknowledgment of service or a defence to the claim (or any part of the claim) and the relevant time for doing so has expired		12.3(1)	

TAB 9 PROCEDURAL TABLES

	Form No	CPR Rule	PD
Claimant may only obtain **judgment in default of defence**:		12.3(2)	
(a) where an acknowledgment of service has been filed but a defence has not been filed			
(b) on a counterclaim made under CPR 20.4, where a defence has not been filed			
and, in either case, the relevant time for doing so has expired			
Default judgment may not be obtained:		12.3(3)	
(a) where the defendant has applied:			
(i) to have the claim struck out under CPR 3.4			
(ii) for summary judgment under CPR Pt 24			
(b) where the defendant has satisfied the whole claim (including costs) on which the claimant is seeking judgment			
(c) in any other case where a PD provides that the claimant may not obtain default judgment			12, paras 1.1 and 1.3
(d) where the claimant is seeking judgment on a claim for money and the defendant has filed or served an admission with a request for time to pay			
In the absence of proof of valid service a claimant is not entitled to judgment in default under CPR 12.3 and the court has to set aside a judgment obtained where there is no such proof: *Shiblaq v Sadikoglu* [2003] hearing date 25 July (BLD 2807032773) Comm Ct			12 para 4.1
Where the claim form is served by the claimant, the claimant may not obtain default judgment unless a certificate of service has been filed.		6.17	
Where service is deemed to have been effected and judgment entered pursuant to the deemed service, the fact that the defendant had no actual knowledge of the issue of the claim does not give him an absolute right to have judgment set aside. Whether to set aside will be within the discretion of the Court: *Akram v Adam* (2004) Times, 29 December, CA.			
Where a claimant was in a position to enter judgment in default, due to a technical error or omission by the defendant, but knew the defendant had a real prospect of successfully defending the claim and of getting a default judgment set aside, he put himself at risk of an adverse costs order if he nevertheless entered judgment: *Roundstone Nurseries Ltd v Stephenson Holdings Ltd* [2009] EWHC 1431 (TCC), [2009] All ER (D) 72 (Jul).			

		Form No	CPR Rule	PD
4. Where permission is required to obtain default judgment (for procedure see 6 below)				
Applications in accordance with CPR Pt 23 will have to be made for **permission** to enter default judgment (rather than being able to obtain such judgment by filing a form of request) in the following circumstances:				
(a)	where although the default judgment sought is for money or the delivery of goods, the claimant claims (and does not abandon) any other remedy		12.4(2)	
(b)	where the default judgment sought is for costs other than fixed costs		12.9	
(c)	claims against a child or protected person		12.10(a)(i)	
(d)	tort claim by one spouse or civil partner against the other		12.10(a)(ii)	
(e)	delivery up of goods where defendant not allowed alternative of paying value		12.4(2)	
(f)	where judgment is sought for failure to file an acknowledgment of service against:		12.10(b)	
	(i) defendant served out of jurisdiction without permission under CPR 6.32(1), 6.32(2) or 6.33(2)			
	(ii) defendant domiciled in Scotland, Northern Ireland or any other Convention country or Member State			
	(iii) a State			12, para 4.4
	(iv) diplomatic agent with immunity			
	(v) persons or organisations having immunity			
5. Procedure – permission not required				
Permission will not be required where claim is for only:				
(a)	a specified sum of money			
(b)	an amount of money to be decided by the court			
(c)	delivery of goods with alternative of paying their value		12.5(1)	
Judgment in default is obtained by filing the relevant practice form in which the claimant may specify the date or rate of payment. If neither are specified the judgment will provide for immediate payment				
Where the sum of money is specified use		N205A or N225		
Where the sum of money is to be decided by the court use		N205B or N227		
Where the judgment entered is for an amount of money to be decided by the				

TAB 9 PROCEDURAL TABLES

	Form No	CPR Rule	PD
court, directions are likely to be given and allocation may be made to a track.			
Allocation to track is appropriate where the claim if defended would have been allocated to the small claims track or if the amount payable is genuinely disputed on substantial grounds or the dispute is not suitable to be dealt with at a disposal hearing	N154, N155, N157		26, para 12.3
If a claimant files a request for judgment which includes an amount of money to be decided by the court in accordance with rules 12.4 and 12.5 and the money is a designated money claim (defined in the Preface to these tables) the court will transfer the claim to the preferred court (again, defined in the Preface to these tables) upon receipt of the request for judgment.		12.5A	
All matters as to the quantification of damages including causation remain at issue at the disposal hearing; see *Lunnun v Singh* [1999] All ER (D) 718 and **CPR** 12.7 [3].			
A 'disposal hearing' is a hearing which will not normally last more than 30 minutes and the court will not normally hear oral evidence and the court may either assess damages or give directions. Unless the claimant has served written evidence at least 3 days prior the court must not assess damages except where the claim has been allocated to the small claims track.			26, para 12.4
Where the claim is for delivery of goods or their value, the default judgment will be for delivery of the goods and in default for payment of their value to be decided by the court and for costs	N205B or N227	12.5(4)	
Where the claim is against more than one defendant and default judgment is sought against one only, see		12.8	
Interest may be included to date of judgment (see **TAB 8** para 7) but if the necessary requirements have not been satisfied its amount will have to be decided by the court (see also para 2 above of this TAB)		12.6(1) and (2)	
Where in proceeding against **the Crown** a default judgment is sought see		12.4(4)	
6. Procedure where permission is required to obtain default judgment		12.10	
The application must be in accordance with CPR Pt 23 and judgment will be such as the court thinks the claimant is entitled to on his statement of case	N244	12.11(1)	
Any evidence relied on by the claimant in support of his application need not be served on a party who has failed to file an acknowledgment of service		12.11(2)	
For evidence required:			
(a) on application (or request), see			12, para 4.1

		Form No	CPR Rule	PD
(b)	on application against a child or protected party, or in tort between spouses or civil partners, see		12.11(3)	12, para 4.2 (as to child or patient)
(c)	on application where service was outside without permission:			
	(i) in Scotland or Northern Ireland in accordance with rule 6.32(1), or			
	(ii) outside the United Kingdom in accordance with rule 6.33(1) or 6.33(2)			
	And service has not been acknowledged (evidence must be by affidavit) see		12.11(4)	12, paras 4.3 and 4.5
(d)	on application against a State (the evidence must be by affidavit), see		12.11(5)	12, para 4.4
(e)	on delivery of goods (without alternative of payment), see			12, para 4.6
Where the defendant is an individual the claimant must provide the defendant's date of birth (if known) in Part C of the application form			12.4(2)	
On all applications save for those referred to in (c) or (d) above, notice must be given in accordance with CPR Pt 23				12, para 5.1
7. Procedure for obtaining a default judgment for costs				
A default judgment for fixed costs may be obtained by filing a request in the relevant practice form			12.9(1)	
If any other type of costs are claimed, application must be made. On such an application judgment shall be for an amount to be decided by the court		N244	Part 23	
8. Setting aside or varying default judgment				
An application to set aside will be made by filing		N244		
If judgment has been **wrongly entered** the court **must** set it aside. It remains mandatory however long the delay before the application to set aside is made: *Credit Agricole Indosuez v Unicof Ltd* (2003) Times, 4 February)			13.2	
In any other case the court may set aside or vary a judgment entered under CPR Pt 12 if:				
(a)	the defendant has a real prospect of successfully defending the claim or			
(b)	it appears to the court that there is some good reason why:			
	(i) the judgment should be set aside or varied, or		13.3(1)	
	(ii) the defendant should be allowed to defend the claim		13.3(2)	

TABLE 10—SUMMARY JUDGMENT

TAB 10

	Form No	CPR Rule	PD
1. Preliminary			
1.1 See paras **CPR 24** and **CPR PD 24**. Note in particular their availability to claimants and defendants and:		Part 24	24
• if a litigant wishes to **avoid allocation**, the application for summary judgment should be lodged prior to completion of the allocation questionnaire. The fact that it has been issued should be clearly stated in the reply to section D, with a request that allocation not take place prior to the hearing of the application			
The indication that there is an intention to apply for summary judgment in the immediate future may well not prevent allocation			
• the application notice should draw the attention of the respondent to the requirement that if he wishes **to rely on written evidence** he must file and serve it at least 7 days prior to the hearing of the application. This should be done prominently (see precedents BCCP C[597]–BCCP C[600])		24.5(1)	24, para 2(5)
1.2 If the respondent fails to comply he can still rely on any document filed by him in the case that has been verified by a statement of truth		32.6	
1.3 The court of its own initiative may order an application for summary judgment to be made under its general powers of management		24.4(3) and 5(3) 3.3(1)	
1.4 For special provision where the claim is **for specific performance**, see para **CPR 24 [9]**			24, para 7.1
1.5 No application can be made for summary judgment against the Crown until after the period for filing a defence specified in r 15.4		24.4(1A)	
1.6 Where the claimant has failed to comply with the Practice Direction (Pre-Action Conduct) or any relevant pre-action protocol an application for summary judgment will not normally be entertained before a defence has been filed or the time for doing so has expired			24, para 2(6)
2. Grounds			
2.1 The court may give summary judgment **against a claimant or defendant** on the whole of a claim or on a particular issue if:		24.2	
(a) it considers that:			

TAB 10 PROCEDURAL TABLES

	Form No	CPR Rule	PD
(i) the **claimant has no real prospect** of succeeding on the claim or issue, or			
(ii) the **defendant has no real prospect** of successfully defending the claim or issue, and			
(b) there is no other **compelling reason** why the case or issue should be disposed of at trial			
2.2 The test for summary judgment is not whether the case is bound to fail (*Peter Robt Crafft v Camden London Borough Council* (2000) LTL, 24 October, CA), but the court should not conduct a mini-trial to establish whether summary disposal is appropriate: *Swain v Hillman* [2001] 1 All ER 91, CA. The criterion to be applied by the judge is not one of probability but of the absence of reality: see *Supablast (Nationwide) Ltd v Story Rail Ltd* [2010] EWHC 56 (TCC), [2010] All ER (D) 133 (Jan) An application for summary judgment may be based on a point of law, the evidence (or lack of it), or a combination of both			24, para 1.3
3. Grounds – special cases			
• For **set-offs and counterclaims** as defences, see para **CPR 24 [7]** Where the claim is suitable for summary judgment but there is a defence of set-off which has a reasonable prospect a court may well grant summary judgment but subject to the decision on the defence of set-off with execution stayed until the trial of that defence or further order of the court			
4. Availability of summary judgment			
• The court may give summary judgment **against a claimant** in any type of proceedings		24.3(1)	
• The court may give summary judgment **against a defendant** in any type of proceedings, except:			
(a) proceedings for possession of **residential premises** against:			
(i) a mortgagor, or			
(ii) a tenant or tenant holding over whose occupancy has protection within the meaning of the Rent Act 1977 or Housing Act 1988, and			
(b) proceedings for an Admiralty claim in rem			
5. Procedure			
5.1 Timing			
An application for summary judgment should be made promptly, but leave of court is required to issue the application			

	Form No	CPR Rule	PD
before the defendant against whom summary judgment is sought has filed:			
(a) an acknowledgement of service, or			
(b) a defence,			
unless a Practice Direction provides otherwise		24.4(1)	
If the claimant applies for summary judgment before the person against whom summary judgment is sought has filed a defence, that defendant does not need to file a defence before the hearing of the application		24.4(2)	
Where a claimant has not complied with any relevant pre-action protocol summary judgment cannot normally be sought until a defence has been filed or the time for so doing has expired			
5.2 Form of application			
Precedents of applications by claimant and defendant can be found at **BCCP** C[597] and **BCCP** C[599]. For practice forms of application see	PF 11 and 12		
The application notice must include a statement that it is an application for summary judgment made under CPR Pt 24 and why the applicant seeks the order			24, para 2(2)
The application notice or the evidence contained, referred to or served with it must:			
(a) identify any point of law or provision in a document on which the applicant relies, and/or			
(b) state that it is made because the applicant believes that on the evidence the respondent has no real prospect of succeeding on the claim or issue (as the case may be) or of successfully defending the claim			
In either case state the applicant knows of no reason why the disposal of the claim or issue should await trial			24, para 2(3)
The application must identify any written evidence on which the applicant relies which is not contained in the application notice			24, para 2(4)
The application notice should bring to the respondent's attention the requirement of filing and serving any written evidence on which he relies at least 7 days before the hearing of the summary judgment application		24.5(1)	24, para 2(5)
5.3 Issue and service			
Upon issue, a date will be fixed for the hearing. The time allocated will usually be in accordance with the **time estimate** given by the applicant. It is important that sufficient time is allowed. If the time originally estimated becomes inadequate having regard to the evidence filed by the respondent, the court should be so			

TAB 10 PROCEDURAL TABLES

	Form No	CPR Rule	PD
informed and re-listing sought with an increased time estimate. Such re-listing may well require an application but the court should be asked to deal with it without a hearing. The delay caused by re-listing is well worth accepting to obtain adequate time to make the application			
The respondent (or the parties if the hearing is fixed of the court's own initiative) must be given at least **14 days' notice** of: (a) the date fixed for the hearing, and (b) the issues that the court will be asked to decide at the hearing		24.4(3)	
A copy of the application notice must be served as soon as practicable after filing and in time to give the notice required		23.7	
Where the application for summary judgment is made much later than is normally the case the court will be especially vigilant in applying the 'no real prospect of success' test: *James E Mc-Cabe Ltd v Scottish Courage Ltd* [2006] EWHC 538 (Comm), [2006] All ER (D) 409 (Mar)			
5.4 Evidence			
The applicant's evidence will be filed as part of or with the application. The statement should be as concise as possible and the temptation to anticipate and answer the respondent's arguments should be resisted; that can be done by filing evidence in reply			
If the respondent wishes to rely on written evidence at the hearing he must: (a) file the written evidence, and (b) serve copies on every party at least 7 days prior to the hearing		24.5(1)	
If the applicant wishes to rely on written evidence in reply he must: (a) file the written evidence, and (b) serve a copy on the respondent at least 3 days before the hearing		24.5(2)	
• For the time for filing evidence where the hearing has been fixed on the court's initiative, see		24.5(3)	
• The Rules do not require evidence already filed to be filed again or evidence already served to be served again		24.5(4)	
• A party may rely on any statement of case or application notice as evidence provided it is verified by a statement of truth		Part 22	
6. The hearing			
6.1 Time is likely to be short and care must be taken to take up less than half the time available for the presentation of the application, leaving time for a short			

	Form No	CPR Rule	PD
reply. In this way the respondent can be properly limited to his proper share of the allotted time. Time has to be left for the court's deliberation and delivery of judgment			
6.2 A skeleton argument (with copies for each party and the court) will be appropriate in all but the most simple application. Copies of any authorities relied on should also be available as well as the original report			
The skeleton argument and authorities should be filed in advance of the hearing in the hope that the court will have the time to read them before the hearing			
Copies of the order sought should also be available			
6.3 The hearing will be before a Master or district judge but he may direct that the application be heard by a High Court Judge (in the High Court) or a circuit judge (in a county court). The court should avoid embarking on a mini-trial in advance of the trial particularly where the case involves the presentation of evidence and cross-examination to assess its strength: *Somerset-Leeke v Kay Trustees Ltd* [2002] BLD 0407022528, 3 July, Ch. See also *North East Lincolnshire Borough Council v Millennium Park (Grimsby) Ltd* (2002) Times, 31 October, CA.			24, para 3
The court may, perhaps must, have regard to considerations of efficient use of resources as is done in the delivery of every other public service: see *Sutradhar v Natural Environment Research Council* [2006] UKHL 33, [2006] 4 All ER 490 per Lord Hoffmann at 42.			
A factual dispute need not prevent summary judgment: *Miller v Shires* [2006] EWCA Civ 1386, [2007] PNLR 273 where summary judgment was given in professional negligence action arising out of a disputed road traffic claim; see further *Hussein v Clydesdale Bank plc* (2012) (Unreported) discussed by David Lytton in his article 'seeking summary judgment in disputes over facts' in (2012) Sol Jo, 13 November at page 10.			
For summary judgment in intellectual property legislation see *Bolton Pharmaceuticals Co 100 Ltd v Doncaster Pharmaceuticals Group Ltd* [2006] EWCA Civ 661, [2006] All ER (D) 389 (May)			
6.4 For summary judgment at trial by the use by the trial judge of his powers under CPR 24.2(a)(ii) see *James v Evans* [2000] 42 EG 173, CA and CPR 24 [4A]			
7. The order			
7.1 The orders that the court may make include: (a) judgment on the claim			

TAB 10   PROCEDURAL TABLES

	Form No	CPR Rule	PD
(b) the striking out or dismissal of the claim			
(c) the dismissal of the application			
(d) a conditional order			24, para 5.1
7.2 The court may make a conditional order if it considers the claim or defence may succeed but it is improbable that it will do so. Such an order may require a party:			24, para 4
(a) to pay money into court, or			
(b) to take a specified step in relation to his claim or defence			
and will provide that the party's claim be dismissed or his statement of case be struck out if he does not comply			24, para 5.2
The court may make an order for security for costs, when determining an application for summary judgment, under CPR 24.6 provided the principles applicable under CPR 25.13 were borne in mind: *Allen v Bloomsbury Publishing plc* [2011] EWHC 770 (Ch), [2011] All ER (D) 213 (Mar).			
In the case of *Jacobs UK Ltd v Skidmore, Owings and Merrill LLP* [2008] EWHC 2847 (TCC), [2008] All ER (D) 258 (Nov) Coulson J gave very pertinent guidance as to the evidence required to obtain summary judgment in various different types of claims and as to the various heads of damage within such claims. He also stated that where applications do not succeed but a condition is made (see preceding paragraph) they could lead the way to settlement. For further guidance see article by Janna Purdie in (2008) NLJ 5 December, page 1713.			
An application for summary judgment is capable of being made as a tactical step aimed at achieving an order whereby the defendant is given leave to defend, or to continue to defend, conditional on a payment into court and in the hope that a favourable judicial comment may be obtained on the likely outcome of the case. Such a tactical step has its risks, particularly as to costs, but may be fruitful. See *Antonio Gramsci Shipping Corpn v Recoletos Ltd* [2010] All ER (D) 241 (May) or for further consideration see article 'Early point scoring counts' by Catherine Reeves in 2010, NLJ, 25 June, at page 902.			
Conditions should not be imposed if a party has no prospect of complying with them: *Chapple v Williams* [1999] CPLR 731, CA			
7.3 If the case is to continue the court may give **directions** for the final hearing, the service of a defence and the management of the case, and in practice will do so		24.6	24, para 10

	Form No	CPR Rule	PD
7.4 For **practice forms** of orders under CPR Pt 24, see	PF 13 and 14		
For **judgment** under part 24, see Forms (these are High Court forms but can be adapted)	No 44 and 44A		
8. Costs			
Where judgment is given for a specified sum, fixed costs may be awarded. Where the court is disposed to give costs, other than fixed costs, the court is likely to summarily assess them. If the court is to be asked for costs, and not merely fixed costs, a costs schedule should be filed and served on the other party at least 24 hours before the date fixed for the hearing		45.4, Table 2 44.13(1)	24.9
If the order made does not mention costs no party is entitled to costs relating to that order			

TABLE 10A—LOW VALUE PERSONAL INJURY CLAIMS IN ROAD TRAFFIC ACCIDENTS

TAB 10A

	Form No	CPR Rule	PD
Proposed expansion of the RTA portal			
The Ministry of Justice has confirmed (see report in (2013) NLJ, 8 January, page 2) that the expansion of the RTA portal, presently covering RTA claims (ie those including damages for personal injury, valued by the claimant at not more than £10,000) will not be implemented on 1 April 2013 but will be delayed. The proposed expansion is to £25,000 in RTA cases and also by the inclusion of employers and public liability claims up to £25,000.			
It is confirmed in (2013) Gazette, 4 March, page 1 that the Justice Secretary stated that the new protocols extending the portals scheme will be implemented from the end of July 2013.			
Preliminary - framework			
This new claims procedure with its own forms replacing pleadings has been in place since 30 April 2010; it applies basically to claims including personal injury which occurred on or after 30 April 2010 valued at not more than £10,000 on a full liability basis (see para 2 below).			RTA Protocol, para 4.1
The Road Traffic Accident Portal is an information exchange which was set up to speed up claims and has been 100% funded by a levy contribution from insurers. The board that runs this scheme is equally divided between insurers and claimants and has voted that costs be split equally between the insurers and the claimants. The board also indicated that until that is achieved the increase of the maximum value of claims falling within the portal scheme to £15,000 would be premature.			
The procedure comprises 3 stages:			
• Stage 1: The claim notification stage governed by the Pre-Action Protocol for Low Value Personal Injury Claims in Road Traffic Accidents started by service of the Claim Notification Form ('CNF')			RTA Protocol, para 6
• Stage 2 for the exchange of medical evidence and of offers is governed by the Protocol and it begins with the Stage 2 Settlement Pack which must be within 15 days of the claimant approving the final medical report and agreeing to rely on the prognosis in it.			RTA Protocol, para 7

	Form No	CPR Rule	PD
• Stage 3 governed by PD 8B - 'Stage 3 procedure' where the parties are not able to agree the amount of the damages having followed the Protocol procedure. This is started by the issue of a claim form in a county court normally for hearing by a district judge.			8B
Note that there are specific provisions where: (a) the claimant is a child and a settlement has been agreed; (b) the RTA Protocol cannot be complied with before the expiry of the limitation; (c) costs are fixed costs and payable in stages - there is a provision for an interim payment; (d) electronic communication - RTA Protocol, para 5 - the address for electronic communication with the defendant can be found at http ://www.rtaclaimsprocess.org.uk. The claimant will give a contact address in the CNF. Subject only to PD 6.1(2) below where the Protocol requires information to be sent to a party it must be sent electronically.		45.18 (as to fixed costs)	8B, para 6.1 RTA Protocol, paras 5.7-5.8 RTA Protocol, para 5
Claims that occur on or after 30 April 2010 fall outside or leave the procedure if (amongst other matters): (a) liability is not admitted; (b) there is an allegation of contributory negligence other than an admitted failure to wear a seat belt; (c) there is a failure in completion and return of the CNF response; (d) the claim is valued at less that £1,000.			
At present there are no decisions to provide guidance so the rules stand for themselves.			
1. Changes are made by the 52nd update to the Civil Procedure Rules with effect from 30 April 2010 by the insertion of:			
1.1 The Pre-Action Protocol for Low Value Personal Injury Claims in Road Traffic Accidents ('the RTA Protocol') setting out three stages; see **PRO 10** in *Volume 1*.			
1.2 Practice Direction 8B - the RTA Protocol - Stage 3 procedure			
1.3 CPR 36, Section II (36.16-36.22 - RTA Protocol offers to settle) and CPR 45.16-45.28 (new fixed costs provisions)			
1.4 Consequential amendments, in particular those to CPR 36.1, 36.2(2)(b) and 3.3(4) as to offers to settle.			

	Form No	CPR Rule	PD
1A With effect form 1 October 2011 the CPR 57th update has amended the RTA Protocol at para 7.55, as to the contents of the Part B sealed envelope of the Stage 3 pack, so **any** Part 36 offers and counter-offers are to be included.			
1B The Ministry of Justice had outlined plans to extend the upper limit of the Road Traffic Accident Portal scheme from £10,000 to £25,000 and to extend it to include public and employer liability cases. It is also proposed to cut the maximum fixed fee (currently £1,200) for cases going through the portal. The proposed cut is from £1,200 to £500 'from the end of April 2013' (2013) Sol Jo, 5 March at page 4.			
2. The **RTA Protocol** applies where:			
(1) a claim for damages arises from as road traffic accident (RTA) on or after 30 **April 2010;**			
(2) the claim includes damages in respect of **personal injuries;**			
(3) the claimant's valuation of the claim on a full liability basis including pecuniary loss, but excluding interest, is **not more than £10,000** (the upper limit); and			
(4) if proceedings were started the **small claims track** would not be the normal track for the claim.			RTA Protocol, para 4.1
• A claim may include **vehicle-related damages** defined as:			RTA Protocol, paras 1.1(6) and 4.3
(a) pre-accident value of the vehicle;			
(b) vehicle repair;			
(c) vehicle insurance excess;			
(d) vehicle hire			
but these are excluded for the purpose of para 4.1			
• As to **electronic communication** between the parties and the provision of e-mail addresses see:			RTA Protocol, para 5.1-5.2
Where the Protocol requires information to be sent to a party (subject only to para 6.1(2) - the defendant-only CNF) it must be sent electronically.			RTA Protocol, para 5.1
2.1 Where the claimant gives notice to the defendant that the claims is unsuitable for the RTA protocol (eg complex issues) the claim will no longer continue under the Protocol. If, however, the court when considering costs considers that the claimant acted unreasonably it will award no more than the fixed costs under CPR 45.18. It is considered that the extension of the scheme (see this TAB at 1B above) would result in a significant increase in cases dropping out.			RTA Protocol, para 7.67
2.2 It is reported by Deborah Evans, the chief executive of the Association of Per-			

	Form No	CPR Rule	PD
sonal Injury Lawyers (APIL), in an article in (2012) NLJ, 8 June that exit rates from the RTA portal are already high — 47%; some of course will be due to settlements.			
• For action to be taken by the defendant when the claimant is unrepresented see:			RTA Protocol, para 5.10
3. The aims of the RTA Protocol are:			
(1) the defendant pays damages and costs using the process set out in the Protocol without the need for the claimant to start proceedings;			
(2) damages are paid within a reasonable time; and			
(3) the claimant's legal representative receives the fixed costs set out at the end of each stage in this Protocol.			RTA Protocol, para 3.1
4. TIME TABLE STAGE 1			
4.1 The **start** of the process is when the claimant sends, duly completed:			
(1) the **claim notification form** (CNF) electronically to the defendant's insurers;	RTA 1		RTA Protocol, para 6.1(1)
(2) the **'defendant only CNF'** to the defendant by first class post.	RTA 2		RTA Protocol, para 6.1(2)
• Where there is a claim for vehicle related damage see			RTA Protocol, para 6.4
• Where the claimant is a child see			RTA Protocol, para 6.5
• As to the statement of truth see			RTA Protocol, para 6.6
• As to rehabilitation see			RTA Protocol, para 6.7
As to 'duly completed' the majority of the boxes are mandatory and the form will be rejected if there are any blanks. 'Not known by the claimant' will be a sufficient answer to achieve acceptance but may result in the defendant deciding that the claim should not continue under the Protocol because he has been given inadequate mandatory information. The claimant must make 'a reasonable attempt' to complete the boxes not marked as mandatory.		45.24(2)(a)	RTA Protocol, para 6.8
If the claimant does not use the form CNF and starts proceedings under Part 7 he will 'fail to comply' with the Protocol and if he succeeds the court may order the defendant to pay no more than the fixed costs and disbursements in CPR 45.18 and CPR 45.30.		45.24(2)(c)	
4.2 By way of response the defendant must send to the claimant an electronic **acknowledgement the next day after receipt of the CNF** and **within 15 days** (30 days in an MIB case) must send the duly completed **Insurer Response** section of the CNF ('the CNF response') to the claimant.			RTA Protocol, para 6.10 and 6.11

	Form No	CPR Rule	PD
4.3 Before the end of stage 1 the defendant must apply to the Compensation Recovery Unit (CRU) for a certificate of recoverable benefits.			RTA Protocol, para 6.12
4.4 Where the defendant:			
(1) **alleges contributory negligence** (except for the claimant's admitted failure to wear a seatbelt);			RTA Protocol, para 6.1(1)
(2) **does not respond;**			RTA Protocol, para 6.1(2)
(3) **does not admit liability** (brief reasons must be given);			
(4) notifies the claimant there is inadequate mandatory information or that the small claims track would be the normal track for the claim;			RTA Protocol, paras 6.15 and 6.16
the claim will no longer continue under the RTA Protocol but will proceed under the Pre-Action Protocol for personal injury claims.			
4.5 Unless the claimant is a child, where liability is admitted or is admitted and the only contributory negligence relates to the admitted failure to use seat belts, **within 10 days** after sending the CNF response, the defendant must pay the **Stage 1 fixed costs (CPR 45.18).**			RTA Protocol, para 6.18
• For position of claimant in default of payment see			RTA Protocol, para 6.19
5. TIME TABLE - STAGE 2			
5.1 **Within 15 days of the claimant approving the final medical report** and agreeing to rely on the prognosis in that report the claimant should send to the defendant a **Stage 2 Settlement Pack** comprising:			
(a) the Stage 2 Settlement Pack Form;			
(b) a medical report or reports (see paras 7.1-7.7 and 7.24-7.25);			
(c) evidence of pecuniary loss; and			
(d) evidence of disbursements.			
If the defendant alleges contributory negligence because of the claimant's failure to wear a seatbelt the Pack must also contain a suggestion of the percentage reduction (which may be 0%) in the amount of damages.	RTA 5		RTA Protocol, para 7.26
Once the medical report has been sent to the defendant the claimant cannot challenge its factual accuracy.			RTA Protocol, para 7.2
• For **interim payments** see			RTA Protocol, paras 7.8-7.15 and 7.21-7.23
• For **vehicle-related damage** - 'additional damages' see			RTA Protocol, paras 7.16 and 7.46
• For request for **interim payment where the claimant is a child** see			RTA Protocol, paras 7.19-7.20

	Form No	CPR Rule	PD
The defendant has **35 days** - '**the total consideration period**' for the consideration of the Stage 2 Settlement Pack, made up of up to 15 days for its consideration ('**the initial consideration period**') and the remainder of the total consideration period for further negotiation ('**the negotiation period**'). These periods are capable of extension by agreement between the parties.			RTA Protocol, paras 7.28-7.29
5.3 Where a party makes an offer 5 days or less before the end of the total consideration period and any agreed extension there will be a further period of 5 days after the end of the period for consideration. During this period (the further consideration period) no further offers can be made by either party.			RTA Protocol, para 7.30
5.4 Within the **initial consideration period** (or any agreed extension) the defendant must either:			
(a) **accept the offer** made by the claimant in the Stage 2 Settlement Pack; or			
(b) make a **counter offer** using that form.			RTA Protocol, para 7.31
For the required contents of the counter offer see:			RTA Protocol, paras 7.34-7.35
• For the position where the defendant gives notice within the initial consideration period that the small claims track would be the normal track or withdraws the admission of causation see			RTA Protocol, para 7.32
• Where the defendant does not respond during the initial consideration period (or any agreed extension) the claim will not continue under the Protocol and the claimant may issue proceedings under CPR Part 7: see			RTA Protocol, para 7.33
5.5 Where a counter offer is made by the defendant (see para 5.4 above) the claimant has until the end of the total consideration period or further consideration period to accept or decline the counter offer.			RTA Protocol, para 7.36
5.6 Any offer to settle at any stage by either party will automatically include and cannot exclude:			
(a) the Stage 2 fixed costs in rule 45.18;			
(b) an agreement in principle to pay disbursements;			
• For withdrawal of offers after the consideration period see			RTA Protocol, para 7.39
5.7 Upon **settlement** (except where the claimant is a child or where the provision as to deductible benefits applies) the defendant must pay:			
(a) the agreed damages less any:			

	Form No	CPR Rule	PD
(i) deductible amount which is payable to the CRU; and (ii) previous interim payment; (b) any unpaid Stage 1 fixed costs in rule 45.18; (c) the Stage 2 fixed costs in rule 45.18; (d) the relevant disbursements allowed in accordance with rule 45.19; and within 10 days of the end of the relevant period in paragraphs 7.28 to 7.30 during which the parties agreed a settlement (7.40) or within 10 days of agreeing to pay the claim and additional damages (7.53).			RTA Protocol, paras 7.40 and 7.53
5.8 For situations where there are **partial settlements** - original damages not agreed but additional damages agreed, or original damages agreed and additional damages not agreed see			RTA Protocol, paras 7.49-7.50
In both instances provision is made for payment of the agreed part. In particular note that where it is the additional damages that are not agreed the claimant may start proceedings under Part 7 in relation to the additional damages.			RTA Protocol, para 7.51
5.9 Where the parties **do not reach agreement** on: (1) the original damages within the period specified (see 2.2 above); or (2) the original damages and where relevant any additional damages within the period specified, the **claimant must send to the defendant the Court Proceedings Pack (Part A and Part B)** which must since 1 October 2011 contain: (a) in Part A the schedule of the claimant's losses and the defendant's responses comprising only the figures specified in sub-paragraphs (1) and (2) above together with the supporting comments and evidence from both parties on any disputed heads of damage; and (b) in part B the final offer and counter-offer from the Stage 2 Settlement Pack Form and where relevant, the offer and any final counter-offer made.	RTA 6 and RTA 7		RTA Protocol, para 7.55
• Comments in the Court Proceedings Pack must not raise matters not raised in the Stage 2 Settlement Pack Form.			RTA Protocol, para 7.57
• Where the claim has become or is complicated the claimant may decide not to proceed further under the RTA Protocol and rely on persuading the court at the even-			

	Form No	CPR Rule	PD
tual hearing that it was a reasonable step to take and so avoid the limitation on costs.			RTA Protocol, para 7.67
• If the defendant considers there is non-compliance in the Court Proceedings Pack it must be returned to the claimant within 5 days with an explanation of why it does not comply.			RTA Protocol, para 7.58
• Where the defendant intends to nominate a legal representative to accept service he should give his name and address.			RTA Protocol, para 7.59
• Where the defendant fails to return the court proceedings pack within the permitted time the claimant should assume the defendant has no further comments to make.			RTA Protocol, para 7.60
• For non-settlement payment by the defendant to the claimant (except where the claimant is a child) see This effects an automatic interim payment to be made within 15 days of receiving the Court Proceedings Pack from the claimant. The payment comprises: (1) the final offer of damages made by the defendant in the Court Proceedings Pack (less any amount payable to the CRU and any previous interim payment); (2) any unpaid Stage 1 fixed costs; (3) the Stage 2 fixed costs; (4) agreed disbursements or if not agreed the amount the defendant considers reasonable.			RTA Protocol, paras 7.61-7.66
6. TIME TABLE STAGE 3			
Practice Direction 8B - RTA Protocol - Stage 3 Procedure			
6.1 The court is involved in the procedure for the first time at this stage which occurs where: (1) the parties have followed the RTA Protocol but have not been able to agree on the damages to be paid; or (2) the claimant is a child, settlement has been agreed but the approval of the settlement by the court is required; or (3) completion of the RTA Protocol is not possible before the expiry of the limitation period.			8B, para 1
• A claim under this PD must be started in the county court and will normally be heard by a district judge.			

	Form No	CPR Rule	PD
6.2 The claim is to be made under the Part 8 procedure, as modified by this PD, but the following provisions of Part 8 are disapplied:			
(1) rule 8.2A (issue of claim form without naming defendants);			
(2) rule 8.3 (acknowledgment of service);			
(3) rule 8.5 (filing and serving written evidence);			
(4) rule 8.6 (evidence - general);			
(5) rule 8.7 (Part 20 claims);			
(6) rule 8.8 (procedure where defendant objects to use of the Part 8 procedure); and			
(7) rule 8.9(c).			
6.3 The application is for the court to determine the amount of the damages and must be started by claim form which must state:			8B, para 2
(1) that the claimant has followed the procedure set out in the RTA Protocol;			
(2) the date when the Court Proceedings Pack (Part A and Part B) form was sent to the defendant (this provision does not apply where the claimant if a child and the application is for a settlement hearing);			
(3) whether the claimant wants the claim to be determined by the court on the papers (except where a party is a child) or at a Stage 3 hearing;			
(4) where the claimant seeks a settlement hearing or a Stage 3 hearing, the dates which the claimant requests should be avoided; and			
(5) the value of the claim.			8B, para 5
6.4 As to the filing and service of **written evidence**, in addition to the claim form the claimant must file and serve:			8B, para 6.1
(1) the Court Proceedings Pack (Part A) Form;			
(2) the Court Proceedings Pack (Part B) Form (the claimant and defendant's final offers) in a sealed envelope (to be opened after the decision);			
(3) copies of medical reports;			
(4) evidence of special damages			
(5) evidence of disbursements (for example the cost of any medical report) in accordance with CPR 45.19(2); and			
There are additional documents to be included if the claim is for approval of a settlement reached on behalf of a child.			

	Form No	CPR Rule	PD
Note in particular (save where the claim is for a child settlement hearing) that the Court Proceedings Pack (Part B) (which contains the parties' 'final offers') must be filed in a sealed envelope.			8B, para 6.1(2)
Only the documents listed above can be put before the court (unless the court otherwise orders). These are all the documents that both parties have seen.			8B, para 7
6.5 For **evidence - general** see para 7 of the PD and in particular note that if the court considers: (1) further evidence must be provided by any party; (2) the claim is not suitable to continue under the Stage 3 procedure, the court will order that the claim continue under Part 7, allocate to a track and give directions (in this event Stage 3 fixed costs will not be allowed).			8B, para 7.2

6.6 The **acknowledgment of service** must state whether the defendant:
 (1) (a) contests the amount of the damages claimed;
      (b) contests the making of an order for damages;
      (c) disputes the court's jurisdiction; or
      (d) objects to the use of the Stage 3 procedure;
 (2) wants the claim to be determined by the court on the papers or at the hearing.			

• Where the defendant objects to the use of Stage 3 he must give reasons in the acknowledgment			
The acknowledgment of service must be filed **not more than 14 days after service of the claim form** and with: (1) any notice of funding; and (2) as soon as possible thereafter a certificate of recoverable benefits.	N210B	36.15(e)(1)	8B, para 8
6.7 For **dismissal of the claim** because of the defendant's opposition see			8B, para 9
For the **withdrawal of an RTA protocol** offer with the necessary permission of the court see			8B, para 10
the claim will not be allocated and so no allocation questionnaire is necessary.			
6.8 **The court will assess the damages:** (1) on the papers; or (2) at **a Stage 3 hearing** where the claimant so requests in the claim or the defendant so requests in the acknowledgment of service or the court itself so orders. (The court is likely to list the hearing for 30 minutes unless representations are made requesting a lon-			

	Form No	CPR Rule	PD
ger period; probably 1 hour would be the maximum.)			
• The court will give the parties at least 21 days notice of the date of paper determination or the Stage 3 hearing.			
• An up to date certificate of recoverable benefits must be filed by the defendant at least 5 days prior to the hearing if the total of the benefits have increased since final offers.			8B, para 11
The hearing will be confined to submissions and the court is unlikely to be greatly influenced by the citation of awards by county courts which of course are not in any way binding but decisions and the JSB Guidelines may be useful to establish the parameters. Copies should be available for the court and the opponent.			
6.9 As to **settlements** at Stage 2 and at Stage 3 where the **claimant is a child** see			8B, paras 12 and 13
7.1 As to **adjournments** see			8B, para 14
7.2 As to **appeals** where the determination has been on paper see			8B, para 15
7.3 As to **limitation** see			8B, para 16
8. OFFERS TO SETTLE			
8.1 An RTA Protocol offer must:			
(1) be set out in the Court Proceedings Pack (Part B) form; and		36.17	
(2) contain the final total amount of the offer from both parties.			
• It will be deemed to have been made on the first business day after this form (Parts A and B) is sent to the defendant.		36.18	
8.2 The amount of the RTA protocol offer must not be disclosed to the court until the termination of the case and any other offer must not be communicated to the court at all.		36.20	
8.3 The RTA offer is treated as exclusive of interest and is only of consequence for the costs of the Stage 3 procedure (see CPR 45.29) and not in respect of any appeal costs.		36.19	
8.4 The costs consequences are:			
(1) where the **judgment is less than or equal to** the defendant's RTA Protocol offer - the court will order **the claimant to pay** the fixed costs in CPR 45.38 (see below) and interest on those costs from the date of the offer;		36.21(2)	
(2) where the judgment **is more than** the defendant's RTA Protocol offer **but less than** the claimant's RTA Protocol offer the court will order the **defendant to**			

	Form No	CPR Rule	PD
pay the claimant's fixed costs in rule CPR 45.32 (see below);		36.21(3)	
(3) where the judgment is **equal to or more than** the claimant's RTA Protocol offer the court will order the **defendant to pay:**			
(a) interest on the whole of damages awarded at a rate not exceeding 10% above base rate for some or all of the period specified starting with the date specified in CPR 36.18 (the first business day after the Court Proceedings Pack (Part A and Part B) is sent to the defendant;			
(b) the fixed costs specified in CPR 45.32 and interest on those costs at a rate not exceeding 10% above base rate		36.21(4)	
• The amount of the judgment is less than the RTA Protocol offer where the judgment is less than that offer once deductible amounts identified in the judgment are deducted (see CPR 35.15(1)(d)).		36.22	
9. COSTS - CPR 45.16-45.28			
9.1 The only costs allowed are (**reductions are proposed**):			
(1) **fixed costs** in CPR 45.18;			
(2) **disbursements** in accordance with CPR 45.19;			
9.2 The amount of the fixed costs are:			
Stage 1 fixed costs £400			
Stage 2 fixed costs £800			
Stage 3 - Type A fixed costs (legal representative costs) £250			
Type B fixed costs (advocate's costs) £250			
Type C fixed costs (advice on child's claim) £150		45.18	
• The court will not award more or less than these amounts except where there is failure to comply with or election not to continue with the RTA Protocol.		45.18	
• Where the claimant lives in the area specified in the Costs PD and instructs a legal representative who practises in that area an addition of 12.5% will be recoverable in respect of Stage 1 and 2 and Stage 3A costs		45.18	Costs PD, para 25A.6
• VAT may be added when appropriate and will be recoverable in addition to the fixed costs		45.19	
9.3 The **disbursements** set out in CPR 45.30 may be allowed by the court			

	Form No	CPR Rule	PD
which must not allow any other type of disbursement. Note in particular the costs of obtaining:			
(i) medical records;			
(ii) a medical report or reports as provided for in the RTA Protocol;			
(iii) an engineer's report;			
(iv) a search of the records of the Driver and Vehicle Licensing Authority, Motor Insurance Database.		45.19(2)(a)	
And also note the court fees in respect of the Stage 3 Procedure are all recoverable as are other disbursements arisen due to a particular feature of the dispute.		45.19(2)(d) and (e)	
9.4 Where the claimant obtains judgment for an amount **more than the defendant's RTA Protocol offer** the court will order the **defendant to pay:**			
(1) where not already paid by the defendant, the Stage 1 and 2 fixed costs;			
(2) where the claim is determined:			
(i) on the papers, Stage 3 Type A fixed costs;			
(ii) at a Stage 3 hearing, Stage 3 Type A and B fixed costs; or			
(iii) at a Stage 3 hearing and the claimant is a child, Type A, B and C fixed costs;			
(3) disbursements allowed in accordance with CPR 45.30; and		45.20	
• For the costs consequence of the claimant not complying with the RTA Protocol or electing not to do so see		45.24	
• For the position where the parties settle after a claim has been started under Part 8 in accordance with PD 8B see		45.25	
• For the position where parties have treated an offer as made under Part 36 and the offer was so expressed but in fact could not have been framed to fall within Part 36 see *Howell v Lees-Millais* [2011] EWCA Civ 786, [2011] All ER (D) 48 (Jul) where applying the overriding objective the Court held, as to costs, that the offer should have Part 36 effect.			
9.5 Where the claimant obtains judgment for an amount **equal to or less than the defendant's RTA Protocol offer** the court will order the **claimant to pay:**			
(1) where the claim is determined			

	Form No	CPR Rule	PD
(i) on the papers, Stage 3 Type A fixed costs; or			
(ii) at a hearing, Stage 3 Type A and B fixed costs;			
(2) disbursements allowed in accordance with CPR 45.19; and		45.26	
9.6 For the costs position on the **adjournment** of a hearing see		45.27	
9.7 For provisions where the claimant is a **child** and:			
(1) there is a settlement at Stage 2, see		45.21	
(2) where there is a settlement at Stage 3, see		45.22	
(3) where the court orders the claim is not suitable to be determined under the Stage 3 procedure, see		45.23	
Note in particular: • a hearing is always necessary in a child settlement case to obain the court's approval of the proposed settlement; • if the settlement is approved the defendant will be ordered to pay the claimant's costs which will include £250 in respect of counsel's fee for attending the settlement hearing; • article 'Settling infant costs' by Lisa Wright in (2011) NLJ, 15 April, page 543.			
10. Review after one year			
For the success of the scheme, the cases that reach Stage 3 and the government's paper 'Solving disputes in the court' see an article 'Hit the road' by District Judge Exton in (2011) Sol Jo, 7 June, page 21 which provide interesting and useful information.			

TABLE 11—DEFENCE AND REPLY

TAB 11

	Form No	CPR Rule	PD
1. Contents of defence			
Where the defendant is an individual, and the claim form does not contain an address at which he resides or carries on business, or provides an incorrect address, the defendant must provide such an address for service, which must be within the United Kingdom, including a postcode. He must also provide his date of birth		16.5(8)	16, para 10.6
The defendant must state:			
(a) which of the allegations is denied and if so why, and his version of events if it is different			
(b) which allegations he is unable to admit or deny and requires the claimant to prove, and			
(c) which allegations he admits		16.5(1) and (2)	
The defendant must also:			16, para 11.1
(a) if he disputes the claimant's statement of value, state why and, if he is able, give his own statement of value			
(b) if he defends in a representative capacity, state what that capacity is			
(c) if the defendant has not filed an acknowledgment of service, give an address for service			
The defence must be verified by a **statement of truth**			
If the claim is for **personal injuries** and the claimant has attached a medical report and/or a schedule of past and future losses, the defendant must comply with; a counter-schedule of expenses and losses must be verified by a statement of case			16, para 12.1 and 22 para 1.5
If the defendant relies on the expiry of any relevant **limitation period** he must give details of it: see			16, para 13.1
If the defence is one of **tender**, see		37.3	37, para 2
If the defendant relies on any provision or right arising under the **Human Rights Act 1998**, see			16, para 15.1
The **defence may include**:			
(a) any point of law on which the defence is based			
(b) names of any witnesses			
(c) supporting documents (including expert's report)			
This is the same right enjoyed by the claimant when drafting his particulars of claim, and for comment see **TAB 1**			

TAB 11 PROCEDURAL TABLES

	Form No	CPR Rule	PD
para 7, ante-penultimate paragraph			
2. Consequences of defence failing to deal with allegations			
A defendant who fails to deal with an allegation shall be taken to admit that allegation, save that:		16.5(5)	
(a) where the claim includes a money claim, a defendant shall be taken to require that any allegation relating to the amount of money claimed be proved unless he expressly admits the allegation		16.5(4)	
(b) a defendant who:			
(i) fails to deal with an allegation, but			
(ii) has set out in his defence the nature of his case in relation to the issue to which the allegation is relevant, shall be taken to require that allegation to be proved		16.5(3)	
3. Effect of filing a defence			
Once a defence has been filed, judgment in default cannot be entered and the court will issue **Allocation Questionnaires** unless it dispenses with them		26.3(1)	
If the claim is for a specified amount and the defendant is an individual, the proceedings will be **automatically transferred** to the defendant's home court unless:		26.2	
(a) the claim was commenced in the defendant's home court			
(b) the claim has been transferred to another defendant's home court			
4. Reply			
If the claimant wished to file a reply to the defence he must:		15.8	
(a) file his reply when he files his **Allocation Questionnaire,** and			
(b) serve his reply on the other parties at the same time as he files it			
The claimant will wish to file a reply when the defence raises new issues, although if he fails to do so he will not be taken as admitting matters raised in the defence		16.7	

TABLE 12—COUNTERCLAIMS, CLAIMS FOR CONTRIBUTION OF INDEMNITY AND OTHER ADDITIONAL CLAIMS

TAB 12

	Form No	CPR Rule	PD
1. Preliminary			
Part 20 applies to a counterclaim and also to any additional claim. A counterclaim is a claim by the defendant against the claimant, whereas additional claims are claims by the defendant against persons other than the claimant and include a claim by one defendant against another and a claim by a defendant against a person who is not already a party (a Third Party).			
2. Description of parties			
See CPR PD 20, para 7 and note in particular:			
(a) if a defendant makes an additional claim against a single additional party that party should be referred to as the Third Party and if he makes separate additional claims against two additional parties (not jointly) they should be referred to as the Third and Fourth Party;			
(b) if the defendant makes a counterclaim against the claimant and additional party the claimant remains as 'Claimant' and the additional party should be referred to as the 'Third Party'.			
PD 20, para 7 contains an exhaustive list of situations and provides examples.			20, para 7
3. The Crown			
In a claim by the Crown for taxes, duties or penalties the defendant cannot make a counterclaim or other Part 20 claim or raise a defence of set off.			
In any other claim by the Crown the defendant cannot make a counterclaim or other Part 20 claim or raise a defence of set off which is based on a claim for the repayment of taxes, duties or penalties.			
In proceedings by the Crown in the name of the Attorney General no counterclaim or other Part 20 claim can be made or defence of set off raised without the permission of the court.			
If the Crown is sued or sues in the name of a Government department no counterclaim or other Part 20 claim can be made or defence of set off raised without the permission of the court unless the subject-matter refers to that department.			

TAB 12 PROCEDURAL TABLES

	Form No	CPR Rule	PD
PART A – COUNTERCLAIMS			
4. A counterclaim against the claimant			
Permission is needed to bring a counter-claim against a claimant brought under Part 8 but otherwise **no permission is required, provided the particulars of the counterclaim are filed with the defence.**			
Permission is required to bring a coun-terclaim after a defence has been filed.		20.4(1) and (2)	
If permission has to be sought an appli-cation under CPR 23 will be necessary and it must be supported by evidence and an explanation for the delay	N244	20.4(2)	20, paras 2.1–2.3
A copy of the proposed counterclaim must be filed with the application			20, para 1.2
4A. Counterclaim against a person other than the claimant			
If it is proposed to counter claim against some person other than the claimant ap-plication must be made to the court to add that person as an additional party. The application may be made without notice unless the court otherwise orders		20.5(1) and (2)	
PD 20, para 1 requires the application for permission of the court required by CPR 20.5(1) to be filed with a copy of the proposed additional claim and PD 20, para 2 requires the application to be supported by evidence setting out the matters listed at (1)-(4) in the paragraph, explaining any delay and providing a timetable of the proceedings to date.			20, paras 1 and 2
When making the order adding the addi-tional party under CPR 20.5(1) the court will give directions for the management of the case.		20.5(3)	
5. Procedure for counterclaims			
The defence and counterclaim should be contained in the same document, as should any reply and defence to counter-claim. the counterclaim is made by filing particulars of it with copies for service. Guidance notes are issued by the court, they are forms:	N211A for claimants, N211C for defendants		20, para 6
A counterclaim will be treated as a claim for the purposes of CPR and must com-ply with the Part 16 "Statement of Case"			20, para 3
A counterclaim must be verified by a statement of truth			20, para 4
A fee is payable to the court on the filing of a counterclaim as if it were a claim.			
If the counterclaim is against an addi-tional party (not the claimant) added as a party by order under CPR 20.5 above the copy claim form served must be ac-companied by: (a) a form for defending the counter-claim; (b) a form for admitting the counter-claim;			

	Form No	CPR Rule	PD
(c) a form for acknowledging service;			
(d) a copy of every statement of case that has already been served in the proceedings and such other documents as the court may direct.		20.12	
The additional party on whom a counterclaim is served pursuant to CPR 20.5(1) becomes a party to the action as soon as he is served with the additional counterclaim.			
6. Responding to a counterclaim			
The acknowledgment of service provisions in CPR 10 do not apply to a claimant who wishes to defend the counterclaim.		20.4(3)	
If the claimant wishes to defend, he must file a defence not later than 14 days after service of the counterclaim.		15.4(1)(a) and (b)	
An additional party added as a Third Party (defendant to the counterclaim), who has acknowledged service must file a defence no later than 28 days from service but if no acknowledgment has been filed no later than 14 days form service.			
Judgment in default (Part 12) applies to a counterclaim but not other additional claims		20.3(3)	20, para 3
Each defendant to a counterclaim may serve or file an admission and CPR 14 applies to judgment on such an admission		14.3, 20.3(4)	
7. Subsequent management when a defence to counterclaim is filed			
The allocation of the claim will include the counterclaim and the court will give directions that the claim and counterclaim will, so far as practicable, be managed together (where a party has been added under CPR 20.5(1) (above) the court will give directions.		20.13	
PART B – DEFENDANT'S ADDITIONAL CLAIM FOR CONTRIBUTION OR INDEMNITY FROM A CO-DEFENDANT			
8. Terms			
'Contribution' – a right of someone to recover from a third party all or part of the amount which he himself is liable to pay.			
'Indemnity' – a right of someone to recover from a third party the whole of the amount which he himself is liable to.		2.2	Glossary
9. Availability			
The permission of the court to claim contribution or indemnity from a co-defendant is only required if the claim is proceedings under Part 8.		8.7	
Otherwise a claim may be made by any defendant who has filed an acknowledgment of service or defence, against a per-			

TAB 12   PROCEDURAL TABLES

	Form No	CPR Rule	PD
son who is already a party to the proceedings, provided he files and service it:		20.6(1)	
(a) with his defence; or			
(b) if the claim for contribution or indemnity is against a party added to the claim later, within 28 days after the party files his defence.			
If neither of these alternatives is satisfied the court's permission will need to be obtained.		20.6(2)	
10. Procedure			
The additional claimant (defendant in the main claim) makes the claim for contribution or indemnity by:		8.7	
(a) filing a notice containing a statement of the nature and grounds of his claim; and			
(b) serving it on his co-defendant in the main claim.			
Service of the notice is as for the service of a claim.		20.3(1)	
11. Response to the notice			
The requirements of acknowledgment and of defence apply but there is no provision for judgment on the contribution or indemnity notice to be entered in default.		20.3(1) and (3)	
If the notice is admitted in writing in whole or in part the claimant may apply for judgment on the admission against his co-defendant in the main suit.		20.3(4)	
12. Case management			
On the filing of a defence to the notice the court will list a case management hearing and give appropriate directions. In the normal way the claim and the contribution or indemnity proceedings will be managed together. This is not however invariably so – see Part D of this TAB below.		20.13(2)	20, para 5
PART C – OTHER ADDITIONAL CLAIMS			
13. Definition			
These claims which may be for any remedy are governed by CPR 20.7. This applies to any additional claim except:			
(a) a counterclaim only against an existing party; and			
(b) a claim for contribution or indemnity made in accordance with CPR 20.6; see art B of this TAB.		20.7	
A peson who is the defendant to such an additional claim and who is not already a party may himself make an additional claim against any other person (whether or not already a party).		20.2(1)(c)	
14. Necessity of permission			
Permission to issue will be required if the case is proceeding under Part 8.			

	Form No	CPR Rule	PD
Otherwise a defendant may make an additional claim without permission, provided it is issued before or at the same time as he files his defence, but may only do so at any other time with the court's permission.		20.7(3)	
When permission is required the application may be made without notice, unless the court otherwise directs, and should be filed with a copy of the proposed additional claim and with supporting evidence.		20.7(5)	
The supporting evidence should include the statements required by CPR PD 20, para 2.1(1)-(4) and explain any delay and provide a timetable of the proceedings to date.			20, paras 1 and 2
15. Issue and service			
An additional claim is treated as if it were a claim except when otherwise provided in Part 20.		20.3(1)	
The additional claimant will file the additional claim form and, if they are separate, the particulars of claim with copies for the court, each additional defendant and each party to the main claim. The additional claimant must pay the court fee.			
If permission to issue is necessary see para 14 of this TAB above.			
The additional claim is made when the court issues the claim form.			
The additional claim, if made without the permission of the court, must be served on the person against whom it is made 14 days after the date on which the additional claim was issued by the court.			
When the court gives permission to issue it will at the same time give directions as to service.			
When the additional claim form is served on a person who is not already a party to the proceedings it must be served with			
(a) a form for defending the claim;			
(b) a form for admitting the claim;			
(c) a form for acknowledging service;			
(d) a copy of			
(i) every statement of case already service in the proceedings;			
(ii) any other documents as the court directs.		20.12(1)	
In all instances a copy of the additional claim form must be served on every existing party.		20.12(2)	
16. Responding to an additional claim			
The forms of acknowledgment and defence should be completed and filed: the defence should be filed no later than 14			

TAB 12 PROCEDURAL TABLES

	Form No	CPR Rule	PD
days from service unless service has been acknowledged in which case the defence should be filed no later than 28 days from service.			
If the additional claim is not a counter-claim or a claim by a defendant for indemnity or contribution against another defendant under CPR 20.6, and the party against whom the additional claims has been made fails to file an acknowledgment of service or a defence, he is:			
(a) deemed to admit the additional claim;			
(b) bound by any relevant judgment or decision in the proceedings.		20.11(2)(a)	
If default judgment is given against the additional claimant, the additional claimant may enter default judgment in respect of the additional claim provided: (a) he has satisfied the default judgment entered against him; (b) he wishes to obtain a remedy other than a contribution or indemnity.		22.11(2)(b) 22.11(3)(a)	
Unless both these provisions are satisfied an application for the court's permission to enter judgment must be made. Unless the court otherwise directs the application may be made without notice.		20.11(4)	
The court can at any time set aside or vary a default judgment made under 20.11(2)(b).		20.11(5)	

TABLE 13—ALLOCATION

TAB 13

	Form No	CPR Rule	PD
1. Allocation principles			
The court, in considering whether to allocation a claim, will have regard to the matters set out in CPR 26.8(1)(a)–(i)		26.8(1)	
The **financial value** of the claim is to be assessed by the court but it must disregard:		26.8(2)	
(a) any amount not in dispute			
(b) any claim for interest			
(c) any claim for costs			
(d) any contributory negligence			
Where the court believes the amount claimed is excessive it can make an order directing the claimant to justify the amount			26A, para 7.3(2)
When there is more than one money claim the court will generally regard the largest of them as determining the financial value of the claims. See			26A, para 7.7
In deciding whether **any amount is not in dispute** the court will apply the following general principles:			
(a) any amount not admitted is disputed			
(b) any part of the claim for which judgment has been entered is not in dispute			
(c) any specific sum claimed as a distinct item which the defendant admits is not in dispute			
(d) any sum offered and accepted for a distinct part of the claim is not in dispute			26A, para 7.4
A claimant can limit his claim to bring it within the financial limits of the small claims track or even to reduce the court fees payable: *Khiaban v Beard* [2003] EWCA Civ 358, [2003] 3 All ER 362, [2003] All ER (D) 111 (Mar)			
2. Re-allocation			
Where a party is dissatisfied with the allocation order he may appeal or apply to the court to re-allocate. He should appeal if the allocation was effected at a hearing at which he was present or had notice; but otherwise should apply for re-allocation	N244		26A, para 11.1(1)
Where there has been a change of circumstances the court can re-allocate on application or on its own initiative. See *Maguire v Molin* [2002] EWCA Civ 1083, [2002] 4 All ER 325 as to the wide discretion enjoyed when deciding whether to reallocate and the matters to be taken into account. See also CPR			

TAB 13 PROCEDURAL TABLES

	Form No	CPR Rule	PD
26.10[1] for further consideration of this case			26A, para 11.1(2)
3. Draft directions			
An attempt should be made by the parties to agree directions, with sensible time limits, for the court's consideration.			27, paras 9 and 10 (small claims), 28, para 9 (fast track)
For a comprehensive order for case management directions in the multi-track see Form PF 52			
4. Costs on small claims and fast track			
Costs incurred before and after allocation shall be governed by the rules of the track to which the claim is allocated except where a court or a practice direction provides otherwise.		44.9(2)	

TABLE 14—APPLICATIONS

TAB 14

	Form No	CPR Rule	PD
1. Preliminary			
See **CPR 23 [1]–CPR 23 [12]** and in particular note:			
1.1 An application should be made as soon as it becomes apparent that an application is necessary or desirable and the general rule is that an applicant must file an application notice unless the application may be made without such notice by operation of a rule or practice direction or the court dispenses with the requirement; see *R (Simmons) v Bolton Metropolitan Borough Council* [2011] EWHC 2729 (Admin).		23.13	23A, para 2.7
1.2 CPR PD 23:			
(a) requires parties, whenever possible, to make an application so that it can be considered at any hearing that has been fixed or is about to be fixed			23A, para 2.8
(b) the parties should anticipate that, at the hearing of the application, the court may wish to review the conduct of the case as a whole and give any necessary directions and be ready to assist in so doing			23A, para 9
(c) important specific applications should not be made at a pre-trial review unless there is more than adequate time for the judge to be able to deal with an additional important application: *Omni Laboratories Inc v Eden energy Ltd* [2011] EWHC 2169 (TCC), [2011] All ER (D) 92 (Aug).			
1.3 All applications made before a claim is commenced should be made under Part 23			23A, para 5
1.4 An application for **further particulars** under Part 18 will only be justified if they will narrow or dispose of an issue or help a court to do so			
In *Lexi Holdings (in administration) v Pannone and Partners* [2010] EWHC 1416 (Ch), 18 June the judge held that the appropriate tests on applications for further information are 'necessity' and 'proportionality' in relation to the applicant's ability to prepare its own case and to understand the case it has to meet.		18.1	
In *National Grid Electricity Transmission plc v ABB* [2012] EWHC 869 (Ch), [2012] All ER (D) 92 (Apr) Roth J stated 'The Part 18 procedure should not be used to force a defendant, in adversarial litigation, to provide what amounts to fragmentary witness evidence			

TAB 14   PROCEDURAL TABLES

	Form No	CPR Rule	PD
at the behest of the claimant at an earlier state in the proceedings'. See further paras 61–80 of his judgment and the article by Mary Blyth in (2012) NLJ, 7 September, page 1105.			
1.5.1 For applications for **interim remedies and security for costs** see CPR 25 and in particular for **interim payments** CPR 25.6 (general procedure) and CPR 25.7 (conditions to be satisfied). The court before ordering an interim payment on the ground that the claimant would at trial obtain judgment for a substantial sum of money against the defendant (CPR 25.7(1)) has to be satisfied on the balance of probabilities that, on the material available, the claimant would obtain judgment for a substantial amount: *Revenue and Customs Comrs v GKN Group* [2012] All ER (D) 107 (Feb). Useful guidance as to the proportion of the anticipated final judgment it is reasonable to award by way of interim payment is provided in *Spillman v Bradfield Riding Centre* [2007] EWHC 89 (QB) [200] All ER (D) 59 (Feb), 6 February. The 'reasonable proportion in that case was 75%.			
The determination of the amount must be in accordance with CPR 25.7(2) and (3) rather than a consideration of the purpose for which the payment is sought.			
The relationship between interim payments (IPOs) and the allocation of losses to periodical payments is considered in *Eeles v Cobham Hire Services Ltd* [2009] EWCA Civ 204, [2009] PIQR P273, Civil Procedure News, 7 April 2009 and see articles 'A clearer future' by Stephen Hazelton in Sol Jo (2009) 26 May, page 6 and 'Interim Solutions' by David Oldham in Sol Jo (2009) 16 December, page 15			
Note most recently the application of the Eeles principles in *FP v Taunton and Somerset NHS Trust* [2009] EWHC 1965 (QB), 110 BMLR 164 and *Johnson (by her mother and litigation friend) v Compton-Cooke* [2009] EWHC 2582 (QB), [2009] All ER (D) 214 (Oct) and in *Brown v Emery* [2010] EWHC 388 (QB), 4 March		25.6 and 25.7	
1.5.2 An application by a defendant for **security for costs** should be made using form N244 and written evidence in support is required. It is good practice to request security by letter before making the application.		25.12	
1.5.3 The written evidence should have attached the request and any reply and also a bill of costs showing costs to date and costs to be incurred. The bill should preferably be in the form of Precedent H at CPR PD 48.			

	Form No	CPR Rule	PD
1.5.4 In an application for security for costs made under CPR 3.1(3) or 3.1(5) or when the court is considering making such an order of its own motion it should apply the principles under CPR 25.12 and 25.13: per Moore Bick LJ in *Huscroft v P & O Ferries Ltd* [2010] EWCA Civ 1483, [2011] All ER 762; for detailed consideration see article 'Cost control' by Bernard Pressman in (2011) NLJ, 1 July, page 915.			
1.5.5 The court may make the order if having regard to all the circumstances of the case it is just to do so, and that either one of the conditions set out in CPR 23.13(2)(a)-(g) applies or an enactment permits the court to require security.		23.13	
1.6 For freezing injunctions to support or assist in relation to an order of security for costs see s 37 of the Senior Courts Act 1981 and *Rajvel Construction Ltd v Bestville Properties Ltd* (2011) 7 September, QBD, Coulson J and see also *Riva Bella SA v Tamsen Yachts GmbH* [2011] EWHC 2338 (Comm) where the applicant was in contempt and the court exercised its discretion under RSC Ord 52r1 in its favour.			
1.7 For **amendment after expiry of the limitation period** the court has to compare the essential facts as pleaded in the exisitng cause of action and the essential facts in the proposed cause of action. If they are the same there is no new claim for the purpose of the Limitation Act 1980, s 35(2): *Revenue and Customs Comrs v Noorasa Begum* [2010] EWHC 1799 (Admin); see also CPR 17.4.			
1.8 The general rule is that hearings are in public but **a hearing may be in private** if it falls within the list set out at (a)-(g) of CPR 39.2(3). The court is required by CPD PD 39A, para 1.5 to list hearings that fall within (1)-(10) of that sub-paragraph in private in the first instance.			
1.9 Pre-action applications in designated money claims: an application in a designated money claim made before the claim has started may be made in any county court (CPR 23.2(4A)).			
2. Definitions			
"Application notice" means a document in which the applicant states his intention to seek a court order		23.1	
Practice Form N244 may be used and it is sensible to do so	N244		
"Respondent" means (a) the person against whom the order is sought and (b) such other person as the court may direct			
3. Filing, notice and service			

TAB 14 PROCEDURAL TABLES

	Form No	CPR Rule	PD
An application must be made by **filing an application notice** unless a Rule, Practice Direction or the court permits an application without such filing or dispenses with it		23.3	
If a copy of the application is to be served it must be accompanied by: (a) a copy of any written evidence in support, and (b) a copy of any draft order which the applicant has attached to his application			
If an application is served but the period of notice is shorter than required the court may direct that in the circumstances sufficient notice has been given and hear the application		23.7(4)	
4. Contents of application notice			
An application notice must state: (a) what order the applicant is seeking, and (b) briefly, why the applicant is seeking the order		23.6	
The formal matters set out in CPR PD 23 must also be included; note that where the applicant is not already a party address for service including a postcode has to be shown			23A, para 2.1
The application must be signed and be verified by a statement of truth if it is wished to rely on matters set out in the application notice as evidence		22.1(a)	
Except in the most simple case the applicant should bring a **draft order** to the hearing and it is good practice to attach a draft of the order to the application form	N244		
If the application is intended to be made to a judge the application should so state			23A, para 2.6
Where the hearing is not likely to last more than one day the parties must file and serve statements of costs on each other at least 24 hours before the time fixed for the hearing. This provision does not apply to mortgage possession proceedings	N260		Costs PD, para 13.5
5. Evidence			
The evidence is generally given by **witness statements** unless the court, a Practice Direction or other enactment requires otherwise. If Form N244 is used, and only one statement is to be relied upon, it can conveniently be set out in Part C of the Form		32.6(1)	
A party may also rely at the hearing of the application on matters set out: (a) in his statement of case, or (b) in his application notice provided the statement or notice is verified by a statement of truth		32.6(2)	

	Form No	CPR Rule	PD
If the respondent wishes to rely on evidence that has not yet been served he should serve it as soon as possible and in any event in accordance with any directions the court has given			23A, para 9.4
If the applicant wishes to file evidence in reply it should also be served as soon as possible and in accordance with any directions given			23A, para 9.5
The court will often need to be satisfied by evidence of the facts that are relied upon in support of or in opposition to the application			23A, para 9.1
6. Application without service of notice			
An application may be made without service only:			23A, para 3
(a) where there is exceptional urgency			
(b) where the overriding objective is best furthered by doing so			
(c) by consent of all the parties			
(d) with the permission of the court			
(e) where a date for hearing has been fixed and a party wishes to make an application and there is insufficient time: see final paragraph of part 3 of this Table, above			23A, para 2.10
(f) where a court order, Rule or Practice Direction permits			
Where the court has disposed of an application without service of the application notice, the application, any evidence in support and the order must be served			
The order must contain a statement of the right to make an **application to set aside or vary the order**		23.9	
The time for making such an application to set aside or vary must be made **within 7 days** after the date on which the order was served on the person making the application		23.10	
7. Applications dealt with without a hearing			
The court may deal with an application without a hearing if:		23.8	
(a) the parties agree as to the terms of the order sought			
(b) the parties agree that the court should dispose of the application without a hearing, or			
(c) the court does not consider that a hearing would be appropriate			
Where the application is for an order in terms that have been agreed the provisions of CPR 40.6 (5)-(7) and PD 40B paras 3 and 11 must be observed		40.6(5)-(7)	40B, paras 3 and 11
Note: Under a court's duty to manage cases there is included "dealing with the case without the parties needing to attend court"		1.4	

TAB 14 PROCEDURAL TABLES

	Form No	CPR Rule	PD
When CPR 23.8(c) applies (ie the court considers a hearing not appropriate) the court will treat the application as if it were proposing to make an order on its own initiative. Accordingly, any party affected may apply within 7 days of service to have the order set aside, varied or stayed and the order must set out this right			
If the court does not agree to dispose of the application without a hearing the court will list the application for hearing and give any necessary directions			23A, para 2.4
8. The hearing			
It is essential for the applicant to have provided for a **sufficient time** allowance for his application to be properly heard			
CPR PD 39A, para 5.1 requires that at any hearing a written statement containing the following information to be provided for the court: (a) the name and address of each advocate; (b) his qualification or entitlement to act as an advocate; and (c) the party for whom he so acts.			39A, para 5.1

TABLE 15—DISCLOSURE AND INSPECTION

TAB 15

	Form No	CPR Rule	PD
1. Preliminary			
1.1 Normal disclosure is limited to 'standard disclosure' see para 2 below and the search for documents is limited to that which is reasonable and proportionate. The parties from the outset must decide what is proportionate and what are the real issues in the case and limit disclosure accordingly see CPR 31 [5]			
1.2 Part 31 does not apply to small claims		27.2(1)(b)	
1.3 A party discloses a document by stating that document exists or has existed		31.2	
1.4 '**Document**' means anything in which information is recorded and '**copy**' means anything onto which information in a document has been copied by any means		31.4	
1.5 The definition extends to electronic documents of which a non-exclusive list is contained in the Practice Direction to which reference should be made where **electronic disclosure** is being considered. It has been suggested, see Gazette (2007) 18 October, page 1, that judges need special e-disclosure training to equip them to interpret the broadly drafted rules. It may well be that the bulk of the judiciary agree with this view. For the vital importance of having the right 'tools' for e-disclosure and discovery and the costs considerations see article by Dr JC Scholtes 'Digging with the right tools' in Sol Jo (2009) 3 February, page 18 and article by Tracey Stretton 'Endless Possibilities' in Sol Jo Expert Witness Supplement, Spring 2009.			31A, para 2A.1–2A.5
There is no duty on parties to preserve documents before proceedings are commenced but after that the situation radically changes. See *Earles v Barclays Bank plc* [2009] EWHC 2500 (QB), [2009] All ER (D) 179 (Oct), (2009) Times, 20 October as to this in relation to electronic data and CPR PD 31B, para 7.			31B, para 7
For 'reasonable search' for disclosure of electronic documents see *Digicel (St Lucia) Ltd v Cable & Wireless plc* [2008] EWHC 2522 (Ch), 23 October, Morgan J and article 'A shock to the system' by Sautter and Church, (2009) NLJ 23 January, page 111 and 'In search of reasonableness' by Chris Paley-Menzies (2009) NLJ, 29 May, page 792. It is to be noted that £2m and nearly 7,000 hours of legal time did not achieve a word search that was considered 'rea-			

TAB 15 PROCEDURAL TABLES

	Form No	CPR Rule	PD
sonable'. See also CPR PD 31B, paras 20–24.			31B, paras 20–24
The duty of disclosure continues throughout the proceedings and see PD 31B, para 7 as to electronic documents.		31.11	31A, para 1.3
1.6 Only in a very exceptional case will a party be ordered to deliver witness statements before receiving disclosure from the other party: *Watford Petroleum Ltd v Interoil Trading SA* [2003] EWCA Civ 1417, [2003] All ER (D) 175 (Sep)			
1.7 The legal representative of a party giving disclosure must 'endeavour to ensure that the person making the disclosure statement . . . understands the duty of disclosure under Part 31'			31A, para 4.4
1.8 In a claim of privilege based on the **'without prejudice' rule** the crucial consideration is whether or not in the course of negotiations the parties contemplated or might reasonably have contemplated litigation if they could not agree: *Barnetson v Framlington Group Ltd* [2007] EWCA Civ 502, [2007] 3 All ER 1054. See also *Stax Claimants v The Bank of Nova Scotia Channel Islands Ltd* [2007] EWHC 1153 (Ch), [2007] All ER (D) 215 (May), [2007] LS Gazette, 2 August, page 28 and *Galliford Try Construction Ltd v Mott Macdonald Ltd* [2008] EWHC 603 (TCC), [2008] All ER (D) 30 (Apr).			
1.9 For the consequence of revealing part of a privileged document or some privileged documents relevant to an issue see *Fulham Leisure Holdings Ltd v Nicholson Graham and Jones* [2006] EWHC 158 (Ch), [2006] 2 All ER 599 and 1.13 below.			
1.10 For disclosure of without prejudice offers made by the parties during **mediation** see *Earl of Malmesbury v Strutt and Parker* [2008] EWHC 616 (QB), [2008] All ER (D) 339 (Apr) where the parties agreed the judge should know the offers made and *Cumbria Waste Management Ltd and Lakeland Waste Management Ltd v Baines Wilson* [2008] EWHC 786 (QB), [2008] BLR 330 where one party to the mediation would not waive privilege and the judge refused to order disclosure to preserve the freedom enjoyed by negotiators. For full discussion of the position see article by Tony Allen, 'Enforced Security', NLJ, 16 May 2008, page 688			
1.11 For **litigation privilege** see *London Pipeline & Storage Ltd v Total UK* [2008] EWHC 1729 (Comm), [2008] All ER (D) 294 (Jul).			
1.12 For **legal professional privilege** see *Three Rivers District Council v Bank of England (No 6)* [2005] 1 AC 610 as to			

	Form No	CPR Rule	PD
the extent of the communication between solicitor and client covered by legal professional privilege; and see *BBGP Managing General Partner Ltd v Babcock Brown Global Partners* [2010] All ER (D) 42 (Oct), (Ch) for extensive consideration of the principles in a substantial and involved case with many parties.			
1.13 For the question of breach of **confidentiality** see *Napier and Irwin Mitchell v Pressdram* [2009] EWCA Civ 443, where the Court of Appeal refused to recognise it 'to protect' the interests of a solicitor against whom an adverse finding has been made by the Law Society adjudication panel. See further as to disclosure of confidential documents *Croft House Care Ltd v Durham County Council* [2010] All ER (D) 12 (May) where the court indicated that where a document had been found to be confidential it still had to decide whether discovery would give rise to a breach of that confidence. It was decided that, balancing the right of third parties to confidentiality against the necessity for the documents to be provided for the purpose of a fair trial, the material should be disclosed: see further Civil Court News, September 2010, page 1.			
1.14 The long established rule, that evidence of **pre-contract negotiation** is inadmissible when a contract is being interpreted was upheld but somewhat undermined by the obiter statements of the House of Lords in *Chartbrook v Persimmon Homes* [2009] UKHL 38, [2009] 3 WLR 267 which regarded them as *prima facie* admissible where they provide background which is potentially relevant. For the acceptance of evidence of 'market practice' (as opposed to trade usage) to assist the court to gain a full understanding of the background to the construction of a written contract see *Cream v Cenkos Secrities plc* [2010] EWCA Civ 1444, [2010] All ER (D) 212 (Dec).			
1.15 For **waiver of privilege** and the question of consequential further disclosure see *Fulham Leisure Holding Ltd v Nicholson Graham and Jones* [2006] EWHC 158 (Ch); *Dore v Leicester County Council* [2010] EWHC 34 (Ch); and article 'Selective disclosure' by Preece and Vannelli, (2010) Sol Jo, 23 March, page 13; and 1.9 above.			
A party that refers the court to a term of an offer made by it pursuant to CPR 36 waives its 'without prejudice' privilege and enables the remaining terms of the offer to be brought to the court's attention: *Virgin Atlantic Airways Ltd v Jet Airways* (2013) Times, 7 February (Ch).			
1.16 **Electronic disclosure**			

TAB 15   PROCEDURAL TABLES

	Form No	CPR Rule	PD
Practice Direction 31B is expressed to 'encourage and assist the parties reach agreement in relation to the **disclosure of electronic documents** in a proportionate and cost effective manner.			31B, para 1.2
Failure to comply with the rules as to such disclosure may result in costs penalties, even on a successful party, or strike out; see *Earles v Barclays Bank plc* [2009] EWHC 2500 (QB), [2009] All ER (D) 179 (Oct) where because of its deficiencies the successful defendant was awarded only 25% of its costs even before PD 31B came into force. Part of the reduction was however because the defendant had incurred more expensive legal representation than the case merited.			
Unless the court otherwise orders the PD only applies to:			
(a) proceedings that are (or are likely to be) allocated to **the multi track**;			31B, para 1.3
(b) proceedings started **on or after 1 October 2010** – paragraphs 2A.2 to 2A.5 of PD 31A continues to apply to proceedings issued before that date.			31B, para 1.4
For definitions, see:			
'Data Sampling'			31B, para 1.5(1)
'Disclosure Date'			31B, para 1.5(2)
'Electronic Document'			31B, para 1.5(3)
'Electronic Image'			31B, para 1.5(4)
'Electronic Documents Questionnaire' which means the questionnaire in the Schedule to the PD			
'Keyword Search'			31B, para 1.5(5)
'Metadata'			31B, para 1.5(6)
'Native Electronic Document'			31B, para 1.5(7)
'Optical Character Recognition (OCR)'			31B, para 1.5(8)
PD 31B requires the parties to keep in mind the general principles of:			31B, para 1.5(9)
• efficient management to minimise costs;			
• use of technology for document management;			
• giving effect to the overriding objective;			
• making documents available for inspection in a way that it gives the other party the same ability to access etc the documents as the providing party;			
• only documents relevant to the proceedings should be disclosed.			31B, para 1.6
As soon as litigation is contemplated clients must be notified of the need to **preserve disclosable documents** including electronic documents that would otherwise be deleted. The EDQ (see below)			

	Form No	CPR Rule	PD
specifically asks if an instruction to preserve documents has been given.			31B, para 1.7
PD 31B makes further provision for:			
• discussions (which are mandatory) between the parties before the first CMC in relation to the use of technology and disclosure (a list of the issues that have to be discussed is set out in the PD);			31B, paras 1.8 and 1.9
• the Electronic Documents Questionnaire (its use is not mandatory but it must be used if the court so orders);			31B, paras 1.10-1.13
• preparation for the first CMC;			31B, paras 1.14-1.16
• the reasonable search;			31B, paras 1.20-1.24
• keyword and other automated searches;			31B, paras 1.25-1.27
• disclosure of metadata;			31B, paras 1.28-1.29
• list of documents. Note in particular that the Form N265 may be amended to accommodate the sub-paragraphs CPR 31, paras 30(2)-(7);			31B, para 1.30
• provision of Disclosure Data in electronic form;			31B, para 1.31
• provision of electronic copies of disclosed documents. Note in particular that the parties should co-operate at an early stage about the format in which Electronic Documents are to be provided for inspection;			31B, paras 1.32-1.35
• specialised technology.			31B, para 1.36
The **Electronic Documents Questionnaire** is annexed to PD 31B; the answers to the questionnaire must be verified by a statement of truth.			31B, para 1.11
If the parties indicate that the cannot agree as to disclosure of Electronic Documents the court will give written directions at a separate hearing and when doing so will consider making an order for completion and exchange of all or part of the Electronic Document Questionnaire.			31B, para 1.15
The person signing the questionnaire should attend the first case management conference and any subsequent hearing at which disclosure is likely to be considered.			31B, para 1.16
The onus is on the parties to monitor the costs of e-disclosure and to keep them to a proportionate level.			
2. Standard disclosure			
Richard Langley in an article 'Ignorance isn't bliss' in (2011) NLJ, 14 January, page 69 presents a convincing argument			

TAB 15 PROCEDURAL TABLES

	Form No	CPR Rule	PD
in favour of the abolition of standard disclosure.			
2.1 Standard disclosure requires a party to disclose only:			
(a) documents on which he relies and			
(b) documents which-			
(i) adversely affect his own case			
(ii) adversely affect another party's case			
(iii) support another party's case and			
(c) documents he is required to disclose by a practice direction		31.6	31A, para 1.1
2.2 In all cases to which CPR 31.5(2) does not apply (see below):		31.5(1)	
(a) an order to give disclosure, unless otherwise directed, is an order to give standard disclosure;			
(b) the court may dispense with or limit standard disclosure;			
(c) the parties may agree in writing to dispense with or limit standard disclosure.			
2.3 Unless the court otherwise directs in all multi-track claims (other than those which include a claim for personal injuries) the provisions of CPR 31.5(2)-(8) will apply.		31.5(2)— (8)	31A, para 1.4
To the extent that the documents disclosed are electronic the Practice Direction 31B-Disclosure of electronic Documents will apply		31.5(9)	
2.4 When giving standard disclosure a party must make **reasonable search** for documents within CPR 36.6(b) and (c): see para 2.1 above and see also the guidance given as to this by Jacob, Rix and Pill LJJ in *Nichia Corpn v Argos Ltd* [2007] EWCA Civ 741, [2007] All ER (D) 299 (Jul). For reasonable search and electronic documents see para 1, sub-para 4 above		31.7(1)	
The factors relevant in deciding reasonableness include:			
(a) the number of documents			
(b) the nature and complexity of the proceedings			
(c) ease and expense of retrieval			
(d) significance of documents likely to be located		31.7(2)	31A, para 2
2.5 The duty to disclose is limited to those documents which are or have been in a party's control but in *North Shore Ventures Ltd v Anstead Holdings Inc* [2012] EWCA Civ 11 the Court stressed the necessity of having regard to the 'true relationship between the litigant and the related third party' for docu-			

	Form No	CPR Rule	PD
ments could be within the control of a litigant even where it did not have a right to possession. This decision is of importance where group companies are concerned.		31.8	
3. Procedure for standard disclosure			
3.1 Each party must make and serve on every other party a list of documents in the relevant practice form	N265	31.10(2)	31A, para 3
The list is divided into 3 sections, which follow the enclosure statement:			
(a) first, documents which the party has within his control and does not object to produce;			
(b) second, documents which the party has within his control but objects to the other party inspecting;			
(c) third, documents that the party has had within his control but are no longer within his control.			
3.2 The list must indicate:			
(a) the documents in respect of which it is claimed there is a right or duty to withhold inspect and			
(b) those documents which are no longer in the party's control and what has happened to them		31.10(4)	31A, paras 4, 5 and 6; 6.1 and 6.2
For the disclosure of copies that have been marked see		31.9	
For the disclosure of electronic documents see			31A, para 2A.1 2A.5
3.3 The list must include a **disclosure statement**. The solicitor for a party must try to ensure his client or the person signing on the client's behalf understands the duty of disclosure			31A, para 4.4
3.4 For the form of the statement see		31.10(6)	31A, para 4.2 and annex
For the ability to amend form N265 where a party is giving disclosure of documents see			31B, para 30
For the person by whom the statement is to be made see		31.10(6) and (7)	31A, para 4.2 and 4.3
For signature by an insurer or the Motor Insurers' Bureau see			31A, para 4.7
3.5 For withholding disclosure on the ground that disclosure would damage the **public interest** see		31.19(1) and(2)	
3.6 The parties may agree or the court may direct that disclosure or inspection, or both, shall take place in stages; typically where a split trial has been ordered		31.13	
4. The right of inspection of a disclosed document			
4.1 A party to whom a party has disclosed a document has a right to inspect it except where:			

TAB 15   PROCEDURAL TABLES

		Form No	CPR Rule	PD
(a)	the document is no longer in the control of the party who disclosed it (see CPR 31.8)		31.3(1)(a)	
(b)	the party disclosing the document has a right or duty to withhold inspection of it (see CPR 31.19)		31.3(1)(b)	
(c)	the party considers it would be disproportionate to the issues provided he has so indicated in his disclosure statement		31.3(c), 31.3(2)	
(d)	where rule 78.26 applies, ie evidence arising out of mediation of certain cross-border disputes – see further Section III CPR – Mediation Directive at **CPR 78.23** to **CPR 78.28.**		31.3(d)	
4.2 For the right to inspect **documents referred to in statements of case etc** see			31.14(1)	
For the right to inspect a document referred to in a witness statement being displaced by a claim of privilege see *Expandable Ltd v Rubin* [2008] EWCA Civ 59, [2008] All ER (D) 148 (Feb), (2008) NLJ, 29 February, page 332 where the court held as to the sufficiency of 'mention' that the document in question doesn't have to be relied upon, referred to in any particular way or for any particular purpose. See also Civil Litigation Brief, Sol Jo (2008) 25 March, page 22.				
See further for disclosure of documents mentioned in witness statements the judgment of Nicol J in *Webster v Ridgeway Foundation School Governors* [2009] EWHC 1140 (QB), (2009) Sol Jo (no 22) 31, where limitations on the right to disclosure of such documents, including questions of proportionality, relevance, redaction, interference with private lives and Article 8 of the European Convention on Human Rights 1950, were fully considered.				
Exhibits attached to a witness statement were held not to be protected from discovery in *Accident Exchanges Ltd v Autofocus Ltd* [2009] EWHC 3304 (QB) because they comprised material collected by the witness on which he might be called to give evidence: see also note by Stephen Gold (2010) NLJ 19 February, page 261.				
4.3 For inspection of documents any document mentioned in an expert's report which has not already been disclosed in the proceedings etc see			31.14(2)	31A, para 7.1 and 7.2
5. Specific disclosure or inspection				
5.1 The court may make an order for **specific disclosure** requiring a party to do one or more of				
(a)	disclosing documents or classes of documents specified in the order			

	Form No	CPR Rule	PD
(b)　　carrying out a search to the extent stated in the order			
(c)　　disclosing any documents located as a result of that search			
5.2 The court may make an order for **specific inspection** requiring a party to permit inspection of a documents referred to in CPR 31.3(2): (see para 4.1 above as to inspection considered disproportionate)		31.12	31A, para 5.1-5.5
5.3 The application will be made in accordance with Part 23 and even if the order is granted costs may be reserved until the court can evaluate the evidential value of material obtained (see CPR 31.12[1] and [2]	N244		
6. Inspection and copying of documents			
6.1 Where a party has a right of inspection he must give written notice of his wish to inspection and such inspection must be permitted and more than 7 days after the date on which the notice was received		31.15(a) and (b)	
6.2 A party may request a copy of a document and if he also undertakes to pay reasonable copying charges he must be supplied with a copy not more than 7 days after receipt of the request			
6.3 For the right or duty to **withhold inspection** see		31.15(c)	
For discussion of refusal of inspection by reason of privilege see CPR 31 [2] –[15]		31.19(3)-(7)	
For use of **privileged documents inadvertently disclosed** see		31.20	
7. Relationship of disclosure and strike out			
A court will be reluctant to strike out the particulars of claim of a case arguably so speculative as to be an abuse of process before ordering disclosure under Part 31 so that the claimant can see if it has an arguable case; *Arsenal Football Club plc v Elite Sports Distribution Ltd* [2002] EWHC 3057 (Ch), [2002] FSR 450, [2003] 07 LS Gaz R 36.			
8. Disclosure before the start of proceedings			
8.1 This is now available in all proceedings see CPR 31.16[1]			
Where there has been a breach of the pre-action protocol, the defendant should be put on written notice that unless there is a compliance within, say, 14 days an application for pre-action disclosure will be made			
8.2 The application is made by application notice and must be supported by evidence; see *Lawrence v Metropolitan Police Comr* [2006] EWCA Civ 425.	N244	25.4 31.16(2)	
The statement to be relied on should provide:			
(a)　　brief circumstances of the claim;			

TAB 15 PROCEDURAL TABLES

	Form No	CPR Rule	PD
(b) the date of the letter of claim and any acknowledgment;			
(c) the date of expiry of the protocol period and details of any breaches			
There should be attached to the statement			
(a) copy correspondence between the parties			
(b) a draft order requiring the defendant to file a statement with time limits for compliance and a schedule of the documents sought			
(c) a statement of costs			
8.3 The court can only make an order for pre-action disclosure if there is a real prospect in principle of such an order being **fair to the parties** if litigation was commenced, or of assisting the parties **to avoid litigation** or of **saving costs** in any event; *Black v Sumitomo Corpn* [2001] EWCA Civ 1819, [2002] 1 WLR 1562 recently followed in *Hands v Morrison Construction Services* [2006] EWHC 2018 (Ch)		31.16(3)(d)	
8.4 When hearing an application for pre-action disclosure the courts should be hesitant about deciding substantive issues in the anticipated proceedings: *Rose v Lynx Express Ltd* [2004] EWCA Civ 447, (2004) Times, 23 April. See also *Total E & P Soudan SA v Edmonds* [2007] EWCA Civ 50, [2007] All ER (D) 303 (Jan) and *Hutchinson 3G (UK) Ltd v O2 (UK) Ltd* [2008] EWHC 50 (Comm), [2008] All ER (D) 80 (Jan), 18 January			
8.5 For the **form of the order** if granted see		31.16(4) and (5)	
8.6 For **precedents** see BCCP D[21] and BCCP D[22]			
8.7 A costs order against the respondent would only be appropriate where it was clearly unreasonable to oppose the application or where the manner of the opposition was so unreasonable as to make it appropriate to require him to bear the whole of both parties' costs. For a case where unreasonable opposition was found see *Bermuda International Securities Ltd v KPMG* [2001] EWCA Civ 26.			
9. Orders for disclosure against a person not a party			
9.1 Such orders are now available in all proceedings see **CPR 31.17**[1] and, by way of example, *Ixis Corporate and Investment Bank v WestLB AG* [2007] EWHC 1748 (Comm), [2007] All ER (D) 276 (Jul) (see final para of 9.3 below)		37.17	
9.2 Application is made by application notice and must be supported by evidence	N244	25.4 31.17(2)	

	Form No	CPR Rule	PD
9.3 The court may only make the order for disclosure against a non party where:			
(a) the documents of which disclosure is sought are likely to support the case of the applicant or adversely affect the case of one of the other parties to the proceedings and			
(b) disclosure is necessary to dispose fairly of the claim or to save costs		31.17(3)	
9.4 For the **form of the order** see		31.17(4) and (5)	
9.5 For **precedents** see BCCP D[23]-BCCP D[24]			
9.6 For **costs** of non party pre-commencement disclosure and orders for disclosure see CPR 48.2 at para **CPR 48.2**			

TABLE 16—EXPERT EVIDENCE

TAB 16

	Form No	CPR Rule	PD
1. Preliminary			
See **CPR 35 [1]–CPR 35 [8]** and note in particular:			
(a) the only provisions of CPR Pt 35 that apply to **small claims** are:			
(i) CPR 35.1 – duty to restrict expert evidence			
(ii) CPR 35.3 – experts – overriding duty to the court			
(iii) CPR 35.7 – court power to direct evidence to be by a single joint expert			
(iv) CPR 35.8 – instructions to single joint expert			
(b) the **pre-action protocol for personal injury claims** encourages and promotes voluntary disclosure of medical reports but failure to disclose the report of an expert instructed in accordance with the protocol (who is not a jointly instructed expert) does not constitute non-compliance with the protocol: *Carlson v Townsend* [2001] EWCA Civ 511, [2001] 3 All ER 663. In this case the expert was jointly selected by the parties but instructed by the claimant alone			
(c) a party who obtains expert evidence without an appropriate direction from the court does so at his own risk as to costs unless he has complied with the pre-action protocol			
2. Powers and duties of the court			
No party shall call an expert to give oral evidence or put an expert's report in evidence without the **permission of the court**. A party can seek such permission by application in which he must provide an estimate of the costs of the proposed expert evidence and identify:	N244	35.4(1) and (2)	
(a) the field in which expert evidence is required and the issues which the expert evidence will address, and			
(b) when practicable, the name of the proposed expert			
The order granting permission may specify the issues that the expert evidence should address.			
An '**expert**' is a person who has been instructed to give or prepare expert evidence; for the purpose of proceedings			

TAB 16 PROCEDURAL TABLES

	Form No	CPR Rule	PD
where the instructions are given by two or more parties to the proceedings (including the claimant) he will be a '**single joint expert**'.		35.2(1) and (2)	
The court's order will relate only to the expert or expert field identified and it may limit the amount of the expert's fees and expenses that may be recovered from any other party		35.4(3) and (4)	
Where a claim has been allocated to the small claims track or fast track permission will normally be for only one expert on a particular issue		35.4(3A), 35.7	Protocol annexed to CPR 35, at para 7
Where an order requires an act to be done by an expert, or otherwise affects him, the party instructing the expert must serve a copy of the order on the expert. If the expert is jointly instructed the claimant must serve the order			35, para 8
It is provided that expert evidence **shall be restricted** to that which is reasonably required to resolve the proceedings. This places a duty on the court and the court may exclude expert evidence if it would not be helpful in resolving any issue justly: *Barings plc v Coopers & Lybrand* (2001) Times, 7 March and *Clifford v Chief Constable of the Hertford Constabulary* [2008] EWHC 2549 (QB), [2008] All ER (D) 254 per Wyn Williams J. It is interesting to compare with that approach the course adopted by the court in *Stewart v Glaze* [2009] EWHC 704 (QB), 153 Sol Jo (no 16) 28 where it was stated that the expert accident reconstruction evidence provided a useful means of testing the factual evidence and the inferences to be drawn from it. That however was the limit of its use. This followed the principles set out in *Liddell v Middleton* [1996] PIQR P36. The Court of Appeal in *Heyward v Plymouth Hospital Trust* (2005) Times, 2 August held is was 'sensible and proportionate' to limit expert evidence to one consultant psychiatrist for each party in a relatively small claim for psychiatric injury.		35.1	
3. Experts' reports			
Expert evidence is to be given in a **written report** unless the court directs otherwise and if a claim is on the small claims track or the fast track the court will not direct an expert to attend a hearing unless it is necessary to do so in the interests of justice		35.5	
The requirement for the **form and content of expert's reports** are set out in Practice Direction 35 and the provisions of the Rule. See also the Protocol for the Instruction of Experts to give Evidence in Civil Claims at **CPR 35 PRO**. In particular note that the experts' reports must contain statement that they:			

	Form No	CPR Rule	PD
(i) understand their duty to the court and have complied and will continue to comply with it; and			
(ii) are aware of the requirements of Part 35 and PD 35, the protocol for the instruction of experts to give evidence in civil claims and the practice direction on pre-action conduct.		35.10	35, para 3.1 and para 13.5 of the Protocol
When giving evidence at court an expert could be cross-examined as to his knowledge of the requirements and his understanding of his duty.			
In *Guntrip* (see above this TAB, section 2) the Court of Appeal stated that because the expert's duty is to the court the expert must notify the court as soon as possible if he is unable to support causation. See further 'Expert Shopping discovered' by Simon Jones (2012) Sol Jo Expert Witness Summer Supplement.			
As to the form of statement of truth for experts, see			35, para 3.3
The wording is mandatory and must not be modified. See also the Protocol for the Instruction of Experts to Give Evidence in Civil Claims, para 13 – Contents of Experts' Reports			
Solicitors who instruct experts must check reports to ensure the statement of truth and that of awareness exactly complies with the requirements of the rule and the PD.			
The expert's duty is to help the court on matters within his expertise; this is paramount and overrides any obligation experts owe to those from whom they have received instructions or by whom they are paid.			
The danger of an expert losing sight of this is provided by the decision of Roderick Evans J in *Williams v Jervis* [2008] EWHC 2346 (QB) in which he described the expert as looking at the claim 'through the prism of his own disbelief'.			
The expert's report must be addressed to the court. It has been suggested that the CPR seek to transform the role of experts from party champions to what are in effect court assistants. This is the subject of argument.		35.3	35, para 2.2
4. Report by a single joint expert			
Where two or more parties wish to submit expert evidence on a particular issue, the court may direct that evidence on that issue is to be given by a single joint expert. The use of single experts is encouraged by the rules. The pre-action protocol for personal injury cases, at paras 3.17-3.19, requires a party to nominate a list of one or more experts he wishes to instruct and gives the other party 14 days to object to some or all of			

TAB 16 PROCEDURAL TABLES

	Form No	CPR Rule	PD
the experts nominated. On the **multi-track**, unless the parties agree, the court will not of its own initiative direct that there shall be a joint expert without holding a case management conference		35.7(1)	35, para 7 29, para 4.13
Machinery is provided by the rules for **selection of the joint expert** where the parties cannot agree		35.7(2)	
For the position where there is a relationship between the proposed expert and one of the parties, see *Liverpool Roman Catholic Archdiocesan Trust v Goldberg (No 2)* [2001] 4 All ER 950, Ch Div			
A single joint expert will typically be appointed in a claim of low value containing a simple issue on quantum or in a more complex case on a minor issue			
If it is necessary to **challenge the report of a jointly instructed expert**, guidance has been provided by:			
LORD WOOLF CJ in *Daniels v Walker* [2000] 1 WLR 1382, CA and in *Peet v Mid-Kent Healthcare NHS Trust* [2001] EWCA Civ 1703, [2002] 3 All ER 688; and NEUBERGER J in *Cosgrove v Pattison* (2001) Times, 13 February and in *Layland v Fairview New Homes plc* [2002] EWHC 1350 (Ch), [2002] All ER (D) 102 (Jul)			
The report of an expert separately instructed without the permission of the court can be exhibited to an application seeking permission for a court order permitting instruction of a separate expert. Guidance is given for the court's consideration when deciding whether to order a single joint expert.		35.7	35, para 7
5. Instructions to a single joint expert			
Any relevant **"instructing party"** may (provided the court has given a direction under r 35.7 for a single joint expert) **give instructions** to the expert and must at the same time send a copy of the instructions to the other relevant parties		35.8(1) and (2)	
The court may give directions as to the expert's fees and expenses and as to any inspection, examination or experiment which the expert wishes to carry out		35.8(3)	
The court may limit fees and expenses and give directions for the amount fixed to be paid into court by some or all of the relevant parties.		35.8(4)	
Unless the court otherwise directs the relevant parties are jointly and severally liable for the payment of the expert's fees and expenses		35.8(5)	
6. Written questions to experts			
A party may put written questions about an expert's report, which must be proportionate, to: (a) an expert instructed by another party or			

	Form No	CPR Rule	PD
(b) a single joint expert appointed under rule 35.7		35.6(1)	
This can only be done once, must be within **28 days** of service of the expert's report and be only for the purpose of clarification of the report, unless the other party agrees or the court gives permission: see *Mutch v Allen* [2001] EWCA Civ 76, [2001] All ER (D) 121 (Jan)		35.6(2)	
When questions are sent to the expert a copy of the questions should be sent to the other party			35, para 6.1
The party instructing the expert must pay the expert's fee for answering any question put under 35.6 but this does not affect who shall ultimately be ordered to pay the expert's fees			35, para 6.2
The answers when received will be treated as part of the report		35.6(3)	
If the expert does not answer the court may order: (a) that the evidence of the expert cannot be relied on, and/or (b) that the party may not recover the fees and expenses of that expert from any other party		35.6(4)	
Separate Experts **7. Discussions between experts**			
The court may direct that there be a discussion between the experts and may specify the issues to be discussed. Unless directed by the court discussions are not mandatory.		35.12(1) and (2)	35, para 9.1
The court may also direct that after the discussion the experts prepare a statement for the court showing those issues on which: (a) they agree and (b) they disagree, with a summary of their reasons for disagreeing		35.12(3)	
Such discussions are without prejudice' and cannot be the subject of cross-examination at the trial unless all parties agree.		35.12(4)	
8. Failure to disclose expert's report			
This will prevent the use of the expert's report at trial or calling the expert to give oral evidence unless the court gives permission. It is necessary that the client gives instructions for the report to be disclosed. .		35.13	
9. Expert's right to ask court for directions			
Experts may file written requests for directions to assist them in carrying out their functions and unless the court otherwise orders must provide copies of the proposed requests for directions: (a) to the party instructing them at least 7 days before filing; and			

TAB 16 PROCEDURAL TABLES

	Form No	CPR Rule	PD
(b) to all other parties at least 4 days before filing.		35.14	
10. Joint Expert – attendance at trial			
There should be no need for the report of a single joint expert to be amplified or tested by cross-examination. His report was the evidence: *Peet v Mid-Kent Health Care Trust* [2001] EWCA Civ 1703, [2002] 3 All ER 688, [2002] 1 WLR 210. The court has a discretion to allow a joint expert to be cross-examined: see *Peet,* above and *Sara Austin v Oxford City Council* [2002] LTL, 14 June, QBD			
11. Experts – difficulties as to trial date			
See *Rollinson v Kimberly Clark Ltd* (1999) Times, 22 June, CA and *Matthews v Tarmac Brick and Tiles Ltd* (1999) 54 BMLR 139, CA		35.10(4)	
12. Costs liability of expert and his liability for negligence			
In *Phillips v Symes* [2004] EWHC 2330 (Ch), [2005] 4 All ER 519, [2005] 2 All ER (Comm) 538 it was held that the Court had power to make a costs order against an expert who by his evidence caused significant expense by reckless disregard of his duties to the court			
An expert witness who provides expert evidence to the court does not now enjoy immunity from civil suit in negligence in relation to evidence given to the court or for views expressed in anticipation of court proceedings: *Jones v Kaney* [2011] UKSC 13, [2011] All ER (D) 346 (Mar). It would appear that the abolition of the immunity of experts will take effect from November 2005, the date of the act by the defendant which was in issue in this case. The decision does not affect the continued enjoyment by experts of absolute privilege from claims in defamation nor does it undermine the immunity of other witnesses in respect of litigation.			
13. Instructions to experts – disclosure			
Once the expert's report is disclosed a court will not order disclosure of the instructions unless it is satisfied there are reasonable grounds for considering that the statement of instructions given to the expert was inaccurate: *Lucas v Barking, Havering and Redbridge Hospitals NHS Trust* [2003] EWCA Civ 1102, [2003] 4 All ER 720, [2004] 1 WLR 220		35.10(4)	
CPR do require the substance of all material on the basis of which the report was written to be disclosed and expressly provide that the instructions given to him are not privileged. An expert's earlier or draft reports remain privileged: *Jackson v Marley Davenport Ltd* [2004] EWCA Civ 1225, (2004) Times, 7 October		35.10(4)	

	Form No	CPR Rule	PD
Where a party is given the court's permission to adduce expert evidence, but that expert is not named, he is entitled to reject the report of the expert first instructed, if he wishes to do so, and instruct another expert without any further permission from the court: *Vasiliou v Hajigeorgiou* [2005] EWCA Civ 236, (2005) Times, 22 March			
14. Protocols			
In particular note the Protocol for the Instruction of Experts to give Evidence in civil claims			35
Further note:			
(a) Pre-action protocol for personal injuries, paras 2.11, 2.12 and 3.14–3.21, also Annex C – "Letter of Instruction to Medical Expert"			
(b) Pre-action protocol for clinical disputes, paras 4.1–4.3			
(c) Pre-action protocol for construction and engineering disputes, paras 3, 4.1 and 4.3.1			
(d) Pre action protocol for professional negligence, paras B2.2, B7.1–B7.3 and C6.1–C6.4			
(e) Pre-action protocol for housing repair cases, paras 9.11, 9.18 and Annex C 'Letter of Instruction to Expert'			
(f) The Practice Direction Pre-action Conduct, para 9.4 and Annex C			

TABLE 17—SMALL CLAIMS

TAB 17

	Form No	CPR Rule	PD
1. Preliminary			
A party may be represented by a **lay representative** at the hearing of a small claim (but not after judgment or on any appeal) provided the party is present throughout: Lay Representatives (Rights of Audience) Order 1999. The lay representative is in the same position as a lawyer at the hearing in that he can address the court, call witnesses and examine them, cross-examine witnesses called by the other party and present documents to the court. Any person may act as a lay representative; a corporate party can appear by a lay representative ((or by an officer or employee); the lay representative may charge his client for so acting. It is irrelevant whether the lay representative is also a witness. The court has a discretion to hear a lay representative in circumstances precluded by the order. A McKenzie friend is allowed to help by taking notes, quietly prompting the litigant and offering advice and guidance; McKenzie friends do not have a right of audience or to conduct litigation. There can lawfully be payment by the litigant to the McKenzie friend. Careful note must be taken of the Practice Guidance: McKenzie Friends (Civil and Family Courts) which is reproduced at **CPR PG 39** in *Volume 1*.			27, para 3
Since 2007 HMCTS has provided a free mediation service for small claims, usually by telephone. In 2010, 11,000 cases were mediated with a settlement rate of 70%. References to mediation of suitable cases is made when at least one party states that he wishes to use the service.			
For a period of 6 months from October 2012 a pilot scheme will operate at CC-MCC (Salford) for designated money claims where both parties are willing to mediate (road traffic accidents and personal injury claims are excluded) — see **CPR PD 51H** — Small Claims Mediation Services: pilot scheme.			
Annex B of the **Practice Direction (Pre-Action Conduct)** sets out the specific information that should be provided in a debt claim by a claimant who is a business against a defendant who is an individual. In appropriate cases this should be meticulously complied with			
For normal scope of small claims track see "Allocation" Procedural Table **TAB 13** and **CPR 26.6** and for allocation fees payable see **TAB 13** at part 2, 4th para		26.6	

TAB 17 PROCEDURAL TABLES

	Form No	CPR Rule	PD
The parties may **consent to the allocation** to the small claims track of a claim which exceeds the value limits for the track. The small claims track costs provisions will apply unless the parties agree that fast track costs provisions shall apply		26.7(3), 27.14(5)	
Judicial case management of a small claim will usually comprise only the issue of Allocation Questionnaires and directions given by a district judge when allocating to track. There is considerable scope for case management by the parties			
On the claimant filing an allocation questionnaire or it being dispensed with or where there is automatic allocation the claimant (or defendant if the action is proceeding on the counterclaim alone) has to pay a fee of £40 if the claim is on the small claims track and exceeds £1,500.			
Before allocating the claim to the small claims track and giving directions for a hearing the court may require any party to give further information about that party's case. Further, a party may ask the court to give particular directions about the conduct of the case			27, paras 2.3 and 2.4
In deciding whether to make an order for the exchange of witness statements the court will have regard to:			
(a) whether either or both of the parties are represented;			
(b) the amount in dispute;			
(c) nature of dispute;			
(d) whether statements can be avoided by a request for information;			
(e) the need to avoid undue formality, cost or delay.			27, para 2.5
It should be noted that in Appendix A of the Practice Direction it is indicated that the court will normally require statements in road traffic cases			27, Appendix A
2. Preliminary hearing			
Notice of allocation will be sent out either with notice of a preliminary hearing or of a final hearing with directions for the parties to carry out. The court can give notice that it proposes to deal with the claim without a hearing but this is rarely done		27.4, 27.4(1)(c)	
The court may hold a preliminary hearing only:		27.6	
(a) where:			
(i) it considers special directions are necessary to ensure a fair hearing, and			
(ii) it appears necessary for a party to attend at court to ensure he understands			

	Form No	CPR Rule	PD
what he must do to comply with the special directions, or			
(b) to enable it to dispose of the claim on the basis that one or other of the parties has no real prospect of success at a final hearing, or			
(c) to strike out a statement of case or part of a statement of case which discloses no reasonable grounds for bringing or defending the claim			
The parties will be given 14 days' notice of the preliminary hearing and the court can, with the agreement of the parties, treat the preliminary hearing as the final hearing		27.6(3) and (4)	
The court must have regard to the desirability of limiting the expense to the parties of attending court		27.6(2)	
In practice a preliminary hearing will only very rarely be directed and then only because the complexity of the claim makes it unlikely that justice can be done between the litigants, especially if unrepresented, without explaining to them what will be expected of them in preparation and at the final hearing			
3. Directions			
At or after the preliminary hearing the court will fix the date of the final hearing, inform the parties of the time allowed for the final hearing and give directions		27.6(5)	
Where a preliminary hearing is not held the court will give directions which will be sent out with the allocation notice. The parties will be informed, at the same time, of the date the hearing is to take place and the time allowed			
Alternatively, but rarely, the court having given special directions will consider what further directions are to be given no later than 28 days after the date the special directions were given		27.4	
The court will be concerned not only to give appropriate directions but to ensure that they are complied with prior to the hearing as the next occasion that the case is considered will almost certainly be the date of the hearing. The danger of adjournments and applications for costs because of unreasonable behaviour are all too apparent			
When giving directions, the court will have available details of the information and documentation the court usually needs in particular types of case set out in Appendix A of **CPR PD 27**. These are: (a) Road traffic claims			

TAB 17 PROCEDURAL TABLES

	Form No	CPR Rule	PD
(b) Building disputes, repairs, goods sold and similar contractual claims			
(c) Landlord and tenant claims			
(d) Breach of duty claims (negligence, deficient professional services and the like)			27
The court will also have available the Standard Directions in Appendix B and Special Directions in Appendix C			
The Standard Directions include the encouragement of the parties to meet with a view to settling the claim or narrowing the issues			
If the parties have submitted proposed directions the court may well make those directions–perhaps with some additions or amendments, particularly if they are agreed by all parties. Otherwise it is virtually inevitable that the court will choose the most appropriate of the pro forma it has available, add special directions and, where the observance of a direction is vital either to doing justice or to dealing with the case in the time allotted, impose **sanctions for default.**			
If a Defence to Counterclaim, or more rarely a Reply, is necessary the court will order it			27, para 2.4
Sanctions to enforce compliance with the directions will vary depending on representation or otherwise. Where the parties are represented, a direction "that in default of due compliance the defaulting party's case do stand struck out and the other party be able to proceed accordingly" might well be appropriate but if the parties are unrepresented it is probably too draconian and a more appropriate direction would be that "default in compliance is likely to lead to an adjournment of the hearing and consideration by the court of an appropriate costs order"			
4. Parts of the rules that do not apply on small claims track			
The following parts of the CPR do not apply to small claims:			
(a) CPR Pt 25 – interim remedies (except interim injunctions)			
(b) CPR Pt 31 – disclosure and inspection			
(c) CPR Pt 32 – evidence (except CPR 32.1, power for court to control evidence)			
(d) CPR Pt 33 – miscellaneous rules as to evidence			
(e) CPR Pt 35 – experts and assessors (except CPR 35.1 – duty to restrict expert evidence; CPR 35.3 – experts overriding duty to the court; CPR 35.7 – court's power to order evidence			

	Form No	CPR Rule	PD
by a joint expert; and CPR 35.8 – instructions to single joint expert)			
(f) Subject to the court's right of its own initiative to order a party to provide further information (see 27.2(3), Part 18 – Further information			
(g) CPR Pt 36 – offers to settle			
(h) CPR Pt 39 – hearings (except the general rule that hearings are to be in public)		27.2	
5. Expert evidence			
No expert can give evidence, oral or written, without the permission of the court. If directing expert evidence the court will order joint instructions if possible. A specimen direction appears in Appendix C to the Practice Direction. Where the parties are both in person, letters of instructions may be beyond them and an additional direction may be necessary that they jointly seek the assistance of, perhaps, the Citizens Advice Bureau in complying with the direction		27.5	27, Appendix C, Form F
6. Disposal without a hearing			
This is only possible if all the parties agree		27.10	
7. The hearing			
The Rules provide:			
(a) the court may adopt any procedure it considers fair			
(b) the hearing will be informal			
(c) strict rules of evidence do not apply			
(d) the court need not take evidence on oath			
(e) the court may limit cross-examination, and			
(f) the court must give reasons for its decision		27.4	27, para 4.3
A hearing fee is payable by the claimant (or the defendant if the action is proceeding solely on the counterclaim) varying in amount from £35 for a claim not exceeding £300 and £245 for a claim exceeding £3,000 but not exceeding £10,000. The fee will be refunded in full if at least 7 days before the hearing date the court received written notice of settlement or discontinuance.			
Guidance for litigants in person is comprehensively (5 pages) provided in forms EX342.	EX342		
For the place of hearing, whether the hearing be in public or in private, the putting of questions by the court, limiting cross-examination, recording evidence and giving reasons, etc, see			27, paras 4 and 5
Witness statements to stand as evidence in chief, **skeleton arguments** and the			

TAB 17 PROCEDURAL TABLES

	Form No	CPR Rule	PD
smallest possible, but properly paginated, **bundles of documents** are essential tools to enable an advocate, lay or qualified, to make the most of the limited time that will be allowed for presentation; see Appendices A, B and C			27, Appendices
For the consequences of **a party failing to attend** a hearing without proper notice, see		27.9(2)–(4)	27, para 6
For the position where a **party does not attend but has**		27.9(1)	
(a) **given at least 7 days' notice to the court** and the other party that he will not attend;			
(b) has served on the other party at least 7 days before the hearing any other documents he has which he has filed with the court; and			
(c) in his written notice to the court has confirmed his compliance with paras (a) and (b) above			
8. The court's powers on the small claims track			
The court may grant any final remedy which it could grant if the proceedings were in the fast track or multi-track. It can award damages (limited to £5,000, unless the parties have consented to allocation to this track under CPR 26.7(3)) and interest, grant an injunction or make a declaration. Its powers to award costs are limited		27.3, 27.14	
9. Costs			
The court may only award on the claim or any appeal:			
(a) court fees (in whole or part)			
(b) fixed costs on issue			
(c) where the claim includes a claim for an injunction or declaration, up to £260 for legal advice and assistance			
(d) expenses which a party or witness has reasonably incurred travelling to and from the hearing and staying away from home to attend the hearing (in whole or part)			
(e) loss of earnings or loss of leave for the party and his witnesses up to £90 per day each for attending the hearing or staying away from home to attend the hearing			
(f) experts' fees not exceeding £750			
(g) such further costs as the court may assess by the summary procedure and order to be paid by a party who has behaved unreasonably		27.14	27 para 7
(h) the stage 1 and where relevant stage 2 fixed costs in rule 45.29 (Pre–action Protocol for low			

	Form No	CPR Rule	PD
value personal injury claims in RTA), provided the requirements of CPR 27.14(2)(h)(i)-(iv) are satisfied			
(i) in an appeal, the cost of any approved transcript reasonably incurred.			
The limits on costs also apply to any fee or reward charged by a lay representative: Courts and Legal Services Act 1990 s 11		27.14(4)	
Any order for costs made before the allocation to the small claims track will not be effected by the allocation		44.11(1)	
The cost of an engineer's report in a motor collision claim can only be recovered as damages if the extent of damage or the costs of repair is in issue but could in an appropriate case be recovered as costs: *Mistry v NE Computing* [1997] Current Law Digest May page 19: County Court			
Where a claim has not yet been allocated to track but would if allocated be appropriate for the small claims track the 'no costs' rule should apply prior to allocation: *Voice and Script International v Alghafar* (2003) LTL, 8 May, CA. This proposition had previously been accepted in *Woodings v BT plc* (2003) LTL, 17 March, but here the judge found although the case was of small value it was complicated and would have been allocated to the multi-track			
But see *Panchal v Maguire* [2006] 1 CL 59 where it was held disposal costs were in the discretion of the trial judge if there has been no allocation to the small claims track and *Lee v Birmingham city Council* [2008] EWCA Civ 891 at **TAB 13**, para 7 above.			
Where a claim is allocated to the small claims track and subsequently re-allocated to another track the provisions as to costs on the small claims track will cease to apply from the date of re-allocation. The court has power to order otherwise (see CPR 44.11) but may well not do so unless it is dealt with in the order of re-allocation: *Tibble v SIG plc* [2012] EWCA Civ 518, [2012] All ER (D) 134 (Apr), discussed by Stephen Gold in 'Civil way' (2012) NLJ, 25 May, page 711.		27.15	
Where one of the parties has behaved **unreasonably** the court may order such further costs as it may assess summarily. If the claim is one where an application is to be made for costs on this basis there should be prepared:		27.14(2)(g)	
(i) a schedule of the costs claimed			
(ii) schedule of the unreasonable behaviour			

TAB 17 PROCEDURAL TABLES

	Form No	CPR Rule	PD
A party's rejection of an offer in settlement will not of itself constitute unreasonable behaviour under para 2(d) but the court may take it into consideration when applying the unreasonable test		27.14(3)	
It will be rare that one particular failing will be enough to establish unreasonable behaviour and it is more likely to be the cumulative effect of an uncooperative attitude. The schedule may include, for example, some of the following:			
(a) failure to respond to a letter before action			
(b) failure to respond to a letter offering a choice of experts and to a suggestion that there be a joint instruction to an independent expert			
(c) failure to comply with directions			
(d) failure to provide requested information			
(e) failure to respond to an offer of settlement or rejecting it unreasonably			
(f) the fact that the party applying for costs achieved a better result than that proposed by him in his offer of settlement			
(g) failure to respond to the submission of proposed directions for the consideration of the court			
(h) failure to supply a copy of his Allocation Questionnaire and the documents attached to it			
(i) telephoning the night before the hearing with a suggestion that parties should talk about it			
(j) pursuing a hopeless case; see *Performing Right Society Ltd v Floravant* [2006] 1 CL 62			
(k) failing to attend the hearing or to give notice of his intention not to attend			
10. Setting aside judgment and rehearing			
A party who was not present or represented at the hearing and has not given written notice to the court may nevertheless apply to set aside the judgment and for the rehearing of the claim			
The application must be made not more than 14 days after the day on which the notice of judgment was served on him		27.11(1) and (2)	
The court may grant such an application only if the applicant:			
(a) had good reason for not attending or being represented at the hearing, and			
(b) he has a reasonable prospect of success at the hearing			
For 'good reason' see *Brazil v Brazil* [2002] EWCA Civ 1135, (2002) Times,			

	Form No	CPR Rule	PD
18 October, CA where the defendant's illiteracy was regarded a significant factor		27.11(3)	
If the judgment is set aside the court must fix a date for the rehearing or rehear it immediately. In practice the court will rarely have sufficient time to deal with the rehearing immediately		27.11(4)	
11. Appeal			
CPR Pt 52 and the accompanying Practice Direction deal with appeals; see in particular CPR PD 52, paras 5.8A–5.8D.			52 para 5.8A–5.8D
Where the court dealt with the claim subject to the appeal without a hearing or after the party gave notice under CPR 27.9 that he would not be attending and requesting the court to deal with the case in his absence, permission to appeal should be sought from the appeal court. If permission to appeal is sought by the unsuccessful party at the conclusion of the small claims hearing the court should give reasons if permission is not granted	N460		27 para 8.2
Where permission to appeal is granted and the appeal itself allowed, the appeal court will, if it is possible, dispose of the case there and then. It may do so without hearing further evidence			27 para 8.3
The 'no costs' rule does now apply on an appeal		27.14(2)	
Hearings will be tape-recorded by the court. A party can obtain a transcript on payment of the proper transcriber's charges			27, para 5.1
For the provision of transcripts at public expense see			52, paras 5.17–5.18
12. Allocation to small claims track in a patents county court			
Since 1 October 2012 holders of copyright, trade mark and design rights have been able to make claims, of value up to £10,000, at an informal hearing and without the need for legal representation.			63, Section V, para 32

TABLE 18—FAST TRACK

TAB 18

	Form No	CPR Rule	PD
1. Preliminary			
It must be continually borne in mind that the three most important effects of allocation to this track are:			
(a) the **length of time** will effectively be limited to **one day** – this will include the opening and, if any, closing speeches, judgment and summary assessment of costs. The court will use its powers to avoid loss of time, eg by dispensing with an opening or limiting cross-examination, but the parties will be anxious to ensure the case finishes in the day because the trial costs recoverable do not increase if the case runs into an extra day		35.7, 35.5(2)	27, para 7.2(4)(b)
(b) besides the limitations on **expert evidence** contained in CPR 26.6(5) and (6) the court on this track will generally direct that expert evidence is given by a single joint expert. Further expert evidence will be by written report unless the attendance of the expert at the hearing is necessary in the interests of justice		35.5	
(c) **costs** will be summarily assessed at the conclusion of the case unless there is good reason not to do so. Generally the mere fact that costs are high will not be regarded as a sufficient reason. Summary assessment is unlikely to be generous in the face of arguments about proportionality and this has to be borne in mind in deciding how much work can be justified in the preparation of a fast track case. Success can be soured by a failure to recover the bulk of the costs incurred			Costs PD, paras 13.2 and 13.5
For fast track trials a party's statement of costs for summary judgment must be filed and served as soon as possible but not less than 2 days before the hearing.			
2. Scope of the fast track			
The fast track is the normal track for any claim for which the small claims track is not the normal track and which has a financial value of not more than £25,000, provided:			
(a) the court considers the trial is not likely to last longer than one day, and			

TAB 18 PROCEDURAL TABLES

		Form No	CPR Rule	PD
(b)	oral expert evidence will be limited to:		26.6(5)	
	(i) one expert per party in relation to any expert field, and			
	(ii) expert evidence in two expert fields			
Note:				
•	Where there is a Part 20 claim to be tried with the claim, it is the total time that is likely for the trial of both claims that is determinative			26, para 9.1(3)(e)
•	A claim may be allocated to and remain on the fast track although there is to be a split trial. Before a party seeks a split trial careful consideration should be given to the statements made by the court in *DHL Air Ltd v Wells* [2003] EWCA Civ 1743, (2003) Times, 14 November			
•	As to allocation of claims in which judgment has been given for an amount to be determined by the court see **TAB 19** post, para 1			26, paras 12.1–12.6
3. Directions				
The same form of **Directions Questionnaire** is appropriate for all levels of case and the information required is to enable the court to allocate to the appropriate track and to give appropriate directions. Completion of the form is particularly important on the fast track because in many fast track cases it will be the only contact between the litigants and the court until the completion of the Pre-trial Checklist shortly before the trial window. In some cases the court may direct that Pre-trial Checklist are dispensed with making the proper completion of the Directions Questionnaire even more important		N150		
The parties are, of course, required to help the court to further the overriding objective of dealing with cases justly but this does not prevent the different parties to a case having differing views of the appropriate track. It is understandably easier for the defendant, who is likely to be found to blame in some degree, to feel that justice requires the case to be dealt with on the fast track so that the time spent on the case will be less and the trial costs will be limited, than for a claimant, with an excellent prospect of success, who would wish for a greater length of time to be spent on the case with oral expert evidence and a longer time allowed for the trial				
The Directions Questionnaire should be used by both parties to present their differing views to the court as persuasively				

	Form No	CPR Rule	PD
as possible provided they fully discharge their duty to co-operate with the court and each other to achieve a trial of the issues in dispute in a manner that is consistent with the overriding objective		1.3, 1.4(2)(a)	
Obviously, if there is an issue as to whether the value exceeds £10,000 (£1,000 if the claim is for personal injuries) or £25,000, authorities on quantum with appropriate references should be sent with the Questionnaire			
The court may find it necessary to hold an allocation hearing but generally will be reluctant to do so and will allocate on the information it has available. Consequent upon the increase in the fast track limit to £25,000 allocation hearings may well increase as some claims will need to be allocated to the multi-track as the trial will take more than one day.			26, para 6
Upon the court allocating to the fast track, the court will give directions for the management of the case and will set a timetable for the steps to be taken between directions and the trial:			
(a) it will fix a trial date or a "trial window" of not more than 3 weeks. The standard time between directions and trial will not be more than 30 weeks		28.2(2) and (3)	
(b) the matters to be dealt with in the directions given will include:			
(i) disclosure of documents			
(ii) service of witness statements			
(iii) expert evidence		28.3(1)	
Reference should be made to **CPR PD** 28 for detailed guidance on directions on allocation and note should particularly be taken of para 3.2 which provides that regard will be had to the extent to which the Practice Direction (Pre-Action Conduct) or pre-action protocol has, or had not, been complied with			28.3
(c) if the court decides not to order standard disclosure it may:			
(i) direct no disclosure take place; or			
(ii) specify the documents or classes of documents that the parties must disclose		28.3(2)	
In the Appendix to CPR PD 28 the Fast Track Standard Directions are set out			
The allocation stage is the prime point in the case at which the court will exercise its powers of management. It is essential for justice to be achieved speedily, and with proportionate costs, for the preparation of the case to start properly and promptly and for a clear timetable to be set with achievable time limits which will result in the trial taking place not			

TAB 18 PROCEDURAL TABLES

	Form No	CPR Rule	PD
more than 30 weeks from the giving of directions			
The court will give careful consideration to directions submitted by the parties particularly if they are agreed. The solicitors for the parties are likely to know more about the facts of the case and to have a grasp of detail that the court cannot hope to achieve. The parties will be aware that the basic timetable the court will have in mind will be:			
(a) Disclosure 4 weeks			
(b) Exchange of witness statements 10 weeks			
(c) Exchange of expert's reports 14 weeks			
(d) Pre-trial Check Lists to be sent out by the court 20 weeks			
(e) Pre-trial Check Lists to be filed 22 weeks			
(f) Hearing 30 weeks			
When considering the Directions Questionnaires the district judge will have available to him a tick-box form to assist him to make the necessary directions quickly and to produce a degree of consistency and compliance with the Court Service technology (see **BCCP C[12]** for such a form)			
Proposed directions should be drafted keeping in mind the layout and order of the tick-box form which will be before the district judge. It must be made clear whether the directions are agreed or not and if not it will be useful to indicate why			
All necessary documents should be attached to the Allocation Questionnaire and copies of the completed Directions Questionnaire and attachments should be served on the other parties. In a straightforward case it may be appropriate to seek a direction that Pre-Trial Check Lists be dispensed with			
Costs estimates must be filed and served with the Pre-Trial Check List but no longer with the Directions Questionnaire; a copy must be served by each solicitor acting on his client's behalf; for the importance see *Leigh v Michelin Tyre plc* [2003] EWCA Civ 1766, (2003) Times, 16 December and PD 43 section 6, particularly 6.5A			Costs PD, paras 6.1–6.6
If a party fails to file a directions questionnaire the court may give such directions as is considers necessary.		26.5(5)	
A directions questionnaire fee of £220 is payable by the claimant except where the case is proceeding on a counterclaim alone, when it is payable by the defendant			
4. Expert evidence on the fast track			

	Form No	CPR Rule	PD
For expert evidence generally see Procedural Table **TAB 16**		Part 35	35
The section "Experts" in part D of the Questionnaire must be carefully completed and a copy of any report referred to attached. The Questionnaire asks whether it is thought that the attendance of the expert at trial to give oral evidence is necessary. If it is thought necessary this should be carefully answered. It is not enough merely to say that the report is not agreed as the court will expect to know what parts are in issue and what effect in money terms the disputed points will have. The court will have to consider whether it is proportionate to allow oral expert evidence bearing in mind that there is a real risk that such permission, if granted, will lengthen the trial and put allocation to the fast track in doubt			
The court will lean very strongly towards an appointment of a **single joint expert**. The PD states 'where possible matters requiring expert evidence should be dealt with by only one expert' and sets out the matters the court should take into account when considering whether to permit expert evidence and whether that evidence should be from a single joint expert. In a personal injury case hopefully observance of the relevant protocol will have resulted in the agreement of a suitable joint expert and a report from that expert enabling the court merely to order that expert's report shall be admissible as evidence and perhaps further ordering that the joint expert do update his report for the trial			
It is still unhappily the case that experts' reports are often obtained without observance of the relevant protocol or, if there is no applicable protocol, without observing the spirit of the protocols. If that is the case the argument that the report has unfortunately been obtained without observance of the protocol but is in existence and it would be a waste of money to instruct a further expert is unlikely to have a sympathetic reception			
It is far more likely that the court will order that there be a joint expert's report and the costs of the original report obtained be not recoverable. In the same way if a defendant has studiously ignored invitations to join in the appointment of a joint expert but then makes application seeking permission to have his own expert's report, unless he can show good grounds for disputing parts of the report obtained by his opponent, he is likely to be left with the right only to ask questions of the expert who has already reported. Even if he is permitted to obtain his own report it is likely to be on terms that he bear the costs either of the original report or that he will bear			

TAB 18 PROCEDURAL TABLES

	Form No	CPR Rule	PD
the costs of obtaining his own report whatever the outcome of the case.			
The single joint expert is so vital to the fast track that parties who fail to seek such an appointment or to respond to proposals for such an appointment do so at their peril			
5. Applications			
Applications are often required to enforce compliance with directions and even if parties and their advisers are diligent in their preparation and observance of the timetable applications may be necessary. Further investigation may necessitate an application to add or substitute a party or to amend a statement of case; these are the sort of applications which the applicant will hope the court will deal with without a hearing, although the party not served may apply within 7 days to have the order set aside or varied	N244	Part 23, 23.10	28, para 5.1
An adjournment because of failure to comply with directions is a matter of last resort and the court will be prepared to re-timetable on the tightest basis that is possible with sanctions for non-compliance to ensure the case can be heard and completed on the trial date. Even if this is impossible the court is likely to make as much progress as possible on the day fixed, perhaps by dealing with liability only or dealing with such issues as are ready on the basis that the costs of the necessary further hearing will be paid by the party in default. If postponement is necessary either in whole or in part, it will be for the shortest possible time. See *Elliot Group Ltd v Algeco SAS* [2010] EWHC 409 (TCC), 1 March 2010 (Coulson J).			28, para 5.4(1), (2) and (5)
The application for an adjournment by a litigant in person raises difficulties but useful guidance is available in *Fox v Graham Group Ltd* (2001) Times, 3 August, NEUBERGER J			
Useful guidance can be found as to an application to amend pleadings when such amendment will delay the trial, in the judgment of Walker J in *EDO Technology Ltd v Campaign to Smash EDO* [2006] EWHC 598 (QB), (2006) Times, 24 May although it is not a fast track case. See also *Davies v Wm Morrison Supermarkets plc* [2007] EWCA Civ 594 – again, not a fast track case			
6. Pre-trial Check List			
Unless they have been dispensed with, Pre-trial Check Lists will be sent out by the court and the parties are required to return them by the date specified in the directions which will not be more than 8 weeks before the trial date or the beginning of the trial period.	N170	28.5	

	Form No	CPR Rule	PD
Where no party files a checklist the court will make an order requiring a checklist to be filed within 7 days from service of the order. If the order is not complied with the claim, defence and any counter-claim will be automatically struck out without further order of the court.	N171	28.5(3)	28, paras 6.1–6.5 and 51B, para 2(3)–(5)
If a party files a completed pre-trial checklist but another party does not or fails to give all the required information or the court considers a direction hearing is necessary, the court may give such directions as it thinks appropriate.		28.5(4)	
The court has power to fix a listing hearing if it thinks a hearing is necessary to ensure proper preparation for the trial			
This will only be done rarely because of the proximity of the trial and the power of the court to control evidence by giving directions.		32.1	
For the sanctions that will apply on filing a pre-trial check list without the appropriate fee or with a cheque that is dishonoured see		3.7, 3.7A and 3.7B	3B
The rules do not require the parties to exchange copies of the check lists before they are filed but they may be encouraged to do so			28, para 6.4
If the directions given include permission to use expert evidence it will say whether that is to be by oral evidence or report and shall name the expert			28, para 7.2(a)
If directions are not given the court must confirm the trial date, specify the place of the trial and give a time estimate all on the basis that the trial will be completed on the same day as it commences. Notice of the hearing will be sent at least three weeks before the hearing date unless the parties have agreed to accept shorter notice	N172		28, para 7.1
The parties should agree directions and file a draft of the proposed terms for the court's consideration. The agreed directions should include provision as to evidence, a trial timetable and time estimate, preparation of a trial bundle and any other matters needed to prepare the case for trial			28, para 7.2
If a party requires any order at this stage he must lodge an application, with the appropriate fee and a draft order, when returning the completed Check List	N244		
As to the requirement of a costs estimate with the pre-trial check list see final para of section 3 above			Costs PD, paras 6.1–6.6
As to the requirement for filing a statement of costs, which must be at least 2 days before the trial, see			Costs PD, para 13.5(4)
A hearing fee is payable by the claimant, unless the case is proceeding on a counterclaim, of £545. If the court receives			

TAB 18 PROCEDURAL TABLES

	Form No	CPR Rule	PD
notice in writing that the case is settled or discontinued the following percentage refunds will be made:		Civil Proceedings Fees Order 2008 (SI 2008/1053)	
(a) 100% more than 28 days before			
(b) 75% between 28 and 14 days before			
(c) 50% between 14 and 7 days (including the 14th day) before			
(d) Fewer than 7 days before, no refund			
7. The trial			
Unless there are applications returnable after the court's consideration of the Pre-trial Check List, the only remaining opportunity for judicial management is at the commencement of the trial. Despite time restraints it is regrettably the case that either during the trial or immediately before it commences there are frequently last minute applications to amend, to adduce evidence not disclosed in accordance with the directions made on allocation or to introduce documents which have come to light at a late stage			
The court must deal with them but the applicant should be extremely cautious before taking up time allotted to the trial by making such an application. It may prevent the trial being completed within the time available and the costs arising from the case being adjourned part heard may well have to be paid by the applicant whether or not he is successful in the trial			
If a trial is not finished on the day it is listed the Rules contemplate that the judge will normally sit on the next court date to complete it. This is often impracticable where the trial is before a district judge who will already have a list for the following day			28, para 8.6
The judge will generally have read the trial bundle and may dispense with an opening address and the parties should anticipate that:			28, para 8.2
(a) the trial will be conducted in accordance with orders previously made		28.7	
(b) witness statements will stand as evidence in chief		32.3(2)	28, para 8.4(2)
(c) the court will exercise its power to control evidence and to restrict cross-examination		32.1	28, para 8.4(1)
(d) the court will confirm any timetable already given or, if there is not one, set its own			28, para 8.3
These trial management directions form an essential part of the active management required by the judge to further the overriding objective		1.4	
For the right of litigants to have reasonable assistance from a lay person (a			

	Form No	CPR Rule	PD
McKenzie Friend, an 'MF') who may (i) provide moral support, take notes, help with case papers and (ii) quietly give advice, see CPR PG 39 - McKenzie Friends (Civil and Family courts) and in particular note CPR PG 39.6 as to the right of audience or to conduct litigation granted by the court and the circumstances that will be taken into account by the court when dealing with an application to grant such a right.			
The trial must not be allowed to "drift" and the completion of the evidence must be at such a time as will allow brief closing speeches, delivery of judgment and assessment of costs			
Save in the most exceptional case the judge should decide which party's case is more likely to be correct: *Cooper v Floor Cleaning Machines Ltd* [2003] EWCA Civ 1649, (2003) Times, 24 October where an appeal was allowed against a decision in a road traffic case dismissing both claim and counterclaim on the ground that neither had discharged the burden of proof.			
Guidance on the type of medical evidence required to demonstrate that a party has been unable to attend and participate in a hearing, such that an adjournment would have been justified, was given in *Levy (Trustee in Bankruptcy of Errol Weston Ellis-Carr) v Ellis-Carr* [2012] EWHC 63 (Ch). The court stated 'evidence should identify the medical attendant and give details of his familiarity with a party's medical condition, detailing all recent consultations; identify with particularity the patient's condition and the features of that condition preventing participation in the trial process; provide a reasoned prognosis; and give the court confidence that the evidence expressed was an independent opinion following proper examination'. The judgment of Norris J in this case has been expressly approved by the Court of Appeal in *Forrester Ketley & Co v Brent* [2012] CA Civ, 21 February.			
8. Costs			
If an order for payment of costs is made, the judge will normally summarily assess the costs in accordance with CPR 44.7 and CPR Pt 46			
Note:			
• The advocate's fee for the trial is fixed depending on the size of the claim (these trial fees have been increased from 1 October 2007)			
They are presently:		45.38	
• Claim value not more that £3,000–£485			

TAB 18 PROCEDURAL TABLES

	Form No	CPR Rule	PD
• Claim value more than £3,000 but not more than £10,000–£690			
• Claim value more than £10,000 but not more than £15,000–£1,035			
• For proceedings issued on or after 6 April 2009 more than £15,000–£1,650			
These fees do not include VAT on the advocate's fee, nor any disbursements			
• The fee for an instructing solicitor at the trial is also fixed but will be subject to the court's view of whether the attendance was necessary. It is presently £345		45.39	
• Parties must, at least 24 hours before the hearing, file and serve written statements of the costs claimed. The form N260 was introduced in 2009 and is to be revised under the Jackson reforms.	N260		
Fast track trial costs will not apply to a case dealt with at a disposal hearing (see **TAB 19**, para 1, penultimate sub-para) whatever the financial value of the claim			26, para 12.5(2)
For the position where costs are awarded to a litigant in person see **TAB 25**, General section at 1.12.3.			
For the position where the successful party forgets to ask for costs see **TAB 19**, para 10			

TABLE 19—MULTI-TRACK

TAB 19

	Form No	CPR Rule	PD
Preliminary			
List of contents of Preliminary section of TAB 19			
1.1 Allocation, fee and CMC (1.1.1-1.1.4)			
1.2 Claims management companies			
1.3 Prohibition of purchase of consumer credit claims			
1.4 Disposal hearings			
1.5 Bank charges litigation			
1.6 Industrial deafness claims			
1.7 Mesothelioma, asbestosis and pleural plaques (1.7.1-1.7.15)			
1.7A Test for causation in clinical negligence claims			
1.8 Tracing of employers in asbestos related cases (1.8.1-1.8.4)			
1.9 Declaration of non-liability			
1.10 Periodical payments as part of damages award and the assessment of damages for future losses (1.10.1–1.10.2)			
1.11 Claimant's right to pay for private care			
1.12 Cost of hospice care			
1.13 Right of local authority, with interest in 'break-down' of damages awarded, to intervene			
1.14 Hearings in private – necessity of application			
1.15 Management of claims where there is an allegation that the road traffic accident had been staged			
1.16 Delay in bringing case to trial			
1.17 Liability of parent company for the negligence of its subsidiary			
1.18 'Use best endeavours'			
1.19 Electronic technology			
1.20 Foreseeability			
Preliminary section			
1.1.1 See **CPR 29 [1]–CPR 29 [2]** and note in particular that the multi-track is the normal track for any claim for which the small claims track or the fast track is not the normal track		26.6(6)	
1.1.2 Part 8 claims are treated as allocated to the multi-track and, accordingly, CPR Pt 26 does not apply (note, however, allocation of possession claims)		8.9, 55.9	55A, para 6.1
1.1.3 An allocation fee is payable			

TAB 19 PROCEDURAL TABLES

	Form No	CPR Rule	PD
1.1.4 The fixing of a case management conference and/or a pre-trial review features frequently in judicial case management on this track. It is to be noted that, on 23 April 2007, Part 2 of the Compensation Act 2006 came fully into force and a whole range of claims-related activities came within the regulated sector for the first time. It is now an offence for a person to provide regulated claims management services in the course of a business unless he is authorised, exempt from the requirement or the requirement of authorisation has been specifically waived. For the regulation of claims management companies, see article by Gordon Exall, Sol Jo, 8 April 2008, page 20.			
1.2 Authorised claims management companies are required to pay an initial fee and an annual fee based on turnover, and at January 2010 the Claims Management Regulator regulated over 2,500 businesses. See article 'Clean up your act' (2009) Sol Jo, 27 October, page 12 by David Bywater.			
The Gazette for 21 July 2010 reported that the turnover of authorised claim management companies was £581m for the last financial year with £377m from the personal injury sector.			
It was reported in the Gazette for 13 April 2012 that the Ministry of Justice has closed 1 in 5 of claims management companies in the last year. 734 businesses ceased to be authorised to the end of March. At April 2012 there were 3,018 authorised businesses. See further as to proposed 'complete ban on inducement advertising' by the Ministry of Justice reported in (2012) NLJ, 17 August, page 1064.			
The Ministry of Justice propose to increase fees for claims management companies and remove the cap on annual fees for companies working in personal injury and financial services; details are set out in Sol Jo for 13 November 2012 at page 3.			
The handling of complaints against claims management companies is to be transferred from the Ministry of Justice to the Legal Ombudsman on a date, not yet specified, in 2013.			
1.3 Solicitors are not allowed to purchase consumer credit claims from claims managers: Sol Jo (2009) 18 August, page 3.			
1.4 Where **damages are to be determined** by the court after the making of **a 'relevant order'** and the financial value of the claim exceeds the small claim limit it will not be allocated to track unless			

	Form No	CPR Rule	PD
(a) the amount payable is genuinely disputed; or			
(b) the dispute is not suitable for disposal hearing			
However, as a **disposal hearing** is not expected to take longer than 30 minutes and no oral evidence is expected to be taken, allocation will take place in all but the simplest case to either fast track or multi track whichever is appropriate.			
A master or district judge has jurisdiction irrespective of value			26, para 12.1-12.6
1.5 For a review of the **bank charges litigation** and appeals to the High Court to lift a stay on the ground of hardship to a bank customer see *Rutherford v HSBC Bank plc* [2009] EWHC 733 (Blair J), 6 April 2009. The battle over unauthorised overdraft charges has been resolved now in favour of the banks; see *Office of Fair Trading v Abbey National* [2009] UKSC 6, [2009] 3 WLR 1215, [2009] NLJR 1702 leaving 'millions' of stayed cases to be resolved individually in the absence of settlement, withdrawal or admission.			
1.6 A decision of the Supreme Court in *Baker v Quantum Clothing Group* [2011] UKSC 17, [2011] All ER (D) 137 (Apr) on industrial deafness should be particularly noted because it over-ruled Court of Appeal authority in *Larner v British Steel* [1993] 4 All ER 102 as to the interpretation of s 29 of the Factories Act 1961. For discussion see article in (2011) NLJ, 24 June, page 872 by Robert Leary entitled 'Loud & clear'.			
1.7.1 Parties concerned with claims arising because the claimant has or claims he has, contracted **mesothelioma** from exposure to asbestos dust would have been aware of the 'fast track' scheme operated by Senior Master Steven Whitaker at the Royal Courts of Justice, Strand, London WC2A 2LL. Most of the hearings were by telephone and the scheme covered the whole country. The scheme operated most of the provisions of the 'show cause' procedure that came into force on 6 April 2008 (see next sub-paragraph) and from that date the Masters of the QBD have operated the 'show cause' procedure			
1.7.2 For the 'show cause' procedure in claims for compensation for mesothelioma see as to issue and the procedure **TAB 1** section 6(c), last sub-paragraph above			
1.7.3 It is essential in asbestos cases to be aware of the various such conditions:			
pleura – thin membrane covering the lungs			

TAB 19   PROCEDURAL TABLES

	Form No	CPR Rule	PD
pleural plaques – thickening of lining of lungs; indicate asbestos exposure but are symptom free			
pleural thickening – can restrict the expansion of the lungs; can be due to various causes			
asbestosis – fibrosis of the lung due to exposure to asbestos			
mesothelioma – cancer of the pleura caused by exposure to asbestos			
lung cancer – can be due to a number of causes, frequently smoking, but can also be caused by exposure to asbestos.			
1.7.4 See generally article 'Smokescreen' by Christopher Moore (2009) Sol Jo Summer Expert Supplement, page 16.			
1.7.5 The Compensation Act 2006 which deals with damages for mesothelioma and the problem of multiple employments came into force on 26 July 2006. The Act restored the 'Fairchild principle' of joint and several liability between mesothelioma defendants.			
1.7.6 It is sufficient to show that tortious exposure materially increased the risk of contracting mesothelioma in the sense that the risk was more than minimal. Section 3 of the 2006 Act reflects the common law requirement of causation by reference to a material increase in risk.			
In *Sienkiewicz v Greif (UK) Ltd and Knowsley Metropolitan Borough Council v Willmore* [2011] UKSC 10, (2011) Gazette, 15 March the leading judgment, was given by Lord Phillips who stated: 'Liability for mesothelioma falls on anyone who materially increased the risk of the victim contracting the disease.' He rejected the 'doubles the risk' test as a basis of deciding what constitutes a material increase of risk and said the question of whether the exposure to asbestos was de minimis was a question for the judge to decide on the facts of the case. Lord Browne stated that it will be very difficult for defendants to establish that a risk is de minimis. For detailed discussion see article 'No fighting back' by Jonathan de Rohan in (2011) NLJ, 18 March, page 386.			
Asbestos claims in cases where there has been a low level of exposure depend on whether the defendant could (at the time) have known that such low levels would have such consequences: see *Williams v University of Birmingham* [2011] EWCA Civ 1242, [2011] All ER (D) 29 (Nov) and *Willmore v Knowsley Metropolitan Borough Council* [2011] UKSC 10, [2011] 2 All ER 857 and for discussion see article by Elizabeth Carley in (2012) NLJ, 13 January, page 55 entitled 'Divided loyalties?'.			

	Form No	CPR Rule	PD
1.7.7 As to liability in mesothelioma cases arising on an exposure basis see *BAI (Run off) Ltd v Durham* [2012] UKSC 14, (2012) Sol Jo LR, 3 April, page 31, (2012) NLJ, 6 April, page 502. Liability is triggered under an employer's liability policy at the time of the negligent exposure to asbestos and resultant inhalation although at that time there is no actionable injury.			
1.7.8 The range of damages for mesothelioma cases is given in the JSB Guidelines 10th edition as from £35,000 to £83,750, and for discussion see articles by Simon Allan in (2012) Gazette, 15 March and by Alan McKenna in (2012) Sol Jo, 27 March, page 15. See also the judgment of Swift J in *Ball v Secretary of State for Energy and Climate Change* [2012] EWHC 145 (QB).			
1.7.9 The court in *Drake and Starkey (executrices of the estate of James Thomas Wilson decd) v Foster Wheeler Ltd* [2010] EWHC 2004 (QB) held the injured claimant could recover 'the reasonable value of gratuitous services rendered by voluntary care' and went on to hold that the recovery of hospice care was also recoverable – the damages for this aspect of the claim to be paid direct to the hospice; for a report see (2010) Sol Jo, 17 August, page 29 and Sol Jo 'Update: Personal Injury' (2010) Sol Jo, 28 September, page 27.			
1.7.10 By its decision in *Rothwell v Chemical & Insulating Co Ltd, Re Pleural Plaques Litigation and Johnston v NEI International Combustion Ltd* [2007] UKHL 39, [2007] All ER (D) 224 (Oct) the House of Lords decided that pleural plaques after exposure to asbestos dust do not give rise to actionable damage. However, in his article in NLJ (2007) 9 November, Colin McCaul QC strongly argues 'Pleural plaques are still alive and kicking'.			
1.7.11 An Act of the Scottish Parliament makes pleural plaques a compensatory condition and an application for Judicial Review by a group of leading insurers has been successfully resisted in the Court of Session. This appeal decision was itself the subject of an appeal but in *AXA General Insurance v The Lord Advocate* [2011] UKSC 46, [2011] All ER (D) 101 (Oct) the justices held that the Scottish Parliament was within its legislative competence in passing a new law restoring the rights to compensation of pleural plaques victims; see report Human Rights Updater, October 2011, page 15.			
1.7.12 The government has issued a statement that it will not legislate to overturn the decision in *Johnston v NEI* (above) which upheld the finding that			

TAB 19 PROCEDURAL TABLES

	Form No	CPR Rule	PD
pleural plaques do not constitute damage.			
1.7.13 In February 2010 the Justice Secretary announced that anyone who has instigated a claim in respect of pleural plaques before the House of Lords decision in *Johnston* (above) in October 2007 will be entitled to a one-off payment of £5,000 but without additional payment for costs; see article in (2010) NLJ, 16 April, 'Unequal victims' by Richard Scorer.			
1.7.14 Section 48 of the Legal Aid, Sentencing and Punishment of Offenders Act 2012 (LASPO) exempts diffuse mesothelioma cases from the success fees and insurance premium provisions until the Lord Chancellor has carried out and published a review of their likely effect on such proceedings. Such fees accordingly remain recoverable in this type of claim. This means ATE insurance and success fees will continue to be recoverable in these cases after April 2013 (the LASPO implementation date).			48, paras 2.1–2.2
1.7.15 The justice minister in a written statement (reported in the Gazette, 8 January 2013, page 3) indicated that the government intends to consult on the introduction of 'fixed legal fees for mesothelioma claims, a dedicated pre-action protocol for those claims as an electronic portal on which the claims will be registered'. The consultation is to be issued in the Spring 2013.			
1.7A The courts have been prepared to depart from the 'but for' test for the establishment of causation in negligence cases, in clinical negligence claims where it can be established that the defendant's negligence made a 'material contribution' to the damage suffered; see *Telles v South West Strategic Health Authority* [2008] EWHC 292 (QB), [2008] All ER (D) 389 (Feb) discussed by Chris Pamplin in his article 'Cause & effect' in (2012) NLJ, 23 November, page 1471.			
1.8.1 The Department for Work and Pensions has issued a consultation paper on setting up an Employees' Liability Tracing Office which will manage a database of employers' liability policy and has also set out plans for a compensation fund of last resort, the Employers' Liability Insurance Bureau. On 28 July 2011 it was reported in the Gazette that this is still being considered but no date for its introduction has been fixed.			
1.8.2 At present claimants in asbestos-related disease cases must forgo a portion of their compensation where the employer's insurer can no longer be traced.			
1.8.3 The government has assured people suffering from asbestos-related			

	Form No	CPR Rule	PD
disease that a fund of last resort is still a matter of negotiation with the insurance industry about setting up a fund for victims who cannot trace insurers. This was reported in the Gazette for (2012) 13 January: a report called for its creation over 2 years ago.			
It appears that those who have been diagnosed with mesothelioma before 25 July 2012 who cannot trace their employers' insurer will still not receive any compensation. For a critical review of the position see an article 'Room for improvement' by Karl Tonks in (2012) NLJ, 7 September, at page 1111.			
1.9 For the extremely unusual situation where the party who would normally be the defendant issues proceedings seeking a declaration of non-liability, ie a negative declaration, see *Toropdar v D (a minor by his litigation friend)* [2009] EWHC 567 (QB), 20 March 2009.			
1.10.1 Since 1 April 2005 courts have had the power to impose **periodical payments** rather than a conventional lump sum for all items of future care. Such awards should be linked to an earning based index rather than the Index of Retails Prices: *Thompstone v Tameside and Glossop Acute Services NHS Trust and other appeals* [2008] EWCA Civ 5, [2008] All ER (D) 72 (Jan). A model form is set out in the *Tombstone* case and the court's attitude to the costs of complying with the terms of the order is set out in *Long v Norwich Union Insurance Ltd* [2009] EWHC 715 (QB), 6 April.			
1.10.2 The assessment of **damages for future losses** is an exercise requiring the calculation of what award will compensate, in money terms, the claimant for his loss of earnings for his working life and the costs of other services, typically care, until death. The annual amount is the multiplicand and the number of years that the loss will be suffered is the multiplier. Allowance has to be made for the interest that will be earned on the capital sum awarded as it depletes over the period of the multiplier. Inflation is, of course, a significant factor.			
This allowance is the '**discount rate**' and the Lord Chancellor is vested with the power to fix that rate by s 1 of the Damages Act 1996; it is presently 2.5%.			
This rate is considered too high and this view is supported by the decision of the Privy Council in *Simon v Helmot* [2012] UKPC 5, [2012] All ER (D) 215 (Mar) an appeal from the Guernsey courts which are not bound by the 2,.5% rule.			
Where periodical payments are ordered for future losses the problem is less significant. The Lord Chancellor is conducting a review of the discount rate			

143

TAB 19   PROCEDURAL TABLES

	Form No	CPR Rule	PD
after first consulting. A detailed review of the decision in *Simon* above, the situation at present and the likely change is provided by Patrick Allen in an article 'The right target' in (2012) NLJ, 27 April, page 565. The consultation is reported to end on 30 October 2012, see (2012) NLJ, 10 August, page 1037. See further an article entitled 'The discount rate: seeking to square the circle' by Richard Evans in (2013) NLJ, 22 January, page 13.			
1.11 A claimant has the **right to pay for care** even when state funding is available and the cost can properly be included in a claim for damages: *Peters v East Midlands Strategic Health Authority* [2009] EWCA Civ 145, [2010] 1LR (QB) 48, [2009] PIQR Q1. It was made clear that this principle has nothing to do with mitigation of costs. For the consideration of the necessary machinery to prevent a subsequent application for public funding see the judgment of Dyson LJ, paras 57-16 and also article in Sol Jo Personal Injury Focus, April 2007, page 9, 'Victims Choice' by Jamie Clark. See also 1.7.9 above.			
1.12 Damages for the cost of hospice care were held to be recoverable in *Drake v Foster Wheeler Ltd* [2010] EWHC 2004 (QB), [2010] All ER (D) 29 (Aug): these were to be held in trust for, or paid direct to, the hospice. The patient had contracted mesothelioma when employed by the defendant and was cared for at the hospice.			
1.13 A local authority's financial interest in whether damages are to be paid, to a person in its care, by way of a lump sum or periodical payments justify it being joined in the assessment of damages proceedings: *Nottingham County Council v Bottomley and East Midlands Strategic Health Authority* [2010] EWCA Civ 726.			
1.14 Proceedings are always to be held in public unless otherwise stated. There is no power in listing officers to list hearings in private without the supervision of the appropriate judge. Proceedings are only given a private character when they were so listed. It is the duty of parties and their advisers to make an application for proceedings to be conducted in private if that was what the party or parties intend to achieve: *North Shore Venture Ltd v Anstead Holdings* (2011) Times, 22 April, Ch.			
1.15 Guidance was given as to case management and preparation of cases where there is an allegation of a conspiracy to claim compensation by 'staging' a road traffic accident: *Locke v Stuart and Axa Corporate Solutions Services Ltd* [2011] EWHC 399 (QB).			

	Form No	CPR Rule	PD
1.16 In *Morrissey v McNicholas* [2011] EWHC 2738 (QB), [2011] All ER (D) 210 (Oct) the court held that the claimant ought to have progressed his libel action but that to strike out the action would be disproportionate – delay was of some 3 years.			
1.17 The Court of Appeal in *Chandler v Cape plc* [2012] EWCA Civ 525, [2012] All ER (D) 105 (Apr) ruled that parent companies may owe a direct duty of care to employees of its subsidiary company in respect of their personal safety; for discussion see (2012) Sol Jo, 15 May, pages 12–13, article by Alan McKenna; (2012) NLJ, 8 June, page 766, article by Rob Weir QC and Vijay Gamaphy and (2012) NLJ, 29 June, page 867 article by Malclolm Dowden entitled 'Parents know best'.			
1.18 A contractual term to use best endeavours may require the expenditure of additional monies and taking on extra expenses: *Jet2com Ltd v Blackpool Airport Ltd* [2012] EWCA Civ 417, [2012] All ER (D) 24 (Apr) discussed in (2012) NLJ, 27 July, page 997 by Caroline Kehoe and Joanne Keillor in an article entitled 'In it for the long haul?'.			
1.19 For cost saving by the use of electronic technology such as 'date ordered indexing and page numbering' of documentation see note in (2012) NLJ 9 November, page 1384			
1.20 'Reasonably foreseeable'. In *John Grimes Partnership v Gubbins* [2013] EWCA Civ 37 it was held that a delay of 15 months by consulting engineers that delayed a development project rendered them liable for loss resulting from a fall in property prices which was 'reasonably foreseeable' at the start of the recession. It made no difference that their fee was only £15,000.			
1. Evidence			
1.1 The relevant provision of the CPR are:			
Part 32, rules 32.1-32.20: Evidence			
Part 33, rules 33.1-33.9: Miscellaneous rules about evidence			
Part 34, rules 34.1-34.24: Witness depositions and evidence for foreign courts.			
1.2 In particular note:			
for investigation of issues to which factual evidence may be directed, identifying witness and limiting length or format of statements		32.2(3)	
for witness statements – form		32.8	
for witness summaries		32.9	
for affidavit evidence		32.15-32.17	32, paras 6-10
for notice to admit facts		32.18	

TAB 19 PROCEDURAL TABLES

	Form No	CPR Rule	PD
for notice to admit or produce documents		32.19	
for notice of intention to rely on hearsay evidence and circumstances in which such notice is not required		33.2-33.3	
1.3 Annex 3 to PD 32 provides video conferencing (VCF) guidance and paragraphs 15-21 specifically deal with cases where VCF is to be used for taking of evidence. The permission of the court will be necessary: for a case where such permission was given see *Polanski v Conde Nast Publications Ltd* [2005] UKHL 10, [2005] 1 All ER 945.		32.3	
1.4 For an article giving very careful and useful guidance on evidence and trials see (2010) NLJ, 29 October, page 1485, 'The new litigation landscape' by Jovita Vassallo. The article in addition to the provisions set out above deals with the preparation of a witness for the pressure of the court room.			
1.5 There remains the problem for the practitioner of how far it is proper to go in preparation of a witness for cross-examination. The fact that a witness statement will usually stand as his evidence will frequently justify an attempt to ask some supplementary questions prior to cross-examination to give time for the witness to settle himself.			
For the distinction between 'preparation' or 'familiarisation' (which is ethical) and 'coaching' (which is not) see *R v Homodau* [2005] EWCA Crim 177 — a criminal case providing guidelines for civil proceedings; see also an article 'Witness familiarisation' by Penny Cooper in (2012) Sol Jo, 26 June, page 10 and an article by Mark Solon 'Abramovich at trial' in (2012) NLJ, 28 September, page 1201.			
2. Case management – general provisions			
When drafting case management directions the starting point should be any relevant model directions and standard directions which can be found online at w ww.justice.gov.uk/courts/procedure-rules/ civil, adapted as appropriate.		29.1	
When it allocates a case to the multi-track the court will:		29.2	
(a) give **directions for management and set a timetable** (normally in the type of case that would have been suitable for the fast track save for the value of the claim exceeding the fast track limit or the number of witnesses making it unlikely it will finish in a day), or			
(b) fix:			
(i) a **case management conference**, or			
(ii) a **pre-trial review**			

	Form No	CPR Rule	PD
or both and give case management directions			
If the court decides only to give directions it can fix a case management conference or a pre-trial review subsequently at any time after allocation		29.3	
The court will **fix the trial date or trial period** as soon as possible		29.2(2)	
Case management will generally be dealt with by: (a) a Master in cases proceeding in the Royal Courts of Justice (b) a district judge in cases proceeding in a High Court District Registry (c) by a district judge (usually) or by a circuit judge in cases proceeding in a county court			29, para 3.10
The conference will be held at the Royal Courts of Justice when the case is proceeding there but otherwise will normally be held at a Civil Trial Centre			29, para 3.1
The court may fix the conference hearing because it thinks it **necessary or desirable** and, when the necessity arises because of the deficiency of a party or his legal representative, will usually impose a **sanction** such as bearing the costs of all parties attending the hearing		3.8	29, para 3.6
A party in default would be advised to make good the deficiency that has occurred and seek to avoid the hearing by submitting agreed directions for the court's consideration, hopefully making the hearing unnecessary			
The parties must endeavour to agree appropriate directions and submit agreed directions, or their respective proposals to the court at least seven days before any case management conference. Where the court approves agreed directions, or issues its own directions, the parties will be so notified by the court and the case management conference will be vacated.		29.4	
When a hearing of the conference is fixed the court will give the parties at least 3 days' notice (7 days if the hearing is a pre-trial review)			29, para 3.3
The parties should consider what directions should be sought and if a party requires a direction that is not routine and it is likely to be opposed he should **issue an application** to be heard at the case management conference. If the hearing of the application is likely to extend the time necessary for the hearing, that extra time should be sought even if this can only be at a fresh hearing date	N244		29, paras 3.5 and 5.8
3. Directions			
See first the provisions of Part 2 of this TAB			

TAB 19   PROCEDURAL TABLES

	Form No	CPR Rule	PD
The **agreed directions** put before the court must:			
(a) set a **timetable** by reference to calendar dates			
(b) include a date or period for the **trial**			
(c) include provision for **disclosure**			
(d) include provision about **factual and expert evidence**; the provision about expert evidence may be that none is necessary			29, para 4.7(1)-(12)
It is specifically provided that disclosure may:			
(a) be limited to standard disclosure or less than that, and/or			
(b) be the supply of copies without a list and that a disclosure statement is dispensed with; but if it is not dispensed with it must provide that it be served			29, para 4.7(3)
If it is appropriate, the agreed directions should include provision for:			
(a) a reply or amended statement of case			
(b) dates for provision of further evidence and for questions to and replies by experts			
(c) disclosure of evidence			
(d) use of single joint expert or exchange (simultaneous or consequential) of expert evidence and discussion between experts			29, para 4.8(4)
Even if the court does not approve the agreed directions it will take them into account when giving its own directions, hopefully without a hearing			
If the parties have agreed directions a covering letter can usefully seek to deal with any reservations or concerns of the court that can be anticipated. If a "split" trial is sought the covering letter should explain why it is appropriate, not simply that it will save costs but what costs will be saved and how the saved costs will exceed those of the extra hearing that may be necessary			
Where the court is giving directions on its own initiative without holding a case management conference see PD 29, para 4.10 and in particular note 4.10(a) as to requiring in appropriate cases that the parties consider ADR			29, para 4.10
Where the court is proposing of its own initiative to make a direction for a joint expert or to appoint an assessor, unless the parties have consented in writing, it must list a case management conference			29, para 4.13
For direction, in clinical negligence cases, for exchange of scholarly literature to be relied on see *Wardlaw v Farrar* [2003] EWCA Civ 1719, [2003] 4 All ER 1358n, (2003) Times, 5 December			

	Form No	CPR Rule	PD
For the appropriate procedure and directions in **low velocity impact** cases see **TAB 15**, paras 15 and 16 above and *Casey v Cartwright* [2006] EWCA Civ 1280, [2006] All ER (D) 72 (Oct); in particular that the defendant who wishes to raise the causation issue should notify all other parties in writing, should raise the issue in the defence and within 21 days of the defence serve a statement showing the grounds and evidence on which the issue is raised			
The parties should raise any question of a **structured settlement** during case management			29 para 3A
4. Case management conferences			
must attend case management conferences and pre-trial reviews			
(a) familiar with the case			
(b) with sufficient authority to deal with issues that may arise			
If a party has a legal representative, a representative:		29.3(2)	29, para 5.2
The court may require a party to attend		3.1(2)(c)	
These provisions must be kept foremost in mind when counsel or agents are being instructed to attend			
The inadequacy of the person attending or who has instructions will be likely to result in a wasted costs order			29, para 5.2(3)
The court will make arrangements to ensure that applications and other hearings "are listed promptly to avoid delay . . ."			29, para 3.9
There may be hearings that can conveniently be heard by telephone conference but many case management conferences will not normally be suitable because of their length and complexity			
The **topics likely to be considered** at a case management conference include:			
(a) clarifying the claim			
(b) any necessary amendments			
(c) disclosure			
(d) the expert evidence reasonably required			
(e) disclosure of factual evidence			
(f) further information and questions to experts			
(g) split trials and preliminary issues			29, para 5.3
The court will also fix a timetable including, where appropriate, a further case management conference, a pre-trial review and a trial date or trial period			29, para 5.4
CPR PD 29 underlines that a party who obtains **expert evidence before obtaining a direction** does so at **his own risk as to costs,** except where the evidence was obtained in accordance with a pre-action protocol			29, para 5.5

TAB 19   PROCEDURAL TABLES

	Form No	CPR Rule	PD
To assist the court the parties and their legal advisers should:			29, para 5.6
(a) ensure that all documents that the court is likely to want to see (including witness statements and experts' reports) are brought to the hearing			
(b) consider whether the parties should attend			
(c) consider whether a case summary will be useful, and			
(d) consider what orders each wishes to be made and give notice of them to the other parties			
Some courts issue with the notice of the case management appointment a letter setting out **the court's specific requirements** as to attendance, information, etc			
Where a split trial is being considered the court will be primarily concerned whether it will save costs without causing prejudice or unfairness: *Ajinomoto Sweeteners Europe SAS v Asda Stores Ltd* [2009] EWHC 781 (QB), [2009] FSR 687.			
A case summary:			
(a) should be designed to assist the court to understand and deal with the questions before it			
(b) should set out a brief chronology of the claim, the issues of fact which are agreed or in dispute and the evidence needed to decide them			
(c) should normally not exceed 500 words in length, and			
(d) should be prepared by the claimant and agreed with the other parties if possible			29, para 5.7
The case summary should be lodged in good time before the hearing; every effort should be made to ensure it is **before the district judge so that he can read it before the hearing**			
For guidance in the case management and preparation of cases which involve an allegation hat there has been a conspiracy to obtain damages following a staged road traffic 'accident' see *Locke v Stuart and AXA Corporate Solicitors* [2011] EWHC 399. It is also to be noted that insurers making such allegations have to do so with care and legal advisers should only make such allegations on proper grounds. Particular care should be taken with trial bundles as to the appearance of the names of persons alleged to have been party to the fraud. Proper evidential grounds on which to found the allegation have to be in existence and available.			
Whilst the court has power after trial to strike out an exaggerated claim (see CPR			

	Form No	CPR Rule	PD
3.4(2)(b)) in reality there is little or no prospect of obtaining such an order: *Fairclough Homes Ltd v Summers* [2012] UKSC 26, [2012] All ER (D) 179 (Jun) discussed by Dominic Regan in an article 'Damaged!' in (2012) NLJ, 29 June. See also (2012) Sol Jo, 3 July at page 2 an article 'A shady business' by Michael Brace in (2012) NLJ, 20 July, page 960.			
5. Variation			
A party dissatisfied with a direction or order should **appeal** (if he was present or had notice of the hearing) or apply to the court to **reconsider its decision**			29, para 6.3(1) and (2)
If he does not do so (**within 14 days of service**) he will be assumed to be content with the direction			29, para 6.2(2)
Reconsideration will usually be by a judge of the same level as the judge who gave the directions or made the order. The court will give at least 3 days' notice of the hearing			29, para 6.3(4)
Where there has been a change of circumstances since the order the court may vary or set aside a directions on application or of its own motion			29, para 6.4
For procedure **where the parties agree about changes,** see		29.5	29, para 6.5
and note in particular an application to the court is necessary for varying a date fixed for: (a) a case management conference (b) a pre-trial review (c) the return of a Pre-trial Check List (d) the trial (e) the trial period or any date for doing any act which would necessitate the change of any of these dates.		29.5(2)	
On an appeal from an order made at a Case Management Conference the court will normally only interfere if the judge at first instance has exceeded 'the generous ambit within which reasonable disagreement is possible': *Clyde & Co LLP v New Look Interiors of Marlow Ltd* [2009] EWHC 173 (QB), [2009] All ER (D) 70 (Feb), NLJ Law Digest 20 February 2009, page 278.			
6. Pre-trial Check List			
The court will send out the Pre-trial Check Lists (unless it has been dispensed with by order or direction) for return by the date filed by the court. If one party fails to return the Check List properly completed or if the court considers it necessary it will fix a date for a listing hearing			
The fee on the filing of a Listing Questionnaire is £110	N170	29.6(1), 29.6(4)	29, para 8.1

TAB 19 PROCEDURAL TABLES

	Form No	CPR Rule	PD
If no party files a Check List the court will order that the claim and any counterclaim will be struck out unless a Check List is filed within 7 days of service of the order		29.6(3)	29, para 8.3
On receipt of the parties' completed Check Lists the court may decide to hold a pre-trial review or cancel any pre-trial review that has previously been ordered that is considered unnecessary		29.7	
The parties should seek agreed directions and seek an agreed order. The agreed directions should include provision about:			
(a) evidence and in particular expert evidence			
(b) a trial timetable and time estimate			
(c) the preparation for a trial bundle			
(d) any other matter necessary to prepare the case for trial			29, para 9.2
A direction as to **expert evidence** will (unless it has been done previously) give permission to use expert evidence, indicate whether the permission is for oral evidence or reports or both and will name the experts concerned			29, para 9.2(4)
The court will fix or confirm the trial date or period, give a time estimate and fix the place of trial			29, para 9.1
The Pre-trial Check List assumes that each party required to complete it has complied with all directions that have been given and is ready for trial. If directions are required the party applying for them must send the appropriate application, with the fee payable and a draft order with the completed Check List	N244		
6A. Trial date			
As soon as practicable after the filing of completed checklists, the hearing of a listing hearing or a pre-trial review being held the court will confirm the date for trial or the week within which the trial is to begin		29.8(c)(1)	
7. Trial bundles			
Unless the court otherwise orders, the claimant must file the trial bundle not more than 7 days nor less than 3 days before the start of the trial			
Unless the court orders otherwise, the trial bundle should include a copy of:			
(a) the claim form and all statements of case			
(b) a case summary and/or chronology where appropriate			
(c) requests for further information and responses to the requests			
(d) all witnesses statements to be relied on as evidence			

	Form No	CPR Rule	PD
(e) any witness summaries			
(f) any notices of intention to rely on hearsay evidence under CPR 32.2			
(g) any notices of intention to rely on evidence (such as a plan, photograph, etc) under CPR 33.6 which is not:			
(i) contained in a witness statement, affidavit or experts' report			
(ii) being given orally at trial			
(iii) hearsay evidence under CPR 33.2			
(h) any medical reports and responses to them			
(i) any experts' reports and responses to them			
(j) any order giving directions as to the conduct of the trial, and			39A, paras 3(1) and (2)
(k) any other necessary documents			
See also as to trial bundles. In *Smales v Lea* [2011] EWCA Civ 1325, (2011) Times, 21 November the Court of Appeal warned that sanctions would be imposed for failure to exclude extraneous documents, see per Lord Neuberger MR at paras 53–56.		39.5	39A, paras 3.3–3.10
It is not necessary to give a hearsay notice of intention to rely on hearsay evidence contained in an agreed court bundle: *Charnock v Rowan* [2012] EWCA Civ 2, [2012] All ER (D) 105 (Jan). It is open to a party to give written notice of objection to admissibility; see (2012) NLJ, 8 June, Civil Way by Stephen Gold, page 77.			
See also an article 'Benchmarks: good on paper' by Paul Waterworth (2009) Gazette 28 January, page 16 on the preparation an importance of trial bundles.			
Fro the preparation of a separate bundle, where that is appropriate, or the experts' reports and answers to questions to be included in the trial bundle see article by Mark Solon entitled 'Expert preparation' in NLJ (2010) 25 June, page 906.			
7A. Bundles of authorities			
The Court of Appeal in *TW v A City Council* [2011] EWCA Civ 17, (2010) Times, 25 January, reminded practitioners that if an authority is reported in the Law Reports, published by the Incorporated Council it is that report that should be used. Subsequently the Lord Chief Justice has issued 'Practice Direction: Citation of Authorities (2012)' [2012] All ER (D) 190 (Mar) which has application to all courts, civil and criminal, below the Supreme Court.			
8. The trial			

TAB 19   PROCEDURAL TABLES

	Form No	CPR Rule	PD
Vacating a trial date that has been fixed is often described as a 'last resort' but that statement relates to a situation that has arisen because of failure to comply with case management directions: *Collins v Gordon* [2008] EWCA Civ 110, 21 January.			29, para 7.4(6)
For detailed consideration of appropriate principles to be applied by the court when considering applications to postpone a trial or adjourn a trial see *Elliott Group Ltd v GECC UK* [2010] EWHC 409 where Coulson J considered fully the earlier decisions in *Boyd and Hutchinson v Foenander* [2003] EWCA Civ 1516, 23 October and *Fitzroy Robinson Ltd v Mentmore Towers Ltd* [2009] EWHC 3070 (TCC), 26 November, an earlier decision of Coulson J. In *Elliott* some adjustments to the timetable were granted but the application to adjourn was refused as the case could properly and fairly be prepared in the time remaining before the trial date.			
For applications to adjourn the trial on grounds of ill-health see **TAB 18**, part 8 (last para) above.			
For consideration of the use of closed material procedure see **TAB 1**, Preliminary section at 1.15.			
For the approach of the court to last-minute applications to amend a party's pleadings see *Swain-Mason v Mills & Reeve (a firm)* [2011] EWCA Civ 14, (2011) Times, 15 February where it reiterated that the applicant had to show the strength of its new case and why justice to all parties required the amendment. In this case the application to amend was made at the trial and was allowed after a successful appeal to the Court of Appeal after refusal.			
A hearing fee of £1,090 is payable; the provisions for percentage refunds are the same as for cases on the fast track, see **TAB 18**, section 6, final paragraph.			
For the principles which the court will apply when faced with an application for an expedited or speedy trial see *Intervet (UK) Ltd v Merial* [2009] EWHC 1965 (Pat).			
A case allocated to the multi-track can only be tried by a **Master or district judge**, subject to any Practice Direction: (a) In the High Court if			
(i) the case is proceeding under CPR Pt 8, or		8.9(c)	2B, para 11.1(a)
(ii) the case has been allocated under CPR Pt 26, with the consent of the parties			

	Form No	CPR Rule	PD
Note:			
• The consent of the parties is required for the determination of a preliminary issue by a Master or district judge			2B, para 4.1
• A Master or district judge can assess the damages or sum due under a judgment without limit, but note *Sandry v Jones* (2000) Times, 3 August, CA			2B, para 4.2
• As to proceedings under the Inheritance (Provision for Family and Dependants) Act 1975 and s 14 of the Trusts for Land and Appointment of Trustees Act 1996, see			2B, para 3.2
(b) In the county court if:			
(i) the case is treated as being allocated to the multi-track under CPR 8.9(c) and Table 2 of the Practice Direction to CPR Pt 8 except those claims listed in para 11.1(a) of the Practice Direction to CPR Pt 2			
(ii) the proceedings are for the recovery of land			2B, para 11.1(b)
(iii) with the permission of the Designated Civil Judge			2B, para 11.1(d)
Note:			
• The position as to assessment of damages is the same as in the High Court (see above) but subject to the approval of the Designated Civil Judge, in some circuits or areas at least, pursuant to CPR PD 26, para 12.6			2B, para 11.1(c)
• The position of proceedings under the Inheritance (Provision for Family and Dependants) Act 1975 and s 14 of the Trusts of Land and Appointment of Trustees Act 1996 is as in the High Court and see High Court and County Courts Jurisdiction Order 1991			
• A district judge may not hear appeals under s 204 of the Housing Act 1996 which deals with homelessness			2B, para 4.2
Trials on the multi-track are not subject to:			
(a) time limits (compare small claims track and fast track)		27.14 46.2	
(b) costs limits (compare small claims track and fast track)			26, paras 8.1 and 9.3
The rules of evidence apply to multi-track trials (compare small claims track)		27.8(3)	
The court will nevertheless seek to deal with cases **expeditiously and fairly** and may:		1.1(2)(d)	

TAB 19   PROCEDURAL TABLES

		Form No	CPR Rule	PD
(i)	dispense with an opening address having read the papers in advance			29, para 10.2
(ii)	enforce or set a timetable			29, para 10.3
(iii)	direct statements and reports to stand as evidence		32.5(2)	29, para 10.4
(iv)	control evidence and restrict cross-examination		32.1	29, para 10.4
where such steps would be **proportionate**				
Rights of audience are governed by the Legal Services Act 2007 (relevant extracts are reproduced at **III SOL [52]** to **III SOL [64]** in *Volume 2*. Note that: Part 3 of the 2007 Act deals with Reserved Legal Activities Part 8 contains Miscellaneous Provisions about Lawyers, etc Schedule 2 deals with the Reserved Legal Activities Schedule 3 deals with Exempt Persons Schedule 5 deals with Authorised Persons				
To obtain rights of audience in the higher civil courts, solicitors and registered European Lawyers (RELs) must obtain a Higher Courts (Civil Advocacy) Qualification pursuant to the **Solicitors Higher Rights of Audience Regulations 2011**. The 2011 Regulations replace the Higher Courts Qualification Regulations 2000 and 2010 but do contain transitional provisions. The 2011 Regulations are assessment based.				
For the right of litigants to have reasonable assistance from a lay person (a **McKenzie Friend**, an 'MF') who may (i) provide moral support, take notes, help with case papers and (ii) quietly give advice, see CPR PG 39 – McKenzie Friends (Civil and Family courts) and in particular note CPR PG 39.6 as to the right of audience or to conduct litigation granted by the court and the circumstances that will be taken into account by the court when dealing with an application to grant such a right.				
The greatest "blow" to the claimant's advocate will be the dispensing with an opening. The use and quality of a **skeleton argument**, lodged in advance of the trial, are vital. For the contents of a skeleton argument see *Tombstone Ltd v Raja* [2008] EWCA Civ 1444 at [125]-[128] per Mummery LJ and in particular that it should be used to aid advocacy and not as a substitute for it. In this case the skeleton argument extended to 110 pages with a further 64 pages of appendices! See also *Midgulf International Ltd v Groupe Chemique Tunisien* [2010] EWC Civ 66, [2010] All ER (D) 114 (Feb) where Toulson LJ expressed strong disapproval of the 'volume of papers'				

	Form No	CPR Rule	PD
with which the Court was presented by the appellants. The original skeleton argument ran to 132 pages and there were over 100 authorities with 5 volumes of authorities! There was a supplemental skeleton of 30 pages.			
The first draft prepared will usually be improved if pruned by a half when it is finalised, a **list of any authorities** what will be referred to should be incorporated and copies of the authorities must be available. Note Practice Direction: Citation of Authorities (2012) issued by the Lord Chief Justice[2012] All ER (D) 190 (Mar). 'Advocates should always be ready with authority in support of a submission and must not rely on their beliefs or opinions'.			
CPR PD 52A, Section 5 deals with skeleton arguments to assist the Court of Appeal; the guidance given is of general application and should be followed.			
The Court of Appeal when delivering a reserved judgment in *TW v A City Council* (20110 TImes, 25 January reminded the profession that relevant authorities should be copied from the Law Reports published by the Incorporated council of Law Reporting.			
It is generally helpful for the skeleton argument to cross-refer to the evidence and to be accompanied by a chronology.			
In a trial where the order sought is complex, consideration should be given to annexing a **draft order**. Great care must be taken when so doing to avoid giving offence. If there is any doubt about its value it should be retained until after judgment has been delivered			
In multi-track trials oral expert evidence will be more frequent than in fast track trials. In the case of *Clifford v Chief Constable of the Hertfordshire Constabulary* [2008] EWHC 2549 (QB), [2008] All ER (D) 254 Wyn Williams J refused to admit expert evidence as he did not see how it would assist in the determination of the main issue in the case which was one of pure fact to be determined by factual evidence. See also **TAB 16**, Expert Evidence, above.		35.5(2)	
An order will usually have been made for experts to meet and, if not agreed, to prepare a statement of the issues on which they agree and those in which they disagree and why. The **experts' statement** is vital in setting the parameters for cross-examination of the experts		35.12(3)	
Where the issue of **causation** is argued before the judge and the parties put to him two or more competing arguments as to the way the event occurred which might be uncommon but not improbable, the judge, having eliminated all			

TAB 19 PROCEDURAL TABLES

	Form No	CPR Rule	PD
causes of the damage save one, could properly ask himself on the balance of probabilities whether that one remaining cause was the cause of the action: *Ide v ATB Sales Ltd and Lexus Financial Services v Russell* [2008] EWCA Civ 424, [2008] AlL ER (D) 374 (Apr).			
For causation in clinical negligence actions where there are several possible causes of injury see *Bailey (by her father and litigation friend) v Ministry of Defence* [2008] EWCA Civ 883, [2009] 1 WLR 1052 and article in Sol Jo (2008) 21 October and (2009) 23 June, page 27			
For the attitude of the court to applications for a **witness protection order** whereby the evidence of certain witnesses be heard in private and restrictions imposed on the disclosure of their identities see *Cherney v Deripaska* [2012] EWCA Civ 1235, 156 Sol Jo (no 37) 31. The trial judge's refusal of the order was upheld. The Court of Appeal stated that the question was not one of discretion, either an order was necessary or it was not.		39.2(3) and (4)	
In cases, such as tripping cases, where the precise location and physical defects are important **accurate sketch plans and photographs** can be crucial: see *Manning v Stylianou* [2006] EWCA Civ 1655 and article at (2007) Sol Jo, 25 May, page 662. See also *Hunte v Bottomley and Sons Ltd* (2007) Times, 21 November, CA			
For the evidential value of plans already in existence in **boundary disputes** and for consideration of the relevant factors in that type of case see *Huntley v Armes* [2010] EWCA Civ 396, [2010] 12 May, Sol Jo, and for a detailed consideration see article 'The great divide' by Marc Glover in Sol Jo, Property Focus June 2010, page 8			
If there is an opportunity to prepare a typed "**skeleton closing**" it is prudent for the defendant's advocate to produce one. It is essential that this is brief, and leaves clear scope for fleshing out in closing speech			
Save in exceptional cases a party should not provide a document to the judge without the other party being provided with a copy or being given the opportunity to make representations about it; *Lloyds Bank plc v Cassidy* (2005) Times, 11 January, CA			
As to public perception of bias, **recusal** of himself by the judge and applications to the judge to withdraw see *AWG Group Ltd v Morrison* [2006] EWCA Civ 6, [2006] 1 All ER 967 and article by Louis Flannery [2006] 156 NLJ, 17 February, p 278 and also see *Howell v Lees Millais* [2007] EWCA Civ 720, [2007] All ER (D) 64 (Jul) where the			

	Form No	CPR Rule	PD
judge concerned had had personal dealings with a firm of solicitors at to his taking up some form of consultancy. The judge declined to stand down but his refusal was overturned by the Court of Appeal. The case was subsequently referred to the Office for Judicial Complaints at the instance of the Lord Chief Justice. This case is the subject of a further article by Louise Flannery at [2007] 15 NLJ, page 2746. The judge was reprimanded by the Lord Chief Justice as a result of the reference to the OJC.			
The court will not ordinarily uphold an objection based on the judge's receipt, whilst at the Bar, of instructions to act for or against any party, solicitor or advocate now before him: *Locabail (UK) Ltd v Bayfield Properties Ltd* [2000] 1 All ER 65, CA; and see also *Mireskandari v Associated Newspapers Ltd* [2010] EWHC 967 (QB), [2010] All ER (D) 06 (May).			
A judge should always reveal before the hearing anything that might give rise to an application to recuse himself: see *Re A (Family Proceedings: Recusal of judge)* (2010) Times, 23 October, and note the judgment of Thorpe LJ.			
It is not part of counsel's duty nor is it appropriate for counsel to influence a decision by a lay client as to whether to waive his right to object to a judge in his case because of an appearance of bias; *Smith v Kvaerner Cementation Foundations Ltd* [2006] EWCA Civ 242, (2006) Times, 11 April, CA			
Where there is real ground for doubt that doubt should be resolved in favour of recusal: *Ansar v Lloyds TSB plc (No 2)* [2006] All ER (D) 277 (Jul)			
The court is unlikely to look favourably on claims of judicial bias after the complainant has awaited the outcome of the case and found it to be unwelcome: *Steadman-Byrne v Amjad* [2007] EWCA Civ 625, (2007) Times, 30 July, per Sedley J. The appeal in this case was nevertheless allowed, the judge having indicated a clear view having heard only one party to the case.			
There was no argument by the respondent that the appellant was estopped from filing an appeal notice by reason of his failure to take objection promptly upon the bias being apparent but the court obviously adverted to the possibility of an argument that an estoppel had arisen or that the apparent bias had been waived			
A useful authority is to be found in the employment case of *Ezsias v North Glamorgan NHS Trust* [2007] EWCA Civ 330, [2007] 4 All ER 940 where the judge at a pre-hearing review expressed her view in such conclusive terms that it			

TAB 19 PROCEDURAL TABLES

	Form No	CPR Rule	PD
was reasonable for a fair-minded and informed observer to take the view that the judge had a closed mind as to the claimant's prospects of success. The Court of Appeal upheld the EAT's decision to set aside the decision, subsequently made by the judge, striking out the appeal on the basis that it had no reasonable prospect of success on the ground of bias, ie the possible perception by a fair-minded observer that the forum had already made up its mind.			
In a more recent employment case, *Pan v West LB AG* UKEAT/0308/11/DM, [2011] All ER (D) 100 (Aug) the Court of Appeal stated that it was established law that the test to be applied in determining bias was whether the fair-minded and informed observer, having considered the facts, would conclude that there was a real possibility that the tribunal was biased.			
A clear manifestation of bias should be drawn to the attention of the court immediately to avoid any argument that the appearance of bias had been waived and in the interest of administration of justice: *Locabail (UK) Ltd v Bayfield Properties Ltd (leave to appeal)* [2000] QB 451; also *Baker v Quantum Clothing Group* [2009] EWCA Civ 566, [2009] All ER (D) 75 (Jun), where the application for re-hearing on the ground of apparent bias were made after the judgment had been reserved.			
For a case where the allegation of apparent bias 'plainly resulted from the extreme bitterness of the dispute between the parties' see *Thompson v Collins* [2009] EWCA Civ 525, [2009] All ER (D) 67 (Apr).			
In *El Farargy v El Farargy* (2007) Times, 23 November, CA the judge made remarks in a directions hearing which resulted in an application for him to recuse himself. The applicant maintained that the remarks betrayed apparent bias. The judge refused to do so but his decision was reversed by the Court of Appeal which found the judge to have crossed the line between the tolerable and the impermissible. Ward LJ observed that it was invidious for a judge to sit in judgment of his own conduct. Where the circumstances permitted, first an informal approach should be made to the judge inviting recusal. This would provide a judge who denies the complaint with the opportunity either to pass the case to a colleague or to invite another judge to make the decision on the application.			
For criticism of Ward LJ's guidance see article 'The *El Farargy* postscript' by Craig Barlow and Jason Hadden, NLJ, 22 February 2008, pages 278-280.			

	Form No	CPR Rule	PD
The Immigration Appeal case *Helow v Secretary of State for the Home Department* [2008] UKHL 62, [2008] 1 WLR 2416, (2008) Times, 5 November involved an allegation of bias and want of impartiality and was reported under the heading 'Partisan magazine did not influence judge'. The appeal failed but the speech of Lord Mance is of considerable interest			
More recently see *R (Kaur) v Institute of Legal Executives Appeal Tribunal* [2011] EWCA Civ 1168 and the detailed consideration of the decision by Nicholas Dobson in an article entitled 'Automatic disqualification and apparent bias' in (2012) Gazette, 9 February, page 18.			
For guidance on circumstances which justify a **lawyer's withdrawal** from a case see *R v Ulcay* [2007] EWCA Crim 2379, [2008] 1 All ER 547; *R v O'Hare* [2006] EWCA Crim 471, [2006] All ER (D) 155 (Mar); and *Re Boodhoo (wasted costs order)* [2007] EWCA Crim 14, [2007] All ER 762n.			
In the case of *Ulcay* both counsel and solicitors successfully applied to withdraw from the case. Subsequently new counsel and solicitors appeared on behalf of the defendant but, after what they regarded as an adjournment for an inadequate time to prepare, they withdrew form the case because of insufficient time to prepare. Both counsel and solicitors followed advice given by their professional body but the advice was stated to be wrong by the court, which felt strongly that the lawyers were professionally obliged by their duty to the court to "soldier on" and do their best to comply with orders of the court. The judgment of the court was given by Sir Igor Judge and he made it clear that Code of Conduct 2007, rule 2.01(b) did not require a solicitor to refuse to act or cease to act in these circumstances			
The **burden of proof** on the parties is such that it is for the claimant on the balance of probabilities to prove that there is a prima facie case and once that is established the defendant has the evidential burden of showing that the prima case has been displaced. For a detailed exposition of the position see the judgment of Pill LJ in *Dawkins v Carnival plc (t/a P & O Cruises)* [2011] EWCA Civ 1237, [2012] 1 Lloyd's Rep 1, [2011] All ER (D) 85 (Dec) and for a review of the implications see article entitled 'Thrills and spills' in (2011) NLJ, 9 December at page 1693 by Keith Dawkins.			
As to summary judgment at trial see *James v Evans* [2000] 3 EGLR 1, CA.			
As to a submission of **no case to answer** and whether an election as to the calling			

TAB 19 PROCEDURAL TABLES

	Form No	CPR Rule	PD
of evidence should be required see *Boyce v Wyatt Engineering* [2001] EWCA Civ 692, (2001) Times, 14 June and *Miller (t/a Waterloo Plant) v Cawley* [2002] EWCA Civ 1100, (2002) Times, 6 September; also *Youssif v Jordan* [2003] EWCA Civ 1852, (2004) Times, 22 January and *Sutradhar v Natural Environmental Research Council* [2004] EWCA Civ 175, (2004) Times, 19 March affd [2006] UKHL 33, [2006] 4 All ER 490. More recently *Benham Ltd v Kithira Investments* [2005] CLY 493 and *Graham v Chorley Borough Council* [2006] EWCA Civ 92, (2006) Times, 20 March			
As to the submission of no case to answer and the putting of the defence to its election see *Graham v Chorley Borough Council* [2006] EWCA Civ 92, (2006) Times, 20 March			
As to an application at trial to argue an **unpleaded point** see *Dupont de Nemours v St Dupont (No 2)* [2003] 05 LS Gaz R 32			
As to the effect of **interference by the judge** during the trial see *Alpha Lettings Ltd v Neptune Research and Development Inc* [2003] EWCA Civ 704, [2003] All ER (D) 273 (May), CA and the statement of Sir Thomas Bingham MR referred to that 'the English tradition sanctions and even encourages a measure of disclosure by the judge of his current thinking . . . '			
For the risk that arises from a judge's lengthy interrogation of witnesses see *Southwark London Borough Council v Kofi-Adu* [2006] EWCA Civ 281, (2006) Times, 1 June			
The Court of Appeal in *Malik v Kalyan* (2010) Times, 1 April, per Rimer LJ, stated 'It is usually good practice for a judge trying a civil claim to see where a line of cross-examination was, or might be, going before stopping it.' The case was remitted to the judge for a retrial on the basis that he would hear further cross-examination from which he might reconsider his findings and conclusions.			
A **hearing fee** of £1,090 is payable by the claimant (or the defendant if the action is proceeding solely on the counterclaim). The provisions for refund on settlement or discontinuance are the same as on the Fast Track; see **TAB 18**, para 6, final sub-paragraph.			
It must be faced that there can be a degree of **delay** that can make a fair trial unachievable. The human rights argument can be followed from a consideration of the decision in *Lehtinden v Finland (No 2)* Application No 4561804 [2009] ECHR 45618/04, Hg 31 March 2007. The proceedings lasted 9 years and 10 months which was found to be			

	Form No	CPR Rule	PD
excessive and a breach of Art 6(1) of the Convention. An award of £4,000 pecuniary damage was made.			
The number of **litigants in person**, now known as self-represented parties, has increased considerably and is expected to continue doing so; see Civil Justice Council report 'Access to justice for Litigants in person', October 2011. For the problems that arise see article 'Going it alone' by Simon Love and Tom Hunter in (2011) NLJ, 23 November, page 1639. Note also the discussion there of **vexatious litigants** and the leading authority *Bhamjee v Forsdick* [2003] EWCA Civ 113, [2003] All ER (D) 429 (Jul).			
8A. Judgment			
The requirement to make thorough **findings of fact** is such that failure to do so will result in a flawed judgment that requires re-hearing: *Gabriel v Kirklees Metropolitan Council* [2004] EWCA Civ 345, [2004] BLR 441, (2004) Times, 12 April			
For the duty on judges to give reasons for their decisions see *Flannery v Halifax Estate Agency Ltd* [2000] 1 All ER 373 per Henry LJ. If at the end of a judgment it appears the judge has failed to deal with a material point it is the advocates' duty to draw the omission to the court's attention and request clarification or a supplemental judgment: *Re S (omission from judgment; duty of counsel)* (2007) Times, 2 July. See also *Re A (a child) (duty to seek reasons)* (2007) Times, 16 October, CA below			
A judge can alter his judgment at any time before it is perfected and entered; that is, in effect, by the sealing of the order giving effect to the judgment (which would now be pursuant to CPR 40.2(2)(b)): *Re Barrell Enterprises* [1973] 1 WLR 19, CA; *Pittalis v Sherefettin* [1986] QB 868, CA (decisions prior to CPR but unaffected by them); *Stewart v Engel* [2000] 3 All ER 518, CA and *Paulin v Paulin* [2009] EWCA Civ 221, [2009] All ER (D) 187 (Mar). Reference should be made to the judgments in *Pittalis* (see above) for the procedure to be adopted and to the judgment of Wilson LJ in *Paulin* above for a detailed consideration of those principles. See also New Law Journal 27 March 2009, page 475 and an article in the same journal on 17 July 2009 at page 1015 entitled 'Reverse gear' by Shantanu Majumdar.			
In *Earl of Malmesbury v Strutt & Parker* [2007] EWHC 2199 (QB), [2007] All ER (D) 103 (Oct) the court expressed the view that there should be 'strong reasons' before the judge's jurisdiction to alter his judgment was exer-			

TAB 19 PROCEDURAL TABLES

	Form No	CPR Rule	PD
cised. Earlier cases had made the existence of 'exceptional circumstances' as the pre-condition. The jurisdiction, on either pre-condition, should only be exercised where it was clear to the judge without prolonged enquiry that his conclusion was wrong.			
A judge has an unlimited jurisdiction to amplify his reasons for the decision at any time: *Re T (a child: contact)* [2002] EWCA Civ 1736, [2003] 1 FCR 303 and *Paulin* (see above).			
A party cannot return to the trial judge and seek to have the re-opening of a final decision. In effect it would be asking him to hear an appeal from himself that he has no power to do. This remains the case if the judge's order was founded on a settlement agreed between the parties after advice: *Roult v North West Strategic Health Authority* [2009] EWCA Civ 444, [2009] PIQR P322.			
If a trial judge decides a claim on one of two or more points a party is not entitled to a decision on the other points that have been made academic by his finding: *Palfrey v Wilson* [2007] EWCA Civ 94, (2007) Times, 5 March			
Only in most exceptional circumstances should counsel ask a judge to reconsider a point of substance after the draft judgment has been sent out: *Egan v Motor Services (Bath) Ltd* [2007] EWCA Civ 1002, (2007) Times, 24 December, CA			
In *R (on the application of Edwards) v Environment Agency* [2008] UKHL 22, [2008] 1 WLR 1587 copies of draft speeches were provided in confidence with a request that counsel check them for 'error and ambiguity'. Lord Hoffmann said: 'The purpose of the disclosure of draft speeches to counsel is to obtain their help in correcting misprints, inadvertent errors of fact or ambiguities of expression. It is not to enable them to re-argue the case.'			
Not only are draft judgments circulated in confidence but all communications in response are covered by the same principle; for the difficulties that arose when confidence was broken by one of the responses being circulated beyond the court see *R (Mohamed) v Secretary of State for Foreign and Commonwealth Affairs* [2010] EWCA Civ 158, [2010] 4 All ER 177, where the result was that the original paragraphs that had been circulated and subsequently amended, were made public on the Court waiving confidentiality.			
The Court of Appeal in *Mohamed* (previous para) stated that where a draft judgment is circulated a copy of any submission by a party seeking correction must be sent to all other parties at the same time as it is lodged with the Court.			40E

	Form No	CPR Rule	PD
Besides circulating its draft judgment the court may also, on occasions, circulate a draft order and invite submissions on it: see for example *Owens v Noble* [2010] Gazette LR, 25 March, page 25 and 1 April, page 17, CA. An issue of fraud was remitted for determination and the issues included whether the remission should be to the original trial judge and as to the costs of the appeal. Remission to the trial judge was upheld there being no exceptional circumstances to the contrary.			
The judge may alter **an ex parte judgment** whether given immediately or after judgment has been reserved so long as the alterations are restricted to punctuation, syntax and grammar or to amplify reasons or give clarification (*Shirt v Shirt* [2012] All ER (D) 212 (Mar)) but not to meet criticisms of it made in appeal grounds (*Brewer v Mann* [2012] All ER (D) 197 (Mar)).			
In *Owens v Noble* (above) the Court of Appeal clarified the correct procedure when it is alleged that a deceit had been practised on the court below. Where fresh evidence is adduced to the Court of Appeal tending to show the trial judge had been deliberately misled, the Court will only allow the appeal and order a retrial where either the fraud was admitted or was incontrovertible. If this is not the case the usual course would be for the issue of fraud to be tried before a decision was made on whether the established judgment should be set aside.			
The Court followed the 'usual course' and *Noble v Owens* [2011] EWHC 534 (QB) was heard before the original trial judge to find whether the claimant had obtained inflated damages by overstating his injuries at the original trial. The evidence relied on to establish that this was the case was surveillance evidence obtained some 8 months after the trial. It was found that the claimant has not misstated the degree of his disability. For a detailed consideration of this hearing see (2011) NLJ, 6 May, page 623 where the article 'Under surveillance' by Lisa Sullivan appears. It must be stressed that a final judgment is normally final which provides certainty in litigation.			
For the Practice Direction as to Reserved Judgments given in:			
(a) Court of Appeal (Civil Division) and			
(b) Queen's Bench Division and Chancery Division at the Royal Courts of Justice see			40E (as substituted with effect from 1 October 2008)
In *McKeowen v British Horse Racing Authority* [2010] EWHC 508 (Admin), 12 March 2010 (Stadler J) it was stated that although a judge had jurisdiction to			

TAB 19 PROCEDURAL TABLES

	Form No	CPR Rule	PD
make substantive changes to a judgment circulated to the parties in draft, even going so far as to reverse his decision, he would only exercise the jurisdiction to do so in exceptional circumstances following the case of *Robinson v Bird* [2003] EWCA Civ 1820.			
A judge who has sent a draft judgment to the parties still retains jurisdiction to alter its substance but should invite submissions on the point at issue; *Robinson v Bird* [2004] EWCA Civ 126			
See further CPR 40.3 [2] and the cases cited and considered there.			
Parties engaged in meaningful settlement discussions between the reserving and the delivery of judgment must tell the court of the discussions: *Gurney Consulting Engineers v Gleeds Health and Safety Ltd* [2006] EWHC 536 (TCC), (2006) Times, 24 April			
Although county court judges should be encouraged to give short judgments they must grapple with conflicts in the evidence of witnesses and sufficiently deal with the fundamental issues so as to explain how they arrived at their decision: *Baird v Thurrock Borough Council* [2005] EWCA Civ 1499, (2005) Times, 15 November			
A judgment takes effect from the date it was given or made or such later date as the court shall specify. An interesting use of the ability to defer the date the judgment takes effect is to be found in *Halabi v Camden London Borough Council* [2008] EWHC 322 (Ch), (2008) Times, 25 March, a case concerning an application to annul a bankruptcy order under the 'debts paid' provision.		40.7	
CPR 3.1(7) does not empower a judge to hear an appeal from himself in respect of a final order (see *SAS Institute Inc v World Programming Ltd* [2010] EWHC 3012 (Ch), [2010] All ER (D) 243 (Nov)) nor permit any party to ask any judge to review his own decision because of the happening of some subsequent event: *Roult (by Angela Holt) v North West Strategic Health Authority* [2009] EWCA Civ 444, [2009] PIQR P322, where it was held the rule could not be used to revoke a judge's approval to a final settlement for the future care costs of the appellant. The court indicated that CPR 3.1(7) was essentially applicable to case management decisions.			
For the effect of **delay** in giving judgment see *Bond v Dunster Properties Ltd* (2011) Gazette LR, 12 May 20, CA where there was a delay of 22 months between the date the hearing was concluded and the date of judgment. It was held that the delay did not render the judge's conclusions on the issues, that were the subject of the appeal, unsafe.			

	Form No	CPR Rule	PD
The delay was however severely criticised.			
In *Zapello v Chief Constable of Sussex* [2010] EWCA Civ 1417 the civil trial judge reserved judgment and the order contained standard wording notifying the parties that they need not attend court, for the handing down of the judgment, if consequential matters had been agreed after seeing the draft judgment. The judge rejected the claim and, in the claimant's absence, awarded costs to the defendant. On appeal by the claimant the Court of Appeal held that the notice was not sufficient to make it clear to the claimant that he should attend court where there was no agreement as to costs. In the circumstance the costs issue should have been adjourned.			
A court has no power to vary the terms of a settlement agreement in the schedule of a Tomlin order: *Community Care North East (a partnership) v Durham County Council* [2010] EWHC 959 (QB), [2010] All ER (D) 09 (Jun), (2010) NLJ, 18 June, page 877.			
8B. The advocate and the judgment			
As to advice given by an advocate at the door of the court, typically as to the acceptance or rejection of an offer, see *Moy v Pettman Smith (a firm)* [2005] 1 All ER 903, (2004) Times, 4 February, HL and *Walker v Chruszcz* [2006] EWHC 64 (QB), [2006] All ER (D) 224 (Jan) where an allegation by the client that he had been pressured into settling his claim at an undervalue at the door of the court failed; the availability of a detailed attendance note contributed significantly to the court's decision			
If an appeal is likely to be considered in cases of doubt counsel must ask the judge for amplification of the reasons where that could solve an issue: *Re A (a child)(duty to seek reasons)* (2007) Times, 16 October, CA			
If a judgment appears to be incomplete or deficient counsel is obliged to invite the judge to expand or supplement it rather than rely on the deficiency to found an appeal: *Re L-B (reversal of judgment)* [2012] EWCA Civ 984, [2013] 1 FLR 209, [2012] Fam Law 1318.			
When considering an appeal it is salutary to bear in mind the standard of the court in *Vaughan v Vaughan* [2007] EWCA Civ 1085, [2007] All ER (D) 43 (Nov):			
"It is sometimes easy to think that an appeal is from a judgment. But it is not, it is from an order. A judgment may have contained an error and a change of circumstances may have invalidated some of its important assumptions but it			

TAB 19 PROCEDURAL TABLES

	Form No	CPR Rule	PD
does not follow that the order should be set aside upon appellate review."			
Advocates do not have immunity from suit in respect of acts concerned with the conduct of litigation: *Arthur JS Hall & Co (a firm) v Simons* [2002] 1 AC 615, HL, a decision which had retrospective effect: *Awoyomi v Radford* [2007] EWHC 1671 (Admin), (2007) Times, 23 July, QB and *McFaddens (a firm) v Platford* [2009] EWHC 126 (TCC), [2009] All ER (D) 257 (Jan). In *McFaddens* the judge reviewed the roles and responsibilities of the barrister and solicitor and the question of whether the solicitor is entitled to rely on counsel's advice.			
8C. Retrial or fresh action			
If fraud is admitted or very clear evidence is found, an appeal on the ground that the trial judge was deliberately misled is the appropriate course rather than the commencement of a fresh action. The appeal will result in a new trial being ordered: see *Owens v Noble* [2010] EWCA Civ 224, 10 March. This is subject to the fresh evidence not being reasonably available to the party aggrieved at the time of the hearing: see *HJ Heinz & Co Ltd v EFL Inc* [2010] EWHC 1203 (Comm), [2010] All ER (D) 01 (Jun).			
Where the fresh evidence as to fraud is contested the appropriate course is for a trial of the issue to be ordered before the judgment obtained is set aside or the appeal dismissed.			
In *Zurich Insurance Co plc v Hayward* [2011] EWCA Civ 641, [2011] All ER (D) 280 (May) the claimants started proceedings to set aside a Tomlin order by which the defendant's personal injury claim had been settled after the claimants in the defence had contended the claim was exaggerated. Subsequently the claimants obtained fresh evidence that the original claim had been fraudulent. An application was filed by the defendant (ie the original claimant) to strike out the claim as an abuse of process as 'res judicata' applied. On appeal the application was dismissed and the action to set aside the Tomlin order allowed to proceed; however the reasoning of the appeal judges differed. For detailed consideration see article 'Skeleton argument' in (2011) NLJ, 15 July, page 976 by Patrick Limb QC who was counsel for *Zurich* in the case.			
In *Kojima v HSBC Bank plc* [2011] EWHC 611, [2011] All ER (D) 249 (Mar) the judge stated that once the court had finally determined a case or part of it considerations such as a material change of circumstances and the judge being misled would generally not			

	Form No	CPR Rule	PD
overcome the overriding public interest in finality. The dissatisfied party would be left only with any rights of appeal available to him. The fact that the claimant had been a litigant in person at the time of the final order did not alter the position.			
The court does have jurisdiction to strike out a statement of case under CPR 3.4(2) for abuse of process even after the trial of the action: see *Fairclough Homes Ltd v Summers* [2012] UKSC 26, [2012] All ER (D) 179 (Jun). The power however is one to be exercised only in exceptional circumstances. This case involved surveillance obtained and the Court declined to exercise this power and held the claimant was entitled to some damages.			
In *Hussain v Hussain* [2012] EWCA Civ 1367, [2012] All ER (D) 224 (Oct) the claimant was the injured driver of the car into which the defendant drove. The trial judge found that the claimant was a party to a fraud to obtain monies for a fabricated personal injury. The Court of Appeal allowed the appeal, drawing a distinction between evidence that related to the reliability of the claimant's recollection and that of taking part in a fraud. For discussion see article 'Hold the cynicism' by David Sawtell in (2013) NLJ 4 January, page 11. In cases such as this the Court of Appeal has made it clear that defendants are obliged to plead in unequivocal terms and with proper particulars what is being alleged and whether it is fraud.			
8D. Personal injury interest rates			

•   Damages for pain and suffering and loss of amenities – 2% (*Birkett v Hayes* [1982] 1 WLR 816, [1982] 2 All ER 710)
 	
•   Special damage (special account rate). After 7 years at 6% fixed at:
 	
  1 February 2009 3%
 	
  1 June 2009 1.5%
 	
  1 July 2009 0.5%
 	
•   Continuing special damages
 	
  Half the appropriate rate from date of the injury until trial. There are conflicting decisions whether half the rate or the full rate is appropriate where the damage has ceased before trial.
 	
  Benefits are disregarded when calculating interest on special damage.			

See 'Practice points: personal injury interest calculation' by Andrew Morgan in (2013) Gazette, 14 January, page 19; also the 7th edn of Ogden's tables published on 10 October 2011 and reviewed			

TAB 19 PROCEDURAL TABLES

	Form No	CPR Rule	PD
by David Regan in (2011) Sol Jo, 15 November, page 17 in an article entitled 'Setting the table'.			
8E. Supply of court documents to a non-party			
The only documents of which a non-party may obtain copies without permission are:			
(a) a statement of case (but not any documents filed with it or attached to it); and			
(b) a judgment or order made or given in public (whether or not after a hearing).		5.4C	
The principle of **open justice**, where documents have been placed before a judge and referred to in the course of proceedings, generally requires that access to them be permitted where it is sought for a proper journalistic purpose: see per Toulson LJ in *R (on the application of Guardian News & Media Ltd) v City of Westminster Magistrates' Court* [2012] EWCA Civ 420, [2012] All ER (D) 18 (Apr).			
9. Costs			
The starting point is for the court to identify the successful party and then to decide having regard to all the circumstances whether it is right to depart from the general rule that the unsuccessful party should be ordered to pay the costs of the successful party: see *Multiplex Construction (UK) Ltd v Cleveland Bridge (UK) Ltd (No 7)* [2008] EWHC 2280 (TCC) per Jackson J, approved in *Fox v Foundation Piling* [2011] EWCA Civ 790.			
Multiplex was also considered in detail by Ramsay J in *Mears v Leeds City Council* [2011] EWHC 2694 (TCC) before applying a discount of 65% to the costs of the successful claimant to reflect the significant costs of issues on which the defendant had succeeded; for discussion see Gazette (2012) 29 march 'Legal update: costs' by Masood Ahmed.		44.3(4)	
If costs are ordered the judge may order that they be subject to detailed assessment or may proceed to assess them summarily at the conclusion of the trial		44.7	
It is unlikely that the parties in a case of any substance will be eager for summary assessment, but schedules of costs should be prepared and, at any rate, brought to the trial even if they are not filed and exchanged			
If there is a trial on liability only the judge is not required to make an immediate decision on costs at that stage but may, at his discretion, postpone making a costs order until quantum has been finally determined: *Shepherds Investments Ltd v Walters* [2007] EWCA Civ			

	Form No	CPR Rule	PD
292, [2007] All ER (D) 40 (Apr). But for a different approach where the claim was not only for a sum of money see *Experience Hendrix LLC v Times Newspapers Ltd* [2008] EWHC 458 (Ch), [2008] All ER (D) 146 (Mar).			
Where a party made an offer of settlement in accordance with CPR 36.21 and it was rejected but was more favourable than the eventual judgment of the court, the court will order costs on an indemnity basis and/or interest on damages at a higher rate from the date of rejection unless it is unjust to do so; *Mamidoil-Jetoil Greek Petroleum Co SA v Okta Crude Oil Refinery AD* (2002) Times, 27 December.			
For the court's attitude to costs where although the claimant has succeeded the court is satisfied he had exaggerated his personal injury claim; see *Painting v University of Oxford* [2005] EWCA Civ 161, (2005) Times, 15 February and *Hall v Stone* [2007] EWCA Civ 1354.		44.3(5)(d)	
The problem of exaggeration by the claimant was very recently considered by the court in *Midland Packaging Ltd v HW Chartered Accountants* [2010] EWHC B16 (Mercantile) where there were Part 36 offers exchanged and the claimant obtained judgment for a sum exceeding the defendant's offer. The judge found that, amongst other factors, the claimant had substantially exaggerated the claims. The judge followed the Court of Appeal decision in *Straker v Tudor Rose* (see **TAB 20** below, paragraph 14.3) that the judge must identify the successful party and then consider whether there were reasons for departing from the general rule that a successful party was entitled to have his costs paid by the other party. The judge found there were good reasons and awarded the defendant a proportion of its costs (75%) from the date of its final offer.			
Morton v Portal Ltd [2010] EWHC 1804 (Ch) was a substantial case in which exaggeration was strongly argued on the issue of costs. The court referred to its power under CPR 44.3(5)(a) and CPR 44.3(2)(b) and stated that the court's power to disallow costs of an issue cannot have been intended to apply merely because a genuine claim was overestimated. The court drew a clear distinction between 'exaggeration' and 'concoction'. In this case the court had not heard evidence and expressed the view that in those circumstances where the sums involved were too large to justify a broad brush approach it was desirable that the matters alleged were dealt with by a costs judge as part of a detailed assessment.		44.3(2)(b) and 44.3(5)(a)	

TAB 19   PROCEDURAL TABLES

	Form No	CPR Rule	PD
For the consequences of a misguided attempt to establish that the claimant had exaggerated her medical condition and to pursue that argument through cross-examination see *Clarke v Maltby* [2010] EWHC 1856 (Ch), [2010] All ER (D) 253 (Jul).			
Where a personal injury claimant has exaggerated her claim but had still beaten the defendant's payment in (or Part 36 offer) the right order was held to be 'no order for costs' in *Widlake v BAA Ltd* [2009] EWCA Civ 1256, 153 Sol Jo (no 45) 29. See also the subsequent case *Sulaman v Axa and Direct Line* [2009] EWCA Civ 1331, [2009] All ER (D) 116 (Dec) where the decision in *Widlake* above was cited. In the circumstances of this case two thirds of the claimant's costs were disallowed, she being found to have lied during the trial. For discussion see NLJ (2009) 22 December, page 5 and note the appeal was dismissed with Sedley LJ dissenting expressing the view that it was disproportionate to deprive the appellant of two-thirds of her costs. For a discussion of the costs trends in such cases see article 'Spinning a yarn' by Gless and Goddard in (2010) NLJ, 19 February, page 267 and for a review of the cases including those referred to above see article by Jonathan Upton entitled 'Lying litigants beware!' (2010) NLJ 19 March, page 418.			
The fraudulent claims and the decisions of the Supreme Court in *Fairclough Homes Ltd v Summers* [2012] UKSC 26, [2012] 4 All ER 317, [2012] 1 WLR 2004 and the comments on the decision in *Ul-Haq v Shah* [2009] EWCA Civ 542, [2010] 1 All ER 73, [2009] RTR 352 see further **TAB 17A**, para 2.6 (above).			
See also an article 'Knocked down' by Andrew Trott in Sol Jo Personal Focus, (2010) April, page 12 and the consideration of the cases *Singh v CS O'Shea & Son Ltd* [2009] EWHC 1251 (QB) and *Kirk v Walton* [2009] EWHC 703 (QB) it contains, and 'The one that got away' by Roger Andre in (2011) Sol Jo, 25 January, page 17.			
For the exceptional position of cases concerning an insurance contract see *Axa General Insurance Ltd v Gottlieb* [2005] EWCA Civ 112, [2005] 1 All ER (Comm) 445, [2005] Lloyd's Rep IR 369, (2005) Times, 3 March. In effect the common law rule in insurance claims is that if the insured makes a claim found to be fraudulent he will not be able to recover for the part of the claim that could honestly be claimed; see also *Aviva Insurance Ltd v Brown* [2011] EWHC 362 (QB), [2012] Lloyd's Rep IR 211 and *Sharon's Bakers (Europe) Ltd v*			

	Form No	CPR Rule	PD
AXA Insurance UK plc [2011] EWHC 210 (Comm), [2012] Lloyd's Rep IR 164, [2011] NLJR 256.			
If the claimant's 'exaggeration' was no more than to put his claim rather high, a defendant who had failed to make an effective and admissible offer could not be regarded as a winner.			
For the court's attitude to the successful party's costs where it is found he was in breach of a pre-action protocol see *Straker v Tudor Rose* [2007] EWCA Civ 368, 151 Sol Jo LB 571. It is the responsibility of the claimant's solicitor to ensure the claim is not issued prematurely			
For the courts' attitude to costs involving **fraud** see *Cheltenham Borough Council v Laird* CA (Civ), 4 February 2010 where the defendant successfully defended an action for fraudulent misrepresentation but was awarded only 65% of costs as she failed on several issues.		44.4	
See *Zurich Insurance Co plc v Hayward* [2011] EWCA Civ 641, [2011] All ER (D) 280 (May) at section 8C (penultimate paragraph) of this TAB and note further that it could not be said that with reasonable diligence the insurers could have uncovered the fraud before the settlement of the first action. See also for detailed discussion the article 'No leg to stand on' by Robert Dickinson in (2011) NLJ, 1 July, page 904.			
See *Fiona Trust & Holdiay Corpn v Yuri Privalou* [2011] EWHC 664 (Comm) where the court made no order for costs in favour of the claimant because the parties and the witnesses had been dishonest.			
The Court has on occasion granted permission for contempt proceedings, eg *Caerphilly County Borough Council v Hughes* [2005] (personal injury fraud) and *Kirk v Walton* [2008] EWHC 1799 (QB) (personal injury exaggeration), cases quoted by Roger Andre in 'The one that got away' (2011) Sol Jo, 25 January, page 17. See also *Lane v Shah* [2011] All ER (D) 23 (Oct), DC (falsifying statements to inflate claim). The claimant was sentenced to 6 months and her husband and daughter each to 3 months. The early release provisions of the Criminal Justice Act 2003, s 258(2) operate, after one half of the term, unconditionally.			
See further *Brighton & Hove Bus and Coach Ltd v Brooks* [2011] EWHC 2504 (Admin), [2011] All ER (D) 146 (Oct) and *Havering London Borough Council v Bowyer, Jones and Bowyer* [2012] EWHC 2237 (Admin). In the latter case sentences of 4 months, 2 months and one month were imposed and the court applied *South Wales Fire*			

TAB 19 PROCEDURAL TABLES

	Form No	CPR Rule	PD
and Rescue Service v Smith [2011] EWHC 1749 (Admin), [2011] All ER (D) 39 (Oct).			
A litigant who is found to be in contempt is so found for knowing what he said was false and that the statement would be likely to interfere with the course of justice; see for example *Nield v Loveday* [2011] EWHC 2324 (Admin), 123 BMLR 132, [2011] All ER (D) 139 (Jul) and the consideration of the case in 'Legal Update: personal injury (2011) Gazette, 6 October, page 16 by Simon Allen who underlines the dangers of verifying documents by a statement of truth. In this case the defendant was imprisoned for 9 months. A helpful consideration of committal for contempt of court for dishonesty in personal injury claims is provided by Roger Cooper in (2012) Sol Jo, 10 January, page 23, 'Road traffic update'. See also consideration of the appropriate sentence for a fraudulent personal injury claim in a contrived motor collision in *Liverpool Victoria Insurance Co Ltd v Bashir* [2012] QB (Adm) 28 February.			
In a commercial case where each party has claims and asserts that there is a balance due to him, the party who is held to be entitled to a payment will generally be regarded as the winner and the starting point as to costs will be the general rule that a successful party is entitled to an order for costs: *Multiplex Constructions (UK) Ltd v Cleveland Bridge UK Ltd* [2008] EWHC 2280 (TCC), (2008) NLJ Law Digest 20 October, page 1473. see also *Pindell Ltd v Airasia Berhad* [2010] EWHC 3238 (Comm), [2010] All ER (D) 123 (Dec) and **TAB 25** below.			
For the effect of conduct on costs both as to disallowance in whole or part and as to the discretion to grant indemnity costs see *Bank of Tokyo-Mitsubishi UFJ Ltd v Baskian Gida Senayi Ve Pazarlama AS* [2009] EWHC 1696 (Ch), Briggs J, [2009] All ER (D) 159 (Jul), (2009) Law Digest 24 July, page 1066 and the cases referred to in the judgment.			
As to **indemnity costs**, the court has a wide discretion, and for the factors to be taken into account by the court when considering whether it is appropriate to award them see *Noorani v Calver* [2009] EWHC 592 (QB), 153 Sol Jo (no 13) 27, [2009] All ER (D) 274 (Mar), Coulson J and see also an article considering the Buncefield litigation in 2008 by Boylan, Francis and Brierly in NLJ (2009) 31 July, page 1081, entitled 'Counting the Total cost'.		44.3	
An order for indemnity costs is only appropriate where 'there was some conduct			

	Form No	CPR Rule	PD
or some circumstance which took the case out of the norm': *Excelsior Commercial & Industrial Ltd v Salisbury, Hamer Aspden & Johnson (a firm)* [2002] EWCA Civ 879, [2002] All ER (D) 39 (Jun), paras 12, 19 and 32.			
This reasoning was repeated by the court in *R (on the application of Rawlinson and Hunter Trustees SA) v Central Criminal Court* [2012] EWHC 3218 (Admin), [2012] NLJR 1503. In this case the court further observed that the abandonment of issues ought not to be discouraged by the award of indemnity costs where a concession was made.			
In *Barr v Biffa Waste Services Ltd (No 4)* [2011] EWHC 1107 (TCC) the Court stated a claimant pursuing a case fairly assessed as 'speculative, weak, opportunist or thin' was vulnerable to an order for indemnity costs if it failed. Coulson J revisited the issue of indemnity costs in *D Morgan plc v Mace and Jones (a firm)(No 3)* [2011] EWHC 26 (TCC) where he rejected most of the defendant's points in favour of such an order and found the defendant's other points insignificant. He refused the defendant's application.			
The TCC has re-iterated the principles on which the court will make an order in *Southwark London Borough Council v IBM UK Ltd* [2011] EWHC 653 (TCC), [2011] All ER (D) 261 (Mar).			
In the article 'Can pursuing a doomed case justify indemnity costs?' (2012) Sol Jo, 3 April, page 14, Ian McConkey and Stephen Gorman review the relevant cases and consider the effect of Part 36 offers. Note in particular *Talbot Design (Seale) Ltd v RJ Canning* [2011] EWHC 3418 (QB).			
For consideration of **non-party costs** orders under Supreme Court Act 1981 see *Dymocks Franchise Supplies (NSW) Pty Ltd v Todd* [2004] UKPC 39, [2005] 4 All ER 195 where Lord Brown identified the principles and *BE Studios v Smith & Williamson* (2005) Times, 16 December where Evans-Lombe J held that impropriety was not a pre-requisite of liability and *Dolphin Quays Development Ltd v Mills* [2008] EWCA Civ 385, [2008] 4 All ER 58 where the court said such orders will always be exceptional and that the ultimate question will be whether or not it is just to make an order.			
The High Court in *Thomson v Berkhamsted Collegiate School* [2009] EWHC 2374 (QB), [2009] NLJR 1440 did find it just to make an order against the parents of the claimant who was seeking damages of nearly £1 million against his former school for failing to			

175

TAB 19 PROCEDURAL TABLES

	Form No	CPR Rule	PD
prevent him being bullied but dropped his case two weeks before the trial. The judge found there was evidence that the parents were not merely funders but directly concerned with the facts of the case. The judge followed the principles set out in *Dymocks* (above). Thomson is of considerable importance for the defendants obtained an order for disclosure of the correspondence between the claimant's solicitor and the third parties: see articles 'Once bitten twice shy' (2009) Sol Jo, 10 November, page 6 by Nick Gilkies and 'School of Thought' (2009) NLJ, 12 November, page 1571 by Nina Unthank. The third parties were joined in the action for the purpose of costs only.			
In *Systemcare (UK) Ltd v Services Design Technology Ltd* [2011] All ER (D) 83 (May) the claimant successfully pursued a claim against the first defendant after the expenditure of considerable money on legal costs. The first defendant then became insolvent. The litigation was held to be without merit and without justification by the first defendant. The second defendant was the managing director and 90% shareholder of the first defendant. The claimant then successfully applied to make the director a second defendant for the purpose of obtaining a non-party costs order against him pursuant to s 51 of the Senior Courts Act 1981; his application for the order was also successful.			
It is good practice where it is likely that a third party costs order will be sought to give early notice of that to the third party: for a case where a third party costs order was made despite the failure to give such notice see *Farrell and Short v Birmingham City Council and Direct Accident Management Services Ltd* [2009] All ER (D) 172 (Jun), CA, the trial judge being satisfied that no prejudice had been suffered as there was no evidence that if notice had been given the third party would have acted differently.			
There is no formal procedure in relation to orders ancillary to applications for non-party costs. Blake J in *Thompson* above stated that ancillary orders that the court considered necessary, eg disclosure, skeleton arguments etc, are made pursuant to the courts' inherent jurisdiction with regard to the overriding objective.			
When the court has ordered a party to pay costs it may order an amount to be paid on account before the costs are assessed. The court has a broad discretion as to this: *Mars UK Ltd v Tecknowledge Ltd (No 2)* [2000] FSR 138, [1999] 2 Costs LR 44 (Ch) and *Dyson Ltd v Hoover Ltd* [2003] EWHC 624 (Ch),			

	Form No	CPR Rule	PD
[2004] 2 All ER 1042, [2004] 1 WLR 126; see also article in Butterworths Costs Newsletter Vol 1, Issue 2, page 6.		44.3(8)	
For consideration of "exceptional" see *Lingfield Properties (Darlington) Ltd v Padgett Lavender Associates* [2008] EWHC 2795 (QB), [2008] All ER (D) 162 (Nov) where the court stated the meaning was 'no more than outside the ordinary run of cases which parties pursue for their own benefit and at their own expense'. See also **TAB 25**, part C, para 11.7 et seq below			
It is interesting to note that in the *Dolphin Quays* case, see above, it was stated that an important factor in the exercise of the discretion to award costs against a non-party was the availability of **security for costs**. The discretion is likely to be exercised more readily in favour of the successful litigant if security was not available at all or only to an inadequate level			
It was held by the court in *Alan Phillips Associates Ltd v Dowling (Terence Edward) (t/a The Joseph Dowling Partnership)* [2007] EWCA Civ 64, [2007] BLR 151 that the third party director had conducted his affairs through the claimant company in such a way that it would be unjust for him to rely on the existence of two separate legal entities to avoid liability for costs.			
A voluntary Code of Conduct for third party litigation funders was approved in November 2011.			
For the position where a **litigant in person obtains an order for costs** see **TAB 25**, General section at 1.12.3.			
9A. Orders in respect of pro bono representation			
For orders under s 194(3) of the Legal Services Act 2007 in respect of pro bono representation, see		44.3C	
The Master of the Rolls, The Deputy Head of Civil Justice and the Solicitor General commend the work of the Access to Justice Foundation and strongly encourage the legal profession to support it: see the article in Civil Court News, 2010, Issue 3, page 18 and the article in the same issue by Toby Brown, Officer of the Access to Justice Foundation ' Pro bono costs – new money for justice'. Further guidance is to be found in his article in the Gazette (2010) 18 November: 'Practice points: pro bono costs'. See further **TAB 25** at 'General', paras 1.11.1-1.11.6.			
9B. Interest on costs			
See **TAB 25** General notes 1.42 and also CPR 44.3(6)(g) and *Powell v Hereford Health Authority* [2002] EWCA Civ			

TAB 19 PROCEDURAL TABLES

	Form No	CPR Rule	PD
1786, [2003] 3 All ER 253 as to the power to specify the dates between which interest should run which may include a period prior to judgment.		44.3(6)(g)	
10. Slip rule			
This has been held to cover forgetting to ask for costs; for a decision where its limits were considered see *SmithKline Beecham plc v Apotex Europe Ltd* [2005] EWHC 1655 (Ch), [2006] 2 All ER 53, [2006] 1 WLR 872 (the subsequent appeals in this case do not relate to the slip rule)		40.12(1)	
The provision in CPR 40.12 was considered in *R + V Versischerung AG v Risk Insurance and Reinsurance Solutions SA* [2007] EWHC 79 (Comm), (2007) Times, 26 February and the court made it clear that the rule cannot be used to correct errors of substance, nor in an attempt to add or detract from the order made. It does no more than to enable the correction of typing errors or matters that were genuine slips or mistakes.			
The court in *Leo Pharma A/S Leo Laboratories Ltd v Sandoz Ltd* [2010] EWHC 1911 reiterated that the slip rule will not be used to correct errors in orders unless they are to correct an accidental slip or omission which does not affect the courts true intention. For detailed discussion see article 'Snafu solutions' by Joanne Williams in (2010) Sol Jo, 20 October, page 17; matters deliberately included by the parties in the order did not amount to accidental slips or omissions.			
The dicta in *Leo Pharma* above was distinguished in *Riva Bella SA v Tamsen Yachts GmbH* [2011] EWHC 2338 (Comm), [2011] All ER (D) 41 (Sep) on the basis that the slip rule could be used to amend an order so as to give effect to the intention of the court. see article by Maria Kell in (2011) NLJ, 11 November, page 1'552.			
11. Vacating hearings			
Solicitors and counsel have a duty to inform the court as soon as it is known a hearing will not proceed. See *Tasyurdu v Immigration Appeal Tribunal* [2003] EWCA Civ 447, Times, 16 April			
Where the hearing is to be vacated by reason of a settlement reached by the parties, the settlement agreement needs to be carefully drafted; reference to article 'Compromising position' by Graham Reid in (2010) NLJ, 12 November, page 1559 and the guidance it gives may well be found rewarding.			
12. Interim non-disclosure orders, prohibition on reporting the fact of proceedings			

	Form No	CPR Rule	PD
12.1 Such orders restrain the publication of information and may exceptionally prohibit publication of the names of a party or the parties and/or details of the subject-matter of the proceedings and 'in the rarest of cases' prohibit the reporting of the fact of proceedings (a super injunction).			
12.2 Relevant provisions include:			
Human Rights Act 1998 (HRA), s 12 in particular sub-s (3) which requires the applicant to satisfy the court that it is likely to be established at trial that publication should not be allowed.			
Article 8 of the European Convention on Human Rights ('the Convention') which grants a right to respect for private and family life.			
Article 10 of the Convention which protects freedom of expression.			
• Neither Article 8 nor Article 120 has precedence over the other.			
12.3 The relevant CPR provisions are:			
CPR 25.3 Interim remedies			
CPR PD 25A Interim injunctions (1)-(5)			
CPR PD 51F Non-disclosure injunctions information collection pilot scheme			
In addition see			
The report of the Committee on Super Injunctions Anonymised Injunctions and Open Justice – headed by Lord Neuberger MR dated 20 May 2011			
Practice Guidance: Interim Non-Disclosure Orders issued as guidance (not as a Practice Direction) by the Master of the Rolls which sets out the law at 1 August 2011.			
12.4 Relevant principles include:			
'Open justice' is a fundamental principle and the general rule is that hearings and judgments are heard and delivered in public: further any order made is open to the public: see *North Shore Ventures Ltd v Anstead Holdings* (2011) Times, 22 April; *Pink Floyd Music Ltd v EMI Records* [2010] EWCA Civ 1429 and *F & C Investments (Holdings) Ltd v Barthelemy* [2011] EWHC 1851 (Ch).			
The burden of establishing any derogation from the principle lies with the person seeking them and can only be established in exceptional circumstances where they are strictly necessary as measures to secure the proper administration of justice.			
Interim non-disclosure orders which contain derogations from the principle of open justice cannot be granted just because the parties agree to them.			
Anonymity will only be granted where it is strictly necessary and only to that ex-			

TAB 19 PROCEDURAL TABLES

	Form No	CPR Rule	PD
tent: see Practice Guidance on Non-Disclosure Order, para 12.			
12.5 Derogations from the principle of open justice include, but are not limited to:			
(a) an order that the hearing be held wholly or partly in private;			
(b) an order that the names of one or more of the parties to be not disclosed; whether or not an anonymity order has been made, a judgment available to the public should normally be given and a copy of the court order should be available to the public although some editing of the judgment or order might be necessary;			
(c) an order that access to documents on the court file be restricted (under rule 5.4C of the inherent jurisdiction);			
(d) an order that the provision of documents to third parties be restricted (under Practice Direction 25A, para 9.2); and			
(e) an order prohibiting disclosure of the existence of the proceedings or the order; see CPR PD 51F – Non-disclosure Injunctions Information Collection Pilot Scheme.			
12.6 If the applicant for interim relief surmounts the hurdle of satisfying the court that it is likely to be established at trial that publication should not be allowed (see para 12.4 above) the court has to decide whether the information in question is private and that the claimant has a reasonable expectation of privacy under Art 8 (see para 12.3 above).			
If so satisfied the court has to perform a balancing exercise between Art 8 rights (ie privacy) of the claimant and the Art 10 right of the defendant (that publication is in the public interest and not just of interest to the public: *DFT v TFD* [2010] EWHC 2335 (QB), [2010] All ER (D) 103 (Oct)) and see *Ferdinand v MGN Ltd* [2011] EWHC 2454 (QB), [2011] All ER (D) 4 (Oct) where it was found to be appropriate in the circumstances to favour the defendant's right of expression. This is not an exercise of discretion, see para 11 of the Practice Guidance.			
Useful guidance, when considering whether the publication of information said to be private should be permitted, is provided by the judgments in *BUQ v HRE* [2012] All ER (D) 78 (Apr) and *SKA v CRH* [2012] EWHC 766 (QB), [2012] All ER (D) 216 (Mar).			
12.7 For consideration of the principles to be applied by the court when considering an application for a departure			

	Form No	CPR Rule	PD
from the principle, balancing the right to open justice with the right to respect for private lives, see the judgment of Lord Neuberger MR in *JIH v News Group Newspapers Ltd* [2010] EWCA Civ 42, [2010] 2 All ER 324, [2011] 1 WLR 1645 where the judgment of Tugendhat J was overturned and the parties were allowed to retain anonymity until trial or further order. The court stated it was for the judge to decide after perusal of the papers if any claimed restriction in publication was justified and he would have to be satisfied that:			
(a) the facts and circumstances were sufficiently strong to justify encroaching on the open justice rule by restraining the extent to which the proceedings could be reported; and			
(b) if so, that the restrictions on publication were fashioned so as to satisfy the need for encroachment in a way which minimised the extent of any restrictions.			
Each case turns on its facts. The onus is on the applicant seeking departure from the general principle of open justice.			
For a clear list of the principles to be applied see the case report in (2011) NLJ, 11 February, page 211 of *JIH* above in this para and for a decision where those principles were considered and applied see *CVB v MGN Ltd* [2012] EWHC 1148 (QB), Tugendhat J.			
Most recently the Court in *McLaren v News Group Ltd* (2012) Gazette LR, 20 September, page 20 ruled that a sexual relationship was of the essence of private life giving a reasonable expectation of privacy but the claimant's public position, when considered in the balancing exercise, caused that balance to fall in favour of the defendant's legitimate interest in publishing its story. The application for an interim injunction was refused. The court adopted the definition in *Spelman v Express Newspapers* [2012] All ER (D) 51 (Mar) of 'a public figure' and having found the claimant fell within it was satisfied he also fell within the category of those from whom the public could reasonably expect a higher standard of behaviour.			
12.8 So-called 'super injunctions', which are restricted to 'the rarest cases', are those which prohibit the publication of the very fact of proceedings; often it is a pre-emptive measure as there is a story about to be published.			
12.9 By reason of the 'Spycatcher' doctrine an injunction against a news organisation binds all others which know about it until the case is decided or settled. The doctrine is not confined to news organisations and any person who			

TAB 19 PROCEDURAL TABLES

	Form No	CPR Rule	PD
knowing of the court's order reveals the information protected and thereby thwarts the purpose of the order is liable to punishment for contempt of court.			
12.10 The report of the Committee on Super-Injunctions (see 12.3 above, highlights of which are to be found in (20110 Sol Jo, 24 May, page 3) acknowledges the difficulty of enforcing super-injunctions where details are published on websites. The court has to decide whether the information in question was private and the claimant has a reasonable expectation of privacy under Art 8 ECHR (see previous para).			
12.11 The situation, where people are permitted to litigate anonymously but the public has access to a public judgment with such information as the judge decides is appropriate has been described by Barbara Hewson in an article entitled 'Suing Anon' in (2011) Sol Jo, 8 February, page 9 as one which 'Celebrity clients may prefer . . . but not the tabloid press'.			
12.12 In *Donald v Ntuli (Guardian News & Media Ltd intervening)* [2010] EWCA Civ 1276, [2011] 1 WLR 294, [2010] 46 LS Gaz R the court upheld an injunction prohibiting publication of the fact of the relationship between the parties but ruled that the parties must be named; Maurice Kay LJ stated an anonymity order could only be justified where identification 'might have serious consequences' for a person's life.			
See also *Spelman (by his litigation friends) v Express Newspapers* [2012] EWHC 239 (QB), [2012] All ER (D) 91 (Feb) where the court granted an injunction restraining the publication of sensitive information but did not take the 'exceptional course' of anonymising the proceedings.			
12.13 For procedure see CPR 39.2(4) and CPR PD 25A and the judgment referred to and the report of *Ntuli v Donald* (see above) in (2010) Gazette, 2 December, page 14 but **above all see the Practice Guidance** referred to above at 12.3 of this TAB, at paras 17 et seq.			
12.14 It is to be noted that anonymity orders cannot be obtained merely by consent application (see per Lord Neuberger in *JIH v News Group Newspapers Ltd* (above)) and also that they can be made in favour of a witness.			
12.15 The problem that arises when an anonymised injunction is undermined by the use of parliamentary privilege is highlighted by the cases of *Goodwin v NGN (VBN interested party)* [2011] EWHC 1437 (QC), Tugendhat J [2011] All ER (D) 45 (Jun) and that concerning Ryan Giggs; see article in (2011) Sol Jo 14 June, page 3 'Judge			

	Form No	CPR Rule	PD
warns MPs over privilege abuse'. The report of 20 May 2011 (above) urges the use of caution in considering whether to make use of the privilege to undermine an injunction granted by the court.			
12.16 Both the Master of the Rolls and the Lord Chief Justice when commenting on the report of 20 May said an MP's statement in Parliament was no justification for lifting an anonymity order.			
12.17 Other factors considered by the court in these applications for injunctions against publication include **blackmail** (a very strong factor but extremely difficult to assess on a paper application); see the report of the statement read to the court on behalf of the applicant in the case of *Giggs, CTB v News Group Newspapers*, which accepted 'there was no basis' in the allegation' (2011) Times, 16 December) and the **harmful effect on the claimant's children,** which was considered by the Court of Appeal in *ETK v News Group Newspapers Ltd* [2011] EWCA Civ 439, [2011] All ER (D) 197 (Apr), Human Rights Updater (2011) April, Issue 106, page 7.			
The Court of Appeal stated that the judge had been wrong to conclude that the harmful effect on the claimant's children could not 'tip the balance'. It was not however a factor of limitless importance that would prevail over all other considerations.			
12.18 For the recommended practice regarding any application for interim injunctive relief in civil proceedings to restrain an interim non-disclosure order see **Practice Guidance: Interim Non-Disclosure Orders,** issued as guidance by the Master of the Rolls. In particular note that: (a) The applicant should prepare (see para 17 of the Practice Guidance): (i) the application/claim form; (ii) a witness statement or statements justifying the need for an order; (iii) legal submissions; (iv) a draft order; (v) an Explanatory Note (see para 33 of the Practice Guidance). (b) The respondents and any non-parties to be served with the order are entitled to advance notice of the application hearing and to be served with the notice and supporting documents prior to the hearing. Failure to give ad-			

TAB 19 PROCEDURAL TABLES

	Form No	CPR Rule	PD
vance notice will have to be justified on 'clear and cogent evidence', by compelling reasons; see paras 18-23 of the Guidance.			
(c) Where an applicant is to provide advance notice of an application to a non-party or where the applicant notifies a non-party of the order, material supplied to the non-party shall be supplied upon receipt of an irrevocable undertaking to the court that the material and information . . . will only be used for the purpose of the proceedings (see paras 24-28 of the Practice Guidance).			
12.19 From 1 August 2011 to 30 September 2012 the Ministry of Justice monitored applications for non disclosure injunctions at the High Court and Court of Appeal. Under the Practice Direction data relating to any injunctions covered by s 12 of the HRA 1998 (freedom of expression) was recorded. Details included whether notice of the application has been given. This has lapsed and is replaced by CPR PD 40F — see next sub-para. No changes to it were made.			
12.20 With effect from 10 October 2012 a scheme for recording and transmission to the Ministry of Justice for analysis of certain data in relation to publication of private or confidential information is provided by Practice Direction 40F — Non-disclosure Injunctions Information Collection Scheme.			40F
13. Live text based communications from court			
By *Practice Guidance* [2011] 1 WLR 61, Sen Cts, Lord Justice Judge (LCJ) gave interim guidance as to the use of such communications during the course of trials for the purpose of fair and accurate reporting. This guidance was revised by the Lord Chief Justice in December 2011 by the issue of Practice Guidance: The Use of Text-Based Forms of Communication (including Twitter) for Court for the Purposes of Fair and Accurate Reporting. The general principle is that the court must be satisfied that they do not pose a danger to the administration of justice in the particular case. The court proceedings must be those open to the public and limited to the part not subject to reporting restrictions.			
Applications can, subject to these matters, be made for the court to permit their use but journalists and legal commentators will not need to make an application. The Supreme Court's policy on text based communications from court rooms by a member of the public or a member of a legal team is that it is permissible subject to exceptions. Use of			

	Form No	CPR Rule	PD
mobile phones in a court room is prohibited; see 'Policy on the use of text based communications (Supreme Court)'.			39A.6
The basis on which the Supreme Court adopted this policy is that cases before it do not involve interaction with witnesses or jurors.			
See also [2011] 1 All ER 604, SC.			
The Lord Chief Justice's guidance is reproduced in the editorial note to CPR PD 39A, para 6 in Volume 1 (see para **CPR PD 39A.6 [2]**).			
14. General damages and the 10% increase			
In *Simmons v Castle* [2012] EWCA Civ 1039 the judgment was used to announce formally that there would be a 10% increase in general damages awarded in most tort actions where judgment is given after 1 April 2013; for considered opinion see article entitled 'The next step' by Kate Parker in (2012) NLJ, 7 September, page 1115.			
The Court of Appeal however reviewed the application of the 10% uplift in damages in personal injury cases upon an application made by the Associated British Insurers.			
It held that from 1 April 2013 'the proper level of general damages in all civil claim for: (i) pain and suffering; (ii) loss of amenity; (iii) physical inconvenience and discomfort; (iv) social discredit (v) mental distress; or (vi) loss of society of relatives, will be 10% higher than previously, unless the claimant falls within s 44(6) of LASPO. It therefore follows that, if the action now under appeal had been the subject of a judgment after 1 April 2013, then (unless the claimant had entered into a CFA before that date) the proper award of general damages would be 10% higher than that agreed in this case, namely £22,000 rather than £20,000'.			
• LASPO is the Legal Aid and Punishment of Offenders Act 2010 • A claimant will fall within s 44(6) of LASPO if he entered a Conditional Fee Agreement (CFA) before 1 April 2013 specifically for the purposes of the provision of advocacy or litigation services in connection with the matter that is the subject of the proceedings in which the costs order was made or advocacy or litigation services were			

TAB 19   PROCEDURAL TABLES

	Form No	CPR Rule	PD
provided under the agreement in connection with the matter before 1 April 2013.			
• The extra 10% applies to general damages awarded in both tort and contract cases.			
• At the re-hearing ([2012] EWCA Civ 1288) the court held that 'the primary purpose' of the 10% increase was as a counter-balance to depriving claimants of their ability to recover success fees and also-after-event insurance premiums.			
• The CFA will still exist but as a private matter between solicitor and his own client.			
A reading of the article by Nigel Poole QC in Sol Jo (2012) October Bar Focus page 13 entitled 'Confusion and uncertainty for claimants' will help to alert litigants and their lawyers to yet a new bundle of uncertainties.			

TABLE 20—OFFERS TO SETTLE

TAB 20

	Form No	CPR Rule	PD
1. Preliminary			
1.1 A party can make an offer to settle in any form he chooses but it will not have Part 36 consequences unless the Part 36 requirements are fulfilled. It will fall to be considered under CPR r44.3 if they are not		36.1(2)	
1.2 The party who makes an offer is the 'offeror' and the party to whom the offer is made is the 'offeree'		36.3(1)	
1.3 The provisions of CPR 36 do not apply to claims allocated to the small claims track		27.2(1)(g)	
1.4 The new CPR 36.14(1A) as to the meaning of '**more advantageous**' applies to offers to settle made on or after 1 October 2011.		36.14(1A)	
1.5 For a detailed consideration of Part 36 and the scope for its improvement see the article by David di Mambro in (2013) NIJ, 25 January, page 66.			
2. Form and content of a Part 36 offer			
The requirements for an offer to have Part 36 consequences are that it **must**:	N242A as amended 1 October 2011 (not mandatory)	36.2	36A, para 1.1 36B – Notice of offer to settle – Part 36
(i) be in writing		36.2(a)	
(ii) state on its face it is intended to have the consequences of Section 1 of Part 36		36.2(b)	
(iii) specify a period of not less than 21 days within which the defendant will be liable for the claimant's costs in accordance with rule 36.10 if the offer is accepted. Form N242A provides that the period must be within 21 days of service but the rule itself does not specify the event from which the 21 day period is to run. It is to be noted that in *C v D* [2010] EWHC 2940 (Ch); and on appeal [2011] EWCA Civ 726 the offer letter stated the offer would remain open 'for 21 days from the date of the offer letter' but the question of the starting date was not the subject of comment by the judge. It is preferable to express the offer as to run from service and if possible to use Form 242A.		36.2(c)	
In *PHI Group Ltd v Robert West Consulting Ltd* [2012] EWCA Civ 588 the Court of Appeal upheld the trial judge who had decided that because the of-			

TAB 20 PROCEDURAL TABLES

		Form No	CPR Rule	PD
	fer did not specify a period of not less than 21 days, or any period, in compliance with CPR 36.2 (2)(c) it was not a Part 36 offer. the Court of Appeal decision was made after the court had considered the decision in *C v D* above.			
(iv)	state whether it relates to the whole of the claim or to part of it or an issue that arises in it and if so to which part or issue, and		36.2(d)	
(v)	state whether it takes into account any counterclaim		36.2(e)	
But note				
•	Lloyd LJ in *PHI Group Ltd* (see above) stated 'It is only properly called a Pt 36 offer if it is made in accordance with the rule'; see article by Clive Thomas entitled 'The write path' in (2012) NLJ, 19 October, page 1319 for consideration and discussion. It seems apparent that the **safest course is to follow the words of the section.**			
•	'relevant period' is defined by r 36.3(1)(c).			
•	requirement (iii) above as to at least 21 days being allowed for acceptance of the offer does not apply if the offer is made less than 21 days before the start of the trial		36.2(3)	
•	additional information is required to be contained in an offer that relates to: (i) future pecuniary loss in a personal injury claim –see r 36.5 (ii) offer to settle provisional damages claim – see r 36.6 (iii) deduction of benefits see r 36.15		36.2(4)	
•	an offeror can make a Part 36 offer solely as to liability		36.2(5)	
•	a Part 36 offer may be made by a defendant in respect of a claim and counterclaim and that remains the case even if the counterclaim has not yet been pleaded: *AF v BG* [2009] EWCA Civ 757, [2009] All ER (D) 249 (Jul). Acceptance will have Part 36 consequences.			
•	where a party is legally represented notice of an offer, acceptance, withdrawal or change of terms must be served on the legal representative			36A, para 1.2
•	the question of whether a Part 36 offer may specify that it will lapse at the end of the relevant period is not specifically dealt			

	Form No	CPR Rule	PD
with in Part 36 but in *C v D* (above in this TAB) the Court of Appeal held that time limited offers do not fall within CPR 36 for such offers must remain in force and be capable of acceptance until withdrawn in accordance with CPR 36.9(2). The Court of Appeal reversed the decision at first instance, not because it took a different view of the effect of Part 36, but on the construction of the offer, holding that the letter was not a time limited offer. It is apparent from the decision that if an offer to settle is made expressly as a Part 36 offer and the Part 36 requirements are in form and substance generally satisfied, the court will be slow to interpret it in such a way as to prevent it being a Part 36 offer. See further articles by Darren Sylvester in (2011) NLJ, 15 July, page 985 entitled 'Part & parcel' and by Rehana Azib in (2011) NLJ, 29 July, page 1047 entitled 'An offer you can't refuse' (see para 2(iii) above in this TAB).		36.3(5)-(7)	
In *Howell v Lees Millais* [2011] EWCA Civ 786, [2011] All ER (D) 48 (Jul) the Master of the Rolls indicated a 'benevolent approach' be taken to offers that looked like Part 36 offers. See discussion of this and other very recent cases by Dominic Regan in (2012) NLJ, 17 February, page 254.			
Nothing in Part 36 prevents a party making an offer to settle in whatever way it chooses but if it does not comply with rule 36.2 it will not have the costs consequences specified in rules 36.10, 36.11 and 36.14. See CPR 44.3 and *French v Groupama Insurance Co Ltd* [2011] EWCA Civ 1119 discussed by Masood Ahmed in 'Legal Update: offers to settle' (2011) Gazette, 24 November, page 18.			
• It was held in *Trewlis v Groupama Insurance Co Ltd* [2012] EWHC 3 (TCC) that where an offer letter did not comply with CPR 36.2 it was not a Part 36 offer; the reasoning of Rix LJ in *C v D* (see above this TAB) was applied.			
• See further in *Carillon JM Ltd v PHI Group Ltd* [2012] EWHC 1581 (QB) per Akenhead J at para 15 of his judgment.			

TAB 20   PROCEDURAL TABLES

	Form No	CPR Rule	PD
• See also *F & C Alternative Investments (Holdings) Ltd v Barthelemy* [2012] EWCA Civ 843 where the Court of Appeal said that to make an award of indemnity costs and enhanced interest by analogy with Part 36 where the offer did not comply with that part was indirectly extending it beyond its expressed ambit; for discussion see article by Ross Risby in (2012) Sol Jo, 7 August, page 13 entitled 'Adhering to the spirit of Part 36'.			
The Court of Appeal in *Soloman v Cromwell Group plc, Oliver v Doughty* [2011] EWCA Civ 1584, [2011] All ER (D) 148 (Dec) stated that CPR 44.12A (Costs only proceedings) applies both to cases settled under CPR Part 36 and to those settled without recourse to it. General provisions have to give way to specific ones; section 11 of CPR 45 contains rules specifically directed to a narrow class of cases to the exclusion of other rules that have general rules for routine cases.			
The terms of CPR 36 as a whole clearly intend that costs incurred in contemplation of proceedings are to be regarded as 'costs of the proceedings' for the purposes of CPR 36.10(1).			
3. Time for making a Part 36 offer			
A Part 36 offer can be made:			
(i) at any time including before proceedings have been commenced			
(ii) in any appeal proceedings.		36.3(2)	
If the Part 36 offer is made before proceedings, to avoid later argument, it should make it clear that the offeror will on acceptance either pay the offeree's costs or will require his costs to be paid by the offeree. To fail to do so is likely to result in the type of cases considered by Francesca Kaye in her article 'All inclusive' in (2011) Sol Jo, 20 September, page 19.			
4. Interest			
A Part 36 offer will be treated as inclusive of interest until the time given for acceptance expires or, if made less than 21 days before the start of the trial, a date 21 days after the offer was made		36.3(3)	
5. Costs of an appeal from a final decision			
A Part 36 offer will only have Part 36 consequences in respect of the proceedings in which it is made and not in relation to costs of an appeal from the final decision in the proceedings. A further			

	Form No	CPR Rule	PD
Part 36 offer can be made in respect of the appeal.		36.3(4)	
6. Withdrawal of Part 36 offer or change of terms			
Withdrawal or the imposition of less advantageous terms requires the permission of the court within the relevant period (see last note in section 2 above) but outside the relevant period permission is not required provided the offeree has not previously served notice of acceptance. Written notice must be given to the offeree and should: (i) refer to the date on which the Part 36 offer was made; (ii) refer to the terms of the offer; and (iii) use words 'which bring home to the offeree that the offer has been withdrawn'.			
For detailed discussion see articles by Christopher Gutteridge entitled 'Compromised position' in (2010) Sol Jo, 190 August, page 10 and by Pertoldi and McIntosh entitled 'Open 24 hours' in (2010) NLJ, 13 August, page 1146.			
A withdrawn offer loses the automatic costs protection of Part 36 but any extant offer may not do so: see *Epsom College v Pierse Contracting Ltd* [2011] EWCA Civ 1449 where there had been multiple offers and also *SG (a minor, by his mother and litigation friend) v Hewitt* [2012] EWCA Civ 1053, [2012] All ER (D) 16 (Aug) considered by Jonathan Aspinall in (2012) NLJ, 7 September, page 1113 in an article entitled 'A question of timing'.		36.3(5)-(7) 36.14(6)(a)	
Where the permission of the court is needed to withdraw or change the terms of an offer application should be made (other than to the trial judge) by Part 23 application or at a trial or other hearing.	N244		36A, para 2.2
6A. Multiple offers			
A party can make as many offers as he wishes and the making of a subsequent offer does not supersede any earlier offers that have not been withdrawn, They will all remain individually capable of acceptance even if the offeree has rejected the offer subsequently accepted: see *Gibbons v Manchester City Council and LG Blower Specialist Bricklayers Ltd v Reeves (joined appeals)* [2010] EWCA Civ 726, [2010] 1 WLR 2081, [2010] All ER (D) 218 (Jun).			
7. Defendant's offer			
Save in personal injury claims for future pecuniary loss and in claims for provisional damages a Part 36 offer by the defendant to pay a sum of money must be an offer to pay a single sum of money and to be treated as a Part 36 offer it must be to pay it in not later than 14			

TAB 20   PROCEDURAL TABLES

	Form No	CPR Rule	PD
days following the date of the acceptance.			
If a defendant is not able to pay within 14 days he will not be able to make an offer with Part 36 effect but he can make an open offer or an offer made without prejudice save as to costs to which the court must have regard under CPR 44.3 and CPR 44.5(3)(a)(ii)		36.4	
8. Time when a Part 36 offer is made			
A Part 36 offer is effective when served on the offeree and a change of terms is effective from such service (provided any necessary permission has been obtained to make the change – see Section 6 above)		36.7	
9. Clarification of Part 36 offer			
Within 7 days of the offer being made the offeree may request clarification and if not given within 7 days, unless the trial has started, apply for an order that it be provided	N244	36.8(1) and (2)	
If the court makes an order it must specify the date when the Part 36 offer is to be treated as having been made		36.8(3)	
10. Acceptance of a Part 36 offer			
10.1 Unless the court's permission to accept (see 10.2 below) is required a Part 36 **may be accepted at any time, by serving written notice of acceptance on the offeror and filing it at the court, unless the offeror serves notice of withdrawal on the offeree.** It has to be remembered that an offer not withdrawn can be accepted outside the relevant period. Express notice of withdrawal must be given if the offer is not to be left open for acceptance		36.9(1) and (2) 36.10(5)	36A, para 3.1
Further that remains the position even if the offer is first rejected; there can be subsequent acceptance (up to withdrawal). Similarly a counter offer does not prevent acceptance of the original offer. The making of a further offer does not mean that an earlier offer cannot still be accepted. See generally *Gibbons v Manchester City Council and LG Blower Specialist Bricklayers Ltd v Reeves (joined appeals)* [2010] EWCA Civ 726, [2010] 1 WLR 2081.			
The necessity to withdraw offers immediately and in writing if the circumstances of a case change is stressed by Deborah Edwards in an article 'Seeking Settlement' in NLJ 16 January 2009, page 58 and by Dominic Regan in his article in (2012) NLJ, 17 February, page 254			
The dangers of failing to withdraw a Part 36 offer and the unforeseen consequences that can then occur are explained by Simon Edwards in his article 'Approach with caution' in Sol Jo (2012) 31 January, page 15.			

	Form No	CPR Rule	PD
For consideration of the argument that although a Part 36 offer had not been withdrawn it had been extinguished see *Mahmood v Elmi* [2011] EWHC 1933 (QB), 29 July where the argument failed.			
For the acceptance of a claim for **provisional damages** see		36.6(5)	
A Part 36 offer cannot be accepted by a claimant whose claim has been struck out for failure to comply with an 'unless' order: *Joyce v West Bus Coach Services* (2012) Times, 21 May (QB).			
For the acceptance of an offer which includes the payment of any part of the **damages by periodical payments** see		36.15(7)	41B
• **Acceptance out of time without permission will result in the default position as to costs applying** so that the offeror will be entitled to costs from the end of the relevant period (defined in CPR 36.3(1)).If the default position is not to be accepted an application to the court will be necessary seeking some other costs order. It is likely that it will be difficult to persuade the court to depart from the default position: see *Matthews v Metal Improvements Co Inc* [2007] EWCA Civ 215, 151 Sol Jo LB 396 and *Lumb v Hampsey* [2011] EWHC 2808 (QB), 11 October. The test is whether it would be 'unjust' for the claimant to have costs for the period after the time for acceptance had passed. The court did 'otherwise order' on appeal in *SG (a minor by his mother and litigation friend) v Hewitt* [2012] EWCA Civ 1053, [2012] All ER (D) 16 (Aug) where the injury was a head injury and the offer (which was not withdrawn) was made at the pre-action stage and when the prognosis was unclear. In reaching its decision to award costs to the claimant for the whole of the period (including the part of it that occurred after the expiry of the relevant period for acceptance the court had regard to the case of *Matthews* (above) and stressed that costs decisions are facts sensitive; for discussion see article 'Back to Normal' in (2012) Gazette, 15 November, page 20 by Masood Ahmed. It is to be noted both parties agreed that the approach of the court to such appeals appears from *Summit Property Ltd v Pitmans (a firm)* [2001] EWCA Civ 2020, [2002] CPLR 97.			

TAB 20 PROCEDURAL TABLES

	Form No	CPR Rule	PD
The decision in *Hewitt* (above) was considered by Simon Gibbs in an article entitled 'Fair costs outcomes and the late part 36 offers' (2012) Sol Jo, 20 October, page 19.			
See also **TAB 19**, part 14 (above)			
The court also '**otherwise ordered**' in *Kunaka v Barclays Bank plc* [2010] EWCA Civ 1035 where the claimant who accepted late was a litigant in person. The bank urged the claimant to accept an offer previously rejected; when he did so the Bank sought costs as he had accepted out of time. See also *Thompson v Bruce* [2011] All ER (D) 213 (Jun) and (2011) NLJ, 15 July, page 984 'Civil Way' by DJ Stephen Gold and see the article 'Carver's last stand?' by James Arrowsmith in (2011) NLJ, 9 September, page 1213 and the cases discussed in the article.			
In *Raggett v Governors of Preston Catholic College* [2012] EWHC 3641 (QB) the argument that the court should 'otherwise order' because the claim could not have been reasonably assessed, failed: for discussion see (2013) Sol Jo, 8 January, page 4, but in *Smith v Trafford Housing Trust* [2012] EWHC 3320 (Ch) the court took a wider view of what would be unjust and did otherwise order: see 'Costly consequences' by Tom Bell in (2013) NLJ, 8 February, page 135.			
The offer in *Thompson v Bruce* [2011] EWHC 1730 (QB), [2011] All ER (D) 213 (Jun) was one that required the approval of the court as the claimants were aged 9 and 10. The court on a purposive construction held that 'proceedings' in CPR 36.10 included steps prior to issue which would normally be allowed in formal assessment. For consideration of whether the costs payable to the offeror in the default position should be on standard or indemnity basis see *Fitzpatrick Contractors Ltd v Tyco Fire and Integrated Solutions (UK) Ltd* [2009] EWHC 274 (Ch), 123 Con LR 69 (Coulson J), 20 February.		36.10(5)	
• It is not permissible to make what purports to be a CPR 36 offer which limits the amount of costs to be payable in the event of acceptance. For consideration whether the making of a Calder-			

	Form No	CPR Rule	PD
bank offer would achieve the offeror's aim see article 'Upside down?' by Dominic Regan in (2011) NLJ, 21 October, page 1429 and the decision in *Hall v Stone* [2007] EWCA Civ 1354.			
A conditional interim payment in *Ali v Stagecoach* [2011] EWCA Civ 1494 was not regarded as an offer because it was not intended to achieve finality.			
• Acceptance on behalf of a child or protected party is not valid unless the court has approved the settlement: *Brennan v ECO Composing Ltd* [2006] EWHC 3153 (QB), [2007] 1 WLR 773. It is to be noted that for counsel's fees for attending an approval hearing to be recoverable there must be some complexity in the case justifying the instruction of counsel: see *Dockerill (by her mother and litigation friend) v Tullett and conjoined appeals* [2012] EWCA Civ 184.			
• Acceptance is by service of written notice of acceptance on the offeror. A copy is to be filed with the court where the case is proceeding.			
• Where a Part 36 offer, acceptance or notice of withdrawal or change of terms is to be served on a party who is legally represented, the documents to be served must be served on the legal representative.		36.9(1)	36A.3
10.2 The court's permission to accept a Part 36 where:			
(i) where acceptance is by one or more, but not all, defendants and r 36.12(4) applies			
(ii) the relevant period has expired and further deductible amounts have been paid to the claimant since the date of the offer –see r 36.15(3)(b)			
(iii) an apportionment is required between claims arising under Fatal Accidents Act 1976 and the Law Reform (Miscellaneous) Provisions Act – see r 41.3A or			
(iv) the trial has started			
Note			
Unless the parties agree a Part 36 offer may not be accepted after the end of the trial but before judgment is handed down		36.9(3)-(5)	
10.3 The court's permission is sought by application under part 23 or at a trial or hearing but not before the judge allocated in advance to conduct the trial	N244		36A, para 3.2

TAB 20   PROCEDURAL TABLES

	Form No	CPR Rule	PD
10.4 For consideration of whether the acceptance of a Part 36 claim creates an enforceable contract and the effect of the Law of Property (Miscellaneous Provisions) Act 1989, s 2, see *Orton v Collins* [2007] EWHC 803 (Ch), [2007] 3 All ER 863. The claimant tried to escape from the acceptance of a Part 36 offer on he ground that it amounted to a disposition of land and the acceptance by the defendant contravened s 2 of the 1989 Act. The argument was rejected by the court so that the claimant was bound by the acceptance.			
11. The acceptance of a Part 36 offer by one or more, but not all, defendants			
This is dealt with in		36.12	
12. Restrictions on disclosure of a Part 36 offer			
A Part 36 offer will be treated as 'without prejudice except as to costs'.			
Its existence must not be communicated to the trial judge or to the judge (if any) allocated in advance to conduct the trial unless the case has been decided.		36.13(1) and (2)	
It follows that the existence of the offer (but not its amount) can be brought to the attention of the court on an interlocutory application			
The prohibition of disclosure to the judge does not apply			
(i) when the defence is one of tender before claim			
(ii) where the proceedings have been stayed following acceptance of a Part 36 offer (see r 36.11 and section 13 of this TAB below)			
(iii) where the offeror and offeree agree in writing it should not apply			
13. The effect of acceptance of a Part 36 offer			
13.1 If a Part 36 offer is accepted the claim will be stayed		36.11(1)	
13.2 If the acceptance relates to the **whole claim** the stay will be upon the terms of the offer		36.11(2)	
13.3 If the offer accepted relates to only **part of the claim:**			
(i) that part of the claim will be stayed upon the terms offer and			
(ii) unless the claimant within the relevant period abandons the balance of the claim (see r36.10(2)), and unless the parties have agreed costs the liability for costs will be decided by the court		36.11(3)	
13.4 If the approval of the court is required before a settlement can be binding the acceptance of the Part 36 offer			

	Form No	CPR Rule	PD
will take effect only when that approval has been given		36.11(4)	
13.5 Notwithstanding the stay the court can deal with the enforcement of the terms of the Part 36 offer and can deal with the costs (including interest on costs) of the proceedings		36.11(5)	
13.6 Unless the parties otherwise agree a single sum of money offered and accepted must be paid within 14 days of acceptance and if not so paid the offeree can enter judgment for the same If the court makes an order for provisional damages or for periodical payments time for payment will be 14 days from service of the order, unless the court otherwise orders		36.11(6) and (7)	
13.7 Where a Part 36 offer accepted is not for payment of a single sum if it is not honoured the receiving party can apply to enforce the agreed terms and is not required to commence a new claim for this purpose. Where the settlement involves transfers of an interest in land, note *Orton v Collins* [2007] EWHC 803 (Ch), [2007] 3 All ER 863.		36.11(8)	
14. The costs consequences of acceptance of a Part 36 offer and costs consequences following judgment are set out in r 36.10 and r 36.14 respectively.			
If the acceptance is within the relevant period, unless the court otherwise orders, the claimant will be entitled to the costs up to the date the notice of acceptance was served on the offeror: this is in effect the equivalent of a costs order on a standard basis. This means the claimant is entitled to 100% of the costs allowed on detailed assessment. The costs judge has no power to vary the order but in an appropriate case he may disallow entire sections of the bill if the costs were unreasonably incurred: *Lahey v Pirelli Tyres* [2007] EWCA Civ 91, [2007] NLJR 294, [2007] PIQR P292.			

TABLE 21—RECOVERY OF POSSESSION OF LAND – CLAIMS BY LANDLORD, MORTGAGEE, LICENSOR, PERSON ENTITLED TO POSSESSION AGAINST TRESPASSERS

TAB 21

See 1 below for general provisions applicable to **possession claims**

See 2 below for particular provisions for **residential tenanted property**

See 3 below for particular provisions for **land subject to mortgage**

See 3A below for particular provisions for **possession proceeding online** by landlords and mortgagees

See 4 below for particular provisions for **claims against trespassers**

	Form No	CPR Rule	PD
Preliminary			
Part 7 Chapter 2 — 'Social Housing: Tenure Reform' of the Localism Act 2011 came into force on 1 April 2012 and will not apply to an assured shorthold tenancy that was granted before that day or to one arising on the coming to an end of an assured shorthold tenancy granted before that day.			
Section 163 of the Act (assured shorthold tenancy following demoted or family intervention housing) has inserted ss 20C and 20D into the Housing Act 1988. Section 164 (assured shorthold tenancy: notice requirements) inserts s 1A and 1B into s 21 of the Housing Act 1988 incorporating a requirement that the court may not make an order for possession unless the landlord has given 6 months notice in writing that he does not propose to grant another tenancy on the expiry of the fixed term tenancy and supplied specified information to the tenant BUT these provisions apply only to a shorthold tenancy of a dwelling in England if:			
(a) it is for a fixed term certain of not less than 2 years; and			
(b) the landlord is a private provider of social housing.			
The 'private provider of social housing' would be what has hitherto been terms a 'housing association'.			
The requirement is additional to that whereby the landlord has to give to the tenant two months' notice in writing stating that he requires possession of the dwelling house: Housing Act 1988, s 21(1)(b).			
The notice may be given before or on the day on which the tenancy comes to an end: Housing Act 1988, s 21(2).			

TAB 21   PROCEDURAL TABLES

	Form No	CPR Rule	PD
For detailed consideration see articles by Jon Holbrook 'In a fix' in (2012) NLJ, 29 June, page 863 and 'In a fix (2)' in (2012) NLJ, 13 July, page 930.			
1. General provisions that apply to all such claims			
Interpretation			
For definition of:			
"a possession claim", see		55.1(a)	
"a possession claim against trespassers"			
note, in particular, this does not include a claim against a tenant or sub-tenant whether the tenancy has been terminated or not and see		55.1(b)	
"mortgage" note this includes a legal and equitable mortgage and see		55.1(c)	
"the 1985 Act" means Housing Act 1985, see		55.1(d)	
"the 1988 Act" means Housing Act 1988, see		55.1(e)	
"a demotion claim" means a claim by a landlord for an order under s 82A of the 1985 Act or s 6A of the 1988 Act ("a demotion order")		55.1(f)	
"a demoted tenancy" means a tenancy created by virtue of a demotion order		55.1(g)	
"a suspension claim" means a claim made by a landlord for an order under section 121A of the 1985 Act		55.1(h)	
1.1 The general provisions do not apply to:			
(a) claims for accelerated possession of property let on an assured shorthold tenancy		55.2(2)(b)	
(b) claims for an interim possession order made under the Criminal Justice and Public Order Act 1994, which are at present dealt with under CPR Pt 55 Section III except where the court otherwise orders or Section III so provides		55.2(2)(c)	
(c) where a claim is for a demotion claim only; Section III of Part 65 applies			
(d) claims for possession of business premises but where the letting is of a mixed business and residential premises: see *Pirabkaran v Patel* (2006) Times, 19 July, CA and *Broadway Investments Hackney Ltd v Grant* [2006] EWCA Civ 1709, [2006] All ER (D) 304 (Dec), [2007] L&TR 11; *Thomas v Ken Thomas Ltd* [2006] EWCA Civ 1504, 151 Sol Jo LB 1396; and *Tan v Sitkowski* [2007]			

	Form No	CPR Rule	PD
	EWCA Civ 30, [2007] 1 WLR 1628. These cases strongly support the statement that such mixed tenancies will normally be governed by the Landlord and Tenant Act 1954. For detailed discussion, see NLJ 11 May 2007, page 669.		
(e)	agreements made between owners and occupiers of caravan parks where mobile homes are sited are governed by the Mobile Homes Act 1983; for consideration of the protection given see (2011) NLJ, 13 May, page 657, article by Andy Creer and John de Waal entitled 'Mobile restrictions'. In England the only issues that remain with the courts (as opposed to Residential Property Tribunals) are termination of the pitch licence and regaining possession.		
	Jurisdiction in respect of the Mobile Homes Act 1983 has been transferred to Residential Property Tribunals: The Mobile Homes Act 1983 (Jurisdiction of Residential Property Tribunals) (England) Order 2011, SI 2011/1005.		
	The provisions of the Mobile Homes Act 1983 now apply to land in England occupied by a local authority as a caravan site providing accommodation for gypsies and travellers.		
(f)	a **house-boat** placed on a supporting platform in a harbour was held not to be part of the plot on which the platform stood so that a tenancy or licence of the plot would not extend to the house-boat: *Tristmere Ltd v Mew* [2011] EWCA Civ 912, [2011] All ER (D) 278 (Jul).		
(g)	The Supreme Court in *Mexfield Housing Corpn Ltd v Berrisford* [2011] UKSC 52 followed the decision in *Prudential Assurance Co Ltd v London Residuary Body* [1992] 2 AC 386, HL holding that an leasehold estate must have a fixed maximum term. It went on to find that the effect that the flat was held by the responded for an **uncertain duration** (being for life) was that it was converted by s 149 of the Law of Property Act 1925 into a lease for 90 years determinable by one month's notice after her death or pursuant to paras 5. or 6 of the agreement. For a detailed consideration of the decision and its consequences (including those on the entitlement to housing benefit) see article entitled 'Legal Wonderland' by Ben		

TAB 21 PROCEDURAL TABLES

	Form No	CPR Rule	PD
Chataway in (2011) Sol Jo, 29 November, page 13.			
The situation arose when the Housing Association purchased the home of the defendant, when she was unable to pay the mortgage, and allowed her to remain in occupation under an 'occupancy agreement'. It is understood the defendants have very large numbers of properties covered by the same standard form of agreement.			
Note that the general provisions apply subject to any enactment or Practice Direction setting out special provisions for a particular type of claim		55.2(2)(a)	
If a claim by a tenant of residential premises against the landlord seeks an order for repairs or other work to be done to those premises see CPR 16.3(4)-(7)			
1.1A Localism Act 2011: local authority tenancies			
From 1 April 2012 Part 7, Chapter 2 of this Act entitled 'Social Housing Tenure Reform' has been in force. The contents of Chapter 2 are outside the scope of this TAB but it is important to be aware of its contents.			
By ss 154–155 of the 2011 Act local authorities can provide a new form of secure tenancy for a fixed term; these tenancies are called **flexible tenancies**. This has been achieved by the insertion of ss 107A to 107E after s 106 of the Housing Act 1985. When such a tenancy is granted the landlord has a mandatory right to possession.			
These provisions and many of the other changes do not affect tenancies which have come into force prior to 1 April 2012.			
A flexible tenancy must be for a term certain for not less than 2 years (s 107A(2)a) of the Housing Act 1985) and a prior written notice that it is to be a flexibly secure tenancy and setting out the express terms of the tenancy must be given; the prospective protective tenant has the right to seek review of the landlord's decision as to the length of term of the tenancy: Housing Act 1985, s 107B.			
Flexible tenancies are not required to be made by deed and it is not required that they be entered in the register of the title to the property.			
On the expiry of the term of a flexibly tenancy a statutory periodic tenancy will arise: Housing Act 1985, s 86. But the landlord will have a mandatory right to possession provided it complies with two pre-conditions:			

	Form No	CPR Rule	PD
(i) the landlord must give not less than 6 months written notice that it does not propose to grant another tenancy and give the reasons for this and also inform the tenant of his right to seek a review of that decision (Housing Act 1985, s 107D) and the time limit (21 days) for doing so; and			
(ii) the landlord must give not less than 2 months written notice that it requires possession. This notice can be given before or on the day the tenancy comes to an end (Housing Act 1985, s 107D(5)).			
Landlords may continue to operate an introductory tenancy scheme for a probationary year subject to notice requirements that a flexible tenancy will follow. The probationary period is not to be taken as part of the period of at least 2 years for the flexible tenancy.			
During the flexible fixed term the tenant is secure subject to the normal statutory possession provisions that can be used against a secure periodic tenant: Housing Act 1985, s 107D(10).			
Sections 158 and 159 and Schedule 14 of the 2011 Act deal with the transfer of secure and assured tenancies; s 160 deals with succession to secure tenancies and s 161 deals with succession to assured tenancies.			
For the provisions of s 164 as to notice requirements as to assured shorthold tenancies of social housing see **TAB 23** below.			
For a detailed discussion of the housing provisions of the 2011 Act including those outlined above see article by James Driscoll 'All change for social housing?' in (2012) NLJ, 20 January, page 90 and Jon Holbrook 'In a fix?' in (2012) NLJ, 29 June, page 868.			
1.1B Housing associations — fixed term assured shorthold tenancies			
Housing Act 1988 already allows landlords to grant fixed-term assured shorthold tenancies and the Regulatory Framework for Social Housing in England from April 2012 sanctions the grant of assured shorthold tenancies providing they are for a minimum fixed term of 5 years, or exceptionally for a minimum fixed term of no less than 2 years. The prospective shorthold tenant is given an ability to complain both about the length and about the type of tenancy.			
To obtain possession under the mandatory right to possession the landlord has to give a 6 months notice and a 2 months notice: see **TAB 23** below, 'Preliminary' section. The provisions are set out and considered in detail by Jon Holbrook in an article 'In a fix (2)?' in			

TAB 21 PROCEDURAL TABLES

	Form No	CPR Rule	PD
(2012) NLJ, 13 July at page 930.			
1.2 High Court or county court			
The claim may only be started in the High Court if:			
(a) there are complicated disputes of fact			
(b) there are points of law of general importance or			
(c) the claim is against trespassers and there is a substantial risk of public disturbance or of serious harm to persons or property which properly require immediate determination			
Note:			
• Value of the property and the amount of any financial claim whilst relevant will not alone normally justify starting the claim in the High Court			55A, para 1.4
• If a claim is started in the High Court the claimant must file with the claim a certificate, stating the reason for bringing the claim in that court, verified by a statement of truth		55.3(2)	
• If a claim is wrongly started in the High Court the court will normally either strike it out or transfer it to the county court			55A, para 1.2
• Where the claim form includes a demotion claim it must be started in the county court for the district in which the land is situated			55A, para 1.9
On starting possession proceedings the fee payable (unless PCOL is used) is:			
in the High Court £465			
in the county court £175 unless the Possession Claims Online website is used when the fee is £100.			
The fees remain the same if there is additionally or alternatively a money claim.			
Possession claims should normally be brought in the county court			55A, para 1.1
1.3 Starting the claim			
If the claim is started in the county court it must be the county court for **the district in which the land is situated** unless an enactment provides otherwise		55.3(1)	
For the **electronic issue** of certain possession claims see		55.10A	55B
The **claim form** must be in the form set out in Table 1 to **CPR PD 4** and be verified by a statement of truth	N5		55A, para 1.5
The claim form or the particulars of claim must contain a statement notifying the court whether or not Sections III and IV of the Practice Direction (Pre-action Conduct) or any relevant protocol has been complied with.			Pre-action Conduct, para 9.7

	Form No	CPR Rule	PD
Where the claim is for relief against forfeiture, the form to be used is:	N5A		
Where the claim is for a claim for possession of property held on assured shorthold tenancy the form to be used if using the accelerated procedure is	N5B		
Possession Claims Online (PCOL) is now in operation nationally; it is a web-based method of seeking possession which is, it is understood, used mainly by lenders, council and social landlords seeking possession of residential properties. Customers are able to set up direct debit arrangements for the payment of court fees. Unlike MCOL all possession claims will still have to have a hearing even if uncontested. The PCOL website sets out the 'specified courts' at which PCOL operates and the date from which it will be available in each specified court			
The PCOL website means the website http ://www.possessionclaim.gov.uk which is accessed via the Courts Services website at h ttp://www.hmcourts-service.gov.u k			
The relevant information and procedural requirements are set out in Practice Direction 55B			
Although the use is understood to be as set out above PCOL may be used by any landlord or lender.			
See 3A below 'Possession Claims Online'			55B
1.4 Particulars of claim			
In a possession claim the particulars must:			55A, para 2.1
(a) identify the land to which the claim relates			
(b) state whether the claim relates to residential property			
(c) state the ground on which possession is claimed			
(d) give full details about any mortgage or tenancy agreement and			
(e) give details of every person who to the best of the claimant's knowledge, is in possession of the property	N119 (rented residential)		
See also CPR 16 "Statement of Case" – precise statement of facts, interest, etc	N120 (mortgaged residential)		
The particulars of claim must be filed and served with the claim form	N121 (trespassers)	55.4	
1.5 The hearing date			
The court will fix a date for the hearing when it issues the claim form		55.1	
Where the **claim is against trespassers** service of the claim form, particulars of claim and any witness statement must be:			

TAB 21 PROCEDURAL TABLES

	Form No	CPR Rule	PD
(a) not less than 5 days before the hearing date where the property is residential			
(b) not less than 2 days before the hearing in the case of other land		55.5(2)	
In all other possession claims:			
(a) the hearing date will be not less than 28 days from the date of issue of the claim form		55.5(3)(a)	
(b) the standard period during issue of the claim form and the hearing will be not more than 8 weeks, and			
(c) the defendant must be served with the claim form and particulars of claim not less than 21 days before the hearing date		55.5(3)(b) and (c)	
Note:			
• The time may be extended or shortened by the court and particular instances when the exercise of this power should be considered are set out in:		3.1(2)(a)	55A, para 3.2
• The court will serve on the claimant or his solicitors **"notice of issue"**. This will specify the date of issue and details of the hearing. The notice draws attention to the time limits for service of the claimant's witness statements	N206B		
By reason of s 42 Finance Act 2003 the following changes have been in the effect of s 14 Stamp Duty Act 1891			
(a) Courts should disregard the requirements of s 14 of the Stamp Duty Act 1891 in respect of any land transaction completed after 30 November 2003 except where it was pursuant to a contract entered into before 10 July 2003			
(b) Except in the case of leases granted by Registered Social Landlords the requirements of s 14 of the Stamp Duty Act 1891 will continue to apply to all land transactions completed before 1 December 2003			
(c) The requirements of s 14 of the Stamp Duty Act 1891 will not apply to any leases granted by Registered Social Landlords (RSLs) on or after 1 January 2000. The requirements of s 14 of the Stamp Duty Act 1891 will continue to apply to leases granted by RSLs before this date			
1.6 The defendant's response			
An acknowledgement of service is not required and CPR Pt 10 does not apply		55.7(1)	
For notes for defendant in claim for possession of rented residential premises see	N7A		

	Form No	CPR Rule	PD
In a possession claim against trespassers the defendant need not file a defence		55.7(2)	
In any other possession claims where the defendant fails to file a defence within 14 days after service of the claim form he can nevertheless take part in any hearing but his failure is relevant as to costs		55.7(3)	
Default judgment is not available		55.7(4)	
For general form of defence to CPR Pt 55 claims, see	N11		
1.7 The hearing			
At the hearing the court may decide the claim or give directions		55.8(1)	
There is a Legal Services Commission direction whereby there should be available a duty solicitor in all county courts on the days on which possession proceedings are heard: 'possession days'. This is not always achieved.			
Where the claim is genuinely disputed on substantial grounds the court will give directions that include allocation		55.8(2)	
Unless the court allocates to the fast track or multi-track or the court otherwise orders any fact that needs to be proved by **the evidence of witnesses** at the hearing, **may be proved by evidence in writing.** In a possession claim against trespassers all witness statements must be filed and served with the claim form and in other cases all witness statements must be filed and served at least 2 days before the hearing.		55.8(4) and (5)	
Where the claimant serves the claim form and particulars of claim there must be produced at the hearing a certificate of service of these documents and rule 6.17(2)(a) shall not apply		55.8(6)	
Where a claimant realises there is a genuine dispute on substantial grounds he should seek to avoid the expense of the first hearing which is only likely to have a time allocation of 5 minutes. If directions can be agreed dealing with allocation and management they should be submitted to the court in good time for consideration, with a request that the first hearing is vacated if the district judge is able to make the proposed directions or such other directions as he feels appropriate			
If the first hearing is to be effective to dispose of the claim, preparation should be such as to enable all relevant matters to be dealt with in the limited time available			
Each party should whenever possible include all the evidence he wishes to present in his statement of case verified by a statement of truth			55A, para 5.1
For the admission of hearsay evidence and reliance on it by the court at the			

TAB 21 PROCEDURAL TABLES

	Form No	CPR Rule	PD
hearing see *Solon South West Housing Association Ltd v James* [2004] EWCA Civ 1847, [2005] HLR 24			
1.8 Allocation			
When the court decides the track for a possession claim the matters to which the court shall have regard include:			
(a) the matters in CPR 26.8 as modified by the relevant Practice Direction			
(b) the amount of any arrears of rent or mortgage instalments			
(c) the importance to the defendant of retaining possession of the land, and			
(d) the importance of vacant possession to the claimant			
(e) if applicable, the alleged conduct of the defendant		55.9(1)	
The financial value of the property will not necessarily be the most important factor and the court may direct a possession claim to be deal with on the fast track even though the value of the property exceeds £25,000			
The court will only allocate possession claims to the small claims track if the parties agree. If there is such agreement and allocation, costs shall be as if the claim were on the fast track save that the trial costs will be in the discretion of the court but shall not exceed the fast track trial costs applicable where the value of the claim is up to £3,000		55.9(2) and (3)	26, para 8.1(1)(c)
The parties can agree that the last provision as to costs shall not apply and that the costs shall be those recoverable on the trial of a small claim		55.9(4)	
2. Claims for possession of residential property let on a tenancy			
2.1 Preliminary			
It is essential for the efficient conduct of possession claims for residential tenancies to keep a set of the up-to-date version of all notices that have to be served. This is both to ensure that the claimant uses the appropriate form and also, when acting for the defendant, to check whether the landlord has used the correct form			
Careful attention must be paid to the **Protocol for possession claims based on rent arrears** by local authorities, social landlords and housing administration trusts which have all since 2 October 2006 been required to give a tenant 5 chances to pay the arrears before the court makes a possession order. Additionally:			
the tenant must be kept informed of what is happening (para 4)			

	Form No	CPR Rule	PD
the landlord must seek to obtain payment through the tenant's benefits (para 5)			
the landlord must work with the tenant to resolve benefit difficulties (paras 6 and 7)			
If a landlord fails to give notice to the tenant of an address in England and Wales at which notices (including notices in proceedings) may be served to the landlord by the tenant, any rent, service or administration charge otherwise due from the tenant to the landlord shall be treated for all purposes as not being due at any time before the landlord does comply with the requirement: Landlord and Tenant Act 1987, s 48. Oral notice is not sufficient but as to sufficiency of written notices see *Rogan v Woodfield Building Services Ltd* (1994) 27 HLR 78. [1995] 1 EGLR 72.			
Once s 48 has been complied with the rent and other payments not previously due become payable in their entirety: *Dallhold Estate UK Pty Ltd v Lindsay Trading* [1994] 17 EG 148, CA.			
The agent of the landlord has no standing to bring proceedings: *Chesters v Abebrese* [1997] Lawtel, 18 July			
A claim which is not a claim for possession may be brought under Section I of Part 55 if it is started in the same claim form as a claim for possession which must be brought in accordance with Section I		55.2(1)	55A, para 1.7
County courts have the power to accept undertakings as part of an order adjourning proceedings: *Hastings Housing Association v Ellis* [2007] EWCA Civ 1238, (2007) Sol Jo, 23 November, page 1475. Great care should be taken in drafting undertakings: see *Hiscox Syndicates Ltd v The Pinnacle Ltd* [2008] All ER (D) 193 (Jan), (2008) Times, 6 February as to degrees of endeavour and also article 'Best Endeavours' by Sara Partington and Kirk Page at (2008) NLJ, 10 October, page 1407 where the cases of *Rhodia International Holdings Ltd v Huntsman International LLC* [2007] EWHC 292 (Comm), [2007] 2 All ER (Comm) 577 and *Ryanair Ltd v SR Technics Ireland Ltd* [2007] EWHC 3089 (QB), [2007] All ER (D) 264 (Dec) are fully discussed.			
The most recent guidance as to the meaning of 'best endeavours' and 'reasonable endeavours' is to be found in the case of *Jet2.com Ltd v Blackpool Airport Ltd* [2011] EWHC 1529 (Comm), [2011] All ER (D) 06 (Jul) – not a possession case. The case is considered by Caroline Kehoe in (2011) NLJ, 14 October, page 1412 in an article entitled 'Coming to terms', which also generally			

TAB 21 PROCEDURAL TABLES

	Form No	CPR Rule	PD
reviews cases concerning 'reasonable endeavours' clauses and obligations to act in 'good faith'.			
The common law of negligence imposes no general duty to warn another of impending danger and that remains the position where the relationship of landlord and tenant exists between the parties: *Mitchell v Glasgow City Council* [2009] UKHL 11, [2009] All ER (D) 182 (Feb).			
Care must be taken to distinguish service occupiers from tenants; the position has been clarified by the judgment in *Wragg v Surrey County Council* [2008] EWCA Civ 19, [2008] HLR 464 where countryside rangers were held to be service occupiers. See (2008) Sol Jo, 19 February, page 4, and 13 May, page 26.			
CLA Information Guide 'Dealing with rent problems' provides useful advice, phone numbers and website addresses: 'Community legal advice' is a free and confidential service paid for by Legal Aid – 0845 345 4 345; http://www.community legaladvice.org.uk.			
2.1A The following dates are important for **private sector tenancies:**			
(a) Only tenancies created **before 15 January 1989** can be tenancies protected by the Rent Act 1977 **(regulated tenancies)**			
A regulated tenancy is any protected or statutory tenancy under the 1977 Act and is so defined in s 18(1) of that Act			
(b) Tenancies created on or after **15 January 1989 (subject to satisfying the qualifying conditions)** are **assured or assured shorthold tenancies** depending whether the formalities required to create an assured shorthold were complied with			
(c) Since **28 February 1997** almost all new tenancies are **assured shorthold tenancies** unless the landlord deliberately creates an **assured tenancy**			
The annual rental threshold for assured shorthold tenancies was £25,000 but from 1 October 2010 has been increased in England only to £100,000; see Assured Tenancies (Amendment) (England) Order 2010, SI 2010/908. It is to be noted that it was held in *Hughes v Borodex Ltd* (2010) Times, 26 May that a tenant lost her protection by carrying out improvements which resulted in the rent of the property exceeding the assured protected tenancy limit.			
The requirement of compliance with s 20 of the Housing Act 1988 to create an assured shorthold tenancy has ceased since 28 February 1997			

	Form No	CPR Rule	PD
Useful guidance for tenants with private landlords who have tenancy difficulties is provided by Community Legal Advice Information Guide C1 'Dealing with rent problems if you rent privately'. CLA telephone number is 0845 345 4 345, and web address is http://www.community legaladvice.org.uk.			
Note:			
• The county court has no jurisdiction under s 7 of the 1988 Act to make a **possession order by consent** unless the judge is satisfied after investigation that the requirements are met: *Gil v Baygreen Properties Ltd* [2002] EWCA Civ 1340, (2002) Times, 17 July			
2.1B Public sector lettings and pre-15 January 1989 housing association tenancies are generally secure tenancies governed by Housing Act 1985 and described as **secure tenancies**			
• Social landlords (such as local authorities, Registered Social landlords and Housing action Trusts) making a possession claim based solely on rent arrears must have regard to the Protocol for Possession Claims Based on Rent Arrears. The Protocol provides: 'Courts should take into account whether this protocol has been followed when considering what orders to make'			
2.1C "Tolerated trespassers" were former secure tenants allowed to remain in occupation after the date given for delivery of possession in an outright possession order or after the making of a possession order with its enforcement suspended on terms in Form N28 or who remained in possession because the order for possession had not been enforced by the landlord. From 20 May 2009 the Housing and Regeneration Act 2008, s 299 and Sch 11 and the Housing (Replacement of Terminated Tenancies) (England) Order 2009, SI 2009/1262 and a similar order for Wales (SI 2009/1260):			
(a) prevent tenants becoming tolerated trespassers by providing that tenancies (whether they be secure, assured, introductory or demoted) end only on **execution under a possession order**, unless the tenant has given notice to quit or surrendered the tenancy;			
(b) give replacement tenancies to those who were tolerated trespassers on 20 May 2009 unless they had entered into any form of new tenancy with their landlord. The replacement tenancy will be of the			

TAB 21   PROCEDURAL TABLES

	Form No	CPR Rule	PD
same type as the original tenancy or as near to it as possible;			
(c) treat the possession order as applying to the replacement order;			
(d) enable the court when dealing with a claim arising from the breach of tenancy agreement or the breach of the statutory tenancy to treat the new tenancy and the original tenancy as being one continuous and uninterrupted tenancy.			
Consider the article 'Righting a housing wrong' by Francis Davey in NLJ, 9 May 2008, page 656 which deals also with the new 'replacement tenancies' for tolerated trespassers who remain in occupation, the provisions of the 2008 Act having come into effect.			
The position of a potential successor to a deceased tolerated trespasser was not addressed by the Housing and Regulatory Reform Act 2008 but in *Austin v London Borough of Southwark* [2010] UKSC 28 it was unanimously decided that potential successors of deceased tolerated trespassers could apply to postpone the date of possession and revive the tenancy under s 85(2) of the Housing Act 1985. The application would have to be under the original possession proceedings and its success or otherwise would depend on the discretion of the county court judge. For consideration of the case of *Austin* and the background to it from the decision (now discredited) in *Thompson v Elmbridge Borough Council* [1987] 1 WLR 1425 to the judgment of Lord Hope and Lady Hale in *Austin* see article by Charlotte Collins and Giles Peaker in (2010) Sol Jo, 13 July, page 16 and see also (2010) NLJ, 2 July, page 914. If the tenancy is revived and the survivor satisfies the necessary conditions he will succeed to the tenancy.			
2.1D It should be noted that the survivor of a same-sex partnership has the same entitlement as a spouse to succeed on the tenant's death as a statutory tenant: *Ghaidan v Godin-Mendoza* [2004] UKHL 30, [2004] 2 AC 557			
But note the relationship must be one of 'mutual lifetime commitment': *Nutting v Southern District Housing Group Ltd* (2005) Times, 5 January, ChD			
Section 160 of the Localism Act 2011 (which came into force on 1 April 2012) inserted s 86A into the Housing Act 1985. This provides a person is qualified to succeed to a secured tenancy if:			
(1) he occupied the house as his only or principal home at the time of the tenant's death <u>and</u> is the tenant's spouse or partner;			

	Form No	CPR Rule	PD
(2) if at the time of the tenant's death the house is not occupied by a spouse or civil partner of the tenant as his only or principal home and the tenancy expressly provides that some other person other than such a spouse or civil partner shall succeed to the tenancy			
• the provisions do not apply if the deceased tenant was a successor as defined in s 88 of HA 1985: HA 1985, s 87A(3) and (4).			
• for the purposes of HA 1985, s 87A a person living with the tenant as the tenant's wife or husband is to be treated as the tenant's spouse and a person who was living with the tenant as if they were civil partners is to be treated as the tenant's civil partner.			
The Supreme Court in *Solihull Metropolitan Borough Council v Hickin* [2012] UKSC 39, (2012) Times, 16 August upheld the decision of the Court of Appeal that when one of two joint tenants under a secure tenancy died the surviving tenant became the sole tenant and the tenancy could not pass to a third party pursuant to statutory provisions that created rights of succession for resident family members upon the death of a secure tenant.			
The Localism Act 2011, s 161 amends HA 1985, s 17 as to the succession to assured tenancies with effect from 1 April 2012. Section 17(1) applies to all assured tenancies unless the deceased tenant was himself a successor tenant.			
Section 17(1A), (1B) and (1C) apply only where the landlord is a private registered landlord of social housing and the tenancy is an assured tenancy for a fixed term of not less than 2 years and provided the deceased tenant was not himself a successor. HA 1985, s 17(1E) applies where the deceased tenant was a successor and only in the limited circumstances set out.			
Section 160 (secure tenancies) and s 161 (assured tenancies) or the Localism Act 2011 do not apply to a tenancy granted before 1 April 2012 or arising by virtue of HA 1985, s 86 or HA 1988, s 5 (periodic tenancy arising on termination of a fixed term).			
2.1E A clause in a tenancy agreement providing that the local housing authority could vary the terms of the agreement if the majority of the tenant's representatives agreed was held to be incompatible with the local authority's statutory right to vary tenancies unilaterally under the provisions of the Housing Act 1985, s 103; *R v Basildon District Council* [2005] EWCA Civ 475.			

TAB 21 PROCEDURAL TABLES

	Form No	CPR Rule	PD
It should be noted that a social landlord does not have the power to vary the terms of a tenancy unilaterally under s 103: *Peabody Trust (Governors of the v Reeve* (2008) Times, 9 June, Ch.			
2.1F Difficulties experienced by the Court in reconciling disability discrimination law and housing law were resolved by the House of Lords in *Lewisham London Borough Council v Malcolm (ECHR intervening)* [2008] UKHL 43, [2008] 1 AC 1399. For detailed discussion of the decision (with which Baroness Hale dissented) see articles by Ann Bevington (2008) Sol Jo, 29 July, page 17, by Spencer Keen (2008) NLJ, 5 September and by Rosenthal and Duckworth (2008) NLJ, 19 September, page 1286. The decision is not discussed here as it was reversed by the insertion of a new definition of discrimination arising from disability in s 15 of the Equality Act 2010. It is however worth stressing that it is no longer relevant whether others without disability or with a different disability would have been treated in the same way.			
Section 15 provides a new cause of action if there is unfavourable treatment in consequence of a person's disability and the onus is on the landlord to show that the treatment is a proportionate means of achieving a legitimate objective. This is, of course, in line with article 8 ECHR. It is still a defence if the person alleged to be discrimination did not know and could not reasonably have been expected to know that the tenant had a disability: s 15(2).			
See further 'Benchmarks: disability discrimination' by District Judge Anson in (2011) Gazette, 26 May, page 23.			
2.1G There can only be one succession to a secure tenancy (see Housing Act 1985, s 87) and s 88(1)(g) of the 1985 Act defines succession to include a joint tenant becoming the sole tenant: note *Birmingham City Council v Walker* [2007] UKHL 22, [2007] 2 AC 262 which makes it apparent that the provisions concerning secure tenants relate only to events that happened after the tenancy became secure			
2.1H Following a succession to a secure tenancy pursuant to s 89 Housing Act 1985 a landlord is entitled to seek possession under ground 18 of Sch 2 if the succession results in the under occupation of the property. For the conditions that have to be satisfied and that the date of trial is the relevant date see *Wandsworth London Borough Council v Randall* [2007] EWCA Civ 1126, [2007] 46 EG 176 (CS). In this case the successor's mother and half-sister moved into			

	Form No	CPR Rule	PD
the property (a 4-bedroomed house) between succession and the hearing; as the hearing date was the relevant one a one-bedroomed flat was held not to be suitable alternative accommodation			
2.1I An express term in a document, described as a 'licence', that it does not create a secure tenancy will not of itself be sufficient to prevent the creation of a secure tenancy: *Langridge v Mansfield District Council* [2008] EWCA Civ 264, [2008] HLR 541.			
2.1J For the obligations of a local authority to provide housing for minors under s 20 of the Children Act 1989 and generally see article 'There's no place like home' by Bloom and Markus in NLJ (2009) 3 July, page 953.			
2.1K For the fine distinction between 'notifying' and 'informing' see *Ali v Birmingham City Council* [2009] EWCA Civ 1279 and article by Nicholas Dobson in (2010) NLJ 29 January, page 133.			
2.2 Particulars of claim			
In addition to the general requirements (see 1.4, above) if the claim includes a claim for non-payment of rent the particulars of claim must set out:	N119	55.4	55A, para 2.1
(a) the amount due at the start of the proceedings			
(b) in schedule form, the dates and amounts of all payments due and payments made for a period of two years immediately preceding the date of issue, or if the first date of default was less than two years prior to issue from the first date of default and a running total			
If the claimant wishes to rely on a history of arrears for longer than two years he should state this in his particulars and exhibit a full or longer schedule to a witness statement			
(c) the daily rate of any rent and interest			
(d) any previous steps taken to recover the arrears of rent with full details of any court proceedings, and			
(e) any relevant information about the defendant's circumstances, in particular:			
(i) whether the defendant is in receipt of social security benefits, and			
(ii) whether any payments are made on his behalf directly to the claimant under the Social Security Contributions and Benefits Act 1992			55A, para 2.3 and 3A
If the claimant knows of any person (including a mortgagee) entitled to claim			

TAB 21   PROCEDURAL TABLES

	Form No	CPR Rule	PD
relief against forfeiture as underlessee under s 146(4) of the Law of Property Act 1925 (or in accordance with s 38 of the Supreme Court Act 1981, or s 138(9C) of the County Courts Act 1984):			
(a) the particulars of claim must state the name and address of that person, and			
(b) the claimant must file a copy of the particulars of claim for service on him			55A, para 2.4
If the claim for possession relates to the conduct of the tenant, the particulars of claim must state details of the conduct alleged			55A, para 2.4A
If the claim for possession relies on a statutory ground or grounds for possession the particulars of claim must specify them			55A, para 2.4B
These are guidance notes on completing particulars of claim form (rented residential premises)	N119A		
2.3 Service of the claim form			
The general provisions as to service apply and note in particular the requirement of a certificate of service where the claimant serves the claim form		Part 6 55.8(6)	
2.4 The hearing date			
See general provisions, 1.5 above			
2.5 The defendant's response			
See general provisions, 1.6 above			
For form of defence see	N11R		
A landlord is not obliged to forfeit a lease for a fixed term to mitigate his loss by seeking a new tenant if the tenant stops paying the rent and vacates; *Reichman v Beveridge* [2006] EWCA Civ 1659, (2007) Times, 4 January, [2007] HLR 354. See article by Sebastien Kokelaar NLJ 2007, 20 April, page 545 for further discussion			
2.6 The hearing			
The hearing date given on issue will be for a hearing in chambers generally before a district judge with a time estimate of 5 minutes. Whenever possible the parties should include the evidence they wish to give in their statements of case verified by a statement of truth			55A, para 5.1
Where relevant the **claimant's evidence** should include the amount of any arrears calculated to the date of the hearing (if necessary specifying a daily rate of arrears)			55A, para 5.2
If the case has not been allocated to fast track or multi-track unless the court otherwise orders any fact may be proved by written evidence verified by a statement of truth.		55.8(3)	55A, para 5.4

	Form No	CPR Rule	PD
Witness statements must be served 2 days prior to the hearing but this does not prevent oral evidence or further written evidence on the day to update the position, eg typically last minute payments in reduction of arrears			55A, para 5.2
At the hearing there is no time or necessity for an opening address but a **"pro forma"** can be completed and handed to the court (a copy having been given to the defendant prior to the hearing) in a rent arrears case showing:			
(a) The date the tenancy commenced			
(b) The occupants (including ages of children)			
(c) The current rent (C/R) and if part of this is paid by Housing Benefit (H/B) the rebated rent			
(d) The current arrears (C/A) and if they include any arrears of H/B			
(e) The date and method of service of the notice			
(f) The order sought			
(g) The details known of the defendant's financial position			
Where relevant the **defendant's evidence** should include:			
(a) the amount of any outstanding housing benefit or social security payments and			
(b) details of any claims for benefit made but not yet determined, and			
(c) details of any appeals or review applications against benefit refusal			55A, para 5.3
Where the court has to be satisfied that it is **"reasonable"** to make an order the defendant should include in his evidence the reasons the arrears have arisen, the effect that a possession order would have, the availability of any alternative accommodation and any proposals he has (and is financially able to maintain) to clear the arrears by instalments.			
For a recent judicial consideration of 'reasonableness' see the judgment of Rimer LJ in *Whitehouse v Lee* [2009] EWCA Civ 375, [2009] 31 EG 74, a case on the Rent Act 1977 in which the test under s 98 is 'reasonableness' and see also the article 'Listening to reason' by Julian Sidoli del Ceno in (2009) Sol Jo, 28 July, page 8.			
The court has to be satisfied it is reasonable to make the order for possession where the ground on which the order is sought is a discretionary ground ie for secure tenancies the grounds 1-8; see Housing Act 1985, s 84, or for assured tenancies grounds 8-17 in Schedule 2, Housing Act 1988			
A case which strongly underlines the importance of the court itself being satis-			

TAB 21 PROCEDURAL TABLES

	Form No	CPR Rule	PD
fied on this point is *London Borough of Hounslow v McBride* [1999] 31 HLR 143, CA. The simple assent to a suspended possession is not an admission of the landlord's grounds and any such order obtained 'by consent' will be set aside. Setting aside may be achieved on appeal or on an application for judicial review.			
An instructive case where the court held that the tenant's breaches of the tenancy agreement (conviction for drug offences) were not such as to make it unreasonable for a possession order to be made in respect of the defendant's tenancy of sheltered accommodation: see *North Devon Homes Ltd v Batchelor* [2008] EWCA Civ 840, 152 Sol Jo (no 30) 31.			
For the balancing exercise to be performed when the tenant's right to buy competes with the landlord's possession claim, see *Basildon District Council v Wahlen* [2006] EWCA Civ 326, (2006) Times, 7 April, CA.			
See also *Manchester City Council v Benjamin* [2008] EWCA Civ 189, [2008] All ER (D) 185 (Mar), (2008) Gazette, 28 March, page 20 a case where the landlord's notice seeking possession was on the ground that the property was more extensive than the tenant reasonably required. Here the balancing exercise came down in favour of the local authority. The court noted that if the tenant became a secure tenant of an alternative property she would have a right to buy the new property.			
It was held in *Islington London Borough Council v Honeygan-Green* [2008] UKHL 70 that on the revival of a secure tenancy, after the tenant had become a tolerated trespasser but before possession was given, its covenants were to be treated as having been continuously in existence even during the limbo period. This included an accrued right to buy under s 124 of the Housing Act 1985 and the tenant did not need to begin the right-to-buy process again by service of a fresh notice. If this gives the tenant an unfair advantage (eg a purchase price well below the market price) the court could in the exercise of its discretion under HA 1985, s 85 make it a condition of discharging the possession order that the tenant could not pursue the right to buy. This would leave the tenant to serve a fresh notice.			
The relevant parts of the Housing and Regeneration Act 2008 have been brought into effect, so that former tolerated trespassers, in the main, will be given replacement tenancies which the court may treat as one continuous tenancy. It may still be possible to prevent giving the tenant and unfair advantage			

	Form No	CPR Rule	PD
from his delay; probably the fall in property prices had made the problem academic, however.			
On 1 October 2010 the Equality Act 2010 was in the main brought into force in respect of conduct on or after this date and pre-Act decisions will need to be reconsidered in the light of the new test it provides for 'discrimination arising from disability'. Section 15 of the Act creates a new cause of action in respect of such discrimination and it is clearly intended to reverse the decision in *Malcolm* which was the government's expressed intention; see para 2.1F of this TAB above.			
It is only in exceptional circumstances that the power to adjourn a hearing to enable a tenant to reduce his rent arrears below 8 weeks so that Ground 8 of Part 1 of Sch 2 to the Housing Act 1988 will not apply. The fact that the arrears were due to maladministration by a housing benefit authority was not such an exceptional circumstance: *North British Housing Association Ltd v Matthews* [2004] EWCA Civ 1736, (2005) Times, 11 January			
An uncleared cheque can be treated as payment for the purpose of arrears calculations: *Day v Coltrane* [2003] EWCA Civ 342, [2003] All ER (D) 210 (Mar)			
2.7 Directions			
If the court is satisfied that the claim is **genuinely disputed** on substantial grounds the court will not decide the claim but will give case management directions including allocation		55.8	
2.8 Orders			
For forms of order, outright and suspended and postponed, see	N26, N28, N28A		55A, para 10
Where an order for possession is made on a mandatory ground this should be noted on the court file: *Diab v Countryside Rentals 1 plc* [2001] All ER (D) 119 (Jul)			
For the appropriate form of possession order for arrears of rent when the **tenant is insolvent** see *Sharples v Places for People Homes* [2011] EWCA Civ 813, [2011] All ER 170 (Jul).			
The rulings in that case are succinctly set out by Stephen Gold in (2011) NLJ, 2 September, page 117 in his article 'Civil way'.			
Note *Norwich City Council v Famuyiwa* [2005] EWCA Civ 1770, (2005) Times, 24 January where it was stated where the judge found it reasonable to make a possession order he should consider whether the position could be controlled by postponing the date for possession on appropriate terms			

TAB 21   PROCEDURAL TABLES

	Form No	CPR Rule	PD
Note also the order and suspended order for possession on forfeiture for rent arrears	N27, N27A		
As to the effect of possession orders against **secure tenants suspended** in the terms of N28 (in contrast to the pre-CPR form N28) see *Harlow District Council v Hall* [2006] EWCA Civ 156, [2006] 1 WLR 2116 where it was held that the effect of a suspended possession order in the existing form terminated the tenancy so that the tenant became a tolerated trespasser even if he kept to the terms of the suspended order			
In *Bristol City Council v Hassan* [2006] EWCA Civ 656, [2006] 22 EG 176 (CS) the Court of Appeal concluded nothing in Housing Act 1985 s 85 fettered the court's discretion to make such order for **postponement** as it thought fit and that a judge was not obliged to set an absolute date to be specified in the order			
This was particularly significant when the arrears are paid by Housing benefit which in practice is paid 4 weekly			
Brooke LJ stated it was lawful to make an order in terms that are now set out in form N28A			
Subsequently the House of Lords held in *Knowsley Housing Trust v White* [2008] UKHL 70, [2009] 1 AC 636 that the position of assured tenants was not the same as that of secure tenants as their tenancy did not come to an end on breach of a suspended order but only when that order was executed.			
The discrepancy between the two types of tenancy was put to an end on 20 May 2009 when the provisions considered in para 2.1C above were brought into effect.			
As a result of the coming into force of the Housing and Regeneration Act 2008 (see 2.1C above of this TAB) tenancies, whether they be secure or assured and whether the possession order be suspended or postponed, remain in force until execution. Which of the two alternative orders should the court be urged to make? From the tenant's point of view a postponed order will be preferable because the landlord will have to apply to the court for a date to be fixed which gives the court the opportunity to consider whether to fix a date or list the application for a hearing. From the landlord's point of view a suspended order will be preferable for a warrant can be issued upon default and it is up to the tenant to apply to suspend it. For detailed consideration of the point see article by Caroline Waterworth entitled 'Suspend or postpone' in (2011) NLJ, 4 February, page 161.			

	Form No	CPR Rule	PD
In an article entitled 'Suspend or post-pone' in (2011) NLJ, 25 February, page 270, Robin Enford extols that benefit of a postponed possession order by reason of it providing the court with a further opportunity to exercise its discretion.			
2.9 Orders fixing a date for possession where the court has made an order post-poning the date for possession of a se-cure or an assured tenancy	N28A		55A, section IV
It must be remembered on making a possession order that the court may im-pose an additional condition, eg that the defendant comply with the tenancy con-ditions until possession is given up. See further article in New Law Journal, 13 April 2007, page 505, 'Re-thinking possession orders' by Holbrook and Bill-ingham			
The tenancy will remain in being not-withstanding the making of an order for possession postponing the date for pos-session, until execution under the posses-sion order			
If there is default at least 14 days and not more than 3 months before applying for an order the claimant must give writ-ten notice to the defendant			55A, para 10.3
For the contents of the notice see			55A, para 10.4
In his reply to the notice the defendant must: (a) where he disputes the stated ar-rears, provide details of payments or credits made; (b) where he agrees the stated arrears, explain why payments have not been made			55A, para 10.5
The claimant's application for an or-der fixing the date upon which the de-fendant has to give up possession must be made by Part 23 application notice. The application must state whether the defendant has any outstanding housing benefit claims			55A, para 10.6
The documents to be filed with the ap-plication are listed in			55A, para 10.7
The rules dealing with applications with-out notice, service and the right to set aside do not apply			55A, para 10.8
The application will be referred to the District Judge who will normally deter-mine the application without a hearing by fixing the date for possession as the next working day but otherwise will fix a hearing date and direct service of the application and supporting evidence but for a case where the court found there was a triable issue as to breach of one or more of the conditions of the postpone-ment see *Wandsworth London Bor-ough Council v Whibley* [2008] EWCA Civ 1259, (2008) Times, 25 November			55A, para 10.9

TAB 21 PROCEDURAL TABLES

	Form No	CPR Rule	PD
The court cannot review the finding that it was reasonable to make the order			55A, para 10.10
2.10 Costs			
Unless the court otherwise orders, the order will be for fixed costs where one of the grounds for possession is arrears of rent, whether or not the order for possession is suspended, if the defendant has not delivered a defence or counter-claim nor otherwise denied liability or has delivered a defence limited to his proposals for payment of the rent arrears		45.1(2)(c), (d) and (f)	
The fixed costs at present are £301.75 (£175 court fee; £69.25 commencement costs and £57.50 costs on entry of judgment); see article 'Short Changed' [2007] NLJ 4 May by Francis Davey. The tenancy agreement may provide that the tenant will pay the landlord's costs and this will normally entitle the landlord to recover reasonable costs (but not more than reasonable costs) and not fixed costs: *Church Comrs v Ibrahim* [1997] 1 EGLR 13, [1997] 03 EG 136, CA		45.2A and 45.4A	
2.11 Human Rights			
The decision of the Supreme Court in *Manchester City Council v Pinnock* [2010] UKSC 45, [2010] All ER (D) 42 (Nov) as to the effect of Article 8(1) of the ECHR (right to respect for one's home) and s 6 of the Human Rights Act 1998 (making it unlawful for a public authority to act incompatibly with a Convention right) on the right to possession of the public authority owner against the occupier, where no defence is available to the occupier under the UK national law, represents at least a plateau in this conflict which has lasted over a decade.			
Pinnock having been the subject of a single judgment, delivered by Lord Neuberger on behalf of the 9 judge court, and after the decision of the ECtHR in *Kay v United Kingdom (Application No 37341/06)* the plateau it represents is thought sufficiently secure to justify starting the review of the position with *Doherty v Birmingham City Council* [2008] UKHL 57 and its consideration of the decision in *Lambeth London Borough Council v Kay* [2006] UKHL 10, [2006] 2 AC 465. The progress of the issue over the preceding years can of course be found in the 2009 edition of this work in **TAB 22**, paras 2.11 and 2.12.			
Article 8(2) of the ECHR allows public authorities to interfere with the Article 8(1) right to one's home so far as it is 'lawful and necessary in a democratic society in the interests of . . . ', amongst other things, 'the rights and freedom of others'.			

	Form No	CPR Rule	PD
It in effect requires a balancing exercise which is described as a 'proportionality test'.			
In *Doherty* (above) which was decided prior to the ECtHR decision in *Kay v United Kingdom* (above), it was decided that the procedure followed by a public authority under domestic law would in most cases automatically supply the jurisdiction required by Article 8(2) of the ECHR. This being subject to the proviso that a challenge could be made to the making of a possession order in the county court, so far as the limits on the jurisdiction permitted, if the defendant could exceptionally show: (a) a seriously arguable point is raised that the law that enables the court to make the possession order is incompatible with its jurisdiction under the Human Rights Act 1998; (b) if the defendant wishes to challenge the decision of a public authority as an improper exercise of its powers on the ground that it was 'a decision that no reasonable person would consider justifiable' per Lord Hope in *Lambeth London Borough Council v Kay* (see above); gateway (b) the public law gateway.			
In *Doherty*, Lords Hope, Rodger and Walker (of the five law Lords sitting) indicated that the county court judges should continue to follow the guidance given in *Kay*, as more fully explained there in the opinion of Lord Hope.			
The minority view of the House of Lords as to this in *Kay*, expressed by Lord Bingham, was to the effect that the personal circumstances of the occupier should be taken into account to achieve compliance with the Human Rights Act 1998 (see above, the first paragraph of 2.11 of this TAB). It was made clear in *Doherty* that gateways (a) and (b) above were modifications made to the decision in *Qazi* by the majority in *Kay* to accommodate the decision in Connors (for these cases see above). For an extremely informative note and commentary on the case of *Doherty* see Human Rights Updater published by LexisNexis UK (2008) October, Issue 81 at page 13.			
The pressure on the stance of the domestic courts as set out in *Doherty* (above) by statements and decisions by ECHR as to breaches of Article 8 as for example in *Cann v United Kingdom (Application No 19009/04)* (2008) Times, 23 May. ECHR when the court stated:			

TAB 21 PROCEDURAL TABLES

	Form No	CPR Rule	PD
'The loss of one's house is the most extreme form of interference with the right to respect for her home. Any person at risk of an interference of this magnitude should in principle be able to have the proportionality of the measure determined by an independent tribunal.'			
And in *Cosic v Croatia* Application No 28261/06 [2009] ECHR 28261/06, where the European Court held that a possession order against an occupier whose lease had expired and who had no security was in violation of Article 8. This underlines the conflict between the domestic courts and the European Court. The degree of conflict was considered by Annette Cafferkey in her article 'Seeking Possession' in (2009) NLJ, 27 November, page 1651.			
This pressure culminated in the decision of the ECtHR in *Kay v United Kigndom* (App No 37341/06) in September 2010 which rejected the argument that the gateway (b) defence is limited to conventional public law grounds (ie no reasonable person would consider it justifiable) and held that personal circumstances should be taken into account (the minority view in *Kay* in the House of Lords). The ECHR allowed the appeal on the basis that the county court was wrong to strike out the article 8 defences put forward by the claimants.			
The court stated that in *McCann* (see above) it had agreed with the minority of the House of Lords in their ruling on *Kay v Lambeth London Borough Council* in 2006 (above):			
'In conclusion, the *Kay* applicants' challenge to the decision to strike out their article 8 defences failed because it was not possible **at that time** to challenge the decision of a local authority to seek a possession order on the basis of the alleged disproportionality of that decision in light of personal circumstances.'			
The only relevant decision of the UK courts on the point since *Kay* to account for the use by the ECHR of the words 'at that time' is the decision in *Doherty* (see above). That decision however did not approve the minority view in *Kay* or hold the gateway (b) defence could be based on personal circumstances in a proportionality consideration. Pending clarification, the position was uncertain.			
Clarification has been provided by the Supreme Court when it delivered judgment in *Manchester City Council v Pinnock* [2010] UKSC 45 where Lord Neuberger giving the judgment of the court stated that to be compatible with Article 8 a court, when considernig whether to make a possession order in respect of a defendant's **home** in favour of a public body, which has a right to possession,			

	Form No	CPR Rule	PD
has to have the power to assess the proportionality of making the order. This reflected the decision of the ECtHR in **Kay** above and reversed precedent that held the county court could not consider proportionality.			
The Article 8 defence need only be considered by the court if it is first raised by the occupier and it will only be in an exceptional case where the domestic law justifies an outright order that Article 8 will justify either the refusal of an order or its suspension (the use of the word 'exceptional' provides a means by which the court can filter out hopeless cases).			
The court (county court), if an Article 8 point is raised, should initially consider it summarily and if it is satisfied that, even if the facts relied upon are established, it would not succeed, it should be dismissed. If the court is satisfied that it might affect the order to be made the point should be further entertained.			
The court's powers when considering the point extends to investigating itself the facts relied on by the claimant landlord to justify the taking or the continuance of the proceedings and also to investigating the facts relevant to the proportionality of the order. The court can determine any issue of fact and hear any evidence necessary for it to do so.			
The court clarified that the judgment applies to all local authority landlords including, presumably, non-government bodies providing social housing, but **does not apply to private landlords.**			
Manchester City Council v Pinnock (above) concerned a **demoted tenancy** at the second stage (ie subsequent to the demotion hearing); s 143D(2) of the Housing Act 1996 states: 'The court must make an order for possession unless the procedure under ss 143E and 143F have not been allowed.' The Supreme Court has applied the section but as qualified by proportionality. See further section 2.12 of the TAB.			
In *Manchester City Council v Pinnock (No 2)* [2011] UKSC 6 the Supreme Court concluded it should make its own order for possession rather than remitting the case. Judgment was given for possession.			
For a consideration of the question of whether mandatory rights to possession have ceased to be mandatory see article by Jon Holbrook in (2010) NLJ, 3 December, page 1663 entitled 'Trouble at mill' and keep in mind that whilst private landlords are not covered by the Human Rights Act 1998 the county court is.			

TAB 21 PROCEDURAL TABLES

	Form No	CPR Rule	PD
Doubts as to whether a registered social landlord is to be treated as a functional public authority were resolved by the decision of the Court of Appeal in *R (on the application of Weaver) v London and Quadrant Housing Trust (Equality and Human Rights Commission intervening)* [2009] EWCA Civ 587, [2009] 25 EG 137 (CS).			
This decision means that registered social landlords ('registered providers') are public authorities for the purposes of s 6 of the Human Rights Act 1998 when acting as landlords, albeit there will be some such bodies which exceptionally are not by reason of not meeting the criteria set out by Lord Nicholls in *Aston Cantlow and Wilmcote with Billesley Parochial Church Council v Wallbank* [2004] 1 AC 546. See generally article by Louise Curtis 'All Change' (2009) New Law Journal 17 July, page 1019.			
The Supreme Court has refused permission to appeal the decision of the Court of Appeal in the *Weaver* case, see last para above; Sol Jo (2009) 19 November, page 5.			
The effect of *Weaver* on the exchange of tenancies can be seen in *R (on the application of McIntyre) v Gentoo Group* [2010] EWHC 5 (Admin), [2010] All ER (D) 01 (Jan), (2010) Sol Jo, 12 January, page 2 and 19 January, page 29 where it was held that the requirement of clearance of 'elderly' rent arrears before the Housing Association's consent could be given was unlawful in public law. The tenant's application for judicial review was dismissed because judicial review is a remedy of last resort and other remedies were available and had not been used. For further consideration and discussion see article by Giles Parker in (2010) Sol Jo, 16 February, page 6 entitled 'Who holds the keys?'			
The legal chairman of the Equality and Human Rights Commission is quoted in the (2010) Sol Jo, 9 November as saying:			
'Today's judgment does not prevent social landlords from evicting a tenant. What it does mean is that such decisions will not be taken lightly — tenants will have the right to have the reasonableness and proportionality of that decision heard by the courts.'			
2.12 Human rights — demoted tenancies and the future of proportionality in respect of other types of tenancy			
The position of demoted tenants has been clarified by the Supreme Court in *Pinnock v Manchester City Corporation* [2010] UKSC 45 and *Kay v United Kingdom (Application No 37341/06)* (2010) Times, 18 Octber, ECHR relating			

	Form No	CPR Rule	PD
to demoted tenancies (ss 143A-143M of the Housing Act 1996) and the impact of the Human Rights Act 1998 on the right of such tenants who enjoy only limited security. Lord Neuberger in giving the judgment of the Court in Pinnock made it clear that a county court judge who is asked to make a possession order against a demoted tenant pursuant to s 143D(2) of the Housing Act 1996 could consider whether it is proportionate to make the order sought, and in view of this the demoted tenancy regime is compatible with Article 8 of the European Convention on Human Rights.		65.11-65.20	
A demoted tenancy arises under s 82A of the Housing Act 1985 which enables an application to be made by local authorities and social landlords against a secure tenant for the tenancy to be terminated and replaced by a demoted tenancy. The application is to the court which must be satisfied that there has been or is threatened to be anti-social conduct or unlawful use of the premises and that it is reasonable to make the order. If the court was satisfied that it should make the order, clearly that would present a considerable obstacle to a defence of lack of proportionality providing an Article 8 defence in any subsequent proceeding affecting the demoted tenancy. In *Pinnock*, itself a demoted tenancy case, having found it should consider the Article 8 defence the Supreme Court decided the county court had acted proportionately.			
This brings home the difficulty facing the occupier but it seems certain such defences will be attempted not only in respect of demoted tenancies but also in cases concerning introductory tenancies and where there is no security of tenure. Similarly non-government bodies providing social housing may well see Article 8 relied on by occupiers who are faced with a possession claim on mandatory grounds (eg cases of 8 weeks rent arrears in a Housing Association tenancy).			
The conjoined Appeals in *London Borough of Hounslow v Powell, Leeds City Council v Hall and Birmingham City Council v Frisby* [2010] EWCA Civ 336, (2011) Times, 1 March were determined by the Supreme Court [2011] UKSC 8, [2011] All ER (D) 255 (Feb) and it has been confirmed the position that a local authority seeking possession of a property which is a person's home must observe the right to respect for the home, Article 8 of the ECHR, and have the power to consider whether the order proposed to be made would be proportionate. Cases where the tenant has been **housed as a homeless person** under Part VII of the Housing Act 1996 or is an **introductory tenant** under s 127 of			

TAB 21 PROCEDURAL TABLES

	Form No	CPR Rule	PD
the Housing Act 1996 are included in this.			
Per Lord Hope in *Powell* at para 34: ' . . . I would hold that these propositions apply as much in principle to homelessness cases as they do to demoted tenancies'.			
The observations as to s 89(1) of the Housing Act 1980 which removed from the court the discretion which it had at common law to make a suspended order for possession with whatever length of postponement it thought fit should also be noted. Whether it will be subject to a declaration of incompatibility in the future remains to be seen.			
Further reading is provided by articles which consider the decision in Pinnock and the probable ways ahead by Giles Parker entitled 'Future Battleground' in (2010) Sol Jo, 30 November, page 13; Annette Cafferkey entitled 'A substantial shift?' in (2010) NLJ, 19 November, page 1604; and Nicholas Dobson entitled 'Beating a path' in (2010) NLJ, 26 November, page 1639. This list is in no sense exhaustive.			
For further reading after the decision in *Powell v Hounslow London Borough Concil* [2011] UKSC 8 see (2011) NLJ, 15 April, page 57, article entitled 'Valuable possession: Take 2' by Madge-Wyld and Salmon; (2011) NLJ, 6 May, page 617 'Valuable possession: a right to reply' by Jon Holbrook; (2011) Sol Jo, 31 May, page 27 'Update: housing' by Giles Peaker; (2011) NLJ, 27 May, page 279 'A ticking time bomb?' by David Cowan. This list is in no sense exhaustive.			
The present legal position in relation to claims for possession by a local authority of the house held by a demoted tenant can be summarised as: • the court has power to assess the proportionality of making the order; • generally Article 8 ECHR need only be considered by the court if raised in the proceeding by or on behalf of the residential occupier; • if an Article 8 point is raised it should be considered summarily and if the court is satisfied that even if the facts relied on were established the point would not succeed, it should be dismissed; • only if the court is satisfied the point could affect the order it should be entertained; • each of the two steps in relation to demoted tenancies (ie demotion and subsequent claim for possession) engage Article 8;			

		Form No	CPR Rule	PD
•	at Stage 1 the court has to (a) consider the facts and (b) be satisfied it is reasonable to make the order – almost impossible to conceive that Article 8 would not be satisfied;			
•	at Stage 2 (the claim for possession against the demoted tenant) the court is required by s 143D(2) to make an order unless it finds the statutory procedure (under s 143E and s 143F of the Housing Act 1996) has not been followed;			
•	a demoted tenant could seek judicial review of the local authority/landlords both to bring and continue proceedings on the basis that is was contrary to Article 8, it being disproportionate;			
•	in the light of the ability to seek judicial review the statutory review grounds of the court can be expanded so that it is able to consider for itself the grounds found by the local authority/landlord and those that had subsequently arisen and make its own finding on them;			
•	s 143D(2) should be construed to allow the court to consider and, if appropriate, give effect to, any Article 8 defence raised by the defendant/tenant;			
•	s 7(1)(b) of the Human Rights Act 1998 gives a county court judge jurisdiction to deal with the defence relying on Article 8 and to consider whether it was proportionate to make the order sought pursuant to s 143D and to investigate and make findings on any relevant matters of fact;			
•	the demoted tenancy regime is compatible with Article 8;			
•	if the court is satisfied it is proportionate to make the order it should do so; if not it could refuse the possession order or extend the time allowed for giving possession (purely on a time basis or by providing it shall only take effect in the breach of a condition imposed);			
•	see the cautionary words of Lord Neuberger in his judgment in *Pinnock* as to the support that can be given to the local authority/landlord's decision, where the defendant has no rights to occupation in domestic law, by its duties in relation to the distribution and management of the housing stock; see also per Lord Hope in *Powell* at para 35.			

TAB 21 PROCEDURAL TABLES

	Form No	CPR Rule	PD
• *Kryvitska and Kryvitsky v Ukraine (Application No 30856/03)* unreported December 2 2010 ECHR referred to in the conjoined appeals considered above confirms that vindication of the local authority's ownership rights and its duty in relation to the allocation and management of its housing stock together be sufficient to satisfy the legitimate aim requirement. This being so in the majority of cases there will be no need for the local authority to explain and justify its reasons for seeking a possession order. The court need only be concerned where the occupier's personal circumstances may make the order for possession disproportionate: see also *Salford v Mullen* [2010] EWCA Civ 336, [2011] 1 All ER 119 at paras 67 and 77.			
• Where the local authority's decision to seek possession was proportionate and the review panel's decision was reasonable so that when the claim was filed the tenant had no defence there remains the question of whether there were any personal circumstances at the time of the hearing which would make a possession order disproportionate. In *Southend-on-Sea Borough Council v Armour* [2012] EWHC 000 (Admin) the Court of Appeal upheld the decision of the trial judge that at the time of the trial there had been a period of approximately 12 months where the tenant had been of good behaviour and observed the terms of the tenancy which would make a possession order disproportionate. For discussion see article entitled 'A Judicial chink?' by Nicholas Dobson in (2012) NLJ, 7 December, page 1524.			
• A proportionality defence can be put forward with a public law 'gateway b' defence. The latter would test the lawfulness of the local authority's decision and if it were found to be lawful its proportionality would then be tested.			
• The Supreme Court in the conjoined appeals referred to above found the reasoning in Pinnock should apply to **introductory tenancies** and in general terms all other types of permitted occupiers who are not secure tenants.			
• The Court of Apeal in two cases (*Corby v Scott* [2012] EWCA Civ 276 and *West Housing Association v Haycroft* (a related appeal))			

	Form No	CPR Rule	PD
said that in the circumstances of introductory or 'starter' tenancies it would only be in exceptional cases that the courts would consider article 8. In both appeals the leading judgment was given by Lord Neuberger.			
2.13 Homeless			
Intentionally homeless families are entitled to temporary accommodation for a period of time that gives 'a reasonable opportunity to find their own accommodation'; s 190 Housing Act 1996. That period should take into account the particular needs and circumstances of the individual and not the cost and other demands on the resources of the local authority: *R (on the application of Colville) v Richmond-on-Thames London Borough Council* [2006] EWCA Civ 718, [2006] 4 All ER 917, [2006] 1 WLR 2808			
Under s 177(1) of the Housing Act 1996 victims of domestic violence are automatically treated as homeless and have a priority entitlement to housing. In *Yemshaw v Hounslow London Borough Council* [2011] UKSC 3, [2011] WLR (D) 18 Lady Hale stated 'physical violence is not the only natural meaning of the word "violence"; another is strength or intensity of emotion, fervour and passion'. Effectively, physiological abuse will fall within the definition of violence in s 177(1) as a result of this decision.			
When considering the suitability of accommodation offered to homeless people regard should be had by the court to any proposed adaptations or alterations: *Boreh v London Borough of Ealing* [2008] EWCA Civ 1176, [2008] All ER (D) 291 (Oct).			
In *Manchester City Council v Moran* [2009] UKHL 36, [2009] 1 WLR 1506 it was held that women living in a refuge, whether or not they were evicted, and families living in overcrowded accommodation awaiting council housing, were to be regarded as homeless (as opposed to intentionally homeless) within the provisions of the Housing Act 1996. The definitions of homelessness are contained in ss 175 and 177 of that Act.			
Accommodation provided under s 192 of the Housing Act 1996 in a women's refuge or similar is a staging post along the way to permanent accommodation and in the light of this finding in *Moran* (see above) the court was 'inclined to accept' that the decision in *R v Ealing London Borough Council, ex p Sidhu* [1982] 8 LGR 534, 2 HLR 45 that a women's refuge was not 'accommodation' could not stand in the light of the decisions in *R v Hillingdon Bor-*			

TAB 21 PROCEDURAL TABLES

	Form No	CPR Rule	PD
ough Council, *ex p Puhlhofer* [1986] AC 484 and *R v Brent London Borough Council, ex p Awua* [1996] AC 55.			
A proportionality defence is available, subject to the facts, where possession is sought against a person housed by the local authority under Part VII of the Housnig Act 1996.			
2.14 Court's procedure when dealing with a proportionality defence			
Lord Hope in *Powell v Hounslow London Borough Council* [2011] UKSC 8 (see above) stated: 'Where the case passed th threshold test of being seriously arguable, the court must consider whether the possession order was a proportionate means of achieving a legitimate aim.'			
2.15 The tenant's insolvency			
Section 285(3) of the Insolvency Act 1986 does not preclude the making of an order for possession: see *Sharples v Places for People Homes London Ltd* [2011] EWCA Civ 83, [2011] All ER (D) 170 (Jul). Here under ground 8 set out in Sch 2 to the Housing Act 1986 — sent more than 8 weeks in arrears. For further consideration see article 'At the Sharples end?' (2011) NLJ, 16 September, page 1242 by Christopher Warenius.			
3. Mortgage possession claims relating to residential property			
3.1 Preliminary			
On 19 November 2008 a pre-action protocol for residential mortgage possession claims was brought into force. It covers:			
(i) first mortgages			
(ii) subsequent mortgages whether or not regulated under the Consumer Credit Act 1974			
Para 1.1 of the Preamble to the protocol states that the Protocol describes the behaviour the court will expect of the parties prior to the start of a possession claim within its scope			
Its provisions include:			
(i) a possession order being postponed where the borrower has taken or will take steps to market the property at an appropriate price in accordance with professional advice			
(ii) the parties to discuss the cause of the arrears, the borrower's financial position and proposals for payment of the arrears			
(iii) where appropriate lender to refer the borrower to independent debt advice			
(iv) the lender to give written reasons within 10 days for rejecting any			

	Form No	CPR Rule	PD
proposal by the borrower for payment			
The protocol gives good reasons for not starting possession proceedings in paragraph 6 of the Protocol and it is provided at 6.4: 'Where the lender decides not to postpone the start of a possession claim it should inform the borrower of the reasons for this decision at least 5 business days before starting proceedings.'			
For consideration of the effectiveness of this protocol see article 'Stemming a rising tide?' by Bailey and Williams in NLJ 13 February 2009, page 221 and 'Vulture funds prey on hard-up homeowners' by James Charles (2009) Times, 4 July, page 72			
The Government has introduced the following schemes to advise and assist borrowers: (a) Support for Mortgage Interest (SMI) whereby homeowners receiving Income Support or certain other benefits can claim an additional element, called Support for Mortgage Interest, on eligible capital up to £200,000 after 13 weeks from claiming benefit. (b) Mortgage Rescue Scheme (MRS) for homeowners who would be eligible for help under the homeless legislation from their local authority on repossession. (c) Homeowners Mortgage Support (HMS) which is a Government guaranteed scheme enabling deferment of a proportion of mortgage interest on experiencing a substantial loss of income. The deferment can be for up to 2 years and the income deferred will have to be paid by the borrower eventually. The eligibility requirements are numerous and detailed. The total principal amount of loans secured on the home must not be more that £400,000. More information about the schemes can be obtained from http://www.direct.gov.uk.			
The Administration of Justice Acts 1970 (s 36) and 1973 (s 8) give powers to the court where the principal sum can be paid by the mortgagor by instalments or otherwise be deferred in whole or in part. See **III REA [22]–III REA [23.6]** in Volume 2. The powers are not available where the principal sum is to be paid on a fixed date or on demand (subject to any collateral agreement to accept instalment payments)			

TAB 21 PROCEDURAL TABLES

	Form No	CPR Rule	PD
If the mortgage is one to which the Consumer Credit Act 1974 applies, the defendant may make an application for a time order in his defence or by application on notice. The £25,000 ceiling for regulation under the CCA 1974 having been abolished from 6 April 2008 agreements, including second mortgages of residential property, made by an individual after 6 April 2008, will be covered by the Act irrespective of the amount borrowed. The time order provisions under s 129 accordingly apply to such second mortgages.			
An agreement for business purposes for over £25,000 will be exempt from regulation under CCA 1974, s 16.			
It is to be noted in respect of mortgages and agreements governed by the CCA that 'Rule 78' clauses whereby on early redemption a calculation is made of the total interest to the end of the original term and only a partial rebate given are void by reason of the Unfair Terms in Consumer Contracts Regulations 1999, SI 1999/2083. Overpayments can be reclaimed: *Evans v Cherrytree Finance Ltd* (13 April 2007, unreported). For further discussion see article 'Unfair Windfalls' by Paul Beevers, NLJ, 28 February 2008, page 317.			
For an unsuccessful attempt to invoke the CCA see *Southern Pacific Mortgage Ltd v Heath* [2009] EWCA Civ 1135, [2009] NLJR 1581, (2009) Times, 20 November where the then limit of £25,000 was exceeded by the payment off of a previous mortgage in favour of another lender of about £19,000 and the provision of £9,000 to the defendant. The Court of Appeal held they were not to be treated as two separate agreements. See further the article 'Time to wipe the slate clean?' by Paul Healey in NLJ (2010) 30 April, page 614.			
Buy to let mortgages will be exempt form the provisions of the CCA 1974.			
Regulation and administration of first residential mortgages will continue to be dealt with by the Financial Services Authority under the provisions of the Financial Services and Markets Act 2000 and not the CCA 1974.			
See further NLJ, 14 and 21 March 2008, page 411.			55A, para 7.1
The effect of a **forged legal mortgage over jointly owned property** (ie where the signature of one but not both of the borrowers is forged) is to vest in the lender an equitable charge over the interest of the borrower who did genuinely sign. The remedy available to the lender is to apply as an equitable chargee for an order for sale under s 14 of the Trusts of Land and Appointment of			

	Form No	CPR Rule	PD
Trustees Act 1996: *Edwards v Bank of Scotland* [2010] EWHC 652 (Ch).			
Where the re-mortgage of a jointly owned property is vitiated by the undue influence of the husband, it nevertheless operates as an equitable charge under s 14 (see immediately preceding para above) on the husband's share: see *Hewett v First Plus Financial Group Ltd* [2010] EWCA Civ 312.			
This table does not deal with **chattel mortgages** obtained by use of a security bill of sale. The relevant statutes are the Consumer Credit Act 1974, the Bills of Sale Act 1878 and the Bills of Sale (Amendment) Act 1882. It is vital to appreciate that in the event of default and the expiry of a default notice no court order is required before the chattel (usually a car) is seised and the lender has only to wait five days before selling the chattel. There is a very useful article by Paul Beevers in NLJ, 11 April 2008, page 507 which sets out the possible steps open to the borrower and above all stresses the urgency of acting appropriately.			7B
Where, to avoid a possession order in favour of the lenders, the owner sells pursuant to a 'sell to rent back' arrangement and is subsequently faced with a claim for possession see **TAB 23** section 4 below.			
3.2 Particulars of claim			
In addition to the general requirements (see 1.4, above) and in particular the necessity of the lender dealing with protocol compliance including handing to the judge two completed copies of form N123 with the statement of truth duly completed and providing an explanation for any failures to comply with the protocol apparent from the answers to the questions in the form.	N123		55A, para 2.1
If the claim is a possession claim by a mortgagee, the particulars of claim must also set out:	N120		55A, para 2.5
(a) if the claim relates to residential property whether: (i) a land charge of Class F has been registered under s 2(7) of the Matrimonial Homes Act 1967 (ii) a notice registered under ss 2(8) or 8(3) of the Matrimonial Homes Act 1983 has been entered and on whose behalf, or (iii) a notice under s 31(10) of the Family Law Act 1996 has been registered and on whose behalf, and if so, that the claimant will serve notice of the claim on the persons on whose			

TAB 21 PROCEDURAL TABLES

	Form No	CPR Rule	PD
behalf the land charge is registered or the notice or caution entered			
(b) the state of the mortgage account by including:			
(i) the amount of:			
the advance			
any periodic repayment, and			
any payment of interest required to be made			
(ii) the amount which would have to be paid (after taking into account any adjustment for early settlement) in order to redeem the mortgage at a stated date not more than 14 days after the claim started specifying the amount of solicitor's costs and administration charges which would be payable			
(iii) if the loan which is secured by the mortgage is a regulated consumer credit agreement, the total amount outstanding under the terms of the mortgage, and			
(iv) the rate of interest payable:			
at the commencement of the mortgage			
immediately before any arrears referred to in paragraph (3) accrued			
at the commencement of the proceedings			
(c) if the claim is brought because of failure to pay the periodic payments when due:			
(i) in schedule form, the dates and amounts of all payments due and payments made under the mortgage agreement or mortgage deed for a period of two years immediately preceding the date of issue or if the first date of default was less than two years before the date of issue from the date of default and a running total			
If the claimant wishes to rely on a history of arrears longer that two years he should state this on his particulars and exhibit a full (or longer) schedule to a witness statement			
(ii) give details of:			
any other payments required to be made as a term			

		Form No	CPR Rule	PD
	of the mortgage (such as for insurance premiums, legal costs, default interest, penalties, administrative or other charges)			
	any sums claimed and stating the nature and amount of each such charge; and whether any of these payments is in arrears and whether or not it is included in the amount of any periodic payment			
(d)	whether or not the loan which is secured by the mortgage is a regulated consumer credit agreement and, if so, specify the date on which any notice required by ss 76 or 87 of the Consumer Credit Act 1974 was given			
(e)	if appropriate details that show the property is not one to which s 141 of the Consumer Credit Act 1974 applies			
(f)	any relevant information about the defendant's circumstances, in particular:			
	(i) whether the defendant is in receipt of social security benefits, and			
	(ii) whether any payments are made on his behalf directly to the claimant under the Social Security Contributions and Benefits Act 1992			
(g)	give details of any tenancy entered into between the mortgagor and mortgagee (including any notices served), and			
(h)	state any previous steps which the claimant has taken to recover the money secured by the mortgage or the mortgaged property and, in the case of court proceedings, state:			
	(i) the dates when the claim started and concluded, and			
	(ii) the dates and terms of any orders made			
(i)	unless it is included in the claim form a statement explaining the steps that have been taken to comply with the Protocol for Possession Claims based on Mortgage or Home Purchase Plan Arrears in respect of Residential Property and dealing with compliance with any other relevant protocol including sections III and IV of the Pre-Action Conduct protocol.			
3.3 Service of the claim form				
The general rules as to service apply:				

TAB 21 PROCEDURAL TABLES

	Form No	CPR Rule	PD
If a class F land charge has been registered or a notice entered, service must also be effected on the person who caused this to be registered or entered		Part 6	
Where the claimant serves, a certificate of service must be produced at the hearing and CPR 6.14(2)(a) as to the filing of a certificate of service does not apply		55.8(6)	
3.4 Hearing date			
The general rules apply (see 1.5, above) and the date given on issue will be for a hearing in chambers generally before a district judge with a time estimate of 5 minutes			
The claimant must send a notice to the property addressed to 'the tenant or occupier' to the housing department of the relevant local authority and to any other registered proprietor (other than the claimant) of a registered charge over the property within 5 days of receiving notification of the date of the hearing by the court giving the prescribed information and produce a copy at the hearing and prove service. The notices must contain the information set out in sub-ss (3) and (3A) respectively.		55.10(1)-(4)	
An unauthorised tenant of residential property may apply to the court for the order for possession to be suspended: see 3.6A of this TAB.		55.10(4A)	
3.5 Defendant's response			
See general provision, 1.6 above			
For form of defence, see	N11M		
For notes for defendant in mortgage possession claim of residential premises see	N7		
3.6 The hearing			
The date given on issue will be for a hearing before a district judge in chambers			
Since January 2010 when implementation of the Legal Services Act 2007 took place, representation of the claimant lender can only be by a solicitor's agent if that person is instructed and supervised by an authorised person and is accordingly an exempt person under Schedule 3 of the 2007 Act. This presents considerable difficulties for a person who is a self-employed agent employed by a third party agency company. CPR PD 39A, para 5.1 requires that at any hearing the advocate should provide written information as to their identity, qualification and for whom they appear. Such a form should be available for production if required and evidence of instruction and supervision by an authorised person should also be available if it is challenged.			

	Form No	CPR Rule	PD
Wherever possible the parties should include their evidence in a statement of case verified by a statement of truth			55A, para 5.1
The **claimant's evidence** should include the amount of mortgage arrears and interest on those arrears. These amounts should if possible be calculated up to the date of the hearing (if necessary by specifying a daily rate or arrears and interest)			
Such evidence can be brought up to date orally at the hearing			55A, para 5.2
Subject to this updating, if the case has not been allocated to fast or multi-track, any fact may be proved by written statements		55.8(3)	
Witness statements must be served 2 days prior to the hearing.		55.8(4)	
The claimant **must** bring to the hearing two copies of **form N123** as to compliance with the mortgage arrears pre-action protocol. One of these is to be handed to the defendant and the other to the judge at the hearing. No documents are to be attached to the form and none are required at the hearing. The object of the document is to avoid the court having to look beyond it unless it is challenged. The claimant or their solicitor has to complete a statement of truth.	N123		
At the hearing there is no time or necessity for an opening but a **"pro forma"** can be completed and handed to the court (a copy having been given to the defendant prior to the hearing) showing:			
(a) the date of the mortgage and the amount advanced			
(b) any further advance			
(c) the date of notice to the occupiers			
(d) the current instalment (and whether any part is paid by social security)			
(e) the amount of arrears			
(f) the balance outstanding			
(g) any information as to the value of the property			
(h) details of the occupants			
(i) the order(s) sought			
The court will have before it the claimant's statement of case, the form N123 and any witnesses' statements and will expect the production of:			
(a) **clear search** under the Land Charges Acts (unregistered land) or the Land Registration Acts (registered land) showing that no class F land charge has been registered under s 2(7) of the Matrimonial Homes Act 1967 or notice registered under s 2(8) or 8(3) of the Matrimonial Homes Act 1967			

TAB 21   PROCEDURAL TABLES

	Form No	CPR Rule	PD
or under s 31(10) of the Family Law Act 1996, and			
(b) an official copy of the register			
If it is relevant the defendant should give evidence of:			
(a) the amount of any social security or housing benefit payments relevant to the mortgage arrears, and			
(b) the status of:			
(i) any outstanding claims for social security or housing benefit and			
(ii) any outstanding applications to appeal or review social security or housing benefit decisions			
The defendant should also give evidence of:			
(a) his ability to pay the current instalments			
(b) his proposal for clearing the arrears – with a supporting financial statement showing it is a realistic proposal			
(c) why the court should be satisfied he is likely to pay the arrears of instalments within a reasonable time			
'Reasonable' can extend to the whole of the remaining period of the mortgage term: *Cheltenham and Gloucester Building Society v Norgan* [1996] 1 All ER 449; *Solon South West Housing Association Ltd v James* [2004] EWCA Civ 1847			
The court does not have to take formal evidence from the defendant: *Cheltenham and Gloucester Building Society v Grant* (1994) 26 HLR 703			
The court does not have the power to alter the contract between the borrower and the lender and for that reason will only very rarely make an order postponing possession on terms that do not provide for payment of the current monthly instalments. It is the case that the court has power to do so for it is not altering the contractual requirements but merely postponing the date for possession under the Administration of Justice Acts 1970 and 1973.			
The court may:			
(a) grant an **outright possession order**, or			
(b) grant a **suspended possession order** and in either case	N26		
(c) grant a **money judgment** for the balance outstanding but if the possession order is suspended the will stay execution of the money judgment on terms	N31		

	Form No	CPR Rule	PD
• if the arrears are consolidated after the suspended order is made but the borrower again falls into arrears the lender may issue a warrant for possession under the order already obtained: *Zinda v Bank of Scotland (No 2)* [2011] EWCA Civ 206. The borrower could apply under s 36(4) of the Administration of Justice Act 1970 to vary or revoke the conditions in the suspended order or apply to suspend it.			
(d) **adjourn** the proceedings under CPR 3.1 or the court's inherent jurisdiction but before doing so the court would require adequate evidence of the borrower's proposed means of repayment: *Cheval Bridging Finance v Bhasisn* [2008] EWCA Civ 1613, [2009] All ER (D) 143 (Apr) and see article 'Beg, borrow or steal' by Edward Peters in New Law Journal, 13 March 2009, page 381. District judges are prepared to adjourn to ensure the protocol is properly followed: see feature in Sol Jo (2009) 8 September, page 2.			
The claimant is **not** likely to seek an order for **costs** but will prefer to rely on its contractual rights to costs. The CPR are believed to preserve the legal position as set out in *Gomba Holdings (UK) Ltd v Minories Finance Ltd (No 2)* [1993] Ch 171, [1992] 4 All ER 588, CA. See further *Marchmont Investments Ltd v BFO SA* [2006] EWHC 1990 (Ch), [2006] All ER (D) 49 (Jul) where an order was made for the borrower to pay the lender's costs in accordance with the terms of the mortgage deed: see also *Adamson v Halifax* [2002] EWCA Civ 1134, [2003] 4 All ER 423		48.3	
If the claim is not made out it will be dismissed			
3.6A Possession claims by a mortgagee against persons other than the mortgagor			
In *Cook v Mortgage Business plc and other cases* [2012] EWCA Civ 17 the Court of Appeal held that the rights of a mortgagee, who had advanced monies for the purchase of a property by the borrower from a vendor who on completion immediately rented it back prevailed on default of the mortgage payments over those of the vendor/tenant.			
Where private landlords have their property repossessed, their tenants are normally evicted with very little notice. The government has the intention to give such tenants 'an extra layer of protec-			

TAB 21 PROCEDURAL TABLES

	Form No	CPR Rule	PD
tion' under government plans: 'Lender Repossession of Residential Property: Protection of Tenants'.			
For the difficulties facing the mortgagee claiming possession against an occupier who is not a mortgagor, see article by Robin Powell entitled 'Repossession claims against third parties' Sol Jo, 17 June 2008, page 8 and the cases referred to in it.			
The **Mortgage Repossessions (Protection of Tenants) Act 2010** which was enacted on 8 April 2010 was brought into effect on 1 October 2010 together with the Dwelling Houses (Execution of Possession Orders by Mortgagees) Regulations 2010, SI 2010/1809. Limited protection is given to assured or Rent Act **tenants whose tenancy is not binding upon the lender.** The court will on the application of the tenant be able to stay or postpone the delivery of possession for up to 2 months from (it would appear) the date of the tenant's application provided that:	N244	55.10(4A)	
(a) this was not done at the time the possession order was made; and			
(b) the tenants has not asked the mortgagee (lender) to give an undertaking in writing not to enforce the order for two months and such an undertaking has not been given.			
The court has to have regard to the circumstances of the tenant and whether the tenant is in breach of his tenancy agreement and the reason for any breach. The court may make the suspension conditional upon payments being made to the lender during the period of suspension.			
The insertion of a new paragraph 4A in CPR 55.10 enables the unprotected tenant to make the application for suspension of the lender's order for possession.			
3.7 Directions			
If the court is satisfied the claim is genuinely disputed substantial grounds it is unlikely to dispose of it but then give case management directions including allocation		55.8(2)	
3.8 Sale of the property			
For the lender's general duty to take reasonable care to obtain the best reasonably available price, see *Michael v Miller* [2004] EWCA Civ 282, [2004] 2 P & CR D12, [2004] 2 EGLR 151 and article entitled 'Fair play' in (2009) Sol Jo 11 August, page 19 by Christopher Berry.			
Where the borrower relies on a prospective sale to avoid a 28 day possession order he will find useful authority in the decision in *Target Home Loans v Cloth-*			

	Form No	CPR Rule	PD
ier [1994] 1 All ER 439, CA and the statement of Nolan LJ: " . . . is there a prospect of an early sale? If so is it better in the interests of all that it be effected by the defendant and his wife or by the mortgage company?" He concluded an order for possession in 3 months was appropriate. In *Royal Trust of Canada v Markham* (1975) 1 WLR per Sir John Pennycuick 'likelihood' was said to be a question of fact to be determined by the judge on the evidence			
For a case where there was a sale to a closely connected company see *Bradford & Bingley plc v Ross* [2005] EWCA Civ 394, (2005) Times, 2 May			
For consideration of a bank's position when it is a mortgagee see *Francis v Barclays Bank plc* [2004] EWHC 2787 (Ch), [2004] 51 EG 88 (CS)			
For a case where the lender had mixed motives for exercising the power of sale see *Meretz Investments v ACP Ltd* (2006) Times, 27 April, CA and also see *Meretz Investment NV v ACP Ltd* (2008) Times, 2 January, CA where an attempt was made to pursue a cause of action in the tort of conspiracy. This failed, the lender's exercise of its power of sale was lawful and further there were no unlawful means employed			
The exercise of a power of sale after default by the borrower was held not to infringe the borrower's rights under art 1 of the First Protocol to the European Convention on Human Rights in *Horsham Properties Group Ltd v Clark and another (Secretary of State intervening)* [2008] EWHC 2327 (Ch), [2008] All ER (D) 58 (Oct), (2008) Times, 29 October			
For a case where the lender's security was extinguished under the provisions of the Limitation Act 1980 see *Ashe v National Westminster Bank plc* [2007] EWHC 494 (Ch), [2007] All ER (D) 227 (Mar). [2007] 2 P & CR 525. This was a case where the mortgage deed gave the lender an immediate right to possession which was not dependent on any default by the borrower or restricted by any term of the deed. Further, more than 12 years had elapsed since any payment had been made by the borrower. For useful discussions of this case see article 'Watching the Clock' by Sarah Greer, NLJ, 18 April 2008, page 548 and article 'Lenders beware – do not delay or you will pay', Sol Jo, 15 April 2008, page 12. Where a borrower sought to dispute the validity of a suspended possession order after 15 years the judge was held on			

TAB 21 PROCEDURAL TABLES

	Form No	CPR Rule	PD
appeal to have been correct in dismissing the application: *Abbey National plc v Miller* [2007] EWCA Civ 138, [2007] All ER (D) 118 (Feb)			
A lender (mortgagee) can sell the mortgaged property in the exercise of the power of sale contained in the mortgage deed and the statutory power of sale, with the effect of over-reaching the borrower's rights, without any court order. In *Horsham Properties Group Ltd v Clark* (see preceding paragraph) the lenders appointed a receiver who sold the property to the claimant who claimed possession from the defendant borrower who was in default of the mortgage covenants. It was held that s 36 of the Administration of Justice Act 1970 did not apply as its provisions only affect claims for possession by lenders and the claimant was not a lender. This procedure is common in buy-to-let mortgage enforcements. See articles in NLJ by Tony Poole, 2 and 9 January 2009 and by Sarah Greer, entitled 'Urgent Review' 20 February 2009; also by James Charles referred to at 3.1 of this TAB, fifth paragraph. It is to be noted that where the sale realised a sufficient sum to discharge the mortgage debt the mortgage ceased to subsist. A human rights defence also failed. The decision in *Ropaigealach v Barclays Bank plc* [2000] 1 QB 26 was followed.			
Statutory reform of the position has been prepared.			
An article by John Carter in (2012) Sol Jo, 18 September, page 18 entitled 'Acting for buyers of repossessed property' provides useful guidance for those acting for purchasers of such properties.			
3.9 Recovery of shortfall			
For the purposes of ss 8 and 20 of the Limitation Act the date at which a building society's right accrued to recover the shortfall from the borrowers after the sale of the security was the date when the borrowers defaulted in monthly instalment payments so that the right to recover the monies (ie the principal) accrued; s 20(1)(b) Limitation Act 1980. Mortgage deeds commonly provide the principal becomes due upon 2 months default in repayments; *West Bromwich Building Society v Wilkinson* [2005] UKHL 44, [2005] 4 All ER 97, [2005] 1 WLR 2303			
Section 29(5) of the Act provides that a fresh limitation period will arise from the date the debtor 'acknowledges the claim' but s 29(7) provides that once the limitation period has expired acknowledgement will not revive the debt. As to what amounts to an acknowledgement see *Bradford & Bingley plc v Rashid* [2006] UKHL 37, (2006) Times, 14 July,			

	Form No	CPR Rule	PD
HL and note the views expressed there of acknowledgements in without prejudice correspondence; and *Ashcroft v Bradford & Bingley plc* [2010] EWCA Civ 223 where monthly payments in reduction of mortgage shortfall debt (made during the period of primary limitation) would amount to a part payment and start time running afresh. See also article by Daniel Lewis 'Owning Up' Sol Jo, 23 November 2007, page 1484.			
Mortgage interest paid by the Benefit agency revived the limitation period as the agency was acting as the agent for the borrower within the statutory framework even though the borrower had no direct control over the agency: *Bradford & Bingley Building Society v Cutler* (2008) Times, 22 February, CA.			
3.10 Clearance of arrears and subsequent default			
If in mortgage possession proceedings where a suspended order for possession has been made the borrower clears the arrears but later again falls into arrears on a strict construction of the form of possession order and on the authority of *Greyhound Guarantee v Caulfield* [1981] CLY 1808 a claimant may simply apply for a warrant but it may be considered more appropriate to apply for permission to enforce the possession order or to start fresh proceedings based on the new default although this will give the borrower the opportunity to apply in good time for the opportunity to remedy the breach			
3.11 The effect of bankruptcy of the borrower			
If his interest in the home does not exceed £1,000 no sale may be ordered or charge imposed on the property			
If no charge is obtained or other action taken within 3 years the property reverts to the bankrupt			
If a charge is applied for and obtained or other action taken within 3 years any increase in value after that date will accrue to the bankrupt and not his estate			
For detailed discussion see article by Professor Gareth Miller [2006] NLJ, 31 March, p 535			
3.12 Where a charge has been imposed on a bankrupt's home an application by the trustee more than 12 years later is not statute barred: *Doodes v Gotham* [2006] EWCA Civ 1080, (2006) Times, 14 August, CA			
3.13 For the application of s 33A of the Insolvency Act 1986 on an application by a trustee under s 14 of the Trusts of Land and Appointment of Trustees Act 1996 see *Nicholls v Lan* [2006] EWHC 1255 (Ch), (2006) Times, 4 August, CA			

TAB 21 PROCEDURAL TABLES

	Form No	CPR Rule	PD
3A. Possession proceedings online by landlords and mortgagees			
3A1. Preliminary			
The ability to start certain possession cases under CPR 55 electronically by use of the 'Possession Cases Online' (PCOL) website is limited to 'specified county courts'. Where the claim has been so started further steps in the claim may be taken electronically. The claimant is required to have an address for service in the United Kingdom and the defendant has an address for service in England and Wales. The claimant must be able to provide a post code for the property.			55B, para 1.1
'PCOL website' means the website http://www.possessionclaim.gov.uk which may be accessed through the courts service website http://www.hmcourts-service.gov.uk			
'Specified court' means a county court specified on the PCOL website as one for which Possession Cases Online is available.			55B, para 1.2
As to payment of **fees and exemption** from payment of fees see			55B, para 4
Presently the fee on starting proceedings for the recovery of land in county court brought by PCOL is £100, ie a discount of £75 per claim			
As to '**statement of truth**' see CPR PD 55B para 8 in particular note any statement of case must be verified by a statement of truth and this applies to online claims, defences and application notices.			55B, para 8
As to **signature** note CPR PD para 9 that provides this may be a person entering his name on an online form.			55B, para 9
3A2. Claims which may be started using PCOL			
A claim under section 1 of part 55 which includes a claim for possession of residential property within the district of a specified court which is brought by:			
(a) a landlord against a tenant solely on the ground of arrears of rent (but not a claim for forfeiture of a lease) or			
(b) a mortgagee against a mortgagor solely on the ground of default in payment of sums due under a mortgage.			
The claim cannot seek any remedy, other than possession, except for arrears of rent or money due under a mortgage, interest and costs and each party must have an address for service in England and Wales.			55B, para 5.1(4)
Note:			
(i) the claimant must be able to specify the postcode of the property			55B, para 5.1(5)

		Form No	CPR Rule	PD
(ii)	a claim against a child or pro-tected person under PCOL			55B, para 5
3A3. Starting a claim using PCOL				
3A3.1 A claimant can start a claim by				
(a)	completing an online claim form at the PCOL website			
(b)	paying the issue fee electronically at the PCOL website or by other means approved by the court's ser-vice			
(c)	the particulars of claim **must be included in the online form** but it is not necessary to file a copy of the tenancy agreement, mortgage deed or agreement.			55B, paras 6.1 and 6.2
(d)	where the possession claim relates to residential property and relies on statutory ground or grounds the claimant must specify in section 4(a) of the online claim form the ground or grounds relied upon.			55B, para 6.2A
3A3.2 The particulars of claim must in-clude a **history of tenancy or mortgage account** in schedule form setting out the information required by PD 55B para 6.3(1) and (2) but if the claimant has provided the defendant with:				
(a)	the information required by MCOB (Mortgagees: Conduct of Business Rules) 13.4.1 and 11.4.4; or			
(b)	in schedule form the information required by PD 55B para 6.3A(2);			
the claimant instead of complying with PD 55B para 6.3 may include in the particulars of claim a **summary only** of the arrears containing the information re-quired by PD 55B para 6.3B(1)-(3).				
Note: MCOB provisions may be found at http://www.fsahandbook.info/FSA/html/handbook/MCOB/13				55B, paras 6.3A and 6.3B
3A3.3 Where the particulars of claim include a summary only (see above) the claimant must				
(a)	serve on the defendant not more than 7 days after issue a full, up to date history of arrears contain-ing at least the information re-quired by para 6.3 of PF 55B (see above) **and**			
(b)	either			
	(i)	make a witness statement confirming that he has com-plied with 6.3A(1) or (2) (see last preceding sub-para of this TAB) including and exhibiting the full arrears history or		
	(ii)	verify by way of oral evi-dence at the hearing that he has so complied and pro-		

TAB 21 PROCEDURAL TABLES

	Form No	CPR Rule	PD
duce and verify the full arrears history			55B, para 6.3C
Note:			
• CPR 55.8(4) requires all witness statements to be filed and served at least 2 days prior to the hearing		55.8(4)	
• for requirement of the claimant if history of arrears of more than 2 years is relied upon see			55B, para 6.4
• the claim shall be deemed to be served on the fifth day after the claim was issued whether or not that day is a business day			55B, para 6.5
• for date the claim is brought for purposes of Limitation Act 1980 see			55B, para 6.6
• for the action to be taken by the court on issue see			55B, para 6.7
3A4. Defence and counterclaim			
3A4.1 A defendant wishing to defend or make a counterclaim to a claim issued using PCOL may file a written defence or defend or make a counterclaim (to be filed with the defence) by			
(a) filing the relevant written form, or			
(b) completing the relevant online form at the PCOL website and, if the defendant is making a counterclaim, paying the appropriate fee electronically at the PCOL website or other approved means.			55B, para 7.1(1)
The defendant who completes the relevant online form must not send a hard copy to the court.			55B, para 7.2
Note:			
• as to effect of acknowledgement of receipt sent to the court by the defendant see			55B, para 7.3
• as to date of filing of the defence form and steps that will be taken by the court see			55B, paras 7.4 and 7.5
3A5. Communication with the court electronically			
When a claim is brought using PCOL the parties may communicate with the court messaging service electronically but the provisions of PD 55B, para 10 must be observed			55B, para 10
3A6. Electronic application			
Certain applications in relation to a possession claim started online may be made ('online applications'); the provisions of PD 55B, para 11 must be observed			55B, para 11
3A7. Viewing the case record			
There are facilities for the parties or their representatives to view the case record; for the provisions see			55B, para 14
4. Claims against trespassers			
4.1 Preliminary			

	Form No	CPR Rule	PD
A claim against trespassers is one for recovery of land which the claimant alleges is occupied only by a person or persons who entered or remained on the land without the consent of the person entitled to possession of the land			
It **does not include a claim against a tenant or sub-tenant** whether his tenancy has been terminated or not		55.1(b)	
In the case of *Bradford v James* [2008] EWCA Civ 837, 152 Sol Jo (no 30) 32 Mummery LJ observed 'calamitous neighbour disputes' should be made the subject of mediation because by the time neighbours get to court it is often too late for court-based ADR and mediation schemes to have much effect.			
Section 6(1) of the Criminal law Act 1977 prevents the physical eviction of trespassers (as opposed to preventing them re-entering if they have left the premises vacant) but sub-section 6(1) does not apply to 'a person who is a displaced residential occupier or a protected intending occupier of the premises in question . . .'.			
See further (2011) Sol Jo, 29 November, page 27 'Landlord and tenant update' by Tessa Shepperson and in particular that although a trespasser, who falls within the exception, commits a criminal offence by remaining in the property after being told to leave the position of the displaced occupier is fraught with difficulty. From 1 September 2012, however, see part 5 of this TAB below.			
Where the claimant does not know the name of a person in occupation or possession of the land the claim must be brought against **"persons unknown"** in additions to any named defendant		55.3(4)	
The claim form must be in the form annexed to the Practice Direction	N5	55.3(5)	
This table does not deal with applications for **"interim possession orders"**. These were introduced by the Criminal Justice and Public Order Act 1994 (ss 75–76) and are dealt with under CPR 55, Section III. See **TAB 24**			
Although the defendant (in a claim for possession against trespassers) is not required to file a defence, a form of defence should be served with the claim form so he can do so if he wishes: see CPR 55.3[3], ante		55.7(2) 55.3(5)	
A possession order by reference to an anticipated trespass can only be made in exceptional circumstances: *Secretary of State for the Environment, Food and Rural Affairs v Drury* [2004] EWCA Civ 200, (2004) Times, 15 March			
The Court of Appeal in *Secretary of State for Environment, Food and Ru-*			

TAB 21   PROCEDURAL TABLES

	Form No	CPR Rule	PD
ral Affairs v Meier [2009] UKSC 11, [2009] 1 WLR 2780, [2009] 49 EG 70 (CS) held that possession orders can only be made in respect of a plot of land occupied by the defendant and not in respect of separate plots not occupied. It did uphold injunctions preventing the defendant occupying these plots. The case of *Drury* above was relied on by the unsuccessful claimant but rejected as incorrect. For discussion see (2009) NLJ 8 December, page 4.			
Where a landowner is seeking damages for temporary trespass see *Sinclair v Gavaghan* [2007] EWHC 2256 (Ch). The approach of the court in such cases is to assess what payment would have been arrived at between the parties for the temporary use of he claimant's land. The court will invariably grant an injunction requiring the defendant to stop trespassing			
In *JA Pye (Oxford) Ltd v United Kingdom (Application No 44302/02)* (2007) 23 BHRC 405 it was held that Art 1, 1st protocol of the ECHR (right to peaceful enjoyment) was not infringed by domestic law enabling a squatter to obtain title by 12 years' adverse possession. Note, however, the new system for acquiring registered land by adverse possession is set out in Sch 6 to the Registered Land Act 2002, which does not have retrospective effect, which gives the squatter the right to apply for registration after 10 years' adverse possession but on notice to the registered owner who then has 2 years to regularise the position: see *Baxter v Mannion* [2011] EWCA Civ 120, [2011] All ER (D) 235 (Feb).			
4.2 Start of proceedings and particular of claim			
In addition to the general requirements (see 1.3 and 1.4, above) the particulars of claim must state the claimant's interest in the land or the basis of his rights to claim possession and the circumstances it has been occupied without his licence or consent	N121		55A, para 2.6
4.3 The hearing date			
See 1.5 above and the court's power to extend or shorten time		3.1(2)(a)	55A, para 3.2
4.4 The defendant's response			
An acknowledgment of service is not required and the defendant need not file a defence. Form N11 should be used if a defence is filed	N11	55.7(1) and (2)	
4.5 Service			
Where a possession claim against trespassers the claim has been issued against persons unknown:		55.6	
(a) the claim form			
(b) the particulars of claim and			

	Form No	CPR Rule	PD
(c)　　any witness statements			
must be served by:			
(a)　　attaching them to the main door or some other part of the land so that they are clearly visible and if practicable, inserting copies in a transparent envelope addressed to "the occupiers" through the letter box, or			
(b)　　placing stakes on the land in places where they are clearly visible and attaching them in a transparent envelope addressed to "the occupiers"			
The transparent envelopes and the stakes will have to be supplied by the claimant			55A, para 4.1
In *Sunset Street Properties Ltd v Persons Unknown* [2011] EWHC 3432 (Ch), [2011] All ER (D) 72 (Dec), a case involving the accelerated possession procedure, it was held that the form of service specified in CPR 55.6 or by the court was not the only form of service that would be good service although the notice given was found to be inadequate: see article by Siobhan Jones entitled 'Make yourself at home?' in (2012) NLJ, 10 February, page 207. Permission to appeal was granted but the case settled before the appeal hearing.			
See below under 4.6 as to shortening the time for service			
4.6 The hearing			
All witness statements on which the claimant relies must have been filed and served with the claim form		55.8(5)	
The time periods for service may be shortened, particularly where there have been assaults, threats or damage			55A, paras 3.1 and 3.2
Where the claimant effected service he must produce at the hearing a certificate of service		55.8(6)	
At the hearing the court may decide the case or give case management directions			
The court does not have power under s 89 Housing Act 1980 nor under any other provision in that Act to give trespassers time to vacate: *Boyland and Son Ltd v Rand* [2007] EWCA Civ 1860, (2007) Times, 18 January			
4.7 Enforcement			
A judgment or order of a county court for possession of land made in a possession claim against trespassers may be enforced in the High Court or county court: High Court and County Courts Jurisdiction (Amendment No 2) Order 2001			
4.8 Liability for injury suffered by a trespasser			
See the judgment of the House of Lords in *Tomlinson v Congleton Bor-*			

TAB 21 PROCEDURAL TABLES

	Form No	CPR Rule	PD
ough Council [2003] UKHL 47, [2004] 1 AC 46, [2003] 3 All ER 1122 where the claimant was willingly running an obvious risk.			
5. The Legal Aid, Sentencing and Punishment of Offenders Act 2012 became law on 1 May 2012 and its scope is not limited by a requirement that an existing occupier has been displaced. It is to be particularly noted that squatting in commercial property has not been criminalised.			
The Act came into force (as to this provision) on 1 September 2012 and people squatting in residential premises without the owner's permission commit a criminal offence. See further an article by Lucy McCormick entitled 'Enforcing the new squatting offence' in (2012) Sol Jo, 18 September, page 11 and an article entitled 'Your place or mine?' by Mark Tempest in (2012) NLJ, 28 September, page 1209. The maximum sentence is 6 months imprisonment and/or a £5,000 fine.			

TABLE 22—ACCELERATED POSSESSION PROCEDURE – HOUSING ACT 1988 S 21

TAB 22

		Form No	CPR Rule	PD
1. Availability				
(a)	The claimant may bring a possession claim under this section of this Part where:			
	(i) the claim is brought under s 21 of the 1988 Act to recover possession of residential property let under an assured shorthold tenancy (an AST), and			
	(ii) all the conditions listed in CPR 55.12 are satisfied			
(b)	The claim must be started in the county court for the district in which the property is situated			
(c)	The claim must be brought by the landlord and not, for example, by the landlord's letting agent: *Chester Accommodation Agency Ltd v Abebrese* (1997) Times, 28 July, CA		55.11	
For notes for claimant in an accelerated possession claims see		N5C		
2. Conditions in CPR 55.12				
(a)	the tenancy and any agreement for the tenancy were entered into on or after 15 January 1989			
(b)	the only purpose is to recover possession and no other claim is made			
(c)	the tenancy did not immediately follow an assured tenancy which was not an assured shorthold tenancy			
(d)	the tenancy fulfilled the conditions provided by ss 19A or 20(1)(a) to (c) of the 1988 Act			
(e)	the tenancy:			
	(i) was the subject of a written agreement			
	(ii) arises by virtue of s 5 of the 1988 Act but follows a tenancy that was the subject of a written agreement, or			
	(iii) relates to the same or substantially the same property let to the same tenant and on the same terms (though not necessarily as to rent or duration) as a tenancy which was the subject of a written agreement, and			

TAB 22 PROCEDURAL TABLES

	Form No	CPR Rule	PD
(f) a notice in accordance with ss 21(1), terminating an AST on the expiry of a fixed term, or 21(4), terminating a periodic AST was given to the tenant in writing			
The **notice under s 21(1)** must be in writing and give to the tenant not less than two months notice that the landlord requires possession of the house. It may be given at any time during the currency of the tenancy including the last day or more frequently at the beginning of the tenancy. It is not necessary to specify a date for possession but a notice that contains one is not invalidated. Possession cannot be sought before the expiration of the 6 month period: *Lower Street Properties v Jones* [1996] HLR 877, CA, but see criticism in (2010) Sol Jo, 16 November, article by Peter Glover. The landlord cannot serve a notice if he has not complied with the Tenancy Deposit Scheme			
The **s 21(4) notice** must be in writing and specify a date after which possession is required. The date specified must be in the last day of a period of the tenancy and be not earlier than 2 months after the date the notice was given. As to 'the last day of a period of a tenancy' see *Fernandez v McDonald* [2003] EWCA Civ 1219, [2003] 4 All ER 1033. However the decision in *Lower Street Properties Ltd v Jones* (see above, immediately preceding paragraph) remains good law (see *Notting Hill Housing Trust v Roomus*, below) so that a formula for ascertaining the date can be used to ensure if the date is wrong the landlord will be entitled to possession. An appropriate formula is 'this notice will expire at the end of the period of your tenancy that will end next after the expiry of 2 months from the service of this notice upon you'. The Court of Appeal in the case of *Bradford Community Housing Ltd v Hussain and Kauser* [2009] EWCA Civ 763 held a notice containing both a date and a 'catch-all' provision was just as good at law as a notice properly calculated in accordance with the provisions of the tenancy. For detailed discussion see article 'Terminating assured shorthold tenancies' New Law Journal 13 October 2006, page 2001, by Andrew Williams and an article by Michael Walsh in (2008) NLJ, 24 October, page 1482 entitled 'Section 21 or bust'. The use of such a clause, however, will not assist the claimant who issues the claim before the notice has, as a matter of law, expired			
It must always be remembered that if the first day of the period is on, say, the 14th, the period will expire one day before that date, ie on the 13th			

	Form No	CPR Rule	PD
See *Notting Hill Housing Trust v Roomus* [2006] EWCA Civ 407, [2006] All ER (D) 432 (Mar), [2007] HLR 2 where it was held that 'at the end of the tenancy' means 'after the end of the tenancy' so that the s 21 notice was valid			
See also *Church Commissioners v Meya* [2006] EWCA Civ 821, [2006] All ER (D) 234 (Jun) where the importance of when rent was last payable under the fixed term, in establishing the periods of the periodic tenancy, was confirmed by the court			
Note			
• As to condition (d) section 19A relates to tenancies entered into on or after 28 February 1997 and section 20(1)(a)–(c) to those assured tenancies not within s 19A (because they were entered into before 28 February 1997)			
• If the tenancy is a demoted short-hold tenancy only the conditions in 1(b) and 1(f) need to be satisfied			
• Arrears of rent cannot be claimed in accelerated possession proceedings		55.12(1)(b)	
3. The claim form			
(a) must be in the form set out in the relevant Practice Direction, and			
(b) (i) must contain such information and			
(ii) must be accompanied by such documents as are required by that form			
All relevant sections of the form must be completed. The form is such that if correctly completed all the requirements of CPR 55.12 will be addressed			
The court will serve the claim form by first class post or an alternative service which provides for delivery the next working day	N5B (as amended 1 October 2011)	55.13	
It should particularly be noted that section 7B of form N5B sets out requirements as to the multiple occupancy lettings and as to any deposit taken and calls for evidence that those requirements have been satisfied.			
4. The defence			
Any defence should be in the form set out in the Practice Direction	N11B (as amended 1 October 2011)	55.14	
Where the assured tenancy was granted to the tenant as part of a 'sell to rent back' arrangement where the tenant had entered into the arrangement to avoid a possession order in favour of lenders, the availability of a defence of proprietary			

TAB 22 PROCEDURAL TABLES

	Form No	CPR Rule	PD
estoppel should be considered: see article by Rawdon Crozier in (2009) Gazette, 14 May, page 27.			
A defendant must file his defence within 14 days after service of the claim form if he wishes:			
(a) to oppose the claim			
(b) seek a postponement of possession in accordance with CPR 55.18			
On receipt of the defence the court will:			
(a) send a copy to the claimant, and			
(b) refer the claim and defence to a judge		55.15(1)	
Where the period for filing a defence has expired and no defence has been filed:		55.15(2)	
(a) the claimant may file a written request for an order for possession, and		55.15(3)	
(b) the court will refer that request to a judge			
If the defence is out of time but received before the landlord's written request is received the court may still consider the defence			
5. Consideration of the claim			
After considering the claim and any defence, the judge will:		55.16	
(a) make an **order for possession without a hearing**	N26A	55.17	
(b) where he is not satisfied as to service of the claim form or that the claimant has established his right to possession under s 21 of the Housing Act 1985 the judge will:		55.16(1)(b)	
(i) direct that a date be **fixed for a hearing**, and			
(ii) give any appropriate case management directions, or		55.16(1)(c)	
(c) **strike out the claim** if the claim form discloses no reasonable grounds for bringing the claim			
The court will give all parties not less than 14 days' notice of a hearing		55.16(3)	
Where a claim is struck out:			
(a) the court will serve its reasons for striking out the claim with the order, and			
(b) the claimant may apply to restore the claim within 28 days after the date the order was served on him		55.16(4)	
6. Postponement of possession		55.18	
Where the defendant seeks postponement of possession on the ground of **exceptional hardship** under s 89 of the Housing Act 1980, the judge may direct a hearing of that issue		55.18(1)	
Where the judge directs a hearing:			

	Form No	CPR Rule	PD
(a) the hearing must be held before the date of which possession is to be given up, and			
(b) the judge will direct how many days' notice the parties must be given of that hearing		55.18(2)	
Where the judge is satisfied on a hearing directed that exceptional hardship would be caused by requiring possession to be given up by that date in the order of possession, he may vary the date on which possession must be given up		55.18(3)	
In a claim in which the judge is satisfied that the defendant has shown exceptional hardship, he will only postpone possession without directing a hearing under CPR 55.18(1) if:			55A, para 8.1
(a) he considers that possession should be given up 6 weeks after the date of the order or, if the defendant has requested postponement to an earlier date, on that date, and			
(b) the claimant indicated on his claim form that he would be content for the court to make such an order without a hearing			
In all other cases if the defendant seeks a postponement of possession under s 89 of the Housing Act 1980, the judge will direct a hearing under CPR 55.18(1)			
If at that hearing, the judge is satisfied that exception hardship would be caused by requiring possession to be given up by the date in the order possession, he may vary that order under CPR 55.18(3) so that possession is to be given up at a later date			
That later date may be no later than 6 weeks after the making of the order for possession on the papers (see s 89 of the Housing Act 1980)			
6A. Article 8 and squatters			
The defence by the occupants, who were squatters, that they enjoyed the protection of Article 8 as to eviction was raised in *Malik v Persons Unknown, Reynolds and Matthews* in the Central London Court on 17 July 2012 and is considered by Lucy McCormick in her article in Sol Jo Property Focus for December 2012 page 23.			
HHJ Walden-Smith found that 'as the court is a public authority and the land is being occupied as a home, Art 8 is capable of application even though the landowner is a private individual and the occupiers are trespassers'.			
Both parties have been given permission to appeal (the judge found that the making of a possession order would not be disproportionate and the appeal is expected to be heard early in 2013.			

TAB 22 PROCEDURAL TABLES

	Form No	CPR Rule	PD
It can be said that it would take exceptional facts to enable the adverse occupiers to succeed.			
7. Setting aside or varying		55.19	
The court may:			
(a) on application by a party within 14 days of service of the order, or			
(b) of its own initiative, **set aside or vary any order made** under CPR 55.17			

TABLE 23—INTERIM POSSESSION ORDERS – RECOVERY OF POSSESSION OF LAND FROM TRESPASSERS

TAB 23

	Form No	CPR Rule	PD
1. Preliminary			
1.1 An interim possession order (IPO) is one made under rules of court for the bringing of summary proceedings for possession of premises which are occupied by trespassers; s 75 (4) of the Criminal Justice and Public Order Act 1994 (the 1994 Act)			
1.2 A person who is **present on premises as a trespasser at any time during the currency of an IPO** commits an offence unless:			
(a) he leaves the premises within 24 hours of the time of service of the IPO and does not return or			
(b) a copy of the order was not fixed to the premises in accordance with rules of the court; s76(2) and (3) of the 1994 Act			
1.3 A person who leaves the premises after service of the IPO commits an offence if he **re-enters or tries to re-enter within the period of one year** beginning with the date of service of the IPO s 76(4) of the 1994 Act			
Notes			
• The claim must be started in the county court in which the land is situated unless there are circumstances which justify starting the claim in the High Court see TAB 22 paras 1.2 and 1.3			
• Where claimant does not know the name of a person in occupation the claim must be brought against person unknown see TAB 22 para 4.1			
• For full text of ss 75 and 76 see CPR 55.20[2] and 55.20[3]			
• A constable in uniform may arrest without warrant any person is or whom he reasonable suspects to be, guilty of an offence under s76			
• The offences are **criminal offences**			
• For the penalties see s75(3) and 76(5) of the 1994 Act			
2. Conditions for use			
2.1 An application for an IPO can be made if:			

TAB 23   PROCEDURAL TABLES

		Form No	CPR Rule	PD
(a)	the only claim is against trespassers for recovery of possession of premises			
(b)	the claimant has an immediate right to possession and has had such a right throughout the period of alleged unlawful occupation, and			
(c)	the claim is made within 28 days of the date the claimant first knew or ought to have known that the defendant (or one of them) was in occupation			
(d)	the defendant did not enter the premises or remain on them with the consent of a person who, at the time the consent was given, had an immediate right to possession			
Note • **premises** means a building, a self-contained part of a building or the land ancillary to it			55.21	
3.The application and its issue				
3.1 The claimant must file:				
(a)	claim form in specified form	N5		
(b)	application in specified form	N130	55.22(2)	55A, para 9.1
(c)	written evidence		55.22(3)	55A, para 9.2
Note • **the written evidence must be by the applicant** or if the applicant is a body corporate a duly authorised officer • a statement of truth by the maker is necessary • it must be stated in the claim form whether Section III and IV of the Practice Direction (Pre-action Conduct) or any relevant protocol have been complied with			55.22(4)	Pre-action Conduct, para 9.7
3.2 The court will issue the claim form and the application and set a hearing date after the hearing of the application. This will be as soon as practicable but **not less than 3 days after the application.**			55.22(5)	
4. Undertakings				
The claimant on issue will have set out the undertakings he gives in support of his application. These will be considered by the court on the hearing.			55.25(1)	
These undertakings are set out in CPR 55.25(1) (a) and (b) and are for the benefit of the defendant against whom the claim does not succeed				
5. Service				
5.1 Within **24 hours of issue** the claimant must serve on the defendant:				
(a)	the claim form			

	Form No	CPR Rule	PD
(b) the application form with evidence in support			
(c) a blank form of defendant's witness statement		55.23(1)	
5.2 Service must be served in accordance with CPR 55.6(a) see TAB 22 para 4.5. However the Court in *Sun Street Properties Ltd v Persons Unknown* [2011] EWHC 3432 (Ch), (2012) Times, 16 January held that the form of service required for possession claims involving the accelerated procedure against trespassers was not limited to that specified in rule 55.6, although it found the notice that had been given to be grossly inadequate.		55.23(2)	
5.3 At or before the hearing the claimant must file a certificate of service of the documents set out in 5.1 above		55.23(3)	
6. Defendant's response			
The defendant can at any time before the hearing file a witness statement in response to the application	N133		55A, para 9.2
7. The hearing of the application			
7.1 The court will **make an IPO** if	N134		55A, para 9.2
(a) the claimant has –			
(i) filed a certificate of service (para 5.3)			
(ii) proved service to the satisfaction of the court and			
(b) (i) the conditions set out in r 55.21(1) are satisfied (see para 2.1 above) and			
(ii) any undertakings given by the claimant as a condition of making the order are adequate		55.25(2)	
Note			
The IPO will require the defendant to vacate the premises specified in the claim form within 24 hours of service	N134	55.25(3)	
7.2 On making the IPO the court will **set a date for the hearing of the claim for possession** which will be not less than 7 days after the date the IPO was made		55.25(4)	
7.3 When the court **does not make an IPO** the court will			
(a) set a date for the hearing of the claim			
(b) give directions for the future conduct of the claim and			
(c) subject to such directions the claim shall proceed in accordance with Section II of CPR 55 (see TAB 22 para 4)		55.25(5)	
8. Service of the IPO			

TAB 23 PROCEDURAL TABLES

	Form No	CPR Rule	PD
8.1 Within 48 hours after it is sealed the claimant must serve the IPO with copies of the claim form and the written evidence in support. Service must be effected in accordance with CPR 55.6(a) (see TAB 22 para 4.5)		55.26(1) and (2) 55.26(3)	
8.2 If not served in accordance within the 48 hour time limit, the claimant can apply to the court for directions for the claim for possession to continue under Section I of Part 55		55.26(4)	
9. Application to set aside the IPO			
9.1 If the defendant has left the premises he may apply on grounds of urgency for the IPO to be set aside before the date of the hearing of the claim. The application must be supported by a witness statement		55.28(1) and (2)	
9.2 The court will give directions as to service and hearing of the application		55.28(3)	
9.3 The application to set aside will thereafter be dealt with by the court in accordance with CPR 55.28 (4) –(6)		55.28(4)–(6)	
9.4 Where notice of the application to set aside is ordered to be given the court may treat the hearing of the application to set aside as the hearing of the claim		55.28(7)	
10. The hearing of the claim			
10.1 Before the hearing the claimant must file a certificate of service of the documents specified in CPR 55.26(2)		55.27(1)	
10.2 The IPO will expire on the date of the hearing		55.27(2)	
10.3 At the hearing the court can make any order it considers appropriate, in particular may (a) make a final order for possession (b) dismiss the application for possession (c) give direction for the claim to continue under CPR 55 section I (d) enforce any of the claimants' undertakings		55.27(3)	
Note • the claimant must serve any order or directions unless the court otherwise orders		55.27(4)	
• a warrant for possession (see TAB 35 may be issued at any time after the making of the order for possession to enforce the order see CCR Ord 24 r6			
• the warrant for possession will be executed by the bailiff (county court) or the sheriff (High Court) contrast the IPO which is enforced as a criminal offence by the police			

TABLE 24—ANTI-SOCIAL BEHAVIOUR ORDERS UNDER THE CRIME AND DISORDER ACT 1998

TAB 24

	Form No	CPR Rule	PD
1. Preliminary			
1.1 The insertion made by the Police Reform Act 2002 in the Crime and Disorder Act 1998 enables applications for an **anti-social behaviour order** (ASBO) to be made in the county court. Previously jurisdiction to make such orders was conferred only on magistrates courts		65.21(1)	
1.2 The amendments came into force on 1 April 2003 and further amendments have been made by the Anti-Social Behaviour Act 2003.			
1.3 Amendments made to Part 65 in relation to gang-related violence in respect of persons aged 14 to 17 came into force on 9 January 2012 (not the subject of this TAB).			
1.4 Applications to the court for anti-social behaviour orders can only be made by **relevant authorities** and are made pursuant to s 1B of the 1998 Act. Applications for interim orders are made pursuant to s 1D.			
A district judge has jurisdiction to make an order under s 1B or s 1D of the Crime and Disorder Act 1998 (anti-social behaviour)			65, para 8.1A
Note that a **freestanding application** cannot be made (s 1B(1)) and there must be principal proceedings in existence to which the person against whom the order is sought is a party or is joined as a party (freestanding applications would have to be made in the Magistrates' Court)			
Note A relevant authority cannot seek an anti-social behaviour order on behalf of individuals: *Dalichi UK Ltd v Stop Huntington Animal Cruelty* (2003) Times, 22 October and for a precedent of particulars of claim where the individuals are second claimants and the first claimants claim under the Protection from Harassment Act 1997 see **BCCP L[907]**		65.21(1)	
Note			
In *W v DPP* [2005 EWCA Civ 1333, (2005) Times, 20 June it was held that a clause in an anti-social behaviour order prohibiting the defendant from 'committing any criminal offence' was too wide and accordingly unenforceable			
In *R (Stanley) v Metropolitan Police Comr* [2004] EWHC 229 (Admin),			

TAB 24 PROCEDURAL TABLES

	Form No	CPR Rule	PD
(2004) Times, 22 October it was held publicity was necessary for an anti-social behaviour order to operate and that photographs, names and at least partial addresses were a necessary part of such publicity			
Further in *R (on the application of Lonergan) v Lewes Crown Court* [2005] EWHC 457 (Admin), [2005] 2 All ER 362 it was held that the inclusion of a curfew term in an anti-social behaviour order was not legally objectionable as it was prohibitory in nature and necessary for prevention and protection			
In *Hewlett v Holding* (2006) Times, 8 February it was held that secret surveillance can be harassment. It would seem likely it would also be considered anti-social behaviour			
In *Conn v Sunderland City Council* (2007) Times, 23 November, CA, (2007) NLJ, 16 November, page 1613 (a claim under the Protection from Harassment Act 1997) the court indicated that the boundary between unattractive and unreasonable conduct and oppressive and unacceptable conduct is whether the conduct was of such gravity as to justify the sanction of criminal law			
In *R v Gowan* [2007] EWCA Crim 1360 the court held an ASBO could not be used to protect a wife with whom the offender had been living and in future would be cohabiting as she lived in the same household as him			
Note There is inevitably overlap with the power to grant an anti-social behaviour injunction (ASBI) under Housing Act 1996 s 153A			
In most cases a local authority should seek to restrain anti-social behaviour by use of its powers under the 1998 Act (ASBO) rather than under s 222(1)(a) of the Local Government Act 1972 by way of injunction: *Birmingham City Council v Shafi* [2008] EWCA Civ 1186, [2009] 3 All ER 127.			
2. Definitions			
'the 1998 Act' means the Crime and Disorder Act 1998		65.21(2)(a)	
'relevant authority' means:			
(a) the council for the local government area			
(aa) in relation to England, a county council			
(b) the chief officer of any police force maintained for a police area			
(c) the chief constable of the British Transport Police Force			
(d) any person registered under section 1 of the Housing Act 1996 as a social landlord who pro-			

	Form No	CPR Rule	PD
vides or manages any houses or hostels in a local government area or			
(e) a housing action trust established by order in pursuance of s 62 of the Housing Act 1988		65.21(2)(b)	
There is a power to add other bodies by statutory instrument			
'the principal proceedings' means any proceedings in a county court		65.21(2)(c)	
'relevant persons' see s1(1B) of the 1998 Act			
Note			
• **premises** means a building, a self-contained part of a building or the land ancillary to it		55.21	
3. Conditions to be established for grant of an Anti-Social Behaviour Order			
3.1 The following conditions have to be fulfilled by virtue of s1 of the 1998 Act with respect to a person aged 10 or over:			
(a) that person has acted, since 1 April 1999, in an anti-social manner, that is in a manner that caused or was likely to cause harassment, alarm or distress to one or more persons not of the same household as himself and			
(b) that such an order is necessary to protect relevant persons from further anti-social acts			
3.2 The application for an order must be accompanied by **written evidence** that must **include evidence** that the **consultation requirement** of s 1E of the 1998 Act has been complied with. There are different requirements for councils and for local authorities (s 1E(2)), the police (s 1E(3)) and other relevant authorities (s 1E(4)); see **III ANSB [15]** and *McC v Wigan Metropolitan Borough Council* [2004] Legal Action, 31 January. A consultation certificate duly signed will be sufficient evidence of compliance		65.25	
3.3 An order can be sought in the county court only against an adult. In courts within a pilot scheme that commenced on 1 October 2004 and operated until 30 September 2006 applications could be made to join a child in existing proceedings and if the child was joined an order under s 1B(4) could be made against him. The scheme was not extended.			
3.4 The court must ignore any behaviour prior to 1 April 1999 and any act which the defendant shows was reasonable in the circumstances: s 1(5) of the 1998 Act.			
3.5 Evidence of anti-social behaviour after the making of the application is			

TAB 24   PROCEDURAL TABLES

	Form No	CPR Rule	PD
admissible: *Birmingham City Council v Dixon* [2009] EWHC 7612 (Admin), (2009) Times, 13 April, Div Ct.			
4. Application where the relevant authority is party to the principal proceedings (Crime and Disorder Act 1998, s 1B(2))			
4.1 Where the relevant authority is the claimant in the principal proceedings and considers that another party to the proceedings is a person against whom an application for an ASBO could reasonably be made, the application must be made in the claim form		65.22(1)(a)	
4.2 Where the relevant authority is a defendant in the principal proceedings the application must be made by application notice (Part 23) filed with the defence		65.22(1)(b)	
4.3 Where the circumstances that lead to the application only becoming known after filing the claim form or the defence the application must be made by application notice issued as soon as possible.		65.22(2)	
4.4 The application made by application notice must normally be on notice to the person against whom the order is sought		65.22(3)	
5. Application by relevant authority to join a party in the principal proceedings (Crime and Disorder Act 1998, s 1B(3A) and (3B)			
5.1 Such an application under 1B(3B) of the 1998 Act by a relevant authority who is a party in the principal proceedings and considers the person's anti-social acts are material in he principal proceedings must be made -			
(a) in accordance with Section 1 of CPR 19		19.4	
(b) in the same application notice as the application for an order under 1B(4) of the 1998 Act (an anti-social behaviour order) and			
(c) as soon as possible after the relevant authority considers the criteria for making the anti-social behaviour order are met	N244	65.23(1)	
5.2 The application notice must contain -			
(a) the relevant authority's reasons for claiming that the person's anti-social behaviour acts are material in relation to the principal proceedings and			
(b) the details of the anti-social acts alleged		65.23(2)	
5.3 The application should normally be made on notice to the person against whom the order is sought		65.23(3)	

	Form No	CPR Rule	PD
5.4 A person must not be joined unless his anti-social acts are material to the principal proceedings: s 1B(3C)			
6. Applications where the relevant authority is not a party in the principal proceedings (Crime and Disorder Act 1998, s 1B(3))			
6.1 An application to be made a party by a relevant authority, that considers it would be reasonable to apply for an ASBO against a person who is a party, may be made in accordance with Part 19 and the application for an anti-social behaviour order must be made in the same proceedings	N244	65.24(1)	
6.2 The application must be made as soon as possible after the authority became aware of the principal proceedings and should normally be made on notice to the person against whom the order is sought		65.24(2)	
6.3 An application by a relevant authority to join a person to the principal proceedings may only be made against a person aged 18 or over			65, para 13.2
7. Procedure for claims			
(see paras 4, 5 and 6 above)			
7.1 The application will be by claim form or, if the case falls within para 5 or para 6 above, by application notice			
7.1A Unless the nature of the principal proceedings requires those proceedings to start in another court, it is appropriate to commence proceedings in the defendant's home court			
7.2 The application for an order under s 1B(4) of the 1998 Act must be supported by written evidence which must include that s 1E of the 1998 Act (that is the consultancy requirements) has been complied with. The evidence must be verified by a statement of truth		65.25	
7.3 A hearing date will be given on issue and the court will prepare notices of the hearing for all parties			
7.4 The defendant must be served with the application, the notice of the hearing and a copy of the witness statement not less than 3 clear days before the hearing and because of the serious nature of the application personal service should be effected			
7A. Application for an Interim Order (Crime and Disorder Act 1998, s 1D)			
7A.1 Such an application must be made in accordance with CPR Part 25			
7A.2 The application should normally be made in the claim for or application notice seeking the order and on notice to the person against whom the order is sought		65.26	

TAB 24 PROCEDURAL TABLES

	Form No	CPR Rule	PD
Note *R (on the application of M) v Lord Chancellor* [2004] EWCA Civ 312, [2004] 2 All ER 531, (2004) Times, 31 March where it was held that an interim anti-social behaviour order made without notice when necessary for a limited period did not contravene the right to a fair trial under Art 6 of European Convention on Human Rights. The order is not effective until served personally and the fact that the defendant could apply for review or discharge and further that the order would contain provision for a return date or a date fixed for hearing the full application made it impossible to say it affected human rights. See also *R (on the application of Stanley, Marshall and Kelly) v Metropolitan Police Comr* [2004] EWHC 2229 (Admin), 168 JP 623			
7A.3 The order must be for a fixed period and, if still in force, end with the determination of the main application (s 1D(4) of the 1998 Act)			
7A.4 The comments of the Court of Appeal in *Moat Housing Group South Ltd v Harris* [2005] EWCA Civ 287, [2005] 2 FLR 551 give guidance and a clear call for caution when dealing with applications that were not on notice and were of an intrusive nature. Without notice applications should be made only in wholly exceptional circumstances			
8. The hearing and the order made			
8.1 The court must be satisfied that the defendant acted in an anti-social manner (see the notes to para 1 and para 3.1 of this table). The court must be satisfied to a criminal standard although not necessarily that the acts were done with intent to cause harassment alarm or distress: *R (on the application of McCann) v Crown Court at Manchester* [2002] UKHL 39, [2003] 1 AC 787, [2002] 4 All ER 593. See also **III ANSB [13.4]** for further discussion but note that the civil standard of proof has been held to be appropriate to injunction applications under s 3 of the Harassment Act 1997: *Jones v Hipgrave* [2004] EWHC 2901 (QB), (2005) Times, 11 January, albeit a different view was expressed in *Birmingham City Council v Shafti* (see this TAB, 1, preliminary to the final paragraph) by a majority of the Court of Appeal in respect of an application for an injunction under s 222(1)(a) of the Local Government Act 1972.			
8.2 The civil rules of evidence apply and note May LJ's judgment in *R (on the application of Cleary) v Highbury Corner Magistrates' Court* [2006] EWHC 1869 (Admin), [2007] 1 All ER 270. Although this is a decision of the Divisional Court it is likely to be relevant in any proceedings where anti-social behav-			

	Form No	CPR Rule	PD
iour is the basis of the claim and the evidence relied on to prove the behaviour is, in whole or in part, anonymous hearsay evidence. The judgment cautioned the courts as to the weight to be given to such evidence and stressed the value of credible direct evidence. See further [2007] NLJ 22 June 'Fighting Back', an article by Chris Cuddihee, and the response to it by Robin Denford in [2007] NLJ 17 August, page 1184 where reference is made to *Solon South West Housing Association v James* [2004] EWCA Civ 1847, [2004] All ER (D) 328 (Dec)			
8.3 An anti-social behaviour order shall have effect for a period (not less than 2 years) specified in the order or until further order; s 1B(7) of the 1998 Act The terms of the order must be pronounced in open court and a written order must accurately set out the order pronounced			
8.4 Except with the consent of the parties no anti-social behaviour order shall be discharged before the end of the period of 2 years beginning with the date of service of the order s 1B(6) of the 1998 Act. A person for whose benefit an ASBO has been obtained cannot waive it, in this case by inviting the defendant into the house, because the order was also for the benefit of others: *Anthony Lee v Accent Foundation Ltd* [2007] 151 Sol Jo LB 806			
8.5 Subject to the last provision (no discharge for 2 years unless by consent of parties) the applicant or defendant may apply for the anti-social behaviour order to be varied or discharged by s 1B(5) of the 1998 Act An application to extend the order for less than 2 years can only be appropriate if it is the applicant's case that it is not necessary to have a further period as long as the minimum period of 2 years: *Leeds City Council v RG* [2007] EWHC 1612 (Admin), [2007] All ER (D) 114 (Jul), (2007) Times, 11 September, QB, Div Ct			
8.6 A modified form of **Penal Notice** must be endorsed on the order made warning the defendant that any breach of the terms of the order will be a criminal offence. The order must be clear and specific in its terms and be both necessary and proportionate			
8.7 Careful drafting of the order is essential as to the terms of the prohibition, duration and the definition of any specified area. Consideration should be given to attaching a plan showing any area specified			
8.8 An example of an anti-social behaviour order being too wide to be enforced is provided by *W v DPP* [2005] EWCA			

TAB 24 PROCEDURAL TABLES

	Form No	CPR Rule	PD
Civ 1333, (2005) Times, 20 June, Div Ct; the ban was against "committing any criminal offence"			
8.9 It was held in *R (on the application of Gosport Borough Council) v Farnham Magistrates Court* [2006] EWHC 3047 (Admin) that if nobody was present to be harassed, alarmed or distressed an order could not be made.			
8.10 The PD on pre-action conduct sets out permitted behaviour by a business creditor seeking repayment of a debt due to it from the debtor. It may inform the debtor of how the money claimed can be paid and can contact the debtor to discuss possible repayment options and provide contact details of agencies that provide free independent advice. In *Ferguson v British Gas Trading Ltd* [2009] EWCA Civ 46, [2009] 3 All ER 304 it was held on appeal, against the refusal to strike out, that letters threatening to terminate gas supply, to start legal proceedings and to report to credit agencies were capable, if sufficiently grave, of amounting to harassment. The court rejected the argument that a large corporation could not be guilty of harassment.			
In *S&D Property Investments Ltd v Nisbett* [2009] EWHC 1726 (Ch) the judge accepted that, in this debt recovery case, calling at the debtor's house and shouting abuse amounted to harassment and awarded damages of £7,000; see article 'Run for your money' by Roddy MacLeod in Sol Jo, 3 August 2010, page 6.			
8.11 It was held in *Mitchell v Glasgow City Council* [2009] UKHL 11, [2009] All ER (D) 182 (Feb) that public authorities who take action against perpetrators of violence and anti-social behaviour are safeguarded from legal proceedings arising from their failure to warn those who might be at risk of a criminal attack in response to the local authority's actions. See also Human Rights Updater (2009) Issue 85 (March), page 5.			
9. Service			
An interim anti-social behaviour order must be personally served on the defendant and may be varied or discharged at any time			65, section IV, para 13.1
An anti-social behaviour order must be served on the defendant personally			
10. Offence			
10.1 If without reasonable excuse a person does anything which he is prohibited from doing in an anti-social behaviour order he is guilty of an offence – see s 1(10) of the 1998 Act			
10.2 On summary conviction the maximum term of imprisonment is 6 months			

	Form No	CPR Rule	PD
and on conviction on indictment the maximum term is 5 years. In either case the defendant can be fined as an alternative or additionally			
10.3 Proceedings may be brought by -			
(a) a council which is a relevant authority			
(b) the council for the local government area in which the person resides or appears to reside: s 1(10A) of the 1998 Act			
See also section 2 of this **TAB**			

CHANGE OF SOLICITOR

TAB 24A

	Form No	CPR	PD
1. Preliminary			
For the importance that the court attaches to the freedom of a litigant to instruct the lawyer of his choice see *British Sky Broadcasting Group plc v Virgin Media Communications Ltd (formerly NTL Communications Ltd)* [2008] EWCA Civ 612, [2008] 4 All ER 1026, [2008] 1 WLR 2854			
See CPR Pt 6 and the Practice Direction to CPR Pt 6 as to the necessity of establishing the address for service of a party who is being represented by a solicitor			
See also the General Notes to CPR Pt 42 at para **CPR 42 [1]**			
Where a party has provided the business address of his solicitor as his address for service, that address will remain the address for service until CPR Pt 42 (Change of Solicitor) is complied with			
2. Failure to comply with CPR Pt 42		42.1	42, para 1(1)
The solicitor whose business address has been given will be considered as still acting until compliance			
Rules 6.7 and 6.23 contain provisions about service on the business address of a solicitor			
3. When notice is required			
Notice is required when:		42.2	
(a) there is a change of solicitor			
(b) where a party appoints a solicitor having previously acted in person (except where the solicitor is only employed as an advocate at a hearing)			42, para 1(3)
(c) where a party who was previously represented by a solicitor intends to act in person			
4. Procedure			
The party or his new solicitor must serve notice of change on every other party and, where appropriate, the former solicitor and then file notice of change		42.2(2)	
The notice filed at the court should be in the prescribed form which includes a statement that notice of the change has been served on all parties and any former solicitor and gives a new address for service	N434	42.2(3) and (4)	
Note:			
see below			
The court cannot order a party to appoint new solicitors: *SMC Engineering (Bristol) Ltd v Fraser* (2001) Times, 26 January, CA			

	Form No	CPR	PD
Where an order is made under r 42.3 that a solicitor has ceased to act or under r 42.4 declaring the solicitor has ceased to be the solicitor for the party, that party must give a new address for service to comply with CPR 6.23(1) and CPR 6.24. The address must be within the UK or where a solicitor is acting an address in the UK or any other EEA state.		6.23(2)(a)	42, para 5.1
, etc			
Where the certificate of a LSC funded litigant or an assisted person is revoked or discharged, the solicitor who acted for that person will cease to be the solicitor acting			
The solicitor must give notice of the revocation or discharge to the court, the other parties and to counsel		42.2(6)(a)	
If the former funded or assisted person wishes to continue any solicitor appointed must comply with CPR 42.2 or if a solicitor is not appointed the party must give an address for service within the United Kingdom			
(Rules 6.23 and 6.24 contain provisions about a party's address for service)		42.2(6)(b)	42, para 2.4
6. Order that a solicitor has ceased to act			
A solicitor may apply for an order that he has ceased to be the solicitor acting for a party		42.3	
The application must be served on the party, unless the court otherwise orders and must be supported by evidence	N244, PF 149		
Where the court makes the order it must be served on all parties and a certificate of service filed	PF 150	42.3(3)	
The solicitor will still be considered the party's solicitor until the order is filed and served in accordance with CPR 42.3(3); see note immediately below		42.2(5)	42, para 1.2
Note:			
The application for an order must not be served on the other parties, service is only to be effected on the party who was formerly the client			
It has been held to be appropriate in a simple case for the application to be made in writing by letter: *Miller v Allied Sainif (UK)* (2000) Times, 31 October, NEUBERGER J so that the costs of an attendance at court can be avoided			
There are differing views as to whether costs would have to be sought by separate action against the client. In many courts costs are ordered on the pragmatic view			

	Form No	CPR	PD
that this saves the expense of further proceedings		42.3(3)	70, para 4
Where solicitors are plainly unwilling to continue to act due to a serious breakdown in their relationship with their client they cannot be forced to continue acting and an order will be made removing them form the record: *UCB Bank plc v Hedworth* [2002] All ER (D) 173 (Dec)			
, the retainer having been terminated on reasonable grounds they were entitled to be paid for work done and to be reimbursed for disbursements incurred prior to the termination. For a decision based on the terms and limits of a solicitor's retainer see *Tom Hoskins plc v EMW Law (a firm)* [2010] EWHC 479, [2010] All ER (D) 54 (Apr).			
7. Removal of solicitor who has ceased to act on the application of another party			
See **CPR 42.4** and note the court has an inherent power to remove a solicitor where facts exist which give rise to a reasonable lay apprehension of bias: *Re L (minors) (care proceedings: cohabiting solicitors)* [2000] 1 WLR 100			
8. Solicitor ceasing to act by reason of death, etc			
For application for declaratory order see	PF 147		
For declaratory order see	PF 148		
9. Solicitor ceasing to act by reason of conflict etc			
which prevented solicitors acting for two clients with conflicting interests is not limited to conflicts in the same transaction. An injunction was granted to the claimants preventing the defendants acting			
Hilton v Barker Booth and Eastwood (a firm) (2005) Times, 4 February, HL			
10. New address for service			
Where the court makes an order under r 42.3 (that a solicitor has ceased to act) or under r 42.4 (declaration that a solicitor has ceased to be a solicitor for the party) the party for whom the solicitor was acting must give a new address for service to comply with rr 6.23(1) and 6.24.			42, para 5.1

TABLE 25—APPEALS TO A CIRCUIT JUDGE FROM A DISTRICT JUDGE IN A COUNTY COURT OR AN APPEAL TO A HIGH COURT JUDGE FROM THE COUNTY COURT OR FROM A MASTER/ DISTRICT JUDGE IN THE HIGH COURT

TAB 25

	Form No	CPR Rule	PD
Preliminary			
The 59th amendments to the CPR and PDs have replaced PD 52 with 5 new PDs supplementing CPR 52; these are PD 52A to PD 52E. These will apply to all appeals where: (a)　the appeal notice was filed; or (b)　permission to appeal was given, on or after 1 October 2012.			52A, para 8.1
The new PDs are:			
PD 52A　General provisions			
PD 52B　Appeals in county courts and the High Court			
PD 52C　Appeals to the Court of Appeal			
PD 52D　Statutory appeals and Appeals subject to specific provision			
PD 52E　Appeals by way of case stated			
For guidance on appeal documentation see also BCCP F — Appeals, F[15]-[17] and F[201].			
1. Destinations			
1.1 For definitions of the terms and abbreviations used in the tables in the TAB see		52.1	52A, para 3.4
1.2 Destination tables are set out in the table following para 3.5; see			52A, para 3
1.3 Where the appeal is of a final or interim decision and any necessary permission has been obtained the appeal: (a)　from a district judge of the county court (save for final appeals in Part 7 claims and specialist claims allocated to the multi-track) is to a circuit judge; (b)　from a Master or district judge of the High Court it to a High Court judge (save for final appeals in Part 7 claims and specialist claims allocated to the multi-track).			

TAB 25   PROCEDURAL TABLES

	Form No	CPR Rule	PD
1.4 For a definition of 'final decision' for appeals purposes, with examples, see			52A, paras 3.6–3.8
1.5 The Designated Civil Judge in consultation with the Presiding Judge has the responsibility for allocating appeals from decisions of district judges.			52A, para 4.5
2. Permission			
2.1 Permission is not required to appeal against:			
(a) a committal order;			
(b) a refusal to grant habeas corpus;			
(c) a secure accommodation order under s 25 of the Children Act 1989.			
2.2 An application for permission to appeal may be made to the lower court at the hearing where the decision intended to appeal was given.			
Where the lower court refuses or where no application is made by the lower court by the appeal court it must be accompanied by the appropriate fee or a fee remission application or certificate	N161 or N162 (small claims)	52.3(2)	52A, para 4.1
• where the time for filing an appellant's notice has expired the appellant must include an application for extension of time within the appellant's notice including the reason for delay and the steps taken prior to making the application. This may be dealt with at or without a hearing. If dealt with without a hearing an application to vary or set aside may be made within 14 days of service of the order.			52A, paras 3.2–3.3
• for appeals in connection with case management decisions see			52A, para 4.6
2.3 Where the appeal court, without a hearing, refuses permission to appeal a further application may be made requesting that the decision be reconsidered at a hearing. The request must be filed within 7 days after service of the notice of refusal.		52.3(4) and (5)	
2.4 Permission to appeal may only be given:			
(a) if it is considered to have a real prospect of success; or			
(b) for some other compelling reason.		52.3(6)	
• If an appeal is seriously contemplated the best course is to seek permission immediately after judgment is delivered. A note should be carefully taken of the reasons given whether or not permission is given.			
• Before leaving the court the Appeals Action Checklist at BCCP F[200] should be precisely followed.			

	Form No	CPR Rule	PD
2.5 The district judge granting or refusing permission should complete Form N460.			
2.6 If leave is granted and that grant is to be challenged it will be too late to do this at the hearing of the appeal when considerable work will have been done.			
2.7 If permission is granted but on terms that the prospective appellant wishes to challenge he should apply to the appeal court for permission rather than making an application to challenge the terms to which objection is taken.			
2.8 Applications to set aside the grant of permission have to 'clear a high hurdle' to succeed.			
3. Appeal notices			
3.1 Where an appellant seeks permission to appeal it must be requested in the **appellant's notice.**		52.4(1)	
3.2 His notice must be **filed** at the appeal court within such period as may be directed by the lower court or where the lower court gives no direction, within 21 days after the decision appealed.		52.4(2)	
3.3 Unless the appeal court otherwise orders an appellant's notice must be served: (a) as soon as practicable; and (b) in any event no later that 7 days after it is filed.			
Any application made in the appeal should be included with the appellant's notice.			
Where the applicant qualifies for fee remission, any application for a transcript of the judgment of the lower court at the public expense should be made with the appellant's notice.			52B, para 4.8
Where an unsuccessful defendant does not appeal a new party may apply for permission to appeal.			
3.3A The appellant must file a certificate of service of the notice as soon as practicable after service.			52B, para 6.1
3.4 A respondent may file and serve a **respondent's notice** and must do so if: (a) he seeks permission to appeal from the appeal court; or (b) he wishes to ask the appeal court to uphold the order of the lower court for different or additional grounds to those it has given.		52.5(1) and (2)	
3.5 When the respondent seeks permission form the appeal court it may be requested in the respondent's notice.		52.5(3)	
3.6 For the time limit for **filing** a respondent's notice when the time has not been fixed by the lower court, see		52.5(4) and (5)	
3.7 Unless the court otherwise orders the respondent's notice must be **served** on			

TAB 25   PROCEDURAL TABLES

	Form No	CPR Rule	PD
the appellant and any other respondent as soon as possible and in any event not later that 7 days after it is filed.		52.5(6)	
3.8 The documents to be filed with the appellant's notice are listed at:			52B, para 4.2
3.9 If the High Court judge or circuit judge refuses permission to appeal at the oral hearing there is no further appeal — Access to Justice Act 1999, s 54(4).			
4. Variation of time			
An application to vary the time for filing an appeal notice must be made to the appeal court. The parties cannot agree to extend any date or time limit.		52.6	52B, Section 3
5. Stay			
Unless the appeal court or lower court otherwise orders, an appeal shall not operate as a stay of any order or decision of the lower court.			
6. Amendment			
An appeal notice may not be amended without the permission of the appeal court.			
7. Striking-out etc of the appeal notice			
The appeal court may:			
(a) strike out the whole or any part of an appeal notice;			
(b) set aside permission to appeal in whole or in part;			
(c) impose or vary conditions in which an appeal may be brought.		52.9	
• The court will only exercise these powers where there is a compelling reason for doing so.			
• Where a person was present when permission was given he may not subsequently request the court to exercise any of these powers.			
8A Orders to limit the recoverable costs of an appeal			
In any proceedings where at first instance costs recovery is normally limited or excluded, an appeal court can order that the recoverable costs of an appeal will be limited to such extent as the court specifies.		52.9A	
The appeal court must have regard to CPR 52.9(2) and (3) when considering its order.			
8 Appeal court powers			
8.1 In relation to an appeal the appeal court has all the powers of the lower court.			
8.2 The appeal court has power to:			
(a) affirm, set aside or vary any order or judgment made or given by the lower court;			
(b) refer any claim or issue for determination by the lower court;			

		Form No	CPR Rule	PD
(c)	order a new trial or hearing;			
(d)	make orders for the payment of interest;			
(e)	make a costs order.		52.10	
•	For appeals in respect of claims tried with a jury, see		52.10(3)	
•	For the exercise by the court of its powers in relation to an order of the lower court, see		52.10(4)	
•	Where the court considers the application or the application notice is totally without merit, see		52.10(5) and (6)	
•	For dismissal of applications and appeals by consent, allowing unopposed applications on paper and appeals involving children or protected parties, see			52A, Section 6
9 Principles for determination of appeals				
9.1 Every appeal will be limited to a review of the lower court unless:				
(a)	a practice direction makes a different provision;			
(b)	the court thinks it better for a rehearing to be held.			
9.2 Unless it otherwise orders the appeal court will not receive:				
(a)	oral evidence; or			
(b)	evidence which was not before the lower court.			
9.3 The court will allow an appeal where the decision was:				
(a)	wrong;			
(b)	unjust because of a serious procedural defect or other irregularity.			
9.4 The appeal court may draw such inferences of fact as it considers justified on the evidence.				
9.5 A party may not rely on a matter not contained in his appeal notice unless the court gives permission.			52.11	
10 Venue for appeals and filing of notices and applications				
Appeals within a county court, from a county court and appeals within the High Court to a judge of the High Court must be brought in the appropriate appeal centre and all other notices (including any respondent's notice) and applications must be filed at that appeal centre.				
The venue for an appeal within a county court will be determined by the Designated Civil Judge and may be different from the appeal centre.				
The tables at the end of PD 52B list the Appeal Centres.				
11 Conduct of the appeal				
11.1 Service of the appellant's notice — see para 3.3 of this TAB				

TAB 25 PROCEDURAL TABLES

	Form No	CPR Rule	PD
11.2 Except where the claim is allocated to the small claims track the appellant must obtain a transcript or other record of reasons and must comply with sub-paras (a), (b) and (c) of PD 52B, para 6.2.			52B, para 6.2
11.3 As soon as practicable, but in any event within 35 days of filing the appellant's notice, the appellant must file an **appeal bundle** containing only documents relevant to the appeal duly paginated and indexed.			52B, para 6.3
11.4 Unless the court otherwise orders the documents must include the documents listed in PD 52B, para 6.4(1) and consideration should also be given to the documents listed in PD 52B, para 6.4(2) subject to relevance.			52B, para 6.4
11.5 A copy of the appeal bundle must be served on each respondent:			
(a) where permission was given by the lower court at the same time as filing the appeal bundle; or			
(b) if permission was granted by the appeal court as soon as possible and in any event within 14 days of the grant of permission; or			
(c) if the application for permission is to be heard on the same occasion as the hearing date, as soon as practicable and in any event within 14 days after notification of the hearing date.			52B, para 6.5
12 Part 36 offers and payments			
Generally such offers or payments must not be disclosed to any judge of the appeal court who is to hear or determine an application for permission or an appeal. For exceptional circumstances, see		52.12(2) and (3)	
13 Determination of applications			
13.1 Applications made in the appeal, including applications for permission to the lower court at the hearing or in the appeal notice may be determined with or without a hearing.		52.3(2)(a) and 52.5(3)	52B, para 7.1
13.2 where a court refuses an application for permission without a hearing the applicant may request the application to be reconsidered as a hearing. If any other application is determined without a hearing any party affected may apply to have the order set aside or varied.			52B, paras 7.2 and 7.3
13.3 Any request or application under this section must be made within 7 days of service of notice of the determination. A copy must be served on all other parties at the same time. The court will give directions for the determination of the application.			52B, para 7.4
14 The hearing			
14.1 For the court's powers see para 8 of this TAB.			

	Form No	CPR Rule	PD
14.2 For the principles to be applied by the court in the determination of appeals see para 9 of this TAB.			
Subject to any order of the court the parties should only file and serve **skeleton arguments:**			
(a) when there are sufficiently complex issues of fact or law			
(b) they would assist the court in respects not readily apparent form the appeal papers.			52B, para 8.3
But if skeleton arguments are to be served, see:			52A, Section 5
For the **respondent's attendance at permission hearings** see			52B, para 8.1

TABLE 26—COURT OF APPEAL

TAB 26

	Form No	CPR Rule	PD
1. Preliminary			
1.1 Relevant documents must be filed in the Civil Appeals Office Registry, Room E 307, Royal Courts of Justice, Strand London WC2A 2LL			52C, para 3(2)
1.1A An appellant's notice, a respondent's notice and an application notice may be filed by e-mail using the e-mail account specified in the 'Guidelines for Filing by E-mail' where those guidelines permit it. For website details see 1.1B below			
1.1B Provision is made for certain notices to be filed electronically at the Court of Appeal, Civil Division using the online forms service on the Court of Appeal, Civil Division website at http://www.civilappeals.gov.uk			
1.2 All documents required to be served must be served by the parties; an order to dispense with service of the appellant's notice must be made in the appeal notice or thereafter by application under Part 23.			52C, paras 7.1–7.3
Evidence in support of any application made in an appellant's notice must be filed and served with the appellant's notice.			
1.3 A court officer assigned to the Civil Appeals Office who is a barrister or solicitor may with the consent of the Master of Rolls (and subject to review on the request of a party) deal with -			
(a) any matter incidental to any proceedings in the Court of Appeal			
(b) other matters where there is no substantial dispute			
(c) dismissal of an appeal or application for failure to comply with any order, rule or practice direction		52.16(2)	
A Court officer may not decide an application for:			
(a) permission to appeal			
(b) bail pending an appeal			
(c) an injunction			
(d) a stay (save in limited circumstances)		52.16(3)	
1.4 At the request of a party filed within 7 days after service of notice of the decision, a hearing will be held to reconsider a decision of a court officer or a single judge without a hearing		52.16(5), (6) and (6A)	
1.5 Substantial changes in civil appeal procedure came into effect in 30 June			

TAB 26 PROCEDURAL TABLES

	Form No	CPR Rule	PD
2004 and on 29 June 2004 the Court of Appeal handed down a Practice Note to explain and give notice of the substantial changes to PD 52.			
1.6 The necessity for everyone who practised and appeared before the Court of Appeal to understand the new regime and comply with it have been made clear. The costs and consequences of failure to do so were stressed			
1.7 It was reported in April 2012 that an automatic mediation pilot for personal injury and contract claims worth up to £100,000 has been started at the Court of Appeal. Pro bono legal advisers can be arranged, for litigants in person who qualify, by Law Works Mediation.			
1.8 The court may make directions and they will prevail over the provisions of PD 52C			52C, para 2
1A. Definitions			
Practice Direction 52C contains definitions of: 'appeal notice' 'appellant's notice' 'hearing date' 'listing window notification' 'replacement skeleton argument'			52C, para 1
2. Permission to Appeal			
2.1 Permission to appeal is required from a decision of a judge in the county court or of the High Court except where the appeal is against (a) a committal order (b) a refusal to grant habeas corpus (c) a secure accommodation order made under s25 of the Children Act 1989		52.3(1)	
2.2 Application can be made (a) to the lower court at the hearing of decision sought to be appealed or (b) to the appeal court in an appeal notice		52.3(2)	
For time limit for an appellant's notice see para 2.8 below in this TAB and also see		52.4(2)	
For time limits for a respondent's notice see		52.5(4) and (5)	
Where a decision has been made to appeal or that an appeal is likely application should be made to the lower court. If the application to appeal is refused by the lower court a further application for permission may be made to the appeal court in an appellant's notice		52.3(3)	
2.3 Permission is required from the Court of Appeal for all appeals to that court from a decision of a county court or the High Court which was itself made on appeal		52.13(1)	

	Form No	CPR Rule	PD
2.4 If permission is to be sought to appeal because of the failure of the judge to give reasons for his decision it would be prudent first to consider the practice set out in *English v Emery Reimold and Strick Ltd* [2002] EWCA Civ 605, [2002] 3 All ER 385			
2.5 Applications for leave to appeal are not to be listed to suit the convenience of counsel even if the appeal was to follow if permission was granted.			
2.6 It is only in exceptional circumstances that permission would be given for a second appeal. See Dyson LJ's guidance as to rule 52.13(2)(a) and (b)		52.13(2)(a) and (b)	
Unless			
(a) the appeal court or the lower court otherwise orders; or			
(b) the appeal is from the Asylum and Immigration Tribunal,			
an appeal does not operate as a stay of any order or decision of the lower court.			
2.7 For the principles to be applied when an application is made to the Court of Appeal for stay of enforcement proceedings pending an appeal to the Court of Appeal against an order of the trial judge see *Gater Assets Ltd v Nak Naftogaz Ukrainy* [2008] EWCA Civ 1051, 8 August (Mummery LJ)		52.7	
2.8 Guidance was given by the Court of Appeal in *Hutchinson (formerly known as WER) v Popdog Ltd (formerly known as REW)* [2011] All ER (D) 178 (Dec) on when permission to appeal would be granted where the appeal would be purely academic between the parties.			
2.9 For the jurisdiction to suspend an order which falls within s 89(1) of the Housing Act 1980 see *Admiral Taverns (Cygnet) Ltd v Daniel* [2008] EWCA Civ 1501 discussed at **CPR 52.7 [1]** above.			
3. Filing of Appellant's Notice and documents to accompany			
3.1 The appellant must complete and file the appellant's notice. It must be accompanied by the appropriate fee or a fee remission certificate.	N161		
An application to the appeal court incidental to the appeal (including for a stay of execution) must be included in the appeal or thereafter in a separate Part 23 application notice. The provisions of Part 23 apply to such an application			
3.2 The appellant's notice must be filed with the documents specified in **CPR PD 52C, para 3.**			52C, para 3(3)-(6)
3.3 The grounds of appeal must identify what in the judgment of the court below is:			

TAB 26 PROCEDURAL TABLES

	Form No	CPR Rule	PD
(i) wrong; (ii) unjust because of a serious procedural or other irregularity, as required by CPR 52.11(3).		52.11(3)	52C, Section 2, para 5
The reasons why must be confined to the skeleton argument.			
If the appellant is unable to provide any necessary documents in time he must complete the appeal notice on the basis of available documents seeking permission to amend the notice when they are available.			
The appeal questionnaire filed in the Court of Appeal, Civil Division on behalf of the appellant must contain the time estimate for the hearing of the appeal. This must be filed and served within 14 days after the listing window notification.			52C, Section 6, para 23
For the court fee payable on filing the appellant's notice see		SCFO fee 9.1	
3.4 Where the **time for filing an appellant's notice has expired** the appellant must include in his notice when filed an application for an extension of time and give the reasons for the delay and the steps taken prior to the application being made.			52C, para 4
• The time limit for filing an appeal to the Court of Appeal is 21 days (including Saturdays, Sundays and Bank holidays) after the date of the decision appealed against.			
3A. Respondent's notice			
A respondent may file and serve a respondent's notice.		52.5(1)	
A respondent who seeks permission to appeal from the court of appeal or wishes to ask the appeal court to uphold the order of the lower court for reasons different or additional to those given by the lower court **must** file a respondent's notice.		52.5(2)	52C, para 8
Where the respondent is seeking permission to appeal from the appeal court it **must** be requested in the respondent's notice.		52.5(3)	
For the time for filing of the respondent's notice see		52.5(4) and (5)	
Unless the appeal court otherwise orders the respondent's notice must be served as soon as practicable and in any event not later than 7 days after it is filed.		52.5(6)	
• Where the respondent is not challenging the order appealed he does not need permission from the appeal court.			
A respondent must, within 14 days of filing the notice, lodge and serve on all			

	Form No	CPR Rule	PD
parties a skeleton argument unless he is not represented			52C, paras 9 and 13
A respondent must file with his notice:			
(a) two additional copies of his notice for the court; and			
(b) one copy each for the appellant and any other respondents.			52C, para 10
as to applications with the respondent's notice see			52C, paras 11 and 12
4. Procedure where permission is being sought from the Court of Appeal			
4.1 Where the appellant is applying for permission in the appellant's notice he must, within 14 days of filing the appeal notice, lodge a bundle containing only those documents which are necessary for the court to determine that application.			52C, para 14
The bundle must be paginated in chronological order and have an index in the front.			
4.2 Within 7 days after service of a notice that permission has been refused without a hearing, the appellant may file a request for the decision to be reconsidered at an oral hearing at the appeal court and must serve a copy of the request statement on the respondent at the same time. The hearing may be before the same judge who refused leave on paper.			52C, para 15
If the appellant is to be represented at the permission hearing his advocate must at least 4 days before the hearing file a brief written statement of the points to be made and the reasons why permission should be granted.			52C, para 16(1)
Although the respondent is given notice of the hearing he is not expected to attend unless so directed. If he is so directed the appellant must supply him with copy documents.			52C, paras 16(2) and (3) and 19 and 20
Where a judge of the Court of Appeal or of the High Court, a Designated Civil Judge or a Specialist Circuit Judge refuses permission without a hearing he may, if he considers the application is totally without merit, make an order that its refusal cannot be reconsidered at a hearing.		52.3(4A)(a)-(b)	
As to re-opening a final determination refusing permission by the Court of Appeal see the criteria in **CPR 52.17**.		52.17	
4.3 When permission is granted, the Civil Appeals Office sends:			
(a) notification of listing window or of hearing			
(b) notification of hear by date			
(c) a copy of the order granting permission			
(d) the court's directions			
(e) appeal questionnaire			

TAB 26 PROCEDURAL TABLES

	Form No	CPR Rule	PD
4.4 For judicial review appeals see:		52.15	
For judicial review and statutory review see Part 54			
4.5 For the position where the appellant is funded by the Legal Services Commission see:			52C, para 17
4.6 For the position when limited permission is granted see:			52C, para 18
5. Procedure when permission obtained or is not necessary			
5.1 Section 5 of PD 52C sets out in detail the timetable for the conduct of an appeal after the date of the listing window notification (that is the letter sent by the Civil Appeals Office notifying the parties of the window within which their appeal is likely to be heard).			52C, section 5
The timetable is divided into 2 parts: (a) listing window notification to lodging bundle; (b) steps to be taken once hearing date is fixed: lodging bundles, supplemental skeletons and bundles of authorities.			
Each part is divided into 3 columns, the third of which cross-references each step to the relevant provision of the PD.			
Multiple appeals: If two or more appeals are pending in the same or related proceedings the parties must seek directions as to whether they should be heard together of consecutively by the same judges and should attempt to agree a single appeal bundle or set of bundles for all the appeals.			52C, para 25
Expedition: The court will deal with requests for expedition without a hearing. The request must be made by letter succinctly setting out the grounds and must be marked for the immediate attention of the court and be copied to the other parties to the appeal.			
If time is short an e-mail can be sent and in extreme urgency the party should use the telephone procedure set out in sub-para (3) of:			52C, para 26
6. Preparation of Bundles			
The importance of precise compliance with the requirements of the Practice Direction cannot be overstated. Failure to do so is likely to result in costs sanctions and consideration of dismissal for non compliance			
The appellant must lodge an **appeal bundle** which must include only relevant documents and which is paginated and in chronological order with an index at the front. The PD lists those documents that must be included and also those which may be included.			52C, para 27(1)

	Form No	CPR Rule	PD
Original material should not be included as the bundles will be destroyed at the conclusion of proceedings.			52C, para 27(2)-(5)
7. Listing and hear by dates			
7.1 Management of the list will be dealt with by the listing officer under the direction of the master. The Civil Appeals list of the Court of Appeal is divided into: • the applications list • the appeals list • the expedited list • the stand out list • the special fixtures list (for special provisions for this list see CPR 52, para 15.9A) • the second fixtures list • the short warned list (for special provisions for this list see CPR 52, para 5.9)			
7.2 Requests for directions (whether as to listing or other matters) should be made to the Civil Appeals Office			
7.2A The hear-by date is the last day of the listing window.			52C, para 22
7.3 After consultation with any opposing advocate, the appellant's advocate must file a **bundle of photocopies of the authorities** relied on by the parties. The requirements of CPR PD 52C, para 29(2)-(5) must be complied with			
7.4 A **skeleton argument** must comply with the provision of PD 52A, Section 5 and must: (a) not normally exceed 25 pages (excluding front and back sheets); (b) be printed on A4 paper at not less than 12 point font and 1.5 line spacing.			52C, para 31
A **supplementary skeleton argument** on which a party wishes to rely must be lodged and served as soon as practicable and must be accompanied by a request for permission setting out the reasons why it is necessary and why it could not reasonably have been lodged earlier. It is only exceptionally that a supplementary skeleton argument lodged later than 7 days before the hearing will be allowed to be used.			52C, para 32
7.5 An appeal notice may not be amended without the leave of the court.		52.8	52C, para 30
The appellant cannot present the Court of Appeal with a totally new argument not stated in the grounds of appeal when the point had not been taken below.			
All documents that are needed for the appeal hearing must be filed at least 7 days prior to the hearing			

TAB 26 PROCEDURAL TABLES

	Form No	CPR Rule	PD
8. The fact that a **Part 36 offer** (or a per-April 2007 payment into court) has been made must not be disclosed to any judge of the appeal court who is to hear or determine:			
(a) an application for permission to appeal, or			
(b) an appeal until all questions (other than costs) have been determined		52.12(1)	
CPR 52.12(1) above does not:			
(a) apply if the Part 36 offer or payment into court is relevant to the substance of the appeal;		52.12(2)	
(b) prevent disclosure of any application in the appeal proceedings if disclosure of the fact that a Part 36 offer or payment into court has been made is properly relevant to the matter to be decided		52.12(3)	
Note rule 36.3 has the effect that a Part 36 offer made in proceedings at first instance will not have consequences in any appeal proceedings. Therefore, a fresh Part 36 offer needs to be made in appeal proceedings. However, rule 52.12 applies to a Part 36 offer whether made in the original proceedings or in the appeal			
9. Video-link facility at the Court of Appeal			
Where counsel are to present short appointments, particularly where considerable travelling time will be involved, they should consider whether the use of the video-link facility would be appropriate.			
10. Court of Appeal – general civil restraint order			
The Court of Appeal has power when making a general civil restraint order to prevent proceedings being brought in the county court as well as in the High Court and the Court of Appeal.			
10A. Declaratory Relief			
The jurisdiction of the Court of Appeal to grant declaratory relief is fully examined in the case of *Rolls Royce plc v Unite* [2009] EWCA Civ 387, [2010] 1 WLR 318, [2010] ICR 1 and in particular by Wall LJ in paras 14 to 28 of his judgment.			
11. Checklists			
11.1 For a checklist for filing papers in the Court of Appeal, see **BCCP Division F**			
11.2 For guidance on appeal documentation, see **BCCP Division F.**			
12. New Evidence			
CPR 52.11(2) provides that an appeal court subject to the CPR will not			

	Form No	CPR Rule	PD
(a) fresh oral evidence			
(b) evidence which was not before the lower court unless the court otherwise orders			
13. Reserved Judgments			
The practice direction supplementing Part 40 (Reserved Judgments) contains provisions relating to reserved judgments			
14. Costs			
When the court makes an order for costs the general rule is that the unsuccessful party will be ordered to pay the costs of the successful party but the court may make a different order.			

TABLE 27—APPEAL TO THE SUPREME COURT

TAB 27

Steps to be taken	Form No	Supreme Court Rules 2009	Supreme Court Practice Directions
[Either (*Where permission to appeal has been granted by the Supreme Court*):			
Notice of intention to proceed			
1. Appellant files notice of intention to proceed with appeal.		r 18(1)	SC PD 3 para 3.4.1
Note: within 14 days of the grant by the Supreme Court of permission to appeal.			SC PD 3 para 3.4.1
Fee on filing of notice of intention to proceed: £800.			SC PD 7 Annex 2
2. Application for permission, which stands as notice of appeal, is re-sealed.			SC PD 3 para 3.4.1
3. Appellant serves copy of notice of appeal on: (1) each Respondent; (2) any recognised intervener; (3) any person who was an intervener in the court below.		r 18(2)	
4. Appellant files: (1) original notice of appeal with 7 copies; and (2) certificate of service.		r 18(2)	SC PD 3 para 3.4.1
Extension of time			
5. *Where he is unable to file notice within the 14 day time limit*, Appellant applies in Form 2 for an extension of time.	2		SC PD 3 para 3.4.2
Respondent's views must be sought and communicated to the Registry.			SC PD 3 para 3.4.2
6. Registrar considers application and either refuses or grants it (if granted case proceeds as an appeal step 10 applies).			SC PD 3 para 3.4.1
Or (*where permission from the Supreme Court is not required*):			
Notice of appeal			
7. Appellant prepares notice of appeal in Form 1 which:	1	r 19(1)	SC PD 4 paras 4.2.1, 4.2.2
(1) must be legible on A4 paper, securely bound on the left, using both sides of the paper;			SC PD 4 para 4.2.1
(2) should include the neutral citation of the judgment appealed against and the references of any law report in the courts below;			SC PD 4 para 4.2.3
(3) must be signed by the appellant or his agent.			SC PD 4 para 4.2.2
8. Appellant serves copy of notice of appeal on:	1	r 20	SC PD 4 para 4.2.15

TAB 27 PROCEDURAL TABLES

Steps to be taken	Form No	Supreme Court Rules 2009	Supreme Court Practice Directions
(1) each Respondent or his solicitor;			
(2) any recognised intervener; and			
(3) any person who was an intervener in the court below.			
Time: before filing.			SC PD 4 para 4.2.15
9. Appellant files in Registry:			
(1) original notice of appeal and 3 copies;	1		SC PD 4 para 4.3.2
(2) certificate of service; giving the full name and address of the Respondents or their agents) either in Form 1 and signed or separately;	1		SC PD 4 para 4.2.15
(3) *If permission to appeal was granted by the court below*: a copy of the order appealed from; and			SC PD 4 para 4.3.2
(4) *if separate from the order*: a copy of the order granting permission to appeal to the Supreme Court.			SC PD 4 para 4.3.2
Fee on filing of notice of appeal: £1,600.			SC PD 7 Annex 2
Time: Within 42 days of the date of the order or decision of the court below, unless other time limits apply.]			SC PD 2 para 2.1.12
Acknowledgment			
10. Respondent serves acknowledgment in Form 3 on:	3	r 21	SC PD 4 para 4.6.2
(1) appellant;			
(2) any other Respondent; and			
(3) any person who was an intervener in the court below or whose submissions were taken into account.			
Time: before filing.			
11. Respondent files:			SC PD 4 para 4.6.1
(1) acknowledgment in Form 3 with 3 copies; and			SC PD 4 para 4.6.3
(2) certificate of service (giving the full name and address of the persons served) either in Form 3 and signed or separately.			SC PD 4 para 4.6.2
Fee on acknowledgment: £320.			SC PD 7 Annex 2
Time: within 14 days after service on him of the notice of appeal.		r 21	SC PD 4 para 4.6.1
Security for costs			
12. *If he seeks security for costs*: Respondent makes application *(see applications below at step 28 below)*.		r 36	
Public funding			
In any appeal where public funding is required:			

Steps to be taken	Form No	Supreme Court Rules 2009	Supreme Court Practice Directions
13. Party desiring public funding:			SC PD 8 para 8.12.1
(1) applies in England and Wales, to the relevant authority;			
(2) gives notice in writing of application to:			
(i) the Registrar; and			
(ii) the other parties to the appeal.			SC PD 8 para 8.12.3
If public funding is granted:			
14. Party obtaining public funding files copy of certificate in Registry.			SC PD 8 para 8.12.2
Interveners			
If outside party wishes to intervene and take part in an appeal:			
15. Intervener makes application for permission to intervene (see applications at step 28 below).	2	r 26	SC PD 6 para 6.9.1
16. Court considers application on paper and grants or refuses it.		r 26(2)	
Preparation of Statement of Facts and Issues and Appendix of documents			
17. Appellant prepares Statement of Facts and Issues and submits it to respondent for agreement.	—	r 22	SC PD 5 para 5.1.3
The agreed Statement of Facts and Issues:			SC PD 5 para 5.1.3
(1) sets out the relevant facts;			
(2) sets out those items which are disputed;			
(3) contains references to every law report of the proceedings below;			
(4) states the duration of the proceedings below; and			
(5) is signed by all parties.			
18. Appellant prepares Appendix of documents (where necessary in several parts) containing in this order:	—	r 22	SC PD 5 para 5.1.4
(1) the order appealed against;			
(2) *if separate,* the order refusing permission to appeal to the Supreme Court;			
(3) the official transcript of the judgment of the court below;			
(4) the final order(s) of all other courts below;			
(5) the official transcript of the final judgment(s) of all other courts below;			
(6) *where necessary for understanding the legal issues and the argument:* the relevant documents filed in the courts below;			
(7) *where necessary for understanding the legal issues and the argument:*			

TAB 27 PROCEDURAL TABLES

Steps to be taken	Form No	Supreme Court Rules 2009	Supreme Court Practice Directions
the relevant documents and correspondence relating to the appeal.			
Filing of Statement of Facts and Issues and Appendix			
19. Appellant files:		r 22	SC PD 5 para 5.2.6
(1) original and 7 copies of Statement of Facts and Issues;			
(2) 8 copies of Part 1 of the Appendix;			
(3) 10 copies of each subsequent part of the Appendix.			
Fee on filing Statement and Appendix: £4,820.			SC PD 7 Annex 2
Time: Within 112 days of filing notice of appeal or notice of intention to proceed.			SC PD 5 para 5.2.1
Extension of time for filing Statement of Facts and Issues and Appendix			
If unable to file the statement and appendix within the time limit:			
20. Appellant files application (for applications see step 28 below) explaining in detail why extension required and including the Respondent's view.	2	r 5	SC PD 5 paras 5.2.3, 5.2.5
Registrar considers application and grants or refuses it.			SC PD 5 paras 5.2.4, 5.2.5
Setting hearing date			
21. Parties notify Registrar that the appeal is ready to list and provide a time estimate.		r 22(3)	SC PD 6 para 6.2.1
Time: Within 7 days after filing the Statement of Facts and Issues and the Appendix.			
Note: Parties are encouraged to offer agreed dates at an early stage and there is no need to wait until after filing the SFI.			
22. Registrar informs parties of likely date of hearing of appeal.		r 22(3)	
Filing and exchange of cases			
23. Appellant:		r 22	SC PD 6 para 6.3.9
(1) files original and 2 copies of his case, a succinct statement of his argument omitting material contained in the Statement of Facts and Issues; and			
(2) serves case on all Respondents.			
Time: No later than 6 weeks before the proposed date of the hearing.			SC PD 6 para 6.3.9
24. Respondent and any other party filing a case (for example, an intervener or advocate to the court):			SC PD 6 para 6.3.10
(1) files original and 2 copies of his case, a succinct statement of his argument omitting material con-			

Steps to be taken	Form No	Supreme Court Rules 2009	Supreme Court Practice Directions
tained in the Statement of Facts and Issues; and			
(2) serves case on all Respondents.			
Time: No later than 4 weeks before the proposed date of the hearing.			SC PD 6 para 6.3.10
Grouping of appeals			
25. Registrar may direct that appeals raising the same or similar issues are heard either together or consecutively by the court constituted of the same Justices and may give any consequential directions that appear appropriate.		r 32	SC PD 8 para 8.2.1
Filing core volumes			
26. Appellant files 10 copies of every case and 10 core volumes each containing in the following order copies of:		r 23	SC PD 6 paras 6.4.1, 6.4.3
(1) notice of appeal (Form 1);			
(2) notice of cross-appeal (if any) and any Respondent's notice of objection or acknowledgment;			
(3) any order made by Supreme Court granting permission, or as to costs or terms;			
(4) Statement of Facts and Issues;			
(5) Appellant's and Respondent's cases (and the case of an intervener or advocate to the court, if any);			
(6) Part 1 of Appendix;			
(7) index to the authorities' volumes.			
Time: After exchange of cases and not later than 14 days before the proposed date of hearing.			SC PD 6 para 6.4.1
Filing of authorities for hearing			
27. Appellant prepares copies of any authorities he requires.			SC PD 6 para 6.5.1
Respondent provides Appellant with 10 copies of any authorities which he requires.			SC PD 6 para 6.5.1
Appellant files 10 copies of the joint set of authorities.		r 24	SC PD 6 para 6.5.1
Time: At the same time as the core volumes are filed.			SC PD 6 para 6.5.1
Procedural applications		r 30	SC PD 7 para 7.1.1
28. Applicant prepares:			
(1) application in the prescribed form which:	2	r 30(2)(a)	SC PD 7 paras 7.1.2, 7.1.3
(a) sets out the reasons for making the application;			
(b) states what order is sought; and			
(c) briefly why it is sought; and			
(2) evidence in support.		r 30(2)(b)	SC PD 7 para 7.1.3

TAB 27 PROCEDURAL TABLES

Steps to be taken	Form No	Supreme Court Rules 2009	Supreme Court Practice Directions
29. Applicant serves copy of application and evidence in support on all other parties.		r 30(3)	SC PD 7 para 7.1.2
Time: before filing.		r 30(3)	SC PD 7 para 7.1.2
30. Applicant files:		r 30(3)	
(1) original application and 3 copies including:			SC PD 7 para 7.1.7
(a) signed certificate of service; and			
(b) indication as to whether the other parties consent or refuse to consent to the application;			
(2) evidence in support.			SC PD 7 para 7.1.3
Fee: £350.* (*£800 for application to intervene in an appeal)			SC PD 7 Annex 2
Time: as soon as it becomes apparent that an application is necessary or expedient.			SC PD 7 para 7.1.1
If he wishes to oppose application:			
31. Party serves notice of objection in the prescribed form in Form 3 on the applicant and any other parties.	3	r 30(4)	
Time: Before filing.		r 30(4)	SC PD 7 para 7.1.4
32. Party objecting files original notice of objection and 3 copies including certificate of service.		r 30(4)	SC PD 7 para 7.1.4, 7.1.7
Fee: £150.			SC PD 7 Annex 2
Time: within 7 days after service of the application.		r 30(4)	SC PD 7 para 7.1.4
33. Wherever possible: Court considers applications without a hearing.			SC PD 7 para 7.1.6
34. If application is opposed it is referred to a Panel of Justices and may be decided with or without an oral hearing.			SC PD 7 para 7.1.6
Death of party			
35. If a party to appeal dies before hearing: immediate notice of the death must be given in writing to the Registrar and to the other parties.			SC PD 8 para 8.4.1
36. Application to substitute new party served on all other parties.			SC PD 8 para 8.4.2
Time: Before application filed.			SC PD 8 para 8.4.2
37. Application to substitute new party filed explaining circumstances and endorsed with a certificate of service on all other parties.			SC PD 8 paras 8.4.2, 8.4.4
Fee: £350.			SC PD 7 Annex 2
Time: within 42 days of the date of notice of death.			SC PD 8 para 8.4.2

Steps to be taken	Form No	Supreme Court Rules 2009	Supreme Court Practice Directions
38. *If the death takes place after the case for the deceased person has been filed but before the appeal has been heard:* Appellant files supplemental case setting out the information about the newly-added parties.			SC PD 8 para 8.4.3
Time: Immediately on death of party.			
Bankruptcy of party			
If a party is adjudicated bankrupt or a corporate body is ordered to be wound up:			
39. Party's solicitor gives immediate notice in writing to the other parties and to the Registrar together with certified copy of the bankruptcy or winding up order.			SC PD 8 para 8.1.1
40. Bankrupt party (or his trustee in bankruptcy) or liquidator files application to pursue the appeal (an appeal cannot proceed until the application has been approved).			SC PD 8 para 8.1.2
Fee: £350.			SC PD 7 Annex 2
Time: within 42 days of the date of the notice.			SC PD 8 para 8.1.2
41. Court makes order.			
Withdrawal of appeal			
42. *If he wishes to withdraw appeal before it has been listed for hearing:* Appellant writes		r 34	SC PD 8 para 8.16.3
(1) to all the Respondents; and then to			
(2) the Registrar, including the consent of the Respondents confirming that costs have been agreed.			
43. *If he wishes to withdraw an appeal that has been listed for hearing:* Appellant:	2		SC PD 8 para 8.16.4
(1) serves application *(see applications at steps 28–34 above)* on Respondent for his consent;			
(2) files application for an order including whether or not the Respondents have consented and a certificate of service, submissions on costs and, where appropriate, indicating how any security money should be disposed			
Fee: £350.			SC PD 7 Annex 2
44. Court may set aside or vary the order appealed from by consent and without an oral hearing, if satisfied that it is appropriate so to do.		r 34(2)	
Specialist advisers			
45. Any party may apply to the Registrar in writing, for specialist advisers to attend the hearing.		r 35	SC PD 8 para 8.13.1
Judgment and order for costs			

TAB 27 PROCEDURAL TABLES

Steps to be taken	Form No	Supreme Court Rules 2009	Supreme Court Practice Directions
46. Court gives judgment on a day notified usually one week in advance.		r 28	SC PD 6 para 6.8.1
47. Registry notifies parties of date of judgment.			
Draft Order			
48. Registrar prepares draft of the order and may invite counsel to comment on the draft.		r 29(5)	SC PD 6 para 6.8.6
49. Parties return draft order either approved or with amendments.			SC PD 7 para 7.4.1
Time: no later than 2 days after receipt (unless otherwise directed) .			SC PD 7 para 7.4.1
Repayment of security for costs			
If he is not ordered to pay costs of appeal:			
50. Any money paid into Security Fund is returned to Appellant.			
Time: after final order has been issued.			

TABLE 28—APPEAL TO THE
JUDICIAL COMMITTEE OF THE PRIVY COUNCIL

TAB 28

Steps to be taken	Form No	Judicial Committee Rules 2009	Judicial Committee of the Privy Council Practice Directions
[Either (*where permission of the Judicial Committee of the Privy Council was required*):			
Notice of intention to proceed			
1. Appellant files notice of intention to proceed with appeal. *For fee see PD 7 Annex 2.*		r 17	JCPC PD 3 para 3.1.7 JCPC PD 7 Annex 2
Time: within 14 days of the grant by the Judicial Committee of permission to appeal.		r 17(1)(c)	JCPC PD 3 para 3.1.7
2. Registry re-seals application for permission to appeal which stands as the notice of appeal.		r 17(2)	JCPC PD 3 para 3.1.7
3. Appellant serves copy of re-sealed notice of appeal on: (1) each Respondent; (2) any recognised intervener; (3) any person who was an intervener in the court below.		r 17(2)	JCPC PD 3 para 3.1.7
4. Appellant files: (1) re-sealed notice of appeal with 7 copies; and (2) certificate of service.		r 18(2)	JCPC PD 3 para 3.1.7
Notice of appeal			
Or (*where permission of the Judicial Committee is not required*):			
5. Appellant serves a copy of the notice of appeal on each Respondent.		r 18	JCPC PD 4 paras 4.2.6
Time: before filing notice of appeal.			
6. Appellant files in Registry: (1) original and 3 copies of notice of appeal in Form 1; (2) certificate of service (giving the full name and address of the Respondents or their agents) either included in Form 1 and signed or separate certificate of service; (3) copy of the order appealed from; and	1	r 18	JCPC PD 4 paras 4.3.1, 4.3.2

TAB 28 PROCEDURAL TABLES

Steps to be taken	Form No	Judicial Committee Rules 2009	Judicial Committee of the Privy Council Practice Directions
(4) *if separate*, copy of the order granting permission to appeal.			
For fee see PD 7 Annex 2.			JCPC PD 7 Annex 2
Time: within 56 days of the date of the order or decision of the court below or (if later) from the date of the order or decision of that court granting permission.]			JCPC PD 4 para 4.3.1
Application to be treated as a financially assisted person			
7. *If he has been granted, or has applied for, assistance from public funds in his own jurisdiction, or his means are such that payment of a prescribed fee would involve undue financial hardship* Appellant files:		r 38(1)	JCPC PD 7 paras 7.2.1, 7.12.1
(1) application to be treated as a financially assisted person; and			JCPC PD 7 para 7.12.1
(2) sworn or credible evidence as to the applicant's means.			
8. *If application is accepted*, Registrar certifies that the Appellant is to be treated as a financially assisted person.			JCPC PD 7 paras 7.12.1
Where a certificate has effect, the Appellant will be entitled to remission or reduction of any liability for fees payable under the Rules.			JCPC PD 7 paras 7.12.2
Acknowledgment by Respondent			
9. *If he intends to participate:* each Respondent prepares notice in Form 3 on A4 paper, securely fastened, using both sides of the paper.	3	r 19(1)	JCPC PD 4 para 4.6.1
10. Respondent serves copy of Form 3 on:		r 19(2)	JCPC PD 4 para 4.6.2
(1) the Appellant; and			
(2) any other Respondent.			
11. Respondent files original Form 3 including certificate of service (giving the full name and address of the persons served) and 3 copies.			JCPC PD 4 paras 4.6.2, 4.6.3
For fee see PD 7 Annex 2.			JCPC PD 7 Annex 2
Time: within 21 days after service of the notice of appeal.			JCPC PD 4 para 4.6.1
Withdrawal of appeal			
12. *If he wishes to withdraw appeal before it has been listed for hearing:* Appellant writes:		r 33	JCPC PD 7 para 7.16.1
(1) to all the Respondents for their consent;			JCPC PD 7 para 7.16.2
(2) to the Registrar, stating that the parties to the appeal have agreed the costs of the appeal.			JCPC PD 7 para 7.16.2
13. Respondent writes to the Registrar confirming agreement to the withdrawal			

Steps to be taken	Form No	Judicial Committee Rules 2009	Judicial Committee of the Privy Council Practice Directions
of the appeal and that the costs have been agreed.			JCPC PD 7 para 7.16.3
14. *If he wishes to withdraw an appeal that has been listed for hearing:* Appellant:			JCPC PD 7 para 7.16.3 4
(1) serves application on Respondent for his consent;			JCPC PD 7 para 7.16.4
(2) files application for an order (see applications at step 15 below) including whether or not the Respondent has consented, certificate of service, submissions on costs and, where appropriate, indicating how any security money should be disposed of.			JCPC PD 7 para 7.16.4
Fee on filing application: £100.			JCPC PD 7 Annex 2
15. Court may set aside or vary the order appealed from by consent and without an oral hearing, if satisfied that it is appropriate so to do.		r 33(2)	
Incidental applications			
16. Applicant prepares:		r 31	JCPC PD 7 para 7.1.1
(1) application in Form 2 stating:	2	r 31(2)(a)	JCPC PD 7 paras 7.1.2, 7.1.3
(a) what order the applicant is seeking;			
(b) briefly why the applicant is seeking the order; and			
(c) the reasons for making the application;			
(2) evidence in support.		r 31(2)(b)	JCPC PD 7 paras 7.1.2, 7.1.3
17. Applicant serves copy of application and evidence in support on all other parties.		r 31(1)	JCPC PD 7 para 7.1.2
Time: before filing.		r 31(1)	JCPC PD 7 para 7.1.2
18. Applicant files:			
(1) original application and 3 copies;			
application must bear a certificate of service; and			
must indicate whether the other parties consent to or refuse to consent to the application; and			JCPC PD 7 para 7.1.7
(2) evidence in support.			
Fee: £100.			JCPC PD 7 Annex 2
Time: as soon as it becomes apparent that an application is necessary or expedient.			JCPC PD 7 para 7.1.1
19. *If he wishes to oppose application* Party serves notice of objection in Form 3 on:	3	r 31(3)	JCPC PD 7 para 7.1.4

TAB 28   PROCEDURAL TABLES

Steps to be taken	Form No	Judicial Committee Rules 2009	Judicial Committee of the Privy Council Practice Directions
(1) the applicant; and			
(2) any other parties.			
20. Party files:		r 31(3)	JCPC PD 7 paras 7.1.4, 7.1.7
(1) original notice of objection and 3 copies;			
(2) *where appropriate:* certificate of service.			
Fee: £70.			JCPC PD 7 Annex 2
Time: within 14 days after service of the application.		r 31(3)	JCPC PD 7 paras 7.1.4
21. Wherever possible Judicial Committee considers applications without a hearing.			JCPC PD 7 para 7.1.6
22. If application opposed it is referred to a Panel unless Registrar otherwise directs and may be decided with or without an oral hearing.			JCPC PD 7 para 7.1.6
Registrar refuses to accept a document			
23. Registrar may refuse to accept a document if:			JCPC PD 2 paras 2.1.10, 2.1.11
(1) it is illegible; or			
(2) it fails to comply with the rules or Practice Direction.			
Registrar considers application and grants or refuses it.			JCPC PD 5 paras 5.2.4, 5.2.5
Setting hearing date			
24. Parties notify Registrar that the appeal is ready to list and provide a time estimate.		r 22(3)	JCPC PD 6 para 6.2.1
Time: Within 7 days after filing the Statement of Facts and Issues and the Appendix.			
Note: Parties are encouraged to offer agreed dates at an early stage and there is no need to wait until after the SFI is filed.			
25. Registrar informs parties of likely date of hearing of appeal.		r 22(3)	
Filing and exchange of cases			
26. Appellant:	12, 13	r 22	JCPC PD 6 para 6.3.9
(1) files original and 2 copies of his case, a succinct statement of his argument omitting material contained in the Statement of Facts and Issues; and			
(2) serves case on all Respondents.			
Transmission of record			
27. Appellant arranges for the proper officer of court appealed from to have the record:	30	r 20(1)	

Steps to be taken	Form No	Judicial Committee Rules 2009	Judicial Committee of the Privy Council Practice Directions
(1) certified by the proper officer of the court below;			
(2) transmitted to Registrar;			
(3) reproduced.			
Time: Without delay when permission to appeal has been granted or a notice of appeal has been filed.		r 20(1)	
28. Proper officer of court appealed from transmits record to Registrar.			
29. Parties inspect record and agree contents of reproduced record.	30	r 20(3)	
Appellant delay in transmitting the record etc			
30. *If appellant fails to have record transmitted promptly or takes no step in prosecution of appeal:* Registrar may give appropriate directions and dismiss appeal.		r 8(2)	
Statement of Facts and Issues			
31. Appellant drafts statement of facts and issues and précis of case and submits them to every Respondent for approval. The précis should be agreed by every Respondent before filing.	33	r 21(1)	JCPC PD 5 paras 5.1.7, 5.1.8
The statement of facts and issues must:		r 21(2)	JCPC PD 5 paras 5.1.7, 5.2.5
(1) set out relevant facts and issues;			
(2) *if the parties cannot agree as to any matter:* set out what items are disputed;			
(3) contain references to every law report of the proceedings below;			
(4) state the duration of the proceedings below.			JCPC PD 5 para 5.1.7
32. Appellant files:			
(1) original statement and 10 copies;			JCPC PD 5 para 5.2.5
(2) précis of the case on no more than 1 side of A4 paper (in Arial point 12).			JCPC PD 5 para 5.1.8
Time: within 42 days after the filing of the notice of intention to proceed or the notice of appeal.		r 21(1)	
Fee on filing Statement and Appendix: £4,820.			JCPC PD 7 Annex 2
Time: Within 112 days of filing notice of appeal or notice of intention to proceed.			JCPC PD 7 Annex 2
Extension of time for filing Statement of Facts and Issues and Appendix			
If unable to file the statement and appendix within the time limit:			
33. Appellant files application (for applications see step 28 below) explaining in detail why extension required and including the Respondent's view.	2	r 5	JCPC PD 5 paras 5.2.3, 5.2.5

TAB 28 PROCEDURAL TABLES

Steps to be taken	Form No	Judicial Committee Rules 2009	Judicial Committee of the Privy Council Practice Directions
Hearing date			
34. Parties notify Registrar that the appeal is ready to list and specify the number of hours that their respective counsel estimate to be necessary for their oral submissions.		r 22(1)	JCPC PD 6 para 6.2.1
Time: within 14 days after the filing of the Statement of Facts and Issues.		r 22(1)	JCPC PD 6 para 6.2.1
35. Registrar informs parties of the date fixed for the hearing.		r 22(2)	JCPC PD 6 para 6.2.1
Death of party			
36. *If a party to an appeal dies before the hearing:* immediate notice of the death must be given in writing to the Registrar and to the other parties.			JCPC PD 7 para 7.6.1
Time: Immediately as appeal cannot proceed until a new party has been appointed to represent the deceased person's interest.			JCPC PD 7 para 7.6.1
37. Application to substitute new party served on all other parties.	32		JCPC PD 7 para 7.6.2
Time: Before application filed.			JCPC PD 7 para 7.6.2
38. Application to substitute new party filed explaining circumstances and indorsed with a certificate of service on all other parties.			JCPC PD 7 para 7.6.2
Fee: £100.			JCPC PD 7 Annex 2
Time: within 42 days of the date of notice of death.			JCPC PD 7 para 7.6.2
39. *If the death takes place after the case for the deceased person has been filed but before the appeal has been heard:* Appellant files supplemental case setting out the information about the newly-added parties.			JCPC PD 7 para 7.6.3
Change of agent			
If any party to appeal, or other matter changes his agent:			
40. Party or new agent gives notice in writing of change to Registrar and to former agent.		r 40	
Time: when the agent is changed.			
Filing and exchange of appellant's and Respondent's cases			
41. Appellant prepares case and			
(1) files original and 2 copies; and	34, 35		JCPC PD 6 para 6.3.9
(2) serves sufficient copies on the Respondent.			JCPC PD 6 paras 6.2.3, 6.3.10, 6.3.11
The number of copies served on the Respondent should be enough to meet the requirements of coun-			

Steps to be taken	Form No	Judicial Committee Rules 2009	Judicial Committee of the Privy Council Practice Directions
sel and agents and should not usually exceed 8.			JCPC PD 6 para 6.3.11
For fee on see PD 7 Annex 2.			JCPC PD 7 Annex 2
Time: at least 6 weeks before the hearing date.		r 23(1)	JCPC PD 6 para 6.3.9
42. Each Respondent prepares case and:			JCPC PD 6 para 6.2.3
(1) serves it on the Appellant and files original and 2 copies at the Registry; and			JCPC PD 6 paras 6.2.3, 6.3.9
(2) serves sufficient copies on the other Respondents.			JCPC PD 6 paras 6.2.3, 6.3.10, 6.3.11
The number of copies of cases exchanged should be enough to meet the requirements of counsel and agents and should not usually exceed 8.			JCPC PD 6 para 6.3.11
Fee on filing case: £370.			JCPC PD 7 Annex 2
Time: at least 4 weeks before the hearing date.		r 23(3)	JCPC PD 6 para 6.3.9
Authorities			
43. Appellant prepares 10 copies of any authorities he requires.:		r 24	JCPC PD 6 para 6.4.1
44. Respondent provides appellant with 10 copies of any authorities he requires.			
Appellant files 10 copies of the joint set of authorities and 10 copies of every case.		r 24	JCPC PD 6 paras 6.4.1, 6.3.14
Time: at least 14 days before the hearing.			JCPC PD 6 para 6.4.1
Hearing of appeal		r 28	
45. Provisional dates are agreed with the parties well in advance of the hearing.			JCPC PD 6 para 6.5.1
46. Court sends formal notification of the hearing to the agents.			
Time: shortly before the hearing.			JCPC PD 6 para 6.5.1
47. Parties attend on appointed day for hearing of appeal. Not more than two Counsel will be heard on behalf of a party (or a single counsel on behalf of an intervener permitted to make oral submissions).			JCPC PD 6 para 6.5.5
48. Judicial Committee may, at the end of the hearing:			
(1) reserve judgment; or			
(2) deliver judgment with reasons; or			
(3) deliver judgment but reserve their reasons.			
If judgment or reasons reserved:			
49. Registrar notifies parties of day appointed by Judicial Committee for deliv-			

TAB 28   PROCEDURAL TABLES

Steps to be taken	Form No	Judicial Committee Rules 2009	Judicial Committee of the Privy Council Practice Directions
ery of judgment or reasons in open court.		r 29	JCPC PD 6 para 6.7.1.1
The judgment, when delivered, will usually contain directions as to costs.			
50. Registrar draws up Order in Council embodying report of Judicial Committee to Her Majesty on the appeal (ie, the effect of the judgment) and arranges the submission of the report to Her Majesty in Council, or draws Judicial Committee's order.	38–43	r 30	
51. Registrar sends draft Order to parties for approval.		r 30(1)	
52. Parties return draft Order approved or with comments.		r 30(1)	
Assessment of costs			
53. Where the Judicial Committee has made an order for costs: Receiving party submits claim for costs to the Registrar in the required form with the required particulars and information.		r 45(1)	JCPC PD 8 paras 7, 9
Fee: 2.5% of sum claimed and 2.5% of the sum allowed.			JCPC PD 7 Annex 2
Time: within 3 months beginning with the date on which the costs order was made.		r 45(1)	
54. Receiving party serves a copy of a claim for costs on the paying party.		r 45(3)	
55. Paying party may (or if the bill is above £20,000, must) file and serve points of dispute.		r 45(4)	
Time: within 21 days beginning with the day on which a claim for costs is served.		r 45(5)	JCPC PD 8 para 15.1
56. Receiving party files and serves response.			JCPC PD 8 para 15.1
Time: within 14 days beginning with the day on which points of dispute are served.			
57. Registrar gives notice of the day and time appointed for assessment to all those entitled to be heard at the assessment.			JCPC PD 8 para 15.3
Time: at least 21 days before the day appointed.			JCPC PD 8 para 15.3
58. A Costs Judge conducts detailed assessment.		r 46	JCPC PD 8 para 1.1
59. Parties attend on appointed day before a Costs Judge.			
The amount allowed is inserted in the order determining the appeal.		r 50	
If assessment is not completed before the Order or Order in Council is made, the amount allowed may be certified subsequently.		r 50	
Fee: 2.5% of sum claimed and 2.5% of the sum allowed.			JCPC PD 7 Annex 2

Steps to be taken	Form No	Judicial Committee Rules 2009	Judicial Committee of the Privy Council Practice Directions
60. *If any party is dissatisfied with the assessment:* Party dissatisfied with the assessment appeals from decision of costs officer to Judicial Committee by incidental application (see steps 16–22 above).		r 51	
Fee on appeal against a decision made on assessment of costs: £150.			
Time: within 14 days after the decision of the costs officer.		r 51	JCPC PD 8 para 18.3
Issue of Order in Council			
61. Registrar:			
(1) inserts in Order in Council:			
(a) amount of assessed costs; and			
(b) any direction by Judicial Committee as to any security filed by appellant; and		rr 30, 50	
(2) arranges printing, signing and sealing of Order in Council.			
62. Registrar sends original Order in Council to court appealed from and copies are sent to parties.			
63. Registrar pays out any security in accordance with Order in Council.			

COURT GUIDES

ADMIRALTY
AND COMMERCIAL COURTS GUIDE

TABLE OF CONTENTS

Introduction.. CPR 61 ACG Intro 1
Section A   Preliminary ....CPR 61 ACG A1
Section B   Commencement, Transfer and Removal..............CPR 61 ACG B1
Section C   Particulars of Claim, Defence and Reply ....CPR 61 ACG C1
Section D   Case Management in the Commercial Court ....CPR 61 ACG D1
Section E   Disclosure....................................CPR 61 ACG E1
Section F   Applications ....CPR 61 ACG F1
Section G   Alternative Dispute Resolution ("ADR").............CPR 61 ACG G1
Section H   Evidence for Trial..............................CPR 61 ACG H1
Section J   Trial .... CPR 61 ACG J1
Section K   After Trial....................................CPR 61 ACG K1
Section L   Multi-party Disputes............................CPR 61 ACG L1
Section M   Litigants in person ....CPR 61 ACG M1
Section N   Admiralty ....CPR 61 ACG N1
Section O   Arbitration ....CPR 61 ACG O1
Section P   Miscellaneous.................................CPR 61 ACG P1
Appendix 1   CPR Part 58 (Commercial Court), and Part 61
               (Admiralty Court); Practice Directions 58 and 61 .CPR 61 ACG App 1 [1]
Appendix 2   CPR Part 62 (Arbitration); Practice Direction 62. .CPR 61 ACG App 2 [1]
Appendix 3   Procedure for issue of claim form when Registry
               closed .... CPR 61 ACG App 3
Appendix 4   Statements of case............................ CPR 61 ACG App 4
Appendix 5   Forms of freezing injunction and search order.....CPR 61 ACG App 5.1
Appendix 6   Case management information sheet .... CPR 61 ACG App 6
Appendix 7   Draft ADR order .... CPR 61 ACG App 7
Appendix 8   Standard pre-trial timetable .... CPR 61 ACG App 8
Appendix 9   Skeleton arguments, chronologies and indices ..... CPR 61 ACG App 9
Appendix 10   Preparation of bundles .... CPR 61 ACG App 10
Appendix 11   Expert evidence............................. CPR 61 ACG App 11
Appendix 12   Progress monitoring information sheet........... CPR 61 ACG App 12
Appendix 13   Pre-trial checklist .... CPR 61 ACG App 13
Appendix 14   Video conferencing guidance .... CPR 61 ACG App 14
Appendix 15   Service out of the jurisdiction: related practice..... CPR 61 ACG App 15
Appendix 16   Security for costs: related practice .... CPR 61 ACG App 16
Appendix 17   Commercial Court User E-mail Guidance .... CPR 61 ACG App 17
Appendix 18   Commercial Court e-working Scheme .... CPR 61 ACG App 18
Appendix 19   Guidance on practical steps for transferring cases to
               London Mercantile Court and to the
               Mercantile Courts.......................... CPR 61 ACG App 19
Addresses and contact details .... CPR 61 ACG Add 1
Forms.. CPR 61 ACG Form 1

INTRODUCTION

CPR 61 ACG Intro 1

This edition of the Admiralty & Commercial Court Guide largely reflects suggestions for improvement made by users since the publication of the 2009 edition. Most of the changes made are points of detail. The Guide incorporates the recent Practice Directions on Arbitration Appeals, E-disclosure and the Electronic Working Scheme. It also reflects the recommendations made in the Jackson Report in relation to docketing. On a practical level users should take note of the provisions relating to lists of issues (D6.1), skeleton arguments (Appendix 9.1 and 9.2(d)), core bundles (Appendix 10.4) and bundles of authorities (F13.4). We are grateful to our colleagues for their assistance in revising the Guide, and in particular to Mr Justice Hamblen who drew together the comments of practitioners through the Users CPR/Guide sub-committee which he chairs.

The Guide is intended to promote the efficient conduct of litigation in the Admiralty and Commercial Courts. It does not provide a complete blueprint for litigation and should be seen as providing guidance to be adopted flexibly and adapted to the exigencies of the particular case. It should not be understood to override in any way the Civil Procedure Rules or Practice Directions made under them, or as fettering the discretion of the judges.

We try to keep the Guide up to date, and suggestions for its improvement are always welcome.

The Hon Mr Justice David Steel

The Admiralty Judge

The Hon Mrs. Justice Gloster DBE

Judge in charge of the Commercial Court

A. PRELIMINARY

A1 The procedural framework

CPR 61 ACG A1

A1.1 Proceedings in the Commercial Court are governed by the Civil Procedure Rules ("CPR") and Practice Directions. CPR Part 58 and its associated Practice Direction deal specifically with the Commercial Court. Part 61 deals with the Admiralty Court and Part 62 deals with arbitration applications. Parts 58 and 61 and their associated Practice Directions are set out in Appendix 1; Rule 62 and its associated Practice Direction is set out in Appendix 2.

A1.2 The Admiralty and Commercial Courts Guide is published with the approval of the Lord Chief Justice and the Head of Civil Justice in consultation with the Judges of the Admiralty and Commercial Courts and with the advice and support of the Admiralty Court and Commercial Court Users Committees. It is intended to provide guidance about the conduct of proceedings in the Admiralty and Commercial Courts and, within the framework of the Civil Procedure Rules and Practice Directions, to establish the practice to be followed in those Courts.

A1.3 It is important to understand what the Guide is and what it is not. It provides guidance without prejudice to the provisions of the CPR and the Practice Directions. It is not itself a Practice Direction and does not constrain in any way how the judges might exercise their discretion under the Rules and Practice Directions in accordance with the overriding objective.

A1.4 Thus, the requirements of the Guide are designed to ensure effective management of proceedings in the Admiralty and Commercial Courts. On matters for which specific provision is not made by the Guide, the parties, their solicitors and counsel will be expected to act reasonably and in accordance with the spirit of the Guide.

A1.5 Pre-trial matters in the Admiralty and Commercial Courts are dealt with by the judges of those Courts: 58PD section 1.2.

A1.6 The Court expects a high level of co-operation and realism from the legal representatives of the parties. This applies to dealings (including correspondence) between legal representatives as well as to dealings with the Court.

A1.7 In order to avoid excessive repetition, the Guide has been written by reference to proceedings in the Commercial Court. Practitioners should treat the guidance as applicable to proceedings in the Admiralty Court unless the content of Part 61 or Section N of this Guide ("Admiralty") specifically requires otherwise.

A1.8 Parties may communicate with by e-mail with the Commercial and Admiralty Courts on certain matters. Those matters are defined and the required procedures (which must be observed) are set out in Appendix 17.

A1.9 On 1 April 2009 the Commercial Court started an electronic working pilot scheme under PD Electronic Working Pilot Scheme. On 1 April 2010 the pilot scheme was replaced with the Electronic Working Scheme as set out in Practice Direction 5C. The Scheme may be used to start claims pursuant to Part 7, Part 8 and Part 20 and also Arbitration claims and Admiralty proceedings as appropriate in the Admiralty and Commercial Court. Full details of the scheme and the text of the Practice Direction can be found at Appendix 18. Information about the scheme can also be found on the Commercial Court website: www.hmCourts-service.gov.uk /infoabout/admiralcomm/.

A2 The Admiralty and Commercial Registry; the Commercial Court Listing office

CPR 61 ACG A2

A2.1 The administrative office for the Admiralty Court and the Commercial Court is the Admiralty & Commercial Registry ("the Registry") which is located at 7 Rolls Building, Fetter Lane, London EC4A 1NL. The Commercial Court Listing Office ("the Listing Office") is located at the same address.

A2.2 It is important that there is close liaison between legal representatives of the parties and both the Registry and the Listing Office. All communications by one party with the Registry and/or Listing Office should be copied to other parties.

A3 The Commercial Court Users Committee

CPR 61 ACG A3

A3.1 The success of the Court's ability to meet the special problems and continually changing needs of the commercial community depends in part upon a steady flow of information and constructive suggestions between the Court, litigants and professional advisers.

A3.2 The Commercial Court Users Committee has assisted in this process for many years, and it is expected to continue to do so. All concerned with the Court are encouraged to make the fullest use of this important channel of communication. Correspondence raising matters for the consideration of the Committee or suggestions for changes or improvements to the Guide should be addressed to the Clerk to the Commercial Court, 7 Rolls Building, Fetter Lane, London, EC4A 1NL or sent by email to ComCt.Listing@hmcts.gsi.gov.uk.

A4 Specialist associations

CPR 61 ACG A4

A4.1 There are a number of associations of legal representatives which liaise closely with the Commercial Court. These will also play an important part in helping to ensure that the Court remains responsive to the "overriding objective".

A4.2 The associations include the Commercial Bar Association ("COMBAR"), the London Common Law and Commercial Bar Association ("LCLCBA"), the City of London Law Society, the London Solicitors Litigation Association, the Commercial Litigators' Forum and the Admiralty Solicitors Group.

B. COMMENCEMENT, TRANSFER AND REMOVAL

B1 Commercial cases

CPR 61 ACG B1

B1.1 Rule 58.1(2) describes a "commercial claim" as follows:

"any claim arising out of the transaction of trade and commerce and includes any claim relating to -

(a)   a business document or contract;

(b)   the export or import of goods;

(c)   the carriage of goods by land, sea, air or pipeline;

(d)   the exploitation of oil and gas reserves or other natural resources;

(e)   insurance and re-insurance;

(f)   banking and financial services;

(g)   the operation of markets and exchanges;

(h)   the purchase and sale of commodities;

(i)   the construction of ships;

(j)   business agency; and

(k)   arbitration."

B2 Starting a case in the Commercial Court

CPR 61 ACG B2

B2.1 Except for arbitration applications which are governed by the provisions of CPR Part 62 and section O of the Guide, the case will be begun by a claim form under Part 7 or Part 8.

B2.2 Save where otherwise specified, references in this Guide to a claim form are to a Part 7 claim form.

B2.3 The Commercial Court may give a fixed date for trial (see section D16), but it does not give a fixed date for a hearing when it issues a claim. Rules 7.9 and 7.10 and their associated Practice Directions do not apply to the Commercial Court.

B2.4 A request for the issue of a Part 7 or a Part 8 claim form may be made by fax at certain times when the Registry is closed to the public: PD58 2.2. The procedure is set out in Appendix 3. Further details may be obtained from the Commercial Court website (www.hmcourts-service.gov.uk/infoabout/admiralcomm) or from the Registry. The fax number is 020 7947 6245.

B2.5 The Commercial Court may give a fixed date for trial (see section D16), but it does not give a fixed date for a hearing when it issues a claim. Rules 7.9 and 7.10 and their associated practice directions do not apply to the Commercial Court.

B3 Pre-Action Protocols

CPR 61 ACG B3

B3.1 The Practice Direction – Protocols applies to actions in the Commercial Court and usually it should be observed, although it is sometimes necessary or proper to start proceedings without following the procedures there contemplated: for example, where delays in starting proceedings might prompt forum-shopping in other jurisdictions. There is no approved protocol for actions in the Commercial Court generally, but cases in the Commercial Court are sometimes covered by an approved protocol, such as the Professional Negligence Pre-Action Protocol.

B3.2 Subject to complying with the Practice Direction and any applicable approved protocol, the parties to proceedings in the Commercial Court are not required, or generally expected, to engage in elaborate or expensive pre-action procedures, and restraint is encouraged.

B3.3 Thus, the letter of claim should be concise and it is usually sufficient to explain the proposed claim(s), identifying key dates, so as to enable the potential defendant to understand and to investigate the allegations. Only essential documents need be supplied, and the period specified for a response should not be longer than one month without good reason.

B3.4 A potential defendant should respond to a letter of claim concisely and only essential documents need by supplied. It should often be possible to respond sufficiently within the 21 days referred to in para 4.4 of the Practice Direction for acknowledgment of the letter of claim. The Practice Direction (para 4.3(c)) requires a potential defendant to give reasons if he requires longer to respond than the period specified in the letter of claim, and even if the period specified is longer than one month, a potential defendant who needs longer should explain the reasons when acknowledging the letter of claim.

B4 Part 7 claims

The form

CPR 61 ACG B4

B4.1 A claimant starting proceedings in the Commercial Court must use practice form N1(CC) for Part 7 claims: PD58 section 2.4.

Marking

B4.2 In accordance with PD58 section 2.3 the claim form should be marked in the top right hand corner with the words "Queen's Bench Division, Commercial Court", and on the issue of the claim form out of the Registry the case will be entered in the Commercial List. Marking the claim form in this way complies sufficiently with PD7 section 3.6(3).

Statement of value

B4.3 Rule 16.3, which provides for a statement of value to be included in the claim form, does not apply in the Commercial Court: rule 58.5(2).

Particulars of claim and the claim form

B4.4 Although particulars of claim may be served with the claim form, this is not a requirement in the Commercial Court. However, if the particulars of claim are not contained in or served with the claim form, the claim form must contain a statement that if an acknowledgment of service is filed indicating an intention to defend the claim, particulars of claim will follow: rule 58.5(1)(a).

B4.5 If particulars of claim do not accompany the claim form they must be served within 28 days after the defendant has filed an acknowledgment of service indicating an intention to defend the claim: rule 58.5(1)(c).

B4.6 The three forms specified in rule 7.8(1) must be served with the claim form. One of these is a form for acknowledging service: rule 58.5(1)(b).

Statement of truth

B4.7 (a) A claim form must be verified by a statement of truth: rule 22.1. Unless the Court otherwise orders, any amendment to a claim form must also be verified: rule 22.1(2).

(b) The required form of statement of truth is set out at PD7 section 7.2.

(c) A claim form will remain effective even where not verified by a statement of truth, unless it is struck out: PD22 section 4.1.

(d) In certain cases the statement of truth may be signed by a person other than the party on whose behalf it is served or its legal representative: section C1.8-1.9.

Trial without service of particulars of claim or a defence

B4.8 The attention of the parties and their legal representatives is drawn to rule 58.11 which allows the Court to order (before or after the issue of a claim form) that the case shall proceed without the filing or service of particulars of claim or defence or of any other statement of case. This facility is to be used with caution. It is unlikely to be appropriate unless all the issues have already been clearly defined in previous exchanges between the parties either in the course of a pre-claim form application or in previous correspondence and then only when the issues are of law or construction.

Interest

B4.9 The claim form (and not only the particulars of claim) must comply with the requirements of rules 16.4(1)(b) and 16.4(2) concerning interest: rule 58.5(3).

B4.10 References to particulars of claim in rule 12.6(1)(a) (referring to claims for interest where there is a default judgment) and rule 14.14(1)(a) (referring to claims for interest where there is a judgment on admissions) may be treated as references to the claim form: rules 58.8(2) and 58.9(3).

B5 Part 8 claims

Form

CPR 61 ACG B5

B5.1 A claimant who wishes to commence a claim under CPR Part 8 must use practice form N208(CC): PD58 section 2.4.

B5.2 Attention is drawn to the requirement in rule 8.2(a) that where a claimant uses the Part 8 procedure his claim form must state that Part 8 applies. Similarly, PD7 section 3.3 requires that the claim form state (if it be the case) that the claimant wishes his claim to proceed under Part 8 or that the claim is required to proceed under Part 8.

Marking and statement of truth

B5.3 Sections B3.2 (marking) and B3.7 (statement of truth) also apply to a claim form issued under Part 8.

Time for filing evidence in opposition to a Part 8 claim

B5.4 A defendant to a Part 8 claim who wishes to rely on written evidence must file and serve it within 28 days after filing an acknowledgment of service: rule 58.12.

B6 Part 20 claims

Form

CPR 61 ACG B6

B6.1 Adapted versions of the Part 20 claim form and acknowledgment of service (Practice Forms no. N211 and N213) and of the related Notes to Part 20 claimant and Part 20 defendant have been approved for use in the Commercial Court.

B7 Service of the claim form

Service by the parties

CPR 61 ACG B7

B7.1 Claim forms issued in the Commercial List are to be served by the parties, not by the Registry: PD58 section 9.

Methods of service

B7.2 Methods of service are set out in CPR Part 6, which is supplemented by a Practice Direction.

B7.3 PD6 sections 2.1 and 3.1 concern service by document exchange and other means, including fax and other electronic means. There are specific provisions about when a solicitor acting for a party may be served.

Applications for extension of time

B7.4 Applications for an extension of time in which to serve a claim form are governed by rule 7.6. Rule 7.6(3)(a), which refers to service of the claim form by the Court, does not apply in the Commercial Court.

B7.5 The evidence required on an application for an extension of time is set out in PD7 section 8.2. In an appropriate case it may be presented by an application notice verified by a statement of truth and without a separate witness statement: rule 32.6(2).

Certificate of service

B7.6 When the claimant has served the claim form he must file a certificate of service: rule 6.14(2). Satisfaction of this requirement is relevant, in particular, to the claimant's ability to obtain judgment in default (see Part 12) and to the right of a non-party to search for, inspect and take a copy of the claim form under rule 5.4(2)(a).

B8 Service of the claim form out of the jurisdiction

CPR 61 ACG B8

B8.1 Service of claim forms outside the jurisdiction without permission is governed by rules 6.32–6.35, and where rule 6.35(5) applies by PD6B.

B8.2 Applications for permission to serve a claim form out of the jurisdiction are governed by rules 6.36 and 6.37 and PD6B. A Guide to the appropriate practice is set out in Appendix 15.

B8.3 Service of process in some foreign countries may take a long time to complete; it is therefore important that solicitors take prompt steps to effect service.

B9 Acknowledgment of service

Part 7 claims

CPR 61 ACG B9

B9.1 (a) A defendant must file an acknowledgment of service in every case: rule 58.6(1). An adapted version of practice form N9 (which includes the acknowledgment of service) has been approved for use in the Commercial Court.

(b) The period for filing an acknowledgment of service is calculated from the service of the claim form, whether or not particulars of claim are contained in or accompany the claim form or are to follow service of the claim form. Rule 9.1(2), which provides that in certain circumstances the defendant need not respond to the claim until particulars of claim have been served on him, does not apply: rule 58.6(1).

Part 8 claims

B9.2 (a) A defendant must file an acknowledgment of service in every case: rule 58.6(1). An adapted version of practice form N210 (acknowledgment of service of a Part 8 claim form) has been approved for use in the Commercial Court. A copy of this practice form (Form N210(CC)) is included at the end of the Guide, together with adapted versions of the notes for claimants and defendants on completing and replying to a Part 8 claim form.

(b) The time for filing an acknowledgment of service is calculated from the service of the claim form.

Acknowledgment of service in a claim against a firm

B9.3 (a) PD10 section 4.4 allows an acknowledgment of service to be signed on behalf of a partnership by any of the partners or a person having the control or management of the partnership business, whether he be a partner or not.

(b) However, attention is drawn to Schedule 1 to the CPR which includes, with modifications, provisions previously contained in RSC Order 81 concerning acknowledgment of service by a person served as a partner who denies his liability as such. (see also the note at the end of CPR Part 10).

Time for filing acknowledgment of service

B9.4 (a) Except in the circumstances described in section B9.4(b) and B9.4(c), or is otherwise ordered by the Court, the period for filing an acknowledgment of service is 14 days after service of the claim form.

(b) If the claim form has been served out of the jurisdiction without the permission of the Court under rules 6.32 and 33 the time for filing an acknowledgment of service is governed by rule 6.35, save that in all cases time runs from the service of the claim form: rule 58.6(3).

(c) If the claim form has been served out of the jurisdiction with the permission of the Court under rule 6.36 the time for filing an acknowledgment of service is governed by rule 6.37.5, see Practice Direction B supplementing rule 6 and the table to which it refers, save that in all cases time runs from the service of the claim form: rule 58.6(3).

B10 Disputing the Court's jurisdiction

Part 7 claims

CPR 61 ACG B10

B10.1 (a) If the defendant intends to dispute the Court's jurisdiction or contend that the Court should not exercise its jurisdiction he must

(i)   file an acknowledgment of service - rule 11(2); and

(ii)   issue an application notice seeking the appropriate relief.

(b) An application to dispute the Court's jurisdiction must be made within 28 days after filing an acknowledgment of service: rule 58.7(2)

(c) If the defendant wishes to rely on written evidence in support of that application, he must file and serve that evidence when he issues the application. In an appropriate case it may be presented by an application notice verified by a statement of truth and without a separate witness statement: CPR32.6(2).

(d) The parties to that application should consider at the time of the application or as soon as possible thereafter whether the application is a 'heavy application' within Section F6.1 likely to last more than half a day but for which the automatic timetable provisions in PD 58 para 13.2 and F6.3 – F6.5 will not for any reason be appropriate. If any party considers that special timetabling is required otherwise than in accordance with those automatic provisions it should at once so inform all other parties and the Listing Office. Unless a timetable covering those matters covered by Section F6.3 to F6.5 can be agreed forthwith, the applicant must without delay inform the Listing Office that a directions hearing will be required. For the purposes of such a hearing all parties must by 1pm on the day before that hearing lodge with the Listing Office a brief summary of the issues of fact and law likely to arise on the application, a list of witnesses of fact whose witness statements or affidavits are likely to be adduced by that party, a list of expert witnesses on whose report that party intends to reply, an estimate of how long the hearing will take and how much pre-hearing reading will be required by the judge and a proposed pre-hearing timetable.

(e) If the defendant makes an application under rule 11(1), the claimant is not bound to serve particulars of claim until that application has been disposed of: rule 58.7(3).

Part 8 claims

B10.2 (a) The provisions of section B10.1(a)–(c) also apply in the case of Part 8 claims.

(b) If the defendant makes an application under rule 11(1), he is not bound to serve any written evidence on which he wishes to rely in opposition to the substantive claim until that application has been disposed of: rule 11.9.

Effect of an application challenging the jurisdiction

B10.3 An acknowledgment of service of a Part 7 or Part 8 claim form which is followed by an application challenging the jurisdiction under Part 11 does not constitute a submission by the defendant to the jurisdiction: rules 11(3) and 11(7).

B10.4 If an application under Part 11 is unsuccessful, and the Court then considers giving directions for filing and serving statements of case (in the case of a Part 7 claim) or evidence (in the case of a Part 8 claim), a defendant does not submit to the jurisdiction merely by asking for time to serve and file his statement of case or evidence, as the case may be.

B11 Default judgment

CPR 61 ACG B11

B11.1 Default judgment is governed by Part 12 and PD12. However, because in the Commercial Court the period for filing the acknowledgment of service is calculated from service of the claim form, the reference to "particulars of claim" in PD12 section 4.1(1) should be read as referring to the claim form: PD58 section 6(1).

B12 Admissions

CPR 61 ACG B12

B12.1 (a) Admissions are governed by CPR Part 14, and PD14, except that the references to "particulars of claim" in PD14 sections 2.1, 3.1 and 3.2 should be read as referring to the claim form: PD58 section 6(2).

(b) Adapted versions of the practice forms of admission (practice forms no. N9A and no. N9C) have been approved for use in the Commercial Court.

B13 Transfer of cases into and out of the Commercial List

CPR 61 ACG B13

B13.1 The procedure for transfer and removal is set out in PD58 section 4. All such applications must be made to the Commercial Court: rule 30.5(3).

B13.2 Although an order to transfer a case to the Commercial List may be made at any stage, any application for such an order should normally be made at an early stage in the proceedings. It might be appropriate for some cases to be brought in a Mercantile Court and managed in its early stages in a Mercantile Court before being transferred to the Commercial List

B13.3 Transfer to the Commercial List may be ordered for limited purposes only, but a transferred case will normally remain in the Commercial List until its conclusion.

B13.4 An order transferring a case out of the Commercial List may be made at any stage, but will not usually be made after a pre-trial timetable has been fixed at the case management conference (see section D8).

B13.5 Some commercial cases may more suitably, or as suitably, be dealt with in one of the Mercantile Courts or the London Mercantile Court. Parties should consider whether it would be more appropriate to begin proceedings in one of those Courts and the Commercial Judge may on his own initiative order the case to be transferred there. Guidance on practical steps for transferring cases to the London Mercantile Court and to the Mercantile Courts is contained in a Guidance Note at Appendix 19.

C. PARTICULARS OF CLAIM, DEFENCE AND REPLY

C1 Form, content, serving and filing

CPR 61 ACG C1

C1.1 (a) Particulars of claim, the defence and any reply must be set out in separate consecutively numbered paragraphs and be as brief and concise as possible. They should not set out evidence. They should also comply with Appendix 4 to the Guide.

(b) Statements of case should be limited to 25 pages in length. The Court will give permission for a longer statement of case to be served where a party shows good reasons for doing so, and if it does the Court might require that a summary of the statement of case is also served. Any application to serve a statement of case longer than 25 pages should be made on paper to the Court briefly stating the reasons for exceeding the 25 page limit.

(c) It is seldom necessary for the proper understanding of the statement of case to include substantial parts of a lengthy document, but if this is necessary the passages in question should be set out in a schedule rather than in the body of the case.

(d) The document must be signed by the individual person or persons who drafted it, not, in the case of a solicitor, in the name of the firm alone.

(e) Documents should be in the form stipulated in the Practice Direction to CPR part 5, including that there should be numbered paragraphs and numbered pages.

C1.2 (a) Particulars of claim, the defence and also any reply must comply with the provisions of rules 16.4 and 16.5, save that rules 16.5(6) and 16.5(8) do not apply.

(b) The requirements of PD16 section 7.4 - 8.1 (which relate to claims based upon oral agreements, agreements by conduct and Consumer Credit Agreements and to reliance upon evidence of certain matters under the Civil Evidence Act 1968) should be treated as applying to the defence and reply as well as to the particulars of claim.

(c)

(i)   full and specific details should be given of any allegation of fraud, dishonesty, malice or illegality; and

(ii)   where an inference of fraud or dishonesty is alleged, the facts on the basis of which the inference is alleged must be fully set out.

(d) Any legislative provision upon which an allegation is based must be clearly identified and the basis of its application explained.

(e) Any provision of The Human Rights Act 1998 (including the Convention) on which a party relies in support of its case must be clearly identified and the basis of its application explained.

(f) Any principle of foreign law or foreign legislative provision upon which a party's case is based must be clearly identified and the basis of its application explained.

(g) It is important that if a defendant or Part 20 defendant wishes to advance by way of defence or defence to counterclaim a positive case on causation, mitigation or quantification of damages, proper details of that case should be included in the defence or Part 20 defence at the outset or, if not then available, as early as possible thereafter.

C1.3 (a) PD16 section 7.3 relating to a claim based upon a written agreement should be treated as also applying to the defence, unless the claim and the defence are based on the same agreement.

(b) In most cases attaching documents to or serving documents with a statement of case does not promote the efficient conduct of the proceedings and should be avoided.

(c) If documents are to be served at the same time as a statement of case they should normally be served separately from rather than attached to the statement of case.

(d) Only those documents which are obviously of critical importance and necessary for a proper understanding of the statement of case should be attached to or served with it. The statement of case must itself refer to the fact that documents are attached to or served with it.

(e) An expert's report should not be attached to the statement of case and should not be filed with the statement of case at the Registry. A party must obtain permission from the Court in order to adduce expert evidence at trial and therefore any party which serves an expert's report without obtaining such permission does so at his own risk as to costs.

(f) Notwithstanding PD16 section 7.3(1), a true copy of the complete written agreement may be made available at any hearing unless the Court orders otherwise.

Adapted versions of the practice forms of defence and counterclaim have been approved for use in the Commercial Court.

Statement of truth

C1.4 Particulars of claim, a defence and any reply must be verified by a statement of truth: rule 22.1. So too must any amendment, unless the Court otherwise orders: rule 22.1(2); see also section C5.4.

C1.5 The required form of statement of truth is as follows:

(i)   for particulars of claim, as set out in PD7 section 7.2 or PD16 section 3.4;

(ii)   for a defence, as set out in PD15 section 2.2 or PD16 section 12.2;

(iii)   for a reply the statement of truth should follow the form for the particulars of claim, but substituting the word "reply" for the words "particulars of claim" (see PD22 section 2.1).

C1.6 Rule 22.1(5), (6) and (8) and PD22 section 3 state who may sign a statement of truth. For example, if insurers are conducting proceedings on behalf of many claimants or defendants a statement of truth may be signed by a senior person responsible for the case at a lead insurer, but

(i)   the person signing must specify the capacity in which he signs;

(ii)   the statement of truth must be a statement that the lead insurer believes that the facts stated in the document are true; and

(iii)   the Court may order that a statement of truth also be signed by one or more of the parties.

See PD22 section 3.6B

C1.7 A statement of case remains effective (although it may not be relied on as evidence) even where it is not verified by a statement of truth, unless it is struck out: PD22 section section 4.1-4.3.

Service

C1.8 All statements of case are served by the parties, not by the Court: PD58 section 9.

Filing

C1.9 The statements of case filed with the Court form part of the permanent record of the Court.

C2 Serving and filing particulars of claim

CPR 61 ACG C2

C2.1 Subject to any contrary order of the Court and unless particulars of claim are contained in or accompany the claim form

(i)   the period for serving particulars of claim is 28 days after filing an acknowledgment of service: rule 58.5(1)(c);

(ii)   the parties may agree extensions of the period for serving the particulars of claim. However, any such agreement and brief reasons must be evidenced in writing and notified to the Court, addressed to the Listing office: PD58 section 7.1;

C2.2 The Court may make an order overriding any agreement by the parties varying a time limit: PD58 section 7.2.

C2.3 The claimant must serve the particulars of claim on all other parties. A copy of the claim form will be filed at the Registry on issue. If the claimant serves particulars of claim separately from the claim form he must file a copy within 7 days of service together with a certificate of service: rule 7.4(3).

C3 Serving and filing a defence

CPR 61 ACG C3

C3.1 The defendant must serve the defence on all other parties and must at the same time file a copy with the Court.

C3.2 (a)

(i)   If the defendant files an acknowledgment of service which indicates an intention to defend the period for serving and filing a defence is 28 days after service of the particulars of claim, subject to the provisions of rule 15.4(2). (See also Appendix 15 for cases where the claim form has been served out of the jurisdiction).

(ii)   If the defendant files an acknowledgement of service stating that he wishes to dispute the Court's jurisdiction, the period for serving and filing a defence is 28 days after filing of the acknowledgement of service (unless an application to challenge the jurisdiction is made on or before that date, in which case no defence need be served before the hearing of the application: see CPR 11(7) and (9)).

(b) The defendant and the claimant may agree that the period for serving and filing a defence shall be extended by up to 28 days: rule 15.5(1). However, any such agreement and brief reasons must be evidenced in writing and notified to the Court, addressed to the Case Management Unit: PD58 section 7.1;

(c) An application to the Court is required for any further extension. If the parties are able to agree that a further extension should be granted, a draft consent order should be provided together with a brief explanation of the reasons for the extension.

C3.3 The general power to agree variations to time limits contained in rule 2.11 and PD58 section 7.1 enables parties to agree extensions of the period for serving and filing a defence that exceed 28 days. The length of extension must in all cases be specified, and any such agreement must be evidenced in writing and comply with the requirements of section C2.1.

C3.4 The claimant must notify the Listing Office by letter when all defendants who intend to serve a defence have done so. This information is material to the fixing of the case management conference (see section D3.1).

C4 Serving and filing a reply

CPR 61 ACG C4

C4.1 Subject to section C4.3, the period for serving and filing a reply (or any accompanying defence to counterclaim) is 21 days after service of the defence: rule 58.10(1).

C4.2 A claimant who does not file a reply does not admit what is pleaded in the defence and a claimant who files a reply that does not deal with something pleaded in the defence is not taken to admit it. A reply should be served only when necessary and then only plead what is necessary: it should not repeat what is pleaded in the particulars of claim.

C4.3 (a) A reply must be filed at the same time as it is served: rule15.8(b); rule 15.8(a) does not apply in proceedings in the Commercial List.

(b) The reply should be served before case management information sheets are provided to the Court (see section D8.5). In the normal case, this will allow the parties to consider any reply before completing the case management information sheet, and allow time for the preparation of the case memorandum and the list of issues each of which is required for the case management conference (see sections D5-D7).

C4.4 In some cases, more than 21 days may be needed for the preparation, service and filing of a reply. In such cases an application should be made on paper for an extension of time and for a postponement of the case management conference. The procedure to be followed when making an application on paper is set out in section F4. If the parties are able to agree that a further extension should be granted, a draft consent order should be provided together with a brief explanation of the reasons for the extension.

C4.5 Any reply must be served by the claimant on all other parties: rule 58.10(1).

C5 Amendment

CPR 61 ACG C5

C5.1 (a) Amendments to a statement of case must show the original text, unless the Court orders otherwise: PD58 section 8.

(b) Amendments may be shown by using footnotes or marginal notes, provided they identify precisely where and when an amendment has been made.

(c) Unless the Court so orders, there is no need to show amendments by colour-coding.

(d) If there have been extensive amendments it may be desirable to prepare a fresh copy of the statement of case. However, a copy of the statement of case showing where and when amendments have been made must also be made available.

C5.2 All amendments to any statement of case must be verified by a statement of truth unless the Court orders otherwise: rule 22.1(2).

C5.3 Questions of amendment, and consequential amendment, should wherever possible be dealt with by consent. A party should consent to a proposed amendment unless he has substantial grounds for objecting to it.

C5.4 Late amendments should be avoided and may be disallowed.

D. CASE MANAGEMENT IN THE COMMERCIAL COURT

D1 Generally

CPR 61 ACG D1

D1.1 All proceedings in the Commercial List will be subject to management by the Court.

D1.2 All proceedings in the Commercial List are automatically allocated to the multi-track and consequently Part 26 and the rules relating to allocation do not apply: rule 58.13(1).

D1.3 Except for rule 29.3(2) (legal representatives to attend case management conferences and pre-trial reviews) and rule 29.5 (variation of case management timetable), Part 29 does not apply to proceedings in the Commercial List: rule 58.13(2).

D1.4 If a party has a legal representative, all case management conferences must be attended by such a representative who is familiar with the case and has sufficient authority to deal with any issues that are likely to arise: rule 29.3(2)

Editorial note

See Heavy and Complex Cases at para.2A–18.1, above.

D2 Key features of case management in the Commercial Court

CPR 61 ACG D2

D2 Case management is governed by rule 58.13 and PD58 section 10. In a normal commercial case commenced by a Part 7 claim form, case management will include the following 12 key features:

(1)   statements of case will be exchanged within fixed or monitored time periods;

(2) a case memorandum, a list of issues and a case management bundle will be produced at an early point in the case;

(3) the case memorandum, list of issues and case management bundle will be amended and updated or revised on a running basis throughout the life of the case and will be used by the Court at every stage of the case. In particular the list of issues will be used as a tool to define what factual and expert evidence is necessary and the scope of disclosure;

(4) the Court itself will approve or settle the list of issues and may require the further assistance of the parties and their legal representatives in order to do so.

(5) a mandatory case management conference will be held shortly after statements of case have been served, if not before (and preceded by the parties lodging case management information sheets identifying their views on the requirements of the case);

(6) at the case management conference the Court will (as necessary) discuss the issues in the case and the requirements of the case with the advocates retained in the case. The Court will set a pre-trial timetable and give any other directions as may be appropriate;

(7) after statements of case have been served, each of the parties may serve a disclosure schedule (see further E2.3 below). At the first case management conference, the Court will discuss with the advocates retained in the case by reference to the list of issues the strategy for disclosure with a view to ensuring that disclosure and searches for documents are proportionate to the importance of the issues in the case to which the disclosure relates and avoiding subsequent applications for specific disclosure;

(8) before the progress monitoring date the parties will report to the Court, using a progress monitoring information sheet, the extent of their compliance with the pre-trial timetable;

(9) on or shortly after the progress monitoring date a judge will (without a hearing) consider progress and give such further directions as he thinks appropriate;

(10) if at the progress monitoring date all parties have indicated that they will be ready for trial, all parties will complete a pre-trial checklist;

(11) in many cases there will be a pre-trial review; In such cases the parties will be required to prepare a trial timetable for consideration by the Court;

(12) throughout the case there will be regular reviews of the estimated length of trial, including how much pre trial reading should be undertaken by the judge.

D3 Fixing a case management conference

CPR 61 ACG D3

D3.1 A mandatory case management conference will normally take place on the first available date 6 weeks after all defendants who intend to serve a defence have done so. This will normally allow time for the preparation and service of any reply (see section C4).

D3.2 (a) If proceedings have been started by service of a Part 7 claim form, the claimant must take steps to fix the date for the case management conference with the Listing Office in co-operation with the other parties within 14 days of the date when all defendants who intend to file and serve a defence have done so: PD58 section 10.2(a). The parties should bear in mind the need to allow time for the preparation and service of any reply.

(b) If proceedings have been begun by service of a Part 8 claim form, the claimant must take steps to fix a date for the case management conference with the Listing Office in co-operation with the other parties within 14 days of the date when all defendants who wish to serve evidence have done so: PD58 section 10.2(b).

D3.3 (a) In accordance with section C3 the Registry will expect a defence to be served and filed by the latest of

(i)   28 days after service of particulars of claim (as certified by the certificate of service); or

(ii)   any extended date for serving and filing a defence as notified to the Court in writing following agreement between the parties; or

(iii) any extended date for serving and filing a defence as ordered by the Court on an application.

(b) If within 28 days after the latest of these dates has passed for each defendant, the parties have not taken steps to fix the date for the case management conference, the Listing Office will inform the Judge in Charge of the List, and at his direction will take steps to fix a date for the case management conference without further reference to the parties.

D3.4 If the proceedings have been transferred to the Commercial List, the claimant must apply for a case management conference within 14 days of the date of the order transferring them, unless the judge held, or gave directions for, a case management conference when he made the order transferring the proceedings: PD58 section 10.3.

D3.5 If the claimant fails to make an application as required by the rules, any other party may apply for a case management conference: PD58 section 10.5.

D3.6 (a) In some cases it may be appropriate for a case management conference to take place at an earlier date.

(b) Any party may apply to the Court in writing at an earlier time for a case management conference: PD58 section 10.4. A request by any party for an early case management conference should be made in writing to the Judge in Charge of the List, on notice to all other parties, at the earliest possible opportunity.

D3.7 If before the date on which the case management conference would be held in accordance with section D3 there is a hearing in the case at which the parties are represented, the business of the case management conference will normally be transacted at that hearing and there will be no separate case management conference.

D3.8 The Court may fix a case management conference at any time on its own initiative. If it does so, the Court will normally give at least 7 days notice to the parties: PD58 section 10.6.

D3.9 A case management conference may not be postponed or adjourned without an order of the Court.

D4 Designated judge

CPR 61 ACG D4

D4.1 An application for the assignment of a designated judge to a case may be made in circumstances where any or all of the following factors:

(i)   the size of or complexity of the case,

(ii)   the fact that it has the potential to give rise to numerous pre-trial applications,

(iii) there is a likelihood that specific assignment will give rise to a substantial saving in costs,

(iv)   the same or similar issues arise in other cases

(v)   other case management considerations

indicate that assignment to a specific judge at the start of the case, or at some subsequent date, is appropriate.

D4.2 An application for the appointment of a designated judge should be made in writing to the Judge in Charge of the List at the time of fixing the case management conference. In appropriate cases the Court may assign a designated judge regardless of whether an application is made.

D4.3 If an order is made for allocation to a designated judge, the designated judge will preside at all subsequent pre-trial case management conferences and other hearings. Normally all applications in the case, other than applications for an interim payment, will be determined by the designated judge and he will be the trial judge.

D4.4 In all cases the Commercial Court Listing Office will endeavour to ensure a degree of judicial continuity. To assist in this, where a previous application in the case has been determined by a judge of the Commercial Court whether at a hearing or on paper, the parties should indicate clearly when lodging the papers, the identity of the judge who last considered the matter, so that so far as reasonably practicable, the papers can be placed before that judge.

D5 Case memorandum

CPR 61 ACG D5

D5.1 In order that the judge conducting the case management conference may be informed of the general nature of the case and the issues which are expected to arise, after service of the defence and any reply the solicitors and counsel for each party shall draft an agreed case memorandum.

D5.2 The case memorandum should contain:

(i)   a short and uncontroversial description of what the case is about; and

(ii)   a very short and uncontroversial summary of the material procedural history of the case.

D5.3 Unless otherwise ordered, the solicitors for the claimant are to be responsible for producing and filing the case memorandum, and where appropriate for revising it.

D5.4 The case memorandum should not refer to any application for an interim payment, to any order for an interim payment, to any voluntary interim payment, or to any payment or offer under CPR Part 36 or Part 37.

D5.5 (a) It should be clearly understood that the only purpose of the case memorandum is to help the judge understand broadly what the case is about. The case memorandum does not play any part in the trial. It is unnecessary, therefore, for parties to be unduly concerned about the precise terms in which it is drafted, provided it contains a reasonably fair and balanced description of the case. Above all the parties must do their best to spend as little time as practicable in drafting and negotiating the wording of the memorandum and keep clearly in mind the need to limit costs.

(b) Accordingly, in all but the most exceptional cases it should be possible for the parties to draft an agreed case memorandum. However, if it proves impossible to do so, the claimant must draft the case memorandum and send a copy to the defendant. The defendant may provide its comments to the Court (with a copy to the claimant) separately.

(c) The failure of the parties to agree a case memorandum is a matter which the Court may wish to take into account when dealing with the costs of the case management conference.

D6 List of issues

CPR 61 ACG D6

D6.1 After service of the defence (and any reply), the solicitors and counsel for each party shall produce a list of the key issues in the case. The list should include the main issues of both fact and law. The list should identify the principal issues in a structured manner, such as by reference to headings or chapters. Long lists of detailed issues should be avoided, and sub-issues should be identified only when there is a specific purpose in doing so. A separate section of the document should list what is common ground between the parties (or any of them, specifying which).

D6.2 (a) The list of issues is intended to be a neutral document for use as a case management tool at all stages of the case by the parties and the Court. Neither party should attempt to draft the list in terms which advance one party's case over that of another.

(b) It is unnecessary, therefore, for parties to be unduly concerned about the precise terms in which the list of issues is drafted, provided it presents the structure of the case in a reasonably fair and balanced way. Above all the parties must do their best to spend as little time as practicable in drafting and negotiating the wording of the list of issues and keep clearly in mind the need to limit costs.

(c) Accordingly, in most cases it should be possible for the parties to draft an agreed list of issues. However, if it proves impossible to do so, the claimant must draft the list and send a copy to the defendant. The defendant may provide its comments or alternative suggested list to the Court (with a copy to the claimant) separately.

D6.3 (a) A draft (or drafts) of the list of issues is to be available to the Court prior to the first case management conference. It is intended that at that stage the draft list should be in a general form, identifying the key issues and the structure of the parties' contentions, rather than setting out all detailed sub-issues..

(b) At the first case management conference and any subsequent case management conferences which take place, the Court will review and settle the draft list of issues with a view to refining it and identifying important sub-issues as appropriate and as required in order to manage the case. Accordingly the list of issues may be developed, by expansion or reduction as the case progresses.

D6.4 The list of issues will be used by the Court and the parties as a case management tool as the case progresses to determine such matters as the scope of disclosure and of factual and expert evidence and to consider whether issues should be determined summarily or preliminary issues should be determined.

D6.5 The list of issues is a tool for case management purposes and is not intended to supersede the pleadings which remain the primary source for each party's case. If at any stage of the proceedings, any question arises as to the accuracy of the list of issues, it will be necessary to consult the pleadings, in order to determine what issues arise.

D7 Case management bundle

Preparation

CPR 61 ACG D7

D7.1 Before the case management conference (see sections D3 and D8), a case management bundle should be prepared by the solicitors for the claimant: PD58 section 10.8.

Contents

D7.2 The case management bundle should contain the documents listed below (where the documents have been created by the relevant time):

(i)   the claim form;

(ii)   all statements of case (excluding schedules), except that, if a summary has been prepared, the bundle should contain the summary, not the full statement of case;

(iii)   the case memorandum (see section D5);

(iv)   the list of issues (see section D6);

GUIDES

(v)   the case management information sheets and the pre-trial timetable if one has already been established (see sections D8.5 and D8.9);

(vi)   the principal orders in the case;

(vii) any agreement in writing made by the parties to disclose documents without making a list or any agreement in writing that disclosure (or inspection or both) shall take place in stages.

See generally PD58 section 10.8.

D7.3 It is also useful for the case management bundle to include all disclosure schedules stating what search each party intends to make pursuant to Rule 31.7 when giving standard disclosure of electronic and other documents and what search he expects of the other party (or parties).

D7.4 The case management bundle should not include a copy of any order for an interim payment.

Lodging the case management bundle

D7.5 The case management bundle should be lodged with the Listing Office at least 7 days before the (first) case management conference (or earlier hearing at which the parties are represented and at which the business of the case management conference may be transacted: see section D3.7) and thereafter in accordance with the rules for lodging bundles set out below (see sections F5.4, 5.7, 5.9, 6.4 and 6.6 and M2.5). In general (unless the court otherwise orders) the case management bundle prepared for the court will be returned to the claimant's solicitors after each hearing.

Preparation and upkeep

D7.6 The claimant (or other party responsible for the preparation and upkeep of the case management bundle), in consultation with the other parties, must revise and update the case management bundle as the case proceeds: PD58 section 10.9.

D8 Case Management Conference

Application to postpone the case management conference

CPR 61 ACG D8

D8.1 (a) An application to postpone the case management conference must be made within 21 days after all defendants who intend to serve a defence have done so.

(b) The application will be dealt with on paper unless the Court considers it appropriate to direct an oral hearing.

Attendance at the case management conference

D8.2 Clients need not attend a case management conference unless the Court otherwise orders. A representative who has conduct of the case must attend from each firm of solicitors instructed in the case. At least one of the advocates retained in the case on behalf of each party should also attend.

D8.3 (a) The case management conference is a very significant stage in the case. Although parties are encouraged to agree proposals for directions for the consideration of the Court, directions will not normally be made by consent without the need for attendance.

(b) The general rule in the Commercial Court, as the Commercial and Admiralty Courts Guide makes clear, is that there must be an oral Case Management Conference (CMC) at Court.

(c) However, there are cases which are out of the ordinary where it may be possible to dispense with an oral hearing if the issues are straightforward and the costs of an oral hearing cannot be justified.

(d) In such a case, if the parties wish to ask the Court to consider holding the CMC on paper, they must lodge all the appropriate documents (see D8.3(e)) by no later than 12 noon on the Tuesday of the week in which the CMC is fixed for the Friday. That timing will be strictly enforced. If all the papers are not provided by that time, the CMC must be expected to go forward to an oral hearing. If the failure to lodge the papers is due to the fault of one party and it is for that reason an oral CMC takes place, that party will be at risk as to costs.

(e) Where a CMC is sought on paper the parties must lodge with the papers (which will include the Case Management bundle with the information sheets fully completed by each party), a draft Order and draft list of issues (both agreed by the parties) for consideration by the Judge and a statement signed by each advocate:

(i)   confirming that the parties have considered and discussed all the relevant issues and brought to the Court's attention anything that was unusual; and

(ii)   setting out information about any steps that had been taken to resolve the dispute by ADR, any future plans for ADR or an explanation as to why ADR would not be appropriate.

(iii)   giving a time estimate for the trial, specifically stating how much pre-trial reading by the judge will be required.

(f) In the ordinary course of things it would be unlikely that any case involving expert evidence or preliminary issues would be suitable for a CMC on paper. In cases involving expert evidence, the Court is anxious to give particular scrutiny to that evidence, given the cost such evidence usually involves and the need to focus that evidence. In cases where preliminary issues are sought, the Court will need to examine the formulation of those issues and discuss whether they are really appropriate.

Applications

D8.4 (a) If by the time of the case management conference a party wishes to apply for an order in respect of a matter not covered by Questions (1)-(19) in the case management information sheet, the application should be made at the case management conference.

(b) In some cases notice of such an application may be given in the case management information sheet itself: see section D8.5(c).

(c) In all other cases the applicant should ensure that an application notice and any supporting evidence is filed and served in time to enable the application to be heard at the case management conference.

Materials: case management information sheet and case management bundle

D8.5 (a) All parties attending a case management conference must complete a case management information sheet: PD58 section 10.7. A standard form of case management information sheet is set out in Appendix 6. The information sheet is intended to include reference to all applications which the parties would wish to make at a case management conference.

(b) A completed case management information sheet must be provided by each party to the Court (and copied to all other parties) at least 7 days before the case management conference.

(c) Applications not covered by the standard questions raised in the case management information sheet should be entered under Question (20). No other application notice is necessary if written evidence will not be involved and the 7 day notice given by entering the application on the information sheet will in all the circumstances be sufficient to enable all other parties to deal with the application.

D8.6 The case management bundle must be provided to the Court at least 7 days before the case management conference: PD58 section 10.8.

The hearing

D8.7 The Court's power to give directions at the case management conference is to be found in rules 3.1 and 58.13(4). At the case management conference the judge will:

(i)   discuss the issues in the case by reference to the draft list of issues, and settle a list of issues;

(ii)   discuss the requirements of the case (including issues of disclosure by reference to the disclosure schedule or schedules), with the advocates retained in the case;

(iii)   fix the entire pre-trial timetable, or, if that is not practicable, fix as much of the pre-trial timetable as possible; and

(iv)   in appropriate cases make an ADR order.

D8.8 At the Case Management Conference, and again at the Pre-Trial Review, active consideration will be given, by reference to the list of issues, to the possibility of the trial or summary determination of a preliminary issue or issues the resolution of which is likely to shorten the proceedings. An example is a relatively short question of law which can be tried without significant delay (though the implications of a possible appeal for the remainder of the case cannot be lost sight of). The Court may suggest the trial of a preliminary issue, but it will rarely make an order without the concurrence of at least one of the parties. Active consideration will also be given to whether any issues are suitable for summary determination pursuant to CPR Part 24.

D8.9 (a) Rules 3.1(2) and 58.13(4) enable the Court at the case management conference to stay the proceedings while the parties try to settle the case by alternative means. The case management information sheet requires the parties to indicate whether a stay for such purposes is sought.

(b) In an appropriate case an ADR order may be made without a stay of proceedings. The parties should consider carefully whether it may be possible to provide for ADR in the pre-trial timetable without affecting the date of trial.

(c) Where a stay has been granted for a fixed period for the purposes of ADR the Court has power to extend it. If an extension of the stay is desired by all parties, a judge will normally be prepared to deal with an application for such an extension if it is made before the expiry of the stay by letter from the legal representatives of one of the parties. The letter should confirm that all parties consent to the application.

(d) An extension will not normally be granted for more than four weeks unless clear reasons are given to justify a longer period, but more than one extension may be granted.

The pre-trial timetable

D8.10 The pre-trial timetable will normally include:

(i)   a progress monitoring date (see section D12 below); and

(ii)   a direction that the parties attend upon the Clerk to the Commercial Court to obtain a fixed date for trial.

Variations to the pre-trial timetable

D8.11(a) The parties may agree minor variations to the time periods set out in the pre-trial timetable without the case needing to be brought back to the Court provided that the variation

(i)   will not jeopardise the date fixed for trial;

(ii)   does not relate to the progress monitoring date; and

(iii)   does not provide for the completion after the progress monitoring date of any step which was previously scheduled to have been completed by that date.

(b) The Court should be informed in writing of any such agreement.

D8.12 If in any case it becomes apparent that variations to the pre-trial timetable are required which do not fall within section D8.11 above; the parties should apply to have the case management conference reconvened immediately. The parties should not wait until the progress monitoring date.

D9 Case management conference: Part 8 claims

CPR 61 ACG D9

D9.1 In a case commenced by the issue of a Part 8 claim form, a case management conference will normally take place on the first available date 6 weeks after service and filing of the defendant's evidence. At that case management conference the Court will make such pre-trial directions as are necessary, adapting (where useful in the context of the particular claim) those of the case management procedures used for a claim commenced by the issue of a Part 7 claim form.

D10 Case management conference: Part 20 claims

CPR 61 ACG D10

D10.1 Wherever possible, any party who intends to make a Part 20 claim should do so before the hearing of the case management conference dealing with the main claim.

D10.2 Where permission to make a Part 20 claim is required it should be sought at the case management conference in the main claim.

D10.3 If the Part 20 claim is confined to a counterclaim by a defendant against a claimant alone, the Court will give directions in the Part 20 claim at the case management conference in the main claim.

D10.4 If the Part 20 claim is not confined to a counterclaim by a defendant against a claimant alone, the case management conference in the main claim will be reconvened on the first available date 6 weeks after service by the defendant of the new party or parties to the proceedings.

D10.5 All parties to the proceedings (i.e. the parties to the main claim and the parties to the Part 20 claim) must attend the reconvened case management conference. There will not be a separate case management conference for the Part 20 claim alone.

D10.6 In any case involving a Part 20 claim the Court will give case management directions at the same case management conferences as it gives directions for the main claim: PD58 section 12. The Court will therefore normally only give case management directions at hearings attended by all parties to the proceedings.

D10.7 The provisions of D10.4, D10.5 and D10.6 apply equally to Part 20 claims brought by parties who are not also parties to the main claim.

D11 Management throughout the case

CPR 61 ACG D11

D11.1 The Court will continue to take an active role in the management of the case throughout its progress to trial. Parties should be ready at all times to provide the Court with such information and assistance as it may require for that purpose.

D12 Progress monitoring

Fixing the progress monitoring date

CPR 61 ACG D12

D12.1 The progress monitoring date will be fixed at the case management conference and will normally be after the date in the pre-trial timetable for exchange of witness statements and expert reports.

Progress monitoring information sheet

D12.2 At least 3 days (i.e. three clear days) before the progress monitoring date the parties must each send to the Case Management Unit (with a copy to all other parties) a progress monitoring information sheet to inform the Court:

(i) whether they have complied with the pre-trial timetable, and if they have not, the respects in which they have not; and

(ii) whether they will be ready for a trial commencing on the fixed date specified in the pre-trial timetable, and if they will not be ready, why they will not be ready.

D12.3 A standard form of progress monitoring information sheet is set out in Appendix 12.

D12.4 The progress monitoring information sheets are referred to the Judge in Charge of the List.

D12.5 Upon considering progress monitoring information sheet, the Court may, particularly if there has been significant non-compliance with the pre-trial timetable, direct a date by which further information sheet are to be sent to the Court

D13 Reconvening the case management conference

CPR 61 ACG D13

D13.1 If in the view of the Court the information given in the progress monitoring sheets justifies this course, the Court may direct that the case management conference be reconvened.

D13.2 At a reconvened hearing of the case management conference the Court may make such orders and give such directions as it considers appropriate. If the Court is of the view that due to the failure of the parties or any of them to comply with the case management timetable the trial cannot be fairly and efficiently conducted on the date fixed, it may vacate the trial date and make such order for costs as is appropriate.

D14 Pre-trial checklist

CPR 61 ACG D14

D14.1 Not later than three weeks before the date fixed for trial each party must send to the Listing Office (with a copy to all other parties) a completed checklist confirming final details for trial (a "pre-trial checklist") in the form set out in Appendix 13.

D15 Further information

CPR 61 ACG D15

D15.1 (a) If a party declines to provide further information requested under Part 18, the solicitors or counsel who are to appear at the application for the parties concerned must communicate directly with each other in an attempt to reach agreement before any application is made to the Court.

(b) No application for an order that a party provide further information will normally be listed for hearing without prior written confirmation from the applicant that the requirements of this section D15.1(a) have been complied with.

(c) The Court will only order further information to be provided if satisfied that the information requested is strictly necessary to understand another party's case.

D15.2 Because it falls within the definition of a statement of case (see rule 2.3(1)) a response providing further information under CPR Part 18 must be verified by a statement of truth.

D16 Fixed trial dates

CPR 61 ACG D16

D16.1 Most cases will be given fixed trial dates immediately after the pre-trial timetable has been set at the case management conference.

D16.2 A fixed date for trial is given on the understanding that if previous fixtures have been substantially underestimated or other urgent matters need to be heard, the trial may be delayed. Where such delay might cause particular inconvenience to witnesses or others involved in the trial, the Clerk to the Commercial Court should be informed well in advance of the fixed date.

D17 Estimates of length of trial

CPR 61 ACG D17

D17.1 At the case management conference an estimate will be made of the minimum and maximum lengths of the trial. The estimate should include time for pre-trial reading by the judge and specify what time has been allowed for that purpose. The estimate will appear in the pre-trial timetable and will be the basis on which a date for trial will be fixed.

D17.2 The Court examines with particular care longer estimates, and will wish to consider with the assistance of advocates whether in the case of particularly long trials all the issues in the trial should be heard at the same hearing: see section J2.

D17.3 If a party subsequently instructs new advocate(s) to appear on its behalf at the trial, the Listing Office should be notified of that fact within 14 days. Advocates newly instructed should review the estimate of the minimum and maximum lengths of the trial, and submit to the Listing Office a signed note revising or confirming the estimate as appropriate.

D17.4 A confirmed estimate of the minimum and maximum lengths of the trial, signed by the advocates who are to appear at the trial, should be attached to the pre-trial checklist.

D17.5 It is the duty of all advocates who are to appear at the trial to seek agreement, if possible, on the estimated minimum and maximum lengths of trial.

D17.6 The provisional estimate and (after it is given) the confirmed estimate must be kept under review by the advocates who are to appear at the trial. If at any stage an estimate needs to be revised, a signed revised estimate (whether agreed or not) should be submitted by the advocates to the Clerk to the Commercial Court.

D17.7 Accurate estimation of trial length is of great importance to the efficient functioning of the Court. The Court will be Guided by, but will not necessarily accept, the estimates given by the parties.

D18 Pre-Trial Review and trial timetable

CPR 61 ACG D18

D18.1 The Court will order a pre-trial review in any case in which it considers it appropriate to do so.

D18.2 A pre-trial review will normally take place between 8 and 4 weeks before the date fixed for trial, but might be earlier in particularly long or complex cases.

D18.3 Whenever possible the pre-trial review will be conducted by the trial judge. It should be attended by the advocates who are to appear at the trial: PD58 section 11.2.

D18.4 Before the pre-trial review or, if there is not to be one, not later than 7 days before the trial is due to commence, the parties must attempt to agree a timetable for the trial providing for oral submissions, examinations in chief (if any) and cross-examination of witnesses of fact and expert witnesses: PD58 section 11.3. The claimant must file a copy of the draft timetable at least two days before the date fixed for the pre-trial review; any differences of view should be clearly identified and briefly explained: PD58 section 11.4. At the pre-trial review the judge may set a timetable for the trial and give such other directions for the conduct of the trial as he considers appropriate.

D19 Orders

D19.1 (a) Except for orders made by the Court on its own initiative under rule 3.3, and unless the Court otherwise orders, every judgment or order will be drawn up by the parties and rule 40.3 is modified accordingly: rule 58.15(1).

(b) Consent orders are to be drawn up in accordance with the procedure described in section F9.

(c) All other orders are to be drawn up in draft by the parties and should:

(i)   be dated in the draft with the date of the judge's decision.

(ii)   bear the name of the judge who made the order (after the designation "Commercial Court";

(iii)   state (after the name of the judge) whether the order was made in public, in private (see section F1.7 below) or on paper.

The claimant is to have responsibility for drafting the order, unless it was made on the application of another party in which case that other party is to have the responsibility. Orders for submission to judges, or for scaling will not be accepted without the information set out in sub-paragraphs (c)(i) to (iii) above.

(d) Two copies of the draft, signed by the parties themselves, or by their solicitors or counsel, must be lodged with the Registry **within five days** of the decision of the Court reflected in the draft.

D19.2 If the Court orders that an act be done by a certain date without specifying a time for compliance, the latest time for compliance is 4.30 p.m. on the day in question.

D19.3 Orders that are required to be served must be served by the parties, unless the Court otherwise directs.

E. DISCLOSURE

E1 Generally

CPR 61 ACG E1

E1.1 The Court will seek to ensure that disclosure is no wider than appropriate. Anything wider than standard disclosure will need to be justified.

E1.2 The obligations imposed by an order for disclosure continue until the proceedings come to an end. If, after a list of documents has been prepared and served, the existence (present or past) of further documents to which the order applies comes to the attention of the disclosing party, that party must prepare and serve a supplemental list.

E1.3 When making standard disclosure, a party is required to make a reasonable search for documents and state in his disclosure statement any limits that he has placed upon his search on the grounds that it would be unreasonable: rule 31.7.

E2 Procedure in advance of disclosure

CPR 61 ACG E2

E2.1 At the first case management conference the Court will normally wish to consider, one or more of the following:

(i)   ordering standard disclosure: rule 31.5(1);

(ii)   dispensing with or limiting standard disclosure: rule 31.5(2);

(iii)   ordering sample disclosure;

(iv)   ordering disclosure in stages;

(v)   ordering disclosure otherwise than by service of a list of documents, for example, by service of copy documents; and

(vi)   ordering specific disclosure: rule 31.12.

E2.2 Among other things the court will normally wish to consider, by reference to the list of issues, the scope of disclosure and whether standard disclosure or some other form of disclosure as outlined in CPR 31.5(4) is appropriate in the case. The reference to standard disclosure is to standard disclosure as defined by rule 31.6. Where standard disclosure is ordered a party is required to disclose only:

(i)   the documents on which he relies; and

(ii)   documents which -

–   adversely affect his own case;

–   adversely affect another party's case; or

–   support another party's case; and

(iii)   documents which he is required to disclose by any relevant Practice Direction.

E2.3 In all cases which come before the Court after 16 April 2013 the provisions of CPR 31.5(3)-(8) will apply. In particular parties are expected to comply with the provisions for service of disclosure statements, and attempts to agree the ambit of disclosure in advance of the case management conference (CPR 31.5(3)). Further in the case of complex litigation the Court will normally be assisted by a disclosure schedule produced by each party, indicating (by reference to categories of documents, the location of documents and the period of time covered by the documentation and otherwise) what documentation the party recognises should be covered by disclosure, and whether he intends to place any, and if so what, limits upon his search on the basis that it would be unreasonable. The court will normally invite the observations of other parties upon the proposals in a disclosure schedule with a view to determining the proper extent of disclosure and any proper limits upon the search for documents before the parties make disclosure. Disclosure schedules may be dispensed with if they are unnecessary or disproportionate in the particular case. Where no disclosure schedule is produced a statement to this effect should be included in the parties' Case Management Information Sheets before Q1. The Court will then consider with the parties at the Case Management Conference whether disclosure schedules should be prepared.

E2.4 The parties should indicate in the Case Management Information Sheets the position as to the ambit of disclosure agreed or contended for. A party who contends that to search for a category or class of document would be unreasonable should also indicate this in his case management information sheet.

E2.5 All parties should have regard to issues which may specifically arise concerning electronic data and documents in accordance with PD31B (October 2010). In summary:

(a) Rule 31.4 contains a broad definition of "document". This extends to Electronic Documents. "Electronic Document" means any document held in electronic form. It includes, for example, e-mail and other electronic communications such as text messages and voicemail, word-processed documents and databases, and documents stored on portable devices such as memory sticks and mobile phones. In addition to documents that are readily accessible from computer systems and other electronic devices and media, it includes documents that are stored on servers and back-up systems and documents that have been deleted. It also includes Metadata and other embedded data which is not typically visible on screen or a print out.

When considering disclosure of Electronic Documents, the parties and their legal representatives should bear in mind the following general principles—

(1) Electronic Documents should be managed efficiently in order to minimise the cost incurred;

(2) technology should be used in order to ensure that document management activities are undertaken efficiently and effectively;

(3) disclosure should be given in a manner which gives effect to the overriding objective;

(4) Electronic Documents should generally be made available for inspection in a form which allows the party receiving the documents the same ability to access, search, review and display the documents as the party giving disclosure; and

(5) disclosure of Electronic Documents which are of no relevance to the proceedings may place an excessive burden in time and cost on the party to whom disclosure is given.

(b) As soon as litigation is contemplated, the parties' legal representatives must notify their clients of the need to preserve disclosable documents. The documents to be preserved include Electronic Documents which would otherwise be deleted in accordance with a document retention policy or otherwise deleted in the ordinary course of business.

(c) The parties and their legal representatives must, before the first case management conference, discuss the use of technology in the management of Electronic Documents and the conduct of proceedings, in particular for the purpose of—

(1) creating lists of documents to be disclosed;

(2) giving disclosure by providing documents and information regarding documents in electronic format; and

(3) presenting documents and other material to the Court at the trial.

The parties and their legal representatives must also, before the first case management conference, discuss the disclosure of Electronic Documents. In some cases (for example heavy and complex cases) it may be appropriate to begin discussions before proceedings are commenced. The discussions should include (where appropriate) the following matters—

(1) the categories of Electronic Documents within the parties' control, the computer systems, electronic devices and media on which any relevant documents may be held, storage systems and document retention policies;

(2) the scope of the reasonable search for Electronic Documents required by rule 31.7;

(3) the tools and techniques (if any) which should be considered to reduce the burden and cost of disclosure of Electronic Documents, including—

    (a) limiting disclosure of documents or certain categories of documents to particular date ranges, to particular custodians of documents, or to particular types of documents;

    (b) the use of agreed Keyword Searches;

    (c) the use of agreed software tools;

    (d) the methods to be used to identify duplicate documents;

    (e) the use of Data Sampling;

    (f) the methods to be used to identify privileged documents and other non-disclosable documents, to redact documents (where redaction is appropriate), and for dealing with privileged or other documents which have been inadvertently disclosed; and

(g)   the use of a staged approach to the disclosure of Electronic Documents;

(4)   the preservation of Electronic Documents, with a view to preventing loss of such documents before the trial;

(5)   the exchange of data relating to Electronic Documents in an agreed electronic format using agreed fields;

(6)   the formats in which Electronic Documents are to be provided on inspection and the methods to be used;

(7)   the basis of charging for or sharing the cost of the provision of Electronic Documents, and whether any arrangements for charging or sharing of costs are final or are subject to re-allocation in accordance with any order for costs subsequently made; and

(8)   whether it would be appropriate to use the services of a neutral electronic repository for storage of Electronic Documents.

(d) In some cases the parties may find it helpful to exchange the Electronic Documents questionnaire provided for in CPR 31.22 and CPR PD31B in order to provide information to each other in relation to the scope, extent and most suitable format for disclosure of Electronic Documents in the proceedings.

(e) The documents submitted to the Court in advance of the first case management conference should include a summary of the matters on which the parties agree in relation to the disclosure of Electronic Documents and a summary of the matters on which they disagree. The person signing the Electronic Documents Questionnaire should attend the first case management conference, and any subsequent hearing at which disclosure is likely to be considered.

(f) If at any time it becomes apparent that the parties are unable to reach agreement in relation to the disclosure of Electronic Documents, the parties should seek directions from the Court at the earliest practical date.

Regard should be had to PD31B for the detailed provisions as to the Court's approach in matters regarding electronic disclosure and the requirements of searching and listing Electronic Documents.

E3 Disclosure procedure

CPR 61 ACG E3

E3.1 In order to comply with rule 31.10(3) (which requires the list to identify the documents in a convenient order and manner and as concisely as possible) it will normally be necessary to list the documents in date order, to number them consecutively and to give each a concise description. In some cases, it will be useful to give each document a "Bates number" identifying the party disclosing it (such as C101 or D(1) 202). However, where there is a large number of documents all falling within a particular category the disclosing party may (unless otherwise ordered) list those documents as a category rather than individually.

E3.2 Each party to the proceedings must serve a separate list of documents. This applies even if two or more parties are represented by the same firm of solicitors.

E3.3 If the physical structure of a file may be of evidential value (e.g. a placing or chartering file) solicitors should make one complete copy of the file in the form in which they received it before any documents are removed for the purpose of giving disclosure or inspection.

E3.4 Unless the Court directs otherwise, the disclosure statement must comply with the requirements of rules 31.7(3) and 31.10(6). In particular, it should

(i)   expressly state that the disclosing party believes the extent of the search to have been reasonable in all the circumstances; and

(ii)   draw attention to any particular limitations on the extent of the search adopted for reasons of proportionality and give the reasons why they were adopted.

E3.5 The disclosure statement for standard disclosure should begin with the following words:

"[I/we], [name(s)] state that [I/we] have carried out a reasonable and proportionate search to locate all the documents which [I am/here name the party is] required to disclose under [the order made by the Court or the agreement in writing made between the parties] on the [] day of [] 20[]."

E3.6 The disclosure statement for standard disclosure should end with the following certificate:

"[I/we] certify that [I/we] understand the duty of disclosure and to the best of [my/our] knowledge [I have/here name the party has] carried out that duty. [I/we] certify that the list above is a complete list of all documents which are or have been in [my/here name the party's] control and which [I am/here name the party is] obliged under [the said order or the said agreement in writing] to disclose."

E3.7 An adapted version of practice form N265 (list of documents: standard disclosure) has been approved for use in the Commercial Court. The Court may at any stage order that a disclosure statement be verified by affidavit.

E3.8 (a) For the purposes of PD31 section 4.3 the Court will normally regard as an appropriate person any person who is in a position responsibly and authoritatively to search for the documents required to be disclosed by that party and to make the statements contained in the disclosure statement concerning the documents which must be disclosed by that party

(b) A legal representative may in certain cases be an appropriate person.

(c) An explanation why the person is considered an appropriate person must still be given in the disclosure statement.

(d) A person holding an office or position in the disclosing party but who is not in a position responsibly and authoritatively to make the statements contained in the disclosure statement will not be regarded as an appropriate person to make the disclosure statement of the party.

(e) The Court may of its own initiative or on application require that a disclosure statement also be signed by another appropriate person.

E4 Specific disclosure

CPR 61 ACG E4

E4.1 Specific disclosure is defined by rule 31.12(2).

E4.2 An order for specific disclosure under rule 31.12 may in an appropriate case direct a party to carry out a thorough search for any documents which it is reasonable to suppose may adversely affect his own case or support the case of the party applying for disclosure or which may lead to a train of enquiry which has either of these consequences and to disclose any documents located as a result of that search: PD31 section 5.5.

E4.3 Where an application is made for specific disclosure the party from whom disclosure is sought should provide to the applicant and to the Court information as to the factors listed in E2.5(d) above and its documents retention policy, to the extent such information is relevant to the application. At the hearing of the application, the Court may take into account the factors listed in E2.5(d) as well as the width of the request and the conduct of the parties.

E4.4 The Court may at any stage order that specific disclosure be verified by affidavit or witness statement.

E4.5 Applications for ship's papers are provided for in rule 58.14.

E5 Authenticity

CPR 61 ACG E5

E5.1 (a) Where the authenticity of any document disclosed to a party is not admitted, that party must serve notice that the document must be proved at trial in accordance with CPR 32.19. Such notice must be served by the latest date for serving witness statements or within 7 days of disclosure of the document, whichever is later.

(b) Where, apart from the authenticity of the document itself, the date upon which a document or an entry in it is stated to have been made or the person by whom the document states that it or any entry in it was made or any other feature of the document is to be challenged at the trial on grounds which may require a witness to be called at the trial to support the contents of the document, such challenge

(i)   must be raised in good time in advance of the trial to enable such witness or witnesses to be called;

(ii)   the grounds of challenge must be explicitly identified in the skeleton argument or outline submissions in advance of the trial.

(c) Where, due to the late disclosure of a document it or its contents or character cannot practicably be challenged within the time limits prescribed in (a) or (b), the challenge may only be raised with the permission of the Court and having regard to the Overriding Objective (CPR 1.1).

F. APPLICATIONS

F1 Generally

CPR 61 ACG F1

F1.1 (a) Applications are governed by CPR Part 23 and PD23 as modified by rule 58 and PD58. As a result

(i)   PD23 section 1 and 2.3-2.6 do not apply;

(ii)   PD23 section 2.8 and 2.10 apply only if the proposed (additional) application will not increase the time estimate (including the estimate for the judge's pre-hearing reading time) already given for the hearing for which a date has been fixed; and

(iii)   PD23 section 3 is subject in all cases to the judge's agreeing that the application may proceed without an application notice being served.

(b) An adapted version of practice form N244 (application notice) has been approved for use in the Commercial Court.

F1.2 An application for a consent order must include a draft of the proposed order signed on behalf of all parties to whom it relates: PD58 section 14.1.

F1.3 The requirement in PD23 section 12.1 that a draft order be supplied on disk does not apply in the Commercial Court since orders are generally drawn up by the parties: PD58 section 14.2.

Service

F1.4 Application notices are served by the parties, not by the Court: PD58 section 9.

Evidence

F1.5 (a) Particular attention is drawn to PD23 section 9.1 which points out that even where no specific requirement for evidence is set out in the Rules or Practice Directions the Court will in practice often need to be satisfied by evidence of the facts that are relied on in support of, or in opposition to, the application.

(b) Where convenient the written evidence relied on in support of an application may be included in the application notice, which may be lengthened for this purpose: see Rule 32.6(2).

Time for service of evidence

F1.6 The time allowed for the service of evidence in relation to applications is governed by PD58 section 13.

Hearings

F1.7 (a) Applications (other than arbitration applications) will be heard in public in accordance with rule 39.2, save where otherwise ordered.

(b) With certain exceptions, arbitration applications will normally be heard in private: rule 62.10(3). See section O.

(c) An application without notice for a freezing injunction or a search order will often need to be heard in private in the interests of justice and therefore be heard in private: see rule 39.2(3)

F1.8 Parties should pay particular attention to PD23 section 2.9 which warns of the need to anticipate the Court's wish to review the conduct of the case and give further management directions. The parties should be ready to give the Court their assistance and should be able to answer any questions that the Court may ask for this purpose.

F1.9 PD23 section 6.1-6.5 and section 7 deal with the hearing of applications by telephone (other than an urgent application out of Court hours) and the hearing of applications using video-conferencing facilities. These methods may be considered when an application needs to be made before a particular Commercial Judge who is currently on circuit. In most other cases applications are more conveniently dealt with in person.

F2 Applications without notice

CPR 61 ACG F2

F2.1 All applications should be made on notice, even if that notice has to be short, unless

(i)   any rule or Practice Direction provides that the application may be made without notice; or

(ii)   there are good reasons for making the application without notice, for example, because notice would or might defeat the object of the application.

F2.2 Where an application without notice does not involve the giving of undertakings to the Court, it will normally be made and dealt with on paper, as, for example, applications for permission to serve a claim form out of the jurisdiction, and applications for an extension of time in which to serve a claim form.

F2.3 Any application for an interim injunction or similar remedy will require an oral hearing.

F2.4 (a) A party wishing to make an application without notice which requires an oral hearing before a judge should contact the Clerk to the Commercial Court at the earliest opportunity.

(b) If a party wishes to make an application without notice at a time when no commercial judge is available he should apply to the Queen's Bench Judge in Chambers (see section P1.1).

F2.5 On all applications without notice it is the duty of the applicant and those representing him:

(i)   to make full and frank disclosure of all matters relevant to the application;

(ii)   to ensure that a note of the hearing of the without notice application, the evidence and skeleton argument in support of it and any order made all be served with the order or as soon as possible thereafter.

F2.6 The papers lodged for the application should include two copies of a draft of the order sought. Save in exceptional circumstances where time does not permit, all the evidence relied upon in support of the application and any other relevant documents must be lodged in advance with the Clerk to the Commercial Court. If the application is urgent, the Clerk to the Commercial Court should be informed of the fact and of the reasons for the urgency. Counsel's estimate of reading time likely to be required by the Court should also be provided.

F3 Expedited applications

CPR 61 ACG F3

F3.1 The Court will expedite the hearing of an application on notice in cases of sufficient urgency and importance.

F3.2 Where a party wishes to make an expedited application a request should be made to the Clerk to the Commercial Court on notice to all other parties.

F4 Paper applications

CPR 61 ACG F4

F4.1 (a) Although contested applications are usually best determined at an oral hearing, some applications may be suitable for determination on paper.

(b) Attention is drawn to the provisions of rule 23.8 and PD23 section 11. If the applicant considers that the application is suitable for determination on paper, he should ensure before lodging the papers with the Court

(i)   that the application notice together with any supporting evidence has been served on the respondent;

(ii)   that the respondent has been allowed the appropriate period of time in which to serve written submissions and evidence in opposition (save in cases of urgency that will ordinarily be at least three clear days);

(iii)   that any evidence in reply has been served on the respondent; and

(iv)   that there is included in the papers

    (A)   the written consent of the respondent to the disposal of the application without a hearing; or

    (B)   a statement by the applicant of the grounds on which he seeks to have the application disposed of without a hearing, together with confirmation that the application and a copy of the grounds for disposing of without a hearing have been served on the respondent and a statement of when they were served.

(c) Where a previous application in the case has been determined by a judge of the Commercial Court whether at a hearing or on paper, it is helpful for the application to indicate clearly when lodging the papers, the identity of the judge who last considered the matter, so that so far as reasonably practicable, the papers can be placed before that judge.

(d) A respondent served with a non-urgent application which is requested to be determined on paper should respond by letter within three clear days of the date of service on him of the application stating whether or not he consents to the application being disposed of without a hearing. If he so consents he should at the same time serve any written submissions and evidence in opposition or, if further time is needed, he should state how much further time and the grounds upon which further time is required. If he does not so consent he should state his reasons. The letter should be sent (by email where possible) to the applicant and all other parties concerned in the application at the same time as it is sent to the Court.

(e) Only in exceptional cases (or where a rule specifically so provides) will the Court dispose of an application without a hearing in the absence of the respondent's consent.

F4.2 (a) Certain applications relating to the management of proceedings may conveniently be made in correspondence without issuing an application notice.

(b) It must be clearly understood that such applications are not applications without notice and the applicant must therefore ensure that a copy of the letter making the application is sent to all other parties to the proceedings.

(c) Accordingly, the following procedure should be followed when making an application of this kind:

(i)   the applicant should first ascertain whether the application is opposed by the other parties;

(ii)   if it is, the applicant should apply to the Court by letter stating the nature of the order which it seeks and the grounds on which the application is made;

(iii)   a copy of the letter should be sent (by e-mail where possible, copied to the Court) to all other parties at the same time as it is sent to the Court and it should be stated that this has been done;

(iv)   any other party wishing to make representations should do so by letter within two days (i.e. two clear days) of the date of the applicant's letter of application, unless a more prompt response is requested by or on behalf of the Court. The representations should be sent (by email where possible) to the applicant and all other parties at the same time as they are sent to the Court;

(v)   the Court will advise its decision by letter to the applicant. The applicant must forthwith copy the Court's letter to all other parties, by email where possible.

F5 Ordinary applications

CPR 61 ACG F5

F5.1 Applications likely to require an oral hearing lasting half a day or less are regarded as "ordinary" applications.

F5.2 Ordinary applications will generally be heard on Fridays, but may be heard on other days. Where possible, the Listing Office will have regard to the availability of advocates when fixing hearing dates.

F5.3 (a) The timetable for ordinary applications (including ordinary summary judgment applications) is set out in PD58 section 13.1 and is as follows:

(i)   evidence in support must be filed and served with the application;

(ii)   evidence in answer must be filed and served within 14 days thereafter;

(iii)   evidence in reply (if any) must be filed and served within 7 days thereafter.

(b) This timetable may be abridged or extended by agreement between the parties provided that any date fixed for the hearing of the application is not affected: PD58 section 13.4. In appropriate cases, this timetable may be abridged by the Court.

F5.4 An application bundle (see section F11) and the case management bundle must be lodged with the Listing Office by 1 p.m. one clear day before the date fixed for the hearing together with a letter from the Applicant's solicitors confirming or updating the time estimate for the hearing and the reading time required for the judge. The applicant on any application must be willing to provide a copy of the application bundle (not just the index) at the same time as it is lodged with the court if appropriate undertakings in relation to costs have been provided by the respondent's solicitors.

F5.5 Save in very short and simple cases, skeleton arguments must be provided by all parties. These must be lodged with the Listing Office and served on the advocates for all other parties to the application by 1 p.m. on the day before the date fixed for the hearing (i.e. the immediately preceding day) together with an estimate of the reading time likely to be required by the Court. Guidelines on the preparation of skeleton arguments are set out in Part 1 of Appendix 9.

F5.7 Thus, for an application estimated for a half day or less and due to be heard on a Friday:

(i)　　the application bundle and case management bundle must be lodged by 1 p.m. on Wednesday; and

(ii)　　skeleton arguments must be lodged by 1 p.m. on Thursday.

If, for reasons outside the reasonable control of the advocate a skeleton argument cannot be delivered to the Listing Office by 1pm, the clerk of the judge hearing the application should be informed before 1pm and the skeleton argument should be delivered direct to the clerk of the judge listed to hear the application and in any event not later than 4pm the day before the hearing.

F5.8 The applicant should, as a matter of course, provide all other parties to the application with a copy of the application bundle at the cost of the receiving party. Further copies should be supplied on request, again at the cost of the receiving party.

F5.9 Problems with the lodging of bundles or skeleton arguments should be notified to the Clerk to the Commercial Court as far in advance as possible. If the application bundle, case management bundle or skeleton argument is not lodged by the time specified, the application may be stood out of the list without further warning.

F6 Heavy applications

CPR 61 ACG F6

F6.1 Applications likely to require an oral hearing lasting more than half a day are regarded as "heavy" applications.

F6.2 Heavy applications normally involve a greater volume of evidence and other documents and more extensive issues. They accordingly require a longer lead-time for preparation and exchange of evidence. Where possible the Listing Office will have regard to the availability of advocates when fixing hearing dates.

F6.3 The timetable for heavy applications (including heavy summary judgment applications) is set out in PD58 section 13.2 and is as follows:

(i)　　evidence in support must be filed and served with the application;

(ii)　　evidence in answer must be filed and served within 28 days thereafter;

(iii)　　evidence in reply (if any) must be filed and served as soon as possible, and in any event within 14 days of service of the evidence in answer.

F6.4 An application bundle (see section F11) and case management bundle must be lodged with the Listing Office by 4 p.m. two days (i.e. two clear days) before the date fixed for the hearing (or if earlier 4 p.m. before the first day of the required reading period) together with a reading list and an estimate for the reading time likely to be required by the court (see further paragraphs F6.5 and F8.1 below) and a letter from the Applicant's solicitors confirming or updating the time estimate for the hearing. The applicant on any application must be willing to provide a copy of the application bundle (not just the index) at the same time as it is lodged with the court if appropriate undertakings in relation to costs have been provided by the respondent's solicitor.

F6.5 Skeleton arguments must be lodged with the Listing Office and served on the advocates for all other parties to the application as follows:

(i)   applicant's skeleton argument (with reading list and time estimate, a chronology unless one is unnecessary, and with a dramatis personae if one is warranted), by 4 p.m. two days (i.e. two clear days) before the hearing (or if earlier 4 p.m. before the first day of the required reading period);

(ii)   respondent's skeleton argument (with reading list and time estimate), by 4 p.m. one day **after** the **day on which the applicant's skeleton argument is required to be lodged**.

Guidelines on the preparation of skeleton arguments are set out in Part 1 of Appendix 9.

F6.6 Thus, for an application estimated for more than half a day with an estimated reading time of 1 day and due to be heard on a Thursday:

(i)   the application bundle, case management bundle and the applicant's skeleton argument must be lodged by 4 p.m. on Monday;

(ii)   the respondent's skeleton argument must be lodged by 4 p.m. on Tuesday.

F6.7 The applicant must, as a matter of course, provide all other parties to the application with a copy of the application bundle at the cost of the receiving party. Further copies must be supplied on request, again at the cost of the receiving party.

F6.8 Problems with the lodging of bundles or skeleton arguments should be notified to the Clerk to the Commercial Court as far in advance as possible. If the application bundle, case management bundle or skeleton argument is not lodged by the time specified, the application may be stood out of the list without further warning.

F7 Evidence

F7.1 Although evidence may be given by affidavit, it should generally be given by witness statement, except where it can conveniently be given in the application notice (see Rule 32.6(2) and except where PD32 requires evidence to be given on affidavit (as, for example, in the case of an application for a freezing injunction or a search order: PD32 section 1.4). In other cases the Court may order that evidence be given by affidavit: PD32 section 1.4(1) and 1.6.

F7.2 Witness statements and affidavits must comply with the requirements of PD32, save that photocopy documents should be used unless the Court orders otherwise.

F7.3 (a) Witness statements must be verified by a statement of truth signed by the maker of the statement: rule 22.1.

(b) At hearings other than trial an applicant may rely on the application notice itself, and a party may rely on his statement of case, if the application notice or statement of case (as the case may be) is verified by a statement of truth: rule 32.6(2).

(c) A statement of truth in an application notice may also be signed as indicated in sections C1.8 and C1.9 above.

F7.4 Proceedings for contempt of Court may be brought against a person who makes, or causes to be made, a false statement in a witness statement (or any other document verified by a statement of truth) without an honest belief in its truth: rule 32.14(1).

F8 Reading time

CPR 61 ACG F8

F8.1 (a) It is essential for the efficient conduct of the Court's business that the parties inform the Court of the reading required in order to enable the judge to dispose of the application within the time allowed for the hearing and of the time likely to be required for that purpose. Accordingly

(i)   in the case of all heavy applications each party must lodge with the Listing Office together with its skeleton argument a reading list with an estimate of the time likely to be required by the Court for reading;

(ii)   in the case of all other applications each party must lodge with the Listing Office by 1pm on the day before the date fixed for the hearing of an application (ie the immediately preceding day) a reading list with an estimate of the time required to complete the reading;

(iii) each reading list should identify the material on both sides which the Court needs to read.

(iv)   if possible, the parties should provide the reading list in an agreed document.

(b) Failure to comply with these requirements may result in the adjournment of the hearing.

F9 Applications disposed of by consent

CPR 61 ACG F9

F9.1 (a) Consent orders may be submitted to the Court in draft for approval and initialling without the need for attendance.

(b) Two copies of the draft, one of which (or a counterpart) must be signed on behalf of all parties to whom it relates, should be lodged at the Registry. The copies should be undated. The order will be dated with the date on which the judge initials it, but that does not prevent the parties acting on their agreement immediately if they wish.

(c) The parties should act promptly in lodging the copies at the Registry. If it is important that the orders are made by a particular date, that fact (and the reasons for it) should be notified in writing to the Registry.

F9.2 For the avoidance of doubt, this procedure is not normally available in relation to a case management conference or a pre-trial review. Whether or not the parties are agreed as between themselves on the directions that the Court should be asked to consider giving at a case management conference or a pre-trial review, attendance will normally be required. See section D8.3.

F9.3 Where an order provides a time by which something is to be done the order should wherever possible state the particular date by which the thing is to be done rather than specify a period of time from a particular date or event: rule 2.9.

F10 Hearing dates, time estimates and time limits

CPR 61 ACG F10

F10.1 Dates for the hearing of applications to be attended by advocates are normally fixed after discussion with the counsel's clerks or with the solicitor concerned.

F10.2 The efficient working of the Court depends on accurate estimates of the time needed for the oral hearing of an application including a considered estimate of the judge's pre-hearing reading. Over-estimating can be as wasteful as under-estimating.

F10.3 Subject to section F10.4, the Clerk to the Commercial Court will not accept or act on time estimates for the oral hearing of applications where those estimates exceed the following maxima:

Application to set aside service:	4 hours

Application for summary judgment:	4 hours
Application to set aside or vary interim remedy:	4 hours
Application to set aside or vary default judgment:	2 hours
Application to amend statement of case:	1 hour
Application for specific disclosure:	1 hour
Application for security for costs:	1 hour

F10.4 A longer listing time will only be granted upon application in writing specifying the additional time required and giving reasons why it is required. A copy of the written application should be sent to the advocates for all other parties in the case at the same time as it is sent to the Listing Office.

F10.5 (a) Not later than five days before the date fixed for the hearing the applicant must provide the Listing Office with his current estimate of the time required to dispose of the application.

(b) If at any time either party considers that there is a material risk that the hearing of the application will exceed the time currently allowed it must inform the Listing Office immediately.

F10.6 (a) All time estimates should be given on the assumption that the judge will have read in advance the skeleton arguments and the documents identified in the reading list. In this connection attention is drawn to section F8.

(b) A time estimate for an ordinary application should allow time for judgment and consequential matters; a time estimate for a heavy application should not.

F10.7 Save in the situation referred to at section F10.8, a separate estimate must be given for each application, including any application issued after, but to be heard at the same time as, another application.

F10.8 A separate estimate need not be given for any application issued after, but to be heard at the same time as, another application where the advocate in the case certifies in writing that

(i)   the determination of the application first issued will necessarily determine the application issued subsequently; or

(ii)   the matters raised in the application issued subsequently are not contested.

F10.9 If it is found at the hearing that the time required for the hearing has been significantly underestimated, the judge hearing the application may adjourn the matter and may make any special costs orders (including orders for the immediate payment of costs and wasted costs orders) as may be appropriate.

F10.10 Failure to comply with the requirements for lodging bundles for the application will normally result in the application not being heard on the date fixed at the expense of the party in default (see further sections F5.9 and F6.8 above). An order for immediate payment of costs may be made.

F11 Application bundles

CPR 61 ACG F11

F11.1 (a) Attention is drawn to Appendix 10, which deals with the preparation of bundles.

(b) Bundles for use on applications may be compiled in any convenient manner but must contain the following documents (preferably in separate sections in the following order):

(i)   a copy of the application notice;

(ii)   a draft of the order which the applicant seeks;

(iii)   a copy of the statements of case;

(iv)   copies of any previous orders which are relevant to the application;

(v)   copies of the witness statements and affidavits filed in support of, or in opposition to, the application, together with any exhibits.

(c) Copies of the statements of case and of previous orders in the action should be provided in a separate section of the bundle. They should not be exhibited to witness statements.

(d) Witness statements and affidavits previously filed in the same proceedings should be included in the bundle at a convenient location. They should not be exhibited to witness statements.

(e) Where for the purpose of the application it is likely to be necessary for the Court to read in chronological order correspondence or other documents located as exhibits to different affidavits or witness statements, copies of such documents should be filed and paged in chronological order in a separate composite bundle or bundles which should be agreed between the parties. If time does not permit agreement on the contents of the composite bundle, it is the responsibility of the applicant to prepare the composite bundle and to lodge it with the Listing Office by 4pm two clear days before the hearing in the case of heavy applications and one clear day before the hearing in the case of all other applications.

F12 Chronologies, indices and dramatis personae

CPR 61 ACG F12

F12.1 For most applications it is of assistance for the applicant to provide a chronology which should be cross-referenced to the documents. Dramatis personae are often useful as well.

F12.2 Guidelines on the preparation of chronologies and indices are set out in Part 2 of Appendix 9.

F13 Authorities

CPR 61 ACG F13

F13.1 On some applications there will be key authorities that it would be useful for the judge to read before the oral hearing of the application. Copies of these authorities should be provided with the skeleton arguments.

F13.2 It is also desirable for bundles of the authorities on which the parties wish to rely to be provided to the judge hearing the application as soon as possible after skeleton arguments have been exchanged.

F13.3 Authorities should only be cited when they contain some principle of law relevant to an issue arising on the application and where their substance is not to be found in the decision of a Court of higher authority.

F13.4

(a)   Save exceptionally (e.g. when to do otherwise would involve ending a bundle in mid-case), bundles of authorities should not exceed 300 pages in length.

(b)   Bundles of authorities should (save where there is good reason otherwise) be printed/copied double sided and be made up as follows:

(i)   Where the authority is reported, PDF copies or photo copies of the original report with the head-note;

(ii)   Where the authority is unreported, the official transcript where available (e.g. the printable RTF version which is available on Bailii).

F14 Costs

CPR 61 ACG F14

F14.1 Costs are dealt with generally at section J13.

F14.2 Reference should also be made to the rules governing the summary assessment of costs for shorter hearings contained in Parts 43 and 44. Active consideration will generally be given by the Court to adopting the summary assessment procedure in all cases where the schedule of costs of the successful party is no more than £100,000, but the parties should always be prepared for the Court to assess costs summarily even where the costs exceed this amount.

F14.3 In carrying out a summary assessment of costs, the Court may have regard amongst other matters to:

(i)   advice from a Commercial Costs Judge or from the Chief Costs Judge on costs of specialist solicitors and counsel;

(ii)   any survey published by the London Solicitors Litigation Association showing the average hourly expense rate for solicitors in London;

(iii)   any information provided to the Court at its request by one or more of the specialist associations (referred to at section A4.2) on average charges by specialist solicitors and counsel.

F14.4 Reference should also be made to CPR 44.3(8). Active consideration will generally be given by the Court to making an order for a payment on account of costs if they are not assessed summarily.

F15 Interim injunctions

Generally

CPR 61 ACG F15

F15.1 (a) Applications for interim injunctions are governed by CPR Part 25.

(b) Applications must be made on notice in accordance with the procedure set out in CPR Part 23 unless there are good reasons for proceeding without notice.

F15.2 A party who wishes to make an application for an interim injunction must give the Clerk to the Commercial Court as much notice as possible.

F15.3 (a) Except when the application is so urgent that there has not been any opportunity to do so, the applicant must issue his claim form and obtain the evidence on which he wishes to rely in support of the application before making the application.

(b) On applications of any weight, and unless the urgency means that this is not possible, the applicant should provide the Court at the earliest opportunity with a skeleton argument.

(c) An affidavit, and not a witness statement, is required on an application for a freezing order or a search order: PD25 section 3.1.

Fortification of undertakings

F15.4 (a) Where the applicant for an interim remedy is not able to show sufficient assets within the jurisdiction of the Court to provide substance to the undertakings given, particularly the undertaking in damages, he may be required to reinforce his undertakings by providing security.

(b) Security will be ordered in such form as the judge decides is appropriate but may, for example, take the form of a payment into Court, a bond issued by an insurance company or a first demand guarantee or standby credit issued by a first-class bank.

(c) In an appropriate case the judge may order a payment to be made to the applicant's solicitors to be held by them as officers of the Court pending further order. Sometimes the undertaking of a parent company may be acceptable.

Form of order

F15.5 Standard forms of wording for freezing injunctions and search orders are set out in Appendix 5. The forms have been adapted for use in the Commercial Court. These examples may be modified as appropriate in any particular case. Any modification to the form by an applicant should be expressly referred to the Judge's attention at the application hearing.

F15.6 A phrase indicating that an interim remedy is to remain in force until judgment or further order means that it remains in force until the delivery of a final judgment. If an interim remedy continuing after judgment is required, say until judgment has been satisfied, an application to that effect must be made (see further section K1).

F15.7 It is good practice to draft an order for an interim remedy so that it includes a proviso which permits acts which would otherwise be a breach of the order to be done with the written consent of the solicitor of the other party or parties. This enables the parties to agree in effect to variations (or the discharge) of the order without the necessity of coming back to the Court.

Freezing injunctions

F15.8 (a) Freezing injunctions made on an application without notice will provide for a return date, unless the judge otherwise orders: PD25 section 5.1(3). In the usual course, the return date given will be a Friday (unless a date for a case management conference has already been fixed, in which event the return date given will in the usual course be that date).

(b) If, after service or notification of the injunction, one or more of the parties considers that more than 15 minutes will be required to deal with the matter on the return date the Listing Office should be informed forthwith and in any event no later than 4 p.m. on the Wednesday before the Friday fixed as the return date.

(c) If the parties agree, the return date may be postponed to a later date on which all parties will be ready to deal with any substantive issues. In this event, an agreed form of order continuing the injunction to the postponed return date should be submitted for consideration by a judge and if the order is made in the terms submitted there will be no need for the parties to attend on the day originally fixed as the return date.

(d) In such a case the defendant and any other interested party will continue to have liberty to apply to vary or set aside the order.

F15.9 A provision for the defendant to give notice of any application to discharge or vary the order is usually included as a matter of convenience but it is not proper to attempt to fetter the right of the defendant to apply without notice or on short notice if need be.

F15.10 As regards freezing orders in respect of assets outside the jurisdiction, the standard wording in relation to effects on third parties should normally incorporate wording to enable overseas branches of banks or similar institutions which have offices within the jurisdiction to comply with what they reasonably believe to be their obligations under the laws of the country where the assets are located or under the proper law of the relevant banking or other contract relating to such assets.

F15.11 Any bank or third party served with, notified of or affected by a freezing injunction may apply to the Court without notice to any party for directions, or notify the Court in writing without notice to any party, in the event that the order affects or may affect the position of the bank or third party under legislation, regulations or procedures aimed to prevent money laundering.

Search orders

F15.12 Attention is drawn to the detailed requirements in respect of search orders set out in PD25 section 7.1-8.3. The applicant for the search order will normally be required to undertake not to inform any third party of the search order or of the case until after a specified date.

Applications to discharge or vary freezing injunctions and search orders

F15.13 Applications to discharge or vary freezing injunctions and search orders are treated as matters of urgency for listing purposes. Those representing applicants for discharge or variation should ascertain before a date is fixed for the hearing whether, having regard to the evidence which they wish to adduce, the claimant would wish to adduce further evidence in opposition. If so, all reasonable steps must be taken by all parties to agree upon the earliest practicable date at which they can be ready for the hearing, so as to avoid the last minute need to vacate a fixed date. In cases of difficulty the matter should be referred to a judge who may be able to suggest temporary solutions pending the hearing.

F15.14 If a freezing injunction or a search order is discharged on an application to discharge or vary, or on the return date, the judge will consider whether it is appropriate that he should assess damages at once and direct immediate payment by the applicant. Where the judge considers that the hearing for the assessment of damages should be postponed to a future date he will give such case management directions as may be appropriate for the assessment hearing, including, if necessary, disclosure of documents and exchange of witness statements and experts' reports.

Applications under section 25 of the Civil Jurisdiction and Judgments Act 1982

F15.15 A Part 8 claim form (rather than an application notice: cf. rule 25.4(2)) must be used for an application under section 25 of the Civil Jurisdiction and Judgments Act 1982 ("Interim relief in England and Wales and Northern Ireland in the absence of substantive proceedings"). The modified Part 8 procedure used in the Commercial Court is referred to at section B4 above.

F16 Security for costs

CPR 61 ACG F16

F16.1 Applications for security for costs are governed by rules 25.12-14.

F16.2 The applicable practice is set out in Appendix 16.

G. ALTERNATIVE DISPUTE RESOLUTION ("ADR")

G1 Generally

CPR 61 ACG G1

G1.1 While emphasising its primary role as a forum for deciding commercial cases, the Commercial Court encourages parties to consider the use of ADR (such as, but not confined to, mediation and conciliation) as an alternative means of resolving disputes or particular issues.

G1.2 Whilst the Commercial Court remains an entirely appropriate forum for resolving most of the disputes which are entered in the Commercial List, the view of the Commercial Court is that the settlement of disputes by means of ADR:

(i)   significantly helps parties to save costs;

(ii)   saves parties the delay of litigation in reaching finality in their disputes;

(iii)   enables parties to achieve settlement of their disputes while preserving their existing commercial relationships and market reputation;

(iv)   provides parties with a wider range of solutions than those offered by litigation; and

(v)   is likely to make a substantial contribution to the more efficient use of judicial resources.

G1.3 The Commercial Judges will in appropriate cases invite the parties to consider whether their dispute, or particular issues in it, could be resolved through ADR.

G1.4 Legal representatives in all cases should consider with their clients and the other parties concerned the possibility of attempting to resolve the dispute or particular issues by ADR and should ensure that their clients are fully informed as to the most cost effective means of resolving their dispute.

G1.5 Parties who consider that ADR might be an appropriate means of resolving the dispute or particular issues in the dispute may apply for directions at any stage, including before service of the defence and before the case management conference.

G1.6 At the case management conference if it should appear to the judge that the case before him or any of the issues arising in it are particularly appropriate for an attempt at settlement by means of ADR but that the parties have not previously attempted settlement by such means, he may invite the parties to use ADR.

G1.7 The judge may, if he considers it appropriate, adjourn the case for a specified period of time to encourage and enable the parties to use ADR. He may for this purpose extend the time for compliance by the parties or any of them with any requirement under the rules, the Guide or any order of the Court. The judge in making an order providing for ADR will normally take into account, when considering at what point in the pre-trial timetable there should be compliance with such an order, such matters as the costs likely to be incurred at each stage in the pre-trial timetable if the claim is not settled, the costs of a mediation or other means of dispute resolution, how far the prospects of a successful mediation or other means of dispute resolution are likely to be enhanced by completion of pleadings, disclosure of documents, provision of further information under CPR 18, exchange of factual witness statements or exchange of experts' reports.

G1.8 The Judge may further consider in an appropriate case making an ADR order in the terms set out in Appendix 7.

G1.9 (a) The Clerk to the Commercial Court keeps some published information on individuals and bodies that offer ADR and arbitration services. If the parties are unable to agree upon a neutral individual or panel of individuals to act as a mediator or give an early neutral evaluation, the normal form of ADR order set out in Appendix 7 contains at paragraph 3 a mandatory requirement that the case management conference should be restored to enable the Court to facilitate agreement on a neutral or panel of neutrals. In order to avoid the cost of a restored case management hearing, the parties may agree to send to the Court their respective list of available neutrals, so as to enable the judge to suggest a name from those lists. In any other case the parties may by consent refer to the judge for assistance in reaching such agreement.

(b) The Court will not recommend any individual or body to act as a mediator or arbitrator.

G1.10 At the case management conference or at any other hearing in the course of which the judge makes an order providing for ADR he may make such order as to the costs that the parties may incur by reason of their using or attempting to use ADR as may in all the circumstances seem appropriate. The orders for costs are normally costs in the case, meaning that if the claim is not settled, the costs of the ADR procedures, will follow the ultimate event, or that each side shall bear its own costs of those procedures if the case is not settled.

G1.11 In some cases it may be appropriate that an ADR order should be made following judgment if application is made for permission to appeal. In such cases the Court may adjourn the application for permission to appeal while making an ADR order providing for ADR procedures to be completed within a specified time and, failing settlement with that period, for the application for permission to appeal to be restored.

G1.12 At the case management conference the Court may consider that an order directed to encouraging bilateral negotiations between the parties' respective legal representatives is likely to be a more cost-effective and productive route to settlement then can be offered by a formal ADR or ENE Order. In such a case the Court will set a date by which there is to be a meeting between respective solicitors and their respective clients' officials responsible for decision-taking in relation to the case in question.

G2 Early neutral evaluation

CPR 61 ACG G2

G2.1 In appropriate cases and with the agreement of all parties the Court will provide a without-prejudice, non-binding, early neutral evaluation ("ENE") of a dispute or of particular issues.

G2.2 The approval of the Judge in Charge of the List must be obtained before any ENE is undertaken.

G2.3 If, after discussion with the advocates representing the parties, it appears to a judge that an ENE is likely to assist in the resolution of the dispute or of particular issues, he will, with the agreement of the parties, refer the matter to the Judge in Charge of the List.

G2.4 (a) The Judge in Charge of the List will nominate a Judge to conduct the ENE.

(b) The judge who is to conduct the ENE will give such directions for its preparation and conduct as he considers appropriate.

G2.5 The judge who conducts the ENE will take no further part in the case, either for the purpose of the hearing of applications or as the judge at trial, unless the parties agree otherwise.

H. EVIDENCE FOR TRIAL

H1 Witnesses of fact

Preparation and form of witness statements

CPR 61 ACG H1

H1.1 Witness statements must comply with the requirements of PD32. The following points are also emphasised:

(i)   the function of a witness statement is to set out in writing the evidence in chief of the witness; as far as possible, therefore, the statement should be in the witness's own words;

(ii)   it should be as concise as the circumstances of the case allow without omitting any significant matters;

(iii)   it should not contain lengthy quotations from documents;

(iv)   it is seldom necessary to exhibit documents to a witness statement;

(v)   it should not engage in (legal or other) argument;

(vi)   it must indicate which of the statements made in it are made from the witness's own knowledge and which are made on information or belief, giving the source for any statement made on information or belief;

(vii) it must contain a statement by the witness that he believes the matters stated in it are true; proceedings for contempt of Court may be brought against a person if he makes, or causes to be made, a false statement in a witness statement without an honest belief in its truth: rule 32.14(1);

(viii) it must comply with any direction of the Court about its length.

H1.2 It is usually convenient for a witness statement to follow the chronological sequence of events or matters dealt with (32PD19.2). It is helpful for it to indicate to which issue in the list of issues the particular passage in the witness statement relates, either by a heading in the statement or in a marginal notation or by some other convenient method.

H1.3 It is improper to put pressure of any kind on a witness to give anything other than his own account of the matters with which his statement deals. It is also improper to serve a witness statement which is known to be false or which it is known the maker does not in all respects actually believe to be true.

Fluency of witnesses

H1.4 If a witness is not sufficiently fluent in English to give his evidence in English, the witness statement should be in the witness's own language and a translation provided.

H1.5 If a witness is not fluent in English but can make himself understood in broken English and can understand written English, the statement need not be in his own words provided that these matters are indicated in the statement itself. It must however be written so as to express as accurately as possible the substance of his evidence.

Witness statement as evidence in chief

H1.6 (a) Where a witness is called to give oral evidence, his witness statement is to stand as his evidence in chief unless the Court orders otherwise: rule 32.5(2).

(b) In an appropriate case the trial judge may direct that the whole or any part of a witness's evidence in chief is to be given orally. Notice of any such application for such an order should be given as early as is reasonably convenient. It is usually reasonable for any such application to be made at a pre-trial review if one is held..

Additional evidence from a witness

H1.7 (a) A witness giving oral evidence at trial may with the permission of the Court amplify his witness statement and give evidence in relation to new matters which have arisen since the witness statement was served: rule 32.5(3). Permission will be given only if the Court considers that there is good reason not to confine the evidence of the witness to the contents of his witness statement: rule 32.5(4).

(b) A supplemental witness statement should normally be served where the witness proposes materially to add to, alter, correct or retract from what is in his original statement. Permission will be required for the service of a supplemental statement. Such application should be made at the pre-trial review or, if there is no pre-trial review, as early as possible before the start of the trial. If application is made at any later stage, the applicant must provide compelling evidence explaining its delay in adducing such evidence.

(c) It is the duty of all parties to ensure that the statements of all factual witnesses intended to be called or whose statements are to be tendered as hearsay statements should be exchanged simultaneously unless the Court has otherwise ordered. Witnesses additional to those whose statements have been initially exchanged may only be called with the permission of the Court which will not normally be given unless prompt application is made supported by compelling evidence explaining the late introduction of that witness's evidence.

Notice of decision not to call a witness

H1.8 (a) If a party decides not to call to give oral evidence at trial a witness whose statement has been served but wishes to rely upon the evidence, he must put in the statement as hearsay evidence unless the Court otherwise orders: rule 32.5. If he proposes to put the evidence in as hearsay evidence, reference should be made to rule 33.2.

(b) If the party who has served the statement does not put it in as hearsay evidence, any other party may do so: rule 32.5(5).

Witness summonses

H1.9 (a) Rules 34.2-34.8 deal with witness summonses, including a summons for a witness to attend Court or to produce documents in advance of the date fixed for trial.

(b) Witness summonses are served by the parties, not the Court.

H2 Expert witnesses

Application for permission to call an expert witness

CPR 61 ACG H2

H2.1 Any application for permission to call an expert witness or serve an expert's report should normally be made at the case management conference. The party applying for such permission will be expected to provide an estimate of the costs of the proposed expert evidence, identify to which issue or issues in the list of issues the proposed expert evidence relates, and to propose any amendments to the list of issues that might be required for this purpose. The court may specify in the order the issues which the expert should address and may limit the length of an expert report.

H2.2 Parties should bear in mind that expert evidence can lead to unnecessary expense and they should be prepared to consider the use of single joint experts in appropriate cases. In many cases the use of single joint experts is not appropriate and each party will generally be given permission to call one expert in each field requiring expert evidence. These are referred to in the Guide as "separate experts".

H2.3 When the use of a single joint expert is contemplated, the Court will expect the parties to co-operate in developing, and agreeing to the greatest possible extent, terms of reference for that expert. In most cases the terms of reference will (in particular) identify in detail what the expert is asked to do, identify any documentary materials he is asked to consider and specify any assumptions he is asked to make.

Provisions of general application in relation to expert evidence

H2.4 The provisions set out in Appendix 11 to the Guide apply to all aspects of expert evidence (including expert reports, meetings of experts and expert evidence given orally) unless the Court orders otherwise. Parties should ensure that they are drawn to the attention of any experts they instruct at the earliest opportunity.

Form and content of expert's reports

H2.5 Expert's reports must comply with the requirements of PD35 sections 1 and 2.

H2.6(a) In stating the substance of all material instructions on the basis of which his report is written as required by rule 35.10(3) and PD35 section 1.2(8) an expert witness should state the facts or assumptions upon which his opinion is based.

(b) The expert must make it clear which, if any, of the facts stated are within his own direct knowledge.

(c) If a stated assumption is, in the opinion of the expert witness, unreasonable or unlikely he should state that clearly.

(d) The expert's report must be limited to matters relevant to the issue or issues in the list of issues to which the relevant expert evidence relates and for which permission to call such expert evidence has been given.

H2.7 It is useful if a report contains a glossary of significant technical terms.

H2.8 Where the evidence of an expert, such as a surveyor, assessor, adjuster, or other investigator is to be relied upon for the purpose of establishing primary facts, such as the condition of a ship or other property as found by him at a particular time, as well as for the purpose of deploying his expertise to express an opinion on any matter related to or in connection with the primary facts, that part of his evidence which is to be relied upon to establish the primary facts, is to be treated as factual evidence to be incorporated into a factual witness statement to be exchanged in accordance with the order for the exchange of factual witness statements. The purpose of this practice is to avoid postponing disclosure of a party's factual evidence until service of expert reports.

Statement of truth

H2.9 (a) The report must be signed by the expert and must contain a statement of truth in accordance with Part 35.

(b) Proceedings for contempt of Court may be brought against a person if he makes, or causes to be made, without an honest belief in its truth, a false statement in an expert's report verified in the manner set out in this section.

Request by an expert to the Court for directions

H2.10 An expert may file with the Court a written request for directions to assist him in carrying out his function as expert, but

(i)   at least 7 days before he does so (or such shorter period as the Court may direct) he should provide a copy of his proposed request to the party instructing him; and

(ii)   at least 4 days before he does so (or such shorter period as the Court may direct) he should provide a copy of his proposed request to all other parties.

Exchange of reports

H2.11 In appropriate cases the Court will direct that the reports of expert witnesses be exchanged sequentially rather than simultaneously. The sequential exchange of expert reports may in many cases save time and costs by helping to focus the contents of responsive reports upon true rather than assumed issues of expert evidence and by avoiding repetition of detailed factual material as to which there is no real issue. Sequential exchange is likely to be particularly effective where experts are giving evidence of foreign law or are forensic accountants.This is an issue that the Court will normally wish to consider at the case management conference.

Meetings of expert witnesses

H2.12 The Court will normally direct a meeting or meetings of expert witnesses before trial. Sometimes it may be useful for there to be further meetings during the trial itself.

H2.13 The purposes of a meeting of experts are to give the experts the opportunity

(i)   to discuss the expert issues;

(ii)   to decide, with the benefit of that discussion, on which expert issues they share or can come to share the same expert opinion and on which expert issues there remains a difference of expert opinion between them (and what that difference is).

H2.14 Subject to section H2.16 below, the content of the discussion between the experts at or in connection with a meeting is without prejudice and shall not be referred to at the trial unless the parties so agree: rule 35.12(4).

H2.15 Subject to any directions of the Court, the procedure to be adopted at a meeting of experts is a matter for the experts themselves, not the parties or their legal representatives.

H2.16 Neither the parties nor their legal representatives should seek to restrict the freedom of experts to identify and acknowledge the expert issues on which they agree at, or following further consideration after, meetings of experts.

H2.17 Unless the Court orders otherwise, at or following any meeting the experts should prepare a joint memorandum for the Court recording:

(i)   the fact that they have met and discussed the expert issues;

(ii)   the issues on which they agree;

(iii)   the issues on which they disagree; and

(iv)   a brief summary of the reasons for their disagreement.

H2.18 If experts reach agreement on an issue that agreement shall not bind the parties unless they expressly agree to be bound by it.

Written questions to experts

H2.19 (a) Under rule 35.6 a party may, without the permission of the Court, put written questions to an expert instructed by another party (or to a single joint expert) about his report. Unless the Court gives permission or the other party agrees, such questions must be for the purpose only of clarifying the report.

(b) The Court will pay close attention to the use of this procedure (especially where separate experts are instructed) to ensure that it remains an instrument for the helpful exchange of information. The Court will not allow it to interfere with the procedure for an exchange of professional opinion at a meeting of experts, or to inhibit that exchange of professional opinion. In cases where (for example) questions that are oppressive in number or content are put, or questions are put for any purpose other than clarification of the report, the Court will not hesitate to disallow the questions and to make an appropriate order for costs against the party putting them.

Documents referred to in experts' reports

H2.20 Unless they have already been provided on inspection of documents at the stage of disclosure, copies of any photographs, plans, analyses, measurements, survey reports or other similar documents relied on by an expert witness as well as copies of any unpublished sources must be provided to all parties at the same time as his report.

H2.21 (a) Rule 31.14(e) provides that (subject to rule 35.10(4)) a party may inspect a document mentioned in an expert's report. In a commercial case an expert's report will frequently, and helpfully, list all or many of the relevant previous papers (published or unpublished) or books written by the expert or to which the expert has contributed. Requiring inspection of this material may often be unrealistic, and the collating and copying burden could be huge.

(b) Accordingly, a party wishing to inspect a document in an expert report should (failing agreement) make an application to the Court. The Court will not permit inspection unless it is satisfied that it is necessary for the just disposal of the case and that the document is not reasonably available to the party making the application from an alternative source.

Trial

H2.22 At trial the evidence of expert witnesses is usually taken as a block, after the evidence of witnesses of fact has been given. The introduction of additional expert evidence after the commencement of the trial can have a severely disruptive effect.

Not only is it likely to make necessary additional expert evidence in response, but it may also lead to applications for further disclosure of documents and also to applications to call further factual evidence from witnesses whose statements have not previously been exchanged. Accordingly, experts' supplementary reports must be completed and exchanged not later than the progress monitoring date and the introduction of additional expert evidence after that date will only be permitted upon application to the trial judge and if there are very strong grounds for admitting it.

H3 Evidence by video link

CPR 61 ACG H3

H3.1 In an appropriate case permission may be given for the evidence of a witness to be given by video link. If permission is given the Court will give directions for the conduct of this part of the trial.

H3.2 The party seeking permission to call evidence by video link should prepare and serve on all parties and lodge with the Court a memorandum dealing with the matters outlined in the Video Conferencing Guidance contained in Annex 3 to PD32 (see Appendix 14) and setting out precisely what arrangements are proposed. Where the proposal involves transmission from a location with no existing video-link facility, experience shows that questions of feasibility, timing and cost will require particularly close investigation.

H3.3 An application for permission to call evidence by video link should be made, if possible, at the case management conference or, at the latest, at any pre-trial review. However, an application may be made at an even later stage if necessary. Particular attention should be given to the taking of evidence by video link whenever a proposed witness will have to travel from a substantial distance abroad and his evidence is likely to last no more than half a day.

H3.4 In considering whether to give permission for evidence to be given in this way the Court will be concerned in particular to balance any potential savings of costs against the inability to observe the witness at first hand when giving evidence.

H4 Taking evidence abroad

CPR 61 ACG H4

H4.1 In an appropriate case permission may be given for the evidence of a witness to be taken abroad. CPR Part 34 contains provisions for the taking of evidence by deposition, and the issue of letters of request.

H4.2 In a very exceptional case, and subject in particular to all necessary approvals being obtained and diplomatic requirements being satisfied, the Court may be willing to conduct part of the proceedings abroad. However, if there is any reasonable opportunity for the witness to give evidence by video link, the Court is unlikely to take that course.

J. TRIAL

J1 Expedited trial

CPR 61 ACG J1

J1.1 The Commercial Court is able to provide an expedited trial in cases of sufficient urgency and importance.

J1.2 A party seeking an expedited trial should apply to the Judge in Charge of the Commercial List on notice to all parties at the earliest possible opportunity. The application should normally be made after issue and service of the claim form but before service of particulars of claim.

J2 Trials of issues

CPR 61 ACG J2

J2.1 The Court may direct a separate trial of any issue under rule 3.1(2)(i). It will sometimes be advantageous to have a separate trial of particular issues with other issues being heard either by the same judge or by another judge of the Commercial Court or in another Court or tribunal. For example, where liability is tried first in the Commercial Court, the assessment of damages can be referred to a Master, or the parties may choose to ask an arbitrator to decide them. The same approach can be applied to other factual questions.

J2.2 Under rule 3.1(2)(j), (k) and (l) the Court may decide the order in which issues are to be tried, may exclude an issue from consideration and may dismiss or give judgment on a claim after a decision on a preliminary issue. The Court is likely to consider this by reference to the list of issues. Particularly in long trials, it will sometimes be advantageous to exercise these powers, and accordingly hear the evidence relevant to some issues before moving on to the evidence relevant to others; and the judge will sometimes decide some issues before moving on to hear the evidence relevant to other issues.

J3 Documents for trial

CPR 61 ACG J3

J3.1 Bundles of documents for the trial must be prepared in accordance with Appendix 10.

J3.2 The number, content and organisation of the trial bundles must be approved by the advocates with the conduct of the trial.

J3.3 Apart from certain specified documents, trial bundles should include only necessary documents: 39APD3.2(11). Consideration must always be given to what documents are and are not relevant and necessary. Where the Court is of the opinion that costs have been wasted by the copying of unnecessary documents it will have no hesitation in making a special order for costs against the person responsible.

J3.4 The number content and organisation of the trial bundles should be agreed in accordance with the following procedure:

(i)   the claimant must submit proposals to all other parties at least 6 weeks before the date fixed for trial; and

(ii)   the other parties must submit details of additions they require and any suggestions for revision of the claimant's proposals to the claimant at least 4 weeks before the date fixed for trial.

This information must be supplied in a form that will be most convenient for the recipient to understand and respond to. The form to be used should be discussed between the parties before the details are supplied.

J3.5 (a) It is the responsibility of the claimant's legal representative to prepare and lodge the agreed trial bundles: see 39APD34.

(b) If another party wishes to put before the Court a bundle that the claimant regards as unnecessary he must prepare and lodge it himself.

J3.6 (a) Preparation of the trial bundles must be completed not later than 10 days before the date for service of skeleton arguments under paragraph J6 below unless the court orders otherwise.

(b) Any party preparing a trial bundle should, as a matter of course, provide all other parties who are to take part in the trial with a copy, at the cost of the receiving party: 39APD3.10. Further copies should be supplied on request, again at the cost of the receiving party.

J3.7 Unless the court orders otherwise, a full set of the trial bundles must be lodged with the Listing Office by the start of the designated reading period (see J6.2 below) and in any event at least 7 days before the date fixed for trial.

J3.8 If bundles are lodged late, this may result in the trial not commencing on the date fixed, at the expense of the party in default. An order for immediate payment of costs may be made.

J3.9 If oral evidence is to be given at trial, the claimant should provide a clean unmarked set of all relevant trial bundles for use in the witness box: 39APD3.10 The claimant is responsible for ensuring that these bundles are kept up to date throughout the trial.

J4 Information technology at trial

CPR 61 ACG J4

J4.1 The use of information technology at trial is encouraged where it is likely substantially to save time and cost or to increase accuracy.

J4.2 If any party considers that it might be advantageous to make use of information technology in preparation for, or at, trial, the matter should be raised at the first case management conference. This is particularly important if it is considered that document handling systems would assist disclosure and inspection of documents or the use of documents at trial. In any event, at the first case management conference, even if neither party itself raises the use of information technology, the parties must expect the Court to consider its use, including its use in relation to trial bundles.

J4.3 Where information technology is to be used for the purposes of presenting the case at trial the same system must be used by all parties and must be made available to the Court. In deciding whether and to what extent information technology should be used at the trial the Court will have regard to the financial resources of the parties and will consider whether it is appropriate that, having regard to the parties' unequal financial resources, it is appropriate that the party applying for the use of such information technology should initially bear the cost subject to the Court's ultimate order as to the overall costs following judgment.

J5 Reading lists, authorities and trial timetable

CPR 61 ACG J5

J5.1 Unless the court orders otherwise, a single reading list approved by all advocates must be lodged with the Listing Office not later than the time at which the Claimant's skeleton argument is lodged under paragraph J6 below.

J5.2 (a) If any party objects to the judge reading any document in advance of the trial, the objection and its grounds should be clearly stated in a letter accompanying the trial bundles and in the skeleton argument of that party.

(b) Parties should consider in particular whether they have any objection to the judge's reading the witness statements before the trial.

(c) In the absence of objection, the judge will be free to read the witness statements and documents in advance.

J5.3 (a) A composite bundle of the authorities referred to in the skeleton arguments should be lodged with the Listing Office as soon as possible after skeleton arguments have been exchanged.

(b) Unless otherwise agreed, the preparation of the bundle of authorities is the responsibility of the claimant, who should provide copies to all other parties. Advocates should liaise in relation to the production of bundles of authorities to ensure that the same authority does not appear in more than one bundle.

J5.4 Cases which are unreported and which are also not included in the index of Judgments of the Commercial Court and Admiralty Court of England and Wales should normally only be cited where the advocate is ready to give an assurance that the transcript contains a statement of some relevant principle of law of which the substance, as distinct from some mere choice of phraseology, is not to be found in any judgment that has appeared in one of the general or specialised series of law reports. The index of Judgments of the Commercial Court and Admiralty Court of England and Wales can be found at www.hmscourt-service.gov.uk/infoabout/admiralcomm/index.htm via the link to "Searchable index of court cases" (at bottom of the box on right hand side of Commercial Court and Admiralty Court).

J5.5 (a) When lodging the reading list the claimant should also lodge a trial timetable.

(b) A trial timetable may have been fixed by the judge at the pre-trial review (section D18.4 above). If it has not, a trial timetable should be prepared by the advocate(s) for the claimant after consultation with the advocate(s) for all other parties.

(c) If there are differences of view between the advocate(s) for the claimant and the advocate(s) for other parties, these should be shown.

(d) The trial timetable will provide for oral submissions, witness evidence and expert evidence over the course of the trial. On the first day of the trial the judge may fix the trial timetable, subject to any further order.

(e) The Court may restrict evidence or submissions to ensure compliance with the trial timetable.

J6 Skeleton arguments etc. at trial

CPR 61 ACG J6

J6.1 Written skeleton arguments should be prepared by each party. Guidelines on the preparation of skeleton arguments are set out in Part 1 of Appendix 9.

J6.2 Unless otherwise ordered, the skeleton arguments should be served on all other parties and lodged with the Court as follows:

(i)   by the claimant, not later than 1 p.m. on the earlier of either the day before the reading period for the trial (set out in the CMC Order or as subsequently amended by Pre Trial Order/checklist or otherwise) commences or two days (i.e. two clear days) before the start of the trial;

(ii)   by each of the defendants, not later than 1 p.m. after the day on which the applicant's skeleton argument is required to be served.

J6.3 Advocates are reminded that the timetable and the requisite reading time should be discussed between the advocates, that a careful estimate should be given at the time of the pre-trial checklist/review and any change in the estimates for trial or reading time should be promptly notified to the Commercial Court Office.

J6.4 The claimant should provide a chronology with his skeleton argument. Indices (i.e. documents that collate key references on particular points, or a substantive list of the contents of a particular bundle or bundles) and dramatis personae should also be provided where these are likely to be useful. Guidelines on the preparation of chronologies and indices are set out in Part 2 of Appendix 9.

J6.5 So far as possible skeleton arguments should be limited in length to 50 pages. Where the advocate or advocates for trial consider that it is not possible to comply with that limit, the matter should be discussed with the trial judge at the pre-trial review or in correspondence.

J7 Trial sitting days and hearing trials in public

CPR 61 ACG J7

J7.1 Trial sitting days will not normally include Fridays.

J7.2 Where it is necessary in order to accommodate hearing evidence from certain witnesses or types of witness, the Court may agree to sit outside normal hours.

J7.3 The general rule is that a hearing is to be in public: rule 39.2(1).

J8 Oral opening statements at trial

CPR 61 ACG J8

J8.1 Oral opening statements should as far as possible be uncontroversial and in any event no longer than the circumstances require. Even in a very heavy case, oral opening statements may be very short. There remains some confusion amongst advocates as to what is necessary to adduce a document other than a witness statement or expert report in evidence. Whereas there can be no doubt that any disclosed document can be relied on as evidence of the facts contained in it or as evidence of its existence or the use to which it was put, see Civil Evidence Act 1995 S.2(4) and CPR 32.19 the mere inclusion of a document in the agreed trial bundles does not in itself mean that it is being adduced in evidence by either party: see Appendix 10. For this to happen either the parties must agree that the document in question is to be treated as put in evidence by one or other of them and the judge so informed or they must actively adduce the document in evidence by some other means. This might be done by counsel inviting the judge to read the document relied upon before the calling of oral evidence. The appropriate procedure will be a matter for the judgment of the advocates in each case. However, whichever course is adopted, it will not normally be appropriate for reliance to be placed in final speeches on any document, not already specifically adduced in evidence by one of the means described.

J8.2 At the conclusion of the opening statement for the claimant the advocates for each of the other parties will usually each be invited to make a short opening statement.

J9 Applications in the course of trial

CPR 61 ACG J9

J9.1 It will not normally be necessary for an application notice to be issued for an application which is to be made during the course of the trial, but all other parties should be given adequate notice of the intention to apply.

J9.2 Unless the judge directs otherwise the parties should prepare skeleton arguments for the hearing of the application.

J10 Oral closing submissions at trial

CPR 61 ACG J10

J10.1 All parties will be expected to make oral closing submissions, whether or not closing submissions have been made in writing. It is a matter for the advocate to consider how in all the circumstances these oral submissions should be presented.

J10.2 Unless the trial judge directs otherwise, the claimant will make his oral closing submissions first, followed by the defendant(s) in the order in which they appear on the claim form with the claimant having a right of reply.

J11 Written closing submissions at trial

CPR 61 ACG J11

J11.1 (a) In a more substantial trial, the Court will normally also require closing submissions in writing before oral closing submissions.

(b) In such a case the Court will normally allow an appropriate period of time after the conclusion of the evidence to allow the preparation of these submissions.

(c) Even in a less substantial trial the Court will normally require a skeleton argument on matters of law.

J12 Judgment

CPR 61 ACG J12

J12.1 (a) When judgment is reserved the judge may deliver judgment orally or by handing down a written judgment.

(b) If the judge intends to hand down a written judgment a copy of the draft text marked

"Draft Judgment"

and bearing the rubric

"This is a judgment to which the Practice Direction supplementing CPR Part 40 applies. It will be handed down on   at
In Court No   . This Judgment is confidential to the parties and their legal representatives and accordingly neither the draft itself nor its substance may be disclosed to any other person or used in the public domain. The parties must take all reasonable steps to ensure that its confidentiality is preserved. No action is to be taken (other than internally) in response to the draft, before judgment has been formally pronounced. A breach of any of these obligations may be treated as a contempt of Court. The official version of the judgment will be available from the <u>Courts Recording and Transcription Unit</u> of the Royal Courts of Justice once it has been approved by the judge.

The Court is likely to wish to hand down its judgment in an approved final form. Counsel should therefore submit any list of typing corrections and other obvious errors in writing (Nil returns are required) to the clerk to   , by fax to 020 7947   or via email at   , by   on   , so that changes can be incorporated, if the judge accepts them, in the handed down judgment."

will normally be supplied to the advocates one clear day before the judgment is to be delivered.

(c) Advocates should inform the judge's clerk not later than noon on the day before judgment is to be handed down of any typographical or other errors of a similar nature which the judge might wish to correct. This facility is confined to the correction of textual mistakes and is not to be used as the occasion for attempting to persuade the judge to change the decision on matters of substance.

(d) The requirement to treat the text as confidential must be strictly observed. Failure to do so amounts to a contempt of Court.

J12.2 (a) Judgment is not delivered until it is formally pronounced in open Court.

(b) Copies of the approved judgment will be made available to the parties, to law reporters and to any other person wanting a copy.

(c) The judge may direct that the written judgment stand as the definitive record and that no transcript need be made. Any editorial corrections made at the time of handing down will be incorporated in an approved official text as soon as possible, and the approved official text, so marked, will be available from the Mechanical Recording Department.

J12.3 If at the time of pronouncement of the judgment any party wishes to apply for permission to appeal to the Court of Appeal, that application should be supported by written draft grounds of appeal.

J12.4 Orders on Judgment should be drawn up in accordance with, and contain the information referred to in section D19.1(c) above.

J13 Costs

CPR 61 ACG J13

J13.1 The rules governing the award and assessment of costs are contained in CPR Parts 43 to 48.

J13.2 The summary assessment procedure provided for in Parts 43 and 44 also applies to trials lasting one day or less.

J14 Interest

CPR 61 ACG J14

J14.1 Historically the Commercial Court has generally awarded interest at base rate plus one percent unless that was shown to be unfair to one party or the other or to be otherwise inappropriate. In the light of recent interest rate developments there is no presumption that base rate plus one percent is the appropriate measure of a commercial rate of interest.

K. AFTER TRIAL

K1 Continuation, variation and discharge of interim remedies and undertakings

CPR 61 ACG K1

K1.1 (a) Applications to continue, vary or discharge interim remedies or undertakings should be made to a Commercial Judge, even after trial.

(b) If a party wishes to continue a freezing injunction after trial or judgment, care should be taken to ensure that the application is made before the existing freezing injunction has expired.

K2 Accounts and enquiries

CPR 61 ACG K2

K2.1 The Court may order that accounts and inquiries be referred to a judge of the Technology and Construction Court or to a Master. Alternatively, the parties may choose to refer the matter to arbitration.

K3 Enforcement

CPR 61 ACG K3

K3.1 Unless the Court orders otherwise, all proceedings for the enforcement of any judgment or order for the payment of money given or made in the Commercial Court will be referred automatically to a master of the Queen's Bench Division or a district judge: PD58 section 1.2(2).

K3.2 Applications in connection with the enforcement of a judgment or order for the payment of money should accordingly be directed to the Registry which will allocate them to the Admiralty Registrar or to one of the Queen's Bench masters as appropriate.

K4 Assessment of damages or interest after a default judgment

CPR 61 ACG K4

K4.1 Unless the Court orders otherwise, the assessment of damages or interest following the entry of a default judgment for damages or interest to be assessed will be carried out by the Admiralty Registrar or one of the Queen's Bench masters to whom the case is allocated by the Registry.

L. MULTI-PARTY DISPUTES
L1 Early consideration

CPR 61 ACG L1

L1.1 Cases which involve, or are expected to involve, a large number of claimants or defendants require close case management from the earliest point. The same is true where there are, or are likely to be, a large number of separate cases involving the same or similar issues. Both classes of case are referred to as "multi-party" disputes.

L1.2 (a) The Judge in Charge of the List should be informed as soon as it becomes apparent that a multi-party dispute exists or is likely to exist and an early application for directions should be made.

(b) In an appropriate case an application for directions may be made before issue of a claim form. In some cases it may be appropriate for an application to be made without notice in the first instance.

L2 Available procedures

CPR 61 ACG L2

L2.1 In some cases it may be appropriate for the Court to make a Group Litigation Order under Part 19 of the Rules. In other cases it may be more convenient for the Court to exercise its general powers of management. These include powers

(i)   to dispense with statements of case;

(ii)   to direct parties to serve outline statements of case;

(iii)   to direct that cases be consolidated or managed and tried together;

(iv)   to direct that certain cases or issues be determined before others and to stay other proceedings in the meantime;

(v)   to advance or put back the usual time for pre-trial steps to be taken (for example the disclosure of documents by one or more parties or a payment into Court).

L2.2 Attention is drawn to the provisions of Section III of Part 19, rules 19.10-19.15 and the Practice Direction supplementing Section III of Part 19. Practitioners should note that the provisions of Section III of Part 19 give the Court additional powers to manage disputes involving multiple claimants or defendants. They should also note that a Group Litigation Order may not be made without the consent of the Lord Chief Justice: PD19B section 3.3(1).

L2.3 An application for a Group Litigation Order should be made in the first instance to the Judge in Charge of the List: PD19B section 3.5.

M. LITIGANTS IN PERSON
M1 The litigant in person

CPR 61 ACG M1

M1.1 Litigants in person appear less often in the Commercial Court than in some other Courts. Their position requires special consideration.

M2 Represented parties

CPR 61 ACG M2

M2.1 Where a litigant in person is involved in a case the Court will expect solicitors and counsel for other parties to do what they reasonably can to ensure that he has a fair opportunity to prepare and put his case.

M2.2 The duty of an advocate to ensure that the Court is informed of all relevant decisions and legislative provisions of which he is aware (whether favourable to his case or not) and to bring any procedural irregularity to the attention of the Court during the hearing is of particular importance in a case where a litigant in person is involved.

M2.3 Further, the Court will expect solicitors and counsel appearing for other parties to ensure that the case memorandum, the list of issues and all necessary bundles are prepared and provided to the Court in accordance with the Guide, even where the litigant in person is unwilling or unable to participate.

M2.4 If the claimant is a litigant in person the judge at the case management conference will normally direct which of the parties is to have responsibility for the preparation and upkeep of the case management bundle.

M2.5 At the case management conference the Court may give directions relating to the costs of providing application bundles, trial bundles and, if applicable, transcripts of hearings to the litigant in person.

M3 Companies without representation

CPR 61 ACG M3

M3.1 Although rule 39.6 allows a company or other corporation with the permission of the Court to be represented at trial by an employee, the complexity of most cases in the Commercial Court makes that unsuitable. Accordingly, permission is likely to be given only in unusual circumstances.

N. ADMIRALTY

N1 General

CPR 61 ACG N1

N1.1 Proceedings in the Admiralty Court are dealt with in Part 61 and its associated Practice Direction.

N1.2 The Admiralty & Commercial Courts Guide has been prepared in consultation with the Admiralty Judge. It has been adopted to provide guidance about the conduct of proceedings in the Admiralty Court. The Guide must be followed in the Admiralty Court unless the content of Part 61, its associated Practice Direction or the terms of this section N require otherwise.

N1.3 One significant area of difference between practice in the Commercial Court and practice in the Admiralty Court is that many interlocutory applications are heard by the Admiralty Registrar who has all the powers of the Admiralty judge save as provided otherwise: rule 61.1 (4).

N2 The Admiralty Court Committee

CPR 61 ACG N2

N2.1 The Admiralty Court Committee provides a specific forum for contact and consultation between the Admiralty Court and its users. Its meetings are usually held in conjunction with the Commercial Court Users Committee. Any correspondence should be addressed to the Deputy Admiralty Marshal, 7 Rolls Building, Fetter Lane, London, EC4A 1NL.

N3 Commencement of proceedings, service of Statements of Case and associated matters

CPR 61 ACG N3

N3.1 Sections B and C of this Guide apply to all Admiralty claims except:

(i)   a claim in rem;

(ii)   a collision claim; and

(iii)   a limitation claim.

N4 Commencement and early stages of a claim in rem

CPR 61 ACG N4

N4.1 The early stages of an in rem claim differ from those of other claims. The procedure is governed generally by rule 61.3 and PD61 sections 3.1-3.11.

N4.2 In addition, the following sections of the Guide apply to claims in rem: B4.3, B4.7 – B4.11, B7.4 – B7.6, C1.1 - C1.6, C1.8 and C2.1 (ii) - C5.4.

N4.3 Subject to PD61 section 3.7, section C1.7 of the Guide also applies to claims in rem.

N4.4 After an acknowledgement of service has been filed a claim in rem follows the procedure applicable to a claim proceeding in the Commercial List, save that the Claimant is allowed 75 days in which to serve his particulars of claim: PD61 section 3.10.

N5 The early stages of a Collision Claim

CPR 61 ACG N5

N5.1 Where a collision claim is commenced in rem, the general procedure applicable to claims in rem applies subject to rule 61.4 and PD61 sections 4.1–4.5.

N5.2 Where a collision claim is not commenced in rem the general procedure applicable to claims proceeding in the Commercial List applies subject to rule 61.4 and PD61 sections 4.1–4.5.

N5.3 Service of a claim form out of the jurisdiction in a collision claim (other than a claim in rem) is permitted in the circumstances identified in rule 61.4(7) only and the procedure set out in Appendix 15 of the Guide should be adapted accordingly.

N5.4 One particular feature of a collision action is that the parties must prepare and file a Collision Statement of Case. Prior to the coming into force of Part 61, a Collision Statement of Case was known as a Preliminary Act and the law relating to Preliminary Acts continues to apply to Collision Statements of Case: PD61 section 4.5.

N5.5 The provisions of Appendix 4 apply to part 2 of a Collision Statement of Case (but not to part 1).

N5.6 Every party is required, so far as it is able, to provide full and complete answers to the questions contained in part 1 of the Collision Statement of Case. The answers should descend to a reasonable level of particularity.

N5.7 The answers to the questions contained in part 1 are treated as admissions made by the party answering the questions and leave to amend such answers will be granted only in exceptional circumstances. As to the principles applicable to the amendment of particulars of claim in a collision claim reference should be made to the judgment of Gross J. in The Topaz [2003] 2 Lloyd's Rep 19.

N6 The early stages of a Limitation Claim

CPR 61 ACG N6

N6.1 The procedure governing the early stages of a limitation claim differs significantly from the procedure relating to other claims and is contained in rule 61.11 and PD61 section 10.1.

N6.2 Service of a limitation claim form out of the jurisdiction is permitted in the circumstances identified in rule 61.11 (5) only and the procedure set out in Appendix 15 of the Guide should be adapted accordingly.

N7 Issue of documents when the Registry is closed

CPR 61 ACG N7

N7.1 When the Registry is closed (and only when it is closed) an Admiralty claim form may be issued on the following designated fax machine: 020 7947 6245 and only on that machine.

N7.2 The procedure to be followed is set out in Appendix 3 of the Guide.

N7.3 The issue of an Admiralty claim form in accordance with the procedure set out in Appendix 3 shall have the same effect for all purposes as a claim form issued in accordance with the relevant provisions of rule 61 and PD61.

N7.4 When the Registry is closed (and only when it is closed) a notice requesting a caution against release may be filed on the following designated fax machine: 020 7947 6245 and only on that machine. This machine is manned 24 hours a day by Court security staff (telephone 020 7947 6260).

N7.5 The notice requesting the caution should be transmitted with a note in the following form for ease of identification by security staff:

"CAUTION AGAINST RELEASE

Please find notice requesting caution against release of the . . . *(name ship/identify cargo)* . . . for filing in the Admiralty & Commercial Registry."

N7.6 The notice must be in Admiralty Form No ADM11 and signed by a solicitor acting on behalf of the applicant.

N7.7 Subject to the provisions of sections N7.9 and N7.10 below, the filing of the notice takes place when the fax is recorded as having been received.

N7.8 When the Registry is next open to the public, the filing solicitor or his agent shall attend and deliver to the Registry the document which was transmitted by fax together with the transmission report. Upon satisfying himself that the document delivered fully accords with the document received by the Registry, the Court officer shall stamp the document delivered with the time and date on which the notice was received, enter the same in the caution register and retain the same with the faxed copy.

N7.9 Unless otherwise ordered by the Court, the stamped notice shall be conclusive proof that the notice was filed at the time and on the date stated.

N7.10 If the filing solicitor does not comply with the foregoing procedure, or if the notice is not stamped, the notice shall be deemed never to have been filed.

N8 Case Management

CPR 61 ACG N8

N8.1 The case management provisions of the Guide apply to Admiralty claims save that:

(i)   In Admiralty claims the case management provisions of the Guide are supplemented by PD61 sections 2.1-2.3 which make provision for the early classification and streaming of cases;

(ii)   In a collision case the claimant should apply for a case management conference within 7 days after the last Collision Statement of Case is filed;

(iii) In a limitation claim where the right to limit is not admitted and the claimant seeks a general limitation decree, the claimant must, within 7 days after the date of the filing of the defence of the defendant last served or the expiry of the time for doing so, apply to the Admiralty Registrar for a case management conference: PD61 section 10.7;

(iv)   In a collision claim or a limitation claim a mandatory case management conference will normally take place on the first available date 5 weeks after the date when the claimant is required to take steps to fix a date for the case management conference;

(v)   In a limitation claim, case management directions are initially given by the Registrar: PD61 section 10.8;

(vi)   In the Admiralty Court, the Case Management Information Sheet should be in the form in Appendix 6 of this Guide but should also include the following questions:

1.   Do any of the issues contained in the List of Issues involve questions of navigation or other particular matters of an essentially Admiralty nature which require the trial to be before the Admiralty Judge?

2.   Is the case suitable to be tried before a Deputy Judge nominated by the Admiralty Judge?

3.   Do you consider that the Court should sit with nautical or other assessors? If you intend to ask that the Court sit with one or more assessors who is not a Trinity Master, please state the reasons for such an application.

N9 Evidence

CPR 61 ACG N9

N9.1 In collision claims, section H1.5 and Appendix 8 are subject to the proviso that experience has shown that it is usually desirable for the main elements of a witness' evidence in chief to be adduced orally.

Authenticity

N9.2 (a) Where the authenticity of any document disclosed to a party is not admitted, that party must serve notice that the document must be proved at trial in accordance with CPR 32.19. Such notice must be served by the latest date for serving witness statements or within 7 days of disclosure of the document, whichever is later.

(b) Where, apart from the authenticity of the document itself, the date upon which a document or an entry in it is stated to have been made or the person by whom the document states that it or any entry in it was made or any other feature of the document is to be challenged at the trial on grounds which may require a witness to be called at the trial to support the contents of the document, such challenge

(i)   must be raised in good time in advance of the trial to enable such witness or witnesses to be called;

(ii)   the grounds of challenge must be explicitly identified in the skeleton argument or outline submissions in advance of the trial.

(c) Where, due to the late disclosure of a document it or its contents or character cannot practically be challenged within the time limits prescribed in (a) or (b), the challenge may only be raised with the permission of the Court and having regard to the Overriding Objective (CPR 1.1).

Skeleton arguments in Collision Claims

N9.3 In collision claims the skeleton argument of each party must be accompanied by a plot or plots of that party's case or alternative cases as to the navigation of vessels during and leading to the collision. All plots must contain a sufficient indication of the assumptions used in the preparation of the plot.

N10 Split trials, accounts, enquiries and enforcement

CPR 61 ACG N10

N10.1 In collision claims it is usual for liability to be tried first and for the assessment of damages and interest to be referred to the Admiralty Registrar.

N10.2 Where the Admiralty Court refers an account, enquiry or enforcement, it will usually refer the matter to the Admiralty Registrar.

N11 Release of vessels out of hours

CPR 61 ACG N11

N11.1 This section makes provision for release from arrest when the Registry is closed.

N11.2 An application for release under rule 61.8(4)(c) or (d) may, when the Registry is closed, be made in, and only in, the following manner:

(i)   The solicitor for the arrestor or the other party applying must telephone the security staff at the Royal Courts of Justice (020 7947 6260) and ask to be contacted by the Admiralty Marshal, who will then respond as soon as practicably possible;

(ii)   Upon being contacted by the Admiralty Marshal the solicitor must give oral instructions for the release and an oral undertaking to pay the fees and expenses of the Admiralty Marshal as required in Form No ADM 12;

(iii)   The arrestor or other party applying must then send a written request and undertaking on Form No ADM 12 by fax to a number given by the Admiralty Marshal;

(iv)   The solicitor must provide written consent to the release from all persons who have entered cautions against release (and from the arrestor if the arrestor is not the party applying) by sending such consents by fax to the number supplied by the Admiralty Marshal;

(v)   Upon the Admiralty Marshal being satisfied that no cautions against release are in force, or that all persons who have entered cautions against release, and if necessary the arrestor, have given their written consent to the release, the Admiralty Marshal shall effect the release as soon as practicable.

N11.3 Practitioners should note that the Admiralty Marshal is not formally on call and therefore at times may not be available to assist. Similarly the practicalities of releasing a ship in some localities may involve the services of others who may not be available outside Court hours.

N11.4 This service is offered to practitioners for use during reasonable hours and on the basis that if the Admiralty Marshal is available and can be contacted he will use his best endeavours to effect instructions to release but without guarantee as to their success.

N12 Use of postal facilities in the Registry

CPR 61 ACG N12

N12.1 Applications together with the requisite documents may be posted to:

The Admiralty and Commercial Registry,
7 Rolls Building,
Fetter Lane,
London EC4A 1NL.

N12.2 In addition to the classes of business for which the use of postal facilities is permitted by the CPR or the Commercial Court Guide, the filing of the following classes of documents is also permitted in Admiralty matters:

(i)   Requests for cautions;

(ii) Collision Statements of Case.

N12.3 (a) Documents sent by post for filing must be accompanied by two copies of a list of the documents sent and an envelope properly addressed to the sender.

(b) On receipt of the documents in the Registry, the Court officer will, if the circumstances are such that had the documents been presented personally they would have been filed, cause them to be filed and will, by post, notify the sender that this has been done. If the documents would not have been accepted if presented personally the Court officer will not file them but will retain them in the Registry for collection by the sender and will, by post, so inform the sender.

(c) When documents received through the post are filed by the Court officer they will be sealed and entered as filed on the date on which they were received in the Registry.

N13 Insurance of arrested property

CPR 61 ACG N13

N13.1 The Marshal will not insure any arrested property for the benefit of parties at any time during the period of arrest (whether before or after the lodging of an application for sale, if any).

N13.2 The Marshal will use his best endeavours (but without any legal liability for failure to do so) to advise all parties known to him as being on the record in actions in rem against the arrested property, including those who have filed cautions against release of that property, before any such property moves or is moved beyond the area covered by the usual port risks policy.

N13.3 In these circumstances, practitioners' attention is drawn to the necessity of considering the questions of insuring against port risks for the amount of their clients' interest in any property arrested in an Admiralty action and the inclusion in any policy of a "Held Covered" clause in case the ship moves or is moved outside the area covered by the usual port risks policy. The usual port risks policy provides, among other things, for a ship to be moved or towed from one berth to another up to a distance of five miles within the port where she is lying.

N14 Assessors

CPR 61 ACG N14

N14.1 In collision claims and other cases involving issues of navigation and seamanship, the Admiralty Court usually sits with assessors. The parties are not permitted to call expert evidence on such matters without the leave of the Court: rule 61.13.

N14.2 Parties are reminded of the practice with regard to the disclosure of any answers to the Court's questions and the opportunity for comment on them as set out in the Judgment of Gross J. in *The Global Mariner* [2005] 1 Lloyd's Rep 699 at p 702.

N14.3 Provision is made in rule 35.15 for assessors' remuneration. Provisions for assessors remuneration are set out in QB Practice Direction [2007] 1 WLR 2508. The usual practice is for the Court to seek an undertaking from the claimant to pay the remuneration on demand after the case has concluded.

O. ARBITRATION

O1 Arbitration claims

CPR 61 ACG O1

O1.1 (a) Applications to the Court under the Arbitration Acts 1950 – 1996 and other applications relating to arbitrations are known as "arbitration claims".

(b) The procedure applicable to arbitration claims is to be found in Part 62 and its associated Practice Direction. Separate provision is made

(i)   by Section I for claims relating to arbitrations to which the Arbitration Act 1996 applies;

(ii)   by Section II for claims relating to arbitrations to which the Arbitration Acts 1950 – 1979 ("the old law") apply; and

(iii)   by Section III for enforcement proceedings.

(c) For a full definition of the expression "arbitration claim" see rule 62.2(1) (claims under the 1996 Act) and rule 62.11(2) (claims under the old law).

(d) Part 58 applies to arbitration claims in the Commercial Court insofar as no specific provision is made by Part 62: rule 62.1(3).

Claims under the Arbitration Act 1996

O2 Starting an arbitration claim

CPR 61 ACG O2

O2.1 Subject to section O2.3 an arbitration claim must be started by the issue of an arbitration claim form in accordance with the Part 8 procedure: rule 62.3(1).

O2.2 The claim form must be substantially in the form set out in Appendix A to Practice Direction 62: PD62 section 2.2.

O2.3 An application to stay proceedings under section 9 of the Arbitration Act 1996 must be made by application notice in the proceedings: rule 62.3(2).

O2.4 Where a question arises as to whether an arbitration agreement is null and void, inoperative or incapable of being performed the Court may deal with it in the same way as provided by rule 62.8(3) which applies where a question arises as to whether an arbitration agreement has been concluded or the dispute which is the subject matter of the proceedings falls within the terms of such an agreement.

O3 The arbitration claim form

CPR 61 ACG O3

O3.1 The arbitration claim form must contain, among other things, a concise statement of the remedy claimed and, if an award is challenged, the grounds for that challenge: rule 62.4(1).

O3.2 Reference in the arbitration claim form to a witness statement or affidavit filed in support of the claim is not sufficient to comply with the requirements of rule 62.4(1).

O4 Service of the arbitration claim form

CPR 61 ACG O4

O4.1 An arbitration claim form issued in the Admiralty & Commercial Registry must be served by the claimant.

04.2 (a) The rules governing service of the claim form are set out in Part 6 of the Civil Procedure Rules.

(b) Unless the Court orders otherwise an arbitration claim form must be served on the defendant within 1 month from the date of issue: rule 62.4(2).

04.3 (a) An arbitration claim form may be served out of the jurisdiction with the permission of the Court: rule 62.5(1).

(b) Rules 6.40 – 6.46 apply to the service of an arbitration claim form out of the jurisdiction: rule 62.5(3).

04.4 The Court may exercise its powers under rules 6.15 and/or 6.37(5)(b) to permit service of an arbitration claim form on a party at the address of the solicitor or other representative acting for him in the arbitration: PD62 section 3.1.

04.5 The claimant must file a certificate of service within 7 days of serving the arbitration claim form: PD62 section 3.2.

05 Acknowledgment of service

CPR 61 ACG O5

05.1 (a) A defendant must file an acknowledgment of service of the arbitration claim form in every case: rule 58.6(1).

(b) An adapted version of practice form N210 (acknowledgment of service of a Part 8 claim form) has been approved for use in the Commercial Court.

05.2 The time for filing an acknowledgment of service is calculated from the service of the arbitration claim form.

06 Standard directions

CPR 61 ACG O6

06.1 The directions set out in PD62 sections 6.2-6.7 apply unless the Court orders otherwise.

06.2 The claimant should apply for a hearing date as soon as possible after issuing an arbitration claim form or (in the case of an appeal) obtaining permission to appeal.

06.3 A defendant who wishes to rely on evidence in opposition to the claim must file and serve his evidence within 21 days after the date by which he was required to acknowledge service: PD62 section 6.2.

06.4 A claimant who wishes to rely on evidence in response to evidence served by the defendant must file and serve his evidence within 7 days after the service of the defendant's evidence: PD62 section 6.3.

06.5 An application for directions in a pending arbitration claim should be made by application notice under Part 23. Where an arbitration application involves recognition and/or enforcement of an agreement to arbitrate and that application is challenged on the grounds that the parties to the application were not bound by an agreement to arbitrate, it will usually be necessary for the Court to resolve that issue in order to determine the application. For this purpose it may be necessary for there to be disclosure of documents and/or factual and/or expert evidence. In that event, it is the responsibility of those advising the applicant to liaise with the other party and to arrange with the Listing office for a case management conference to be listed as early as possible to enable the Court to give directions as to the steps to be taken before the hearing of the application.

06.6 PD62 paragraphs 6.6 and 6.7 provide for the Claimant's skeleton to be served not later than 2 days before the hearing date and the Respondent's skeleton to be served not later than the day before the hearing date. However:

(a) In relation to hearings of appeals in which permission to appeal has been granted, see paragraph O8.2 below and in relation to applications under section 68 see paragraph O8.8A below;

(b) Where an application (other than one mentioned in (a) above) is likely to last more than half a day the Respondent's skeleton should be served one clear day before the hearing date, consistently with the Commercial Court practice for heavy applications.

07 Interim remedies

CPR 61 ACG O7

07.1 An application for an interim remedy under section 44 of the Arbitration Act 1996 must be made in an arbitration claim form: PD62 section 8.1.

08 Challenging the award

Challenge by way of appeal

CPR 61 ACG O8

08.1 The procedures applicable to applications for permission to appeal and bundles of documents for any substantive appeal have been revised with effect from 1 October 2010. All applications for permission to appeal should comply with paragraph 12 of the revised Arbitration Practice Direction which requires that:

(1)   Where a party seeks permission to appeal to the Court on a question of law arising out of an arbitration award, the arbitration claim form must, in addition to complying with rule 62.4(1)—

  (i)   identify the question of law;

  (ii)   state the grounds (but not the argument) on which the party challenges the award and contends that permission should be given;

  (iii)   be accompanied by a skeleton argument in support of the application in accordance with paragraph 12.2; and

  (iv)   append the award.

(2)   Subject to paragraph (3), the skeleton argument —

  (i)   must be printed in 12 point font, with 1½ line spacing,

  (ii)   should not exceed 15 pages in length and

  (iii)   must contain an estimate of how long the Court is likely to need to deal with the application on the papers.

(3)   If the skeleton argument exceeds 15 pages in length the author must write to the Court explaining why that is necessary.

(4)   Written evidence may be filed in support of the application only if it is necessary to show (insofar as that is not apparent from the award itself):

  (i)   that the determination of the question raised by the appeal will substantially affect the rights of one or more of the parties;

  (ii)   that the question is one which the tribunal was asked to determine;

  (iii)   that the question is one of general public importance;

  (iv)   that it is just and proper in all the circumstances for the Court to determine the question raised by the appeal.

Any such evidence must be filed and served with the arbitration claim form.

(5)   Unless there is a dispute whether the question raised by the appeal is one which the tribunal was asked to determine, no arbitration documents may be put before the Court other than:

  (i)   the award; and

(ii)   any document (such as the contract or the relevant parts thereof) which is referred to in the award and which the Court needs to read to determine a question of law arising out of the award.

("arbitration documents" means documents adduced in or produced for the purposes of the arbitration.)

(6)   A respondent who wishes to oppose an application for permission to appeal must file a respondent's notice which:

(i)   sets out the grounds (but not the argument) on which the respondent opposes the application; and

(ii)   states whether the respondent wishes to contend that the award should be upheld for reasons not expressed (or not fully expressed) in the award and, if so, states those reasons (but not the argument).

(7)   The respondent's notice must be filed and served within 21 days after the date on which the respondent was required to acknowledge service and must be accompanied by a skeleton argument in support which complies with paragraph (2) above.

(8)   Written evidence in opposition to the application should be filed only if it complies with the requirements of paragraph (4) above. Any such evidence must be filed and served with the respondent's notice.

(9)   The applicant may file and serve evidence or argument in reply only if it is necessary to do so. Any such evidence or argument must be as brief as possible and must be filed and served within 7 days after service of the respondent's notice.

(10)   If either party wishes to invite the Court to consider arbitration documents other than those specified in paragraph (5) above the counsel or solicitor responsible for settling the application documents must write to the Court explaining why that is necessary.

(11)   If a party or its representative fails to comply with the requirements of paragraphs (1) to (9) the Court may penalise that party or representative in costs.

(12)   The Court will normally determine applications for permission to appeal without an oral hearing but may direct otherwise, particularly with a view to saving time (including Court time) or costs.

(13)   Where the Court considers that an oral hearing is required, it may give such further directions as are necessary.

(14)   Where the Court refuses an application for permission to appeal without an oral hearing, it will provide brief reasons.

(15)   The bundle for the hearing of any appeal should contain only the claim form, the respondent's notice, the arbitration documents referred to in paragraph (5), the order granting permission to appeal and the skeleton arguments.

08.2 If permission to appeal is granted skeleton arguments should be served in accordance with the timetable for applications in section F above.

08.3 [No longer used]

08.4 [No longer used]

08.5 [No longer used]

Challenging an award for serious irregularity

08.6 (a) An arbitration claim challenging an award on the ground of serious irregularity under section 68 of the 1996 Act is appropriate only in cases where there are grounds for thinking

(i)   that an irregularity has occurred which

(ii)   has caused or will cause substantial injustice to the party making the challenge.

(b) An application challenging an award on the ground of serious irregularity should therefore not be regarded as an alternative to, or a means of supporting, an application for permission to appeal.

08.7 The challenge to the award must be supported by evidence of the circumstances on which the claimant relies as giving rise to the irregularity complained of and the nature of the injustice which has been or will be caused to him.

08.8 If the nature of the challenge itself or the evidence filed in support of it leads the court to consider that the claim has no real prospect of success, the court may exercise its powers under rule 3.3(4) and/or rule 23.8(c) to dismiss the application without a hearing. If a respondent considers that the case is one in which the court could appropriately deal with the application without a hearing it should within 21 days file a respondent's notice to that effect together with a skeleton argument (not exceeding 15 pages) and any evidence relied upon. The applicant may file a skeleton/evidence in reply within 7 days of service of the respondent's notice and skeleton argument. Where the court makes an order dismissing the application without a hearing the applicant will have the right to apply to the court to set aside the order and to seek directions for the hearing of the application. If such application is made and dismissed after a hearing the court may consider whether it is appropriate to award costs on an indemnity basis.

08.8A Skeleton arguments for the hearing of the challenge should be served in accordance with the timetable for applications in section F above.

Multiple claims

08.9 If the arbitration claim form includes both a challenge to an award by way of appeal and a challenge on the ground of serious irregularity, the applications should be set out in separate sections of the arbitration claim form and the grounds on which they are made separately identified.

08.10 In such cases the papers will be placed before a judge to consider how the applications may most appropriately be disposed of. It is usually more appropriate to dispose of the application to set aside or remit the award before considering the application for permission to appeal.

09 Time limits

CPR 61 ACG O9

09.1 An application to challenge an award under sections 67 or 68 of the 1996 Act or to appeal under section 69 of the Act must be brought within 28 days of the date of the award: see section 70(3).

09.2 The Court has power to vary the period of 28 days fixed by section 70(3) of the 1996 Act: rule 62.9(1). However, it is important that any challenge to an award be pursued without delay and the Court will require cogent reasons for extending time.

09.3 An application to extend time made before the expiry of the period of 28 days must be made in a Part 23 application notice, but the application notice need not be served on any other party: rule 62.9(2) and PD62 section 11.1(1).

09.4 An application to extend time made after the expiry of the period of 28 days must be made in the arbitration claim form in which the applicant is seeking substantive relief: rule 62.9(3)(a).

09.5 An application to vary the period of 28 days will normally be determined without a hearing and prior to the consideration of the substantive application: PD62 section 10.2.

Claims under the Arbitration Acts 1950 - 1979

010 Starting an arbitration claim

CPR 61 ACG O10

010.1 Subject to section 010.2 an arbitration claim must be started by the issue of an arbitration claim form in accordance with the Part 8 procedure: rule 62.13(1).

010.2 The claim form must be substantially in the form set out in Appendix A to PD62 section 2.2.

010.3 An application to stay proceedings on the grounds of an arbitration agreement must be made by application notice in the proceedings: rule 62.13(2).

011 The arbitration claim form

CPR 61 ACG O11

011.1 An arbitration claim form must state the grounds of the claim or appeal: rule 62.15(5)(a).

011.2 Reference in the arbitration claim form to the witness statement or affidavit filed in support of the claim is not sufficient to comply with the requirements of rule 62.15(5)(a).

012 Service of the arbitration claim form

CPR 61 ACG O12

012.1 An arbitration claim form issued in the Admiralty & Commercial Registry must be served by the claimant.

012.2 The rules governing service of the claim form are set out in Part 6 of the Civil Procedure Rules.

012.3 (a) An arbitration claim form may be served out of the jurisdiction with the permission of the Court: rule 62.16(1).

(b) Rules 6.40 – 6.46 apply to the service of an arbitration claim form out of the jurisdiction: rule 62.16(4).

012.4 Although not expressly covered by PD62, the Court may in an appropriate case exercise its powers under rule 6.15 and/or 6.37(5) to permit service of an arbitration claim form on a party at the address of the solicitor or other representative acting for him in the arbitration.

012.5 The claimant must file a certificate of service within 7 days of serving the claim form.

013 Acknowledgment of service

CPR 61 ACG O13

013.1 (a) A defendant must file an acknowledgment of service in every case: rule 58.6(1).

(b) An adapted version of practice form N210 (acknowledgment of service of a Part 8 claim form) has been approved for use in the Commercial Court.

013.2 The time for filing an acknowledgment of service is calculated from the service of the arbitration claim form.

014 Standard directions

CPR 61 ACG O14

014.1 Where the claim or appeal is based on written evidence, a copy of that evidence must be served with the arbitration claim form: rule 62.15(5)(b).

014.2 Where the claim or appeal is made with the consent of the arbitrator or umpire or other parties, a copy of every written consent must be served with the arbitration claim form: rule 62.15(5)(c).

014.3 An application for directions in a pending arbitration claim should be made by application notice under Part 23.

015 Interim remedies

CPR 61 ACG O15

015.1 An application for an interim remedy under section 12(6) of the 1950 Act must be made in accordance with Part 25.

015.2 The application must be made by arbitration claim form.

015.3 A claim under section 12(4) of the 1950 Act for an order for the issue of a witness summons to compel the attendance of a witness before an arbitrator or umpire where the attendance of the witness is required within the district of a District Registry may be started in that Registry: rule 62.14.

016 Challenging the award

Challenge by way of appeal

CPR 61 ACG O16

016.1 A party wishing to appeal against the award of an arbitrator or umpire must file and serve with the arbitration claim form a statement of the grounds for the appeal, specifying the relevant part(s) of the award and reasons: rule 62.15(6).

016.2 A party seeking permission to appeal must also file and serve with the arbitration claim form any written evidence in support of the contention that the question of law concerns a term of the contract or an event which is not "one off": rule 62.15(6).

016.3 Any written evidence in reply must be filed and served not less than 2 days before the hearing of the application for permission to appeal: rule 62.15(7).

016.4 A party who wishes to contend that the award should be upheld for reasons other than those set out in the award and reasons must file and serve on the claimant a notice specifying the grounds of his contention not less than 2 days before the hearing of the application for permission to appeal: rule 62.15(8).

016.5 Applications for permission to appeal will be heard orally, but will not normally be listed for longer than half an hour. Skeleton arguments should be lodged.

Claims to set aside or remit the award

016.6 A claim to set aside or remit an award on the grounds of misconduct should not be regarded as an alternative to, or a means of supporting, an application for permission to appeal.

016.7 The directions set out in PD62 sections 6.2-6.7 should be followed unless the Court orders otherwise.

Multiple claims

016.8 If the arbitration claim form includes both an appeal and an application to set aside or remit the award, the applications should be set out in separate sections of the arbitration claim form and the grounds on which they are made separately identified.

016.9 The Court may direct that one application be heard before the other or may direct that they be heard together, as may be appropriate. It is usually more appropriate to dispose of the application to set aside or remit the award before considering the application for permission to appeal.

O17 Time limits

CPR 61 ACG O17

017.1 (a) Time limits governing claims under the 1950 and 1979 Acts are set out in rule 62.15.

(b) Different time limits apply to different claims. It is important to consult rule 62.15 to ensure that applications are made within the time prescribed.

(c) The Court has power under rule 3.1(2) to vary the time limits prescribed by rule 62.15, but will require cogent reasons for doing so.

O18 Provisions applicable to all arbitrations

Enforcement of awards

CPR 61 ACG O18

018.1 All applications for permission to enforce awards are governed by Section III of Part 62: rule 62.17.

018.2 An application for permission to enforce an award in the same manner as a judgment may be made without notice, but the Court may direct that the arbitration claim form be served, in which case the application will continue as an arbitration claim in accordance with the procedure set out in Section I: rule 62.18(1)–(3).

018.3 An application for permission to enforce an award in the same manner as a judgment must be supported written evidence in accordance with rule 62.18(6).

018.4 (a) Two copies of the draft order must accompany the application.

(b) If the claimant wishes to enter judgment, the form of the judgment must correspond to the terms of the award.

(c) The defendant has the right to apply to the Court to set aside an order made without notice giving permission to enforce the award and the order itself must state in terms

(i)   that the defendant may apply to set it aside within 14 days after service of the order or, if the order is to be served out of the jurisdiction, within such other period as the Court may set; and

(ii)   that it may not be enforced until after the end of that period or any application by the defendant to set it aside has been finally disposed of: rule 62.18(9) and (10).

Matters of general application

O19 Transfer of arbitration claims

CPR 61 ACG O19

019.1 An arbitration claim which raises no significant point of arbitration law or practice will normally be transferred

(i)   if a rent-review arbitration, to the Chancery Division;

(ii)   if a construction or engineering arbitration, to the Technology and Construction Court.

019.2 Salvage arbitrations will normally be transferred to the Admiralty Court.

020 Appointment of a Commercial Judge as sole arbitrator or umpire

CPR 61 ACG O20

020.1 Section 93 of the Arbitration Act 1996 provides for the appointment of a Commercial Judge as sole arbitrator or umpire. The Act limits the circumstances in which a Judge may accept such an appointment.

020.2 Enquiries should be directed to the Judge in Charge of the Commercial List or the Clerk to the Commercial Court.

P. MISCELLANEOUS

P1 Out of hours emergency arrangements

CPR 61 ACG P1

P1.1 (a) When the Listing office is closed, solicitors or counsel's clerks should in an emergency contact the Clerk to the Queen'[s Bench Judge in Chambers by telephone through the security desk at the Royal Courts of Justice: PD58 section 2.2.

(b) The telephone number of the security desk is included in the list of addresses and contact details at the end of the Guide.

P1.2 When the Listing Office is closed an urgent hearing will initially be dealt with by the Queen's Bench Judge in Chambers who may dispose of the application himself or make orders allowing the matter to come before a Commercial Judge at the first available opportunity.

P2 Index of decisions of the Commercial and Admiralty Courts

CPR 61 ACG P2

P2.1 An Index has been prepared on a subject-matter basis of unreported Commercial Court and Admiralty Court judgments from 1995 onwards. The Index is updated regularly.

P2.2 The Index is provided as a service to litigants and to the legal profession, and to assist the Commercial Court and the Admiralty Court to maintain reasonable consistency of approach in those areas of law and procedure most frequently before them.

P2.3 The index of Judgments of Commercial Court and Admiralty Court of England and Wales is available to all Internet users and can be found at www.hmcourts-service.gov.uk/infoabout/admiralcomm/index.htm via the link to "Searchable index of court cases" (at bottom of the box on right hand side of Commercial Court and Admiralty Court).

P2.4 The judgments referred to in the Index are kept in the Registry. They may be consulted there.

P2.5 Copies of the judgments referred to in the Index may be obtained from the Registry (or where there is difficulty, from the clerk to the judge) unless the judgment is in the form of a transcript, in which case copies should be obtained from the shorthand writers or other transcript agency.

APPENDICES
APPENDIX 1

CPR 61 ACG App 1

Comprises Part 58 CPR and PD 58 Commercial Court) and Part 61 CPR and PD 61 (Admiralty Court), which can be found at:

Part 58: www.justice.gov.uk/courts/procedure-rules/civil/rules/part58

PD 58: www.justice.gov.uk/courts/procedure-rules/civil/rules/pd_part58#id4524 487

Part 61: www.justice.gov.uk/courts/procedure-rules/civil/rules/part61

PD61: www.justice.gov.uk/courts/procedure-rules/civil/rules/pd_part61

APPENDIX 2
CIVIL PROCEDURE RULES

CPR 61 ACG App 2

Comprises Part 62 CPR and PD 62 (Arbitration), which can be found at:

Part 62: www.justice.gov.uk/courts/procedure-rules/civil/rules/part62

PD 62: www.justice.gov.uk/courts/procedure-rules/civil/rules/pd_part62#id4524 496

APPENDIX 3
PROCEDURE FOR ISSUE OF CLAIM FORM WHEN REGISTRY CLOSED

CPR 61 ACG App 3

(See section B2.4 of the Guide.)

Procedure

The procedure is as follows:

1. The claim form must be signed by a solicitor acting on behalf of the claimant, and must not require the permission of the Court for its issue (unless such permission has already been given).

2. The solicitor causing the claim form to be issued ("the issuing solicitor") must

    (i)   endorse on the claim form the endorsement shown below and sign that endorsement;

    (ii) send a copy of the claim form so endorsed to the Registry by fax for issue under this section; and

    (iii) when he has received a transmission report stating that the transmission of the claim form to the Registry was completed in full and the time and the date of the transmission, complete and sign the certificate shown below.

3. When the Registry is next open to the public after the issue of a claim form in accordance with this procedure the issuing solicitor or his agent shall attend and deliver to the Registry the document which was transmitted by fax (including the endorsement and the certificate), or if that document has been

served, a true and certified copy of it, together with as many copies as the Registry shall require and the transmission report.

4.   When the proper officer at the Registry has checked and is satisfied that the document delivered under paragraph 3 fully accords with the document received under paragraph 2, and that all proper fees for issue have been paid, he shall allocate a number to the case, and seal, mark as "original" and date the claim form with the date on which it was issued (being, as indicated below, the date when the fax is recorded at the Registry as having been received).

5.   As soon as practicable thereafter the issuing solicitor shall inform any person served with the unsealed claim form of the case number, and (on request) shall serve any such person with a copy of the claim form sealed and dated under paragraph 4 above (at such address in England and Wales as the person may request) and the person may, without paying a fee, inspect and take copies of the documents lodged at the Registry under paragraphs 2 and 3 above.

Effect of issue following request by fax.

The issue of a claim form in accordance with this procedure takes place when the fax is recorded at the Registry as having been received, and the claim form bearing the endorsement shall have the same effect for all purposes as a claim form issued under CPR Part 7 [or 8, as the case may be]. Unless otherwise ordered the sealed version of the claim form retained by the Registry shall be conclusive proof that the claim form was issued at the time and on the date stated. If the procedure set out in this Appendix is not complied with, the Court may declare (on its own initiative or on application) that the claim form shall be treated as not having been issued.

Endorsement

A claim form issued pursuant to a request by fax must be endorsed as follows:

"1.   This claim form is issued under paragraph 2.2 of Practice Direction 58 and may be served notwithstanding that it does not bear the seal of the Court.

2.   A true copy of this claim form and endorsement has been transmitted to the Admiralty and Commercial Registry, 7 Rolls Building, Fetter Lane London, EC4A 1NL, at the time and date certified below by the solicitor whose name appears below ("the issuing solicitor").

3.   It is the duty of the issuing solicitor or his agent to attend at the Registry when it is next open to the public for the claim form to be sealed.

4.   Any person upon whom this unsealed claim form is served

(a)   will be notified by the issuing solicitor of the number of the case;

(b)   may require the issuing solicitor to serve a copy of the sealed claim form at an address in England and Wales; and

(c)   may inspect without charge the documents which have been lodged at the Registry by the undersigned solicitor.

5.   I, the issuing solicitor, undertake to the Court, to the defendants named in this claim form, and to any other person upon whom this claim form may be served:

(a)   that the statement in paragraph 2 above is correct;

(b)   that the time and date given in the certificate with this endorsement are correct;

(c)   that this claim form is a claim form which may be issued under section 2.2 and Appendix A of Practice Direction 58;

(d)   that I will comply in all respects with the requirements of Appendix A of Practice Direction 58;

(e)   that I will indemnify any person served with the claim form before it is sealed against any loss suffered as a result of the claim form being or becoming invalid in accordance with Appendix A of Practice Direction 58.

(Signed)

Solicitor for the claimant"

[**Note:** the endorsement may be signed in the name of the firm of solicitors rather than an individual solicitor, or by solicitors' agents in their capacity as agents acting on behalf of their professional clients.]

Certificate

An issuing solicitor must sign a certificate in the following form:

"I certify that I have received a transmission report confirming that the transmission of a copy of this claim form to the Registry by fax was fully completed and that the time and date of transmission to the Registry were [enter the time and date shown on the transmission report].

Dated

(Signed)

Solicitor for the claimant."

[**Note:** the certificate may be signed in the name of the firm of solicitors rather than an individual solicitor, or by solicitors' agents in their capacity as agents acting on behalf of their professional clients]

APPENDIX 4
STATEMENTS OF CASE

CPR 61 ACG App 4

The following principles apply to all statements of case and should, as far as possible, also be observed when drafting a Part 8 claim form, which will not contain, or be followed by, particulars of claim:

1.   The document must be as brief and concise as possible.

2.   The document must be set out in separate consecutively numbered paragraphs and sub-paragraphs.

3.   So far as possible each paragraph or sub-paragraph should contain no more than one allegation.

4.   The document must deal with the case on a point by point basis to allow a point by point response.

5.   Where particulars are given of any allegation or reasons given for a denial, the allegation or denial should be stated first and the particulars or reasons for it listed one by one in separate numbered sub-paragraphs.

6.   A party wishing to advance a positive case should set that case out in the document; a simple denial is not sufficient.

7.   Any matter which, if not stated, might take another party by surprise should be stated.

8.   Where they will assist:

   (i)   headings should be used; and

   (ii)   abbreviations and definitions should be established and used, and a glossary annexed.

9.   Contentious headings, abbreviations and definitions should not be used. Every effort should be made to ensure that headings, abbreviations and definitions are in a form that will enable them to be adopted without issue by the other parties.

10. Particulars of primary allegations should be stated as particulars and not as primary allegations.

11. If it is necessary to rely upon a substantial amount of detailed factual information or lengthy particulars in support of an allegation, these should be set out in schedules or appendices.

12. Particular care should be taken to set out only those factual allegations which are necessary to support the case. Evidence should not be included.

13. A response to particulars set out in a schedule should be set out in a corresponding schedule.

14. If it is necessary for the proper understanding of the statement of case to include substantial parts of a lengthy document the passages in question should be set out in a schedule rather than in the body of the case.

15. Contentious paraphrasing should be avoided.

16. The document must be signed by the individual person or persons who drafted it, not, in the case of a solicitor, in the name of the firm alone.

17. The document must not be longer than 25 pages unless the Court has given permission for a longer document.

APPENDIX 5
FORMS OF FREEZING INJUNCTION AND SEARCH ORDER

adapted for use in the Commercial Court

CPR 61 ACG App 5.1

IN THE HIGH COURT OF JUSTICE

QUEEN'S BENCH DIVISION

Before The Honourable Mr Justice [   ]

Claim No.

BETWEEN

Claimant(s)/Applicant(s)

- and –

Defendant(s)/Respondent(s)

PENAL NOTICE

If you [   ][1] disobey this order you may be held to be in contempt of Court and may be imprisoned, fined or have your assets seized.

Any other person who knows of this order and does anything which helps or permits the Respondent to breach the terms of this order may also be held to be in contempt of Court and may be imprisoned, fined or have their assets seized.

This order

1. This is a Freezing Injunction made against [   ] ("the Respondent") on [   ] by Mr Justice [   ]

on the application of [   ] ("the Applicant"). The Judge read the Affidavits listed in Schedule A and accepted the undertakings set out in Schedule B at the end of this Order.

2.   This order was made at a hearing without notice to the Respondent. The Respondent has a right to apply to the Court to vary or discharge the order – see paragraph 13 below.

3.   There will be a further hearing in respect of this order on [
            ] ("the return date").[2]

4.   If there is more than one Respondent-

    (a)   unless otherwise stated, references in this order to "the Respondent" mean both or all of them; and

    (b)   this order is effective against any Respondent on whom it is served or who is given notice of it.

Freezing injunction

[For injunction limited to assets in England and Wales]

5.   Until after the return date or further order of the Court, the Respondent must not remove from England and Wales or in any way dispose of, deal with or diminish the value of any of his assets which are in England and Wales up to the value of £.

[For worldwide injunction]

5.   Until the return date or further order of the Court, the Respondent must not-

    (1)   remove from England and Wales any of his assets which are in England and Wales up to the value of £   ; or

    (2)   in any way dispose of, deal with or diminish the value of any of his assets whether they are in or outside England and Wales up to the same value.

[For either form of injunction]

6.   Paragraph 5 applies to all the Respondent's assets whether or not they are in his own name, whether they are solely or jointly owned [and whether the Respondent is interested in them legally, beneficially or otherwise][3]. For the purpose of this order the Respondent's assets include any asset which he has the power, directly or indirectly, to dispose of or deal with as if it were his own. The Respondent is to be regarded as having such power if a third party holds or controls the asset in accordance with his direct or indirect instructions.

7.   This prohibition includes the following assets in particular-

    (a)   the property known as [title/address] or the net sale money after payment of any mortgages if it has been sold;

    (b)   the property and assets of the Respondent's business [known as [name]] [carried on at [address]] or the sale money if any of them have been sold; and

    (c)   any money in the account numbered [account number] at [title/address].

(d)   any interest under any trust or similar entity including any interest which can arise by virtue of the exercise of any power of appointment, discretion or otherwise howsoever.

[For injunction limited to assets in England and Wales]

8.   If the total value free of charges or other securities ("unencumbered value") of the Respondent's assets in England and Wales exceeds £   , the Respondent may remove any of those assets from England and Wales or may dispose of or deal with them so long as the total unencumbered value of his assets still in England and Wales remains above £.

[For worldwide injunction]

(1)   If the total value free of charges or other securities ("unencumbered value") of the Respondent's assets in England and Wales exceeds £, the Respondent may remove any of those assets from England and Wales or may dispose of or deal with them so long as the total unencumbered value of the Respondent's assets still in England and Wales remains above £   .

(2)   If the total unencumbered value of the Respondent's assets in England and Wales does not exceed £, the Respondent must not remove any of those assets from England and Wales and must not dispose of or deal with any of them. If the Respondent has other assets outside England and Wales, he may dispose of or deal with those assets outside England and Wales so long as the total unencumbered value of all his assets whether in or outside England and Wales remains above £.

Provision of information

(1)   Unless paragraph (2) applies, the Respondent must [within hours of service of this order] and to the best of his ability inform the Applicant's solicitors of all his assets [in England and Wales] [worldwide] [exceeding £   in value][4] whether in his own name or not and whether solely or jointly owned, giving the value, location and details of all such assets.

(2)   If the provision of any of this information is likely to incriminate the Respondent, he may be entitled to refuse to provide it, but is recommended to take legal advice before refusing to provide the information. Wrongful refusal to provide the information is contempt of Court and may render the Respondent liable to be imprisoned, fined or have his assets seized.

10.   Within [   ] working days after being served with this order, the Respondent must swear and serve on the Applicant's solicitors an affidavit setting out the above information.
[5]

Exceptions to this order

11.

(1)   This order does not prohibit the Respondent from spending £ a week towards his ordinary living expenses and also £ [or a reasonable sum] on legal advice and representation.

[But before spending any money the Respondent must tell the Applicant's legal representatives where the money is to come from.]

[(2)   This order does not prohibit the Respondent from dealing with or disposing of any of his assets in the ordinary and proper course of business, but before doing so the Respondent must tell the Applicant's legal representatives.]

(3)   The Respondent may agree with the Applicant's legal representatives that the above spending limits should be increased or that this order should be varied in any other respect, but any agreement must be in writing.

(4)   The order will cease to have effect if the Respondent-

    (a)   provides security by paying the sum of £ into Court, to be held to the order of the Court; or

    (b)   makes provision for security in that sum by another method agreed with the Applicant's legal representatives.

Costs

12.   The costs of this application are reserved to the judge hearing the application on the return date.

Variation or discharge of this order

13.   Anyone served with or notified of this order may apply to the Court at any time to vary or discharge this order (or so much of it as affects that person), but they must first inform the Applicant's solicitors. If any evidence is to be relied upon in support of the application, the substance of it must be communicated in writing to the Applicant's solicitors in advance.

Interpretation of this order

14.   A Respondent who is an individual who is ordered not to do something must not do it himself or in any other way. He must not do it through others acting on his behalf or on his instructions or with his encouragement.

15.   A Respondent which is not an individual which is ordered not to do something must not do it itself or by its directors, officers, partners, employees or agents or in any other way.

Parties other than the applicant and respondent

16.   **Effect of this order**

It is a contempt of Court for any person notified of this order knowingly to assist in or permit a breach of this order. Any person doing so may be imprisoned, fined or have their assets seized.

17.   **Set off by banks**

This injunction does not prevent any bank from exercising any right of set off it may have in respect of any facility which it gave to the respondent before it was notified of this order.

18.   **Withdrawals by the Respondent**

No bank need enquire as to the application or proposed application of any money withdrawn by the Respondent if the withdrawal appears to be permitted by this order.

[For worldwide injunction]

19.   **Persons outside England and Wales**

(1)   Except as provided in paragraph (2) below, the terms of this order do not affect or concern anyone outside the jurisdiction of this Court.

(2)   The terms of this order will affect the following persons in a country or state outside the jurisdiction of this Court -

    (a)   the Respondent or his officer or agent appointed by power of attorney;

    (b)   any person who-

        (i)   is subject to the jurisdiction of this Court;

        (ii)   has been given written notice of this order at his residence or place of business within the jurisdiction of this Court; and

        (iii)   is able to prevent acts or omissions outside the jurisdiction of this Court which constitute or assist in a breach of the terms of this order; and

    (c)   any other person, only to the extent that this order is declared enforceable by or is enforced by a Court in that country or state.

[For worldwide injunction]

20.   **Assets located outside England and Wales**

Nothing in this order shall, in respect of assets located outside England and Wales, prevent any third party from complying with-

(1)   what it reasonably believes to be its obligations, contractual or otherwise, under the laws and obligations of the country or state in which those assets are situated or under the proper law of any contract between itself and the Respondent; and

(2)   any orders of the Courts of that country or state, provided that reasonable notice of any application for such an order is given to the Applicant's solicitors.

Communications with the Court

All communications to the Court about this order should be sent to the Admiralty and Commercial Court Listing Office, 7 Rolls Building, Fetter Lane, London, EC4A 1NL quoting the case number. The telephone number is 020 7947 6826.

The offices are open between 10 a.m. and 4.30 p.m. Monday to Friday.

Schedule A Affidavits

The Applicant relied on the following affidavits-

[name]	[number of affida-vit]	[date sworn]	[filed on behalf of]
(1)			
(2)			

Schedule B Undertakings given to the Court by the applicant

(1)   If the Court later finds that this order has caused loss to the Respondent, and decides that the Respondent should be compensated for that loss, the Applicant will comply with any order the Court may make.

[(2)   The Applicant will-

   (a)   on or before *[date]* cause a written guarantee in the sum of £ to be issued from a bank with a place of business within England or Wales, in respect of any order the Court may make pursuant to paragraph (1) above; and

   (b)   immediately upon issue of the guarantee, cause a copy of it to be served on the Respondent.]

(3)   As soon as practicable the Applicant will issue and serve a claim form [in the form of the draft produced to the Court] [claiming the appropriate relief].

(4)   The Applicant will [swear and file an affidavit] [cause an affidavit to be sworn and filed] [substantially in the terms of the draft affidavit produced to the Court] [confirming the substance of what was said to the Court by the Applicant's counsel/solicitors].

(5)   The Applicant will serve upon the Respondent [together with this order] [as soon as practicable]-

   (i)   copies of the affidavits and exhibits containing the evidence relied upon by the Applicant, and any other documents provided to the Court on the making of the application;

   (ii)   the claim form; and

   (iii)   an application notice for continuation of the order.

[(6)   Anyone notified of this order will be given a copy of it by the Applicant's legal representatives.]

(7)   The Applicant will pay the reasonable costs of anyone other than the Respondent which have been incurred as a result of this order including the costs of finding out whether that person holds any of the Respondent's assets and if the Court later finds that this order has caused such person loss, and decides that such person should be compensated for that loss, the Applicant will comply with any order the Court may make.

(8)   If this order ceases to have effect (for example, if the Respondent provides security or the Applicant does not provide a bank guarantee as provided for above) the Applicant will immediately take all reasonable steps to inform in writing anyone to whom he has given notice of this order, or who he has reasonable grounds for supposing may act upon this order, that it has ceased to have effect.

[(9)   The Applicant will not without the permission of the Court use any Information obtained as a result of this order for the purpose of any civil or criminal proceedings, either in England and Wales or in any other jurisdiction, other than this claim.]

[(10)   The Applicant will not without the permission of the Court seek to enforce this order in any country outside England and Wales [or seek an order of a similar nature including orders conferring a charge or other security against the Respondent or the Respondent's assets].][6]

NAME AND ADDRESS OF APPLICANT'S LEGAL REPRESENTATIVES

The Applicant's legal representatives are-

[Name, address, reference, fax and telephone numbers both in and out of office hours and e-mail]

---

1   Insert name of Respondent(s).

2   In the Commercial Court, usually 14 days after the injunction was granted, particularly where parties are outside the jurisdiction

3   Whether this wider wording should be included in relation to the Order and/or the provision of information will be considered on a case by case basis—see generally *JSC BTA Bank v Kythreotis and Others* **[2010] EWCA Civ 1436**.

4   In most cases, careful consideration will need to be given to inserting a lower limit of say £10,000 or equivalent below which value assets need not be disclosed.

5   Consideration should also be given to amalgamating paragraphs 9 and 10 of the draft Order, so as to require only one disclosure exercise, verified by Affidavit.

6   Unless the Court directs otherwise this paragraph should be included in Orders for worldwide freezing injunctions.

CPR 61 ACG App 5.2

Search Order

SEARCH ORDER
IN THE HIGH COURT OF JUSTICE
QUEEN'S BENCH DIVISION

COMMERCIAL COURT

Before The Honourable Mr Justice [   ]

Claim No.

BETWEEN

Claimant(s)/Applicant(s)

- and –

Defendant(s)/Respondent(s)

PENAL NOTICE

If you [   ]¹ disobey this order you may be held to be in contempt of Court and may be imprisoned, fined or have your assets seized.

Any other person who knows of this order and does anything which helps or permits the Respondent to breach the terms of this order may also be held to be in contempt of Court and may be imprisoned, fined or have their assets seized.

This order

1.   This is a Search Order made against [   ] ("the Respondent") on [   ] by Mr Justice [   ] on the application of [   ] ("the Applicant"). The Judge read the Affidavits listed in Schedule F and accepted the undertakings set out in Schedules C, D and E at the end of this order.

2.   This order was made at a hearing without notice to the Respondent. The Respondent has a right to apply to the Court to vary or discharge the order – see paragraph 27 below.

3   There will be a further hearing in respect of this order on [   ] ("the return date").

4.   If there is more than one Respondent-

   (a)   unless otherwise stated, references in this order to "the Respondent" mean both or all of them; and

   (b)   this order is effective against any Respondent on whom it is served or who is given notice of it.

5.   This order must be complied with by-

   (a)   the Respondent;

   (b)   any director, officer, partner or responsible employee of the Respondent; and

   (c)   if the Respondent is an individual, any other person having responsible control of the premises to be searched.

The search

6.   The Respondent must permit the following persons[2] -

   (a)   [   ] ("the Supervising Solicitor);

   (b)   [   ], a solicitor in the firm of [   ], the Applicant's solicitors; and

   (c)   up to [   ] other persons[3] being [their identity or capacity] accompanying them, (together "the search party"), to enter the premises mentioned in Schedule A to this order and any other premises of the Respondent disclosed under paragraph 18 below and any vehicles under the Respondent's control on or around the premises ("the premises") so that they can search for, inspect, photograph or photocopy, and deliver into the safekeeping of the Applicant's solicitors all the documents and articles which are listed in Schedule B to this order ("the listed items").

7.   Having permitted the search party to enter the premises, the Respondent must allow the search party to remain on the premises until the search is complete. In the event that it becomes necessary for any of those persons to leave the premises before the search is complete, the Respondent must allow them to re-enter the premises immediately upon their seeking re-entry on the same or the following day in order to complete the search.

Restrictions on search

8.   This order may not be carried out at the same time as a police search warrant.

9.   Before the Respondent allows anybody onto the premises to carry out this order, he is entitled to have the Supervising Solicitor explain to him what it means in everyday language.

10.   The Respondent is entitled to seek legal advice and to ask the Court to vary or discharge this order. Whilst doing so, he may ask the Supervising Solicitor

to delay starting the search for up to 2 hours or such other longer period as the Supervising Solicitor may permit. However, the Respondent must-

(a)   comply with the terms of paragraph 27 below;

(b)   not disturb or remove any listed items; and

(c)   permit the Supervising Solicitor to enter, but not start to search.

Provision of information

11.   Before permitting entry to the premises by any person other than the Supervising Solicitor, the Respondent may, for a short time (not to exceed two hours, unless the Supervising Solicitor agrees to a longer period), gather together any documents he believes may be [incriminating or][4] privileged and hand them to the Supervising Solicitor for him to assess whether they are [incriminating or] privileged as claimed.

(a)   If the Supervising Solicitor decides that the Respondent is entitled to withhold production of any of the documents on the ground that they are privileged or incriminating, he will exclude them from the search and record them on a list for inclusion in his report and return them to the respondent.

(b)   If the Supervising Solicitor believes that the Respondent may be entitled to withhold production of the whole or any part of a document on the ground that it or part of it may be privileged or incriminating, or if the respondent claims to be entitled to withhold production on those grounds, the Supervising Solicitor will exclude it from the search and retain it in his possession pending further order of the court.

12.   If the Respondent wishes to take legal advice and gather documents as permitted, he must first inform the Supervising Solicitor and keep him informed of the steps being taken.

Provision of information

13.   No item may be removed from the premises until a list of the items to be removed has been prepared, and a copy of the list has been supplied to the Respondent, and he has been given a reasonable opportunity to check the list.

14.   The premises must not be searched, and items must not be removed from them, except in the presence of the Respondent.

15.   If the Supervising Solicitor is satisfied that full compliance with paragraphs 13 or 14 is not practicable, he may permit the search to proceed and items to be removed without fully complying with them.

Delivery up of articles/documents

16.   The Respondent must immediately hand over to the Applicant's solicitors any of the listed items, which are in his possession or under his control, save for any computer or hard disk integral to any computer. Any items the subject of a dispute as to whether they are listed items must immediately be handed over to the Supervising Solicitor for safe keeping pending resolution of the dispute or further order of the Court.

17.   The Respondent must immediately give the search party effective access to the computers on the premises, with all necessary passwords, to enable the computers to be searched. If they contain any listed items the Respondent

must cause the listed items to be displayed so that they can be read and copied.[5] The Respondent must provide the Applicant's Solicitors with copies of all listed items contained in the computers. All reasonable steps shall be taken by the Applicant and the Applicant's solicitors to ensure that no damage is done to any computer or data. The Applicant and his representatives may not themselves search the Respondent's computers unless they have sufficient expertise to do so without damaging the Respondent's system.

Provision of information

18. The Respondent must immediately inform the Applicant's Solicitors (in the presence of the Supervising Solicitor) so far as he is aware-

    (a)   where all the listed items are;

    (b)   the name and address of everyone who has supplied him, or offered to supply him, with listed items;

    (c)   the name and address of everyone to whom he has supplied, or offered to supply, listed items; and

    (d)   full details of the dates and quantities of every such supply and offer.

19. Within [   ] working days after being served with this order the Respondent must swear and serve an affidavit setting out the above information.[6]

Prohibited acts

20. Except for the purpose of obtaining legal advice, the Respondent must not directly or indirectly inform anyone of these proceedings or of the contents of this order, or warn anyone that proceedings have been or may be brought against him by the Applicant until 4.30 p.m. on the return date or further order of the Court.

21. Until 4.30 p.m. on the return date the Respondent must not destroy, tamper with, cancel or part with possession, power, custody or control of the listed items otherwise than in accordance with the terms of this order.

22. [Insert any negative injunctions.]

23. [Insert any further order]

Costs

24. The costs of this application are reserved to the judge hearing the application on the return date.

Restrictions on service

25. This order may only be served between [   ] a.m./p.m. and
    [   ] a.m./p.m. [and on a weekday].[7]

26. This order must be served by the Supervising Solicitor, and paragraph 6 of the order must be carried out in his presence and under his supervision.

Variation and discharge of this order

27.   Anyone served with or notified of this order may apply to the Court at any time to vary or discharge this order (or so much of it as affects that person), but they must first inform the Applicant's solicitors. If any evidence is to be relied upon in support of the application, the substance of it must be communicated in writing to the Applicant's solicitors in advance.

Interpretation of this order

28.   Any requirement that something shall be done to or in the presence of the Respondent means-

(a)   if there is more than one Respondent, to or in the presence of any one of them; and

(b)   if a Respondent is not an individual, to or in the presence of a director, officer, partner or responsible employee.

29.   A Respondent who is an individual who is ordered not to do something must not do it himself or in any other way. He must not do it through others acting on his behalf or on his instructions or with his encouragement.

30.   A Respondent which is not an individual which is ordered not to do something must not do it itself or by its directors, officers, partners, employees or agents or in any other way.

Communications with the Court

All communications to the Court about this order should be sent to the Admiralty and Commercial Court Listing Office, 7 Rolls Building, Fetter Lane, London EC4A 1NL quoting the case number. The telephone number is 020 7947 6826.

The offices are open between 10 a.m. and 4.30 p.m. Monday to Friday.

Schedule A The premises

Schedule B The listed items

Schedule C Undertakings given to the Court by the applicant

(1)   If the Court later finds that this order or carrying it out has caused loss to the Respondent, and decides that the Respondent should be compensated for that loss, the Applicant will comply with any order the Court may make. Further if the carrying out of this order has been in breach of the terms of this order or otherwise in a manner inconsistent with the Applicant's solicitors' duties as officers of the Court, the Applicant will comply with any order for damages the Court may make.

[(2)   As soon as practicable the Applicant will issue a claim form [in the form of the draft produced to the Court] [claiming the appropriate relief].]

(3)   The Applicant will [swear and file an affidavit] [cause an affidavit to be sworn and filed] [substantially in the terms of the draft affidavit produced to the Court] [confirming the substance of what was said to the Court by the Applicant's counsel/solicitors].

(4)   The Applicant will not, without the permission of the Court use any information or documents obtained as a result of carrying out this order nor

inform anyone else of these proceedings except for the purposes of these proceedings (including adding further Respondents) or commencing civil proceedings in relation to the same or related subject matter to these proceedings until after the return date.

[(5) The Applicant will maintain pending further order the sum of £ [ ] in an account controlled by the Applicant's solicitors.]

[(6) The Applicant will insure the items removed from the premises.]

Schedule D Undertakings given by the applicant's solicitors

(1) The Applicant's solicitors will provide to the Supervising Solicitor for service on the Respondent-

(i) a service copy of this order;

(ii) the claim form (with defendant's response pack) or, if not issued, the draft produced to the Court;

(iii) an application for hearing on the return date;

(iv) copies of the affidavits *[or draft affidavits]* and exhibits capable of being copied containing the evidence relied upon by the applicant;

(v) a note of any allegation of fact made orally to the Court where such allegation is not contained in the affidavits or draft affidavits read by the judge; and

(vi) a copy of the skeleton argument produced to the Court by the Applicant's [counsel/solicitors].

(2) The Applicants' solicitors will answer at once to the best of their ability any question whether a particular Item is a listed item.

(3) Subject as provided below the Applicant's solicitors will retain in their own safe keeping all items obtained as a result of this order until the Court directs otherwise.

(4) The Applicant's solicitors will return the originals of all documents obtained as a result of this order (except original documents which belong to the Applicant) as soon as possible and in any event within [two] working days of their removal.

Schedule E Undertakings given by the supervising solicitor

(1) The Supervising Solicitor will use his best endeavours to serve this order upon the Respondent and at the same time to serve upon the Respondent the other documents required to be served and referred to in paragraph (1) of Schedule D.

(2) The Supervising Solicitor will offer to explain to the person served with the order its meaning and effect fairly and in everyday language, and to inform him of his right to take legal advice (such advice to include an explanation that the Respondent may be entitled to avail himself of [the privilege against self-incrimination or] [legal professional privilege]) and to apply to vary or discharge this order as mentioned in paragraph 27 above.

(3) The Supervising Solicitor will retain in the safe keeping of his firm all items retained by him as a result of this order until the Court directs otherwise.

(4) Unless and until the court otherwise orders, or unless otherwise necessary to comply with any duty to the court pursuant to this order, the Supervising

Solicitor shall not disclose to any person any information relating to those items, and shall keep the existence of such items confidential.

(5) Within [48] hours of completion of the search the Supervising Solicitor will make and provide to the Applicant's solicitors, the Respondent or his solicitors and to the judge who made this order (for the purposes of the Court file) a written report on the carrying out of the order.

Schedule F Affidavits

The Applicant relied on the following affidavits-

[name]	[number of affidavit]	[date sworn]	[filed on behalf of]

(1)

(2) *NAME AND ADDRESS OF APPLICANT'S SOLICITORS*

The Applicant's solicitors are-

[Name, address, reference, fax and telephone numbers both in and out of office hours.]

---

1   Insert name of Respondent.

2   Where the premises are likely to be occupied by an unaccompanied woman and the Supervising Solicitor is a man, at least one of the persons accompanying him should be a woman.

3   None of these persons should be people who could gain personally or commercially from anything they might read or see on the premises, unless their presence is essential.

4   References to incriminating documents should be omitted from orders made in intellectual property proceedings, where the privilege against self-incrimination does not apply – see paragraph 8.4 of the Practice Direction.

5   If it is envisaged that the Respondent's computers are to be imaged (i.e. the hard drives are to be copied wholesale, thereby reproducing listed items and other items indiscriminately), special provision needs to be made and independent computer specialists need to be appointed, who should be required to give undertakings to the Court.

6   The period should ordinarily be longer than the period in paragraph (2) of Schedule D, if any of the information is likely to be included in listed items taken away of which the Respondent does not have copies.

7   Normally, the order should be served in the morning (not before 9.30 a.m.) and on a weekday to enable the Respondent more readily to obtain legal advice.

APPENDIX 6
CASE MANAGEMENT INFORMATION SHEET

CPR 61 ACG App 6

The information supplied should be printed in bold characters

Case Management Information Sheet

Party lodging information sheet:

Name of solicitors:

Name(s) of advocates for trial:

[Note: This Sheet should normally be completed with the involvement of the advocate(s) instructed for trial. If the claimant is a litigant in person this fact should be noted at the foot of the sheet and proposals made as to which party is to have responsibility for the preparation and upkeep of the case management bundle.]

(1) Please confirm the nature of your dispute (for statistical purposes) by ticking the appropriate box or boxes below:

Commercial Court claims: disputes relating to:

☐ arbitration applications and appeals

☐ aviation

☐ carriage of goods by land, sea, air or pipeline

☐ commercial fraud

☐ corporate or business acquisition agreements

☐ general commercial contracts and arrangements, including agency agreements

☐ insurance and/or reinsurance

☐ oil and gas and other natural resources

☐ physical commodity trading

☐ professional negligence claims

☐ provision of financial services

☐ sale of goods

☐ shipping – charter party dispute

☐ shipping – construction

☐ shipping – financing

☐ shipping – cargo

☐ transactions on commodity exchanges

☐ transactions on financial markets or relating to securities and/or banking transactions

Admiralty Court claims: shipping and/or maritime disputes relating to:

☐ arrest

☐ cargo claims

☐ collision

☐ general average

☐ personal injury

☐ salvage

☐ ship mortgage

☐ other

(2) Please state the value of your claim.

(3) Please state how many foreign parties (if any) are involved.

(4) Please state whether the CMC is suitable for hearing by a deputy.

(5) Is it agreed that standard disclosure is appropriate? If so by what date can you give standard disclosure? If standard disclosure is not agreed and you consider that a different ambit of disclosure is appropriate, please specify.

(6) In relation to standard disclosure, do you contend in relation to any category or class of document under rule 31.6(b) that to search for that category or class would be unreasonable? If so, what is the category or class and on what grounds do you so contend?

(7) Is specific disclosure required on any issue? If so, please specify.

(8) By what dates can you (a) give specific disclosure or (b) comply with a special disclosure order?

(9) May the time periods for inspection at rule 31.15 require adjustment, and if so by how much?

(10) Are amendments to or is information about any statement of case required? If yes, please give brief details of what is required.

(11) Can you make any additional admissions? If yes, please give brief details of the additional admissions.

(12) Are any of the issues in the case suitable for trial as preliminary issues?

(13)

(a)   On the evidence of how many witnesses of fact do you intend to rely at trial (subject to the directions of the Court)? Please give their names, or explain why this is not being done.

(b)   By what date can you serve signed witness statements?

(c)   How many of these witnesses of fact do you intend to call to give oral evidence at trial (subject to the directions of the Court)? Please give their names, or explain why this is not being done.

(d)   Will interpreters be required for any witness?

(e)   Do you wish any witness to give oral evidence by video link? Please give his or her name, or explain why this is not being done. Please state the country and city from which the witness will be asked to give evidence by video link.

(14)

(a)   On what issues may expert evidence be required?

(b)   What is the estimated cost of the proposed expert evidence?

(c)   Is this a case in which the use of a single joint expert might be suitable (see rule 35.7)?

(d)   On the evidence of how many expert witnesses do you intend to rely at trial (subject to the directions of the Court)? Please give their names, or explain why this is not being done. Please identify each expert's field of expertise.

(e)   By what date can you serve signed expert reports?

(f)   When will the experts be available for a meeting or meetings of experts?

(g)   How many of these expert witnesses do you intend to call to give oral evidence at trial (subject to the directions of the Court)? Please give their names, or explain why this is not being done.

(h)   Will interpreters be required for any expert witness?

(i)   Do you wish any expert witness to give oral evidence by video link? Please give his or her name, or explain why this is not being done. Please state the country and city from which the witness will be asked to give evidence by video link.

(15) What are the advocates' present provisional estimates of (i) the minimum and maximum lengths of the trial (ii) the pre-reading time likely to be required for the judge?

(16) What is the earliest date by which you believe you can be ready for trial?

(17) Is this a case in which a pre-trial review is likely to be useful?

(18) Is there any way in which the Court can assist the parties to resolve their dispute or particular issues in it without the need for a trial or a full trial?

(19)

(a)   Might some form of Alternative Dispute Resolution procedure assist to resolve or narrow the dispute or particular issues in it?

(b)   Has the question at (a) been considered between the client and legal representatives (including the advocate(s) retained)?

(c)   Has the question at (a) been explored with the other parties in the case?

(d)   Do you request that the case is adjourned while the parties try to settle the case by Alternative Dispute Resolution or other means?

(e)   Would an ADR order in the form of Appendix 7 to the Commercial Court Guide be appropriate?

(f)   Are any other special directions needed to allow for Alternative Dispute Resolution?

(20) What other applications will you wish to make at the Case Management Conference?

(21) Does provision need to be made in the pre-trial timetable for any application or procedural step not otherwise dealt with above? If yes, please specify the application or procedural step.

(22) Are there, or are there likely in due course to be, any related proceedings (e.g. a Part 20 claim)? Please give brief details.

(23) Please indicate whether it is considered that the case is unsuitable for trial by a deputy judge. If the case is considered to be unsuitable please give reasons for this view.

(24) Please indicate whether it is considered that the case should be allocated to a designated judge. If so please give reasons for this view and write to the Judge in Charge of the List in accordance with D4.2.

[Signature of solicitors]

Note: This information sheet must be lodged with the Clerk to the Commercial Court at least 7 days before the Case Management Conference (with a copy to all other parties): see section D8.5 of the Commercial Court Guide.

APPENDIX 7
DRAFT ADR ORDER

CPR 61 ACG App 7

1. On or before [*] the parties shall exchange lists of 3 neutral individuals who are available to conduct ADR procedures in this case prior to [*]. Each party may [in addition] [in the alternative] provide a list identifying the constitution of one or more panels of neutral individuals who are available to conduct ADR procedures in this case prior to [*].

2. On or before [*] the parties shall in good faith endeavour to agree a neutral individual or panel from the lists so exchanged and provided.

3. Failing such agreement by [*] the Case Management Conference will be restored to enable the Court to facilitate agreement on a neutral individual or panel.

4. The parties shall take such serious steps as they may be advised to resolve their disputes by ADR procedures before the neutral individual or panel so chosen by no later than [*].

5. If the case is not finally settled, the parties shall inform the Court by letter prior to [disclosure of documents/exchange of witness statements/exchange of experts' reports] what steps towards ADR have been taken and (without prejudice to matters of privilege) why such steps have failed. If the parties have failed to initiate ADR procedures the Case Management Conference is to be restored for further consideration of the case.

6. [Costs].

Note: The term "ADR procedures" is deliberately used in the draft ADR order. This is in order to emphasise that (save where otherwise provided) the parties are free to use the ADR procedure that they regard as most suitable, be it mediation, early neutral evaluation, non-binding arbitration etc.

APPENDIX 8
STANDARD PRE-TRIAL TIMETABLE

CPR 61 ACG App 8

1. [Standard disclosure is to be made by [*], with inspection [*] days after notice.]

2. Signed statements of witnesses of fact, and hearsay notices where required by rule 33.2, are to be exchanged not later than [*].

3. Unless otherwise ordered, witness statements are to stand as the evidence in chief of the witness at trial.

4. Signed reports of experts

(i)   are to be confined to one expert for each party from each of the following fields of expertise: [*];

(ii)   are to be confined to the following issues: [*];

(iii)   are to be exchanged [sequentially/simultaneously];

(iv)   are to be exchanged not later than [date or dates for each report in each field of expertise].

5. Meeting of experts

(i)   The meeting of experts is to be by [*];

(ii)   The joint memorandum of the experts is to be completed by [*];

(iii)   Any short supplemental expert reports are to be exchanged [sequentially/simultaneously] by not later than [date or dates for each supplemental report].

6. [If the experts' reports cannot be agreed, the parties are to be at liberty to call expert witnesses at the trial, limited to those experts whose reports have been exchanged pursuant to 4. above.]

[Or: The parties are to be at liberty to apply to call as expert witnesses at the trial those experts whose reports they have exchanged pursuant to 4. above, such application to be made not earlier than [*] and not later than [*].]

7. Preparation of trial bundles to be completed in accordance with Appendix 10 to the Commercial Court Guide by not later than [*].

8. The provisional estimated length of the trial is [*]. This includes [*] pre-trial reading time.

9. Within [*] days the parties are to attend on the Clerk to the Commercial Court to fix the date for trial which shall be not before [*].

10. The progress monitoring date is [*]. Each party is to lodge a completed progress monitoring information sheet with the Clerk to the Commercial Court at least 3 days before the progress monitoring date (with a copy to all other parties).

11. Each party is to lodge a completed pre-trial checklist not later than 3 weeks before the date fixed for trial.

12. [There is to be a pre-trial review not earlier than [*] and not later than [*]].

13. Save as varied by this order or further order, the practice and procedures set out in the Admiralty & Commercial Courts Guide are to be followed.

14. Costs in the case.

15. Liberty to restore the Case Management Conference.

APPENDIX 9
SKELETON ARGUMENTS, CHRONOLOGIES AND INDICES
Part 1 Skeleton arguments

CPR 61 ACG App 9

1. A skeleton argument is intended to identify both for the parties and the Court those points which are, and are not, in issue and the nature of the argument in relation to those points that are in issue. It is not a substitute for oral argument.

2. Skeleton arguments must therefore

(a) identify concisely:

   (i)   the nature of the case generally and the background facts insofar as they are relevant to the matter before the Court;

   (ii) the propositions of law relied on with references to the relevant authorities;

   (iii) the submissions of fact to be made with references to the evidence;

(b) be in numbered paragraphs and state the name of the advocate(s) who prepared them; and

(c) avoid arguing the case at length;

(d) be prepared in a format which is easily legible. No skeleton should be served in a font smaller than 12 point and with line spacing of less than 1.5.

Part 2 Chronologies and Indices

3. As far as possible chronologies and indices should not be prepared in a tendentious form. The ideal is that the Court and the parties should have a single point of reference that all find useful and are happy to work with.

4. Where there is disagreement about a particular event or description, it is useful if that fact is indicated in neutral terms and the competing versions shortly stated.

5. If time and circumstances allow its preparation, a chronology or index to which all parties have contributed and agreed can be invaluable.

6. Chronologies and indices once prepared can be easily updated and are of continuing usefulness throughout the life of the case.

APPENDIX 10
PREPARATION OF BUNDLES

CPR 61 ACG App 10

1. The preparation of bundles requires a high level of co-operation between legal representatives for all parties. It is the duty of all legal representatives to co-operate to this high level.

2. Bundles should be prepared as follows:

(i)   No more than one copy of any one document should be included, unless there is good reason for doing otherwise;

(ii) Contemporaneous documents, and correspondence, should be included in chronological order;

(iii) Where a contract or similar document is central to the case it may be included in a separate place provided that a page is inserted in the chronological run of documents to indicate

(A) the place the contract or similar document would have appeared had it appeared chronologically and

(B) where it may be found instead;

(iv) Documents in manuscript, or not fully legible, should be transcribed; the transcription should be marked and placed adjacent to the document transcribed;

(v) Documents in a foreign language should be translated; the translation should be marked and placed adjacent to the document transcribed; the translation should be agreed, or, if it cannot be agreed, each party's proposed translation should be included;

(vi) If a document has to be read across rather than down the page, it should be so placed in the bundle as to ensure that the top of the text is nearest the spine;

(vii) No bundle should contain more than 300 pages;

(viii) Bundles should not be overfilled, and should allow sufficient room for later insertions. Subject to this, the size of file used should not be a size that is larger than necessary for the present and anticipated contents;

(ix) Bundles should be paginated, in the bottom right hand corner and in a form that can clearly be distinguished from any existing pagination on the document;

(x) Bundles should be indexed, save that a chronological bundle of contemporaneous documents need not be indexed if an index is unlikely to be useful;

(xi) Bundles should be numbered and named on the outside and on the inside front cover, the label to include the short title of the case, and a description of the bundle (including its number, where relevant).

3. Documents within bundles should be marked as follows:

(i) When copy documents from exhibits have been included in the bundle(s), then unless clearly unnecessary, the copy of the affidavit or witness statement to which the documents were exhibited should be marked in the right hand margin (in manuscript if need be) to show where the document referred to may be found in the bundle(s).

(ii) Unless clearly unnecessary, where copy documents in a bundle are taken from the disclosure of more than one party the documents should be marked in the top right hand corner (in manuscript if need be) to show from which party's disclosure the copy document has been taken;

(iii) Where there is a reference in a statement of case or witness statement to a document which is contained in the trial bundles a note should be made in the margin (if necessary in manuscript) identifying the place where that document is to be found. Unless otherwise agreed this is the responsibility of the party tendering the statement of case or witness statement.

4. For the trial a handy-sized core bundle should be provided containing the really important documents in the case. The documents in this bundle should be paginated, but each page should also bear its bundle and page number reference in the main bundles. It is particularly important to allow sufficient room for later insertions (see paragraph 2(viii) above). The core bundle should be prepared and provided at the latest by the time of the lodging of the first trial skeleton.

5. Large documents, such as plans, should be placed in an easily accessible file.

6. (a) When agreeing bundles for trial, legal representatives should bear in mind the effect of the Civil Evidence Act 1995 and of rules 33.2(3) (notice requiring proof of authenticity) and 32.19 (hearsay notices).

(b) Pursuant to those provisions, documents which have not been the subject of a notice served in accordance with rule 32.19(2) (requiring proof of authenticity) will be admissible as evidence of the truth of their contents even if there has been non-compliance with the notice requirements of s. 2(1) of the 1995 Act and rule 33.2 (see s. 2(4) of the Act). Accordingly, save for documents in respect of which there has been a timely notice to prove authenticity, all documents in the trial bundle will be admissible in evidence without more.

(c) The fact that documents in the trial bundle are admissible in evidence does not mean that all such documents form part of the evidence in the trial. It is the trial advocate's responsibility to indicate clearly to the Court before closing his or her case the written evidence which forms part of that case. This should be done in the written opening statement or in the oral opening statement if the document is then available. Documents which have not previously been put in evidence before the closure of the parties' cases should not normally be referred to as evidence in the course of final speeches.

APPENDIX 11
EXPERT EVIDENCE - REQUIREMENTS OF GENERAL APPLICATION

CPR 61 ACG App 11

1. It is the duty of an expert to help the Court on the matters within his expertise: rule 35.3(1). This duty is paramount and overrides any obligation to the person from whom the expert has received instructions or by whom he is paid: rule 35.3(2).

2. Expert evidence presented to the Court should be, and should be seen to be, the independent product of the expert uninfluenced by the pressures of litigation.

3. An expert witness should provide independent assistance to the Court by way of objective unbiased opinion in relation to matters within his expertise. An expert witness should never assume the role of an advocate.

4. An expert witness should not omit to consider material facts which could detract from his concluded opinion.

5. An expert witness should make it clear when a particular question or issue falls outside his expertise.

6. If an expert's opinion is not properly researched because he considers that insufficient data is available, this must be stated in his report with an indication that the opinion is no more than a provisional one.

7. In a case where an expert witness who has prepared a report is unable to confirm that the report contains the truth, the whole truth and nothing but the truth without some qualification, that qualification must be stated in the report.

8. If, after exchange of reports, an expert witness changes his view on a material matter having read another expert's report or for any other reason, such change of view should be communicated in writing (through the party's legal representatives) to the other side without delay, and when appropriate to the Court.

APPENDIX 12
PROGRESS MONITORING INFORMATION SHEET

CPR 61 ACG App 12

The information supplied should be printed in bold characters

[SHORT TITLE OF CASE and FOLIO NUMBER]

Fixed trial date/provisional range of dates for trial specified in the pre-trial timetable:

Party lodging information sheet:

Name of solicitors:

Name(s) of advocates for trial:

[Note: this information sheet should normally be completed with the involvement of the advocate(s) instructed for trial]

(1) Have you complied with the pre-trial timetable in all respects?

(2) If you have not complied, in what respects have you not complied?

(3) Will you be ready for a trial commencing on the fixed date (or, where applicable, within the provisional range of dates) specified in the pre-trial timetable?

(4) If you will not be ready, why will you not be ready?

[Signature of solicitors]

Note: This information sheet must be lodged with the Listing Office at least 3 days before the progress monitoring date (with a copy to all other parties): see section D12.2 of the Guide.

APPENDIX 13
PRE-TRIAL CHECKLIST

CPR 61 ACG App 13

The information supplied should be printed in bold characters

[SHORT TITLE OF CASE and FOLIO NUMBER]

a.   Trial date:

b.   Party lodging checklist:

c.   Name of solicitors:

d.   Name(s) of advocates for trial:

[**Note:** this checklist should normally be completed with the involvement of the advocate(s) instructed for trial]

1. Have you completed preparation of trial bundles in accordance with Appendix 10 to the Commercial Court Guide?

2. If not, when will the preparation of the trial bundles be completed?

3. Which witnesses of fact do you intend to call?

4. Which expert witness(es) do you intend to call (if directions for expert evidence have been given)?

5. Will an interpreter be required for any witness and if so, have any necessary directions already been given?

6. Have directions been given for any witness to give evidence by video link? If so, have all necessary arrangements been made?

7. What are the advocates' confirmed estimates of (i) the minimum and maximum lengths of the trial (ii) the pre-reading time likely to be required for the judge?? (A confirmed estimate of length signed by the advocates should be attached).

8. What is your estimate of costs already incurred and to be incurred at trial?

[Signature of solicitors]

APPENDIX 14

CPR 61 ACG App 14

The Video Conferencing Guidance contained in this Appendix reproduces the Guidance in Annex 3 of Practice Direction—Evidence, which can be found at: www.justice.gov.uk/courts/procedure-rules/civil/rules/pd_part32#IDA3PCKC.

APPENDIX 15
SERVICE OUT OF THE JURISDICTION: RELATED PRACTICE
Service out of the jurisdiction without permission

CPR 61 ACG App 15

1. (a) Before issuing a claim form or seeking permission to serve out of the jurisdiction, it is necessary to consider whether the jurisdiction of the Eng-

lish Courts is affected by the Civil Jurisdiction and Judgments Act 1982. Where each claim in the claim form is a claim which the Court has by virtue of the Civil Jurisdiction and Judgments Act 1982 power to hear and determine, service of the claim form out of the jurisdiction may be effected without permission provided that, in the case of service in Scotland or Northern Ireland, the relevant requirements of rules 6.32 and 6.34 are satisfied; and, in the case of service out of the United Kingdom, the relevant requirements of rules 6.33 and 6.34 are satisfied.

These requirements include the requirement to file with the claim form a notice containing a statement of the grounds on which the claimant is entitled to serve the claim form out of the jurisdiction and to serve a copy of that notice with the claim form. In the case of service out of the jurisdiction of the United Kingdom, paragraph 2.1 of PD6B requires the notice to be in the form of practice form N510 in order to comply with rule 6.34. Rule 6.34(2) provides that, if the claimant fails to file such a notice, the consequence is that the claim form may only be served once the claimant has filed the requisite notice or if the Court gives permission.

(b) Because of the significance of (amongst other things) the concept of "first seisure" in the context of Council Regulation (EC) No 44/2001 of 22 December 2001 on jurisdiction and the recognition and enforcement of judgments in civil and commercial matters ("the Judgment Regulation"), it is very important that the statement as to the grounds upon which the claimant is entitled to serve the claim form out of the jurisdiction is accurate and made with care. If entitlement to serve out of the jurisdiction without leave is wrongly asserted, a claimant may be ordered to pay the costs of a defendant's application to strike out the claim or set aside serve of the claim form on an indemnity basis.

(c) Rule 6.35 sets out the time periods during which a defendant must respond to a claim form where permission was not required for service, depending on whether the defendant is:

(i)   in Scotland or Northern Ireland;

(ii)   in a Member State or a Convention Territory; or

(iii)   elsewhere.

Paragraph 6 of PDB sets out the periods for responding in the case of defendants served elsewhere.

These provisions are subject to the modifications set out in rule 58 in relation to Commercial Court Cases, including, but not limited to:

(i)   that a defendant must file an acknowledgement of service in every case; and

(ii)   that the time periods provided by rule 6.35 apply after service of the claim form.

Application for permission: statement in support

2. (a) The grounds upon which a claimant may apply for the Court's permission to serve a claim form out of the jurisdiction pursuant to rule 6.36 (in circumstances where neither rule 6.32 nor rule 6.33 applies) are set out in paragraph 3.1 of PDB.

(b) An application for permission under rule 6.36 must set out:

(i)   the ground in PD6B relied on as giving the Court jurisdiction to order service out, together with a summary of the facts relied on as bringing the case within each such paragraph;

(ii)   where the application is made in respect of a claim referred to in paragraph 3.1(3) of PD6B, the grounds on which the claimant believes that there is between the claimant and the defendant a real issue which it is reasonable for the Court to try;

(iii)   the belief of the claimant that the claim has a reasonable prospect of success; and

(iv)   the defendant's address or, if not known, in what place or country the defendant is or is likely to be found.

(c) The claimant should also present evidence of the considerations relied upon as showing that the case is a proper one in which to subject a party outside the jurisdiction to proceedings within it (stating the grounds of belief and sources of information); exhibit copies of the documents referred to and any other significant documents; and draw attention to any features which might reasonably be thought to weigh against the making of the order sought. Where convenient the written evidence should be included in the form of application notice, rather than in a separate witness statement. The form of application notice may be extended for this purpose.

Application for permission: copies of draft order

3. (a) specify the periods within which the defendant must:

(i)   file an acknowledgement of service;

(ii)   serve or file an admission;

(iii)   file a defence; and

(b) set out any other directions sought by the claimant as to:

(i)   the method of service;

(ii)   the terms of any order sought giving permission to serve other documents out of the jurisdiction;

The relevant periods referred to in sub-paragraphs (a)(i)–(iii) above are specified in paragraphs 6.1–6.6 of PDB, and in the Table at the end of that Practice Direction.

Application for permission: copy or draft of claim form

4. A copy or draft of the claim form which the applicant intends to issue and serve must be provided to the judge who will usually initial it. If the endorsement to the claim form includes causes of action or claims not covered by the grounds on which permission to serve out of the jurisdiction can properly be granted, permission will be refused unless the draft is amended to restrict it to proper claims. Where the application is for the issue of a concurrent claim form, the documents submitted must also include a copy of the original claim form.

Arbitration matters

5. Service out of the jurisdiction in arbitration matters is governed by Part 62. As to the 1968 Convention on Jurisdiction in the context of arbitration, see Article 1(4), which applies rules 6.40 – 6.46. The Judgment Regulation does not apply to "arbitration" (see Article 1.(2)(d), but what proceedings fall within the category of arbitration and what do not, may be a difficult question: see The Front Comor, 10 February 2009, Case C-185/07.

Practice under rules 6.32 and 6.33

6. (a) Although a Part 7 claim form may contain or be accompanied by particulars of claim, there is no need for it to do so and in many cases particulars of claim will be served after the claim form: rule 58.5.

(b) A defendant should acknowledge service in every case: rule 58.6(1).

(c) The period for filing an acknowledgment of service will be calculated from the service of the claim form, whether or not particulars of claim are to follow: rule 58.6.

(d) The periods for filing an acknowledgement of service and a defence are set out respectively in rule 6.35(2) (in relation to claim forms served in Scotland and Northern Ireland); in rule 6.35(3) (in relation to claim forms served pursuant to rule 6.33 on a defendant in a Convention Territory within Europe or a Member State); in rule 6.35(4) (in relation to claim forms served pursuant to rule 6.33 on a defendant in a Convention Territory outside Europe); and in paragraphs 6.1, 6.3, 6.4 and the Table in PDB in relation to claim forms served pursuant to rule 6.33 on a defendant in a country elsewhere: rule 6.35(5).

Practice under rule 6.36

7. (a) Although a Part 7 claim form may contain or be accompanied by particulars of claim, there is no need for it to do so and in many cases particulars of claim will be served after the claim form: rule 58.5. If the claim form states that particulars of claim are to follow, there is no need to obtain further permission to serve out of the jurisdiction: rule 6.38(2).

However, permission must be obtained to serve any other document out of the jurisdiction: rule 6.38(2); other than in cases where the defendant has given an address for service in Scotland and Northern Ireland: rule 6.38(3).

(b) A defendant should acknowledge service in every case: rule 58.6(1).

(c) The periods for filing an acknowledgment of service will be calculated from the service of the claim form, whether or not particulars of claim are to follow: rule 58.6.

(d) The period for serving, and filing, particulars of claim (where they were not contained in the claim form and did not accompany the claim form) will be calculated from acknowledgment of service: rule 58.5(1)(c).

(e) The period for serving and filing the defence will be calculated from service of the particulars of claim: rule 58.10(2).

8. Time for serving and filing a defence is calculated:

(a) where the Particulars of Claim are served with the claim form, to be calculated by reference to the number of days listed in the Table in PDB plus an additional 14 days after service of the particulars of claim: paragraph 6.4 of PDB.

(b) where the Particulars of Claim are served after the acknowledgement of service, 28 days from the service of the Particulars of Claim.

9. There is some uncertainty whether the Court's powers under rule 6.37 and rule 6.40 to give directions about the "method" of service include a specific power to make an order for service of documents to which Section IV of Part 6 applies by an alternative method (e.g. service on solicitors within the jurisdiction or service on a party by email); see the Notes in the 2010 Edition of Civil Procedure Rules Part 6 at paras 6.15.1 and 6.15.7. To date, the Commercial and Admiralty Court Judges have taken the view that they do have such power and, in appropriate cases, have made orders providing for alternative methods of service, in cases where the criteria for serving the claim form out of the jurisdiction are satisfied. However, in circumstances where such alternative service is not permitted by the law of the country in which the defendant is to be served, rule 6.40(3) and (4) would appear to prevent such orders being made.

Practice under rule 6.41 – service in accordance with the Service Regulation

10. If a party wishes to effect service of the claim form or other document in accordance with the Service Regulation, then the procedure to be adopted differs depending upon whether service is being made pursuant to rule 6.33 (service of the claim form, and other documents, out of the jurisdiction where the permission of the Court is not required), or whether it is being made pursuant to rules 6.36 and 6.37 (service of the claim form, and other documents, out of the jurisdiction where the permission of the Court is required).

11. In the former case (service without permission), the claimant must file the relevant documents referred to in rule 6.41(2) with the Registry. If the documents are in order, the relevant Court officer will seal the claim form and forward the documents to the Senior Master of the Queen's Bench Division in accordance with rule 6.41(3).

12. In the latter case (service with permission), the claimant must first obtain permission from a judge to serve the relevant documents out of the jurisdiction, together with a direction pursuant to rule 6.37 that one, or the, method of service

is to be in accordance with the Service Regulation. Once such an order has been made, the relevant Court officer will seal the claim form and forward the documents to the Senior Master in accordance with rule 6.41(3).

13. In either case, once the documents have been forwarded by the Registry to the Senior Master, any queries thereafter about the progress of such service should be directed to the Senior Master.

APPENDIX 16
SECURITY FOR COSTS: RELATED PRACTICE
First applications

CPR 61 ACG App 16

1. First applications for security for costs should not be made later than at the Case Management Conference and in any event any application should not be left until close to the trial date. Delay to the prejudice of the other party or the administration of justice might well cause the application to fail, as will any use of the application to harass the other party. Where it is intended to make an application for security at the Case Management Conference the procedure, and timetable for evidence, for an ordinary application must be followed (see section F5 of the Guide).

Successive applications

2. Successive applications for security can be granted where the circumstances warrant. If a claimant wishes to seek to preclude any further application it is incumbent on him to make that clear.

Evidence

3. An affidavit or witness statement in support of an application for security for costs should deal not only with the residence of the claimant (or other respondent to the application) and the location of his assets but also with the practical difficulties (if any) of enforcing an order for costs against him.

Investigation of the merits of the case

4. Investigation of the merits of the case on an application for security is strongly discouraged. It is usually only in those cases where it can be shown without detailed investigation of evidence or law that the claim is certain or almost certain to succeed or fail will the merits be taken into consideration.

Undertaking by the applicant

5. In appropriate cases an order for security for costs may only be made on terms that the applicant gives an undertaking to comply with any order that the Court may make if the Court later finds that the order for security for costs has caused loss to the claimant and that the claimant should be compensated for such loss. Such undertakings are intended to compensate claimants in cases where no order for costs is ultimately made in favour of the applicant.

Stay of proceedings

6. It is not usually convenient or appropriate to order an automatic stay of the proceedings pending the provision of the security. It leads to delay and may disrupt the preparation of the case for trial, or other hearing. Experience has shown that it is usually better to give the claimant (or other relevant party) a reasonable time

within which to provide the security and the other party liberty to apply to the Court in the event of default. This enables the Court to put the claimant to his election and then, if appropriate, to dismiss the case.

Amount of security

7. Where the dispute on an application for security for costs relates to the correct evaluation of the amount of costs likely to be allowed to a successful defendant on an assessment of costs, parties should consider whether it would be advantageous for the judge hearing the application to sit with a Costs Judge as an informal assessor. The judge himself may take such an initiative.

APPENDIX 17
COMMERCIAL COURT USER E-MAIL GUIDANCE
Introduction

CPR 61 ACG App 17

1. This guidance sets out how parties may communicate by e-mail with the Commercial and Admiralty Courts on certain matters.

Restrictions

2. A party should not use e-mail to take any step in a claim which requires a fee to be paid for that step. If a party sends by e-mail a document for which a fee is payable upon filing, the document will be treated as not having been filed.

3. Where a party sends or lodges a document by e mail he should still comply with any rule or Practice Direction requiring the document to be served on any other person.

4. Nothing in this guidance requires any person to accept service of a document by e-mail.

The subject line

5. The subject line of the e-mail should contain only the following information which should be in the following order:

a.   First, the proper title of the claim (abbreviated as necessary) with the claimant named first and the defendant named second; unless the action is an Admiralty action, the name of the ship should not be used:

b.   Second, the claim number.

Form and content of the e-mail

6. Correspondence and documents may be sent either as text or attachments, except that documents required to be in a practice form should be sent in that form as attachments using one of the formats specified in paragraph 17.

7. Parties must not use e-mail to send any document which exceeds 40 pages in the aggregate of normal typescript in length or 2 MB whichever is the smaller. Documents may not be subdivided to comply with this requirement.

8. Where a party files a document by e-mail, he should not send a hard copy in addition, unless there are good reasons for so doing or the Court requires. An e-mail to the address ComCt.Listing@hmcts.gsi.gov.uk or ComCt.Registry@hmcts.gsi.gov.uk will provide an automatic receipt.[1]

9. Parties are advised to bear in mind when sending correspondence or documents of a confidential or sensitive nature that the security of e-mails cannot be guaranteed.

10. Where a time limit applies, it remains the responsibility of the party to ensure that the document is filed in time. Parties are advised to allow for delays or downtime on their server.

Attachments

11. Attachments should be in one of the following formats:

a.   Microsoft Word viewer/reader (.doc) in Word 1997 or later format

b.   Rich Text Format as (.rtf) files

c.   Plain/Formatted Text as (.txt) files

d.   Hypertext documents as (.htm) files

e.   Adobe Acrobat as (.pdf) files minimum viewer version 4

Receipt of e-mail by the Court

12. If an e-mail is sent before 4.30 p.m on a business day it will be treated as having been received on that day. If it is sent after 4.30 p.m it will be treated as having been received on the next day the Court office is open.

13 If a response to the subject matter of the e-mail is not received within a reasonable period, the sender should assume that the Court has not received it and should send the e-mail again (forwarding the original), or file the document (with a copy of the email) by another means.

14. Parties should not telephone to enquire as to the receipt of an e-mail. They should observe the procedure set out in paragraph 15.

Replies to e-mails sent to the Court

15. The Court will normally send any reply by e-mail to documents or correspondence sent by e-mail.

a.   All replies will be sent to the e-mail address from which the e-mail has been sent. If the sender wishes the reply to be copied to other parties or to another e-mail address used by the sender of the message, such e-mail addresses must be specified in the copy line.

b.   The Court will not send copies to clients or others not on the record; the copy line must therefore not contain the addresses of such persons.

c.   The e-mail should also contain in the body of the e-mail the name and telephone number of the sender.

Note: It is important that each firm or set of chambers considers putting in place a system to deal with the absence of the individual who has sent the e-mail and to whom the Court will ordinarily reply. Two possible solutions are:

a.   A central mail box within each firm, either from which the e-mail is sent to the Court (and which will therefore receive the reply) or to which it is copied by the individual sender who sends it direct to the Court (and who will receive a copy of the reply);

b.   a second individual e-mail address within the firm to which the reply will be copied so that any reply can be monitored.

It must be for each firm and set of chambers to devise its own system.

Communication with the Clerk to a Commercial Judge

16. No documents or correspondence should be sent by e-mail to the Clerk to a Commercial Judge dealing with a case, unless:

a. an arrangement is made with the Clerk in each specific instance in which e-mail is to be used;

b. if such an arrangement is made, the e-mail must be copied to the appropriate Listing Office Address,, The Registry Address, or the Admiralty Marshal Address, as the case may be.

---

[1]   The automated response from the List Office and the Registry will now say: "Your e-mail has been received by the Commercial Court Listing Office/Registry and appropriate action is being taken. Provided the document is not one for which a fee is payable upon filing and is no more than 40 pages, please do not send hard copies of this e-mail, unless requested to do so."

APPENDIX 18
ELECTRONIC WORKING
Introduction

CPR 61 ACG App 18

1. On 1 April 2009 the Commercial Court began a electronic working pilot scheme. It allowed claims to be brought by issuing a claim form electronically, other documents to be filed electronically in those cases and an electronic Court file to be used and inspected.

2. On 1 April 2010 the pilot scheme was replaced with the Electronic Working Scheme as set out in Practice Direction 5C. The Scheme may be used to start claims pursuant to Part 7, Part 8 and Part 20 and also Arbitration claims and Admiralty proceedings as appropriate in the Admiralty and Commercial Court.

Operation of the scheme

3. The electronic scheme operates 24 hours every day and so claim forms can be issued and documents can be filed in cases to which the scheme applies outside normal Court office opening hours. However, the scheme is not operated (i) during planned "down-time" and (ii) during "unplanned down-time". See PD 1.2(2). If the scheme is not operating, claim forms can be issued outside normal Court hours by fax.: see PD 58 2.2, and para B2.4 and Appendix 3 of the Guide.

Fees

4. Under the scheme fees may be paid by any method which HMCS may permit. It is intended that it should soon be possible to do so by credit or debit card.

Forms

5. All forms filed at Court under the scheme must be in PDF format, and where they are available, the PDF forms created for the scheme must be used. If necessary forms must be converted into PDF format before they are filed. See PD para 4.1, 4.2, 4.3.

Starting claims

6. The procedure for starting a claim under the scheme is set out in PD para 6. The Court will enter on the claim form as the issue date the date when the claim form was received by the Court electronically: PD para 6.4. A claim form is issued on the date entered on the form by the Court: CPR 7.2(2).

Defendants

7. Where a claim is started electronically, a defendant may file documents electronically. Any fees (for example, payable by a defendants making a counter-claim or an application) must be paid when and in the manner stipulated by the Court. See para 4 above, and PD para 7.

Statements of truth and signatures

8. Attention is drawn to paras 8 and 9 of the PD, which deal with statements of truth and signatures.

Hard copies of documents

9. All trial bundles must be filed in hard copy format; PD para 14.

10. The need for paper copy bundles to be filed in relation to applications is addressed in PD para 13.

CPR 61 ACG App 18 [1]

PRACTICE DIRECTION—ELECTRONIC WORKING PILOT can be found at: www.just ice.gov.uk/courts/procedure-rules/civil/rules/pd_part05c.

Editorial Note: The text of the Electronic Working Pilot Scheme Practice Direction can be found at para **CPR PD 5B**

APPENDIX 19
GUIDANCE ON PRACTICAL STEPS FOR TRANSFERRING CASES TO THE MERCANTILE COURTS

CPR 61 ACG App 19

1. If a case is suitable for transfer to a Mercantile Court, either party can apply to the Commercial Judge prior to the CMC for transfer or, if no such application is made, the Commercial Judge will normally consider this with the parties at the CMC. He will expect the parties to have considered this issue prior to the CMC. Among the factors that the parties should consider are the size and complexity of the claim, the location of the parties and their legal advisers and the convenience of the witnesses. If transfer is contemplated, the parties should also contact the appropriate Listing Officer (at the telephone numbers set out at paragraph 9) to ascertain likely trial dates.

2. If the case is one that is suitable for transfer and a decision is made to transfer prior to the CMC, the Commercial Judge will order that the case be transferred to a Mercantile Court and the CMC will take place at the Mercantile Court.

3. If the case is one that is suitable for transfer and a decision is made to transfer at the CMC, the Commercial Judge will, in order to save the costs of a further hearing in the Mercantile Court, usually make all the directions with the appropriate timetable down to trial in the same way as if the case were to remain in the Commercial Court, including a direction to fix the trial date through the appropriate Listing Officer (see paragraph 9 below) within a specified period of time. If, as is usually the case, it is thought desirable to give the parties time to try and settle the case through direct negotiation or ADR, this will be built into the timetable.

4. The Commercial Judge will consider the time at which transfer is to take place and this must be specified in the Order. The Commercial Judge will decide whether he considers a PTR or further CMC appears necessary at that stage.

5. The Order must be drawn up in the usual way and lodged with the Commercial Registry in 7 Rolls Building, Fetter Lane.

(a)   If the draft Order was not initialled in Court by the Judge, the Order will then be sent to the Judge who made the Order to be approved. That normally takes 3-4 days

(b)   If the draft Order was initialled in Court by the Judge at the hearing, the Order can be brought straight up to the Registry to be sealed.

6. Once the Order comes back, the Registry will put the Order in the various out trays for the solicitors clerks to collect. If the Order was sent in via the post, then the Registry will return it via the post or, if the firm of solicitors are not one of the regular users, the Registry will inform them of the procedure as to how to collect the Order.

7. Once the Order is sealed, the transfer from the Commercial Court is during normal circumstances effected by the Registry within one week; the transfer is effected by the Registry sending the Court file and the Order to the Mercantile Court as the case may be. The Registry will also inform all parties on record once the case has been transferred.

8. The Mercantile Court will then receive all the papers which were on the Commercial Court file and they will give the case one of their own numbers and inform the parties.

9. The case will then continue in exactly the same way as if at the Commercial Court save that the hearing date must be fixed with the Listing Office at the Mercantile Court within the time limit specified in the Order. The parties must contact the specialist Listing Officer at the Court to which the case has been transferred. The telephone and fax numbers of the Listing Officers for the specialist list are:

London Mercantile Court:
020 7947 6826
Fax 020 7947 7670
E-mail: comct.listing@hmcourts-service.gsi.gov.uk

Birmingham:
0121 681 3035
Fax 0121 250 6730
E-mail: birmingham.mercantile@hmcourts-service.gsi.gov.uk

Bristol:
0117 910 6706
Fax 0117 910 6727
E-mail: bristolmercantilelisting@hmcourts-service.gsi.gov.uk

Leeds:
0113 306 2461
Fax 0113 306 2392
E-mail: e-filing@leeds.countycourt.gsi.gov.uk

Newcastle:
0191 201 2047
Fax 0191 201 2000
E-mail: hearings@newcastle.countycourt.gsi.gov.uk

Liverpool/Manchester:
0161 240 5307
Fax 0161 240 5398

E-mail: highcourtspecialisthearings@manchester.countycourt.gsi.gov.uk

Wales and Chester:
02920 376483
Fax 02920 376475
E-mail: hearings@cardiff.countycourt.gsi.gov.uk

Parties are asked to speak to the specialist Listing Officers who will tell them of the facilities available at other Courts.

11. The Commercial Court monitors compliance with its Orders through the provision of progress monitoring information sheets which have to be provided by the Progress Monitoring Date specified in the Order. The standard directions for the Mercantile Courts provide for a Progress Monitoring Date; such a date should therefore be provided for in any Order. The Mercantile Courts monitor progress in accordance with paragraph 8 of the Mercantile Courts Practice Direction supplemental to Part 59. A PTR (either in Court or by telephone conference) may be held in the Mercantile Courts if the parties make a request or the Mercantile Judge so directs.

12. The parties are expected to keep the Listing Officer of the Court to which the case is transferred apprised of any settlement of the case. Where the Commercial Judge has not made all the directions or the parties need to make an application either orally or in writing, then the appropriate directions will be considered and made by the Mercantile Judge.

ADDRESSES AND CONTACT DETAILS

CPR 61 ACG Add 1

As of October 2011 the Admiralty and Commercial issue and listing offices and the Admiralty Marshal are now in the Rolls Building.

The address for all of these is now:

7 Rolls Building,
Fetter Lane,
London, EC4A 1NL

The individual telephone and fax numbers are as follows:

The Admiralty Marshal:
Tel: 020 7947 6111
Fax: 020 7947 7671

The Admiralty & Commercial Registry:
Tel: 020 7947 6112
Fax: 020 7947 6245
DX 160040 Strand 4

The Admiralty & Commercial Court Listing office:
Tel: 020 7947 6826
Fax: 020 7947 7670
DX 160040 Strand 4

The Secretary to the Commercial Court Committee:
Mr James Kelly
Tel: 020 7947 6826
Fax: 020 7947 7670
DX 160040 Strand 4

Out of hours emergency number:

(Security Office at Royal Courts of Justice):
020 7947 6260

Fax number for the procedure under sections B3.11 and B4.4 of the Guide for the issue of claim forms when the Registry is closed: 020 7947 6245.

THE CHANCERY GUIDE

January 2013

TABLE OF CONTENTS

Preface	....	CHG Pref 1
General Note	....	CHG Pref 1 [1]
Chapter 1	Introductory	CHG 1.1
Section A	General Civil Work..................................	CHG 1.2
Chapter 2	Starting Proceedings, Allocation and Statements of Case.	CHG 2.1
Chapter 3	The Court's Case Management Powers	CHG 3.1
Chapter 4	Disclosure of Documents and Expert Evidence	CHG 4.1
Chapter 5	Applications	CHG 5.1
Chapter 6	Listing Arrangements	CHG 6.1
Chapter 7	Preparation for Hearings	CHG 7.1
Chapter 8	Conduct of a Trial	CHG 8.1
Chapter 9	Judgments, Orders and Proceedings after Judgment.....	CHG 9.1
Chapter 10	Appeals..	CHG 10.1
Chapter 11	Costs..	CHG 11.1
Chapter 12	Chancery Business outside London..................	CHG 12.1
Chapter 13	County Courts	CHG 13.1
Chapter 14	Use of Information Technology	CHG 14.1
Chapter 15	Miscellaneous Matters	CHG 15.1
Chapter 16	Suggestions for Improvement and Court Users' Committees	CHG 16.1
Chapter 17	Alternative Dispute Resolution.....................	CHG 17.1
Section B	Specialist Work...................................	CHG 18.1
Chapter 18	Introduction to the Specialist Work of the Chancery Division	CHG 18.1
Chapter 19	The Bankruptcy Court	CHG 19.1
Chapter 20	The Companies Court	CHG 20.1
Chapter 21	Mortgage Claims	CHG 21.1
Chapter 22	Partnership Claims and Receivers..................	CHG 22.1
Chapter 23	The Patents Court and Trade Marks etc	CHG 23.1
Chapter 24	Probate and Inheritance Claims	CHG 24.1
Chapter 25	Trusts	CHG 25.1
Appendix 1	Addresses and other Contact Details	CHG App 1.1
Appendix 2	Guidelines on Statements of Case..................	CHG App 2.1
Appendix 3	Case Management Directions.......................	CHG App 3.1
Appendix 4		CHG App 4
	Part 1: Judge's Application Information Form	CHG App 4
	Part 2: Written Evidence Lodgment Form.................	CHG App 4
Appendix 5	Correspondence with Chancery Masters	CHG App 5.1
Appendix 6	Guidelines on Bundles	CHG App 6.1
Appendix 7	Guidelines on Skeleton Arguments, Chronologies, Indices and Reading Lists..................................	CHG App 7.1
Appendix 8	Delivery of Documents in Chancery Chambers	CHG App 8.1
Appendix 9	Guidelines on Witness Statements	CHG App 9.1
Appendix 10	A Guide for Receivers in the Chancery Division	CHG App 10.1
Appendix 11	Lloyd's Names' Estate Applications: Forms	CHG App 11.1
Appendix 12	Practice Note: Remuneration of Judicial Trustees	CHG App 12.1
Appendix 13	Transfer of Cases to Chancery Trial Centres	CHG App 13.1
Appendix 14	Guidelines on Forms of Order	CHG App 14.1
Appendix 15	Chancery Business at Central London Civil Justice Centre...	CHG App 15.1

ABBREVIATIONS USED IN THIS GUIDE:

Civil Procedure Rules	CPR
HM Courts Service	HMCS
Practice Direction supplementing a Civil Procedure Rule	PD
Rules of the Supreme Court 1965	RSC
Pre-trial review	PTR
Part 1	CPR Part 1
rule 1.1	CPR Part 1 rule 1.1
PD 52	PD supplementing CPR Part 52

The Civil Procedure Rules (comprising rules, practice directions, pre-action protocols and forms) are published by the Stationery Office. They are also published on the Justice website: http://www.justice.gov.uk/about/hmcts/index.htm. This Guide will also be found on the Chancery Division section of the Justice website: http://www.justice.gov.uk/courts/rcj-rolls-building/chancery-division.

(1)   Please note that references to the CPR within this guide have been adapted to comply with COURT FORMS house style. Thus, references to rule 1.1 are referred to as CPR 1.1.

(2)   See note 1 above. References to PD 52 are referred to as CPR PD 52.

PREFACE

CHG Pref 1

This is the seventh edition of the Chancery Guide. Its preparation was initiated by Sir Andrew Morritt, my predecessor as Chancellor, who retired as head of the Division in January 2013 after heading the Division with conspicuous distinction for the previous 12 years.

This edition has been produced under the supervision of Sir Launcelot Henderson. Revision of the Guide is a time consuming task, requiring considerable patience and dedication over a lengthy period. I am extremely grateful to Sir Launcelot for bringing this edition to completion. He has been assisted by many others, including, in particular, the Chancery judges and specialist circuit judges, Chief Master Winegarten and Master Teverson, Chief Registrar Baister and Registrar Barber, Steven Rogers (Associate), Vicky Bell (HMCTS), Doug Bell (Chancery Clerk of the Lists), Matt Smith (HMCTS), and the Chancery Bar Association (especially Malcolm Davis-White QC, Katherine McQuail and Mark West).

The publication of this edition follows the move of the Division, together with the Commercial Court and the Technology and Construction Court, to the purpose built Rolls Building. As the largest business court complex in the world, with 31 court rooms, 55 conference rooms, and modern high quality facilities, it is an appropriate contemporary venue for conduct of the national and international work of the Division.

This new edition of the Guide contains changes reflecting the move to the Rolls Building. Other notable changes concern the use of IT, the new scheme for electronic filing of most skeletons for hearings in the Rolls Building, points of practice and procedure relating to applications, particularly in the Applications Court, the practice and procedure before Masters and in the Bankruptcy and Companies Courts, Tomlin Orders, appeals, litigants in person, the Central London Civil Justice Centre, and Chancery business outside London.

Other important procedural changes will affect the practice and work of the Division in the foreseeable future. In particular, aspects of Sir Rupert Jackson's Civil Justice review will shortly come into effect. Furthermore, it seems entirely appropriate, following the Division's move to the Rolls' Building, to have a thorough review of the current practices and procedures for the conduct of business in the Chancery Division, to ensure that those procedures are appropriate for current times. I have, therefore, asked Mr Justice Briggs to take charge of such a review (the Chancery Modernisation Review). He will be assisted by Mr Justice Newey and will have the benefit of an expert advisory panel. It is anticipated that the review will be completed, following public consultation, by the end of this year.

Sir Terence Etherton

Chancellor of the High Court

January 2013

CHAPTER 1: INTRODUCTORY
About the Chancery Division

CHG 1.1

1.1 The Chancery Division is one of the three parts, or Divisions, of the High Court of Justice. The other two are the Queen's Bench Division and the Family Division. The head of the Chancery Division is the Chancellor of the High Court ("the Chancellor"). There are currently 18 High Court judges attached to the Division. In addition, in the Royal Courts of Justice, Rolls Building in London, there are six judges who are referred to as Masters (one of whom is the Chief Master), and five judges who are referred to as Bankruptcy Registrars (one of whom is the Chief Registrar). In the District Registries (see Chapter 12) the work done by Masters in London is performed by District Judges. References in this Guide to a Master include, in the case of proceedings in a District Registry, references to a District Judge. Deputies sit on a regular basis for both judges and Masters. Any reference to a judge or Master in the Guide includes a reference to a person sitting as a deputy.

CHG 1.2

1.2 The Chancery Division undertakes civil work of many kinds, including specialist work such as companies, patents and contentious probate. The range of cases heard in the Chancery Division is wide and varied. The major part of the case-load today involves business or property disputes of one kind or another. Often these are complex and involve substantial sums of money.

CHG 1.3

1.3 Judges of the Chancery Division also sit as judges of the Court of Protection; in the Upper Tribunal (particularly the Tax Chamber) and in the Competition Appeal Tribunal. This Guide does not cover any of those courts or tribunals.

CHG 1.4

1.4 In many types of case (e.g. claims for professional negligence against solicitors, accountants, valuers or other professionals) the claimant has a choice whether to bring the claim in the Chancery Division or elsewhere in the High Court. But there are other types of case which, in the High Court, must be brought in the Chancery Division including claims (other than claims in the Commercial Court) relating to the application of Articles 101 and 102 of the Treaty on the Functioning of the European Union (TFEU) and the equivalent provisions in the Competition Act 1998. The specialist work of the Chancery Division is dealt with in Section B of this Guide. There are also certain claims which must be started in the Chancery Division either in the High Court or in a District Registry where there is a Chancery District Registry or in the Central London Civil Justice Centre (Chancery List).

CHG 1.4 [1]

Although claims against valuers and surveyors can be issued in the Chancery Division, in many cases they are likely to be transferred to the Queens Bench or an appropriate county court, on the footing that the specialist skills of the judges of the Chancery Division are not required for that class of business.

About this Guide

CHG 1.5

1.5 The aim of this Guide is to provide additional practical information not already contained in the CPR or the PDs supplementing them. Litigants and their advisers are expected to be familiar with the CPR and the PDs. This Guide should be used in conjunction with them. It is not the function of this Guide to summarise the CPR or the PDs, nor should it be regarded as a substitute for them.

CHG 1.6

1.6 This Guide does not have the status of a Practice Direction. So it does not have the force of law. But failure to comply with this Guide may influence the way in which the court exercises its powers under the CPR, including the making of adverse costs orders. In case of any conflict between this Guide and a rule or Practice Direction, the rule or Practice Direction prevails.

CHG 1.7

1.7 This Guide is published as part of a series of guides to various civil courts. Where information is more readily available in another guide, this Guide may simply refer to it. A separate book contains Practice Forms for use in the Chancery Division and in the Queen's Bench Division. Some of the forms most commonly used in the Chancery Division are found in the Appendices to this Guide. Forms may also be downloaded from the Justice website and may be found in the main procedural reference books.

CHG 1.8

1.8 Section A of this Guide is concerned with general civil work. Section B deals with specialist work. Some subjects are covered in more detail in the Appendices, and Appendix 1 sets out some contact details which may be useful.

CHG 1.9

1.9 Material which used to be contained in the Chancery Division Practice Directions and which remains relevant has been incorporated into either Section A or Section B of this Guide, as appropriate.

CHG 1.10

1.10 A reference in this Guide to a Part is to that Part of the CPR, to a rule is to the relevant rule in the CPR, unless otherwise stated, and to PD [number] is to the PD supplementing the Part so numbered. If there is more than one PD to a Part, the PDs are distinguished by letter (eg PDs 7A to 7E). The PD about costs, supplementing CPR Parts 43 to 48, is called the Costs PD[1].

CHG 1.11

1.11 This Guide states the position as at 31 January 2013. During the currency of the Guide, and even in some cases before publication, there are likely to be changes in matters covered in the text, including room numbers and other contact details; these should be checked as necessary. The Guide will be kept under review in the light of practical experience and of changes to the rules and practice directions. Any comments on the text of the Guide are welcome and should be addressed to the clerk to the Chancellor.

CHG 1.12

1.12 The text of the Guide is also to be found, together with other Court Guides and other useful information concerning the administration of justice in the Chancery

Division and elsewhere, on the Justice website. Amendments will appear on the Guide on the website as appropriate at: http://www.justice.gov.uk/courts/rcj-rolls-building/chancery-division. The Guide is also printed in the main procedural referen ce books.

---

1. Note that from 1 April 2013, the CPR costs provisions are re-organised and amended so that the substantive costs provisions are now found in CPR Pt 44 to CPR Pt 47 and their accompanying practice directions: see Civil Procedure (Amendment) Rules 2013, SI 2013/262. For the practice directions see the Justice website at www.justice.gov.uk.

SECTION A GENERAL CIVIL WORK

CHAPTER 2 STARTING PROCEEDINGS, ALLOCATION AND STATEMENTS OF CASE

Key Rules: CPR Parts 7, 8, 9, 10, 15, 16, 18, 20, 26 and CPR Schedule 1

Before starting a claim

CHG 2.1

2.1 Before issuing a claim parties should consider the PD on Pre-Action Conduct and any relevant Pre-Action protocols. The PD applies only to claims begun as a Part 7 or Part 8 claim. It does not therefore apply to claims which are started by some other means (eg petition). The court will not expect the PD to be complied with where:

(1)   telling the other potential party in advance would defeat the purpose of the application (e.g an application for a freezing order);
(2)   the application involves the making of representation orders so that non-parties may be bound by the outcome (eg pension cases);
(3)   there is no other party for the applicant to engage with (eg an application to the Court by trustees for directions);
(4)   the application results from agreement following negotiation (eg a variation of trust);
(5)   the urgency of the application is such that it is not practicable to comply; or
(6)   the claimant follows a statutory or other formal pre-action procedure.

CHG 2.2

2.2 In other cases the court will consider the extent to which the PD and any relevant Pre-Action Protocol has been complied with.

How to start a claim

CHG 2.3

2.3 Claims are issued out of the High Court of Justice, Chancery Division, either in the Royal Courts of Justice, Rolls Building or in a District Registry. There is no Production Centre for Chancery claims.

CHG 2.3 [1]

The Electronic Working Pilot Scheme is currently in abeyance. Further discussions are in train in order to promote electronic working in the future.

CHG 2.4

2.4 The claim form must be issued either as a Part 7 claim under Part 7, or as a Part 8 claim under the alternative procedure for claims in Part 8.

CHG 2.5

2.5 When issuing proceedings, the general rule is that the title of the claim should contain only the names of the parties to the proceedings. There are seven exceptions to this: (a) proceedings relating to the administration of an estate, which should be entitled "In the estate of AB deceased" (some cases relating to the estates of deceased Lloyd's names require additional wording: see paragraph 25.29 below); (b) contentious probate proceedings, which should be entitled "In the estate of AB deceased (probate)"; (c) proceedings under the Inheritance (Provision for Family and Dependants) Act 1975, which should be entitled "In the Matter of the Inheritance (Provision for Family and Dependants) Act 1975"; (d) proceedings relating to pension schemes, which may be entitled "In the Matter of the [] Pension Scheme"; (e) proceedings in the Companies Court are entitled in the matter of the relevant company or other person and of the relevant legislation: see paragraph 20.5; (f) a claim form to which Section I of CPR Part 63 applies (patents and registered designs) must be marked 'Chancery Division Patents Court' or 'Patents County Court', as the case may be, below the title of the court in which it is issued (CPR PD 63 para 3.1(a)); and (g) a claim form to which Section II of CPR Part 63 applies (eg copyright, registered trade marks, Community trade marks and other intellectual property rights) must, except for claims started in a patents county court, be marked 'Intellectual Property' below the title of the court in which it is issued (CPR PD 63 para 17). (See also paragraph 23.5.)

Service

CHG 2.6

2.6 Part 6 applies to the service of documents, including claim forms. Unless the claimant notifies the court that they wish to serve the claim form, or the court directs otherwise, it will be served by the court. Many solicitors, however, will prefer to serve the claim form themselves and will notify the court that they wish to do so.

Allocation

CHG 2.7

2.7 The vast majority of claims issued, and all those retained, in the Chancery Division will be either expressly allocated to the multi-track or in the case of Part 8 claims, deemed to be allocated to that track. Chapter 13 deals with transfer to county courts.

Statements of case

CHG 2.8

2.8 In addition to the matters which PD 16 requires to be set out specifically in the particulars of claim, a party must set out in any statement of case:

(1)   full particulars of any allegation of fraud, dishonesty, malice or illegality; and
(2)   where any inference of fraud or dishonesty is alleged, the facts on the basis of which the inference is alleged.

CHG 2.9

2.9 A party should not set out allegations of fraud or dishonesty unless there is credible material to support the contentions made. Setting out such matters without such material being available may result in the particular allegations being struck out and may result in wasted costs orders being made against the legal advisers responsible.

CHG 2.9 [1]

Following the decision of the House of Lords in *Medcalf v Mardell* [2002] UKHL 27, [2003] 1 AC 120, [2002] 3 All ER 721 allegations of fraud or dishonesty can be properly pleaded providing that there is material available which, even if not admissible, is of such a character as to lead responsible legal advisers exercising an objective professional judgment to conclude that such allegations can properly be based upon that material.

CHG 2.10

2.10 In the preparation of statements of case, the guidelines in Appendix 2 should be followed.

CHG 2.11

2.11 The guidelines apply to: the claim form (unless no particulars are given in it); particulars of claim; defence; additional claims under Part 20; reply to a defence; and a response to a request for further information under Part 18.

CHG 2.12

2.12 Parties should not attach copies of documents or any expert's report to their statement of case if they are bulky.

CHG 2.13

2.13 Notwithstanding rule 15.8, claimants should if possible serve any reply before they file their allocation questionnaire. This will enable other parties to consider the reply before they file their allocation questionnaire. However, the deadline for filing the reply is that in rule 15.8.

Part 8 claims

CHG 2.14

2.14 This procedure is appropriate in particular where there is no substantial dispute of fact, such as where the case raises only questions of the construction of a document or a statute. Additionally, PD 8 Section B lists a large number of particular claims which must be brought under Part 8. Other rules also require the Part 8 procedure to be used. Of particular relevance will be applications to enforce charging orders by sale, claims under the Inheritance (Provision for Family and Dependants) Act 1975, proceedings relating to solicitors and certain proceedings under the Companies Act 2006 (PD 49 para 5). Subject to jurisdiction, applications to enforce charging orders are now issued in the court in which the charging order was made. Proceedings to enforce charging orders made in any Division of the High Court and the Court of Appeal are issued in the Chancery Division.

CHG 2.14 [1]

In practice many applications to enforce charging orders over land will continue to be issued and heard in the Chancery Division. County Court jurisdiction is limited to those cases where the amount owing in respect of the charging order does not exceed the county court limit (currently £30,000). It follows that any application to enforce a charging order obtained in the county court in respect of a debt exceeding £30,000 will still fall to be issued in the Chancery Division. Such a claim, however, if straightforward, is likely to be transferred to a local county court (often the court where the charging order was made) and that court clothed with jurisdiction pursuant to s 40(2) of the County Courts Act. This practice will in most cases cease to be necessary when projected changes in the County Court's equity jurisdiction are brought into effect.

CHG 2.15

2.15 Part 8 also provides for a claim form to be issued without naming a defendant with the permission of the court. No separate application for permission is required where personal representatives seek permission to distribute the estate of a deceased Lloyd's name nor for applications under section 48 of the Administration of Justice Act 1985 (see further Chapter 25 - Trusts). Likewise, no separate permission is required where an application is made under PD Part 64.1(A) for the approval by the court of a specific transaction to be entered into by trustees. Where permission is needed, it is to be sought by application notice under Part 23. The application should be listed before a Master.

CHG 2.16

2.16 Part 8 claims will generally be disposed of on written evidence. Key features of the CPR Part 8 procedure are:

(1)   no particulars of claim
(2)   no defence
(3)   no allocation questionnaire
(4)   no judgment in default
(5)   normally no oral evidence.

CHG 2.17

2.17 Defendants who wish to contest a Part 8 claim or to take part in the proceedings should complete and file the acknowledgment of service in form N210 which accompanies the claim form. Alternatively the information required to be contained in the acknowledgment of service can be provided by letter. Any objection to the use of the Part 8 procedure must be made at that time. A party who does not wish to contest a claim should indicate that fact on the form acknowledging service or by letter.

CHG 2.17 [1]
The current Form N210 does make provision for a party to indicate his or her intention not to contest.

CHG 2.18

2.18 Claimants must file the written evidence, namely evidence by witness statement, on which they intend to rely with the claim form. Defendants are required to file and serve their evidence when they file their acknowledgment of service, namely within 14 days after service of the claim form (rule 8.5(3)). By paragraph 7.5 of PD 8, a defendant's time for filing evidence may be extended by written agreement for not more than 14 days from the filing of the acknowledgment of service. Any such agreement must be filed with the court by the defendant at the same time as they file an acknowledgment of service. The claimant has 14 days for filing evidence in reply but this period may be extended by written agreement for not more than 28 days from service of the defendant's evidence. Again, any such agreement must be filed with the court. Any longer extension either for the defendant or the claimant requires an application to the court. It is recognised that in substantial matters the time limits for evidence in Part 8 may be burdensome upon defendants and in such matters the court will normally be willing to grant a reasonable extension. If the parties are in agreement that such an extension should be granted the application should be made in writing by letter. The parties should at all times act co-operatively.

CHG 2.18 [1]
Attention is drawn to the need to file with the acknowledgment of service any agreement for an extension of time for filing evidence. This is often overlooked.

CHG 2.19

2.19 Defendants who acknowledge service but do not intend to file evidence should notify the court in writing when they file their acknowledgment of service that they do not intend to file evidence. This enables the court to know what each defendant's intention is when it considers the file.

CHG 2.20

2.20 The general rule is that the court file will be considered by the court after the time for acknowledgment of service has expired, or, if the time for serving the defendant's evidence has been extended, after the expiry of that period. There are exceptions to this rule (including some claims under the Variations of Trusts Act 1958 and cases where a party has applied for summary judgment).

CHG 2.21

2.21 In some cases if the papers are in order the court will not require any oral hearing, but will be able to deal with the matter on paper by making a final order. In other cases the court will direct that the Part 8 claim is listed either for a disposal hearing or for a case management conference.

CHAPTER 3 THE COURT'S CASE MANAGEMENT POWERS

Key Rules: CPR rule 1.4, and CPR Parts 3, 18, 19, 26, 29, 31, 39

CHG 3.1

3.1 A key feature of the CPR is that cases are closely monitored by the court. Case management by the court includes: identifying disputed issues at an early stage; fixing timetables; dealing with as many aspects of the case as possible on the same occasion; controlling costs; disposing of cases summarily where they disclose no case or defence; dealing with the case without the parties having to attend court; and giving directions to ensure that the trial of a case proceeds quickly and efficiently.

CHG 3.1 [1]

A cardinal feature of the changes in the rules with effect from 1 April 2013 is that the court will take a much more active role in respect of costs management and cost s budgeting in multitrack cases. In the majority of cases the parties will now have to work to budgets either agreed between the parties or determined by the court. The directions given will, necessarily, reflect those budgets.

CHG 3.2

3.2 The rules require the parties themselves to help the court to further the overriding objective. Accordingly the court will expect the parties to co-operate with each other. Failure to do so may attract adverse costs consequences.

CHG 3.3

3.3 The court will expect the parties to co-operate with each other. Where appropriate the court will encourage the parties to use alternative dispute resolution (on which see Chapter 17) or otherwise help them settle the case. In particular, the court will readily grant a short stay at allocation or at any other stage to accommodate mediation or any other form of settlement negotiations. The court will not, however, normally, grant an open-ended stay for such purposes and if, for any reason, a lengthy stay is granted it will be on terms that the parties report to the court on a regular basis in respect of their negotiations.

CHG 3.4

3.4 In the Chancery Division case management is normally carried out by the Master, but a judge may be nominated by the Chancellor to hear the case and to deal with the case management where it is appropriate due to the size or complexity of the case or for other reasons. A request by any or all parties for such a nomination should be addressed to the clerk to the Chancellor.

Directions

CHG 3.5

3.5 It is expected that parties and their advisers will try to agree proposals for management of the case at the allocation stage in accordance with rule 29.4 and paragraphs 4.6 to 4.8 of PD 29. In particular, the parties must act co-operatively and seek to agree directions and a list of the issues to be tried. The court will approve the parties' proposals, if they are suitable, and give directions accordingly without a hearing. If it does not approve the agreed directions it may give modified directions or its own directions or, more usually, direct a case management conference. If the parties cannot agree directions then each party should put forward its own proposals for the future management of the case for consideration by the court. Electronic copies should be available so that any necessary changes can be made quickly. Draft orders commonly made by the Masters on allocation and at case management conferences are set out at Appendix 3, and parties drafting proposed directions for submission to a Master on allocation or at a case management conference should have regard to and make use, as appropriate, of those draft orders.

CHG 3.6

3.6 If parties do not, at the allocation stage, agree or attempt to agree directions and if, in consequence, the court is unable to give directions without ordering a case management conference, the parties should not expect to recover any costs in respect of such a case management conference. It will not generally be acceptable for the parties in their Allocation questionnaires to indicate that they have not suggested or agreed draft directions (using the form at Appendix 3). If by the time limited for the filing of Allocation Questionnaires directions are still the subject of discussion, the Master should be alerted to this in the Allocation Questionnaire and given a time by which draft directions will be filed. If a party seeks an unusual or non-routine order they should provide a short explanation for the court with the Allocation Questionnaire. Similarly if the parties seek permission to adduce expert evidence and the reason for this is not obvious they should provide an agreed explanation for use by the court.

CHG 3.6 [1]

The Guide, as indeed the CPR, emphasises the parties' duty to co-operate with each other and the court in respect of the management of claims. Failure to co-operate and to put forward sensible case management proposals will result only in delay and in a refusal by the court to allow one or both parties their costs.

CHG 3.7

3.7 In many claims the court will give directions without holding a case management conference.

CHG 3.7 [1]

Consequent upon the courts involvement in costs management and budgeting, it is unlikely that it will now be possible to give directions in very many cases without a hearing. It will only be where budgets are agreed and where, therefore, the court is not required to investigate the proposed budgets that 'paper' directions are likely to be possible.

CHG 3.8

3.8 Any party who considers that a case management conference should be held before any directions are given should so state in their allocation questionnaire (or, in the case of a Part 8 claim, inform the court in writing) and give reasons why they consider that a case management conference is required. When filing an allocation questionnaire a party is also requested to lodge a form giving their time estimate for any case management conference and specifying any dates or times inconvenient for the holding of a case management conference.

CHG 3.9

3.9 Wherever possible, the advocate(s) instructed or expected to be instructed to appear at the trial should attend any hearing at which case management directions are likely to be given. To this end the court when ordering a case management conference, otherwise than upon allocation, will normally send out questionnaires to the parties in respect of their availability. Parties must not, however, expect that a case management conference will be held in abeyance for a substantial length of time in order to accommodate the advocates' convenience.

CHG 3.10

3.10 Case management conferences are intended to deal with the general management of the case. They are not an opportunity to make controversial interim applications without appropriate notice to the opposing party. Accordingly, as provided by paragraph 5.8(1) of PD 29, where a party wishes to obtain an order not routinely made at a case management conference (such as an order for specific disclosure or summary disposal) such application should be made by separate Part 23 application to be heard at the case management conference and the case management conference should be listed for a sufficient period of time to allow the application to be heard. Where parties fail to comply with this paragraph it is highly unlikely that the court will entertain, other than by consent, an application which is not of a routine nature. It is the obligation of the parties to ensure that a realistic time estimate for any hearing is given to the court.

CHG 3.10 [1]

It will now be very important for parties attending CMCs to provide the court prior to the CMC with information by way of position statements or skeleton arguments as to any differences between them as to their prospective budgets. Budgets and directions go hand in hand and the court cannot determine one without the other.

CHG 3.11

3.11 Even where routine orders are sought (i.e. orders falling within the topics set out in paragraph 5.3 of PD 29) care should be taken to ensure that the opposing party is given notice of the orders intended to be sought.

Case management bundle

CHG 3.12

3.12 Parties should consider the compiling of a permanent case management bundle containing a neutral case summary, the statements of case and court orders, updated as necessary during the progress of the case. The court may direct the compiling of such a bundle in an appropriate case.

CHG 3.12 [1]

This is a new idea in the Chancery Division but reflects an established practice in the Commercial Court.

Applications for information and disclosure

CHG 3.13

3.13 Before a party applies to the court for an order that another party provides them with any further information or specific disclosure of documents they must communicate directly with the other party in an attempt to reach agreement or narrow the issues before the matter is raised with the court. If not satisfied that the parties have taken steps to reach agreement or narrow the issues, the court will normally require such steps to be taken before hearing the application.

Preliminary issues

CHG 3.14

3.14 Costs can sometimes be saved by identifying decisive issues, or potentially decisive issues, and ordering that they are tried first. The decision of one issue, although not itself decisive of the whole case, may enable the parties to settle the remainder of the dispute. In such cases a preliminary issue may be appropriate.

CHG 3.15

3.15 At the allocation stage, at any case management conference and again at any PTR, consideration will be given to the possibility of the trial of preliminary issues the resolution of which is likely to shorten proceedings. The court may suggest the trial of a preliminary issue, but it will rarely make an order without the concurrence of at least one of the parties.

CHG 3.15 [1]

If at a case management conference one party intends to seek the trial of preliminary issues it is good practice to issue a separate application supported by evidence in respect of that question so that the court has before it all necessary material. An application for a preliminary issue should not be regarded as an order to be made routinely at a case management conference.

Group Litigation Orders

CHG 3.16

3.16 Under rule 19.11, where there are likely to be a number of claims giving rise to common or related issues of fact or law, the court may make a Group Litigation Order ("GLO") for their case management. Such orders may be appropriate in Chancery proceedings and there are a number in existence. A list of GLOs is published on the Justice website (www.justice.gov.uk). An application for a GLO is m ade under Part 23. The procedure is set out in PD 19B Group Litigation, which pro vides that the application should be made to the Chief Master, except for claims in a specialist list (such as the business of the Patents Court), when the application should be made to the senior judge of that list.

CHG 3.17

3.17 Claimants wishing to join in group litigation should issue proceedings in the normal way and should then apply (by letter) to be entered on the Group Register set up by a GLO. Where the Register is kept in the Chancery Division at the Rolls Building, it is kept by Mrs VC Bell, Chancery Lawyer (Room D01–010, tel. 020 7947 6080). Any initial enquiries regarding GLOs may be addressed to her.

Trial timetable

CHG 3.18

3.18 The judge at trial, or sometimes at the PTR, may determine the timetable for the trial. The advocates for the parties should be ready to assist the court in this respect if so required. The time estimate given for the trial should have been based on an approximate forecast of the trial timetable (including any time needed for pre-reading by the trial judge) and must be reviewed by each party at the stage of the PTR and as preparation for trial proceeds thereafter. If that review requires a change in the estimate the other parties' advocates and the court must be informed.

CHG 3.19

3.19 When a trial timetable is set by the court, it will ordinarily fix the time for the oral submissions and factual and expert evidence, and it may do so in greater or lesser detail. Trial timetables are always subject to any further order by the trial judge.

Pre-Trial Review

CHG 3.20

3.20 The court has power to direct that a PTR be held (see rule 29.7). This power will normally be exercised in cases estimated to take more than 10 days and in other cases where the circumstances warrant it, the court may direct that a PTR be held (see rule 29.7).

CHG 3.21

3.21 Such a PTR will normally be heard by a judge. The date and time should be fixed with the Chancery Judges' Listing Officer. If the trial judge has already been nominated, the application will if possible be heard by that judge. The advocates' clerks must attend the Chancery Judges' Listing Officer in sufficient time so that the PTR can be fixed between four and eight weeks before the trial date.

CHG 3.22

3.22 A PTR should be attended by advocates who are to represent the parties at the trial. Any unrepresented party should also attend.

CHG 3.23

3.23 Not less than 7 days before the date fixed for the PTR the claimant, or another party if so directed by the court, must circulate a list of matters to be considered at the PTR, including proposals as to how the case should be tried, to the other parties, who must respond with their comments at least 2 days before the PTR.

CHG 3.24

3.24 The claimant, or another party if so directed by the court, should deliver a bundle containing the lists of matters to be considered and proposals served by the parties on each other and the trial timetable, together with the results of the discussions between the parties as to those matters, and any other documents the court is likely to need in order to deal with the PTR, to the Chancery Judges' Listing Office by 10 am on the day before the day fixed for the hearing of the PTR.

CHG 3.25

3.25 At the PTR the court will review the state of preparation of the case, and deal with outstanding procedural matters, not limited to those apparent from the lists of matters lodged by the parties. The court may give directions as to how the case is to be tried, including directions as to the order in which witnesses are to be called (for example all witnesses of fact before all expert witnesses) or as to the time to be allowed for particular stages in the trial.

CHG 3.25 [1]

In practice and because it is rare for the trial judge to be known sufficiently early for him or her to deal with a PTR, parties often prefer that in lieu of a PTR there is a final case management conference close to trial at which the Master (who is likely to be familiar with the case) can give any final directions. The Master, however, will not set a trial timetable.

CHAPTER 4 DISCLOSURE OF DOCUMENTS AND EXPERT EVIDENCE

Key Rules: CPR Parts 18, 29, 31, 35; CPR PD 31 and CPR PD 35

CHG 4.1

4.1 As part of its management of a case, the court will give directions about the disclosure of documents and any expert evidence. An application for specific disclosure should be made by a specific Part 23 application and is not to be regarded as a matter routinely dealt with at a case management conference.

CHG 4.2

4.2 Although applications for disclosure pursuant to *Norwich Pharmacal v Customs and Excise Commissioners* [1974] AC 133 [1973] 2 All ER 943 HL may be made under Part 7 or Part 8 (as the case may be), nevertheless if the application is or is thought likely to be uncontested the court may entertain in the alternative an application under Part 23 supported by evidence.

Disclosure of documents

CHG 4.3

4.3 Under the CPR, the normal order for disclosure is an order for standard disclosure, which requires disclosure of:

(1)   a party's own documents - that is, the documents on which a party relies;
(2)   adverse documents - that is, documents which adversely affect their or another party's case or support another party's case; and
(3)   required documents - that is, documents which a PD requires them to disclose.

CHG 4.4

4.4 Since disclosure can be very expensive, the parties should consider methods by which the expense can be limited. In relation to the disclosure of electronic documents, it is essential that careful attention be given to CPR PD 31B— Disclosure of Electronic Documents, as soon as litigation is contemplated and throughout the process of preparation for trial. CPR PD 31B applies to all proceedings started on or after October 1 2010 which are, or are likely to be, allocated to the multi-track (see too CPR PD 31A para 2A.2).

CHG 4.4 [1]

The new rule changes in force from 1 April 2013 no longer make standard disclosure a default position and set out a menu of orders designed to limit and thereby reduce the cost of disclosure. In many cases, however, the needs of justice will still require that standard disclosure remains the appropriate order.

CHG 4.5

4.5 The court may also make an order for specific disclosure going beyond the limits of standard disclosure if it is satisfied that standard disclosure is inadequate.

CHG 4.6

4.6 The court will not make such an order readily. One of the clear principles underlying the CPR is that the burden and cost of disclosure should be reduced. The court will, therefore, seek to ensure that any specific disclosure ordered is proportionate In the sense that its cost does not outweigh the likely benefits to be obtained from such disclosure. The court will, accordingly, seek to tailor the order for disclosure to the requirements of the particular case. The financial position of the parties, the importance of the case and the complexity of the issues will be taken into account when considering whether more than standard disclosure should be ordered.

CHG 4.7

4.7 If specific disclosure is sought, the parties should give careful thought to the ways in which such disclosure can be limited, for example by requiring disclosure in stages or by requiring disclosure simply of sufficient documents to show a specified matter and so on. They should also consider whether the need for disclosure could be avoided by requiring a party to provide information under Part 18.

Expert evidence

General

CHG 4.8

4.8 Part 35 contains particular provisions designed to limit the amount of expert evidence to be placed before the court and to reinforce the obligation of impartiality which is imposed upon an expert witness. The key question now in relation to expert evidence is the question as to what added value such evidence will provide to the court in its determination of a given case.

CHG 4.9

4.9 Fundamentally, Part 35 states that expert evidence must be restricted to what is reasonably required to resolve the proceedings and makes provision for the court to direct that expert evidence is given by a single joint expert. The parties should consider from the outset of the proceedings whether appointment of a single joint expert is appropriate.

Duties of an expert

CHG 4.10

4.10 It is the duty of an expert to help the court on the matters within their expertise; this duty overrides any obligation to the person from whom the expert has received instructions or by whom they are paid (rule 35.3). Attention is drawn to PD 35 and the Protocol for the Instruction of Experts which sets out the duties of an expert and the form and contents of an expert's report.

CHG 4.10 [1]

Experts must be careful, when accepting instructions, to have regard to potential conflicts of interest. An expert who fails to fulfil his or her duty, or who acts in circumstances of conflict, can be the subject of a wasted costs order.

Single joint expert

CHG 4.11

4.11 The introduction to PD 35 states that, where possible, matters requiring expert evidence should be dealt with by a single expert.

CHG 4.12

4.12 In very many cases it is possible for the question of expert evidence to be dealt with by a single expert. The factors which the court will take into account in deciding whether there should be a single expert include those listed in CPR PD 35 paragraph 7. Single experts are, for example, often appropriate to deal with questions of quantum in cases where the primary issues are as to liability. Likewise, where expert evidence is required in order to acquaint the court with matters of expert fact, as opposed to opinion, a single expert will usually be appropriate. There remains, however, a substantial body of cases where liability will turn upon expert opinion evidence or where quantum is a primary issue and where it will be appropriate for the parties to instruct their own experts. For example, in cases where the issue for determination is whether a party acted in accordance with proper professional standards, it will often be of value to the court to hear the opinions of more than one expert as to the proper standard in order that the court becomes acquainted with the range of views existing upon the question and in order that the evidence can be tested in cross-examination.

CHG 4.13

4.13 It is not necessarily a sufficient objection to the making by the court of an order for a single joint expert that the parties have already appointed their own experts. An order for a single joint expert does not prevent a party from having their own expert to advise them, but they may well be unable to recover the cost of employing their own expert from the other party. The duty of an expert who is called to give evidence is to help the court.

CHG 4.14

4.14 When the use of a single joint expert is contemplated the court will expect the parties to co-operate in developing, and agreeing to the greatest possible extent, terms of reference for the expert. In most cases the terms of reference will (in particular) detail what the expert is asked to do, identify any documentary material they are asked to consider and specify any assumptions they are asked to make.

More than one expert - exchange of reports

CHG 4.15

4.15 In an appropriate case the court will direct that experts' reports are delivered sequentially. Sequential reports may, for example, be appropriate if the service of the first expert's report would help to define and limit the issues on which such evidence may be relevant.

Discussion between experts

CHG 4.16

4.16 The court will normally direct discussion between experts before trial. Sometimes it may be useful for there to be further discussions during the trial itself. The purpose of these discussions is to give the experts the opportunity:

(1)   to discuss the expert issues; and
(2)   to identify the expert issues on which they share the same opinion and those on which there remains a difference of opinion between them (and what that difference is).

CHG 4.17

4.17 Unless the court otherwise directs, the procedure to be adopted at these discussions is a matter for the experts. It may be sufficient if the discussion takes place by telephone.

CHG 4.18

4.18 Parties must not seek to restrict their expert's participation in any discussion directed by the court, but they are not bound by any agreement on any issue reached by their expert unless they expressly so agree.

Written questions to experts

CHG 4.19

4.19 It is emphasised that this procedure is only for the purpose (generally) of seeking clarification of an expert's report where the other party is unable to understand it. Written questions going beyond this can only be put with the agreement of the parties or with the permission of the court. The procedure of putting written questions to experts is not intended to interfere with the procedure for an exchange of professional opinion in discussions between experts or to inhibit that exchange of professional opinion. If questions that are oppressive in number or content are put or questions are put without permission for any purpose other than clarification of an expert's report, the court will not hesitate to disallow the questions and to make an appropriate order for costs against the party putting them.

Request by an expert to the court for directions

CHG 4.20

4.20 An expert may file with the court a written request for directions to assist them in carrying out their function as expert: rule 35.14. Copies of any such request must be provided to the parties in accordance with rule 35.14(2) save where the court orders otherwise. The expert should guard against accidentally informing the court about, or about matters connected with, communications or potential communications between the parties that are without prejudice or privileged. The expert may properly be privy to the content of these communications because the expert has been asked to assist the party instructing him or her to evaluate them.

Assessors

CHG 4.21

4.21 Under rule 35.15 the court may appoint an assessor to assist it in relation to any matter in which the assessor has skill and experience. The report of the assessor is made available to the parties. The remuneration of the assessor is determined by the court and forms part of the costs of the proceedings.

CHAPTER 5 APPLICATIONS

Key Rules: CPR Part 23 and CPR Part 25, CPR PD 23A and CPR PD 25A

CHG 5.1

5.1 This Chapter deals with applications to a judge, including applications for interim remedies, and applications to a Master. As regards the practical arrangements for making, listing and adjourning applications, the Chapter is primarily concerned with hearings at the Royal Courts of Justice, Rolls Building. Hearings before Chancery judges and District Judges outside London are dealt with in Chapter 12.

CHG 5.2

5.2 It is most important that only applications which need to be heard by a judge (e.g. most applications for an injunction) should be made to a judge. Any procedural application (e.g. for directions) should be made to a Master unless there is some special reason for making it to a judge. Otherwise the application may be dismissed with costs. If an application is to be made to a judge, the application notice should state that it is a judge's application. If an application which should have been made to a Master is made to a judge, the judge may refuse to hear it.

CHG 5.3

5.3 Part 23 contains rules as to how an application may be made. In some circumstances it may be dealt with without a hearing, or by a telephone hearing.

Applications without notice

CHG 5.4

5.4 Generally it is wrong to make an application without giving prior notice to the respondent. There are, however, three classes of exceptions.

(1)   First, there are cases where the giving of notice might frustrate the order (e.g. a search order) or where there is such urgency that there has not been time to give notice. Even in an urgent case, however, the applicant should notify the respondent informally of the application if possible, unless secrecy is essential.

(2)   Second, there are some procedural applications normally made without notice relating to such matters as service out of the jurisdiction, service, extension of the validity of claim forms, permission to issue writs of possession etc. All of these are properly made without notice the rules usually expressly provide that the absent party will be entitled to apply to set aside or vary any order provided that application is so made within a given number of days of service of the order. A defendant who wishes to dispute the jurisdiction of the court, following service out of the jurisdiction, should apply to the court under CPR Part 11.

(3)   Third, there are cases in which the respondent can only be identified by description and not by name.

An application made without giving notice which does not fall within the classes of cases where absence of notice is justified may be dismissed or adjourned until proper notice has been given.

Applications without a hearing

CHG 5.5

5.5 Part 23 makes provision for applications to be dealt with without a hearing. This is a useful provision in a case where the parties consent to the terms of the order sought or agree that a hearing is not necessary (often putting in written representations by letter or otherwise). It is also a useful provision in a case where, although the parties have not agreed to dispense with a hearing and the order is not consented to, the order sought by the application is, essentially, non-contentious. In the latter case, the order made will be treated as being made on the court's own initiative and will set out the right of any party affected by the application who has not been heard to apply to vary or set aside the order.

CHG 5.6

5.6 These provisions should not be used to deal with contentious matters without notice to the opposing party and without a hearing. Usually, this will result in delay since the court will simply order a hearing. It may also give rise to adverse costs orders. It will normally be wrong to seek an order which imposes sanctions in the event of non-compliance without notice and without a hearing. An application seeking such an order may well be dismissed.

Applications to a judge

CHG 5.7

5.7 If an application is made to a judge in existing proceedings, e.g. for an injunction, it should be made by application notice. This is called an Interim Application. Normally 3 clear days' notice to the other party is required but in an emergency or for other good reason the application can be made without giving notice, or the full 3 days' notice, to the other side. Permission to serve on short notice may be obtained on application without notice to the Interim Applications judge. Such permission will not be given by the Master. Except in an emergency a party notifies the court of their wish to bring an application by delivering the requisite documents to the Chancery Judges' Listing Office (ground floor, Rolls Building) and paying the appropriate fee. They should at the same time deliver a completed 'Judge's Application Information Form' in the form set out in Appendix 4. An application will only be listed if (a) two copies of the claim form and (b) two copies of the application notice (one stamped with the appropriate fee) are lodged with the Chancery Judges' Listing Office before 12 noon on the working day before the date for which notice of the application has been given. Any party seeking an order should submit an electronic draft of that order attached to an email addressed to chanceryinterimorders@hmcts.gsi.gov.uk. The emails and orders should sufficiently identify the case (not necessarily the full name) and should be in Word (.doc) format.

CHG 5.8

5.8 The current practice is that one Judge combines the functions of Interim Applications judge and Companies judge. The judge's name will be found in the Daily Cause List.

CHG 5.9

5.9 The Interim Applications judge is available to hear applications each working day in term and an application notice can be served for any working day in term except the last. If the volume of applications requires it, any other judge who is available to assist with Interim Applications will hear such applications as the Interim Applications judge may direct. Special arrangements are made for hearing applications out of hours and in vacation, for which see paragraphs 5.41 to 5.47 below.

CHG 5.10

5.10 An application should not be listed before the Interim Applications Judge if it is suitable for hearing by a Master or Registrar. The mere fact that it is urgent is not enough, because both Masters and Registrars are available to hear urgent applications. If an application which should be heard by a Master or Registrar is listed before the Interim Applications Judge, the judge may refuse to hear it.

CHG 5.11

5.11 **An application should not be listed before the Interim Applications Judge unless the overall time required to deal with the application is two hours or less. The two hour maximum includes the judge's pre-reading time, time in court and time for judgment.**

CHG 5.12

5.12 If the overall time required to deal with an application is likely to exceed two hours the application should be heard as an application by order (see paragraphs 5.14 and 5.20). If an application is listed before the Interim Applications Judge and it becomes apparent (either on the day of the hearing or beforehand) that the overall time required to deal with it is likely to exceed two hours the Chancery Judges' Listing Officer (or, in appropriate cases, the clerk to the Interim Applications Judge) must be notified immediately.

CHG 5.13

5.13 Every skeleton argument must begin with an estimate of the time required for pre-reading and an estimate of the time required in court (including time for judgment). It is essential that these time estimates are realistic, and take account of the fact that the judge will usually have no prior acquaintance with the case.

CHG 5.14

5.10 At the beginning of each day's hearing the Interim Applications Judge calls on each of the applications to be made that day in turn. This enables the judge to establish the identity of the parties, their state of readiness, their estimates of the duration of the hearing, and where relevant the degree of urgency of the case. On completion of this process, the judge decides the order in which the applications will be heard and gives any other directions that may be necessary. Sometimes cases are released to other judges at this point. If a case is likely to take two hours or more (including pre-reading and oral delivery of judgment), the judge will usually order that it is given a subsequent fixed date for hearing and hear any application for a court order to last until the application is heard fully.

CHG 5.15

5.15 Where an application is to be heard as an application by order the solicitors or the clerks to counsel concerned should apply to the Chancery Judges' Listing Office for a date for the hearing. Before so doing there must be lodged with the Chancery Judges' Listing Office a certificate signed by the advocate stating the estimated length of the hearing.

CHG 5.16

5.16 Parties and their representatives should arrive at least ten minutes before the court sits. This will assist the usher to take a note of the names of those proposing to address the court and any revised estimate of the hearing time. This information is given to the judge before he or she sits. Parties should also allow time before the court sits to agree any form of order with any other party if this has not already been done. If the form of the order is not agreed before the court sits, the parties may have to wait until there is a convenient break in the list before they can ask the court to make any agreed order. If an application, not being an Interim Application by Order, is adjourned the Associate in attendance will notify the Chancery Judges' Listing Office of the date to which it has been adjourned so that it may be relisted for the new date.

CHG 5.17

5.17 If an application is adjourned to a later date the applicant must:

(1)   remove all bundles for the current hearing from the court unless otherwise directed by the Judge;

(2)   ensure that all papers and bundles required for the adjourned hearing are lodged with the Chancery Judges' Listing Office, ground floor, Rolls Building, no later than one working day before the return date; and

(3)   ensure that the adjourned hearing has been re-listed on the correct day when the papers are re-lodged with the Listing Office.

Without Notice Applications

CHG 5.18

5.18 If a return date is given on an interim injunction (or any other remedy granted by the Judge) the applicant must ensure that an application notice for the return date is issued and served on the other parties (normally at least 3 working days before the return date); and that an up to date hearing bundle for use by the judge is lodged in accordance with paragraph 5.17 above. This bundle must include copies of the interim injunction or order, the issued application for the relief originally granted, and the issued application notice for the return date. Failure to comply with these requirements may lead to delay in dealing with the application or costs sanctions.

Agreed Adjournment of Interim Applications

CHG 5.19

5.19 If all parties to an Interim Application agree, it can be adjourned for not more than 14 days by counsel's clerks or solicitors attending the Chancery Judges' Listing Officer on the ground floor, Rolls Building, at any time before 4pm on the day before the hearing of the application and producing consents signed by solicitors or counsel for all parties agreeing to the adjournment. A litigant in person must attend before the Chancery Judges' Listing Officer as well as signing a consent. This procedure may not be used for more than three successive adjournments and no adjournment may be made by this procedure to the last two days of any term.

Interim Applications by Order by agreement

CHG 5.20

5.20 This procedure should also be used where the parties agree that the application will take two hours or more and that, in consequence, the application should be adjourned to be heard as an Interim Application by Order. In that event, the consents set out above should also contain an agreed timetable for the filing of evidence or confirmation that no further evidence is to be filed. Any application arising from the failure of a party to abide by the timetable and any application to extend the timetable must be made to the judge.

CHG 5.21

5.21 Undertakings given to the court may be continued unchanged over any adjournment. If, however, on an adjournment an undertaking is to be varied or a new undertaking given then that must be dealt with by the court.

Applications without notice

CHG 5.22

5.22 On all applications made in the absence of the respondent the applicant and their legal representatives owe a duty to the court to disclose all matters relevant to the application. This includes matters of fact or law which are or may be adverse to the applicant. If made orally, the disclosure must be confirmed by witness statement or affidavit. The applicant or their legal representatives must specifically direct the court to passages in the evidence which disclose matters adverse to the application. This duty also applies to litigants in person. If there is a failure to comply with this duty and an order is made, the court may subsequently set aside the order on this ground alone.

CHG 5.23

5.23 A party wishing to apply urgently to a judge for remedies without notice to the respondent must notify the clerk to the Interim Applications Judge by telephone. Where such an urgent application is made, two copies of the order sought and a completed Judge's Application Information Form in the form in Appendix 4 should, where possible, be included with the papers handed to the judge's clerk. Where an application is very urgent and the Interim Applications Judge is unable to hear it promptly, it may be heard by any judge who is available, though the request for this must be made to the clerk to the Interim Applications Judge, or, in default, to the Chancery Judges' Listing Officer. Every effort should be made to issue the claim form before the application is made. If this is not practicable, the party making the application must give an undertaking to the court to issue the claim form forthwith even if the court makes no order, unless the court orders otherwise. A party making an urgent application must ensure that all necessary fees are paid.

CHG 5.24

5.24 A party wishing to make an application without notice should give as much advance warning to the court as possible. If the overall time required to deal with the application (including pre-reading) is likely to exceed two hours arrangements for the listing of the application should be made with the Chancery Judges' Listing Officer.

Freezing Injunctions and Search Orders

CHG 5.25

5.25 The grant of freezing injunctions (both domestic and world-wide) and search orders is a staple feature of the work of the Chancery Division. Applications for such orders are almost invariably made without notice in the first instance; and in a proper case the court will sit in private in order to hear them. Where such an application is to be listed, two copies of the order sought, together with the application notice, should be lodged with the Chancery Judges' Listing Office. If the application is to be made in private, it will be listed as 'Application without notice' without naming the parties. The judge will consider, in each case, whether publicity might defeat the object of the hearing and, if it would, will hear the application in private.

Period for which an injunction or an order appointing a receiver is granted if the application was without notice

CHG 5.26

5.26 When an application for an injunction is heard without notice, and the judge decides that an injunction should be granted, it will normally be granted for a limited period only - usually not more than seven days. The same applies to an interim order appointing a receiver. The applicant will be required to give the respondent notice of their intention to apply to the court at the expiration of that period for the order to be continued. In the meantime the respondent will be entitled to apply, though generally only after giving notice to the applicant, for the order to be varied or discharged.

Opposed applications without notice

CHG 5.27

5.27 These are applications of which proper notice has not been given to the respondents but which are made in the presence of both parties in advance of a full hearing of the application. The judge may impose time limits on the parties if, having regard to the pressure of business or for any other reason, the judge considers it appropriate to do so. On these applications, the judge may, in an appropriate case, make an order which will have effect until trial or further order as if proper notice had been given.

Implied cross-undertakings in damages

CHG 5.28

5.28 Often the party against whom an injunction is sought gives to the court an undertaking which avoids the need for the court to grant the injunction. In these cases, there is an implied undertaking in damages by the party applying for the injunction in favour of the other. The position is less clear where the party applying for the injunction also gives an undertaking to the court. The parties should consider and, if necessary, raise with the judge whether the party in whose favour the undertaking is given must give a cross-undertaking in damages in those circumstances. Consideration should also be given to the question whether a cross-undertaking should be given in favour of a person who is not a respondent to the application.

Orders on applications

CHG 5.29

5.29 Any party seeking an order in the Interim Applications court should submit an electronic draft of that order (including backsheet with the solicitor's name and reference) attached to an email addressed to: chanceryinterimorders@hmcts.gsi.gov.uk The emails and orders should be named with a version of the name of the case sufficient to identify it (not necessarily the full name), and should be in Word (.doc) format, and in no circumstances in PDF format.

Form of order when continuing an injunction

CHG 5.30

5.30 An order ("the new order"), the effect of which is to continue an injunction granted by an earlier order ("the original order"), may be drawn up in either of the following ways:

(a)   by writing out in full in the new order the terms of the injunction granted by the original order, amended to give effect to a new expiry date or event; or

(b)   by ordering in the new order that the injunction contained (in a specific paragraph or paragraphs) in the annexed original order is to continue until the new expiry date or event (and annexing the original order);

CHG 5.31

5.31 In general, the better practice is that indicated in 5.30 (a) above, as it expresses in the clearest possible way by reference to a single document exactly what it is that the party restrained is prevented from doing in the period of the continuation.

CHG 5.32

5.32 The practice indicated in 5.30 (b) is also acceptable, but can be cumbersome, particularly where an order is continued several times or where the original order is itself bulky and much of it no longer relevant.

CHG 5.33

5.33 Whilst it is also possible, in principle, to continue an injunction simply by ordering in the new order that the injunction contained (in a specific paragraph or paragraphs) of the original order is to continue until the new expiry date or event (without annexing the original order), this practice has the disadvantage that it is not possible for the party restrained and third parties to see what activities are prevented without cross-referring to another document (which may or may not have been served). This may also give rise to difficulties of enforcement. It is particularly inadvisable to use this form where a litigant in person is involved.

CHG 5.34

5.34 In drafting the new order, consideration should always be given to whether a penal notice should be included.

CHG 5.35

5.35 Care should be taken not to "continue" paragraphs which do not need to be continued because they have been carried out or are no longer appropriate, such as orders requiring information or documents to be disclosed.

CHG 5.36

5.36 It is good practice to recite in the new order that the original order has been made.

Consents by parties not attending hearing

CHG 5.37

5.37 It is commonly the case that on an interim application the respondent does not appear either in person or by solicitors or counsel but the applicant seeks a consent order based upon a letter of consent from the respondent or their solicitors or a draft statement of agreed terms signed by the respondent's solicitors. This causes no difficulty where the agreed relief falls wholly within the relief claimed in the application notice.

CHG 5.38

5.38 If, however, the agreed relief goes outside that which is claimed in the application notice or even in the claim form or when undertakings are offered then difficulties can arise. A procedure has been established for this purpose to be applied to all applications in the Chancery Division.

CHG 5.39

5.39 Subject always to the discretion of the court, no order will be made in such cases unless a consent signed by or on behalf of the respondent to an application is put before the court in accordance with the following provisions:

(1) Where there are solicitors on the record for the respondent the court will normally accept as sufficient a written consent signed by those solicitors on their headed notepaper.

(2) Where there are solicitors for the respondent who are not on the record, the court will normally accept as sufficient a written consent signed by those solicitors on their headed notepaper only if in the consent (or some other document) the solicitors certify that they have fully explained to the respondent the effect of the order and that the respondent appeared to have understood the explanation.

(3) Where there is a written consent signed by a respondent acting in person the court will not normally accept it as sufficient unless the court is satisfied that the respondent understands the effect of the order either by reason of the circumstances (for example the respondent is himself a solicitor or barrister) or by means of other material (for example, the respondent's consent is given in reply to a letter explaining in simple terms the effect of the order).

(4) Where the respondent offers any undertaking to the court (a) the document containing the undertaking must be signed by the respondent personally, (b) solicitors must certify on their headed notepaper that the signature is that of the respondent and (c) if the case falls within (2) or (3) above, solicitors must certify that they have explained to the respondent the consequences of giving the undertaking and that the respondent appeared to understand the explanation.

Bundles and Skeleton Arguments

CHG 5.40

5.40 See Chapter 7 below.

Out of hours emergency arrangements

CHG 5.41

5.41 An application should not be made out of hours unless it is essential. An explanation will be required as to why it was not made or could not be made during normal court hours. Applications made during legal vacations must also constitute vacation business.

CHG 5.42

5.42 There is always a Duty Chancery Judge available to hear urgent out of hours applications. The following is a summary of the procedure:

(1) All requests for the Duty Chancery Judge to hear urgent matters are to be made through the judge's clerk. There may be occasions when the Duty Chancery Judge is not immediately available. The clerk will be able to inform the applicant of the judge's likely availability.

(2)   Initial contact should be through the Royal Courts of Justice (tel: 020 7947 6260), who should be requested to contact the Duty Chancery Judge's clerk. The applicant must give a telephone number for the return call.

(3)   When the clerk contacts the applicant, he or she will need to know:

(a)   the name of the party on whose behalf the application is to be made;

(b)   the name of the person who is to make the application and their status (counsel or solicitor);

(c)   the nature of the application;

(d)   the degree of urgency; and

(e)   contact telephone numbers for the persons involved in the application.

(4)   The Duty Judge will indicate to his or her clerk whether he or she is prepared to deal with the matter by telephone or whether it will be necessary for the matter to be dealt with by a hearing, in court or elsewhere. The clerk will inform the applicant and make the necessary arrangements. The Duty Judge will also indicate how any necessary papers are to be delivered (whether physically or by fax or e-mail)

(5)   Applications for interim injunctions will only be heard by telephone where the applicant is represented by counsel or solicitors (PD 25, Interim Injunctions, paragraph 4.5 (5)).

CHG 5.43

5.43 Which judge will, in appropriate cases, hear an out of hours application varies according to when the application is made.

(1)   Weekdays. Out of hours duty, during term time, is the responsibility of the Interim Applications Judge. The judge is normally available from 4.15pm until 10.15am Monday to Thursday.

(2)   Weekends. A Duty Chancery Judge is nominated by rota for weekends, commencing 4.15pm Friday until 10.15am Monday.

(3)   Vacation. The Vacation Judge also undertakes out of hours applications.

CHG 5.44

5.44 Sealing orders out of hours. In normal circumstances it is not possible to issue a sealed order out of hours. The judge may direct the applicant to lodge a draft of the order made with the Issue Section (ground floor, Rolls Building) by 10 am on the following working day.

CHG 5.45

5.45 County court matters and matters proceeding out of London. Similar arrangements exist for making urgent applications out of hours in county court matters in certain parts of England and Wales and High Court matters proceeding in Chancery District Registries. The pager numbers for regional Urgent Business Officers are given in Appendix 1 to this Guide.

Vacation arrangements

CHG 5.46

5.46 There is a Chancery Judge available to hear applications in vacation. Applications must generally constitute vacation business in that, in particular, they require to be immediately or promptly heard.

CHG 5.47

5.47 In the Long Vacation, two Vacation judges sit each day to hear vacation business. In other vacations there is one Vacation judge. Mondays and Thursdays are made available for urgent Interim Applications on notice. The judge is available on the remaining days for urgent business.

Applications to a Master

CHG 5.48

5.48 Applications to a Master should be made by application notice. Application notices are issued by the Masters' Appointments Section (ground floor, Rolls Building). (There are special arrangements for a CPR Part 23 application that is required to be heard as a matter of urgency—see Paragraph 6.33 below). It is important that application notices are lodged at or addressed to Masters' Appointments, Ground Floor, Rolls Building, 7 Rolls Buildings, Fetter Lane, London, EC4A 1NL and not to a more generalised address such as 'Chancery Division, Rolls Building', or 'Chancery Division, Royal Courts of Justice' as otherwise the listing of the application may be delayed or the application may be wrongly listed before a judge. If the Master has already directed a case management conference the parties should ensure that all applications in the proceedings are properly issued and listed to be heard at the case management conference. If the available listed time is likely to be insufficient to give directions and hear any application the parties should co-operate and invite the court to arrange a longer appointment. It is the duty of the parties to seek to agree directions if possible and to provide a draft of the order for consideration by the Master.

CHG 5.48 [1]

As a matter of practice applications which are sought to be listed at a case management conference or at another existing hearing will be considered by the Master prior to such listing in order that the Master can be satisfied that adequate time is available.

CHG 5.49

5.49 Applications to a Master estimated to last in excess of two hours will require serious co-operation between the parties and will require the Master's directions before they are listed. The Master will normally give his permission to list such an application on condition that there is compliance with directions given by the Master.

CHG 5.49 [1]

Deputy Masters will not give permission for an appointment in excess of two hours. If, therefore, the assigned Master (see 6.28) is not available then either the party seeking to issue the application should await the Master's availability, or, in case of urgency, apply to another permanent Master.

CHG 5.50

5.50 Those directions are likely to require:

(1)   that the applicant agrees the time estimate (see below) with their opponent;
(2)   that, if the time allowed subsequently becomes insufficient, the court is informed and a new and longer appointment given;
(3)   that the parties agree an appropriate timetable for filing evidence such that the hearing will be effective on the date listed;
(4)   that positive confirmation is to be given to the Master five working days before the hearing date that the hearing remains effective; and
(5)   that, in the event of settlement, the Master be informed of that fact, as soon as possible.

CHG 5.51

5.51 The agreed time estimate must identify separately the time for the Master to pre-read any documents required to be pre-read; the hearing time of the application and the time to give any judgment at the conclusion of the hearing. The time for judgment should also take into account any further time that may be required for the Master to assess costs, and for any application for permission to appeal.

CHG 5.52

5.52 Failure to comply with the Master's directions given in respect of the listing of an appointment in excess of two hours may result, depending upon the circumstances, in the application not being heard or in adverse costs orders being made.

CHG 5.53

5.53 On any matter of substance, the Master is likely to require a bundle and skeleton arguments to be provided before the hearing, as detailed in paragraphs 7.40 to 7.50 below. Where directions are given in respect of an application to which paragraph 5.49 applies, the provision of a bundle and skeleton arguments should form part of the agreed timetable.

CHG 5.54

5.54 The Masters are normally available to hear short oral applications without notice between 2.15 pm and 2.45 pm (for the procedure to be followed see paragraph 6.31 below). Such applications are intended for straightforward procedural matters that are capable of being disposed of within 5 to 10 minutes and do not require significant reading or investigation into the substance of the case. An example of a suitable matter might be an application for permission to serve a witness summary. Such applications should not be used for matters which should be dealt with on notice and are likely if notice were given to be contentious.

CHG 5.55

5.55 Letters should not be used in place of a Part 23 application, and parties should be particularly careful to keep any correspondence with the Masters to a minimum and to ensure that opposing parties receive copies of any correspondence. Failure in this regard will mean that the Master will refuse to deal with the correspondence. Correspondence should state that it has been copied to the other parties (or should state why it has not been copied). Unless the matter is one of urgency correspondence and any other documents should be sent by post. If, in a case of real urgency, a letter is sent by fax, it should not be followed by a hard copy, unless it contains an original document which needs to be filed. Further guidance is set out in the Chief Master's Practice Note reproduced at Appendix 5.

CHG 5.56

5.56 There is no distinction between term time and vacation so far as business before the Chancery Masters is concerned. They will deal with all types of business throughout the year. When a Master is on holiday, his or her list will normally be taken by a deputy Master.

Applications for payment out of court

CHG 5.57

5.57 Applications under CPR PD 37 for payment out of money held in court must be made by CPR Part 23 Application Notice (Form N244). The required documents should be sent to the Miscellaneous Payments Clerk—Masters' Appointments/Case Management Section. The following must be included:

(1)   the reasons why the payment should be made (in Part C of the application notice)

(2)   any relevant documents such as birth, marriage or death certificate, title deeds etc. (exhibited to the application notice)

(3)   a statement whether or not anyone else has any claim to the money (in the Statement of Truth)

(4)   bank details, ie the name and address of the relevant bank/building society branch, its Sort Code, and the Account Title and Number; and

(5)   the court fee.

CHG 5.58

5.58 If there is a dispute as to entitlement to money in court, the Master may order the matter to proceed by Part 8 claim (see paragraph 2.14 above). In all other cases the Master will consider the file without a hearing and make an order for payment and/or sign the appropriate payment schedule.

CHAPTER 6 LISTING ARRANGEMENTS

Key Rules: CPR Part 29 and CPR Part 39

CHG 6.1

6.1 This Chapter deals with listing arrangements for hearings before judges and Masters in the Rolls Building, Royal Courts of Justice.

Hearings before judges

Responsibility for listing

CHG 6.2

6.2 Subject to the direction of the Chancellor, the Chancery Judges' Listing Officer, ground floor, Rolls Building has overall responsibility for listing. All applications relating to listing should, in the first instance, be made to the Chancery Judges' Listing Officer, who will refer matters, as necessary, to a judge. Any party dissatisfied with any decision of the Chancery Judges' Listing Officer may, on one clear day's notice to all other parties, apply to the Interim Applications judge. Any such application should be made within seven days of the decision of the Chancery Judges' Listing Officer and be arranged through the Chancery Judges' Listing Office.

CHG 6.3

6.3 There are three main lists in the Chancery Division: the Trial List, the Interim Hearings List and the General List. In addition there is a separate Patents List which is also controlled on a day-to-day basis by the Chancery Judges' Listing Officer in Room WG4 (see Chapter 23).

The Trial List

CHG 6.4

6.4 This comprises a list of all trials to be heard with witnesses.

CHG 6.4 [1]

There are 3 "Listing Categories":

Category "A" being claims of great substance and/or difficulty and/or of public importance, which will be heard only by a High Court Judge. The court must be satisfied that the claim meets the criteria of this category.

Category "B" being claims of substance and/or difficulty, which will be heard either by a High Court Judge (if available) or a Deputy appointed under s 9 of the Senior Courts Act 1981 (**II SCA [9]**).

Category "C" being other claims, which will generally be heard by a Deputy High Court Judge appointed under s 9 of the Senior Courts Act 1981 (**II SCA [9]**).

The Interim Hearings List

CHG 6.5

6.5 This list comprises interim applications and appeals from Masters.

The General List

CHG 6.6

6.6 This list comprises other matters including bankruptcy applications, Part 8 proceedings, applications for judgment and all company matters.

Listing of Cases in the Trial List

CHG 6.7

6.7 The procedure for listing Chancery cases to be heard in the Rolls Building and listed in the Trial List is that at an early stage in the claim the court will give directions with a view to fixing the period during which the case will be heard. In a Part 7 claim that period (the Trial Window) will be determined by the court either when the case is allocated or subsequently at a case management conference or other directions hearing. In a Part 8 claim covered by this procedure, that is to say a Part 8 claim to be heard with witnesses, similar directions will be given when the Part 8 claim is listed for preliminary directions or for a case management conference. It is only in a small minority of Part 8 claims that the claim is tried by a judge in the Trial List and the Trial Window procedure applies. The bulk of Part 8 claims are heard on written evidence either by the Master or by the judge. Additionally, many Part 8 claims, even where oral evidence is to be called, will be heard by the Master pursuant to the jurisdiction set out in paragraph 4.1 of PD 2B Allocation of Cases to Levels of Judiciary.

CHG 6.7 [1]

Many Part 7 cases will fall at the margin between cases which ought to be transferred to a County Court, given a category C listing, or, by consent of the parties, tried by the Master. In that circumstance the court will allocate as between these possibilities, having regard to the wishes of the parties, the availability of judicial resources and the potential date that matters could be brought to trial either in the county court, or before the Master or on the basis of a category C marking. If matters proceed before the Master then the Master will fix a date in his list rather than allocating a trial window.

CHG 6.8

6.8 In determining the Trial Window the court will have regard to the listing constraints created by the existing court list and will determine a Trial Window which provides the parties with enough time to complete their preparations for trial. A Trial Window, once fixed, will not readily be altered. A list of current Trial Windows is published on the HMCS website. When determining the Trial Window the court will direct that one party, normally the claimant, makes an appointment to attend on the Chancery Judges' Listing Officer (ground floor, Rolls Building) to fix a trial date within the Trial Window, by such date as may be specified in the order and gives notice of that appointment to all other parties. It is to be understood that an order to attend on the Chancery Judges' Listing Officer imposes a strict obligation of compliance, without which the Trial Window that has been given may be lost.

CHG 6.9

6.9 At the listing appointment, the Chancery Judges' Listing Officer will take account, insofar as it is practical to do so, of any difficulties the parties may have as to the availability of counsel, experts and witnesses. The Chancery Judges' Listing Officer will, nevertheless, try to ensure the speedy disposal of the trial by arranging a firm trial date as soon as possible within the Trial Window. If a Case Summary has been prepared (see PD 29 paragraphs 5.6 and 5.7) the claimant must produce a copy at the listing appointment together with a copy of the particulars of claim and any orders relevant to the fixing of the trial date. If, exceptionally, at the listing appointment, it appears to the Chancery Judges' Listing Officer that a trial date cannot be provided by the court within the Trial Window, he may fix the trial date outside the Trial Window at the first available date.

CHG 6.10

6.10 A party wishing to appeal a date allocated by the Chancery Judge's Listing Officer must, within 7 days of the allocation, make an application to the Interim Applications judge. The application notice should be filed in the Chancery Judges' Listing Office and served, giving one clear day's notice to the other parties.

CHG 6.11

6.11 A trial date once fixed will, like a Trial Window, only rarely be altered or vacated. An application to adjourn a trial date will normally be made to the Interim Applications judge (see further paragraph 7.39). A contested application may however be entertained by the Master if, for example, on the hearing of an Interim Application or case management conference it becomes clear that the trial date cannot stand without injustice to one or both parties.

CHG 6.11 [1]

A discrete application to vacate a trial date or alter a trial window will also be entertained by the Master if it is made well in advance of the date of trial or of the commencement of the window in question.

Cases in the General and Interim Hearings Lists

CHG 6.12

6.12 Any matters for which no date has been arranged will be liable to appear in the list for hearing with no warning save that given by the next day's cause list: see paragraph 6.17 below.

Estimate of duration

CHG 6.13

6.13 If after a case is listed the estimated length of the hearing is varied, or if the case is settled, withdrawn or discontinued, the solicitors for the parties must forthwith inform the Chancery Judges' Listing Officer in writing. Failure so to do may result in an adverse costs order being made. If the case is settled but the parties wish the Master to make a consent order, the solicitor must notify the Chancery Judges' Listing Officer in writing, whereupon he will take the case out of the list and notify the Master. The Master may then make the consent order.

CHG 6.14

6.14 Seven days before the date for the hearing, the claimant's solicitors must inform the Chancery Judges' Listing Officer whether there is any variation in the estimate of duration, and, in particular, whether the case is likely to be disposed of in some summary way. If the claimant is a litigant in person, this must be done by the solicitor for the first-named defendant who has instructed a solicitor. If a summary disposal is likely, the solicitor must keep the Chancery Judges' Listing Officer informed of any developments as soon as they occur.

Applications after listing for hearing

CHG 6.15

6.15 Where a case has been listed for hearing and because of the timing of the hearing an application needs to be made as a matter of urgency, parties should first consult the Masters' Appointments Section (ground floor, Rolls Building) as to the availability of the assigned Master or, in an appropriate case, applying to the Master himself. Provision can be made for urgent applications to be dealt with in the fortnightly urgent applications list (see further paragraph 6.33). Parties should not list an application before the Interim Applications judge without first consulting the Masters' Appointments Section. If (and only if) a Master cannot hear the application in good time, the application may be made to the Interim Applications judge.

Appeals

CHG 6.16

6.16 All appeals for hearing by High Court judges in the Division are issued by the Chancery Judges' Listing Office, ground floor, Rolls Building. Enquiries relating to such appeals are to be made in the first instance to that Office, except as provided by paragraph 6.18 below.

Daily list of cases

CHG 6.17

6.17 This list, known as the Daily Cause List, is available on the Justice website: h ttp://www.justice.gov.uk, and is also posted electronically each afternoon on the g round floor, Rolls Building.

Listing of Particular Business

CHG 6.18

6.18 Appeals from Masters

(1)   Appeals from Masters, where permission has been given, will appear in the Interim Hearings List. Such appeals (stamped with the appropriate fee) must be filed with the Chancery Judges' Listing Officer, ground floor, Rolls Building. When an appeal is filed an appeal number will be allocated and any future order will bear both the original claim number and the appeal number. On being satisfied that the case has been placed in the Interim Hearings List, solicitors should forthwith inform the Chancery Judges' Listing Officer whether they intend to instruct counsel and, if so, the name or names of counsel.

(2)   Any order made on appeal from a Master will be placed on the court file. However, practitioners should co-operate by ensuring that a copy of any relevant order is available to the Master at any subsequent hearing.

CHG 6.18 [1]

Because, on an appeal, a new appeal file is created by the court, it must not be assumed that papers relating to the appeal will reach the main court file. It is for this reason that it is very helpful if parties ensure that any documents pertaining to an appeal which may be relevant to the future progress of the case are brought to the attention of the Master at or before any subsequent hearing.

CHG 6.19

6.19 Applications for permission to appeal from Masters

Applications for permission to appeal from a decision of a Master (stamped with the appropriate fee) must be lodged in the Chancery Judges' Listing Office (ground floor, Rolls Building). If permission to appeal is granted the appeal will appear in the Interim Hearings List and the procedure set out above will apply.

CHG 6.20

6.20 Bankruptcy Appeals

Notice of appeal from the decision of a Registrar or of a county court should be lodged in the Chancery Judges' Listing Office (ground floor, Rolls Building). The appeal will be entered in the Interim Hearings List, usually with a fixed date. The date of the hearing will be fixed by the Chancery Judges' Listing Officer in the usual way.

CHG 6.21

6.21 Bankruptcy Applications

All originating applications to the judge should be lodged in the Chancery Judges' Listing Office (ground floor, Rolls Building). Urgent applications without notice for: (i) the committal of any person to prison for contempt; or, (ii) injunctions or the modification or discharge of injunctions will be passed directly to the clerk to the Interim Applications Judge for hearing by that judge. All applications on notice for (i) and (ii) above, and applications referred to the judge by the Registrar, will be listed by the Chancery Judges' Listing Officer. Applications estimated not to exceed two hours will be heard by the Interim Applications judge. The Chancery Judges' Listing Officer is to give at least three clear days' notice of the hearing to the applicant and to any respondent who attended before the Registrar. Applications over two hours will be placed in the General List and listed accordingly.

CHG 6.22

6.22 Companies Court

Matters for hearing before the Companies judge, such as applications for an administration order, applications for approval by the court of schemes of arrangement and applications for the appointment of provisional liquidators, may be issued for hearing on any working day in term time (other than the last day of each term). Unopposed applications for the approval of schemes of arrangement will sometimes be heard by a judge before the start of normal sittings. Other applications may be dealt with by the Interim Applications judge as Companies judge. Applications or petitions which are estimated to exceed two hours are liable to be stood over to a date to be fixed by the Chancery Judges' Listing Officer. Urgent applications will also be dealt with by the Interim Applications judge. Applications and petitions referred to the judge by the Registrar will be placed in the General List and listed accordingly.

CHG 6.23

6.23 Applications referred to the judge

Applications referred by the Master to the judge will be added to the Interim Hearings List. The power to refer applications made to the Master and in respect of which the Master has jurisdiction is now very sparingly exercised. The proper use of judicial resources dictates that where the Master has jurisdiction in respect of an application he should ordinarily exercise that jurisdiction. The same principles apply to Registrars.

CHG 6.24

6.24 Judge's Applications

Reference should be made to Chapter 5.

CHG 6.25

6.25 Short Applications

An application for judgment in default made to a judge (because the Master has no jurisdiction) should be made to the Interim Applications Judge.

CHG 6.26

6.26 Summary Judgment

Where an application for summary judgment includes an application for an injunction or a declaration, it usually has to be made to a judge because in most cases the Master cannot grant an injunction or make a declaration save in terms agreed by the parties. In such cases the application should be made returnable before the judge instead of the Master and will be listed in the General List. The return date to be inserted in the application notice should be a Monday at least 14 clear days after the application notice has been served. The application notice should be issued in the Chancery Judges' Listing Office (ground floor, Rolls Building) when there must be lodged two copies of the application notice and the witness statements or affidavits in support together with their exhibits. On the return date the application will normally be adjourned to a date to be fixed if the hearing is likely to take longer than thirty minutes and appropriate directions will be given. The adjourned date will be fixed in the usual way through the Chancery Judges' Listing Officer, and a certificate signed by an advocate as to the estimated length of the hearing must be lodged with the Chancery Judges' Listing Officer.

If the applicant informs the Chancery Judges' Listing Officer at the time of issue of an application notice for summary judgment returnable before a judge that directions have been agreed, or are not necessary, the application will be listed for a substantive hearing without being listed for directions.

If, subsequent to issue, the parties agree directions the Chancery Judges' Listing Officer will, on application, re-list the application for a substantive hearing and any directions hearing will be vacated. Time estimates should be agreed.

CHG 6.27

6.27 Variation of Trusts: Application to a judge

Applications under the Variation of Trusts Act 1958 for a hearing before the judge may be listed for hearing in the General List without any direction by a Master on the lodgement in the Chancery Judges' Listing Office (ground floor, Rolls Building) of a certificate signed by advocates for all the parties, stating (i) that the evidence is complete and has been filed; (ii) that the application is ready for hearing and (iii) the estimated length of the hearing.

Hearings before masters

Assignment of cases before Masters

CHG 6.28

6.28 Claims issued after 21 March 2012 are, as a general rule, allocated to the Chancery Masters by a letter of the alphabet. That letter is to be found after the prefix letters HC (which indicate High Court Chancery) and the first two digits (which indicate the year). For example, in HC12A00001 the letter A indicates the Master.

The assigned Masters are identified as follows:

Chief Master Winegarten   A

Master Bragge	B
Master Bowles	C
Master Price	D
Master Teverson	E
Master Marsh	F

(Before 21 March 2012 claims were, as a general rule, allocated by reference to the last digit of the claim number. These claims are retained to the original Master; those ending with the digit 8 are being dealt with by Master Marsh and those ending with the digit 9 by Chief Master Winegarten.)

Applications by the Official Solicitor under rule 21.13 to be appointed a guardian of a child's estate are normally dealt with by the Chief Master. All applications for a Group Litigation Order in the Chancery Division have to be made to the Chief Master: see paragraph 3.16.

CHG 6.28 [1]

Master Winegarten has now retired and pending his replacement his work is dealt with by Master Bragge, with the assistance of deputies.

CHG 6.29

6.29 An important exception to the general rule is that all registered trade mark claims are assigned to Master Bragge. Practitioners must, therefore, ensure, both at the date of issue of proceedings and when any application is to be made, that the court staff are aware that the claim is a registered trade mark claim and that, irrespective of the claim number, the claim and any application in the claim is assigned to and should be listed before Master Bragge. Each month in term time a day or more is usually set aside in Master Bragge's list specifically for trade mark applications and practitioners should, if possible, seek to have applications listed on that day. If the provisions of this paragraph are ignored and an application in a registered trade mark claim is listed other than before Master Bragge, it is likely that the Master before whom it is listed will refuse to hear it. If Master Bragge is away it is to be expected that the claim will be heard by the Deputy sitting for him.

CHG 6.30

6.30 In addition, from time to time, the Chief Master assigns particular classes of case to particular Masters. This will normally relate to managed litigation where the particular parties will be aware that their cases have been specifically assigned.

Oral applications without notice

CHG 6.31

6.31 Masters are normally available to hear short oral applications without notice between 2.15 pm and 2.45 pm on working days. Notice should be given to the Master's Appointments Section (ground floor, Rolls Building), or by telephone or fax, by 4.30 pm on the previous working day (except in cases of real emergency when notice may be given at any time) so that the file will be before the Master. If this procedure is not followed the Master will be likely to refuse to deal with the application. The Master will expect notice of such an application to have been given in an appropriate case to the other party. This procedure must not be used as a substitute for cases where the issue and service of an Application Notice is appropriate.

CHG 6.32

6.32 If the assigned Master is not available on any particular day, the applicant will be informed and (except in cases of emergency) asked to come when the assigned Master is next available. Applications will only be heard by another Master in cases of emergency or when the assigned Master is on vacation.

Listing arrangements for urgent applications to Masters

CHG 6.33

6.33 There is a fortnightly 'urgent applications' list for urgent Masters' business. It is held from 11.00–1.00 and 2.15–4.30 on every other Wednesday. One Master (in rotation) will take this list (whether or not he is the assigned Master for the case). The following requirements must be observed:

(1)   applicants must certify on the application notice when issued as follows 'I hereby certify that this is urgent business, and cannot await a hearing before the assigned Master in its due turn, because (*specify reasons*). [signed] [dated].' If appropriate, the reasons for urgency may be attached in a covering letter;

(2)   application notices must be issued and served in the usual way;

(3)   an application should not be so listed unless the overall time required to deal with the application is two hours or less. The two hour maximum includes pre-reading, time in court, time for judgment and costs assessment;

(4)   the directions set out in this Guide relating to delivery of bundles and skeleton arguments will apply;

(5)   In the event of a settlement, the Court Office must be informed as soon as possible to allow the listing time to be available for the efficient disposal of other urgent business;

(6)   failure to comply with these arrangements may result in the Master refusing to hear the application and/or in an adverse costs order being made. If the Master is not satisfied that the matter was urgent the case may be put back by him Into the assigned Master's ordinary list to come on for hearing in its due turn;

(7)   this procedure is not to be understood as a substitute for the existing arrangements for listing applications for extensions of time or for 'without notice' applications, in respect of which the existing arrangements will continue to apply; and

(8)   these arrangements do not apply to registered trade mark claims, which continue to be dealt with by Master Bragge in the normal way (see paragraph 6.29 above).

CHG 6.33 [1]

Current experience is that this list is not fully used and that parties, in preference, still seek to list urgent applications before the assigned Masters. Weight of business means that this will not continue to be viable and that the urgent list should be regarded as the first port of call for genuinely urgent business.

CHG 6.34

6.34 See also Chapter 5, paragraphs 5.48 to 5.55 (Applications to Masters).

CHAPTER 7 PREPARATION FOR HEARINGS
Key Rules: CPR Part 29 and CPR Part 39

CHG 7.1

7.1 This Chapter contains guidance on the preparation of cases for hearings before judges and Masters. Guidelines about the conduct of trials are given in Chapter 8 of this Guide. The preparation of witness statements is also covered in Chapter 8.

Hearings before judges

CHG 7.2

7.2 To ensure court time is used efficiently there must be adequate preparation of cases before the hearing. This covers, among other things, the preparation and exchange of skeleton arguments, compiling bundles of documents and dealing out of court with queries which need not concern the court. The parties should also use their best endeavours to agree before any hearing what are the issues or the main issues.

CHG 7.2 [1]

In accordance with Court of Appeal practice the court should be informed at the earliest possible date of any settlement, so that judicial reading time is not wasted. Likewise, if it appears that a case is likely to settle then the court should be kept informed of that fact.

Estimates

CHG 7.3

7.3 Realistic estimates of the length of time a hearing is expected to take must be given.

CHG 7.4

7.4 In estimating the length of a hearing, sufficient time must be allowed for pre-reading any documents required to be read, the length of oral submissions, the time required to examine witnesses (if any), and, if appropriate, an immediate judgment, together with the summary assessment of costs, in cases where that may arise, and any application for permission to appeal.

CHG 7.5

7.5 Except as mentioned below, a written estimate signed by the advocates for all the parties is required in the case of any hearing before a judge. This should be delivered to the Chancery Judges' Listing Officer:

(1)   in the case of a trial, on the application to fix the trial date; and
(2)   in any other case, as soon as possible after the application notice or case papers have been lodged with the Chancery Judges' Listing Office.

CHG 7.6

7.6 If the estimate given in the application notice for an application to the Interim Applications Judge (other than applications by order) or for an application listed before the Companies judge requires to be revised, the revised estimate should be given to the court as soon as practicable, and in any event orally when the application is called on.

Changes in Estimate

CHG 7.7

7.7 The parties must inform the court immediately of any material change in a time estimate. They should keep each other informed of any such change. In any event a further time estimate signed by the advocates to the parties must be lodged when bundles are lodged (see paragraph 7.30 below).

Inaccurate estimates

CHG 7.8

7.8 Where estimates prove inaccurate, a hearing may have to be adjourned to a later date and the party responsible for the adjournment is likely to be ordered to pay the costs thrown away.

Bundles

CHG 7.9

7.9 Bundles of documents for use in court will generally be required for all hearings if more than 25 pages are involved (and may be appropriate even if fewer pages are involved). The efficient preparation of bundles of documents is very important. Where bundles have been properly prepared, the case will be easier to understand and present, and time and costs are likely to be saved. Where documents are copied unnecessarily or bundled incompetently the cost may be disallowed.

CHG 7.10

7.10 Where the provisions of this Guide as to the preparation or delivery of bundles are not followed, the bundle may be rejected by the court or be made the subject of a special costs order.

CHG 7.11

7.11 The claimant or applicant (as the case may be) should begin preparation of the bundles in sufficient time to enable:

(1)   the bundles to be agreed with the other parties (so far as possible);
(2)   references to the bundles to be used in skeleton arguments; and
(3)   the bundles to be delivered to the court at the required time.

CHG 7.12

7.12 The representatives for all parties involved must co-operate in agreeing bundles for use in court. The court and the advocates should all have exactly the same bundles.

CHG 7.13

7.13 When agreeing bundles for trial, the parties should establish through their legal representatives, and record in correspondence, whether the agreement of bundles:

(1)   extends no further than agreement of the composition and preparation of the bundles; or

(2)   includes agreement that the documents in the bundles are authentic (see rule 32.19); or

(3)   includes agreement that the documents may be treated as evidence of the facts stated in them.

The court will normally expect parties to agree that the documents, or at any rate the great majority of them, may be treated as evidence of the facts stated in them. A party not willing to agree should, when the trial bundles are lodged, write a letter to the court (with a copy to all other parties) stating that it is not willing to agree, and explaining why.

CHG 7.14

7.14 Detailed guidelines on the preparation of bundles are set out in Appendix 6, in addition to those in PD 39, Miscellaneous Provisions relating to Hearings, paragraph 3. These must always be followed unless there is good reason not to do so. Particular attention is drawn to the need to consider the preparation of a core bundle.

CHG 7.15

7.15 The general rule is that the claimant/applicant must ensure that one copy of a properly prepared bundle is delivered at the Chancery Judges' Listing Office not less than three clear days (and not more than seven days) before a trial or application by order. However, the court may direct the delivery of bundles earlier than this. Where oral evidence is to be given an additional copy of the bundle must be available in court for the use of the witnesses. In the case of bundles to be used on judge's Applications (other than applications by order) the bundles must be delivered to the clerk to the Interim Applications Judge by 10am on the morning preceding the day of the hearing unless the court directs otherwise. A bundle delivered to the court should always be in final form and parties should not make a request to alter the bundle after it has been delivered to the court save for good reason.

CHG 7.16

7.16 If the case is one which does not require the preparation of a bundle, the advocate should check before the hearing starts that all the documents to which he or she wishes to refer and which ought to have been filed have been filed, and, if possible, indicate to the Associate or in court support staff which they are.

CHG 7.17

7.17 Bundles provided for the use of the court should be removed promptly after the conclusion of the hearing unless the court directs otherwise.

Skeleton Arguments

CHG 7.18

7.18 The general rule is that for the purpose of all hearings before a judge skeleton arguments should be prepared. The exceptions to this general rule are where the application does not warrant one, for example because it is likely to be short, or where the application is so urgent that preparation of a skeleton argument is impracticable or where an application is ineffective and the order is agreed by all parties (see also paragraph 25.12 relating to applications under the Variation of Trusts Act 1958).

CHG 7.19

7.19 In an appropriate case the court may direct sequential rather than simultaneous delivery of skeleton arguments.

Time for delivery of skeleton arguments

CHG 7.20

7.20 In the more substantial matters (e.g. trials and applications by order) – subject to any contrary direction not less than two clear days before the date or first date on which the application or trial is due to come on for hearing; or, if earlier, one clear day before the trial judge is due to begin pre-reading.

CHG 7.21

7.21 On judge's applications without notice - with the papers which the judge is asked to read on the application.

CHG 7.22

7.22 On all other applications to a judge, including interim applications - as soon as possible and not later than 10am on the day preceding the hearing. If a skeleton argument is delivered on the day of the hearing, the judge may not have time to read it before the hearing.

CHG 7.23

7.23 Preparation of skeleton arguments should not be left until notice is given that the case is to be heard. Notice may be given that the case is to be heard the next day.

Place to which skeleton arguments should be delivered

CHG 7.24

7.24 If the name of the judge is not known, or the judge is a Deputy Judge, skeleton arguments should be delivered to the Chancery Judges' Listing Office (ground floor, Rolls Building).

CHG 7.25

7.25 If the name of the judge (other than a Deputy Judge) is known, skeleton arguments should be delivered to the judge's clerk.

CHG 7.26

7.26 Parties should always ask the judge's clerk whether the judge wishes to receive an electronic copy of the skeleton argument by e-mail and, if so, the e-mail address to which the skeleton argument should be sent.

Filing of skeleton arguments by email at the Rolls Building

CHG 7.26A

7.26A From 29 October 2012 a pilot scheme operated at the Rolls Building requiring the lodging by email of skeleton arguments for most hearings where they were up to 25 pages in length. The Judges of the Chancery Division have now decided that the scheme should continue permanently at the Rolls Building. The relevant mailboxes are:

chancery.applications.skeletons@hmcts.gsi.gov.uk: for skeletons for use in the Applications Court; and

chancery.general.skeletons@hmcts.gsi.gov.uk: for all other skeletons.

For further details of the scheme, see paragraph 14.9 below.

Content of skeleton arguments

CHG 7.27

7.27 Appendix 7 contains guidelines which should be followed on the content of skeleton arguments and chronologies, as well as indices and reading lists. Every skeleton argument prepared by an advocate should state at the end his or her name, professional address and contact details (email and telephone).

CHG 7.28

7.28 In most cases before a judge, a list of the persons involved in the facts of the case, a chronology and a list of issues will also be required. The chronology and list of issues should be agreed where possible. The claimant/applicant is responsible for preparing the list of persons involved and the chronology, and they should deliver these and their list of issues (if required) to the court with their skeleton argument.

CHG 7.29

7.29 Unless the court gives any other direction, the parties shall, as between themselves, arrange for the delivery, exchange, or sequential service of skeleton arguments and any list of persons involved, list of issues or chronology. Where there are no such arrangements, all such documents should, where possible, be given to the other parties (if any) in sufficient time before the hearing to enable them properly to consider them.

Reading lists and time estimates

CHG 7.30

7.30 When lodging the agreed bundles, or as soon as practicable thereafter, there should also be lodged a further agreed time estimate, together with an agreed reading list and an agreed time estimate in respect of that reading list. The time estimates and reading list must be signed by the advocates for the parties. Failing agreement as to the time estimates or reading list then separate reading lists and time estimates must be submitted signed by the appropriate advocate. See Appendix 7 as to reading lists.

Failure to lodge bundles or skeleton arguments on time

CHG 7.31

7.31 Failure to lodge skeleton arguments and bundles in accordance with this Guide may result in:

(1)   the matter not being heard on the date in question;
(2)   the costs of preparation being disallowed; and
(3)   an adverse costs order being made.

CHG 7.32

7.32 In the Rolls Building, a log will be maintained of all late skeletons and bundles. The log will regularly be inspected by the Chancellor who will consider such further action as may be appropriate in relation to any recurrent failure by any chambers, barrister, or solicitors firm to comply with the requirements of the CPR and the Guide.

Authorities

CHG 7.33

7.33 Authorities are usually supplied as photocopies. Photocopies of authorities should be of full and not reduced size. Unless copies of authorities are provided, lists of authorities should be supplied to the usher or in court support staff by 9am on the first day of the hearing. Delivery of skeleton arguments does not relieve parties of their duty to deliver lists of authorities to the usher or in court support staff by the time stated.

CHG 7.34

7.34 Advocates should always endeavour to agree and supply a single joint bundle of authorities. If separate bundles have to be provided, every effort should be made to avoid duplication of authorities, or the provision of different reports of the same authority without good reason. Only if such co-operation is impractical, advocates should exchange lists of authorities by 4pm on the day before the hearing. Any failure in this regard which has the effect of increasing the length of a hearing or of giving rise to delay in the hearing of an application may give rise to an adverse costs order.

CHG 7.35

7.35 Excessive citation of authority should be avoided and practitioners must have full regard to *Practice Direction (Citation of Authorities)* [2012] 1 WLR 780. In particular, the citation of authority should be restricted to the expression of legal principle rather than the application of such principle to particular facts. Practitioners must also, when citing authority, seek to ensure that their citations comply with *Practice Direction (Judgments: Neutral Citations)* [2002] 1 WLR 346.

Oral Argument

CHG 7.36

7.36 The court may indicate the issues on which it wishes to be addressed and those on which it wishes to be addressed only briefly.

Documents and Authorities

CHG 7.37

7.37 Only the key part of any document or authority should be read aloud in court.

CHG 7.38

7.38 At any hearing, handing in written material designed to reduce or remove the need for the court to take a manuscript note will assist the court and save time. Any such material should also be available for the judge in electronic form.

Adjournments

CHG 7.39

7.39 As a timetable for the case will have been fixed at an early stage, applications for adjournment of a trial should only be necessary where there has been a change of circumstances not known when the timetable was fixed. Once a trial has been fixed it will rarely be adjourned.

When to apply

(1)   A party who seeks to have a hearing before a judge adjourned must inform the Chancery Judges' Listing Officer of their application as soon as possible.
(2)   Applications for an adjournment immediately before a hearing begins should be avoided as they take up valuable time which could be used for dealing with effective business and, if successful, they may result in a loss of court time altogether.

How to apply

(3)   If the application is agreed, the parties should, in writing, apply to the Chancery Judges' Listing Officer. The Officer will consult the judge nominated for such matters. The judge may grant the application on conditions and give directions as to a new hearing date. But the judge may direct that the application be listed for a hearing and that all parties attend.
(4)   If the adjournment is opposed the party asking for it should apply to the judge nominated for such matters or to the judge to whom the matter has been allocated. A hearing should be arranged, at the first opportunity, through the Chancery Judges' Listing Office.
(5)   A short summary of the reasons for the adjournment should be delivered to the Chancery Judges' Listing Office, where possible by 12 noon on the day before the application is made. Where an application for an adjournment is made on medical grounds, the court will normally require a witness statement and/or medical evidence. The medical evidence should at least take the form of a medical certificate or doctor's letter. In other cases a witness statement may not be required.
(6)   The party requesting an adjournment will, in general, be expected to show that they have conducted their own case diligently. Parties should take all reasonable steps to ensure that their cases are adequately prepared in sufficient time to enable a hearing before the court to proceed. Likewise, they should take reasonable steps to prepare and serve any document (including any written evidence) required to be served on any other party in sufficient time to enable the other party similarly to be adequately prepared.
(7)   If a failure to take reasonable steps necessitates an adjournment, the court may disallow costs as between solicitor and client, or order the person responsible to pay the costs under rule 48.7, or dismiss the application, or make any other order (including an order for the payment of costs on an indemnity basis).
(8)   A trial date may, on occasion, also be vacated by the Master in the circumstances envisaged in paragraph 6.11.

CHG 7.39 [1]
An application to vacate a trial will be entertained by the Master if made well in advance of the trial window.

Hearings before Masters and Registrars

CHG 7.40

7.40 As in the case of hearings before judges, there must be adequate preparation of cases prior to a hearing before the Masters and Registrars. Parties must ensure when issuing applications to be heard by the Masters and Registrars that time estimates are realistic and make proper allowance for the time taken to pre-read any documents required to be read, give judgment and deal with the summary assessment of costs and any application for permission to appeal. The parties must inform the court and all other parties immediately of any material change in a time estimate. Where estimates prove inaccurate, the hearing may have to be adjourned to a later date and the party responsible for the adjournment is likely to be ordered to pay the costs thrown away.

CHG 7.40 [1]

It is good practice and to be encouraged to indicate when issuing and listing an application to identify the pre-reading time and the hearing time separately so that provision for pre-reading can be built into the Masters' lists. This will, or should, eradicate under listing and reduce the number of cases which have to be taken out the list with consequent wasted expense to the parties as well as wasted court resources.

CHG 7.41

7.41 In the case of a hearing before a Master or Registrar which is listed for one hour or more and in any other hearing before a Master or Registrar such as a case management conference, where a bundle would assist, a bundle should be provided.

CHG 7.42

7.42 Bundles must be provided for a trial or equivalent hearing (such as an account or inquiry or a Part 8 claim with oral evidence) which is listed before a Master or a Registrar. Such bundles must comply with Appendix 6 and contain or be accompanied by a reading list and an estimate of reading time as set out in paragraph 7.30 above.

CHG 7.43

7.43 Parties should always ask whether the Master or Registrar wishes to receive an electronic copy of the skeleton argument by e-mail and, if so, the e-mail address to which the skeleton argument should be sent.

CHG 7.44

7.44 Bundles provided for the use of the Master or Registrars should be removed promptly after the conclusion of the hearing unless the Master or Registrar directs otherwise.

Delivery of bundles for hearings before Masters

CHG 7.45

7.45

(1)   Bundles should be delivered to Masters' Appointments, ground floor, Rolls Building, not less than 2 (and not more than 7) clear working days before the hearing. They should be clearly marked "For hearing on . . . . [date] before Master . . . . " They must not be taken to the Registry Issue Section or the Chancery Judges' Listing Office, and no document required for any hearing must be taken to the RCJ or Rolls Building post room. Documents delivered to the wrong place are unlikely to reach the Master in time for the hearing, resulting in probable postponement and the party responsible for the adjournment is likely to be ordered to pay the costs thrown away.
(2)   Detailed guidance on where to deliver documents in the Rolls Building is at Appendix 8.
(3)   Where no bundle is provided for the use of the Master, but a party intends to rely on the exhibits to a witness statement or affidavit, that party must ensure that those documents are filed with the court in sufficient time to be

available to be read by the Master in advance of the hearing. Documents filed less than 10 days before a hearing must be taken to Masters' Appointments, ground floor, Rolls Building, for filing and marked "For hearing on . . . . *[date]* before Master . . . ." (Documents filed before that time should be filed in the Issue Section, ground floor, Rolls Building, in the normal way). Exhibits should not be placed in lever arch files but should be fastened securely, for example by treasury tags.

Delivery of bundles for hearings before Bankruptcy Registrars

CHG 7.46

7.46 Bundles should be delivered to the Registrars' Enquiries Office (1st Floor, Rolls Building) not less than 2 (and not more than 7) clear working days before the hearing. The should be clearly marked "For hearing on . . . . *[date]* before Registrar . . . ."

Delivery of bundles for hearings before Companies Court Registrars

CHG 7.47

7.47 Bundles should be delivered to the Registrars' Enquiries Office (1st Floor, Rolls Building) not less than 2 (and not more than 7) clear working days before the hearing. They should be clearly marked "For hearing on . . . . *[date]* before Registrar . . . ."

Late delivery of bundles for hearings before Masters and Registrars

CHG 7.48

7.48 Parties delivering bundles should note that a log will be kept recording the time of their delivery to the Registrars' Enquiries Office and Masters' Appointments. Any failure to comply with these requirements which results in the postponement of a hearing may render that party liable to pay the costs occasioned by the adjournment.

Note: Bundles for hearings before a Chancery judge must be delivered to the Chancery Judges' Listing Office (ground floor, Rolls Building).

Skeleton arguments

CHG 7.49

7.49 Skeleton arguments should normally be prepared in respect of any application before the Master or Registrar of one or more hours' duration and certainly for any trial or similar hearing. They are to be delivered to the same place and at the same time as bundles. The contents of the skeleton argument should be in accordance with Appendix 7.

CHG 7.50

7.50 Where a skeleton argument is required, photocopies of any authorities to be relied upon should accompany the skeleton argument.

CHG 7.51

7.51 If pursuant to the e-mail protocol for communications with the Chancery Division (paragraph 14.8 below), a skeleton argument is sent electronically, then the provisions of the protocol as well as the time limits set out above must be followed. In particular, any authorities relied on should not be attached to the electronic version of the skeleton argument; but should be delivered in hard form and, where it would assist, be accompanied by a copy of the skeleton argument in hard form.

CHG 7.52

7.52 Failure to deliver skeleton arguments or bundles in accordance with this Guide is likely to result in the matter not being heard on the date fixed, the costs of preparation being disallowed and an adverse costs order being made.

Compromise or settlement of hearings

CHG 7.53

7.53 When hearings before Masters are compromised or settled, Masters' Appointments (ground floor, Rolls Building) should be informed in writing immediately and in any event no later than 4pm on the day preceding the hearing. In the case of substantial hearings involving pre-reading Masters' Appointments should be informed immediately if it appears likely that a hearing will be ineffective, with a request that the Master is immediately notified. Written notification must similarly be given to the Registrars' Enquiries Office (1st floor, Rolls Building) for bankruptcy and companies hearings. Failure to notify and consequent waste of court time may result in an adverse costs order being made.

CHG 7.53 [1]

It is helpful to the court, in the event that a case appears to the parties to be likely to settle if, in respect of any substantial matter, the court is informed of that likelihood as soon as it arises.

CHAPTER 8 CONDUCT OF A TRIAL

Key Rules: CPR Part 32 and CPR Part 39

CHG 8.1

8.1 An important aim of all concerned must be to ensure that at trial court time is used as efficiently as possible. Thorough preparation of the case prior to trial is the key to this.

CHG 8.2

8.2 Chapter 7 of this Guide applies to preparation for a trial as well as for other hearings in court. This Chapter contains matters which principally affect trials.

Time limits

CHG 8.3

8.3 The court may, either at the outset of the trial or at any time thereafter, fix time limits for oral submissions, and the examination and cross-examination of witnesses. (See paragraphs 3.18 - 19.)

Oral Submissions

CHG 8.4

8.4 In general, and subject to any direction to the contrary by the trial judge, there should be a short opening statement on behalf of the claimant, at the conclusion of which the judge may invite short opening statements on behalf of the other parties.

CHG 8.5

8.5 Unless notified otherwise, advocates should assume that the judge will have read their skeleton arguments and the principal documents referred to in the reading list lodged in advance of the hearing (see paragraph 7.30). The judge will state at an early stage how much he or she has read and what arrangements are to be made about reading any documents not already read, for which an adjournment of the trial after opening speeches may be appropriate. If the judge needs to read any documents additional to those mentioned in the reading list lodged in advance of the hearing, a list should be provided during the opening.

CHG 8.6

8.6 It is normally convenient for any outstanding procedural matters to be dealt with in the course of, or immediately after, the opening statements.

CHG 8.7

8.7 After the evidence is concluded, and subject to any direction to the contrary by the trial judge, oral closing submissions will be made on behalf of the claimant first, followed by the defendant(s) in the order in which they appear on the claim form, followed by a reply on behalf of the claimant. In a lengthy and complex case each party should provide written summaries of their closing submissions.

CHG 8.8

8.8 The court may require the written summaries to set out the principal findings of fact for which a party contends.

Witness Statements

CHG 8.9

8.9 In the preparation of witness statements for use at trial, the guidelines in Appendix 9 should be followed.

CHG 8.10

8.10 If a witness wishes to deal with matters not dealt with in the original witness statement a supplementary witness statement should be prepared and served on the other parties, as soon as possible Permission is required to adduce a supplementary witness statement at trial if any other party objects to it. This need not be sought before service; it can be sought at a case management conference if convenient or, if need be, at trial.

CHG 8.11

8.11 Witnesses are expected to have re-read their witness statements shortly before they are called to give evidence.

CHG 8.12

8.12 Where a party decides not to call a witness whose witness statement has been served to give oral evidence at trial, prompt notice of this decision should be given to all other parties. The party should make plain when they give this notice whether he or she proposes to put, or seek to put, the witness statement in as hearsay evidence. If they do not put the witness statement in as hearsay evidence, rule 32.5(5) allows any other party to put it in as hearsay evidence.

CHG 8.13

8.13 Facilities may be available to assist parties or witnesses with special needs, whether as regards access to the court, or audibility in court, or otherwise. The Chancery Judges' Listing Office should be notified of any such needs prior to the hearing. The Rolls Building Management Team (tel 020 7947 7899) can also assist with parking, access etc. Similar facilities may be available at courts outside the Rolls Building.

Expert Evidence

CHG 8.14

8.14 The trial judge may disallow expert evidence which either is not relevant for any reason, or which the judge regards as excessive and disproportionate in all the circumstances, even though permission for the evidence has been given.

CHG 8.15

8.15 The evidence of experts (or of the experts on a particular topic) is commonly taken together at the same time and after the factual evidence has been given. If this is to be done it should be agreed by the parties before the trial and should be raised with the judge at the PTR, if there is one, or otherwise at the start of the trial. Expert evidence should as far as possible be given by reference to the reports exchanged.

Physical exhibits

CHG 8.16

8.16 Some cases involve a number of physical exhibits. The parties should try to agree the exhibits in advance and their system of labelling. Where it would be desirable, they should agree a scheme of display (e.g. on a board with labels readable from a distance). Where witness statements refer to these, a note in the margin (which can be handwritten) of the exhibit number should be added.

CHAPTER 9 JUDGMENTS, ORDERS AND PROCEEDINGS AFTER JUDGMENT

Key Rules: CPR Part 40, and CPR PD 40A, CPR PD 40B, CPR PD 40D AND CPR PD 40E

Judgments

CHG 9.1

9.1 Where judgment is reserved, the judge will normally deliver his or her judgment by handing down the written text without reading it out in open court. Where this course is adopted, the advocates will be supplied with the full text of the draft judgment in advance of delivery. In such cases, the advocates should familiarise themselves with the text of the judgment and be ready to deal with any points which may arise when judgment is delivered. The parties should seek to agree any consequential orders: see CPR PD 40E paragraph 4.1.

CHG 9.2

9.2 The text may be shown, in confidence, to the parties, but only for the purpose of obtaining instructions and on the strict understanding that the judgment, or its effect, is not to be disclosed to any other person, or used in the public domain, and that no action is taken (other than internally) in response to the judgment. Advocates should notify the judge's clerk of any obvious errors or omissions: see CPR PD 40E paragraph 3.1.

CHG 9.3

9.3 The judgment does not take effect until formally delivered in court, when, if requested and so far as practicable, it will be made available to the law reporters and the press. The judge will normally direct that the written judgment may be used for all purposes as the text of the judgment, and that no transcript of the judgment need be made. Where such a direction is made, copies of a judgment delivered in the Rolls Building may be obtained from the Court Recording and Transcription Unit in the Royal Courts of Justice (see Appendix 1). Elsewhere, the court will supply a copy.

CHG 9.3 [1]

Paragraphs 9.1 to 9.3 apply also to reserved judgments given by the Masters. Where a reserved judgment is delivered to the parties prior to the judgment being formally handed down and prior to any order implementing the judgment being drawn the parties will sometimes seek to persuade the Judge or Master to reopen his or her judgment. Such applications are to be discouraged and, while jurisdiction exists, will only be acceded to in very rare cases. Because the judgment does not take effect until formal handing down, but is until that time regarded as a draft, time does not begin to run for purposes of any appeal or application in relation to appeal until formal handing down has taken place (see further the note at **CHG 10.11 [1]**).

CHG 9.4

9.4 If the parties have agreed the form of the order and any consequential orders, and have supplied the judge with a draft, judgment may be handed down without the need for an attendance.

Orders

CHG 9.5

9.5 It may often be possible for the court to prepare and seal an order more quickly if a draft of the order is handed in. Speed may be particularly important where the order involves the grant of an interim injunction or the appointment of a receiver without notice. In all but the most simple cases a draft order should be prepared and brought to the hearing.

CHG 9.6

9.6 The court may direct the parties to agree and sign a draft order. Where the proceedings are in the Rolls Building, the draft order should, when agreed and signed, be delivered (if it is a judge's order) to the relevant judge's clerk or (if it is a Master's order) to the Master's clerk (ground floor, Rolls Building). In the case of any dispute or difficulty as to the contents of the order, the parties should mention the matter to the judge or Master who heard the application and should do so with expedition.

CHG 9.7

9.7 Where a draft or an agreed statement of the terms of an order exists in electronic form, it is often helpful if the draft or agreed statement is provided to the court by e-mail or on a digital storage device as well as in hard copy, particularly if the order needs to be drawn quickly. Any digital storage device supplied for this purpose must be new and newly-formatted before writing the material on it so as to minimise the risk of transferring a computer virus. The current word processing system used by the Chancery Associates is Microsoft Windows 2003. Enquiries regarding the provision of digital storage devices should be made of the Associate responsible for drawing the order in question.

CHG 9.8

9.8 Any party seeking an order in the Interim Applications court must submit an electronic draft of that order: see paragraph 5.29.

CHG 9.9

9.9 Further guidance on the drafting of orders by the parties may be found in Appendix 14.

Drafting and Service of Orders

CHG 9.10

9.10 Orders will be drawn up by the court, unless the judge or Master directs that no order be drawn. Unless a contrary order is made, or the party concerned has asked to serve the order, a sealed order will be sent by the court to each party.

CHG 9.11

9.11 Where a particular order is required to be served personally, the party concerned (see above) will be responsible for service.

Forms of Order

CHG 9.12

9.12 Recitals will be kept to a minimum and the body of the order will be confined to setting out the decision of the court and the directions required to give effect to it. If upon receipt of an order any party is of the view that it is not drawn up in such a way as to give effect to the decision of the court, prompt notice must be given to the Associate concerned (5th floor, Rolls Building) and to all other parties setting out the reasons for dissatisfaction. If the differences cannot be resolved, the objecting party may apply on notice for the order to be amended and should do so promptly.

Copies of Orders

CHG 9.13

9.13 Copies of orders may be obtained from the File Management Section (ground floor, Rolls Building) upon payment of the appropriate fee.

Consent Orders

CHG 9.14

9.14 All consent orders filed in Chancery Chambers and in respect of which a fee has been paid are referred to the Master for approval before the order is sealed. Such orders should be delivered to Masters' Appointments (ground floor, Rolls Building).

Consents by parties not attending the hearing.

CHG 9.15

9.15 This is covered in paragraphs 5.37-5.39 above.

Tomlin Orders

CHG 9.16

9.16

"And the parties having agreed to the terms set out in the attached schedule

IT IS BY CONSENT ORDERED

That all further proceedings in this claim be stayed except for the purpose of carrying such terms into effect

AND for that purpose the parties have permission to apply".

9.16 Where proceedings are to be stayed on agreed terms to be scheduled to the order, the draft order should be drawn so as to read, with any appropriate provision in respect of costs, as follows:

Any direction for:

(1)   payment of money out of court, or
(2)   payment and assessment of costs

should be contained in the body of the order and not in the schedule.

This form of order is called a "Tomlin Order". If the order refers to a confidential schedule or agreement, this must be filed with the order but with a prominent request that it be treated as a confidential document not open to inspection to be retained in a sealed envelope on the court file and marked "Not to be inspected without the permission of the Master or judge".

Note that it is not the normal practice of the judges of the Chancery Division to inspect schedules or agreements annexed to Tomlin Orders. The judge who makes the order undertakes no responsibility for the scheduled terms and cannot be taken to have approved them.

CHG 9.16 [1]

In many cases the court will be prepared to approve a consent order in Tomlin form; the order simply recording that terms have been agreed in a particular and identifiable document without the necessity for lodgement of that document.

Proceedings after judgment

CHG 9.17

9.17 Proceedings under judgments and orders in the Chancery Division are now regulated by PD 40 Accounts, Inquiries etc., PD40B Judgments and Orders, and PD40D Court's Powers in relation to Land etc.

Directions

CHG 9.18

9.18 Where a judgment or order directs further proceedings or steps, such as accounts or inquiries, it will often give directions as to how the accounts and inquiries are to be conducted, for example:

for accounts

(1)   who is to lodge the account and within what period;
(2)   within what period objection is to be made; and
(3)   arrangements for inspection of vouchers or other relevant documents;

for inquiries

(4)   whether the inquiry is to proceed on written evidence or with statements of case;
(5)   directions for service of such evidence or statements; and
(6)   directions as to disclosure.

CHG 9.19

9.19 If directions are not given in the judgment or order an application should be made to the assigned Master as soon as possible asking for such directions. The application notice should specify the directions sought. Before making the application, applicants should write to the other parties setting out the directions they seek and inviting their response within 14 days. The application to the court should not be made until after the expiry of that period unless there is some special urgency. The application must state that the other parties have been consulted and have attached to it copies of the applicant's letter to the other parties and of any response from them. The Master will then consider what directions are appropriate. In complex cases the Master may direct a case management conference.

CHG 9.20

9.20 If any inquiry is estimated to last more than two days and involves very large sums of money or strongly contested issues of fact or difficult points of law, the Master may direct that it be heard by a judge. The parties are under an obligation to consider whether in any particular case the inquiry is more suitable to be heard by a judge and should assist the Master in this. Accounts, however long they are estimated to take, will normally be heard by the Master. The Master is likely to want to give detailed directions in connection with the account and the form of it.

CHG 9.20 [1]

Parties should always consider very carefully the appropriate directions which are needed to bring to a resolution the issues raised in an account. Without very careful thought by the parties and the court there are serious dangers that an account will become cumbersome, inordinately expensive and wholly disproportionate to the matters in issue.

Registration of judgments

CHG 9.21

9.21 Under the Register of Judgments, Orders and Fines Regulations 2005, money judgments in claims commenced in the High Court after 6th April 2006 (unless exempt) are registered with the Registrar of Judgments, Orders and Fines. Returns are sent to the Registrar by the court. In non-contested cases (judgments in default or on admission) registration is immediate. In contested cases the judgment is not registered unless steps are taken to enforce it under Part 70 or Part 71.

CHG 9.22

9.22 Judgments which are the subject of an appeal under Part 52 are not registered until the appeal has been determined. The court officer responsible for returns (Andrew Pooley, 5th floor, Rolls Building, tel 0207 947 6528) should be informed if permission to appeal is granted after a judgment has been registered, and he should also be informed when an application is made under Part 70 or Part 71.

CHG 9.23

9.23 If the judgment debt is satisfied, the judgment has been set aside or reversed, or the amount of the debt increases as a result of the issue of a final costs certificate or an increase in the amount of the debt as a consequence of enforcement proceedings, the court officer responsible for returns (as above) should be notified.

CHAPTER 10 APPEALS

Key Rules: CPR Part 52 and CPR PD 52A, CPR PD 52B, CPR PD 52D, CPR PD (Insolvency Proceedings), Part 4, Paragraph 19: Appeals; CPR PD (Directors' Disqualification Proceedings) Paras 35.1–35.2

General

CHG 10.1

10.1 This Chapter is concerned with the following appeals affecting the Chancery Division:

(1)   appeals within the ordinary work of the Division, from Masters to High Court judges;

(2)   insolvency appeals from High Court Registrars and from county courts to High Court judges;

(3)   appeals to High Court judges in the Chancery Division from orders in claims proceeding in a county court; and

(4)   statutory appeals to the Chancery Division.

Proceedings under the Companies Acts (and other legislation relating to companies and limited liability partnerships) are specialist proceedings for the purposes of CPR 49 and therefore as regards the destination of appeals. In those cases appeals from final decisions by a Registrar of the Companies Court go direct to the Court of Appeal: see the table in CPR PD 52A paragraph 3.5. Such appeals are not covered in this Chapter. Most appeals from tribunals are now dealt with by the Upper Tribunal, which is not covered by this Guide. Appeals from some other bodies (eg the Comptroller of Patents) still lie to the court.

CHG 10.2

10.2 This Chapter does not deal with appeals from High Court judges of the Division, except as regards permission to appeal, and as to giving notice to the court of an appeal in a contempt case. It does not deal with appeals in the course of the detailed assessment of costs.

CHG 10.3

10.3 The detailed procedure for appeals is set out in Part 52 and in PD 52, and in the PD relating to Insolvency Proceedings, to which reference should be made. This Chapter only refers to some of the salient points.

Permission to appeal

CHG 10.4

10.4 Permission to appeal is required in all cases except: (a) appeals against committal orders, and (b) certain statutory appeals. Permission to appeal will be given only where the court considers that the appeal would have a real prospect of success or there is some other compelling reason why the appeal should be heard (rule 52.3(6)). An application for permission to appeal may be made to the lower court, but only if it is made at the hearing at which the decision to be appealed was made. However, the court has power to adjourn that hearing for the purpose of considering any application for permission to appeal. If the lower court refuses permission, or permission is not applied for to the lower court, an application may be made to the appeal court by Appellant's Notice.

CHG 10.5

10.5 An application to the appeal court for permission may be dealt with without a hearing, but if refused without a hearing the applicant is normally entitled to request that it be reconsidered at a hearing. If, however, the judge who refuses permission considers that the application is totally without merit, he or she may refuse permission for the application to be reconsidered. Notice of the hearing is often given to the respondent; the respondent may submit written representations or attend the hearing but will not usually be awarded any costs of so doing even if permission to appeal is refused. The judge who hears the oral application will usually be the same judge who dealt with the application on the papers.

CHG 10.6

10.6 Guidance for litigants in relation to appeals to the High Court is available by way of a Guide to High Court Appeals which may be obtained from the Chancery Judges' Listing Office, ground floor, Rolls Building.

CHG 10.7

10.7 A party who wishes to appeal to the High Court must lodge, with the appellant's notice, the documents set out in CPR PD 52B paragraph 4.2. The remaining documents which are required to make up the appeal bundle, including a transcript of the judgment under appeal, must be filed within 35 days. This period may be extended by a judge, who will consider any application for an extension on paper. If there is a delay in obtaining a transcript of the judgment to be appealed, the appellant should try to obtain a note of the judgment, which the lawyers representing any party at the hearing below ought to be able to provide, at least as an interim measure before a transcript is obtained.

CHG 10.8

10.8 If the documents required for consideration of an application for permission to appeal to the High Court have not been lodged, despite any extension which has been allowed, the case may be listed for oral hearing in the Dismissal List, for the appellant to show cause why the case should not be dismissed. The respondent will not normally be notified of such a hearing.

CHG 10.8 [1]

Where a reserved judgment is sent to the parties in writing (as is now common practice) it will be sent as a draft so that time will not begin to run for appeal on receipt but only when the judgment is formally handed down. If the order to be made resultant upon the judgment is agreed then the parties will often not have to attend the handing down of judgment. If there is no agreement then judgment will be handed down at a hearing and time will begin to run from the date of that hearing. The court may also hand down judgment in the absence of the parties and then adjourn the hearing and extend time for any application for permission to appeal in order to allow application for permission to appeal to be made on the restored hearing.

Stay

CHG 10.9

10.9 Unless the lower court or the appeal court orders otherwise, an appeal does not operate as a stay of any order or decision of the lower court. A stay of execution may be applied for in the appellant's notice. If it is, it may be dealt with on paper. If the stay is required as a matter of great urgency, or before the appellant's notice can be filed, an application should be made to the Interim Applications Judge.

Appeals from Masters in cases proceeding in the Chancery Division

CHG 10.10

10.10 If permitted, an appeal from a decision of a Master in a case proceeding in the Chancery Division usually lies to a High Court judge of the Division. An appeal from a final decision of a Master in a Part 7 claim allocated to the multi-track lies direct to the Court of Appeal.

CHG 10.10 [1]

In some instances an appeal from the Master will lie directly to the Court of Appeal. Those cases are where a Part 7 claim has been allocated to the multi track and tried by the Master with the consent of the parties, or where the Master has determined an account or an inquiry within a Part 7 Claim; where a Part 8 claim is tried by the Master but where, unusually, that claim has been expressly allocated to the multi track; and where the Master directs that the appeal be transferred directly to the Court of Appeal pursuant to CPR 52.14 (important point of principle or practice).

Provisions exist under paragraph 5.17 of the Practice Direction to CPR 52 for the court to order the provision of transcripts of judgments and of evidence at public expense. Application can be made either at the hearing to which the proposed transcript relates or by subsequent application. In respect of applications for transcripts of judgments an order will be made if the court is satisfied that the order is justified by the applicant's financial circumstances. In respect of transcripts of evidence the court will also have to be satisfied that the proposed appeal to which the application relates has reasonable prospects of success.

Insolvency appeals

CHG 10.11

10.11 An appeal lies from a county court (Circuit or District Judge) or a High Court Registrar in bankruptcy or Company insolvency matters to a High Court judge of the Chancery Division. An appeal against a decision of a District Judge sitting in a county court must be lodged at an Appeal Centre on the same circuit as that county court. Permission to appeal is required. Additional guidance for litigants in insolvency appeals is available on the MOJ website www.justice.gov.uk/courts/rcj-rolls-building/chancery-division/appeals.

CHG 10.12

10.12 Appeals in proceedings under the Company Directors Disqualification Act 1986 are treated as being in insolvency proceedings.

Appeals from orders made in county court claims

CHG 10.13

10.13 An appeal against a decision of a Circuit Judge in a claim proceeding in a county court lies to the High Court, unless, either, the decision is a final decision in a claim allocated to the multi-track or in specialist proceedings to which rule 49 applies, or the decision is itself on an appeal. In either of these cases the appeal lies direct to the Court of Appeal. This does not apply, however, where the allocation to the multi-track is deemed, rather than the result of a specific order, so that in cases begun by a Part 8 claim form, even though they are deemed to be so allocated, appeals lie to the High Court. The general rules as to the requirement for permission described above apply to these appeals. Any appeal to the High Court must be lodged at an Appeal Centre on the same circuit as the county court where the order under appeal was made. A full list of appeal centres is set out in Table B of CPR PD 52B.

Statutory appeals

CHG 10.14

10.14 The Chancery Division hears a variety of appeals and cases stated under statute from decisions of tribunals and other persons. Some of these are listed or referred to in PD 52D, but this is not exhaustive. However, most appeals from tribunals are now dealt with by the Upper Tier Tribunal.

Appeals to the Court of Appeal: permission to appeal

CHG 10.15

10.15 An appeal lies from a judgment of a High Court judge of the Division to the Court of Appeal (unless an enactment makes it final and unappealable), but permission is required in all cases except where the order is for committal. Permission may be granted by the High Court judge, if applied for at the hearing at which the decision to be appealed was made, unless the order of the High Court judge was itself on an appeal (other than an appeal from the Comptroller of Patents), in which case permission may only be granted by the Court of Appeal.

Appeals in cases of contempt of court

CHG 10.16

10.16 Appellant's notices which by CPR PD 52D paragraph 9.1 are required to be served on 'the court from whose order or decision the appeal is brought' may be served, in the case of appeals from the Chancery Division, on the Chief Master of the Chancery Division; service may be effected by leaving a copy of the notice of appeal with the Chancery Judges' Listing Office, ground floor, Rolls Building.

Dismissal by consent

CHG 10.17

10.17 The practice is as set out in CPR PD 52A paragraph 6, for all appeals. Where the appeal is proceeding in the High Court a document signed by all parties or their legal representatives must be lodged with the Chancery Judges' Listing Office (ground floor, Rolls Building), requesting dismissal of the appeal. The appeal can be dismissed without any hearing by an order made in the name of the Chancellor. Any orders with directions as to costs will be drawn by the Chancery Associates.

CHAPTER 11 COSTS

Key Rules: CPR Part 43 to CPR Part 48 and the PD supplementing them[1]

CHG 11.1

11.1 This Chapter does not set out to do more than refer to some salient points on costs relevant to proceedings in the Chancery Division. In particular it does not deal with the processes of detailed assessment or appeals in relation to such assessments. In this Chapter the "paying party" is the party by whom the costs are to be paid; and the "receiving party" is the party to whom the costs are to be paid.

CHG 11.2

11.2 A number of provisions in respect of costs in the CPR and in the PD supplementing Parts 43 to 48 (Costs PD) are likely to be relevant to Chancery proceedings:

(1)   *Informing the client of costs orders*: Solicitors have a duty to tell their clients, within 7 days, if an order for costs is made against them and they were not present at the hearing. Solicitors must also tell anyone else who has instructed them to act on the case or who is liable to pay their fees. They must inform these persons how the order came to be made (rule 44.2; Costs PD, paragraph 7.1).

(2)   *Providing the court with estimates of costs*: The court can order a party to file an estimate of costs and to serve it on the other parties. (Costs PD, paragraph 6.3). This is to assist the court in deciding what case management orders to make and also to inform other parties as to their potential liability for costs. In addition, represented parties must file estimates of costs when they file their allocation questionnaire or any listing questionnaire (Costs PD, paragraph 6.4).

(3)   *Summary assessment of costs*: An outline of these provisions is given below. Their effect is that in the majority of contested hearings lasting no more than a day the court will decide, at the end of the hearing, not only who is to pay the costs but also how much those costs should be, and will order them to be paid, usually within 14 days. As a result the paying party will have to pay the costs at an early stage.

(4)   *Interim orders for costs*: Where the court decides immediately who is to pay particular costs, but does not assess the costs summarily, for example after a trial lasting more than a day, so that the final amount of costs payable has to be fixed by a detailed assessment, the court may (and usually will) order the paying party to pay a sum or sums on account of the ultimate liability for costs.

(5)   *Interest on costs*: The court has power to award interest on costs from a date before the date of the order, so compensating the receiving party for the delay between incurring the costs and receiving a payment in respect of them from the paying party.

(6)   *Costs capping orders*: The court has power to make an order limiting the amount of future costs (including disbursements) which a party may recover under a subsequent costs order in that party's favour, if the conditions in CPR 44.18(5) are satisfied. For the relevant criteria and procedure, see CPR 44.18 to CPR 44.20 and Costs PD, sections 23A and (in relation to proceedings concerning trust funds) 23B.

CHG 11.2 [1]

As from 1 April 2013 the court will, in the majority of cases, also be closely involved in costs management and costs budgeting in respect of multitrack litigation. See further **CHG 3.10 [1]** above.

Summary Assessment

CHG 11.3

11.3 The court will generally make a summary assessment of costs whenever the hearing lasts for less than one day. The judge or Master who heard the application or other hearing (which will include a trial, or the hearing of a Part 8 Claim, lasting less than a day) carries out the summary assessment. The court may decide not to assess costs summarily either because it orders the costs to be "costs in the case" or because it considers the case to be otherwise inappropriate for summary assessment, typically because substantial issues arise as to the amount of the costs claimed. Costs payable to a party funded by the Legal Services Commission cannot be assessed summarily.

CHG 11.3 [1]

Where costs are substantial and not suitable for summary assessment the court will very often exercise its power to order the payment of a sum of money by way of an interim order and upon account of the costs to which the receiving party will ultimately be entitled.

CHG 11.4

11.4 In order that the court can assess costs summarily at the end of the hearing each party who intends to claim costs must, no later than 24 hours before the time fixed for the hearing, serve on the other party, and file with the court, his or her statement of costs. Paragraph 13.5 of the Costs PD contains requirements about the information to be included in this statement, and the form of the statement. Failure by a party to file and serve his or her statement of costs as required by paragraph 13.5 of the Costs PD will be taken into account by the court in deciding what order to make about costs and could result in a reduced assessment, in no order being made as to costs, or in the party being penalised in respect of the costs of any further hearing or detailed assessment hearing which may be required as a result of the party's failure.

CHG 11.5

11.5 Where the receiving party is funded by the Legal Services Commission the court cannot assess costs summarily. It is not, however, prevented from assessing costs summarily by the fact that the paying party is so funded. A summary assessment of costs payable by a person funded by the Legal Services Commission is not by itself a determination of the amount of those costs which the funded party is to pay (as to which see section 11 of the Access to Justice Act 1999 and regulation 10 of the Community Legal Services (Costs) Regulations 2000). Ordinarily, where costs are summarily assessed and ordered to be paid by a funded person the order will provide that the determination of any amount which the person who is or was in receipt of services funded by the Legal Services Commission is to pay shall be dealt with in accordance with regulation 10 of the Regulations.

Basis of assessment

CHG 11.6

11.6 The amount of costs to be paid by one person to another can be determined on the standard basis or the indemnity basis. The basis to be used is determined when the court decides that a person should pay the costs of another. The usual basis is the standard basis and this is the basis that will apply if the order does not specify the basis of assessment. Costs that are unreasonably incurred or are unreasonable in amount are not allowed on either basis.

CHG 11.7

11.7 On the standard basis the court only allows costs which are proportionate to the matters in issue. If it has any doubt as to whether the costs were reasonably incurred or reasonable and proportionate in amount, it resolves the doubt in favour of the paying party. The concept of proportionality will always require the court to consider whether the costs which have been incurred were warranted having regard to the issues involved. A successful party who incurs costs which are disproportionate to the issues involved and upon which they have succeeded will only recover an amount of costs which the court considers to have been proportionate to those issues.

CHG 11.8

11.8 On the indemnity basis the court resolves any doubt it may have as to whether the costs were reasonably incurred or were reasonable in amount in favour of the receiving party.

CHG 11.8 [1]

Where costs are ordered on the indemnity basis the amounts recovered are not limited to amounts which are proportionate.

CHG 11.9

11.9 The court must take into account all the circumstances, including the parties' conduct and the other matters mentioned in rule 44.5. Indemnity costs are not confined to cases of improper or reprehensible conduct. They may be awarded where something takes the case out of the norm. They will not, however, usually be awarded unless there has been conduct by the paying party which the court regards as unreasonable or unless the case falls within rule 48.4 (costs payable to a trustee or personal representative out of the relevant trust fund or estate) (see paragraph 11.14 below).

Time for payment

CHG 11.10

11.10 A party must normally pay costs which are awarded against them and summarily assessed within 14 days of the assessment. But the court can extend that time (rules 44.8, 3.1(2)(a)). The court may therefore direct payment by instalments, or defer the liability to pay costs until the end of the proceedings so that the costs can then be set against any costs or judgment to which the paying party then becomes entitled.

Consent orders, and cases where only costs are in issue

CHG 11.11

11.11

(1)   If the parties have agreed the amount of costs, they do not need to file a statement of the costs, and summary assessment is unnecessary.

(2)   If the parties to an application are able to agree an order by consent without the parties attending they should also agree a figure for costs to be inserted in the order or agree that there should be no order as to costs.

(3)   If the costs position cannot be agreed then the parties will have to attend on the appointment but unless good reason can be shown for the failure of the parties to deal with costs as set out above no costs will be allowed for that

attendance. The court finds it most unsatisfactory if parties agree the terms of a consent order but not the provision for costs. Depending on the facts and circumstances, the court may not be able to decide on the question of costs without hearing the application fully, but it is not likely to be consistent with the overriding objective to allow the necessary amount of court time to the dispute on costs in such a case. The court may then have to decide the costs issue on a broad brush approach, making an order against one party or the other only if it is clear, without spending too much time on it, that such an order would be appropriate, and otherwise making no order as to the costs.

Funding arrangements

CHG 11.12

11.12 Funding arrangements are defined in CPR 43.2(1)(k). If a claimant has entered into a funding arrangement before starting proceedings they must file notice of the arrangement when they issue the claim form or, if the court is to serve the claim form, file sufficient copies of the notice for service by the court. A claimant who enters into a funding arrangement on or after starting the proceedings must file and serve notice within seven days of entering the funding arrangement.

CHG 11.13

11.13 The court should be informed, on any application for the payment of costs, if any party has entered into a funding arrangement. The court can then consider whether, in the light of that arrangement, to stay the payment of any costs which have been summarily assessed until the end of the action, or to decline to order the payment of costs on account under rule 44.3(8).

Other provisions

CHG 11.14

11.14 Parts 45 to 48, and the Costs PD, contain provisions regarding:

(1)   special cases in which costs are payable;
(2)   wasted costs;
(3)   fixed costs (these are payable for instance if judgment for a sum of money is given in default); and
(4)   detailed assessment.

In the context of Chancery litigation attention is drawn to rule 48.2 (Costs orders in favour of or against non-parties); rule 48.3 (Amount of costs where costs are payable pursuant to a contract) (see further Costs PD paragraph 50 and see also Chapter 21 - Mortgage Claims); and rule 48.4 and Costs PD paragraph 50A (Limitations on court's power to award costs in favour of trustee or personal representative). Reference may also be made to Chapter 25 as regards costs orders in trust litigation.

---

1 Note that from 1 April 2013, the CPR costs provisions are re-organised and amended so that the substantive costs provisions are now found in CPR Pt 44 to CPR Pt 47 and their accompanying practice directions: see Civil Procedure (Amendment) Rules 2013, SI 2013/262. For the practice directions see the Justice website at www.justice.gov.uk.

CHAPTER 12 CHANCERY BUSINESS OUTSIDE LONDON
General
CHG 12.1

12.1 Many Chancery cases are heard outside London. There are ten Chancery District Registries: Birmingham, Bristol, Caernarfon, Cardiff, Leeds, Liverpool, Manchester, Mold, Newcastle-upon-Tyne, and Preston. Chancery judges with jurisdiction to hear High Court cases sit regularly at these centres.

CHG 12.2

12.2 Outside London, county courts have exclusive jurisdiction in bankruptcy, and proceedings in bankruptcy must therefore be brought in the relevant county court which has bankruptcy jurisdiction rather than in the District Registries.

Judges
CHG 12.3

12.3 Two Chancery judges supervise the arrangements for the hearing of Chancery cases out of London. Mr Justice Morgan is the Chancery Supervising Judge for Wales and the Western and Midland Regions. Mr Justice Briggs, as Vice-Chancellor of the County Palatine of Lancaster, is the Chancery Supervising Judge for the Northern Region (which now includes Chester) and the North Eastern Region. Both these judges regularly take substantial Chancery matters for hearing outside London. Mr Justice Morgan sits regularly in Birmingham, Bristol and Cardiff, but if appropriate will sit elsewhere in the relevant areas. Mr Justice Briggs sits regularly in Manchester, Liverpool, Leeds and Newcastle, and may sit in Preston or in other court centres in either Region (e.g. Carlisle or Sheffield) if business so requires.

CHG 12.3 [1]

Mr Justice Morgan is now the supervising judge for the Western Wales and Midland circuits and Mr Justice Norris is Vice-Chancellor of the County Palatine.

CHG 12.4

12.4 There are also Specialist Circuit judges who have the authority to exercise the powers of a judge of the Chancery Division (under section 9 of the Senior Courts Act 1981, therefore known as section 9 judges) and who normally sit out of London. They exercise a general Chancery jurisdiction, subject to exceptions. Those exceptions are proceedings directly concerning revenue, and proceedings before the Patents Court constituted as part of the Chancery Division under section 96 of the Patents Act 1977.

CHG 12.5

12.5 Currently the Circuit judges who sit regularly in Chancery matters out of London are:

Judge McCahill QC (Bristol)

Judge Purle QC (Birmingham)

Judge David Cooke (Birmingham)

Judge Simon Barker QC (Birmingham)

Judge Jarman QC (Cardiff)

Judge Pelling QC (Manchester, Liverpool and Preston)

Judge Behrens (Leeds and Newcastle)

Judge Kaye QC (Leeds and Newcastle)

Judge Hodge QC (Manchester, Liverpool and Preston)

Judges Hegarty QC and Waksman QC (who are the local Mercantile judges based in Manchester and Liverpool) and Judges Raynor QC and Stephen Davies and Bird also assist in the disposal of Chancery business on the Northern Region. So also, in the North-Eastern Region, does Judge Langan QC who is the Mercantile judge for Leeds and Newcastle. The Chancery, Mercantile and TCC judges assist each other in Birmingham, Bristol and Cardiff as well. Judge Havelock-Allan QC, the Mercantile Judge in Bristol, is also authorised to sit as a Chancery Judge. All the judges who sit at the Cardiff Civil Justice Centre (Judges Jarman QC, Keyser QC and Seys-Llewellyn QC) are authorised to sit as Chancery judges.

CHG 12.6

12.6 In addition certain other Circuit judges and some Recorders or Queen's Counsel are authorised to take Chancery cases on the same basis.

Trials

CHG 12.7

12.7 If a Chancery case is proceeding in any District Registry other than a Chancery District Registry, the case should normally be transferred to the appropriate Chancery District Registry upon the first occasion the case comes before the court. Guidelines about transfer of cases are contained in Appendix 13.

CHG 12.8

12.8 The venue of a Chancery trial out of London will normally be one of the centres mentioned above. However in appropriate circumstances (e.g. because of the number or age of local witnesses, the need for a site visit, or travel problems) arrangements can be made for a Chancery judge to sit elsewhere. In the Northern Region (which now includes Chester) there is a presumption that Chancery cases issued in the Liverpool District Registry will be tried in Liverpool. All other Chancery cases in the Northern Region will be heard in Manchester, although, exceptionally, and for good reason, Chancery cases may be listed for trial in Chester or Preston. In Wales Chancery cases are normally heard in Cardiff or Swansea, although arrangements can be made for trials at other venues.

CHG 12.9

12.9 In cases of great difficulty or importance the trial may be by a High Court judge. Arrangements can also be made in exceptional circumstances for a High Court judge to deal with any of the matters excepted from the jurisdiction of an authorised Circuit judge. Such a judge may be one of the Chancery judges other than Morgan or Briggs JJ.

CHG 12.10

12.10 Where it is desired that a case be heard by a specialist Chancery judge outside one of the normal Chancery Centres, or be taken by a High Court judge, inquiries should normally be made in the first instance to the Listing Officer for the nearest Chancery District Registry on the relevant circuit. If the need arises, inquiries can also be made to the clerk to Mr Justice Morgan or the clerk to Mr Justice Briggs, as the case may be. If no relevant clerk is available, inquiries should be made to the Chancery Judges' Listing Officer (ground floor, Rolls Building) in London. The clerks' contact numbers are in Appendix 1.

Applications

CHG 12.11

12.11 Subject to the following paragraphs any application should normally be made to a District Judge (unless it relates to a matter which a District Judge does not have power to hear).

CHG 12.12

12.12 A District Judge may of his or her own initiative (for instance because of the complexity of the matter or the need for specialist attention) direct that an application be referred to a High Court judge or an authorised Circuit Judge.

CHG 12.13

12.13 If all or any of the parties consider that the matter should be dealt with by a judge (High Court or Circuit), the parties or any of them may arrange that the matter be listed on one of the ordinary application days (see paragraph 12.14 below). The District Judges, who will consult where necessary with one of the Chancery judges (High Court or Circuit), are usually available by post or telephone to give guidance on procedural matters, for example the court before which the matter should come or whether the matter may be dealt with in writing.

Application Days before a judge

CHG 12.14

12.14 Applications days are listed regularly before a judge, when applications and short appeals, including all interim matters are heard. Normally all matters will be called into court at the commencement of the day in order to work out a running order unless a specific time for the application has been given. Matters will be heard without the court going into private session unless good reason is shown. Rights of audience are unaffected.

CHG 12.15

12.15 Application days are: as required in Birmingham, Friday in Bristol and Friday in Cardiff. There are no fixed application days in Birmingham, but application days are listed with sufficient frequency to ensure that normal business can be accommodated, and urgent applications are listed flexibly, if necessary before normal sitting hours. Parties should liaise with the listing officer to identify the next available time. Short urgent applications in Bristol can also be heard at other times.

Applicants for emergency injunctions in Bristol should, if possible, supply the court with a completed Telephone Checklist form in advance of the hearing. This form, as well as guidance on the operation of the Bristol Chancery Applications List, is available on the Courts/Courts finder page (search for Bristol Civil Justice Centre) on www.justice.gov.uk or from the Chancery Clerk.

In the Northern Region application days are on Friday of each week in Manchester, although there are special arrangements for appropriate Liverpool applications to be listed before the Specialist Chancery District Judges in Liverpool. In Leeds and

Newcastle Chancery and Mercantile application days are combined. In Leeds applications are heard on Fridays. In Newcastle there is at least one application day each month, on a Friday. An application which needs to be heard urgently may be made, by telephone or in person, on a day other than the regular applications day: the Listing Officer for the relevant centre should be approached as soon as possible when the need for an urgent hearing arises.

Applications out of hours and telephone applications

CHG 12.16

12.16 These are governed by the general rules, save that in the case of applications out of hours, the party applying should contact the relevant court office. The main relevant contact numbers are set out in Appendix 1. In case of difficulty, contact the Royal Courts of Justice, on the number given in Appendix 1.

CHG 12.16 [1]

In the district registries, but not in the Royal Courts of Justice, the bulk of procedural applications will as from 6th April 2007 be made, subject to contrary direction by the court, by way of telephone hearing.

Agreed interim orders

CHG 12.17

12.17 Normally a hearing will not be necessary. The procedure is as in the general rules.

CHG 12.18

12.18 A judge is unlikely to agree to more than two consent adjournments of an interim application. Applications to vacate a trial date will require substantial justification and a hearing, normally before the trial judge.

Local Listing Arrangements

CHG 12.19

12.19 Listing arrangements may vary at different centres, depending on availability of judges and courtrooms. The current details are described below.

Birmingham: Listing

CHG 12.20

12.20 There is a flexible arrangement whereby any of the specialist judges may direct that a particular case in their own list (normally not one involving complex specialist issues of law) is suitable for trial before any specialist judge, whatever his or her primary field. Parties may be asked for their views on this at a CMC, and are free to volunteer such views at any time. This may result in an earlier hearing date. An alternative in the Chancery list (normally only for cases of 3 days or less) is that with the agreement of the parties, the court may allocate a case both a first fixture and an earlier date on which it is listed as second fixture, to be called on if the case first fixed for that date settles. In such cases the parties must prepare for trial on the assumption that the second fixture may be effective. The court office will give as much notice as possible (normally seven days, and, in any event, three days) if the second fixture is to be called on.

Bristol: Listing

CHG 12.21

12.21 All cases are allocated a fixed starting date. No reserve list is operated. However, every case listed for trial will have a pre-trial review at least 6 weeks before the trial date. This review often identifies cases likely to settle. Parties in other cases which are ready for trial in the same period are then contacted and given the opportunity to take up any time made available by the settlement. Any discussions concerning listing should be with the Chancery Listing clerk in Bristol.

Cardiff: Reserve Listing

CHG 12.22

12.22 Judge Jarman QC sits both as a Chancery judge and a judge of the Technology and Construction Court. His list contains both categories of case. All cases are allocated a fixed starting date but some are first and some reserve fixtures. Other judges are called upon in the event of both first and reserve fixtures being effective. Any discussions concerning listing should be with the Chancery Listing clerk in Cardiff.

Manchester, Liverpool and Preston

CHG 12.23

12.23 The Shared List

When sitting at the same court centre, Judge Hodge QC and Judge Pelling QC will assist each other in the disposal of their respective daily lists. If necessary and if they are available at the relevant court centre, Judge Hegarty QC and Judge Waksman QC (who are the local Mercantile judges), and other circuit judges will assist in the disposal of business. Listing for all Chancery matters in Manchester, Liverpool and Preston is dealt with from Manchester.

Multiple Fixtures

Given the very high settlement rate multiple fixtures may be arranged for a particular date. In the unlikely event that a case has to be stood out of the list, a new date will be given.

Liverpool business

Judges Hodge QC and Pelling QC hear trials of Chancery actions issued by Liverpool District Registry at Liverpool Civil and Family Courts. Applications to be heard by them in cases issued by Liverpool District Registry, other than applications by order, will be heard on Applications Day in Manchester. Applications by order in Liverpool cases will be listed if possible in Liverpool. District Judge hearings in Chancery actions issued by Liverpool District Registry are listed by and heard at Liverpool Civil and Family Courts.

Leeds and Newcastle

CHG 12.24

12.24 When sitting at the same time in Leeds or Newcastle Judge Behrens, Judge Langan QC and Judge Kaye QC will assist each other in the disposal of their respective daily lists. The Chancery and Mercantile Court lists are run on a shared basis in both Leeds and Newcastle.

Chancery Business in the North: Further Guidance

CHG 12.25

12.25

(1)   A guide to Chancery business in the North East can be found at Appendix 16.
(2)   The website of the Northern Chancery Bar Association (www.nchba.co.uk) contains guidance and relevant practice notes relating to Chancery business in the North of England.

GUIDES

CHAPTER 13 COUNTY COURTS

Key Rules: CPR Part 30; PD 7A, paragraphs 2.1–2.10

Unified procedure

CHG 13.1

13.1 A key feature of the civil justice reforms is the introduction of a unified procedure for the High Court and for county courts. The procedure to be followed in both courts is therefore the same.

Chancery cases brought in the county court

CHG 13.2

13.2 Any county court has jurisdiction to hear a Chancery case, subject to three principal exceptions: (1) a probate claim in a county court must be brought in a county court where there is a Chancery District Registry or the Central London Civil Justice Centre: CPR part 57.2(3); (2) an intellectual property claim must be brought in any such county court or in the Patents County Court: CPR Part 63.13 and PD 63 paragraph 16. Claims relating to patents, registered designs, semiconductor topography rights and plant varieties may only be brought in the Patents County Court; (3) insolvency proceedings may only be brought in a county court which has insolvency jurisdiction.

CHG 13.2 [1]

Regard must also be had to the jurisdictional limits of the county court in respect of equity cases and also to the fact that under certain statutes jurisdiction in respect of particular matters of a Chancery nature is limited to the High Court. The jurisdictional limits of the county court in equity are likely to be subject to substantial increase following a recent Ministry of Justice consultation.

CHG 13.3

13.3 If a case of a Chancery nature is brought in any county court, the claim form should be marked "Chancery Business" in the top left hand corner: CPR PD 7A para 2.5.

CHG 13.4

13.4 If a Chancery case is brought in a county court which does not coincide with a Chancery District Registry, consideration ought to be given at an early stage to whether it needs to have specialist case management or a specialist trial judge, because of the nature of the issues. If it needs either, then it may be necessary to transfer the case to a county court at a Chancery District Registry. If there are good reasons against such a transfer, for example because of the distance involved and the convenience of parties or witnesses, then it may be possible, with enough notice, to arrange that the trial is heard by a Recorder with Chancery experience or even by a Chancery Circuit judge. Guidance has been given to District Judges by the Chancery supervising judges as to the circumstances and types of case in respect of which either a transfer or a special arrangement for trial by a judge or Recorder with specialist experience may be appropriate. These guidelines are reprinted in Appendix 13.

Transfer to a county court

CHG 13.5

13.5 Any Chancery case which does not require to be heard by a High Court judge, and falls within the jurisdiction of the county courts, may be transferred to a county court. Parties should expect that either the Master or the judge will consider whether a claim started in the High Court should be transferred to a county court. The High Court has power to transfer a case to a county court even where that court would not otherwise have had jurisdiction. The criteria for transfer are set out in CPR rule 30.3(2). The Master will in particular consider whether proceedings seeking an order for sale of property outside Greater London should be transferred to the local county court. Where a case has been so transferred, the papers must be marked "Chancery Business" so as to ensure, so far as possible, suitable listing.

CHG 13.5 [1]

Section 40 of the County Courts Act 1984 does not restrict cases which can be transferred out to those falling within the county court jurisdiction. Subject to specific statutory provisions, any case can be transferred to the county court by the High Court and the County Court will thereby be clothed with jurisdiction. The Masters will frequently exercise their powers to transfer out and to clothe the county court with jurisdiction, particularly where a transfer can be made to a county court where chancery expertise is known to exist, or where proceedings have only been brought in the High Court for jurisdictional reasons but where the case is otherwise appropriate to the county court. In appropriate cases smaller intellectual property cases will be transferred to the Patents County Court.

CHG 13.6

13.6 If the case is one of a specifically Chancery nature a transfer from the High Court will ordinarily be to the Central London Civil Justice Centre (Chancery List) ('the CLCJC') where cases are heard by specialist Chancery Circuit judges or Recorders and a continuous Chancery List is maintained, unless the parties prefer a transfer to a local county court which coincides with a Chancery District Registry.

CHG 13.6 [1]

A note dealing with the practice of Chancery Business at the Central London County Court is to be found at para **CHG CLCC**, printed after this Guide. Notwithstanding the note, care should be taken to consider whether Claims fall within the original jurisdiction of the County Court before issuing such a claim in the County Court.

CHG 13.7

13.7 If a claim is transferred to a county court at the allocation stage no other directions will usually be given and all case management will be left to the county court.

CHG 13.8

13.8 The Chancery List at the CLCJC is managed by the Business Section at 26 Park Crescent, London W1N 4HT. The telephone number of the section manager is set out in Appendix 1. A guide to the Chancery List may be obtained from the section manager and is reproduced at Appendix 15.

CHG 13.9

13.9 As an alternative to starting the case in the Chancery Division and transferring to the CLCJC a case (if appropriate to be started there) may be started at the CLCJC and a request made there for it to be transferred to the Chancery List. The request will receive judicial consideration and a transfer will be made if appropriate.

CHG 13.10

13.10 It should be noted that only in very limited circumstances may freezing orders or search orders be granted in the county court. If necessary, an application may be made in the High Court in aid of the county court proceedings if such an order is to be sought in a case where it cannot be granted in the county court.

CHG 13.11

13.11 Practitioners should continue to take care that Chancery cases requiring chancery expertise are dealt with in a county court with a Chancery District Registry.

Patents County Court

CHG 13.12

13.12 See Chapter 23 below and the Patents Court and Patents County Court Guide (details of which are given in paragraph 23.3).

CHAPTER 14 USE OF INFORMATION TECHNOLOGY

Key Rules: CPR 1.4, CPR PD 5B; CPR Pt 6; CPR PD 6A, CPR PD 31B, CPR PD 32, Annex 3

General

CHG 14.1

14.1 The CPR contain certain provisions about the use of information technology ('IT') in the conduct of cases. No standard practice has evolved or been prescribed for the use of IT in civil cases, but it is possible to identify certain areas in which electronic techniques may be used which should encourage the efficient and economical conduct of litigation.

CHG 14.1 [1]

As from 1st April 2010 and although the take up is, as yet, small provisions as to electronic working are in operation in the Chancery Division and a new practice direction relating to electronic working now applies (see para **CPR PD 5C** above).

CHG 14.2

14.2 Since not all litigants have equal access to IT facilities and techniques, use of IT (otherwise than in cases where the rules or practice directions permit it) is acceptable only if no party to the case will be unfairly prejudiced and its use will save time or money.

CHG 14.3

14.3 In any case in which it is proposed to use IT in the preparation, management and presentation of a case in a manner which is not provided for by the CPR, it may be necessary for directions to be given by the judge who is to hear the case. While it may be satisfactory for parties and their solicitors to agree to a particular application of IT (for example, using modern software to deal with extensive disclosure of emails and other digitally stored documents), techniques to deal with the preparation of documents for use in court, in effect by way of electronic bundles, are likely to need the agreement of the judge. The Chancery Division, as a general practice, would encourage the digitisation of the documents in a document-heavy case, with a view to having a largely or partially paperless trial. However, individual judicial preferences may vary as to the extent to which this is acceptable in any given case. Accordingly if it is intended to adopt that technique, it will be desirable for a judge to be nominated to conduct the case at an early stage so that he or she can approve and control the process. Where a nomination is desired, application should be made to the Chancellor in writing by letter addressed to his clerk for a judge to be nominated.

CHG 14.4

14.4 In every case in which it is proposed to use IT, the first step will be for the solicitors for all parties to determine whether it is possible to establish a common protocol for the electronic exchange and management of information. One example of this is the TeCSA IT Protocol, which can be found at http://www.tecsa.org.uk/it_protocol. The CPR's underlying policy of co-operation and collaboration is particularly important in this context. In a large case the parties must facilitate the task of the judge by providing any additional help and IT know-how, including, for example, demonstrations, which he or she may require in order to control the case properly.

CHG 14.5

14.5 The judges of the Chancery Division and their clerks are equipped with computers running Windows XP3 and Microsoft Office 2003 (including Word 2003). To avoid compatibility problems it is preferable that text files to be provided for use by a judge or clerk be provided in a format compatible with Word 2003. Although the judges' computers can read the newer .docx format, it is inconvenient to have documents submitted in that format and documents should be submitted in .doc format (or the equivalent for the other Office programmes). PDF documents are also acceptable, though not preferred if .doc format is available, and should not be used for skeleton arguments or written submissions.

Provision of information on digital storage devices: Skeleton arguments etc

CHG 14.6

14.6 Particular arrangements are made for the lodging of skeleton arguments in digital form—see below. Longer skeleton arguments, chronologies, witness statements, experts' reports and other documents (if available in digital form) should be provided on digital storage devices (or by email) if the judge requests it. Enquiry should be made of the judge's clerk for this purpose. Digital storage devices provided to judges must be checked for virus contamination and be clean. Transcripts are now always available digitally. If a written final submission contains a lot of references to transcript evidence, and where the complexity of the case justifies it, consideration should be given to inserting clickable links to transcript references in a digital version of the submission.

Email communications with the Chancery Division

CHG 14.7

14.7 A protocol for email communications with the Chancery Division sets out how parties may communicate by e-mail on certain matters, and can be found at http://www.justice.gov.uk. The protocol applies CPR PD 5B on electronic communication and filing of documents in respect of specified documents: longer skeleton arguments, chronologies, reading lists, lists of issues, lists of authorities (but not the authorities themselves) and lists of key persons involved in the case sent in advance of a hearing. The protocol sets out the relevant email addresses, which are also to be found in Appendix 1. The clerk to the judge concerned should be contacted to find out whether the judge will accept other documents by email and whether documents should be sent by email direct to the judge's clerk's email address.

Skeleton arguments—particular arrangements

CHG 14.8

14.8 Subject to the exception mentioned below, all skeletons of 25 pages and fewer for hearings in the Rolls Building should be filed by email to the appropriate address:

chancery.applications.skeletons@hmcts.gsi.gov.uk for skeletons for use in the Applications Court; and

chancery.general.skeletons@hmcts.gsi.gov.uk for all other skeletons.

The following principles should be observed:

(1)   These email boxes should be used for skeleton arguments only and not for any other documents. Any other documents are likely to be ignored. The only exceptions are:

      (a)   in the case of the Applications Court mailbox, a short indication that a case is going to be ineffective in the event of that becoming apparent late on the previous day or early on the morning of the hearing; and

      (b)   a short reading list.

(2)   Any skeleton arguments of more than 25 pages should be provided in hard copy.

(3)   The digital copy should be in .doc format (preferred) or .docx format; but should not be in .pdf format.

(4)   All emails should have the following in the subject matter line of the enclosing email and in the following order: the name of the case (in short form) and case number; the name of the judge (if known); and the date of the hearing if known or the hearing window where it is not.

(5)   In the Applications Court a fresh skeleton should be emailed in respect of any adjourned hearing even if it has not changed in form since the earlier hearing; and it should be clearly re-dated.

(6)   If a supplemental or amended skeleton is lodged, the attention of the relevant judge's clerk should be drawn to that lodgement (preferably by direct email) so that it is not overlooked.

(7)   Any skeleton lodged in accordance with the above rules need not thereafter be provided in hard copy, unless the court otherwise directs.

(8)   If the skeleton supports a hearing in private, and if the privacy considerations make it undesirable for the skeleton to be transmitted by email (which may not always be the case), it may be lodged in hard copy form with the Chancery Judges' Listing Office, or with the judge's clerk (if known).

(9)   This direction applies only to skeleton arguments filed in support of forthcoming hearings. It does not apply to skeleton arguments filed in support of appeals where a hearing may not necessarily take place, or in support of any other application where there is no forthcoming hearing. Those skeletons should be lodged in hard copy.

(10)   The above email boxes will be cleared of all skeletons over 14 days old at any given time.

Transcripts

CHG 14.9

14.9 The various shorthand writers provide a number of different transcript services. These range from an immediately displayed transcript which follows the evidence almost as it is given to provision of transcripts of a day's proceedings one or two days in arrears. The use of transcripts in trials is always of assistance if they can be justified on the ground of cost, and in long cases they are almost a necessity. If an instantaneous service is proposed, inquiries should be made of the judge's clerk, and sufficient time for the installation of the equipment necessary and for any familiarisation on the part of the judge with the system should be found. If special transcript-handling software is to be used by the parties, consideration should be given to making the software available to the judge, though it will not be possible to load software (as opposed to the text of transcripts) on a judge's computer.

CHG 14.10

14.10 If the shorthand writers make transcripts available in digital form (and nearly all do) the judge should be provided with a digital version of the transcripts as they become available if he or she requires them.

Fax communications

CHG 14.11

14.11 The use of fax in the service of documents is now authorised by rule 5.5 (1)(a) and 5PD paragraph 5. It should be noted in particular that where a party files a document by fax they must not send a hard copy in addition; and that faxes should not be used to send letters or documents of a routine or non-urgent nature.

CHG 14.12

14.12 Each of the judges sitting in the Chancery Division may be reached by fax if the occasion warrants it. The respective judges' clerks' telephone and fax numbers are set out in Appendix 1. Where the name of the judge is not known, short documents may be sent to the Chancery Judges' Listing Office, whose fax number is also given in Appendix 1. Written evidence should not be sent by fax to this number. All fax messages should have a cover sheet setting out the name of the case, the case number and the judge's name, if known.

CHG 14.12 [1]

Fax messages are commonly sent to the Masters (fax 020 7947 7422). Parties should have particular regard to the Chief Master's Note relating to correspondence with the court.

Telephone hearings

CHG 14.13

14.13 Applications may be heard by telephone, if the court so orders, but normally only if all parties entitled to be given notice agree, and none of them intends to be present in person. Special provisions apply where the applicant or another party is a litigant in person: see CPR PD 23A paragraph 6.3 and CPR PD 25A paragraph 4.5 (Interim Injunctions). Guidance on other aspects of telephone hearings, and in particular how to set them up, is contained in CPR PD 23A paragraph 6.9. When putting that guidance into practice once an order has been made for a hearing to take place by a telephone conference call, the following points may be useful:

(1)   A telephone hearing may be set up by calling the BT Legal Call Centre on 0800 778877. The caller's name and EB account number will have to be given. The court service account number is EB-26724. Other telecommunications providers may also be able to offer the same facility.
(2)   The names and telephone numbers of the participants in the hearing including the judge must be provided.
(3)   The co-ordinator should be told the date, time and likely approximate duration of the hearing.
(4)   The name and address of the court and the court case reference should be given, for delivery of the tape of the hearing.
(5)   Then tell the court that the hearing has been arranged.

It is necessary to ensure that all participants in the hearing have all documents that it may be necessary for any of them to refer to by the time the hearing begins.

CHG 14.13 [1]

In Chancery District Registries telephone hearings have, as from 6 April 2007, been the 'default' position in respect of many procedural applications. This does not apply to the High Court at the Royal Courts of Justice, where a telephone hearing will not generally be regarded appropriate to a contentious application, such as an application for summary disposal or a fully contested application for specific disclosure; nor for a hearing of any great length. Such hearings will often, however, be of value in dealing with relatively routine case management matters.

Video-conferencing

CHG 14.14

14.14 The court may allow evidence to be taken using video-conferencing facilities: rule 32.3. Experience has shown that normally taking evidence by this means is comparatively straightforward, but its suitability may depend on the particular witness, and the case, and on such matters as the volume and nature of documents which need to be referred to in the course of the evidence.

CHG 14.15

14.15 A video link may also be used for an application, or otherwise in the course of any hearing.

CHG 14.16

14.16 Annex 3 to PD 32 (Video Conferencing Guidance) provides further detail on the manner in which video conferencing facilities are to be used in civil proceedings.

CHG 14.17

14.17 Video conferencing facilities are available in all courts in the Rolls Building. Some are specially, and permanently, equipped. Others are served by movable equipment. Attention is drawn to the following matters:

(1)   Permission to use video conferencing during a hearing should be obtained as early as possible in the proceedings. If all parties are agreed that the use of video conferencing is appropriate, then a hearing may not be necessary to obtain such permission.

(2)   Arrangements should be made for using the video conferencing facilities with the Chancery Judges' Listing Office or the individual identified on the web communications page referred to above at www.justice.gov.uk.

(3)   The permanently equipped courts are better for longer video conferencing s essions. The temporarily equipped courts are adequate for shorter ones. The parties should consider whether the length and nature of the evidence requ ires one or the other, and communicate with the court accordingly.

CHAPTER 15 MISCELLANEOUS MATTERS

Key Rules: CPR Part 39; CPR PD 39A: Miscellaneous Provisions relating to Hearings

Litigants in person

CHG 15.1

15.1 The provisions of this Guide in general apply to litigants in person. Thus, for example, litigants in person should:

(1)   prepare a written summary of their argument in the same circumstances as those in which a represented party is required to produce a skeleton argument;

(2)   prepare a bundle of documents in the same way that a represented party is required to produce a bundle of documents;

(3)   be prepared to put forward their argument within a limited time if they are directed to do so by the court; and

(4)   if making an application in the absence of the respondent, comply with the duty of full and frank disclosure (see para 5.22).

CHG 15.2

15.2 This means that litigants in person should identify in advance of the hearing those points which they consider to be their strongest points, and that they should put those points at the forefront of their oral and written submissions to the court.

CHG 15.3

15.3 It is not the function of court officials to give legal advice. However, subject to that, they will do their best to assist any litigant. Litigants in person who need further assistance should contact the Community Legal Advice (CLA) through their Information Points. The CLA is developing local networks of people giving legal assistance such as law centres, local solicitors or the Citizens' Advice Bureaux. CLA Information Points are being set up in libraries and other public places. Litigants can telephone the CLA helpline to find their nearest CLA Information Point on 0845 345 4345.

CHG 15.4

15.4 There is no Citizens' Advice Bureau in the Rolls Building, but the Royal Courts of Justice Advice Bureau off the main hall at the Royal Courts of Justice is open from Monday to Friday from 10am to 12.30pm and from 2pm to 4.30pm. The bureau is run by lawyers in conjunction with the Citizens' Advice Bureau and is independent of the court. Appointments must be booked. Call 0207 947 7771 or 0844 856 3534 or (for calls from mobile phones) 03004568341. The bureau also operates a drop-in Bankruptcy Court advice desk on Monday to Friday (10am–2.30pm) in Room TM1.03, 1st Floor, Thomas More Building. In appropriate cases the bureau may be able to refer a case to the Bar Pro Bono Unit (http://www.barpr obono.org.uk) which also administers the Personal Insolvency Litigation Advice and Representation Scheme ('PILARS').

CHG 15.5

15.5 Where a litigant in person is the applicant, the court may ask one of the represented parties to open the matter briefly and impartially, and to summarise the issues.

CHG 15.6

15.6 It is the duty of an advocate to ensure that the court is informed of all relevant decisions and enactments of which the advocate is aware (whether favourable or not to his or her case) and to draw the court's attention to any material irregularity.

CHG 15.7

15.7 Representatives for other parties must treat litigants in person with consideration. Before the case starts they should where possible be given photocopies of any authorities which are to be cited in addition to the skeleton argument. They should be asked to give their names to the usher or in court support staff if they have not already done so. Representatives for other parties should explain the court's order after the hearing if the litigant in person does not appear to understand it.

CHG 15.8

15.8 If a litigant in person wishes to give oral evidence he or she will generally be required to do so from the witness box in the same manner as any other witness of fact.

CHG 15.9

15.9 A litigant in person must give an address for service in England or Wales. If he or she is a claimant, the address will be in the claim form or other document by which the proceedings are brought. If he or she is a defendant, it will be in the acknowledgment of service form which he or she must send to the court on being served with the proceedings. It is essential that any change of address should be notified in writing to Chancery Chambers and to all other parties to the case.

CHG 15.10

15.10 Notice of hearing dates will be given by post to litigants at the address shown in the court file. A litigant in person will generally be given a fixed date for trial on application. A litigant in person who wishes to apply for a fixed date should ask the Chancery Judges' Listing Office for a copy of its Guidance Notes for litigants in person.

Assistance to litigants in person

CHG 15.11

15.11 A litigant who is acting in person may be assisted at a hearing by another person, often referred to as a McKenzie friend (see *McKenzie v McKenzie* [1971] P 33). The litigant must be present at the hearing. If the hearing is in private, it is a matter of discretion for the court whether such an assistant is allowed to attend the hearing. That may depend, among other things, on the nature of the proceedings.

CHG 15.12

15.12 The McKenzie friend is allowed to help by taking notes, quietly prompting the litigant and offering advice and suggestions to the litigant. The court can, and sometimes does, permit the McKenzie friend to address the court on behalf of the litigant, by making an order to that effect under Schedule 3 paragraph 2 of the Legal

Services Act 2007). Although applications are considered on a case by case basis, the Chancery Division will usually follow the guidance contained in *Practice Note (McKenzie friends: Civil and Family Courts)* [2010] 1 WLR 1881. Different considerations may apply where the person seeking the right of audience is acting for remuneration and any applicant should be prepared to disclose whether he or she is acting for remuneration and if so how the remuneration is calculated.

CHG 15.12 [1]

There is a strong presumption that the court will allow a litigant assistance by a McKenzie friend provided that the person behaves responsibly and does not seek to go beyond that which he is allowed to do (see 15.12). This Practice Guidance is set out in this volume at para **CPR PG 39**.

CHG 15.13

15.13 The Personal Support Unit ('PSU') at the Royal Courts of Justice, Room M104) on the first floor, opposite courts 5 and 6, tel: 020 7073 1703, open Monday to Friday, 9.30 am to 4.30 pm , offers personal support for litigants in person, witnesses and others. The PSU also operates at the Birmingham, Manchester, Liverpool and Cardiff Civil Justice Centres, the Principal Registry of the Family Division and the Wandsworth County Court. The PSU will sometimes be able to accompany litigants into court to provide emotional support and give other guidance, but it does not give legal advice.

Representation on behalf of companies

CHG 15.14

15.14 Rule 39.6 allows a company or other corporation to be represented at trial by an employee if the employee has been authorised by the company or corporation to appear on its behalf and the court gives permission. Paragraph 5 of PD 39 describes what is needed to obtain permission from the court for this purpose and mentions some of the considerations relevant to the grant or refusal of permission.

Robed and unrobed hearings

CHG 15.15

15.15 Judges wear robes for all hearings. Robes are not worn at hearings before Masters unless the Cause List is marked otherwise. Robes are worn at the following hearings before Bankruptcy and Companies Court Registrars: public examinations of bankrupts and of directors or other officers of companies; applications for discharge from bankruptcy or for suspension of such discharge; all proceedings under the Company Directors Disqualification Act 1986; petitions to wind up companies; final hearings of petitions for the reduction of capital of companies. District judges wear robes for trials and winding up petitions. Barristers wear robes for all trials and appeals and in any case where the liberty of the subject is at stake. Current guidance for barristers may be found on the Bar Council's website at http://www.barcouncil.org.uk.

CHG 15.15 [1]

Masters, who did not previously robe, now robe for trials and for hearings analogous to trials, such as accounts and inquiries, or when sitting in open court and the expectation will be that counsel and solicitors will, themselves, robe accordingly.

Solicitors' rights of audience

CHG 15.16

15.16 At hearings in chambers before 26 April 1999 solicitors had general rights of audience. The fact that a matter which would then have been heard in chambers is now heard in public under Part 39 does not affect rights of audience, so in such matters as would have been heard in chambers previously, the general right of audience for solicitors continues to apply. Such cases included appeals from Masters, applications for summary judgment, and those concerned with pleadings, security for costs and the like, pre-trial reviews, and applications concerned with the administration of a deceased person's estate, a trust or a charity. They did not include applications in what is now the Interim Applications List or the Companies Court, nor appeals from county courts or insolvency appeals. Solicitors do, however, have general rights of audience in personal insolvency matters; this is not affected by whether the hearing is in public or private.

CHG 15.17

15.17 If a solicitor who does not have the appropriate special right of audience wishes to be heard in a case which is not one which, before 26 April 1999, would have been heard in chambers nor a personal insolvency case, an application may be made for the grant of a special right of audience before the particular court and for the particular proceedings under Schedule 3 paragraph 2 of the Legal Services Act 2007.

Recording at hearings

CHG 15.18

15.18 In the Rolls Building it is normal to record all proceedings which take place in court before a judge until 6pm. For hearings which take place in private, the recording to equipment will not normally be turned off but a note will be made on the computer log to the effect that the hearing (or relevant part of it) is in private. If any party wishes different arrangements to be made, this should be raised with the judge (through his or her clerk) before the start of the hearing.

CHG 15.19

15.19 At hearings before Masters, it is not normally practicable to record anything other than any oral evidence and the judgment, but these will be recorded.

CHG 15.19 [1]

The normal practice, in fact, is for the entirety of any hearing before a judge to be recorded. Before the Master, the current practice has until recently been as set out in 15.19. With the introduction of new technology, however, all, or almost all, hearings are now recorded. In cases where, for any reason, recording does not take place it will be the responsibility of the advocates or parties to make and agree a note for the Master's approval in the event of an appeal. Now that permission to appeal is required in all appeals, it is essential that a note or transcript of the lower court's judgment is available whenever permission is sought from the appeal court. See the note to 10.10 as to the availability of transcripts at public expense.

CHG 15.20

15.20 No party or member of the public may use recording equipment without the court's permission.

CHG 15.20 [1]

To reflect the availability of mobile email, social media (such as Twitter) and internet enabled laptops, guidance has recently been given by the Lord Chief Justice as to the use of such live text-based forms of communication in the court room. Litigants and court users should consult that guidance before seeking to use any such forms of communication in court and should, in any event, seek judicial permission before such forms of communication are brought into use. The guidance is reproduced in this Volume at para **CPR PD 39A.6 [2]**.

CHAPTER 16 SUGGESTIONS FOR IMPROVEMENT AND COURT USERS' COMMITTEES

CHG 16.1

16.1 Suggestions for improvements in this Guide or in the practice or procedure of the Chancery Division are welcome. Unless they fall within the remit of the committees mentioned at paras 16.2 to 16.7 below, they should be sent to the clerk to the Chancellor.

Chancery Division Court Users' Committee

CHG 16.2

16.2 The Chancery Division Court Users' Committee's function is to review, as may from time to time be required, the practice and procedure of all courts forming part of the Chancery Division, to ensure that they continue to provide a just, economical and expeditious system for the resolution of disputes. The Chancellor is the chairman. Its membership includes judges, a Master, barristers, solicitors and other representatives of court staff and users. Meetings are held three times a year, and more often if necessary. Suggestions for points to be considered by the Committee should be sent to the clerk to the Chancellor.

Bankruptcy and Companies Court Users' Committee

CHG 16.3

16.3 Proposals for changes in insolvency matters fall within the remit of the Bankruptcy and Companies Court Users' Committee unless they relate to the Insolvency Rules 1986. The members of the Bankruptcy and Companies Court Users' Committee include members of the Bar, the Law Society, the Insolvency Service and the Society of Practitioners of Insolvency. Meetings are held three times a year, and more often if necessary. Suggestions for points to be considered by the Committee should be sent to the clerk to the Chancellor.

Insolvency Rules Committee

CHG 16.4

16.4 The Insolvency Rules Committee must be consulted before any changes to the Insolvency Rules 1986 are made. The Chairman of the Insolvency Rules Committee is Mr Justice David Richards. Proposals for changes in the Rules should be sent to The Insolvency Service, Room 502, PO Box 203, 21 Bloomsbury Street, London WC1B 3QW, with a copy to the clerk to Mr Justice David Richards.

Intellectual Property Court Users' Committee

CHG 16.5

16.5 This considers the problems and concerns of intellectual property litigation generally. Membership of the committee includes the Patent judges and a representative of each of the Patent Bar Association, the Intellectual Property Lawyers Association, the Chartered Institute of Patent Attorneys, the Institute of Trade Mark Attorneys and the Trade Marks Designs and Patents Federation. It will also include one or more other Chancery judges. The Chairman is Mr. Justice Floyd. Anyone having views concerning the improvement of intellectual property litigation is invited to make his or her views known to the committee, preferably through the relevant professional representative on the committee.

Pension Litigation Court Users' Committee

CHG 16.6

16.6 This consists of a judge and a Master, two barristers and two solicitors. Its Chairman is Mr. Justice Warren. Any suggestions for consideration by the committee should be sent to the clerk to Mr. Justice Warren.

Court Users' Committees outside London

CHG 16.7

16.7 There are several Court Users' Committees relating to Chancery work outside London. They are as follows:

(1)   *The Northern Region and the North-Eastern Region Court Users Committees*: the Northern Region Chancery Court Users' Committee, which meets in Manchester; the Leeds Chancery and Mercantile Court Users' Committee; and the Newcastle Joint Chancery Mercantile and TCC Court Users' Committee. Each of these meets two or three times a year, and has a membership including judges, court staff, barristers and solicitors. The Vice-Chancellor of the County Palatine of Lancaster chairs these three Committees, and the Vice-Chancellor's clerk acts as secretary to each Committee. All communications should be to the clerk.

(2)   *The Western Region, Wales and Midland Region Court User Committees*: these circuit committees normally meet three or four times per year. They have a membership including judges, court staff, barristers and solicitors.

(a)   *Western Region*: Judge McCahill QC chairs the committee in Bristol (or Mr Justice Morgan when there), Mrs Liz Bodman acts as secretary. All communications should be addressed to her at Bristol Civil Justice Centre, 2 Redcliff Street, Bristol BS1 6GR.

(b)   *Wales*: Judge Jarman QC chairs the committee in Cardiff (or Mr Justice Morgan when there), the Diary Manager, Annette Parsons acts as secretary. All communications should be addressed to her at Cardiff Civil Justice Centre, 2 Park Street, Cardiff, CF1 1ET.

(c)   *Midland Region*: Judge Purle QC chairs the committee in Birmingham (or Mr Justice Morgan when there), the Chancery Listing Officer, acts as secretary. All communications should be addressed to him at Chancery Listing Section, Birmingham Civil Justice Centre, 33 Bull Street, Birmingham, B4 6DS.

CHAPTER 17 ALTERNATIVE DISPUTE RESOLUTION

Key Rules: CPR rules 3.1 and 26.4, CPR PD 26 paragraph 3

CHG 17.1

17.1 While emphasising the primary role of the court as a forum for deciding cases, the court encourages parties to consider the use of ADR (such as, but not confined to, mediation and conciliation) as a possible means of resolving disputes or particular issues.

CHG 17.2

17.2 The settlement of disputes by means of ADR can:

(1)   significantly help litigants to save costs;
(2)   save litigants the delay of litigation in reaching finality in their disputes;
(3)   enable litigants to achieve settlement of their disputes while preserving their existing commercial relationships and market reputation;
(4)   provide litigants with a wider range of solutions than those offered by litigation; and
(5)   make a substantial contribution to the more efficient use of judicial resources.

CHG 17.3

17.3 The court will in an appropriate case invite the parties to consider whether their dispute, or particular issues in it, could be resolved through ADR. In particular, it is to be expected that the judge or Master at any case management conference will inquire what steps can usefully be taken to resolve the dispute by settlement discussion, alternative dispute resolution or other means. The parties should be in a position to tell the court what steps have been taken or are proposed to be taken. The court may also adjourn the case for a specified period of time to encourage and enable the parties to use ADR and for this purpose extend the time for compliance by the parties or any of them with any requirement under the CPR or this Guide or any order of the court. The court may make such order as to the costs that the parties may incur by reason of the adjournment or their using or attempting to use ADR as may in all the circumstances seem appropriate.

CHG 17.3 [1]

It is now clear that a court cannot require parties to use ADR. The court can in appropriate cases provide robust encouragement to the parties to go to ADR and costs consequences may arise if a party refuses unreasonably to go to ADR or behaves unreasonably during or in respect of ADR.

CHG 17.4

17.4 Legal representatives in all cases should consider with their clients and the other parties concerned the possibility of attempting to resolve the dispute or particular issues by ADR and they should ensure that their clients are fully informed as to the most cost effective means of resolving their dispute.

CHG 17.5

17.5 Parties who consider that ADR might be an appropriate means of resolving their dispute, or particular issues in the dispute, may apply for directions at any stage.

CHG 17.6

17.6 The Clerk to the Commercial Court keeps some published information as to individuals and bodies that offer ADR services: see paragraph G1.9 of the Admiralty and Commercial Courts Guide. (The list also includes individuals and bodies that offer arbitration services.) If the parties are unable to agree upon a neutral individual, or panel of individuals, for ADR, they may refer to the judge for assistance, though the court will not recommend any particular body or individual to act as mediator or arbitrator.

CHG 17.6 [1]

There are as indicated now many arbitral and mediation bodies and individuals, as well as organisations such as IDRAS (Improving Dispute Resolution Advisory Service), which offer and assist on a specialist basis in the provision of ADR. Full listings are outside the scope of this work.

SECTION B SPECIALIST WORK

CHAPTER 18 INTRODUCTION TO THE SPECIALIST WORK OF THE CHANCERY DIVISION

CHG 18.1

18.1 As explained in Chapter 1 of this Guide, some proceedings in the High Court must be brought in the Chancery Division. These matters include:

(1)   claims for the sale, exchange or partition of land, or the raising of charges on land;

(2)   mortgage claims;

(3)   claims relating to the execution of trusts;

(4)   claims relating to the administration of the estates of deceased persons;

(5)   bankruptcy matters;

(6)   claims for the dissolution of partnerships or the taking of partnership or other accounts;

(7)   claims for the rectification, setting aside or cancellation of deeds or other instruments in writing;

(8)   contentious probate business;

(9)   claims relating to patents, trade marks, registered designs, copyright or design right;

(10)   claims for the appointment of a guardian of a minor's estate;

(11)   jurisdiction under the Companies Acts 1985 and the Insolvency Act 1986 relating to companies;

(12)   some revenue matters;

(13)   claims relating to charities;

(14)   some proceedings under the Solicitors Act 1974;

(15)   proceedings under the Landlord and Tenant Acts 1927 (Part I), 1954 (Part II) and 1987 and the Leasehold Reform Act 1967;

(16)   proceedings (other than those in the Commercial Court) relating to the application of Articles 101 and 102 of the Treaty on the Functioning of the European Union and the equivalent provisions of the Competition Act 1998; and

(17)   proceedings under other miscellaneous statutory jurisdictions.

CHG 18.1 [1]

Virtually all proceedings under the Landlord and Tenant Act 1954 and 1987 and the Leasehold Reform Act 1967 are now dealt with exclusively by the county court. Such proceedings can only be commenced in the High Court if the Claimant can certify that the case is suitable for High Court proceedings having regard to the criteria set out in the practice direction supplementing Part 56. Likewise proceedings for possession, including mortgage possession claims, can only be commenced in the High Court on the basis of appropriate certification (see Part 55 and the practice direction thereto) (see further under Chapter 21 of the Guide).

CHG 18.2

18.2 There is concurrent jurisdiction with the Family Division under the Inheritance (Provision for Family and Dependants) Act 1975.

CHG 18.3

18.3 Certain appeals lie to the Chancery Division under statute. These are dealt with in paragraph 10.14. Intellectual property appeals are covered in Chapters 23 and the Patents Court Guide.

CHG 18.4

18.4 The Chancery judges are among the nominated judges of the Court of Protection but this Guide does not deal with the Court of Protection. Chancery judges also sit in the Upper Tribunal and the Competition Appeal Tribunal; but this Guide does not deal with those.

CHAPTER 19 THE BANKRUPTCY COURT

Key Rules: CPR PD - Insolvency Proceedings; Insolvency Rules 1986 ('The Insolvency Rules')

CHG 19.1

19.1 The Bankruptcy Court (ie the High Court sitting in bankruptcy) is part of the Chancery Division and disposes of proceedings relating to insolvent individuals arising under Parts 7A to XI of the Insolvency Act 1986 and related legislation. These include applications for interim orders to support an individual voluntary arrangement, applications to set aside a statutory demand, bankruptcy petitions and various applications concerned with the realisation and distribution of the assets of individuals who have been adjudged bankrupt, as well as proceedings concerning the administration in bankruptcy of the insolvent estate of a deceased person. The procedure in the Bankruptcy Court is governed by the Insolvency Rules and CPR PD - Insolvency Proceedings. Appeals in bankruptcy matters are covered in Chapter 10.

CHG 19.2

19.2 Proceedings in the Bankruptcy Court are issued on the ground floor, Rolls Building and are dealt with by the Registrars in Bankruptcy, not the Masters. Proceedings under Parts X to XI of the Insolvency Act 1986 should be entitled "IN BANKRUPTCY": see CPR PD (Insolvency Proceedings) paragraph 4.3. All insolvency proceedings are allocated to the multi-track.

CHG 19.3

19.3 Certain matters, such as applications for injunctions or for committal for contempt, must be heard by a Judge. They are listed in CPR PD (Insolvency Proceedings) paragraph 3.3. A judge is available to hear such matters each day in term time and applications may be listed for any such day. The judge will normally also be hearing the interim applications list for the day, but one or more other judges may be available to assist if necessary. A Registrar is also available to hear urgent applications.

CHG 19.4

19.4 The Registrar may refer or adjourn proceedings to the judge, having regard to the complexity of the proceedings, whether the proceedings raise new or controversial points of law, the likely date and length of the hearing, and public interest in the proceedings: see CPR PD (Insolvency Proceedings) paragraph 3.4, and the availability of relevant specialist expertise. When proceedings have been referred or adjourned to the judge, interim applications and applications for directions or case management will be listed before a judge, except where liberty to apply to the Registrar has been given.

CHG 19.5

19.5 There are prescribed forms for use in connection with all types of statutory demand and of petitions for bankruptcy orders. Every other type of application is now made using Form 7.1A (the former distinction in the Insolvency Rules between originating and ordinary applications having been abolished).

Statutory demands

CHG 19.6

19.6 All applications to set aside a statutory demand are referred initially to a Registrar. The application may be dismissed by the court without a hearing if it fails to disclose sufficient grounds (see Insolvency Rules, r 6.5(14). If it is not dismissed summarily, it will be allocated a hearing date when the Registrar may either dispose of it summarily or give directions for its disposal at a later date. Such directions will commonly include an order for the filing and service of written evidence and a listing certificate (see paragraph 19.13 below).

Bankruptcy petitions

CHG 19.7

19.7 The court will not normally allow more than one bankruptcy petition to be presented against an individual at any one time.

CHG 19.8

19.8 In cases where the statutory demand relied on has not been personally served on the debtor or where execution of the debt has been returned unsatisfied in whole or in part, the permission of the Registrar is in practice required before a petition may be presented to the court. For service of statutory demands see CPR PD (Insolvency Proceedings) paragraphs 13.1–13.4.

CHG 19.9

19.9 On presentation to the court a bankruptcy petition is given a distinctive number. The details of the name and address of the petitioner, of their solicitors and of the debtor are entered on a computerised record which may be searched by attendance on the ground floor of the Rolls Building. It will also be endorsed with a hearing date which may be extended on application without notice if the petitioner has been unable to serve the petition on the debtor before the hearing date (see Insolvency Rules r 6.28 and CPR PD (Insolvency Proceedings) para 14.6.

CHG 19.10

19.10 A debtor who intends to oppose the making of a bankruptcy order should file and serve a written notice in the prescribed form stating their grounds for opposing the petition not less than five business days before the hearing date. The court may give such further directions as to the filing of evidence and of listing certificates (see paragraph 19.13 below) as it considers appropriate to the disposal of the petition.

Other applications

CHG 19.11

19.11 Many different types of application may be made to the court for the purpose of the administration of the estate and affairs of a bankrupt individual or insolvent person who is subject to an individual voluntary arrangement (IVA). These may involve such matters as the examination of the bankrupt or of persons having knowledge of their affairs, the realisation of assets in their estate and the determination of disputes regarding the validity of a creditor's claim to dividend or entitlement to vote at a creditors' meeting. Such applications will be given a hearing date when the Registrar will give such directions as are appropriate to the type of case, which may include directions for the filing and service of written evidence, for the cross-examination of witnesses and for the filing of listing certificates (see paragraph 19.13 below).

Orders without attendance

CHG 19.12

19.12 In suitable cases the court will normally be prepared to make orders under Part VIII of the Act (interim orders for IVAs) and consent orders without attendance by the parties. Details of these types of order and of the relevant procedure to follow are set out in CPR PD (Insolvency Proceedings) paragraphs 16.1–16.8.

Listing certificates

CHG 19.13

19.13 In order to prevent waste of the court's time each party to insolvency proceedings may be required by the court to file a listing certificate in which they will be required to certify whether the directions previously given by the court have been complied with, whether and by whom they will be represented at the final hearing, their estimate of the time required for such hearing and their representative's dates to avoid. On the filing of the certificates in any particular case the court will fix a date for the final hearing of the case and notify the parties.

Preparation for hearings before the Registrars

CHG 19.14

19.14 Paragraphs 7.40 to 7.52 apply to hearings before the Bankruptcy Registrars. Skeleton arguments and bundles should be delivered to the clerks' room, 1st Floor, Rolls Building.

General information

CHG 19.15

19.15 Inspection of the court file in any insolvency proceedings is governed by the Insolvency Rules r 7.31A.

CHG 19.16

19.16 The following publications regarding practice and procedure in the Bankruptcy Court are available free from the public counters, ground floor, Rolls Building.

(1)   I wish to make myself bankrupt—what do I do?
(2)   Court fees for personal bankrupts.
(3)   Bankruptcy Court Guide.
(4)   "I wish to set aside a statutory demand—what do I do?"
(5)   "I wish to file a notice of opposition—what do I do?"
(6)   "I wish to apply to annul a bankruptcy order—what do I do?"
(7)   I wish to apply for my Certificate of Discharge from Bankruptcy— what do I do?
(8)   Insolvency Practice Direction.
(9)   Practice Statement—the fixing and approval of the remuneration of appointees (2004).

Electronic copies of the above guides are available on the HMCTS website.

CHAPTER 20 THE COMPANIES COURT

Key Rules: CPR PD 49A—Applications Under The Companies Acts And Related Legislation; CPR PD (Insolvency Proceedings); Insolvency Rules 1986; Insolvent Companies (Disqualification Of Unfit Directors) Proceedings Rules 1987; CPR PD (Directors Disqualification Proceedings)

CHG 20.1

20.1 The Companies Court is a part of the Chancery Division. Applications in the High Court under the Companies Act 2006, the Financial Services and Markets Act 2002, the Insolvency Act 1986 in relation to companies registered in England and Wales, and the Company Directors Disqualification Act 1986, must be commenced in the Companies Court. Proceedings concerning insolvent partnerships, under the Insolvent Partnerships Order 1994, are also brought in the Companies Court (unlike proceedings against partners separately, which, if the partner is an individual, are brought in bankruptcy). Many other kinds of application are brought in the Companies Court. Appeals in Companies Court matters are dealt with in Chapter 10.

CHG 20.2

20.2 Applications, other than in insolvency, are governed by the Civil Procedure Rules and PD 49 - Applications under the Companies Acts and related legislation.

CHG 20.3

20.3 Applications in insolvency relating to companies (and to insolvent partnerships) are governed by the Insolvency Rules and PD - Insolvency Proceedings.

CHG 20.4

20.4 Proceedings under the Company Directors Disqualification Act 1986 are governed by the Insolvent Companies (Disqualification of Unfit Directors) Proceedings Rules 1987 and PD - Directors Disqualification Proceedings.

CHG 20.5

20.5 Proceedings in the Companies Court under a particular statute should be entitled accordingly, thus:

"In the matter of [name and registration number of the company] And in the matter of the Companies Act 2006 [and of any other statute as appropriate]"

"In the matter of [name of the relevant company] And in the matter of the Company Directors Disqualification Act 1986"

"In the matter of [name of the debtor] And in the matter of the Insolvency Act 1986 [and of any appropriate order, such as the Insolvent Partnerships Order 1994]"

CHG 20.6

20.6 The Companies Court has a separate administrative procedure. Proceedings are issued in the Companies Court, and they are dealt with by the Registrars.

CHG 20.7

20.7 Petitions for winding up, petitions for confirmation by the court of reduction of capital, applications for validation orders and interim applications for directions in proceedings by shareholders are among the principal matters heard by the Registrars. A limited category of applications of a routine or administrative nature may be dealt with by the member of court staff in charge of the winding up list: see CPR PD (Insolvency Proceedings) paragraph 12.1.

CHG 20.8

20.8 Certain matters such as applications for an administration order under Part II of the Insolvency Act 1986, applications for approval by the court of schemes of arrangement and applications for the appointment of provisional liquidators must be heard by a judge. A judge is available to hear companies matters each day in term time, and applications to be heard by that judge may be listed for any such day. Unopposed applications for the approval of schemes of arrangement will sometimes be heard by a judge before the start of normal sittings. Other applications may be dealt with by the Interim Applications Judge as Companies judge. The Registrar may refer or adjourn proceedings to the judge in accordance with the criteria set out in paragraph 19.4 above.

Preparation for hearings before the Registrars

CHG 20.9

20.9 Paragraphs 7.40 to 7.52 apply to hearings before the Registrars of the Companies Court. Skeleton arguments and bundles should be delivered to the clerks' room, 1st floor, Rolls Building.

Companies entering Administration

CHG 20.10

20.10 The statutory regime for administrations is now found in the Insolvency Act 1986, schedule B1, which should be read with the substituted Part 2 of the Insolvency Rules 1986. Administrations commenced by petition before 15 September 2003 and administrations of certain bodies (building societies, insolvent partnerships, limited liability partnerships, certain insurers, and public utility companies listed in Section 249(1)(a) – (d) of the Enterprise Act 2002) continue to be governed by Part II of the Insolvency Act 1986 (or enacted before the introduction of Schedule B1) and the former Part 2 of the Insolvency Rules 1986.

Accordingly, there are now three procedural routes into administration: by court order; by notice filed at court by the holder of a qualifying floating charge; or by notice filed at court by the company or its directors. Administration creates a statutory moratorium and allows the affairs, business and property of the company to be managed by an administrator.

Court Order

CHG 20.11

20.11 An application to the court for an administration order must be commenced by the prescribed form of application (Form 2.1B) and must be supported by a witness statement. The Insolvency Act and Rules specify the information which must be included in the witness statement: see in particular Insolvency Rules rule 2.4. The application may be made by the company, its directors, one or more creditors, the designated officer for a magistrates' court (in relation to a fine) or any combination of the above. The application will be listed before a judge.

CHG 20.12

20.12 Where a pre-arranged sale of the business is envisaged consideration should be given to the extent of the information to be provided to the court on the making of the application. Attention is drawn in this respect to Statement of Insolvency Practice 16, issued under procedures agreed between the insolvency regulatory authorities acting through the Joint Insolvency Committee (JIC).

Out of court

CHG 20.13

20.13 The holder of a qualifying floating charge, the company or its directors, may appoint an administrator without going through the court process. The appointment becomes effective when a notice of appointment in the prescribed form accompanied by the administrator's consent to act and a statement by them that in their opinion the purpose of the administration is likely to be achieved has been filed with the court. CPR 2.19 makes special provision for filing notice of appointment by fax or email out of business hours. (Form 2.7B). The designated fax number and email address for filing a notice in the Royal Courts of Justice are published on the Insolvency Service website. The fax number is 020 7947 6607 and the email address is: rcjcompanies.orders@hmcts.gsi.gov.uk.

Extension of administration order

CHG 20.14

20.14 Where it is necessary to apply to court for an extension of an administration order, the application should be made in good time. In the absence of special circumstances, the application should be made not less than one month before the end of the administration. The evidence in support of any late application must explain why the application is being made late. If the application is made within the last month of the administration the court will consider whether any part of the costs should be disallowed as an expense of the administration (see CPR PD (Insolvency Proceedings) paragraph 10.1).

Schemes of arrangement

CHG 20.15

20.15 A scheme under Part 26 of the Companies Act 2006 can be proposed whether or not a company is in liquidation. It is necessary to obtain the sanction of the court to a scheme which has been approved by the requisite majority of members or creditors of each class at separately convened meetings directed by the court. If the company is insolvent the objective of the scheme may be more simply and economically achieved by a company voluntary arrangement under Part I of the Act. However, a scheme under Part 26 has the advantage that the court may approve the distribution of assets otherwise than in accordance with creditors' strict legal rights.

CHG 20.16

20.16 The application for an order to convene meetings of members or creditors under section 896 is made by a CPR Part 8 claim form. The application will usually be heard by a Registrar, unless it is thought that issues of difficulty may arise, in which case it can be heard by a judge. The relevant practice is set out in *Practice Statement (Companies: Schemes of Arrangements)* [2002] 1 WLR 1345.

CHG 20.17

20.17 A The application to sanction a scheme of arrangement, once approved by members or creditors by the statutory majority, is made by the original claim form.

The hearing of the application at which the sanction of the court is sought will be before a judge. If the application also seeks confirmation of a reduction of capital, there will first be an application to the Registrar for directions. In other cases the application will go straight to a judge.

Winding-up petitions

CHG 20.18

20.18 Proceedings to wind up a company are commenced by presenting a petition to the court. The presentation of a winding up petition can cause substantial damage to a company. A winding up petition should not be presented when it is known that there is a real dispute about the debt. Practitioners should make reasonable enquiries from their client as to the existence of any such dispute. The court may order a petitioner to pay the company's costs of a petition based on a disputed debt on the indemnity basis.

CHG 20.19

20.19 Before presenting a winding up petition the creditor must conduct a search to ensure that no petition is already pending. Save in exceptional circumstances a second petition should not be presented while a prior petition is pending. A petitioner who presents a second petition in such circumstances does so at risk as to costs: see PD – Insolvency Proceedings, paragraph 11.1.

CHG 20.20

20.20 The Insolvency Act and Rules contain detailed guidance on the form and content of a winding up petition: see in particular PD – Insolvency Proceedings, paragraph 11.2. Note too the requirement that the statement of truth verifying the petition should be made no more than 10 business days before it is issued (paragraph 11.3). If there is an interval of more than 10 business days the court will usually require re-verification.

CHG 20.21

20.21 When a winding up petition is presented to either the Companies Court, a Chancery District Registry or a county court having jurisdiction, particulars including the name of the company and the petitioner's solicitors are entered in a computerised register. This is called the Central Registry of Winding Up Petitions. It may be searched by personal attendance at the ground floor, Rolls Building, or by telephone on 0906 754 0043.

CHG 20.22

20.22 The requirement to advertise the petition (Insolvency Rules, r 4.11(2)(b)) is mandatory, and designed to ensure that the class remedy of winding up by the court is made available to all creditors, and is not used simply as a means of putting improper pressure on the company to pay the petitioner's debt or costs: see CPR PD (Insolvency Proceedings) paragraph 11.5. Failure to comply with the rule, without good reason accepted by the court, may lead to the summary dismissal of the petition on the return date (Insolvency Rules, r 4.11(6)). If the court, in its discretion, grants an adjournment, this will be on condition that the petition is advertised in due time for the adjourned hearing. No further adjournment for the purpose of advertisement will normally be granted.

CHG 20.23

20.23 Copies of every notice gazetted in connection with a winding up petition (or, where this is not practicable, a description of the form and content of the advertisement) must be lodged with the court as soon as possible after publication and in any event not later than five business days before the hearing of the petition. This rule applies even if the advertisement is defective in some way or if the petitioner decides not to pursue the petition.

CHG 20.24

20.24 If an order is made restraining advertisement while an application is made to the court to stop the proceedings, the case is listed in the Daily Cause List by number only so that the name of the company is not given.

Proceedings for relief from unfairly prejudicial conduct under the Companies Act 2006, section 994

CHG 20.25

20.25 Petitions under the Companies Act 2006, section 994, are liable to involve extensive factual enquiry and many of the measures summarised in Section A of this Guide which are designed to avoid unnecessary cost and delay are particularly relevant to them. Procedure is governed by the Companies (Unfair Prejudice Applications) Proceedings Rules 2009 (SI 2009/2469).

CHG 20.26

20.26 Where applications are brought in the Companies Court and in a related case in the Chancery Division at the same time, special arrangements can be made on request to the Chancery Judges' Listing Officer for the applications to be heard by the same judge.

Applications for permission to act as director of a company with a prohibited name

CHG 20.27

20.27 Section 216 of the Insolvency Act 1986 restricts the use of a company name by any person who was a director or shadow director of the company in the 12 month period ending with the day before it went into insolvent liquidation— except with the permission of the court: Section 216(3).

CHG 20.28

20.28 The application for permission is governed by the Insolvency Rules 1986, rr 4.226 to 4.230. These rules provide for certain exceptions to the prohibition. The application for permission is made by application in Form 7.1A supported by a witness statement.

CHG 20.29

20.29 By r 4.227A(2) the court may call upon the liquidator for a report of the circumstances in which the company became insolvent and the extent of the applicant's apparent responsibility. However if the liquidator consents to the application it is helpful if their views are put before the court at the outset. The Registrar who then hears the application may be prepared to grant it at the first hearing.

CHG 20.30

20.30 At least 14 days' notice should be given to the Secretary of State and/or the Official Receiver.

General

CHG 20.31

20.31 Inspection of the court file in any insolvency proceedings is governed by the Insolvency Rules r 31A.

CHG 20.32

20.32 The following publication is available from the public counters, ground floor, Rolls Building:

(1)   I wish to apply to extend time for Registration of a Charge or to rectify a mis-statement or omission.

CHG 20.33

20.33 For restoration to the register of a company which has been dissolved or struck off, see the Treasury Solicitor's website at: www.tsol.gov.uk/Publications/S cheme_Publications/company_restorations_Oct_2011.pdf.

CHAPTER 21 MORTGAGE CLAIMS

Key Rules: CPR Pt 55 and CPR Pt 73 and the PDs supplementing them

CHG 21.1

21.1 Under Part 55 mortgage possession claims commenced since 15 October 2001, whether in respect of residential or commercial property, are generally heard in the county courts. The only exceptions to this are (a) a relatively small number of cases where either the county court has no jurisdiction or where the claimant can certify, verified by a statement of truth, exceptional reasons for bringing the claim in the High Court and (b) any remaining transitional cases, i.e. mortgage possession claims commenced before 15 October 2001, and proceedings to enforce charging orders commenced prior to 25 March 2002, as to which directions should be sought from the assigned Master.

CHG 21.1 [1]

As regards enforcement of charging orders see paragraph 21.4 as to the limited jurisdiction of the county court and the consequent residual jurisdiction of the High Court.

CHG 21.2

21.2 Attention is drawn to the Pre-Action Protocol for Possession Claims based on Mortgage or Home Purchase Plan Arrears in respect of Residential Property. Parties should be able, if requested by the court, to explain the actions that they have taken to comply with this protocol. Form N123 contains a Mortgage Protocol Pre-action Checklist.

CHG 21.3

21.3 PD 55 emphasises that High Court possession claims are to be regarded as exceptional and that while the value of the property and the size of the claim may well be relevant circumstances they will not, taken alone, normally justify the issue of proceedings in the High Court. High Court proceedings may, however, be justified where there are complicated disputes of fact or where a claim gives rise to points of law of general importance; or where the County Court has no jurisdiction in respect of particular relief sought. Where a mortgage possession claim is issued in the High Court it is assigned to the Chancery Division. The provisions of Part 55 will apply to it.

CHG 21.4

21.4 The most common instance where, notwithstanding Part 55, the Chancery Division will retain jurisdiction in a mortgage possession case is where proceedings are brought seeking an order for sale under an equitable charge, ordinarily that created by a charging order, but where part of the relief claimed ancillary to the order for sale is an order for possession. Although rule 73.10 now provides that proceedings to enforce charging orders by sale should be made in the court in which the charging order was made, that provision is expressly subject to that court having jurisdiction. Except in cases which have been transferred from the High Court to the county court the jurisdiction of a county court to enforce a charge is confined to those cases where the amount secured by the charge falls within the relevant county court limit which is still £30,000, although the Government has decided in principle to increase it to £350,000). It follows that in many cases where judgments have been obtained in county courts and charging orders made enforcement will nonetheless require proceedings in the High Court.

CHG 21.4 [1]

In straightforward cases, where, because of the amount secured by the charging order, primary jurisdiction is given to the High Court, the court will very often transfer the case to a local county court, clothing that court with jurisdiction pursuant to s 40(2) of the County Courts Act 1984. This will be particularly the case if the charging order has been made in the county court in respect of a judgment of the county court.

CHG 21.5

21.5 Such proceedings, as well as proceedings to enforce charging orders made in other Divisions of the High Court, are assigned to the Chancery Division. The evidence required in support of such proceedings is that set out in paragraph 4.3 of PD 73.

CHG 21.6

21.6 The Chancery Division retains its jurisdiction in respect of redemption and foreclosure of mortgages and kindred matters.

CHG 21.7

21.7 Rule 48.3 and paragraph 50 of the Costs PD (Amount of costs where costs are payable under a contract) are of particular relevance to mortgage claims[1].

---

1 Note that from 1 April 2013, the CPR costs provisions are re-organised and amended so that the substantive costs provisions are now found in CPR Pt 44 to CPR Pt 47 and their accompanying practice directions: see Civil Procedure (Amendment) Rules 2013, SI 2013/262. For the practice directions see the Justice website at www.justice.gov.uk.

CHAPTER 22 PARTNERSHIP CLAIMS AND RECEIVERS

Key Rules: CPR Part 69, CPR PD 24 and CPR PD 40A

Partnership claims

CHG 22.1

22.1 In claims for or arising out of the dissolution of a partnership often the only matters in dispute between the partners are matters of accounting. In such cases there will be no trial. The court will, if appropriate, make a summary order under paragraph 6 of PD 24 for the taking of an account. This will be taken before the Master.

CHG 22.2

22.2 Only if there is a dispute as to the existence of a partnership (whether it is claimed that there never was a partnership or that the partnership is still continuing and has not been dissolved) or if there is a material dispute as to the terms of the partnership (e.g. as to the profit sharing ratios) will there be a trial, at which the judge will decide those issues. In such cases there will be a two stage procedure with the judge deciding these issues at the trial and ordering the winding up of the partnership which will involve the taking of the partnership accounts by the Master (see PD 40 Accounts, Inquiries etc.).

CHG 22.3

22.3 In some cases and in order to reduce costs, it may be appropriate for the parties to invite the Master to determine factual issues as a preliminary to the account, eg issues as to terms of the partnership or assets comprised in it. At any case management conference it will be particularly important to identify the issues to be determined before an effective account or inquiry can be made. The court will not simply order accounts and inquiries without identifying the issues.

CHG 22.3 [1]

It is often the case that the Master will also, by agreement of the parties, resolve the question as to the existence or otherwise of the partnership and (whether by agreement or within the context of an account or inquiry) any other question relating to the partnership. It is very rare for partnership cases to go to trial before the Judge.

CHG 22.4

22.4 The expense of taking an account in court is usually wholly disproportionate to the amount at stake. Parties are strongly encouraged to refer disputes on accounts to a jointly instructed accountant for determination or mediation.

CHG 22.5

22.5 The functions of a receiver in a partnership action are limited. Unlike the liquidator of a company it is the receiver's duty to wind up the partnership. The receiver's primary function is to get in the debts and preserve the assets pending winding up by the court and the receiver has no power of sale without the permission of the court.

Receivers

CHG 22.6

22.6 The procedure for the appointment of receivers by the court is comprehensively governed by CPR Part 69 and CPR PD 69. Guidance for receivers in the

Chancery Division is available on request from the Associates or the Chancery Operations Manager. The guidance is also reproduced at Appendix 10. Particular attention should be paid to the question of the receiver's remuneration and the fact that it must be authorised on the basis specified in an order of the court.

CHAPTER 23 THE PATENTS COURT AND INTELLECTUAL PROPERTY CLAIMS

Key Rules: CPR Part 63 and CPR PD 63 - Patents, etc

CHG 23.1

23.1 The matters assigned to the Patents Court are essentially all those concerned with patents, registered designs, semiconductor topography rights and plant varieties. CPR Part 63 and PD 63 deal with its particular procedures, and other intellectual property claims. Appeals in patent, design and trade mark cases are governed by Part 52 (see CPR 63.16); reference should be made to Chapter 10 for the general procedure as regards such appeals.

CHG 23.2

23.2 The procedure of the Patents Court is broadly that of the Chancery Division as a whole, but there are important differences.

CHG 23.3

23.3 The Patents Court has its own Court Guide which is available on the Justice website (www.justice.gov.uk/guidance/courts-and-tribunals/courts/patents-court/index.htm) and can also be found in Section 2F of Volume 2 of the White Book. That Guide must be consulted for guidance as to the procedure in the Patents Court and the Patents County Court.

CHG 23.4

23.4 The Court's diary can be accessed on its website. The Patents Court will endeavour, if the parties so desire and the case is urgent, to sit in September.

Registered trademarks and other intellectual property rights

CHG 23.5

23.5 CPR 63.13 and paragraphs 16 to 24 of PD 63 apply to claims relating to matters arising out of the Trade Marks Act 1994 and other intellectual property rights (such as copyright, passing off, design rights, etc.) as set out in paragraph 16 of PD 63. Claims under the Trade Marks Act 1994 must be brought in the Chancery Division. Among the Chancery Masters trade mark cases are assigned to Master Bragge. Cases not specifically assigned to the Patents Court may be heard by any judge of the Division, and may also be heard in certain Chancery District Registries (see PD 63 paragraphs 16 and 21.1).

CHG 23.6

23.6 Appeals from decisions of the Registrar of Trade Marks are brought to the Chancery Division as a whole, not the Patents Court. Permission to appeal is not required.

CHAPTER 24 PROBATE AND INHERITANCE CLAIMS

Key Rules: CPR Part 57 and CPR PD 57

Probate

CHG 24.1

24.1 In general, contentious probate proceedings follow the same pattern as an ordinary claim but there are important differences and Part 57 and PD 57 should be carefully studied. All probate claims are allocated to the multi-track. Particular regard should be had to the following:

(1)   The claim form must be issued out of the Issue Section in the Rolls Building or out of the Chancery District Registries, or if the claim is suitable to be heard in the county court, a county court where there is also a Chancery District Registry, or the Central London Civil Justice Centre Chancery List.

(2)   A defendant must file an acknowledgment of service. An additional 14 days is provided for doing so.

(3)   Save where the court orders otherwise, the parties must at the outset of proceedings lodge all testamentary documents in their possession and control with the court. At the same time parties must file written evidence describing any testamentary document of the deceased of which they have knowledge, stating, if any such document is not in the party's possession or control, the name and address, if known, of the person in whose possession or under whose control the document is. In the case of a claimant, these materials must be lodged at the time when the claim form is issued. In the case of a defendant, these materials must be lodged when service is acknowledged. If these requirements are not complied with it is likely that the claim will not be issued and, correspondingly, that the acknowledgment of service will not be permitted to be lodged.

(4)   The court will generally ensure that all persons with any potential interest in the proceedings are joined as parties or served with notice under Part 19.8A.

(5)   A default judgment cannot be obtained in a probate claim. Where, however, no defendant acknowledges service or files a defence, the claimant may apply for an order that the claim proceed to trial and seek a direction that the claim be tried on written evidence.

(6)   If an order pronouncing for a will in solemn form is sought under CPR Part 24, the evidence in support must include written evidence proving due execution of the will. In such a case, if a defendant has given notice under CPR 57.7(5) that they raise no positive case but require that the will be proved in solemn form and that, to that end, they wish to cross examine the attesting witnesses, then the claimant's application for summary judgment is subject to the right of such a defendant to require the attesting witnesses to attend for cross examination.

(7)   A defendant who wishes to do more than test the validity of the will by cross examining the attesting witnesses must set up by counterclaim their positive case in order to enable the court to make an appropriate finding or declaration as to which is the valid will, or whether a person died intestate or as the case may be.

(8)   The proceedings may not be discontinued without permission. Even if they are compromised, it will usually be necessary to have an order stating to whom the grant is to be made, either under rule 57.11 (leading to a grant in common form), or after a trial on written evidence under paragraph 6.1(1) of PD 57 (leading to a grant in solemn form) or under section 49 of the Administration of Justice Act 1985 and paragraph 6.1(3) of PD 57 (again leading to a grant in solemn form). Practitioners should refer to PF38CH and adapt as appropriate.

CHG 24.1 [1]

The original jurisdiction of the county court, even the Central London County Court [Central London Civil Justice Centre], or a county court where there is a Chancery District Registry, is limited by section 32 of the County Courts Act 1984 to the limited class of cases falling within that section – see further note **CPR 57.2 [1]** to Part 57. The High Court has power, however, under section 40(2) of the County Courts Act to transfer contentious probate claims commenced in the High Court to the county court, if appropriate, and that power is now more readily exercised than hitherto.

CHG 24.1 [2]

Failure to lodge all testamentary documents will result in the court refusing to approve any settlement of the claim until such time as the relevant documents have been lodged.

CHG 24.2

24.2 When the court orders trial of a contentious probate claim on written evidence, or where the court is asked to pronounce in solemn form under Part 24, it is normally necessary for an attesting witness to sign a witness statement or swear an affidavit of due execution of any will or codicil sought to be admitted to probate. The will or codicil is at that stage in the court's possession and cannot be handed out of court for use as an exhibit to the witness statement or affidavit, so that the attesting witness has to attend at the Rolls Building or the District Registry at which the documents are lodged.

CHG 24.3

24.3 Where an attesting witness is unable to attend the Rolls Building or the appropriate District Registry in order to sign his or her witness statement or swear his or her affidavit in the presence of an officer of the court, the solicitor concerned may request from Masters' Appointments (ground floor, Rolls Building) or from the District Registry, a photographic copy of the will or codicil in question. This will be certified as authentic by the court and may be exhibited to the witness statement or affidavit of due execution in lieu of the original. The witness statement or affidavit must in that case state that the exhibited document is an authenticated copy of the document signed in the witness' presence.

CHG 24.4

24.4 When a probate claim started in the Rolls Building is transferred to or listed for trial at a court outside London, the solicitor for the party responsible for preparing the court bundle must write to Masters' Appointments (ground floor, Rolls Building) and request that the testamentary documents be forwarded to the appropriate District Registry.

CHG 24.5

24.5 If a disputed will is required for forensic examination an application should be made under Part 23. The court will require to be satisfied that the examiner is suitably qualified and can give undertakings for the safe-keeping and preservation of the will, and that the proposed methods of examination will not damage the will.

Inheritance (Provision for Family and Dependants) Act 1975

CHG 24.6

24.6 Claims under the Inheritance (Provision for Family and Dependants) Act 1975 in the Chancery Division will be allocated to the Multi-Track and are issued by way of a Part 8 claim. Ordinarily they will be tried by the Master unless an order is made transferring the claim to a county court for trial. They are governed by Section IV of CPR Part 57 and Section IV of CPR PD 57.

CHG 24.7

24.7 The written evidence filed by the claimant with the claim form must exhibit an official copy of the grant of probate or letters of administration together with every testamentary document in respect of which probate or letters of administration was granted.

CHG 24.7 [1]

There is authority that an application under the Inheritance Act 1975 can only be commenced after a grant of representation has been made. This may cause difficulty, where the validity of a will is disputed (and where therefore there is no final grant of representation) and it is desired to bring a 1975 Act claim either in conjunction with or in the alternative to a claim for probate. In these circumstances the grant of representation by way of the appointment of an administrator pending suit may resolve the jurisdictional difficulty. To avoid difficulties, however, it is probably better practice to deal with the grant of representation before bringing 1975 Act proceedings.

CHG 24.8

24.8 A defendant must file and serve acknowledgment of service not later than 21 days after service of the Part 8 claim form. Any written evidence (subject to any extension agreed or directed) must likewise be served and filed no later than 21 days after service.

CHG 24.9

24.9 The personal representatives of the deceased are necessary defendants to a claim under the 1975 Act and the written evidence filed by a defendant who is a personal representative must comply with paragraph 16 of PD 57..

CHG 24.10

24.10 On the hearing of a claim under the 1975 Act, the personal representatives must produce the original grant of representation to the deceased's estate. If the court makes an order under the Act, the original grant together with a sealed copy of the order must, under paragraph 18.2 of PD 57, be sent to the Principal Registry of the Family Division, First Avenue House, 42-49 High Holborn, London WC1V 6NP for a memorandum of the order to be endorsed on or permanently annexed to the grant.

CHG 24.11

24.11 Where claims under the 1975 Act are compromised the consent order filed must comply with paragraph 9.16 of this Guide.

CHG 24.11 [1]

Paragraph 9.15 no longer deals with the 1975 Act. The reference, however, is to the requirement, found in paragraph 18.3 of the PD supporting Part 57, that where an order is made compromising a 1975 Act Claim then that order should contain a requirement that a memorandum of the order should be endorsed on or annexed to the grant of representation

and that a copy of the order be sent to the Principal Registry for the order to be endorsed or annexed.
_____

CHAPTER 25 TRUSTS

Key Rules: CPR Part 8; CPR Part 19; CPR Part 64; CPR PD 64A and CPR PD 64B

Introduction

CHG 25.1

25.1 This Chapter contains material about a number of aspects of proceedings concerning trusts, the estates of deceased persons (other than probate claims) and charities.

CHG 25.2

25.2 The topics covered in this Chapter are (a) applications by trustees for directions and related matters; (b) the Variation of Trusts Act 1958; (c) section 48 of the Administration of Justice Act 1985; (d) vesting orders as regards property in Scotland; (e) trustees under a disability; (f) lodgement of funds; (g) the estates of deceased Lloyd's Names; and (h) judicial trustees.

Trustees' applications for directions

CHG 25.3

26.3 Applications to the court by trustees for directions in relation to the administration of a trust or charity, or by personal representatives in relation to a deceased person's estate, are to be brought by Part 8 claim form, and are governed by Part 64, and its PDs; rule 8.2A is also relevant.

CHG 25.4

25.4 Where the remedy sought is the approval of a sale, purchase, compromise or other transaction by a trustee, the claim form may be issued under rule 8.2A without naming a defendant. In all other cases, permission to issue the claim form under rule 8.2A is required. Case management directions will be given where the court grants an application to issue the claim form under rule 8.2A.

Proceeding without a hearing

CHG 25.5

25.5 The court will always consider whether it is possible to deal with the application on paper without a hearing.

CHG 25.6

25.6 Cases in which the directions can be given without a hearing include those where personal representatives apply to be allowed to distribute the estate of a deceased Lloyd's name, following the decision in *Re Yorke (deceased)* [1997] 4 All ER 907 (see paragraphs 25.26-31 below), as well as applications under section 48 of the Administration of Justice Act 1985 (see paragraphs 25.15-20 below).

Representation Orders

CHG 25.7

25.7 It is not necessary to make representation orders under rule 19.7 on an application for directions, and sometimes it would not be possible, for lack of separate representatives among the parties of all relevant classes of beneficiaries, but such orders can be useful in an appropriate case and they are sometimes made.

Costs

CHG 25.8

> 25.8 Normally the trustees' costs of a proper application will be allowed out of the trust fund, on an indemnity basis, as will the assessed (or agreed) costs of beneficiaries joined as defendants, subject to their conduct of the proceedings having been proper and reasonable.

CHG 25.8 [1]

In some cases the court will go further and make a prospective costs order in favour of the trustees in respect of their costs of the litigation for which directions have been sought. Such a costs order will provide for the trustees' costs to be paid out of the trust fund.

Prospective costs orders

CHG 25.9

> 25.9 In proceedings brought by one or more beneficiaries against trustees, the court has power to direct that the beneficiaries be indemnified out of the trust fund in any event for any costs incurred by them and any costs which they may be ordered to pay to any other party, known as a prospective costs order: see *McDonald v. Horn* [1995] 1 All ER 961. Such an order may provide for payments out of the trust fund from time to time on account of the indemnity so that the beneficiaries' costs may be paid on an interim basis. Applications for prospective costs orders should be made on notice to the trustees. The court will require to be satisfied that there are matters which need to be investigated. How far the court will wish to go into that question, and in what way it should be done, will depend on the circumstances of the particular case. The order may be expressed to cover costs incurred only up to a particular stage in the proceedings, so that the application has to be renewed, if necessary, in the light of what has occurred in the proceedings in the meantime: see CPR PD 64A paragraphs 6.1–6.8, to which is annexed a model form of order.

Charity trustees' applications for permission to bring proceedings

CHG 25.10

> 25.10 In the case of a charitable trust, if the Charity Commission refuses its consent to the trustees applying to the court for directions, under Charities Act 2011 Section 115(2), and also refuses to give the trustees the directions under its own powers, for example under Sections 105 or 110, the trustees may apply to the court under Section 115(5). On such an application, which may be dealt with on paper, the judge may call for a statement from the Charity Commission of its reasons for refusing permission, if not already apparent from the papers. The court may require the trustees to attend before deciding whether to grant permission for the proceedings. It is possible to require notice of the hearing to be given to the Attorney-General, but this would not normally be appropriate.

Variation of Trusts Act 1958

CHG 25.11

> 25.11 An application under the Variation of Trusts Act 1958 should be made by a Part 8 claim form. As to listing of such applications see paragraph 6.27. The Master will not consider the file without an application. Evidence is dealt with by PD 64 para 4.

CHG 25.12

> 25.12 Where any children or unborn beneficiaries will be affected by an arrangement under the Act, evidence must normally be before the court which shows that

their litigation friends (in the case of children) or the trustees (in the case of unborns) support the arrangement as being for their benefit, and exhibits a written opinion to this effect. In complicated cases a written opinion is usually essential to the understanding of the litigation friends and the trustees, and to the consideration by the court of the merits and fiscal consequences of the arrangement. If the written opinion was given on formal instructions, those instructions must be exhibited. Otherwise the opinion must state fully the basis on which it was given. The opinion must be given by the advocate who will appear on the hearing of the application. A skeleton argument may not be needed where a written opinion has been put in evidence and no matters not appearing from the instructions or the opinion are to be relied on.

CHG 25.13

25.13 Where the interests of two or more children, or two or more of the children and unborn beneficiaries, are similar, a single written opinion will suffice; and no written opinion is required in respect of those who fall within the proviso to section 1(1) of the Act (discretionary interests under protective trusts). Further, in proper cases the requirement of a written opinion may at any stage be dispensed with by the Master or the judge.

CHG 25.13 [1]

Applications for the removal of protective trusts where the interest of the principal beneficiary has not failed or determined can, unlike other applications under the Variation of Trusts Act 1958, be heard by the Master.

CHG 25.14

25.14 Where parties are represented by the same solicitors and counsel from the same Chambers the court is unlikely to assess costs summarily, or to dispense with an assessment on the basis that they have been agreed, unless either the case is a clear one or the value of the trust fund is such that a detailed assessment of costs would be disproportionate.

Applications under section 48 of the Administration of Justice Act 1985

CHG 25.15

25.15 Applications under section 48 of the Administration of Justice Act 1985 should be made by Part 8 Claim Form without naming a defendant, under rule 8.2A. No separate application for permission under rule 8.2A need be made. The claim should be supported by a witness statement or affidavit to which are exhibited: (a) copies of all relevant documents; (b) instructions to a person with a 10-year High Court qualification within the meaning of the Courts and Legal Services Act 1990 ("the qualified person"); (c) the qualified person's opinion; and (d) draft terms of the desired order. The application should not seek a decision of the court on the construction of any instrument.

CHG 25.16

25.16 The witness statement or affidavit (or exhibits thereto) should state: (a) the reason for the application (b) the names of all persons who are, or may be, affected by the order sought; (c) all surrounding circumstances admissible and relevant in construing the document; (d) the date of qualification of the qualified person and his or her experience in the construction of trust documents; (e) the approximate value of the fund or property in question; (f) whether it is known to the applicant that a dispute exists and, if so, details of such dispute and (g) what steps are proposed to be taken in reliance on the opinion.

CHG 25.17

25.17 When the file is placed before the Master he will consider whether the evidence is complete and if it is send the file to the judge.

CHG 25.18

25.18 The judge will consider the papers and, if necessary, direct service of notices under rule 19.8A or request such further information as he or she may desire. If the judge is satisfied that the order sought is appropriate, the order will be made and sent to the claimant.

CHG 25.19

25.19 If following service of notices under rule 19.8A any acknowledgment of service is received, the claimant must apply to the Master (on notice to the parties who have so acknowledged service) for directions. If the claimant desires to pursue the application to the court, in the ordinary case the Master will direct that the case proceeds as a Part 8 claim.

CHG 25.20

25.20 If on the hearing of the claim the judge is of the opinion that any party who entered an acknowledgment of service has no reasonably tenable argument contrary to the qualified person's opinion, in the exercise of his or her discretion he or she may order such party to pay any costs thrown away, or part thereof.

Vesting orders - property in Scotland

CHG 25.21

25.21 In applications for vesting orders under the Trustee Act 1925 any investments or property situate in Scotland should be set out in a separate schedule to the claim form, and the claim form should ask that the trustees may have permission to apply for a vesting order in Scotland in respect thereto.

CHG 25.22

25.22 The form of the order to be made in such cases will (with any necessary variation) be as follows:

"It is ordered that the [] as Trustees have permission to take all steps that may be necessary to obtain a vesting order in Scotland relating to [the securities] specified in the schedule herein."

Disability of Trustee

CHG 25.23

25.23 There must be medical evidence showing incapacity to act as a trustee at the date of issue of the claim form and that the incapacity is continuing at the date of signing the witness statement or swearing the affidavit. The witness statement or affidavit should also show incapacity to execute transfers, where a vesting order of stocks and shares is asked for.

CHG 25.24

25.24 The trustee under disability should be made a defendant to the claim but need not be served unless he or she is sole trustee or has a beneficial interest.

Lodgement of Funds

CHG 25.25

25.25 Mortgagees wishing to lodge surplus proceeds of sale in court under s.63 of the Trustee Act 1925 must in their witness statement or affidavit, and in addition to the matters set out in 37PD 6.1, set out the steps they have taken to fulfil their obligation under s.105 of the Law of Property Act 1925 to pay other incumbrancers (if any) and the mortgagor and why those steps have not been successful. Failure to do so will usually result in their application being rejected by the court

Estates of Deceased Lloyd's Names

CHG 25.26

25.26 The procedure concerning the estates of deceased Lloyd's names is governed by a Practice Statement [2001] 3 All ER 765. Before invoking the procedure, practitioners should consider with care whether it is still necessary to do so following the approval by the High Court on 25 June 2009, under Section 111 of the Financial Services and Markets Act 2000, of a scheme transferring to Equitas Insurance Ltd the legal liabilities under English law of Names in respect of the years 1992 and earlier: see the judgment of Blackburne J in *Re the Names at Lloyd's for the 1992 and Prior Years of Account* [2009] EWHC 1595 (Ch).

CHG 25.27

25.27 Personal representatives who still wish to apply to the court for permission to distribute the estate of a deceased Lloyd's Name following *Re Yorke (deceased)* [1997] 4 All ER 907, or trustees who wish to administer any will trusts arising in such an estate, may, until further notice and if appropriate in the particular estate, adopt the following procedure.

CHG 25.28

25.28 The procedure will be appropriate where:

(1)   the only, or only substantial, reason for delaying distribution of the estate is the possibility of personal liability to Lloyd's creditors;

(2)   all liabilities of the estate in respect of syndicates of which the Name was a member for the years 1992 and earlier (if any) were reinsured (whether directly or indirectly) into the Equitas group and

(3)   all liabilities of the estate in respect of syndicates of which the Name was a member for the years 1993 and later (if any) arise in respect of syndicates which have closed by reinsurance in the usual way or are protected by the terms of an Estate Protection Plan issued by Centrewrite Limited or are protected by the terms of EXEAT insurance cover provided by Centrewrite Limited.

CHG 25.28 [1]

Where cases do not fall within the foregoing paragraph, the practice nonetheless is for a procedure analogous to that provided for by the Practice Statement to be adopted and for evidence to be lodged sufficient to satisfy the court that the estate is protected from potential

Lloyd's liabilities and therefore that the estate can be distributed without any reservation to meet such liabilities.

CHG 25.29

25.29 In these circumstances personal representatives (and, if applicable, trustees) may apply by a Part 8 Claim Form headed "In the Matter of the Estate of [] deceased (a Lloyd's Estate) and In the Matter of the Practice Direction dated May 25 2001" for permission to distribute the estate (and, if applicable, to administer the will trusts) on the footing that no or no further provision need be made for Lloyd's creditors. Ordinarily, the claim form need not name any other party. It may be issued in this form without a separate application for permission under rule 8.2A.

CHG 25.30

25.30 The claim should be supported by a witness statement or an affidavit substantially in the form set out in Appendix 11 adapted as necessary to the particular circumstances and accompanied by a draft of the desired order substantially in the form also set out in Appendix 11. If the amount of costs has been agreed with the residuary beneficiaries (or, if the costs are not to be taken from residue, with the beneficiaries affected) their signed consent to those costs should also be submitted. If the Claimants are inviting the court to make a summary assessment they should submit a statement of costs in the form specified in the Costs PD. If in his or her discretion the Master (or outside London the District Judge) thinks fit, he or she will summarily assess the costs but with permission for the paying party to apply within 14 days of service of the order on them to vary or discharge the summary assessment. Subject to the foregoing, the order will provide for a detailed assessment unless subsequently agreed.

CHG 25.31

25.31 The application will be considered in the first instance by the Master who, if satisfied that the order should be made, may make the order without requiring the attendance of the applicants, and the court will send it to them. If not so satisfied, the Master may give directions for the further disposal of the application.

Judicial Trustees

CHG 25.32

25.32 Judicial trustees are appointed by the court under the Judicial Trustees Act 1896, in accordance with the Judicial Trustee Rules 1983. An application for the appointment of a judicial trustee should be made by Part 8 claim (or, if in an existing claim, by an application notice in that claim) which must be served (subject to any directions by the court) on every existing trustee who is not an applicant and on such of the beneficiaries as the applicant thinks fit. Once appointed, a judicial trustee may obtain non-contentious directions from the assigned Master informally by letter, without the need for a Part 23 application (unless the court directs otherwise). Applications for directions can be sought from the court as to the trust or its administration by rule 8 of the Judicial Trustee Rules.

CHG 25.32 [1]

Judicial Trustee are rarely appointed. They may be appropriate in a case where it is envisaged both that the trust will subsist for a lengthy period and where the circumstances of the trust are complex and will, or may, require regular intervention by, or directions from the court.

Having regard to Article 6 of the European Convention on Human Rights great care must be taken in respect of informal access to the assigned Master for directions. If, as between the Judicial Trustee and the beneficiaries or the beneficiary to which the directions relate, the matter is at all contentious it would be inappropriate to deal with the matter without proper notice to the beneficiaries or beneficiary and without giving those persons an opportunity to be heard. Further, if arising out of any informal guidance given, any contentious application falls to be made, it would be inappropriate for the Master who had given that guidance to be asked to further adjudicate. In those circumstances the Master should be asked to direct that the application be heard by another Master.

CHG 25.33

25.33 Where it is proposed to appoint the Official Solicitor as judicial trustee, inquiries must first be made to his office for confirmation that he is prepared to act if appointed. The Official Solicitor will not be required to give security.

CHG 25.34

25.34 A judicial trustee is entitled under rule 11 of the 1983 rules to such remuneration as is reasonable in respect of work reasonably performed. Applications for payment by the trustee must be by letter to the court, submitted with the accounts. A Practice Note issued by the Chief Chancery Master, with the authority of the Vice-Chancellor, on 1 July 2003 sets out the best practice to be followed in determining the amount of remuneration. The Practice Note mirrors the position regarding receivers' remuneration under CPR rule 69.7 and is reproduced at Appendix 12.

APPENDICES

APPENDIX 1: ADDRESSES AND OTHER CONTACT DETAILS
1. Clerks to the Chancery Judges
CHG App 1.1

(all numbers to be preceded by 020 and by 7947, except where indicated)

Clerk to:	telephone	fax
The Chancellor	6412	
Mr Justice Peter Smith	6183	
Mr Justice David Richards	7419	
Mr Justice Mann	7964	
Mr Justice Warren	7260	
Mr Justice Briggs	6741	
Mr Justice Henderson	6669	
Mr Justice Morgan	6419	
Mr Justice Norris	1728	
Mr Justice Barling	6675	
Mr Justice Floyd	7073 1740	
Mr Justice Sales	6657	
Mrs Justice Proudman	6671	
Mr Justice Arnold	7073 1789	
Mr Justice Roth	6589	
Mr Justice Vos	7606	
Mr Justice Newey	7467	
Mr Justice Hildyard	6039	
Mrs Justice Asplin	7071 5766	

Chancery Judges Clerks Fax Numbers: 0870 761 7696.

2. E-mail communications

CHG App 1.2

The e-mail protocol sets out how parties may communicate by e-mail on certain matters with the Chancery Division, and can be found at: http://www.justice.gov.uk /guidance/courts-and-tribunals/courts/chancery-division/email-communications. htm.

The relevant e-mail addresses are:

(a)   For skeleton arguments for hearings within the scheme operating at the Rolls Building (see paragraph 14.9):
  (i)   Skeleton arguments for use in the Applications Court: chancery.applications.skeletons@hmcts.gsi.gov.uk
  (ii)   All other skeletons: chancery.general.skeletons@hmcts.gsi.gov.uk

(b)   For other skeleton arguments, chronologies, reading lists, lists of issues, lists of authorities (but not the authorities themselves) and lists of the persons involved in the facts of the case sent in advance of a hearing:
Judge:
mailto://rcjchancery.judgeslisting@hmcts.gsi.gov.uk
[Note: The clerk to the Judge concerned should be contacted to find out whether other documents will be accepted by e-mail, and whether documents should be sent direct to the judge's clerk's e-mail address.]
Chancery Master:
chancery.mastersappointments@hmcts.gsi.gov.uk
Companies and High Court Bankruptcy Registrar:
Rcjcompanies.orders@hmcts.gsi.gov.uk
County Court Bankruptcy Registrar:
RCJBankCLCCDJhearings@hmcts.gsi.gov.uk

(c)   For the agreed terms of an Order which is ready to be sealed following the conclusion of a hearing:
Judge:
rcjchancery.ordersandaccounts@hmcts.gsi.gov.uk
Chancery Master:
rcjchancery.ordersandaccounts@hmcts.gsi.gov.uk
Companies and High Court Bankruptcy Registrar:
rcjbankruptcy.registrarshearings@hmcts.gsi.gov.uk
County Court Bankruptcy Registrar:
RCJBankCLCCDJhearings@hmcts.gsi.gov.uk

3. At the Royal Courts of Justice, Rolls Building

CHG App 1.3

(All telephone extension numbers and fax numbers should be prefixed by 020 7947 unless otherwise specified)

HIGH COURT BANKRUPTCY AND COMPANIES

Ground Floor

High Court Bankruptcy and Companies Operational Manager (7472)

Companies Schemes and Reductions of Capital (6727)

High Court Bankruptcy and Companies Issue Section:

Issue of all Debtors' Bankruptcy petitions over £100,000, issue of all Creditors' Bankruptcy petitions, applications to set aside statutory demands, applications for Interim Orders, issue of all Winding Up Petitions. Filing affidavits, witness statements and documents In relation to Companies and Bankruptcy except Winding Up, applications for certificates of discharge in bankruptcy (6294)

All other Companies Court applications (6102)

Central Index (0906 754 0043)

Winding up Section:

All file and case management, including where it results in orders relating to the Winding Up Court.

Filing of documents for the Winding Up procedure (6516)

Registrars Hearings:

High Court Bankruptcy and Companies Registrars' orders (6731)

File Management:

High Court Bankruptcy File Inspections, and Office copies. Requesting bankruptcy and companies files, for applications without notice to be made in Chambers (6175)

1ST FLOOR

HEARING ROOM 7 Chief Registrar Baister

HEARING ROOM 8 Registrar Derrett

HEARING ROOM 9 Registrar Nicholls

HEARING ROOM 10 Registrar Barber

HEARING ROOM 11 Registrar Jones

Registrars Enquiries office

GROUND FLOOR

CHANCERY CHAMBERS

Ground Floor

Issue Section:

Issue and amendment of all Chancery process including Patents County Court Claims, filing affidavits and witness statements (save those lodged within two days of a hearing before a Master which are to be filed with the Masters' Appointment Section); filing acknowledgements of service, searches of cause book and transfers in (7754/7783) Patents County Court Clerk and Section Manager (6571)

Masters' Appointments:

Issue of Masters' applications, including applications without notice to Masters; filing affidavits and witness statements in proceedings before Masters (only if filed within two working days of hearing before the Master); skeleton arguments, applications to serve out of jurisdiction; filing stop notices; filing testamentary documents in contested probate cases; filing grants lodged under Part 57; filing affidavits relating to funds paid into court under the Trustee Act 1925, Compulsory Purchase Act 1965 and the Lands Clauses Consolidation Act 1845. Manager (6095); Clerks to Chancery Masters (6702/7391);

File Management:

Applications for office copy documents, including orders, transfers out, Notice of Change and Certificates of Service. Manager (6083) Admin Clerk (6148)

1st Floor

HEARING ROOM 3 Chief Master Winegarten

HEARING ROOM 6 Master Bragge

HEARING ROOM 4 Master Bowles

HEARING ROOM 1 Master Price

HEARING ROOM 5 Master Teverson

HEARING ROOM 2 Master Marsh

Room D01-010 Lawyer, Chancery Chambers (6080)

Room D01-007 Personal Assistant (Masters) (6777)

Ground Floor

Chancery Judges' Listing Office (6690) Fax (0870 739 5869)

High Court Appeals Office (6778)

Video-conferencing requests (7887)

Consultation room requests (6585)

5th Floor

Chancery Associates:

Preparation of all Chancery Orders and Companies and Bankruptcy Court Orders; small payments; bills of costs for assessment; settlement of payment and lodgement schedules; accounts of receivers, judicial trustees, guardians and administrators; applications relating to security set by the court; matters arising out of accounts and inquiries ordered by the court (6733);

Manager in Court Support/Usher (6322) (room no 55)

4. Additional numbers

Additional numbers at the Royal Courts of Justice, Rolls Building

CHG App 1.4

(Prefaced by 020 7947 unless otherwise specified)

RCJG Switchboard (6000/6818)

Rolls Security Office (7000)

Rolls First Aid (7000)

Additional numbers at the Royal Courts of Justice but outside the Rolls Building

(Prefaced by 020 7947 unless otherwise specified)

Officer in charge of Courts and Recording Transcription Unit (6154)

RCJ Advice Bureau (0845 120 3715 or 020 7947 6880; fax 020 7947 7167)

Personal Support Unit (7701)

RCJ Security Office (6260)

5. London, outside the Royal Courts of Justice

CHG App 1.5

Central London Civil Justice Centre: see Appendix 15

6. Outside London

CHG App 1.6

The following are the court addresses, telephone and fax numbers for the courts at which there are regular Chancery sittings outside London:

Birmingham:

The Priory Courts,
33 Bull Street,
Birmingham B4 6DS.
Telephone: 0121-681-3033.
Fax: 0121-681-3121.

Bristol:

Bristol Civil Justice Centre
Bristol Civil Justice Centre
2 Redcliff Street
Bristol BS1 6GR DX95903 Bristol 3

Telephone: General switchboard: 0117 3664800
Specialist Jurisdiction Listing Officer: 0117 3664860
Chancery Clerk: 0117 3664868
Fax: 0117 3664801
e-mail: bristolchancerylisting@hmcts.gsi.gov.uk
bristolchanceryjudgeskeletons@hmcts.gsi.gov.uk

Cardiff:

The Civil Justice Centre,
2 Park Street,
Cardiff CF1 1ET.
Telephone: 02920 376412.
Fax: 02920 376475
Email: hearings@cardiffcountycourt.gsi.gov.uk
Skeletons: cardiffcjcskeletons@hmcourts-service.gsi.gov.uk

Leeds:

The Court House,
1 Oxford Row,
Leeds LS1 3BG.
Telephone: 0113-283-0040.
Fax: 0113-244-8507.

Liverpool:

35 Vernon Street
Liverpool
Merseyside L2 2BX
DX 702600 Liverpool
Tel: 0151 296 2449 or 2550
Email: efilings@liverpool.countycourt.gsi.gov.uk

Manchester:

Manchester Civil Justice Centre
1 Bridge Street West
Manchester Greater Manchester M60 9DJ
DX 72483 Manchester 44
Telephone: Listing: 0161 240 5223/5224
Chancery: 0161 240 5225/5226/5227
Insolvency: 0161 240 5228/5229
Fax: 0161 240 5398
Email: manchester.chancery@hmcts.gsi.gov.uk

Newcastle:

The Law Courts,
Quayside,
Newcastle-upon-Tyne NE1 3LB.
Telephone: 0191-201-2000.
Fax: 0191-201-2001.

Preston:

The Law Courts,
Openshaw Place,
Ringway,
Preston PR1 2LL.
Telephone: 01772-832300.
Fax: 01772-832476.

In some centres resources do not permit the listing telephone numbers to be attended personally at all times. In cases of urgency, solicitors, counsel and counsel's clerks may come into the Chancery Court and leave messages with the member of staff sitting in court.

Urgent court business officer pager numbers for out of hours applications:

Birmingham (Midland Region):

West Side: 07699-618079

East Side: 07699-618078

Bristol: 07699-618088

Cardiff: 07699-618086

Manchester and Liverpool: 07699-618080

Preston: 07699-618081

Newcastle: 01399-618083

Leeds and Bradford: 01399-618082

In case of difficulty out of hours, contact the Royal Courts of Justice on 020 7947 6260.

APPENDIX 2: GUIDELINES ON STATEMENTS OF CASE

CHG App 2.1

1. The document must be as brief and concise as possible.

CHG App 2.2

2. The document must be set out in separate consecutively numbered paragraphs and sub-paragraphs.

CHG App 2.3

3. So far as possible each paragraph or sub-paragraph should contain no more than one allegation.

CHG App 2.4

4. The document should deal with the case on a point by point basis, to allow a point by point response.

CHG App 2.5

5. Where the CPR require a party to give particulars of an allegation or reasons for a denial (see rule 16.5(2)), the allegation or denial should be stated first and then the particulars or reasons listed one by one in separate numbered sub-paragraphs.

CHG App 2.6

6. A party wishing to advance a positive case must identify that case in the document; a simple denial is not sufficient.

CHG App 2.7

7. Any matter which if not stated might take another party by surprise should be stated.

CHG App 2.8

8. Where they will assist, headings, abbreviations and definitions should be used and a glossary annexed.

CHG App 2.9

9. Contentious headings, abbreviations, paraphrasing and definitions should not be used; every effort should be made to ensure that headings, abbreviations and definitions are in a form that will enable them to be adopted without issue by the other parties.

CHG App 2.10

10. Particulars of primary allegations should be stated as particulars and not as primary allegations.

CHG App 2.11

11. Schedules or appendices should be used if this would be helpful, for example where lengthy particulars are necessary.

CHG App 2.12

12. The names of any witness to be called may be given, and necessary documents (including an expert's report) can be attached or served contemporaneously if not bulky (PD 16; Guide paragraph 2.11). Otherwise evidence should not be included.

CHG App 2.13

13. A response to particulars stated in a schedule should be stated in a corresponding schedule.

CHG App 2.14

14. Lengthy extracts from a document should not be set out. If an extract has to be included, it should be placed in a schedule.

CHG App 2.15

15. The document must be signed by the individual person or persons who drafted it, and not, in the case of a solicitor, in the name of the firm only. It must be accompanied by a Statement of Truth.

APPENDIX 3: DRAFT CASE MANAGEMENT DIRECTIONS
MULTI-TRACK CLAIMS

CHG App 3

Claim No.

IT IS ORDERED

1. Allocation to multi-track

() that this claim is allocated to the multi-track.

2. Transfer of claims, including transfer from Part 8

() that the claim be transferred to:

(a)   the. . . . . Division of the High Court;
(b)   the. . . . . District Registry;
(c)   the. . . . . [Central London] Civil Justice Centre [Chancery List].

(...) that the issue(s). . . . . (*define issue(s)*) be transferred to
. . . . (*one of (a) to (c) above*) for determination.

(...) that the. . . . . (*party*) apply by. . . . . (*date*) to a Judge of
the Technology and Construction Court [*or other Specialist List*] for an Order to
transfer the claim to that Court.

(...) that the claim. . . . . (*title and claim number*) commenced in [the
. . . . County Court] [the District Registry of. . . . .], be
transferred from that Court to the Chancery Division of the High Court.

(...) that this claim shall continue as if commenced under Part 7 and shall be
allocated to the multi-track.

3. Alternative dispute resolution

This claim be stayed until. . . . . [*one month*] for the parties to try to
settle the dispute by alternative dispute resolution or other means. The parties
shall notify the Court in writing at the end of that period whether settlement has
been reached.

The parties shall at the same time lodge *either*:

(a)   (if a settlement has been reached) a draft consent Order signed by all
        parties; *or*
(b)   (if no settlement has been reached) a statement of agreed directions signed
        by all parties or (in the absence of agreed directions) statements of the
        parties' respective proposed directions.
        (i)   a statement of agreed directions signed by all parties or (in the
                absence of agreed directions) statements of the parties' respective
                proposed directions;
        (ii)   the parties' Disclosure Reports; and
        (iii)   the parties' Costs Budgets.

4. Probate cases only

(...) that the. . . . . [*party*] file [his] [her] witness statement or affidavit of
testamentary scripts and lodge any testamentary script at the Chancery Chambers,
Case Management Section, The Rolls Building, 7 Rolls Building, Fetter Lane,
London, EC4A 1NL [. . . . . District Registry] by. . . . . (*date*).

5. Case summary

(...) that [each party] [the. . . . . (*party*)] by. . . . . (*date*) prepare and serve a case summary [not exceeding. . . . . words] on all other parties, to be agreed by. . . . . (*date*) and filed by . . . . (*date*) and if it is not agreed by that date the parties shall file their own case summaries.

6. Trial date

(...) that the trial of the claim/issue(s) take place between. . . . . (*date*) and. . . . . (*date*) ("the trial window").

(...) that the. . . . . (*party*) shall make an appointment to attend on the Listing Officer (The Rolls Building, 7 Rolls Building, Fetter Lane, London, EC4A 1NL; Tel. 020 7947 6690; Fax No. 0870 739 5869; email: rcjchancery.judgeslisting@hmcts.gsi.gov.uk) to fix a trial date within the trial window, such appointment to be not later than. . . . . (*date*) and give notice of the appointment to all other parties.

(...) that

(i) the claim be entered in the [Trial List] [General List], with a listing category of . . . . [A] [B] [C], with a time estimate of . . . . days/weeks
(ii) the trial take place in London (*or* identify venue).

7. Pre Trial Review

(Add if case is estimated to last more than 10 days or if appropriate:)

(...) [the trial being estimated to last more than 10 days] that there be a Pre Trial Review on a date to be arranged by the Listing Officer [in conjunction with the parties] [to take place shortly before the trial and, if possible, in front of the Judge who will be conducting the trial] at which, except for urgent matters in the meantime, the Court will hear any further applications for Orders.

8. All directions agreed

(If the parties have sent in a full list of agreed directions which are satisfactory, use this paragraph. A case management conference may then not be required:)

(...) The parties having agreed the following directions it is by consent ordered: ...

9. Some directions agreed

(If the parties have agreed some directions which are satisfactory, use this paragraph:)

(...) The parties having agreed the following directions it is by consent ordered:

10. Case management conference etc

(...) that there be a [further] case management conference before the Master in Hearing Room . . . , First Floor, The Rolls Building, 7 Rolls Building, Fetter Lane, London, EC4A 1NL on. . . . . (*date*) at. . . . . o'clock (of . . . . hours/minutes duration).

(...) that there shall be a case management conference (of. . . . . hours/minutes duration). In order for the Court to fix a date the parties are to complete the accompanying questionnaire and file it by. . . . . (*date*).

(...) that the. . . . . (*party*) apply for an appointment for a [further] case management conference by. . . . . (*date*).

(...) At the case management conference, except for urgent matters in the meantime, the Court will hear any further applications for Orders and any party must file an Application Notice for any such Orders and serve it and supporting evidence (if any) by. . . . . (*date*).

11. Case [and Costs] Management conference

(...) that there be a Case [and Costs] Management conference before the Master in Hearing Room . . . , First Floor, The Rolls Building, 7 Rolls Building, Fetter Lane, London EC4A 1NL on. . . . . (*date*) at. . . . . o'clock (of . . . . hours/minutes duration).

(*Note: reference should be made to paragraph 28*)

12. Amendments to statement of case

(...) that the. . . . . (*party*) has permission to amend [his] [her] state-ment of case as in the copy on the Court file [initialled by the Master].

(...) that the amended statement of case be verified by a statement of truth.

(...) that the amended statement of case be filed by. . . . . (*date*).

(...) that [the amended statement of case be served by. . . . . (*date*).] [service of the amended statement of case be dispensed with].

(...) that any consequential amendments to other statements of case be filed and served by. . . . . (*date*)

(...) that the costs of and consequential to the amendment to the statement of case [shall be paid by. . . . . (*party*) in any event] [are assessed in the sum of £. . . . . and are to be paid by. . . . . (*party*)][within . . . . (*time*)].

13. Addition of parties etc.

(...) that the. . . . . (*party*) has permission:

(a)   to [add] [substitute] [remove]. . . . . (*name of party*) as a . . . . (*party*) and
(b)   to amend [his] [her] statement of case in accordance with the copy on the Court file [initialled by the Master].

and that the amended statement of case be verified by a statement of truth.

(...) that the amended statement of case be:

(a)   filed by. . . . . (*date*);
(b)   served on. . . . . (*new party, existing parties or removed party, as appropriate*), by. . . . . (*date*).

(...) that a copy of this Order be served on. . . . . (*new party, existing parties or removed party, as appropriate*), by. . . . . (*date*).

(...) that any consequential amendments to other statements of case be filed and served by. . . . . (*date*).

(...) that the costs of and consequential to the amendment to the statement of case [shall be paid by the. . . . . (*party*) in any event] [are assessed in the sum of £. . . . . and are to be paid by the. . . . . (*party*)].

14. Consolidation

(...) that this claim be consolidated with claim number. . . . . (*number and title of claim*), the lead claim to be claim number. . . . . [The title to the consolidated case shall be as set out in the Schedule to this Order].

15. Trial of issue

(...) that the issue of. . . . . (*define issue*) be tried as follows:

(a) with the consent of the parties, before a Master
-   (i) on. . . . . (*date*) in Hearing Room . . . , First Floor, The Rolls Building, 7 Rolls Building, Fetter Lane, London, EC4A 1NL;
-   (ii) with a time estimate of. . . . . (*hours*),
-   (iii) with the filing of listing questionnaires dispensed with, *or*

(b) before a Judge
-   (i) with the trial of the issue to take place between. . . . . (*date*) and. . . . . (*date*) ("the trial window")
-   (ii) with the. . . . . (*party*) to make an appointment to attend on the Listing Officer (The Rolls Building, 7 Rolls Building, Fetter Lane, London, EC4A 1NL; Tel: 020 7947 6690; Fax No: 020 7947 7345) to fix a trial date within the trial window, such appointment to be not later than. . . . . (*date*) and to give notice of the appointment to all other parties.
-   (iii) with the issue to be entered in the [Trial List] [General List], with a listing category of . . . . [A] [B] [C], and a time estimate of. . . . . days/ weeks and to take place in London (*or* identify venue).

16. Further information

(...) that the. . . . . (*party*) provide by. . . . . (*date*) the [further information] [clarification] sought in the request dated. . . . . (*date*) [initialled by the Master].

(...) that any request for [further information] [clarification] shall be served by . . . . [*date*].

17. Disclosure of documents

(...) that disclosure is dispensed with.

(...) that [*party*] disclose the documents on which it relies and at the same time request any specific disclosure that it requires from any other party.

(...) [that each party shall give disclosure on an issue by issue basis.]

(...) [that each party disclose any documents which it is reasonable to suppose may contain information which enables that party to advance its own case or to damage that of any other party, or which leads to an inquiry which has either of those consequences.]

(...) [that [*party*] give standard disclosure.]

(...) [*such other order in relation to disclosure as the court is asked to consider appropriate, including if appropriate in relation to electronic documents*] **Please set out the order proposed**

***Notes*:**

(a) The court will consider the disclosure reports provided by the parties and decide which of the disclosure options set out in CPR 31.5(7) should apply to this claim. Proposals put forward by the parties will be taken into account in making that decision.

*(b) **A list of issues**, preferably agreed, should be attached to the draft directions so as to assist the court in determining any order to be made in relation to disclosure.*

18. Inspection of documents

(...) that any requests for inspection or copies of disclosed documents shall be made within. . . . . days after service of the list and shall be responded to within [7] days of receipt of the request.

19. Preservation of property

(...) that the. . . . . (*party*) preserve. . . . . (*give details of relevant property*) until trial of the claim or further Order *or other remedy under CPR 25.1(1).*

20. Witness statements

(...) that each party serve on every other party the witness statement of the oral evidence which the party serving the statement intends to rely on in relation to [any issues of fact] [the following issues of fact. . . . . (*define issues*)] to be decided at the trial, those statements [and any notices of intention to rely on hearsay evidence] to be

(a) exchanged by. . . . . (*date*) or
(b) served by. . . . . (*party*) by. . . . . (*date*) and by
. . . . (*party*) by. . . . . (*date*)

provided that before exchange the parties shall liaise with a view to agreeing a method of identification of any documents referred to in any such witness statement.

(...) that the. . . . . (*party*) has permission to serve a witness summary relating to the evidence of. . . . . (*name*) of. . . . . (*address*) [on every other party by] [to be served on. . . . . (*party*)/exchanged at the same time as exchange of witness statements].

(**Note:** *The parties should consider the court's power in CPR 32.2(3)*)

21. No expert evidence

(...) no expert evidence being necessary, that [no party has permission to call or rely on expert evidence] [permission to call or rely on expert evidence is refused].

22. Single expert

(...) that evidence be given by the report of a single expert in the field of . . . . (*define field*) instructed jointly by the parties, on the issue of . . . . (*define issue*) [and [his] [her] fees shall be limited to £ . . . .].

(...) that if the parties are unable to agree [by. . . . . (*date*)] who that expert is to be and about the payment of [his] [her] fees any party may apply for further directions.

() that unless the parties agree in writing or the Court orders otherwise, the fees and expenses of the single expert shall be paid to [him] [her] by the parties equally.

(...) that each party give [his] [her] instructions to the single expert by . . . . (*date*).

(...) that the report of the single expert be filed and served by [him] [her] on the parties by. . . . . (*date*).

(...) that no party may recover from another party more than £. . . . . for the fees and expenses of the expert.

(...) that the evidence of the expert be given at the trial by [written report] [oral evidence] of the expert.

23. Separate Experts

(...) that each party has permission to adduce [oral] expert evidence in the field of. . . . . (*specify*) [limited to. . . . . expert(s) [per party] [on each side].

(...) (*where practicable*) that the experts shall be . . . . (*specify name*)
And . . . . (*specify name*)

(...) that the experts' reports shall be exchanged by. . . . . (*date*).

(...) that the experts shall hold a discussion for the purpose of:

(a)   identifying the issues, if any, between them; and
(b)   where possible, reaching agreement on those issues.

(...) that the experts shall by. . . . . [*specify date after discussion*]
prepare and file a statement for the Court showing:

(a)   those issues on which they are agreed; and
(b)   those issues on which they disagree and a summary of their reasons for
        disagreeing.

(...) No party shall be entitled to recover by way of costs from any other party more
than £. . . . . for the fees or expenses of an expert.

Note: *to assist the court in determining what order should be made in relation to
expert evidence, the parties should attach a **list of issues**, preferably agreed.*

24. Definition and reduction of issues

(...) that by. . . . . (*date*) the parties list and discuss the issues in the
claim [including the experts' reports and statements] and attempt to define and
narrow the issues [including those issues the subject of discussion by the experts].

25. Trial bundle and skeleton arguments

(...) that not earlier than 7 days or later than 3 days before the date fixed for trial the
Claimant shall file with the Chancery Listing Office a trial bundle for the use of the
Judge in accordance with Appendix 6 of the Chancery Guide.

(...) that skeleton arguments and chronologies shall be filed not less than 2 clear
days before the date fixed for trial in accordance with Appendix 7 of the Chancery
Guide.

26. Settlement

(...) that If the claim or part of the claim is settled the parties must immediately
inform the Court, whether or not it is then possible to file a draft Consent Order to
give effect to the settlement.

27. Compliance with Directions

(...) that the parties shall by. . . . . (*date*) notify the Court in writing that
they have fully complied with all directions or state:

(a)   with which directions they have not complied;
(b)   why they have not complied; and
(c)   what steps they are taking to comply with the outstanding directions in time
        for the trial.

If the Court does not receive such notification or if the steps proposed to comply
with outstanding directions are considered by the Court unsatisfactory, the Court
may order a hearing (and may make appropriate orders as to costs against a party
in default).

28. Costs Management

(...) [*where budgets have been agreed*] the parties having agreed and filed budgets,
the court makes a costs management order which records that agreement.

(...) [*where budgets have been filed and exchanged but have not been agreed in
whole or in part*] that there be a case and costs management conference before the
Master in Hearing Room . . . First Floor, The Rolls Building, 7 Rolls Building, Fetter
Lane, London EC4A 1NL on . . . . (*date*) at . . . . o'clock
(of . . . . hours/minutes duration).

(...) [*where a Case and Costs Management Conference is ordered*] at least 5 working days before the Case and Costs Management Conference the claimant must file with the court, and send copies to all other parties, the following documents:

(a)   a case summary and list of issues,

(b)   a one page summary of Precedent H of all parties' budgets to enable the court to undertake comparison of the budgets, in the form set out below.*

(...) (*Set out any other proposed directions with regard to budgets*)

(**Note:** *If budgets are not agreed the court may direct a Costs Management Conference*)

29. Costs

(...) that the costs of this application be [costs in the case][. . . . .]

* *Form of summary of Precedent H*

Phase	Claimant	1st defendant	2nd defendant	3rd defendant	TOTAL
Pre-action					
Issue/pleadings					
CMC					
Disclosure					
Witness statements					
Experts' reports					
PTR					
Trial preparation					
Trial					
ADR					
Contingencies					
TOTAL					

APPENDIX 4

Part 1: Judge's application information form

CHG App 4

Title as in claim form

Application Information

1.   [- DATE APPLICATION TO BE HEARD -]

2.   DETAILS OF SOLICITOR/PARTY LODGING THE APPLICATION

    a.   [Name]

    b.   [Address]

    c.   [Telephone No.]

    d.   [Reference]

    e.   [Acting for Claimant(s)/Defendant(s)]

3.   DETAILS OF COUNSEL/OR OTHER ADVOCATE

    a.   [Name]

    b.   [Address of Chambers/Firm]

    c.   [Telephone No.]

4.   DETAILS OF OTHER PART(Y'S)(IES') SOLICITORS

    a.   [Name]

    b.   [Address]

    c.   [Telephone No.]

    d.   [Reference]

    [Acting for Claimant(s)/Defendant(s)]

GUIDES

APPENDIX 5 CORRESPONDENCE WITH CHANCERY MASTERS – PRACTICE NOTE

CHG App 5

(1)   One of the consequences of the new Rules and Practice Directions has been a significant increase in letters to the Court from parties and their solicitors. This imposes a heavy extra burden on the staff and Masters. It also means that court files have to be moved more often, which itself gives rise to problems. It would therefore be greatly appreciated if parties and solicitors involved in litigation before the Chancery Masters had regard to the following points.

(2)   When corresponding, please consider carefully (a) whether your letter is really necessary and (b) if it is who the correct addressee should be. Only address letters to the Master if the letter needs to be seen by him. If not address the letter to his clerk.

(3)   Faxes should not be used to send letters or documents of a routine or non-urgent nature. Where a party files a document by fax he must not send a hard copy in addition. (If, exceptionally, a fax has included a document the original of which needs to go on the court file, then a hard copy enclosing the original may be sent and it should be marked clearly "confirmation of fax").

(4)   As a general rule all correspondence, whether letter or fax, must be copied to the other parties. Correspondence should therefore state that it has been copied to the other parties (or else it should state that it has not been and explain why).

(5)   Correspondence should not be used in place of a Part 23 application (which requires payment of a fee, a draft order and a statement of truth).

J Winegarten

Chief Chancery Master

July 2009

APPENDIX 6: GUIDELINES ON BUNDLES

Bundles of documents must comply with paragraph 3 of PD 39 Miscellaneous Provisions relating to Hearings. These guidelines are additional to those requirements, and they should be followed wherever possible.

CHG App 6.1

1. The preparation of bundles requires co-operation between the legal representatives for all parties, and in many cases a high level of co-operation. It is the duty of all legal representatives to co-operate to the necessary level. Where a party is a litigant in person, it is also that party's duty to co-operate as necessary with the other parties' legal representatives.

CHG App 6.2

2. Bundles should be prepared in accordance with the following guidance.

Avoidance of duplication

CHG App 6.3

3. No more than one copy of any one document should be included, unless there is good reason for doing otherwise. One such reason may be the use of a separate core bundle.

CHG App 6.4

4. If the same document is included in the chronological bundles and is also an exhibit to an affidavit or witness statement, it should be included in the chronological bundle and where it would otherwise appear as an exhibit a sheet should instead be inserted. This sheet should state the page and bundle number in the chronological bundles where the document can be found.

CHG App 6.5

5. Where the court considers that costs have been wasted by copying unnecessary documents, a special costs order may be made against the relevant person. In no circumstances should rival bundles be presented to the court.

Chronological order and organisation

CHG App 6.6

6. In general documents should be arranged in date order starting with the earliest document.

CHG App 6.7

7. If a contract or other transactional document is central to the case it may be included in a separate place provided that a page is inserted in the chronological run of documents to indicate where it would have appeared chronologically and where it is to be found instead. Alternatively transactional documents may be placed in a separate bundle as a category.

Pagination

CHG App 6.8

8. This is covered by paragraph 3 of the PD, but it is permissible, instead of numbering the whole bundle, to number documents separately within tabs. An exception to consecutive page numbering arises in the case of the core bundle. For this it may be preferable to retain the original numbering with each bundle represented by a separate divider.

CHG App 6.9

9. Page numbers should be inserted in bold figures, at the bottom of the page and in a form that can clearly be distinguished from any other pagination on the document.

Format and presentation

CHG App 6.10

10. Where possible, the documents should be in A4 format. Where a document has to be read across rather than down the page, it should so be placed in the bundle as to ensure that the top of the text starts nearest the spine.

CHG App 6.11

11. Where any marking or writing in colour on a document is important, for example on a conveyancing plan, the document must be copied in colour or marked up correctly in colour.

CHG App 6.12

12. Documents in manuscript, or not easily legible, should be transcribed; the transcription should be marked and placed adjacent to the document transcribed.

CHG App 6.13

13. Documents in a foreign language should be translated; the translation should be marked and placed adjacent to the document translated; the translation should be agreed or, if it cannot be agreed, each party's proposed translation should be included.

CHG App 6.14

14. The size of any bundle should be tailored to its contents. There is no point having a large lever-arch file with just a few pages inside. On the other hand bundles should not be overloaded as they tend to break. No bundle should contain more than 300 pages.

CHG App 6.15

15. Binders and files must be strong enough to withstand heavy use.

CHG App 6.16

16. Large documents, such as plans, should be placed in an easily accessible file. If they will need to be opened up often, it may be sensible for the file to be larger than A4 size.

Indices and labels

CHG App 6.17

17. Indices should, if possible, be on a single sheet. It is not necessary to waste space with the full heading of the action. Documents should be identified briefly but properly, e.g. "AGS3 - Defendants Accounts".

CHG App 6.18

18. Outer labels should use large and clearly visible lettering, e.g. "A. Pleadings." The full title of the action and solicitors' names and addresses should be omitted. A label should be used on the front as well as on the spine.

CHG App 6.19

19. It is important that a label should also be stuck on to the front inside cover of a file, in such a way that it can be clearly seen even when the file is open.

Staples etc.

CHG App 6.20

20. All staples, heavy metal clips etc. should be removed.

Statements of case

CHG App 6.21

21. Statements of case should be assembled in 'chapter' form, ie claim form followed by particulars of claim, followed by further information, irrespective of date.

CHG App 6.22

22. Redundant documents, eg particulars of claim overtaken by amendments, requests for further information recited in the answers given, should generally be excluded. Backsheets to statements of case should also be omitted.

Witness statements, affidavits and expert reports

CHG App 6.23

23. Where there are witness statements, affidavits and/or expert reports from two or more parties, each party's witness statements etc. should, in large cases, be contained in separate bundles.

CHG App 6.24

24. The copies of the witness statements, affidavits and expert reports in the bundles should have written on them, next to the reference to any document, the reference to that document in the bundles. This can be done in manuscript.

CHG App 6.25

25. Documents referred to in, or exhibited to, witness statements, affidavits and expert reports should be put in a separate bundle and not placed behind the statement concerned, so that the reader can see both the text of the statement and the document referred to at the same time.

CHG App 6.26

26. Backsheets to affidavits and witness statements should be omitted.

New Documents

CHG App 6.27

27. Before a new document is introduced into bundles which have already been delivered to the court - indeed before it is copied - steps should be taken to ensure that it carries an appropriate bundle/page number, so that it can be added to the court documents. It should not be stapled, and it should be prepared with punch holes for immediate inclusion in the binders in use.

CHG App 6.28

28. If it is expected that a large number of miscellaneous new documents will from time to time be introduced, there should be a special tabbed empty loose-leaf file for that purpose. It is conventional to label this file "X". An index should be produced for this file, updated as necessary.

Inter-Solicitor Correspondence

CHG App 6.29

29. It is seldom that all inter-solicitor correspondence is required. Only those letters which are likely to be referred to should be copied. They should normally be placed in a separate bundle.

Core bundle

CHG App 6.30

30. Where the volume of documents needed to be included in the bundles, and the nature of the case, makes it sensible, a separate core bundle should be prepared for the trial, containing those documents likely to be referred to most frequently.

Basis of agreement of bundles

CHG App 6.31

31. See Chapter 7, paragraph 13.

Photocopy authorities

CHG App 6.32

32. See Chapter 7, paragraphs 33 to 35.

APPENDIX 7:GUIDELINES ON SKELETON ARGUMENTS, CHRONOLOGIES, INDICES AND READING LISTS

Skeleton arguments

CHG App 7.1

1. A skeleton argument is intended to identify both for the parties and the court those points which are, and those that are not, in issue, and the nature of the argument in relation to those points which are in issue. It is not a substitute for oral argument.

CHG App 7.2

2. Every skeleton argument should therefore:

(1) identify concisely:
  (a) the nature of the case generally, and the background facts insofar as they are relevant to the matter before the court;
  (b) the propositions of law relied on with references to the relevant authorities;
  (c) the submissions of fact to be made with reference to the evidence;
(2) be as brief as the nature of the issues allows - it should not normally exceed 20 pages of double-spaced A4 paper and in many cases it should be much shorter than this;
(3) be in numbered paragraphs and state the name (and contact details) of the advocate(s) who prepared it;
(4) avoid arguing the case at length;
(5) avoid formality and make use of abbreviations, eg C for Claimant, A/345 for bundle A page 345, 1.1.95 for 1st January 1995 etc.

CHG App 7.3

3. Paragraph 1 also applies to written summaries of opening speeches and final speeches. Even though in a large case these may necessarily be longer, they should still be as brief as the case allows.

Reading lists

CHG App 7.4

4. The documents which the Judge should if possible read before the hearing may be identified in a skeleton argument, but must in any event be listed in a separate reading list, if possible agreed between the advocates, which must be lodged with the agreed bundles, together with an estimate, if possible agreed, of the time required for the reading.

Chronologies and indices

CHG App 7.5

5. Chronologies and indices should be non contentious and agreed with the other parties if possible. If there is a material dispute about any event stated in the chronology, that should be stated in neutral terms and the competing versions shortly stated.

CHG App 7.6

6. If time and circumstances allow its preparation, a chronology or index to which all parties have contributed and agreed can be invaluable.

CHG App 7.7

7. Chronologies and indices once prepared can be easily updated and may be of continuing usefulness throughout the case.

APPENDIX 8 DELIVERY OF DOCUMENTS IN CHANCERY CHAMBERS

1. Delivery of documents for Masters' hearings

CHG App 8.1

(a)   Deliver bundles and skeletons (if required) to Masters' Appointments, Ground Floor, Rolls Building, at least 2 and not more than 7 clear working days before the hearing.

(b)   Mark clearly "for hearing on . . . . *(date)* before Master . . . .

(c)   Insert a reading list and estimate of reading time if appropriate.

(d)   Bundles may be presented in ring binders or lever arch files, or as appropriate.

(e)   Documents for Masters' hearings should not be taken direct to the Master's room unless in any particular case the Master has directed otherwise.

(f)   Documents required for Masters' hearings should never be taken to (i) the Issue Section (Ground Floor, Rolls Building); (ii) the Chancery Judges' Listing Office (Ground Floor, Rolls Building) or (iii) the RCJ Post Room—if they are they may well not reach the Master in time.

Note: Documents required for hearings before a Chancery Judge must not be delivered to the Issue Section or Masters' Appointments. They must be delivered to the Chancery Judges' Listing Office (Ground Floor, Rolls Building).

CHG App 8.1 [1]

After the move to the Rolls Building bundles for Masters hearings should be lodged with the Masters' Appointments Section, Ground Floor Rolls Building. Bundles for judges hearings should be lodged with Chancery Judges Listing, Ground Floor, Rolls Building.

2. Filing of documents

CHG App 8.2

(a)   Take or send documents required to be filed (ie placed on the Court file, either under the CPR or under an Order of the Court (eg statements of case, defences, allocation questionnaires, some witness statements)) to the Issue Section (Ground Floor, Rolls Building).

(b)   But documents (e.g. witness statements, exhibits) required to be filed which are needed for a Masters' hearing within 10 working days must be delivered for filing to Masters' Appointments, Ground Floor, Rolls Building not the Issue Section.

(c)   If bulky, use treasury tags, not files or ring binders.

APPENDIX 9: GUIDELINES ON WITNESS STATEMENTS

CHG App 9.1

1. The function of a witness statement is to set out in writing the evidence in chief of the maker of the statement. Accordingly witness statements should, so far as possible, be expressed in the witness's own words. This guideline applies unless the perception or recollection of the witness of the events in question is not in issue.

CHG App 9.2

2. Witness statements should be as concise as the circumstances of the case allow. They should be written in consecutively numbered paragraphs. They should present the evidence in an orderly and readily comprehensible manner. They must be signed by the witness, and contain a statement that he or she believes that the facts stated in his or her witness statement are true. They must indicate which of the statements made are made from the witness's own knowledge and which are made on information and belief, giving the source of the information or basis for the belief.

CHG App 9.3

3. Inadmissible material should not be included. Irrelevant material should likewise not be included.

CHG App 9.4

4. Any party on whom a witness statement is served who objects to the relevance or admissibility of material contained in a witness statement should notify the other party of their objection within 28 days after service of the witness statement in question and the parties concerned should attempt to resolve the matter as soon as possible. If it is not possible to resolve the matter, the party who objects should make an appropriate application, normally at the PTR, if there is one, or otherwise at trial.

CHG App 9.5

5. It is incumbent on solicitors and counsel not to allow the costs of preparation of witness statements to be unnecessarily increased by over-elaboration of the statements. Any unnecessary elaboration may be the subject of a special order as to costs.

CHG App 9.6

6. Witness statements must contain the truth, the whole truth and nothing but the truth on the issues covered. Great care must be taken in the preparation of witness statements. No pressure of any kind should be placed on a witness to give other than a true and complete account of his or her evidence. It is improper to serve a witness statement which is known to be false or which the maker does not in all respects actually believe to be true. In addition, a professional adviser may be under an obligation to check where practicable the truth of facts stated in a witness statement if he or she is put on enquiry as to their truth. If a party discovers that a witness statement which they have served is incorrect they must inform the other parties immediately.

CHG App 9.7

7. A witness statement should simply cover those issues, but only those issues, on which the party serving the statement wishes that witness to give evidence in chief.

Thus it is not, for example, the function of a witness statement to provide a commentary on the documents in the trial bundle, nor to set out quotations from such documents, nor to engage in matters of argument. Witness statements should not deal with other matters merely because they may arise in the course of the trial.

CHG App 9.8

8. Witness statements very often refer to documents. If there could be any doubt as to what document is being referred to, or if the document has not previously been made available on disclosure, it may be helpful for the document to be exhibited to the witness statement. If, to assist reference to the documents, the documents referred to are exhibited to the witness statement, they should nevertheless not be included in trial bundles in that form: see Appendix 6 paragraph 4. If (as is normally preferable) the documents referred to in the witness statement are not exhibited, care should be taken in identifying them, for example by reference to the lists of documents exchanged on disclosure. In preparation for trial, it will be necessary to insert cross-references to the trial bundles so as to identify the documents: see Appendix 6 paragraph 24.

CHG App 9.9

9. If a witness is not sufficiently fluent in English to give his or her evidence in English, the witness statement should be in the witness' own language and a translation provided. If a witness is not fluent in English but can make himself or herself understood in broken English and can understand written English, the statement need not be in his or her own words provided that these matters are indicated in the statement itself. It must however be written so as to express as accurately as possible the substance of his or her evidence.

APPENDIX 10: A GUIDE FOR RECEIVERS IN THE CHANCERY DIVISION

CHG App 10.1

(1)   This guide sets out brief notes on the procedure to be followed after an order has been made appointing a receiver in the Chancery Division. The procedure is now governed by CPR Part 69 and CPR PD 69.

(2)   Appendix C contains notes on the main powers and duties of a receiver and a copy should be passed to the receiver.

Action on the Appointment of a Receiver (CPR 69.6; CPR PD 69 paragraphs 6.1–6.3, 8.1–8.3)

CHG App 10.2

(3)   Where an order has been made appointing a receiver, it is generally necessary to apply for directions, by application notice under CPR Part 23. CPR PD 69 paras 6.1–6.3 lists the matters on which directions will usually be given. A draft order should normally be submitted with the application notice.

(4)   The application for directions should normally be made immediately after the making of the order appointing the receiver, especially where security has to be given within a limited time (see below). Only if the order appointing the receiver appoints him or her by name and gives full directions as to accounts and security will an application for directions not be necessary.

(5)   The receiver may of course apply to the Master at any time for other directions as necessary. Where the directions are unlikely to be contentious or important to the parties this may be done by letter (see Part 69 PD 8).

Giving Security (CPR 69.5; CPR PD 69 paragraphs 7.1–7.3).

CHG App 10.3

(6)   The order appointing a receiver will normally include directions in relation to security, and will specify the date by which security is to be given. It is therefore important to obtain an early date for the directions hearing. If security is not completed within the time specified the receivership may be terminated and it will then be necessary for an application to be made to renew it. To avoid this, if it seems likely that security will not be given in time an application should be made at the directions hearing for an extension of time to give security.

(7)   When the amount of the security has been settled, a guarantee in Form PF 30 CH (Appendix A) must (unless the receiver is a licensed insolvency practitioner covered by bond, which has been extended to cover the appointment) be prepared and entered into with one of the four main clearing banks or the insurance company listed in Appendix B.

(8)   The guarantee must then be engrossed and executed, ie signed by the receiver and signed and sealed by the bank or insurance company. It should then be lodged in the Masters' Appointments Section, Ground Floor, Rolls Building, 7 Rolls Building, Fetter Lane, London, EC4A 1NL. It will then be signed by the Master and endorsed with a certificate of completion of security and placed on the court file. Where security is given by bond, written evidence of the extended bond and the sufficiency of its cover must be filed at the above address in accordance with the requirements of CPR PD 69 para 7.3(1).

(9)   If the amount of the security given is subsequently increased or decreased, an endorsement is made to the original guarantee.

Receiver's Remuneration (CPR 69.7; CPR PD 69 paragraphs 9.1–9.6)

CHG App 10.4

(10)   A receiver may only charge for his or her services if the court permits it and specifies the basis on which the receiver is to be remunerated. Unless the court directs the remuneration to be fixed by reference to some fixed scale, or percentage of rents collected, it will determine the amount in accordance with the criteria set out in rule 69.7(4).

Receiver's Accounts (CPR 69.8; CPR PD 69 paragraphs 10.1–10.3).

CHG App 10.5

(11)   If directions as to the receiver's accounts have not been given in the order appointing the receiver, such directions must be obtained at the directions hearing.
(12)   Normally accounts are prepared half-yearly and must be delivered within a month of the end of the accounting period.
(13)   Generally accounts need only be presented to the court if any party receiving them serves notice on the receiver, under rule 69.8(3), that they object to any item in the accounts.

Discharge of Receiver and Cancellation of Security (CPR 69.10, CPR 69.11)

CHG App 10.6

(14)   When a receiver has completed his or her duties, the receiver or any party should apply for an order discharging the receiver and cancelling the security.
(15)   When an order for cancellation of a receiver's security has been made, any guarantee and the duplicate order appointing the receiver are endorsed to that effect.
(16)   The endorsed guarantee and duplicate order should then be taken to the bank or insurance company by the solicitors for cancellation and return of any outstanding premium.

Appendix A to Guide for Receivers: Guarantee for receiver's acts and defaults

CHG App 10.7

IN THE HIGH COURT OF JUSTICE
CHANCERY DIVISION

[TITLE]

I, (*Name*). of (*address*), the Receiver [and manager] appointed by Order dated..(*date*) (*or* proposed to be appointed) in this claim hereby undertake to the Court duly to account for all money and property received by me as such Receiver [and manager] at such times and in such manner in all respects as the Court directs.

And we.. (*name(s) of surety or sureties*) hereby [jointly and severally[2]] undertake with the Court and guarantee to be answerable for any default by..(*name*) as such Receiver [and manager] and upon such default to pay to any person or persons or otherwise as the Court directs any sum or sums not exceeding £..in total that may from time to time be certified by [a Master of the Supreme Court][a District Judge] to be due from. . . . . (*name*) as Receiver [and manager] and we submit to the jurisdiction of the Court in this action to determine any claim made under this undertaking.

Dated this . . . . . day of . . . . 20. . . . . .

Signed sealed and delivered by the above named . . . . in the presence of

or

The Common Seal of . . . . was hereunto affixed in the presence of:-

(Signature of receiver)

(Seal of surety with appropriate signature or signatures)

---

¹   Adapted from Form PF 30CH.
²   Omit these words in the case of a guarantee or other company.

Appendix B to Guide for Receivers: Guarantees for Personal Applicants

CHG App 10.8

The insurance company detailed below is willing to act as surety

Name of company	Address to be shown on and for correspondence:
Zurich GSG Limited	Hawthorn Hall
	Hall Road
	Wilmslow
	Cheshire SK9 5BZ

Appendix C to Guide for Receivers: The Powers and Duties of a Receiver

CHG App 10.9

(1)   The main function of a receiver appointed by the court is to protect the assets received by him or her pending the court proceedings. The following notes set out some of the more important powers and duties a receiver should be aware of.

(2)   A receiver must obtain the permission of the court (which may be contained in the order appointing him) before he or she can:

(a)   bring, defend or compromise legal proceedings
(b)   pay a debt (other than in a partnership claim)
(c)   compromise a claim
(d)   purchase or sell assets other than in the normal course of business
(e)   grant obtain or surrender a lease or purchase or sell real property (even in the course of managing a business); since the appointment of a receiver is an equitable remedy it does not confer on the receiver any title to land: unless the legal owner is prepared to join in the conveyance or lease the receiver would in any case have to obtain a vesting order under section 47 or section 50 of the Trustee Act 1925.
(f)   borrow money

    (g)   carry on or close down or sell a business

    (h)   employ additional staff in the course of managing a business

    (i)   carry out repairs to property costing more than £1000 in any one accounting year

(3)   Receivers should ensure that they have insurance (if any) transferred into their own names and should consider the adequacy of the insurance cover

(4)   Receivers are not entitled to instruct their own solicitors without the express permission of the court.

(5)   Receivers should seek the court's directions on any question of doubt which arises in the course of the receivership

(6)   Receivers should bear in mind that their function as receiver does not include the preparation of partnership accounts and they cannot include fees for such work in their remuneration as receiver.

(7)   Unless expressly authorised by the court (whether in the Order appointing them or otherwise) the receivers must not part with assets in their hands, whether to the person appointing them or otherwise. If the receiver has completed his or her functions as receiver before the disputes between the parties have been resolved in the proceedings, the receiver should normally apply to be discharged on lodging into court the money he or she is holding.

APPENDIX 11: LLOYD'S NAMES' ESTATE APPLICATIONS: FORMS

Form of witness statement

CHG App 11

[Heading as in claim form]

1. We are the personal representatives of the estate of the above-named Deceased ("the Deceased") who died on [. . . . .]. We obtained [a grant of probate] [letters of administration] out of the [. . . . .] Registry on [. . . . .] and a copy of the grant [and the Deceased's will dated [. . . . .]] is now produced and shown to us marked ". 1". We make this witness statement in support of our application for permission to distribute the Deceased's estate [and to administer the will trusts of which we will be the Trustees following administration.]. This witness statement contains facts and matters which, unless otherwise stated, are within our own knowledge obtained in acting in the administration of the estate. We believe them to be true.

2. The Deceased was before his death an underwriting member of Lloyd's of London whose underwriting activities are treated as having ceased on [. . . . .]. The estate was sworn for probate purposes at £[. . . . . . .]. We are now in a position to complete the administration of the estate and to distribute it to the beneficiaries but we do not wish to do so [or to constitute the will trusts] without the authority of the Court because of the existence of possible contingent claims arising out of the Deceased's underwriting liabilities for which we might be liable.

3. The position concerning the Deceased's Lloyd's liabilities is as follows:

3.1 [The Deceased's liabilities in respect of the years of account 1992 and earlier were reinsured into Equitas as part of the Lloyd's settlement. There is now produced and shown to us marked ".2" a copy of the certificate or statement of reinsurance into Equitas].

3.2 [The syndicates in which the Deceased participated in the years of account 1993 and later have [closed by reinsurance in the usual way] [are the subject of an Estate Protection Plan issued to the Deceased by Centrewrite Limited] [are protected by an EXEAT policy obtained by the Claimants from Centrewrite Limited].

4. There is now produced and shown to us marked ".3" a copy of a letter dated [. . . . .] from the estate's Lloyd's agents confirming that [all] the syndicates have been reinsured to close [with the exception of [. . . . .] which syndicate is protected by [the Estate Protection Plan] [the EXEAT policy]] and confirming that in the case of failure of a reinsuring syndicate to honour its obligations, the primary liability to a creditor will fall on Lloyd's Central Fund. [A copy of the [Estate Protection Plan and Annual Certificate] [EXEAT policy] is now produced and shown to us marked ".4".]

5. The Claimants believe that the interests of any Lloyd's claimant are reasonably secured by virtue of the fact that all the Lloyd's syndicates in which the Deceased participated have either been closed ultimately by reinsurance to close (in respect of any open years prior to 1992 originally into the Equitas group) or, in respect of subsequent years [have all closed by reinsurance] [are protected by the Estate Protection Plan] [are protected by the EXEAT policy.] [The [Estate Protection Plan] [EXEAT policy] is provided by Centrewrite Limited which is a wholly-owned subsidiary of Lloyd's and the beneficiary of an undertaking by Lloyd's to maintain its solvency. We have no reason to doubt the solvency of Centrewrite. A copy of the latest report and accounts of Centrewrite Limited is now produced and shown to us marked ". 6".]

6. [Explain why it is still considered prudent to seek the protection of a *Re Yorke* order: see paragraph 25.26 of this Guide.]

7. As appears from the schedule now produced and shown to us marked ".7" in which we summarise the assets and liabilities of the estate, we have paid all the debts of the Deceased known to us (apart from the costs and expenses associated with the final administration of the estate) and we have also advertised for and dealt with all claimants in accordance with s.27 of the Trustee Act 1925 [or if not explain why].

8. We know of no special reason or circumstance which might give rise to doubt whether the provision described above can reasonably be regarded as adequate provision for potential claims against the estate and we ask for permission to distribute accordingly.

Form of order

[Heading as in claim form]

ON THE APPLICATION of the Claimants by Part 8 Claim Form dated [ ]

UPON READING the written evidence filed

IT IS ORDERED THAT:

1.   the Claimants as [the personal representatives of the estate ("the Estate") of the above named deceased ("the Deceased")] [and] [the trustees of the trusts of the Deceased's will dated [. . . . .]("the Will")] have permission to [distribute the Estate] [and] [administer the trusts of the Will and distribute capital and income in accordance with such trusts] without making any retention or further provision in respect of any contract of insurance or reinsurance under-written by the Deceased in the course of his business as an underwriting member of Lloyd's of London

2.   the costs of the Claimants of this application [either in the agreed sum of £. . . . . . .] [or summarily assessed in the sum of £. . . . . . [assessed in the sum of £. . . . . .] (with permission to [the residuary beneficiaries] [name beneficiaries] to apply within 14 days after service of this order on them for the variation or discharge of this summary assessment] [or subject to detailed assessment on the indemnity basis if not agreed by or on behalf of [the residuary beneficiaries] name beneficiaries]] be raised and paid or retained out of the Estate in due course of administration.

APPENDIX 12 PRACTICE NOTE: REMUNERATION OF JUDICIAL TRUSTEES

CHG App 12

(1) When dealing with the assignment of remuneration to a judicial trustee under section 1(5) of the Judicial Trustees Act 1896 and rule 11 of the Judicial Trustee Rules 1983 the court will consider directions as to remuneration based on the common form of order set out below, subject to such modifications as may be required in any particular case.

(2) In general the court when considering reasonable remuneration for the purposes of rule 11(1)(a) will need to be satisfied as to the basis upon which the remuneration is claimed, that it is justified and that the amount is reasonable and proportionate and within the limit of 15% of the capital value of the trust property specified in the rule.

(3) The court may, before determining the amount of remuneration, require the judicial trustee to provide further information, alternatively refer the matter to a costs judge for him to assess remuneration.

(4) When an application is made to the court for the appointment of a judicial trustee or when the court gives directions under rule 8 practitioners should produce to the court a draft order which should take account of the common form of order

Draft paragraphs of order

[IT IS ORDERED]

. . . . that the remuneration of the Judicial Trustee shall be in such amount as may be approved from time to time by this court upon application for payment on examination of his accounts

. . . . that the Judicial Trustees accounts shall be endorsed by him with a certificate of the approximate capital value of the trust property at the commencement of the year of account

. . . . that every application for payment by the Judicial Trustee shall be in the form of a letter to the court (with a copy to the beneficiaries) which shall (a) set out the basis of the claim to remuneration, the scales or rates of any professional charges, the work done and time spent, any information concerning the complexity of the trusteeship that may be relied on and any other matters which the court shall be invited by the Judicial Trustee to take into account and (b) certify that he considers that the claim for remuneration is reasonable and proportionate

J. Winegarten

Chief Chancery Master 1st July 2003

With the authority of the Vice-Chancellor

APPENDIX 13 TRANSFER OF CASES TO CHANCERY TRIAL CENTRES

CHG App 13

1. Matters that ought normally to be transferred to a Chancery trial centre. Careful consideration should be given to whether the case should be transferred to a District Registry or a county court or whether arrangements should simply be made for the case to be heard in a different trial centre.

Proceedings under the Companies Acts;

Other disputes among company shareholders;

Corporate insolvency proceedings (except for winding up petitions by creditors);

Personal insolvency proceedings (except for bankruptcy petitions, interim orders and applications to set aside statutory demands);

Directors' disqualification proceedings (but note that the transferee court must have jurisdiction under the Company Directors Disqualification Act 1986);

Claims within CPR Part 56 (Landlord and Tenant Claims and Miscellaneous Provisions about Land) other than applications under section 24 or section 38(4) of the Landlord and Tenant Act 1954 or under the Access to Neighbouring Land Act 1992;

Probate claims, or claims for the rectification of wills, substitution and removal of personal representatives within CPR Part 57 (probate claims ought not to be started outside a Chancery county court in any event);

Proceedings relating to the estate of a deceased person, to trusts or to charities within CPR Part 64;

Proceedings under section 14 of the Trusts of Land and Appointment of Trustees Act 1996 (though a simple case of a joint property dispute, where there is little or no dispute as to the beneficial shares, may best be dealt with at the home county court);

Proceedings relating to intellectual property, including passing-off;

Proceedings relating to land, easements, covenants or contracts relating to land where an injunction, specific performance or declaration is sought or where there are substantial or complex issues (though not all injunction cases are appropriate for transfer, e.g. housing disrepair cases and many neighbour disputes);

Proceedings for breach of a restrictive covenant, breach of trust or breach of fiduciary duty where an injunction is sought or where there are substantial or complex issues;

Claims for rescission on the grounds of undue influence or other equitable grounds, or for rectification of a document;

Claims relating to membership of, exclusion from, or dissolution of, a club or other unincorporated association;

Other claims – for instance for professional negligence or for breach of contract – which involve issues of trust, company, intellectual property, land or conveyancing law or procedure;

Claims for the dissolution of partnerships or the taking of partnership accounts;

Matters other than those listed above, where an account is one of the remedies sought and the issues likely to arise on the account are substantial or complex.

2. Matters which ought not normally to be transferred

Proceedings relating to residential tenancies;

Proceedings relating to residential mortgages (unless a serious issue arises, for example, as to the occupation rights of a third party and as to whether the mortgagee's rights prevail over those of such a third party);

Claims to enforce a charging order;

Applications under section 24 of the Landlord and Tenant Act 1954;

Applications under section 38(4) of the Landlord and Tenant Act 1954;

Applications under the Access to Neighbouring Land Act 1992;

Proceedings under the Inheritance (Provision for Family and Dependants) Act 1975.

APPENDIX 14 GUIDELINES ON DRAFTING ORDERS
Title and Parties

CHG App 14

In the heading to the title the name and judicial title of the Judge should appear followed by the date of the Order immediately below the words "Chancery Division". If the Judge sat in private the words "sitting in private" should be added after the Judge's name.

Normally all the parties should be listed. Apart from the exceptions set out in Paragraph 2.5 of the Chancery Guide there is no need to recite Statutes, deeds etc in the Title.

Recitals

The Order should begin with a recital as to how the matter got before the Court (e.g. Upon the Application of . . . by Notice dated . . . .)

There should be a recital as to who the Court heard.

There may be a recital that the Court "read the written evidence filed". The words "And upon reading the evidence recorded on the Court File as having been read" are no longer relevant since nothing is now recorded on the Court File as having been read. On an Application without notice there should be a recital of the evidence before the Court – this would usually be in a Schedule.

Consent orders

If the order is an order made by consent it must bear the words "By consent".

Order

The paragraphs should be consecutively numbered.

If the order directs a payment into or out of court after the direction the words 'as directed in the attached payment/lodgement schedule' should appear. In such a case a payment or lodgement schedule should be drawn by the Associate

If a party applied for permission to appeal at the hearing the order must state –

(a)   whether or not the judgment or order is final;
(b)   whether an appeal lies from the judgment or order and, if so, to which appeal court;
(c)   whether the court gave permission to appeal; and
(d)   if not, the appropriate appeal court to which any further application for permission to appeal may be made.

If the applicant wishes to serve the order, a provision should be included in the order to that effect. This will cut out the need to secure an undertaking to serve when the order is collected after it is entered.

Backsheet

All Orders should have backsheets which should-

–   Show the name of the Judge and date of the Order immediately below the words Chancery Division as in the title.
–   Give the Claim Number

There is no need to recite all parties on the backsheet. It suffices to give the name of the First Claimant and the First Defendant

The backsheet should record how the Order is to be served. If it is intended that the Court should serve the Order the words "The Court sent sealed copies of this Order to" should appear under the word Order and the names, addresses (including DX address) and references of the Solicitors or litigants in person to whom it is to be sent given. If it is intended that one of the parties should serve then under the word Order the words "The Court sent this Order and sealed copies for service to" followed by the name and address etc of the party who is to effect service should appear.

Further guidance

Further guidance is contained in PD 40B

APPENDIX 15 CHANCERY BUSINESS AT CENTRAL LONDON CIVIL JUSTICE CENTRE

(Revised) May 2012

Central London Civil Justice Centre

Chancery Business Contact Details – at a glance

Addresses

CHG App 15

(1) For County Court Offices, District Judges and all fee remittances:

(NB This is the Court's official postal address)

13-14 Park Crescent

London W1B 1HT

(2) For Trial Centre, Circuit Judges, and Chancery Section office:

26 Park Crescent

London W1N 4HT

DX 97325 Regents Park 2

FAX 08703 305717 (All Chancery matters)

020 7917 5000 (Option 5) Chancery Section (for all general matters) and Chancery Listings before a District Judge

020 7917 5000 (Option 6) Chancery Listings before a Circuit Judge

TEL 020 7917 7821 or

020 7917 7889 Chancery Section (for all general matters)

020 7917 7938 (ONLY for transcripts of Trial Centre hearings)

020 7917 5107 (ONLY for transcripts of DJ hearings)

E-MAIL chance.clerk@hmcts.gsi.gov.uk

(All general enquiries and communications)

CentralLondonCJSKEL@hmcts.gsi.gov.uk

(ONLY for skeleton arguments for Circuit Judge hearings)

CentralLondonDJSKEL@hmcts.gsi.gov.uk (ONLY for skeleton arguments for District Judge hearings)

Contacts

Clerk to HH Judge Marc Dight (Senior Chancery Judge)

Mr Matthew Carr: matthew.carr@hmcts.gsi.gov.uk

Chancery Manager Miss Ramona Persad: chance.clerk@hmcts.gsi.gov.uk

Operations Manager (formerly the Court Manager) Ms Sue Bennett: chance.clerk@hmcts.gsi.gov.uk

Introduction

The High Court transfers an increasing number of Chancery cases to the Central London Civil Justice Centre ("CLCJC") at 26 Park Crescent, London W1. Two specialist Chancery Senior Circuit Judges have been appointed to maintain CLCJC as a centre for Chancery business. CLCJC therefore handles not only Chancery cases commenced in the County Court, but also cases commenced in the High Court but regarded as suitable for conduct at CLCJC, either by agreement of the parties (see s 23 County Courts Act 1984) or by the High Court, which may decide to transfer the matter to CLCJC on its own initiative under Section 40(2) of that Act.

In addition, any significant Chancery case in a County Court in the London area will be transferred to CLCJC Chancery List for trial, and any lengthy or complex cases from any County Court on the South Eastern Circuit or elsewhere may also be transferred. Litigants may wish to consider commencing such cases at CLCJC in the first place.

Suitable High Court cases may also be tried by one of the specialist Chancery Senior Circuit Judges sitting at CLCJC as a High Court judge under s. 9 [Senior Courts] Act 1981.

1. The Chancery List at Central London

1.1 The business of the Chancery List at CLCJC now comprises business from the three sources mentioned above, ie:

1.1.1 cases transferred from the Chancery Division of the High Court; cases are often transferred at a very early stage;

1.1.2 cases transferred from other county courts on the SE Circuit, because of complexity or length (an estimated trial of two days or more); and

1.1.3 Chancery claims issued in the Central London County Court.

1.2 All business of the Chancery List is identified by a unique case number. Formerly, this started 'CHY', but after recent IT changes, it will now take the form '1CL1***' (claims issued in the Chancery List during 2011 and '2CL1*****' (claims issued in the Chancery List in 2012), where the number '1' after 'CL' identifies the claim as being Chancery.

1.3 A list of the kinds of case which are suitable for the Chancery List appears at Annex A. The following should be noted.

1.3.1 Since 2001 the court has had original jurisdiction in contentious probate matters pursuant to CPR Part 57.2.

1.3.2 The court has only limited original jurisdiction in matters relating to companies. However where CLCJC has no original jurisdiction, appropriate cases can, by arrangement, be directed by the High Court to be heard at CLCJC by one of the Specialist Chancery Judges sitting as a High Court Judge, authorised under s 9 of the [Senior Courts] Act 1981.

1.3.3 The court's original jurisdiction in trust, equity and partnership matters is currently technically limited to £30,000 under the County Courts Act 1984. However it is commonplace for higher value cases to be transferred to CLCJC from the High Court, or for the parties to agree to confer extended jurisdiction (see Paragraph 1.5 below).

1.4 Claims may be issued in the Chancery List if the Claimant thinks it appropriate. The claim form must be clearly marked "Chancery Business". If it later appears that the case is unsuitable for the Chancery List it will be transferred back to the General List by a judge. Otherwise, cases from the above sources may be identified as suitable for the Chancery List at any stage. At this point they will be transferred into the Chancery List, (subject to the approval of a Chancery judge if the transfer order is not made by a specialist Chancery judge), and allocated a Chancery list number in the form "2CL1****".

1.5 It is open to parties to increase the court's jurisdiction beyond the current limits under the County Courts Act 1984 by filing a signed joint memorandum of consent pursuant to s 23 of the Act. This can be a useful way of obtaining an earlier hearing in an urgent case which is suitable for trial by a specialist Circuit Judge.

2. The Court House

2.1 CLCJC is located in two buildings in Park Crescent, London W1.

2.2 The Trial Centre is at 26 Park Crescent London W1N 4HT, at the western end of Park Crescent, (ie nearest to the London Clinic and Harley Street). Trials and applications before Circuit Judges take place here.

2.3 The County Court Offices and the District Judges' Chambers, are on the eastern side of Park Crescent, at 13-14 Park Crescent. London W1B 1HT (which is the court's official postal address). Applications and hearings before District Judges may be heard either here, or at 26 Park Crescent (see Paragraph 3.6 below).

2.4 The nearest Underground stations are Regents Park (on the Bakerloo Line: 2 minutes) and Great Portland Street (on the Metropolitan, Hammersmith and City, and Circle Lines: 5 minutes). Warren Street (Northern Line: 10 minutes) and Baker Street (Jubilee line:10 minutes) are also within walking distance.

3. The Judiciary

3.1 The senior specialist Chancery Circuit Judge is His Honour Judge Marc Dight, who is authorised to sit as a Deputy Judge of the High Court under s 9 of the [Senior Courts] Act 1981. Any communications for his attention should be addressed to his clerk:

Mr Matthew Carr
Clerk to the Senior Chancery Judge
E-Mail: matthew.carr@hmcts.gsi.gov.uk.

3.2 Six other resident and visiting Circuit Judges are generally authorised to hear any Chancery List cases ('Category 2' business). These are HH Judge Edward Bailey, HH Judge John Hand QC, HH Judge Karen Walden-Smith, HH Judge Nick Madge and HH Judge Nigel Gerald.

3.3 In addition there is a panel of Recorders drawn from the Chancery Bar and approved by the Chancellor of the High Court. The Recorders are asked to sit from time to time if the Chancery Circuit Judges are not available, or to relieve pressure on the list. References in this Guide to a "Circuit Judge" include a Recorder unless the context suggests otherwise.

3.4 There are two designated specialist Chancery District Judges: District Judge Margaret Langley and District Judge Barry Lightman. They are based at 13-14 Park Crescent. In addition, District Judge Ruth Fine is authorised to deal with Chancery cases if the state of the lists requires.

3.5 The Chancery District Judges normally deal with Chancery applications and case management in the District Judges' Chancery List, which is heard on Wednesdays and Fridays at 13-14 Park Crescent. However, hearings may take place at other times, or at 26 Park Crescent, according to the state of the list. Litigants should always check the location on the court hearing list. Appointments before Chancery District Judges are made through the District Judges Listings Section.

3.6 It is the policy of the court to ensure that all Chancery List matters are dealt with by a judge of suitable experience. Although not Chancery specialists, a number of the Resident Judges at the court have considerable experience in some Chancery areas (eg landlord and tenant matters). If, at case management, a Senior Chancery Judge considers that because of its nature, a particular case could be efficiently heard by any such other Resident Judge, the case will be marked accordingly ("Category 3" business), and may subsequently be listed before either a Chancery Judge or any other Judge so nominated.

3.7 A party who considers it appropriate, on the grounds of the particular nature, importance or value of the case, may apply to the Senior Chancery Judge (through her clerk) for the case to be reserved to the Senior Chancery Judges' List ("Category 1" business).

4. The Chancery Section and communicating with the Court.

4.1 The Chancery List is administered between both buildings depending at which level of judge you are seeking. In the first instance all enquiries should go to the Chancery Section which is based at 13-14 Park Crescent. Enquiries should be made at the counter on the 1st floor. Queries and applications can be presented in person at the reception desk on the fourth floor at 26 Park Crescent, so long as they do not involve the payment of fees (but note Paragraph 6.6 below with regard to obtaining expedition) if the matter is to be dealt with by a Circuit Judge only. Please note the counter times may vary for general enquiries at particular times of the year, namely the summer period. Please check with the Court first.

4.2 All enquiries and correspondence concerned with the Chancery List should be addressed by post to the postal address of the court to the appropriate listings section:

Central London Civil Justice Centre
13-14 Park Crescent
London W1B 1HT

or sent through the DX system to

DX 97325 Regents Park 2

4.3 The following numbers are dedicated numbers for use of the Chancery List business:

Tel: 020 7917 5000 (Option 5) Chancery Section (for all general matters) and Chancery Listings before a District Judge

020 7917 5000 (Option 6) Chancery Listings before a Circuit Judge

Fax: 08703 305 717

E-mail: chance.clerk@hmcts.gsi.gov.uk

Please note the special fax number. Chancery List communications should not be sent to any other numbers and this number should not be used for any other type of claim.

4.4 The Chancery Section Manager is Miss Ramona Persad. The Chancery Manager is responsible for the Chancery Section, comments and complaints.

Communications should be addressed to CHANCERY MANAGER, at the above address.

4.5 For administrative reasons, all post to CLCJC is received at 13-14 Park Crescent. After sorting, Chancery List post is allocated to staff and should be processed with 3-5 days upon receipt.

4.6 HMCTS has introduced a business centre in Salford known as the County Court Money Claims Centre (CCMCC) who process all specified Part 7 claims from issue to either judgment by default or the return of allocation questionnaires for the General List. Please note that ALL administration for Chancery Business is processed at CLCJC only irrespective of what type the claim is. Please do not send any documentation to the CCMCC.

4.7 All applications requiring a fee to be paid **must** be initiated at 13-14 Park Crescent, whether made by post or in person. After fee processing, Chancery applications are then processed by the Chancery section either by way of listing or referring the Application. If the Application is to be listed before a Circuit Judge, the Application will be sent to Circuit Judge Listings.

4.8 To assist Chancery Section staff to deal correctly and quickly with letters and applications, it is important that **the case's Chancery number, names of the parties and the date of the next fixed hearing are stated <u>prominently on the first page of the letter or application.</u>** If the matter is regarded as urgent this may also be stated: see further Paragraph 6.4 below.

4.9 Communications to the court may be made, and **short** documents (12 pages maximum and not involving payment of fees) may be filed, addressed to the Chancery Manager **by** email to the email address given above. The subject line

must include the Chancery number, the parties' names (abbreviated if necessary), the nature of the document, and the date and time of any forthcoming hearing (see also general guidance in CPR PD 5B supplemental to CPR 5.5).

4.10 Faxed documents (other than skeleton arguments: see (Paragraph 8.3 below) for any Chancery list hearings taking place at 26 Park Crescent must be faxed to 020 7917 7935 to ensure that they reach the Judges' hearing rooms in time.

Faxed Documents for hearings at 13/14 Park Crescent must be faxed to **08703 305 717**.

It is likely that your document will not reach the Judge in time if faxed to the wrong number.

5. Case management

5.1 Subject to the protocols set out in this Guide and to any specific requirements of the Civil Procedure Rules, the Chancery List at CLCJC will follow the practice set out in the Chancery Guide (see Volume II of the White Book).

5.2 When a case is transferred to Central London Chancery List from either a county court or the High Court, directions will usually be given at the transferring court to continue progress towards trial during the transfer period. However, the transferring court cannot make any order fixing a trial date or window at CLCJC. When the file is received at CLCJC, it will be immediately placed before one of the senior Chancery Judges, who will review the existing case management directions (if any), and either give appropriate directions on paper for the further conduct of the matter (which may include giving a listing appointment for trial) or direct an immediate case management conference.

5.3 Case management hearings before a District Judge will usually be held on Wednesdays or Fridays, or by telephone under CPR Pt 23. Case management hearings and applications before a Circuit Judge will usually also be heard on Fridays at 10 am or 2 pm, at 26 Park Crescent, or by telephone under CPR Pt 23.

5.4 The judge may have a telephone list in the morning (at 10 am) or the afternoon (at 2 pm) but not both. Telephone appointments are dealt with strictly by time allocated.

A Note setting out the procedure for arranging a telephone hearing will, where applicable, be attached to the Notice of Hearing issued by the Court. The parties and their advisers should refer to this.

5.5 Matters in the list for attended hearings are dealt with in a convenient order, according to urgency and time estimate.

5.6 Appeals from a Chancery District Judge will normally be listed before one of the specialist Chancery Circuit Judges as part of the normal weekday Chancery List. If a trial is imminent, appropriate time arrangements will be made.

5.7 It is essential that the parties provide accurate time estimates for applications and case management conferences. If hearings overrun their allocated time, telephone hearings will, and attended hearings may, be adjourned, with possible sanctions in costs.

5.8 Parties will usually be asked to provide an agreed minute of case management directions ordered at a hearing, and they can often avoid the need for a hearing by drafting or agreeing proposed directions beforehand. To assist litigants, a form of standard model directions frequently given in Chancery cases (Form MT3(CHY)) is at Annex B. Attention is draw in particular to the procedure for fixing trial dates – see paragraph 7.2 below.

6. Applications

Normal business

6.1 Chancery applications before Circuit Judges are normally heard with case management business, which is listed every Friday. In exceptional cases of urgency (for example an urgent injunction) an appointment may be given for another day and time. Longer hearings (2 hours or more) may be listed in the normal daily trial lists.

6.2 Any routine application in a Chancery case should be made to the Court Office at 13-14 Park Crescent by leaving or posting copies of the Application Notice (one more than the number of parties involved), and the required fee. After issue by the office, the application will be delivered to the Chancery Section, either on the same day or the following morning, and will be dealt with as follows (subject to Paragraphs 6.4 and 6.5) below:

6.2.1 Where a hearing is requested, the Chancery Clerk will ascertain which level of judge the party has requested. If the level of judge is a District Judge, the Chancery Clerk will list on notice applications on the first convenient date on a Wednesday or a Friday. Without notice applications will be referred with the court file to a Chancery District Judge. If the level of judge is a Circuit Judge for on notice applications, the Chancery Clerk will refer the application to the Circuit Judges Listings Section to list for a hearing. If the level of judge is a Circuit Judge for without notice applications, the Chancery Clerk will refer the application with the court file to a Circuit Judge. For applications on notice the court will notify the parties of the date and time of the appointment.

6.2.2 Where the applicant requests that the application be dealt with without a hearing, the Application Notice will be placed before a judge of the appropriate level. If the judge is of the view that a hearing is required, he or she will direct a hearing within an appropriate timescale. The appropriate section (either the Chancery Section or the Circuit Judges Listings Section) will then list the matter and notify the parties of the date and time.

6.2.3 If the judge deals with the matter on paper, he or she will make such order as is considered appropriate in the circumstances. This will not necessarily be the order requested in the application. The court will then notify the parties of the application and of the order which has been made. Any such order will always contain a provision that any party may apply to the court, as provided in the order (usually within 7 days) to have the order set aside or varied.

6.3 Both the Chancery Section and the Circuit Judges Listings Section will endeavour to deal with Chancery Application Notices as set out above, within five working days of their receipt.

Urgent business

Certified urgent business

6.4 Any party making an application which is considered urgent may certify it "**URGENT**" and give brief reasons in a covering letter. The Chancery Section clerk will then give the application such priority as it appears to warrant, and is likely to put it before a Circuit Judge immediately for directions. Parties should note that any abuse of the "urgent" certification may have the result that costs will be disallowed.

Applications within four weeks of trial

6.5 Any application received by the Chancery Section within four weeks before the date fixed for trial will automatically be treated as urgent business. Regardless of the nature of the application or the level of judge which may be suggested by the applicant, the application will be placed immediately before a Circuit Judge for directions. The Judge will then make such order as is considered appropriate to the circumstances.

Voluntary expedited procedure

6.6 Any party wishing to obtain an early appointment for the hearing of an application may use the following procedure.

6.6.1 The applicant should take the Application Notice (and copies) and fee, in person to the Court Office at 13-14 Park Crescent for immediate issue by the Chancery Section, wait whilst the issue is processed and receive back the issued Application Notice and copies.

6.6.2 The issued Application Notice should then be taken in person to the Circuit

Judges Listings Section Office on the fourth floor of 26 Park Crescent.

6.6.3 The Circuit Judges Listings Section clerk will then immediately list the application for hearing whilst the applicant waits, and will list it for hearing on the immediately following Friday if requested by the applicant. Such applications will be listed before a Circuit Judge.

6.6.4 The applicant will then be responsible for service of notice of the appointment on the responding party or parties.

When using this procedure, applicants are reminded that **at least three clear days' notice** to any other party (ie before close of business on Monday) are required if an application is to be heard "with notice" on a Friday. If insufficient notice is given the hearing can, and normally will, take place as an application made "without notice", whether or not the responding party attends. The Judge will make such order as is appropriate in the circumstances.

Extreme urgency

6.7 During normal working hours, emergency applications (ie applications where even the expedited timetable above would be inadequate) can and should be made directly to one of the Senior Chancery Judges. Contact should be made through their clerks (see Paragraphs 3.1 and 3.2) who will make special arrangements appropriate to the circumstances.. There is no facility at the court for dealing with "out of hours" emergency applications. In any such case, litigants should use the emergency "out of hours" service at the Royal Courts of Justice in the Strand (Tel: 020 7947 6000/6260).

7. Listing and Trials

7.1 Fast track Chancery trials will usually be heard by one of the Chancery District Judges. Fast track trials take place on Thursdays, and the Chancery District Judges list their own cases for hearing.

7.2 Multi-track Chancery trials will be given fixed dates in accordance with the usual practice of the CLCJC for multi-track cases. Under the present system, the trial date is set by a telephone listing appointment,

7.2.1 This will be given for a precise time, usually on Tuesday or Wednesday

7.2.2 Prior to the appointment, the court will ascertain (or estimate, if such information has not been given) the likely trial length, and will specify an appropriate trial window.

7.2.3 The parties will be directed to keep the listing appointment, with dates to avoid during the trial window, by telephone either by setting up a telephone conference appointment as under CPR Pt 23, or, if the parties can agree a combined list of dates to avoid, one party may telephone at the relevant time in the usual way.

7.2.4 The trial date will be fixed by the court officer over the telephone, on the basis of the information then available. If the telephone appointment is not set up and the required information is not received by the time stated, the court will proceed to list in any event. No telephone call after the appointment date and time will be considered or otherwise dealt with unless directed by the Court.

7.2.5 In either case a formal notice of hearing will also be sent by post or DX. Thereafter, the hearing date will not be altered except on application on notice to a Circuit Judge.

When drafting case management orders, solicitors and counsel should note that the above is now the usual procedure, and expressions such as "first open date after . . . " are obsolete. The court's standard form listing direction can be found in Annex B.

7.3 Parties should note that the practice in the Chancery List is to give listing appointments at an early stage, as soon as the likely witnesses and trial length can be known. The court is able to fix an appropriate window well in advance to take account of likely trial preparation time, and the early fixing of a trial date has been shown to improve efficient trial management.

7.4 Subject to absences, there are three or four Chancery Circuit Judges available to sit at all times. It is therefore the practice of the Chancery Section to list five cases to be heard in parallel at any time, in the confident expectation that, with settlements and the flexibility of listing arrangements, there will be a Chancery List Judge available to hear all listed Chancery cases. There remains, however the risk that all cases will stand up. In such a situation, every effort is made (including, where possible, the use of a Recorder or of another Resident Judge with appropriate experience) to ensure that no case is adjourned out.

7.5 The CLCJC aims to achieve continuous listing so that cases should not have to be adjourned part heard. The Chancery Section and the Circuit Judges Listings Section pursues this objective. Solicitors and counsel should note, therefore, that if a case overruns its trial estimate the Judge is likely to continue the hearing notwithstanding this, and they should arrange their diary commitments accordingly. A case in the Chancery List will never be adjourned part heard for any significant length of time simply because it has overrun its trial estimate. However, a case which overruns from a Thursday may possibly be adjourned to the following week, to accommodate Friday case management business.

7.6 The parties' time estimates are critical to the objective of providing flexibility and continuous listing for the benefit of all litigants. Time estimates should always be practical and realistic. The parties should note the following:

7.6.1 Time estimates for Chancery cases should, if at all possible, be given in a form which indicates whether or not pre-reading time is included in the estimate (and in any event what pre-reading time requirement is expected) and also whether or not the estimate includes any time for the delivery of an immediate judgment.

7.6.2 In order to accommodate pre-reading, and to minimise waiting by the parties, the Chancery List will operate the following general rule regarding the parties' attendance on the first day, according to the estimated length of the hearing, and, where possible, this will be noted on case management directions:

1 or 2 day case:	10.30 am
3 day case	11.30 am
4 day or more case	2 pm.

If in doubt, the parties can contact the Chancery Section after 4 pm on the day before the hearing, to ascertain when their attendance is required.

7.6.3 Time estimates should assume that witness statements will be taken as read and that consequently no significant time will normally be required for oral evidence in chief. Pre-reading time should be calculated to allow for the reading of witness statements.

7.6.4 The trial judge will not normally expect to pre-read bundles of documents, apart from any key documents indicated as being required for a basic understanding of the case, unless arrangements are specifically made for this. If extensive reading of bundles is required, then the parties' advocates should decide whether this is best done before or during the hearing itself, and should make their time estimates and/or inform the court just before trial, accordingly.

7.6.5 Allowance should be made for any witnesses using interpreters. Experience indicates that the use of an interpreter trebles the length of time for a witness's oral evidence. The evidence of witnesses using a foreign language must carry the appropriate certification as to the witness's understanding, pursuant to the CPR.

7.7 Apart from the above, as a general rule, the parties should assume that, before the hearing, the judge will have been able to read the skeleton arguments, any key documents, and the witness statements, but not bundles of documentary evidence.

7.8 It is the duty of the parties to inform the Chancery Section immediately of any changes in the time estimate of the case.

7.9 Advocates may assume that in Chancery cases, robes will be worn for trials and appeals, and that robes will not be worn for applications, except committal proceedings for contempt of court.

8. Bundles and skeleton arguments

8.1 The practice set out in the Chancery Guide and in CPR part 39 should be followed in respect of bundles and skeleton arguments.

8.2 Bundles and skeleton arguments should be lodged in accordance with case management directions in the case, but at the very latest they **must** be lodged 24 hours prior to the time fixed for any hearing. They should be marked for the attention of the appropriate Listing Section Manager.

8.3 Skeleton arguments should now be filed in accordance with the court's Skeleton Argument Protocol by email to CentralLondonCJSKEL@hmcts.gsi.gov.uk for a Circuit Judge and CentralLondonDJSKEL@hmcts.gsi.gov.uk for a District Judge (unless email is not available to the party). The subject line MUST commence with the Case No (without spaces) followed by case name. If a party has no access to email then skeleton arguments can be filed in person or be sent by fax to 'Reception' at 26 Park Crescent on 020 7917 7940. It is always advisable for a hard copy skeleton argument to be available at the hearing.

9. Authorities

9.1 Bringing photocopies of authorities to court is helpful to the judges and is encouraged. It is also helpful if any bundle of authorities is provided with an index and appropriate tabs, and if bulky, is placed in a ring binder or lever arch file.

9.2 The court has a text book library including most of the usual Chancery, landlord and tenant and mercantile books. It maintains a set of Law Reports, the All England Law Reports, the Weekly Law Reports and an up-to-date set of Halsbury's Statutes and Halsbury's Laws. However, the provision of photocopied extracts from textbooks, especially specialist books, is of great assistance to the court.

10. Orders

10.1 Orders made after a hearing, whether a trial or an application, will be drawn up and dispatched on the same day wherever possible, or within 5 business days.

10.2 In order to assist the court, parties should draw up, in advance of the hearing, a minute of any order that they expect to ask the court to make.

10.3 Where the terms of an order can only be finally decided at the hearing itself, solicitors and counsel should be prepared to draft a minute of the order after the hearing, to be handed in to the court clerk in order to assist the preparation of the sealed order. Alternatively, they may be asked to send in a minute to the court clerk by email, on returning to their office.

10.4 Where a party is granted relief at a hearing in the absence of the other party, the representative of the party obtaining the order should ensure either that the court confirms that it will be able to dispatch the sealed order within 24 hours, or that the judge gives any necessary direction for informing the absent party of the terms of the order in the interim.

10.5 Orders made after consideration of a case on paper will be drawn up and dispatched as soon as possible. However, as orders on hearings take priority, this may take up to a week. Counsel and solicitors should bear in mind the time constraints mentioned here and above at Paragraph 6.1-6.3 when making any application for an order without a hearing. This is especially important if the order sought is time-sensitive; an application for determination at a hearing may be more appropriate.

11. Transcripts

11.1 The court has a digital recording system in every courtroom. In the event of an appeal, therefore, a request should be made for a transcript of the evidence (if needed) and the judgment, if not handed down in writing.

11.2 Parties seeking to obtain a transcript should place an order with an approved member of the transcription panel and submit form EX107 to the court. Any enquiries related to transcripts should be directed in the first place as follows:

For hearings at 26 Park Crescent, to

Circuit Judges Listings Section: 020 7917 5000 (option 6)

For hearings at 13-14 Park Crescent to

Ms June Dodds: 020 7917 5107

12. Central London Chancery Court User Group

12.1 The CLCJC Chancery Court User Group has been re-established, to meet periodically to monitor the operation of the Chancery List.

12.2 The Group comprises representatives from the Chancery and Property Bar Associations, the Property Litigation Association, the Association of Contentious Trust and Probate Solicitors, the Society of Trust and Estate Practitioners, the West London Law Society, the Westminster and Holborn Law Society, and representative local solicitors' firms. Meetings are held every four months and attended by the court's Chancery Judiciary and Chancery Administration Coordinator.

12.3 The group is anxious to be kept informed of how the Chancery List is working in order to ensure that the best possible service can be delivered to meet the needs of users. Complaints, comments, suggestions and ideas for improvement may be communicated through any member of the group. However in the first place it will be useful if suggestions could be sent to either the Chancery Manager (Miss Ramona Persad) or the Senior Chancery Judge (HH Judge Marc Dight) at 26 Park Crescent, London W1B1HT.

(Revised) May 2012

Annex A
Cases suitable for the Chancery List at Central London Civil Justice Centre

Any case in the following list which is either expressly transferred from the High Court or is within the statutory jurisdiction of the County Court, which can be extended by agreement (see s 23 of the County Courts Act 1984)

Note: Where a subject is noted * as being potentially suitable for either the Chancery or the General List, it is for the Claimant's solicitor to choose which is regarded as more appropriate in the first instance. Thereafter, the case will continue in that list unless transferred by the Court on case management, either of its own initiative, or upon application: see Paragraph 1.4 of the Guide

Wills

– Probate disputes
– Interpretation
– Inheritance Act.

Administration of Estates

Trusts

All matters relating to the validity of trusts and their administration but including especially

- Resulting and constructive trusts.
- Home sharing cases, ie *Stack v Dowden* cases: see s.14 of the Trusts of Land Act 1996.
  (However two party cases with no complicating aspect may also be suitable for the General List*).

Land

- Sale of land (including specific performance claims)
- Contracts affecting land
- Disputes as to title
- Boundary disputes
- Land registration
- Right of way and other easements and rights over land
- Adverse possession
- Proprietary estoppel

Landlord & Tenant

Many landlord and tenant matters, and in particular business tenancy disputes under the 1954 Act, are suitable either for the Chancery or the General List.*

The Chancery List is particularly suitable for

- Substantial breach of covenant/forfeiture claims
- Rent review and other valuation matters
- Service charges and management (if not within the exclusive jurisdiction of the LVT.)
- Leasehold enfranchisement.
- Agricultural tenancies

It is less suitable or necessary for

- Residential tenancies
- Housing cases.

Partnership Actions

- Disputes as to the existence, terms, or termination of any partnership
- Administration or winding up of any partnership business.

Company Law

- Shareholders' agreements
- Disputes regarding the running or management of a company
- Breach of directors' duties (fiduciary and contractual)

But **NOT** cases within the exclusive statutory jurisdiction of the Companies Court.

It should also be noted that CLCJC has no jurisdiction in personal insolvency, and therefore has no original company winding up jurisdiction nor in matters depending on that jurisdiction, eg claims to set aside transactions in fraud of creditors under s 423 of the Companies Act 1986. However, such claims can be dealt with at CLCJC as High Court cases by specific authority being conferred on the specialist Chancery Judges, under s 9 of the Senior Courts Act 1981.

Torts

Torts in the property and commercial fields especially trespass, nuisance, and negligence in relation to assets and business or financial matters. (Many such matters will also be suitable for the General List.*)

- Fraud including constructive trusts and tracing

Mortgages, banking and financial matters

Mortgages, charges and securities including banking securities (other than simple mortgage possession cases where no defence is raised other than on the figure), but especially

– *O'Brien* defences.
– Disputes regarding priority of mortgages or charges
– Guarantees and indemnities
– Assignments of choses in action
– Subrogation

Business litigation*

Business disputes may be suitable for either the General List or the Chancery List. The Chancery List may be an appropriate list for business litigation as an alternative to a mercantile list where, in particular, a complex point of legal principle or interpretation of contract may arise.

Injunctions and equitable remedies

All forms of equitable relief, including

– injunction,
– specific performance,
– declarations as to interests,
– tracing, and
– equitable accounting
– Claims in restitution

Professional negligence related to any of the above topics

– including solicitors, surveyors, valuers, architects, accountants, financial advisers.

Annex B
Model standard case management directions for Chancery List cases at Central London Civil Justice Centre: Form MT3 (CHY)

Form MT 3 (CHY)

Case Number:

Parties:

1. Claim allocated to the Multi Track, to proceed as Chancery Business.

2. The parties do give serious consideration to using mediation with a view to reaching an early settlement. The parties may be assisted by reference to the directory of accredited civil mediators which can be found at: http://www.civilmedi ation.justice.gov.uk.

The parties will be expected to provide an explanation if mediation has not been attempted. Costs consequences may follow.

Disclosure

3. Each party shall give to the other parties standard disclosure of documents on Form N265 by 4.00pm on [   ]

4. All requests for inspection of or a copy of a document must be made by 4.00pm on [normally 7 days later]. Copies of requested documents to be supplied by 4 pm on [normally a further 7 days later].

Witness statements

5. The parties shall [serve] [exchange] statements of witnesses of fact by 4.00pm on [   ].

Expert evidence [Use (1) (2) or (3)]

(1) No expert evidence

6. [It being agreed] [The court being of the view] that no expert evidence is required, neither party has permission to rely on expert evidence without further order.

(2) Single joint expert

6. Expert evidence [on the issue of   ] shall be limited to the written report of a single expert [name if available] to be jointly instructed by the parties. Unless the parties agree in writing or the court otherwise orders, the fees and expenses of the single expert shall be paid by the parties equally.

7. Parties are to agree a letter of instruction to the single joint expert by 4 pm on [   ]. Expert to provide a copy of his report to the parties and file his report with the court by 4 pm on [   ].

8. Each party to serve any questions to the single joint expert on the other parties and the single joint expert by 4 pm on [   ]. Expert to respond to such questions by 4 pm on [   ] by serving a copy of his answers on the parties and filing the answers with the court.

9. If the parties cannot agree by 4.00pm on [   ] [who the expert is to be] [the form of the letter of instruction] [the payment of the expert's fees] either party may apply to the court for further directions.

(3) Parties' experts

5. Each party has permission to rely on expert evidence of a [state discipline(s)].

6. Experts' written reports to be served by 4 pm on [   ].

7. Expert reports to be agreed if possible. If not, the experts shall hold without prejudice discussions and prepare and serve a statement of issues agreed and issues not agreed with a summary of the reasons for any disagreement by 4.00pm on [   ].

8. Experts to attend for cross examination at the trial unless agreed by the parties or otherwise ordered by the Court.

View (in appropriate cases)

[]. Parties to co-operate in making arrangements for an early site inspection (aided by the provision of an agreed case summary and core bundle of key documents) by a Circuit Judge (to whom the case will then be reserved)[1].

Listing

[]. The case is to be listed for trial before a Circuit Judge in the period from [   ] to [   ] with a time estimate of [   ] day/s, [including hours] [excluding any] pre-reading time for the court. [*For hearing of 3 days or more:* Parties not to attend until on the first day][2]

[]. There will be a telephone listing appointment on [the first available date after namely] at   . Each party must have dates to avoid for parties, witnesses and advocates. The listing appointment will be conducted as a telephone conference pursuant to PD 26.3; relevant information is attached. The parties are encouraged to agree a list of such dates, in which case one party may phone (without setting up a formal telephone conference) on behalf of all, provided he certifies that all others have agreed.

[]. On receipt of the required information the Court will arrange the date over the phone at the time of the call. If the telephone appointment is not set up and the required information is not received by the time stated, the court will proceed to list,. In either case a formal notice of hearing will also be sent by post or DX. Thereafter, the hearing date will not be altered except on application on notice to a Circuit Judge.

[]. No telephone call after the appointment date and time will be considered or otherwise dealt with unless directed by the Court.

Preparation for trial

[] *If considered necessary, direction for a Pre-Trial Review on an appropriate date, approximately 3-4 weeks before trial date. Provision can be made to vacate the PTR upon receipt of a joint certificate from the parties' solicitors, not less than three days before the PTR that the case is ready for trial and no further directions are required.*]

[] Not less than [3] nor more than [7] days before the date fixed for trial, the Claimant is to prepare and file a trial bundle in accordance with the Practice Direction to Part 39 CPR. [Such trial bundles is to include [a chronology] [a case summary not exceeding   words] [a list of issues].]

[] Skeleton arguments are to be exchanged. Skeleton arguments shall be filed at least [one] clear day before the hearing, and should be filed by email to mailto://C entralLondonCJSKEL@hmcts.gsi.gov.uk in accordance with the court's CJ Skeleton Argument Protocol, unless email is not available to the party.

[] Parties to inform the court immediately if the case should settle.

Costs

18. Costs of this [application] [case management conference] [hearing] be

[   ].

[as appropriate].

Dated:

HH Judge

Mr/Ms Recorder

District Judge

Deputy District Judge

---

1   This direction is for consideration in appropriate cases, namely where the dispute turns wholly or mainly on the interpretation of title deeds and/or plans. It may be employed at any stage of case management if it appears likely to promote early narrowing of the issues and/or assistance with settlement.

2   (1) Trial window will in principle to be one month for each day of estimated length of trial, and will commence about 4 weeks after the projected time of the last step in pre-trial preparation, which will usually be either exchange of witness statements or finalisation of expert evidence.

(2) Attendance on the first day will normally be 11.30 am for a case of 3 days and 2 pm for a hearing of 4 or more days, but the parties may vary this

APPENDIX 16 CHANCERY BUSINESS IN THE NORTH EAST
At a glance
Addresses

CHG App 16

Vice-Chancellor, Mr Justice Briggs

Clerk: Anne Bateman: anne.bateman@hmcts.gsi.gov.uk

Leeds:

Address for High Court District Registry, county court, Circuit Judges, District Judges, fee remittances:

Leeds Combined Court Centre, The Courthouse, 1, Oxford Row, Leeds, LS1 3BG; DX

For general queries on Chancery (or Mercantile or TCC) cases, orders, skeleton arguments, documents for filing on case management hearings or matters for the Friday applications list:

Telephone: 0113 306 2461
Fax: 0870 761 7710
e-mail: orders@leeds.districtregistry.gsi.gov.uk

For queries relating to Chancery/Mercantile/TCC trials, trial dates, trial bundles, and skeleton arguments for trials:

Telephone: 0113 306 2441
Fax: 0870 761 7740
e-mail: hearings@leeds.countycourt.gsi.gov.uk

Contact: Richard Sutherland (Head of Listing)

richard.sutherland@hmcts.gsi.gov.uk

0113 306 2440

Newcastle:

Contact: Phil Lloyd (Diary Manager)

phil.lloyd2@hmcts.gsi.gov.uk

0191 201 2029

If sending skeleton arguments by email, please identify the case name and case number in the subject-line of the email message. Please insert the case name at least in the file name (not just 'skel.doc' or similar as lots of people do (but which is no help to anyone!)). Please send skeleton arguments and drafts in Word format NOT pdf.

Judge in Charge of Specialist Lists in North East

HH Judge Roger Kaye QC

Listing queries or problems may be referred to the judge in charge of the specialist list, or if unavailable, any of the specialist circuit judges.

2. Overview

2.1 Chancery high court jurisdiction is generally exercised in the North East at Leeds and Newcastle (but see also paragraph 2.6 below).

2.2 The guidance set out in this Guide applies equally to chancery business in the North East as in the rest of England and Wales subject to and with the obvious modifications or emphasis mentioned in Chapter 12 or here. Attention is drawn to paragraph 4 below.

2.3 At Leeds there are three specialist circuit judges (Judges Behrens, Langan QC and Kaye QC) who are permanently based there supported by four District Judges nominated for Chancery work: District Judges Jordan, Giles, Saffman and Bedford and suitably ticketed deputy high court judges including Judge Gosnell (the local designated civil judge ('DCJ')). Judge Langan QC is also the Mercantile Court Judge whilst Judge Kaye QC is the Chancery/Mercantile Judge. Judge Langan retires in February 2013. Selection of a specialist Mercantile/TCC judge is underway.

2.4 County court business of a specialist chancery nature is also dealt with by the same specialist judges but can also be dealt with by one of the other circuit judges authorised to hear chancery cases, by suitable ticketed recorders or deputy high court judges, and by the nominated District Judges. County court cases commenced elsewhere may, if they give rise or are likely to give rise to especial difficulty or complexity, be transferred in to the nearest main centre (Leeds or Newcastle) and marked 'Chancery Business'.

2.5 The three specialist judges also visit Newcastle on a regular basis to hear cases both in the High Court and county court there where they are supported by HH Judge Walton, the local DCJ, and by the local District Judges, and by deputies and recorders.

2.6 Where individual circumstances, such as disability or difficulty of travel, render it appropriate, arrangements can be made to have the case (both high court and county court) transferred to a more convenient trial centre for hearing. Application should initially be made to the principal contact at Leeds or Newcastle as the case may be who may refer the matter to the DCJ or to one of the specialist judges.

2.7 Both Leeds and Newcastle operate an integrated system in that the specialist judges are also authorised to hear and determine cases in the QBD proceeding in the Mercantile Court and the Technology and Construction Court (TCC).

3. Points of emphasis

3.1 Court Staff:

3.1.1 Members of the court staff are always willing to help where they can, especially in a genuine emergency. Where parties are represented it is the task of those representing them to prepare the appropriate material for court use (bundles, witness statements, skeleton arguments etc.) and to collate the papers into hearing bundles. Neither the staff, nor for that matter the judge, should, however, be expected to collate large numbers of faxed or e-mailed documents, to print off documents or authorities e-mailed for the judge, or to prepare court bundles, or to amend and insert documents into court bundles at the last minute. Where this appears to be requested on an excessive basis the staff will refer the decision to a senior manager or to the judge. A charge will be levied by HMCTS of 0.50p per page.

3.1.2 Rudeness to court staff is never acceptable.

3.2 Preparation for Hearings

3.2.1 Bundles: Irrespective of whether the hearing is proceeding in the high court or county court and of the length or type of hearing, bundles for use at the hearing including bundles of authorities where appropriate must be agreed and prepared (in accordance with this guide) in advance of the hearing and lodged in time even where no order is made to that effect. See also paragraph 3.1.1 above.

3.2.2 Overlarge bundles, poorly copied documents, bundles not page numbered, documents faxed at the last minute, and late insertions into the bundles will not be accepted unless the judge permits.

3.2.3 Authorities bundles: the authorities should preferably be agreed (to avoid unnecessary waste and duplication), listed in chronological order and the particular passages relied on appropriately marked.

3.2.4 Skeleton Arguments: must also be lodged in advance of the hearing. A guide to their preparation can be found at: http://www.chba.org.uk/__data/assets/pdf_file/0020/93701/ HHJ_Roger_Kaye_QC_paper.pdf

3.2.5 Electronic copies: electronic copies of documents such as skeleton arguments are welcomed. They are not a substitute for hard copies and where submitted should be submitted in Word format, not pdf. See above as to subject line and file name or reference.

3.2.6 Time: subject to any order of the court, the latest time for lodging bundles and skeleton arguments will, save where the case is urgent, be at least two clear days before the hearing. If this is not possible a written explanation by email or letter must be sent to the court.

3.2.7 Time Estimates and Draft Orders: applications or requests (formal or informal) for all hearings should be accompanied by or be preceded by a written time estimate agreed and accepted by all solicitors, counsel and parties in the case together with a draft of the order sought.

3.2.8 Where not agreed, separate time estimates should be submitted. The time estimate must include preparation time (ie time allowed for pre-reading), hearing time, and judgment time. They must be as realistic as possible. It is better to over-estimate than under-estimate. The latter leads invariably to delay and adjourned hearings. If the time estimate changes, the court must always be informed.

3.3 Interim Applications to the Vice-Chancellor or Circuit Judges

3.3.1 Interim applications are held in Leeds every Friday and in Newcastle on one of the Fridays when the judge attends. Dates can be obtained from the court office. When the Vice-Chancellor is in attendance interim applications will usually be listed before him. Otherwise they will be listed before one of the specialist judges or occasionally before a deputy high court judge.

3.3.2 In accordance with the arrangements referred to in paragraph 2.7 above, a typical interim applications list may expect to hear applications in the High Court (Chancery Division and Queen's Bench Division (Mercantile Court and TCC)) and occasionally in case of urgency also specialist business proceeding in the County Court marked 'Chancery Business'. Applications concerning companies where there is an unadvertised winding up petition will generally be listed as 'Re A Company' and will NOT be listed in the general applications list.

3.3.3 Whilst the specialist judges will always do their best to assist, this depends on the number of cases and their estimated and actual time and degree of urgency. Applications in excess of two hours (including the judge's pre-reading time, time in court, and time for judgment (see Guide, paragraph 5.11)) should not be placed in the interim applications list, and if placed there, may expect to be adjourned to another day. Where the list is especially heavy applications shorter than two hours may also occasionally have to be adjourned in this way. Short applications of a wide variety can sometimes also be listed for oral hearing or a telephone conference hearing at 10.00 or even earlier.

3.3.4 Interim applications within the jurisdiction of the district judges are dealt with in their ordinary daily lists or on specially allocated Chancery listing days.

3.4 Extensions of Administration Orders

3.4.1 Applications for extensions of administration orders which are lodged in compliance with the Practice Direction: Insolvency Proceedings (2012) (and paragraph 10 in particular) and which are straightforward may be dealt with on paper by one of the chancery specialist judges provided they are accompanied by

- a skeleton argument from counsel or the responsible partner of the solicitors concerned and
- a draft order.

3.4.2 The supporting skeleton argument should contain a succinct summary of the application, the relevant dates (the date the company went into administration, extensions previously granted, and the date the current administration period expires, the period of extension sought and the reasons). The skeleton argument should also specifically draw attention to any unusual features which will include any request for an extension period in excess of one year.

3.4.3 Practitioners must accept that the judge may still decide that the matter should be dealt with at an oral hearing in the usual way.

3.5 Attendance at Court: Parties and their representatives should attend at court at the designated time. Current security arrangements tend to lead to delay at the commencement of each morning and afternoon session. Allowance for this should be made. Parties and their representatives must not wait to be contacted by the court staff but should make themselves known. If a short adjournment is required, e.g. for negotiations or instructions, the judge must be kept informed.

4. Sanctions

4. It is important to emphasise what is said in paragraph 1.6 of the Guide. This is not a Practice Direction but failure to comply may influence the way cases are managed or dealt with. Accordingly, failure to abide by these requirements (and in particular as regards bundles, skeletons, time estimates and attendance) may, subject to any order of the judge, be expected to be visited in sanctions which may include adjournment of the case, or adverse orders in costs including disallowance of costs.

5. Court Users Committees

5. Court users committees exist at both Leeds and Newcastle. Matters of concern or interest may always be brought to the attention of practitioners via this route. There are usually three meetings each year at each of Leeds and Newcastle chaired by the Vice-Chancellor or the senior chancery judge present. Items for the Agenda, or of concern or queries can be sent to the clerk to the Vice-Chancellor, Mr Justice Briggs (above).

6. Other Useful Local Information

6.1 Local chancery bar representatives of Chancery Bar Association:

6.1.1 Leeds:

Dominic Crossley, Chancery House Chambers, 7, Lisbon Square, Leeds LS1 4LY;

email: dominic.crossley@chanceryhouse.co.uk.

6.1.2 Newcastle:

Stephanie Jarron, Enterprise Chambers, 65 Quayside, Newcastle upon Tyne, NE1 3DE;

email: stephaniejarron@enterprisechambers.com.

6.2 Local Law Society: see

*   www.leedslawsociety.org.uk
*   www.newcastle-lawsoc.org.uk

6.3 Chancery Bar Association: www.chba.org.uk

6.4 Northern Chancery Bar Association: www.nchba.co.uk

THE MERCANTILE COURT GUIDE

CPR 59 MCG

This Guide is published with the approval of the Lord Chief Justice.

CONTENTS

1.	Introduction	CPR 59 MCG 1
2.	Pre-action conduct	CPR 59 MCG 2
3.	Commencement and transfer	CPR 59 MCG 3
4.	Communicating with the Court	CPR 59 MCG 4
5.	Particulars of Claim, Defence and Reply	CPR 59 MCG 5
6.	Case management	CPR 59 MCG 6
7.	ADR	CPR 59 MCG 7
8.	Applications	CPR 59 MCG 8
9.	Injunctions	CPR 59 MCG 9
10.	Disclosure	CPR 59 MCG 10
11.	Witness statements	CPR 59 MCG 11
12.	Expert evidence	CPR 59 MCG 12
13.	The Pre-trial review	CPR 59 MCG 13
14.	The trial	CPR 59 MCG 14
15.	Costs	CPR 59 MCG 15
16.	Litigants in person	CPR 59 MCG 16
17.	Arbitration claims	CPR 59 MCG 17

Appendices

A	Local Mercantile Court Information	CPR 59 MCG App A
B	Case Management Information Sheet	CPR 59 MCG App B
C	Specimen Directions	CPR 59 MCG App C
D	Pre-trial checklist	CPR 59 MCG App D
E	Table of Cross-references	CPR 59 MCG App E

1 INTRODUCTION

CPR 59 MCG 1

1.1 The Mercantile Courts operate in eight regional centres throughout England and Wales as part of the Queens Bench Division of the High Court. They decide business disputes of all kinds apart from those which, because of their size, value or complexity, will be dealt with by the Commercial Court. As well as large cases the Mercantile Courts decide smaller disputes and recognise the importance of these, particularly to smaller and medium sized businesses.

1.2 This Guide explains how to conduct business cases in the Mercantile Courts and it therefore concentrates on the distinctive features of litigation in these Courts. It is not a summary of or a substitute for the Civil Procedure Rules which govern all civil cases. Nor does it replace Part 59 of the CPR which deals specifically with Mercantile Courts, or its Practice Direction ("PD59"). But it is a guide to the practice of these Courts and may be cited, as appropriate, in any Mercantile case.

1.3 By Part 59.1(2) a mercantile claim is one which "relates to a commercial or business matter in a broad sense". This covers most business disputes including cases about:

(a)   business documents and contracts;

(b)   the export, import, carriage and sale of goods;

(c)   insurance and re-insurance;

(c)   banking and financial services; guarantees;

(d)   markets and exchanges; sale of commodities;

(e)   share sale agreements;

(f)   professional negligence in a commercial context (e.g. accountants, financial intermediaries and advisors and solicitors);

(g)   business agency and management agreements;

(h)   restraint of trade;

(i)   injunctions affecting commercial matters, including post-termination of employment;

(j)   confidential information;

(k)   freezing and search orders; and

(l)   arbitration claims, in particular appeals on points of law from, and challenges to, arbitration awards made under the Arbitration Act 1996 and the enforcement of such awards.

1.4   It follows that the range of cases heard in the Mercantile Court is wide. Provided that a case involves a dispute of a genuinely business nature which is fit for the High Court, the Mercantile Court will usually accommodate it. All mercantile judges are authorised to try civil High Court cases generally and will usually accept actions at the margins of the definition into their courts.

1.5   Generally cases in the Mercantile Courts are heard by designated mercantile judges. Other judges with business experience also sit in the Mercantile Courts. Details of each court and each judge are set out in Appendix A. As these details change please check the on line version of this Guide before relying on them.

1.6   Mercantile judges manage Mercantile cases and deal with all interlocutory applications. These are not heard by Masters or District judges (PD59 para. 1.3 (1)). Wherever possible, the trial judge will have dealt with the case at some or all of its earlier stages. This provides continuity and consistency. Once a judgment is obtained enforcement applications are heard by Masters or District judges (PD59 para. 1.3)

1.7   The Judge in charge of the Commercial Court is also the Judge in charge of the Mercantile Courts. The Admiralty and Commercial Courts Guide ("the Commercial Court Guide") may often be of relevance to a claim in the Mercantile Court. If a point is not specifically covered in this Guide, reference should be made to the Commercial Court Guide. However, practitioners should bear in mind that some parts of the Commercial Court Guide are only appropriate for very large cases and there is a particular need to be proportionate in a Mercantile case. Sometimes, the rules governing the two courts are different and these will be identified in this Guide.

1.8   A table of cross-references to relevant Rules, Practice Directions and the Commercial Court Guide is at Appendix E.

1.9   The Court's ability to meet the changing needs of the commercial community depends in part upon a steady flow of information and constructive suggestions between the Court, litigants and professional advisers. Each Mercantile Court has a Users Committee. Users are encouraged to make the fullest use of this important channel of communication. Details of local users committees appear in Appendix A.

1.10   Although the Mercantile Courts serve different regions in England and Wales, their practices and approach are the same. There are some practical differences in the administration of the Mercantile Courts (for example listing) and these are explained in Appendix A.

1.11   The Mercantile Courts seek to operate in a way which gives effect to the overriding objective of dealing with cases justly and proportionately, is streamlined, accessible to non-lawyers and cost effective, promotes the early resolution of disputes where possible and actively manages through to trial the cases which do not settle.

1.12   It is incumbent upon the parties to help the Court to achieve the overriding objective. They should co-operate courteously to achieve resolution at the lowest feasible cost and in the shortest practicable time. They should put their cards on the table from the outset. The Court expects a high level of co-operation and realism from their legal representatives. It discourages over-lengthy or argumentative correspondence. Parties who fail to observe these and other requirements of the overriding objective can expect to be ordered to pay the unnecessary costs incurred.

2. PRE-ACTION CORRESPONDENCE

CPR 59 MCG 2

2.1   The Practice Direction entitled "Pre-Action Conduct" (within White Book Vol. 1 Section C "Pre-Action Conduct and Protocols) applies to actions in the Mercantile Court. It should be observed, although it is sometimes necessary or appropriate to start proceedings without following the procedures set out there, for example, where there is urgency. There is no specific Pre-Action Protocol for the Mercantile Court but some cases which may proceed in that court are covered by an approved protocol, such as the Professional Negligence Pre-Action Protocol. Subject to complying with the Practice Direction and any applicable protocol, the parties to proceedings in the Mercantile Court are not required or expected, to engage in elaborate pre-action procedures, and restraint is encouraged.

2.2   Thus, the letter of claim should be concise and it is usually sufficient to explain the proposed claim and identify key dates and matters, so that the potential defendant can understand and investigate the allegations. Only essential documents need be supplied. A potential defendant should respond to a letter of claim concisely and again, only essential documents need be supplied.

3. COMMENCEMENT AND TRANSFER

Starting a case in the Mercantile Court

CPR 59 MCG 3

3.1   Except for arbitration applications which are governed by the provisions of Part 62, the case will be begun by a claim form under Part 7 or Part 8. All claim forms should be marked "MERCANTILE COURT" (outside London, and after the reference to the appropriate registry) or "LONDON MERCANTILE COURT". Failure to do this may result in non-allocation to that Court or delay in processing the claim. The claim form should be verified by a statement of truth.

3.2   **Part 8 Claims** These are appropriate only where there is no substantial dispute of fact, for example where the case turns on a pure point of law or the interpretation of a contract. All Part 8 Claims should be marked as such.

3.3   **Issue of Claim Forms** In every Court a party may request it to issue the Claim Form in person or by post. In addition, in the London Mercantile Court, a party may request it to issue the claim form electronically. This procedure is governed by PD5C.

3.4   **Particulars of claim and the claim form** Although particulars of claim may be served with the claim form, this is not a requirement in the Mercantile Court. However, if they are not contained in or served with the claim form, (a) they must contain a statement that if an acknowledgment of service is filed indicating an intention to defend the claim, particulars of claim will follow and (b) the particulars of claim must be served within 28 days after the defendant has filed an acknowledgment of service indicating an intention to defend the claim: rule 59.4.

3.5   **Service of the claim form** Claim forms issued in the Mercantile Court are, as elsewhere in the High Court, served by the parties, not by the Court. Methods of service are set out in Part 6, which is supplemented by PD6A and 6B.

3.6 Applications for an extension of time in which to serve a claim form are governed by rule 7.6. The evidence required on such an application is set out in PD7A para. 8.2. In an appropriate case it may be presented by an application notice verified by a statement of truth and without a separate witness statement: rule 32.6(2).

3.7 When the claimant has served the claim form he must file a certificate of service: rule 6.17(2). This is required before a claimant can obtain judgment in default (see Part 12).

3.8 **Acknowledgment of service** A defendant must file an acknowledgment of service in every case: rule 59.5.The period for filing an acknowledgment of service is calculated from the service of the claim form, whether or not particulars of claim are contained in or accompany the claim form or are to follow service of the claim form. Rule 9.1(2), which provides that in certain circumstances the defendant need not respond to the claim until particulars of claim have been served on him, does not apply: rule 59.5.

3.9 The period for filing an acknowledgment of service is 14 days after service of the claim form unless the claim form has been served abroad If it has been served out of the jurisdiction without the permission of the court under rules 6.32 and 33 the time for filing an acknowledgment of service is governed by rule 6.35. If the claim form has been served out of the jurisdiction with the permission of the court under rule 6.36 the time for filing an acknowledgment of service is governed by rule 6.37(5), See PD6B and the table to which it refers: rule 59.5 (3).

3.10 **Service of the claim form out of the jurisdiction** Service of claim forms outside the jurisdiction without permission is governed by rules 6.32-6.35, and, where rule 6.35(5) applies, by PD6B. Applications for permission to serve a claim form out of the jurisdiction are governed by rules 6.36 and 6.37 and PD6B. A guide to the appropriate practice is set out in Appendix 15 of the Commercial Court Guide. Service of process in some foreign countries may take a long time to complete; it is therefore important that solicitors take prompt steps to effect service.

3.11 If the defendant intends to dispute the court's jurisdiction or to contend that the court should not exercise its jurisdiction he must file an acknowledgment of service – rule 11(2); and issue an application notice. An application to dispute the court's jurisdiction must be made within 28 days after filing an acknowledgment of service: rule 59.6. If the defendant wishes to rely on written evidence in support of that application, he must file and serve that evidence when he issues the application. In an appropriate case it may be presented by an application notice verified by a statement of truth and without a separate witness statement: rule 32.6(2).

3.12 If the defendant makes an application under rule 11(1), the claimant is not bound to serve particulars of claim until that application has been disposed of: rule 59.6(3).

3.13 **Effect of an application challenging the jurisdiction** An acknowledgment of service of a Part 7 or Part 8 claim form which is followed by an application challenging the jurisdiction under Part 11 does not constitute a submission by the defendant to the jurisdiction: rules 11(3) and 11(7).

3.14 **Default judgment** Default judgment is governed by Part 12 and PD12. However, because in the Mercantile Court the period for filing the acknowledgment of service is calculated from service of the claim form (PD59 para. 5(2)), the reference to "particulars of claim" in PD12 para. 4.1(1) should be read as referring to the claim form. In addition, if particulars of claim were not served with the claim form and the defendant then fails to acknowledge service, default judgment must be the subject of an application, not a request. It can be made without notice but the Court may direct its service on the defendant: rule 59.7.

Transfer of cases to and from a Mercantile Court.

3.15 The procedure for transfer into the Mercantile Court is set out in rule 59.3 and PD59 para. 4. In respect of applications to transfer other than from the Commercial Court, these can be dealt with only by mercantile judges. A mercantile judge also has the power to transfer such a case into the Mercantile Court of his own motion. If both parties consent to a such transfer into the Mercantile Court, the application may be made by letter. Such applications should be made early in the proceedings.

3.16   If a party wishes to transfer the case from a Mercantile Court to different specialist list other than the Commercial Court, only a judge of that specialist list may grant such transfer. The party seeking transfer should refer the matter first to the mercantile judge because if he considers that transfer is appropriate the judge of the relevant specialist list to which transfer is sought can be informed. In some cases (for example transfer to the TCC) the mercantile judge may also sit as a TCC judge and can permit the transfer directly.

3.17   Permission to transfer any case from the Commercial Court to the Mercantile Court, or vice versa, may be granted only by a judge of the Commercial Court. Guidance about such transfers is contained in a Note at Appendix 19 to the Commercial Court Guide.

3.18   In an exceptional case, it may be appropriate for a case commenced in a particular Mercantile Court to be tried locally by a judge of the Commercial Court. If any party wishes the case to be so tried they should mention the matter to the mercantile judge at the earliest opportunity. The papers will thereafter be referred to the judge in charge of the Commercial Court together with any comments of the mercantile judge as to the appropriateness of trial before a Commercial Court judge. If the judge in charge agrees, the necessary arrangements will be made. In most cases, formal transfer into the Commercial Court (albeit with case management and trial locally) will not be required.

4. COMMUNICATING WITH THE COURT
E-mail

CPR 59 MCG 4

4.1   Although there is no provision for the electronic filing of documents apart from at the London Mercantile Court, parties may communicate with the Court by e-mail where the Mercantile Court concerned provides an e-mail address. But any such communications should not be accompanied by lengthy documents which need to be filed separately. The size limit is 40 pages in total of normal typescript or 2 MB whichever is the smaller. Nor should evidence for a hearing be lodged in this way. For details of Court e-mail addresses, see Appendix A. All e-mails to the Court should be copied to the other parties at the same time.

4.2   In an appropriate case, the judge concerned may provide his own e-mail address so that the parties can communicate directly with him, for example in relation to the submission of skeleton arguments or post-hearing matters. The judge may agree with the parties when they might use that address. The particular e-mail address provided must be treated as strictly confidential. Any communication to the judge must be copied both to the other parties and to the Court on its own e-mail address.

Telephone hearings and paper applications

4.3   Even where there is an application to be decided by the Court it may not be necessary to have a full oral hearing. See section 8, Applications, below.

5. PARTICULARS OF CLAIM, DEFENCE AND REPLY
Form, content, serving and filing statements of case

CPR 59 MCG 5

5.1   Statements of case should be as succinct as possible. They should not set out evidence. They should be limited to 20 pages in length. The court will give permission for a longer statement of case to be served where a party shows good reasons for doing so. Any application to serve a statement of case longer than 20 pages should be made on paper to the court briefly stating the reasons for exceeding that limit. It will rarely be necessary to plead large parts of a lengthy document in the statement of case. If this is necessary the parts should be set out in a schedule not in the body of the case.

5.2   The requirements of PD16.7.4 – 8.1 (which relate to claims based upon oral agreements, agreements by conduct and Consumer Credit Agreements and to reliance upon evidence of certain matters under the Civil Evidence Act 1968) should be treated as applying to the defence and reply as well as to the particulars of claim.

5.3   Full and specific details should be given of any allegation of fraud, dishonesty, malice or illegality. Where an inference of fraud or dishonesty is alleged, the facts on the basis of which the inference is alleged must be fully set out.

5.4   Any legislative provision (including any provision of The Human Rights Act 1998 or the Convention), and any principle or provision of foreign law upon which an allegation is based should be clearly identified and the basis of its application explained.

5.5   If a defendant wishes to advance a positive case on causation, mitigation or quantification of damages, proper details of that case should be included in the defence or Part 20 defence at the outset or, if not then available, as early as possible thereafter.

5.6   **Attaching documents to the Particulars of Claim** PD16.7 para. 3 requiring a copy of the contract to be served with the Particulars of Claim in a claim based upon a written agreement should be treated as also applying to the defence, unless the claim and the defence are based on the same agreement.

5.7   But in most cases attaching documents to or serving documents with a statement of case does not promote the efficient conduct of the proceedings and should be avoided. If documents are to be served at the same time as a statement of case they should normally be served separately from rather than attached to the statement of case. Only those documents which are obviously of critical importance and necessary for a proper understanding of the statement of case should be attached to or served with it. The statement of case should itself refer to the fact that documents are attached to or served with it.

5.8   All statements of case must be verified by a statement of truth.

Serving and filing particulars of claim.

5.9   Subject to any contrary order of the court and unless particulars of claim are contained in or accompany the claim form, the period for serving particulars of claim is 28 days after filing an acknowledgment of service: rule 59.4.(c). The parties may agree extensions of the period for serving the particulars of claim. However, any such agreement and brief reasons for it must be put in writing and notified to the court, addressed to the Court's Listing Office and the court may make an order overriding any agreement by the parties varying a time limit: PD59 para. 6.

5.10   Unless the particulars of claim are contained in the claim form which the Court is to serve, the claimant must serve the particulars of claim on all other parties. A copy of the claim form will be filed at the Court on issue. If the claimant serves particulars of claim separately from the claim form he must file a copy within 7 days of service together with a certificate of service: rule 7.4(3).

Serving and filing a defence

5.11   The defendant must serve the defence on all other parties and must at the same time file a copy with the court. If the defendant files an acknowledgment of service which indicates an intention to defend the period for serving and filing a defence is 28 days after service of the particulars of claim, subject to the provisions of rule 15.4(2). (See 59.9 (2) and also Appendix 15 to the Commercial Court Guide for cases where the claim form has been served out of the jurisdiction).

5.12   The defendant and the claimant may agree that the period for serving and filing a defence shall be extended by up to 28 days: rule 15.5(1). However, any such agreement and brief reasons must be in writing and notified to the court: PD59 para. 6.2. An application to the court is required for any further extension. If the parties are able to agree a further extension, a draft consent order should be provided together with a brief explanation of the reasons for the extension.

Serving and filing a reply

5.13   Any reply must be served and filed within 21 days after service of the defence: rule 59.9. A claimant who does not file a reply does not admit what is pleaded in the defence and a claimant who files a reply that does not deal with something pleaded in the defence is not taken to admit it. A reply is necessary when the Claimant wishes to allege facts (or rely upon a legal provision or argument) which have not been pleaded in the claim. Accordingly, it should not be served simply to repeat what is pleaded in the particulars of claim. Proper consideration should be given to the question of a reply as soon as the defence has been served. The reply should be served before case management information sheets are provided to the Court. This will enable the judge to see all the pleaded issues before the Case Management Conference ("CMC") and will assist the parties in preparing for it. In some cases, more than 21 days may be needed for the service and filing of a reply. In such cases an application should be made on paper for an extension of time and for a postponement of the CMC.

5.14   Any reply must be served by the claimant on all other parties: rule 59.9(1).

Amendment

5.15   Although PD58 para. 8 applies only to the Commercial Court, it (and section C5 of the Commercial Court Guide) should be followed in the Mercantile Court. Accordingly, an amended statement of case should show the original text unless the Court orders otherwise. But amendments may be also be shown by using footnotes or marginal notes, provided they identify precisely where and when an amendment has been made. Unless the court so orders, there is no need to show amendments by colour-coding. If there have been extensive amendments it may be desirable to prepare a clean unmarked copy of the statement of case for ease of reading. However, a copy of the statement of case showing where and when amendments have been made must also be made available. All amendments must be verified by a statement of truth unless the court orders otherwise.

5.16   Questions of amendment, and consequential amendment, should wherever possible be dealt with by consent. A party should consent to a proposed amendment unless he has substantial grounds for objecting to it. A party which considers that an amendment is required should apply for it at the earliest opportunity. Late amendments (especially those sought shortly before, or at trial) should be avoided and may be disallowed.

6 CASE MANAGEMENT IN THE MERCANTILE COURT

General principles of case management

CPR 59 MCG 6

6.1   Where appropriate, the court will take an active role in the management of the case through to trial. Parties should be ready at all times to provide the court with such information and assistance as it may require for that purpose. They are also encouraged to ask the Court to decide applications on paper or by telephone where that is clearly appropriate and where the other party has sufficient time to respond.

6.2   The CMC is a key event in the life of a case. The Court will wish to deal with as many issues as possible at that stage to save time and costs and the parties must be able and willing to assist the Court to achieve this.

6.3   Where parties fail to co-operate with each other or take disproportionate steps or create delay, they may be penalised in costs.

Fixing the Case Management Conference

6.4   The Claimant must apply for a CMC within 14 days of service of the reply or confirmation by the Claimant that no reply is to be served in the case of a Part 7 claim, or within 14 days of service of the Defendant's evidence in a Part 8 claim, or within 14 days of notification of transfer by the receiving court. If the Claimant fails to apply for a CMC any other party may apply or the Court may order a CMC of its own motion. When the Court fixes the CMC it may give directions in relation to it which shall take precedence over any directions set out below.

6.5   Because all interlocutory applications and CMCs are dealt with by the judge, it is essential that practitioners do not seek to list the CMC or any other application before a District Judge as this will lead to delay. Equally, as all mercantile cases are allocated to the multi-track, no allocation questionnaire need be filed. The document relevant to a case's management in the mercantile court is the Case Management Information Sheet, dealt with in paragraph 6.15 below.

6.6   The CMC will be held at a hearing in the usual way unless a different order is made. Any party may apply in writing not later than 3 clear days before the hearing for the CMC to be held by telephone and the Court will then decide on paper whether to proceed in this way or not.

6.7   Where a party is represented, a legal representative familiar with the case and who has sufficient authority to deal with any issues likely to arise must attend. In a heavy or complex case, the retained advocate should attend if possible.

Documents required for the CMC

6.8   Subject to any earlier order of the Court, not less than 7 days before the CMC the parties must file with the Court (a) a Case Management Information Sheet ("CMIS") in the form set in Appendix B and (b) an application notice for any application not covered by an order sought in the CMIS.

6.9   In addition, the Claimant (or other party applying for the CMC) shall also file and serve a case management file containing:

(a)   statements of case;

(b)   a brief summary of what the case is about;

(c)   the list of issues;

(d)   the CMISs;

(e)   draft directions which should as far as possible be agreed with the other party and which may be based upon the template at Appendix C; such directions should also be e-mailed to the Court using the appropriate e-mail address contained in Appendix A;

(f)   a costs budget substantially in the form set out in Precedent HB to PD51G.

6.10   If there is any significant dispute likely to arise at the CMC the parties should also serve written submissions in relation to it, 2 clear days before the hearing and file them by e-mail at the relevant address.

List of Issues

6.11   The list of issues is intended to be an agreed record of the principal issues of fact and law arising in the case and must be prepared before the CMC and after service of the reply (if any). It should be a neutral document to assist the Court and the parties in the management of the case, for example in relation to preliminary issues, the scope of disclosure, witness statements, or expert evidence. Accordingly, it should not be heavily drafted, negotiated or slanted. It is not a statement of case or a substitute for one. The parties must make every effort to agree the list of issues.

6.12   If there is genuine disagreement over the list of issues the parties should produce their own rival lists if possible using one document with the differences highlighted;

6.13   The list(s) of issues should be e-mailed to the Court at the relevant address prior to the CMC and any later hearing where they may be relevant;

6.14   The Court may order the list of issues to be refined or clarified at or after the CMC.

The Case Management Information Sheet

6.15   This is an essential aid to the understanding by the Court (and the other side) as to one party's assessment of how the case is expected to progress to trial, and its cost, along with the evidence to be called. Parties who fail to lodge it can expected to be penalised in costs in an appropriate case. It is in the form at Appendix B.

Costs Budget

6.16   Practice Direction 51G has introduced a pilot costs management scheme in all Mercantile Courts and Technology and Construction Courts which will run until September 2012. Paragraph 3.1 requires that a costs budget in Form HB is filed at the first CMC. This replaces the costs schedule H previously required by section G of the Costs Practice Direction.

6.17   The costs budget should include reasonable allowances for intended activities (eg. disclosure, witness statements, experts), identifiable contingencies (eg. making or resisting particular applications) and disbursements. See PD51G para. 3.2.

6.18   The costs budget is required in advance so that the Court can consider whether or not to make a costs management order and if it does, it will form the basis of that party's costs budget going forward subject to any amendments. See further paragraph 15.4 below.

The Case Management Conference

6.19   At the CMC the Court will give such directions for the management of the case as it considers appropriate. It will consider actively the exercise of its case management powers set out in rules 1.4 (2) and 3.1 and those attending must be prepared to assist in that exercise and be in a position to provide the Court with all necessary information. While the parties need not themselves attend, they may find it useful to do so and in any event they should be easily contactable by their representatives at the time of the CMC.

6.20   The Court is likely to give particular consideration to

(a)   whether any of the issues can be narrowed and if so how, and whether a split trial or trial of preliminary issue is appropriate;

(b)   whether further information should be provided by a party where it has been requested within a reasonable period but declined and the parties' legal representatives have been unable to resolve the issue;

(c)   the scope of disclosure, including electronic disclosure, and where relevant, a summary of the parties' discussions as to the disclosure and inspection of

Electronic Documents (see paragraphs 10.5-10.6 below) and the use of information technology in the management of documents generally;

(d)   whether expert evidence is necessary and if so whether it may be adduced by a single joint expert or if not, by the parties' experts giving their evidence concurrently;

(e)   the extent to which ADR has been considered or attempted;

(f)   whether the parties have co-operated with each over the management of the case thus far;

(g)   whether or not to make a costs management order under PD 51G.

6.21   Accordingly, the parties' representatives must be fully prepared and able, to discuss in detail with the Court the matters referred to above along with any other matters likely to arise. The aim of the Court, in all but the most substantial of cases, is to have one CMC only.

6.22   At the CMC, the Court may fix a trial date and pre-trial review ("PTR") (if appropriate). Parties must therefore have details of availability of witnesses and advocates to hand. Advocates must also be in a position to give a clear and reliable estimate of the length of trial.

6.23   The Court may also decide to fix a Progress Monitoring Date. If it does, it may after that date fix a further CMC or a PTR on its own initiative if no or insufficient information has been provided by the parties or it is otherwise appropriate.

6.24   The parties may not less than 7 days before the CMC submit agreed directions up to trial (in hard copy and by e-mail) and invite the Court to vacate the CMC on that basis. The Court will consider the position on paper and may vacate the hearing, order it to take place by telephone, maintain it or make any other appropriate order. Parties must assume that the hearing will proceed unless notified to the contrary.

6.25   Subject to the discretion of the judge dealing with the CMC, the Court may issue directions agreed and/or ordered at the CMC based upon the electronic version submitted beforehand. This may enable the directions to be issued and sealed at the conclusion of the CMC itself.

Further Case Management Conference

6.26   In some cases it may be necessary to hold a second CMC. In others, the judge may of his own motion wish to discuss some aspect of the case with the parties and may require a telephone or oral hearing. The parties should be prepared to accommodate such hearings.

7 ALTERNATIVE DISPUTE RESOLUTION
ADR generally

CPR 59 MCG 7

7.1   Business cases are often easier to settle than other disputes particularly when the relief sought is confined to the payment of money. Many businesses are able to settle a case by direct discussions or through their lawyers. If this does not work parties are encouraged to consider the use of ADR (such as, but not confined to, mediation) as an alternative means of resolving disputes or particular issues.

7.2   The settlement of disputes by means of ADR saves costs and avoids the delay inherent in litigation. It may also enable the parties to settle their dispute while preserving their existing commercial relationships and market reputation. ADR also provides parties with a wider range of solutions than those offered by litigation.

7.3   Lawyers should in all cases consider with their clients and the other parties concerned the possibility of attempting to resolve the dispute by ADR and should ensure that their clients are fully informed as to the most cost effective means of resolving their dispute.

7.4   Parties who consider that ADR might be an appropriate means of resolving the dispute or particular issues in it may apply for directions at any stage, including before service of the defence and before the CMC, for example to stay the proceedings pending mediation.

7.5   In any ovont, the Court will in appropriate cases invite the parties to consider whether their dispute, or particular issues in it, could be resolved through ADR, especially, but not only, at a CMC. Whenever there is a substantial application being heard by the Court the parties should be prepared to discuss ADR at the conclusion of the hearing.

7.6   The judge may, if he considers it appropriate, adjourn the case for a specified period of time to encourage and enable the parties to use ADR. He may for this purpose extend the time for compliance by the parties with any requirement under the rules, the Guide or any order of the Court. The judge in making an order providing for ADR, will normally take into account, when considering at what point in the pre-trial timetable there should be compliance with such an order, such matters as the costs likely to be incurred at each stage in the pre-trial timetable if the claim is not settled, the costs of a mediation or other means of dispute resolution, and how far the prospects of a successful mediation or other means of dispute resolution are likely to be enhanced by completion of pleadings, disclosure of documents, provision of further information under CPR 18, exchange of factual witness statements or exchange of experts' reports.

7.7   The judge may further consider in an appropriate case making an ADR Order in the terms set out in Appendix 7 of The Commercial Court Guide.

7.8   At the CMC the judge may consider that an order directed to encouraging bilateral negotiations between the parties' respective legal representatives is likely to be a more cost-effective and productive route to settlement then can be offered by a formal ADR Order. In such a case the court will set a date by which there is to be a meeting between respective solicitors and their respective clients' officials responsible for decision-taking in relation to the case in question.

Early neutral evaluation

7.9   In appropriate cases, and with the agreement of all parties the court will provide a without-prejudice, non-binding, early neutral evaluation ("ENE") of a dispute or particular issue. Any party may apply for an ENE and if a mercantile Judge considers that it is appropriate he will give such directions for its preparation and conduct as are appropriate. The judge who conducts the ENE will take no further part in the case, either for the purpose of the hearing of applications or as the judge at trial, unless the parties agree otherwise. An ENE may be conducted entirely on paper, or after a hearing (with or without evidence) although in general such hearings will not be expected to last more than one day. The Judge conducting the ENE will give his conclusion with brief reasons, either orally or in writing. Parties are encouraged to consider ENE as one form of ADR especially where they feel unable to settle the dispute without some formal indication as to where the merits lie, and hence what might be the result at trial.

7.10   Whether it is practicable to make an ENE order at any given mercantile court may depend on the judicial resources then available given that the judge hearing the ENE may thereafter be unable to hear the case.

8 APPLICATIONS TO THE COURT

Generally

CPR 59 MCG 8

8.1   Applications are governed by Part 23 and PD23 as modified by rule 59 and PD59.9 and 10. Any application for an order should include a draft of the order sought. Once an application has been issued by the Court copies will be sent to the party making the application for service, unless the Court has agreed to effect service. The Mercantile Court is conscious of the time and cost of an oral hearing. Accordingly it is willing to consider hearing applications by video-link, telephone or on paper in an appropriate case. It is unlikely to do so in the case of an application for summary judgment/strike out, interim payment, security for costs, injunction (save where it is without notice and urgency dictates it) or other substantial application. The form of application notice enables the applying party to select which mode of determination it seeks, subject thereafter to the agreement of the Court.

Time for service of evidence

8.2   The time allowed for the service of evidence in relation to applications is governed by PD59.9.1 and 9.2. Broadly, except in applications which are going to last more than half a day, evidence in support of an application is to be served with that application, evidence in answer is due within 14 days of service and evidence in reply within 7 days after that.

Applications without notice

8.3   All applications should be made with notice, even if that notice has to be short, unless a rule or Practice Direction provides that the application may be made without notice or there are good reasons for making the application without notice, for example, because notice might defeat the object of the application. Where an application without notice is otherwise appropriate and does not involve the grant of an injunction, it will normally be dealt with by the judge on paper, as, for example, with applications for permission to serve a claim form out of the jurisdiction, and applications for an extension of time in which to serve a claim form. But in any given case the judge may require the applicant to provide clarification or further information by telephone or at a brief hearing.

8.4   On all applications without notice it is the duty of the applicant and those representing him to make full and frank disclosure of all matters relevant to the application.

Expedited applications

8.5   The Court will expedite the hearing of an application on notice in cases of sufficient urgency and importance. Where a party wishes to make an expedited application a request should be made to the court on notice to all other parties.

Video-conferencing

8.6   Most Mercantile Courts have facilities for video conferences. When an applicant wishes to have a matter heard in this way, it should say so in the application and explain why. The other parties should then indicate to the Court as soon as possible after being served whether they agree or not, giving reasons. Even if the parties agree, the Court may still decide that a full oral hearing, or conversely a telephone hearing, is more appropriate. Information about each Court's video conferencing are in Appendix A.

Telephone hearings

8.7   If the Court agrees that an application may be dealt with by telephone, it will normally be for the applicant to arrange the telephone conference which should include the recording of the call.

Paper applications

8.8   Attention is drawn to the provisions of rule 23.8 and PD23A.11. If the applicant considers that the application is suitable for determination on paper, he should ensure before lodging the papers with the court that (a) the application notice together with any supporting evidence has been served on the respondent; (b) the respondent has been allowed the appropriate period of time in which to serve evidence in opposition; (c) any evidence in reply has been served on the respondent; and (d) there is included in the papers the written consent of the respondent to the disposal of the application without a hearing; or a statement by the applicant of the grounds on which he seeks to have the application disposed of without a hearing, together with confirmation that the application and a copy of the grounds for disposing of without a hearing have been served on the respondent and a statement of when they were served.

8.9   The parties may ask the Court to deal with certain matters relating to the management of proceedings in correspondence without the need to issue an application notice. For example, this may be appropriate where the issue is costs only or the working out of figures or particular orders, following a hearing, the timing of certain directions where their substance is already agreed or has been determined or the identity of a single joint expert or mediator. The party making this request shall copy its request the other party at the same time. Subject to any other direction of the Court, the other party shall then have two clear days in which to indicate to the requesting party and to the Court its consent or opposition to matters proceeding in this way. If the Court decides to proceed in this way, it will inform the parties and they shall then make their representations on the matter in issue as directed by the Court. The Court will then decide the matter and issue the appropriate supplemental order.

Bundles and Skeleton Arguments

8.10   An application bundle must be lodged with the Court 2 clear days before the date fixed for the hearing. The applicant should, as a matter of course, provide all other parties to the application with a copy of the application bundle. Appendix 10 of the Commercial Court Guide deals with in detail with the preparation of bundles.

8.11   Skeleton arguments must be provided by all parties. These must be lodged with the Court at least one clear day before the date fixed for the hearing together with an estimate of the reading time likely to be required by the court. Guidelines on the preparation of skeleton arguments are set out in Part 1 of Appendix 9 of the Commercial Court Guide. On some applications there will be key authorities that it would be useful for the judge to read before the oral hearing of the application. Copies of these authorities should be provided with the skeleton arguments. In any event, bundles of the authorities on which the parties wish to rely should be provided to the judge hearing the application as soon as possible after skeleton arguments have been exchanged.

8.12   Both the application bundle and the skeleton arguments are vital advance material for the judge who is to hear the application. If they are not filed, the hearing may be vacated or costs sanctions applied. If there is likely to be a problem with the delivery of the bundle, it is the responsibility of the applicant to inform the Court forthwith and to indicate when it will be filed. Equally it is the responsibility of Counsel to inform the Court if a skeleton argument cannot be filed on time, and why.

8.13   At any stage before the hearing of an application if it appears to the Court that the application bundle and/or skeleton arguments should be filed at an earlier stage it may issue directions to that effect.

8.14   If at any time either party considers that there is a material risk that the hearing of the application will exceed the time currently allowed it must inform the Court immediately. All time estimates should be given on the assumption that the judge will have read in advance the skeleton arguments and the documents identified in the reading list.

8.15   If it is found at the hearing that the time required for the hearing has been significantly underestimated, the judge hearing the application may adjourn the matter and may make any special costs orders (including orders for the immediate payment of costs and wasted costs orders) as may be appropriate.

8.16   On any hearing expected to take up to one day, the judge is likely to assess summarily any costs which a party has been ordered to pay. Such assessments, and related costs matters are dealt with in paragraphs 15.5 to 15.7 below.

9 INJUNCTIONS

Generally

CPR 59 MCG 9

9.1   Applications for interim injunctions are governed by Part 25. They must be made on notice in accordance with the procedure set out in Part 23 unless there are good reasons for proceeding without notice. Except when the application is so urgent that there has not been any opportunity to do so, the applicant must issue his claim form and obtain the evidence on which he wishes to rely in support of the application before making the application.

9.2   On applications of any weight, and unless the urgency means that this is not possible, the applicant should provide the court at the earliest opportunity with a skeleton argument.

Without notice injunctions

9.3   If an injunction is sought without notice, the applicant will be expected the explain the basis for it. Any delay in seeking the injunction may prove fatal. Parties are reminded of the duty to make full and frank disclosure on such applications. If the injunction is granted, the Court will normally fix a return day within, not more than 7 days later. The applicant should endeavour to provide an electronic version of the order sought. It may then be possible for the Court to issue it (with appropriate amendments) at the conclusion of the hearing.

Fortification of undertakings

9.4   Where the applicant for an interim injunction is not able to show sufficient assets within the jurisdiction of the Court to support the undertakings given, particularly the cross-undertaking in damages, he may be required to reinforce his undertakings by providing security. This will be ordered in such form as the judge decides is appropriate but may, for example, take the form of a payment into court, a bond issued by an insurance company or a first demand guarantee or standby credit issued by a first-class bank. In an appropriate case the judge may order a payment to be made to the applicant's solicitors to be held by them as officers of the court pending further order. Sometimes the undertaking of a parent company may be acceptable. Accordingly, any party seeking an injunction must come prepared to deal with the question of providing security.

Freezing injunctions and search orders

9.5   The practice of the Mercantile Court is to follow the practice and procedure of the Commercial Court. See section F15.8 — 15.15 of the Commercial Court Guide. Standard forms of wording for freezing injunctions and search orders are set out in Appendix 5 thereto. They should be followed in the Mercantile Court unless the judge orders otherwise. Accordingly, any draft submitted should be in the form prescribed by Appendix 5. Any departure from the standard form must be specifically drawn to the judge's attention at the hearing.

9.6   Parties are reminded that an affidavit, and not a witness statement, is required on an application for a freezing injunction or a search order. (PD25A para. 3.1) and that the duty of disclosure is especially important in this context.

10 DISCLOSURE

Generally

CPR 59 MCG 10

10.1   The court will seek to ensure that disclosure is no wider than necessary. Anything wider than standard disclosure will need to be justified. When considering disclosure at the first CMC in a substantial case where there is a dispute about the issue, the court will often be assisted by a disclosure schedule produced by each party, indicating (by reference to categories of documents, location of documents and the period of time covered by the documentation and otherwise) which documents the party accepts are covered by standard disclosure, and whether he intends to place any, and if so what, limits upon his search on the basis that it would be unreasonable. The court can then decide the matter after hearing from the other party.

10.2   A party who contends that to search for a category or class of document would be unreasonable (see rule 31.7) should also indicate this in his CMIS (see Appendix B).

10.3   The parties should in any event be prepared to discuss with the Court at the CMC the proper scope of disclosure and how it, and the consequent inspection, might most appropriately be made. This may include using information technology (for example CDs or DVDs) to exchange copy documents and to access them thereafter and at trial.

Electronic Disclosure

10.4   This is now governed by PD31B. The extensive use of information technology in business dealings makes this a particularly relevant provision for mercantile cases. Para. 5 (3) defines an Electronic Document as "any document held in electronic form. It includes, for example, e-mail and other electronic communica tions, such as text messages and voicemail, word-processed documents and databases and documents stored on portable devices such as memory sticks and mobile phones. In addition to documents that are readily accessible from computer systems and other electronic devices and media, it includes documents that are stored on servers and back-up systems and electronic documents that have been deleted. It also includes Metadata and other embedded data which is not typically visible on screen or a print out." Para. 7 requires parties' legal advisers to notify their clients of the need to preserve disclosable documents which include Elec-tronic Documents. Failure to observe this requirement, so that, for example, important documents only emerge at trial, may have serious consequences including the adjournment of a hearing and costs orders against the defaulting party, which may be sought on an indemnity basis.

10.5   The parties should also, prior to the first CMC, discuss any issues that may arise regarding searches for and the preservation of electronic documents. This may involve the categories of Electronic Documents within their control, the computer systems, electronic devices and media on which any relevant documents may be held, the storage systems and document retention policies, the scope of the reasonable search for such documents, the means by which the burden and cost of disclosure might be reduced and the other matters referred to in PD31B para. 9. In general the parties should provide the court with an explicit account of the issues as to retrieval and disclosure of electronic documents which have arisen and where proportionality is in issue each party should provide the court with an informed estimate of the volume of documents involved and the cost of their retrieval and disclosure. They should also co-operate at an early stage as to the format in which electronic copy documents are to be provided on inspection. They should also consider the use of information technology in the conduct of the proceedings generally including the disclosure and inspection and/or copying of non-Electronic Documents — see para. 8.

10.6   Para. 14 requires the parties to submit before the first CMC a document summarising the extent of the parties' agreement on such matters. Where there is disagreement the Court will make the appropriate orders which may include the holding of a further CMC on disclosure and/or the completion of an Electronic Documents Questionnaire.

Specific Disclosure

10.7   An order for specific disclosure under rule 31.12 may direct a party to carry out a thorough search for any documents which it is reasonable to suppose may adversely affect his own case or support the case of the party applying for disclosure or which may lead to a train of enquiry which has either of these consequences and to disclose any documents located as a result of that search: PD31 para. 5.5. Specific disclosure is normally the subject of a separate application but the parties should be prepared to discuss at the CMC whether such an application is likely and if it is, whether any issue relating to particular documents can be conveniently dealt with at the CMC.

11 WITNESS STATEMENTS

Preparation and form of witness statements

CPR 59 MCG 11

11.1   Witness statements must comply with the requirements of PD32. In addition,

(a)   the function of a witness statement is to set out in writing the evidence in chief of the witness; as far as possible, therefore, the statement should be in the witness's own words;

(b)   it should be as concise as the circumstances of the case allow without omitting any significant matters;

(c)   it should not contain lengthy quotations from, or commentaries upon, documents;

(d)   it is seldom necessary to exhibit documents to a witness statement;

(e)   it should not engage in (legal or other) argument;

(f)   it must indicate which of the statements made in it are made from the witness's own knowledge and which are made on information or belief, giving the source for any statement made on information or belief;

(g)   it must contain a statement by the witness that he believes the matters stated in it are true;

(h)   it is usually convenient for a witness statement to follow the chronological sequence of events or matters dealt with (PD32 para. 19.2). It is also helpful for particular topics covered to be indicated by the appropriate heading.

11.2   The copies of witness statements to be inserted into the trial bundle should be annotated with the trial bundle references of the documents to which they refer.

Fluency of witnesses

11.3   If a witness is not sufficiently fluent in English to give his evidence in English, the witness statement should be in the witness's own language and a translation provided. If a witness is not fluent in English but can make himself understood in broken English and can understand written English, the statement need not be in his own words provided that these matters are indicated in the statement itself. It must however be written so as to express as accurately as possible the substance of his evidence.

Additional evidence from a witness

11.4   A witness giving oral evidence at trial may with the permission of the court amplify his witness statement and give evidence in relation to new matters which have arisen since the witness statement was served: rule 32.5(3). Permission will be given only if the Court considers that there is good reason not to confine the evidence of the witness to the contents of his witness statement: rule 32.5(4).

Witness summonses

11.5   If a witness will not voluntarily provide a witness statement and agree to attend Court, the relevant party may wish to serve a summons for the witness to attend court or to produce documents in advance of the date fixed for trial. A witness summons is issued by the Court at the request of the relevant party who must then serve it; but if the summons is to be served within 7 days before the trial, the permission of the Court is needed. See rule 34.2-34.7 and also rule 32.9.

Evidence to be given by video-link

11.6   A witness may give evidence by video-link or by other means other than oral testimony when present at the trial, if the Court permits. (rule 32.3). The Courts which have video-link facilities are listed in Appendix A. Parties seeking to use such facilities should make application at an early stage, preferably at the CMC and in any event no later than the PTR. Detailed guidance is at PD32 Annex 3 and section H3 of the Commercial Court Guide.

12 EXPERT EVIDENCE
Generally

CPR 59 MCG 12

12.1   Any application for permission to call an expert witness or serve an expert's report should normally be made at the CMC when the party applying will be expected to identify the expert's field of expertise and the issue to which the proposed expert evidence relates.

12.2   The parties should always consider whether expert evidence is truly required at all and if it is, whether it can be given by a single joint expert rather than one for each side. If each side is to have its own expert, they should further consider whether the evidence can be given concurrently. See further paragraph 12.7 below. They can expect the Court at the CMC to give detailed consideration to such matters.

12.3   The provisions set out in Appendix 11 to the Commercial Court Guide apply to all aspects of expert evidence (including expert reports, meetings of experts and expert evidence given orally) unless the court orders otherwise. Parties should ensure that they are drawn to the attention of any experts they instruct at the earliest opportunity.

Single Joint Expert

12.4   Such an expert may be particularly appropriate where the claim is of modest value and the instruction of two experts would be disproportionate, the issue is itself a self-contained or subsidiary one or where it consists largely of testing or other analysis which can conveniently be done for all parties by one firm. A single joint expert may be inappropriate where the issue is substantial or complex or where one or both sides have already instructed an expert.

12.5   When the use of a single joint expert is contemplated, the court will expect the parties to co-operate in developing, and agreeing terms of reference for that expert and his fees. In most cases the terms of reference will (in particular) identify in detail what the expert is asked to do, identify any documentary materials he is asked to consider and specify any assumptions he is asked to make.

Exchange of reports

12.6   In appropriate cases the court will direct that the reports of expert witnesses be exchanged sequentially rather than simultaneously. This may in many cases save time and costs by helping to focus the contents of responsive reports upon true rather than assumed issues of expert evidence and by avoiding repetition of detailed factual material as to which there is no real issue. Sequential exchange is likely to be particularly effective where experts are giving evidence of foreign law or are forensic accountants. This is an issue that the court will normally wish to consider at the CMC. The Court will also consider whether it should provide at the outset for the service of supplemental reports where the initial reports were exchanged simultaneously.

Concurrent Evidence

12.7   There is provision in the Mercantile Courts for expert evidence at trial to be taken concurrently, that is to say with both experts in the witness box at the same time, taking part in a structured dialogue with the judge according to a fixed agenda of issues on which they disagree. This enables the judge and the trial advocates to receive the immediate view of both experts on a particular matter and the opportunity for the experts to make points to each other as well as answering questions. There remains the opportunity for the trial advocates to ask questions of the experts in the usual way. It is thought that in an appropriate case this procedure will lead to a saving of time and costs (for example by narrowing issues and avoiding repetition) and a clearer understanding of the real issues between the experts. Therefore, at the CMC and the PTR the parties and the judge will give careful consideration as to whether an order for concurrent evidence should be made.

Meetings of expert witnesses

12.8   The court will normally direct a meeting or meetings of expert witnesses before trial. This will normally follow the exchange of reports. However, in some cases it may be appropriate to direct an initial meeting of experts even before exchange of reports. This may narrow some assumed issues or ensure that both experts are addressing themselves to the precisely the same issues. Sometimes it may be useful for there to be further meetings during the trial itself.

12.9   The purposes of an experts' meeting are to give the experts the opportunity to discuss the expert issues and to decide, with the benefit of that discussion, on which expert issues they share or can come to share the same expert opinion and on which expert issues there remains a difference of expert opinion between them (and what that difference is).

12.10   Unless the court orders otherwise, at or following any meeting the experts should prepare a joint memorandum for the court recording:

(a)   the fact that they have met and discussed the expert issues;

(b)   the issues on which they agree;

(c)   the issues on which they disagree; and

(d)   a brief summary of the reasons for their disagreement.

12.11   If the experts do reach agreement on an issue that agreement will not bind the parties unless they expressly agree to be bound by it.

Written questions to experts

12.12   Under rule 35.6 a party may, without the permission of the court, put written questions to an expert instructed by another party (or to a single joint expert) about his report. Unless the court gives permission or the other party agrees, such questions should be for the purpose only of clarifying the report. The court will pay close attention to the use of this procedure (especially where separate experts are instructed) to ensure that it remains an instrument for the helpful exchange of information.

Trial

12.13   At trial the evidence of expert witnesses is usually taken as a block, after the evidence of witnesses of fact has been given. The introduction of additional expert evidence after the commencement of the trial can have a severely disruptive effect. Not only is it likely to make necessary additional expert evidence in response, but it may also lead to applications for further disclosure of documents and also to applications to call further factual evidence from witnesses whose statements have not previously been exchanged. Accordingly, experts' supplementary reports must be completed and exchanged not later than the progress monitoring date and the introduction of additional expert evidence after that date will only be permitted upon application to the trial judge and if there are very strong grounds for admitting it.

13 THE PRE-TRIAL REVIEW AND TRIAL TIMETABLE

CPR 59 MCG 13

13.1   Where a PTR has been ordered, the Pre-trial Check List (substantially in the form reproduced here as Appendix D) must be filed at Court not less than 7 days before the PTR.

13.2   If no PTR has been ordered, the Pre-trial Check List should be served 6 weeks before the trial date unless otherwise ordered. In such a case, the judge will consider the Pre-trial Check Lists and decide then whether to order a PTR. If he does not, he may on his own initiative give directions for the further preparation of the case or as to the conduct of the trial.

13.3   Where a PTR has been ordered it will be conducted by the trial judge whenever possible. The advocates who will appear at the trial should attend.

13.4   A PTR gives the Court the opportunity to review the case before the trial and the parties the opportunity to ventilate any remaining procedural issues between them. Failure by the parties to mention any matter which ought properly to be dealt with at this stage and which is left to trial may be taken into account when the Court at trial decides what order (including any order for costs) to make.

13.5   The Court will also revisit the time estimate for trial and consider the trial timetable. This should provide for openings, witness evidence, expert evidence and oral closing submissions, over the course of the trial. The trial timetable should be submitted 2 clear days before the PTR.

13.6   The parties may not less than 7 days before the PTR request the Court in writing to vacate it on the basis that there are no issues which fall to be determined or that any such issues have been resolved by consent in the form of agreed directions submitted to the Court at the same time in hard copy and by e-mail. The Court will consider the position on paper and may vacate the PTR, order it to take place by telephone, maintain it or make any other appropriate order. Parties must assume that the hearing will proceed unless notified to the contrary.

14 THE TRIAL

Trial Bundles

CPR 59 MCG 14

14.1   The bundles of documents for the trial should be prepared in accordance with Appendix 10 of the Commercial Court Guide which contains an essential checklist. The number, content and organisation of the trial bundles should be approved by the advocates with the conduct of the trial. They should consist of files with 2 and not 4 rings.

14.2   Parties are reminded that apart from certain specified documents, trial bundles should include only necessary documents: PD39A para. 3.2(11). Consideration must always be given to what documents are and are not relevant and necessary. Where the court is of the opinion that costs have been wasted by the copying of unnecessary documents it will have no hesitation in making a special order for costs against the party responsible.

14.3   The number, content and organisation of the trial bundles should be agreed in accordance with the following procedure, subject to any other direction of the Court:

(a)   the claimant should submit proposals to all other parties at least 4 weeks before the date fixed for trial;

(b)   the other parties should submit details of additions they require and any suggestions for revision of the claimant's proposals to the claimant at least 3 weeks before the date fixed for trial.

14.4   Preparation of the trial bundles should be completed not later than 2 weeks before the date fixed for trial. Parties are reminded of the requirement under PD39A para. 3.9 to agree questions of authenticity and admissibility or summarise their disagreement.

14.5   It is the responsibility of the claimant's legal representative to prepare and lodge the agreed trial bundles: see PD39A para. 3.4. If another party wishes to put before the court a bundle that the claimant regards as unnecessary he must prepare and lodge it himself. Bundles should be lodged with the Court at least 7 days before trial. If bundles are lodged late, this may result in the trial not commencing on the date fixed, at the expense of the party in default. An order for immediate payment of costs may be made.

14.6   If oral evidence is to be given at trial, the claimant should provide a clean unmarked set of all relevant trial bundles for use in the witness box: PD39A para. 3.10. The claimant is responsible for ensuring that these bundles are kept up to date throughout the trial.

Opening Notes

14.7   The Claimant's opening note should outline its case on the issues for trial, highlighting (by reference to trial bundle numbering) the key documents and providing a reading list for the Court with an estimate of how long pre-reading will take. The legal framework for the claim should also be set out although extensive legal argument or citation of authorities is not required at this stage. The Defendant's note should be similarly concise. The timing and mode of service of the notes will have been set at the PTR or by agreement between the parties and the Court. Under normal circumstances such notes must be provided at least 2 clear days before the trial and may be ordered to be sequential.

Opening Speeches

14.8   The Court will usually permit a brief opening speech by the Claimant and a response from the Defendant. This gives the Court and the parties an opportunity to clarify any matters arising out of the opening notes and narrow issues if possible.

Applications

14.9   If it is necessary to make an application for example in relation to evidence it should be made at the earliest point in the trial which may be during opening. Parties should not delay in making such applications on the basis that as the trial progresses they may become unnecessary.

Closing submissions

14.10   The form and timing of closing submissions will be decided in the course of the trial. The usual course particularly in the case of shorter trials, is that the advocates will be expected to make oral closing submissions, either immediately after the evidence has been completed or shortly thereafter. Unless the trial judge directs otherwise, the claimant will make his oral closing submissions first, followed by the defendant in the order in which they appear on the claim form with the claimant having a right of reply.

14.11   In a more substantial trial, the court may well require written closing submissions before oral closing submissions. In such a case the court will normally allow an appropriate period of time after the conclusion of the evidence to allow the preparation of these submissions.

15 COSTS

Generally

CPR 59 MCG 15

15.1   See Part 44. The general rule is that the unsuccessful party will pay the successful party's costs but the judge may make a different order: rule 44.3 (2). Parties should note that their conduct during the proceedings may be taken into account in the ways set out in rule 44.3 (4) and (5). The judge may disallow the costs of, or make a costs order against, any party which has unnecessarily increased costs at any stage.

15.2   Mercantile cases are often complex with a variety of different issues to be decided. Accordingly, the judge may have regard to the outcome on particular issues as well as who has succeeded overall; see rule 44.3 (4) (b).

15.3   The judge has the power to make a wide range of orders to give effect to the merits of the parties' position on costs, including ordering payment of a proportion only of a party's costs or in a fixed amount, or from or until particular dates: rule 44.3 (6).

Costs Management Practice Direction 51G

15.4   If a costs management order is made (see paragraphs 6.16 to 6.18 above) the judge will approve the parties' costs budget. If the costs budget becomes inaccurate later on, the party concerned should produce it to the court on any future case management hearing and before trial and the judge may then approve or not approve any necessary revisions. When the costs are ultimately assessed, the judge conducting the assessment will have regard to the last approved costs budget and will not depart from it without good reason.

Summary Assessment of costs

15.5   The general rule is that if a hearing in the Mercantile Court takes no longer than a day, the judge will assess the costs summarily. If the application disposes of the whole claim, those costs may be summarily assessed, too: PD44 para. 13.2.

15.6   If a party wishes the Court to make a summary assessment of its costs, if the other side is ordered to pay them, it must provide statement of those costs with a detailed schedule, no later than 24 hours before the hearing: PD44 para. 13.5. If this rule is not complied with, the judge may well decline to make an assessment and order that the costs be the subject of a detailed assessment in the usual way.

15.7   The Senior Court Costs Office's Guide to the Summary Assessment of Costs is in the last section of Part 48. Annex 2 to the Guide contains a list of guideline hourly rates for solicitors across England and Wales. This is updated annually. For the latest rates, see: (up date www ref nearer to publication) http://www.justice.go v.uk/courts/rcj-rolls-building/senior-courts-costs-office/guidance

The Court is not bound to limit a party's costs to those rates but they are often regarded as a very useful starting point. Cases justifying higher rates may be where the work has had to be done with real urgency or where the amount at stake or the complexity of the case, is very substantial.

Payment on account of costs

15.8   Even if a summary assessment is not made, for example because of pressure of time or the nature or extent of the disputes over the costs incurred, or because the hearing has exceeded one day, the Court may well order that a payment on account of such costs be made. See rule 44.3 (8). But if it is to do so, it will normally require a document which gives at least some detail as to how the sum claimed is arrived at.

Pro Bono Costs Orders

15.9   If a party had legal representation which was provided free of charge (for example under the Bar Pro Bono Scheme or by the Access to Justice Foundation), the Court may order the other party to pay such costs as it would have ordered against it, had the first party's representation not been free of charge. It can assess such costs or order a detailed assessment in the usual way. The recipient is, however, not the first party but the relevant prescribed charity which arranged the representation. Such orders may not be made against those whose own representation is provided without charge or who are funded by the Legal Services Commission. See s194 of the Legal Services Act 2007, CPR44.3C and PD 43 para. 5.21.

16 LITIGANTS IN PERSON AND COMPANIES WITHOUT REPRESENTATION

CPR 59 MCG 16

16.1   Those bringing or defending claims in the Mercantile Court are sometimes unable to afford legal representation or do not have it for some other reason. Such "litigants in person" require special consideration.

16.2   Where a litigant in person is involved in a case the court will expect solicitors and counsel for other parties to do what they reasonably can to ensure that he has a fair opportunity to prepare and put his case. The duty of an advocate to ensure that the court is informed of all relevant decisions and legislative provisions of which he is aware (whether favourable to his case or not) and to bring any procedural irregularity to the attention of the court during the hearing is of particular importance in a case where a litigant in person is involved.

16.3   Further, the court will expect solicitors and counsel appearing for other parties to ensure that they provide the various documents required for the management of the case and trial, even where the litigant in person is unwilling or unable to participate. If the claimant is a litigant in person the judge at the CMC will normally direct which of the parties is to have responsibility for the preparation and upkeep of the case management bundle. The court may also give directions relating to the costs of providing application bundles, trial bundles and, if applicable, transcripts of hearings to the litigant in person.

16.4   Litigants in person are reminded that if their case is in London, Cardiff or Manchester, they may obtain very helpful support before and during a hearing (though not extending to legal advice or representation) from the court's Personal Support Unit ("PSU"). See its website at http://www.thepsu.org and the individual contact details at Appendix A for those Court centres where the PSU operates. The other parties in the case should remind the litigant in person of this service at those centres if he appears to be unaware of it. The Court's experience is that the involvement of the PSU can be of great assistance to both parties, as well as the judge.

16.5   Litigants in person may also seek the assistance of a "McKenzie friend" who may sit alongside them in court and provide assistance such as taking notes or making quiet suggestions to them. If sought, permission for a McKenzie friend is usually given unless fairness or the interests of justice do not require it. It is less common for the court to grant a right of audience to a particular individual who is not otherwise qualified to act as an advocate although there is power to do so under paragraph 1 (2) of Schedule 3 to the Legal Services Act 2007. It would be exceptional for the court to grant permission where the person concerned is unqualified but holds himself out as providing advocacy services. See generally section 13G in volume 2 of the White Book.

16.6   Although rule 39.6 enable the Court to allow a company or other corporation without legal representation to be represented at trial by an employee, the complexity of cases in the Mercantile Court may make that unsuitable.

17 ARBITRATION CLAIMS

CPR 59 MCG 17

17.1   Applications to the court under the Arbitration Acts 1950 — 1996 and other applications relating to arbitrations are known as "arbitration claims". The procedure applicable to arbitration claims is to be found in Part 62 and PD62. The most common claims are (a) appeals on a point of law against the arbitration award where the parties have provided for this in the contract (b) applications for permission to appeal where they have not (c) applications to set aside the award for serious irregularity and (d) applications to enforce an arbitration award. Almost all arbitration claims are made under the Arbitration Act 1996. Only the Commercial Court, the Technology and Construction Court and the Mercantile Court have jurisdiction to deal with them. The claims dealt with by the Technology and Construction Court will usually relate to construction or similar contracts. Part 59, which deals with the Mercantile Court generally, applies to arbitration claim unless any provision in Part 62 says otherwise: rule 62.1 (3). In general, the Mercantile Court will apply section O of the Commercial Court Guide.

17.2   The automatic directions set out in PD62 para. 6 will apply unless the Court has otherwise ordered.

17.3   Where the claim is for permission to appeal, the detailed procedure set out in PD62 para. 12 will apply. Sometimes a party also seeks to challenge the award on the grounds of serious irregularity. If so, both claims should be made in the same claim form. On receipt of the papers the judge will consider whether such claims should be dealt with together or separately and give appropriate directions or order a hearing to take place to discuss the matter further.

17.4   In the interests of saving costs and of proportionality the Mercantile Courts may be expected to deal informally and robustly with some smaller arbitration claims which seem obviously misconceived.

17.5   Enforcement of awards is governed by rule 62.18. An application to enforce must be made without notice in an arbitration claim form, supported by written evidence and accompanied by two copies of the draft of the order required. If the Court gives permission to enforce the defendant will be given 14 days (more if outside the jurisdiction) to apply to set it aside and no enforcement will take place until the 14 days or longer period expires or any application to set aside is disposed of.

APPENDIX A

CPR 59 MCG App A

Court Addresses and other information

1. London and South East

Address

Rolls Building

7 Rolls Buildings

Fetter Lane

London

England

EC4A 1NL

DX 160040 Strand 4

Judge

His Honour Judge Mackie CBE QC

Clerk — Claire Thomas

Email: mailto://Claire.thomas1@hmcts.gsi.gov.uk

Tel: 020 7947 7205

Listing

Commercial Court Listing

Email: mailto://Comct.listing@hmcts.gsi.gov.uk

Tel: 020 7947 6826

Fax: 020 7947 7670

Users' Committee

Contact the Commercial Court Users Committee

Video-conferencing

Contact: Anita Homji

Tel: 020 7947 7887

E-mail: mailto://anita.homji@hmcts.gsi.gov.uk

PSU (at RCJ)

Room M104 at the Royal Courts of Justice, on the first floor, opposite courts 5 and 6.

Tel: 020 7947 7701/7703

Fax: 020 7947 7702

Email: mailto://rcj@thepsu.org.uk

Hours: 9.30am – 4.30pm, Monday to Friday

2. Midlands (Birmingham)

Address

Birmingham Civil Justice Centre

Priory Courts

33 Bull Street

Birmingham West Midlands

England

B4 6DS

DX 701987 Birmingham 7

Judge

His Honour Judge Brown QC (Court 5 on 2nd floor)

Clerk – Caroline Norman and Alison Wood (court office on 5th floor)

Email: mailto://Birmingham.mercantile@hmcts.gsi.gov.uk

Tel: 0121 681 3035

Fax: 0121 250 6730

Listing

Kevin Print: 0121 250 6229 E-mail as above.

Video-conferencing

Contact diary manager Andrea Lloyd on 0212 681 3120. E-mail address as above.

Users' Committee

Chair: HHJ Brown QC

Bar Representatives: Edward Pepperall at ep@st-philips.com

Steven Reed at mailto://sr@no5.com

Solicitor Representative: Mark Surguy at mailto://MarkSurguy@eversheds.com

PSU

Contact Jimmy Clarke c/o Business Support, Personal Support Unit at above address.

Tel: 0121 250 6354, email http://birmingham@thepsu.org.uk

3. North East (Leeds)

Address

Leeds Combined Court Centre

The Courthouse

1 Oxford Row

Leeds West Yorkshire

England

LS1 3BG

DX 703016 Leeds 6

Judges

His Honour Judge Langan QC

His Honour Judge Kaye QC

Clerk – David Eaton

Email: mailto://david.eaton@hmcts.gsi.gov.uk

Tel: 0113 306 2440/2441

Fax: 0113 306 2393/0113 242 6380

Listing and Video-conferencing

David Eaton at mailto://david.eaton@hmcts.gsi.gov.uk

Users' Committee (combined with Chancery Users)

Chair: Mr Justice Briggs. Contact via: mailto://anne.bateman@hmcts.gsi.gov.uk

4. North East (Newcastle upon Tyne)

Address

Newcastle Combined Court Centre

The Law Courts

The Quayside

Newcastle-upon-Tyne Tyne & Wear

England

NE1 3LA

DX 65127 Newcastle upon Tyne 2

Judges

His Honour Judge Langan QC

His Honour Judge Kaye QC

Clerk – Phil Lloyd

Email: mailto://phil.lloyd2@hmcts.gsi.gov.uk

Tel: 0191 2012029

Fax: 0191 2012001

Listing, video-conferencing and Users' Committee

Details as for Leeds

5. North West (Liverpool)

Address

Liverpool Civil and Family Court

35 Vernon Street

Liverpool Merseyside

England

L2 2BX

DX 702600 Liverpool 5

Judges

His Honour Judge Hegarty QC

His Honour Judge Waksman QC

Listing and Enquiries

Mercantile Manager: Elizabeth Taylor (e-mail available on telephone request)

Email (for filing and enquiries): mailto://e-filing@liverpool.countycourt.gsi.gov.uk

Tel: 0151 296 2449

Fax: 0151 296 2201 (not a dedicated fax so clearly mark "Mercantile Court")

Video-conferencing

Contact: Mark Holmes

Tel: 0151 296 2446

E-mail: mark.holmes@hmcts.gsi.gov.uk

Users Committee

See Manchester below.

PSU

Tel. 0151 296 2296

E-mail: mailto://liverpool@thepsu.org.uk

6. North West (Manchester)

Address

Manchester Civil Justice Centre

1 Bridge Street West

Manchester Greater Manchester

England

M60 9DJ

DX 724783 Manchester 44 Manchester Civil Justice Centre

Judges and Listing

His Honour Judge Hegarty QC

His Honour Judge Waksman QC

Manager of Specialist Listing — Andrew Mattey

Email: mailto://highcourtspecialisthearings@manchester.countycourt.gsi.gov.uk

Tel: 0161 240 5307

Fax: 0161 240 5398/9

Users Committee

Chair: Jeff Lewis

E-mail: mailto://Jeff.Lewis@brabnerscs.com

PSU

Room 2.15 on level 2, Civil Justice Centre

Tel: 0161 240 5037

Fax. 0161 839 5241

E-mail: mailto://manchester@thepsu.org.uk

Hours: 9.30am – 4.30pm, Monday to Friday

7. South West (Bristol)

Address

Bristol Civil Justice Centre

2 Redcliff Street

Bristol England

BS1 6GR

DX 95903 Bristol 3

Judge and Listing

His Honour Judge Havelock-Allan QC (Court 3 on 3rd floor)

Specialist Listing Officers – Vikki Haddock and Laura Turner

Email: mailto://bristolmercantilelisting@hmcts.gsi.gov.uk (Data size limit: 2 MB)

Tel: 0117 366 4866 or 4868

Fax: 0117 366 4801

Video-conferencing

Contact Colin Burton on 0117 366 4825

Users' Committee

Chair: HHJ Havelock-Allan QC: contact via listing officers at e-mail address above.

8. Wales (Cardiff)

Address

Cardiff Civil Justice Centre

2 Park Street

Cardiff CF10 1ET

Canolfan y Llysoedd Sifil Caerdydd

2 Stryd y Parc

Caerdydd CF10 1ET

Judge

His Honour Judge Chambers QC

Clerk – Tracey Davies

Email: mailto://tracey.davies2@hmcts.gsi.gov.uk

Tel: 02920 376412

Fax: 02920 376475

Video-conferencing

Contact: Circuit Judges Listing

Tel: As above

E-mail mailto://hearings@cardiff.countycourt.gsi.gov.uk

PSU

Tel: 02920 343 685

E-mail: mailto://cardiff@thepsu.org.uk

9. Wales (Mold)

Address

Law Courts

Civic Centre

Mold Flintshire

Wales

CH7 1AE

DX 702521 Mold 2

Judge and Listing

His Honour Judge Chambers QC

Listing: Clerk — Julie Holmes/Beth Sear/Tracey Paterson

Tel: 01978 317406

Fax: 01978 358213

Administration: Denise Lloyd

Tel: 01978 317406

Fax: 01978 358213

The Listing is done out of Wrexham, the courtroom is at Mold

Video-conferencing

Contact: Civil listing at Wrexham

Tel no: 01978 317406

E-mail mailto://northwalescivillisting@wrexham.countycourt.gsi.gov.uk

APPENDIX B

CPR 59 MCG App B

Case Management Information Sheet – Mercantile Courts

[Title of Case]

This information sheet must be filed with Mercantile Listing at least 7 days before the Case Management Conference, and copies served on all other parties: see paragraph 7.7 of the Mercantile Courts Practice Direction.

Party filing:

Solicitors:

Advocate(s) for trial:

Date:

Substance of case

1.   What in about 20 words maximum is the case about? Please provide a separate concise list of issues in a complex case.

Parties

2.   Are all parties still effective?

3.   Do you intend to add any further party?

Statements of case

4.   Do you intend to amend your statement of case?

5.   Do you require any "further information" – see CPR 18?

Disclosure

6.   By what date can you give standard disclosure?

7.   Do you contend that to search for any type of document falling within CPR 31.6(b) would be unreasonable within CPR 31.7(2); if so, what type and on what grounds?

8.   Is any specific disclosure required – CPR 31.12?

9.   Is a full disclosure order appropriate?

10.   By what dates could you give:

        (i)   any specific disclosure referred to at 8; and

        (ii)   full disclosure?

Admissions

11.   Can you make any additional admissions?

Preliminary issues

12.   Are any issues suitable for trial as preliminary issues? If yes, which?

Witnesses of fact

13.   On how many witnesses of fact do you intend to rely at the trial (subject to the court's direction)?

14.   Please name them, or explain why you do not.

15.   Which of them will be called to give oral evidence?

16.   When can you serve their witness statements?

17.   Will any require an interpreter?

Expert evidence

18.   Are there issues requiring expert evidence?

19.   If yes, what issues?

20.   Might a single joint expert be suitable on any issues (see CPR 35.7)?

21.   What experts do you intend (subject to the court's direction) to call? Please give the number, their names and expertise.

22.   By what date can you serve signed expert reports?

23.   Should there be meetings of experts of like disciplines, of all disciplines? By when?

24.   Which experts, if any, do you intend not to call at the trial?

25.   Will any require an interpreter?

Trial

26.   What are the advocates' present estimates of the length of the trial?

27.   What is the earliest date that you think the case can be ready for trial?

28.   Where should the trial be held?

29.   Is a Pre-Trial Review advisable?

A.D.R.

30.   Might some form of Alternative Dispute Resolution assist to resolve the dispute or some part of it?

31.   Has this been considered with the client?

32.   Has this been considered with the other parties?

33.   Do you want the case to be stayed pending A.D.R. or other means of settlement — CPR 26.4; or any other directions relating to A.D.R.?

Other applications

34.   What applications, if any, not covered above, will you be making at the conference?

Costs

35.   What, do you estimate, are your costs to date?

36.   What, do you estimate, will be your costs to end of trial?

[Signature of party/solicitor]

APPENDIX C

CPR 59 MCG App C

Case No:

IN THE HIGH COURT OF JUSTICE
QUEEN'S BENCH DIVISION
MANCHESTER DISTRICT REGISTRY
MERCANTILE COURT
HIS HONOUR JUDGE [ ] QC
Sitting as a Judge of the High Court
Hearing date: [ ]
BETWEEN:

Claimant

and

Defen-
dant

ORDER

UPON the Case Management Conference in this matter

AND UPON HEARING [ ] for the Claimant and [ ] for the Defendant

Statements of Case

1.   The Claimant has permission to amend the Particulars of Claim in the form produced to the Court. Any such Amended Particulars of Claim shall be filed and served by [*].

2.   The Defendant has permission to serve an Amended Defence [and Counterclaim] in the form produced to the Court [consequential upon the Amended Particulars of Claim]. Any such Amended Defence [and Counterclaim] shall be filed and served by [*].

3.   [The Claimant has permission to file and serve an Amended Reply [and Defence to Counterclaim] in the form produced to the Court [consequential upon the Amended Defence] [and Counterclaim]. Any such Amended Reply [and Defence to Counterclaim] shall be filed and served by [*].]

4.   The costs of, and occasioned by, the amendments to the [*] shall be paid by [*] in any event, such costs to be assessed on the standard basis by way of detailed assessment if not agreed.

5.   The [*] shall file and serve Replies to the Request for Further Information or Clarification made by the [*] on [date] in relation to the [statement of case] by [*].

Consolidation/Joint management and trial of cases

6.   "This action is to be consolidated [managed and tried] with action number [ ]. The lead action shall be [ ]. From the date of this Order all directions in the lead action shall apply to both actions, unless otherwise stated."

List of Issues

7.   The List of Issues annexed to this Order has been [agreed by the parties] [approved by the Court]. [The List shall be kept updated by the parties and cross-referenced to the statements of case.]

8.   [The parties shall by [date] agree and file with the Court a [comprehensive] list of issues. In the event that they are unable to agree, each party shall file its own proposed list of issues by that date.]

Disclosure

9.   The parties shall give Standard Disclosure by [*]; Inspection on 48 hours' notice shall be completed by [*]. [The parties shall identify and discuss prior to disclosure those categories of documents which they expect to see in other parties' Lists of Documents.]

10.   The parties shall exchange an Electronic Documents Questionnaire by [*]. In the case of difficulty or disagreement, the matter shall be referred to the Court for further directions at the earliest practicable date.]

11.   The [Claimant] [Defendant] [shall give Specific Disclosure of the documents or classes of documents set out [below] [in the schedule attached to this

Order]] [shall carry out a search for the documents set out [below] [in the Schedule annexed to this Order] [in accordance with the following directions: (*)].

12.   Disclosure of all such documents or classes of documents [of any documents located as a result of the search] shall be given by [*]; and Inspection on 48 hours' notice shall be completed by [*]

Witnesses

13.   Signed statements of witnesses of fact and hearsay notices when required by CPR 33.2, shall be exchanged not later than [*]. [A summary of the evidence of the following witness, namely [*] shall be served by [*].]

14.   Unless otherwise ordered, the witness statements shall stand as the evidence in chief of the witnesses at trial.

15.   [The evidence of [*] shall be given by video link at [*] [date or period]. [The Claimant/Defendant shall be responsible for making the necessary arrangements; but the costs thereof will be in the discretion of the Court.]

Experts

Experts called by each party

16.   Each party shall have permission to adduce expert evidence as follows:

(1)   [Number]

(2)   [Expertise]

(3)   [Issue(s) to be covered]

17.   Signed reports of experts shall be exchanged [sequentially as follows: by the Claimant's expert by [*] and by the Defendant's expert by [*]] [simultaneously by [*].]

18.   Experts of like disciplines shall:

(1)   Hold discussions pursuant to CPR 35.12(3) for the purposes of identifying the issues, If any, between them and, where possible, reaching agreement on those issues (or at least narrowing them); and

(2)   Prepare a joint written statement pursuant to CPR 35.12(3), by [*] stating:

(a)   That they have met and discussed the expert issues;

(b)   The issue(s) on which they agree;

(c)   The issues on which they disagree; and

(d)   A brief summary of the reasons for their disagreement.

19.   [The parties may serve short supplemental experts' reports, to be exchanged [sequentially] [simultaneously] by not later than [*]

20.   If the experts' reports cannot be agreed, the parties shall be at liberty to call expert witnesses at the trial, limited to those experts whose reports have been exchanged under this order.

21.   [The experts referred to above shall given their evidence concurrently in accordance with the Guidelines issued for the Manchester Concurrent Evidence Pilot Scheme. In order to assists the Court, both parties shall file with the Court and provide to the experts not later than [ ] clear days before

the trial, an agreed agenda consisting of a list of the issues still in dispute between the experts, in a logical order. Such an agenda will be subject to revision by the Court.]

[or

Single Joint Expert

22. The parties shall have permission to adduce expert evidence in the following field(s) of expertise in the form of a written report by a single joint expert pursuant to CPR 35.7:

    (1)   [Expertise]

    (2)   [Issue(s) to be covered].

23. The parties shall identify and shall if possible give joint instruction to the single joint expert by [*]. In the case of difficulty or disagreement, the matter shall be referred to the Court for directions at the earliest practicable date.

24. The report of the single joint expert shall be produced by [*].

25. Any questions to the expert shall be put to him by [*] and answered by [*].

26. Any party may apply not later than [*] for an order that the expert witness shall give oral evidence at the trial.]

ADR

27. The parties shall engage in ADR procedures as follows:

    (1)   On or before [*] the parties shall exchange lists of 3 neutral individuals who are available to conduct ADR procedures in this case prior to [*]. Each party may [in addition] [in the alternative] provide a list identifying the constitution of one or more panels of neutral individuals who are available to conduct ADR procedures in this case prior to [*].

    (2)   On or before [*] the parties shall in good faith endeavour to agree a neutral individual or panel from the lists so exchanged and provided.

    (3)   Failing such agreement by [*] the parties shall either agree a short list of 3, or shall send to the Court their own lists (limited to 3), so as to enable the Court to select a neutral individual or panel; and all parties shall be bound by that selection.

    (4)   The parties shall take such serious steps as they may be advised to resolve their disputes by ADR procedures before the neutral individual or panel so chosen by no later than [*].

    (5)   If the case is not finally settled, the parties shall inform the Court by letter prior to [disclosure of documents/exchange of witness statements/exchange of experts' reports] what steps towards ADR have been taken and (without prejudice to matters of privilege) why such steps have failed. If the parties have failed to initiate ADR procedures the Case Management Conference shall be restored for further consideration of the case.

           or

28. "In the period [ ] to [ ] the parties shall take such steps as they may be advised to try to settle the dispute by ADR or other means."

     or

29. The case shall be stayed from [*] until [*] so as to enable the parties try to settle the dispute by Alternative Dispute Resolution or by other means.

30. The Claimant/Defendant shall notify the court of the outcome of ADR (i.e. whether or not the case has settled) as soon it is known but in any event by no later than 7 days after [the conclusion of the ADR] [date by reference to end of ADR window].

Trial

31. The trial of this action shall commence on [   ], with a time estimate [ ] days.

Or

32. Each party shall by [*] apply to the Court for a trial date. Such a date to be not before [ ] and not after [ ].

33. [The date fixed shall be provisional until payment of the trial fee. The trial fee shall be paid no later than [ ].]

34. The progress monitoring date is [*]. Each party shall notify the court in writing by that date (with a copy to all other parties) of the progress of the case, including —

    (1) Whether the directions have been complied with in all respects;

    (2) If any directions are outstanding, which of them and why; and

    (3) Whether a further case management conference or a pre-trial review is required.

35. There will be a pre-trial review on [*].

36. Pre-Trial Checklists are to be filed no later than 7 days before the date fixed for the PTR.

37. If the parties consider that the PTR is not necessary they shall inform the Court not less than [3] clear days in advance stating why it is not necessary and enclosing any agreed further directions in relation to the trial. The Judge dealing with the PTR will consider this and inform the parties as soon as practicable thereafter whether the PTR is to go ahead or not and/or make any further appropriate directions in writing.]

38. Trial bundles, including a core bundle, must be agreed, prepared and delivered to counsel not less than 14 days before the trial date, and to the court not less than 7 days before the trial date. The trial bundle shall be in fully functioning, indexed and paginated lever arch files each containing no more than 250 pages. [A core bundle must be provided where the files exceed 5 in number.] Each file shall state the name of the case and (in large figures) its volume number on the spine and on the inside of the front of the file. Files with 4 as opposed to 2 rings shall not be used.

39. The following documents [*] shall be provided to the court electronically as a Word attachment, as well as in hard copy:

    (1) Skeleton arguments shall be served on all other parties, and lodged with the Court by e-mail to the following addresses:

        (a) To [ ] Listing Section at:

        (b) To the Judge if he has permitted the use of his own e-mail address.

(2)   By the Claimant, not later than [*] pm [*] clear days before the start of the trial [hearing];

(3)   By each of the Defendants, not later than [*] pm [*] clear days before the start of the trial [hearing];

(4)   The parties shall also provide to the Court not later than [*] pm [*] clear days before the start of the trial [hearing]:

    (a)   a chronology;

    (b)   a dramatis personae;

    (c)   an agreed reading list; and

    (d)   a composite bundle of the authorities referred to in the skeleton arguments.

Costs

40.   Costs in the case [or otherwise].

41.   [The Court has made a Costs Management Order in this case, and has approved the parties' costs budgets (as amended) as indicated thereon. [in the total sum of £]]

42.   [On [ ] at 10.00am there will be a [telephone] conference in order for the Court to review both parties' costs. 3 clear days before such conference the parties shall exchange their current Forms HB and 2 clear days before the conference they shall exchange and file with the Court (a) any object ions to the other party's Form HB and (b) any reasons for an increase in their own costs shown in their own Form HB.]

DATED this   day of

APPENDIX D

CPR 59 MCG App D

Pre-trial Check List — Mercantile Courts

[Title of Case]

Where a Pre-trial Review has been ordered, this check list must be filed with Mercantile Listing not less than 7 days before the Pre-trial Review, and copies served on all other parties. Where a Pre-trial Review has not been ordered, it must be filed and served not less than 6 weeks before the trial date.

See paragraph 8.2 of the Mercantile Courts Practice Direction.

(a)   Trial Date:
(b)   Whether Pre-trial Review ordered:
(c)   Date of Review:
(d)   Party lodging:
(e)   Solicitors:
(f)   Advocate(s) for trial:
(g)   Date lodged:
[Note: this checklist should normally be completed with the involvement of the advocate(s) instructed for trial.]

1.   Have all the directions made to date been carried out?

2.   If not, what remains to be carried out? When will it be carried out?

3.   Do you intend to take any further steps regarding:

     (i)   statements of case?

     (ii)   disclosure?

     (iii)   witnesses and witness statements?

     (iv)   experts and expert reports?

     If yes in any case, what and by when?

4.   Will the preparation of trial bundles be completed not later than 3 weeks before the date fixed for trial? If not, what is the position?

5.   What witnesses of fact do you intend to call?

6.   (Where directions for expert evidence have been given) what experts do you intend to call?

7.   Is any interpreter needed: for whom?

8.   If a Pre-trial Review has not been ordered, do you think one would be useful?

9.   What are the advocate(s)' confirmed estimates of the minimum and maximum lengths of the trial? A confirmed estimate signed by the advocate(s) and dated must be attached.

10.

     (i)   Might some form of alternative dispute resolution now assist?

     (ii)   Has the question been considered with the client?

     (iii)   Has the question been explored with the other parties to the case?

APPENDIX E
TABLE OF CROSS-REFERENCES

CPR 59 MCG App E

Paragraph in Mercantile Court Guide	CPR	Practice Direction	Paragraph in Commercial Court Guide
INTRODUCTION			
1.3	59.1 (2)		
1.6		59 para. 1.3	
1.12	1.3		
PRE-ACTION CORRESPONDENCE			
2.1		Pre-Action Conduct	
COMMENCEMENT AND TRANSFER			
3.1	22.1 (1)	59 para. 2.2, 7Apara. 7	
3.2	8.1 (2)		
3.3	7.2, 7.12	5C	
3.4	59.4 (1)		
3.5	6	6A, 6B	
3.6	7.6, 32.6 (2)	7A para. 8	

Paragraph in Mercantile Court Guide	CPR	Practice Direction	Paragraph in Commercial Court Guide
3.7	6.17(2), 12		
3.8	59.5	59 para. 5	
3.9	59.5, 6.35, 6.37 (5)	6B	
3.10	6.32-37	6B	App 15
3.11	59.6, 11 (1)and (2), 32.6 (2)		
3.12	59.6 (3)		
3.13	11 (3) and (7)		
3.14	59.7	59 para. 5	
3.15	59.3	59 para. 4	
3.16	30.5 (2) and (3)		
3.17	30.5 (3), 58.4	58 para. 4	App 19
PARTICULARS OF CLAIM, DEFENCE AND REPLY			
5.1	16.4-7		C1, App 4 (save para. 16)
5.2		16 para. 7.4-8.1	C1
5.3		16 para. 8.2	C1.2
5.4			C1.2
5.5			C1.2
5.6		16 para. 7.3	C1.3
5.7			C1.3
5.8	22.1		
5.9	59.4 (c), 2.11	59 para. 6	
5.10	???		
5.11	15.2, 15.4, 15.6 and 59.9 (2)		App 15
5.12	15.5	59 para. 6	
5.13	16.7, 59.9(1)		C4
5.14	59.9. (1)		
5.15		58 para. 8	C5.1-5.2
5.16			C5.3
CASE MANAGEMENT			
6.1	1.4, 3.1, 3.3		D2
6.4		59 para. 7.2 (2)-7.6	
6.7	29.3 (2)		
6.11			D6
6.16		51G	
6.19	1.4(2), 3.1, 59(4)	29 para. 5, 59 para. 7.10	D8.7-8.9
6.22		59 para. 8	
6.23		59 para. 7.10 and 7.11	
6.24		59 para. 7.8 and 7.9	D8.3
ALTERNATIVE DISPUTE RESOLUTION			

Paragraph in Mercantile Court Guide	CPR	Practice Direction	Paragraph in Commercial Court Guide
7.1-7.8	1.4 (2) (e) and (f)		G1, App7
7.9-7.10			G2
APPLICATIONS			
8.1	23	23, 59 paras. 9 and 10	
8.2		59 para. 9.1-9.3	
8.3-8.4			F2
8.8	23.8 and 23.9	23A para. 11	F4
8.10			App 10
8.11			App 9 Pt 1
INJUNCTIONS			
9.1	23, 25.1-25.4	25A	F15.3
9.3			F15.1
9.4			F15.4
9.5		25A paras. 3.1, 6 and 7	F15.8-15, App5
9.6		25A para. 3.1	
DISCLOSURE			
10.1	31	31A	E1.1 and 1.2 and 2.1-2.4
10.2	31.7		E1.3
10.4	31.4	31B	
10.5		31B paras. 8 and 9	E2.5
10.6		31B para. 14	
10.7	31.12	31A paras. 5.1-5.5	
WITNESS STATEMENTS			
11.1	32.4-32.14	32 paras. 1 and 17-25	
11.2			App 10 para. 3 (3)
11.3			H1.4-1.5
11.4	32.5 (3)-(4)		
11.5	32.9, 34.2-7		H1.9
11.6	32.3	32 Annex 3	H3
EXPERT EVIDENCE			
12.1	35.1 and 35.4	35, Protocol for the Instruction of Experts	H2.1
12.2	35.1 and 35.4		H2.2-3
12.3			H2.4 and App11
12.4-12.5	35.7-8	35 para. 7	
12.6			H2.11
12.7			
12.8	35.12	35 para. 9.1	H2.12
12.9	35.12 (1) and (2)	35 para. 9.2	H2.13
12.10	35.12 (3)		H2.14-17
12.11	35.12 (4)-(5)		H2.18

GUIDES

Paragraph in Mercantile Court Guide	CPR	Practice Direction	Paragraph in Commercial Court Guide
12.12	35.6	35 para. 6	
12.13			H2.22
PRE-TRIAL REVIEW AND TRIAL TIMETABLE			
13.2		59 para. 8	
13.3			D18.3
13.5			D18.4
TRIAL			
14.1	39.5	39A para. 3	J3 and App 10
14.2		39A para. 3 (2)	J3.3
14.3			J3.4-3.5
14.4		39A para. 3.9	
14.5		39A para. 3.4	J3.7
14.6		39A para. 3.10	
14.7			J8.1
14.8			J8.2
14.9			J9
14.10			J10
14.11			J11
COSTS			
15.1	44, 44.3 (4)-(6)		
15.2	44.3 (4) (b)		
15.3	44.3 (6)		
15.4		51G	
15.5	44.7	44 para. 13.2	
15.6		44 para. 13.5 and 13.6	
15.7		Guide to the Summary Assessment of Costs	
15.8	44.3 (8)		
LITIGANTS IN PERSON			
16.2			M2.1-2.2
16.3			M2.3-2.4
16.5	Section 13G Vol. 2		
16.6	39.6		
ARBITRATION CLAIMS			
17.1	62, 62.1 (3)	62	O1-05
17.2		62 para. 6	O6
17.3		62 para. 12	O8-09
17.5	62.18		O18

THE PATENTS COURT GUIDE

CPR 63 PCG

Issued December 2012. By authority of the Chancellor of the High Court
Introduction. . . . . **CPR 63 PCG 1**
Allocation . . . . **CPR 63 PCG 2**
The judges of the Patents Court . . . . **CPR 63 PCG 3**
Judges able and willing to sit out of London. **CPR 63 PCG 4**
Intellectual Property Court Users' Committee . . . . **CPR 63 PCG 5**
Statements of Case. . . . . **CPR 63 PCG 6**
Active case management and streamlined procedure . . . . **CPR 63 PCG 7**
Admissions. . . . . **CPR 63 PCG 8**
Alternative Dispute Resolution ('ADR'). . . . . **CPR 63 PCG 9**
Disclosure . . . . **CPR 63 PCG 10**
Arrangements for listing . . . . **CPR 63 PCG 11**
Time estimates and technical complexity ratings . . . . **CPR 63 PCG 12**
Documents and timetable . . . . **CPR 63 PCG 13**
Telephone Applications . . . . **CPR 63 PCG 14**
Jurisdiction of Masters. . . . . **CPR 63 PCG 15**
Consent orders. . . . . **CPR 63 PCG 16**
Draft judgments. . . . . **CPR 63 PCG 17**
Orders following Judgment . . . . **CPR 63 PCG 18**
Appeals from the Comptroller-General of Patents, Designs and Trade
   Marks ("the Comptroller"). . . . . **CPR 63 PCG 19**
Specimen Minute of Order for Directions . . . . **CPR 63 PCG 20**
Annex A: Contact details. . . . . **CPR 63 PCG 21**

GENERAL

1. INTRODUCTION

CPR 63 PCG 1

This guide applies to the Patents Court only. The Patents County Court has its own guide to which users of that court are referred.

The general guidance applicable to matters in the Chancery Division, as set out in the Chancery Guide also applies to patent actions unless specifically mentioned below. 'PD63' refers to the Practice Direction- Patents and Other Intellectual Property Claims which supplements CPR Part 63. Thus practitioners should consult this guide together with the Chancery Guide.

2. ALLOCATION

CPR 63 PCG 2

Actions proceeding in the Patents Court are allocated to the multi-track (Part 63.1(3)). Attention is drawn to Part 63.8 and PD63.5 (case management). With effect from January 2013 claims issued in the Patents Court will receive claim numbers starting 2013HP rather than the current 2013 HC, and similarly for subsequent years.

3. THE JUDGES OF THE PATENTS COURT

CPR 63 PCG 3

The judges of the Patents Court and their clerks are set out in Annex A to this guide, together with their contact details.

Trials of cases with a technical difficulty rating of 4 or 5 will normally be heard by Floyd J or Arnold J or by suitably qualified deputy High Court judges.

4. JUDGES ABLE AND WILLING TO SIT OUT OF LONDON

CPR 63 PCG 4

If the parties so desire, for the purpose of saving time or costs, the Patents Court will sit out of London. Before any approach is made to the Chancery Listing Officer, the parties should discuss between themselves the desirability of such a course. If there is a dispute as to venue, the court will resolve the matter on an application. Where there is no dispute, the Chancery Listing Officer should be contacted as soon as possible so that arrangements can be put in place well before the date of the proposed hearing.

5. INTELLECTUAL PROPERTY COURT USERS' COMMITTEE

CPR 63 PCG 5

This committee (the 'IPCUC') considers the problems and concerns of intellectual property litigators. Membership of the committee includes the judges of the Patents Court and the Patents County Court, representatives of the Intellectual Property Bar Association, the Intellectual Property Lawyers Association, the Chartered Institute of Patent Attorneys, the Institute of Trade Mark Attorneys and the IP Federation. Anyone having views concerning the improvement of intellectual property litigation is invited to make his or her views known to the committee, preferably through the relevant professional representative on the committee. They may also be communicated to the secretary, whose details are in Annex A to this guide.

The Patents County Court also has a Users' Committee which has a membership and general remit similar to the IPCUC. Matters of specific interest to the Patents County Court do arise and are considered by this committee. Its secretary is Alan Johnson, Bristows (100 Victoria Embankment, London EC4Y 0DH Tel: 020 7400 8000 Fax: 020 7400 8050).

PROCEDURE IN THE PATENTS COURT AND PATENTS COUNTY COURT

6. STATEMENTS OF CASE

Time Limits

CPR 63 PCG 6

6.1 In general, the time limits set out in Part 15 apply to litigation of patents and registered designs. However, Part 63.7 modifies Part 15 in respect of the time limits for filing defences and replies.

Content of statements of case

6.2 In general, statements of case (i.e. the pleadings of all parties) must comply with the requirements of Part 16. Furthermore, they should comply with Part 63.6 and PD63.4. Copies of important documents referred to in a statement of case (e.g. an advertisement referred to in a claim of infringement form or documents cited in Grounds of Invalidity) should be served with the statement of case. Where any such document requires translation, a translation should be served at the same time.

Service on the Comptroller

6.3 Parties are reminded of the requirement in Part 63.14(3) that where a remedy is sought that would if granted affect an entry in any United Kingdom Patent Office register (for example the revocation of a patent or reregistered design), they are required to serve on the Comptroller: the claim form, counterclaim or application notice; any other relevant statement of case (including any amended statement of case); and any accompanying documents. In addition, PD63.14.1 requires that when such an order is made, the party in whose favour the order is made must serve it on the Comptroller within 14 days.

Independent validity of claims

6.4 Where one party raises the issue of validity of a patent, the patentee (or other relevant party) should identify which of the claims of the patent are alleged to have independent validity as early as possible.

7. ACTIVE CASE MANAGEMENT AND STREAMLINED PROCEDURE

CPR 63 PCG 7

7.1 The claimant should apply for a case management conference ('CMC') within 14 days of the date when all defendants who intend to file and serve a defence have done so (PD63.5.3). If the claimant fails to do so, then any other party may apply for a CMC (PD63.5.6). Any party may apply in writing for a CMC prior to the above periods. Where a case has been transferred from another division or from another court, the claimant must file for a CMC within 14 days of the transfer (PD63.5.4).

7.2 Almost invariably CMCs in the Patents Court will be conducted by a judge. However, in the limited circumstances set out in PD63.5.2(2) (see also para.15 below), a Master may conduct a CMC. Bundles in accordance with PD63.5.9 should be filed with the court.

7.3 In general, parties should endeavour to agree directions prior to the date fixed for the CMC. Although the court has the right to amend directions which have been agreed, this will only happen where there is manifest reason for doing so.

7.4 In accordance with the overriding objective, the court will actively manage the case. In making any order for directions, the court will consider all relevant matters and have regard to the overriding objective with particular emphasis on proportionality, the financial position of the parties, the degree of complexity of the case, the importance of the case and the amount of money at stake.

7.5 The parties are reminded of their continuing obligation to assist the court to further the overriding objective. Moreover, it is the duty of the parties' advisors to remind litigants of the existence of mediation or other forms of alternative dispute resolution as a possible means to resolve disputes. In particular, the parties should consider:

(a)   The need for and/or scope of any oral testimony from factual or expert witnesses. The court may confine cross-examination to particular issues and to time limits. The parties should consider whether oral testimony of witnesses should be given by video facility.
(b)   The need for, and scope of, any disclosure of documents.
(c)   The need for any experiments, process or product descriptions.
(d)   The need for an oral hearing or whether a decision can be made on the papers. If an oral hearing is considered to be appropriate, the court may order that the hearing be of a fixed duration.
(e)   Whether all issues should be tried together or whether it would be advantageous for one or more issues to be tried in advance of the remaining issues
(f)   Whether there is a need for a document setting out the basic undisputed technology ("technical primer"), and if so, its scope and the steps to be taken to achieve agreement of it.

(g)   Whether a scientific adviser should be appointed.
(h)   The technical complexity of the action. Technical complexity is measured on a scale of 1 to 5, with 1 being the least complex and 5 the most.
(i)   Whether a costs-capping order should be made.
(j)   Whether there should be a stay of proceedings for mediation or other form of alternative dispute resolution.

Streamlined procedure

7.6 Any party may at any time apply to the court for a streamlined procedure in which:

(a)   all factual and expert evidence is in writing;
(b)   there is no requirement to give disclosure of documents;
(c)   there are no experiments;
(d)   cross-examination is only permitted on any topic or topics where it is necessary and is confined to those topics;

or for any variant on the above.

7.7 Prior to applying for a streamlined procedure, the party seeking it should put its proposal to other parties in the proceedings and should endeavour to agree a form of order.

7.8 If the parties agree to a streamlined procedure, the proposed form of order should be put to the judge for approval as a paper application.

8. ADMISSIONS

CPR 63 PCG 8

8.1 With a view to early elimination of non-issues, practitioners are reminded of the necessity of making admissions as soon as possible. This should be done as early as possible, for instance, in a defence or reply. Thus, in a defence, a party may admit the acts complained of or that his article/process has certain of the features of a claim. In a reply a patentee may be able to admit prior publication of cited documents. For the effect of admissions, see Part 14.

8.2 Parties should also consider serving a notice to admit facts in accordance with rule 32.18 for the purpose of identification of points not in dispute. By asking whether or not the defendant disputes that his article/process has certain features of the claim the real dispute can be narrowed. Thus the ambit of disclosure and of witness and expert statements will be narrowed.

8.3 Parties are reminded that when deciding the issue of costs, a court can take into account the conduct of the parties, including whether it was reasonable for a party to contest a particular issue – rule 44.3(5)(b).

8.4 The position should be kept under constant review. If there is any alteration in the admissions that can be made, the identity of the claims said to have independent validity, or the claims alleged to be infringed, that information should be communicated forthwith to the other parties.

9. ALTERNATIVE DISPUTE RESOLUTION ("ADR")

CPR 63 PCG 9

9.1 While emphasising its primary role as a forum for deciding patent and registered design cases, the Patents Court encourages parties to consider the use of ADR (such as, but not confined to, mediation and conciliation) as an alternative means of resolving disputes or particular issues within disputes. A fuller list of the different types of ADR can be found in section 2.12 of the Guide to the Patents County Court.

9.2 Settlement of dispute by ADR has many advantages including significant saving of costs and providing parties with a wider range of solutions than can be offered by litigation. Legal representatives should consider and advise their clients as to the possibility of attempting to resolve the dispute via ADR. In an appropriate case, the Patents Court may adjourn a case for a specified period of time to encourage and enable the parties to use ADR.

10. DISCLOSURE

CPR 63 PCG 10

10.1 Parties are obliged to provide disclosure in accordance with Part 31 as modified by Rule 63.9 and PD63.6.1-6.3.

Process and Product Descriptions

10.2 Where appropriate, parties are encouraged to provide a process and/or product description ('PPD') instead of standard disclosure relating to processes or products which are alleged to infringe or are otherwise relevant to proceedings.

10.3 Subject to 10.5 below, PPDs must be adequate to deal with the nature of the allegation that has been advanced by the other party or parties. The parties have joint responsibility at an early stage to determine the nature of the case advanced so that the PPD is adequate to deal with that case.

10.4 Parties should bear in mind when preparing a PPD that they may be called on to prove it at trial. Any material omission or inaccuracy could result in a costly adjournment with consequential adverse orders, including as to costs. A PPD ought to be accompanied by a signed written statement which:

(i)   states that the person making the statement is personally acquainted with the facts to which the description relates;
(ii)   verifies that the description is a true and complete description of the product or process; and
(iii) contains an acknowledgement by the person making the statement that he may be required to attend court in order to be cross-examined on the contents of the description.

10.5 Insofar as a party is not able to verify that the PPD is a true and complete description of all relevant aspects of his product or process (for example because he does not make certain components in his product and does not know how they work), then the correct course is for the party to verify such parts as he is able, and to serve a disclosure list (which may or may not contain any documents) in relation to the remainder.

Descriptions and drawings of processes or products

10.6 Parties are encouraged to agree descriptions and drawings of processes and/or products which are the subject of infringement proceedings or are alleged to constitute relevant prior art.

Models or apparatus of processes or products

10.7 If a party wishes to adduce a model or apparatus at trial, it should, if practicable, ensure that directions for such are given at the first CMC (PD 63, para 8.1). Parties should endeavour to view and agree the accuracy of such models or apparatus where possible well in advance of the date of trial.

GENERAL MATTERS RELATING TO HEARINGS OF APPLICATIONS AND TRIALS

11. ARRANGEMENTS FOR LISTING

CPR 63 PCG 11

11.1 The Chancery Listing Officer is responsible for the listing of all work of the Patents Court.

11.2 The Chancery Listing Officer and his staff are located in the Rolls Building. The office is open to the public from 10.00 am to 4.30 pm each day. The telephone number is 020 7947 7717 and the fax number is 0870 739 5868.

11.3 Appointments to fix trials and interim applications are dealt with on Tuesdays and Thursdays between 11.00 am and 12.00 noon. The applicant should first obtain an appointment from the Chancery Listing Officer and give 3 clear days' notice to all interested parties of the date and time fixed.

11.4 A party should not seek to list an application or cause the opposing advocate or counsel's clerk to 'pencil in' a date for hearing prior to raising with the proposed respondent the subject-matter of the application so that, where possible, agreement may be reached on the subject-matter of the application. Applicants who fail properly to consult with the respondents prior to listing an application may be met with an adverse costs order.

Short applications

11.5 Short applications (i.e. those estimated to last no more than 1 hour) will usually be heard before the normal court day starts at 10.30 am e.g. at 9.30 or 10 am. These can be issued and the hearing date arranged at any time by attendance at the Chancery Listing Office. Attention is drawn to PD63.5 about the filing of documents and skeleton arguments.

Urgent applications and Without Notice applications

11.6 A party wishing to apply without notice to the respondent(s) should contact the Chancery Listing Office. In cases of emergency in vacation or out of normal court hours, the application should be made to the duty Chancery judge.

September sittings

11.7 The Patents Court and Patents County Court will endeavour, if the parties so desire and the case is urgent, to sit in September.

Interim injunction hearings and expedited trials

11.8 Applicants for interim remedies (in particular, interim injunctions) and respondents are encouraged to consider whether an expedited (speedy) trial would better meet the interests of justice. Applications for expedited trials may be made at any time but should be made as soon as possible and notice given to all parties. Parties are reminded that varying degrees of expedition are possible. Some cases may warrant extreme expedition, others a lesser degree.

11.9 When an application for an interim injunction is made the applicant should, where practicable, make prior investigations with the Chancery Listing Officer about trial dates on an unexpedited and expedited basis having regard to the estimated length of trial.

12. TIME ESTIMATES

CPR 63 PCG 12

12.1 In providing appropriate time estimates, parties must appreciate the need to give realistic and accurate time estimates and ensure that the time estimate includes a discrete reading time for the court to read the papers prior to the hearing of the application or trial. In general, the court will wish to read the skeleton arguments, the patent (where relevant), the prior art (where relevant), expert reports and other key documents (e.g. important witness statements). Advisors should bear in mind the technical difficulty of the case when considering the reading time estimate. The court will consider the imposition of guillotines where time estimates are exceeded.

12.2 Similarly, in proving technical complexity ratings, the parties must appreciate the need to give realistic and accurate estimates of the technical complexity of the case. The technical complexity rating should take account of the complexity of both the patent and the prior art as well as the complexity of the infringement issues and likely evidence.

Revised time estimates

12.3 Where parties and their legal advisors consider that a time estimate that has been provided (e.g. at the CMC) has become unrealistic, they have a duty to notify the new time estimate to the Chancery Listing Office or, where appropriate, the judge's clerk as soon as possible. The same applies to estimates of technical complexity.

13. DOCUMENTS AND TIMETABLE

CPR 63 PCG 13

13.1 Bundling for the hearing of applications and trials is of considerable importance and should be approached intelligently. The general guidance given in Appendix 6 of the Chancery Guide should be followed. Solicitors or patent attorneys who fail to do so may be required to explain why and may be penalised personally in costs.

13.2 If it is known which judge will be taking the hearing, papers for the hearing should be lodged directly with that judge's clerk. If there is insufficient time to lodge hard copies before the deadline, documents of significance (and particularly skeleton arguments) should be supplied by e-mail to the clerk of the judge concerned, followed up by clean hard copies.

13.3 It is the responsibility of both parties to ensure that all relevant documents are lodged with the clerk of the judge who will be taking the hearing by noon two days before the date fixed for hearing unless some longer or shorter period has been ordered by the judge or is prescribed by this guide.

13.4 The judges request that all important documents also be supplied to them on a USB stick in a format convenient for the judge's use (normally the current or a recent version of Microsoft Word for Windows or as a text searchable pdf). These will usually include skeleton arguments, important patents, prior art and drawings, the witness statements and expert reports. More general use of e-bundling is under consideration and a draft protocol for e-bundling which has been prepared by the Intellectual Property Court Users' Committee may be obtained from the clerk to Floyd or Arnold JJ.

13.5 Prior to trial, parties should ensure that they comply with the requirements of PD63.9 concerning the provision of a trial timetable, trial bundle and reading guide for the judge. The trial timetable should be detailed and set out the times and dates that witnesses will be required to give evidence, as well as any days that any witness is unavailable to give evidence.

13.6 Where a technical primer has been produced, the parties should identify those parts which are agreed to form part of the common general knowledge. Usually, this should be done shortly after exchange of expert reports but a reasonable time prior to trial.

13.7 Skeleton arguments should be lodged in time for the judge to read them before an application or trial.

(a)   In the case of applications, this should normally be 10:30am the previous working day (or, in the case of short applications, 3pm)

(b)   In the case of trials, this should normally be at least two working days before commencement of the trial. In substantial cases, a longer period (to be discussed with the clerk to the judge concerned) may be needed.

13.8 Where any party wishes to put documents to a witness in cross-examination, these should generally be supplied to the witness sufficient time in advance so that the witness has time to consider them before giving evidence. Generally, documents for cross-examination should be supplied at least 24 hours before the witness gives evidence. However, more time may be required depending on the nature and number of the documents intended to be relied upon.

13.9 Following the evidence in a substantial trial, a short adjournment may be granted to enable the parties to summarise their arguments in writing before oral argument.

Transcripts

13.10 In trials where a transcript of evidence is being made and supplied to the judge, the transcript should be supplied by e-mail and in hard copy. Where real time transcription is being used, the Court should be provided with a terminal.

14. TELEPHONE APPLICATIONS

CPR 63 PCG 14

14.1 For short (20 minutes or less) matters, the judges of the Patents Court are willing to hear applications by telephone conference in accordance with the Practice Direction under Part 23. The party making the application is responsible for setting up the telephone application and informing the parties, Counsels' clerks and Chancery Listing of the time of the conference call.

14.2 It is possible for the application to be recorded, and if recording by the court rather than by British Telecom (or other service provider) is requested, arrangements should be made with the Chancery Listing Officer. The recording will not be transcribed. The tape will be kept by the clerk to the judge hearing the application for a period of six months. Arrangements for transcription, if needed, must be made by the parties.

14.3 This procedure should be used where it will save costs.

MISCELLANEOUS

15. JURISDICTION OF MASTERS

CPR 63 PCG 15

15.1 Masters have only a limited jurisdiction in patent matters (see PD63.5.2(2)). Generally it is more convenient for consent orders (on paper or in court) to be made by a judge even where a Master has jurisdiction to do so.

15.2 Where a Master makes a consent order disposing of an action which has been fixed, it is the duty of all the parties' representatives to inform the Chancery Listing Officer that the case has settled. Where the validity of the patent was in issue, the United Kingdom Intellectual Property Office ('UKIPO') should also be informed.

16. CONSENT ORDERS

CPR 63 PCG 16

16.1 The court is normally willing to make consent orders without the need for the attendance of any parties. A draft of the agreed order and the written consent of all the parties' respective solicitors or counsel should be supplied to the Chancery Listing Office. Unless the judge considers a hearing is needed, he will make the order in the agreed terms by initialling it. It will be drawn up accordingly and sent to the parties.

17. DRAFT JUDGMENTS

CPR 63 PCG 17

17.1 Many judgments, particularly after a full trial, will be reserved and handed down at a later date, as advised by the Chancery Listing Office. Prior to that, the practice has arisen to provide the parties' legal representatives (or litigants in person) with a copy of the draft judgment for advocates to notify the court of typographical and obvious errors (if any). The text may be shown, in confidence, to the parties, but only for the purpose of obtaining instructions and on the strict understanding that the judgment, or its effect, is not to be disclosed to any other person, or used in the public domain, and that no action is taken (other than internally) in response to the judgment. Reference is invited to PD40E paras 2.1 to 2.9.

18. ORDERS FOLLOWING JUDGMENT

CPR 63 PCG 18

18.1 Where a judgment is made available in draft before being given in open court the parties should, in advance of that occasion, exchange drafts of the desired consequential order. It is highly undesirable that one party should spring a proposal on the other for the first time when judgment is handed down. Where the parties are agreed as to the consequential order and have supplied to the judge a copy of the same signed by all parties or their representatives, attendance at the handing down of the judgment is not necessary.

19. APPEALS FROM THE COMPTROLLER-GENERAL OF PATENTS, DESIGNS AND TRADE MARKS ("THE COMPTROLLER")

Patents

CPR 63 PCG 19

19.1 By virtue of statute, these lie only to the High Court and not the Patents County Court. They are now governed by Part 52 (see Rule 63.16). Permission to appeal is not required. Note that the Comptroller must be served with a Notice of Appeal (Rule 63.16(3)). The appellant has the conduct of the appeal and he or his representative should, within 2 weeks of lodging the appeal, contact the Chancery Listing Officer with a view to arranging a hearing date. The appellant must ensure that the appeal is set down as soon as is reasonably practicable after service of the notice of appeal. Parties are reminded that the provisions about the service of skeleton arguments apply to appeals from the Comptroller.

Registered Designs

19.2 Appeals in registered designs cases go to the Registered Designs Appeal Tribunal. This consists of one of the patent judges sitting as a tribunal. The CPR and PD do not apply to such appeals. Where such an appeal is desired, contact should be made direct with the Chancery Listing Officer.

Trade Marks

19.3 These are assigned to the Chancery Division as a whole, not the Patents Court (Rule 63.16(2)). Permission to appeal is not required.

Appeals on paper only

19.4 The court will hear appeals on paper only if that is what the parties desire. If the appellant is willing for the appeal to be heard on paper only, he should contact the respondent and UKIPO at the earliest opportunity to discover whether such a way of proceeding is agreed. If it is, the Chancery Listing Office should be informed as soon as possible. The parties (and the Chancery Listing Officer if he/she desires) should liaise amongst themselves for early preparation of written submissions and bundles and provide the court with all necessary materials.

SPECIMEN MINUTE OF ORDER FOR DIRECTIONS

Commentary

CPR 63 PCG 20

A draft order is annexed below covering most normal eventualities. The directions are intended only as a guide and are not 'standard directions'. Not all paragraphs will be applicable in every case.

Form of order for directions

CPR 63 PCG 22

AND UPON the parties' legal advisors having advised the litigants of the existence of mediation as a possible means of resolving this claim and counterclaim.

Transfer

1. [This claim and counterclaim be transferred to the Patents County Court.] (If this order is made, no other order will generally be necessary, though it will generally be desirable for procedural orders to be made at this time to save the costs of a further conference in the Patents County Court.)

Service on the Comptroller

2. The [claimants/defendants] shall serve on the Comptroller: (a) the claim form, counterclaim or application notice; (b) any other relevant statement of case (including any amended statement of case); and (c) any accompanying documents of any claim for a remedy which would, if granted, affect an entry in any United Kingdom Patent Office register.

Amendments to statements of case

3. The claimants have permission to amend their claim form shown in red on the copy [annexed to the application notice/as signed by the solicitors for the parties/ annexed hereto] and [to re-serve the same on or before [date]/and that reservice be dispensed with] and that the defendants have permission to serve a consequentially amended defence within [number] days [thereafter/hereafter] and that the claimants have permission to serve a consequentially amended reply (if so advised) within [number] days thereafter.

Further Information and Clarification

4.

(a)   The [claimants/defendants] do on or before [date] serve on the [defendants/ claimants] the further information or clarification of the [specify statement of case] as requested by the [claimants/defendants] by their request served on the [defendants/claimants] on [date] [and/or]

(b)   The [claimants/defendants] do on or before [date] serve on the [defendants/ claimants] [a response to their request for further information] [do answer the requests in their request for further information] or clarification of the [identify statement of case] served on the [defendants/claimants] on [date].

Admissions

5. The [claimants/defendants] do on or before [date] state in writing whether or not they admit the facts specified in the [defendants'/claimants'] notice to admit facts dated [date].

Security

6. The claimants/defendants do provide security for the defendants'/claimants' costs for its claim/counterclaim in the sum of £[state sum] by [paying such sums into court] [specify manner in which security to be given] and that:

(i)   in the meantime the claim [counterclaim] be stayed [and/or];

(ii)   unless security is given as ordered by the above date, the claim [counterclaim] be struck out without further order with the defendants'/claimants' costs of the claim [counterclaim] to be the subject of detailed assessment if not agreed.

Lists of Documents

7.

(a)   The claimants and the defendants respectively do on or before [state date] make and serve on the other of them a list in accordance with form N265 of the documents in their possession custody or control which they are required to disclose in accordance with the obligation of standard disclosure in accordance with Part 31 as modified by paragraph 5 of the Practice Direction - Patents etc. supplementing Part 63.

(b)   In respect of those issues identified in Schedule [number] hereto disclosure shall be limited to those [documents/categories of documents] listed in Schedule [number].

Inspection

8. If any party wishes to inspect or have copies of such documents as are in another party's control, it shall give notice in writing that it wishes to do so and such inspection shall be allowed at all reasonable times upon reasonable notice and any copies shall be provided within [number] working days of the request upon the undertaking of the party requesting the copies to pay the reasonable copying charges.

Experiments

9.

(a)   Where a party desires to establish any fact by experimental proof, including an experiment conducted for the purposes of litigation or otherwise not being an experiment conducted in the normal course of research, that party shall on or before [date] serve on all the other parties a notice stating the facts which it desires to establish and giving full particulars of the experiments proposed to establish them.

(b)   A party upon whom a notice is served under the preceding sub-paragraph shall within [number] days, serve on the party serving the notice a notice stating in respect of each fact whether or not that party admits it.

(c)   Where any fact which a party wishes to establish by experimental proof is not admitted that party shall apply to the court for further directions in respect of such experiments.

[*Or where paragraph 9 of the Practice Direction - Patents etc. supplementing CPR Part 63 has been complied with.*]

9.

(a)   The claimants/defendants are to afford to the other parties an opportunity, if so requested, of inspecting a repetition of the experiments identified in paragraphs [specify them] of the notice[s] of experiments served on [date]. Any such inspection must be requested within [number] days of the date of this order and shall take place within [number] days of the date of the request.

(b)   If any party shall wish to establish any fact in reply to experimental proof that party shall on or before [date] serve on all the other parties a notice stating the facts which it desires to establish and giving full particulars of the experiments proposed to establish them.

(c)   A party upon whom a notice is served under the preceding sub-paragraph shall within [number] days serve on the party serving the notice a notice stating in respect of each fact whether or not that party admits it.

(d)   Where any fact which a party wishes to establish by experimental proof in reply is not admitted the party may apply to the court for further directions in respect of such experiments.

Notice of Models, etc.

10.

(a)   If any party wishes to rely at the trial of this claim and counterclaim upon any model or apparatus, that party shall on or before [date] give notice thereof to all the other parties; shall afford the other parties an opportunity within [number] days of the service of such notice of inspecting the same and shall, if so requested, furnish the other party with copies or illustrations of such model or apparatus.

(b)   No further or other model or apparatus shall be relied upon in evidence by either party save with consent or by permission of the court.

Product or Process Description

11.

(a)   The defendants/claimants do provide a written description together with relevant drawings of the following [product(s)] [process(es)] to the claimants/defendants by [. . . .].
(i)   [description of product or process];
(ii)   [description of product or process];
etc.

(b)   The description served under paragraph (a) shall be accompanied by a signed written statement which shall:
(i)   state that the person making the statement is personally acquainted with the facts to which the description relates;
(ii)   verify that the description is a true and complete description of the product or process; and
(iii)   contain an acknowledgement by the person making the statement that he may be required to attend court in order to be cross-examined on the contents of the description.

Technical Primer

12. The parties shall use their best endeavours to agree on or before [date] a single technical primer setting out the basic undisputed technology and shall on or before [date] indicate which parts of the technical primer are agreed to form part of the common general knowledge.

Scientific Adviser

13. A.B is appointed a scientific adviser to assist the court in this claim and counterclaim, his/her costs to be met in the first instance in equal shares by the parties and to be costs in the claim and counterclaim, subject to any other order of the trial judge.

Written Evidence

14.

(a) Each party shall on or before [date] serve on the other parties [signed] written statements of the oral evidence which the party intends to lead on any issues of fact to be decided at the trial, such statements to stand as the evidence in chief of the witness unless the court otherwise directs;

(b) Each party shall on or before [date] serve on the other parties [signed] written statements of the oral evidence which it intends to lead at trial in answer to facts and matters raised in the witness statements served on it under paragraph (a) and (b) above;

(c) Each party may call up to [number] expert witnesses in this claim and counterclaim provided that the said party:

    (i) supplies the name of such expert to the other parties and to the court on or before [date]; and

    (ii) no later than [date]/[[number days] before the date set for the hearing of this claim and counterclaim] serve upon the other parties a report of each such expert comprising the evidence which that expert intends to give at trial.

    (iii) no later than [date]/[[number of days] before the date set for the hearing of this claim and counterclaim] serve upon the other parties any report of such expert in reply to a report served under paragraph 14(c)(ii) above.

(d) [The claimant shall, with the cooperation of the other parties, arrange for the experts to meet on or before [date] to determine on what issues they agree and on what they disagree and the experts shall before [date] file a report stating where they agree and where they disagree and in the latter case, their reasons for disagreeing].

Civil Evidence Act Notices

15. Each party shall, no later than [date], serve upon the other parties any Civil Evidence Act Notices upon which it intends to rely at trial.

Admissibility of Evidence

16. A party who objects to any statements of any witness being read by the judge prior to the hearing of the trial, shall serve upon each other party a notice in writing to that effect setting out the grounds of the objection.

Non-Compliance

17. Where either party fails to comply with the directions relating to experiments and written evidence it shall not be entitled to adduce evidence to which such directions relate without the permission of the court.

Trial Bundles

18. Each party shall no later than [28] days before the date fixed for the trial of this claim and counterclaim serve upon the other parties a list of all the documents to be included in the trial bundles. The claimants shall no later than [21] days before the date fixed for trial serve upon the defendants . . . sets of the bundles for use at trial.

19. The claimants must file with the court no later than [4] days before the date fixed for the trial:

(i)   the trial bundle; and
(ii)   a reading guide for the judge.

Trial

20. The trial of these proceedings shall be before an assigned judge alone in [London], estimated length [number] days which shall include a pre-trial reading estimate for the judge of [number] days. The technical difficulty rating is [ ].

Liberty to Apply

21. The parties are to be at liberty on three days' notice to apply for further directions and generally.

Costs

22. The costs of this application are to be costs in the claim and counterclaim.

ANNEX A: CONTACT DETAILS

1. The judges of the Patents Court, their clerks and their contact details

Mann J (Clerk: Susan Woolley - tel 020 7947 7964; mailto://Susan.Woolley@hmcts.gsi.gov.uk)

Warren J (Clerk: Elizabeth Collum – tel 020 7947 7260; mailto://Elizabeth.Collum2@hmcts.gsi.gov.uk)

Morgan J (Clerk: Heather Watson – tel 020 7947 6419; mailto://Heather.Watson@hmcts.gsi.gov.uk)

Norris J (Clerk Emma Patrick - tel 020 7073 1728; mailto://Emma.Patrick@hmcts.gsi.gov.uk)

Floyd J [Judge in charge of the Patents Court] (Clerk: Alison Hall – tel 020 7073 1740; mailto://Alison.Hall@hmcts.gsi.gov.uk)

Arnold J (Clerk: Alison Lee – tel 020 7073 1789; mailto://Alison.Lee2@hmcts.gsi.gov.uk)

Roth J (Clerk: Chris Ellis - tel 020 7947 6589; mailto://Chris.Ellis@hmcts.gsi.gov.uk)

Vos J (Clerk: Robin Cliffe - tel 020 7947 7606; mailto://Robin.Cliffe@hmcts.gsi.gov.uk)

2. Secretary of the Intellectual Property Court Users Committee and current contact details

Philip Westmacott, Bristows, 100 Victoria Embankment, London EC4Y ODH Tel: 020 7400 8000 Fax: 020 7400 8050.

THE PATENTS COUNTY COURT GUIDE

CPR 63 PCCG

Issued December 2012. By authority of the Chancellor of the High Court

1. General
    1.1 Introduction ....CPR 63 PCCG 1.1
    1.2 Jurisdiction ....CPR 63 PCCG 1.2
    1.3 Allocation ....CPR 63 PCCG 1.3
    1.4 The judges of the Patents County Court.............CPR 63 PCCG 1.4
    1.5 Judges able and willing to sit out of London ....CPR 63 PCCG 1.5
    Committee ....CPR 63 PCCG 1.6
    1.7 Representation................................CPR 63 PCCG 1.7
    1.8 Appeals ....CPR 63 PCCG 1.8
2. Procedure in the Patents County Court
    2.1 Before issuing proceedings ....CPR 63 PCCG 2.1
    2.2 Issuing proceedings............................CPR 63 PCCG 2.2
    2.3 Service of documents..........................CPR 63 PCCG 2.3
    2.4 Statements of case............................CPR 63 PCCG 2.4
    2.5 Case management ....CPR 63 PCCG 2.5
    2.6 Transfers between the High Court and the Pat-
    ents County Court..............................CPR 63 PCCG 2.6
    2.7 Re-Allocation within the PCC between the multi-track and
    small claims track ....CPR 63 PCCG 2.7
    2.8 Applications ....CPR 63 PCCG 2.8
    2.9 Fast track and expedition ....CPR 63 PCCG 2.9
    2.10 The trial ....CPR 63 PCCG 2.10
    2.11 Costs.....................................CPR 63 PCCG 2.11
    2.12 Alternative Dispute Resolution ....CPR 63 PCCG 2.12
3. General arrangements ....CPR 63 PCCG 3
    3.1 Issuing proceedings and applications ....CPR 63 PCCG 3.1
    3.2 Arrangements for listing ....CPR 63 PCCG 3.2
    3.3 Time estimates for applications...................CPR 63 PCCG 3.3
    3.4 Documents and timetable ....CPR 63 PCCG 3.4
    3.5 Telephone applications ....CPR 63 PCCG 3.5
    3.6 Consent orders ....CPR 63 PCCG 3.6
    3.7 The trial ....CPR 63 PCCG 3.7
    3.8 Draft judgments ....CPR 63 PCCG 3.8
    3.9 Orders following judgment......................CPR 63 PCCG 3.9
    3.10 Enforcement ....CPR 63 PCCG 3.10
    3.11 Contacting the Patents County Court.............CPR 63 PCCG 3.11
    3.12 Information available on the internet ....CPR 63 PCCG 3.12
Annexes
    Annex A Contact details................................CPR 63 PCCG 4
    Annex B Specimen CMC Order ....CPR 63 PCCG 5

GENERAL

1.1 INTRODUCTION

CPR 63 PCCG 1.1

This is the general Guide to the Patents County Court (PCC). It is written for all users of the PCC, whether a litigant in person or a specialist IP litigator.

The Guide aims to help users and potential users of the PCC by explaining how the procedures will operate, providing guidelines where appropriate and dealing with various practical aspects of proceedings before the PCC.

The Patents County Court has a multi-track and a small claims track. The PCC multi-track has a limit on damages of up to £500,000. Costs orders will be made which are proportionate to the nature of the dispute and subject to a cap of no more than £50,000. The small claims track is for suitable claims in the PCC with a value of up to £10,000. Costs orders on the small claims track are highly restricted.

The focus of this Guide is the PCC multi-track. There is a separate Guide for the PCC small claims track.

County courts in general operate three tracks – a multi-track, a fast track under CPR Part 28 and a small claims track. The PCC does not operate a separate Part 28 fast track (see "Fast track and expedition" below).

The Guide cannot be wholly comprehensive of all issues which may arise on the multi-track in the PCC. In circumstances which are not covered by this guide, reference may be made to the Patents Court Guide and the Chancery Guide.

History of the PCC

Following the report of the Committee chaired by Sir Derek Oulton in 1987, the PCC was set up in 1990. The PCC was intended to provide a less costly and less complex alternative to the High Court, Patents Court. The Patents Court is intended to deal with larger and more complex claims.

Based initially in Wood Green in North London, the PCC moved to Park Crescent near Regent's Park in the West End of London in the mid 1990s. In 2002 the court moved to Field House, Breams Buildings, and to St Dunstan's House, Fetter Lane in 2008.

In June 2009, the Intellectual Property Court Users' Committee (IPCUC) published a consultation paper setting out proposals for reform of the PCC and in July 2009 the working party's final report was published. The proposals were adopted in the final report of the Review of Civil Litigation Costs by Lord Justice Jackson and on 1st October 2010 a new set of procedures was implemented in the PCC.

In 2011 the PCC moved to the Rolls Building along with the Chancery Division of the High Court (including the Patents Court), the Commercial Court and the Technology and Construction Court.

Following on from the proposals set out in the Jackson Review and in response to a further recommendation made in the Hargreaves Review, a small claims track within the Patents County Court was set up and came into effect on 1 October 2012.

1.2 ALLOCATION

CPR 63 PCCG 1.2

Most users of the Patents County Court will be concerned with its particular jurisdiction in relation to intellectual property matters indicated below but the court's ordinary jurisdiction as a county court is unaffected (s 287(5) of the Copyright Designs and Patents Act 1988) and there may be other causes of action which may appropriately be brought before it.

The intellectual property jurisdiction of the Patents County Court includes patents, designs (registered and unregistered, Community and UK national), trade marks (UK and Community), passing off, copyright, database right and other rights conferred by the Copyright Designs and Patents Act 1988.

For example, the Patents County Court may hear and determine actions and counterclaims for:

- Infringement of patents, designs, trade marks, copyright and other intellectual property rights

- Revocation or invalidity of patents, registered designs and trade marks
- Amendment of patents
- Declarations of non-infringement
- Determination of entitlement to a patent, design or any other intellectual property
- Employee's compensation in respect of a patented invention
- Unjustified threats of proceedings for infringement of patents, designs or trade marks.

The court will in future be renamed so as to recognise its broad IP jurisdiction.

(a) Legal basis for jurisdiction of the PCC

The Patents County Court is formally part of the Central London County Court but is administered separately at the Rolls Building. The legal basis for the court's IP jurisdiction derives from a number of sources including sections 287(1) and (5) of the Copyright Designs and Patents Act 1988 (which define the "special jurisdiction" and preserve the court's ordinary jurisdiction as a county court), the Patents County Court (Designation and Jurisdiction) Order 1994 (SI 1994/1609), and the High Court and County Courts Jurisdiction Order 1991 (SI 1991/724). The court is a designated Community Trade Mark Court (SI 2006/1027) and Community Designs Court (SI 2005/696). The scope and extent of the court's jurisdiction was addressed in *ALK Abello v Meridian* [2010] EWPCC 014, *National Guild of Removers & Storers Ltd v Christopher Silveria* [2010] EWPCC 015, *Minsterstone Ltd v Be Modern Ltd* [2002] FSR 53 and *McDonald v Graham* [1994] RPC 407.

The "special jurisdiction" covers proceedings relating to patents and designs and proceedings ancillary to or arising out of the same subject matter as those proceedings (s 287(1) 1988 Act). The position of designs is addressed further in the context of the small claims track (below).

For many cases, it is not important to determine whether a case falls within the "special jurisdiction" of the PCC. However the rules differ on some minor respects between cases in the special jurisdiction and otherwise and this is addressed below. It can also be relevant to some aspects of legal representation before the PCC. It has some relevance to the cap on recoverable damages applicable in the PCC because two separate legal instruments were required to bring in the damages cap, one for the special jurisdiction (SI 2011/1402) and one for the ordinary jurisdiction (SI 2011/2222).

Users should be aware that the court's ordinary jurisdiction does not extend to certain equitable claims such as some claims for breach of confidence. However the Patents County Court does have full jurisdiction to handle such matters if they are ancillary to a case within the court's designated jurisdiction under SI 1994/1609 and SI 2005/587 (patents, designs and trade marks), see *Ningbo v Wang* [2012] EWPCC 51.

The small claims track

The jurisdiction of the PCC small claims track is a subset of the normal jurisdiction of the PCC available on the PCC multi-track. CPR r 63.27(1)(a) limits the kinds of intellectual property claim which may be allocated to the PCC small claims track. The PCC small claims track may deal with any IP claim within the jurisdiction of the PCC save for those referred to in r 63.2. In practice this means the small claims track may hear claims relating to copyright, trade marks and passing off, and unregistered designs (UK or Community). Claims relating to patents, registered designs (UK or Community) and plant varieties remain on the PCC multi-track.

The Government's response to the Hargreaves review calling for the introduction of a small claims track in the PCC indicated that it could be useful for copyright, design and possibly trade mark cases. In establishing the small claims track, a view had to be taken about the position of designs in relation to the special and ordinary jurisdiction of the Patents County Court. That is because the small claims track, in which cases come before District Judges and Deputy District Judges, is based on the ordinary jurisdiction of the court and not the special jurisdiction. Designs are referred to without qualification in s 287(1) 1988 Act along with patents, nevertheless it is possible to distinguish between registered designs and unregistered design rights. The former are monopolies which have some similarities to patents, while the latter are closer to copyrights. This essential difference exists for Community designs as well. It is probable that, even if s 287(1) did not exist, the court's ordinary jurisdiction would extend to unregistered design rights (but not to registered designs). The reasoning, whereby copyright falls within the ordinary jurisdiction of the court, applies equally to unregistered design right. Furthermore, the distinction is one which is already reflected in the CPR: see rr. 63.1(1)(a)(ii),(b)(ii), 63.2(1)(a)(ii) and 63.13. Thus unregistered design rights are regarded as falling within the ordinary jurisdiction of the Patents County Court, whether or not they also fall within the special jurisdiction. Registered designs do not fall within the ordinary jurisdiction; they fall only within the special jurisdiction.

(b) Applicable rules of procedure

The rules applicable to proceedings started in or transferred to the Patents County Court are as follows:

* The general Civil Procedure Rules (CPR) provide the framework for proceedings in the Patents County Court as they apply to all civil courts in England and Wales.
* Intellectual Property Claims applies to all intellectual property claims. Part 63 includes rules specific to intellectual property cases and in some areas modifies the general parts of the CPR.
* Practice Direction 63 (PD 63) supplements CPR Part 63.
* Part 63 and PD 63 are arranged in sections as follows:
    * Section I relates to proceedings which concern patents and registered designs (Community or national). It is applicable to proceedings in the Patents County Court which relate to those rights.
    * Section II allocates all other IP cases to particular courts including the Chancery Division, Patents County Court and certain county courts where there is a Chancery District Registry.
    * Section III deals with service of documents and participation by the Comptroller.
    * Section IV does not relate to proceedings in the Patents County Court.
    * Section V relates to all proceedings started in or transferred to the Patents County Court. This section contains the new procedural rules applicable after 1st October 2010.
* Attention is drawn to two other parts of the general CPR which contain provisions specific to the Patents County Court. They are PD 30 paragraphs 9.1 and 9.2 relating to transfers to and from a Patents County Court; Part 45 Section VII Scale Costs for Claims in the Patents County Court and Section 25C of the Costs Practice Direction (CPR Pt 45).

(c) Legal remedies

All the remedies available in the High Court are available in the Patents County Court including preliminary and final injunctions, damages, accounts of profits, delivery up and disclosure. In particular search and seizure (*Anton Piller*) and asset freezing (*Mareva*) orders are available in the Patents County Court (SI 1991/1222). These remedies are available for all cases in the PCC (*Suh v Ryu* [2012] EWPCC 20).

There are two detailed exceptions. The PCC small claims track has the power to order final injunctions (and award damages and other final remedies) but not preliminary injunctions, search and seizure (*Anton Piller*) and asset freezing (*Mareva*) orders (r 63.27(4)). All these remedies are available on the PCC multi-track. The second exception is that, in the multi-track in the PCC, search and seizure and asset freezing orders should only be made by the nominated circuit judge presiding over the PCC or by a High Court judge sitting in the PCC (*Suh v Ryu* [2012] EWPCC 20).

(d) Enforcement

Orders of the PCC are enforced in the same way as any other orders of a county court in England and Wales. Orders for the payment of money can be enforced by obtaining information from judgment debtors (CPR rule 71), making charging orders (CPR rule 73) and in the other ways available under the CPR. The PCC has the power to commit for contempt of court (see *Westwood v Knight* [2012] EWPCC 6). It also has the power to issue a bench warrant to secure attendance at court (*Westwood v Knight* [2012] EWPCC 14).

(e) The cap on damages in the PCC

There is a cap on the damages recoverable in the PCC of £500,000. The same cap also applies to the sum recoverable on an account of profits. The £500,000 figure does not include interest (save for interest due under an agreement) or costs (SI 2011/1402 paragraph 2(2) and SI 2011/2222 paragraph 3(4)). The cap is a limit on the amount or value of the claim for damages (or an account) (SI 2011/1402 paragraph 2(1) and SI 2011/2222 paragraph 2(d) and 3(1)). It is not an automatic cap on the value of the proceedings as a whole (such as the value of any injunction which may be sought).

The claimant may waive any excess claimed over £500,000 (s 288(2) of the 1988 Act, s17 of the County Courts Act 1984 and SI 2011/2222 paragraph 3(2)).

The cap itself may be waived by agreement of the parties (s 288(4) of the 1988 Act and SI 2011/2222 paragraph 3(3)).

1.3 ALLOCATION

CPR 63 PCCG 1.3

The limit on damages available in the Patents County Court provides a clear distinction between that court and the High Court. There is otherwise no sharp dividing line between cases which should be brought in the Patents County Court and actions which should be brought in the High Court.

In deciding between the High Court and the PCC as the court in which to commence a claim, users should bear in mind that the Patents County Court was established to handle the smaller, shorter, less complex, less important, lower value actions and the procedures applicable in the court are designed particularly for cases of that kind. The court aims to provide cheaper, speedier and more informal procedures to ensure that small and medium sized enterprises, and private individuals, are not deterred from innovation by the potential cost of litigation to safeguard their rights. Longer, heavier, more complex, more important and more valuable actions belong in the High Court.

Parties may agree with each other to maintain a case in the Patents County Court if they wish to make use of the procedures available in it. The court will endeavour to accommodate parties in that respect. The court will, however, maintain its list in such a way as to ensure that it maintains access to justice for small and medium sized enterprises.

If a party to litigation in either the Patents County Court or the High Court believes that the other court is a more appropriate forum for the case, they should apply to transfer it. In the Patents County Court an application to transfer to the High Court must be made at or before the case management conference (CPR rule 63.25(4)). There are a number of cases in which the transfer provisions now applicable have been considered. They include *ALK Abello v Meridian* [2010] EWPCC 014, *Caljan Rite-Hite v Solvex* [2011] EWHC 669 (Ch), *A.S.Watson v The Boots Company* [2011] EWPCC 26, *Comic Enterprises v Twentieth Century Fox* [2012] EWPCC 13, *Environmental Recycling v Stillwell* [2012] EWHC 2097 (Pat), *Destra v Comada* [2012] EWPCC 39.

The following guidelines are provided to assist users in determining which of the two courts is suitable:

- Size of the parties. If both sides are small or medium sized enterprises then the case may well be suitable for the Patents County Court. If one party is a small or medium sized enterprise but the other is a larger undertaking then again the case may be suitable for the Patents County Court but other factors ought to be considered such as the value of the claim and its likely complexity.
- The complexity of the claim. The procedure in the Patents County Court is streamlined and trials last no more than 2 days. A trial which would appear to require more time than that even with the streamlined procedure of the Patents County Court is likely to be unsuitable.
- The nature of the evidence. Experiments in a patent case may be admitted in the Patents County Court but a case which will involve substantial complex experimental evidence will be unsuitable for the Patents County Court.
- Conflicting factual evidence. Cross-examination of witnesses will be strictly controlled in the Patents County Court. The court is well able to handle cases involving disputed factual matters such as allegations of prior use in patents and independent design as a defence to copying; but if a large number of witnesses are required the case may be unsuitable for the Patents County Court.
- Value of the claim. Subject to the agreement of the parties, there is a limit on the damages available in the PCC of £500,000. However, assessing the value of a claim is not only concerned with the damages available. Putting a value on a claim is a notoriously difficult exercise, taking into account factors such as possible damages, the value of an injunction and the possible effect on competition in a market if a patent was revoked. As a general rule of thumb, disputes where the value of sales, in the UK, of products protected by the intellectual property in issue (by the owner, licensees and alleged infringer) exceeds £1 million per year are unlikely to be suitable for the Patent County Court in the absence of agreement.

Allocation between the PCC multi-track and small claims track

If the claim has a value of £10,000 or less and if it is concerned with the intellectual property rights applicable in the PCC small claims track (essentially copyright, trade marks and passing off or unregistered design rights (UK or Community)) then that track is likely to be the appropriate track in the PCC. Otherwise the case should proceed on the normal PCC multi-track.

The separate Guide to the PCC small claims track deals with cases proceeding on that track.

1.4 THE JUDGES OF THE PATENTS COUNTY COURT

CPR 63 PCCG 1.4

The patents judge of the Patents County Court is a Specialist Circuit Judge. The judges of the High Court, Patents Court are able to sit as judges of the Patents County Court as necessary. Certain senior members of the Intellectual Property Bar are qualified and able to sit as recorders in the Patents County Court when the need arises.

1.5 JUDGES ABLE AND WILLING TO SIT OUT OF LONDON

CPR 63 PCCG 1.5

If the parties so desire, for the purpose of saving time or costs, the Patents County Court will sit out of London. Before any approach is made to the

Judge's Clerk, the parties should discuss between themselves the desirability of such a course. If there is a dispute as to venue, the court will resolve the matter on an application. Where there is no dispute, the Judge's Clerk should be contacted as soon as possible so that arrangements can be put in place well before the date of the proposed hearing.

COMMITTEE

CPR 63 PCCG 1.6

The Patents County Court has a Users' Committee which considers the problems and concerns of intellectual property litigators in the Patents County Court. Membership of the committee includes the judges of the Patents County Court and of the Patents Court, representatives of each of the Intellectual Property Office, European Patent Office, Intellectual Property Bar Association, IP Chambers Clerks, the Intellectual Property Lawyers Association, the Chartered Institute of Patent Attorneys, the Institute of Trade Mark Attorneys, the IP Federation, the British Copyright Council, the Pro Bono Committees and IP Academics. Anyone having views concerning the improvement of intellectual property litigation in the Patents County Court is invited to make his or her views known to the committee, preferably through the relevant professional representative on the committee or its secretary (contact details are in Annex A).

If matters relate to intellectual property litigation more widely, then this may be a matter for the Intellectual Property Court Users' Committee. Views can be expressed to the Patents County Court Users' Committee, who will refer on matters outside its remit, or direct to representatives of the Intellectual Property Court Users' Committee or its secretary.

1.7 REPRESENTATION

CPR 63 PCCG 1.7

A person may represent themselves in litigation in the PCC as a litigant in person. However, intellectual property matters are often quite complex and cases will often benefit from the assistance of a knowledgeable legal representative.

Patent attorneys, solicitors and trade mark attorneys all have rights to represent clients in the PCC. These professionals may additionally instruct barristers to help prepare the case and/or argue the case in court. In some instances, a barrister may accept instructions directly from the public.

Each of these professions has a different qualification and skill set. So, in some cases, it may be appropriate to instruct more than one legal representative to act as a team.

More information about these different professions can be found at the following Websites:

Chartered Institute of Patent Attorneys - www.cipa.org.ukregarding patent attorneys and patent attorney litigators

Law Society - www.lawsociety.org.uk regarding solicitors; and for IP specialist solici tors the IPLA – www.ipla.org.uk

Institute of Trade Mark Attorneys - www.itma.org.uk regarding trade mark and design litigators

Bar Council - www.barcouncil.org.ukregarding barristers, and for IP specialist barris ters - www.ipba.co.uk

Pro Bono Group) and ILEX Pro Bono Forum. The website is at: www.nationalprobono centre.org.uk.

A litigant wishing to seek pro-bono legal assistance should approach the Citizens Advice Bureau or a Law Centre first. There is a CAB office in the Royal Courts of Justice, Strand, London.

The Patents County Court Users Committee is working with CIPA to look at setting up a CIPA pro bono scheme and also actively considering other ways to widen the availability of pro-bono legal assistance in the Patents County Court.

1.8 APPEALS (RULE 52)

CPR 63 PCCG 1.8

If a party wishes to appeal, permission is generally required. Permission may be sought from the judge making the order or from the court to which the appeal is addressed.

Appeals from the multi-track in the Patents County Court

Depending on the nature of the order being appealed, the destination of an appeal from the multi-track in the PCC is either the Court of Appeal or the High Court. Final orders are appealed to the Court of Appeal whereas interim orders are appealed to the High Court (Chancery Division) (see paragraphs 3 and 4(b) of the Access to Justice Act 1999 (Destination of Appeals) Order 2000 (SI 2000/1071)). Strictly this assumes that the judge making the order in the PCC is a circuit judge or a recorder, but that is the norm in the PCC.

When permission is sought from the judge making the order, the order must identify the route of appeal (CPR Pt 40.2(4)).

Appeals from the PCC small claims track

The destination of an appeal from an interim decision on the PCC small claims track is to the circuit judge in the Patents County Court and the destination of an appeal from a final decision on the PCC small claims track is to the Court of Appeal, since decisions in the PCC small claims track are taken by district judges or deputy district judges (see the Access to Justice Act 1999 (Destination of Appeals) Order 2000 (SI 2000/1071)).

2. PROCEDURE IN THE PATENTS COUNTY COURT

2.1 BEFORE ISSUING PROCEEDINGS

CPR 63 PCCG 2.1

Attention is drawn to the Practice Direction – Pre-Action Conduct (a copy of which can be found at www.justice.gov.uk).

Compliance with this Practice Direction will affect the timetable, once proceedings are issued (see further below). However, as unjustified threats to bring legal proceedings in respect of many IP rights can themselves be subject to litigation, each claimant will have to make their own decision as to whether it is appropriate to write to a prospective defendant to see if matters can be settled before any proceedings are issued.

2.2 ISSUING PROCEEDINGS

CPR 63 PCCG 2.2

The Patents County Court is situated in the Rolls Building in London at the address in Annex A. The issue of claims forms takes place at the public counter at the Rolls Building.

Most proceedings are issued using claim form N1 (form available at www.justice.gov.uk). A claimant should ensure that there is a copy of the claim form for the court and each defendant, as well as a copy for itself.

2.3 SERVICE OF DOCUMENTS

CPR 63 PCCG 2.3

The claim form should be served on the defendant with a response pack. The claim form should be served by the claimant and so the claimant should make sure the defendant's copy of the claim form is obtained from the court at issue.

CPR Part 6 and the associated practice direction deal with service of documents. Attention is also drawn to r 63.14, regarding service on an address for service for a registered right and to when a copy of a document should also be sent to the UK Intellectual Property Office.

The CPR only requires the Acknowledgement of Service to be filed with the Court, although subsequent documents, such as the Defence, should both be filed with the Court and served on the other parties (see r 15.6). In any event it may often be helpful to send a copy of any document filed with the court to the other party, to ensure that those documents are received in a timely manner.

2.4 STATEMENTS OF CASE

(a) Introduction

CPR 63 PCCG 2.4

The statements of case are the documents where each party sets out its case. As discussed below, these need to be full, but not unnecessarily lengthy. Statements of case can stand as evidence at trial in the PCC, where relevant individuals have verified them with a statement of truth, as discussed further below.

(b) Time limits

In general, the time limits set out in Part 15 apply to litigation of all intellectual property rights. However, r 63.22 modifies Part 15 in respect of the time limits for filing defences and replies.

The time limit for filing the defence depends on whether the Particulars of Claim confirms that Pre-Action Conduct practice direction has been complied with (r 63.22(2) and (3)). The time limit is 42 days or 70 days respectively.

The time limit for the reply to defence is 28 days from the service of the defence (r 63.22(4)).

The time limit for a defence to counterclaim is 14 days from service of the counterclaim (r 15.4(1)(a) (since Part 10 does not apply (r20.4(3))). The parties can agree that it will be extended to 28 days and must notify the Court (15.5). (Note this time limit is not dealt with in Part 63 and so is not restricted by r 63.22(6)).

The time limit for the reply to defence to counterclaim is 14 days from the service of the defence (r 63.22(5)).

The parties are not at liberty to extend the time limits set out in r 63.22 without the prior consent of the judge. Applications for any extension of time must be made in good time and set out clear grounds as to why they are required. They are almost always dealt with without a hearing.

(c) Content of statements of case

In general, statements of case (i.e. the pleadings of all parties) must comply with the requirements of Part 16. Furthermore, they should comply with r63.6 and PD 63 paras. 4.1-4.6. Copies of important documents referred to in a statement of case (e.g. an advertisement referred to in a claim for infringement or documents cited in Grounds of Invalidity) should be served with the statement of case. Where any such document requires translation, a translation should be served at the same time.

A particular feature of statements of case in the Patents County Court is that they should comply with r63.20 (1) and must set out concisely all facts and arguments relied on. A key purpose of this requirement is to facilitate the conduct of the case management conference which will be conducted on an issue by issue basis. Therefore the court and the parties need to know what the issues are going to be in sufficient detail for that process to take place. However, attention is drawn to the requirement for the matters to be set out concisely. The parties are invited to raise issues with the court before committing excessive time and resources to the production of unnecessarily lengthy statements of case.

Guidance on the statement of case is as follows:

- In a normal case it is unlikely that legal arguments will need to be set out in any detail in the statement of case, all that is likely to be required is a brief statement of the nature of the argument to be relied on.
- Lengthy expositions of construction of patent claims are unlikely to be necessary or desirable. However the parties will be expected to identify the claims in issue (for infringement and validity) and identify the relevant features of those claims.
- It is likely to be necessary to break down a patent claim into suitable integers in order to explain a case on infringement with reference to specific elements of the alleged infringing product or process. This may be most conveniently done in the form of a table or chart annexed to the statement of case. Points on construction should emerge from this exercise and may need to be identified but lengthy argument on them is not required.
- A submission of lack of novelty of a patent is likely to require a similar approach to infringement (i.e. a claim break down, perhaps in the form of a table, with the claim integers compared with the relevant parts of the prior art disclosure(s) relied upon).
- A case of obviousness of a patent is likely to require a statement addressing the allegedly obvious step(s).
- A specific statement of what facts are said to be relevant and common general knowledge is likely to be necessary. A short summary of the relevant technical background may be helpful.
- Similarity between marks may not require elaboration but in an appropriate case some detail will be necessary, particularly in relation to allegations that goods or services are similar. Parties to trade mark cases should identify the nature and characteristics of the relevant consumer (if relevant).
- A defence of independent design in a copyright case (or similar) will need to be addressed in appropriate detail.

(d) Independent validity of patent claims

Where one party raises the issue of validity of a patent, the patentee (or other relevant party) should identify which of the claims of the patent are alleged to have independent validity in his reply (or defence) to the allegation of invalidity.

(e) Statements of truth

Attention is drawn to r 63.21, which modifies Part 22 in its application to the Patents County Court. The statement of truth must be made by a person with knowledge of the facts alleged (or by persons who between them have such knowledge). If more than one person signs the statement of truth, the individuals should indicate in some suitable manner which parts of the statement of case they are verifying.

Statements of case (or parts of them) suitably verified may be permitted to stand as evidence at trial. The court's permission to do so is required (r 32.6) but will generally be given. This is a matter to raise at the case management conference (see e.g. *Westwood v Knight* [2010] EWPCC 16).

Attention is drawn to r 32.14 which sets out the consequences of verifying a statement of case containing a false statement without an honest belief in its truth, and to the procedures set out in PD 32 para 28.

2.5 CASE MANAGEMENT (R63.23)

CPR 63 PCCG 2.5

The case management conference ("CMC") in the Patents County Court is conducted by a judge. The purpose of the CMC is to manage the conduct of the case in order to bring the proceedings to a trial in a manner proportionate to the nature of the dispute, the financial position of the parties, the degree of complexity of the case, the importance of the case and the amount of money at stake. At the first CMC, the court will identify the issues and decide whether to make orders under paragraph 29.1 of PD 63. These include orders permitting the filing of further material in the case such as witness statements, experts' reports and disclosure and orders permitting cross-examination at trial and skeleton arguments. The trial date will be fixed at the CMC.

(a) Allocation questionnaire

All cases are allocated to the multitrack automatically by operation of r 63.1(3) unless the case is to be allocated to the small claims track in which case r 63.27 applies (see the Guide to the PCC small claims track).

The effect of these provisions means that the Patents County Court generally dispenses with the need for an allocation questionnaire.

(b) The date for the case management conference

The date for the CMC will normally be arranged as follows. The claimant should apply for a CMC within 14 days after all defendants who intend to file and serve a defence have done so. Where a case has been transferred from another court, the claimant should apply for a CMC within 14 days of the transfer. Any party may apply for a CMC at an earlier date than these dates. If the claimant has not applied for a CMC within 14 days then the defendant should do so. In any event the Court can and will aim to fix a date for a CMC if the parties have not done so within a reasonable period. These requirements are mandatory for cases within Section I of Part 63 (essentially patents and registered designs; see PD 63 para 5.3 – 5.7) but should be followed in all cases in the Patents County Court as a matter of efficient case management.

(c) The case management conference

The CMC will be conducted as a hearing in open court. However where all parties consent the court may determine the CMC on paper (r 63.23(3)).

Bundles should be filed with the court at the Rolls Building (full address in Annex A). Although PD 63 para 5.9 applies to the preparation of those bundles, parties must consider the different procedure in the Patents County Court and, where appropriate, include attachments to the statements of case and copies of the documents referred to in the statements of case.

In general, parties should endeavour to agree directions prior to the date fixed for the CMC. Although the court has the right to amend directions which have been agreed, this will only happen where there is manifest reason for doing so.

The CMC is an important part of the procedure because no material may be filed in the case by way of evidence, disclosure or written submissions unless permission is given for it by the judge and the proper time for that permission to be given is the CMC (see e.g. *Westwood v Knight* [2010] EWPCC 16). Save in exceptional circumstances the court will not consider an application by a party to submit material in a case in addition to that ordered at the CMC (r 63.23(2), see e.g. *Liversidge v Owen Mumford* [2012] EWPCC 33 and *Redd v Red Legal* [2012] EWPCC 50).

The basis on which the court will decide whether to permit material to be filed in a case is by applying the cost-benefit test (PD 63 para 29.2(2)) and by giving permission in relation to specific and identified issues only ((PD 63 para 29.2(1)). PD 63 para 29.1 lists the material which the court may order: disclosure of documents, a product or process description, experiments, witness statements, experts' reports, cross-examination at trial, and written submissions or skeleton arguments. The parties need to attend the CMC in a position to assist the court in making appropriate orders on this basis. In particular, the parties should consider:

(a)   The need for and scope of any evidence from factual or expert witnesses. Note the court will consider whether there is sufficient evidence in the statements of case or whether further evidence is required.
(b)   The need for and scope of any oral testimony and cross-examination. Note that the court will confine any permitted cross-examination to particular issues and to time limits.
(c)   The need for, and scope of, any disclosure of documents.
(d)   The need for any experiments, process or product descriptions or supply of any samples.
(e)   The need for written submissions or skeleton arguments.
(f)   The likely timetable up to trial. This may include dates on which disclosure of documents, product and process description and experiments is to take place as well as a schedule for witness statements and experts reports including provisions for any evidence in reply (if required).
(g)   The need for an oral hearing or whether a decision can be made on the papers. If an oral hearing is considered to be appropriate, the court will order that the hearing be of a fixed duration of no more than 2 days.

A specimen CMC order is attached to this Guide at Annex B.

(d) A review of the issues

At the case management conference the court will identify the issues (r63.23(1)). In order to do so the court will generally conduct a brief review of the issues in the case. Often it will be appropriate to produce a list of the issues in the proceedings. These need not be lengthy documents. They should be agreed if possible but rather than incurring cost debating lists of issues before the CMC, the most cost effective approach is generally to leave the argument over to the CMC itself.

(e) Matters arising in particular cases before the PCC

The following specific matters come up regularly and experience so far has shown that the approaches described below may be reasonable and proportionate.

In patent cases:

•   to require the patentee to rely on no more than three independently valid claims; and
•   to require a party challenging validity to rely on no more than three items of prior art.

These limits are intended to be flexible and in an appropriate case they can and have been relaxed. The reference to prior art includes all starting points for the obviousness analysis. In other words it does not encompass a party's general reliance on common general knowledge as part of its case on obviousness but it does include an argument of obviousness over common general knowledge alone.

Also in patent cases, evidence over and above the material in the statement of case may well only be required in relation to common general knowledge and obviousness.

In copyright and unregistered design right cases, if the issues include a defence of independent design, cross-examination and a measure of disclosure is likely to be required.

In registered design cases, there may be no need for cross-examination at all.

In general, if expert evidence is required, it may be possible for that evidence to be given by "in house" experts.

(f) Amendments to the statement of case

On occasions a party may wish to amend its statement of case. If the other parties agree then generally no difficulties arise. If not then the court's permission is needed. This is best sought at the CMC but if the need for amendment arises after the CMC then it can be done by a separate application. In considering whether to permit the amendment the court will consider all the circumstances including proportionality and the cost-benefit test (see *Temple Island v New English Teas* [2011] EWPCC 19).

(g) Expression of a preliminary, non-binding opinion on the merits

If both parties wish the court to do so, if it is likely to assist the parties in reaching a settlement, the PCC is willing to express a preliminary and non-binding opinion on the merits of the case (see *WeightWatchers v Love Bites* [2012] EWPCC 12 and *Fayus v Flying Trade* [2012] EWPCC 43).

(h) Costs in a multi-party case

If the case includes more than one defendant or group of defendants who are separately represented, the parties should consider the question of the likely effect of the costs capping provisions (see *Gimex v Chillbag* [2012] EWPCC 34 and *Liversidge v Owen Mumford (costs)* [2012] EWPCC 40). If in doubt the parties should raise the matter at the CMC.

2.6 TRANSFERS BETWEEN THE HIGH COURT AND THE PCC (RULE 63.18 AND RULES 63.25(4) AND (5))

CPR 63 PCCG 2.6

Applications to transfer a case to the High Court should be made at the case management conference. The court will have regard to the provisions of PD 30 (Transfer) and in particular paragraph 9.1 thereof which relates to transfers between the High Court and Patents County Court. The considerations set out above in the section on Allocation will be taken into account. In addition, in considering an application to transfer to the High Court the following further matters will be taken into account:

- The holder of an intellectual property right who does not wish to incur High Court costs but apprehends that an alleged infringer may seek to have the matter transferred to the High Court, may consider an undertaking to limit the enforcement of their rights; e.g. by foregoing an injunction or by reference to a certain value of sales (cf. *Liversidge v Owen Mumford* [2011] EWPCC 34).
- A defendant seeking transfer to the High Court when the claimant cannot afford the cost of High Court litigation may offer to allow the claimant to withdraw their claim without prejudice to a right to restart litigation and/or without an adverse costs award.

An application to transfer a case to the High Court after the CMC will only be considered in exceptional circumstances.

The High Court has the power to transfer a case before it from the High Court to the Patents County Court. An application for such an order must be made to the High Court, either to a judge or (if appropriate) a Chancery Master (*DKH Retail v Republic* [2012] EWHC 877 (Ch)).

The High Court has no power to order proceedings within the special jurisdiction to be transferred from the Patents County Court (s 289(1) 1988 Act).

2.7 RE-ALLOCATION OF CASES WITHIN THE PCC BETWEEN THE MULTI- TRACK AND THE SMALL CLAIMS TRACK (R 63.27 AND R 26.10)

CPR 63 PCCG 2.7

Even once a case is proceeding on one track in the PCC, the case may subsequently be re-allocated to the other track if it is appropriate to do so. A case will be re-allocated from the small claims track to the multi-track if it emerges that the nature of the claim makes it inappropriate for the small claims track. Circumstances in which it may be appropriate to re-allocate a case between the multi-track and the small claims track could arise if it emerges that the current track is inappropriate having regard to the value of the case or to its complexity or the relief sought.

A claim will not be re-allocated (unless it has to be) if that would cause substantial disruption to the progress of litigation.

2.8 APPLICATIONS (R 63.25)

CPR 63 PCCG 2.8

Any application to the court except for the CMC will be dealt with without a hearing unless the court considers it necessary to hold a hearing (r 63.25(3)). Provisions relating to telephone hearings of applications are set out at paragraph 3.5 below.

Once the application is received by a respondent, by r 63.25(2) the respondent to the application must file and serve on all relevant parties a response within 5 days of service of the application notice. When an application is to be resolved on paper, it is imperative that the applicant tells the court the date on which the application notice was served. This is necessary so that the court can know when the 5 day period provided for by r 63.25(2) has expired. Unless the matter is urgent or for some other good reason, the court will generally not deal with a paper application until it can be seen that the 5 day period provided for by r 63.25(2) has expired.

Applications for judgment in default

These can generally be dealt with as paper applications, provided the application notice has been served on the relevant defendant and the court is informed of the date on which this took place in order to give effect to the 5 day period provided for by r 63.25(2).

2.9 FAST TRACK AND EXPEDITION

CPR 63 PCCG 2.9

. All cases in the Patents County Court are either on the multi-track or the small claims track.

The normal operation of the procedure on the PCC multi-track is intended to ensure that trials and applications are heard and dealt with in a timely fashion. Nevertheless the court can accommodate urgent applications (such as applications for interim remedies) and, when necessary, trials can be dealt with on an expedited (speedy) basis. Applications for expedited trials may be made at any time but should be made as soon as possible and notice given to all parties.

2.10 THE TRIAL (PD 63 PARA 31)

CPR 63 PCCG 2.10

time estimates but the time estimates will not be determinative of the trial timetable. So far as appropriate the court will allocate equal time to the parties. Cross-examination will be strictly controlled.

The court will endeavour to ensure that the trial lasts no more than 2 days. Many cases in the Patents County Court are heard in a single day.

Trial on paper

In an appropriate case and if the parties consent, the PCC is able and willing to conduct a trial entirely on paper (for an example see *Hoffmann v DARE* [2012] EWPCC 2).

2.11 COSTS (RULE 63.23)

CPR 63 PCCG 2.11

25,000 on an inquiry as to damages or account of profits.

Tables A and B of Section 25C of the Costs Practice Direction set out the maximum amount of scale costs which the court will award for each stage of a claim in the Patents County Court.

In the PCC all costs are assessed summarily (r 45.41(3)). In preparing their statement of costs, parties should bear in mind that they will need to explain which stage of the claim the costs were incurred in relation to. The general approach to the summary assessment process is explained in *Westwood v Knight* [2011] EWPCC 11.

The application of an issue based approach to costs in the context of the PCC scales and the cap is addressed in *BOS v Cobra* [2012] EWPCC 44.

For cases which have been transferred to the Patents County Court from elsewhere, either another county court or the High Court, the Patents County Court will deal with costs incurred in proceedings before transfer on a case by case basis. Costs incurred in the High Court before transfer are usually dealt with by being summarily assessed as High Court costs (e.g. *Westwood v Knight* [2011] EWPCC 11).

Costs at the interim stage

At the interim stage costs in the Patents County Court are generally reserved to the conclusion of the trial (r 63.26(1)).When a party has behaved unreasonably the court will make an order for costs at the conclusion of the hearing (r 63.21(2)).

2.12 ALTERNATIVE DISPUTE RESOLUTION

CPR 63 PCCG 2.12

The primary role of the Patents County Court is as a forum for deciding intellectual property rights cases. However, the Patents County Court encourages parties to consider the use of ADR (such as, but not confined to, mediation and conciliation) as an alternative means of resolving disputes or particular issues within disputes.

Settlement of a dispute by ADR has many advantages. It can result in significant saving of costs. It also has the potential to provide the parties with a wider range of solutions than can be offered by litigation. For example, while the solution to litigation is usually limited to "win/lose" on the issues put in front of the court, ADR may provide a creative "win/win" solution, as some forms of ADR can explore other ways for the parties to co-operate. ADR can also explore settlement in several countries at the same time.

Legal representatives should consider and advise their clients as to the possibility of seeking to resolve the dispute via ADR. However not all cases are suitable for settlement this way. In an appropriate case, the Patents County Court has the power to adjourn a case for a specified period of time to encourage and enable the parties to use ADR. At the Case Management Conference, the Patents County Court Judge will ask whether the parties have been advised about ADR and whether an adjournment is being sought. However, this will not usually be a reason to delay the CMC itself.

There are many forms of ADR. Most of these are not free. These include:

(a)   This can involve the use of a third party to see if agreement may be reached or to offer a non-binding opinion on the dispute. Some trade bodies offer conciliation services.

(b)   This involves the appointment of a trained mediator to see whether a legally binding agreement can be negotiated. The parties will usually sign a framework agreement for the procedure of the mediation. Mediation can involve the mediator meeting with both parties together and/ or meeting the parties in separate rooms and shuttling between them.

(c)   This involves the appointment of an arbitrator or private decision maker, under a set of procedural rules. The arbitrator will then make a binding decision on the case. Arbitration replaces the court action, but the decision of the arbitrator is private to the parties. NB since arbitration is a matter private matter between the parties, arbitrators cannot revoke intellectual property rights.

(d)   This involves the appointment of an expert to give an opinion about one or more issues in a dispute. Such opinions are not binding but assist the parties in reaching a settlement of the case.

(e)   This involves the appointment of an expert to make a decision about one or more issues in a dispute. Such decisions can be legally binding, by agreement between the parties.

(f)   The UK IPO runs a scheme to give non-binding opinions on patent infringement and patent validity. The opinion is given on the basis of written papers provided by the party applying for the opinion. The other party has the right to file observations, but does not become a party to proceedings before the IPO. The parties can agree to be bound by the outcome of any such opinion.

3. GENERAL ARRANGEMENTS

3.1 ISSUING PROCEEDINGS AND APPLICATIONS

(a) Issuing proceedings

CPR 63 PCCG 3.1

3.1 Claim forms are issued at the public counter of the Rolls Building (address in Annex A).

The fee for issuing proceedings depends on the nature of the claim, including its value. Guidance may be sought from the Court. Information on the latest court fees can be found at www.justice.gov.uk.

(b) Transferring proceedings to the Patents County Court

Cases transferred to the Patents County Court will be taken to the Rolls Building (address in Annex A).

(c) Issuing interim applications

The issue of all interim process is dealt with at the public counter of the Rolls Building (address in Annex A).

Users are reminded that:

*   The first case management conference (r 63.23) will be conducted at a hearing unless all parties consent to determination on paper.
*   The court will deal with all other applications without a hearing unless it considers one necessary (r 63.25(3)).

The fee will be determined on the face of the application notice when it is issued and prior to consideration (if any) by the court of whether a hearing is necessary. Accordingly applications marked for determination at a hearing will be charged the appropriate fee for a hearing. Applications marked for determination otherwise than at a hearing will be charged the appropriate fee for a paper application.

Personal attendance to issue process

The Fee and the application notice should be taken to the public counter at the Rolls Building. The Application will be issued and returned.

Postal application to issue process

Applications should be sent the address in Annex A. The Clerk will issue and return the application.

3.2 ARRANGEMENTS FOR LISTING

(a) First case management conference (r 63.23)

CPR 63 PCCG 3.2

If the application is for the first case management conference (r 63.23), the date for the hearing will be fixed by liaison with the Chancery Listing Office at the Rolls Building (address in Annex A).

(b) Interim Applications when a hearing has been ordered

For applications marked for determination at a hearing, the court will promptly consider whether a hearing is necessary. If the court considers it necessary to hold a hearing, the date will be fixed by the Chancery Listing Office at the Rolls Building (address in Annex A).

(c) Trials

Trial dates will be fixed at the Case Management Conference (CMC) and parties attending the Case Management Conference should have the necessary information in order to fix a trial date. This may include dates relating to the availability of witnesses and parties as well as the availability of legal representatives.

The trial fee must be paid within 14 days of the trial date being set.

3.3 TIME ESTIMATES FOR APPLICATIONS

CPR 63 PCCG 3.3

The parties must provide time estimates for all applications in respect of which a hearing is sought. Parties must appreciate the need to give a realistic and accurate time estimate and ensure that it includes a discrete reading time for the court to read the papers prior to the hearing of the application.

s Clerk as soon as possible.

3.4 DOCUMENTS AND TRIAL TIMETABLE

CPR 63 PCCG 3.4

The preparation of papers for the hearing of applications and trials is of considerable importance and should be approached intelligently. The general guidance given in Appendix 6 of the Chancery Guide should be followed. Legal representatives and litigants in person who fail to do so may be required to explain why and may be penalised personally in costs.

Papers for the hearing should be lodged directly at the Rolls Building. If there is insufficient time to lodge hard copies before the deadline, faxed documents of significance (and particularly skeleton arguments) should be supplied, followed up by clean hard copies. As an alternative to faxing documents they may, by agreement, be sent by e-mail to the Judge's Clerk.

It is the responsibility of both parties to ensure that all relevant documents are lodged by noon two days before the date fixed for hearing unless some longer or shorter period has been ordered by the judge or is prescribed by this guide.

The judge requests that all important documents also be supplied on a USB stick or via e-mail in a format convenient for the judge's use (normally the current or a recent version of Microsoft Word or as a text searchable pdf). For trial, these will usually include skeleton arguments, important patents and drawings, the witness statements and expert reports.

Prior to trial, parties should ensure that they comply with the requirements of PD 63 para 9 concerning the provision of a trial bundle and reading guide for the judge. Insofar as the trial timetable has not already have been discussed at the CMC and set out in the Order for Directions, the parties should provide a detailed time table setting out the times and dates that witnesses will be required to be available for any cross-examination already ordered.

If they are used, skeleton arguments should be lodged in time for the judge to read them before an application or trial. Any skeleton argument must also be served on the other parties in the case:

(a)   In the case of applications, if a skeleton argument is used, it should normally be filed by 10:30am the previous working day (or, in the case of short applications, 3pm).
(b)   In the case of trials, skeletons may only be used where they have been ordered at the CMC and they should normally be lodged at least two working days before commencement of the trial.

3.5 TELEPHONE APPLICATIONS

CPR 63 PCCG 3.5

The Patents County Court will hear applications by telephone conference in accordance with the Practice Direction under Part 23 and PD 63 para 30.1. The party making the application is responsible for setting up the telephone application and informing the parties, Counsels' clerks (where barristers are instructed) and the Judge's Clerk or the Chancery Listing Office of the time of the conference call.

It is possible for the application to be recorded, and if recording by the court rather than by British Telecom (or other service provider) is requested, arrangements should be made with the Judge's Clerk. The recording will not be transcribed. The tape will be kept by the Judge's Clerk for a period of six months. Arrangements for transcription, if needed, must be made by the parties.

GUIDES

This procedure should be used where it will save costs.

3.6 CONSENT ORDERS

CPR 63 PCCG 3.6

The court is normally willing to make consent orders without the need for the attendance of any parties. A draft of the agreed order and the written consent of all the parties or their respective legal representatives should be supplied to the Judge's Clerk. Unless the judge assigned to hear the application considers a hearing is needed, he or she will make the order in the agreed terms by initialling it. It will be drawn up accordingly and sent to the parties.

3.7 THE TRIAL

CPR 63 PCCG 3.7

The Court will normally hear trials from 10.30am to 4.15pm with a break from 1pm to 2pm for lunch. CMCs and other hearings will normally be heard at 10.30am but may be heard at a different time if appropriate.

If appropriate, arrangements can be made for witnesses to give their oral evidence by video link. This needs to be arranged well in advance with the parties and the court.

Where a transcript of evidence is being made and supplied to the judge, the transcript should be supplied by e-mail and in hard copy.

3.8 DRAFT JUDGMENTS

CPR 63 PCCG 3.8

Many judgments, particularly after a full trial, will be reserved and handed down at a later date, as advised by the Judge's Clerk or the Chancery Listing Office. Where possible the date for handing down the judgment will be set at the CMC. The practice has arisen to provide the parties' legal representatives (or litigants in person) with a copy of the draft judgment for advocates to notify the court of typographical and obvious errors (if any). The text may be shown, in confidence, to the parties, but only for the purpose of obtaining instructions and on the strict understanding that the judgment, or its effect, is not to be disclosed to any other person, or used in the public domain, and that no action is taken (other than internally) in response to the judgment. If the parties would prefer not to be shown the draft judgment on this basis they should inform the court at the time the judgment is reserved.

3.9 ORDERS FOLLOWING JUDGMENT

CPR 63 PCCG 3.9

Where a judgment is made available in draft before being given in open court the parties should, in advance of that occasion, exchange drafts of the desired consequential order. It is highly undesirable that one party should spring a proposal on the other for the first time when judgment is handed down. Where the parties are agreed as to the consequential order and have supplied to the judge a copy of the same signed by all parties or their representatives, attendance at the handing down of the judgment is not necessary.

3.10 ENFORCEMENT

CPR 63 PCCG 3.10

Enforcement of orders is undertaken at the PCC in the Rolls Building. Where appropriate, cases may be transferred elsewhere for enforcement, e.g. to a county court local to the defendant.

3.11 CONTACTING THE PATENTS COUNTY COURT

CPR 63 PCCG 3.11

Contact details for the Patents County Court are in Annex A.

3.12 INFORMATION AVAILABLE ON THE INTERNET

CPR 63 PCCG 3.12

Information about the Patents County Court is available on the Courts website at w ww.justice.gov.uk. The information available includes:

A copy of this Guide and the Guide for the PCC small claims track
The Patents County Court daily list.
A list of the forthcoming trials in the Patents County Court and the details of past trials.
Judgments of the Patents County Court are usually available at the Bailli website (address in Annex A)

ANNEX A
The Patents County Court

CPR 63 PCCG 4

The home of the Patents County Court is in the Rolls Building at this address:

The Rolls Building
7 Rolls Building
Fetter Lane
London   EC4A 1NL
DX160040 Strand 4

The Patents County Court is presided over by a specialist circuit judge. At present Mr Justice Birss supervises the Patents County Court.

The contact details for the Clerk to the Patents County Court are: Christy Irvine Ch risty.Irvine@hmcts.gsi.gov.uk

Tel: 020 77947 6265

Chancery Listing Office

The Chancery Listing Office may be contacted at:

Michael Mcilroy

Chancery Listing Officer

7 Rolls Building
Fetter Lane
London   EC4A 1NL
DX160040 Strand 4
Tel: 020 7947 7717/6690
Team email chanceryjudgeslisting@hmcts.gsi.gov.uk

Whether you contact listing by fax, e-mail or by post please avoid duplication of work by only sending documents once.

Postal application to issue process

Applications should be addressed to the Issue Section at the Rolls Building (address above) and clearly marked Patents County Court.

The public counter

The public counters are on the ground floor of the Rolls Building (address above). The counters are open Monday to Friday (except public holidays) from 10am - 4.30pm.

General Enquiries

A general email address for the Patents County Court is:

patentscountycourt@hmcts.gsi.gov.uk

Apart from the issuing of proceedings, all communications with the Court should be addressed to the Clerk to the Patents County Court.

Enquiries relating to a case which has been allocated to the PCC small claims track may be made to the clerks in the PCC small claims track (see the Guide to the PCC small claims track).

Please note the court staff cannot give legal advice.

Patents County Court Users Committee

The secretary to the PCCUC is Alan Johnson, Bristows, 100 Victoria Embankment, London EC4Y 0DH Tel: 020 7400 8000 Fax: 020 7400 8050 Email: Alan.Johnson@Bristows.com

IP Court Users Committee

The secretary to the IP Court users committee is Philip Westmacott, Bristows, 100 Victoria Embankment, London EC4Y 0DH Tel: 020 7400 8000 Fax: 020 7400 8050 Philip.Westmacott@Bristows.com

Information available on the Internet

Copies of this Guide, the Guide to the Patents County Court Small Claims Track, and other material are available on HM Courts & Tribunal Service's website at www.justice.gov.uk

The Patents County Court daily list appears at the end of the Chancery List on the Daily Court Lists page at www.justice.gov.uk. The full address is

www.justice.gov.uk/courts/court-lists/list-chancery-judges

A link to a diary setting out a list of the forthcoming trials in the Patents County Court as well as a list of recent trials and applications is available at:

www.justice.gov.uk/courts/rcj-rolls-building/patents-county-court

Judgments of the Patents County Court are usually available at the Bailii website:

ANNEX B: SPECIMEN CMC ORDER

CPR 63 PCCG 5

UPON HEARING the Case Management Conference on [date]

UPON the issues being identified in the Schedule to this order

IT IS ORDERED THAT:

Disclosure

1. The parties will make and serve on the other of them a list in accordance with form N265 of the documents in their control which relate to [issue X] by [date]. If any party wishes to inspect or have copies of such documents as are in another party's control it shall give notice in writing that it wishes to do so and such inspection shall be allowed at all reasonable times upon reasonable notice and any copies shall be provided within 14 days of the request, upon the undertaking of the party requesting the copies to pay the reasonable copying charges.

Evidence

2. The statements of case shall stand as evidence in chief in relation to [issue 1, and issue 2].

3. The parties may serve witness statements dealing with [issue X] on or before 4pm on [date].

4. The parties may serve witness statements in reply on or before 4pm on [date].

5. The parties may each serve an expert's report dealing with [issues 3, 4 and 5] on or before 4pm on [date].

6. The parties may serve an expert's report in reply on or before 4pm on [date].

7. The witnesses dealing with [issues 3, 4, 5 and X] may be cross-examined at trial. No other witness will be cross-examined.

Trial

8. The time allocated for the trial is 1 day. The parties are allocated ½ day each.

9. Time estimates for the cross-examination and speeches of the parties will be filed by 4pm on [date]. The court will consider the estimates and allocate time taking them into account.

10. The parties have permission to file skeleton arguments, on or before 4pm on [date].

11. The trial of the Claim shall take place on [date].

12. Judgment in the action shall be handed down on [date].

Costs

13. Costs reserved.

Schedule

List of issues:

(1)   Infringement of claim 5
(2)   Novelty of claim 1 over [citation 1]
(3)   Inventive step of claim 1 over [citation 1]
(4)   Inventive step of claim 1 over [citation 2]
(5)   Inventive step of claim 5 over [citation 2]

GUIDE TO THE PATENTS COUNTY COURT SMALL CLAIMS TRACK

1. GENERAL

1.1 INTRODUCTION

CPR 63 SCT 1.1

This Guide applies to the small claims track within the Patents County Court (PCC). It is written for all users of the PCC, whether a litigant in person or a specialist Intellectual Property (IP) litigator.

The Guide aims to help users and potential users of the small claims track of the PCC by explaining how the procedures will operate, providing guidelines where appropriate and dealing with various practical aspects of proceedings in the small claims track.

The Patents County Court has a multi-track and a small claims track. The small claims track is for suitable claims in the PCC with a value of up to £10,000. Costs orders on the small claims track are highly restricted. The PCC multi-track has a limit on damages of up to £500,000; costs orders will be made which are proportionate to the nature of the dispute, subject to a cap of no more than £50,000. This Guide is concerned specifically with the PCC small claims track. There is a general Patents County Court Guide which addresses proceedings in the multi-track and covers wider matters like the history of the PCC, details of its jurisdiction and the Patents County Court User's Committee.

In circumstances which are not covered by this guide, reference may be made to the Patents County Court Guide, the Patents Court Guide and the Chancery Guide.

1.2 ORIGIN OF THE PCC SMALL CLAIMS TRACK

CPR 63 SCT 1.2

The PCC was set up in 1990. On 1 October 2010 a new set of streamlined procedures was implemented in the PCC and today the PCC it is intended to provide a less costly and less complex forum in which to try intellectual property disputes. It does so using a streamlined form of the multi-track procedure of the Civil Procedure Rules (CPR).

Following on from the proposals set out in the Review of Civil Litigation Costs by Lord Justice Jackson and in response of a further recommendation made in the Hargreaves Review, a small claims track within the Patents County Court was set up. The small claims track came into effect on 1 October 2012.

The small claims track is intended to benefit SMEs and entrepreneurs with the lowest value IP claims, for example, a photographer who finds his image reproduced without consent.

The court will in future be renamed so as to recognise its broad IP jurisdiction.

1.3 JURISDICTION

CPR 63 SCT 1.3

The details of the basis for the legal jurisdiction of the PCC are set out in the Patents County Court Guide.

The PCC small claims track is available only for certain kinds of IP cases. The main kinds of claim which may be brought in the PCC small claims track are concerned with:

- copyright,
- trade marks (UK and Community registered trade marks),
- passing off,
- unregistered design right (UK and Community unregistered design right),

For example the small claims track of the Patents County Court may hear and determine actions for:

- Infringement of copyright
- Infringement of trade mark or passing off
- Infringement of unregistered design right

The PCC small claims track is **not** available for certain intellectual property claims. The main kinds of IP claim which may not be brought in the PCC small claims track are claims concerned with patents, registered designs (including Community registered designs), and plant varieties.

The detailed rules which govern the IP rights which may or may not be taken on the PCC small claims track are paragraph 16.1 of the *Intellectual Property Claims* and rule 63.2 (1) of *Part 63 of the CPR*. IP rights listed in paragraph 16.1 which are not listed in rule 63.2 may be taken on the PCC small claims track.

If the PCC small claims track is not suitable, all IP claims may be brought in the High Court or in the streamlined multi-track of the Patents County Court.

1.4 LEGAL REMEDIES

CPR 63 SCT 1.4

The main remedies available on the PCC small claims track are damages for infringement (or an account of profits) and a final injunction to prevent infringement in future.

Interim remedies such as interim injunctions, search and seizure and asset freezing orders are not available on the small claims track of the PCC. These remedies are available on the streamlined multi-track procedure of the PCC and so, for example, a claimant seeking an interim injunction in the PCC should use the multi-track procedure even if the claim is otherwise suitable for the PCC small claims track.

1.5 APPLICABLE RULES OF PROCEDURE

CPR 63 SCT 1.5

The rules applicable to small claims track proceedings within the Patents County Court are as follows:

- The general Civil Procedure Rules (CPR) provide the framework for proceedings in the Patents County Court as they apply to all civil courts in England and Wales.
- CPR Part 63- Intellectual Property Claims applies to all intellectual property claims. Part 63 includes rules specific to intellectual property cases and in some areas modifies the general parts of the CPR.
- Practice Direction 63 (PD 63) supplements CPR Part 63.
- Attention is drawn to two particular parts of the CPR which contain provisions specific to the PCC small claims track.
  - First is CPR Part 27, which deals with the small claims track in general. It is modified in its application to the PCC small claims track in that interim injunctions are not available.
  - Second are two rules in CPR Part 63 (r 63.27 and r 63.28). Rule 63.27 relates to allocation to the PCC small claims track and r 63.28 clarifies which rules are applicable to the track.

1.6 PROCEDURE

CPR 63 SCT 1.6

The PCC small claims track will follow the standard small claims procedure of the CPR but within the framework of the Patents County Court. The procedure is outlined below.

Part 27 of the CPR set out the procedure for dealing with claims which have been allocated to the small claims track. The CPR include details on the conduct of a small claims track hearing which highlights its accessibility:

- The court may adopt any method of proceeding at a hearing that it considers to be fair.
- Hearings will be informal.
  - The strict rules of evidence do not apply.
  - The court need not take evidence on oath.
  - The court may limit cross-examination.
  - The court must give reasons for its decision (Rule 27.8).

Additionally the court may, if all parties agree, deal with the claim without a hearing i.e. 'on paper' (Rule 27.10).

1.7 ALLOCATION

CPR 63 SCT 1.7

The PCC small claims track is intended to provide a proportionate procedure by which most straightforward IP claims with a financial value of not more that £10,000 can be decided without the need for substantial pre-hearing preparation and the formalities of a traditional trial. The limit on value of £10,000 is the same as the limit applicable for general civil claims on the small claims track.

Allocation of cases between the multi-track and small claims track in the PCC works in the following way.

10,000 and the subject matter relates to one of the appropriate IP rights (usually copyright, trade marks, passing off or unregistered design right).

All claims in the PCC are automatically allocated to the multi-track initially unless the claimant states in the Particulars of Claim that he or she wishes the claim to be allocated to the small claims track. So a claimant who wishes to use the small claims track must say so in writing, as part of the Particulars of Claim (see below).

If the defendant does not object to allocation to the small claims track and assuming the case is suitable, then it will be allocated to the PCC small claims track.

In cases where there is a dispute the court will determine allocation. One example of a dispute may be if the claimant has asked for the case to be allocated to the small claims track but the defendant objects. Another example could be that the claimant not sought allocation to the small claims track but the defendant thinks the case should be a small claim. In these situations, once the dispute has arisen, the court will decide to which track the claim should be allocated.

The value of the claim will be one aspect the court will consider in deciding to allocate a claim to a particular track. It will also consider other factors such as: the likely complexity of the facts, law or evidence; the amount of oral evidence which may be required and the views expressed by the parties. Cases concerned with the validity of registered trade marks are unlikely to be suitable for the small claims track.

Even if the parties have consented to allocation, the case will not be allocated to the PCC small claims track if it is not suitable for that track.

If there is no dispute about allocation, there is no need to file an allocation questionnaire.

If there is a reason to do so at a later stage, the court can re-allocate a case proceeding on one track in the PCC to the other track. Where a claim is re-allocated to the other track, the costs rules applicable to the first track will cease to apply after the claim has been re-allocated and the costs rules on the new track will apply from the date of re-allocation.

1.8 COSTS RECOVERY

CPR 63 SCT 1.8

The general principle that the unsuccessful party will pay the legal costs of the successful party does not apply on the small claims track. In the case of the small claims track, the costs recoverable are highly restricted.

The applicable rule (CPR r 27.14) states that except in certain circumstances . The circumstances in which the court may award sums for costs include: fixed sums in relation to issuing the claim; court fees; certain expenses relating to attending the hearing etc.

Practice Direction (PD) 27 (section 7.1-7.3) sets out the maximum amounts which may be ordered in particular special circumstances. The maximum sum for legal advice and assistance in a claim including an injunction is a sum not exceeding £260 (paragraph 7.2). The maximum amount for the loss of earnings of each party or witness attending a hearing is £90 per day for each person (paragraph 7.3).

1.9 LEGAL REPRESENTATION

CPR 63 SCT 1.9

One way in which costs on the small claims track are kept proportionate to what is at stake is that any party may present his/her own case at a hearing although a lawyer or lay representative (anyone other than a barrister, a solicitor or a legal executive employed by a solicitor) may present it for him/her. A corporate party (business) may be represented by any of its officers or employees.

Patent attorneys, solicitors and trade mark attorneys all have rights to represent clients in the PCC. These professionals may additionally instruct barristers to help prepare/argue the case in court, although this will not normally be suitable if a claim is to be heard upon the low cost small claims track.

More information about qualified legal professionals can be found at the following websites:

- Chartered Institute of Patent Attorneys — www.cipa.org.uk.
- Law Society — www.lawsociety.org.uk (regarding Solicitors).
- Bar Council — www.barcouncil.org.uk (regarding Barristers).
- Institute of Trade Mark Attorneys — www.itma.org.uk.

Where a person bringing or defending a case in the PCC cannot afford to pay for their own legal representative, then they may be eligible to seek free or pro bono advice. The National Pro Bono Centre houses national clearing houses for legal pro bono work delivered in England and Wales: i.e. the Bar Pro Bono Unit, Law Works (the Solicitors' Pro Bono Group) and ILEX Pro Bono Forum. The website is at: www.nationalprobonocentre.org.uk.

A litigant wishing to seek pro-bono legal assistance should approach the Citizens Advice Bureau or a Law Centre first. There is a CAB office in the Royal Courts of Justice, Strand, London.

The Patents County Court Users Committee is working with CIPA to look at setting up a CIPA pro bono scheme and also actively considering other ways to widen the availability of pro-bono legal assistance in the Patents County Court.

1.10 THE JUDGES OF SMALL CLAIMS TRACK OF THE PATENTS COUNTY COURT

CPR 63 SCT 1.10

The judges who sit in the small claims track of the PCC are District Judges and Deputy District Judges. They sit in the Thomas More Building at the address in Annex A. This is close to the main home of the Patents County Court at the Rolls Building.

2. PROCEDURE IN THE SMALL CLAIMS TRACK

2.1 BEFORE ISSUING PROCEEDINGS

CPR 63 SCT 2.1

Attention is drawn to the Practice Direction- Pre-Action Conduct (a copy of which can be found on the HM Courts Service website at www.justice.gov.uk).

Compliance with this Practice Direction will affect the timetable, once proceedings are issued (see further below). However, as unjustified threats to bring legal proceedings in respect of many IP rights can themselves be subject to litigation, each claimant will have to make their own decision as to whether it is appropriate to write to a prospective defendant to see if matters can be settled before any proceedings are issued.

2.2 ISSUING PROCEEDINGS

CPR 63 SCT 2.2

All proceedings should be issued at the public counter in the Rolls Building. The full address details are set out within Annex A.

2.3 SERVICE OF DOCUMENTS

CPR 63 SCT 2.3

The claim form should be served on the defendant with a response pack. The claim form should be served by the claimant and so the claimant should make sure the defendant's copy of the claim form is obtained from the court at issue.

2.4 STATEMENTS OF CASE

Introduction

CPR 63 SCT 2.4

Statements of case are the documents where each party sets out its case. These need to be full, but not unnecessarily lengthy. Statements of case can stand as evidence at trial in the PCC, where relevant individuals have verified them with a statement of truth.

Time limits

The time limits applicable in the PCC are the same whether the case is proceeding on the small claims track or the multi-track.

In general, the time limits set out in Part 15 apply to litigation of all intellectual property rights. However, rule 63.22 modifies Part 15 in respect of the time limits for filing defences and replies.

The time limit for filing the defence depends on whether the Particulars of Claim confirms that Pre-Action Conduct practice direction has been complied with (rule 63.22(2) and (3)). The time limit is 42 days or 70 days respectively.

The time limit for the reply to defence is 28 days from the service of the defence (rule 63.22(4)).

The parties are not at liberty to extend the time limits set out in rule 63.22 without the prior consent of the judge. Applications for any extension of time must be made in good time and set out clear grounds as to why they are required.

Contents

Statements of case within the small claims track must set out concisely all facts and arguments relied on. The case will be assessed on an issue by issue basis, therefore the court needs to know what all the issues are for that process to take place. Guidance on the statement of case is as follows:

- In a normal case it is unlikely that legal arguments will need to be set out in any detail in the statement of case, all that is likely to be required is a brief statement of the nature of the argument to be relied on.
- Similarity between works (in a copyright case) or similarity between marks (in a trade mark case) may not require elaboration but in an appropriate case some detail will be necessary. In 6 trade mark cases the nature and characteristics of the relevant consumer should be identified (if relevant).
- A defence of independent design in a copyright case (or similar) will need to be addressed in appropriate detail.

2.5 CASE MANAGEMENT

CPR 63 SCT 2.5

Case management in the small claims track is governed by CPR r 27.4. After allocation, the court will give directions. The case management in the PCC small claims track will be conducted by a district judge or deputy district judge.

The court will normally give directions on paper without a preliminary hearing, and fix a date for the final hearing. If that is not possible, various alternative orders may be made. One possible order is to fix a date for a preliminary hearing.

The court will not normally allow more than one day for the hearing of a claim.

2.6 EXPERTS (R 27.5)

CPR 63 SCT 2.6

No expert may give evidence, whether written or oral, without the permission of the court.

2.7 PRELIMINARY HEARING (R 27.6)

CPR 63 SCT 2.7

The court may hold a preliminary hearing in an appropriate case. If it decides to do so, the parties will be given at least 14 days notice. At a preliminary hearing the court will fix a date for a final hearing (if that has not already been done), inform the parties of the amount of time allowed for the final hearing and give any appropriate directions.

Preliminary hearings in the small claims track of the PCC will take place at the Thomas More Building (address in Annex A).

2.8 TRANSFERS

CPR 63 SCT 2.8

Cases proceeding in the Patents County Court may (if appropriate) be transferred to the High Court. This is unlikely to be relevant to the small claims track. The general Patents County Court Guide contains information about transfers to the High Court.

2.9 THE TRIAL

CPR 63 SCT 2.9

The general rule is that a small claims hearing will be in public. The judge may decide to hold it in private, or deal with it as a paper hearing if the parties agree.

s room but it may take place in a courtroom. Trials in the small claims track of the PCC will take place at the Thomas More Building (address in Annex A).

Rule 27.8 allows the court to adopt any method of proceeding that it considers to be fair and to limit cross examination. The judge may in particular:

(1)   Ask questions of any witness himself before allowing any other person to do so.
(2)   Ask questions of all or any of the witnesses himself before allowing any other person to ask questions of any witnesses.
(3)   Refuse to allow cross-examination of any witnesses until all the witnesses have given evidence in chief.
(4)   Limit cross examination of a witness to a fixed time or to a particular subject or issue, or both.

A hearing that takes place at the court will be tape recorded by the court. A party may obtain a transcript of such a recording on payment of the proper transcribers' charges.

Provisions are in place to enable a party to give notice that he will not attend a final hearing and sets out the effect of his giving such notice and of not doing so. Nothing in the provisions affect the general power of the court to adjourn a hearing, for example where a party who wishes to attend a hearing on the date fixed cannot do so for a good reason.

2.10 FEES

CPR 63 SCT 2.10

Fees are payable to the court when issuing a claim using the small claims track and on certain other occasions. Guidance Fees is available on the website of HM Courts Service at www.justice.gov.uk.

2.11 ALTERNATIVE DISPUTE RESOLUTION

CPR 63 SCT 2.11

The primary role of the Patents County Court is as a forum for deciding intellectual property rights cases. However, the Patents County Court encourages parties to consider the use of ADR (such as, but not confined to, mediation and conciliation) as an alternative means of resolving disputes or particular issues within disputes.

Settlement of a dispute by ADR has many advantages. It can result in significant saving of costs. It also has the potential to provide the parties with a wider range of solutions than can be offered by litigation. For example, while the solution to litigation is usually limited to "win/lose" on the issues put in front of the court, ADR may provide a creative "win/win" solution, as some forms of ADR can explore other ways for the parties to cooperate. ADR can also explore settlement in several countries at the same time.

Legal representatives should consider and advise their clients as to the possibility of seeking to resolve the dispute via ADR. However, not all cases are suitable for settlement this way. In an appropriate case, the Patents County Court has the power to adjourn a case for a specified period of time to encourage and enable the parties to use ADR. At the Case Management Conference, the Judge will ask whether the parties have been advised about ADR and whether an adjournment is being sought. However, this will not usually be a reason to delay the CMC itself.

There are many forms of ADR. Most of these are not free. These include:

(a)   This can involve the use of a third party to see if agreement may be reached or to offer a non binding opinion on the dispute. Some trade bodies offer conciliation services.

(b)   This involves the appointment of a trained mediator to see whether a legally binding agreement can be negotiated. The parties will usually sign a framework agreement for the procedure of the mediation. Mediation can involve the mediator meeting with both parties together and/or meeting the parties in separate rooms and shuffling between them.

(c)   This involves the appointment of an arbitrator or private decision maker, under a set of procedural rules. The arbitrator will then make a binding decision on the case. Arbitration replaces the court action, but the decision of the arbitrator is private to the parties. NB since arbitration is a private matter between parties, arbitrators cannot revoke intellectual property rights.

(d)   This involves an appointment of an expert to give an opinion about one or more issues in a dispute. Such opinions are not binding but assist the parties in reaching a settlement of the case.

(e)   This involves the appointment of an expert to make a decision about one or more issues in a dispute. Such decisions can be legally binding, by agreement between the parties.

2.12 APPEALS

CPR 63 SCT 2.12

An appeal from an interim decision in the PCC small claims track is to the circuit judge sitting in the PCC. An appeal from a final decision is to the Court of Appeal. An appeal can only be made with permission. Permission can be sought from the judge who made the order in the small claims track or from the court handling any appeal.

ANNEX A CONTACT DETAILS AND ADDRESSES
Patents County Court (Small Claims Track)
The Patents County Court

CPR 63 SCT 3

The home of the Patents County Court is in the Rolls Building at this address:

The Rolls Building
7 Rolls Building
Fetter Lane
London   EC4A 1NL

DX160040 Strand 4

The Patents County Court is supervised by Mr Justice Birss.

The contact details for the Clerk to the Patents County Court are: Christy Irvine Christy.Irvine@hmcts.gsi.gov.uk

The public counter for the PCC small claims track

The public counter for the small claims track of the Patents County Court is on the ground floor of the Rolls Building (address above). It is the same counter which is used for all cases in the Patents County Court. This is the place at which all fees will be paid and all proceedings and applications issued.

The counters are open Monday to Friday (except public holidays) from 10am-4.30pm.

Trials and preliminary hearings in the PCC small claims track

Trials and preliminary hearings in the small claims track of the Patents County Court will take place in the Thomas More Building at this address:

Thomas More Building
Royal Courts of Justice
Strand
London   WC2A 2LL
DX 44450 STRAND
Tel: 020 7947 7387/6187
Fax: 0870 761 7695
Email: PCCsmallclaimstrack@hmcts.gsi.gov.uk

Judges on the PCC small claims track

The judges who will hear cases on the PCC small claims track are District Judge Janet Lambert, District Judge Melissa Clarke and District Judge Charlotte Hart.

The clerks in charge of the PCC small claims track will be the clerks to the District Judges at the Thomas More Building. They can be contacted on the telephone numbers and email address for the PCC small claims track given above.

Two deputy District Judges will also sit on the PCC small claims track: Nicola Solomon and Richard Vary.

Chancery Listing Office

The Chancery Listing Office may be contacted at:

Michael Mcilroy

Chancery Listing Officer

General Enquiries

Enquiries relating to a case which has been allocated to the PCC small claims track may be made to the clerks in the PCC small claims track (see the Guide to the PCC small claims track).

Enquiries relating to the Patents County Court in general may be addressed to the Clerk to the Patents County Court (above).

Please note the court staff cannot give legal advice.

Internet

Copies of this Guide, the general Guide to the Patents County Court and other material are available on HM Courts Service's website at www.justice.gov.uk

THE QUEEN'S BENCH GUIDE

A guide to the working practices of the Queen's Bench Division within the Royal Courts of Justice

TABLE OF CONTENTS

Preface		QBG Pref
1 Introduction		QBG 1.1.1
	1.1 The Guide	QBG 1.1.1
	1.2 The Civil Procedure Rules	QBG 1.2.1
	1.3 The Practice Directions	QBG 1.3.1
	1.4 The Forms	QBG 1.4.1
	1.5 The Queen's Bench Division	QBG 1.5.1
	1.6 The Central Office	QBG 1.6.1
	1.7 The Judiciary	QBG 1.7.1
2 General		QBG 2.1.1
	2.1 Essential matters	QBG 2.1.1
	2.2 Inspection and copies of documents	QBG 2.2.1
	2.3 Time limits	QBG 2.3.1
	2.4 Legal representation	QBG 2.4.1
	2.5 Costs	QBG 2.5.1
	2.6 Court fees	QBG 2.6.1
	2.7 Information technology	QBG 2.7.1
3 Steps before Issue of a Claim Form		QBG 3.1.1
	3.1 Settlement	QBG 3.1.1
	3.2 Disclosure before proceedings are started	QBG 3.2.1
	3.3 Defamation proceedings/offer of amends	QBG 3.3.1
4 Starting Proceedings in the Central Office		QBG 4.1.1
	4.1 Issuing the claim form	QBG 4.1.1
	4.2 Particulars of Claim (POC)	QBG 4.2.1
	4.3 Part 8 Procedure	QBG 4.3.1
	4.4 Service	QBG 4.4.1
5 Response to a Part 7 Claim		QBG 5.1.1
	5.1 General	QBG 5.1.1
	5.2 Acknowledgement of service	QBG 5.2.1
	5.3 Admissions	QBG 5.3.1
	5.4 Defence	QBG 5.4.1
	5.5 Default judgment	QBG 5.5.1
	5.6 Statements of case	QBG 5.6.1
6 Preliminary Case Management		QBG 6.1.1
	6.1 The Practice Master	QBG 6.1.1
	6.2 Assignment to Masters	QBG 6.2.1
	6.3 Listing before Masters	QBG 6.3.1
	6.4 Automatic transfer	QBG 6.4.1
	6.5 Allocation	QBG 6.5.1
	6.6 Alternative dispute resolution ('ADR')	QBG 6.6.1
	6.7 Part 8–alternative procedure for claims	QBG 6.7.1
	6.8 Specific matters which may be dealt with under Part 8	QBG 6.8.1
	6.9 Transfer	QBG 6.9.1
	6.10 Part 20 proceedings	QBG 6.10.1
	6.11 Summary Judgment	QBG 6.11.1
	6.12 Offers to settle and payments into and out of court	QBG 6.12.1
7 Case Management and Interim Remedies		QBG 7.1.1
	7.1 Case management–general	QBG 7.1.1
	7.2 The case management conference	QBG 7.2.1

7.3	Preliminary issues	QBG 7.3.1
7.4	Trial timetable	QBG 7.4.1
7.5	Listing Questionnaire	QBG 7.5.1
7.6	Pre-trial review	QBG 7.6.1
7.7	Requests for further information	QBG 7.7.1
7.8	Disclosure	QBG 7.8.1
7.9	Experts and assessors	QBG 7.9.1
7.10	Evidence	QBG 7.10.1
7.11	Hearings	QBG 7.11.1
7.12	Applications	QBG 7.12.1
7.13	Interim remedies	QBG 7.13.1
7.14	Interlocutory Orders	QBG 7.14.1
8 Defamation Claims		QBG 8.1.1
8.1	Offer to make amends	QBG 8.1.1
8.2	Ruling on meaning	QBG 8.2.1
8.3	Summary disposal	QBG 8.3.1
8.4	Statements read in court	QBG 8.4.1
8 Listing before Judges		QBG 9.1.1
9.1	Responsibility for listing	QBG 9.1.1
9.2	The Lists	QBG 9.2.1
9.3	The Jury List	QBG 9.3.1
9.4	The Trial List	QBG 9.4.1
9.5	The Interim Hearings List	QBG 9.5.1
9.6	General	QBG 9.6.1
9.7	Listing before the Interim Applications Judge	QBG 9.7.1
9.8	The Lists generally	QBG 9.8.1
9.9	Listing Office–general matters	QBG 9.9.1
10 Trial, Judgments and Orders		QBG 10.1.1
10.1	General	QBG 10.1.1
10.2	The Trial	QBG 10.2.1
10.3	Judgments and Orders	QBG 10.3.1
11 Appeals		QBG 11.1.1
11.1	General	QBG 11.1.1
11.2	Permission to appeal	QBG 11.2.1
11.3	Notices	QBG 11.3.1
11.4	Appeals in cases of contempt of court	QBG 11.4.1
12 Enforcement		QBG 12.1.1
12.1	General	QBG 12.1.1
12.2	Writs of execution	QBG 12.2.1
12.3	Interpleader proceedings (RSC Ord 17)	QBG 12.3.1
12.4	Examination of judgment debtor (RSC Ord 48)	QBG 11.4.1
12.5	Third Party Debt Order proceedings (RSC Ord 49)	QBG 12.5.1
12.6	Charging orders (RSC Ord 50)	QBG 12.6.1
12.7	Receivers; equitable execution (RSC Ord 51)	QBG 12.7.1
12.8	Committals, etc. (RSC Ord 52)	QBG 12.8.1
12.9	Execution against property of Foreign or Commonwealth States	QBG 12.9.1
12.10	Recovery of enforcement costs	QBG 12.10.1
12.11	Enforcement of Magistrates' Courts' orders	QBG 12.11.1
12.12	Enforcement of foreign judgments and enforcement of High Court judgments abroad	QBG 12.12.1
13 Miscellaneous		QBG 13.1.1
13.1	Service of foreign process (RSC Ord 69)	QBG 13.1.1
13.2	Rectification of register of deeds of arrangement (RSC Ord 94 r 4)	QBG 13.2.1
13.3	Exercise of jurisdiction under the Representation of the People Acts (RSC Ord 95 r 5)	QBG 13.3.1
13.4	Bills of Sale Acts 1878 and 1882 and the Industrial and Provident	

Societies Act 1967 (RSC Ord 95)...................... QBG 13.4.1
13.5 Enrolment of deeds and other documents .... QBG 13.5.1
13.6 Bail (RSC Ord 79 r 9) .... QBG 13.6.1
13.7 References to the Court of Justice of the European Communities QBG 13.7.1
13.8 Group Litigation Orders 'GLOs' .... QBG 13.8.1
Annex 1 – Fees .... QBG App 1
Annex 2 – Masters' abbreviations .... QBG App 2

PREFACE

Foreword by The Rt. Hon. Sir Igor Judge
President of the Queen's Bench Division

QBG Pref

We live in a new procedural world. Old landmarks have disappeared from view. New features have taken their place. And everyone seems to be speaking a different language. It is easy to become disoriented. Though it is six years since the introduction of the Civil Procedure Rules, much has changed since the publication of the First Edition of this Guide.

This Guide, prepared for those litigating in the Queen's Bench Division of the High Court, particularly in the Central Office, provides a clear and detailed road-map for those who have lost, or are not sure of, the way.

I am sure this Guide will prove invaluable to the many who will, I hope, use it.

An appreciation

With the support and encouragement of Sir Igor Judge, the President of the Queen's Bench Division, this Guide has been prepared for the assistance of all who practise or litigate in the Queen's Bench Division.

The contributions made by the Queen's Bench Masters and the staff of the Central Office have been invaluable but this Guide would not have been completed without the hard work and diligence of Master Fontaine, Bryony Young, Clerk to the Interim Applications Judge and Maxine Fidler, my former Personal Assistant, to all of whom I am indebted.

However, all errors and omissions are mine and I would welcome any comments and suggestions from the Profession and all using this Guide for its improvement.

The Senior Master and Queen's Remembrancer

January 2007

1 INTRODUCTION

A 1.1 The guide

QBG 1.1.1

1.1.1 This Guide has been prepared by the Senior Master, acting under the authority of the Lord Chief Justice, and provides a general explanation of the work and practice of the Queen's Bench Division with particular regard to proceedings started in the Central Office, and is designed to make it easier for parties to use and proceed in the Queen's Bench Division.

QBG 1.1.2

1.1.2 The Guide must be read with the Civil Procedure Rules ('the CPR') and the supporting Practice Directions. Litigants and their advisers are responsible for acquainting themselves with the CPR; it is not the task of this Guide to summarise the CPR, nor should anyone regard it as a substitute for the CPR. It is intended to bring the Guide up to date at regular intervals as necessary.

QBG 1.1.3

1.1.3 The Guide does not have the force of law, but parties using the Queen's Bench Division will be expected to act in accordance with this Guide. Further guidance as to the practice of the Queen's Bench Division may be obtained from the Practice Master (see paragraph 6.1 below).

QBG 1.1.4

1.1.4 It is assumed throughout the Guide that the litigant intends to proceed in the Royal Courts of Justice. For all essential purposes, though, the Guide is equally applicable to the work of the District Registries, which deal with the work of the Queen's Bench Division outside London, but it should be borne in mind that there are some differences.

QBG 1.1.5

1.1.5 The telephone numbers and room numbers quoted in the Guide are correct at the time of going to press.

1.2 The Civil Procedure Rules

QBG 1.2.1

1.2.1 The Overriding Objective set out in Part 1 of the CPR is central to civil proceedings and enables the court to deal with cases justly. To further this aim the work is allocated to one of three tracks - the small claims track, the fast track and the multi-track - so as to dispose of the work in the most appropriate and effective way combined with active case management by the court.

QBG 1.2.2

1.2.2 The CPR are divided into Parts. A particular Part is referred to in the Guide as Part 7, etc., as the case may be. Any particular rule within a Part is referred to as Rule 6.4(2), and so on.

1.3 The Practice Directions

QBG 1.3.1

1.3.1 Each Part - or almost each Part - has an accompanying Practice Direction or Directions, and other Practice Directions deal with matters such as the Pre-Action Protocols and the former Rules of the Supreme Court and the County Court Rules which are scheduled to Part 50.

QBG 1.3.2

1.3.2 The Practice Directions are made pursuant to statute, and have the same authority as do the CPR themselves. However, in case of any conflict between a Rule and a Practice Direction, the Rule will prevail. Each Practice Direction is referred to in the Guide with the number of any Part that it supplements preceding it; for example, the Practice Direction supplementing Part 6 is referred to as the Part 6 Practice Direction. But where there is more than one Practice Direction supplementing a Part it will also be described either by topic, for example, Part 25 Practice Direction - Interim Payments, or where appropriate, the Part 40B Practice Direction.

1.4 Forms

QBG 1.4.1

1.4.1 The Practice Direction supplementing Part 4 (Forms) lists the practice forms that are generally required to be used by or referred to in the CPR, and also those referred to in such of the Rules of the Supreme Court and the County Court Rules as are still in force (see Part 50 of the CPR; Schedules 1 and 2).

QBG 1.4.2

1.4.2 Those listed in Table 1 with a number prefixed by the letter N are forms that are referred to in and generally required to be used by Rules or Practice Directions. Those listed in Table 2 are Practice Forms that may be used as precedents. The Civil Procedure Forms Volume contains a comprehensive set of forms for use in the High Court and the county courts; these are listed under the same numbers that previously identified them.

QBG 1.4.3

1.4.3 The forms may be modified as circumstances in individual cases require, but it is essential that a modified form contains at least as full information or guidance as would have been given if the original form had been used.

QBG 1.4.4

1.4.4 Where the Royal Arms appears on any listed form it must appear on any modification of that form. The same format for the Royal Arms as is used on the listed forms need not be used. All that is necessary is that there is a complete Royal Arms.

QBG 1.4.5

1.4.5 Forms are available from the Court Service website at http://www.hmcourts -service.gov.uk

1.5 The Queen's Bench Division

QBG 1.5.1

1.5.1 The Queen's Bench Division is one of the three divisions of the High Court, together with the Chancery Division and Family Division. A Lord Justice of Appeal, currently Lord Justice Judge has been appointed by the Lord Chief Justice to be the President of the Queen's Bench Division and Lord Justice May has been appointed as Vice-President; a High Court Judge is appointed as Judge in charge of the Lists and is currently Mr Justice Eady.

QBG 1.5.2

1.5.2 Outside London, the work of the Queen's Bench Division is administered in provincial offices known as District Registries. In London, the work is administered in the Central Office at the Royal Courts of Justice. The work in the Central Office of the Queen's Bench Division is the responsibility of the Senior Master, acting under the authority of the President of the Queen's Bench Division.

QBG 1.5.3

1.5.3 The work of the Queen's Bench Division is (with certain exceptions) governed by the CPR. The Administrative Court, the Admiralty Court, the Commercial Court and the Technology and Construction Court are all part of the Queen's Bench Division. However, each does specialised work requiring a distinct procedure that to some extent modifies the CPR. For that reason each has an individual Part of the CPR, its own Practice Direction and (except for the Administrative Court) its own Guide, to which reference should be made by parties wishing to proceed in the specialist courts.

QBG 1.5.4

1.5.4 The work of the Queen's Bench Division consists mainly of claims for;
(1)   damages in respect of:
    (a)   personal injury,
    (b)   negligence,
    (c)   breach of contract,
    (d)   libel and slander (defamation),
    (e)   other tortious acts
    (f)   breach of statutory duty
(2)   non-payment of a debt, and
(3)   possession of land or property.

Proceedings retained to be dealt with in the Central Office of the Queen's Bench Division will almost invariably be multi-track claims.

QBG 1.5.5

1.5.5 In many types of claim - for example claims in respect of negligence by solicitors, accountants, etc. or claims for possession of land - the claimant has a choice whether to bring the claim in the Queen's Bench Division or in the Chancery Division. However, there are certain matters that may be brought only in the Queen's Bench Division, namely:
(1)   High Court Enforcement Officer's interpleader proceedings,
(2)   applications for the enrolment of deeds,
(3)   registration of foreign judgments under the Civil Jurisdictions and Judgments Act 1982 or the European Regulation
(4)   applications for bail in criminal proceedings,
(5)   applications under the Administration of Justice Act 1920 and the Foreign Judgments (Reciprocal Enforcement) Act 1933 and European Regulations.
(6)   registration and satisfaction of Bills of Sale,
(7)   Election Petitions,
(8)   applications for orders to obtain evidence for foreign courts.

1.6 The Central Office

QBG 1.6.1

1.6.1 The information in this and the following paragraph is to be found in the Part 2 Practice Direction at paragraph 2; it is reproduced here for the convenience of litigants. The Central Office is open for business from 10 a.m. to 4.30 p.m. on every day of the year except;

(1)   Saturdays and Sundays,

(2)   Good Friday and the day after Easter Monday,

(3)   Christmas Day and Boxing Day and, if these days are a Friday or Saturday, the Bank Holidays allotted in their place, then 28th December,

(4).   Bank Holidays in England and Wales (under the Banking and Financial Dealings Act 1971), and

(5)   such other days as the Lord Chancellor, with the concurrence or the Lord Chief Justice, the Master of the Rolls, the President of the Family Division and the Chancellor, may direct.

QBG 1.6.2

1.6.2 One of the Masters of the Queen's Bench Division is present on every day on which the Central Office is open for the purpose of superintending the business administered there and giving any directions that may be required on questions of practice and procedure. S/he is normally referred to as the 'Practice Master'. (See paragraph 6.1 below for information about the Practice Master and Masters in general.)

QBG 1.6.3

1.6.3 The Central Office consists of the Action Department, the Masters' Support Unit, the Foreign Process Section, the Masters' Secretary's Department, the Queen's Bench Associates' Department, the Clerk of the Lists, the Registry of the Technology and Construction Court and the Admiralty and Commercial Registry.

QBG 1.6.4

1.6.4 The Action Department deals with the issue of claims, responses to claims, admissions, undefended and summary judgments, enforcement, drawing up certain orders, public searches, provision of copies of court documents, enrolment of deeds and registration of foreign judgments.

QBG 1.6.5

1.6.5 The Masters' Secretary's Department covers three discrete areas of work;

(1)   the Masters' Support Unit, which provides support (a) to the Masters, including assisting with case-management, and (b) to the Senior Master,

(2)   Foreign Process, and

(3)   Investment of Children's Funds.

Also one of the staff acts as the Chief Clerk to the Prescribed Officer for Election Petitions (the Senior Master).

QBG 1.6.6

1.6.6 The Queen's Bench Associates sit in court with the Judges during trials and certain interim hearings. The Chief Associate manages the Queen's Bench Associates and also provides support to the Senior Master as the Queen's Remembrancer. The Associates draw up the orders made in court at trial and those interim orders that the parties do not wish to draw up themselves, or directed by a Master to be drawn by the Court.

QBG 1.6.7

1.6.7 The Clerk of the Lists lists all trials and matters before the Judges (see Section 8 below).

QBG 1.6.8

1.6.8 The Technology and Construction Court deals with claims which involve issues or questions which are technically complex or for which a trial by a Judge of that court is for any other reason desirable (see the Part 49C Practice Direction - Technology and Construction Court).

QBG 1.6.9

1.6.9 The Admiralty and Commercial Court deals mainly with shipping collision claims and claims concerning charters and insurance and commercial arbitrations. See the Commercial Court Guide and the Part 49D Practice Direction – Commercial Court, the Part 49F Practice Direction - Admiralty and the Part 49G Practice Direction – Arbitrations.

1.7 The Judiciary

QBG 1.7.1

1.7.1 The judiciary in the Queen's Bench Division consist of the High Court Judges (The Honourable Mr/Mrs Justice . . . . and addressed in court as my Lord/my Lady) and in the Royal Courts of Justice, the Masters (Master . . . .); in the District Registries the work of the Masters is conducted by District Judges.

QBG 1.7.2

1.7.2 Trials normally take place before a High Court Judge (or Deputy High Court Judge) who may also hear pre-trial reviews and other interim applications. Wherever possible the judge before whom a trial has been fixed will hear any pre-trial review. A High Court Judge will hear applications to commit for contempt of court, applications for injunctions and most appeals from Masters' orders. (See the Practice Direction to Part 2B Allocation of cases to levels of Judiciary, and see paragraphs 7.11 and 7.12 below for more information on hearings and applications.)

QBG 1.7.3

1.7.3 The Masters deal with interim and some pre-action applications, and manage the claims so that they proceed without delay. The Masters' rooms are situated in the East Block of the Royal Courts of Justice. Hearings take place in these rooms or (short hearings only) in the Bear Garden.

QBG 1.7.4

1.7.4 Cases are assigned on issue by a court officer in the Action Department to Masters on a rota basis, and that Master is then known as the assigned Master in relation to that case. (See paragraphs 6.2 and 6.3 below for more information about assignment and the Masters' lists.)

QBG 1.7.5

1.7.5 General enquiries about the business dealt with by the Masters should initially be made in writing to the Masters' Support Unit in Room E16

2 GENERAL

2.1 Essential matters

QBG 2.1.1

2.1.1 Before bringing any proceedings, the intending claimant should think carefully about the implications of so doing. (See Section 3 below about steps to be taken before issuing a claim form.)

QBG 2.1.2

2.1.2 A litigant who is acting in person faces a heavier burden in terms of time and effort than does a litigant who is legally represented, but all litigation calls for a high level of commitment from the parties. No intending claimant should underestimate this.

QBG 2.1.3

2.1.3 The Overriding Objective of the CPR is to deal with cases justly, which means dealing with the claim in a way which is proportionate (amongst other things) to the amount of money involved. However, in all proceedings there are winners and losers; the loser is generally ordered to pay the costs of the winner and the costs of litigation can still be large. The risk of large costs is particularly acute in cases involving expert witnesses, barristers and solicitors. Also, the costs of an interim hearing are almost always summarily assessed and made payable by the unsuccessful party usually within 14 days after the order for costs is made. There may be a number of interim hearings before the trial itself is reached, so the costs must be paid as the claim progresses. (See also paragraph 2.5 Costs below.)

QBG 2.1.4

2.1.4 The intending claimant should also keep in mind that every claim must be proved, unless of course the defendant admits the allegations. There is little point in incurring the risks and expense of litigating if the claim cannot be proved. An intending claimant should therefore be taking steps to obtain statements from his/her prospective witnesses before starting the claim; if s/he delays until later, it may turn out that s/he is in fact unable to obtain the evidence that s/he needs to prove his/her claim. A defendant faces a similar task.

QBG 2.1.5

2.1.5 Any party may, if s/he is to succeed, need an opinion from one or more expert witnesses, such as medical practitioners, engineers, accountants, or as the case may be. However s/he must remember that no expert evidence may be given at trial without the permission of the court. The services of such experts are in great demand, especially as, in some fields of expertise, there are few of them. It may take many months to obtain an opinion, and the cost may be high. (See paragraph 7.9 below for information about experts' evidence.) If the claim is for compensation for personal injuries, the claimant must produce a medical report with his/her particulars of claim.

QBG 2.1.6

2.1.6 The claimant must remember also not to allow the time limit for starting his/her claim to pass (see paragraph 2.3 below for information about time limits).

QBG 2.1.7

2.1.7 Any intending claimant should also have in mind that s/he will usually be required to give standard disclosure of the documents on which s/he relies. Although Rule 31.3(2) makes provision for a party not to be required to disclose documents, if disclosure would be disproportionate to the value of the claim, in complex cases it may still be necessary to disclose relatively large quantities of documents, and this invariably involves much time, effort and expense. (See paragraph 7.8 below for information about disclosure.)

QBG 2.1.8

2.1.8 In many cases the parties will need legal assistance, whether by way of advice, drafting, representation at hearings or otherwise. It is not the function of court staff to give legal advice; however, subject to that, they will do their best to assist any litigant. Litigants in person who need assistance or funding should contact the Community Legal Service through their information points. The CLS are developing local networks of people giving legal assistance such as law centres, local solicitors or the Citizens Advice Bureaux. CLS Information Points are being set up in libraries and other public places. Litigants can telephone the CLS to find their nearest CLS Information Point on 0845 608 1122 or can log on to the CLS website at http://www.justask.org.uk for the CLS directory and for legal information.

QBG 2.1.9

2.1.9 The RCJ Advice Bureau off the Main Hall at the Royal Courts of Justice is open Monday to Friday from 10.00am to 1.00pm and from 2.00pm to 5.00pm. The Bureau is run by lawyers in conjunction with the Citizens Advice Bureau and is independent of the court. It is also a registered Charity No 1050358. The Bureau operates on a 'first come first served' basis, or telephone advice is available on 0845 120 3715 Monday to Friday from 11.00am to 12.00pm and from 3.00pm to 4.00pm.

2.2 Inspection and copies of documents

QBG 2.2.1

2.2.1 Intending claimants must not expect to be able to keep the details of a claim away from public scrutiny. In addition to the right of a party to obtain copies of documents in the proceedings to which s/he is a party from the court record (on payment of the prescribed fee), (see CPR 5.4B), any person may obtain from the court records a copy of a claim form when it has been served, and the particulars of claim but not documents attached to the particulars of claim. This applies to claims issued from 2 October 2006. For claims issued before that date particulars of claim may only be inspected or copied where they are included in or served with the claim form, on request and payment of the appropriate fee. Any judgment or order made in public (whether made at a hearing or without a hearing) may also be obtained from the records of the court on payment of the appropriate fee. Additionally, under CPR 5.4 other specified documents may be obtained with the permission of the court, upon making an application in accordance with Part 23.

QBG 2.2.2

2.2.2 Witness statements used at trial are open to inspection, at the time of the trial, unless the court directs otherwise. Considerations of publicity are often particularly important in deciding whether to commence proceedings in respect of an alleged libel or slander; such a claim may, by its attendant publicity, do more damage than was ever inflicted by the original publication. In such proceedings the claimant may decide to serve his/her particulars of claim separately from the claim form, in which case they are not open to inspection by non-parties, without the permission of the court.

QBG 2.2.3

2.2.3 CPR 5.4(7) gives details of where the court, on application by a party or person identified in the claim form, may restrict inspection and obtaining of copies.

2.3 Time limits

QBG 2.3.1

2.3.1 There are strict time limits that apply to every claim. First, there are time limits fixed by the Limitation Act 1980 [and some other Statutes, such as the Human Rights Act 1998 and the Defamation Act 1996] within which proceedings must be brought. There are circumstances in which the court may extend those time limits, but this should be regarded as exceptional. In all other cases, once the relevant time limit has expired, it is rarely possible to start a claim.

QBG 2.3.2

2.3.2 Secondly, in order to try and bring the proceedings to an early trial date, a timetable will be set with which all parties must comply. Unless the CPR or a Practice Direction provides otherwise, or the court orders otherwise, the timetable may be varied by the written agreement of the parties. However, there are certain 'milestone' events in the timetable for which the parties may not vary the time limits. Examples of these are;

(1)   return of the Allocation Questionnaire/Reply to Defence, which should be returned together with the Allocation Questionnaire

(2)   date for the case management conference

(3)   return of the Pre Trial Checklist

(4)   date fixed for trial.

(5)   Defence when time has elapsed following the days from service of Particulars of Claim on the Defendant (CPR 15.5)

Where parties have extended a time limit by agreement, the party for whom the time has been extended must advise the Registry Section in writing of the appropriate event in the proceedings for which the time has been extended and the new date by which it must be done. For example, if an extension is agreed for the filing of the defence, it is for the defendant to inform the Registry Section.

QBG 2.3.3

2.3.3 The court has power to impose a sanction on any party who fails to comply with a time limit. If the court considers that a prior warning should be given before a sanction is imposed, it will make an 'unless' order; in other words, the court will order that, unless that party performs his/her obligation by the time specified, s/he will be penalised in the manner set out in the order. This may involve the party in default having his/her claim or statement of case struck out and judgment given against him. An Order striking out a claim or statement of case must be applied for after the time specified has expired, as this is not automatic unless the Unless Order so provides.

2.4 Legal representation

QBG 2.4.1

2.4.1 A party may act in person or be represented by a lawyer. A party who is acting in person may be assisted at any hearing by another person (often referred to as a McKenzie friend) subject to the discretion of the Court. The McKenzie friend is allowed to help by taking notes, quietly prompting the litigant and offering advice and suggestions. The litigant however, must conduct his/her own case; the McKenzie friend may not represent him and may only in very exceptional circumstances be allowed to address the court on behalf of the litigant (see s.27(2)(c) of the Courts and Legal Services Act 1990).

QBG 2.4.2

2.4.2 A written statement should be provided to the court at any hearing concerning the representation of the parties in accordance with paragraph 5.1 of the Part 39 Practice Direction (the Court Record Form, found outside the Masters' Rooms or in the Bear Garden).

QBG 2.4.3

2.4.3 At a trial, a company or corporation may be represented by an employee if the company or corporation authorises him to do so and the court gives permission. Where this is to be the case, the permission of the Judge who is to hear the case may be sought informally; paragraph 5 of the Part 39 Practice Direction describes what is needed to obtain permission from the court for this purpose and mentions some of the considerations relevant to the grant or refusal of permission. A further statement concerning representation should be provided in accordance with paragraph 5.2 of the Part 39 Practice Direction.

QBG 2.4.4

2.4.4 Experienced outdoor clerks from solicitors firms are permitted to appear before the Masters. Barristers' clerks may attend before a Master to fix a hearing date for Counsel.

The Personal Support Unit (PSU) is an independent charity, which supports litigants-in-person, witnesses, victims, their family members and other supporters attending the Royal Courts. There are now nearly 100 fully trained and experienced volunteers. Requests vary from the very simple to the complex. Some people just require directions or advice about procedures. Others need to unburden themselves, while others request the moral and emotional support of being accompanied in court. The PSU can be particularly helpful for clients with special needs.

The PSU

Room M104

Royal Courts of Justice

Strand

WC2A 2LL

Tel: 020 7947 7701/3 Fax: 020 7947 7702 email: mailto://rcj@thepsu.co.uk *or:* http://www.thepsu.co.uk.

2.5 Costs

QBG 2.5.1

2.5.1 Costs are dealt with in Parts 43 to 48. There are important provisions in the costs rules, particularly with respect to;
(1)   informing the client of costs orders,
(2)   providing the court with estimates of costs,

(3)   summary assessment of costs,

(4)   interim orders for costs, and

(5)   interest on costs.

QBG 2.5.2

2.5.2 Solicitors have a duty under Rule 44.2 to notify their client within 7 days if an order for costs is made against him in his/her absence. Solicitors must also notify any other person who has instructed them to act in the proceedings or who is liable to pay their fees (such as an insurer, trade union or the Legal Services Commission (LSC)). They must also inform these persons how the order came to be made (paragraphs 7.1 and 7.2 of the Costs Practice Direction).

QBG 2.5.3

2.5.3 The court may at any stage order any party to file an estimate of base costs (substantially in the form of Precedent H in the Schedule of Costs Precedents annexed to the Costs Practice Direction) and serve copies on all the other parties (paragraph 6.3 of the Costs Practice Direction). This will both assist the court in deciding what case management directions to make and inform the other parties as to their potential liability for payment of costs.

QBG 2.5.4

2.5.4 If a party seeks an order for his/her costs, in order to assist the court in making a summary assessment, s/he must prepare a written statement of the costs s/he intends to claim in accordance with paragraph 13.5 of the Costs Practice Direction, following as closely as possible Form N260. In addition, when an Allocation Questionnaire or a Pre Trial Checklist is filed, the party filing it must file and serve an estimate of costs on all the other parties.

QBG 2.5.4 [1]
Editorial Note. For a precedent of estimates of costs see **BCCP E [1501]**.

QBG 2.5.5

2.5.5 If the parties have agreed the amount of costs, they do not need to file a statement of the costs, and summary assessment is unnecessary. Or, where the parties agree a consent order without any party attending on the application, the parties should insert either an agreed figure for costs or that there should be no order for costs in the order (paragraph 13.4 of the Costs Practice Direction).

QBG 2.5.6

2.5.6 Unless the court decides not to order an assessment of costs where, for example, it orders costs to be 'costs in the case', it may either make a summary assessment of costs or order a detailed assessment to take place. The court will generally make a summary assessment of costs at any hearing, which lasts for less than one day;

(1)   'summary assessment' is where the court, when making an order for costs, assesses those costs and orders payment of a sum of money in respect of them, and

(2)   'detailed assessment' is the procedure by which the amount of costs is decided by a Costs Judge or Costs Officer at a later date in accordance with Part 47.

The provision of summary assessment means that the paying party is likely to be paying the costs at an earlier stage than s/he would have done under the previous rules (and see paragraph 2.5.15 below).

QBG 2.5.7

2.5.7 The court will not make a summary assessment of the costs of a receiving party (the party to whom the costs are to be paid) where s/he is;

(1)   a child or patient within the meaning of Part 21 unless the solicitor acting for the child or patient has waived the right to further costs, or

(2)   an assisted person or a person in receipt of funded services under sections 4-11 of the Access to Justice Act 1999.

The costs payable by a party who is an assisted person or a person in receipt of funded services may be summarily assessed as the assessment is not by itself a determination of the assisted person's ability to pay those costs.

QBG 2.5.8

2.5.8 Rule 44.3A prevents the court from assessing an additional liability in respect of a funding agreement before the conclusion of the proceedings. At an interim hearing therefore, the court will assess only the base costs. (See paragraph 14.9 of the Costs Practice Direction for assessing an additional liability and Section 19 for information about funding arrangements.)

QBG 2.5.9

2.5.9 Interim orders for costs; where the court decides immediately who is to pay particular costs, but does not assess the costs summarily, for example after a trial lasting more than a day, so that the final amount of costs payable has to be fixed at a detailed assessment, the court may order the paying party to pay a sum or sums on account of the ultimate liability for costs.

QBG 2.5.10

2.5.10 Interest on costs; the court has power to award interest on costs from a date before the date of the order, so compensating the receiving party for the delay between incurring the costs and receiving payment in respect of them.

QBG 2.5.11

2.5.11 Parties should note that where the court makes an order, which does not mention costs, no party is entitled to costs in relation to that order.

QBG 2.5.12

2.5.12 Rule 44.3 describes the court's discretion as to costs and the circumstances to be taken into account when exercising its discretion. Rules 44.4 and 44.5 set out the basis of assessment and the factors to be taken into account in deciding the amount of costs. (See also Sections 8 and 11 of the Costs Practice Direction.)

QBG 2.5.13

2.5.13 The amount of costs to be paid by one party to another may be ordered to be assessed on the standard basis or on the indemnity basis. The basis to be used is decided when the court decides that a party should pay the costs of another. Costs that are unreasonably incurred or are unreasonable in amount are not allowed on either basis.

QBG 2.5.14

2.5.14 The standard basis is the usual basis for assessment where only costs which are proportionate to the matters in issue, are allowed, and any doubt as to whether the costs were reasonably incurred or reasonable and proportionate in amount is resolved in favour of the paying party. On the indemnity basis, any such doubts are resolved in favour of the receiving party.

QBG 2.5.15

2.5.15 A party must normally pay summarily assessed costs awarded against him within 14 days of the assessment, but the court can extend that time, direct payment by instalments, or defer the liability to pay the costs until the end of the proceedings so that they can then be set off against any costs or judgment to which the paying party becomes entitled.

QBG 2.5.16

2.5.16 Fixed costs relating to default judgments, certain judgments on admissions and summary judgments etc. are set out in Part 45, (see also Section 25 of the Costs Practice Direction). Part 46 relates to fast track costs.

QBG 2.5.17

2.5.17 Part 47 and Sections 28 to 49 of the Costs Practice Direction contain the procedure for detailed assessment together with the default provisions. Precedents A,B,C and D set out in the Schedule of Costs Precedents annexed to the Costs Practice Direction are model forms of bills of costs for detailed assessment. Section 43 deals with costs payable out of the Community Legal Service fund, Section 44 deals with costs payable out of a fund other than the CLS fund and Section 49 deals with costs payable by the LSC. Part 48 and Sections 50 to 56 of the Costs Practice Direction deal with Special Cases, In particular;

(1)   costs payable by or to a child or patient,

(2)   litigants in person, (see CPR 48.6 The costs allowed under this rule must not exceed, except in the case of a disbursement, two-thirds of the amount which would have been allowed if the litigant in person had been represented by a legal representative) and

(3)   wasted costs orders- personal liability of the legal representative.

QBG 2.5.18

2.5.18 Costs only proceedings are dealt with in Rule 44.12A and Section 17 of the Costs Practice Direction. They may be brought in the High Court only where the dispute was of such a value or type that had proceedings been brought they would have been commenced in the High Court. Proceedings are brought under Part 8 by the issue of a Claim Form in the Supreme Court Costs Office at Clifford's Inn, Fetter Lane, London EC4A 1DQ. (See also paragraphs 4.1.16 and 6.8.13 below.)

2.6 Court fees

QBG 2.6.1

2.6.1 The fees payable in the High Court as from 10 January 2006 are set out in Schedule 1 to the Civil Proceedings Fees Order 2004. Fees relating to the Queen's Bench Division are listed in Annex 1 to the Guide.

QBG 2.6.2

2.6.2 In the Royal Courts of Justice fees are paid in the Fees Room E01 and by way of receipt for the fee, it is usually stamped on the document to which they relate.

2.7 Information Technology

QBG 2.7.1

2.7.1 To support the work of the Central Office in operating the provisions of the CPR, and to facilitate effective case management there is a limited computerised system to provide a record of proceedings and to produce some court forms and orders.

QBG 2.7.2

2.7.2 A number of specific applications of information technology have been well developed in recent years; the use of fax, the provision of skeleton arguments on disk and daily transcripts on disk have become more commonplace. Short applications may be dealt with more economically by a conference telephone call, and taking evidence by video link has become more common and the available technology has improved considerably. The CPR contains certain provisions about the use of information technology, for example, Part 6 and the Part 6 Practice Direction deal with service of documents by Fax or other electronic means, the Part 23 Practice Direction refers to telephone hearings and video conferencing, Rule 32.3 allows the use of evidence given by video link and the Part 5 Practice Direction refers to the filing of documents at court by Fax.

QBG 2.7.3

2.7.3 Parties may agree to use information technology in the preparation, management and presentation of a case; however the agreement of the Judge or Master should be sought before providing the court with material in electronic form. Where permission has been given by a specific Master, the material for use at a hearing or in support of an application can be provided on a CD-Rom or in some cases by e-mail. The parties should check with the court which word-processing format should be used. This will normally be Word 6 or in some cases in PDF format.

QBG 2.7.4

2.7.4 A protocol has been prepared as a guide to all persons who are involved in the use of video conferencing equipment in civil proceedings in the High Court. It covers its use in courtrooms where the equipment may be installed, and also the situation where the court assembles in a commercial studio or conference room containing video conferencing equipment. Copies of the Video- conferencing Protocol may be obtained from the Bar Council at a charge of £2.50 to cover expenses.

3 STEPS BEFORE ISSUE OF A CLAIM FORM

3.1 Settlement

QBG 3.1.1

3.1.1 So far as reasonably possible, a claimant should try to resolve his/her claim without litigation. The court is increasingly taking the view that litigation should be a last resort and parties may wish to consider the use of Alternative Dispute Resolution ('ADR'). (See paragraph 6.6 below.)

QBG 3.1.2

3.1.2 There are codes of practice for preliminary negotiations in certain types of claim. These codes of practice are called 'Protocols' and are set out in a schedule to the Protocols Practice Direction to the CPR. Even if there is no protocol that applies to the claim, the parties will nonetheless be expected to comply with the spirit of the Overriding Objective (see paragraph 4 of the Protocols Practice Direction).

QBG 3.1.3

3.1.3 An offer to settle a claim may be made by either party whether before or after a claim is brought. The court will take account of any offer to settle made before proceedings are started when making any order as to costs after proceedings have started.

3.2 Disclosure before proceedings are started

QBG 3.2.1

3.2.1 An intending claimant may need documents to which s/he does not yet have access. If the documents are not disclosed voluntarily, in accordance with the Pre Action Protocols, then Rule 31.16 sets out the provisions for making an application for disclosure of documents before proceedings have started. An Application Notice under Part 23 is required together with the appropriate fee. This may be issued in the Registry Section, Room E07 and will be assigned to a Master for hearing.

QBG 3.2.2

3.2.2 Essentially, the court must be satisfied that the applicant and respondent to the application are likely to be parties when proceedings are brought, that the required documents are those that the respondent would be required to disclose under Rule 31.6 when proceedings are brought and that their early disclosure might dispose of or assist the disposal of anticipated proceedings or save costs.

3.3 Defamation proceedings: Offer of Amends

QBG 3.3.1

3.3.1 Application may be made to the court before a claim is brought for the court's assistance in accepting an offer of amends under section 3 of the Defamation Act 1996. The application is made by Part 8 Claim Form. For more information see paragraph 4.1.15 (Part 8 procedure) and paragraph 8.1 defamation below.

4 STARTING PROCEEDINGS IN THE CENTRAL OFFICE

4.1 Issuing the claim form

QBG 4.1.1

4.1.1 All claims must be started by issuing a Claim Form. The great majority of claims involve a dispute of fact, and the Claim Form should be issued in accordance with Part 7 of the CPR. The Part 8 procedure may be followed in the types of claim described in paragraphs 4.1.14 to 4.1.16 below.

QBG 4.1.2

4.1.2 The requirements for issuing a Claim Form are set out in Part 7 and the Part 7 Practice Direction, the main points of which are summarised in the following paragraphs.

QBG 4.1.3

4.1.3 The Practice Direction at paragraphs 2, 3 and 4 provides information as to;

(1)   where a claim should be started,

(2)   certain matters that must be included in the Claim Form, and

(3)   how the heading of the claim should be set out on the Claim Form.

In defamation cases, Part 53 and the Part 53 Practice Direction sets out matters that should be included in the Claim Form and particulars of claim. See also paragraph 12.7 below.

QBG 4.1.4

4.1.4 Proceedings are started when the court issues a Claim Form, and a Claim Form is issued on the date sealed on the Claim Form by the court. However, where a Claim Form is received in the court office on an earlier date than the date of issue, then, for the purposes of the Limitation Act 1980, the claim is brought on the earlier date (see paragraphs 5.1 to 5.4 of the Part 7 Practice Direction).

QBG 4.1.5

4.1.5 To start proceedings in the Action Department, a claimant must use form N1 (or form N208 for a Part 8 claim) (or a form suitably modified as permitted by Part 4), and should take or send the Claim Form to Room E07, Registry Section, Action Department, Central Office, Royal Courts of Justice, Strand, London WC2A 2LL. If the court is to serve the Claim Form, the claimant must provide sufficient copies for each defendant. The Claimant will be required to provide a Court copy, a Claimant's copy and one copy for each named Defendant. Copies of practice forms relevant to the work of the Action Department (including the Claim Form and Response Pack) are available from that office. Alternatively, claimants may produce their own forms, which may be modified as the circumstances require, provided that all essential information, especially any information or guidance that the form gives to the recipient, is included. (See Part 4 Forms.)

QBG 4.1.6

4.1.6 On issuing the Claim Form, the court will give or send the claimant a notice of issue endorsed with the date of issue of the Claim Form. If the claimant requires the court to serve the Claim Form, the date of posting and deemed date of service will also be endorsed on the notice of issue. Claimants and especially their solicitors who use the Action Department, are encouraged to serve their own documents but must inform the court when service has been effected (see paragraph 4.2.4 in relation to service by the claimant and the certificate of service). For certain types of claims, the notice of issue contains a request for judgment. (See paragraph 5 below for information about default judgments.)

QBG 4.1.7

4.1.7 A Claim Form must be served within 4 months after the date of issue (Rule 7.5) unless it is to be served out of the jurisdiction, when the period is 6 months; and Rule 7.6 and paragraph 7 of the Practice Direction set out how and on what grounds an extension of time for service of the Claim Form may be sought. (See Section 4.2 below about service.)

4.2 Particulars of Claim

QBG 4.2.1

4.2.1 The particulars of claim may be;

(1) included in the Claim Form, (if served as part of the Claim Form they are available to be copied for any person under CPR 5.4 – see para. 2.2 above)

(2) in a separate document served with the Claim Form, or

(3) in a separate document served within 14 days of service of the Claim Form provided that the particulars of claim are served within the latest time for serving the Claim Form.

QBG 4.2.2

4.2.2 A Claim Form that does not include particulars of claim must nonetheless contain a concise statement of the nature of the claim. Any Claim Form and/or Particulars of Claim that

(1) does not comply with the requirements of rule 16.2, or 16.4 or

(2) is garbled or abusive,

will be referred to a Master and is likely to be struck out by the court.

QBG 4.2.3

4.2.3 Where the particulars of claim are neither included in or served with the Claim Form;

(1) the Claim Form must contain a statement that particulars of claim will follow, and

(2) the particulars of claim must be served by the claimant and a copy then filed at the court together with a Certificate of Service (CPR 7.4(3))

However, where a Claim Form is to be served out of the jurisdiction, the particulars of claim, if not included in the claim form, must accompany it. (See paragraph 4.2.13 below.)

QBG 4.2.4

4.2.4 Certain forms must accompany the particulars of claim when they are served on the defendant. These forms are listed in Rule 7.8 and are included in a Response Pack, which is available from the Action Department.

QBG 4.2.5

4.2.5 A party who has entered into a funding arrangement and who wishes to claim an additional liability must give the Court and any other party information about that claim if s/he is to recover the additional liability. Where the funding arrangement has been entered into before proceedings are commenced, the claimant should file a notice of funding in form N251 when the Claim Form is issued.

QBG 4.2.6

4.2.6 Part 22 requires the Claim Form and particulars of claim to be verified by a statement of truth, and where the particulars of claim are not included in the Claim Form itself, these are to be separately verified by a statement of truth; see paragraph 6 of the Part 7 Practice Direction, and the Part 22 Practice Direction.

QBG 4.2.7

4.2.7 Part 16 and the Part 16 Practice Direction deal with statements of case, and in particular the contents of the Claim Form and the particulars of claim. Part 16 does not apply to claims in respect of which the Part 8 alternative procedure for claims is being used. See paragraph 5.6 below for more about statements of case. Note the requirements in relation to personal injury claims, fatal accident claims, hire purchase claims and recovery of land or goods.

4.3 Part 8 procedure

QBG 4.3.1

4.3.1 A claimant may use the Part 8 procedure where;

(1)   s/he seeks the court's decision on a question that is unlikely to involve a substantial dispute of fact, or

(2)   a Rule or Practice Direction requires or permits the use of the Part 8 procedure,

however, the court may at any stage order the claim to continue as if the claimant had not used the Part 8 procedure.

QBG 4.3.2

4.3.2 Certain matters that must be included on the Claim Form when the Part 8 procedure is being used are set out in Rule 8.2. The types of claim for which the Part 8 procedure may be used include;

(1)   a claim by or against a child or patient that has been settled before the commencement of proceedings, the sole purpose of the claim being to obtain the approval of the court to the settlement,

(2)   a claim for provisional damages that has been settled before the commencement of proceedings, the sole purpose of the claim being to obtain a judgment by consent,

(3)   a claim under s. 3 of the Defamation Act 1996 (made other than in existing proceedings), and

(4)   a claim under Rule 44.12A where the parties have agreed all issues before the commencement of proceedings except the amount of costs and an order for costs is required.

QBG 4.3.3

4.3.3 In addition to the provisions of Rule 8.1, attention is drawn also to the Part 8(B) Practice Direction which deals with proceedings brought under 'the Schedule Rules'.

See Paragraph 6.7 below for more information regarding the Part 8 procedure.

4.4 Service

QBG 4.4.1

4.4.1 Service of documents is dealt with in Part 6; Section I (Rules 6.1 to 6.11) contains provisions relating to service generally and Section II (Rules 6.12 to 6.16) contains special provisions relating to service of the Claim Form. Section III (Rules 6.17 to 6.31) deals with service out of the jurisdiction. Some of the more important provisions are described below.

Within the jurisdiction

QBG 4.4.2

4.4.2 The methods by which a document may be served are to be found in Rule 6.2. The court will serve a document that it has issued or prepared unless;

(1)   the party on whose behalf it is to be served notifies the court that s/he wishes to serve it himself,

(2)   the court orders otherwise, or

(3)   a Rule or Practice Direction provides otherwise.

It is anticipated that practitioners familiar with Central Office procedures will wish to continue to serve their own documents.

QBG 4.4.3

4.4.3 Where a party has entered into a funding agreement the notice of funding (form N251) must be served on all the other parties. If a claimant files his/her notice of funding when his/her Claim Form is issued, the Court will serve it on the other parties provided sufficient copies are provided. Otherwise the claimant must serve the notice of funding with the Claim Form. A defendant should file his/her notice of funding with his/her first document, i.e. his/her defence or acknowledgement of service etc. Sufficient copies of the notice should be provided for the Court to serve.

QBG 4.4.4

4.4.4 In all other circumstances a party must serve a notice of funding within 7 days of entering into the funding agreement.

QBG 4.4.5

4.4.5 Where the court has tried to serve a document but has been unable to serve it, the court will send a notice of non-service to the party on whose behalf it was to be served stating the method attempted. On receipt of this notice, the party should take steps to serve the document himself, as the court is under no further duty to effect service. The method of service used by the court will normally be first-class post.

QBG 4.4.6

4.4.6 Where a claimant has served a Claim Form, s/he must file a certificate of service that complies with the provisions of Rule 6.10. The certificate of service must be filed within 7 days of service of the Claim Form, and the claimant may not obtain judgment in default if it has not been filed.

QBG 4.4.7

4.4.7 Information as to how personal service is to be effected and as to service by electronic means is to be found in the Part 6 Practice Direction. Rule 6.6 deals with service on a child or patient.

QBG 4.4.8

4.4.8 A party must give an address for service within the jurisdiction (i.e. in England or Wales). Rule 6.5 contains information as to the address for service.

QBG 4.4.9

4.4.9 A party may make an application for permission to serve a document by an alternative method to those set out in Rule 6.2. The application may be made without notice, and paragraph 9.1 of the Practice Direction sets out the evidence that will be required in support of the application. (Paragraph 7.12 below contains information in relation to applications.)

Out of the jurisdiction

QBG 4.4.10

4.4.10 The provisions for service out of the jurisdiction are contained in Rules 6.17 to 6.31. Rule 6.19 sets out the provisions whereby a Claim Form may be served out of the jurisdiction without the permission of the court, and Rule 6.20 sets out the circumstances where the court's permission is required. Parties should also see the Practice Direction on service out of the jurisdiction.

QBG 4.4.11

4.4.11 A claimant may issue a Claim Form against defendants, one or some of whom appear to be out of the jurisdiction, without first having obtained permission for service out of the jurisdiction, provided that where the Claim Form is not one which may be served without the permission of the court under Rule 6.19, the Claim Form is endorsed by the court that it is 'not for service out of jurisdiction'.

QBG 4.4.12

4.4.12 Where a Claim Form is to be served in accordance with Rule 6.19 it must contain a statement of the grounds on which the claimant is entitled to serve it out of the jurisdiction. (See 6BPD.2). The statement should be as follows;

(1)

'I, (name) state that the High Court of England and Wales has power under the Civil Jurisdiction and Judgments Act 1982 to hear this claim and that no proceedings are pending between the parties in Scotland, Northern Ireland or another Convention territory of any contracting state as defined by section 1(3) of the Act.', or

(2) where the proceedings are those to which Article 16 of Schedule 1, 3C or 4 to the Act refers,

'I, (name) state that the High Court of England and Wales has power under the Civil Jurisdiction and Judgments Act 1982, the claim having as its object rights in rem in immovable property or tenancies in immovable property (or otherwise in accordance with the provisions of Article 16 of Schedule 1, 3C or 4 to that Act) to which Article 16 of Schedule 1, 3C or 4 to that Act applies, to hear the claim and that no proceedings are pending between the parties in Scotland, Northern Ireland or another Convention territory of any contracting state as defined by section 1(3) of the Act.', or

(3) where the defendant is party to an agreement conferring jurisdiction to which Article 17 of Schedule 1, 3C or 4 to that Act applies,

'I, (name) state that the High Court of England and Wales has power under the Civil Jurisdiction and Judgments Act 1982, the defendant being a party to an agreement conferring jurisdiction to which Article 17 of Schedule 1, 3C or 4 to that Act applies, to hear the claim and that no proceedings are pending between the parties in Scotland, Northern Ireland or another Convention territory of any contracting state as defined by section 1(3) of the Act.'.

(4) where the Judgments Regulation applies (except where Articles 22 or 23 of the Regulation, or Rule 6.19(2) applies),

'I, (name) state that the High Court of England and Wales has power under Council Regulation (EC) No 44/2001 of 22nd December 2000 (on jurisdiction and the recognition and enforcement of judgments in civil and commercial matters) to hear this claim and that no proceedings are pending between the parties in Scotland, Northern Ireland or any other Regulation state as defined by section 1(3) of the Civil Jurisdiction and Judgments Act 1982'

(5) where Article 22 of the Judgments Regulation applies,

'I, (name) state that the High Court of England and Wales has power under Council Regulation (EC) No 44/2001 of 22nd December 2000 (on jurisdiction and the recognition and enforcement of judgments in civil and commercial matters), the claim having as its object rights in rem in immovable property or tenancies in immovable property (or otherwise in accordance with the provisions of Article 22 of that Regulation) to which Article 22 of that Regulation applies, to hear this claim and that no proceedings are pending between the parties in Scotland, Northern Ireland or any other Regulation state as defined by section 1(3) of the Civil Jurisdiction and Judgments Act 1982'

(6) where Article 23 of the Judgments Regulation applies,

'I, (name) state that the High Court of England and Wales has power under Council Regulation (EC) No 44/2001 of 22nd December 2000 (on jurisdiction and the recognition and enforcement of judgments in civil and commercial matters), the defendant being party to an agreement conferring jurisdiction to which Article 23 of that Regulation applies, to hear this claim and that no proceedings are pending between the parties in Scotland, Northern Ireland or any other Regulation state as defined by section 1(3) of the Civil Jurisdiction and Judgments Act 1982'

(7) where Rule 6.19(2) applies,

'I, (name) state that the High Court of England and Wales has power to hear this claim under [state the provisions of the relevant enactment] which satisfies the requirements of rule 6.19(2), and that no proceedings are pending between the parties in Scotland, Northern Ireland, or in another Contracting State or Regulation State as defined by section 1(3) of the Civil Jurisdiction and Judgments Act 1982'

QBG 4.4.13

4.4.13 The statement should be signed and have set out the full name of the signatory. If a Claim Form as specified in paragraph 4.2.10 above does not bear the appropriate above statement, the Claim Form will be endorsed 'not for service out of the jurisdiction'.

QBG 4.4.14

4.4.14 An application for an order for permission to issue a Claim Form for service out of the jurisdiction or to serve the Claim Form out of the jurisdiction should be made in accordance with Part 23 (form PF 6(A) may be used). The application must be supported by written evidence, and may be made without notice. The written evidence should state the requirements set out in Rule 6.21(1) and (2).

QBG 4.4.15

4.4.15 An order giving permission for service out of the jurisdiction should be in form PF 6(B) and will;

(1)   specify the country in which, or place at which, service is to be effected, and

(2)   specify the number of days within which the defendant may either

     (a)   file an acknowledgement of service,

     (b)   file or serve an admission, or

     (c)   file a defence to

the claim, and where an acknowledgement of service is filed, specify a further 14 days within which the defendant may file a defence. {This information can be found in the Table in the Practice Direction to Part 6 (6BPD.11}

QBG 4.4.16

4.4.16 Where service is to be effected in a country which requires a translation of the documents to be served, it is the claimant's responsibility to provide the translation of all the documents for each defendant. In every case, it is the claimant's duty to ensure that the Response Pack clearly states the appropriate period for responding to the Claim Form, and form N9, form N1C and other relevant forms must be modified accordingly. Every translation must be accompanied by a statement by the person making it;

(1)   that it is a correct translation, and

(2)   including the person's name, address and qualifications for making the translation.

QBG 4.4.17

4.4.17 The periods for acknowledging service of a Claim Form served out of the jurisdiction are set out in Rule 6.22 and in the Table contained in the Part 6 Section III Practice Direction, and the periods for serving a defence to a Claim Form served out of the jurisdiction are set out in Rule 6.23 and in the Table in the Practice Direction. Rule 6.24 describes the methods of service.

QBG 4.4.18

4.4.18 Where the Claim Form is to be served through;

(1)   the judicial authorities of the country where the Claim Form is to be served,

(2)   a British Consular authority in that country,

(3)   the authority designated under the Hague Convention in respect of that country, or

(4)   the Government of that country, or

(5)   where the court permits service on a State, the Foreign and Commonwealth Office,

(6)   the Receiving Agency designated under Regulation (EC) 1348/2000

the claimant should provide the Senior Master with the following documents by forwarding them to the Foreign Process section, Room E 10;

(a)   a request for service by the chosen method (in form PF 7),

(b)   a sealed copy and a duplicate copy of the Claim Form,

(c)   the Response Pack as referred to in paragraph 4.2.14,

(d)   a translation in duplicate, and the statement referred to in paragraph 4.2.13, and

(e)   any other relevant documents.

QBG 4.4.19

4.4.19 Where service has been requested in accordance with paragraph 4.2.16, the particulars of claim, if not included in the Claim Form, must accompany the

Claim Form (in duplicate). Where the claimant is effecting service of the Claim Form direct (and not as in paragraph 4.2.16) and the Claim Form states that particulars of claim are to follow, the permission of the court is not required to serve the particulars of claim out of the jurisdiction.

QBG 4.4.20

4.4.20 Where an official certificate of service is received in a foreign language, it is the responsibility of the claimant to obtain a translation of the certificate. Where a defendant served out of the jurisdiction fails to attend a hearing, the official certificate of service is evidence of service. Otherwise the claimant may take no further steps against the defendant until written evidence showing that the Claim Form has been duly served is filed.

QBG 4.4.21

4.4.21 Further advice on service out of the jurisdiction may be obtained from the Foreign Process Section, Room E10.

5 RESPONSE TO A PART 7 CLAIM

5.1 General

QBG 5.1.1

5.1.1 Responding to particulars of claim is dealt with in Part 9. A defendant may respond to the service of particulars of claim by;

(1)   filing or serving an admission in accordance with Part 14,

(2)   filing a defence in accordance with Part 15,

(3)   doing both if part only of the claim is admitted, or

(4)   filing an acknowledgement of service in accordance with Part 10.

QBG 5.1.2

5.1.2 Where a defendant receives a Claim Form that states that particulars of claim are to follow, s/he need not respond to the claim until the particulars of claim have been served on him.

QBG 5.1.3

5.1.3 If a defendant fails to;

(1)   file an acknowledgement of service within the time specified in rule 10.3, and

(2)   file a defence within the time specified in Rule 15.4, or

(3)   file or serve an admission in accordance with Part 14

the claimant may obtain default judgment if Part 12 allows it. (See paragraph 5.5 below for information about default judgments.)

5.2 Acknowledgement of service

QBG 5.2.1

5.2.1 Acknowledgements of service are dealt with in Part 10. A defendant may file an acknowledgement of service if;

(1)   s/he is unable to file a defence within the period specified in Rule 15.4, or

(2)   s/he wishes to dispute the court's jurisdiction. (CPR 11.7).

Filing an acknowledgement of service extends the time for filing the defence by 14 days.

QBG 5.2.2

5.2.2 A defendant who wishes to acknowledge service of a Claim Form should do so by using form N9. Rule 10.5 states that the acknowledgement of service must;

(1)   be signed by the defendant or his/her legal representative, and

(2)   include the defendant's address for service which must be within the jurisdiction of the court (CPR 6.5)

The Part 10 Practice Direction contains information relating to the acknowledgement of service and how it may be signed.

5.3 Admissions

QBG 5.3.1

5.3.1 The manner in which a defendant may make an admission of a claim or part of a claim is set out in Rules 14.1 and 14.2, and Rules 14.3 to 14.7 set out how judgment may be obtained on a written admission.

QBG 5.3.2

5.3.2 Included in the Response Pack that will accompany the Claim Form when it is served on the defendant, is an admission form (form N9A for a specified amount and form N9C for an unspecified amount). If the defendant makes an admission and requests time to pay, s/he should complete as fully as possible the statement of means contained in the admission form, or otherwise give in writing the same details of his/her means as could have been given in the admission form.

QBG 5.3.3

5.3.3 Where the defendant has;

(1)   made an admission in respect of a specified sum and requested time to pay, or

(2)   made an admission in respect of an unspecified sum, offered a sum in satisfaction (which is accepted) and requested time to pay,

and the claimant has not accepted the request for time to pay, on receipt of the claimant's notice the court will enter judgment for the amount admitted or offered (less any payments made) to be paid at the time and rate of payment determined by the court.

QBG 5.3.4

5.3.4 Where the defendant has;

(1)   made an admission for an unspecified amount, or

(2)   made an admission for an unspecified amount and offered in satisfaction a sum that the claimant has not accepted,

on receipt of the claimant's request for judgment the court will enter judgment for an amount to be decided by the court and costs.

QBG 5.3.5

5.3.5 The matters that the court will take into account when determining the time and rate of payment are set out in paragraph 5.1 of the Part 14 Practice Direction.

QBG 5.3.6

5.3.6 The court may determine the time and rate of payment with or without a hearing, but, where a hearing is to take place, the proceedings must, where the provisions of Rule 14.12(2) apply, be transferred to the defendant's home court. Where the Claim Form was issued in the Royal Courts of Justice the defendant's home court will be the district registry for the district in which the defendant's address given in the admission form is situated. If there is no such district registry the proceedings will remain in the Royal Courts of Justice.

QBG 5.3.7

5.3.7 The procedure for an application for re-determination of a decision determining the time and rate of payment is to be found in Rule 14.13 and paragraphs 5.3 to 5.6 of the Practice Direction.

QBG 5.3.8

5.3.8 Where judgment has been entered for an amount to be decided by the court and costs, the court will give any directions that it considers appropriate, which may include allocating the case to a track. (See paragraph 6.5 below about allocation.)

QBG 5.3.9

5.3.9 Judgment will not be entered on an admission where;

(1)   the defendant is a child or patient, or

(2)   the claimant is a child or patient and the admission is made in respect of

(a)   a specified amount of money, or

(b)   a sum offered in satisfaction of a claim for an unspecified amount of money.

See Part 21 and the Part 21 Practice Direction, and in particular Rule 21.10 which provides that, where a claim is made by or on behalf of a child or patient or against a child or patient, no settlement, compromise or payment shall be valid, so far as it relates to that person's claim, without the approval of the court.

5.4 Defence

QBG 5.4.1

5.4.1 A defendant who wishes to defend all or part of a claim must file a defence, and if s/he fails to do so, the claimant may obtain default judgment if Part 12 allows it. The time for filing a defence is set out in Rule 15.4.

QBG 5.4.2

5.4.2 A form for defending the claim is included in the Response Pack. The form for defending the claim also contains provision for making a counterclaim. Part 22 requires a defence to be verified by a statement of truth (see the Part 15 Practice Direction, paragraph 2; and see also Part 22 and the Part 22 Practice Direction).

QBG 5.4.3

5.4.3 The parties may, by agreement, extend the period specified in Rule 15.4 for filing a defence by up to 28 days. If the parties do so, the defendant must notify the court in writing of the date by which the defence must be filed. If the Claimant will not agree to extend time for filing of the Defence, or if a Defendant seeks further time beyond 28 days for filing a defence, the Defendant must issue an application (see Part 23) to obtain a court order for further time. A Claimant may consent to such an application.

5.5 Default judgment

QBG 5.5.1

5.5.1 A party may obtain default judgment under Part 12 except in the circumstances set out in Rules 12.2 and 12.3(3) and paragraphs 1.2 and 1.3 of the Part 12 Practice Direction, which list the circumstances where default judgment may not be obtained.

QBG 5.5.2

5.5.2 To obtain default judgment under the circumstances set out in Rules 12.4(1) and 12.9(1), a party may do so by filing a request. A court officer deals with a request and provided s/he is satisfied that the provisions of paragraph 4.1 of the Part 12 Practice Direction have been complied with, s/he will enter the default judgment.

QBG 5.5.3

5.5.3 Default judgment in respect of claims specified in Rules 12.4(2)(a), 12.9 and 12.10 must be obtained by making an application to a Master. The following are some of the types of claim that require an application for default judgment;

(1)   against children and patients,

(2)   for costs (other than fixed costs) only,

(3)   for declaratory relief,

(4)   by one spouse against the other on a claim in tort,

(5)   for delivery up of goods where the defendant is not allowed the alternative of paying their value,

(6)   against the Crown, and

(7)   against a foreign State, diplomatic agents or persons or organisations who enjoy immunity from civil jurisdiction under the provisions of the International Organisations Acts 1968 and 1981.

Paragraph 4 of the Practice Direction provides information about the evidence required in support of an application for default judgment.

QBG 5.5.4

5.5.4 Where default judgment has been obtained for an amount to be decided by the court, the matter will be referred to a Master for directions to be given concerning the management of the case and any date to be fixed for a hearing.

5.6 Statements of Case

QBG 5.6.1

5.6.1 Statements of case are defined in Rule 2.3(1) and comprise the particulars of claim and defence in the main proceedings and any further information given under Part 18 and also in any Part 20 proceedings, and any reply (which is optional); they are dealt with in Part 16. (Part 16 does not apply to claims proceeding under Part 8.)

QBG 5.6.2

5.6.2 The particulars of claim, whether contained in the Claim Form or served separately, should set out the claimant's claim clearly and fully. The same principle applies to the defence.

QBG 5.6.3

5.6.3 Part 16 sets out certain matters which must be included in a statement of case. Paragraphs 8 and 9 of the Part 16 Practice Direction contain matters, which should be included in the particulars of claim in specific types of claim, and paragraph 10 lists matters, which must be set out in the particulars of claim if relied on. In addition to the matters listed in paragraph 10, full particulars of any allegation of dishonesty or malice and, where any inference of fraud or dishonesty is alleged, the basis on which the inference is alleged should also be included. Points of law may be set out in any statement of case. For information in respect of statements of case in defamation claims see the Part 53 Practice Direction.

QBG 5.6.4

5.6.4 In addition to the information contained in Part 16 and the Part 16 Practice Direction, the following guidelines on preparing a statement of case should be followed;

(1)   a statement of case must be as brief and concise as possible and confined to setting out the bald facts and not the evidence of them,

(2)   a statement of case should be set out in separate consecutively numbered paragraphs and sub-paragraphs,

(3)   so far as possible each paragraph or sub-paragraph should contain no more than one allegation,

(4)   the facts and other matters alleged should be set out as far as reasonably possible in chronological order,

(5)   the statement of case should deal with the claim on a point-by-point basis, to allow a point-by-point response,

(6)   where a party is required to give reasons, the allegation should be stated first and then the reasons listed one by one in separate numbered sub-paragraphs,

(7)   a party wishing to advance a positive claim must identify that claim in the statement of case,

(8)   any matter which, if not stated, might take another party by surprise, should be stated,

(9)   where they will assist, headings, abbreviations and definitions should be used and a glossary annexed; contentious headings, abbreviations, para-phrasing and definitions should not be used and every effort should be made to ensure that they are in a form acceptable to the other parties,

(10)   particulars of primary allegations should be stated as particulars and not as primary allegations,

(11)   schedules or appendices should be used if this would be helpful, for example where lengthy particulars are necessary, and any response should also be stated in a schedule or appendix,

(12)   any lengthy extracts from documents should be placed in a schedule.

QBG 5.6.5

5.6.5 A statement of case should be verified by a statement of truth. If a party fails to verify his/her statement of case, it will remain effective unless struck out, but that party may not rely on the statement of case as evidence of any of the matters contained in it; a statement of case verified by a statement of truth is advisable as evidence only at hearings other than the trial (see Rule 32.6(2). Any party may apply to the court for an order to strike out a statement of case, which has not been verified.

6 PRELIMINARY CASE MANAGEMENT

6.1 The Practice Master

QBG 6.1.1

6.1.1 On every working day, the Practice Master is available from 10.30a.m. to 1.00p.m. and from 2.00p.m. to 4.30p.m. to answer questions about the practice of the Queen's Bench Division. Usually, one Master takes the Morning Practice, and another Master takes the Afternoon Practice. This will be shown on the Daily Cause List and is also on the notice boards in the Masters' corridors, and on the Listing Notice board outside The Masters Support Unit, Room E16. Also, a board is placed on the door of the Master who is sitting as Practice Master.(NOTE: the Practice Master will finish at 12 noon on those days where the High Court Enforcement Officers Interpleader list is listed- this usually takes place on the first Monday in each month).

QBG 6.1.2

6.1.2 The Practice Master cannot give advice, whether about a given case or about the law generally, s/he is there simply to answer general questions about the CPR and practice governing the work of the Queen's Bench Division, and can deal with any consent order, notwithstanding that the claim in which it is to be made has been assigned to another Master. The Practice Master may grant stays of execution and deal with urgent applications, which do not require notice to be given to the respondent. It is unnecessary to make an appointment to see the Practice Master and litigants are generally seen in order of arrival.

6.2 Assignment to Masters

QBG 6.2.1

6.2.1 A claim issued in the Central Office will normally be assigned upon issue to a particular Master as the procedural judge responsible for managing the claim. The Registry Section of the Action Department will endorse the name of the Assigned Master on the Claim Form. However, assignment may be triggered at an earlier stage, for example, by one of the following events;

(1)   an application for pre-action disclosure under Rule 31.16,

(2)   an application for an interim remedy before the commencement of a claim or where there is no relevant claim (Part 25).

It occasionally happens that a claim is assigned to a Master who may have an 'interest' in the claim. In such cases the Senior Master will re-assign the claim to another Master.

QBG 6.2.2

6.2.2 Where either an application notice or Part 8 Claim Form is issued which requires a hearing date to be given immediately, the Registry will assign a Master and the Masters' Support Unit will give a hearing date.

QBG 6.2.3

6.2.3 The Senior Master may assign a particular Master to a class/group of claims or may re-assign work generally. At present Clinical negligence claims are assigned to Master Ungley and Master Yoxall. Claims for Mesothelioma are assigned to Master Whitaker. In the event of an assigned Master being on leave or for any other reason temporarily absent from the Royal Courts of Justice then the Masters' Support Unit may endorse on the appropriate document the name of another Master.

QBG 6.2.4

6.2.4 A court file will be opened when a Claim Form is issued. The name of the assigned Master will be endorsed on the Court File and entered on the Claim Forms. Any application notice in an assigned claim for hearing before a Master should have the name of the assigned Master entered on it by the solicitors/litigants making the application.

6.3 Listing before Masters

QBG 6.3.1

6.3.1 The Masters' lists consist of;

(1)   the Chambers List - short applications in Rooms E102 and E110 ('the Bear Garden lists'),

(2)   Private Room Appointments, (**using the prescribed PRA form)** and

(3)   the High Court Enforcement Officer's Interpleader applications (formerly Sheriffs' applications).

QBG 6.3.2

6.3.2 Parties attending on all applications before the Masters are requested to complete the Court Record Sheet (form PF48), which will be used to record details of the claim, representation and the nature of the application. Copies of this form may be found in the writing desks in the Masters' corridors and the Bear Garden. The form will be placed on the file when the hearing is concluded.

QBG 6.3.3

6.3.3 Masters will sit each day at 10.30am in the Bear Garden, Rooms E102 and E110 to hear applications in the Chambers Lists (Bear Garden lists). Applications of up to 30 minutes duration are listed at 10.30am, 11.00am and 11.30am. Solicitors and Counsel may attend any application in these lists although the costs of being represented by Counsel may be disallowed if not fully justified. **If the Master considers that the application is likely to take longer than 30 minutes s/he may adjourn it to a private room appointment**. The applicant must then complete the PRA form giving details of the parties' availability as fully as possible. Failure to do so may result in the request form being returned for further information thereby delaying the hearing date. The PRA form is available in the Masters Support Unit, Room E16 and available from the Court Service Website.

QBG 6.3.4

6.3.4 **Hearing dates** for the Chambers Lists (Bear Garden lists) are given by the Masters' Support Unit. The assigned Master gives hearing dates for private room appointments personally. The parties or their legal representatives must inform the Masters' Support Unit of any settlements as soon as possible. All time estimates must be updated as necessary. Any Order made which as a consequence results in a hearing being not required must be notified to the Master by using the Notice of Cancellation form available from the Judgments & Orders Section Room E15 – E17. This should be completed by the parties, and will be sent to the Assigned Master to note in the Diary accordingly.

QBG 6.3.5

6.3.5 Applications in the Chambers Lists (Bear Garden list) may, by agreement or where the application notice has not been served, be transferred for a private room appointment on a date to be specified by the Master, or may be re-listed for another date in the Chambers List. In all other cases an application for a postponement of the hearing date must be made to the Master to whom the claim has been assigned. An application may be re-listed in the Chambers List (Bear Garden list) without permission of a Master if for any reason the application has not been heard or has not been fully disposed of.

QBG 6.3.6

6.3.6 When an application in the Bear Garden list is adjourned by a Master s/he will specify the date to which it is adjourned.

Adjournments

QBG 6.3.7

6.3.7 An application for the adjournment of a private room appointment must be made to the Master who gave the appointment unless the application is by agreement of all parties and the Master approves. The Master will usually require details of parties' availability. Any adjournment will normally be to a new hearing date.

QBG 6.3.8

6.3.8 If the application for an adjournment is opposed by any other party, the party seeking the adjournment must issue an application for an adjournment, if time permits, and must give the court, and all other parties as much notice as possible of such application. Where possible, it is preferable that such application is heard before the date for the hearing. **The Master will not grant an adjournment readily where it is opposed by any other party. Good reason will need to be shown, and if the reason is illness of a party, an original (not a photocopy) medical certificate signed and dated by a medical practitioner, setting out the reasons why attendance at court is not possible, will be required**.

QBG 6.3.9

6.3.9 If an adjournment of a hearing is granted, the Master will usually require details of parties' availability. Any adjournment will normally be to a new hearing date.

QBG 6.3.10

6.3.10 **Where an application for which a Master has given a private room appointment has been settled, it is the duty of the parties or their legal representatives, particularly those who obtained that appointment, to notify the Master immediately.**

QBG 6.3.11

6.3.11 If the Master hearing an application considers that the result might affect the date fixed for a trial, s/he may refer the application to the Judge in Charge of the List. This possibility should be considered when making an application and a request should be included in the application notice asking the Master to refer the application to the Judge.

QBG 6.3.12

6.3.12 If the Master considers that an application should more properly be heard by a Judge, s/he may either during the hearing or before it takes place refer the application to the Interim Applications Judge. Among the circumstances that may make this appropriate are;

(1)   that the time required for the hearing is longer than a Master could ordinarily make available,

(2)   that the application raises issues of unusual difficulty or importance, etc. or

(3)   that the outcome is likely to affect the trial date or window (in which case the referral will be to the Judge in Charge of the Lists).

However, it is emphasised that no single factor or combination of factors is necessarily decisive, and the Master has a complete discretion.

QBG 6.3.13

6.3.13 The High Court Enforcement Officer's first return applications are interpleader applications and are listed at monthly intervals before the Practice Master at 12.00pm on the first Monday of each month.

6.4 Automatic transfer

QBG 6.4.1

6.4.1 Part 26 requires certain claims to be transferred automatically. Where;

(1)   the claim is for a specified amount of money,

(2)   the claim has not been issued in a specialist list,

(3)   the defendant, or one of the defendants, is an individual,

(4)   the claim has not been issued in the individual defendant's home court, and

(5)   the claim has not already been transferred to another individual defendant's home court,

the claim will, on receipt of the defence, be transferred to the individual defendant's home court.

QBG 6.4.2

6.4.2 Where the Claim Form was issued in the Royal Courts of Justice the defendant's home court will be the district registry or county court for the district in which the defendant's address for service as shown on the defence is situated. If there is no such district registry or county court the proceedings will remain in the Royal Courts of Justice. If the claim is against more than one individual defendant, the claim will be transferred to the home court of the defendant who first files his/her defence. (See Section 6.9 below about transfer following an order.)

6.5 Allocation

QBG 6.5.1

6.5.1 When a defence to a claim is received in the Action Department from all the defendants, or from one or more of the defendants and the time for filing a defence has expired, the Action Department Registry will send an Allocation Questionnaire to all parties to an action, unless it has been dispensed with. If an Allocation Questionnaire is dispensed with the appropriate fee is still payable (CPR 26.3.3)

QBG 6.5.2

6.5.2 The Allocation Questionnaire to be used in accordance with Part 26 is form N150. The Allocation Questionnaire will state the time within which it must be filed, which will normally be at least 14 days after the day on which it is deemed served. Where proceedings are automatically transferred to a defendant's home court, notwithstanding that the issuing court will send out the Allocation Questionnaire before transfer, the Allocation Questionnaire should nevertheless be returned to the receiving court, the address for which will be on the covering letter.

QBG 6.5.3

6.5.3 Each party should state in his/her Allocation Questionnaire if there is any reason why the claim should be managed and tried at a court other than the Royal Courts of Justice or the trial centre for a particular district registry. Paragraph 2.6 of the Part 29 Practice Direction sets out certain types of claim that are suitable for trial in the Royal Courts of Justice. Form PF52 will be sent out to parties with the Allocation Questionnaire. Parties are encouraged to agree directions for the management of the claim, in the form of PF 52 or similar as prescribed by the Master.

QBG 6.5.4

6.5.4 Where a party fails to file his/her Allocation Questionnaire within the specified time the court officer will refer the proceedings to the Master for his/her directions. **The Master's directions may include 'the standard unless order', that is that unless the defaulting party files his/her Allocation Questionnaire within 7 days, his/her statement of case will be struck out.**

QBG 6.5.5

6.5.5 Where one but not all of the parties has filed an Allocation Questionnaire the Master may allocate the claim to the multi-track where s/he considers that s/he has sufficient information to do so. Alternatively, the Master may order that an allocation hearing take place and that all or any particular parties must attend. The court officer will then send out a Notice of Allocation Hearing (form N153) giving reasons for the hearing and any other directions.

QBG 6.5.6

6.5.6 Parties requesting a stay to settle the proceedings should do so in their Allocation Questionnaire or otherwise in writing. The court encourages parties to consider the use of ADR (see paragraph 6.6 below). The Master will normally direct the proceedings to be stayed for one month, but parties may by agreement seek an extension of the stay. Paragraph 3 of the Part 26 Practice Direction sets out the procedure for seeking an extension.

QBG 6.5.7

6.5.7 Parties are reminded that an estimate of costs must be filed and served when the Allocation Questionnaire is filed (paragraph 6.4 of the Costs Practice Direction).

QBG 6.5.8

6.5.8 On receipt of the Allocation Questionnaires or on an allocation hearing the Master will allocate the claim to the multi-track or transfer the claim to the appropriate county court. Rule 26.6 sets out the scope of each track. By operation of para 2.1 of Part 7A Practice Direction and Rule 26.6(4), claims proceeding in the Royal Courts of Justice must be allocated to the multi-track.

6.6 Alternative Dispute Resolution ('ADR')

QBG 6.6.1

6.6.1 Parties are encouraged to use ADR (such as, but not confined to, mediation and conciliation) to try to resolve their disputes or particular issues. Legal representatives should consider with their clients and the other parties the possibility of attempting to resolve the dispute or particular issues by ADR and they should ensure that their clients are fully informed as to the most cost effective means of resolving their dispute.

QBG 6.6.2

6.6.2 The settlement of disputes by ADR can;

(1)   significantly reduce parties' costs,

(2)   save parties the delay of litigation in resolving their disputes,

(3)   assist parties to preserve their existing commercial relationships while resolving their disputes, and

(4)   provide a wider range of remedies than those available through litigation.

The Master will, in an appropriate case, invite the parties to consider whether their dispute, or particular issues in it, could be resolved by ADR. The Master may also either stay proceedings for a specified period of time or extend the time for compliance with an order, a Rule or Practice Direction to encourage and enable the parties to use ADR. Parties may apply for directions seeking a stay for ADR at any time.

QBG 6.6.3

6.6.3 Information concerning ADR may be obtained from the National Mediation Helpline, Tel. 0845 60 30 809 http://www.nationalmediationhelpline.com. This is a pilot scheme launched under the auspices of the Department for Constitutional Affairs in March 2005. It is aimed at people with personal injury claims, small claims, business and consumer disputes.

6.7 Part 8 - alternative procedure for claims

QBG 6.7.1

6.7.1 Paragraphs 4.3.14 to 4.3.16 above deal with issuing a Part 8 Claim Form. The alternative procedure set out in Part 8 ('the Part 8 procedure') may not be used if a Practice Direction provides that it does not apply in respect of a particular type of claim. A Rule or Practice Direction may require or permit the use of the Pt 8 procedure and may disapply or modify any of the Pt 8 rules in respect of specified types of proceedings. The Part 8B Practice Direction deals with commencement of proceedings under the Rules of the Supreme Court and the County Court Rules the provisions of which remain in force in Schedules 1 and 2 to the CPR ('the Schedule rules'). The Schedule rules and the Practice Directions supporting them may require certain proceedings to be commenced by the issue of a Part 8 Claim Form with appropriate modifications to the Part 8 procedure.

QBG 6.7.2

6.7.2 The main features of the Part 8 procedure are;

(1)   Part 16 (statements of case) does not apply, but the claimant may be required to file Details of Claim when issuing,

(2)   Part 15 (defence and reply) does not apply,

(3)   judgment in default may not be obtained (Rule 12.2),

(4)   Rules 14.4 to 14.7 (judgment by request on an admission) do not apply,

(5)   a Part 8 claim shall be treated as being allocated to the multi-track

QBG 6.7.3

6.7.3 All Part 8 Claim Forms will be referred to a Master for directions as soon as the Part 8 Claim Form is issued. These may include fixing a hearing date. Where a hearing date is fixed, notice of the hearing date must be served with the Claim Form. Where the Master does not fix a hearing date when the Claim Form is issued s/he will give directions for the disposal of the claim as soon as practicable after the receipt of the acknowledgement of service or as the case may be, the expiry of the period for acknowledging service.

QBG 6.7.4

6.7.4 Where a Part 8 Claim Form has been issued for the purpose of giving effect to a consent order for an award of damages to a child or patient or an award of provisional damages as in paragraph 4.1.15 (1) and (2) above, a draft of the order sought should be attached to the claim form. For more information see paragraphs 6.8.1 to 6.8.8 and 9.3.8 to 9.3.10 below about children and patients, and paragraphs 6.8.12, 9.3.11 and 9.3.12 below about provisional damages.

QBG 6.7.5

6.7.5 A defendant who wishes to respond to a Part 8 Claim Form should acknowledge service of it and may do so either by using form N210 or otherwise in writing giving the following information;

(1)   whether s/he contests the claim, and

(2)   where s/he is seeking a different remedy from that set out in the Claim Form, what that remedy is.

If a defendant does not acknowledge service of the Claim Form within the specified time, s/he may attend the hearing of the claim but may not take part in the hearing unless the court gives permission.

QBG 6.7.6

6.7.6 Rules 8.5 and 8.6 and paragraph 5 of the Part 8 Practice Direction (alternative procedure) deal with evidence to be relied on in Part 8 proceedings; **the claimant's evidence must be filed and served with the Claim Form, and the defendant's evidence (if any) must be filed with his/her acknowledgement of service**. If the defendant files written evidence s/he must at the same time serve it on the other parties. It is helpful to the court if, where the defendant does not intend to rely on written evidence, s/he notifies the court in writing to that effect.

QBG 6.7.7

6.7.7 Where a defendant contends that the Part 8 procedure should not be used, s/he should state the reasons for his/her contention on his/her acknowledgement of service. On receipt of the acknowledgement of service, the Master will give appropriate directions for the future management of the claim.

6.8 Specific matters which may be dealt with under the Part 8 procedure

Settlements on behalf of children and patients

QBG 6.8.1

6.8.1 Part 21 and the Part 21 Practice Direction set out the requirements for litigation by or against children and patients. References in Part 21, the Part 21 Practice Direction and in this guide to;

(1)   'child' means a person under 18, and

(2)   'patient' means a person who by reason of mental disorder within the meaning of the Mental Health Act 1983 is incapable of managing and administering his/her own property and affairs.

No settlement or compromise of a claim by or against a child or patient will be binding unless and until the court has approved it. In addition, a party may not obtain a default judgment against a child or patient without the permission of the court, and may not enter judgment on an admission against a child or patient.

QBG 6.8.2

6.8.2 A patient must have a litigation friend to conduct proceedings on his/her behalf, and so must a child unless the court makes an order permitting the child to act on his/her own behalf. A litigation friend is someone who can fairly and competently conduct proceedings on behalf of the child or patient. S/he must have no interest in the proceedings adverse to that of the child or patient, and all steps s/he takes in the proceedings must be taken for the benefit of the child or patient. Rules 21.5 to 21.8 and paragraphs 2 and 3 of the Practice Direction set out how a person may become a litigation friend.

QBG 6.8.3

6.8.3 Applications for the approval of settlements or compromises of claims by or against a child or patient proceeding in the Central Office are heard by a Master. If the purpose of starting the claim is for the approval of a settlement, a Part 8 Claim Form should be issued in accordance with form PF170(A) which must contain a request for approval of the settlement (or compromise) and, in addition to the details of the claim, must set out the terms of the settlement (or compromise) or must have attached to it a draft consent order. The draft consent order should be in form N292, and should include the child's National Insurance Number, so that the child can be subsequently traced. See paragraph 6 of the Practice Direction for further information which the Master will require.

QBG 6.8.4

6.8.4 Where parties reach a settlement (or compromise) in proceedings started by the issue of a Part 7 Claim Form (where the trial has not started) an application must be made to the Master, or if the amount of the proposed settlement exceeds £ 750,000, to the Judge, in accordance with Part 23 for the approval of the settlement. The application notice should be in form PF170(B) and should have attached to it a draft consent order in form N292. (See CPR 21.10 PD 21 paras 6 & 7) The application notice should be lodged in Room E16. (See Section 7.12 below for information about applications.) If the trial has started, oral application may be made to the trial judge. Applications for approval of a settlement on behalf of a child or patient will normally be heard in public unless the Judge or Master orders otherwise. If a settlement is approved in private, the terms of settlement will be announced in public.

QBG 6.8.5

6.8.5 Paragraph 8 of the Practice Direction gives information about control of money recovered by or on behalf of a child or patient. Paragraph 10 deals with investment of money on behalf of a child and paragraph 11 deals with investment on behalf of a patient. Enquiries concerning investment for a child are dealt with in Room E105.

QBG 6.8.6

6.8.6 In respect of investment on behalf of a child, the litigation friend or his/her legal representative should provide the Master or a Judge with a completed form PF 172 (request for investment). The child's birth certificate should also be provided. When investment directions have been given, the PF172 will then be forwarded to the Court Funds Office for their investment managers to make the appropriate investment. The Court of Protection is responsible for the administration of patients' funds (unless they are small). Paragraph 11 of the Practice Direction gives full information about procedure for investment by the Court of Protection. These procedures may also be used for investment of money on behalf of a child or patient following an award of damages at trial.

QBG 6.8.7

6.8.7 Damages may also be paid to a child or patient by way of a structured settlement. A Judge or Master must approve a structured settlement on behalf of a child or patient. The Court of Protection must also approve a structured settlement on behalf of a patient. (For more information about structured settlements see the Part 40C Practice Direction – Structured Settlements.)

QBG 6.8.8

6.8.8 Control of a child's fund, provided s/he is not also a patient, passes to him when s/he reaches the age of 18 (see paragraph 12.2 of the Practice Direction).

Summary order for possession

QBG 6.8.9

6.8.9 In practice such claims are usually dealt with in the appropriate County Court. Paragraph 1 of Part 55 Practice direction gives details of the limited circumstances where a claim may be brought in the High Court. High Court claims for the possession of land subject to a mortgage will be assigned to the Chancery Division.

Settlements of a provisional damages claim

QBG 6.8.10

6.8.10 A claim for provisional damages may proceed under Part 8 where the Claim Form is issued solely for the purpose of obtaining a consent judgment. The claimant must state in his/her Claim Form in addition to the matters set out in paragraph 4.4 of the Part 16 Practice Direction that the parties have reached agreement and request a consent judgment. A draft order in accordance with paragraph 4.2 of the Part 41 Practice Direction should be attached to the Claim Form. The claimant or his/her legal representative must lodge the case file documents (set out in the draft order) in Room E16. Once the Provisional damages claim has been approved the documents lodged will be compiled into a file and preserved by the Court. For more information about provisional damages claims and orders see Part 41 and the Part 41 Practice Direction, and section 9.3 below.

Costs only proceedings

QBG 6.8.13

6.8.13 Proceedings may be brought under Part 8 where the parties to a dispute have reached a written agreement before proceedings have been started but have been unable to agree an amount of costs. The costs only proceedings may be started by the issue of a Claim Form in the Supreme Court Costs Office at Clifford's Inn, Fetter Lane, London EC4A 1DQ. The Costs Practice Direction at Section 17 sets out in detail the provisions for issue and proceeding with the claim.

6.9 Transfer

QBG 6.9.1

6.9.1 Part 30 and the Part 30 Practice Direction deal with transfer of proceedings, within the High Court, from the High Court to the County Court and be-tween County Courts. The jurisdiction of the High Court to transfer proceedings to the county courts is contained in s. 40 of the County Courts Act 1984 as substituted by s. 2(1) of the Courts and Legal Services Act 1990. Under that section the court has jurisdiction in certain circumstances to strike out claims that should have been started in a county court.

QBG 6.9.2

6.9.2 Rule 30.2 sets out the provisions for the transfer of proceedings between;

(1)   county courts,

(2)   the Royal Courts of Justice and a district registry of the High Court, and

(3)   between district registries.

Rule 30.3 sets out the criteria to which the court will have regard when making an order for transfer. (See paragraph 6.4 above about automatic transfer.)

QBG 6.9.3

6.9.3 The High Court may order proceedings in any Division of the High Court to be transferred to another Division or to or from a specialist list. **An application for the transfer of proceedings to or from a specialist list must be made to a Judge dealing with claims in that list**

QBG 6.9.4

6.9.4 A claim with an estimated value of less than £50,000 may be transferred to a county court, if the county court has jurisdiction, unless it is to proceed in the High Court under an enactment or in a specialist list

QBG 6.9.5

6.9.5 An order for transfer takes effect from the date it is made. When an order for transfer is sealed the court officer will immediately transfer the matter to the receiving court. At the same time, the court officer will also notify all parties of the transfer. An order for transfer to the High Court at the Royal Courts of Justice should state: 'Transfer to the Central Office, Queen's Bench Division, [or as appropriate] at the Royal Courts of Justice.'

QBG 6.9.6

6.9.6 Paragraph 5 of the Part 30 Practice Direction sets out the procedure for appealing an order for transfer. Where an order for transfer is made in the absence of notice given to a party, that party may apply to the court that made the order to have it set aside.

QBG 6.9.7

6.9.7 Where money has been paid into court before an order for transfer is made, the court may direct transfer of the money to the control of the receiving court.

6.10 Part 20 proceedings

QBG 6.10.1

6.10.1 Part 20 deals with (a) counterclaims and (b) other additional claims, being claims for contribution or indemnity and what were formerly called 'third party' claims. A Part 20 claim is treated as a claim for the purpose of the CPR with certain exceptions, for which see Rule 20.3.

QBG 6.10.2

6.10.2 A defendant may make a counterclaim by completing the defence and counterclaim form provided in the Response Pack. The fee for the Counterclaim will depend on the amount claimed, and will therefore be deemed the same as a fee for Issue of Claim (see Fees Annex 1). If the counterclaim is not filed with the defence, the permission of the court is required. Where a counterclaim brings in a new party, the defendant (Part 20 claimant) must apply to the court for an order in form PF 21A adding the new party as defendant.

QBG 6.10.3

6.10.3 A defendant claiming contribution or indemnity from another defendant may do so by filing a notice, in form PF 22, containing a statement of the nature and grounds of his/her claim and serving the notice on the other defendant.

QBG 6.10.4

6.10.4 Any other additional claim may be brought by the issue of a Part 20 Claim Form, N211. If the Part 20 Claim Form is issued at a time other than when the defence is filed, the permission of the court is required. Rule 20.8 deals with service of a Part 20 Claim Form and Rule 20.12 sets out the forms, which must accompany the Part 20 Claim Form.

6.11 Summary judgment

QBG 6.11.1

6.11.1 The court may give summary judgment under Part 24 against a claimant or defendant;

(1)   if it considers that (a) the claimant has no real prospect of succeeding on the claim or issue, or (b) the defendant has no real prospect of successfully defending the claim, and

(2)   there is no other reason why the claim or issue should be disposed of at a trial.

QBG 6.11.2

6.11.2 The court may give summary judgment against a claimant in any type of proceedings, and against a defendant in any type of proceedings except (a) proceedings for possession of residential premises against a mortgagor, or a tenant or person holding over after the end of his/her tenancy where occupancy is protected within the meaning of the Rent Act 1977 or the Housing Act 1988, (b) proceedings for an Admiralty claim in Rem, and (c) contentious probate proceedings. For information about summary disposal of defamation claims see Part 53, the Part 53 Practice Direction and paragraph 12.7 below.

QBG 6.11.3

6.11.3 An application for summary judgment should be made in accordance with Part 23 and the application notice should contain the information set out in paragraph 2 of the Part 24 Practice Direction (parties may use forms PF 11 and PF 12 as precedents). The application notice should be filed and served on the respondent giving at least 14 days notice of the date fixed for the hearing and the issues to be decided at the hearing. Unless the application notice contains all the evidence on which the applicant relies, the application notice should identify that evidence.

QBG 6.11.4

6.11.4 In claims which include a claim for;

(1)   specific performance of an agreement,

(2)   rescission of such an agreement, or

(3)   forfeiture or return of a deposit made under such an agreement,

the application notice and any evidence in support must be served on the defendant not less than 4 days before the hearing. This replaces for such applications the 14 days notice usually required for summary judgment applications (Part 24 Practice Direction paragraph 7).

QBG 6.11.5

6.11.5 The application will normally be listed before a Master unless, for example, an injunction is also sought. In that case the application notice should state that the application is intended to be made to a Judge.

QBG 6.11.6

6.11.6 Where an order made on an application for summary judgment does not dispose of the claim or issue, the court will give case management directions in respect of the claim or issue.

6.12 Offers to settle and payments into and out of court

QBG 6.12.0

6.12.0 From 6 April 2007 new rules will be in force concerning offers to settle and payments into court, and Parts 36 and 37, which deal with these subjects, will be substituted by new Parts 36 and 37. The following notes reflect the position as it will be after the new rules come into force. For the position before 6 April 2007, please see Section 6.12 of the previous edition of the Queen's Bench Guide, and the 2006 Civil Procedure Rules.

QBG 6.12.00

6.12.00 Transitional provisions – the following is a summary. The full details are set out in Practice Direction B supplementing Part 36.

A Part 36 offer or payment valid before 6 April 2007 will continue to be a valid Part 36 offer under the new rules after that date, specifically in relation to costs and the effect of acceptance. It will have the consequences set out in the new Part 36 after that date. Where a Part 36 offer is made before 6 April 2007, if permission of the court was required to accept it before 6 April 2007, then permission of the court will still be required after that date. Any payments into court before 6 April 2007 will be governed by Rule 37.3, and treated as if that payment had been made under a court order (See section 6.12.11 below), except where a Part 36 offer is accepted without needing the court's permission and the defendant agrees that the sum in court may be taken out in satisfaction, in whole or in part, of the offer.

QBG 6.12.1

6.12.1 Part 36 deals with offers to settle. A party may offer to settle a claim at any time, including before commencement of proceedings.. An offer to settle made in accordance with Part 36 will have the costs and other consequences specified in that Part. It must comply with the following:

(1)   Be in writing;

(2)   State on its face that it is intended to have the consequences of Part 36;

(3)   Specify a period of not less than 21 days within which the defendant will be liable for the claimant's costs in accordance with rule 36.10 if the offer is accepted (not applicable if the offer is made less than 21 days before the start of the trial);

(4)   State whether it relates to the whole claim or to part of it or to an issue that arises in it and if so which part or issue;

(5)   State whether it takes into account any counterclaim.

A Part 36 offer may be made using Form N242A.

QBG 6.12.2

6.12.2 The offer may only be withdrawn or its terms changed before the expiry of the time given for acceptance (see (3) above), with the court's permission. After the expiry of that period the party making the offer may withdraw it or change its terms without the court's permission.

QBG 6.12.3

6.12.3 A Part 36 offer is made when received by the offeree. A Part 36 offer is accepted by serving written notice on the offeror. The notice of acceptance must also be filed with the court.

QBG 6.12.4

6.12.4 The times for accepting a Part 36 offer is set out in Rule 36.9. The general rule is that a Part 36 offer or Part 36 payment made more than 21 days before the start of the trial may be accepted at any time without the permission of the court unless the offeror serves notice of withdrawal on the offeree.,.In certain circumstances the permission of the court must be obtained to accept a Part 36 offer, for example where the trial has started, or where the claimant is a child or patient. Rule 36.9(3) sets out all the circumstances where permission is required.

QBG 6.12.5

6.12.5 If the court's permission is required to accept a Part 36 offer, an application must be made in accordance with Part 23 (see Section 7.12 below), which must be dealt with by a judge other than the judge allocated to conduct the trial, unless the parties agree that the trial judge may hear the application.

QBG 6.12.6

6.12.6 When a Part 36 offer is accepted within the relevant period (as defined by Rule 36.3(1)(c)), the general rule is that the claimant will be entitled to his/her costs up to the date of service of the notice of acceptance. Where a Part 36 offer is made less than 21 days before the start of trial, and is accepted, or a Part 36 offer is accepted after expiry of the period given for acceptance, then unless the parties agree the liability for costs, the court will make an order as to costs.

QBG 6.12.7

6.12.7 If a Part 36 offer is accepted, the claim will be stayed, but if approval of the court is required, the stay will take effect only when that approval has been given. Rule 36.11(5) sets out the powers that the court retains after such a stay is in place.

QBG 6.12.8

6.12.8 Rule 36.13 provides that a Part 36 offer will be treated as 'without prejudice except as to costs'. The fact that such an offer has been made must not be communicated to the trial judge, except in certain circumstances set out in Rule 32,13(3). In the Action Department a Part 36 offer, if not accepted, will be kept in a separate file held by the Manager of the Registry Section and not made available to the trial judge until after determination.

QBG 6.12.9

6.12.9 Where a Part 36 offer is not accepted and a trial of the claim takes place, Rule 36.14 sets out the costs consequences where a claimant fails to do better than the Part 36 offer, where a claimant does as well as or better than s/he proposed in his/her Part 36 offer.

QBG 6.12.10

6.12.10 Note that Rule 36.5 contains special provisions relating to claims for damages for personal injury where such a claim includes a claim for future pecuniary loss, and Rule 36.6 contains provisions relating to a claim which includes a claim for provisional damages. Rule 36.15 applies where a payment to a claimant following a Part 36 offer would be a compensation payment under section 1 of the Social Security (Recovery of Benefits) Act 1997, (usually personal injury claims). For the situation where a Part 36 offer is made by one or more, but not all, of a number of defendants, see Rule 36.12.

QBG 6.12.11

6.12.11 Part 37 deals with payments into and out of court, which are now confined to certain limited circumstances (except where any relevant transitional provisions apply):

(1)   Money paid into court under a court order – a party making such a payment must serve notice of this on every other party and file a certificate of service in respect of each such notice.

(2)   Where a defendant wishes to rely on a defence of tender before claim he must make a payment into court of the amount s/he says was tendered.

(3)   Payments into court under enactments – see the Practice Direction to Part 37 at 37PD.4 to 8.

QBG 6.12.12

6.12.12 Money paid into court should be paid by cheque payable to the Accountant General of the Supreme Court. It must be accompanied by a sealed copy of the order providing for the payment in, or of the defence, whichever is applicable, and the Court Funds Office form 100.

QBG 6.12.13

6.12.13 Money into court under a court order or in support of a defence of tender may not be paid out without the court's permission except where a Part 36 offer is accepted without needing the permission of the court and the defendant agrees that a sum paid into court by him or her should be used to satisfy the offer in whole or in part.

QBG 6.12.14

6.12.14 Where permission is required to take funds out of court an application must be made in accordance with Part 23 (see Section 7.12 below). If the court's permission is not required, the requesting party should file a request for payment in Court Funds Office form 201 with the Court Funds Office, accompanied by a statement that the defendant agrees that the money should be used to satisfy the Part 36 offer in Court Funds Office form 202. See the Practice Direction at 37PD.3.5 for the details required to be provided on the form. A party is obliged to notify the court whether s/he is or has been in receipt of Legal Funding by the Legal Services Commission.

7 CASE MANAGEMENT AND INTERIM REMEDIES

7.1 Case management–general

QBG 7.1.1

7.1.1 CPR requires the court to provide a high degree of case management. Case management includes; identifying disputed issues at an early stage; fixing time-tables; dealing with as many aspects of the claim as possible on the same occasion; controlling costs; disposing of proceedings summarily where appropriate; dealing with the applications without a hearing where appropriate; and giving directions to ensure that the trial of a claim proceeds quickly and efficiently. The court will expect the parties to co-operate with each other, and where appropriate, will encourage the parties to use ADR or otherwise help them settle the case.

QBG 7.1.2

7.1.2 Parties and their legal representatives will be expected to do all that they can to agree proposals for the management of the claim in accordance with Rule 29.4 and paragraphs 4.6 to 4.8 of the Part 29 Practice Direction. There is provision in the Allocation Questionnaire for proposing certain directions to be made, otherwise parties may use form PF 50 for making the application (attaching to it the draft form of order in form PF 52) and file it for the Master's approval. If the Master approves the proposals s/he will give directions accordingly.

7.2 The Case Management Conference

QBG 7.2.1

7.2.1 Parties who are unable to agree proposals for the management of the case, should notify the Court of the matters which they are unable to agree.

QBG 7.2.2

7.2.2 Where;

(1)   the parties proposed directions are not approved, or

(2)   parties are unable to agree proposed directions, or

(3)   the Master wishes to make further directions,

the Master will generally either consult the parties or direct that a case management conference be held.

QBG 7.2.3

7.2.3 In relatively straightforward claims, the Court may give directions without holding a case management conference.

QBG 7.2.4

7.2.4 Any party who considers that a case management conference should be held before any directions are given should so state in his/her Allocation Questionnaire, (or in a Part 8 claim should notify the Master in writing), giving his/her reasons and supplying a realistic time estimate for the case management conference, with a list of any dates or times convenient to all parties, or most of them, in form PF 49.

QBG 7.2.5

7.2.5 Where a case management conference has been fixed, parties should ensure that any other applications are listed or made at that hearing. A party applying for directions at the case management conference should use form PF 50 for making their application and attach to it the draft order for directions (form PF 52).

QBG 7.2.6

7.2.6 Parties should consider whether a case summary would assist the Master at the Case Management Conference in dealing with the issues before him or her. Paragraph 5.7 of the Part 29 Practice Direction sets out the provisions for preparation of a case summary.

QBG 7.2.7

7.2.7 It may be appropriate for the advocates instructed or expected to be instructed to appear at the trial to attend any hearing at which case management directions are likely to be given. In any event, the legal representatives who attend the case management conference must be familiar with the case and have sufficient authority to deal with any issues which may arise. Where necessary, the court may order the attendance of a party.

7.3 Preliminary issues

QBG 7.3.1

7.3.1 Costs can sometimes be saved by identifying decisive issues, or potentially decisive issues, and by the Court ordering that they be tried first. The decision of one issue, although not necessarily itself decisive of the claim as a whole, may enable the parties to settle the remainder of the dispute. In such a case, the trial of a preliminary issue may be appropriate.

QBG 7.3.2

7.3.2 At the allocation stage, at any case management conference and again at any pre-trial review, the court will consider whether the trial of a preliminary issue may be helpful. Where such an order is made, the parties and the court should consider whether the costs of the issue should be in the issue or in the claim as a whole.

QBG 7.3.3

7.3.3 Where there is an application for summary judgment, and issues of law or construction may be determined in the respondent's favour, it will usually be in the interests of the parties for such issues to be determined conclusively, rather than that the application should simply be dismissed.

7.4 Trial timetable

QBG 7.4.1

7.4.1 To assist the court to set a trial timetable, a draft timetable should be prepared by the claimant's advocate(s) after consulting the other party's advocates. If there are differing views, those differences should be clearly indicated in the timetable. The draft timetable should be filed with the trial bundle.

QBG 7.4.2

7.4.2 The trial timetable will normally include times for giving evidence (whether of fact or opinion) and for oral submissions during the trial.

QBG 7.4.3

7.4.3 The trial timetable may be fixed at the case management conference, at any pre-trial review or at the beginning of the trial itself.

7.5 Listing Questionnaire (Pre Trial Check List)

QBG 7.5.1

7.5.1 The court will send out a Pre Trial Checklist (N170) to all parties for completion, specifying the date by which it must be returned.

QBG 7.5.2

7.5.2 Paragraph 6.4 of the Costs Practice Direction requires an estimate of costs to be filed and served with the Pre Trial Checklist.

7.6 Pre-trial review

QBG 7.6.1

7.6.1 Where the trial of a claim is estimated to last more than 10 days, or where the circumstances require it, the Master may direct that a pre-trial review ('PTR') should be held. The PTR may be heard by a Master, but more usually is heard by a Judge.

QBG 7.6.2

7.6.2 Application should normally be made to the Queen's Bench Listing Officer for the PTR to be heard by the trial judge (if known), and the applicant should do all that he can to ensure that it is heard between 4 and 8 weeks before the trial date, and in any event long enough before the trial date to allow a realistic time in which to complete any outstanding matters.

QBG 7.6.3

7.6.3 The PTR should be attended by the advocates who are to represent the parties at the trial.

QBG 7.6.4

7.6.4 At least 7 days before the date fixed for the PTR, the applicant must serve the other parties with a list of matters to be considered at the PTR, and those other parties must serve their responses at least 2 days before the PTR. Account must be taken of the answers in any listing questionnaires filed. Realistic proposals must be put forward and if possible agreed as to the time likely to be required for each stage of the trial and as to the order in which witnesses are to be called.

QBG 7.6.5

7.6.5 The applicant should lodge a properly indexed bundle containing the listing questionnaires (if directed to be filed) and the lists of matters and the proposals, together with the results of discussions between the parties, and any other relevant material, in the Queen's Bench Listing Office, Room WG8, by no later than 10.30am on the day before the day fixed for the hearing of the PTR. If the PTR is to take place before a Master and he asks for the bundle in advance, it should be lodged in the Masters' Support Unit, Room E14. Otherwise it should be lodged at the hearing.

QBG 7.6.6

7.6.6 At the PTR, the court will review the parties' state of preparation, deal with any outstanding matters, and give any directions or further directions that may be necessary.

7.6 Requests for further information

QBG 7.7.1

7.7.1 A party seeking further information or clarification under Part 18 should serve a written request on the party from whom the information is sought before making an application to the court. Paragraph 1 of the Part 18 Practice Direction deals with how the request should be made, and paragraph 2 deals with the response. A statement of truth should verify a response. Parties may use form PF 56 for a combined request and reply, if they so wish.

QBG 7.7.2

7.7.2 If a party who has been asked to provide further information or clarification objects or is unable to do so, s/he must notify the party making the request in writing.

QBG 7.7.3

7.7.3 Where it is necessary to apply for an order for further information or clarification the party making the application should set out in or have attached to his/her application notice;

(1)   the text of the order sought specifying the matters on which further information or clarification is sought, and

(2)   whether a request has been made and, if so, the result of that request.

Applicants may use form PF 57 for their application notice.

7.8 Disclosure and Inspection of Documents

Disclosure and inspection of documents involves two stages. First, disclosure of the existence of documents and claiming privilege from inspection for such documents as may attract privilege (e.g. those to which 'legal advice' privilege applies); and secondly, offering facilities to the opposing party for inspection of certain of those documents.

QBG 7.8.1

7.8.1 Under Part 31, there is no longer any general duty to disclose documents. Instead, a party is prevented from relying on any document that s/he has not disclosed, and is required to give inspection of any document to which s/he refers in his/her statement of case or in any witness statement, etc.. The intention is that disclosure should be proportionate to the value of the claim.

QBG 7.8.2

7.8.2 If an order for disclosure is made, unless the contrary is stated, the Court will order standard disclosure, namely disclosure of only;

(1)   the documents on which a party relies,

(2)   the documents that adversely affect his/her own or another party's case,

(3)   the documents that support another party's case, and

(4)   the documents required to be disclosed by a relevant practice direction.

Parties should give standard disclosure by completing form N265 and may list the documents by category.

QBG 7.8.3

7.8.3 The court may either limit or dispense with disclosure (and the parties may agree to do likewise). The court may also order disclosure of specified documents or specified classes of documents. In deciding whether to make any such order for specific disclosure, the court will want to be satisfied that the disclosure is necessary, that the cost of disclosure will not outweigh the benefits of disclosure and that a party's ability to continue the litigation would not be impaired by any such order.

QBG 7.8.4

7.8.4 The court will therefore seek to ensure that any specific disclosure ordered is appropriate to the particular case, taking into account the financial position of the parties, the importance of the case and the complexity of the issues.

QBG 7.8.5

7.8.5 If specific disclosure is sought, a separate application for specific disclosure should be made in accordance with Part 23; it is not a matter that would be routinely dealt with at the CMC. The parties should give careful thought to ways of limiting the burdens of such disclosure, whether by giving disclosure in stages, by dispensing with the need to produce copies of the same document, by requiring disclosure of documents sufficient merely for a limited purpose, or otherwise. They should also consider whether the need for disclosure could be reduced or eliminated by a request for further information.

QBG 7.8.6

7.8.6 A party who has the right to inspect a document should give written notice of his/her wish to inspect to the party disclosing the document. That party must permit inspection not more than 7 days after receipt of the notice.

7.9 Experts and Assessors

QBG 7.9.1

7.9.1 The parties in a claim must bear in mind that under Part 35 no party may call an expert or put in evidence an expert's report without the court's express permission, and the court is under a duty to restrict such evidence to what is reasonably required.

QBG 7.9.2

7.9.2 The duty of an expert called to give evidence is to assist the court. This duty overrides any obligation to the party instructing him or by whom s/he is being paid (see the Part 35 Practice Direction). In fulfilment of this duty, an expert must for instance make it clear if a particular question or issue falls outside his/her expertise or if s/he considers that insufficient information is available on which to express an opinion.

QBG 7.9.3

7.9.3 Before the Master gives permission, s/he must be told the field of expertise of the expert on whose evidence a party wishes to rely and where practicable the identity of the expert. Even then, s/he may, before giving permission, impose a limit on the extent to which the cost of such evidence may be recovered from the other parties in the claim.

QBG 7.9.4

7.9.4 Parties should always consider whether a single expert could be appointed in a particular claim or to deal with a particular issue. Before giving permission for the parties to call separate experts, the Master will always consider whether a single joint expert ought to be used, whether in relation to the issues as a whole or to a particular issue.

QBG 7.9.5

7.9.5 In many cases it is possible for the question of expert evidence or one or more of the areas of expert evidence to be dealt with by a single expert. Single experts are, for example, often appropriate to deal with questions of quantum in cases where primary issues are as to liability. Likewise, where expert evidence is required in order to acquaint the court with matters of expert fact, as opposed to opinion, a single expert will usually be appropriate. There remain, however, a body of cases where liability will turn upon expert opinion evidence and where it will be appropriate for the parties to instruct their own experts. For example, in cases where the issue for determination is as to whether a party acted in accordance with proper professional standards, it will often be of value to the court to hear the opinions of more than one expert as to the proper standard in order that the court becomes acquainted with a range of views existing upon the question and in order that the evidence can be tested in cross-examination.

QBG 7.9.6

7.9.6 It will not be a sufficient ground for objecting to an order for a single joint expert that the parties have already chosen their own experts. An order for a single joint expert does not prevent a party from having his/her own expert to advise him, though that is likely to be at his/her own cost, regardless of the outcome.

QBG 7.9.7

7.9.7 When the use of a single joint expert is being considered, the Master will expect the parties to co-operate in agreeing terms of reference for and instructions to the expert. In most cases, such terms of reference/instructions will include a statement of what the expert is asked to do, will identify any documents that s/he will be asked to consider and will specify any assumptions that s/he is asked to make.

QBG 7.9.8

7.9.8 The court will generally also order that experts in the same field confer on a 'without prejudice' basis, and then report in writing to the parties and the court on the extent of any agreement, giving reasons at least in summary for any continuing disagreement. A direction to 'confer' gives the experts the choice of discussing the matter by telephone or in any other convenient way, as an alternative to attending an actual meeting. Any material change of view of an expert should be communicated in writing to the other parties through their legal representatives, and when appropriate, to the court.

QBG 7.9.9

7.9.9 Written questions may be put to an expert within 28 days after service of his/her report, but must only be for purposes of clarification of the expert's report e.g. when the other party does not understand it. Questions going beyond this can only be put with the agreement of the parties or the Master's permission. The procedure of putting written questions to experts is not intended to interfere with the procedure for an exchange of professional opinion in discussions between experts or to inhibit that exchange of professional opinion. If questions that are oppressive in number or content are put without permission for any purpose other than clarification of the expert's report, the court is likely to disallow the questions and make an appropriate order for costs against the party putting them. (See paragraph 4.3 of the Part 35 Practice Direction with respect to payment of an expert's fees for answering questions under Rule 35.6.)

QBG 7.9.10

7.9.10 An expert may file with the court a written request for directions to assist him in carrying out his/her function as an expert. The expert should guard against accidentally informing the court about, or about matters connected with, communications or potential communications between the parties that are without prejudice or privileged. The expert may properly be asked to be privy to the content of these communications because s/he has been asked to assist the party instructing him to evaluate them.

QBG 7.9.11

7.9.11 Under Rule 35.15 the court may appoint an assessor to assist it in relation to any matter in which the assessor has skill and experience. The report of the assessor is made available to the parties. The remuneration of the assessor is decided by the court and forms part of the costs of the proceedings.

7.10 Evidence

QBG 7.10.1

7.10.1 Evidence is dealt with in the CPR in Parts 32, 33 and 34.

QBG 7.10.2

7.10.2 The most common form of written evidence is a witness statement. The Part 32 Practice Direction at paragraphs 17, 18 and 19 contains information about the heading, body (what it must contain) and format of a witness statement. The witness must sign a statement of truth to verify the witness statement; the wording of the statement of truth is set out in paragraph 20.2 of the Practice Direction.

QBG 7.10.3

7.10.3 A witness statement may be used as evidence in support of an interim application and, where it has been served on any other party to a claim, it may be relied on as a statement of the oral evidence of the witness at the trial. Part 33 contains provisions relating to the use of hearsay evidence in a witness statement.

QBG 7.10.4

7.10.4 In addition to the information and provisions for making a witness statement mentioned in paragraph 7.10.2, the following matters should be borne in mind;

(1)   a witness statement must contain the truth, the whole truth and nothing but the truth on the issues it covers,

(2)   those issues should consist only of the issues on which the party serving the witness statement wishes that witness to give evidence in chief and should not include commentary on the trial bundle or other matters which [may arise during the trial or] may have arisen during the proceedings,

(3)   a witness statement should be as concise as the circumstances allow, inadmissible or irrelevant material should not be included,

(4)   the cost of preparation of an over elaborate witness statement may not be allowed,

(5)   Rule 32.14 states that proceedings for contempt of court may be brought against a person ifs/he makes, or causes to be made, a false statement in a document verified by a statement of truth without an honest belief in its truth,

(6)   If a party discovers that a witness statement, which they have served, is incorrect they must inform the other parties immediately.

QBG 7.10.5

7.10.5 Evidence may also be given by affidavit but unless an affidavit is specifically required either in compliance with a court order, a Rule or Practice Direction, or an enactment, the party putting forward the affidavit may not recover from another party the cost of making an affidavit unless the court so orders.

QBG 7.10.6

7.10.6 The Part 32 Practice Direction at paragraphs 3 to 6 contains information about the heading, body, jurat (the sworn statement which authenticates the affidavit) and the format of an affidavit. The court will normally give directions as to whether a witness statement or, where appropriate, an affidavit is to be filed.

QBG 7.10.7

7.10.7 A statement of case, which has been verified by a statement of truth, and an application notice containing facts which have been verified by a statement of truth may also stand as evidence other than at the trial.

QBG 7.10.8

7.10.8 Evidence by deposition is dealt with in Part 34. A party may apply to a Master for an order for a person to be examined before a hearing takes place (Rule 34.8). Evidence obtained on an examination under that Rule is referred to as a deposition. The Master may order the person to be examined before either a Judge, an examiner of the court or such other person as the court appoints. The Part 34 Practice Direction at paragraph 4 sets out in detail how the examination should take place.

QBG 7.10.9

7.10.9 Provisions relating to applications for evidence by deposition to be taken either;

(1)   in this country for use in a foreign court, or

(2)   abroad for use in proceedings within the jurisdiction

are set out in detail in the Part 34 Practice Direction at paragraphs 5 and 6.

QBG 7.10.10

7.10.10 The procedure for issuing a witness summons is also dealt with in Part 34 and the Practice Direction. A witness summons may require a witness to;

(1)   attend court, or

(2)   produce documents to the court, or

(3)   both,

on either a date fixed for the hearing or another date as the court may direct (but see also Rule 31.17 which may be used when there are areas of contention).

QBG 7.10.11

7.10.11 The court may also issue a witness summons in aid of a court or tribunal which does not have the power to issue a witness summons in relation to the proceedings before it (and see the Part 34 Practice Direction at paragraphs 1, 2 and 3).

QBG 7.10.12

7.10.12 To issue a witness summons, two copies should be filed in the Action Department, Room E07 for sealing; one copy will be retained on the court file.

QBG 7.10.13

7.10.13 A witness summons must be served at least 7 days before the date upon which the witness is required to attend. If this is not possible for any reason, an order must be sought from a Master that a witness summons is binding although it will be served less than 7 days before the date when the witness is required to attend. A Master will usually be prepared to deal with this in Practice, without notice.

QBG 7.10.14

7.10.14 A witness summons will be served by the court unless the party on whose behalf it is issued indicates in writing that s/he wishes to serve it himself. If time is a critical factor, it may be preferable for the party to serve the witness summons. For the method of service see the notes to Part 34 at paragraph 34.6.1.

QBG 7.10.15

7.10.15 At the time of service of the witness summons the witness must be offered 'Conduct money' to defray his or her expenses of coming to, staying at, and returning from the place of the trial. Thus, where the court is to serve, the party on whose behalf it is issued must deposit the amount of conduct money in the court office. For the relevant amounts see the note at Part 34 paragraph 34.7.1.

7.11 Hearings

Hearings generally

Hearings in public/private

QBG 7.11.1

7.11.1 All hearings are in principle open to the public, even though in practice most of the hearings until the trial itself will be attended only by the parties and their representatives. However, in an appropriate case the court may decide to hold a hearing in private. Rule 39.2 lists the circumstances where it may be appropriate to hold a hearing in private. In addition, paragraph 1.5 of the Part 39 Practice Direction sets out certain types of hearings which may be listed in private.

QBG 7.11.2

7.11.2 The court also has the power under section 11 of the Contempt of Court Act 1981 to make an order forbidding publication of any details that might identify one or more of the parties. Such orders are granted only in exceptional cases.

QBG 7.11.3

7.11.3 References in the CPR and Practice Directions to hearings being in public or private do not restrict any existing rights of audience or confer any new rights of audience in respect of applications or proceedings which under the rules previously in force would have been heard in court or chambers respectively. Advocates (and judges) do not wear robes at interim hearings before High Court Judges. Robes are worn for trials and certain other proceedings such as preliminary issues, committals etc. It is not intended that the new routes of appeal should restrict the advocate's right of audience, in that, a solicitor who appeared in a county court matter which is the subject of an appeal to a High Court Judge would normally be allowed to appear at the appeal hearing.

Conduct of the parties

QBG 7.11.4

7.11.4 Parties are reminded that they are expected to act with courtesy and respect for the other parties present and for the proceedings of the court. Punctuality is particularly important; being late for hearings is unfair to the other parties and other court users, as well as being discourteous to them and to the court.

Preparation for hearings

QBG 7.11.5

7.11.5 To ensure court time is used efficiently there must be adequate preparation prior to the hearing. This includes the preparation and exchange of skeleton arguments, the compilation of bundles of documents and the giving of realistic time estimates. Where estimates prove inaccurate, a hearing may have to be adjourned to a later date, and the party responsible for the adjournment is likely to be ordered to pay the costs thrown away.

QBG 7.11.6

7.11.6 The parties should use their best endeavours to agree beforehand the issues, or main issues between them, and must co-operate with the court and each other to enable the court to deal with claims justly; parties may expect to be penalised for failing to do so.

QBG 7.11.7

7.11.7 A bundle of documents must be compiled for the court's use at the trial, and also for hearings before the Interim Applications Judge or a Master where the documents to be referred to total 25 pages or more. The party lodging a trial or hearing bundle should supply identical bundles to all parties and for the use of witnesses. The efficient preparation of bundles is very important. Where bundles have been properly prepared, the claim will be easier to understand and present, and time and costs are likely to be saved. Where documents are copied unnecessarily or bundled incompetently, the costs may be disallowed. Paragraph 3 of the Part 39 Practice Direction sets out in full the requirements for compiling bundles of documents for hearings or trial.

QBG 7.11.8

7.11.8 The trial bundle must be filed not more than 7 and not less than 3 days before the start of the trial. Bundles for a Master's hearing should be brought to the hearing unless it is likely to assist the Master to read the bundle in advance in which case it should be lodged with the Masters' Support Unit or the Master directly 1-3 days in advance. The contents of the trial bundle should be agreed where possible, and it should be made clear whether in addition, they are agreeing that the documents in the bundle are authentic even if not previously disclosed and are evidence of the facts stated in them even if a notice under the Civil Evidence Act 1995 has not been served. If the trial/hearing bundles are extensive and either party wishes the judge to read certain documents in advance of the hearing, a reading list should be provided.

QBG 7.11.9

7.11.9 Lists of authorities for use at trial or at substantial hearings before a Judge should be provided to the usher by 9.00am on the first day of the hearing. For other applications before a Judge, or applications before a Master, copies of the authorities should be included in the bundle or in a separate bundle.

QBG 7.11.10

7.11.10 For trial and most hearings before a Judge, and substantial hearings before a Master, a chronology, a list of the persons involved and a list of the issues should be prepared and filed with the skeleton argument. A chronology should be non-contentious and agreed with the other parties if possible. If there is a material dispute about any event stated in the chronology, that should be stated.

QBG 7.11.11

7.11.11 Skeleton arguments should be prepared, filed and served;

(1)   for trials, not less than 2 days before the trial in the Listing Office, and

(2)   for substantial applications or appeals, not later than 1 day before the hearing in the Listing Office and, where the Master has requested papers in advance of the hearing, in the Masters' Support Unit Room E16 or directly with the Master. Parties should avoid handing skeleton arguments to the other party at the door of the court even for less substantial hearings, so that each party has time to consider the other party's case.

QBG 7.11.12

7.11.12 A skeleton argument should;

(1)   concisely summarise the party's submissions in relation to each of the issues,

(2)   cite the main authorities relied on, which may be attached,

(3)   contain a reading list and an estimate of the time it will take the Judge to read,

(4)   be as brief as the issues allow and not normally be longer than 20 pages of double-spaced A4 paper,

(5)   be divided into numbered paragraphs and paged consecutively,

(6)   avoid formality and use understandable abbreviations, and

(7)   identify any core documents, which it would be helpful to read beforehand.

QBG 7.11.13

7.11.13 Where a party decides not to call a witness whose witness statement has been served, to give oral evidence at trial, prompt notice of this decision should be given to all other parties. The party should also indicate whether s/he proposes to put, or seek to put, the witness statement in as hearsay evidence. If s/he does not, any other party may do so.

Recording of proceedings

QBG 7.11.14

7.11.14 At any hearing, including the trial, any oral evidence, the judgment or decision (including reasons) and any summing up to a jury will be recorded. At hearings before Masters, it is not normally practicable to record anything other than oral evidence and any judgment, but these will be recorded. If a party wishes the whole proceedings to be recorded that party should inform the Master at the start of the hearing. A party to the proceedings may obtain a transcript of the proceedings on payment of the appropriate charge, from the Courts Recording and Transcription Unit, Room WB14. A person who is not a party to the proceedings may not obtain a transcript of a hearing which took place in private without the permission of the court.

QBG 7.11.15

7.11.15 No person or party may use unofficial recording equipment at a hearing without the permission of the court; to do so constitutes a contempt of court.

7.12 Applications

QBG 7.12.1

7.12.1 Applications for court orders are governed by Part 23 and the Part 23 Practice Direction. Rule 23.6 and paragraph 2 of the Part 23 Practice Direction set out the matters an application notice must include. The Part 23 Practice Direction states that form N244 may be used, however, parties may prefer to use form PF244 which is available for use in the Royal Courts of Justice only. To make an application the applicant must file an application notice unless a Rule or Practice Direction permits otherwise or the court dispenses with the requirement for an application notice. Except in cases of extreme urgency, or where giving notice might frustrate the order (as with a search order), an application notice must be served on every party unless a Rule or Practice Direction or a court order dispenses with service (see paragraph 7.12.3 below). A Master will not normally make an order on the basis of correspondence alone.

QBG 7.12.2

7.12.2 Applications for remedies which a Master has jurisdiction to grant should ordinarily be made to a Master. The Part 2 Practice Direction (Allocation of cases to levels of Judiciary) contains information about the types of applications which may be dealt with by Masters and Judges. An application notice for hearing by;

(1)   a Judge should be issued in the Queen's Bench Listing Office, Room WG8, and

(2)   a Master should be issued in the Masters' Support Unit, Room E16,

and wherever possible should be accompanied by a draft in double spacing of the order sought.

QBG 7.12.3

7.12.3 The following are examples of applications which may be heard by a Master where service of the application notice is not required;

(1)   service by an alternative method (Rule 6.8),

(2)   service of a Claim Form out of the jurisdiction (section III of Part 6),

(3)   default judgment under Rule 12.11(4) or (5),

(4)   substituting a party under Rule 19.1(4),

(5)   permission to issue a witness summons under Rule 34.3(2),

(6)   deposition for use in a foreign court (CPR Part 34 Section II),

(7)   Interim Charging Order (CPR Part 73)), and

(8)   Interim Third Party Debt Order (CPR Part 72).

QBG 7.12.4

7.12.4 Paragraph 3 of the Part 23 Practice Direction states in addition that an application may be made without serving an application notice;

(1)   where there is exceptional urgency,

(2)   where the overriding objective is best furthered by doing so,

(3)   by consent of all parties, and

(4)   where a date for a hearing has been fixed and a party wishes to make an application at that hearing but does not have sufficient time to serve an application notice.

With the court's permission an application may also be made without serving an application notice where secrecy is essential.

QBG 7.12.5

7.12.5 Where an application is heard in the absence of one or more of the parties, it is the duty of the party attending to disclose fully all matters relevant to the application, even those matters adverse to the applicant. Failure to do so may result in the order being set aside. In addition any party who has not had notice of a hearing may apply to have the order set aside within 7 days of service of the order made at the hearing.

QBG 7.12.6

7.12.6 Where notice of an application is to be given, the application notice should be served as soon as practicable after issue and, if there is to be a hearing, at least 3 clear days before the hearing date, unless the CPR provides a longer period or for permission for shorter service is obtained from a Master. Where there is insufficient time to serve an application notice, informal notice of the application should be given unless the circumstances of the application require secrecy.

QBG 7.12.7

7.12.7 The court may deal with an application without a hearing if;

(1)   the parties agree the terms of the order sought,

(2)   the parties agree that the application should be dealt with without a hearing, or

(3)   the court does not consider that a hearing would be appropriate.

QBG 7.12.8

7.12.8 The court may deal with an application or part of an application by telephone where it is convenient to do so or in matters of extreme urgency. Applications where there are a number of contested issues or where the hearing is likely to take longer than 45 minutes are not usually suitable for telephone hearings. The hearings most appropriate for a telephone hearing are Case Management Conferences and short applications for, e.g. extensions of time. See paragraph 6 of the Part 23 Practice Direction for the procedure to be followed.

Urgent applications

QBG 7.12.9

7.12.9 Applications of extreme urgency may be made out of hours and will be dealt with by the duty judge. An explanation will be required as to why it was not made or could not be made during normal court hours.

QBG 7.12.10

7.12.10 Initial contact should be made through the Security Office on 020 7947 6260 who will require the applicant's phone number. The clerk to the duty judge will then contact the applicant and will require the following information;

(1)   the name of the party on whose behalf the application is to be made,

(2)   the name and status of the person making the application,

(3)   the nature of the application,

(4)   the degree of urgency, and

(5)   the contact telephone number(s).

QBG 7.12.11

7.12.11 The duty judge will indicate to his/her clerk ifs/he thinks it appropriate for the application to be dealt with by telephone or in court. The clerk will inform the applicant and make the necessary arrangements. Where the duty judge decides to deal with the application by telephone, and the facility is available, it is likely that the judge will require a draft order to be faxed to him. An application for an injunction will be dealt with by telephone only where counsel or solicitors represent the applicant.

QBG 7.12.12

7.12.12 It is not normally possible to seal an order out of hours. The judge is likely to order the applicant to file the application notice and evidence in support on the same or next working day, together with two copies of the order for sealing.

7.13 Interim remedies

QBG 7.13.1

7.13.1 Interim remedies which the court may grant are listed in Rule 25.1. An order for an interim remedy may be made at any time including before proceedings are started and after judgment has been given. Some of the most commonly sought remedies are injunctions, many of which are heard by the Interim Applications Judge.

QBG 7.13.2

7.13.2 Where a Claim has been started, an application on notice for an injunction should be filed in the Listing Office, Room WG8 for a hearing to be listed. If the application is to be made without giving notice to the other parties in the first instance, the Application Notice stamped with the appropriate fee should be brought to the Interim Applications Court, Court 37, together with the evidence in support, a skeleton argument (where appropriate) and two copies of the Order sought. Applications without notice are heard in Court 37 at 10.00am and 2.00pm, and at such other times as the urgency of the application dictates.

QBG 7.13.3

7.13.3 Where an injunction is granted without the other party being present it will normally be for a limited period; a return date 1 to 2 weeks ahead. If the injunction order contains an undertaking to issue a Claim Form, this should be issued before the Application Notice for the return date is filed in Room WG8 prior to service.

QBG 7.13.4

7.13.4 The Part 25 (Interim Injunctions) Practice Direction at paragraph 4 deals fully with making urgent applications and those without notice, and paragraphs 6, 7 and 8 deal specifically with search orders and freezing injunctions, examples of which are annexed to the Practice Direction.

QBG 7.13.5

7.13.5 Certain applications may be heard in private if the judge thinks it appropriate to do so (Rule 39.2(3)). An application to go into private should be made at the outset of the hearing. Certain applications for search orders and freezing injunctions might be appropriate for hearing in private.

QBG 7.13.6

7.13.6 Applications for interim payments are heard by a Master. The application notice should be filed in the Masters' Support Unit, Room E14. The requirements for obtaining an order for an interim payment are fully dealt with in the Part 25 (Interim Payments) Practice Direction.

7.14 Interlocutory Orders

Orders made by the Masters

QBG 7.14.1

7.14.1 In the majority of cases Orders by Masters in the Queen's Bench Division are drawn up by one of the parties, who must then arrange to have this sealed by the Judgment & Orders Section (Room E17) and effect service on all other parties. In a limited number of circumstances, e.g. where an order is made of the court's own initiative, the court will draw up, seal and serve an order.

QBG 7.14.2

7.14.2 Where an application notice has been issued, and there has been a hearing, the Master will endorse the order in handwriting upon the <u>original</u> application notice. (If the original is not at the hearing, the party drawing up the order will have to ask the Master's permission to treat a photocopy as an original). If the parties have provided a draft order, will endorse this, with or without amendment. The application notice would then be endorsed 'Order in the form initialled'. If the hearing is one where there is no application notice, for example a Case Management Conference, then the Master will endorse the order on any Notice of the hearing sent by the court, or will use a draft order provided by one of the parties to endorse the order.

QBG 7.14.3

7.14.3 The Master will usually direct which party should be responsible for drawing up the Order. In the absence of such direction, this will be the party who issued the application to which the order relates, or the Claimant where the order was made in a case management conference. The Master will also direct a date by which the order should be drawn up, sealed and served. If no date is specified, the order must be served within 14 days of the date it was made.

QBG 7.14.4

7.14.4 The party responsible for drawing up the order should lodge with the Judgments & Orders Section:

(i)   The application notice (or other document) endorsed by the Master;

(ii)   Clean copies for sealing, one for each party and one for the court file;

(iii)   Evidence of payment of the court fee

QBG 7.14.5

7.14.5 That party should serve the sealed order upon each other party to the action by the date specified. If not sealed and served by that date, a party will have to obtain the court's permission to file the order out of time, which should be sought from the Practice Master.

QBG 7.14.6

7.14.6 If an order is made without a hearing, then the party making the application must also draw up, file and serve the order in accordance with the procedure set out below.

Orders made by a High Court Judge

QBG 7.14.7

7.14.7 Order made by a Judge on an interim application will, where the parties have legal representation, generally be drawn up in the same way as orders made by the Masters. However, the court will draw, seal and serve orders on behalf of litigants in person, and also orders made in appeal proceedings.

7.15 Civil Restraint Orders

QBG 7.15.1

7.15.1 The power of the court to make civil restraint order ('CROs') is governed by CPR 3.11, however the practice direction to Part 3 (Civil Restraint Orders) sets out the procedure in detail.

QBG 7.15.2

7.15.2 There are 3 types of CRO – limited civil restraint order, extended civil restraint order and general civil restraint order.

QBG 7.15.3

7.15.3 For a limited CRO ('LCRO') to be made, 2 or more findings that a litigant's application is totally without merit must first have been made. An LCRO may by made by a Judge of any court which includes a Master and District Judge. An LCRO restrains the litigant from making any further application in the proceedings in which the LCRO is made and usually remains in effect for the duration of those proceedings.

QBG 7.15.4

7.15.4 An extended CRO ('ECRO') may be made where a litigant has persistently issued claims or made applications which are totally without merit. An ECRO may be made (i) in respect of any court when made by a Judge of the Court of Appeal, (ii) in the High Court or any county court when made by a Judge of the High Court and (iii) in any county court when made by a Designated Civil Judge or his appointed deputy.

QBG 7.15.5

7.15.5 An ECRO restrains the litigant from making any further applications involving or relating to or touching or leading to the proceedings in which the ECRO is made and will be made for a specified period not exceeding 2 years.

QBG 7.15.6

7.15.6 A general CRO ('GCRO') may be made where, despite the existence of an ECRO, a litigant persists in issuing claims and making applications which are totally without merit.

QBG 7.15.7

7.15.7 A GCRO restrains the litigant from issuing any claim or making any application (i) in any court when made by a Judge of the Court of Appeal, (ii) in the High Court or any county court when made by a Judge of the High Court and (iii) in any county court when made by a Designated Civil Judge or his appointed deputy.

QBG 7.15.8

7.15.8 The CRO's provide for the litigant to seek in writing the court's permission to issue any claim or make any application which is restrained by the CRO. Both the CRO's and the practice direction set out in detail how such application is to be made and the consequences of failing to do so.

QBG 7.15.9

7.15.9 An application for a CRO may be made by another party in accordance with the provisions of Part 23, or may be made by the court of its own volition.

8 DEFAMATION CLAIMS

Defamation claims are governed by Part 53 and the Part 53 Practice Direction. Paragraph 2 of the Practice Direction sets out the information which should be included in a statement of case.

8.1 Offer to make amends

QBG 8.1.1

8.1.1 Under section 2 of the Defamation Act 1996 a person who has published a statement alleged to be defamatory of another may offer to make amends ('a section 2 offer'). The section 2 offer must;

(1)   be in writing,

(2)   be expressed to be an offer to make amends under section 2 of the Act, and

(3)   state whether it is a qualified offer, and if so, set out the defamatory meaning in relation to which it is made.

A section 2 offer is an offer;

(1)   to make a suitable correction of the statement complained of and sufficient apology,

(2)   to publish the correction and apology in a manner that is reasonable and practicable in the circumstances, and

(3)   to pay to the aggrieved party compensation (if any) and costs as may be agreed or determined to be payable.

QBG 8.1.2

8.1.2 Where a section 2 offer is accepted by an aggrieved person s/he may not bring or continue defamation proceedings against the person making the offer, but s/he may apply to the court under section 3 of the Act for an order that the other party fulfil his/her offer by taking the agreed steps. If the parties are unable to agree the amount of compensation or costs, the aggrieved party may apply to the court for the amount to be decided. (See para. 3 of the Defamation Practice Direction (Part 53)).

QBG 8.1.3

8.1.3 In the event that the parties are unable to agree on the steps to be taken, the person making the offer may take such steps as s/he thinks appropriate, including making an application for the court's approval of the terms of a statement to be read in Court containing a correction and apology. s/he may also give an undertaking to the court as to the manner of their publication.

QBG 8.1.4

8.1.4 In existing proceedings the above applications may be made in accordance with Part 23, otherwise a Part 8 Claim Form should be issued. The application or claim must be supported by written evidence as set out in the Part 53 Practice Direction at paragraph 3.3, and should be made to a Master. If the application or claim involves the court's approval for a statement to be read in Court, it should be made to the Senior Master. The Claim Form or application notice should be issued or filed in the Masters' Support Unit, Room E16.

8.2 Ruling on meaning

QBG 8.2.1

8.2.1 An application for an order determining whether or not a statement complained of is capable of;

(1)   having any meaning or meanings attributed to it in a statement of case,

(2)   being defamatory of the claimant, or

(3)   bearing any other meaning defamatory of the claimant,

should be made in accordance with Part 23 and may be made at any time after service of the particulars of claim. Paragraphs 4.3 and 4.4 or the Practice Direction state the information which must be included in the application notice and evidence in support.

QBG 8.2.2

8.2.2 The application notice should be filed in the Listing Office, Room WG8, for hearing by the Judge in charge of the Jury list, or another designated Judge.

8.3 Summary disposal

QBG 8.3.1

8.3.1 Section 8 of the Act gives the court power to dispose summarily of the claimant's claim. The court may;

(1)   dismiss the claim if it appears that it has no realistic prospect of success and there is no reason why it should be tried, or

(2)   give judgment for the claimant and grant him summary relief.

QBG 8.3.2

8.3.2 Summary relief includes the following;

(1)   a declaration that the statement was false and defamatory of the claimant,

(2)   an order that the defendant publish or cause to be published a suitable correction and apology,

(3)   damages not exceeding £10,000,

(4)   an order restraining the defendant from publishing or further publishing the matter complained of.

QBG 8.3.3

8.3.3 Applications for summary disposal are dealt with in Rule 53.2 and paragraphs 5.1 to 5.3 of the Part 53 Practice Direction. Substantial claims and those involving the Police authorities or the Media or those seeking an order restraining publication will be dealt with by the Judge in charge of the Jury list or another designated Judge, and the application notice should be filed in the Listing Office, Room WG8. Applications for summary disposal in other defamation claims may be made at first instance to a Master.

QBG 8.3.4

8.3.4 An application notice for summary disposal must state;

(1)   that it is an application for summary disposal made in accordance with section 8 of the Act,

(2)   the matters set out in paragraph 2(3) of the Part 24 Practice Direction, and

(3)   whether or not the defendant has made an offer to make amends under section 2 of the Act, and whether or not it has been withdrawn.

The application may be made at any time after service of the particulars of claim and the provisions of Rule 24.4(1)(a) and (b) do not apply.

QBG 8.3.5

8.3.5 Where the court has made an order for summary relief as in 12.7.9(2) above (specifying the date by which the parties should agree the content, time, manner, form and place of publication of the correction and apology) and the parties are unable to comply within the specified time, the claimant must prepare a summary of the court's judgment and serve it on the other parties within 3 days following the date specified in the order for the content to be agreed by the parties.

QBG 8.3.6

8.3.6 If the parties are unable to agree the summary, they must within 3 days of its receipt, apply to the court by;

(1)   filing an application notice, and

(2)   filing and serving on all the other parties a copy of the summary showing the revisions they wish to make to it.

The court (normally the Judge who delivered the judgment) will then settle the summary.

8.4 Statements read in Court

QBG 8.4.1

8.4.1 Paragraph 6 of the Practice Direction only applies where a party wishes to accept a Part 36 offer, Part 36 payment or other offer of settlement.

QBG 8.4.2

8.4.2 An application for permission to make the statement before a Judge in Court may be made before or after acceptance of the Part 36 offer, Part 36 payment or other offer to settle, and should be made in accordance with Part 23 to the Senior Master, or if s/he is not available, to the Practice Master. The application notice, together with a copy of the statement, should be filed in the Masters' Support Unit, Room E16.

QBG 8.4.3

8.4.3 Where permission has been given, the parties may take a copy of the order to the Listing Office, Room WG8 for the matter to be listed before the Judge in charge of the Jury List for mention. Otherwise, the Action Department will send the court file to the Listing Office for the matter to be listed.

9 LISTING BEFORE JUDGES

9.1 Responsibility for Listing

QBG 9.1.1

9.1.1 At the Case Management Conference hearing the Master will give a period of between one and three months within which the Clerk of the Lists is to arrange the trial. This is known as the 'trial window'. It should normally start on a Monday. The parties (usually counsel's clerks) attend before the Queen's Bench Listing Officer to agree a 'trial period', usually a 3 day period, within which the trial will commence. A Master will not generally order a trial fixture without first consulting the Listing Officer.

QBG 9.1.2

9.1.2 The Clerk of the Lists (Room WG3, Royal Courts of Justice) is in general responsible for listing. All applications relating to listing should in the first instance be made to him. Any party dissatisfied with any decision of the Clerk of the Lists may, on one day's notice to all other parties, apply to the Judge in charge of the List.

QBG 9.1.3

9.1.3 The application should be made within 7 days of the decision of the Clerk of the Lists and should be arranged through the Queen's Bench Listing Office, Room WG5.

9.2 The Lists

QBG 9.2

9.2 There are three Lists, namely;

(1)   the Jury List

(2)   the Trial List, and

(3)   the Interim Hearings List.

The Lists are described below.

QBG 9.2 [1]

There are 3 'Listing Categories':

Category 'A' being claims of great substance and/or difficulty and/or of public importance, which will be heard only by a High Court Judge. The court must be satisfied that the claim meets the criteria of this category. The Master will inform the Judge in charge of the Trial List of the nature of the claim and the reasons for assigning it to this category. A Case Summary (see **CPR PD 29** para 5.7) should be available.

Category 'B' being claims of substance and/or difficulty, which will be heard either by a High Court Judge (if available) or a Deputy appointed under s 9 of the Supreme Court Act 1981 (**II SCA [9]**).

Category 'C' being other claims, which will generally be heard by a Deputy High Court Judge appointed under s 9 of the Supreme Court Act 1981 (**II SCA [9]**).

9.3 The Jury List

QBG 9.3.1

9.3.1 Claims for damages for libel and slander (defamation), fraud, malicious prosecution and false imprisonment will be tried by a Judge and jury unless the court orders trial by a Judge alone.

QBG 9.3.2

9.3.2 Where a claim is being tried by a Judge and jury it is vitally important that the jury should not suffer hardship and inconvenience by having been misled by an incorrect time estimate. It is therefore essential that time estimates given to the court are accurate and realistic.

QBG 9.3.3

9.3.3 Dates for the trial of substantial claims will be fixed by the Listing Office within the trial window after consideration of the parties' views. In such cases the Listing Office may, in addition, impose an alternative reserve date several weeks or months in advance of the trial date, in an endeavour to dispose of claims more quickly and to fill gaps in the List created by frequent settlements. When a reserve date is so allocated a 'cut off' date will be stated by the Clerk of the Lists again, after consideration of any views expressed by the parties and having regard to the complexity of the claim and the commitments of counsel and expert witnesses. On the cut off date a decision will be made by the Clerk of the Lists to break or confirm the reserved date for trial.

QBG 9.3.4

9.3.4 If a party considers that s/he will suffer significant prejudice as the result of the decision of the Clerk of the Lists relating to either a reserved date or the cut off date s/he may apply to the Judge in charge of the Jury List for reversal or variation of the decision, as set out in paragraph 9.1.2 above.

QBG 9.3.5

9.3.5 Jury applications will enter the Interim Warned List not less than two weeks from the date the application notice is filed. Parties may 'offer' a date for hearing the application within the week for which they are warned. Subject to court availability, the application will be listed on the offered date. Any application not reached on the offered date will return to the current Warned List and will be taken from that List as and when required.

QBG 9.3.6

9.3.6 Applications in defamation claims in respect of 'meaning' (for an explanation of 'meaning' see paragraph 4.1 of the Part 53 Practice Direction) may be listed in private on a specific day allocated for such matters.

QBG 9.3.7

9.3.7 Jury applications of length and/or complexity may be fixed by the same manner as set out in paragraph 9.3.6 above. (See the section below on The Trial List for general information about fixing trials).

QBG 9.3.8

9.3.8 Applications for directions and other applications within the Master's jurisdiction should firstly be made to a Master unless;

(1)   a direction has been given for the arranging of a trial date, or

(2)   a date has been fixed or a window given for the trial.

Interim applications made after (1) or (2) above should be made to the Judge. The Master will use his/her discretion to refer a matter to the Judge if s/he thinks it right to do so.

QBG 9.3.9

9.3.9 If a party believes that the Master is very likely to refer the application to the Judge, for example where there is a substantial application to strike out, the matter should first be referred to the Master or Practice Master on notice to the other parties without waiting for a private room appointment. The Master will then decide whether the application should be referred to the Judge.

9.4 The Trial List

QBG 9.4.1

9.4.1 This List consists of trials (other than Jury trials), preliminary questions or issues ordered to be tried and proceedings to commit for contempt of court.

QBG 9.4.2

9.4.2 The Royal Courts of Justice presents unique problems in terms of fixing trial dates. The number of Judges and Masters involved and their geographical location has caused, for the time being at least, a different approach to the fixing of trials in the Chancery and Queen's Bench Divisions.

QBG 9.4.3

9.4.3 The requirement of Judges to go on Circuit, sit in the Criminal Division of the Court of Appeal, deal with cases in the Administrative Court and other lists make it difficult to fix dates for trials before particular Judges. Accordingly the following will only apply to the Listing Offices in the Royal Courts of Justice.

QBG 9.4.4

9.4.4 At as early an interim stage as practicable, the court will give directions with a view to fixing the trial date, week, or other short period within which the trial is to begin (the trial window).

QBG 9.4.5

9.4.5 For that purpose the court may;
(1)   direct that the trial do not begin earlier than a specified date calculated to provide enough time for the parties to complete any necessary preparations for trial, and/or
(2)   direct that the trial date be within a specified period, and/or
(3)   specify the trial date or window.

QBG 9.4.6

9.4.6 If directions under 9.4.5(1) or (2) are given the court will direct the parties to attend upon the Clerk of the Lists in Room WG5 in order to fix the trial date or trial window.

QBG 9.4.7

9.4.7 The claimant must, unless some other party agrees to do so, take out an appointment with the Clerk of the Lists within 7 days of obtaining the direction in paragraph 9.4.6 above. If an appointment is not taken out within the 7 days, the Listing Office will appoint a date for a listing hearing and give notice of the date to all parties.

QBG 9.4.8

9.4.8 At the listing hearing the Clerk of the Lists will take account, in so far as it is practical to do so, of any difficulties the parties may have as to availability of counsel, experts and witnesses. The Clerk of the Lists will, nevertheless, try to ensure the speedy disposal of the trial by arranging a firm trial date as soon as possible within the trial window or, as the case may be, after the 'not before' date directed by the court under paragraph 8.4.5 above. If exceptionally it appears to the Clerk of the Lists at the listing hearing that a trial date cannot be provided within a trial window, s/he may fix the trial date outside the trial period at the first available date. (If a case summary has been prepared (see the Part 29 Practice Direction The Multi-track, paragraphs 5.6 and 5.7) the claimant must produce a copy at the listing hearing together with a copy of particulars of claim and any orders relevant to the fixing of the trial date.)

QBG 9.4.9

9.4.9 The Listing Office will notify the Masters' Support Unit of any trial date or trial window given. In accordance with Rule 29.2(3) notice will also be given to all the parties.

QBG 9.4.10

9.4.10 A party who wishes to appeal a date or window allocated by the Listing Officer must, within 7 days of the notification, make an application to the Judge nominated by each Division to hear such applications. The application notice should be filed in the Listing Office and served, giving one days notice, on the other parties.

9.5 The Interim Hearings List

QBG 9.5.1

9.5.1 This List consists of interim applications, appeals and applications for judgment.

QBG 9.5.2

9.5.2 On each Thursday of Term and on such other days as may be appropriate, the Clerk of the Lists will publish a Warned List showing the matters in the Interim Hearings List that are liable to be heard in the following week. Any matters for which no date has been arranged will be liable to appear in the List for hearing with no warning save that given by the Cause List for the following day, posted each afternoon outside Room WG5.

QBG 9.5.3

9.5.3 Fixtures will only be given in exceptional circumstances. The parties may by agreement 'offer' preferred dates for their matter to be heard, to be taken from the List on designated days, within the week following entry into the Warned List in accordance with Listing Office practice. Matters lasting less than a day are usually offered for two preferred consecutive days and matters lasting more than a day are usually offered for three preferred consecutive days.

9.6 General

QBG 9.6.1

9.6.1 In addition to the matters listed to be heard by individual Judges, the Daily Cause List for each day may list 'unassigned cases'. These are matters from the two Lists to be heard that day but not assigned to a particular Judge. If on any day a matter assigned to a particular Judge proves to be ineffective, s/he will hear an unassigned case. It is hoped that the great majority of unassigned cases will be heard on the day that they are listed but this cannot be absolutely guaranteed. Parties engaged in matters listed as unassigned should attend outside the court where the matter is listed. The Clerk of the Lists will notify them as soon as possible, which Judge is to hear the matter. It is not the practice to list cases as unassigned unless the parties consent and there are no witnesses.

QBG 9.6.2

9.6.2 Appeals from Masters' decisions will appear in the Interim Hearings List. The appeal notice (stamped with the appropriate fee) must be filed in Room WG7. On filing the appeal notice the solicitors should inform the Clerk of the Lists whether they intend to instruct counsel and, if so, the names of counsel.

9.7 Listing before the Interim Applications Judge

QBG 9.7.1

9.7.1 All interim applications on notice to the Interim Applications Judge will initially be entered in a List for hearing. They will be listed for hearing in Room E101 or some other nominated venue on any day of the week. Any matter, which cannot be disposed of with within one hour, will not be taken on the date given for the listed hearing.

QBG 9.7.2

9.7.2 If the parties agree that a matter cannot be disposed of within one hour, the applicant/appellant;

(1)   may, on filing the application notice/notice of appeal, seek to have the matter placed directly into the Interim Hearings Warned List, or

(2)   must as soon as practicable and in any event not later than 24 hours before the hearing date, transfer the matter into the Interim Hearings List.

If the parties do not so agree, or agree less than 24 hours before the hearing date, the parties must attend on that date.

QBG 9.7.3

9.7.3 Matters in the Interim Hearings List will be listed by the Clerk of the Lists in Room WG3, and the parties will be notified by the Listing Office (Room WG5) of the date on which the matter will enter the Warned List. Matters in the Warned List may be listed for hearing at any time on or after that date.

QBG 9.7.4

9.7.4 In order to ensure that a complete set of papers in proper order is available for the Judge to read before the hearing, the parties must in advance of the hearing lodge in room WG4 a bundle, properly paginated in date order, and indexed, containing copies of the following documents;

(1)   the application notice or notice of appeal,

(2)   any statements of case,

(3)   copies of all written evidence (together with copy exhibits) on which any party intends to rely, and

(4)   any relevant order made in the proceedings.

QBG 9.7.5

9.7.5 The bundle should be agreed if possible. In all but simple cases a skeleton argument and, where that would be helpful, a chronology should also be lodged. (See paragraph 8.9.1 and 8.9.2 below in respect of skeleton arguments.)

QBG 9.7.6

9.7.6 Where a date for the hearing has been arranged the bundle must be lodged not later than 3 clear days before the fixed date. For application or appeals where there is no fixed date for hearing, the bundle must be lodged not later than 48 hours after the parties have been notified that the matter is to appear in the Warned List. (For information concerning trial bundles see the Part 39 Practice Direction.)

QBG 9.7.7

9.7.7 Except with the permission of the Judge no document may be used in evidence or relied on unless a copy of it has been included in the bundle referred to in paragraph 8.7.6 above. If any party seeks to rely on written evidence which has not been included in the bundle, that party should lodge the original (with copy exhibits) in Room WG5 in advance of the hearing, or otherwise with the Court Associate before the hearing commences.

QBG 9.7.8

9.7.8 In appeals from Circuit and District Judges the provisions of paragraphs 8.7.4, 8.7.5, 8.7.6 and 8.7.7 should be complied with. In addition, the notes (if any) of reasons given by the Circuit Judge or District Judge, prepared by the Judge, counsel or solicitors should be lodged.

QBG 9.7.9

9.7.9 Subject to the discretion of the Judge, any application or appeal normally made to the Interim Applications Judge may be made in the month of September. In the month of August, except with the permission of a Judge, only appeals in respect of orders;

(1)   to set aside a claim form, or service of a claim form,

(2)   to set aside judgment,

(3)   for stay of execution,

(4)   for any order by consent,

(4)   for permission to enter judgment,

(5)   for approval of settlements or for interim payment,

(6)   for relief from forfeiture,

(7)   for a charging order,

(8)   for a Third Party Debt Order,

(9)   for appointment or discharge of a receiver,

(10)   for relief by way of High Court Enforcement Officer's interpleader,

(11)   for transfer to a county court or for trial by Master, or

(12)   for time where time is running in the month of August,

may be heard, and only applications of real urgency will be dealt with, for example, urgent applications in respect of injunctions, or for possession (under RSC O.113 in Schedule 1 to Part 50).

QBG 9.7.10

9.7.10 It is desirable, where this is practical, that application notices or appeal notices are submitted to the Practice Master or a Judge prior to the hearing of the application or appeal so that they can be marked 'fit for August' or 'fit for vacation'. If they are so marked, then normally the Judge will be prepared to hear the application or appeal in August, if marked 'fit for August' or in September if marked 'fit for vacation'. The application to a Judge to have the papers so marked should normally be made in writing, the application shortly setting out the nature of the application or appeal and the reasons why it should be dealt with in August or in September, as the case may be.

9.8 The Lists generally

QBG 9.8.1

9.8.1 Where a fixed date has been given it is the duty of the parties to keep the Clerk of the Lists fully informed as to the current position of the matter with regard to negotiations for settlement, whether all aspects of the claim are being proceeded with an estimate of the length of the hearing, and so on.

QBG 9.8.2

9.8.2 Applications for adjournments will not be granted except for the most cogent reasons. If an application is made because solicitors were unaware of the state of the List they may be ordered personally to pay the costs of the application.

QBG 9.8.3

9.8.3 A party who seeks to have a hearing before a Judge adjourned must inform the Clerk of the Lists of his/her application as soon as possible. Applications for an adjournment immediately before a hearing begins should be avoided as they take up valuable time, which could be used, for dealing with effective matters and, if successful, may result in court time being wasted.

QBG 9.8.4

9.8.4 If the application is made by agreement, the parties should, in writing, apply to the Clerk of the Lists who will consult the Judge nominated to deal with such matters. The Judge may grant the application on conditions that may include giving directions for a new hearing date.

QBG 9.8.5

9.8.5 If the application is opposed the applicant should apply to either the nominated Judge or the Judge to whom the matter has been allocated. A hearing should then be arranged through the Clerk of the Lists. A short summary of the reasons for the adjournment should be lodged with the Listing Office where possible by 10.30am on the day before the application is to be made. Formal written evidence is not normally required.

QBG 9.8.6

9.8.6 The applicant will be expected to show that s/he has conducted his/her own case diligently. Any party should take all reasonable steps;

(1)   to ensure his/her case is adequately prepared in sufficient time to enable the hearing to proceed, and

(2)   to prepare and serve any document (including any evidence) required to be served on any other party in sufficient time to enable that party also to be prepared.

QBG 9.8.7

9.8.7 If a party or his/her solicitor's failure to take reasonable steps necessitates an adjournment, the court may dismiss the application or make any other order including an order penalising the defaulting party in costs.

9.9 Listing Office - general matters

QBG 9.9.1

9.9.1 To facilitate the efficient listing of proceedings, parties are reminded that skeleton arguments concisely summarising each party's submissions must be prepared and filed with the Listing Office;

(1)   for trials, not less than 3 days before the trial, and

(2)   for substantial applications or appeals, not later than 1 day before the hearing.

QBG 9.9.2

9.9.2 If it is anticipated that a Skeleton Argument will be filed late, a letter of explanation should accompany it which will be shown to the Judge before whom the trial or hearing is to take place.

QBG 9.9.3

9.9.3 For parties' information, the following targets for the disposal of matters in the Lists have been agreed as set out below:

Interim Hearings Warned List within 4 weeks

From date of fixing;

Trials under 5 days within 4 months

Trials over 5 but under 10 days within 6 months

Trials over 10 but under 20 days within 9 months

Trials over 20 days within 12 months.

10 TRIAL, JUDGMENTS AND ORDERS

10.1 General

QBG 10.1.1

10.1.1 The trial of a claim in the Royal Courts of Justice normally takes place before a High Court Judge or a Deputy sitting as a High Court Judge. A Master may assess the damages or sum due to a party under a judgment and, subject to any Practice Direction, may try a claim which is

(1)   treated as being allocated to the multi-track because it is proceeding under Part 8, or

(2)   with the consent of the parties, allocated to the multi-track under Part 26.

QBG 10.1.2

10.1.2 Claims for defamation, malicious prosecution or false imprisonment will be tried by a Judge sitting with a Jury unless the court orders otherwise.

10.2 The Trial

QBG 10.2.1

10.2.1 See paragraph 2.4. above about representation at the trial, and paragraphs 7.11.14 and 7.11.15 above about recording of proceedings.

QBG 10.2.2

10.2.2 Rule 39.3 sets out the consequences of a party's failure to attend the trial and see also paragraph 2 of the Part 39 Practice Direction.

QBG 10.2.3

10.2.3 The Judge may fix a timetable for evidence and submissions if it has not already been fixed. The claimant's advocate will normally begin the trial with a short opening speech, and the Judge may then allow the other party to make a short speech. Each party should provide written summaries of their opening speeches if the points are not covered in their skeleton arguments

QBG 10.2.4

10.2.4 It is normally convenient for any outstanding procedural matters or applications to be dealt with in the course of, or immediately after, the opening speech. In a jury trial such matters would normally be dealt with before the jury is sworn in.

QBG 10.2.5

10.2.5 Unless the court orders otherwise, a witness statement will stand as the evidence in chief of the witness, provided s/he is called to give oral evidence. With the court's permission, a witness may amplify his/her witness statement or give evidence in relation to new matters which have arisen since the witness statement was served on the other parties.

QBG 10.2.6

10.2.6 The Court Associate will be responsible for any exhibits produced as evidence during the trial. After the trial, the exhibits are the responsibility of the party who produced them. Where a number of physical exhibits are involved, it is desirable, if possible, for the parties to agree a system of labelling and the manner of display, beforehand. The Associate will normally draw the Judgment or order made at the trial.

QBG 10.2.7

10.2.7 At a jury trial, it is the parties' responsibility to provide sufficient bundles of documents for the use of the jury.

QBG 10.2.8

10.2.8 Facilities are available to assist parties or witnesses with special needs. The Queen's Bench Listing Office should be notified of any needs or requirements prior to the trial, in writing.

10.3 Judgments and orders

QBG 10.3.1

10.3.1 Part 40 deals with judgments and orders. Rule 40.2 contains the standard requirements of a judgment or order and Rule 40.3 contains provisions about drawing them up, see also paragraph 1 of the Part 40B Practice Direction for more information.

QBG 10.3.2

10.3.2 Provisions concerning consent orders are contained in Rule 40.6 which sets out in paragraph (3) the types of consent judgments and orders that may be sealed and entered by a court officer, provided;

(1)   that none of the parties is a litigant in person, and

(2)   the approval of the court is not required by a Rule, a Practice Direction or an enactment.

Other types of consent order require an application to be made to a Master or Judge for approval. It is common for a respondent to a consent order not to attend the hearing but to provide a written consent. The consent may either be written on the document or contained in a letter, and must be signed by the respondent, or where there are solicitors on record as acting for him, by his/her solicitors. Paragraph 3 of the Part 40B Practice Direction contains further information about consent orders.

QBG 10.3.3

10.3.3 Rule 40.11 sets out the time for complying with a judgment or order, which is 14 days unless the judgment or order specifies otherwise (for example by instalments), or a Rule specifies a different time, or the judgment or proceedings have been stayed.

QBG 10.3.4

10.3.4 The Part 40B Practice Direction contains further information about the effect of non-compliance with a judgment or order (and sets out the penal notice), adjustment of the final judgment sum in respect of interim payments and compensation recovery, and refers to various precedents for types of judgments and orders. See also;

(1)   the Part 40 Practice Direction- Accounts and Enquiries, and

(2)   the Part 40C Practice Direction- Structured Settlements which sets out the procedure to be followed both on settlement and after trial. Precedents for structured settlement orders, Parts 1 and 2, are annexed to the Practice Direction.

QBG 10.3.5

10.3.5 Where judgment is reserved, the Judge may deliver his/her judgment by handing down the written text without reading it out in open court. Where this is the case, the advocates will be supplied with the full text of the judgment in advance of delivery. The advocates should then familiarise themselves with the contents and be ready to deal with any points which may arise when the judgment is delivered. Any direction or requirement as to confidentiality must be complied with.

QBG 10.3.6

10.3.6 The judgment does not take effect until formally delivered in court. If the judgment is to be handed down in writing copies will then be made available to the parties and, if requested and so far as practicable, to the law reporters and the press.

QBG 10.3.7

10.3.7 The Judge will usually direct that the written judgment may be used for all purposes as the text of the judgment, and that no transcript need be made. Where such a direction is made, a copy will be provided to the court's Recording and Transcription Unit, Room WB14, from where further copies may be obtained (and see paragraph 7.11.14 above).

Judgment or order for payment of money on behalf of a child or patient

QBG 10.3.8

10.3.8 The usual order made at trial will make provision for any immediate payment to the litigation friend or his/her legal representative and for the balance of the award to be placed to a special investment account pending application to a Master or District Judge (in the case of a child) or the Court of Protection (in the case of a patient) for investment directions. The order will specify the time within which the application should be made. It should also deal with any interest accrued to the date of Judgment, and or any interest which accrues in the future. An Order should also refer to Majority directions, and decisions on investment of the fund in Court.

QBG 10.3.9

10.3.9 The litigation friend or his/her legal representative should then write to or make an appointment with;

(1)   in the case of a child, the Master or District Judge in accordance with paragraph 6.8.6 above and the Part 21 Practice Direction, or

(2)   in the case of a patient, the Court of Protection in accordance with paragraph 11 of the Part 21 Practice Direction.

QBG 10.3.10

10.3.10 Where after trial the Judge has found in favour of a child or patient, instead of judgment being given, the proposed award of damages may be paid by way of a structured settlement. The structure must be approved by the Judge, and in the case of a patient must also be approved by the Court of Protection. (See also the Part 40C Practice Direction – Structured Settlements.)

Provisional damages

QBG 10.3.11

10.3.11 Rule 41.1 defines an award of provisional damages. Where there is a chance that a claimant may in the future develop a particular disease or deterioration as a result of the event giving rise to the claim, s/he can seek an award of damages for personal injury on the assumption that s/he will not develop the disease or deterioration, with provision for him to make a further application within the time specified in the order, ifs/he does so develop the disease or deterioration.

QBG 10.3.12

10.3.12 The Part 41 Practice Direction gives further information about provisional damages awards and, in particular, about the preservation of the case file for the time specified in the order for making a further application, and the documents to be included in the case file. A precedent for a provisional damages judgment is annexed to the Practice Direction.

11 APPEALS

11.1 General

QBG 11.1.1

11.1.1 Appeals are governed by Part 52 and the Part 52 Practice Direction. The contents of Part 52 are divided into three sections; I - General Rules about Appeals, II - Special Provisions applying to the Court of Appeal, and III - Provisions about reopening Appeals.

QBG 11.1.2

11.1.2 The Practice Direction Is divided into four sections; I - General Provisions about Appeals, II General Provisions about Statutory Appeals and Appeals by way of Case Stated, III - Provisions about Specific Appeals and IV – Provisions about Reopening Appeals.

QBG 11.1.3

11.1.3 The following paragraphs apply to orders made after 2nd May 2000 and are intended only to draw parties' attention to the basic provisions for bringing an appeal in or from the Queen's Bench Division. For further information about these procedures and about other specific types of appeal, parties should refer to Part 52, the Practice Direction and the Civil Appeals Guide.

For the purposes of Part 52 and the Part 52 Practice Direction, except where the meaning indicates otherwise, the term 'Judge' Includes a Master or District Judge.

QBG 11.1.4

11.1.4 Routes of Appeal – An appeal will lie from the decision of:

A District Judge of a county court; to a Circuit Judge

A Master or a District Judge of a District Registry of the High Court; to a High Court Judge

A Circuit Judge; to a High Court Judge

A High Court Judge; to the Court of Appeal,

unless the decision to be appealed is a final decision in a claim allocated to the multi-track or in specialist proceedings (under the Companies Acts 1985 or 1989 or to which Sections I, II or III of Part 57 or any of Parts 58 to 63 apply), in which case the appeal will lie to the Court of Appeal.

QBG 11.1.5

11.1.5 Unless the lower court or the appeal court orders otherwise, filing an Appellant's Notice does not operate as a stay of any order or decision of the lower court. A stay must be specifically sought either in the Appellant's Notice or separately in accordance with Part 23.

11.2 Permission to appeal

QBG 11.2.1

11.2.1 Permission to appeal is required to appeal from a decision of a Judge in a county court or the High Court, except where the appeal is in respect of;

(1)   a committal order,

(2)   a refusal to grant habeas corpus,

(3)   a secure accommodation order made under s 25 of The Children Act 1989,

(4)   certain statutory appeals, or

(5)   where a Practice Direction so provides.

QBG 11.2.2

11.2.2 Applicants are encouraged to seek permission at the hearing at which the decision to be appealed against is made. If it is not, or if it is sought and refused, permission should be sought from the court appealed to ('the appeal court'). Where permission is sought from the appeal court it must be requested in the Appellant's Notice. Permission may be granted, or refused, or granted in part (whether as to a part of the order, a ground of appeal or an issue) and refused as to the rest. (See paragraphs 4.1 to 4.24 of the Practice Direction in respect of permission to appeal.)

QBG 11.2.3

11.2.3 Refusal of permission at a hearing is, effectively, the end of the road (s 54(4) of the Access to Justice Act 1999 and paragraph 4.8 of the Practice Direction), save in extremely rare cases where the Court of Appeal or the High Court may reopen a final appeal or refusal of permission (52.17).

QBG 11.2.4

11.2.4 Where the decision sought to be appealed to the Court of Appeal was itself made on appeal to a county court or the High Court, permission must be sought from the Court of Appeal (52.13(1)). The Court of Appeal will not grant permission unless an important point of principle or practice is involved, or there is some other compelling reason.

QBG 11.2.5

11.2.5 An application for permission to appeal to a High Court Judge is made by filing an Appellant's Notice in the High Court Appeals Listing Office, Room WG7. An application for permission to appeal to the Court of Appeal is made by filing an Appellant's Notice in the Civil Appeals Office Registry, Room E307.

QBG 11.2.6

11.2.6 Before an application for permission can be considered, whether on the papers or at a hearing, the documents in support of the appeal must be lodged. The documents listed at section 11 of the Appellant's Notice should be lodged when the Appellant's Notice is filed. If the appellant needs more time to lodge the documents he/she must complete section 11 to obtain an extension of up to 14 days. This extension may be granted by a court officer. If the appellant is still unable to obtain the documents he/she may apply in writing for a further extension. This may also be granted by a court officer but any subsequent application for an extension must be made to a Judge.

QBG 11.2.7

11.2.7 Where the documents are not lodged in accordance with the extended time period and no further application for an extension is made, the matter will be placed in a Dismissal list before the Judge in charge of the List on notice to the appellant.

QBG 11.2.8

11.2.8 Where permission to appeal is being sought from the Court of Appeal, the Appellant must file the documents set out in paragraph 5.6, 5.6A, 5.9 and 5.12 of the Part 52 practice direction.

QBG 11.2.9

11.2.9 An application for permission is normally first considered on the papers without a hearing, although the application may be listed for a hearing at the outset, if the appellant requests it (52.3.5). Where permission is refused on the papers, the applicant may request that it be reconsidered at a hearing. The request should be made within 7 days of service of the notice of refusal.

QBG 11.2.10

11.2.10 The court will give notice of the permission hearing to the parties. A respondent who volunteers written submissions or attends the permission hearing will not normally be allowed his/her costs. If the court requests submissions from or the attendance of a Respondent, he/she will normally be allowed his/her costs if permission is refused (paragraphs 4.22–4.24 of the Part 52 practice direction).

11.3 Appeal Notices

QBG 11.3.1

11.3.1 Rule 52.4 and paragraph 5 of the Practice Direction deal with the Appellant's Notice. The appellant must file 3 copies of his/her notice at the appeal court either within a period specified by the court appealed from ('the lower court') or, if no such period is specified, within 21 days of the date of the decision appealed from. The notice must be served on each respondent as soon as practicable, and in any event not later than 7 days after it is filed.

QBG 11.3.2

11.3.2 A respondent must file a notice where;

(1)   he/she also wishes to appeal the lower court's decision,

(2)   he/she wishes to uphold the decision of the lower court for different or additional reasons to those given by the lower court, or

(3)   he/she is seeking permission to appeal from the appeal court.

QBG 11.3.3

11.3.3 The Respondent's Notice must be filed either within a period specified by the lower court or, if no such period is specified, within 14 days of;

(1)   the date the respondent is served with the appellant's notice where

   (a)   permission to appeal was given by the lower court or

   (b)   permission to appeal is not required,

(2)   the date the respondent is served with notification that the appeal court has given the appellant permission to appeal, or

(3)   the date the respondent is served with notification that the application for permission to appeal and the appeal itself are to be heard together.

(Paragraph 7 of the Part 52 practice direction deals with the Respondent's Notice.)

QBG 11.3.4

11.3.4 The notices to be used are as follows;

(1)   the Appellant's Notice - form N161, and

(2)   the Respondent's Notice - form N162.

There is a leaflet available from the Listing Office, Room WG7 entitled 'I want to appeal', which provides information about High Court appeals.

11.4 Procedure where permission is obtained

QBG 11.4.1

11.4.1 Where permission to appeal has been granted by the appeal court, the appellant must serve the appeal bundle on each respondent within 7 days of receiving the order giving permission to appeal.

QBG 11.4.2

11.4.2 The Appellant must include in the appeal bundle the Respondent's Notice and a skeleton argument (if any), any relevant transcripts of evidence, any documents which the parties have agreed are relevant and the order granting permission. If the order granting permission was made at an oral hearing, a transcript or note of the judgment should also be lodged. Where permission was refused in respect of a particular issue, any papers relating solely to that issue should be removed from the bundle. See paragraph 15.4 for more information on preparing the appeal bundle.

QBG 11.4.3

11.4.3 The High Court Appeals Office will notify the parties of either the hearing date or of the 'listing window' during which the appeal is likely to be heard. Where the appeal is in the Court of Appeal, the Civil Appeals Office Registry will notify the parties of the 'hear by' date and will send the appellant an Appeal Questionnaire. Paragraph 15.7 contains more information about listing in the Court of Appeal.

QBG 11.4.4

11.4.4 The Appeal Questionnaire must be completed and returned within 14 days of the date of the notification letter. The Appeal Questionnaire must contain the matters set out in paragraphs 6.5 and 6.6 of the Part 52 practice direction.

QBG 11.4.5

11.4.5 In the Court of Appeal, all the papers required for the hearing must be filed at least 7 days before the hearing. For an appeal to the High Court, all papers should be lodged not later than [2 days] before the hearing

11.5 Disposing of applications for permission and appeals where the Appellant does not wish to proceed

QBG 11.5.1

11.5.1 The following does not apply where any party to the proceedings is a child or patient.

QBG 11.5.2

11.5.2 The appellant may request that his/her application or appeal be dismissed. The request must state that the appellant is not a child or patient. If the request includes a statement from the respondent that he/she is not a child or patient and consents to the dismissal order being made without costs, the order will be so made. Otherwise the dismissal order will be made on the basis that the appellant pays the costs of the application or appeal.

11.6 Appeals in cases of contempt of court

QBG 11.6.1

11.6.1 Appellant's Notices which by paragraph 21.4 of the Part 52 Practice Direction (appeals in cases of contempt of court (s.13 of the Administration of Justice Act 1960)) are required to be served on 'the court from whose order or decision the appeal is brought'. In the case of appeals from the Queen's Bench Division, the Senior Master of the Queen's Bench Division should be served but service may be effected by leaving a copy of the Appellant's Notice with the High Court Appeals Office in Room WG7, Royal Courts of Justice, Strand, London WC2A 2LL.

12 ENFORCEMENT

12.1 General

QBG 12.1.1

12.1.1 Enforcement in the High Court is governed by CPR Parts 70 and 74 together with RSC Orders 17, 45 to 47 and 52 as in Schedule 1 to the CPR.

QBG 12.1.2

12.1.2 RSC O. 45 deals with enforcement generally. A judgment or order for payment of money (other than into court) may be enforced by a writ of Fieri Facias, Third Party Debt Order Third Party Debt Order, a Charging Order or the appointment of a receiver. A judgment or order to do or abstain from doing an act may be enforced by a writ of sequestration (with the permission of the court) or an order of committal. A judgment or order for possession of land may be enforced by a writ of possession, and a judgment or order for delivery of goods without the alternative of paying their value by a writ of specific delivery. In each case, where RSC O.45 r.5 applies enforcement may also be by a writ of sequestration or an order of committal.

12.2 Writs of execution

QBG 12.2.1

12.2.1 RSC O.46 deals with writs of execution generally. Rules 2 and 3 set out the circumstances when permission to issue a writ is necessary. Rule 4 contains provisions for making an application for permission. Rule 5 deals with applications for permission to issue a writ of sequestration. RSC O. 47 contains provisions concerning writs of Fieri Facias. Forms of writs of execution may be used as follows:

(1)   writs of Fieri Facias in form Nos. 53 to 63,

(2)   writs of delivery in form Nos. 64 and 65,

(3)   writs of possession in form Nos. 66 and 66A,

(4)   writ of sequestration in form No. 67,

(5)   writ of restitution in form No. 68,

(6)   writ of assistance in form No. 69.

QBG 12.2.2

12.2.2 With certain exceptions, writs of execution issued in the Royal Courts of Justice are executed by the High Court Enforcement Officer. RSC O.46 r.6 sets out the provisions for issue of writs of execution. In the Queen's Bench Division writs of execution are issued in the Central Office in Room E15-E17. Before the Writ can be sealed for issue, a signed praecipe for its issue must be filed in one of forms PF 86 to 90, as appropriate, stamped with the appropriate fee. A copy of the judgment or order requiring enforcement should also be provided.

QBG 12.2.3

12.2.3 On an application for permission to issue a writ of possession under RSC O.45 r.3(2), if the property consists of a house of which various parts are sublet to, or in the occupation of, different persons, the evidence in support should show the nature and length of the notice which has been given to the various occupiers. Where the defendant or any other persons are in actual possession of the premises of which possession is sought, the evidence must contain the following information:

(1)   whether the premises or any part of it is residential,

(2)   if so,

    (a)   what is the rateable value of the residential premises, and

    (b)   whether it is let furnished or unfurnished and, if furnished, the amount of furniture it contains, and

(3)   any other matters that will assist the Master in deciding whether any occupier is protected by the Rent Acts.

QBG 12.2.4

12.2.4 Where a party wishes to enforce a judgment or order expressed in a foreign currency by the issue of a writ of fieri facias, the praecipe and writ of fieri facias must be endorsed with the following certificate:

'I/We certify that the rate current in London for the purchase of (state the unit of foreign currency in which the judgment is expressed) at the close of business on (state the nearest preceding date to the date of issue of the writ of fieri facias) was () to the £ sterling and at this rate the sum of (state amount of the judgment debt in the foreign currency) amounts to £ '.

The schedule to the writ of fieri facias should be amended;

(1)   showing the amount of the judgment or order in the foreign currency at paragraph 1.

(2)   inserting a new paragraph 2. as follows:

'2.   Amount of the sterling equivalent as appears from the certificate endorsed on the praecipe for issue of the writ £ '.

(3)   renumbering the remaining paragraphs accordingly.

The writ of fieri facias wil then be issued for the sterling equivalent of the judgment expressed in foreign currency as appears from the certificate.

QBG 12.2.5

12.2.5 County Court judgments or orders to which Article 8(1) of the High Court and County Courts Jurisdiction Order 1991 applies may be enforced in the High Court, and since 26th April 1999, any County Court judgment for over £600 may be transferred to the High Court for enforcement by a High Court Enforcement Officer (except where it is a judgment arising from a regulated agreement under the Consumer Credit Act).

QBG 12.2.6

12.2.6 The party seeking enforcement should obtain from the appropriate county court a certificate of the judgment of the county court in compliance with CCR O. 22 r.8(1A) (In Schedule 2 to the CPR), setting out details of the judgment or order to be enforced, sealed with the seal of that court and dated and signed by an officer of that court and stating on its face that it is granted for the purpose of enforcing the judgment or order by execution against goods in the High Court. Form N293A is a 'Combined Certificate of Judgment and Request for Writ of Fieri Facias' and should be used.

QBG 12.2.7

12.2.7 A correctly completed form N293A together with a copy should be filed in Room E15-E17 where the court officer will;

(1)   allocate a reference number,

(2)   date seal the Certificate and copy, returning the original to the party and retaining the copy, and

(3)   enter the proceedings in a register kept for that purpose.

The certificate will be treated for enforcement purposes as a High Court judgment and interest at the appropriate rate will run from the date of the Certificate.

QBG 12.2.8

12.2.8 The title of all subsequent documents shall be set out as follows:

'IN THE HIGH COURT OF JUSTICE
QUEEN'S BENCH DIVISION
High Court Claim No.
County Court Claim No.

(Sent from the [   ] County Court by Certificate dated (*date*))

Claimant

Defendant'

When the writ of fieri facias is issued, the Certificate of judgment retained by the party will be date-sealed by the court officer on the bottom left hand corner and endorsed with either the named Enforcement Officer or the District for Enforcement for which the writ is directed.

QBG 12.2.9

12.2.9 The Sheriffs Lodgement Centre at 20 – 21 Tooks Court, London EC4A 1LB provides a service for arranging transfer up of county court judgments. (A helpline is provided on 020 7205 2555)

QBG 12.2.10

12.2.10 It is important to remember in these cases that although any application for a stay of execution may be made to a Master in the High Court by application notice filed in accordance with Part 23, all other applications for enforcement or other relief must be made to the issuing county court. This practice is followed in the district registries with such variations as circumstances require.

QBG 12.2.11

12.2.11 When a writ of execution has been issued in the Royal Courts of Justice it may then be delivered to the Sheriffs Lodgement Centre. Value Added Tax is payable in addition to the High Court Enforcement Officer's fee on the services for which the fee is payable, and must be paid at the time of delivery of the writ. If the goods, chattels and property to be seized in execution are not within Greater London, the High Court Enforcement Officer will direct the writ to a High Court Enforcement Officer who is authorised to act in the appropriate district. Goods, which may not be seized in execution of a writ, are set out in s.138(3A) of the Supreme Court Act 1981 as follows:

(1)   such tools, books, vehicles and other items of equipment as are necessary to that person for use personally by him in his/her employment, business or vocation,

(2)   such clothing, bedding, furniture, household equipment and provisions as are necessary for satisfying the basic domestic needs of that person and his/her family,

(3)   any money, bank notes, bills of exchange, promissory notes, bonds, specialties or securities for money belonging to that person.

QBG 12.2.12

12.2.12 When first executing a writ of fieri facias the High Court Enforcement Officer will deliver to the debtor or leave at each place where execution is levied a notice of seizure in form No 55. This is commonly known as 'walking possession' and the notice explains to the debtor the situation with regard to the goods seized and what s/he then has to do.

QBG 12.2.13

12.2.13 After execution of a writ of execution, the High Court Enforcement Officer will endorse on the writ a statement of the manner in which s/he has executed it and will send a copy of the statement to the party issuing the writ.

12.3 Interpleader proceedings (RSC O.17)

QBG 12.3.1

12.3.1 Where a person is under liability in respect of a debt or property and has been, or expects to be claimed against by two or more persons claiming the same debt or property, if the person under liability does not dispute the debt or claim the property, s/he may apply to the court for relief by way of interpleader, i.e. for the entitlement of the persons claiming the same debt or property to be established in separate proceedings between them.

QBG 12.3.2

12.3.2 Where the High Court Enforcement Officer has seized goods in execution and a person other than the person against whom the writ of execution was issued wishes to claim the goods seized, s/he must give notice of his/her claim to the High Court Enforcement Officer, including in his/her notice a statement of his/her address which will be his/her address for service. The High Court Enforcement Officer will then give notice of that claim to the judgment creditor on whose behalf the goods were seized, in form PF 23. The notice requires the judgment creditor to state whether s/he admits or disputes the claim. The claimant must do so within 7 days of receipt of the High Court Enforcement Officer's notice and may use form PF 24 to do so.

QBG 12.3.3

12.3.3 Where the judgment creditor admits the claim, the High Court Enforcement Officer will withdraw from possession of the goods and may apply under RSC O.17 r.2(4) for an order to restrain a claim being brought against him for having taken possession of the goods. Where the claimant disputes the claim, the High Court Enforcement Officer may apply for interpleader relief. An application for interpleader relief if made in existing proceedings is made by an application in accordance with Part 23, otherwise it is made by the issue of a Part 8 claim form.

QBG 12.3.4

12.3.4 The Master may deal with the claims summarily, or may direct an issue to be tried between the parties in dispute (see RSC O.17 r.5) or make such other order as is appropriate.

12.4 Examination of judgment debtor (Part 71)

QBG 12.4.1

12.4.1 Where a person ('the judgment creditor') has obtained a judgment or order for payment of a sum of money against a person ('the judgment debtor'), the judgment creditor may apply for an order requiring the judgment debtor to attend to be orally examined concerning his assets and means. If the judgment debtor is a company or corporation, the court will order a named officer of the company or corporation to attend for examination. In the case of a judgment or order which is not for payment of a sum of money, the court may make an order for the attendance of the party liable for his examination on such questions as may be specified in the order.

QBG 12.4.2

12.4.2 An application for an order under Part 71 should be made in accordance with Part 23 without notice to any other party. The application must be supported by evidence giving details of the judgment or order, including the amount still owing, and showing that the judgment creditor is entitled to enforce the judgment or order. Where the judgment debtor is a company or corporation the evidence must give details of the officer to be examined. Form PF 98 may be used as a precedent for the evidence in support. Where a judgment creditor has obtained judgments in several different proceedings against the same judgment debtor, only one applica-tion need be made, setting out in the body of the application details of all the judgments on which examination is sought.

QBG 12.4.3

12.4.3 The examination will take place before a Master, Registrar, District Judge or nominated officer, as may be ordered, and will normally be at the court where the least expense will be incurred, usually the county court for the area where the judgment debtor lives. If a different court is requested by the applicant the reason why should be given in the application notice.

QBG 12.4.4

12.4.4 The application notice/evidence should be filed in the Masters' Support Unit Room E16 for consideration by a Master who will, if satisfied, make the or-der sought. Where the examination is to take place in a county court, the judgment creditor should lodge a copy of the order with the county court and obtain an appointment for the examination. If the examination is to take place in the Royal Courts of Justice, the order should be taken to Room E17 where the appointment will be endorsed on the order. In the Central Office the officers are nominated at the discretion of the Senior Master and their names may be obtained from Room E17.

QBG 12.4.5

12.4.5 The order (endorsed with the penal notice as set out in paragraph 9.1 of the Part 40B Practice Direction) together with details of the appointment must be served personally on the judgment debtor or on the officer of the judgment debtor company or corporation to be examined. A judgment debtor should be offered his conduct money, i.e. expenses of travelling to and from the examination and of attending to give evidence.

QBG 12.4.6

12.4.6 The officer conducting the examination will take down, or arrange to have taken down in writing the judgment debtor's statement. The officer will read the statement to the judgment debtor and will ask him or her to sign it. If he or she refuses to do so the officer will sign the statement. If the judgment debtor refuses to answer any question or if any other difficulties arise, the matter will be referred to the Interim Applications Judge in Court 37.

12.5 Third Party Debt Order proceedings (CPR Part 72)

QBG 12.5.1

12.5.1 Where a judgment creditor has obtained a judgment or order for payment of a sum of money against a judgment debtor, and another person ('the Third Party ') is indebted to the judgment debtor, the judgment creditor may apply to the Master for an order that the Third Party pays to the judgment creditor the amount of the debt due to the judgment debtor, or sufficient of it to satisfy the judgment debt.

QBG 12.5.2

12.5.2 The application should be made by filing an application notice in Practice Form N349, verified by a statement of truth, but the application notice need not be served on the judgment debtor. The application will normally be dealt with without a hearing and must be supported by evidence as set out in CPR 72 Practice Direction 1.2. If the Master is satisfied that such an order is appropriate, s/he will make an interim order in form N84 specifying the debt attached and appointing a time for the Third Party and the judgment debtor to attend and show cause why the order should not be made final.

QBG 12.5.3

12.5.3 The Third Party Debt Order to show cause must be served on the Third Party, and on the judgment debtor, in accordance with CPR 72.5. Where the Third Party or the judgment debtor fails to attend the hearing or attends but does not dispute the debt, the Master may make a final Third Party Debt Order against the Third Party under CPR 72.8 in form N85. The final order may be enforced in the same manner as any other order for the payment of money. Where the Third Party or the judgment debtor disputes the debt, the Master may dispose of the matter as set out in CPR 72.8.

QBG 12.5.4

12.5.4 Where the judgment creditor seeks to enforce a judgment expressed in a foreign currency by Third Party Debt Order proceedings, the evidence in support of the application must contain words to the following effect:

'The rate current in London for the purchase of (state the unit of foreign currency in which the judgment is expressed) at the close of business on (state the nearest preceding date to the date of verifying the evidence) was () to the £ sterling, and at this rate the sum of (state the amount of the judgment debt in the foreign currency) amounts to £. . . . . I have obtained this information from (state source) and believe it to be true.'

12.6 Charging Orders (CPR Part 73)

QBG 12.6.1

12.6.1 A judgment creditor may apply for a charging order on the property or assets of the judgment debtor, which will have the effect of providing him with security over the property of the judgment debtor. The High Court has jurisdiction to impose a charging order in the following cases:

(1)   where the property is a fund lodged in the High Court,

(2)   where the order to be enforced is a maintenance order of the High Court, and

(3)   where the judgment or order is made in the High Court and exceeds £5000.

The property and assets of the judgment debtor on which a charge may be imposed by a charging order are specified by s.2 of the Charging Orders Act 1979.

QBG 12.6.2

12.6.2 An interim charging order imposing a charge on land will be drawn in respect of the judgment debtors interest in the land and not the land itself, unless the court orders otherwise. If an interim charging order is made on stocks or shares in more than one company, a separate order must be drawn in respect of each company. A judgment creditor may apply in a single application notice for charging orders over more than one asset, but if the court makes charging orders over more than one asset, there will be separate orders relating to each asset. If the judgment debt is expressed in a foreign currency, the evidence in support of any application for a charging order should contain a similar provision to that set out in paragraph 12.5.4 above.

QBG 12.6.3

12.6.3 The application for a charging order is made to a Master and should be made in Practice Form N379 if the application relates to land, or N380 if the application relates to securities. The application is made without being served and will normally be dealt with without a hearing. If the Master is satisfied that such an order is appropriate, s/he will make an order in form N86 appointing a time for the judgment debtor to attend and show cause why the order should not be made absolute.

QBG 12.6.4

12.6.4 The interim order and the application notice should be served in accordance with CPR 73.5, or otherwise as directed by the Master. After further consideration at the hearing the Master will either make the order Final (with or without modifications) as in form N87, or discharge it. Where the order is discharged or varied, the order of discharge must be served in accordance with CPR 73.9(3).

QBG 12.6.5

12.6.5 CPR 73.7 deals with the effects of a charging order on funds in court, which includes securities held in court.

QBG 12.6.6

12.6.6 Although the court may make a charging order in a foreign currency, to facilitate enforcement it is usually preferable for it to be expressed in sterling. Thus if the foreign debt is in a foreign currency the evidence in support of the application should contain the sterling equivalent and request the charging order to be made in sterling. (See paragraph 12.6.2 above).

Enforcement of Charging Order

QBG 12.6.7

12.6.6 Proceedings for the enforcement of a charging order by sale of the property charged must be begun by a Part 8 Claim Form issued out of the Chancery Division of the High Court or a Chancery district registry unless the High Court has no jurisdiction, in which case application should be made to the appropriate County Court. (RSC O.50 r.9A). The County Court's limit at present is when the amount owing does not exceed £30,000.

12.7 Receivers; equitable execution (CPR Part 69)

QBG 12.7.1

12.7.1 Equitable execution is a process which enables a judgment creditor to obtain payment of the judgment debt where the interest of the judgment debtor in property cannot be seized or reached by ordinary execution.

QBG 12.7.2

12.7.2 An application for appointment of a receiver by way of equitable execution may be made to a Master, who also has jurisdiction to grant an injunction if, and only so far as, the injunction is ancillary or incidental to the order. The procedure follows that set out in RSC O.30 rr.1 to 6, and the application should be made in accordance with Part 23 and the Part 23 Practice Direction as described in the following paragraphs.

QBG 12.7.3

12.7.3 If the judgment creditor seeks an injunction (as in 11.7.2 above) s/he should file his/her application notice based on form No. 82 but setting out in addition the injunction sought, together with a witness statement or affidavit in support stating:

(1)   the date and particulars of the judgment, and that it remains wholly unsatisfied, or to what extent it remains unsatisfied,

(2)   the particulars and result of any execution which has been issued, and the nature of the High Court Enforcement Officer's return (if any),

(3)   that the judgment debtor has no property which can be taken by the ordinary process of execution, (ifs/he has, give reasons showing that legal execution would be futile),

(4)   particulars of the property in respect of which it is proposed to appoint a receiver,

(5)   the name and address of the receiver proposed to be appointed, and that in the deponent's judgments/he is a fit and proper person to be appointed receiver, and

(6)   that the judgment debtor is in financial difficulties [that the immediate appointment of a receiver without the delay of giving security is of great importance] and that the deponent believes that the judgment debtor may assign or dispose of his/her estate or interest in (give details of property) unless restrained from doing so by the order and injunction of the court.

QBG 12.7.4

12.7.4 The judgment creditor need not give notice of this application which will normally be dealt with without a hearing. If the Master is satisfied with the evidence s/he will make an order in form No. 83 for a hearing to take place in respect of the application for the appointment of the receiver and granting an injunction meanwhile.

QBG 12.7.5

12.7.5 If the judgment creditor does not seek an injunction, the application notice should be filed and served together with the evidence in support (as in paragraph 11.7.3 above but without paragraph (6)).

QBG 12.7.6

12.7.6 At the hearing of the application to appoint the receiver, the Master will, if s/he thinks fit, make an order in form No. 84. A copy of the order appointing the receiver shall be served by the judgment creditor on the receiver and all other parties to the proceedings.

QBG 12.7.7

12.7.7 Where a receiver has been ordered to give security under RSC O.30 r.2, the judgment creditor should obtain an appointment before the Master who made the order appointing the receiver, to settle the form and amount of the security. Unless otherwise ordered, the security will be in the form of a guarantee. The judgment creditor should have prepared a draft form of guarantee for the Master to approve at the appointment. Form PF 30CH may be used as a precedent for the guarantee.

QBG 12.7.8

12.7.8 RSC O.30 r.3 deals with the remuneration of the receiver which may either be assessed by the Master or referred to a costs judge. RSC O.30 r.5 contains the provisions for submitting the receiver's accounts.

12.8 Committals, etc. (RSC O.52)

QBG 12.8.1

12.8.1 The court has power to punish contempt of court by an order of committal to prison or by other means. These may be by ordering the payment of a fine, by the issue of a writ of sequestration, or by making a hospital or guardianship order under certain provisions of the Mental Health Act 1983. Committal applications under RSC O.52 r.4 are always dealt with by a High Court Judge. The following provisions apply to applications made under RSC O.52 r.4.

QBG 12.8.2

12.8.2 The application should be made in existing proceedings by filing an application notice. If not in existing proceedings, a Part 8 Claim Form should be issued (see paragraphs 2.1 and 2.2 of the practice direction - Committal Applications). The Claim Form or application notice must contain a prominent notice stating the possible consequences of the court making a committal order. The notice is annexed at the end of the practice direction.

QBG 12.8.3

12.8.3 Evidence in support of a committal application must be by affidavit and, together with the Part 8 Claim Form or application notice, must be served personally on the person sought to be committed giving 14 days notice unless otherwise directed by the court (paragraph 4.2 of the practice direction). A date for the hearing must be obtained from the Listing Office, Room WG8 and endorsed on or served with the Claim Form or application notice.

QBG 12.8.4

12.8.4 Paragraphs 2.5, 2.6 and 3.1 to 3.4 of the Practice Direction deal with the content of the evidence, and serving and filing, and paragraph 4 deals with the hearing date and management of the proceedings.

QBG 12.8.5

12.8.5 Committal proceedings will normally be heard in public, but see RSC O.52 r.6 which sets out certain types of cases which may be heard in private (although brief details of the case must be read out in public) and see paragraph 9 of the Practice Direction.

QBG 12.8.6

12.8.6 Where the court makes a finding of contempt, details of the contempt and of the order or undertaking breached (where appropriate) must be set out in the order. The term of any period of committal must be stated in the order and must not exceed two years. A fine must be expressed as payable to Her Majesty the Queen and the order must state the amount of the fine and the date and time within which it must be paid. A contemnor and his solicitors will be notified separately as to how the fine should be paid. A precedent of the order is in form No. 85 and will normally be drawn by the court.

QBG 12.8.7

12.8.7 When an order for committal to prison is made, the court will issue a warrant to the Tipstaff authorising him to convey the contemnor to the appropriate prison. A copy of the order should be served on the prison governor and the Official Solicitor. RSC O.52 r.8 deals with the discharge of a person committed.

12.9 Execution against property of Foreign or Commonwealth States

QBG 12.9.1

12.9.1 In cases where judgment has been obtained against a foreign or Commonwealth State and it is sought to execute the judgment by a writ of fieri facias, a charging order or a Third Party Debt Order, the following provisions apply:

(1)   Before the writ of fieri facias is issued, the Master must be informed in writing and his/her direction sought. In cases where an application is to be made for a charging order to show cause or a Third Party to show cause, the evidence in support of the application must include a statement that the execution sought is against a foreign or Commonwealth State.

(2)   The Master, having been so informed will, as soon as practicable, inform the Foreign and Commonwealth Office ('FCO') of the application and will not permit the issue of a writ of fieri facias, nor grant an order to show cause until the FCO has been so informed. The Protocol Division of the Head of Diplomatic Missions and International Organisations Unit of the FCO may be contacted by telephone on 020 7008 0991 or by Fax on 020 7008 0978.

(3)   Having regard to all the circumstances of the case, the Master may postpone the decision whether to issue the writ or grant the order to show cause for so long as s/he considers reasonable for the purpose of enabling the FCO to furnish further information relevant to his/her decision, but not for longer than 3 days from the time of his/her contacting the FCO. In the event that no further information is received from the FCO within 24 hours of its being informed, then the writ of fieri facias may be issued or the order to show cause may be sealed without further delay.

12.10 Recovery of enforcement costs

QBG 12.10.1

12.10.1 Subsection (3) of section 15 of the Courts and Legal Services Act 1990 enables a person taking steps to enforce a money judgment in the High Court to recover the costs of any previous attempt to enforce that judgment. Subsection (4) of section 15 excludes costs that the court considers to have been unreasonably incurred.

QBG 12.10.2

12.10.2 The application for an enforcement costs order is made to a Master and should be made in accordance with Part 23 but the application notice need not be served on the judgment debtor. The application will normally be dealt with without a hearing and must be supported by evidence substantially as set out in form PF 205. The deponent should exhibit sufficient vouchers, receipts or other documents as are reasonably necessary to verify the amount of the costs of previous attempts to enforce the judgment.

QBG 12.10.3

12.10.3 If the Master is satisfied that such an order is appropriate, s/he will make an order for payment of the amount of such costs ass/he considers may be recoverable under subsection (3) of section 15. If the amount of such costs is less than that claimed by the judgment creditor, the Master may either disallow the balance or give directions for a detailed assessment or other determination of the balance. If after assessment or other determination it appears that the judgment creditor is entitled to further costs beyond those originally allowed, s/he may issue a further writ of fieri facias or take other lawful steps to enforce those costs. Interest on the costs runs either from the date the Master made the enforcement costs order or from the date of the costs certificate.

12.11 Enforcement of Magistrates' Courts' orders

QBG 12.11.1

12.11.1 The Magistrates' Courts Act 1980, s.87 provides that payment of a sum ordered to be paid on a conviction of a magistrates' court may be enforced by the High Court or a county court (otherwise than by the issue of a writ of fieri facias or other process against goods or by imprisonment or attachment of earnings) as if the sum were due to the clerk of the magistrates' court under a judgment of the High Court or county court, as the case may be.

QBG 12.11.2

12.11.2 In the Central Office, the application is made to a Master and should be made in accordance with Part 23. Where enforcement is sought by a Third Party Debt Order or charging order to show cause, the application will normally be dealt with without a hearing. Otherwise the application notice and evidence in support should be served on the defendant.

QBG 12.11.3

12.11.3 The application must be supported by a witness statement or affidavit in a form appropriate to the type of execution sought and must have exhibited to it the authority of the magistrates' court to take the proceedings which will recite the conviction, the amount outstanding and the nature of the proceedings authorised to be taken (Magistrates Courts Forms Rules 1981, Form 63).

QBG 12.11.4

12.11.4 The application notice and evidence in support together with an additional copy of the exhibit should be filed in Room E15 where it will be assigned a reference number from the register kept for that purpose. The Master according to the type of enforcement sought will then deal with the matter.

QBG 12.11.5

12.11.5 This practice will also be followed in the District Registries with such variations as circumstances may render necessary.

12.12 Enforcement of Foreign Judgments and Enforcement of High Court Judgments Abroad

QBG 12.12.1

12.12.1 CPR 74 deals with enforcement of judgments in different jurisdictions. Section 1 covers enforcement in England & Wales of judgments of foreign courts.

QBG 12.12.2

12.12.2 If a foreign court is not a party to an agreement with this country on mutual recognition and enforcement of judgments, then a fresh action will need to be brought based on that foreign judgment. Such an action can usually be made by a Part 8 claim.

QBG 12.12.3

12.12.3 Section 1 of the rule covers enforcement of judgments of foreign courts covered by the Administration of Justice Act 1933 ('the 1933 Act'), the Foreign

Judgments (Reciprocal Enforcement) Act 1933 ('the 1933 Act'), the Civil Jurisdiction and Judgments Act 1982 ('the 1982 Act') and the Council Regulation (EC)
No. 44/2001 of 22nd December 2000 ('the Judgments Regulation').

QBG 12.12.4

12.12.4 A list of the countries that are covered by each of the various Acts and the
Judgments Regulation is set out in Her Majesty's Court Service 'Notes for
Guidance' on the above Acts and Regulation, which can be obtained from the
Judgments & Orders Section of the Action Department of the Central Office (Room
E17). This also contains the standard forms used and sets out the procedure for
applications for registration.

Reciprocal enforcement; the Administration of Justice Act 1920 the Foreign Judgments (Reciprocal Enforcement) Act 1933, the Civil Jurisdiction and Judgments Act 1982 and the Judgments Regulation.

QBG 12.12.5

12.12.5 CPR 74.4 sets out how an application for registration of a foreign judgment
in the High Court under the 1920, 1933 or 1982 Acts under the Judgments
Regulation may be made. The application should be made without notice being
served on any other party, but the Master may direct that a Part 8 Claim Form
should be issued and served.

QBG 12.12.6

12.12.6 CPR 74.4 (2)-(6) sets out what the evidence in support of the application
should contain or have exhibited to it. The foreign judgment will be registered in the
foreign currency in which it is expressed and must not be converted into Sterling in
the evidence in support. When it comes to enforcing the foreign judgment, the
amount should then be converted in accordance with the instructions set out above
in paragraph 11 in respect of the type of enforcement sought.

QBG 12.12.7

12.12.7 The order giving permission to register the judgment must be drawn up by,
or on behalf of the judgment creditor and will be entered in the Register of
Judgments kept in the Action Department Room E17 of the Central Office for that
purpose. The order will usually contain a direction that the costs of and caused by
the application and the registration be assessed and added to the judgment as
registered. The Order for registration of the judgment must state the matters set out
in CPR 74.6 (3) including the right of the judgment debtor to apply, and the time
within which s/he may do so, to have the registration set aside. The notice must be
served on the judgment debtor in accordance with CPR 74.6 (1).

QBG 12.12.8

12.12.8 An application to set aside the registration of a judgment under CPR 74.7
(1) must be made in accordance with Part 23 and be supported by a witness
statement or affidavit.

QBG 12.12.9

12.12.9 Section 2 of CPR 74 covers enforcement in foreign countries of judgments
of the High Court and County Court of England & Wales. A judgment creditor who
wishes to enforce such a judgment abroad must apply for a certified copy of the
judgment.

QBG 12.12.10

12.12.10 Section 3 of CPR 74 deals with enforcement of UK Judgments in other parts of the UK. A person who wishes to enforce a judgment of the High Court or County Court of England & Wales in another part of the UK may apply for a certified copy of the judgment.

QBG 12.12.11

12.12.11 An application for a certified copy of a judgment entered in the High Court may be made without notice and must be supported by evidence, in accordance with CPR 74.13 for enforcement of High Court and County judgments in foreign countries, and in accordance with CPR 74.17or 18 for enforcement of High Court and County judgments in other parts of the UK. The certified copy will be endorsed with a certificate signed by the Master. The forms of certificate are included in the 'Notes for Guidance' referred to in paragraph 11.12.4 above. Where the application was made under s. 10 of the Foreign Judgments (Reciprocal Enforcement) Act 1933, an additional certificate will be issued and signed by the Master [as in form PF 155.] Judgment creditors who intend to seek enforcement abroad should ensure that their judgment is endorsed as follows:

'This judgment carries interest from (date) at the rate of 8% per annum in accordance with the provisions of the Judgments Act 1838'.

QBG 12.12.12

12.12.12 An application may also be made for registration in the High Court of a judgment given by a court in another part of the UK.

QBG 12.12.13

12.12.13 The certificate must be filed for registration in Room E15 – E17 in the Action Department within 6 months from the date of its issue. Under paragraph 9 of schedule 6 to the Act of 1982 an application may be made to stay the enforcement of the certificate. The application may be made without notice being served on any other party supported by a witness statement or affidavit stating that the applicant is entitled and intends to apply to the judgment court to set aside or stay the judgment.

Applications under s.18 of the Act of 1982; judgment containing non-money provisions: The procedure is set out in CPR 74.16(3).

QBG 12.12.14

12.12.14 The certificates will be entered in the register of certificates in respect of judgments ordered to be registered under CPR 74 PD 3 kept in the Central Office for that purpose.

Enforcement of European Community judgments

QBG 12.12.15

12.12.15 Section 4 of CPR deals with enforcement of European Community judgments in England and Wales, that is, judgments not of the national courts of Member States but rather the judgments of the courts and institutes of the community itself.

QBG 12.12.16

12.12.16 CPR 74.19 An application for registration may be made without notice being served on any other party and must be supported by written evidence containing or having exhibited to it the matters referred to in CPR 74.21 (1).

QBG 12.12.17

12.12.17 The order for registration must contain the information and exhibit the documents required by CPR 74.22. The order for registration will be entered in the register of the Judgments and Orders kept in the Action Department Room E17, Central Office for that purpose. The registration order must be served on every person against whom judgment was given.

QBG 12.12.18

12.12.18 An application to vary or cancel a registration under the provisions of CPR 74.23 shall be made by application notice in accordance with Part 23, supported by written evidence, and must be made within 28 days of service of the registration order.

Enforcement of recommendations etc. under the Merchant Shipping (Liner Conferences) Act 1982

QBG 12.12.19

12.12.19 Applications under s. 9 of the Act of 1982 for registration of a recommendation, determination or award, are dealt with by a Commercial Judge and shall be made by the issue of a Part 8 Claim Form. The application should be supported by evidence in accordance with CPR 74 PD 12.

QBG 12.12.20

12.12.20 The order giving permission to register the recommendation, determination or award must be drawn up by or on behalf of the party making the application, and entered in the register of the recommendations, determinations and awards ordered to be registered under s. 9 of the Act of 1982, directed by the Senior Master to be kept in the Admiralty and Commercial Registry.

Regulation (EC) No. 805/2004 of the European Parliament and of the Council of 21 April 2004 ('the European Enforcement Order')

QBG 12.12.21

12.12.21 The European Enforcement Order (EEO) creates a simplified method of enforcement for uncontested claims throughout the EU member states (except Denmark). Details of the procedure are contained in Section V of Part 74.

QBG 12.12.22

12.12.22 An application for an EEO certificate must be made by Form N219 or N219A depending upon whether the Judgment was by agreement/admission/settlement or in default of defence or objection. The application may be made without notice and will be dealt with without a hearing, unless the Master orders a hearing.

QBG 12.12.23

12.12.23 An application under Article 6(2) of the EEO Regulation for a certificate indicating the lack or limitation of enforceability of an EEO certificate must be made to the court of origin by application in accordance with Part 23.

QBG 12.12.24

12.12.24 An application under Article 10 of the EEO Regulation for rectification or withdrawal of an EEO certificate must be made to the court of origin and may be made by application in accordance with Part 23.

QBG 12.12.25

12.12.25 A person seeking to enforce an EEO in England and Wales must lodge at the court in which enforcement proceedings are to be brought the documents required by Article 20 of the EEO Regulation.

QBG 12.12.26

12.12.26 Where an EEO certificate has been lodged and the judgment debtor applies to stay or limit the enforcement proceedings under Article 23 of the EEO Regulation, such application must be made by application in accordance with Part 23 to the court in which the EEO is being enforced.12.12.27 An application under Article 21 of the EEO Regulation that the court should refuse to enforce an EEO must be made by application in accordance with Part 23 to the court in which the EEO is being enforced.

13 MISCELLANEOUS

13.1 Service of foreign process (CPR 6.32) and Council Regulation (EC) No 1348/2000

QBG 13.1.1

13.1.1 CPR 6.32 applies to the service on a person in England or Wales of any process in connection with civil or commercial proceedings in a foreign court or tribunal, except those countries to which the Service Regulation is applicable (see 12.1.4 below). A request for service is made to the Senior Master from either Her Majesty's Principal Secretary of State for Foreign and Commonwealth Affairs, or where the foreign court or tribunal is in a convention country, from a consular or other authority of that country.

QBG 13.1.2

13.1.2 Where the foreign court or tribunal certifies that the person to be served understands the language of the process, it is not necessary to provide a translation. CPR 6.34 deals with the manner of service; the process may be served through the Bailiff of the county court and the usual practice is for the Senior Master to provide a certificate for the bailiff or county court officer to use. The Senior Master may make an order for service by an alternative method based on the bailiff's certificate.

QBG 13.1.3

13.1.3 When service has been effected, the Senior Master will send a certificate, together with a copy of the process served, (if applicable) to the authority who requested service, stating how service was effected, or why service could not be effected. There is a discretion to charge for the costs of service or attempted service, but recovery is usually sought only where the country requesting service does not provide a reciprocal free service.

QBG 13.1.4

13.1.4 Council Regulation (EC) No 1348/2000 ('the Service Regulation') applies to service on a person in England & Wales of proceedings in from courts in other European Union Member States, and provides a complete code for service of proceedings between member states. The Senior Master is the central body designated under Article 3 of the Regulation. The Regulation can be found at CPR Practice Direction 6.36.

13.2 Rectification of register of deeds of arrangement (RSC O.94 r.4)

QBG 13.2.1

13.2.1 Deeds of arrangement must be registered. The registration office is at the Department of Trade.

QBG 13.2.2

13.2.2 An application for an order as set out in RSC O.94 r.4(1)(a) or (b) must be made to a Master of the Queen's Bench Division. Notice need not be served on any other party and a witness statement must support the application or affidavit as described in rule 4(2).

13.3 Exercise of jurisdiction under the Representation of the People Acts (RSC O.94 r.5)

QBG 13.3.1

13.3.1 RSC O.94 r.5 describes the jurisdiction of the High Court under the above Acts. The practice is governed by the Election Petition Rules 1960 (as amended). The Senior Master is the Prescribed Officer.

QBG 13.3.2

13.3.2 Under Part III of the Representation of the People Act 1983, the result of a parliamentary or local government election may be questioned on the grounds of some irregularity either before or during the election. The provisions of Part III have also been applied to European Parliamentary elections.

QBG 13.3.3

13.3.3 The challenge is made by the issue of an Election Petition

(a)   in respect of a Parliamentary election by one or more electors or

(b)   in respect of a local government election by four or more electors,

or by an unsuccessful or alleged candidate.

The member/councillor whose election is complained of is a Respondent to the petition as is the Returning Officer if his/her conduct is complained of. The petition is issued in the Election Petitions Office, Room E08, normally within 21 days of the election. (although this may be extended in certain circumstances).

QBG 13.3.4

13.3.4 The petition is tried by two High Court Judges of the Queen's Bench Division in respect of Parliamentary elections or by a Commissioner in respect of Local Government elections. The Commissioner must be a lawyer of not less than 10 years standing who neither resides nor practices in the area concerned. The trial usually takes place in the constituency/local government area for which the Election Petition has been issued, although preliminary matters are usually dealt with at the Royal Courts of Justice.

QBG 13.3.5

13.3.5 The election court may confirm the result of the election, or substitute another candidate as the member/councillor, or may order the election to be re-run.

QBG 13.3.6

13.3.6 Applications for remedies under various sections of the Representation of the People Act 1983 are also issued in the Election Petitions Office, and are usually heard by an Election Rota Judge.

QBG 13.3.7

13.3.7 Outside the court offices' opening times, but while the building is still open to the public, election petitions and applications may be left in the letterbox located outside Room E08. When the building is closed, Election Petitions and applications may be left with Security at the Main Entrance, up until midnight on the last day for service.

13.4 Bills of Sale Acts 1878 and 1882 and the Industrial and Provident Societies Act 1967 (RSC O.95)

QBG 13.4.1

13.4.1 Every bill of sale and absolute bill of sale to which the Act of 1878 applies must be registered under s.8 of that Act, within 7 clear days of its making, and, under s.11 of the Act of 1878, the registration of a bill of sale must be renewed at least once every 5 years. The register for the purpose of the Bills of Sale Acts contains the particulars of registered bills of sale and an alphabetical index of the names of the grantors, and is kept in the Action Department in Room E15 – E17.

QBG 13.4.2

13.4.2 An application to register a bill of sale, which is made within the prescribed time, should be made by filing in Room E15-E17 the original bill of sale and any document annexed to it together with a witness statement or affidavit in form PF 179 or PF 180. An application to re-register a bill of sale, which is made within the prescribed time, should be made by filing in Room E15-E17 a witness statement or affidavit in form PF 181.

QBG 13.4.3

13.4.3 An application to rectify;

(1)   an omission to register, by extending the time for registration, or

(2)   an omission or mis-statement of the name, residence or occupation of a person in the register, by correcting the registration,

must be made by witness statement or affidavit to a Master of the Queen's Bench Division. In addition to the matters set out in forms PF 179 or PF 180, the evidence in support must also set out the particulars of the omission and state the grounds on which the application is made.

QBG 13.4.4

13.4.4 Where the residence of the grantor of the bill of sale or the person against whom the process is issued is outside the London bankruptcy district, or where the bill of sale describes the goods as being in a place outside that district, the Central Office will send copies of the bill of sale to the appropriate county court district judge.

QBG 13.4.5

13.4.5 The Master, on being satisfied that the omission or mis-statement of name, residence or occupation of a person in the register was accidental or due to inadvertence, may order the omission or mis-statement to be rectified by the insertion in the register of the correct name, residence or occupation of the person.

QBG 13.4.6

13.4.6 Where the Master is satisfied that the omission to register a bill of sale or a witness statement or affidavit of renewal within the prescribed time was accidental or due to inadvertence, s/he may extend the time for registration on such terms ass/he thinks fit. In order to protect any creditors who have accrued rights of property in the assets in respect of which the bill of sale was granted between the date of the bill and its actual registration, any order to extend the time for registration will normally be made 'without prejudice' to those creditors. The order will be drawn up in form PF 182.

QBG 13.4.7

13.4.7 An application for an order that a memorandum of satisfaction be written on a registered copy of a bill of sale, made without the consent of the person entitled to the benefit of the bill of sale, must be made by the issue of a Part 8 Claim Form. Where the consent of the person entitled to the benefit of the bill of sale has been obtained, the application may be made by a witness statement or affidavit containing that consent and verifying the signature on it. Form PF 183 contains precedents for the evidence and forms of consent. Where the application is made with consent, the evidence need not be served on any other person. If the Master is satisfied on the evidence, s/he will endorse his/her approval on the witness statement or affidavit (an order is not normally drawn up) and send it to Room E17 for a memorandum of satisfaction to be entered on the copy of the Bill in the Registry. If a copy of the bill of sale has been sent to a county court district judge, a notice of satisfaction will be sent to that district judge.

QBG 13.4.8

13.4.8 Where the consent has not been obtained, the Claim Form must be served on the person entitled to the benefit of the bill of sale and must be supported by evidence that the debt (if any) for which the bill of sale was made has been satisfied or discharged.

QBG 13.4.9

13.4.9 An application to restrain removal on sale of goods seized in accordance with RSC O.95 r.3 and under the proviso to s.7 of the Bills of Sale Act (1878) Amendment Act 1882 must be made by the issue of a Part 8 Claim Form for hearing before the Interim Applications Judge.

QBG 13.4.10

13.4.10 Under the Industrial and Provident Societies Act 1967 an application to record an instrument creating a fixed or floating charge on the assets of a registered society or to rectify any omission or mis-statement in it must be made within 14 days beginning with the date of its execution.

QBG 13.4.11

13.4.11 Under RSC O.95 r.5 and in accordance with s.1(5) of the Act of 1967 the court may order;

(1)   that the period for making an application for recording a charge be extended, or

(2)   an omission or mis-statement in such an application be rectified.

The procedure for obtaining an order as in (1) or (2) above is similar to that under s. 14 of the Bills of Sale Act 1878 and must be made by witness statement or affidavit to a Master of the Queen's Bench Division as in paragraph 13.4.3 above and must exhibit a copy of the instrument duly authenticated in the prescribed manner together with any other particulars relating to the charge.

QBG 13.4.12

13.4.12 RSC O.95 r.3 refers to the assignment of book debts; the register of assignments of book debts is kept in Room E15- E17 in the Central Office. An application for registration under s. 344 of the Insolvency Act 1986 should be made in accordance with RSC O.95 r.6(2). Parties may use form PF 186 for their evidence in support. It is helpful if the original assignment is also produced.

13.5 Enrolment of deeds and other documents

QBG 13.5.1

13.5.1 Any deed or document which by virtue of any enactment is required or authorised to be enrolled in the Supreme Court may be enrolled in the Central Office. See the Part 5 Practice Direction at paragraph 6, which fully sets out the procedure for enrolment and contains in an appendix the Enrolment of Deeds (Change of Name) Regulations 1994.

13.6 Bail

QBG 13.6.1

13.6.1 With the coming into force on 5th April 2004 of section 17 of the Criminal Justice Act 2003, the Queen's Bench Division of the High Court no longer has the power to grant bail in criminal proceedings to a defendant in custody who has been refused bail, or to vary the arrangements for bail of an inferior court.

QBG 13.6.2

13.6.2 The limited remaining right of the High Court to grant bail in specific circumstances is exercised by the Administrative Court.

13.7 References to the Court of Justice of the European Communities

QBG 13.7.1

13.7.1 A party wishing to apply for an order under CPR 68 may do so by application before or at the trial or hearing. An application made before the trial or hearing should be made in accordance with Part 23.

QBG 13.7.2

13.7.2 Before making an order for reference, the Court will pay close attention to the terms of Part 68 of the CPR, to form PF 109 and to the 'Guidance of the Court of Justice of the European Communities on References by National Courts for Preliminary Rulings' which may be found in the Practice Direction (ECJ References: Procedure) (1999) 1 WLR 260.

QBG 13.7.3

13.7.3 It is the responsibility of the Court, rather than the parties, to settle the terms of the reference. This should identify as clearly, succinctly and simply as the nature of the case permits the question to which the Court of England & Wales seeks an answer and it is very desirable that language should be used which lends itself readily to translation.

QBG 13.7.4

13.7.4 The referring court should, in a single document scheduled to the order (in form PF 109);

(1)   identify the parties and summarise the nature and history of the prooood lngs,

(2)   summarise the salient facts, indicating whether these are proved or admitted or assumed,

(3)   make reference to the rules of national law (substantive and procedural) relevant to the dispute,

(4)   summarise the contentions of the parties as far as relevant,

(5)   explain why a ruling of the European Court is sought, identifying the EC provisions whose effect is in issue, and

(6)   formulate, without avoidable complexity, the question(s) to which an answer is requested.

QBG 13.7.5

13.7.5 Where the document is in the form of a judgment, passages, which are not relevant to the reference, should be omitted from the text scheduled to the order. Incorporation of appendices, annexes or enclosures as part of the document should be avoided, unless the relevant passages lend themselves readily to translation and are clearly identified.

QBG 13.7.6

13.7.6 When the order of reference has been approved by the Judge and sealed by the court, the order, together with any other necessary documents should be promptly passed to Room F 209 where the Clerk will process the reference for the attention of the Senior Master of the Queen's Bench Division, for transmission to Luxembourg without avoidable delay.

13.8 Group Litigation Orders 'GLOs'

QBG 13.8.1

13.8.1 Section III of Part 19 and the Practice Direction - Group Litigation deal with claims where multiple parties are claimants.

QBG 13.8.2

13.8.2 When considering applying for a GLO, the applicant should contact the Law Society at 113 Chancery Lane, London WC2A 1PL, who may be able to assist in putting the applicant in contact with other parties who may also be interested in applying for a GLO in the same matter.

QBG 13.8.3

13.8.3 The consent of either the Lord Chief Justice or the Vice Chancellor to the GLO is required. In the Queen's Bench Division the application should be made to the Senior Master in accordance with Part 23. If the Senior Master is minded to make the GLO s/he will forward a copy of the application notice and any written evidence to the Lord Chief Justice. The application notice should include the information set out in paragraph 3.2 of the Practice Direction.

QBG 13.8.4

13.8.4 A group register will be set up and maintained by a party to the GLO of all the parties to the group of claims to be managed under the GLO. In order to publicise the GLO when it has been made, a copy should be supplied to the Law Society and to the Senior Master. A record of each GLO made will be maintained in the Central Office in a Nationwide Register of all GLO's notified to the Senior Master.

QBG 13.8.5

13.8.5 The Practice Direction sets out how the group litigation will be managed. In particular, a managing judge will be appointed. The case management directions are likely to direct;

(1) that a 'Group Particulars of Claim' containing the various claims of the claimants on the group register are served,

(2) that one claim proceed as a 'test' claim, and

(3) a cut-off date after which no additions may be made to the group register.

(4) that all documents in the GLO be headed in the name of the Group Litigation name

ANNEX 1
GUIDE TO CIVIL PROCEEDINGS FEES

QBG App 1

The new Civil Proceedings Fees Order combines Supreme Court and county court fees. For details of the fees to be taken, refer to the Fees section, below, at **FEE 1.8**.

ANNEX 2

QBG App 2

The following is a list of the abbreviations commonly used by Masters on endorsements of orders, though there may be some variation as between individual Masters.

A.D.R.	Alternative Dispute Resolution
Aff.	Affidavit
A.M-T	Allocate to multi-track
A.N.	Appointment Notice
App.	Application
A.Q.	Allocation Questionnaire
A.S.	Assessed summarily
B.N.L.T.	By no later than
C.C.	County Court
C.I.A.	Costs in the application
C.I.A.E.	Costs in any event
C.I.C.	Costs in the case
Cl.	Claimant
Col.	Certificate for Counsel
C.M.C.	Case Management Conference
C.O.C.B.	Costs of and caused by
C.R.	Costs reserved
C.T.R.	Costs of today reserved
D./Def	Defendant/Defence

D.A.I/N.A.	Detailed assessment if not agreed
Disc.	Disclosure
Dism.	Dismissed
Disp. C/S.	Dispense with requirement of certificate of service
F.C.	Fixed costs
F.C.O	Final Charging Order
F.I.	Further information
F.O.	Further order
F.O.D.	First open date
I.A.E.	In any event
I.B.	Indemnity basis
Insp.	Inspection
I.T.P.D.O.	Interim Third party Debt Order
J.	Judgment (as in Part 24 applications)
L.A.	Legal Aid
L.A.A.	Legal Aid assessment
L.Q.	Listing Questionnaire
O.	Order
On C.Serv.	On producing certificate of service
O. Exam.	Oral examination
P/C	Particulars of claim
P.D.	Practice direction
Pm.	Permission
Pm. A.	Permission to apply
Pm. R.	Permission to restore
Pm. R.F.D.	Permission to restore for further directions
Pt.	Part
P.R.A.	Private room appointment
R.	Rule
S.A.	Set aside/Special allowance
S.O.J.	Service out of the jurisdiction
S/C	Statement of Case
S.B.	Standard basis
S/T	Statement of truth
Tfr.	Transfer
T.P.D.O.	Third Party Debt Order
W.C.O.	Wasted Costs Order
W.N.	Without notice
W.S.	Witness statement

THE TECHNOLOGY AND CONSTRUCTION COURT GUIDE

Section 1   Introduction ....CPR 60 TCCG 1
Section 2   Pre-Action Protocol ....CPR 60 TCCG 2
Section 3   Commencement and Transfer.....................CPR 60 TCCG 3
Section 4   Access to the Court ....CPR 60 TCCG 4
Section 5   Case management and the First CMC ....CPR 60 TCCG 5
Section 6   Applications after the First CMC...............CPR 60 TCCG 6
Section 7   ADR...CPR 60 TCCG 7
Section 8   Preliminary Issues............................CPR 60 TCCG 8
Section 9   Adjudication Business..........................CPR 60 TCCG 9
Section 10   Arbitration ....CPR 60 TCCG 10
Section 11   Disclosure....................................CPR 60 TCCG 11
Section 12   Witness Statements and Factual Evidence for use at trialCPR 60 TCCG 12
Section 13   Expert Evidence ....CPR 60 TCCG 13
Section 14   The Pre-Trial Review ....CPR 60 TCCG 14
Section 15   The Trial.....................................CPR 60 TCCG 15
Section 16   Costs...CPR 60 TCCG 16
Section 17   Enforcement ....CPR 60 TCCG 17
Section 18   The TCC Judge as Arbitrator...................CPR 60 TCCG 18
Appendix A   Case management information sheet ....CPR 60 TCCG A
Appendix B   Case management directions form ....CPR 60 TCCG B
Appendix C   Pre-trial review questionnaire................CPR 60 TCCG C
Appendix D   Contact details for courts dealing with TCC claims....CPR 60 TCCG D
Appendix E   Draft ADR Order...............................CPR 60 TCCG E
Appendix F   Draft directions order in adjudication enforcement
              proceedings...................................CPR 60 TCCG F
Appendix G   Draft Court Settlement Order ....CPR 60 TCCG G
Appendix H   Amendments in the Second Revision ....CPR 60 TCCG H

Explanatory note: This Second Revision of the Second Edition of the TCC Guide makes the changes identified in Appendix G.

1. INTRODUCTION

1.1 Purpose of Guide

CPR 60 TCCG 1

1.1.1 The Technology and Construction Court ('TCC') Guide is intended to provide straightforward, practical guidance on the conduct of litigation in the TCC. Whilst it is intended to be comprehensive, it naturally concentrates on the most important aspects of such litigation. It therefore cannot cover all the procedural points that may arise. It does, however, describe the main elements of the practice that is likely to be followed in most TCC cases. This Guide does not and cannot add to or amend the CPR or the relevant practice directions. The purpose and function of this Guide is to explain how the substantive law, rules and practice directions are applied in the TCC and cannot affect their proper interpretation and effect: see *Secretary of State for Communities and Local Government v Bovale* [2009] 1 WLR 2274 at [36].

1.1.2 The Guide reflects the flexible framework within which litigation in the TCC is habitually conducted. The guidance set out in the Guide is designed to ensure effective management of proceedings in the TCC. It must always be remembered that, if parties fail to comply with these requirements, the court may impose sanctions including orders for costs.

1.1.3 In respect of those procedural areas for which specific provision is not made in this Guide, the parties, together with their advisors, will be expected to act reasonably and in accordance with both the spirit of the Guide and the overriding objective at CPR Rule 1.1

1.1.4 It is not the function of the Guide to summarise the Civil Procedure Rules ('the CPR'), and it should not be regarded as a substitute for the CPR. The parties and their advisors are expected to familiarise themselves with the CPR and, in particular, to understand the importance of the 'overriding objective' of the CPR. The TCC endeavours to ensure that all its cases are dealt with justly and with proper proportionality. This includes ensuring that the parties are on an equal footing; taking all practicable steps to save expenditure; dealing with the dispute in ways which are proportionate to the size of the claim and cross-claim and the importance of the case to the parties; and managing the case throughout in a way that takes proper account of its complexity and the different financial positions of the parties. The court will also endeavour to ensure expedition, and to allot to each case an appropriate share of the court's resources.

1.1.5 The TCC Guide has been prepared in consultation with the judges of the TCC in London, Cardiff, Birmingham, Manchester and Leeds, and with the advice and support of TECBAR, TeCSA, the Society for Computers and Law and the TCC Users' Committees in London, Cardiff, Birmingham, Manchester, Liverpool and Leeds. The TCC Guide is published with the approval of the Head of Civil Justice and the deputy Head of Civil Justice.

1.2 The CPR

1.2.1 Proceedings in the TCC are governed by the CPR and the supplementary Practice Directions. CPR Part 60 and its associated Practice Direction deal specifically with the practice and procedure of the TCC.

1.2.2 Other parts of the CPR that frequently arise in TCC cases include Part 8 (Alternative Procedure for Claims); Parts 12 and 13 (Default Judgment and Setting Aside); Part 17 (Amendments); Part 20 (Counterclaims and Other Additional Claims); Part 24 (Summary Judgment); Part 25 (Interim Remedies and Security for Costs); Part 26 (Case Management); Part 32 (Evidence); Part 35 (Experts and Assessors) and Part 62 (Arbitration Claims).

1.3 The TCC

1.3.1 What are TCC Claims? CPR Rules 60.1 (2) and (3) provide that a TCC claim is a claim which (i) involves technically complex issues or questions (or for which trial by a TCC judge is desirable) and (ii) has been issued in or transferred into the TCC specialist list. Paragraph 2.1 of the TCC Practice Direction identifies the following as examples of the types of claim which it may be appropriate to bring as TCC claims –

(a)   building or other construction disputes, including claims for the enforcement of the decisions of adjudicators under the Housing Grants, Construction and Regeneration Act 1996;
(b)   engineering disputes;
(c)   claims by and against engineers, architects, surveyors, accountants and other specialised advisors relating to the services they provide;
(d)   claims by and against local authorities relating to their statutory duties concerning the development of land or the construction of buildings;
(e)   claims relating to the design, supply and installation of computers, computer software and related network systems;
(f)   claims relating to the quality of goods sold or hired, and work done, materials supplied or services rendered;
(g)   claims between landlord and tenant for breach of a repairing covenant;
(h)   claims between neighbours, owners and occupiers of land in trespass, nuisance, etc.

(i)   claims relating to the environment (for example, pollution cases);
(j)   claims arising out of fires;
(k)   claims involving taking of accounts where these are complicated; and
(l)   challenges to decisions of arbitrators in construction and engineering disputes including applications for permission to appeal and appeals.

It should be noted that this list is not exhaustive and many other types of claim might well be appropriate for resolution in the TCC. In recent years the range of work in the TCC has become increasingly diverse, and many civil claims which are factually or technically complex are now heard in the TCC. This has included group actions for personal injury and public nuisance, and a number of procurement disputes arising in connection with the Public Contracts Regulations 2006. In addition, the TCC regularly deals with allegations of lawyers' negligence arising in connection with planning, property, construction and other technical disputes and with applications under the Arbitration Act 1996.

1.3.2 The Court. Both the High Court and the county courts deal with TCC business. TCC business is conducted by TCC judges unless a TCC judge directs otherwise: see CPR 60.1(5)(b)(ii).

TCC business in the High Court is conducted by TCC judges who include High Court judges, circuit judges and recorders. Circuit judges and recorders only have jurisdiction to manage and try TCC cases if they have been nominated by the Lord Chancellor pursuant to section 68(1)(a) of the Senior Courts Act 1981 or are authorised to sit in the TCC as High Court judges under section 9 of that Act.

TCC business in the County Court is conducted by TCC judges who include circuit judges and recorders. TCC business may also be conducted by certain district judges ('TCC liaison district judges') provided that: (1) a TCC judge has so directed under CPR 60.1(5)(b)(ii); (2) the designated civil judge for the court has so directed in accordance with the Practice Direction at CPR 2BPD11.1(d).

It should be noted that those circuit judges who have been nominated pursuant to section 68 (1)(a) of the Senior Courts Act 1981 fall into two categories: 'full time' TCC judges and 'part time' TCC judges. 'Full time' TCC judges spend most of their time dealing with TCC business, although they will do other work when there is no TCC business requiring their immediate attention. 'Part time' TCC judges are circuit judges who are only available to sit in the TCC for part of their time. They have substantial responsibilities outside the TCC.

In respect of a court centre where there is no full time TCC judge, the term 'principal TCC judge' is used in this Guide to denote the circuit judge who has principal responsibility for TCC work.

The phrase 'Technology and Construction Court' or 'TCC' or 'the court' is used in this Guide to denote any court which deals with TCC claims. All of the courts which deal with TCC claims form a composite group of courts. When those courts are dealing with TCC business, CPR Part 60, its accompanying Practice Direction and this Guide govern the procedures of those courts. The High Court judge in charge of the TCC ('the Judge in Charge'), although based principally in London, has overall responsibility for the judicial supervision of TCC business in those courts.

1.3.3 The TCC in London. The principal centre for TCC work is the High Court in London at St Dunstan's House, 133-137 Fetter Lane, London, EC4A 1HD. In 2011 the TCC in London will move to the Rolls Building, a new specialist court building off Fetter Lane. The Judge in Charge of the TCC sits principally at St Dunstan's House together with other High Court and circuit judges who are full time TCC judges. Subject to paragraph 3.7.1 below, any communication or enquiry concerning a TCC case, which is proceeding at St Dunstan's House, should be directed to the clerk of the judge who is assigned to that case and, if by email, copied to the TCC Registry. The various contact details for the judges' clerks are set out in Appendix D.

The TCC judges who are based at St Dunstan's House will, when appropriate, sit at court centres outside London.

TCC county court cases in London are brought in (or transferred to) the Central London Civil Justice Centre, 13-14 Park Crescent, London W1N 4HT.

1.3.4 District Registries. TCC claims can be brought in the High Court outside London in any District Registry, although the Practice Direction states that it is preferable that, wherever possible, such claims should be issued in one of the following District Registries: Birmingham, Bristol, Cardiff, Chester, Exeter, Leeds, Liverpool, Newcastle, Nottingham and Manchester. There are currently full-time TCC Judges in Birmingham and Manchester. Contact details are again set out in Appendix D. There are part time TCC judges and/or recorders nominated to deal with TCC business available at most court centres throughout England and Wales.

In a number of regions a 'TCC liaison district judge' has been appointed. It is the function of the TCC liaison district judge:

(a)   To keep other district judges in that region well informed about the role and remit of the TCC (in order that appropriate cases may be transferred to the TCC at an early, rather than late, stage).
(b)   To deal with any queries from colleagues concerning the TCC or cases which might merit transfer to the TCC.
(c)   To deal with any subsidiary matter which a TCC judge directs should be determined by a district judge pursuant to rule 60.1 (5) (b) (ii).
(d)   To deal with urgent applications in TCC cases pursuant to paragraph 7.2 of the Practice Direction (i.e. no TCC judge is available and the matter is of a kind that falls within the district judge's jurisdiction).
(e)   To hear TCC cases when a TCC judge has so directed under CPR 60.1(5)(b)(ii) and when the designated civil judge for the court has so directed in accordance with the Practice Direction at CPR 2BPD11.1(d).

1.3.5 County Courts outside London. TCC claims may also be brought in those county courts which are specified in the Part 60 Practice Direction. The specified county courts are: Birmingham, Bristol, Cardiff, Chester, Exeter, Leeds, Liverpool, Newcastle, Nottingham and Manchester. Contact details are again set out in Appendix D.

Where TCC proceedings are brought in a county court, statements of case and applications should be headed:

'In the . . . County Court

Technology and Construction Court'

1.3.6 The division between High Court and county court TCC cases. As a general rule TCC claims for more than £50,000 are brought in the High Court, whilst claims for lower sums are brought in the county court. However, this is not a rigid dividing line. The monetary threshold for High Court TCC claims tends to be higher in London than in the regions. Regard must also be had to the complexity of the case and all other circumstances. Arbitration claims and claims to enforce or challenge adjudicators are generally (but not invariably) brought in the High Court. The scale of fees differs in the High Court and the county court. This is a factor which should be borne in mind in borderline cases.

1.4 The TCC Users' Committees

1.4.1 The continuing ability of the TCC to meet the changing needs of all those involved in TCC litigation depends in large part upon a close working relationship between the TCC and its users.

1.4.2 London. The Judge in Charge chairs two meetings a year of the London TCC Users' Committee. The judge's clerk acts as secretary to the Committee and takes the minutes of meetings. That Committee is made up of representatives of the London TCC judges, the barristers and solicitors who regularly use the Court, the professional bodies, such as architects, engineers and arbitrators, whose members are affected by the decisions of the Court, and representatives of both employers and contractors' groups.

1.4.3 Outside London. There are similar meetings of TCC Users' Committees in Birmingham, Manchester, Liverpool, Cardiff and Leeds. Each Users' Committee is chaired by the full time TCC judge or the principal TCC judge in that location.

1.4.4 The TCC regards these channels of communication as extremely important and all those who are concerned with the work of the Court are encouraged to make full use of these meetings. Any suggestions or other correspondence raising matters for consideration by the Users' Committee should, in the first instance, be addressed to the clerk to the Judge in Charge at St. Dunstan's House or to the clerk to the appropriate TCC judge outside London.

1.5 Specialist Associations

1.5.1 There are a number of associations of legal representatives which are represented on the Users' Committees and which also liaise closely with the Court. These contacts ensure that the Court remains responsive to the opinions and requirements of the professional users of the Court.

1.5.2 The relevant professional organisations are the TCC Bar Association ('TECBAR') and the TCC Solicitors Association ('TeCSA'). Details of the relevant contacts at these organisations are set out on their respective websites, namely h ttp://www.tecbar.org and http://www.tecsa.org.

2. PRE-ACTION PROTOCOL

2.1: Introduction

CPR 60 TCCG 2

2.1.1 There is a Pre-Action Protocol for Construction and Engineering Disputes. Where the dispute involves a claim against architects, engineers or quantity surveyors, this Protocol prevails over the Professional Negligence Pre-Action Protocol: see paragraph 1.1 of the Protocol for Construction and Engineering Disputes and paragraph A.1 of the Professional Negligence Pre-Action Protocol. The current version of the Construction and Engineering Pre-Action Protocol ('the Protocol') is set out in volume 1 of the White Book at section C.

Editorial note. This Protocol is printed at **PRO 4** in the Protocols section below.

2.1.2 The purpose of the Protocol is to encourage the frank and early exchange of information about the prospective claim and any defence to it; to enable parties to avoid litigation by agreeing a settlement of the claim before the commencement of proceedings; and to support the efficient management of proceedings where litigation cannot be avoided.

2.1.3 Proportionality. The overriding objective (CPR rule 1.1) applies to the pre-action period. The Protocol must not be used as a tactical device to secure advantage for one party or to generate unnecessary costs. In lower value TCC claims (such as those likely to proceed in the county court), the letter of claim and the response should be simple and the costs of both sides should be kept to a modest level. In all cases the costs incurred at the Protocol stage should be proportionate to the complexity of the case and the amount of money which is at stake. The Protocol does not impose a requirement on the parties to produce a detailed pleading as a letter of claim or response or to marshal and disclose all the supporting details and evidence or to provide witness statements or expert reports that may ultimately be required if the case proceeds to litigation. Where a party has serious concerns that the approach of the other party to the Pre-Action Protocol is not proportionate, then it is open for that party to issue a claim form and/or make an application (see paragraph 4.1.5 below) to seek the assistance of the court.

2.2 To Which Claims Does The Protocol Apply?

2.2.1 The court will expect all parties to have complied in substance with the provisions of the Protocol in all construction and engineering disputes. The only exceptions to this are identified in paragraph 2.3 below.

2.2.2 The court regards the Protocol as setting out normal and reasonable pre-action conduct. Accordingly, whilst the Protocol is not mandatory for a number of the claims noted by way of example in paragraph 1.3.1 above, such as computer cases or dilapidations claims, the court would, in the absence of a specific reason to the contrary, expect the Protocol generally to be followed in such cases prior to the commencement of proceedings in the TCC.

2.3 What Are The Exceptions ?

2.3.1 A claimant does not have to comply with the Protocol if his claim:

(a)   is to enforce the decision of an adjudicator;
(b)   includes a claim for interim injunctive relief;
(c)   will be the subject of a claim for summary judgment pursuant to Part 24 of the CPR; or
(d)   relates to the same or substantially the same issues as have been the subject of a recent adjudication or some other formal alternative dispute resolution procedure.

2.3.2 In addition, a claimant need not comply with any part of the Protocol if, by so doing, his claim may become time-barred under the Limitation Act 1980. In those circumstances, a claimant should commence proceedings without complying with the Protocol and must, at the same time, apply for directions as to the timetable and form of procedure to be adopted. The court may order a stay of those proceedings pending completion of the steps set out in the Protocol.

2.4 What Are The Essential Ingredients Of The Protocol ?

2.4.1 The Letter of Claim. The letter of claim must comply with Section 3 of the Protocol. Amongst other things, it must contain a clear summary of the facts on which each claim is based; the basis on which each claim is made; and details of the relief claimed, including a breakdown showing how any damages have been quantified. The claimant must also provide the names of experts already instructed and on whom he intends to rely.

2.4.2 The Defendant's Response. The defendant has 14 days to acknowledge the letter of claim and 28 days (from receipt of the letter of claim) either to take any jurisdiction objection or to respond in substance to the letter of claim. Paragraph 4.3.1 of the Protocol enables the parties to agree an extension of the 28 day period up to a maximum of 3 months. In any case of substance it is quite usual for an extension of time to be agreed for the defendant's response. The letter of response must comply with section 4 of the Protocol. Amongst other things, it must state which claims are accepted, which claims are rejected and on what basis. It must set out any counterclaim to be advanced by the defendant. The defendant should also provide the names of experts who have been instructed and on whom he intends to rely. If the defendant fails either to acknowledge or to respond to the letter of claim in time, the claimant is entitled to commence proceedings.

2.4.3 Pre-action Meeting. The Construction and Engineering Protocol is the only Protocol under the CPR that generally requires the parties to meet, without prejudice, at least once, in order to identify the main issues and the root causes of their disagreement on those issues. The purpose of the meeting is to see whether, and if so how, those issues might be resolved without recourse to litigation or, if litigation is unavoidable, what steps should be taken to ensure that it is conducted in accordance with the overriding objective. At or as a result of the meeting, the parties should consider whether some form of alternative dispute resolution ('ADR') would be more suitable than litigation and if so, they should endeavour to agree which form of ADR to adopt. Although the meeting is 'without prejudice', any party who attended the meeting is at liberty to disclose to the Court at a later stage that the meeting took place; who attended and who refused to attend, together with the grounds for their refusal; and any agreements concluded between the parties.

2.5 What Happens To The Material Generated By The Protocol?

2.5.1 The letter of claim, the defendant's response, and the information relating to attendance (or otherwise) at the meeting are not confidential or 'without prejudice' and can therefore be referred to by the parties in any subsequent litigation. The detail of any discussion at the meeting(s) and/or any note of the meeting cannot be referred to the court unless all parties agree.

2.5.2 Normally the parties should include in the bundle for the first case management conference: (a) the letter of claim, (b) the response, and (c) if the parties agree, any agreed note of the pre-action meeting: see Section 5 below. The documents attached to or enclosed with the letter and the response should not be included in the bundle.

2.6 What If One Party Has Not Complied With The Protocol ?

2.6.1 There can often be a complaint that one or other party has not complied with the Protocol. The court will consider any such complaints once proceedings have been commenced. If the court finds that the claimant has not complied with one part of the Protocol, then the court may stay the proceedings until the steps set out in the Protocol have been taken.

2.6.2 Paragraph 2.3 of the Practice Direction in respect of Protocols (Section C of volume 1 of the White Book) makes plain that the court may make adverse costs orders against a party who has failed to comply with the Protocol. The court will exercise any sanctions available with the object of placing the innocent party in no worse a position than he would have been if the Protocol had been complied with.

2.6.3 The court is unlikely to be concerned with minor infringements of the Protocol or to engage in lengthy debates as to the precise quality of the information provided by one party to the other during the Protocol stages. The court will principally be concerned to ensure that, as a result of the Protocol stage, each party to any subsequent litigation has a clear understanding of the nature of the case that it has to meet at the commencement of those proceedings.

2.7 Costs of compliance with the Protocol.

2.7.1 If compliance with the Protocol results in settlement, the costs incurred will not be recoverable from the paying party, unless this is specifically agreed.

2.7.2 If compliance with the Protocol does not result in settlement, then the costs of the exercise cannot be recovered as costs, unless:

– those costs fall within the principles stated by Sir Robert Megarry V-C in *Re Gibson's Settlement Trusts* [1981] Ch 179; or
– the steps taken in compliance with the Protocol can properly be attributable to the conduct of the action.

3. COMMENCEMENT AND TRANSFER

3.1 Claim Forms

CPR 60 TCCG 3

3.1.1 All proceedings must be started using a claim form under CPR Part 7 or CPR Part 8 or an arbitration claim form under CPR Part 62: see paragraph 10.1 below. All claims allocated to the TCC are assigned to the Multi-Track: see CPR Rule 60.6(1).

3.2 Part 7 Claims

3.2.1 The Part 7 claim form must be marked 'Technology and Construction Court' in the appropriate place on the form.

3.2.2. Particulars of Claim may be served with the claim form, but this is not a mandatory requirement. If the Particulars of Claim are not contained in or served with the claim form, they must be served within 14 days after service of the claim form.

3.2.3 A claim form must be verified by a statement of truth, and this includes any amendment to a claim form, unless the court otherwise orders.

3.3 Part 8 Claims

3.3.1 The Part 8 claim form must be marked 'Technology and Construction Court' in the appropriate place on the form.

3.3.2 A Part 8 claim form will normally be used where there is no substantial dispute of fact, such as the situation where the dispute turns on the construction of the contract or the interpretation of statute. For example, claims challenging the jurisdiction of an adjudicator or the validity of his decision are sometimes brought under Part 8. In those cases the relevant primary facts are often not in dispute. Part 8 claims will generally be disposed of on written evidence and oral submissions.

3.3.3 It is important that, where a claimant uses the Part 8 procedure, his claim form states that Part 8 applies and that the claimant wishes the claim to proceed under Part 8.

3.3.4 A statement of truth is again required on a Part 8 claim form.

3.4 Service

3.4.1 Claim forms issued in the TCC at St Dunstan's House in London are to be served by the claimant, not by the Registry. In some other court centres claim forms are served by the court, unless the claimant specifically requests otherwise.

3.4.2 The different methods of service are set out in CPR Part 6 and the accompanying Practice Direction.

3.4.3 Applications for an extension of time in which to serve a claim form are governed by CPR Rule 7.6 and there are only limited grounds on which such extensions of time are granted. The evidence required on an application for an extension of time is set out in paragraph 8.2 of Practice Direction A supplementing CPR Part 7.

3.4.4 When the claimant has served the claim form, he must file a certificate of service: Rule 6.14 (2). This is necessary if, for instance, the claimant wishes to obtain judgment in default (CPR Part 12).

3.4.5 Applications for permission to serve a claim form out of the jurisdiction are subject to Rules 6.19-6.31 inclusive.

3.5 Acknowledgment of Service

3.5.1 A defendant must file an acknowledgment of service in response to both Part 7 and Part 8 claims. Save in the special circumstances that arise when the claim form has been served out of the jurisdiction, the period for filing an acknowledgment of service is 14 days after service of the claim form.

3.6 Transfer

3.6.1 Proceedings may be transferred from any Division of the High Court or from any specialist list to the TCC pursuant to CPR rule 30.5. The order made by the transferring court should be expressed as being subject to the approval of a TCC judge. The decision whether to accept such a transfer must be made by a TCC judge: see rule 30.5 (3). Many of these applications are uncontested, and may conveniently be dealt with on paper. Transfers from the TCC to other Divisions of the High Court or other specialist lists are also governed by CPR rule 30.5. In London there are quite often transfers between the Commercial Court and the TCC, in order to ensure that cases are dealt with by the most appropriate judge. Outside London there are quite often transfers between the TCC and the mercantile courts.

3.6.2 A TCC claim may be transferred from the High Court to one of the county courts noted above, and from any county court to the High Court, if the criteria stated in CPR Rule 30.3 are satisfied. In ordinary circumstances, proceedings will be transferred from the TCC in the High Court to the TCC in an appropriate county court if the amount of the claim does not exceed £50,000.

3.6.3 Where no TCC judge is available to deal with a TCC claim which has been issued in a district registry or one of the county courts noted above, the claim may be transferred to another district registry or county court or to the High Court TCC in London (depending upon which court is appropriate).

3.6.4 On an application to transfer the case to the TCC from another court or Division of the High Court, there are a number of relevant considerations:

(a)   Is the claim broadly one of the types of claim identified in paragraph 2.1 of the Part 60 Practice Direction?
(b)   Is the financial value of the claim and/or its complexity such that, in accordance with the overriding objective, the case should be transferred into the TCC?
(c)   What effect would transfer have on the likely costs, the speed with which the matter can be resolved, and any other broader questions of convenience for the parties?

3.6.5 On an application to transfer into the TCC, when considering the relative appropriateness of different courts or divisions, the judge will ascertain where and in what areas of judicial expertise and experience the bulk or preponderance of the issues may lie. If there was little significant difference between the appropriateness of the two venues, and the claimant, having started in one court or division, was anxious to remain there, then the application to transfer in by another party is likely to be unsuccessful.

3.6.6 Where a TCC Claim is proceeding in a District Registry and it becomes apparent that the case would merit case management or trial before a High Court judge, the matter should be raised with the TCC judge at the District Registry who will consult the Judge in Charge: see paragraph 3.7.3 below. If the case does merit the involvement of a High Court judge it is not necessary for the case to be transferred to London but rather a High Court judge can in appropriate cases sit outside London to deal with the case in the District Registry.

3.7 Assignment

3.7.1 Where a claim has been issued at or transferred to the TCC in London, the Judge in Charge of the TCC ('the Judge in Charge') shall with the assistance of court staff classify the case either 'HCJ' or 'SCJ' and assign it to a particular TCC judge.

(i)   If the case is classified 'HCJ', it shall be managed by a High Court judge and tried by a High Court judge or a deputy High Court judge.
(ii)   If the case is classified 'SCJ', it shall generally be managed by a senior circuit judge and tried by a senior circuit judge or by a recorder.
(iii) In general the assigned TCC judge who case manages a case will also try that case. Although this continuity of judge is regarded as important, it will sometimes be necessary for there to be a change of assigned judge to case manage or try a case but such changes are kept to a minimum.

3.7.2 When classifying a case 'HCJ' or 'SCJ', the Judge in Charge will take into account the following matters, as well as all the circumstances of the case:

(1)   The size and complexity of the case.

(2)   The nature and importance of any points of law arising.
(3)   The amount of money which is at stake.
(4)   Whether the case is one of public importance.
(5)   Whether the case has an international element or involves overseas parties.
(6)   The limited number of High Court judges and the needs of other court users, both civil and criminal.

The Judge in Charge may change the classification of any case from 'HCJ' to 'SCJ' or from 'SCJ' to 'HCJ', if it becomes appropriate to do so. There will be a band of cases near the borderline between 'HCJ' and 'SCJ', where the classification will be liable to change depending upon the settlement rate of other cases and the availability of judges.

3.7.3 When proceedings are commenced in, or transferred to, the TCC at St Dunstan's House in London, any party to those proceedings may write to the court setting out matters relevant to classification. Any such letter should be clear and concise and should be copied to all other parties. A defendant who wishes to send such a letter should do so as soon as he becomes aware of the proceedings. Any party who believes that a case has been wrongly classified (whether 'HCJ' or 'SCJ') should write to the court promptly setting out his grounds for that belief. All letters referred to in this paragraph are referred to the judge in charge of the TCC or (in his absence) to the other TCC High Court judge for consideration.

3.7.4

(a)   When a TCC case has been assigned to a named High Court judge, all communications about case management should be made to the assigned High Court judge's clerk with email communications copied to the TCC Registry at tcc@hmcourts-service.gsi.gov.uk.
(b)   When a case has been assigned to a named senior circuit judge in the TCC at St Dunstan's House, all communications about case management shall be made to that judge's clerk.
(c)   All communications in respect of the issue of claims or applications and all communications about fees, however, should be sent to the TCC Registry.
(d)   All statements of case and applications should be marked with the name of the assigned judge.

3.7.5 There are currently full time TCC judges at Birmingham and Manchester. There are principal TCC judges at other court centres outside London. TCC cases at these court centres are assigned to judges either (a) by direction of the full time or principal TCC judge or (b) by operation of a rota. It will not generally be appropriate for the Judge in Charge (who is based in London) to consider TCC cases which are commenced in, or transferred to, court centres outside London. Nevertheless, if any TCC case brought in a court centre outside London appears to require management and trial by a High Court judge, then the full time or principal TCC judge at that court centre should refer the case to the Judge in Charge for a decision as to its future management and trial.

3.7.6 When a TCC case has been assigned to a named circuit judge at a court centre other than in London, all communications to the court about the case (save for communications in respect of fees) shall be made to that judge's clerk. All communications in respect of fees should be sent to the relevant registry. All statements of case and applications should be marked with the name of the assigned judge.

3.8 Electronic Working in London

3.8.1 Since 20 July 2009 all TCC claims in the TCC Registry in London can be issued electronically and all proceedings, whether the claims were commenced electronically or by a paper claim form issued after that date, can be continued by taking advantage of the electronic issuing and filing process ('e-working'). It is hoped that in future years eworking in the TCC will be extended to courts outside London.

3.8.2 After a pilot scheme which ended on 31 March 2010, all e-working is now dealt with by Practice Direction 5C to CPR Part 5. A summary of the process is set out below.

3.8.3 Requirements for e-working. To carry out e-working all that is required is an email address and the relevant version of Adobe Acrobat.

3.8.4 Starting a Claim Electronically. To start a claim electronically it is necessary to send an email to mailto://getform@justice.gsi.gov.uk with the relevant form name in the title: eg NI(TCC) for a Part 7 claim form in the TCC. An email will then be received with the necessary blank claim form which can be saved and then used for future use. After completing the form it is sent to mailto://submit@justice.gsi.gov.uk. It is necessary to pay the fee which will generally be by a one off online payment or pay ment from an electronic account set up for that purpose. The claim form is then re ceived as an issued and sealed claim form.

3.8.5 Effect of starting a claim on paper. If a party has started a claim by issuing a claim form after 20 July 2009 then that claim is scanned and an electronic file created so that the same facilities for e-working are available as with a claim which was started by issuing a claim electronically.

3.8.6 Steps after the Claim Form. The claim form contains a number of document keys or links for standard forms to allow the parties to use them to obtain the necessary forms to continue the process eg acknowledgment of service, part 20 claim forms. In addition, by the use of the multipurpose form a party can file any other documents with the court such as pleadings, witness statements or skeleton arguments.

3.8.7 The court process. As all documents issued or filed electronically are automatically filed in the court file there is no requirement for any hard copy documents to be filed with the court except when it is necessary to file a hard copy case management bundle, a bundle for any application and a trial bundle.

3.8.8 Communications with the court. When there is an electronic file, the court will communicate with the parties at one or more nominated email addresses. Parties are also now accepting service by email but this will only apply if they have expressly given consent to service by email. The court would encourage solicitors and the parties to adopt service by email.

3.8.9 Further information on e-working. Parties who require assistance with e-working should contact the TCC Registry in London on 020 7947 6022 or the e-working helpline on 020 8123 0846.

4. ACCESS TO THE COURT

4.1 General Approach

CPR 60 TCCG 4

4.1.1 There may be a number of stages during the case management phase when the parties will make applications to the court for particular orders: see Section 6 below. There will also be the need for the court to give or vary directions, so as to enable the case to progress to trial.

4.1.2 The court is acutely aware of the costs that may be incurred when both parties prepare for an oral hearing in respect of such interlocutory matters and is always prepared to consider alternative, and less expensive, ways in which the parties may seek the court's assistance.

4.1.3 There are certain stages in the case management phase when it will generally be better for the parties to appear before the assigned judge. Those are identified at Section 4.2 below. But there are other stages, and/or particular applications which a party may wish to make, which could conveniently be dealt with by way of a telephone hearing (Section 4.3 below) or by way of a paper application (Section 4.4 below).

4.1.4 Access prior to the issue of proceedings. Under paragraph 4.1 of the Practice Direction supplementing CPR Part 60 it is provided that a party who intends to issue a TCC claim must make any application before the claim form is issued to a TCC judge. This provision allows a party, for instance, to issue an application for pre-action disclosure.

4.1.5 As a party will have issued a TCC claim in circumstances where paragraph 6 of the Pre-Action Protocol for Construction and Engineering Disputes applies (limitation or time bar by complying with the pre-action protocol), this provision does not apply to that situation. The court might however be persuaded to deal with an application concerned with the pre-action protocol process under this provision although it may be necessary to insist on a claim form being issued.

4.1.6 Sometimes parties wish to use the TCC procedures for Early Neutral Evaluation (see section 7.5) or the Court Settlement Process (see section 7.6) prior to issuing a TCC claim, often as part of the pre-action protocol. The court will seek to accommodate the parties' wishes but again may have to insist on a claim form being issued.

4.2 Hearings in Court

4.2.1 First Case Management Conference. The court will normally require the parties to attend an oral hearing for the purposes of the first Case Management Conference. This is because there may be matters which the judge would wish to raise with the parties arising out of the answers to the case management information sheets and the parties' proposed directions: see section 5.4 below. Even in circumstances where the directions and the case management timetable may be capable of being agreed by the parties and the court, the assigned judge may still wish to consider a range of case management matters face-to-face with the parties, including the possibility of ADR. See paragraphs 7.2.3, 7.3.2, 8.1.3, 11.1, 13.3, 13.4 and 16.3.2 below.

4.2.2 Whilst the previous paragraph sets out the ideal position, it is recognised that in low value cases the benefits of personal attendance might be outweighed by the costs involved. This is particularly so at court centres outside London, where the parties may have to travel substantial distances to court. Ultimately, the question whether personal attendance should be dispensed with at any particular case management conference must be decided by the judge, after considering any representations made and the circumstances of that particular case.

4.2.3 Pre-trial Review. It will normally be helpful for the parties to attend before the judge on a Pre-trial Review ('PTR'). It is always preferable for Counsel or other advocates who will be appearing at the trial to attend the PTR. Again, even if the parties can agree beforehand any outstanding directions and the detailed requirements for the management of the trial, it is still of assistance for the judge to raise matters of detailed trial management with the parties at an oral hearing. In appropriate cases, e.g. where the amount in issue is disproportionate to the costs of a full trial, the judge may wish to consider with the parties whether there are other ways in which the dispute might be resolved. See Paragraphs 14.1 to 14.5 below for detailed provisions relating to the PTR.

4.2.4 Interlocutory Applications. Whether or not other interlocutory applications require to be determined at an oral hearing will depend on the nature and effect of the application being made. Disputed applications for interim payments, summary judgment and security for costs will almost always require an oral hearing. Likewise, the resolution of a contested application to enforce an adjudicator's decision will normally be heard orally. At the other end of the scale, applications for extensions of time for the service of pleadings or to comply with other orders of the court can almost always be dealt with by way of a telephone hearing or in writing.

4.3 Telephone Hearings

4.3.1 Depending on the nature of the application and the extent of any dispute between the parties, the Court is content to deal with many case management matters and other interlocutory applications by way of a telephone conference.

4.3.2 Whilst it is not possible to lay down mandatory rules as to what applications should be dealt with in this way (rather than by way of an oral hearing in court), it may be helpful to identify certain situations which commonly arise and which can conveniently be dealt with by way of a telephone conference.

(a) If the location of the court is inconvenient for one or more of the parties, or the value of the claim is low, then the CMC and the PTR could, in the alternative to the procedure set out in Section 4.2 above, take place by way of a telephone conference. The judge's permission for such a procedure would have to be sought in advance.

(b) If the parties are broadly agreed on the orders to be made by the court, but they are in dispute in respect of one or two particular matters, then a telephone hearing is a convenient way in which those outstanding matters can be dealt with by the parties and the assigned judge.

(c) Similarly, specific arguments about costs, once a substantive application has been disposed of, or arguments consequential on a particular judgment or order having been handed down, may also conveniently be dealt with by way of telephone hearing.

(d) Other applications which, depending on their size and importance, may conveniently be dealt with by way of a telephone hearing include limited applications in respect of disclosure and specific applications as to the scope and content of factual or expert evidence exchanged by the parties.

4.3.3 Telephone hearings are not generally suitable for matters which are likely to last for more than an hour, although the judge may be prepared, in an appropriate case, to list a longer application for a telephone hearing.

4.3.4 Practical matters. Telephone hearings can be listed at any time between 8.30 a.m. and 5.30 p.m., subject to the convenience of the parties and the availability of the judge. It is not essential that all parties are on the telephone when those that are not find it more convenient to come to court. Any party, who wishes to have an application dealt with by telephone, should make such request by letter or e-mail to the judge's clerk, sending copies to all other parties. Except in cases of urgency, the judge will allow a period of two working days for the other parties to comment upon that request before deciding whether to deal with the application by telephone.

4.3.5 If permission is given for a telephone hearing, the court will normally indicate which party is to make all the necessary arrangements. In most cases, it will be the applicant. The procedure to be followed in setting up and holding a telephone hearing is generally that set out in section 6 of the Practice Direction 23A supplementing CPR Part 23 and the TCC in London and at Regional Centres are 'telephone conference enabled courts' for the purposes of that section. The party making arrangements for the telephone hearing must ensure that all parties and the judge have a bundle for that hearing with identical pagination.

It is vital that the judge has all the necessary papers, in good time before the telephone conference, in order that it can be conducted efficiently and effectively.

4.4 Paper Applications

4.4.1 CPR rule 23.8 and section 11 of the accompanying Practice Direction enable certain applications to be dealt with in writing. Parties in a TCC case are encouraged to deal with applications in writing, whenever practicable. Applications for abridgments of time, extensions of time and to reduce the trial time estimate can generally be dealt with in writing, as well as all other variations to existing directions which are wholly or largely agreed. Disputes over particular aspects of disclosure and evidence may also be capable of being resolved in this way.

4.4.2 If a party wishes to make an application to the court, it should ask itself the question: 'Can this application be conveniently dealt with in writing?' If it can, then the party should issue the application and make its (short) written submissions both in support of its application and why it should be dealt with on paper. The application, any supporting evidence and the written submissions should be provided to all parties, as well as the court. These must include a draft of the precise order sought. There are some paper applications which can be made without notice to the other party or parties: see CPR 23.4(2), 23.9 and 23.10.

4.4.3 The party against whom the application is made, and any other interested party, should respond within 3 days dealing both with the substantive application and the request for it to be dealt with in writing.

4.4.4 The court can then decide whether or not to deal with the application in writing. If the parties are agreed that the court should deal with it in writing, it will be rare for the court to take a different view. If the parties disagree as to whether or not the application should be dealt with in writing, the court can decide that issue and, if it decides to deal with it in writing can go on to resolve the substantive point on the basis of the parties' written submissions.

4.4.5 Further guidance in respect of paper applications is set out in Section 6.7 below.

4.4.6 It is important for the parties to ensure that all documents provided to the court are also provided to all the other parties, so as to ensure that both the court and the parties are working on the basis of the same documentation. The pagination of any bundle which is provided to the court and the parties must be identical.

4.5 E-mail Communications

4.5.1 Electronic Working under the provisions of CPR Part 5, Practice Direction 5C is available in and the preferred way of working in the TCC in London. In addition general rules relating to communication and filing of documents by e-mail are set out in CPR Part 5, Practice Direction 5B. For Electronic Working, see paragraph 3.8 above.

4.5.2 The judges' clerks all have e-mail addresses identified in Appendix D. They welcome communication from the parties electronically. Parties should preferably file all documents by using Electronic Working in all claims issued in or transferred to the TCC in London since 20 July 2009. In addition, by agreement with the judge's clerk, it is also possible to provide documents to the Court electronically. However, it should be noted that HM Court Service imposes a restriction on the size of any e-mail, including its attachments. Larger attachments can be submitted by CD/DVD.

4.5.3 Depending on the particular circumstances of an individual trial, the assigned judge may ask for an e-mail contact address for each of the parties and may send e-mail communications to that address. In addition, the judge may provide a direct contact e-mail address so that the parties can communicate directly with him out of court hours. In such circumstances, the judge and the parties should agree the times at which the respective e-mail addresses can be used.

4.5.4 Every e-mail communication to and from the judge must be simultaneously copied to all the other parties.

4.6 Video Conferencing

4.6.1 In appropriate cases, particularly where there are important matters in dispute and the parties' representatives are a long distance from one another and/or the court, the hearing may be conducted by way of a Video Conference ('VC'). Prior arrangements will be necessary for any such hearing.

4.6.2 In London, a VC can be arranged through the VC facilities in Court 14A of St Dunstan's House, the VC suite at the Royal Courts of Justice or, when the TCC moves to the Rolls Building in 2011, the facilities in that building. Alternatively, there are a number of other VC suites in the Strand/Fleet Street area which would be suitable. Details of these facilities are available from the judges' clerks.

4.6.3 Outside London, a VC can be arranged at the following TCC courts with the requisite facilities: Birmingham, Bristol, Cardiff, Central London, Chester, Exeter, Leeds, Liverpool, Newcastle-upon-Tyne, Nottingham, Manchester and Winchester.

4.7 Contacting the court out of hours

4.7.1 Occasionally it is necessary to contact a TCC judge out of hours. For example, it may be necessary to apply for an injunction to prevent the commencement of building works which will damage adjoining property; or for an order to preserve evidence. A case may have settled and it may be necessary to inform the judge, before he/she spends an evening or a weekend reading the papers.

4.7.2 At St Dunstan's House and, from 2011, the Rolls Building. RCJ Security has been provided with the telephone numbers and other contact information of all the TCC judges based at St Dunstan's House and of the court manager. If contact is required with a judge out of hours, the initial approach should be to RCJ Security on 0207-947-6000. Security will then contact the judge and/or the court manager and pass on the message or other information. If direct contact with the judge or court manager is required, RCJ Security must be provided with an appropriate contact number. This number will then be passed to the judge and/or the court manager, who will decide whether it is appropriate for him or her to speak directly to the contacting party.

4.7.3 At Other Court Centres. At the Central London Civil Justice Centre and at all court centres outside London there is a court officer who deals with out of hours applications.

4.8 Lodging documents.

4.8.1 In London, in cases issued or transferred-in after 20 July 2009, the preferred way of lodging documents is by the use of Electronic Working: see paragraph 3.8 above.

4.8.2 In other cases in London and in Regional Centres, in general documents should be lodged in hard copy and not sent by email or fax. This causes unnecessary duplication as well as additional work for hard-pressed court staff. Fax communication with the court, in particular, is discouraged. If the court or judge's clerk agrees, some documents may be sent by email but otherwise only if matters are urgent may documents be sent by either email or fax, with a hard copy sent by way of confirmation and marked as such. In certain cases, the court may ask for documents to be submitted in electronic form by email or otherwise, where that is appropriate.

5. CASE MANAGEMENT AND THE FIRST CMC

5.1 General

CPR 60 TCCG 5

5.1.1 The general approach of the TCC to case management is to give directions at the outset and then throughout the proceedings to serve the overriding objective of dealing with cases justly. The judge to whom the case has been assigned has wide case management powers, which will be exercised to ensure that:

–   the real issues are identified early on and remain the focus of the ongoing proceedings;
–   a realistic timetable is ordered which will allow for the fair and prompt resolution of the action;
–   costs are properly controlled and reflect the value of the issues to the parties and their respective financial positions.

5.1.2 In order to assist the judge in the exercise of his case management functions, the parties will be expected to co-operate with one another at all times. See CPR rule 1.3. Costs sanctions may be applied, if the judge concludes that one party is not reasonably co-operating with the other parties.

5.1.3 A hearing at which the judge gives general procedural directions is a case management conference ('CMC'). CMCs are relatively informal and business-like occasions. Representatives sit when addressing the judge.

5.1.4 The following procedures apply in order to facilitate effective case management:

–   Upon commencement of a case in the TCC, it is allocated automatically to the multi-track. The provisions of CPR Part 29 apply to all TCC cases.
–   The TCC encourages a structured exchange of proposals and submissions for CMCs in advance of the hearing, so as to enable the parties to respond on an informed basis to proposals made.
–   The judges of the TCC operate pro-active case management. In order to avoid the parties being taken by surprise by any judicial initiative, the judge will consider giving prior notification of specific or unusual case management proposals to be raised at a case management conference.

5.1.5 The TCC's aim is to ensure that the trial of each case takes place before the judge who has managed the case since the first CMC. Whilst continuity of judge is not always possible, because of the need to double- or triple-book judges, or because cases can sometimes overrun their estimated length through no fault of the parties, this remains an aspiration of case management within the TCC.

5.1.6 To ensure that costs are properly controlled the judge will consider at all stages of case management whether there are ways in which costs can be reduced. If the judge considers that any particular aspect has unnecessarily increased costs, such as prolix pleadings or witness statements, the judge may make a costs order disallowing costs or ordering costs to be paid, either on the basis of a summary assessment, or by giving a direction to the costs judge as to what costs should be disallowed or paid on a detailed assessment: see also paragraph 5.5.5 below.

5.2 The Fixing of the First CMC

5.2.1 Where a claim has been started in the TCC, or where it has been transferred into the TCC, paragraph 8.1 of the Part 60 Practice Direction requires the court to fix the first CMC within 14 days of the earliest of

–   the filing by the defendant of an acknowledgement of service or
–   the filing by the defendant of the defence or
–   the date of the order transferring the case to the TCC.

If some defendants but not others are served with proceedings, the claimant's solicitors should so inform the court and liaise about the fixing of the first CMC.

5.2.2 This means that the first CMC takes place relatively early, sometimes before the defendant has filed a defence. However, if, as will usually be the case, the parties have complied with the protocol (Section 2 above) they will have a good idea of each other's respective positions, and an effective CMC can take place. If, on the other hand, there has been a failure to comply with the protocol, or there are other reasons why the issues are not clearly defined at the outset, then it may be important for the judge to be involved at an early stage.

5.2.3 Despite the foregoing considerations, it is sometimes apparent to the parties that it will be more cost effective to postpone the first CMC until after service of the defence or the defences. If any of the parties wishes to delay the first CMC until then, they can write to the judge's clerk explaining why a delayed CMC is appropriate. If such a request is agreed by the other party or parties, it is likely that the judge will grant the request.

5.3 The Case Management Information Sheet and Other Documents

5.3.1 All parties are expected to complete a detailed response to the case management information sheet sent out by the Registry when the case is commenced/transferred. A copy of a blank case management information sheet is attached as Appendix A. It is important that all parts of the form are completed, particularly those sections (e.g. concerned with estimated costs) that enable the judge to give directions in accordance with the overriding objective.

5.3.2 The Registry will also send out a blank standard directions form to each party. A copy is attached at Appendix B. This sets out the usual directions made on the first CMC. The parties should fill them in, indicating the directions and timetable sought. The parties should return both the questionnaire and the directions form to the court, so that the areas (if any) of potential debate at the CMC can be identified. The parties are encouraged to exchange proposals for directions and the timetable sought, with a view to agreeing the same before the CMC for consideration by the court.

5.3.3 If the case is large or complex, it is helpful for the advocates to prepare a Note to be provided to the judge the day before the CMC which can address the issues in the case, the suggested directions, and the principal areas of dispute between the parties. If such a Note is provided, it is unnecessary for the claimant also to prepare a Case Summary as well.

5.3.4 In smaller cases, a Case Summary for the CMC, explaining briefly the likely issues, can be helpful. Such Case Summaries should be non-contentious and should (if this is possible without incurring disproportionate cost) be agreed between the parties in advance of the hearing.

5.4 Checklist of Matters likely to be considered at the first CMC

5.4.1 The following checklist identifies the matters which the judge is likely to want to consider at the first CMC, although it is not exhaustive:

- The need for, and content of, any further pleadings. This is dealt with in Section 5.5 below.
- The outcome of the Protocol process, and the possible further need for ADR. ADR is dealt with in Section 7 below.
- The desirability of dealing with particular disputes by way of a Preliminary Issue hearing. This is dealt with in Section 8 below.
- Whether the trial should be in stages (e.g. stage 1 liability and causation, stage 2 quantum). In very heavy cases this may be necessary in order to make the trial manageable. In more modest cases, where the quantum evidence will be extensive, a staged trial may be in the interest of all parties.
- The appropriate orders in respect of the disclosure of documents. This is dealt with in Section 11 below.
- The appropriate orders as to the exchange of written witness statements. This is dealt with in Section 12 below. It should be noted that, although it is normal for evidence-in-chief to be given by way of the written statements in the TCC, the judge may direct that evidence about particular disputes (such as what was said at an important meeting) should be given orally without reference to such statements.
- Whether it is appropriate for the parties to rely on expert evidence and, if so, what disciplines of experts should give evidence, and on what issues. This may be coupled with an order relating to the carrying out of inspections, the obtaining of samples, the conducting of experiments, or the performance of calculations. Considerations relating to expert evidence are dealt with in Section 13 below. The parties must be aware that, in accordance with the overriding objective, the judge will only give the parties permission to rely on expert evidence if it is both necessary and appropriate, and, even then, will wish to ensure that the scope of any such evidence is limited as far as possible.
- In certain cases the possibility of making a costs cap order. See Section 16.3 below.
- The appropriate timetable for the taking of the various interlocutory steps noted above, and the fixing of dates for both the PTR and the trial itself (subject to paragraph 5.4.2 below). The parties will therefore need to provide the judge with an estimate for the length of the trial, assuming all issues remain in dispute. Unless there is good reason not to, the trial date will generally be fixed at the first CMC (although this may be more difficult at court centres with only one TCC judge). Therefore, to the extent that there are any relevant concerns as to availability of either witnesses or legal representa-

tives, they need to be brought to the attention of the court on that occasion. The length of time fixed for the trial will depend on the parties' estimates, and also the judge's own view.

If the parties' estimate of trial length subsequently changes, they should inform the clerk of the assigned judge immediately.

5.4.2 The fixing of the trial date at the CMC is usually as a provisional fixture. Therefore no trial fee is payable at this stage. The court should at the same time specify a date upon which the fixture will cease to be 'provisional' and, therefore, the trial fee will become payable. This should ordinarily be two months before the trial date. It should be noted that:

–   if the trial fee is not paid within 14 days of the due date, then the whole claim will be struck out: see CPR rule 3.7 (1) (a) and (4);

–   if the court is notified at least 14 days before the trial date that the case is settled or discontinued, then the trial fee, which has been paid, shall be refunded: see fee 2.2 in Schedule 1 to the Civil Proceedings Fees Order 2004.

For all purposes other than payment of the trial fee, the provisional date fixed at the CMC shall be regarded as a firm date.

5.4.3 Essentially, the judge's aim at the first CMC is to set down a detailed timetable which, in the majority of cases, will ensure that the parties need not return to court until the PTR.

5.5 Further Pleadings

5.5.1 <u>Defence.</u> If no defence has been served prior to the first CMC, then (except in cases where judgment in default is appropriate) the court will usually make an order for service of the defence within a specified period. The defendant must plead its positive case. Bare denials and non-admissions are, save in exceptional circumstances, unacceptable.

5.5.2 <u>Further Information.</u> If the defendant wants to request further information of the Particulars of Claim, the request should, if possible, be formulated prior to the first CMC, so that it can be considered on that occasion. All requests for further information should be kept within reasonable limits, and concentrate on the important parts of the case.

5.5.3 <u>Reply.</u> A reply to the defence is not always necessary. However, where the defendant has raised a positive defence on a particular issue, it may be appropriate for the claimant to set out in a reply how it answers such a defence. If the defendant makes a counterclaim, the claimant's defence to counterclaim and its reply (if any) should be in the same document.

5.5.4 <u>Part 20 Claims.</u> The defendant should, at the first CMC, indicate (so far as possible) any Part 20 claims that it is proposing to make, whether against the claimant or any other party. Part 20 claims are required to be pleaded in the same detail as the original claim. They are a very common feature of TCC cases, because the widespread use of sub-contractors in the UK construction industry often makes it necessary to pass claims down a contractual chain. Defendants are encouraged to start any necessary Part 20 proceedings as soon as possible. It is undesirable for applications to join Part 20 defendants, to be made late in the proceedings.

5.5.5 Costs. If at any stage the judge considers that the way in which the case has been pleaded is likely to lead or has led to inefficiency in the conduct of the proceedings or to unnecessary time or costs being spent, the judge may order that the party should re-plead the whole or part of the case and may make a costs order disallowing costs or ordering costs to be paid, either on the basis of a summary assessment or by giving a direction to the costs judge as to what costs should be disallowed or paid on a detailed assessment: see also paragraph 5.1.6 above and paragraph 12.1.4 below.

5.6 Scott Schedules

5.6.1 It can sometimes be appropriate for elements of the claim, or any Part 20 claim, to be set out by way of a Scott Schedule. For example, claims involving a final account or numerous alleged defects or items of disrepair, may be best formulated in this way, which then allows for a detailed response from the defendant. Sometimes, even where all the damage has been caused by one event, such as a fire, it can be helpful for the individual items of loss and damage to be set out in a Scott Schedule. The secret of an effective Scott Schedule lies in the information that is to be provided. This is defined by the column headings. The judge may give directions for the relevant column headings for any Schedule ordered by the court. It is important that the defendant's responses to any such Schedule are as detailed as possible. Each party's entries on a Scott Schedule should be supported by a statement of truth.

5.6.2 Nevertheless, before any order is made or agreement is reached for the preparation of a Scott Schedule, both the parties and the court should consider whether this course (a) will genuinely lead to a saving of cost and time or (b) will lead to a wastage of costs and effort (because the Scott Schedule will simply be duplicating earlier schedules, pleadings or expert reports). A Scott Schedule should only be ordered by the court, or agreed by the parties, in those cases where it is appropriate and proportionate.

5.6.3 When a Scott Schedule is ordered by the court or agreed by the parties, the format must always be specified. The parties must co-operate in the physical task of preparation. Electronic transfer between the parties of their respective entries in the columns will enable a clear and user-friendly Scott Schedule to be prepared, for the benefit of all involved in the trial.

5.7 Agreement between the Parties

5.7.1 Many, perhaps most, of the required directions at the first CMC may be agreed by the parties. If so, the judge will endeavour to make orders in the terms which have been agreed, unless he considers that the agreed terms fail to take into account important features of the case as a whole, or the principles of the CPR. The agreed terms will always, at the very least, form the starting-point of the judge's consideration of the orders to be made at the CMC. If the agreed terms are submitted to the judge 3 days in advance of the hearing date, it may be possible to avoid the need for a hearing altogether, although it is normally necessary for the Court to consider the case with the parties (either at an oral hearing or by way of a telephone conference) in any event.

5.7.2 The approach outlined in paragraph 5.7.1 above is equally applicable to all other occasions when the parties come before the court with a draft order that is wholly or partly agreed.

5.8 Drawing Up of Orders

5.8.1 Unless the court itself draws up the order, it will direct one party (usually the claimant or applicant) to do so within a specified time. That party must draw up the order and lodge it with the court for approval. Once approved, the order will be stamped by the court and returned to that party for service upon all other parties. The order should refer to the date on which the order was made by stating 'Date order made: [date]'. This date should generally be the date referred to in relation to orders rather than later dates which reflect the process of submission of the draft order, approval by the judge and sealing by the court.

5.9 Further CMC

5.9.1 In an appropriate case, the judge will fix a review CMC, to take place part way through the timetable that has been set down, in order to allow the court to review progress, and to allow the parties to raise any matters arising out of the steps that have been taken up to that point. This will not, however, be ordered automatically.

5.9.2 Each party will be required to give notice in writing to the other parties and the court of any order which it will be seeking at the review CMC, two days in advance of the hearing..

5.10 The Permanent Case Management Bundle

5.10.1 In conjunction with the judge's clerk, the claimant's solicitor is responsible for ensuring that, for the first CMC and at all times thereafter, there is a permanent bundle of copy documents available to the judge, which contains:

- any relevant documents resulting from the Pre-Action Protocol;
- the claim form and all statements of case;
- all orders;
- all completed case management information sheets.

5.10.2 The permanent case management bundle can then be supplemented by the specific documents relevant to any particular application that may be made. Whether these supplementary documents should (a) become a permanent addition to the case management bundle or (b) be set on one side, will depend upon their nature. The permanent case management bundle may remain at court and be marked up by the judge; alternatively, the judge may direct that the permanent case management bundle be maintained at the offices of the claimant's solicitors and provided to the court when required.

6. APPLICATIONS AFTER THE FIRST CMC

6.1 Relevant parts of the CPR

CPR 60 TCCG 6

6.1.1 The basic rules relating to all applications that any party may wish to make are set out in CPR Part 23 and its accompanying Practice Directions.

6.1.2 Part 7 of the Practice Direction accompanying CPR Part 60 is also of particular relevance.

6.2 Application Notice

6.2.1 As a general rule, any party to proceedings in the TCC wishing to make an application of any sort must file an application notice (rule 23.3) and serve that application notice on all relevant parties as soon as practicable after it has been filed (rule 23.4). Application notices should be served by the parties, unless (as happens in some court centres outside London) service is undertaken by the court.

6.2.2 The application notice must set out in clear terms what order is sought and, more briefly, the reasons for seeking that order: see rule 23.6.

6.2.3 The application notice must be served at least 3 days before the hearing at which the Court deals with the application: rule 23.7 (1). Such a short notice period is only appropriate for the most straight-forward type of application.

6.2.4 Most applications, in particular applications for summary judgment under CPR Part 24 or to strike out a statement of case under CPR rule 3.4, will necessitate a much longer notice period than 3 days. In such cases, it is imperative that the applicant obtain a suitable date and time for the hearing of the application from the assigned judge's clerk before the application notice is issued. The applicant must then serve his application notice and evidence in support suffi-ciently far ahead of the date fixed for the hearing of the application for there to be time to enable the respondent to serve evidence in response. Save in exceptional circumstances, there should be a minimum period of 10 working days between the service of the notice (and supporting evidence) and the hearing date. If any party considers that there is insufficient time before the hearing of the application or if the time estimate for the application itself is too short, that party must notify the Judge's clerk and the hearing may then be refixed by agreement.

6.2.5 When considering the application notice, the judge may give directions in writing as to the dates for the provision or exchange of evidence and any written submissions or skeleton arguments for the hearing.

6.3 Evidence in Support

6.3.1 The application notice when it is served must be accompanied by all evidence in support: rule 23.7 (2).

6.3.2 Unless the CPR expressly requires otherwise, evidence will be given by way of witness statements. Such statements must be verified by a statement of truth signed by the maker of the statement: rule 22.1.

6.4 Evidence in opposition and Evidence in reply

6.4.1 Likewise, any evidence in opposition to the application should, unless the rules expressly provide otherwise, be given by way of witness statement verified by a statement of truth.

6.4.2 It is important to ensure that the evidence in opposition to the application is served in good time before the hearing so as to enable:

– the court to read and note up the evidence;
– the applicant to put in any further evidence in reply that may be considered necessary.

Such evidence should be served at least 5 working days before the hearing.

6.4.3 Any evidence in reply should be served not less than 3 working days before the hearing. Again, if there are disputes as to the time taken or to be taken for the preparation of evidence prior to a hearing, or any other matters in respect of a suitable timetable for that hearing, the court will consider the written positions of both parties and decide such disputes on paper. It will not normally be necessary for either a separate application to be issued or a hearing to be held for such a purpose.

6.4.4 If the hearing of an application has to be adjourned because of delays by one or other of the parties in serving evidence, the court is likely to order that party to pay the costs straight away, and to make a summary assessment of those costs.

6.5 Application Bundle

6.5.1 The bundle for the hearing of anything other than the most simple and straightforward application should consist of:

– the permanent case management bundle (see Section 5.8 above);
– the witness statements provided in support of the application, together with any exhibits;
– the witness statements provided in opposition to the application together with exhibits;
– any witness statements in reply, together with exhibits.

6.5.2 The permanent case management bundle will either be with the court or with the claimant's solicitors, depending on the order made at the first CMC: see paragraph 5.9 above. If it is with the claimant's solicitors, it should be provided to the court not less than 2 working days before the hearing. In any event, a paginated bundle (see paragraph 6.5.4 below) containing any material specific to the application should also be provided to the court not less than 2 working days before the hearing, unless otherwise directed by the judge. A failure to comply with this deadline may result in the adjournment of the hearing, and the costs thrown away being paid by the defaulting party.

6.5.3 In all but the simplest applications, the court will expect the parties to provide skeleton arguments and copies of any authorities to be relied on. The form and content of the skeleton argument is principally a matter for the author, although the judge will expect it to identify the issues that arise on the application, the important parts of the evidence relied on, and the applicable legal principles. For detailed guidance as to the form, content and length of skeleton arguments, please see paragraph 7.11.12 of the Queen's Bench Guide; Appendix 3 of the Chancery Guide; and Appendix 9 of the Commercial Court Guide.

6.5.4 For an application that is estimated to last 1/2 day or less, the skeleton should be provided no later than 1 pm on the last working day before the hearing. It should be accompanied by photocopies of the authorities relied on.

6.5.5 For an application that is estimated to last more than 1/2 day, the skeleton should be provided no later than 4 pm one clear working day before the hearing. It should be accompanied by photocopies of the authorities relied on.

6.5.6 The time limits at paragraphs 6.5.4 and 6.5.5 above will be regarded as the latest times by which such skeletons should be provided to the court. Save in exceptional circumstances, no extension to these periods will be permitted.

6.5.7 Pagination. It is generally necessary for there to be a paginated bundle for the hearing. Where the parties have produced skeleton arguments, these should be cross-referred to the bundle page numbers.

6.6 Hearings

6.6.1 Arbitration applications may be heard in private: see CPR rule 62.10. All other applications will be heard in public in accordance with CPR rule 39.2, save where otherwise ordered.

6.6.2 Provided that the application bundle and the skeletons have been lodged in accordance with the time limits set out above, the parties can assume that the court will have a good understanding of the points in issue. However, the court will expect to be taken to particular documents relied on by the parties and will also expect to be addressed on any important legal principles that arise.

6.6.3 It is important that the parties ensure that every application is dealt with in the estimated time period. Since many applications are dealt with on Fridays, it causes major disruption if application hearings are not disposed of within the estimated period. If the parties take too long in making their submissions, the application may be adjourned, part heard, and the Court may impose appropriate costs sanctions.

6.6.4 At the conclusion of the hearing, unless the court itself draws up the order, it will direct the applicant to do so within a specified period.

6.7 Paper Applications

6.7.1 As noted in Section 4 above, some applications may be suitable for determination on paper under the procedure set out in paragraph 4.4 above.

6.7.2 In addition, certain simple applications (particularly in lower value cases) arising out of the management of the proceedings may be capable of being dealt with by correspondence without the need for any formal application or order of the court. This is particularly true of applications to vary procedural orders, which variations are wholly or largely agreed, or proposals to vary the estimated length of the trial. In such cases, the applicant should write to the other parties indicating the nature of its application and to seek their agreement to it. If, however, it emerges that there is an issue to be resolved by the court, then a formal application must be issued and dealt with as a paper application or, possibly, at an oral hearing.

6.8 Consent Orders

6.8.1 Consent Orders may be submitted to the Court in draft for approval without the need for attendance.

6.8.2 Two copies of the draft order should be lodged, at least one of which should be signed. The copies should be undated as the Court will set out the date the order is made: see paragraph 5.8.1 above.

6.8.3 As noted elsewhere, whilst the parties can agree between themselves the orders to be made either at the Case Management Conference or the Pre-Trial Review, it is normally necessary for the Court to consider the case with the parties (either at an oral hearing or by way of a telephone conference) on those occasions in any event.

6.8.4 Generally, when giving directions, the court will endeavour to identify the date by which the relevant step must be taken, and will not simply provide a period during which that task should be performed. The parties should therefore ensure that any proposed consent order also identifies particular dates, rather then periods, by which the relevant steps must be taken.

6.9 Costs

6.9.1 Costs are dealt with generally at Section 16 below.

6.9.2 The costs of any application which took a day or less to be heard and disposed of will be dealt with summarily, unless there is a good reason for the court not to exercise its powers as to the summary assessment of costs.

6.9.3 Accordingly, it is necessary for parties to provide to the court and to one another their draft statements of costs no later than 24 hours before the start of the application hearing. Any costs which are incurred after these draft statements have been prepared, but which have not been allowed for (e.g. because the hearing has exceeded its anticipated length), can be mentioned at the hearing.

7. ALTERNATIVE DISPUTE RESOLUTION

7.1 General

CPR 60 TCCG 7

7.1.1 The court will provide encouragement to the parties to use alternative dispute resolution ('ADR') and will, whenever appropriate, facilitate the use of such a procedure. In this Guide, ADR is taken to mean any process through which the parties attempt to resolve their dispute, which is voluntary. In most cases, ADR takes the form of inter-party negotiations or a mediation conducted by a neutral mediator. Alternative forms of ADR include early neutral evaluation either by a judge or some other neutral person who receives a concise presentation from each party and then provides his or her own evaluation of the case.

7.1.2 Although the TCC is an appropriate forum for the resolution of all IT and construction/engineering disputes, the use of ADR can lead to a significant saving of costs and may result in a settlement which is satisfactory to all parties.

7.1.3 Legal representatives in all TCC cases should ensure that their clients are fully aware of the benefits of ADR and that the use of ADR has been carefully considered prior to the first CMC.

7.2 Timing

7.2.1 ADR may be appropriate before the proceedings have begun or at any subsequent stage. However the later ADR takes place, the more the costs which will have been incurred, often unnecessarily. The timing of ADR needs careful consideration.

7.2.2 The TCC Pre-Action Protocol (Section 2 above) itself provides for a type of ADR, because it requires there to be at least one face-to-face meeting between the parties before the commencement of proceedings. At this meeting, there should be sufficient time to discuss and resolve the dispute. As a result of this procedure having taken place, the court will not necessarily grant a stay of proceedings upon demand and it will always need to be satisfied that an adjournment is actually necessary to enable ADR to take place.

7.2.3 However, at the first CMC, the court will want to be addressed on the parties' views as to the likely efficacy of ADR, the appropriate timing of ADR, and the advantages and disadvantages of a short stay of proceedings to allow ADR to take place. Having considered the representations of the parties, the court may order a short stay to facilitate ADR at that stage. Alternatively, the court may simply encourage the parties to seek ADR and allow for it to occur within the timetable for the resolution of the proceedings set down by the court.

7.2.4 At any stage after the first CMC and prior to the commencement of the trial, the court, will, either on its own initiative or if requested to do so by one or both of the parties, consider afresh the likely efficacy of ADR and whether or not a short stay of the proceedings should be granted, in order to facilitate ADR.

7.3 Procedure

7.3.1 In an appropriate case, the court may indicate the type of ADR that it considers suitable, but the decision in this regard must be made by the parties. In most cases, the appropriate ADR procedure will be mediation.

7.3.2 If at any stage in the proceedings the court considers it appropriate, an ADR order in the terms of Appendix E may be made. If such an order is made at the first CMC, the court may go on to give directions for the conduct of the action up to trial (in the event that the ADR fails). Such directions may include provision for a review CMC.

7.3.3 The court will not ordinarily recommend any individual or body to act as mediator or to perform any other ADR procedure. In the event that the parties fail to agree the identity of a mediator or other neutral person pursuant to an order in the terms of Appendix E, the court may select such a person from the lists provided by the parties. To facilitate this process, the court would also need to be furnished with the CV's of each of the individuals on the lists.

7.3.4 Information as to the types of ADR procedures available and the individuals able to undertake such procedures is available from TeCSA, TECBAR, the Civil Mediation Council, and from some TCC court centres outside London.

7.4 Non-Cooperation

7.4.1 Generally. At the end of the trial, there may be costs arguments on the basis that one or more parties unreasonably refused to take part in ADR. The court will determine such issues having regard to all the circumstances of the particular case. In *Halsey v Milton Keynes General NHS Trust* [2004] EWCA Civ 576; [2004] 1 WLR 3002, the Court of Appeal identified six factors that may be relevant to any such consideration:

(a)   the nature of the dispute;
(b)   the merits of the case;
(c)   the extent to which other settlement methods have been attempted;
(d)   whether the costs of the ADR would be disproportionately high;
(e)   whether any delay in setting up and attending the ADR would have been prejudicial;
(f)   whether the ADR had a reasonable prospect of success.

7.4.2 If an ADR Order Has Been Made. The court will expect each party to co-operate fully with any ADR procedure which takes place following an order of the court. If any other party considers that there has not been proper co-operation in relation to arrangements for mediation or any other ADR procedure, the complaint will be considered by the court and cost orders and/or other sanctions may be ordered against the defaulting party in consequence. However, nothing in this paragraph should be understood as modifying the rights of all parties to mediation or any other ADR procedure to keep confidential all that is said or done in the course of that ADR procedure.

7.5 Early Neutral Evaluation

7.5.1 An early neutral evaluation ('ENE') may be carried out by any appropriately qualified person, whose opinion is likely to be respected by the parties. In an appropriate case, and with the consent of all parties, a TCC judge may provide an early neutral evaluation either in respect of the full case or of particular issues arising within it. Unless the parties otherwise agree the ENE will be produced in writing and will set out conclusions and brief reasons. Such an ENE will not, save with the agreement of the parties, be binding on the parties.

7.5.2 If the parties would like an ENE to be carried out by the court, then they can seek an appropriate order from the assigned judge either at the first CMC or at any time prior to the commencement of the trial.

7.5.3 The assigned judge may choose to do the ENE himself. In such instance, the judge will take no further part in the proceedings once he has produced the ENE, unless the parties expressly agree otherwise. Alternatively, the assigned judge will select another available TCC judge to undertake the ENE.

7.5.4 The judge undertaking the ENE will give appropriate directions for the preparation and conduct of the ENE. These directions will generally be agreed by the parties and may include:

- a stay of the substantive proceedings whilst the ENE is carried out.
- a direction that the ENE is to be carried out entirely on paper with dates for the exchange of submissions.
- a direction that particular documents or information should be provided by a party.
- a direction that there will be an oral hearing (either with or without evidence), with dates for all the necessary steps for submissions, witness statements and expert evidence leading to that hearing. If there is an oral hearing the ENE will generally not last more than one day.
- a statement that the parties agree or do not agree that the ENE procedure and the documents, submissions or evidence produced in relation to the ENE are to be without prejudice, or, alternatively, that the whole or part of those items are not without prejudice and can be referred to at any subsequent trial or hearing.
- a statement whether the parties agree that the judge's evaluation after the ENE process will be binding on the parties or binding in certain circumstances (eg if not disputed within a period) or temporarily binding subject to a final decision in arbitration, litigation or final agreement.

7.6 Court Settlement Process

7.6.1 The Court Settlement Process is a form of mediation carried out by TCC judges. Whilst mediation may be carried out by any appropriately qualified person, in an appropriate case, and with the consent of all parties, a TCC judge may act as a Settlement Judge pursuant to a Court Settlement Order in the terms set out in Appendix G.

7.6.2 If the parties would like to consider the use of the Court Settlement Process or would like further information, they should contact the TCC Registry in London or the TCC Liaison District Judges in the court centres outside London.

7.6.3 Where, following a request from the parties, the assigned TCC judge considers that the parties might be able to achieve an amicable settlement and that a TCC judge is particularly able to assist in achieving that settlement, that judge or another TCC judge, with the agreement of the parties, will make a Court Settlement Order (Appendix G) embodying the parties' agreement and fixing a date for the Court Settlement Conference to take place with an estimated duration proportionate to the issues in the case.

7.6.4 The TCC judge appointed as the Settlement Judge will then conduct the Court Settlement Process in accordance with that Court Settlement Order in a similar manner to that of a mediator. If no settlement is achieved then the case would proceed but, if the assigned judge carried out the Court Settlement Process, then the case would be assigned to another TCC judge. In any event, the Settlement Judge would take no further part in the court proceedings.

8. PRELIMINARY ISSUES
8.1 General

CPR 60 TCCG 8

8.1.1 The hearing of Preliminary Issues ('PI'), at which the court considers and delivers a binding judgment on particular issues in advance of the main trial, can be an extremely cost-effective and efficient way of narrowing the issues between the parties and, in certain cases, of resolving disputes altogether.

8.1.2 Some cases listed in the TCC lend themselves particularly well to this procedure. A PI hearing can address particular points which may be decisive of the whole proceedings; even if that is not the position, it is often possible for a PI hearing to cut down significantly on the scope (and therefore the costs) of the main trial.

8.1.3 At the first CMC the court will expect to be addressed on whether or not there are matters which should be taken by way of Preliminary Issues in advance of the main trial. Subject to paragraph 8.5 below, it is not generally appropriate for the court to make an order for the trial of preliminary issues until after the defence has been served. After the first CMC, and at any time during the litigation, any party is at liberty to raise with any other party the possibility of a PI hearing and the court will consider any application for the hearing of such Preliminary Issues. In many cases, although not invariably, a PI order will be made with the support of all parties.

8.1.4 Whilst, for obvious reasons, it is not possible to set out hard and fast rules for what is and what is not suitable for a PI hearing, the criteria set out in Section 8.2 below should assist the parties in deciding whether or not some or all of the disputes between them will be suitable for a PI hearing.

8.1.5 Drawbacks of preliminary issues in inappropriate cases. If preliminary issues are ordered inappropriately, they can have adverse effect. Evidence may be duplicated. The same witnesses may give evidence before different judges, in the event that there is a switch of assigned judge. Findings may be made at the PI hearing, which are affected by evidence called at the main hearing. The prospect of a PI hearing may delay the commencement of ADR or settlement negotiations. Also two trials are more expensive than one. For all these reasons, any proposal for preliminary issues needs to be examined carefully, so that the benefits and drawbacks can be evaluated. Also the court should give due weight to the views of the parties when deciding whether a PI hearing would be beneficial.

8.1.6 Staged trials. The breaking down of a long trial into stages should be differentiated from the trial of preliminary issues. Sometimes it is sensible for liability (including causation) to be tried before quantum of damages. Occasionally the subject matter of the litigation is so extensive that for reasons of case management the trial needs to be broken down into separate stages.

8.2 Guidelines

8.2.1 The Significance of the Preliminary Issues. The court would expect that any issue proposed as a suitable PI would, if decided in a particular way, be capable of:

– resolving the whole proceedings or a significant element of the proceedings; or
– significantly reducing the scope, and therefore the costs, of the main trial; or
– significantly improving the possibility of a settlement of the whole proceedings.

8.2.2 Oral Evidence. The court would ordinarily expect that, if issues are to be dealt with by way of a PI hearing, there would be either no or relatively limited oral evidence. If extensive oral evidence was required on any proposed PI, then it may not be suitable for a PI hearing. Although it is difficult to give specific guidance on this point, it is generally considered that a PI hearing in a smaller case should not take more than about 2 days, and in a larger and more complex case, should not take more than about 4 days.

8.3 Common Types of Preliminary Issue

The following are commonly resolved by way of a PI hearing:

(a) Disputes as to whether or not there was a binding contract between the parties.

(b) Disputes as to what documents make up or are incorporated within the contract between the parties and disputes as to the contents or relevance of any conversations relied on as having contractual status or effect.

(c) Disputes as to the proper construction of the contract documents or the effect of an exclusion or similar clause.

(d) Disputes as to the correct application of a statute or binding authority to a situation where there is little or no factual dispute.

(e) Disputes as to the existence and/or scope of a statutory duty.

(f) Disputes as to the existence and/or scope of a duty of care at common law in circumstances where there is no or little dispute about the relevant facts.

8.4 Other Possible Preliminary Issues

The following can sometimes be resolved by way of a preliminary issue hearing, although a decision as to whether or not to have such a hearing will always depend on the facts of the individual case:

8.4.1 A Limitation Defence. It is often tempting to have limitation issues resolved in advance of the main trial. This can be a good idea because, if a complex claim is statute-barred, a decision to that effect will lead to a significant saving of costs. However, there is also a risk that extensive evidence relevant to the limitation defence (relating to matters such as when the damage occurred or whether or not there has been deliberate concealment) may also be relevant to the liability issues within the main trial. In such a case, a preliminary issue hearing may lead to a) extensive duplication of evidence and therefore costs and b) give rise to difficulty if the main trial is heard by a different judge.

8.4.2 Causation and 'No Loss' Points. Causation and 'No Loss' points may be suitable for a PI hearing, but again their suitability will diminish if it is necessary for the court to resolve numerous factual disputes as part of the proposed PI hearing. The most appropriate disputes of this type for a PI hearing are those where the defendant contends that, even accepting all the facts alleged by the claimant, the claim must fail by reason of causation or the absence of recoverable loss.

8.4.3 'One-Off' Issues. Issues which do not fall into any obvious category, like economic duress, or misrepresentation, may be suitable for resolution by way of a PI hearing, particularly if the whole case can be shown to turn on them.

8.5 Use of PI as an adjunct to ADR

8.5.1 Sometimes parties wish to resolve their dispute by ADR, but there is one major issue which is a sticking point in any negotiation or mediation. The parties may wish to obtain the court's final decision on that single issue, in the expectation that after that they can resolve their differences without further litigation.

8.5.2 In such a situation the parties may wish to bring proceedings under CPR Part 8, in order to obtain the court's decision on that issue. Such proceedings can be rapidly progressed. Alternatively, if the issue is not suitable for Part 8 proceedings, the parties may bring proceedings under Part 7 and then seek determination of the critical question as a preliminary issue. At the first CMC the position can be explained and the judge can be asked to order early trial of the proposed preliminary issue, possibly without the need for a defence or any further pleadings.

8.6 Precise Wording of PI

8.6.1 If a party wishes to seek a PI hearing, either at the first CMC or thereafter, that party must circulate a precise draft of the proposed preliminary issues to the other parties and to the court well in advance of the relevant hearing.

8.6.2 If the court orders a PI hearing, it is likely to make such an order only by reference to specific and formulated issues, in order to avoid later debate as to the precise scope of the issues that have been ordered. Of course, the parties are at liberty to propose amendments to the issues before the PI hearing itself, but if such later amendments are not agreed by all parties, they are unlikely to be ordered.

8.7 Appeals

8.7.1 When considering whether or not to order a PI hearing, the court will take into account the effect of any possible appeal against the PI judgment, and the concomitant delay caused.

8.7.2 At the time of ordering preliminary issues, both the parties and the court should specifically consider whether, in the event of an appeal against the PI judgment, it is desirable that the trial of the main action should (a) precede or (b) follow such appeal. It should be noted, however, that the first instance court has no power to control the timetable for an appeal. A first instance court's power to extend time under CPR rule 52.4 (2) (a) for filing an appellant's notice is effectively limited to 14 days (see paragraph 5.19 of the Practice direction supplementing Part 52). The question whether an appeal should be (a) expedited or (b) stayed is entirely a matter for the Court of Appeal. Nevertheless, the Court of Appeal will take notice of any 'indication' given by the lower court in this regard.

9. ADJUDICATION BUSINESS

9.1 Introduction

CPR 60 TCCG 9

9.1.1 The TCC is ordinarily the court in which the enforcement of an adjudicator's decision and any other business connected with adjudication is undertaken. Adjudicators' decisions predominantly arise out of adjudications which are governed by the mandatory provisions of the Housing Grants, Construction and Regeneration Act 1996 ('HGCRA'). These provisions apply automatically to any construction contract as defined in the legislation. Some Adjudicators' decisions arise out of standard form contracts which contain adjudication provisions, and others arise from ad-hoc agreements to adjudicate. The TCC enforcement procedure is the same for all kinds of adjudication.

9.1.2 In addition to enforcement applications, declaratory relief is sometimes sought in the TCC at the outset of or during an adjudication in respect of matters such as the jurisdiction of the adjudicator or the validity of the adjudication. This kind of application is dealt with in Paragraph 9.4 below.

9.1.3 The HGCRA provides for a mandatory 28-day period within which the entire adjudication process must be completed, unless a) the referring party agrees to an additional 14 days, or b) both parties agree to a longer period. In consequence, the TCC has moulded a rapid procedure for enforcing an adjudication decision that has not been honoured. Other adjudication proceedings are ordinarily subject to similar rapidity.

9.2 Procedure In Enforcement Proceedings

9.2.1 Unlike arbitration business, there is neither a practice direction nor a claim form concerned with adjudication business. The enforcement proceedings normally seek a monetary judgment so that CPR Part 7 proceedings are usually appropriate. However, if the enforcement proceedings are known to raise a question which is unlikely to involve a substantial dispute of fact and no monetary judgment is sought, CPR Part 8 proceedings may be used instead.

9.2.2 The TCC has fashioned a procedure whereby enforcement applications are dealt with promptly. The details of this procedure are set out below.

9.2.3 The claim form should identify the construction contract, the jurisdiction of the adjudicator, the procedural rules under which the adjudication was conducted, the adjudicator's decision, the relief sought and the grounds for seeking that relief.

9.2.4 The claim form should be accompanied by an application notice that sets out the procedural directions that are sought. Commonly, the claimant's application will seek an abridgement of time for the various procedural steps, and summary judgment under CPR Part 24. The claim form and the application should be accompanied by a witness statement or statements setting out the evidence relied on in support of both the adjudication enforcement claim and the associated procedural application. This evidence should ordinarily include a copy of the adjudicator's decision.

9.2.5 The claim form, application notice and accompanying documents should be lodged in the appropriate registry or court centre clearly marked as being a 'paper without notice adjudication enforcement claim and application for the urgent attention of a TCC judge'. A TCC judge will ordinarily provide directions in connection with the procedural application within 3 working days of the receipt of the application notice at the courts.

9.2.6 The procedural application is dealt with by a TCC judge on paper, without notice. The paper application and the consequent directions should deal with:

(a)   the abridged period of time in which the defendant is to file an acknowledgement of service;
(b)   the time for service by the defendant of any witness statement in opposition to the relief being sought;
(c)   an early return date for the hearing of the summary judgment application and a note of the time required or allowed for that hearing; and
(d)   identification of the judgment, order or other relief being sought at the hearing of the adjudication claim.

The order made at this stage will always give the defendant liberty to apply.

9.2.7 A direction providing that the claim form, supporting evidence and court order providing for the hearing are to be served on the defendant as soon as practicable, or sometimes by a particular date, will ordinarily also be given when the judge deals with the paper procedural application.

9.2.8 The directions will ordinarily provide for an enforcement hearing within 28 days of the directions being made and for the defendant to be given at least 14 days from the date of service for the serving of any evidence in opposition to the adjudication application. In more straightforward cases, the abridged periods may be less.

9.2.9 Draft standard directions of the kind commonly made by the court on a procedural application by the claimant in an action to enforce the decision of an adjudicator are attached as Appendix F.

9.2.10 The claimant should, with the application, provide an estimate of the time needed for the hearing of the application. This estimate will be taken into account by the judge when fixing the date and length of the hearing. The parties should, if possible jointly, communicate any revised time estimate to the court promptly and the judge to whom the case has been allocated will consider whether to refix the hearing date or alter the time period that has been allocated for the hearing.

9.2.11 If the parties cannot agree on the date or time fixed for the hearing, a paper application must be made to the judge to whom the hearing has been allocated for directions.

9.2.12 Parties seeking to enforce adjudication decisions are reminded that they might be able to obtain judgment in default of service of an acknowledgment of service or, if the other party does not file any evidence in response, they might be able to obtain an expedited hearing of the Part 24 application.

9.3 The Enforcement Hearing

9.3.1 Where there is any dispute to be resolved at the hearing, the judge should be provided with copies of the relevant sections of the HGCRA, the adjudication procedural rules under which the adjudication was conducted, the adjudicator's decision and copies of any adjudication provisions in the contract underlying the adjudication.

9.3.2 Subject to any more specific directions given by the court, the parties should lodge, by 4.00 p.m. one clear working day before the hearing, a bundle containing the documents that will be required at the hearing. The parties should also file and serve short skeleton arguments and copies of any authorities which are to be relied on (preferably as an agreed joint bundle), summarising their respective contentions as to why the adjudicator's decision is or is not enforceable or as to any other relief being sought. For a hearing that is expected to last half a day or less, the skeletons should be provided no later than 1 p.m. on the last working day before the hearing. For a hearing that is estimated to last more than half a day, the skeletons should be provided no later than 4 p.m. one clear working day before the hearing.

9.3.3 The parties should be ready to address the court on the limited grounds on which a defendant may resist an application seeking to enforce an adjudicator's decision or on which a court may provide any other relief to any party in relation to an adjudication or an adjudicator's decision.

9.4 Other Proceedings Arising Out Of Adjudication

9.4.1 As noted above, the TCC will also hear any applications for declaratory relief arising out of the commencement of a disputed adjudication. Commonly, these will concern:

(a)   Disputes over the jurisdiction of an adjudicator. It can sometimes be appropriate to seek a declaration as to jurisdiction at the outset of an adjudication, rather than both parties incurring considerable costs in the adjudication itself, only for the jurisdiction point to emerge again at the enforcement hearing.

(b)   Disputes over whether there is a written contract between the parties or, in appropriate cases, whether there is a construction contract within the meaning of the Act.

(c)   Disputes over the permissible scope of the adjudication, and, in particular, whether the matters which the claimant seeks to raise in the adjudication are the subject of a pre-existing dispute between the parties.

9.4.2 Any such application will be immediately assigned to a named judge. In such circumstances, given the probable urgency of the application, the judge will usually require the parties to attend a CMC within 2 working days of the assignment of the case to him, and he will then give the necessary directions to ensure the speedy resolution of the dispute.

9.4.3 It sometimes happens that one party to an adjudication commences enforcement proceedings, whilst the other commences proceedings under Part 8, in order to challenge the validity of the adjudicator's award. This duplication of effort is unnecessary and it involves the parties in extra costs, especially if the two actions are commenced at different court centres. Accordingly there should be sensible discussions between the parties or their lawyers, in order to agree the appropriate venue and also to agree who shall be claimant and who defendant. All the issues raised by each party can and should be raised in a single action.

10. ARBITRATION

10.1 Arbitration Claims in the TCC

CPR 60 TCCG 10

10.1.1 'Arbitration claims' are any application to the court under the Arbitration Act 1996 and any other claim concerned with an arbitration that is referred to in CPR

62.2(1). Common examples of arbitration claims are challenges to an award on grounds of jurisdiction under section 67, challenges to an award for serious irregularity under section 68 or appeals on points of law under section 69 of the Arbitration Act 1996. Arbitration claims may be started in the TCC, as is provided for in paragraph 2.3 of the Practice Direction – Arbitration which supplements CPR Part 62.

10.1.2 In practice, arbitration claims arising out of or connected with a construction or engineering arbitration (or any other arbitration where the subject matter involved one or more of the categories of work set out in paragraph 1.3.1 above) should be started in the TCC. The only arbitration claims that must be started in the Commercial Court are those (increasingly rare) claims to which the old law (i.e. the pre-1996 Act provisions) apply: see CPR rule 62.12.

10.1.3 The TCC follows the practice and procedure for arbitration claims established by CPR Part 62 and (broadly) the practice of the Commercial Court as summarised by Section O of the Admiralty and Commercial Court Guide. In the absence of any specific directions given by the court, the automatic directions set out in section 6 of the Practice Direction supplementing CPR Part 62 govern the procedures to be followed in any arbitration claim from the date of service up to the substantive hearing.

10.2 Leave to appeal

10.2.1 Where a party is seeking to appeal a question of law arising out of an award pursuant to section 69 of the Arbitration Act 1996 and the parties have not in their underlying contract agreed that such an appeal may be brought, the party seeking to appeal must apply for leave to appeal pursuant to sections 69(2), 69(3) and 69(4) of that Act. That application must be included in the arbitration claim form as explained in paragraph 12 of the Practice Direction.

10.2.2 In conformity with the practice of the Commercial Court, the TCC will normally consider any application for permission to appeal on paper after the defendant has had an appropriate opportunity to answer in writing the application being raised.

10.2.3 The claimant must include within the claim form an application for permission to appeal. No separate application notice is required.

10.2.4 The claim form and supporting documents must be served on the defendant. The judge will not consider the merits of the application for permission to appeal until (a) a certificate of service has been filed at the appropriate TCC registry or court centre and (b), subject to any order for specific directions, a further 28 days have elapsed, so as to enable the defendant to file written evidence in opposition. Save in exceptional circumstances, the only material admissible on an application for permission to appeal is (a) the award itself and any documents annexed to or necessary to understand the award and (b) evidence relevant to the issue whether any identified question of law is of general public importance: see the requirements of paragraph 12 of the Practice Direction.

10.2.5 If necessary, the judge dealing with the application will direct an oral hearing with a date for the hearing. That hearing will, ordinarily, consist of brief submissions by each party. The judge dealing with the application will announce his decision in writing or, if a hearing has been directed, at the conclusion of the hearing with brief reasons if the application is refused.

10.2.6 Where the permission has been allowed in part and refused in part:

(a)   Only those questions for which permission has been granted may be raised at the hearing of the appeal.
(b)   Brief reasons will be given for refusing permission in respect of the other questions.

10.2.7 If the application is granted, the judge will fix the date for the appeal, and direct whether the same judge or a different judge shall hear the appeal.

10.3 Appeals where leave to appeal is not required

10.3.1 Parties to a construction contract should check whether they have agreed in the underlying contract that an appeal may be brought without leave, since some construction and engineering standard forms of contract so provide. If that is the case, the appeal may be set down for a substantive hearing without leave being sought. The arbitration claim form should set out the clause or provision which it is contended provides for such agreement and the claim form should be marked 'Arbitration Appeal – Leave not required'.

10.3.2 Where leave is not required, the claimant should identify each question of law that it is contended arises out of the award and which it seeks to raise in an appeal under section 69. If the defendant does not accept that the questions thus identified are questions of law or maintains that they do not arise out of the award or that the appeal on those questions may not be brought for any other reason, then the defendant should notify the claimant and the court of its contentions and apply for a directions hearing before the judge nominated to hear the appeal on a date prior to the date fixed for the hearing of the appeal. Unless the judge hearing the appeal otherwise directs, the appeal will be confined to the questions of law identified in the arbitration claim form.

10.3.3 In an appropriate case, the judge may direct that the question of law to be raised and decided on the appeal should be reworded, so as to identify more accurately the real legal issue between the parties.

10.4 The hearing of the appeal

10.4.1 Parties should ensure that the court is provided only with material that is relevant and admissible to the point of law. This will usually be limited to the award and any documents annexed to the award: see *Hok Sport Ltd v Aintree Racecourse Ltd* [2003] BLR 155 at 160. However, the court should also receive any document referred to in the award, which the court needs to read in order to determine a question of law arising out of the award: see *Kershaw Mechanical Services Ltd v Kendrick Construction Ltd* [2006] EWHC (TCC).

10.4.2 On receiving notice of permission being granted, or on issuing an arbitration claim form in a case where leave to appeal is not required, the parties should notify the court of their joint estimate or differing estimates of the time needed for the hearing of the appeal.

10.4.3 The hearing of the appeal is to be in open court unless an application (with notice) has previously been made that the hearing should be wholly or in part held in private and the court has directed that this course should be followed.

10.5 Section 68 applications – Serious Irregularity

10.5.1 In some arbitration claims arising out of construction and engineering arbitrations, a party will seek to appeal a question of law and, at the same time, seek to challenge the award under section 68 of the Arbitration Act 1996 on the grounds of serious irregularity. This raises questions of procedure, since material may be admissible in a section 68 application which is inadmissible on an application or appeal under section 69. Similarly, it may not be appropriate for all applications to be heard together. A decision is needed as to the order in which the applications should be heard, whether there should be one or more separate hearings to deal with them and whether or not the same judge should deal with all applications. Where a party intends to raise applications under both sections of the Arbitration Act 1996, they should be issued in the same arbitration claim form or in separate claim forms issued together. The court should be informed that separate applications are intended and asked for directions as to how to proceed.

10.5.2 The court will give directions as to how the section 68 and section 69 applications will be dealt with before hearing or determining any application. These directions will normally be given in writing but, where necessary or if such is applied for by a party, the court will hold a directions hearing at which directions will be given. The directions will be given following the service of any documentation by the defendant in answer to all applications raised by the claimant.

10.6 Successive awards and successive applications

10.6.1 Some construction and engineering arbitrations give rise to two or more separate awards issued at different times. Where arbitration applications arise under more than one of these awards, any second or subsequent application, whether arising from the same or a different award, should be referred to the same judge who has heard previous applications. Where more than one judge has heard previous applications, the court should be asked to direct to which judge any subsequent application is to be referred.

10.7 Other applications and Enforcement

10.7.1 All other arbitration claims, and any other matter arising in an appeal or an application concerning alleged serious irregularity, will be dealt with by the TCC in the same manner as is provided for in CPR Part 62, Practice Direction - Arbitration and Section O of The Admiralty and Commercial Courts Guide.

10.7.2 All applications for permission to enforce arbitration awards are governed by Section III of Part 62 (rules 62.17 - 62.19).

10.7.3 An application for permission to enforce an award in the same manner as a judgment or order of the court may be made in an arbitration claim form without notice and must be supported by written evidence in accordance with rule 62.18(6). Two copies of the draft order must accompany the application, and the form of the order sought must correspond to the terms of the award.

10.7.4 An order made without notice giving permission to enforce the award:

(a)   must give the defendant 14 days after service of the order (or longer, if the order is to be served outside the jurisdiction) to apply to set it aside;
(b)   must state that it may not be enforced until after the expiry of the 14 days (or any longer period specified) or until any application to set aside the order has been finally disposed of: rule 62.18(9) and (10).

10.7.5 On considering an application to enforce without notice, the judge may direct that, instead, the arbitration claim form must be served on specified parties, with the result that the application will then continue as an arbitration claim in accordance with the procedure set out in Section I of Part 62: see rule 62.18(1)-(3).

11. DISCLOSURE
11.1 Standard Disclosure

CPR 60 TCCG 11

11.1.1 The appropriate disclosure and inspection orders to be made will normally be considered and made at the first case management conference. This is governed by CPR Part 31 and the Practice Direction supplementing it. This procedure provides for standard disclosure, being disclosure and inspection in accordance with CPR Part 31 of:

(a)   the documents upon which a party relies;
(b)   the documents which adversely affect his or another party's case or support another party's case; and
(c)   the documents which a party is required to disclose by any relevant practice direction.

11.2 Limiting disclosure and the cost of disclosure

11.2.1 In many cases being conducted in the TCC, standard disclosure will not be appropriate. This may for any one or more of the following reasons:

(a)   The amount of documentation may be considerable, given the complexity of the dispute and the underlying contract or contracts, and the process of giving standard disclosure may consequently be disproportionate to the issues and sums in dispute.

(b)   The parties may have many of the documents in common from their previous dealings so that disclosure is not necessary or desirable.

(c)   The parties may have provided informal disclosure and inspection of the majority of these documents, for example when complying with the pre-action Protocol.

(d)   The cost of providing standard disclosure may be disproportionate.

In such cases, the parties should seek to agree upon a more limited form of disclosure or to dispense with formal disclosure altogether. Such an agreement could limit disclosure to specified categories of documents or to such documents as may be specifically applied for.

11.2.2 Where disclosure is to be provided, the parties should consider whether it is necessary for lists of documents to be prepared or whether special arrangements should be agreed as to the form of listing and identifying disclosable documents, the method, timing and location of inspection and the manner of copying or providing copies of documents. Where documents are scattered over several locations, or are located overseas or are in a foreign language, special arrangements will also need to be considered. Thought should also be given to providing disclosure in stages or to reducing the scope of disclosure by providing the relevant material in other forms.

11.2.3 Electronic data and documents give rise to particular problems as to searching, preserving, listing, inspecting and other aspects of discovery and inspection. These problems should be considered and, if necessary made the subject of special directions. Furthermore, in appropriate cases, disclosure, inspection and the provision of copies of hard copies may be undertaken using information technology. Attention is drawn to the relevant provisions in CPR Part 31 and Practice Direction 31B: Disclosure of Electronic Documents and also to the TeCSA IT Protocol which provides guidance in relation to these matters.

11.2.4 All these matters should be agreed between the parties. If it is necessary to raise any of these matters with the court they should be raised, if possible, at the first CMC. If points arise on disclosure after the first CMC, they may well be capable of being dealt with by the court on paper.

11.3 Electronic Service of documents

11.3.1 Parties are encouraged to file documents electronically in the London TCC: see Electronic Working at paragraph 3.8 above. In addition and in other cases, the parties should consult with each other before the first CMC with a view to arranging the service of pleadings, schedules, witness statements, experts' reports, disclosure lists and other documents in electronic form instead of or as well as in hard copy. The parties should also consider whether to maintain a common running index, so that every document which has been exchanged between the parties has a unique reference number. Any agreement reached on these matters should be recorded and made the subject of an order for directions. Where agreement is not possible, the parties should raise these matters for decision at a CMC.

12. WITNESS STATEMENTS AND FACTUAL EVIDENCE FOR USE AT TRIAL

12.1 Witness statements

CPR 60 TCCG 12

12.1.1 Witness statements should be prepared generally in accordance with CPR Part 22.1 (documents verified by a statement of truth) and CPR Part 32 (provisions governing the evidence of witnesses) and their practice directions, particularly paragraphs 17 to 22 of the Practice Direction supplementing CPR Part 32.

12.1.2 Unless otherwise directed by the court, witness statements should <u>not</u> have annexed to them copies of other documents and should <u>not</u> reproduce or paraphrase at length passages from other documents. The only exception arises where a specific document needs to be annexed to the statement in order to make that statement reasonably intelligible.

12.1.3 When preparing witness statements, attention should be paid to the following matters:

(a) Even when prepared by a legal representative or other professional, the witness statement should be, so far as practicable, in the witness's own words.

(b) The witness statement should indicate which matters are within the witness's own knowledge and which are matters of information and belief. Where the witness is stating matters of hearsay or of either information or belief, the source of that evidence should also be stated.

(c) The witness statement must include a statement by the witness that he believes the facts stated to be true.

(d) A witness statement should be no longer than necessary and should not be argumentative.

12.1.4 <u>Costs.</u> If at any stage the judge considers that the way in which witness statements have been prepared is likely to lead or has led to inefficiency in the conduct of the proceedings or to unnecessary time or costs being spent, the judge may order that the witness should re-submit the witness statement in whole or part and may make a costs order disallowing costs or ordering costs to be paid, either on the basis of a summary assessment or by giving a direction to the costs judge as to what costs should be disallowed or paid on a detailed assessment; see paragraph 5.5.5 above.

12.2 Other matters concerned with witness statements

12.2.1 <u>Foreign language.</u> If a witness is not sufficiently fluent in English to give his evidence in English, the witness statement should be in his or her own language and an authenticated translation provided. Where the witness has a broken command of English, the statement may be drafted by others so as to express the witness's evidence as accurately as possible. In that situation, however, the witness statement should indicate that this process of interpolation has occurred and also should explain the extent of the witness's command of English and how and to what parts of the witness statement the process of interpolation has occurred.

12.2.2 <u>Reluctant witness.</u> Sometimes a witness is unwilling or not permitted or is unavailable to provide a witness statement before the trial. The party seeking to adduce this evidence should comply with the provisions of CPR rule 32.9 concerned with the provision of witness summaries.

12.2.3 <u>Hearsay.</u> Parties should keep in mind the need to give appropriate notice of their intention to rely on hearsay evidence or the contents of documents without serving a witness statement from their maker or from the originator of the evidence contained in those documents. The appropriate procedure is contained in CPR rules 33.1 – 33.5.

12.2.4 <u>Supplementary Witness Statements.</u> The general principle is that a witness should set out in their witness statement their complete evidence relevant to the issues in the case. The witness statement should not include evidence on the basis that it might be needed depending on what the other party's witnesses might say. The correct procedure in such cases is for the witness to provide a supplementary witness statement or, as necessary, for a new witness to provide a witness statement limited to responding to particular matters contained in the other party's witness statement and to seek permission accordingly. In some cases it might be appropriate for the court to provide for the service of supplementary witness statements as part of the order at the first case management conference.

12.2.5 <u>Supplementary Evidence in Chief.</u> The relevant witness evidence should be contained in the witness statements, or if appropriate witness summaries, served in advance of the hearing. Where, for whatever reason, this has not happened and the witness has relevant important evidence to give, particularly where the need for such evidence has only become apparent during the trial, the judge has a discretion to permit supplementary evidence in chief.

12.3 Cross-referencing

12.3.1 Where a substantial number of documents will be adduced in evidence or contained in the trial bundles, it is of considerable assistance to the court and to all concerned if the relevant page references are annotated in the margins of the copy witness statements. It is accepted that this is a time-consuming exercise, the need for which will be considered at the PTR, and it will only be ordered where it is both appropriate and proportionate to do so. See further paragraphs 14.5.1 and 15.2.3 below.

12.4 Video link

12.4.1 If any witness (whose witness statement has been served and who is required to give oral evidence) is located outside England and Wales or would find a journey to court inconvenient or impracticable, his evidence might be given via a video link. Thought should be given before the PTR to the question whether this course would be appropriate and proportionate. Such evidence is regularly received by the TCC and facilities for its reception, whether in appropriate court premises or at a convenient venue outside the court building, are now readily available.

12.4.2 Any application for a video link direction and any question relating to the manner in which such evidence is to be given should be dealt with at the PTR. Attention is drawn to the Video-conferencing Protocol set out at Annex 3 to the Practice Direction supplementing CPR Part 32 – Evidence. The procedure described in Annex 3 is followed by the TCC.

13. EXPERT EVIDENCE

13.1 Nature of expert evidence

CPR 60 TCCG 13

13.1.1 Expert evidence is evidence as to matters of a technical or scientific nature and will generally include the opinions of the expert. The quality and reliability of expert evidence will depend upon (a) the experience and the technical or scientific qualifications of the expert and (b) the accuracy of the factual material that is used by the expert for his assessment. Expert evidence is dealt with in detail in CPR Part 35 ('Experts and Assessors') and in the Practice Direction supplementing Part 35. Particular attention should be paid to all these provisions, given the detailed reliance on expert evidence in most TCC actions. Particular attention should also be paid to the 'Protocol for the instruction of experts to give evidence in civil claims' annexed to Practice Direction 35 – Experts and Assessors.

13.1.2 The provisions in CPR Part 35 are concerned with the terms upon which the court may receive expert evidence. These provisions are principally applicable to independently instructed expert witnesses. In cases where a party is a professional or a professional has played a significant part in the subject matter of the action, opinion evidence will almost inevitably be included in the witness statements. Any points arising from such evidence (if they cannot be resolved by agreement) can be dealt with by the judge on an application or at the PTR.

13.2 Control of expert evidence

13.2.1 Expert evidence is frequently needed and used in TCC cases. Experts are often appointed at an early stage. Most types of case heard in the TCC involve more than one expertise and some, even when the dispute is concerned with relatively small sums, involve several different experts. Such disputes include those concerned with building failures and defects, delay and disruption, dilapidations, subsidence caused by tree roots and the supply of software systems. However, given the cost of preparing such evidence, the parties and the court must, from the earliest pre-action phase of a dispute until the conclusion of the trial, seek to make effective and proportionate use of experts. The scope of any expert evidence must be limited to what is necessary for the requirements of the particular case.

13.2.2 At the first CMC, or thereafter, the court may be asked to determine whether the cost of instructing experts is proportionate to the amount at issue in the proceedings, and the importance of the case to the parties. In dealing with any issues of proportionality, the court should be provided with estimates of the experts' costs.

13.2.3 The parties should also be aware that the court has the power to limit the amount of the expert's fees that a party may recover pursuant to CPR 35.4 (4).

13.3 Prior to and at the first CMC

13.3.1 There is an unresolved tension arising from the need for parties to instruct and rely on expert opinions from an early pre-action stage and the need for the court to seek, wherever possible, to reduce the cost of expert evidence by dispensing with it altogether or by encouraging the appointment of jointly instructed experts. This tension arises because the court can only consider directing joint appointments or limiting expert evidence long after a party may have incurred the cost of obtaining expert evidence and have already relied on it. Parties should be aware of this tension. So far as possible, the parties should avoid incurring the costs of expert evidence on uncontroversial matters or matters of the kind referred to in paragraph 13.4.3 below, before the first CMC has been held.

13.3.2 In cases where it is not appropriate for the court to order a single joint expert, it is imperative that, wherever possible, the parties' experts co-operate fully with one another. This is particularly important where tests, surveys, investigations, sample gathering or other technical methods of obtaining primary factual evidence are needed. It is often critical to ensure that any laboratory testing or experiments are carried out by the experts together, pursuant to an agreed procedure. Alternatively, the respective experts may agree that a particular firm or laboratory shall carry out specified tests or analyses on behalf of all parties.

13.3.3 Parties should, where possible, disclose initial or preliminary reports to opposing parties prior to any pre-action protocol meeting, if only on a without prejudice basis. Such early disclosure will assist in early settlement or mediation discussions and in helping the parties to define and confine the issues in dispute with a corresponding saving in costs.

13.3.4 Before and at the first CMC and at each subsequent pre-trial stage of the action, the parties should give careful thought to the following matters:

(a)   The number, disciplines and identity of the expert witnesses they are considering instructing as their own experts or as single joint experts.
(b)   The precise issues which each expert is to address in his/her reports, to discuss without prejudice with opposing parties' experts and give evidence about at the trial.
(c)   The timing of any meeting, agreed statement or report.
(d)   Any appropriate or necessary tests, inspections, sampling or investigations that could be undertaken jointly or in collaboration with other experts. Any such measures should be preceded by a meeting of relevant experts at which an appropriate testing or other protocol is devised. This would cover (i) all matters connected with the process in question and its recording and (ii) the sharing and agreement of any resulting data or evidence.
(e)   Any common method of analysis, investigation or reporting where it is appropriate or proportionate that such should be adopted by all relevant experts. An example of this would be an agreement as to the method to be used to analyse the cause and extent of any relevant period of delay in a construction project, where such is in issue in the case.

(f)   The availability and length of time that experts will realistically require to complete the tasks assigned to them.

13.3.5 In so far as the matters set out in the previous paragraph cannot be agreed, the court will give appropriate directions. In giving permission for the reception of any expert evidence, the court will ordinarily order the exchange of such evidence, with a definition of the expert's area of expertise and a clear description of the issues about which that expert is permitted to give evidence. It is preferable that, at the first CMC or as soon as possible thereafter, the parties should provide the court with the name(s) of their expert(s).

13.4 Single joint experts

13.4.1 An order may be made, at the first CMC or thereafter, that a single joint expert should address particular issues between the parties. Such an order would be made pursuant to CPR Parts 35.7 and 35.8.

13.4.2 Single joint experts are not usually appropriate for the principal liability disputes in a large case, or in a case where considerable sums have been spent on an expert in the pre-action stage. They are generally inappropriate where the issue involves questions of risk assessment or professional competence.

13.4.3 On the other hand, single joint experts can often be appropriate:

(a)   in low value cases, where technical evidence is required but the cost of adversarial expert evidence may be prohibitive;
(b)   where the topic with which the single joint expert's report deals is a separate and self-contained part of the case, such as the valuation of particular heads of claim;
(c)   where there is a subsidiary issue, which requires particular expertise of a relatively uncontroversial nature to resolve;
(d)   where testing or analysis is required, and this can conveniently be done by one laboratory or firm on behalf of all parties.

13.4.4 Where a single joint expert is to be appointed or is to be directed by the court, the parties should attempt to devise a protocol covering all relevant aspects of the appointment (save for those matters specifically provided for by CPR rules 35.6, 35.7 and 35.8).

13.4.5 The matters to be considered should include: any ceiling on fees and disbursements that are to be charged and payable by the parties; how, when and by whom fees will be paid to the expert on an interim basis pending any costs order in the proceedings; how the expert's fees will be secured; how the terms of reference are to be agreed; what is to happen if terms of reference cannot be agreed; how and to whom the jointly appointed expert may address further enquiries and from whom he should seek further information and documents; the timetable for preparing any report or for undertaking any other preparatory step; the possible effect on such timetable of any supplementary or further instructions. Where these matters cannot be agreed, an application to the court, which may often be capable of being dealt with as a paper application, will be necessary.

13.4.6 The usual procedure for a single joint expert will involve:

(a)   The preparation of the expert's instructions. These instructions should clearly identify those issues or matters where the parties are in conflict, whether on the facts or on matters of opinion. If the parties can agree joint instructions, then a single set of instructions should be delivered to the expert. However, rule 35.8 expressly permits separate instructions and these are necessary where joint instructions cannot be agreed
(b)   The preparation of the agreed bundle, which is to be provided to the expert. This bundle must include CPR Part 35, the Practice Direction supplementing Part 35 and the section 13 of the TCC Guide.
(c)   The preparation and production of the expert's report.
(d)   The provision to the expert of any written questions from the parties, which the expert must answer in writing.

13.4.7 In most cases the single joint expert's report, supplemented by any written answers to questions from the parties, will be sufficient for the purposes of the trial. Sometimes, however, it is necessary for a single joint expert to be called to give oral evidence. In those circumstances, the usual practice is for the judge to call the expert and then allow each party the opportunity to cross-examine. Such cross-examination should be conducted with appropriate restraint, since the witness has been instructed by the parties. Where the expert's report is strongly in favour of one party's position, it may be appropriate to allow only the other party to cross-examine.

13.5 Meetings of experts

13.5.1 The desirability of holding without prejudice meetings between experts at all stages of the pre-trial preparation should be kept in mind. The desired outcome of such meetings is to produce a document whose contents are agreed and which defines common positions or each expert's differing position. The purpose of such meetings includes the following:

(a)   to define a party's technical case and to inform opposing parties of the details of that case;
(b)   to clear up confusion and to remedy any lack of information or understanding of a party's technical case in the minds of opposing experts;
(c)   to identify the issues about which any expert is to give evidence;
(d)   to narrow differences and to reach agreement on as many 'expert' issues as possible; and
(e)   to assist in providing an agenda for the trial and for cross examination of expert witnesses, and to limit the scope and length of the trial as much as possible.

13.5.2 In many cases it will be helpful for the parties' respective legal advisors to provide assistance as to the agenda and topics to be discussed at an experts' meeting. However, (save in exceptional circumstances and with the permission of the judge) the legal advisors must not attend the meeting. They must not attempt to dictate what the experts say at the meeting.

13.5.3 Experts' meetings can sometimes usefully take place at the site of the dispute. Thought is needed as to who is to make the necessary arrangements for access, particularly where the site is occupied or in the control of a non-party. Expert meetings are often more productive, if (a) the expert of one party (usually the claimant) is appointed as chairman and (b) the experts exchange in advance agendas listing the topics each wishes to raise and identifying any relevant material which they intend to introduce or rely on during the meeting.

13.5.4 It is generally sensible for the experts to meet at least once before they exchange their reports.

13.6 Experts' Joint Statements

13.6.1 Following the experts' meetings, and pursuant to CPR 35.12 (3), the judge will almost always require the experts to produce a signed statement setting out the issues which have been agreed, and those issues which have not been agreed, together with a short summary of the reasons for their disagreement. In any TCC case in which expert evidence has an important role to play, this statement is a critical document and it must be as clear as possible.

13.6.2 It should be noted that, even where experts have been unable to agree very much, it is of considerable importance that the statement sets out their disagreements and the reasons for them. Such disagreements as formulated in the joint statement are likely to form an important element of the agenda for the trial of the action.

13.6.3 Whilst the parties' legal advisors may assist in identifying issues which the statement should address, those legal advisors must not be involved in either negotiating or drafting the experts' joint statement. Legal advisors should only invite the experts to consider amending any draft joint statement in exceptional circumstances where there are serious concerns that the court may misunderstand or be misled by the terms of that joint statement. Any such concerns should be raised with all experts involved in the joint statement.

13.7 Experts' Reports

13.7.1 It is the duty of an expert to help the court on matters within his expertise. This duty overrides any duty to his client: CPR rule 35.3. Each expert's report must be independent and unbiased. Paragraphs 3(vii), 3.3.1(vi) and 5.5(i) of the Pre-Action Protocol for Construction and Engineering Disputes contain provisions as to experts in TCC cases and accordingly Annex C to the Practice Direction – Pre-Action Conduct does not apply: see paragraphs 9.1 and 9.4 of the Practice Direction – Pre-Action Conduct.

13.7.2 The parties must identify the issues with which each expert should deal in his or her report. Thereafter, it is for the expert to draft and decide upon the detailed contents and format of the report, so as to conform with the Practice Direction supplementing CPR Part 35 and the Protocol for the Instruction of Experts to give Evidence in Civil Claims. It is appropriate, however, for the party instructing an expert to indicate that the report (a) should be as short as is reasonably possible; (b) should not set out copious extracts from other documents; (c) should identify the source of any opinion or data relied upon; and (d) should not annex or exhibit more than is reasonably necessary to support the opinions expressed in the report. In addition, as set out in paragraph 15.2 of the Protocol for the Instruction of Experts to give Evidence in Civil Claims, legal advisors may also invite experts to consider amendments to their reports to ensure accuracy, internal consistency, completeness, relevance to the issues or clarity of reports.

13.8 Presentation of Expert Evidence

13.8.1 The purpose of expert evidence is to assist the court on matters of a technical or scientific nature. Particularly in large and complex cases where the evidence has developed through a number of experts' joint statements and reports, it is often helpful for the expert at the commencement of his or her evidence to provide the court with a summary of their views on the main issues. This can be done orally or by way of a PowerPoint or similar presentation. The purpose is not to introduce new evidence but to explain the existing evidence.

13.8.2 The way in which expert evidence is given is a matter to be considered at the PTR. However where there are a number of experts of different disciplines the court will consider the best way for the expert evidence to be given. It is now quite usual for all expert evidence to follow the completion of the witness evidence from all parties. At that stage there are a number of possible ways of presenting evidence including:

(a)   For one party to call all its expert evidence, followed by each party calling all of its expert evidence.

(b)   For one party to call its expert in a particular discipline, followed by the other parties calling their experts in that discipline. This process would then be repeated for the experts of all disciplines.

(c)   For one party to call its expert or experts to deal with a particular issue, followed by the other parties calling their expert or experts to deal with that issues. This process would then be repeated for all the expert issues.

(d)   For the experts for all parties to be called to give concurrent evidence, colloquially referred to as 'hot-tubbing'. When this method is adopted there is generally a need for experts to be cross-examined on general matters and key issues before they are invited to give evidence concurrently on particular issues. Procedures vary but, for instance, a party may ask its expert to explain his or her view on an issue, then ask the other party's expert for his or her view on that issue and then return to that party's expert for a comment on that view. Alternatively, or in addition, questions may be asked by the judge or the experts themselves may each ask the other questions. The process is often most useful where there are a large number of items to be dealt with and the procedure allows the court to have the evidence on each item dealt with on the same occasion rather than having the evidence divided with the inability to have each expert's views expressed clearly. Frequently, it allows the extent of agreement and reason for disagreement to be seen more clearly. The giving of concurrent evidence may be consented to by the parties and the judge will consider whether, in the absence of consent, any particular method of concurrent evidence is appropriate in the light of the provisions of the CPR.

14. THE PRE-TRIAL REVIEW

14.1 Timing and Attendance

CPR 60 TCCG 14

14.1.1 The Pre-Trial Review ('PTR') will usually be fixed for a date that is 4–6 weeks in advance of the commencement of the trial itself. It is vital that the advocates, who are going to conduct the trial, should attend the PTR and every effort should be made to achieve this. It is usually appropriate for the PTR to be conducted by way of an oral hearing or, at the very least, a telephone conference, so that the judge may raise matters of trial management even if the parties can agree beforehand any outstanding directions and the detailed requirements for the management of the trial. In appropriate cases, e.g. where the amount in issue is disproportionate to the costs of a full trial, the judge may wish to consider with the parties whether there are other ways in which the dispute might be resolved.

14.2 Documents

14.2.1 The parties must complete the PTR Questionnaire (a copy of which is at Appendix C attached) and return it in good time to the court. In addition, the judge may order the parties to provide other documents for the particular purposes of the PTR.

14.2.2 In an appropriate case, the advocates for each party should prepare a Note for the PTR, which addresses:

- any outstanding directions or interlocutory steps still to be taken;
- the issues for determination at the trial;
- the most efficient way in which those issues might be dealt with at the trial, including all questions of timetabling of witnesses.

These Notes should be provided to the court by 4 p.m. one clear working day before the PTR.

14.2.3 The parties should also ensure that, for the PTR, the court has an up-to-date permanent case management bundle, together with a bundle of the evidence (factual and expert) that has been exchanged. This Bundle should also be made available to the court by 4 p.m. one clear day before the PTR.

14.3 Outstanding Directions

14.3.1 It can sometimes be the case that there are still outstanding interlocutory steps to be taken at the time of the PTR. That will usually mean that one, or more, of the parties has not complied with an earlier direction of the court. In that event, the court is likely to require prompt compliance, and may make costs orders to reflect the delays.

14.3.2 Sometimes a party will wish to make an application to be heard at the same time as the PTR. Such a practice is unsatisfactory, because it uses up time allocated for the PTR, and it gives rise to potential uncertainty close to the trial date.

It is always better for a party, if it possibly can, to make all necessary applications well in advance of the PTR. If that is not practicable, the court should be asked to allocate additional time for the PTR, in order to accommodate specific applications. If additional time is not available, such applications will not generally be entertained.

14.4 Issues

14.4.1 The parties should, if possible, provide the judge at the PTR with an agreed list of the main issues for the forthcoming trial (including, where appropriate, a separate list of technical issues to be covered by the experts). The list of issues should not be extensive. It is provided as a working document to assist in the management of the trial and not as a substitute for the pleadings.

14.4.2 If the parties are unable to agree the precise formulation of the issues, they should provide to the court their respective formulations. Because the list of issues should be confined to the main issues the opportunity for disagreement should be minimised. The judge will note the parties' formulations, but, because the issues are those which arise on the pleadings, is unlikely to give a ruling on this matter at the PTR unless the different formulations show that there is a dispute as to the pleaded case.

14.5 Timetabling and Trial Logistics

14.5.1 Much of the PTR will be devoted to a consideration of the appropriate timetable for the trial, and other logistical matters. These will commonly include:

– Directions in respect of oral and written openings.
– Sequence of oral evidence; for example, whether all the factual evidence should be called before the expert evidence.
– Timetabling of oral evidence. To facilitate this exercise, the advocates should, after discussing the matter and whether some evidence can be agreed, provide a draft timetable indicating which witnesses need to be cross-examined and the periods during it is proposed that they should attend. Such timetables are working documents.
– The manner in which expert evidence is to be presented: see paragraph 13.8 above.
– Whether any form of time limits should be imposed. (Since the purpose of time limits is to ensure that that the costs incurred and the resources devoted to the trial are proportionate, this is for the benefit of the parties. The judge will endeavour to secure agreement to any time limits imposed.)
– Directions in respect of the trial bundle: when it should be agreed and lodged; the contents and structure of the bundle; avoidance of duplication; whether witness statements and/or expert reports should be annotated with cross references to page numbers in the main bundle (see paragraph 12.3 above); and similar matters.
– Whether there should be a core bundle; if so how it should be prepared and what it should contain. (The court will order a core bundle in any case where (a) there is substantial documentation and (b) having regard to the issues it is appropriate and proportionate to put the parties to cost of preparing a core bundle).
– Rules governing any email communication during trial between the parties and the court.
– Any directions relating to the use of simultaneous transcription at trial (this subject to agreement between the parties).
– Whether there should be a view by the judge.

14.5.2 The topics identified in paragraph 14.5.1 are discussed in greater detail in section 15 below.

15. THE TRIAL

15.1 Arrangements prior to the trial - witnesses

CPR 60 TCCG 15

15.1.1 Prior to the trial the parties' legal representatives should seek to agree on the following matters, in so far as they have not been resolved at the PTR: the order in which witnesses are to be called to give evidence; which witnesses are not required for cross examination and whose evidence in consequence may be adduced entirely from their witness statements; the timetable for the trial and the length of time each advocate is to be allowed for a brief opening speech. When planning the timetable, it should be noted that trials normally take place on Mondays to Thursdays, since Fridays are reserved for applications.

15.1.2 The witnesses should be notified in advance of the trial as to: (a) when each is required to attend court and (b) the approximate period of time for which he or she will be required to attend.

15.1.3 It is the parties' responsibility to ensure that their respective witnesses are ready to attend court at the appropriate time. It is never satisfactory for witnesses to be interposed, out of their proper place. It would require exceptional circumstances for the trial to be adjourned for any period of time because of the unavailability of a witness.

15.2 Opening notes, trial bundle and oral openings

15.2.1 Opening notes. Unless the court has ordered otherwise, each party's advocate should provide an opening note, which outlines that party's case in relation to each of the issues identified at the PTR. Each opening note should indicate which documents (giving their page numbers in the trial bundle) that party considers that the judge should pre read. The claimant's opening note should include a neutral summary of the background facts, as well as a chronology and cast list. The other parties' opening notes should be shorter and should assume familiarity with the factual background. In general terms, all opening notes should be of modest length and proportionate to the size and complexity of the case. Subject to any specific directions at the PTR, the claimant's opening note should be served two clear working days before the start of the trial; the other parties opening notes should be served by 1 p.m. on the last working day before the trial.

15.2.2 Trial bundles. Subject to any specific directions at the PTR, the trial bundles should be delivered to court at least three working days before the hearing. It is helpful for the party delivering the trial bundles to liaise in advance with the judge's clerk, in order to discuss practical arrangements, particularly when a large number of bundles are to be delivered. The parties should provide for the court an agreed index of all trial bundles. There should also be an index at the front of each bundle. This should be a helpful guide to the contents of that bundle. (An interminable list, itemising every letter or sheet of paper is not a helpful guide. Nor are bland descriptions, such as 'exhibit 'JT3', of much help to the bundle user.) The spines and inside covers of bundles should be clearly labelled with the bundle number and brief description.

15.2.3 As a general rule the trial bundles should be clearly divided between statements of case, orders, contracts, witness statements, expert reports and correspondence/ minutes of meetings. The correspondence/ minutes of meetings should be in a separate bundle or bundles and in chronological order. Documents should only be included, if they are relevant to the issues in the case or helpful as background material. Documents should not be duplicated. Exhibits to witness statements should generally be omitted, since the documents to which the witnesses are referring will be found elsewhere in the bundles. The bundles of contract documents and correspondence/ minutes of meetings should be paginated, so that every page has a discrete number. The other bundles could be dealt with in one of two ways:

– The statements of case, witness statements and expert reports could be placed in bundles and continuously paginated.

– Alternatively, the statements of case, witness statements and expert reports could be placed behind tabbed divider cards, and then the internal numbering of each such document can be used at trial. If the latter course is adopted, it is vital that the internal page numbering of each expert report continues sequentially through the appendices to that report.

The court encourages the parties to provide original copies of expert reports in this way so that any photographs, plans or charts are legible in their original size and, where appropriate, in colour. In such cases sequential numbering of every page including appendices is essential.

The ultimate objective is to create trial bundles, which are user friendly and in which any page can be identified with clarity and brevity (e.g. 'bundle G page 273' or 'defence page 3' or 'Dr Smith page 12'). The core bundle, if there is one (as to which see paragraph 14.5.1 above), will be a separate bundle with its own pagination or contain documents from other bundles retaining the original bundle number behind a divider marked with the bundle number.

15.2.4 <u>Opening speeches.</u> Subject to any directions made at the PTR, each party will be permitted to make an opening speech. These speeches should be prepared and presented on the basis that the judge will have pre-read the opening notes and the documents identified by the parties for pre-reading. The claimant's advocate may wish to highlight the main features of the claimant's case and/or to deal with matters raised in the other parties' opening notes. The other parties' advocates will then make shorter opening speeches, emphasising the main features of their own cases and/or responding to matters raised in the claimant's opening speech.

15.2.5 It is not usually necessary or desirable to embark upon legal argument during opening speeches. It is, however, helpful to foreshadow those legal arguments which (a) explain the relevance of particular parts of the evidence or (b) will assist the judge in following a party's case that is to be presented during the trial.

15.2.6 <u>Narrowing of issues.</u> Experience shows that often the issues between the parties progressively narrow as the trial advances. Sometimes this process begins during the course of opening speeches. Weaker contentions may be abandoned and responses to those contentions may become irrelevant. The advocates will co-operate in focussing their submissions and the evidence on the true issues between the parties, as those issues are thrown into sharper relief by the adversarial process.

15.3 Simultaneous transcription

15.3.1 Many trials in the TCC, including the great majority of the longer trials, are conducted with simultaneous transcripts of the evidence being provided. There are a number of transcribing systems available. It is now common for a system to be used involving simultaneous transcription onto screens situated in court. However, systems involving the production of the transcript in hard or electronic form at the end of the day or even after a longer period of time are also used. The parties must make the necessary arrangements with one of the companies who provide this service. The court can provide a list, on request, of all companies who offer such a service.

15.3.2 In long trials or those which involve any significant amount of detailed or technical evidence, simultaneous transcripts are helpful. Furthermore, they enable all but the shortest trials to be conducted so as to reduce the overall length of the trial appreciably, since the judge does not have to note the evidence or submissions in longhand as the trial proceeds. Finally, a simultaneous transcript makes the task of summarising a case in closing submissions and preparing the judgment somewhat easier. It reduces both the risk of error or omission and the amount of time needed to prepare a reserved judgment.

15.3.3 If possible, the parties should have agreed at or before the PTR whether a simultaneous transcript is to be employed. It is usual for parties to agree to share the cost of a simultaneous transcript as an interim measure pending the assessment or agreement of costs, when this cost is assessable and payable as part of the costs in the case. Sometimes, a party cannot or will not agree to an interim cost sharing arrangement. If so, it is permissible for one party to bear the cost, but the court cannot be provided with a transcript unless all parties have equal access to the transcript. Unlike transcripts for use during an appeal, there is no available means of obtaining from public funds the cost of a transcript for use at the trial.

15.4 Time limits

15.4.1 Generally trials in the TCC are conducted under some form of time limit arrangement. Several variants of time limit arrangements are available, but the TCC has developed the practice of imposing flexible guidelines in the form of directions as to the sharing of the time allotted for the trial. These are not mandatory but an advocate should ordinarily be expected to comply with them.

15.4.2 The practice is, in the usual case, for the court to fix, or for the parties to agree, at the PTR or before trial an overall length of time for the trial and overall lengths of time within that period for the evidence and submissions. The part of those overall lengths of time that will be allocated to each party must then be agreed or directed.

15.4.3 The amount of time to be allotted to each party will not usually be the same. The guide is that each party should have as much time as is reasonably needed for it to present its case and to test and cross examine any opposing case, but no longer.

15.4.4 Before the trial, the parties should agree a running order of the witnesses and the approximate length of time required for each witness. A trial timetable should be provided to the court when the trial starts and, in long trials, regularly updated.

15.4.5 The practice of imposing a strict guillotine on the examination or cross examination of witnesses, is not normally appropriate. Flexibility is encouraged, but the agreed or directed time limits should not ordinarily be exceeded without good reason. It is unfair on a party, if that party's advocate has confined cross-examination to the agreed time limits, but an opposing party then greatly exceeds the corresponding time limits that it has been allocated.

15.4.6 An alternative form of time limit, which is sometimes agreed between the parties and approved by the court, is the 'chess clock arrangement'. The available time is divided equally between the parties, to be used by the parties as they see fit. Thus each side has X hours. One representative on each side operates the chess clock. The judge has discretion 'to stop the clock' in exceptional circumstances. A chess clock arrangement is only practicable in a two-party case.

15.5 Oral evidence

15.5.1 Evidence in chief is ordinarily adduced by the witness confirming on oath the truth and accuracy of the previously served witness statement or statements. A limited number of supplementary oral questions will usually be allowed (a) to give the witness an opportunity to become familiar with the procedure and (b) to cover points omitted by mistake from the witness statement or which have arisen subsequent to its preparation.

15.5.2 In some cases, particularly those involving allegations of dishonest, disreputable or culpable conduct or where significant disputes of fact are not documented or evidenced in writing, it is desirable that the core elements of a witness's evidence-in-chief are given orally. The giving of such evidence orally will often assist the court in assessing the credibility or reliability of a witness.

15.5.3 If any party wishes such evidence to be given orally, a direction should be sought either at the PTR or during the openings to that effect. Where evidence in chief is given orally, the rules relating to the use of witness statements in cross-examination and to the adducing of the statement in evidence at any subsequent stage of the trial remain in force and may be relied on by any party.

15.5.4 It is usual for all evidence of fact from all parties to be adduced before expert evidence and for the experts to give evidence in groups with all experts in a particular discipline giving their evidence in sequence: see paragraph 13.8.2 above for ways for expert evidence to be given. Usually, but not invariably, the order of witnesses will be such that the claimant's witnesses give their evidence first, followed by all the witnesses for each of the other parties in turn. If a party wishes a different order of witnesses to that normally followed, the agreement of the parties or a direction from the judge must be obtained in advance.

15.5.5 In a multi-party case, attention should be given (when the timetable is being discussed) to the order of cross-examination and to the extent to which particular topics will be covered by particular cross-examiners. Where these matters cannot be agreed, the order of cross-examination will (subject to any direction of the judge) follow the order in which the parties are set out in the pleadings. The judge will seek to limit cross examination on a topic which has been covered in detail by a preceding cross examination.

15.5.6 In preparing witness statements and in ascertaining what evidence a witness might give in an original or supplementary witness statement or as supplementary evidence-in-chief, lawyers may discuss the evidence to be given by a witness with that witness. The coaching of witnesses or the suggestion of answers that may be given, either in the preparation of witness statements or before a witness starts to give evidence, is not permitted. In relation to the process of giving evidence, witness familiarisation is permissible, but witness coaching is not. The boundary between witness familiarisation and witness coaching is discussed in the context of criminal proceedings by the Court of Appeal in *R v Momodou* [2005] EWCA Crim 177 at [61]–[62]. Once a witness has started giving evidence, that witness cannot discuss the case or their evidence either with the lawyers or with anyone else until they have finally left the witness box. Occasionally a dispensation is needed (for example, an expert may need to participate in an experts' meeting about some new development). In those circumstances the necessary dispensation will either be agreed between the advocates or ordered by the judge.

15.6 Submissions during the trial

15.6.1 Submissions and legal argument should be kept to a minimum during the course of the trial. Where these are necessary, (a) they should, where possible, take place when a witness is not giving evidence and (b) the judge should be given forewarning of the need for submissions or legal argument. Where possible, the judge will fix a time for these submissions outside the agreed timetable for the evidence.

15.7 Closing submissions

15.7.1 The appropriate form of closing submissions can be determined during the course of the trial. Those submissions may take the form of (a) oral closing speeches or (b) written submission alone or (c) written submissions supplemented by oral closing speeches. In shorter or lower value cases, oral closing speeches immediately after the evidence may be the most cost effective way to proceed. Alternatively, if the evidence finishes in the late afternoon, a direction for written closing submissions to be delivered by specified (early) dates may avoid the cost of a further day's court hearing. In longer and heavier cases the judge may (in consultation with the advocates) set a timetable for the delivery of sequential written submissions (alternatively, an exchange of written submissions) followed by an oral hearing. In giving directions for oral and/or written closing submissions, the judge will have regard to the circumstances of the case and the overriding objective.

15.7.2 It is helpful if, in advance of preparing closing submissions, the parties can agree on the principal topics or issues that are to be covered. It is also helpful for the written and oral submissions of each party to be structured so as to cover those topics in the same order.

15.7.3 It is both customary and helpful for the judge to be provided with a photocopy of each authority and statutory provision that is to be cited in closing submissions.

15.8 Views

15.8.1 It is sometimes necessary or desirable for the judge to be taken to view the subject-matter of the case. In normal circumstances, such a view is best arranged to take place immediately after the openings and before the evidence is called. However, if the subject matter of the case is going to be covered up or altered prior to the trial, the view must be arranged earlier. In that event, it becomes particularly important to avoid a change of judge. Accordingly, the court staff will note on the trial diary the fact that the assigned judge has attended a view. In all subsequent communications between the parties and court concerning trial date, the need to avoid a change of judge must be borne firmly in mind.

15.8.2 The matters viewed by the judge form part of the evidence that is received and may be relied on in deciding the case. However, nothing said during the view to (or in the earshot of) the judge, has any evidential status, unless there has been an agreement or order to that effect.

15.8.3 The parties should agree the arrangements for the view and then make those arrangements themselves. The judge will ordinarily travel to the view unaccompanied and, save in exceptional circumstances when the cost will be shared by all parties, will not require any travelling costs to be met by the parties.

15.9 Judgments

15.9.1 Depending on the length and complexity of the trial, the judge may (a) give judgment orally immediately after closing speeches; (b) give judgment orally on the following day or soon afterwards; or (c) deliver a reserved judgment in writing at a later date.

15.9.2 Where judgment is reserved. The judge will normally indicate at the conclusion of the trial what arrangements will be followed in relation to (a) the making available of any draft reserved judgment and (b) the handing down of the reserved judgment in open court. If a judgment is reserved, it will be handed down as soon as possible. Save in exceptional circumstances, any reserved judgment will be handed down within 3 months of the conclusion of the trial. Any enquiries as to the progress of a reserved judgment should be addressed in the first instance to the judge's clerk, with notice of that enquiry being given to other parties. If concerns remain following the judge's response to the parties, further enquiries or communication should be addressed to the judge in charge of the TCC.

15.9.3 If the judge decides to release a draft judgment in advance of the formal hand down, this draft judgment will be confidential to the parties and their legal advisers. Solicitors and counsel on each side should send to the judge a note (if possible, agreed) of any clerical errors or slips which they note in the judgment. However, this is not to be taken as an opportunity to re-argue the issues in the case.

15.10 Disposal of judge's bundle after conclusion of the case

15.10.1 The judge will have made notes and annotations on the bundle during the course of the trial. Accordingly, the normal practice is that the entire contents of the judge's bundle are disposed of as confidential waste. The empty ring files can be recovered by arrangement with the judge's clerk.

15.10.2 If any party wishes to retrieve from the judge's bundle any particular items of value which it has supplied (e.g. plans or photographs), a request for these items should be made to the judge's clerk promptly at the conclusion of the case. If the judge has not made annotations on those particular items, they will be released to the requesting party.

16. COSTS

16.1 General

CPR 60 TCCG 16

16.1.1 All disputes as to costs will be resolved in accordance with CPR Part 44, and in particular CPR rule 44.3.

16.1.2 The judge's usual approach will be to determine which party can be properly described as 'the successful party', and then to investigate whether there are any good reasons why that party should be deprived of some or all of their costs.

16.1.3 It should be noted that, in view of the complex nature of TCC cases, a consideration of the outcome on particular issues or areas of dispute can sometimes be an appropriate starting point for any decision on costs.

16.1.4 As set out in paragraphs 5.1.6, 5.5.5 and 12.1.4 above, if the judge considers that any particular aspect is likely to or has led to unnecessarily increased costs, the judge may make a costs order disallowing costs or ordering costs to be paid, either on the basis of a summary assessment, or by giving a direction to the costs judge as to what costs should be disallowed or paid on a detailed assessment.

16.2 Summary Assessment of Costs

16.2.1 Interlocutory hearings that last one day or less will usually be the subject of a summary assessment of costs in accordance with CPR 44.7 and section 13 of the Costs Practice Direction. The parties must ensure that their statements of costs, on which the summary assessment will be based, are provided to each other party, and the Court, no later than 24 hours before the hearing in question: see paragraph 6.9.3 above.

16.2.2 The Supreme Court Costs Office Guide to the Summary Assessment of Costs sets out clear advice and guidance as to the principles to be followed in any summary assessment. Generally summary assessment proceeds on the standard basis. In making an assessment on the standard basis, the court will only allow a reasonable amount in respect of costs reasonably incurred and any doubts must be resolved in favour of the paying party.

16.2.3 In arguments about the hourly rates claimed, the judge will have regard to the principles set out by the Court of Appeal in *Wraith v Sheffield Forgemasters Ltd* [1998] 1 WLR 132: i.e. the judge will consider whether the successful party acted reasonably in employing the solicitors who had been instructed and whether the costs they charged were reasonable compared with the broad average of charges made by similar firms practising in the same area.

16.2.4 When considering hourly rates, the judge in the TCC may have regard to any relevant guideline rates.

16.2.5 The court will also consider whether unnecessary work was done or an unnecessary amount of time was spent on the work.

16.2.6 It may be that, because of pressures of time, and/or the nature and extent of the disputes about the level of costs incurred, the court is unable to carry out a satisfactory summary assessment of the costs. In those circumstances, the court will direct that costs be assessed on the standard (or indemnity) basis and will order an amount to be paid on account of costs under CPR Rule 44.3 (8).

16.3 Costs Cap Orders

16.3.1 In exercising case management powers, the judge may make costs cap orders which, in normal circumstances, will be prospective only. He should only do so, however, where there is a real and substantial risk that, without such an order:

(a)   costs will be disproportionately or unreasonably incurred and
(b)   such costs cannot be controlled by conventional case management and a detailed assessment of costs after a trial, and
(c)   it is just to make such an order.

See CPR rule 3.1 and the notes to that rule in the White Book headed 'Prospective costs cap orders'.

16.3.2 The possibility of a costs cap order should be considered at the first CMC. The later such an order is sought, the more difficult it may be to impose an effective costs cap.

16.4 Costs: Miscellaneous

16.4.1 The court may at any stage order any party to file and serve on the other parties an estimate of costs: see CPR rule 3.1 (2) (ll) and section 6 of the Costs Practice Direction. The case management information sheet for the first CMC requires such costs information. This information allows the court properly to exercise its case management functions. In appropriate cases (and where it is proportionate to do so) the judge will exercise his power under paragraph 3 of the Costs Practice Direction to direct the parties to file estimates of costs prepared in such a way as to demonstrate the likely effects of giving or not giving or not giving a particular case management direction.

16.4.2 Pursuant to CPR Rule 44.2 and Section 7 of the Costs Practice Direction, solicitors have a duty to tell their clients within 7 days if an order for costs was made against the clients and they were not present at the hearing, explaining how the order came to be made. They must also give the same information to anyone else who has instructed them to act on the case or who is liable to pay their fees.

17. ENFORCEMENT

17.1 General

CPR 60 TCCG 17

17.1.1 The TCC is concerned with the enforcement of judgments and orders given by the TCC and with the enforcement of adjudicators' decisions and arbitrators' awards. Adjudication and arbitration enforcement have been dealt with in, respectively, sections 9 and 10 above.

17.2 High Court

17.2.1 London. A party wishing to make use of any provision of the CPR concerned with the enforcement of judgments and orders made in the TCC in London can use the TCC Registry in London or any other convenient TCC District Registry listed in Appendix A.

17.2.2 Outside London. Where the judgment or order in respect of which enforcement is sought was made by a judge of the TCC out of London, the party seeking enforcement should use the Registry of the court in which the judgment or order was made.

17.2.3 Where orders are required or sought to support enforcement of a TCC judgment or order, a judge of the TCC is the appropriate judge for that purpose. If available, the judge who gave the relevant judgment or made the relevant order is the appropriate judge to whom all applications should be addressed.

17.3 County Court

17.3.1 A TCC county court judgment (like any other county court judgment):

(a)   if for less than £600, must be enforced in the county court;

(b) if for between £600 and £4999, can be enforced in either the county court or the High Court, at the option of the judgment creditor;

(c) if for £5,000 or more, must be enforced in the High Court.

17.3.2 If a judgment creditor in a TCC county court wishes to transfer any enforcement proceedings to any other county court (whether a TCC county court or not), he must make a written request to do so pursuant to section 2 of the Practice Direction supplementing Part 70. Alternatively, at the end of the trial the successful party may make an oral application to the trial judge to transfer the proceedings to some other specified county court for the purposes of enforcement.

17.4 Enforcement on paper

17.4.1 Where the application or order is unopposed or does not involve any substantial dispute, the necessary order should be sought by way of a paper application.

17.5 Charging Orders and Orders for Sale

17.5.1.One of the most common methods of enforcement involves the making of a charging order over the judgment debtor's property. There are three stages in the process.

17.5.2. The judgment creditor can apply to the TCC for a charging order pursuant to CPR 73.3 and 73.4. The application is in Form N379 in which the judgment creditor must identify the relevant judgment and the property in question. The application is initially dealt with by the judge without a hearing, and he may make an interim charging order imposing a charge over the judgment debtor's interest in the property and fixing a hearing to consider whether or not to make the charging order final.

17.5.3. The interim charging order must be served in accordance with CPR 73.5. If the judgment debtor or any other person objects to the making of a final charging order, then he must set out his objection in accordance with CPR 73.8. There will then be a hearing at which the court will decide whether or not to make the charging order final.

17.5.4. Ultimately, if the judgment remains unsatisfied, the party who has obtained the final charging order may seek an order for the sale of the property in accordance with CPR 73.10. Although paragraph 4.2 of PD 73 might suggest that a claim for an order for sale to enforce a charging order must be started in the Chancery Division, there is no such restriction in the rule itself and practical difficulties have arisen for parties who have obtained a judgment, an interim charging order and a final charging order in the TCC and who do not want to have to transfer or commence fresh proceedings in another division in order to obtain an order for sale. The TCC will, in appropriate circumstances, in accordance with the overriding objective, make orders for sale in such circumstances, particularly if the parties are agreed that is the most convenient cost-effective course: see *Packman Lucas Limited v Mentmore Towers Ltd* [2010] EWHC 1037 (TCC).

17.5.5 In deciding whether or not to make an order for sale, the court will consider, amongst other things, the size of the debt, and the value of the property relative to that debt, the conduct of the parties and the absence of any other enforcement option on the part of the judgment creditor.

18. THE TCC JUDGE AS ARBITRATOR

18.1 General

CPR 60 TCCG 18

18.1.1 Section 93(1) of the Arbitration Act 1996 ('the 1996 Act') provides that a judge of the TCC (previously an Official Referee) may 'if in all the circumstances he thinks fit, accept appointment as a sole arbitrator or as an umpire by or by virtue of an arbitration agreement'. Judges of the TCC may accept appointments as sole arbitrators or umpires pursuant to these statutory provisions. The 1996 Act does not limit the appointments to arbitrations with the seat in England and Wales.

18.1.2 However, a TCC judge cannot accept such an appointment unless the Lord Chief Justice 'has informed him that, having regard to the state of (TCC) business, he can be made available': see section 93(3) of the 1996 Act. In exceptional cases a judge of the TCC may also accept an appointment as a member of a three-member panel of arbitrators if the Lord Chief Justice consents but such arbitrations cannot be under section 93 of the 1996 Act because section 93(6) of the 1996 Act modifies the provisions of the 1996 Act where there is a judge-arbitrator and this could not apply to arbitral tribunals with three arbitrators, one of whom was a judge-arbitrator.

18.1.3 Application should be made in the first instance to the judge whose acceptance of the appointment is sought. If the judge is willing to accept the appointment, he will make application on behalf of the appointing party or parties, through the judge in charge of the TCC, to the Lord Chief Justice for his necessary approval. He will inform the party or parties applying for his appointment once the consent or refusal of consent has been obtained.

18.1.4 Subject to the workload of the court and the consent of the Lord Chief Justice, the TCC judges will generally be willing to accept such requests, particularly in short cases or where an important principle or point of law is concerned. Particular advantages have been noted by both TECBAR and TeCSA in the appointment of a TCC judge to act as arbitrator where the dispute centres on the proper interpretation of a clause or clauses within one of the standard forms of building and engineering contracts.

18.2 Arbitration Management and Fees

18.2.1 Following the appointment of the judge arbitrator, the rules governing the arbitration will be decided upon, or directed, at the First Preliminary Meeting, when other appropriate directions will be given. The judge arbitrator will manage the reference to arbitration in a similar way to a TCC case.

18.2.2 The judge sitting as an arbitrator will sit in a TCC court room (suitably rearranged) unless the parties and the judge arbitrator agree to some other arrangement.

18.2 Fees are payable to the Court Service for the judge arbitrator's services and for any accommodation provided. The appropriate fee for the judge arbitrator, being a daily rate, is published in the Fees Order and should be paid through the TCC Registry.

18.3 Modifications to the Arbitration Act 1996 for judge-arbitrators

18.3.1 As section 93 envisages that appointments of judge-arbitrators will be in arbitrations where the seat of the arbitration is in England and Wales, Schedule 2 of the 1996 Act modifies the provisions of the Act which apply to arbitrations where the seat is in England and Wales.

18.3.2 In relation to arbitrations before judge-arbitrators, paragraph 2 of Schedule 2 to the Arbitration Act 1996 provides that references in Part I of the 1996 Act to 'the court' shall be construed in relation to a judge-arbitrator, or in relation to the appointment of a judge-arbitrator, as references to 'the Court of Appeal'. This means that, for instance, any appeal from a judge-arbitrator under section 69 of the 1996 Act is therefore heard, in the first instance, by the Court of Appeal.

APPENDIX A CASE MANAGEMENT INFORMATION SHEET

CPR 60 TCCG A

This Appendix is the same as Appendix A to the Part 60 Practice Direction.

APPENDIX B CASE MANAGEMENT DIRECTIONS FORM

CPR 60 TCCG B

Action no HT-. . . . .

Delete or amend the following directions, as appropriate to the circumstances of the case.

1. Trial date . . . . For the purposes of payment of the trial fee, but for no other purposes, this date is provisional. This date will cease to be provisional and the trial fee will become payable on . . . [usually be 2 months before the trial date].

2. Estimated length of trial . . . .

3. Directions, if appropriate, (a) for the trial of any preliminary issues or (b) for the trial to be divided into stages . . .

4. This action is to be [consolidated] [managed and tried with] action no . . . The lead action shall be . . . All directions given in the lead action shall apply to both actions, unless otherwise stated.

5. Further statements of case shall be filed and served as follows:

– Defence and any counterclaim by 4 p.m. on . . .
– Reply (if any) and defence to counterclaim (if any) by 4 p.m. on . . .

6. Permission to make the following amendments . . .

7. Disclosure of documents by 5 p.m. on . . . [Standard disclosure dispensed with/ limited/ varied as follows . . .]. Specific directions in respect of electronic disclosure . . .

8. There shall be a Scott Schedule in respect of defects/ items of damage/ other . . .

– The column headings shall be as follows . . .
– Claimant/ defendant to serve Scott Schedule by 5 p.m. on . . .
– Defendant/ claimant to respond to Scott Schedule by 5 p.m. on . . .

9. Signed statements of witnesses of fact to be served by 5 p.m. on . . . [Supplementary statements of witnesses of fact to be served by 5 p.m. on . . .]

10. The parties have permission to call the following expert witnesses in respect of the following issues:

– . . .
– . . .
– . . .

11. In respect of any expert evidence permitted under paragraph 10:

– Directions for carrying out inspections/ taking samples/ conducting experiments/ performance of calculations shall be . . .
– Experts in like fields to hold discussions in accordance with rule 35.12 by . . .
– Experts' statements rule 35.12 (3) to be prepared and filed by 5 p.m. on . . .
– Experts' reports to be served by 5 p.m. on . . .

12. A single joint expert shall be appointed by the parties to report on the following issue(s) . . . . The following directions shall govern the appointment of the single joint expert:

– . . .
– . . .

13. [All documents are being issued and filed in this case by e-working.] or [This case will be continued from the date of this order by all documents being issued and filed by e-working] or [The following documents shall be provided to the court electronically or in computer readable form, as well as in hard copy . . .]

14. A review case management conference shall be held on . . . at . . . a.m./ p.m. Time allowed . . .

15. The pre-trial review shall be held on . . . at . . . a.m./p.m. Time allowed . . .

16. The above dates and time limits may be extended by agreement between the parties. Nevertheless:

- The dates and time limits specified in paragraphs . . . may not be extended by more than . . . days without the permission of the court.
- The dates specified in paragraph 1 (trial) and paragraph 15 (pre-trial review) cannot be varied without the permission of the court.

16. Liberty to restore.

17. Costs in the case.

18. Claimant's solicitors to draw up this order by . . . [Delete if order is to be drawn up by the court.]

Order made on [date]

APPENDIX C PRE-TRIAL REVIEW QUESTIONNAIRE

CPR 60 TCCG C

This Appendix is the same as Appendix C to the Part 60 Practice Direction.

APPENDIX D CONTACT DETAILS FOR TECHNOLOGY AND CONSTRUCTION COURT

CPR 60 TCCG D

The High Court of Justice, Queen's Bench Division, Technology and Construction Court

St Dunstan's House, 133-137 Fetter Lane, London EC4A 1HD

(a) Management

Court Manager: Mr Wilf Lusty (mailto://wilf.lusty@hmcourts-service.gsi.gov.uk)

Registry Managers: Mr Steven Gibbon (mailto://steven.gibbon@hmcourts-service. gsi.gov.uk) and Ms Dawn Rollason (mailto://dawn.rollason@hmcourts-service.gsi.g ov.uk)

Court Manager: Tel: 020 7947 6022

Fax: 020 7947 7428

Registry: Tel: 020 7947 7156

Fax: 020 7947 6465

(b) TCC Judges

Mr Justice Akenhead (Judge in Charge of the TCC from 1 September 2010)

Clerk: Mr Sam Taylor (mailto://sam.taylor1@hmcourts-service.gsi.gov.uk)

Tel: 020 7947 7445

Fax: 020 7947 7436

Mr Justice Ramsey

Clerk: Mr David Hamilton (mailto://david.hamilton5@hmcourts-service.gsi.gov.uk)

Tel: 020 7947 6331

Fax: 020 7947 6803

Mr Justice Coulson

Clerk: Ms Sarah Cox (mailto://sarah.cox@hmcourts-service.gsi.gov.uk)

Tel: 020 7947 6547

Fax: 020 7947 6263

Mr Justice Edwards-Stuart

Clerk: Ms Carole Collins (mailto://carole.collins@hmcourts-service.gsi.gov.uk)

Tel: 020 7947 7205

Fax: 020 7947 6465

His Honour Judge David Wilcox

Clerk: Mr Dan Ward (mailto://Dan.Ward@hmcourts-service.gsi.gov.uk)

Tel: 020 7947 6450

Fax: 020 7947 6465

His Honour Judge John Toulmin CMG QC

Clerk: Ms Valerie Servante (mailto://valerie.servante2@hmcourts-service.gsi.gov.uk)

Tel: 020 7947 6456

Fax: 020 7947 6465

The following High Court Judges may be available, when necessary and by arrangement with the President of the Queen's Bench Division, to sit in the TCC:

Mr Justice Burton

Mr Justice Field

Mr Justice Ouseley

Mr Justice Simon

Mr Justice Christopher Clarke

Mr Justice Teare

Mr Justice Foskett

The following judges are also TCC judges who may be available when necessary and by arrangement with the President of the Queen's Bench Division, to sit in the TCC: His Honour Judge Anthony Thornton QC; His Honour Judge David Mackie QC; Her Honour Judge Anna Guggenheim QC

Birmingham District Registry: Birmingham County Court, 33 Bull Street, Birmingham, West Midlands, B4 6DS

TCC listing and clerk to His Honour Judge David Grant: Peter Duke (mailto://Peter.Duke@hmcourts-service.gsi.gov.uk)

Tel: 0121 681 3181 Fax: 0121 681 3121

TCC Judges:

His Honour Judge David Grant (full time TCC Judge)

Her Honour Judge Frances Kirkham (part time TCC Judge)

His Honour Judge Simon Brown QC (Mercantile Judge)

His Honour Judge Charles Purle QC (Chancery Judge)

His Honour Judge David Cooke

His Honour Martin McKenna

Bristol District Registry: Bristol County Court, TCC Listing Office, Bristol Civil Justice Centre, 2 Redcliff Street, Bristol BS1 6GR

Head of Specialist Listing: Kathryn Everett

Tel: 0117 366 4864

TCC Listing officer: Priya Patel

Tel: 0117 366 4861

Email: mailto://bristoltcclisting@hmcourts-service.gsi.gov.uk

Switchboard Tel: 0117 366 4800

TCC Judges: His Honour Judge Mark Havelock-Allan QC (principal TCC judge);

His Honour Judge Patrick McCahill QC

Cardiff District Registry: Cardiff County Court. Cardiff Civil Justice Centre, 2 Park Street, Cardiff CF10 1 ET

Main switchboard: 02920 376 400 Fax: 02920 376 475 Listing office: 02920 376 412

Circuit Judges Listing Manager: Graham Driver. Tel: 02920 376 483 (mailto://graham.driver@hmcourts-service.gsi.gov.uk)

Specialist Listing Officer: Tracey Davies. Tel: 02920 376 412 (mailto://tracey.davies@hmcourts-service.gsi.gov.uk)

TCC Judges:

His Honour Judge Milwyn Jarman QC (principal TCC judge)

His Honour Judge Nicholas Chambers QC

His Honour Judge Anthony Seys Llewellyn QC

Central London Civil Justice Centre, 26 Park Crescent, London WIN 4HT

TCC/Chancery Section - Manager: Mr Nick Coleman Tel: 0207 917 7821 Fax: 0207 917 7935 Goldfax: 0970 330 571 Email: mailto://chance.clerk@hmcourts-service.gsi.gov.uk

Circuit judge listing: Tel: 020 7917 7932 Email: mailto://hearingsatcentrallondon.countycourt@hmcourts-service.gsi.gov.uk

TCC Judges:

His Honour Judge Brian Knight QC (principal TCC judge);

His Honour Judge Paul Collins CBE;

His Honour Judge Edward Bailey

Chester District Registry: Chester County Court, The Chester Civil Justice Centre, Trident House, Little St John Street, Chester CH1 1SN

Diary Manager: Julie Burgess

E-mail: mailto://Julie.burgess@hmcourts-service.gsi.gov.uk

Tel: 01244 404200 Fax: 01244 404300

TCC Judge:

His Honour Judge Derek Halbert

Exeter District Registry: Exeter County Court, Southernhay Gardens, Exeter, Devon, EX1 1UH

Tel: 01392 415350 Fax: 01392 415645

TCC Judge:

His Honour Judge Barry Cotter QC

Leeds Combined Court Centre, The Courthouse, 1 Oxford Row, Leeds LS1 3BG

High Court Civil Listing Officers: David Eaton

Tel: 0113 306 2440/2441 Fax: 0113 242 6380

e-mail: mailto://david.eaton@hmcourts-service.gsi.gov.uk

TCC Judges:

His Honour Judge John Cockroft (principal TCC judge);

His Honour Judge John Behrens;

His Honour Judge Peter Langan QC;

His Honour Judge Simon Grenfell;

His Honour Judge Simon Hawkesworth QC;

His Honour Judge Kaye QC

Leicester District Registry: Leicester County Court, 90 Wellington Street, Leicester LE1 6HG

Tel: 0116 222 5700 Fax: 0116 222 5763

TCC Judge:

His Honour Judge David Brunning

Liverpool District Registry: Liverpool Combined Court Centre, Liverpool Civil & Family Courts, 35 Vernon Street, Liverpool L2 2BX

TCC listing officer: Jackie Jones Tel: 0151 296 2444 Fax: 0151 295 2201

TCC Judges:

His Honour Judge Graham Platts (principal TCC judge)

His Honour Judge Stephen Stewart QC

His Honour Judge Allan Gore QC

Manchester District Registry: Manchester Civil Justice Centre, 1 Bridge Street West, Manchester M60 9DJ

TCC clerks: Isobel Rich and David Fernandez

Tel: 0161 745 7511

Fax: 0161 745 7202

e-mail: mailto://highcourtspecialisthearings@manchester.countycourt.gsi.gov.uk

TCC Judges

His Honour Judge Philip Raynor QC (full time TCC judge)

His Honour Judge Stephen Davies (full time TCC judge)

The following judges at Manchester are nominated to deal with TCC business: His Honour Judge Brendan Hegarty QC, His Honour Judge David Hodge QC, His Honour Judge Mark Pelling QC and His Honour Judge David Waksman QC.

Mold County Court Law Courts, Civic Centre, Mold, Flintshire, Wales, CH7 1AE

TCC listing officer: Selina Wilkes

Tel: 01352 707405 Fax: 01352 753874

TCC Judges: Will attend from Cardiff when required

Newcastle upon Tyne Combined Court Centre, The Law Courts, Quayside, Newcastle upon Tyne NE1 3LA

Tel: 0191 201 2029

Listing Officer: Mrs Carol Gallagher (mailto://carol.gallagher@hmcourts-service.gsi.gov.uk)

Tel: 0191 201 2047 Fax: 0191 201 2001

TCC Judge: His Honour Judge Christopher Walton; District Judge Atherton

Nottingham District Registry: Nottingham County Court, 60 Canal Street, Nottingham NG1 7EJ

Tel 0115 910 3500 Fax: 0115 910 3510

TCC Judge: His Honour Judge Richard Inglis

Salford District Registry: Salford County Court, Prince William House, Peel Cross Road, Salford M5 4RR

TCC clerks: Isobel Rich and David Fernandez

Tel: 0161 745 7511 Fax: 0161 745 7202 e-mail: mailto://Hearings@salford.countycourt.gsi.gov.uk

TCC Judges: His Honour Judge David Gilliland QC (full time TCC judge); His Honour Judge Phillip Raynor QC (full time TCC judge)

The following judges at Manchester are nominated to deal with TCC business: His Honour Judge Brendan Hegarty QC; His Honour Judge David Hodge QC; His Honour Judge Mark Pelling QC and His Honour Judge David Waksman QC

Sheffield Combined Court Centre, The Law Courts, 50 West Bar, Sheffield S3 8PH

Tel: 0114 281 2419 Fax: 0114 281 2585

TCC Judge: His Honour Judge John Bullimore

Winchester Combined Court Centre, The Law Courts, Winchester, Hampshire, SO23 9EL

Diary Manager: Mr Wayne Hacking

e-mail mailto://wayne.hacking@hmcourts-service.gsi.gov.uk

Tel: 023 8021 3254

Civil Listing Officer: Mrs Karen Hart

mailto://Karen.hart@hmcourts-service.gsi.gov.uk)

Tel: 01962 814113 Switchboard: 01962 814100 Fax: 01962 814260

TCC Judge: His Honour Judge Iain Hughes QC

APPENDIX E DRAFT ADR ORDER

1. By [*date/time*] the parties shall exchange lists of three neutral individuals who have indicated their availability to conduct a mediation or ENE or other form of ADR in this case prior to [*date*].

2. By [*date/time*] the parties shall agree an individual from the exchanged lists to conduct the mediation or ENE or other form of ADR by [*date*]. If the parties are unable to agree on the neutral individual, they will apply to the Court in writing by [*date/time*] and the Court will choose one of the listed individuals to conduct the mediation or ENE or other form of ADR.

3. There will be a stay of the proceedings until [*date/time*] to allow the mediation or ENE or other form of ADR to take place. On or before that date, the Court shall be informed as to whether or not the case has been finally settled. If it has not been finally settled, the parties will:

(a)   comply with all outstanding directions made by the Court;
(b)   attend for a review CMC on [*date/time*].

Order made on [*date*]

APPENDIX F DRAFT DIRECTIONS IN ADJUDICATION ENFORCEMENT PROCEEDINGS

CPR 60 TCCG F

Upon reading the Claim Form, Particulars of Claim, the Claimant's without notice application dated [*date*] and the evidence in support thereof

IT IS ORDERED THAT:

1. The Claimant's solicitor shall [as soon as practicable after receipt of this Order]/[by 4pm on [*date*]] serve upon the Defendant

(a)   The Claim Form and Response Pack
(b)   This Order
(c)   The Claimant's Application Pursuant to Part 24 and the Claimant's evidence in support.

2. The time for the Defendant to file its Acknowledgment of Service is abridged to [ ] days from the date of service. If the Defendant fails to lodge its Acknowledgment of Service within this abridged time, judgement in default can be entered.

3. The Claimant hereby has permission to issue an application pursuant to CPR Part 24 without an Acknowledgment of Service or Defence having been filed.

4. The Part 24 application will be heard on [*date*] at [*time am/pm*] at [*location*]. Estimated Length of Hearing: [*hours*]. Any change to the estimate by a party shall be notified to the court seven days before the hearing.

5. Any further evidence in relation to the Part 24 Application shall be served and filed

(a)   By the Defendant, by [*date*]
(b)   By the Claimant, in response to that of the Defendant, by [*date*]

and in either case no later than 4.00pm upon that day.

6. The Claimant's solicitor shall file a paginated bundle comprising

(a)   The witness statements provided in support of the application, together with any exhibits;
(b)   The witness statements provided in opposition to the application together with exhibits;
(c)   Any witness statements in reply, together with exhibits;

This bundle is to be provided no later than [*time*] on [*date*].

7. The parties shall file and serve skeleton arguments by no later than [*date*]. The parties shall lodge a joint bundle of photocopies of relevant authorities with the skeleton arguments.

8. The costs of and incidental to these directions are reserved to the Part 24 hearing. Permission to apply in respect of such costs in the absence of such hearing.

9. The parties have permission to apply to the court on two working days' written notice to the other to seek to set aside or vary these directions.

APPENDIX G DRAFT COURT SETTLEMENT ORDER

Court Settlement

CPR 60 TCCG G

1. The Court Settlement Process under this Order is a confidential, voluntary and non-binding dispute resolution process in which the Settlement Judge assists the Parties in reaching an amicable settlement at a Court Settlement Conference.

2. This Order provides for the process by which the Court assists in the resolution of the disputes in the Proceedings. This Order is made by consent of the Parties with a view to achieving the amicable settlement of such disputes. It is agreed that the Settlement Judge may vary this Order at any time as he thinks appropriate or in accordance with the agreement of the Parties.

3. The following definitions shall apply:

(1)   The Parties shall be [names]
(2)   The Proceedings are [identify]
(3)   The Settlement Judge is [name]

The Court Settlement Process

4. The Settlement Judge may conduct the Court Settlement Process in such manner, as the Judge considers appropriate, taking into account the circumstances of the case, the wishes of the Parties and the overriding objective in Part 1 of the Civil Procedure Rules. A Preliminary Court Settlement Conference shall be held, either in person or in some other convenient manner, at which the Parties and the Settlement Judge shall determine, in general terms, the procedure to be adopted for the Court Settlement Process, the venue of the Court Settlement Conference, the estimated duration of the Court Settlement Conference and the material which will be read by the Settlement Judge in advance of the Court Settlement Conference.

5. Unless the Parties otherwise agree, during the Court Settlement Conference the Settlement Judge may communicate with the Parties together or with any Party separately, including private meetings at which the Settlement Judge may express views on the disputes. Each Party shall cooperate with the Settlement Judge. A Party may request a private meeting with the Settlement Judge at any time during the Court Settlement Conference. The Parties shall give full assistance to enable the Court Settlement Conference to proceed and be concluded within the time stipulated by the Settlement Judge.

6. In advance of the Court Settlement Conference, each Party shall notify the Settlement Judge and the other Party or Parties of the names and the role of all persons involved in the Court Settlement Conference. Each Party shall nominate a person having full authority to settle the disputes.

7. No offers or promises or agreements shall have any legal effect unless and until they are included in a written agreement signed by representatives of all Parties (the "Settlement Agreement").

8. If the Court Settlement Conference does not lead to a Settlement Agreement, the Settlement Judge may, if requested by the Parties, send the Parties such assessment setting out his views on such matters as the Parties shall request, which may include, for instance, his views on the disputes, his views on prospects of success on individual issues, the likely outcome of the case and what would be an appropriate settlement. Such assessment shall be confidential to the parties and may not be used or referred to in any subsequent proceedings.

Termination of the Settlement Process

9. The Court Settlement Process shall come to end upon the signing of a Settlement Agreement by the Parties in respect of the disputes or when the Settlement Judge so directs or upon written notification by any Party at any time to the Settlement Judge and the other Party or Parties that the Court Settlement Process is terminated.

Confidentiality

10. The Court Settlement Process is private and confidential. Every document, communication or other form of information disclosed, made or produced by any Party specifically for the purpose of the Court Settlement Process shall be treated as being disclosed on a privileged and without prejudice basis and no privilege or confidentiality shall be waived by such disclosure.

11. Nothing said or done during the course of the Court Settlement Process is intended to or shall in any way affect the rights or prejudice the position of the Parties to the dispute in the Proceedings or any subsequent arbitration, adjudication or litigation. If the Settlement Judge is told by a Party that information is being provided to the Settlement Judge in confidence, the Settlement Judge will not disclose that information to any other Party in the course of the Court Settlement Process or to any other person at any time.

Costs

12. Unless otherwise agreed, each Party shall bear its own costs and shall share equally the Court costs of the Court Settlement Process.

Settlement Judge's Role in Subsequent Proceedings

13. The Settlement Judge shall from the date of this Order not take any further part in the Proceedings nor in any subsequent proceedings arising out of the Court Settlement Process and no party shall be entitled to call the Settlement Judge as a witness in any subsequent adjudication, arbitration or judicial proceedings arising out of or connected with the Court Settlement Process.

Exclusion of Liability

14. For the avoidance of doubt, the Parties agree that the Settlement Judge shall have the same immunity from suit in relation to a Court Settlement Process as the Settlement Judge would have if acting otherwise as a Judge in the Proceedings.

Particular Directions

15. A Court Settlement Conference shall take place on [*date*] at [*place*] commencing at [*time*].

16. If by [*date*] the Parties have not concluded a settlement agreement, the matter shall be listed on the first available date before an appropriate judge who shall be allocated for the future management and trial of the Proceedings.

17. The Court Settlement Process shall proceed on the basis of such documents as might be determined at the Preliminary Court Settlement Conference and which may include the documents filed in the court proceedings and further documents critical to the understanding of the issues in the dispute and the positions of the Parties.

APPENDIX H MAIN AMENDMENTS MADE IN THE SECOND REVISION TO THE SECOND EDITION

CPR 60 TCCG H

Item	Paragraph	Comment
1	1.1.1	The role of the Guide has been explained in the light of the decision in *Secretary of State for Communities and Local Government v Bovale* [2009] 1 WLR 2274 at [36]. The text has generally been reviewed for compliance with this decision.
2	1.3.1	This paragraph has been amended to include further categories of cases which are now commonly brought in the TCC
3	1.3.2 and 1.3.4(e)	This paragraph now includes the ability of TCC Liaison District Judges to hear TCC cases in the County Court if nominated by a TCC judge and the Designated Civil Judge. This is an interim solution, pending any statutory amendments being made, to reflect the second part of recommendation 6(iii) at Chapter 29 of the Jackson Report.
4	1.3.3, 4.6.2 and 4.7.2	Amendment to reflect the move of the London TCC from St Dunstan's House to the Rolls Building in early 2011.
5	2.3.2	Change to provision on proportionality to reflect the Jackson Report at paragraph 4.10 of Chapter 35 and current role of the court.
6	3.4.3	This emphasises the limited grounds for applications for extension of time to serve a claim form under CPR 7.6
7	3.6.4 to 3.6.6	Additional explanation has been added as to the grounds for transfer to the TCC and the basis for transfer from a District Registry to London in the light of *Neath Port Talbot CBC v Currie* [2008] EWHC 1508 (TCC).
8	3.7.1	This paragraph has been amended to reflect the allocation of cases in the TCC with the recent appointment of TCC High Court judges and authorisations under s.9 of the Senior Courts Act 1981, compared to the position of specialist circuit judges and recorders nominated under s.68 of the Senior Courts Act 1981.
9	3.7.4	This paragraph has been amended to deal with the means of communication with TCC High Court judges
10	3.8	A new section on Electronic Working has been added in the light of the practice in the TCC since 20 July 2009 and Practice Direction 5C.
11	4.1.4 to 4.1.6	These new paragraphs deal with access to the TCC for pre-action applications under para. 4.1 of PD60 and refers to the current practice in relation to the pre-action protocol and applications for ADR in the TCC.

Item	Paragraph	Comment
12	4.3.4 and 4.3.5	Modification to the provisions for telephone hearing to indicate willingness to have some parties heard by telephone and other parties to attend in person.
13	4.4.2	An addition has been made to deal with paper applications made without notice.
14	4.5.1 and 4.5.2	These paragraphs on Email communication have been amended to reflect the preference for electronic Working in London.
15	4.6.2	Amends the provision relating to availability of Video Conferencing in London
16	4.8.1 and 4.8.2	Lodging of documents in London has been amended to reflect the preference for Electronic Working. In addition, in other cases, a provision has been added to discourage documents being sent by fax.
17	5.1.6	An amendment has been made to reflect recommendation 6(i) of the Jackson Report.
18	5.5.5	An amendment has been made to reflect recommendation 6(i) of the Jackson Report.
19	5.7.1	A provision has been added to remind parties that even if directions for the first CMC are agreed a hearing may be need to deal with other matters. This would include ADR.
20	5.8.1	A provision has been added to require 'Date order made' to be added to orders to avoid confusion between the date of the hearing, dated when the draft order was submitted, date order approved by the judge and date order sealed.
21	6.7.1 and 6.7.2	These have been amended to reflect the advantage of paper applications rather than oral hearings.
22	6.8.1 and 6.8.2	Amendments to reflect the change to 'Date order made' in paragraph 5.8.1
23	7.1.1 and 7.2.1	Minor amendments to reflect the breadth of ADR and the need for early ADR. This also reflects recommendation 6(iv) of the Jackson Report and the King's College Report 'Mediating Construction Disputes: An Evaluation of Existing Practice'.
24	7.5.4	The provision for ENE has been expanded to alert parties to matters that need to be considered, in the light of experience.
25	7.6	The provision for the Court Settlement Process has now been added after the successful completion of the Pilot Scheme and the approval for the process to be a permanent part of TCC procedure. The use of this process particularly in small claims also reflects recommendation 6(iv) of the Jackson Report.
26	9.2.5	The provision for the assignment of an adjudication enforcement application to a named judge has been deleted as experience shows that flexibility of listing is needed for these urgent applications.
27	9.2.7	The provision has been amended to reflect the usual adjudication enforcement direction to serve the claim form as soon as practicable.
28	9.2.12	A paragraph has been added to remind parties that default remedies or shortened time periods may be appro-

Item	Paragraph	Comment
		priate where the party opposing adjudication enforcement applications takes no part or a limited part in the proceedings.
29	9.3.2	A change has been made so that authorities are served with skeleton arguments rather than with bundles.
30	10.2.4	The provision for permission to appeal in arbitrations has been amended to reflect the fact that directions are often given when the arbitration claim is issued and to provide for "documents necessary to understand the award" to be referred to.
31	11.2.3	Reference is made to the Practice Direction 31B: Disclosure of Electronic Documents.
32	11.3.1	Amendment to the provision relating to service using information technology to reflect modern practice and Electronic Working in London.
33	12.1.4	An amendment has been made to reflect recommendation 6(i) of the Jackson Report.
34	12.2.4 and 12.2.5	An amendment has been made to reflect the comments at paragraphs 2.5 and 2.6 of Chapter 29 of the Jackson Report.
35	13.6.3, 13.7.1 and 13.7.2	These have been amended to reflect the Protocol for the Instruction or Experts and to deal with the extent to which lawyers can be involved in commenting on experts' joints statements and reports
36	13.8.1 and 13.8.2	These have been amended to reflect the growing practice of short presentations by experts at the start of their evidence and the use of 'concurrent-evidence' (colloquially known as 'hot-tubbing') in TCC cases.
37	14.1.1	A provision has been added, similar to that at 5.7.1 for the first CMC, to remind parties that even if directions for the PTR are agreed a hearing may be need to deal with other matters. This would include ADR.
38	14.4.1 to 1.4.3.	Amendments have been made to reflect recommendation 6(ii) of the Jackson Report.
39	14.5.1	Amendments have been made to the matters to be considered at the PTR to reflect the provisional nature of the trial timetable and the need to consider how expert evidence will be presented.
40	15.2.3	The provision as to bundles has been amended so that bundle numbers are included on the front cover of the bundle and so that original copies of expert reports, fully paginated, are included because photocopies of photographs, plans etc are rarely easy to read.
41	15.5.6	The provisions as to lawyers' contact with witnesses when preparing witness statements have been made clear as have the questions of witness coaching/familiarisation. The current reference to Momodou might be thought to prevent contact with witnesses in civil claims where it is prevented in criminal proceedings.
42	16.1.4	Amendments have been made to reflect recommendation 6(ii) of the Jackson Report.

Item	Paragraph	Comment
43	16.2.4	An amendment has been made to delete the reference to TecSA guideline rates as these are no longer produced.
44	17.5	Addition of a section on Charging Orders and Orders for Sale to reflect the increased use of these methods of enforcement in the TCC and the decision in *Packman Lucas Limited v Mentmore Towers Ltd* [2010] EWHC 1037 (TCC).
45	18.1.1, 18.1.2 and 18.1.4	Amendments are made to the circumstances in which TCC judges can be appointed as judge-arbitrators to reflect s.93 of the Arbitration Act 1996 and the current practice of permitting TCC judges to sit as arbitrators in limited circumstances.
46	18.3	Amendments to reflect the way in which the Arbitration Act 1996 is amended when a judge-arbitrator is appointed under s.93.
47	Appendix B	The standard directions on the case management conference have been amended to provide that the court has to deal with the extent of Electronic Working and that the order should state "Date order made".
48	Appendix D	The list of TCC judges and their contact details have been amended.
49	Appendix E	The draft ADR order has been amended to reflect the breadth of ADR methods
50	Appendix F	The standard adjudication enforcement directions have been amended to reflect possible applications for judgments in default, changes to time estimates, the need for fixed dates and the change to authorities being produced with skeleton arguments (see amendment to 9.3.2 above)
51	Appendix G	This contains a draft Court Settlement Order
52	Appendix H	The addition of this appendix setting out the main amendments to this revision of the TCC Guide.